A-Z GREATER MAN

CW00676377

CONTENTS

Key to Map Pages	2-3
Large Scale City & Town Centres	4-9
Map Pages	10-133
Postcode Map	134-135
Road Map	136-137
Index to Streets, Towns, Villages, & selected Places of Interest	138-237
Index to Hospitals & Hospices	238-239
Rail Connections Map	240

REFERENCE

Motorway M60

Primary Route A580

A Road A577

B Road B6194

Dual Carriageway

One-way Street
Traffic flow on A Roads is also indicated by a heavy line on the driver's left.

Road Under Construction
Opening dates are correct at time of publication

Proposed Road

Pedestrianized Road

Restricted Access

Track & Footpath

Residential Walkway

Railway — Station, East Lancashire Railway Station, Level Crossing, Tunnel

Metrolink (LRT)
The boarding of Metrolink trams at stops may be limited to a single direction, indicated by the arrow — Stop

Built-up Area — REGENCY CLOSE

Local Authority Boundary

National Park Boundary

Posttown Boundary

Postcode Boundary (within Posttown)

Map Continuation 90 — Large Scale Centres 4

Airport

Car Park (selected)

Church or Chapel

Cycleway (selected)

Fire Station

Hospital

House Numbers (A & B Roads only) 13 8

Information Centre

National Grid Reference 390

Park & Ride (Train or Tram) P+R

Police Station

Post Office

Speed Camera with Speed Limit 30
Fixed Cameras and long term road works cameras
Symbols do not indicate camera direction

Toilet: without facilities for the Disabled
with facilities for the Disabled
Disabled use only

Viewpoint

Educational Establishment

Hospital or Healthcare Building

Industrial Building

Leisure or Recreational Facility

Place of Interest

Public Building

Shopping Centre or Market

Other Selected Buildings

SCALE

Map Pages 4-9
1:9,500 6⅔ inches (16.93cm) to 1 mile 10.52cm to 1km
0 ⅛ ¼ ⅜ Mile
0 100 200 300 400 500 Metres

Map Pages 10-133
1:19,000 3⅓ inches (8.47cm) to 1 mile 5.26cm to 1km
0 ¼ ½ ¾ Mile
0 250 500 750 Metres 1 Kilometre

Copyright of Geographers' A-Z Map Company Limited

Fairfield Road, Borough Green, Sevenoaks, Kent TN15 8PP
Telephone: 01732 781000 (Enquiries & Trade Sales)
01732 783422 (Retail Sales)

www.az.co.uk

Edition 5 2012

Ordnance Survey

KEY TO MAP PAGES

Leyland
Tarleton
Croston
Euxton
CHORLEY
Eccleston
Rufford
CHARNOCK RICHARD
BLACKBURN WITH DARWEN
DARWEN
LARGE SCALE 7 BOLTON TOWN CENTRE
LARGE SCALE 9 WIGAN TOWN CENTRE
Belmont Resr.
Belmont
Edgworth
10
RAMSBOTTOM
Charnock Richard
Weld Bank
Coppull
18
19
Adlington
Rivington
20
21
BOLTON WEST
Horwich
Dimple
Turton Bottoms
Egerton
22
Horrocks Fold
Eagley
23
Bradshaw
Astley Bridge
Hawkshaw
Holcombe Brook
24
Tottington
Harwood
Walshaw
Burscough
Leeds & Liverpool Canal
Parbold
Shevington Moor
Appley Bridge
32
33
Roby Mill
Shevington
Gathurst
STANDISH
34
Red Rock
Thorn Hill
Blackrod
35
Aspull
Marylebone
36
Bottom o' th' Moor
37
Lostock Junction
Wingates
Barrow Bridge
BOLTON
38
39
Breightmet
Daubhill
Burnden
Starling
Ainsworth
40
Little Lever
RADCLIFFE
ORMSKIRK
SKELMERSDALE
50
Up Holland
51
Orrell
Higher End
Crawford
Lamberhead Grn.
WIGAN
52
Top Lock
53
Ince-in-Makerfield
Hindley
Platt Bridge
Westhoughton
54
Daisy Hill
55
Over Hulton
Atherton
Hindley Green
FARNWORTH
56
57
Walkden
Little Hulton
Tyldesley
Kearsley
58
Clifton
Longshaw
Rainford
68
Billinge
69
Garswood
Moss Bank
Chadwick Green
Landgate
70
Bamfurlong
Bryn Gates
Abram
71
Ashton-In-Makerfield
Bickershaw
72
Westleigh
LEIGH
73
Higher Folds
Pennington
Lowton Common
Astley
74
Worsley
75
Boothstown
Swinton
76
Eccles
KIRKBY
ST. HELENS
Knowsley
Prescot
Haydock
86
Golborne
87
NEWTON-LE-WILLOWS
Collins Green
Lowton
Glazebury
Twiss Green
88
89
Culcheth
Croft
90
Irlam
91
Davyhulme
Flixton
92
URMSTON
Trafford Park
Burtonwood
BURTONWOOD
Huyton
Cadishead
Glazebrook
102
Rixton
Warburton
103
Carrington
Partington
Mossbrow
104
Ashton upon Mersey
Woodhouses
Broadheath
Timperley
LIVERPOOL
WIDNES
WARRINGTON
Halewood
Oughtrington
Lymm
112
Dunham Woodhouses
113
ALTRINCHAM
114
Hale
Bowdon
Broomedge
Manchester Ship Canal
Bridgewater Canal
Appleton Thorn
Speke
LIVERPOOL JOHN LENNON AIRPORT
RUNCORN
High Legh
Bucklow Hill
LARGE SCALE 6 ALTRINCHAM TOWN CENTRE
RIVER MERSEY
Mobberley
132
133
KNUTSFORD
ELLESMERE PORT
Frodsham
River Weaver
Budworth Mere
Pick Mere
CHESTER
Helsby
NORTHWICH
Weaverham
DELAMERE FOREST PARK
Davenham
M6
M61
M62
M56
M57
M58
M60
M65
M53
SCALE
0 1 2 3 4 5 Miles
0 1 2 3 4 5 6 7 Kilometres

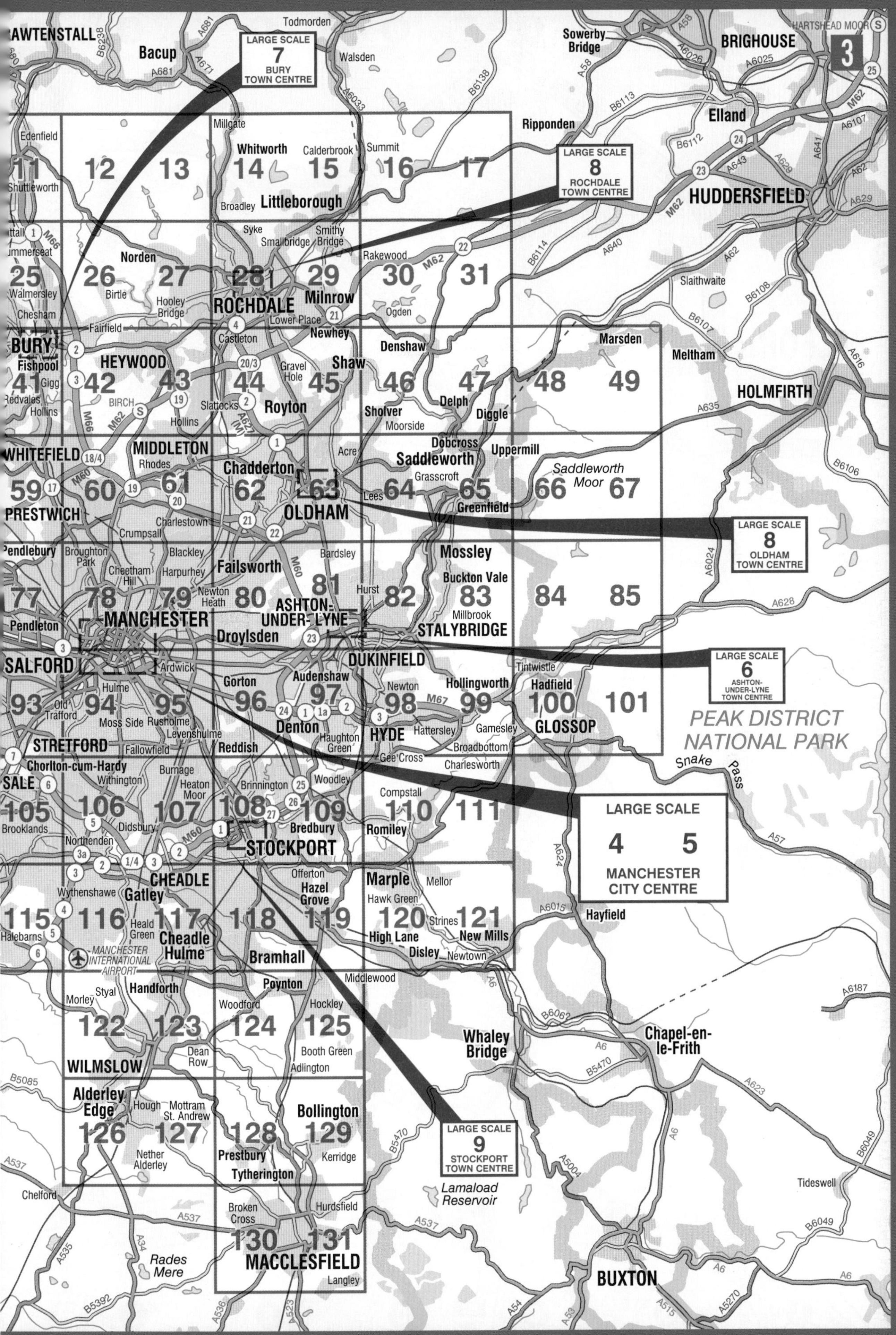
RAWTENSTALL
Bacup
Todmorden
Walsden
Sowerby Bridge
HARTSHEAD MOOR
BRIGHOUSE
LARGE SCALE 7 BURY TOWN CENTRE
Elland
Ripponden
Millgate
LARGE SCALE 8 ROCHDALE TOWN CENTRE
HUDDERSFIELD
Edenfield
Shuttleworth
Whitworth
Calderbrook
Summit
Broadley
Littleborough
Syke
Smallbridge
Smithy Bridge
Rakewood
Norden
Birtle
Hooley Bridge
ROCHDALE
Milnrow
Ogden
Slaithwaite
Walmersley
Chesham
Fairfield
Lower Place
Newhey
Castleton
BURY
Fishpool
Gigg
Redvales
Hollins
HEYWOOD
BIRCH
Gravel Hole
Shaw
Denshaw
Marsden
Meltham
Royton
Slattocks
Sholver
Moorside
Delph
Diggle
HOLMFIRTH
WHITEFIELD
MIDDLETON
Rhodes
Chadderton
Acre
Dobcross
Saddleworth
Uppermill
Grasscroft
Saddleworth Moor
PRESTWICH
Lees
OLDHAM
Greenfield
Charlestown
Crumpsall
LARGE SCALE 8 OLDHAM TOWN CENTRE
Pendlebury
Broughton Park
Cheetham Hill
Blackley
Harpurhey
Failsworth
Bardsley
Mossley
Newton Heath
Hurst
Buckton Vale
Millbrook
ASHTON-UNDER-LYNE
STALYBRIDGE
Pendleton
MANCHESTER
Droylsden
SALFORD
Ardwick
DUKINFIELD
Tintwistle
LARGE SCALE 6 ASHTON-UNDER-LYNE TOWN CENTRE
Gorton
Audenshaw
Newton
Hollingworth
Hadfield
Hulme
Old Trafford
Moss Side
Rusholme
Levenshulme
Denton
HYDE
Hattersley
Gamesley
GLOSSOP
PEAK DISTRICT NATIONAL PARK
STRETFORD
Fallowfield
Reddish
Haughton Green
Gee Cross
Broadbottom
Charlesworth
Snake Pass
Chorlton-cum-Hardy
Burnage
Withington
SALE
Heaton Moor
Brinnington
Woodley
Compstall
LARGE SCALE 4 5 MANCHESTER CITY CENTRE
Brooklands
Didsbury
Bredbury
Romiley
Northenden
STOCKPORT
CHEADLE
Offerton
Hazel Grove
Marple
Mellor
Hawk Green
Wythenshawe
Gatley
Heald Green
Cheadle Hulme
Strines
High Lane
Disley
New Mills
Newtown
Hayfield
Halebarns
MANCHESTER INTERNATIONAL AIRPORT
Bramhall
Middlewood
Morley
Styal
Handforth
Poynton
Woodford
Hockley
Whaley Bridge
Chapel-en-le-Frith
Dean Row
Booth Green
Adlington
WILMSLOW
Alderley Edge
Hough
Mottram St. Andrew
Bollington
LARGE SCALE 9 STOCKPORT TOWN CENTRE
Nether Alderley
Prestbury
Kerridge
Tytherington
Lamaload Reservoir
Tideswell
Chelford
Broken Cross
Hurdsfield
Rades Mere
MACCLESFIELD
Langley
BUXTON
11 12 13 14 15 16 17
25 26 27 28 29 30 31
41 42 43 44 45 46 47 48 49
59 60 61 62 63 64 65 66 67
77 78 79 80 81 82 83 84 85
93 94 95 96 97 98 99 100 101
105 106 107 108 109 110 111
115 116 117 118 119 120 121
122 123 124 125
126 127 128 129
130 131

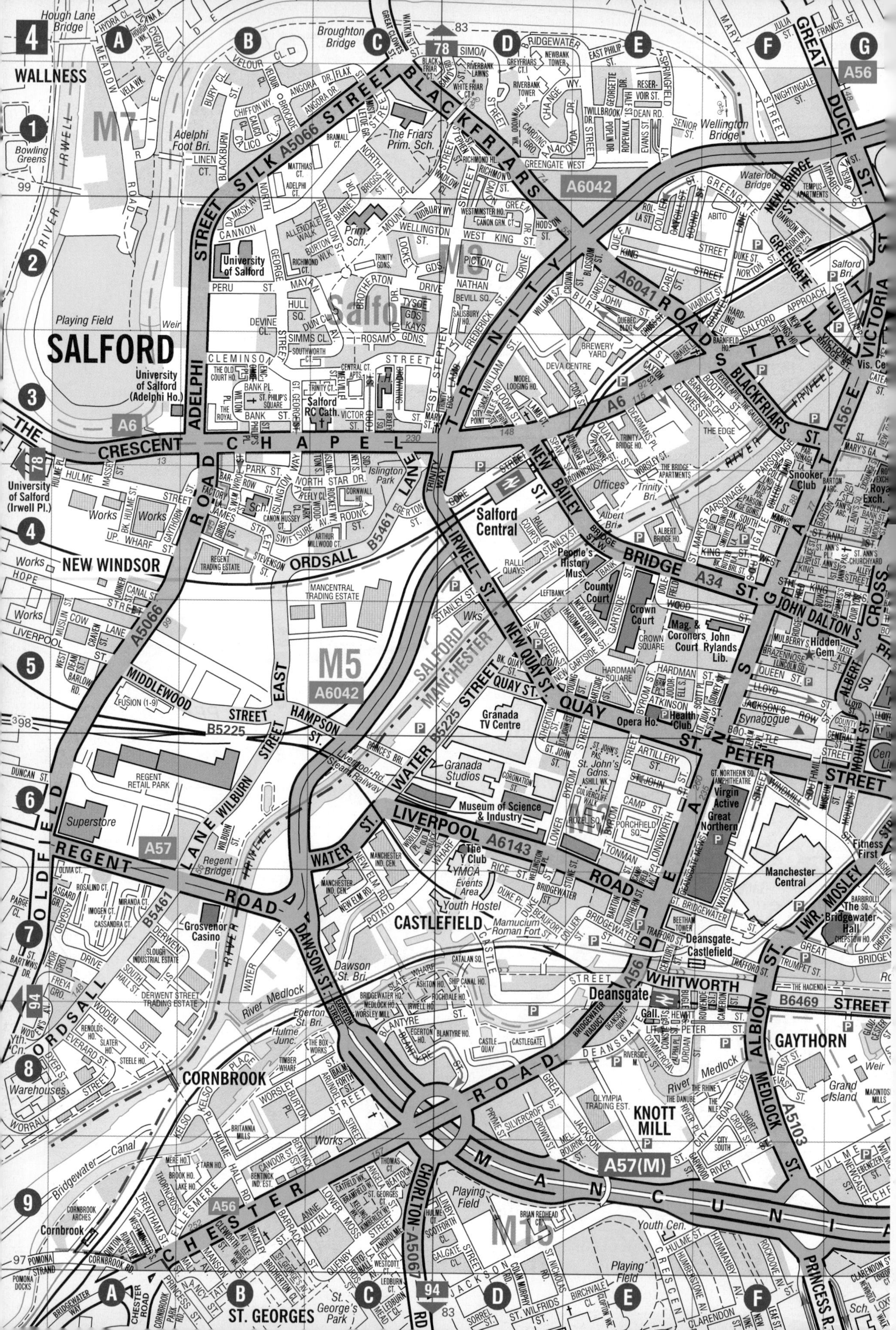
WALLNESS
SALFORD
M7
M3
M5
M15
Salford
University of Salford
University of Salford (Adelphi Ho.)
University of Salford (Irwell Pl.)
Playing Field
Bowling Greens
Adelphi Foot Bri.
Hough Lane Bridge
Broughton Bridge
Wellington Bridge
Waterloo Bridge
Salford Bri.
The Friars Prim. Sch.
Salford RC Cath.
NEW WINDSOR
Islington Park
Salford Central
People's History Mus.
County Court
Crown Court
Mag. & Coroners Court
John Rylands Lib.
Hidden Gem
Granada TV Centre
Granada Studios
Museum of Science & Industry
CASTLEFIELD
Mamucium Roman Fort
Youth Hostel
YMCA
Deansgate-Castlefield
Deansgate
Great Northern
Manchester Central
The Bridgewater Hall
Opera Ho.
Synagogue
Snooker Club
Royal Exch.
Fitness First
REGENT RETAIL PARK
Superstore
MANCENTRAL TRADING ESTATE
REGENT TRADING ESTATE
Grosvenor Casino
SLOUGH INDUSTRIAL ESTATE
DERWENT STREET TRADING ESTATE
OLYMPIA TRADING EST.
KNOTT MILL
GAYTHORN
Grand Island
CORNBROOK
Cornbrook
ST. GEORGES
St. George's Park
Youth Cen.
Hulme Junc.
River Medlock
River Irwell
Bridgewater Canal
Liverpool Rd. Steam Railway
SALFORD MANCHESTER
THE CRESCENT
CHAPEL STREET
BLACKFRIARS ROAD
TRINITY WAY
SILK STREET
ADELPHI STREET
ORDSALL LANE
REGENT ROAD
LIVERPOOL ROAD
QUAY STREET
BRIDGE STREET
DEANSGATE
WHITWORTH STREET
PETER STREET
ALBION STREET
CHESTER ROAD
MANCUNIAN WAY
A6
A6042
A6041
A5066
A56
A57
A57(M)
A34
A6143
B5225
B5461
B6469
A5067
A5103
78
94
83
99
98
97

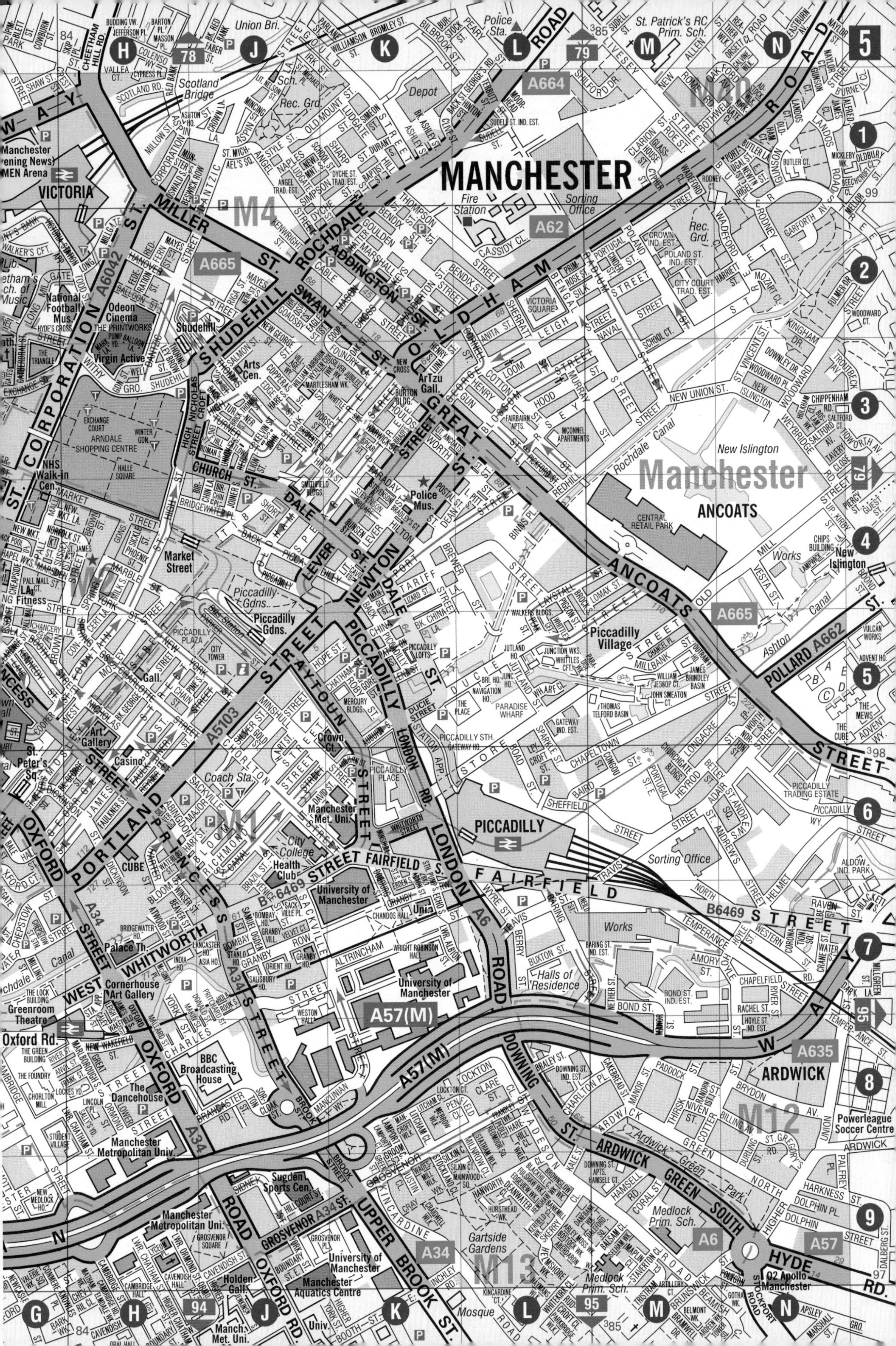
5
H
J
K
L
M
N
G
1
2
3
4
5
6
7
8
9
78
79
94
95
MANCHESTER
Manchester
M4
M1
M12
M13
A664
A665
A62
A6042
A5103
A34
A6
A57(M)
A635
A662
A57
B6469
VICTORIA
PICCADILLY
Oxford Rd.
ANCOATS
ARDWICK
New Islington
Manchester Evening News MEN Arena
National Football Mus.
Odeon Cinema
THE PRINTWORKS
Virgin Active
Shudehill
Arts Cen.
ARNDALE SHOPPING CENTRE
EXCHANGE COURT
HALLE SQUARE
NHS Walk-in Cen.
Market Street
Piccadilly Gdns.
PICCADILLY PLAZA
CITY TOWER
Art Gallery
Casino
St. Peter's Sq.
Coach Sta.
Crown Ct.
PICCADILLY PLACE
Manchester Met. Uni.
City College
Health Club
University of Manchester
Palace Th.
CUBE
Cornerhouse Art Gallery
Greenroom Theatre
BBC Broadcasting House
The Dancehouse
Manchester Metropolitan Univ.
Manchester Metropolitan Uni.
Sugden Sports Cen.
Holden Gall.
University of Manchester Aquatics Centre
Gartside Gardens
Medlock Prim. Sch.
O2 Apollo Manchester
Powerleague Soccer Centre
Piccadilly Village
PARADISE WHARF
CENTRAL RETAIL PARK
VICTORIA SQUARE
Fire Station
Sorting Office
Police Sta.
Police Mus.
ArTzu Gall.
Depot
Rec. Grd.
Scotland Bridge
Union Bri.
St. Patrick's RC Prim. Sch.
Works
Halls of Residence
PICCADILLY TRADING ESTATE
Rochdale Canal
Ashton Canal
CORPORATION ST.
MILLER ST.
SHUDEHILL
ROCHDALE ROAD
OLDHAM ROAD
GREAT ANCOATS STREET
OLDHAM STREET
PORTLAND STREET
PRINCESS STREET
OXFORD ROAD
OXFORD STREET
WHITWORTH STREET
WEST
LONDON ROAD
DOWNING STREET
ARDWICK GREEN SOUTH
HYDE RD.
UPPER BROOK ST.
FAIRFIELD STREET
POLLARD STREET
CHURCH ST.
DALE ST.
PICCADILLY
NEWTON STREET
LEVER ST.
DUCIE ST.
GROSVENOR ST.
STOCKPORT ROAD

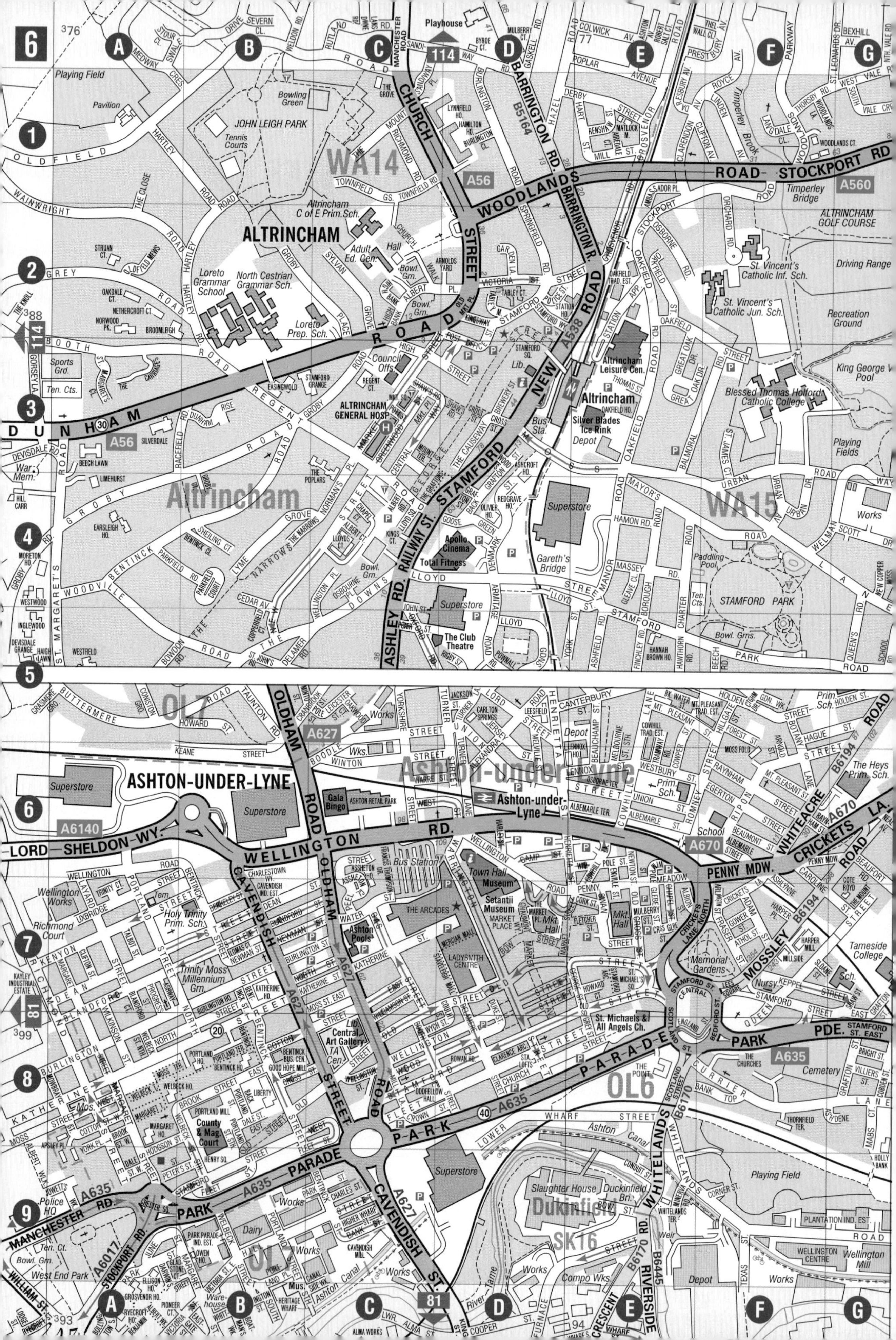
A
B
C
D
E
F
G
1
2
3
4
5
6
7
8
9
376
Playhouse
114
Playing Field
Pavilion
Bowling Green
JOHN LEIGH PARK
Tennis Courts
OLDFIELD
WAINWRIGHT
THE CLOSE
HARTLEY
GREY ROAD
CHURCH
WA14
TOWNFIELD
RICHMOND RD.
Altrincham C of E Prim.Sch.
ALTRINCHAM
Adult Ed. Cen.
Hall
Loreto Grammar School
North Cestrian Grammar Sch.
Loreto Prep. Sch.
STRUAN CT.
OLDFIELD MEWS
OAKDALE CT.
NETHERCROFT CT.
NORWOOD PK.
BROOMLEIGH
THE KNOLL
388
BOOTH
Sports Grd.
Ten. Cts.
GORSEY LA.
MARGARET'S
THE CARRIAGES
EASINGWOLD
STAMFORD GRANGE
D U N H A M
30
A56
SILVERDALE
DEVISDALE RD.
War Mem.
BEECH LAWN
LIMEHURST
HILL CARR
RACEFIELD RD.
REGENT
Council Offs.
REGENT CT.
ALTRINCHAM GENERAL HOSP.
MARKET ST.
THE POPLARS
Altrincham
GROBY
EARSLEIGH HO.
BENTINCK
MORETON HO.
WESTWOOD
INGLEWOOD
DEVISDALE GRANGE
HAIGH LAWN
WESTFIELD
ST. MARGARET'S
WOODVILLE
PARKFIELD RD.
PARKFIELD COURT
LYME
HARROWS
THE NARROWS
NORMAN'S
CEDAR AV.
BOWDON ROAD
THE DOWNS
WELLINGTON PL.
OSBORNE PL.
Bowl. Grn.
KINGS CT.
LLOYDS CT.
ASHLEY RD.
RAILWAY ST.
STAMFORD
NEW
A538 ROAD
Apollo Cinema
Total Fitness
Superstore
The Club Theatre
LLOYD
DENMARK
GOOSE GREEN
ARMITAGE
POWNALL
RIGBY ST.
WOODLANDS
B5164
BARRINGTON RD.
SPRINGFIELD
VICTORIA ST.
TABLEY ST.
STAMFORD SQ.
Lib.
POST OFFICE
Bus Sta.
Altrincham
Altrincham Leisure Cen.
Silver Blades Ice Rink
Depot
OAKFIELD
OAKFIELD TRAD. EST.
STATION APP.
STOCKPORT RD.
GREAT OAK DR.
BALMORAL
MAYOR'S RD.
HAMON RD.
MASSEY
MANOR
BOROUGH RD.
Gareth's Bridge
GLEAVE CL.
CHARTER
FINCHLEY RD.
HAWTHORN
HANNAH BROWN HO.
ASHFIELD RD.
YORK
BEECH
PARK
QUEEN'S
SCHOOL
ROAD
COLWICK AV.
POPLAR AVENUE
DERBY
HART
RENSHAW
MATLOCK M.
MILL ST.
GROSVENOR
CLARENDON
CLIFTON AV.
LINDEN AV.
Timperley Brook
ROYCE
PRESTBURY AV.
PARKWAY
BEXHILL AV.
ST. LEONARDS DR.
WEST VALE
THORSBY RD.
LANGDALE CL.
WOODLANDS CT.
ROAD
STOCKPORT RD
A560
Timperley Bridge
ALTRINCHAM GOLF COURSE
Driving Range
St. Vincent's Catholic Inf. Sch.
St. Vincent's Catholic Jun. Sch.
Recreation Ground
King George V Pool
Blessed Thomas Holford Catholic College
Playing Fields
ST. JAMES CT.
URBAN RD.
URBAN DR.
WA15
Works
WELMAN
SCOTT
Paddling Pool
Ten. Cts.
STAMFORD PARK
Bowl. Grns.
NEW COPPER MOSS
BUTTERMERE
GRASMERE GRO.
CONISTON
OL7
HOWARD ST.
TAUNTON RD.
KEANE STREET
OLDHAM
A627
Works
Wks.
YORKSHIRE
STREET
BOODLE
WINTON
JACKSON ST.
CARLTON SPRINGS
LORD
LEESFIELD
HENRIETTA
CANTERBURY ST.
Depot
BEAUCHAMP ST.
MELBOURNE
Ashton-under-Lyne
Superstore
ASHTON-UNDER-LYNE
Superstore
Gala Bingo
ASHTON RETAIL PARK
WARRE ST.
WEST
Ashton-under-Lyne
ALBEMARLE TER.
A6140
LORD SHELDON WY.
WELLINGTON RD.
CAVENDISH
WELLINGTON
Wellington Works
Richmond Court
Holy Trinity Prim. Sch.
Trinity Moss Millennium Grn.
KAYLEY INDUSTRIAL ESTATE
81
399
Bus Station
THE ARCADES
Town Hall Museum
Setantii Museum
MARKET PLACE
Mkt. Hall
Ashton Pools
LADYSMITH CENTRE
Central Art Gallery
TA Cen.
Lib.
20
County & Mag. Court
PORTLAND MILL
St. Michaels & All Angels Ch.
PARADE
A635
OL6
PARK
40
Police HQ
MANCHESTER RD.
Ten. Ct.
Bowl. Grn.
West End Park
WILLIAM ST.
A6017
STOCKPORT RD.
Works
Dairy
Ware-house
CAVENDISH MILL
Ashton Canal
81
ALMA WORKS
393
WHARF STREET
LOWER
Superstore
Slaughter House
Duckinfield Bri.
Dukinfield
SK16
River Tame
Compo Wks.
B6170 RD.
CRESCENT
RIVERSIDE
B6445
WHITELANDS
SCOTLAND ST.
B6170
CURRIER
BANK TOP
Playing Field
Depot
Works
WELLINGTON CENTRE
Wellington Mill
PLANTATION IND. EST.
THE CHURCHES
Cemetery
THORNFIELD TER.
ASHDENE
MABS CT.
Memorial Gardens
Tameside College
PENNY MDW.
CRICKETS LA.
A670
WHITEACRE
B6194
The Heys Prim. Sch.
MOSSLEY
PARK PDE.
STAMFORD ST. EAST
Prim. Sch.
School
Prim. Sch.
HOLDEN ST.
BOTANY
HAGUE
ARNOLD
MOSS FOLD
RAYNHAM
EGERTON
RIPON
BEAUMONT
STAMFORD ST.
CENTRAL
ENGLAND ST.
BEDFORD ST.
QUEEN
Sch.
Nursy
KEPPEL

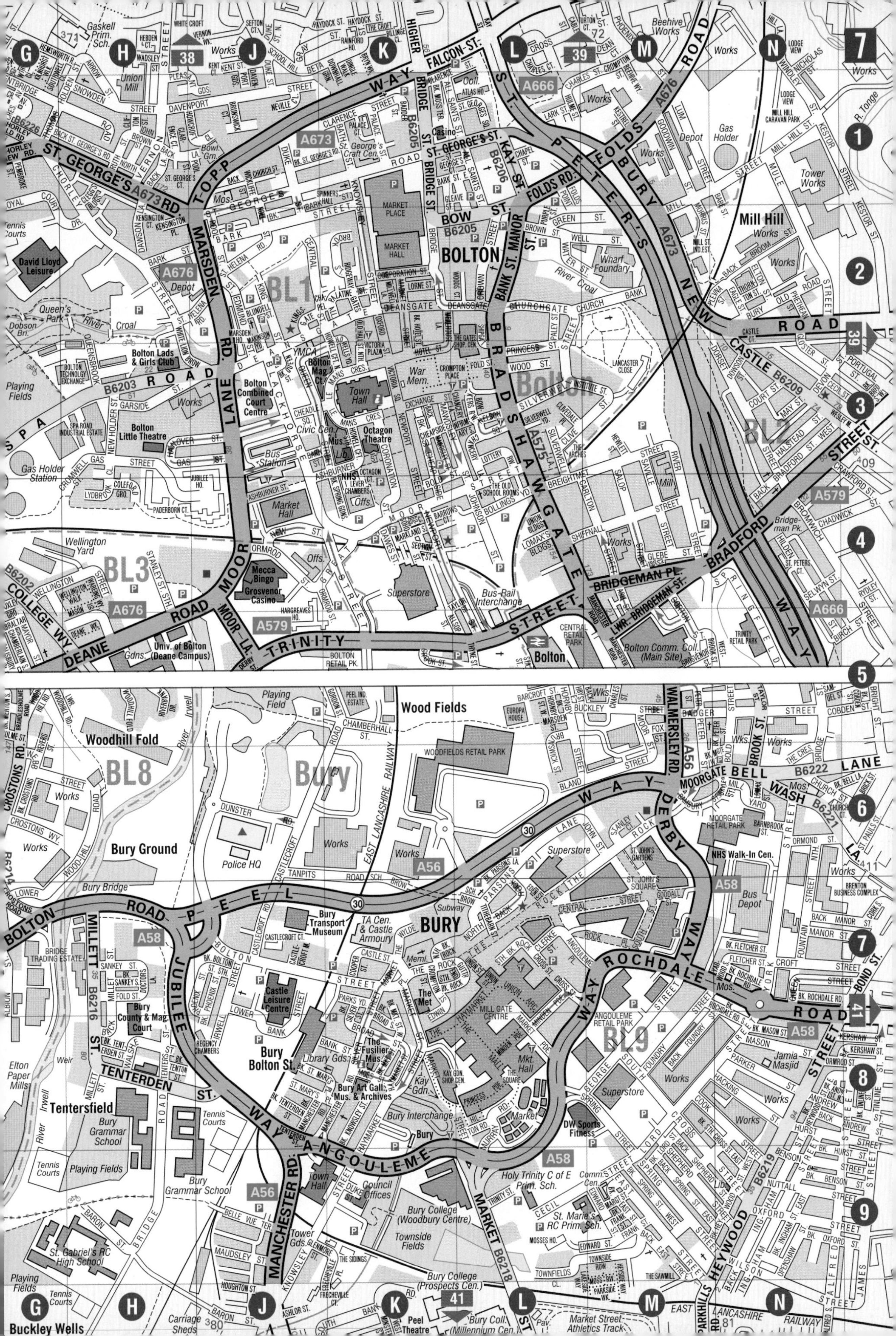

BOLTON
BL1
BL2
BL3
Bolton
Market Place
Market Hall
Town Hall
Octagon Theatre
Bolton Combined Court Centre
Bolton Little Theatre
Bolton Lads & Girls Club
David Lloyd Leisure
Queen's Park
River Croal
Mill Hill
Tower Works
Wharf Foundry
Gas Holder
Gas Holder Station
Mecca Bingo
Grosvenor Casino
Univ. of Bolton (Deane Campus)
Superstore
Bus-Rail Interchange
Bolton
Central Retail Park
Bolton Comm. Coll. (Main Site)
Trinity Retail Park
Bolton Retail Pk.
Playing Fields
Wellington Yard
Spa Road Industrial Estate
ST. GEORGE'S RD.
TOPP WAY
MARSDEN RD.
MOOR LANE
DEANE ROAD
TRINITY STREET
BRADSHAWGATE
ST. PETER'S WAY
BURY NEW ROAD
CASTLE ROAD
BRADFORD STREET
A666
A673
A676
A579
A575
B6205
B6206
B6209
B6226
B6202
B6203
38
39
BURY
BL8
BL9
Bury
Woodhill Fold
Wood Fields
Woodfields Retail Park
Bury Ground
Bury Bridge
Police HQ
Bury Transport Museum
TA Cen. & Castle Armoury
Castle Leisure Centre
Bury County & Mag. Court
Bury Bolton St.
Library Gds.
The Fusiliers Mus.
Bury Art Gall. Mus. & Archives
Bury Interchange
Mill Gate Centre
Mkt. Hall
Angouleme Retail Park
Superstore
DW Sports Fitness
NHS Walk-In Cen.
Bus Depot
Moorgate Retail Park
Brenton Business Complex
Jamia Masjid
Tentersfield
Bury Grammar School
Elton Paper Mills
River Irwell
Town Hall
Council Offices
Bury College (Woodbury Centre)
Townside Fields
Bury College (Prospects Cen.)
Holy Trinity C of E Prim. Sch.
St. Marie's RC Prim. Sch.
St. Gabriel's RC High School
Buckley Wells
Carriage Sheds
Peel Theatre
Market Street Athletics Track
EAST LANCASHIRE RAILWAY
PEEL WAY
BOLTON ROAD
JUBILEE WAY
ANGOULEME WAY
DERBY WAY
ROCHDALE ROAD
MANCHESTER RD.
WALMERSLEY RD.
HEYWOOD STREET
A56
A58
B6216
B6218
B6219
B6221
B6222
41
G
H
J
K
L
M
N
1
2
3
4
5
6
7
8
9

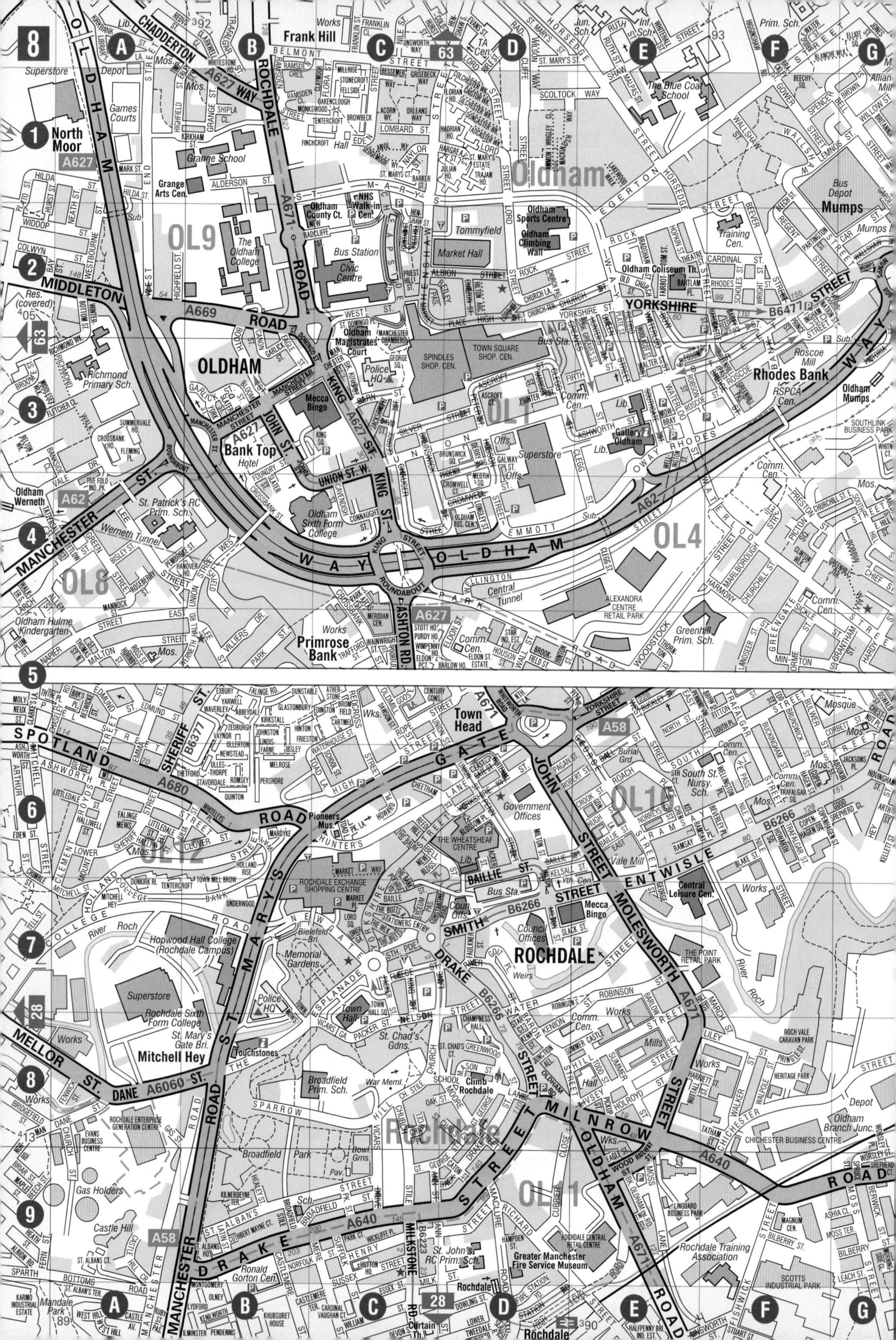
A
B
C
D
E
F
G
1
2
3
4
5
6
7
8
9
63
28
Frank Hill
North Moor
A627
Superstore
Depot
Games Courts
Grange School
Grange Arts Cen.
OL9
The Oldham College
CHADDERTON
ROCHDALE ROAD
A627 WAY
A671
OLDHAM WAY
MIDDLETON ROAD
A669
Res. (covered)
Richmond Primary Sch.
OLDHAM
Oldham County Ct.
NHS Walk-in Cen.
Bus Station
Civic Centre
Tommyfield
Market Hall
Oldham Sports Centre
Oldham Climbing Wall
Oldham
The Blue Coat School
Training Cen.
Bus Depot
Mumps
Oldham Coliseum Th.
YORKSHIRE STREET
B6477
Oldham Magistrates Court
Police HQ
SPINDLES SHOP. CEN.
TOWN SQUARE SHOP. CEN.
Bus Sta.
Comm. Cen.
Lib.
Gallery Oldham
OL1
Rhodes Bank
Roscoe Mill
RSPCA Cen.
Oldham Mumps
SOUTHLINK BUSINESS PARK
Mecca Bingo
Bank Top
Hotel
A627 KING ST.
MANCHESTER STREET
UNION ST. W.
Superstore
Oldham Sixth Form College
Oldham Werneth
A62
MANCHESTER ST.
St. Patrick's RC Prim. Sch.
Werneth Tunnel
OL8
OL4
Central Tunnel
ALEXANDRA CENTRE RETAIL PARK
Greenhill Prim. Sch.
Oldham Hulme Kindergarten
Works
Primrose Bank
MERIDIAN CEN.
ASHTON RD.
A627
Comm. Cen.
SPOTLAND
A680
ROAD
SHERIFF ST.
B6377
OL12
Town Head
A671
GATE
YORKSHIRE STREET
A58
JOHN STREET
Pioneers Mus.
ROCHDALE EXCHANGE SHOPPING CENTRE
THE WHEATSHEAF CENTRE
Government Offices
OL16
South St. Nursy. Sch.
Comm. Cen.
Mosque
B6266
ENTWISLE
Vale Mill
Central Leisure Cen.
Works
River Roch
Hopwood Hall College (Rochdale Campus)
Memorial Gardens
Bus Sta.
Coun. Offs.
SMITH STREET
Mecca Bingo
Council Offices
ROCHDALE
Weirs
THE POINT RETAIL PARK
MOLESWORTH
Superstore
Rochdale Sixth Form College
St. Mary's Gate Bri.
Mitchell Hey
Police HQ
Town Hall
Touchstones
St. Chad's Gdns.
War Meml.
Broadfield Prim. Sch.
Climb Rochdale
MELLOR ST.
DANE
A6060 ST.
ST. MARY'S
MANCHESTER ROAD
ROCHDALE ENTERPRISE GENERATION CENTRE
EVANS BUSINESS CENTRE
Gas Holders
Castle Hill
Broadfield Park
Bowl. Grns.
Rochdale
DRAKE STREET
B6266
MILNROW
OLDHAM
A671
A640
OL11
Comm. Cen.
Works
Mills
Hall
ROCH VALE CARAVAN PARK
HERITAGE PARK
Depot
Oldham Branch Junc.
CHICHESTER BUSINESS CENTRE
LINGUARD BUSINESS PARK
MAGNUM CEN.
Rochdale Training Association
SCOTTS INDUSTRIAL PARK
ROCHDALE CENTRAL RETAIL CENTRE
Greater Manchester Fire Service Museum
St. John's RC Prim. Sch.
Ronald Gorton Cen.
A640
B6223
MILKSTONE RD.
Curtain Th.
Rochdale
KARMO INDUSTRIAL ESTATE
Mandale Park
A58
HALFPENNY BRI. IND. EST.

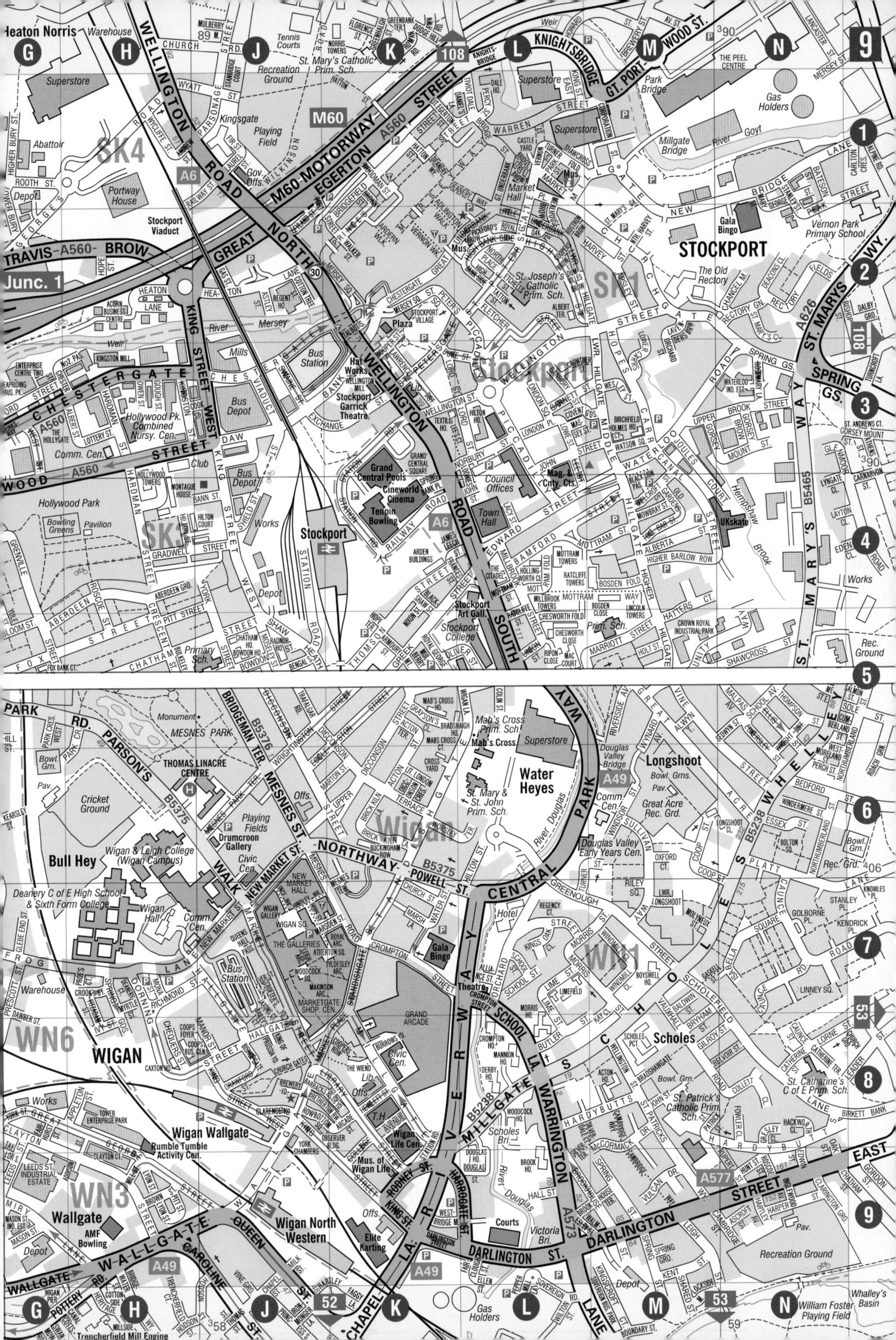
9
Heaton Norris
Warehouse
Superstore
Abattoir
SK4
Portway House
Stockport Viaduct
TRAVIS A560 BROW
Junc. 1
M60 MOTORWAY
EGERTON STREET
A560
GREAT NORTH ROAD
WELLINGTON ROAD NORTH
WELLINGTON ROAD SOUTH
KNIGHTSBRIDGE
GT. PORTWOOD ST.
Recreation Ground
St. Mary's Catholic Prim. Sch.
Tennis Courts
Kingsgate
Playing Field
Gov. Offs.
The Peel Centre
Park Bridge
Gas Holders
River Goyt
Millgate Bridge
Market Hall
Mus.
Gala Bingo
Vernon Park Primary School
STOCKPORT
The Old Rectory
St. Joseph's Catholic Prim. Sch.
SK1
Stockport
Plaza
Bus Station
Hat Works
Stockport Garrick Theatre
River Mersey
Weir
Mills
Bus Depot
Hollywood Pk. Combined Nursy. Cen.
CHESTERGATE
KING STREET WEST
Comm. Cen.
Club
Hollywood Park
Bowling Greens
Pavilion
SK3
Works
Grand Central Pools
Cineworld Cinema
Tenpin Bowling
Stockport
Council Offices
Town Hall
Mag. & Cnty. Cts.
UKskate
Hempshaw Brook
Depot
Stockport Art Gall.
Stockport College
Prim. Sch.
Primary Sch.
Crown Royal Industrial Park
Rec. Ground
ST. MARY'S WAY
B5465
A626
A6
Works
108
M60
A6
30
PARK
MESNES PARK
Monument
PARSON'S WALK
THOMAS LINACRE CENTRE
Cricket Ground
Bull Hey
Wigan & Leigh College (Wigan Campus)
Deanery C of E High School & Sixth Form College
Wigan Hall
Comm. Cen.
Playing Fields
Drumcroon Gallery
Civic Cen.
Wigan
NORTHWAY
POWELL ST.
B5375
B5376
Mab's Cross Prim. Sch.
Mab's Cross
Superstore
Water Heyes
St. Mary & St. John Prim. Sch.
River Douglas
CENTRAL PARK WAY
A49
Douglas Valley Bridge
Longshoot
Great Acre Rec. Grd.
Douglas Valley Early Years Cen.
WN1
WN6
WIGAN
Bus Station
New Market Hall
Wigan Gallery
The Galleries
Marketgate Shop. Cen.
Gala Bingo
Grand Arcade
Civic Cen.
Lib.
Offs.
T.H.
Wigan Life Cen.
Mus. of Wigan Life
Theatre
Hotel
SCHOOL LA.
WARRINGTON LA.
MILLGATE
B5238
Scholes Bri.
Courts
Victoria Bri.
Scholes
St. Patrick's Catholic Prim. Sch.
St. Catharine's C of E Prim. Sch.
Recreation Ground
DARLINGTON STREET
A577
A573
Wigan Wallgate
Rumble Tumble Activity Cen.
Works
WN3
Wallgate
AMF Bowling
Depot
WALLGATE
Wigan North Western
Elite Karting
Gas Holders
Depot
William Foster Playing Field
Whalley's Basin
Trencherfield Mill Engine
52
53
G H J K L M N
1 2 3 4 5 6 7 8 9

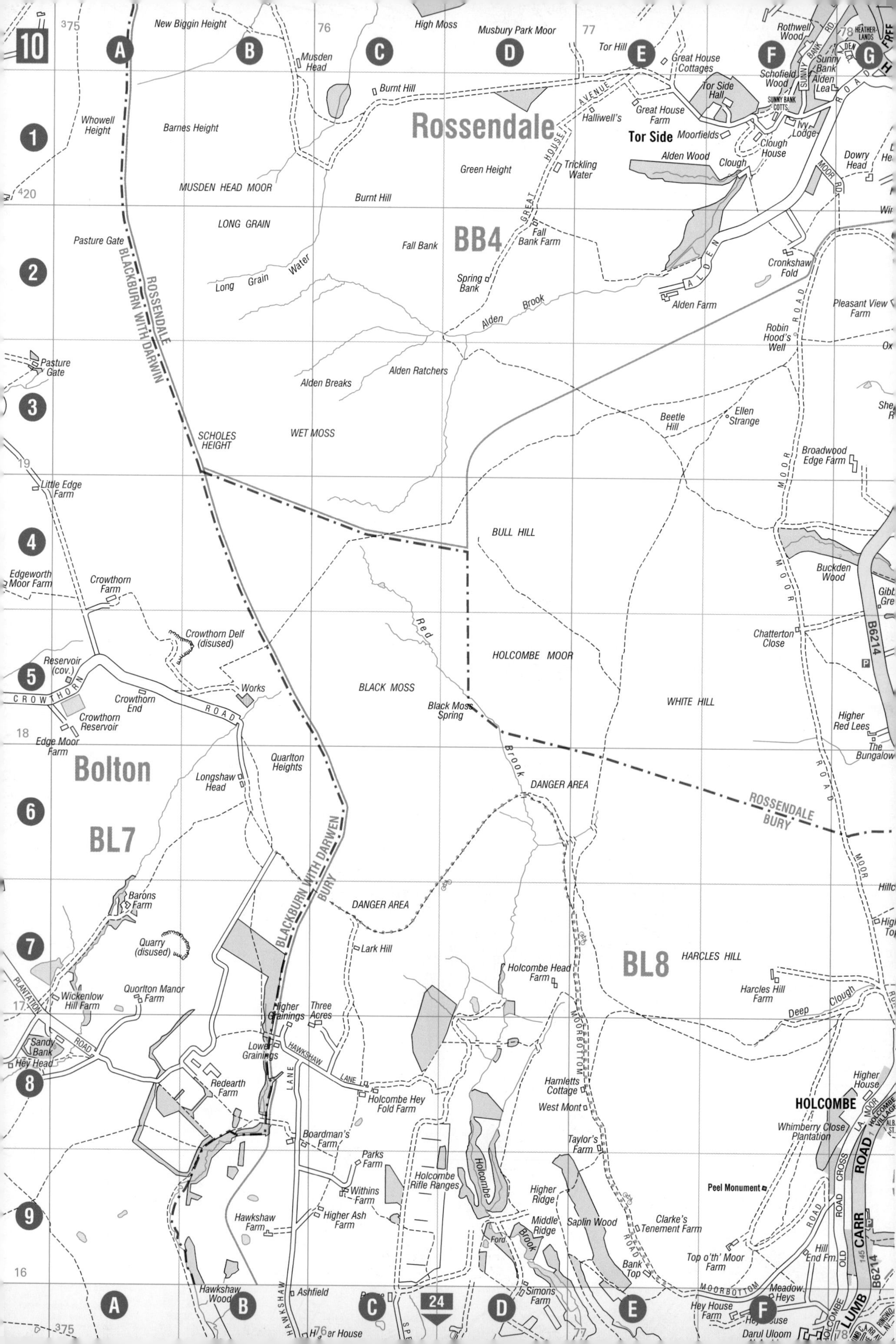

New Biggin Height
High Moss
Musbury Park Moor
Tor Hill
Great House Cottages
Rothwell Wood
Heatherlands
Musden Head
Burnt Hill
Schofield Wood
Sunny Bank
Alden Lea
Tor Side Hall
Whowell Height
Barnes Height
Rossendale
Halliwell's
Great House Farm
Sunny Bank Cotts.
Tor Side
Moorfields
Ivy Lodge
Clough House
Alden Wood
Clough
Trickling Water
Green Height
Dowry Head
MUSDEN HEAD MOOR
Burnt Hill
LONG GRAIN
Pasture Gate
Fall Bank
BB4
Fall Bank Farm
Long Grain Water
Spring Bank
Cronkshaw Fold
Alden Brook
Alden Farm
Pleasant View Farm
Robin Hood's Well
Pasture Gate
Alden Ratchers
Alden Breaks
Beetle Hill
Ellen Strange
SCHOLES HEIGHT
WET MOSS
Broadwood Edge Farm
Little Edge Farm
BULL HILL
Buckden Wood
Edgeworth Moor Farm
Crowthorn Farm
Crowthorn Delf (disused)
HOLCOMBE MOOR
Chatterton Close
Reservoir (cov.)
Works
BLACK MOSS
Black Moss Spring
WHITE HILL
Crowthorn End
CROWTHORN ROAD
Crowthorn Reservoir
Higher Red Lees
Edge Moor Farm
Red Brook
The Bungalow
Bolton
Quarlton Heights
Longshaw Head
DANGER AREA
ROSSENDALE
BURY
BL7
BLACKBURN WITH DARWEN
BURY
Barons Farm
DANGER AREA
Lark Hill
Quarry (disused)
BL8
HARCLES HILL
Holcombe Head Farm
Wickenlow Hill Farm
Quorlton Manor Farm
PLANTATION ROAD
Harcles Hill Farm
Higher Grainings
Three Acres
Deep Clough
Sandy Bank
Lower Grainings
HAWKSHAW LANE
Hey Head
Redearth Farm
Hamletts Cottage
Higher House
Holcombe Hey Fold Farm
West Mont
HOLCOMBE
Whimberry Close Plantation
Boardman's Farm
Taylor's Farm
Parks Farm
Holcombe Rifle Ranges
Holcombe
Peel Monument
Withins Farm
Higher Ridge
Hawkshaw Farm
Higher Ash Farm
Middle Ridge
Saplin Wood
Clarke's Tenement Farm
Ford
Brook
MOORBOTTOM ROAD
Hill End Fm.
Top o'th' Moor Farm
Bank Top
CARR ROAD
B6214
Hawkshaw Wood
Ashfield
Simons Farm
MOORBOTTOM
Meadow Heys
Hey House Farm
Darul Uloom
24
BLACKBURN WITH DARWIN
ROSSENDALE
MOOR ROAD
GREAT HOUSE AVENUE
ALDEN ROAD
LUMB
CROSS LANE
OLD ROAD
A B C D E F G
1 2 3 4 5 6 7 8 9
375 76 77 78
20 19 18 17 16

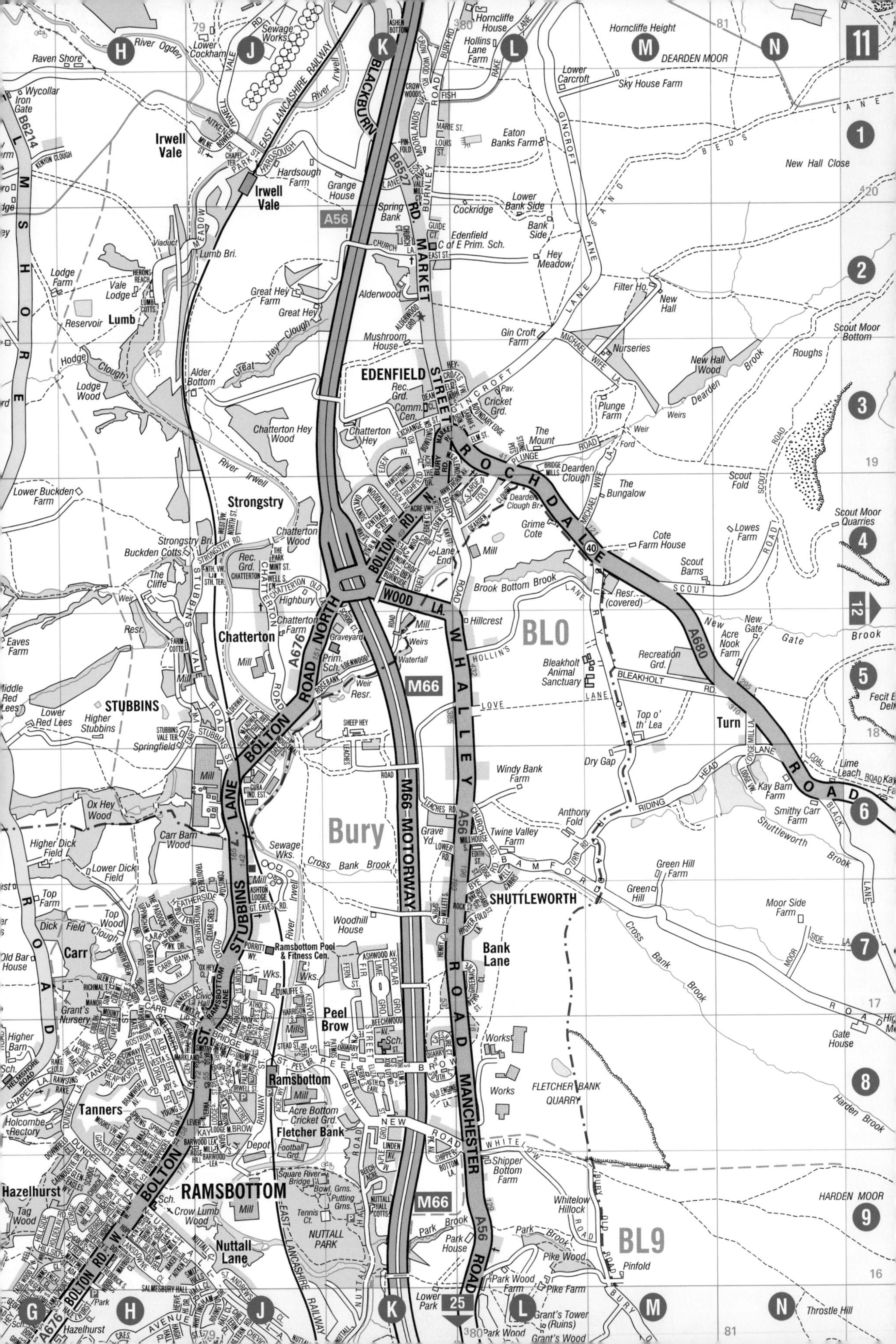

Irwell Vale
Lumb
Edenfield
Strongstry
Chatterton
Stubbins
Bury
BL0
BL9
Shuttleworth
Bank Lane
Peel Brow
Ramsbottom
Carr
Tanners
Hazelhurst
Nuttall Lane
Turn
Horncliffe Height
Dearden Moor
Harden Moor
Fletcher Bank Quarry
Nuttall Park
M66 Motorway
A56
A676
A680
B6527
B6214
Blackburn Rd.
Market Street
Rochdale Road
Bolton Road North
Manchester Road
Whalley Road
River Irwell
River Ogden
East Lancashire Railway
New Hall Close
Scout Moor Bottom
Scout Moor Quarries
Ramsbottom Pool & Fitness Cen.
Bleakholt Animal Sanctuary

12
25

Higher Mount Pleasant
COWPE LOWE
Higher Tippet
Far Fold
BOTTOM'S ROW
MILL COTTS.
Lwr. Boarsgreave Farm
Boarsgreave
Higher Boarsgreave
SAND BEDS LANE
Brown Hill Close
Black Hill
Pike Hill
Puss Height
Lower Fold
Cowpe Hall Farm
Cowpe Brook
Rossendale
BB4
New Hall Close
Back o' th' Lowe
Cowpe Reservoir
Willow Field
Horncliffe Close
Scout Moor Brook
Weirs
Wicken Slack
Waugh's Well
Foe Edge
Scout Moor Bottom
Scout Moor High Level Reservoir
Weir
Cragg High Level Tank
Roughs
Tottington Higher End Moor
Cowpe Moss
Moss Top
SCOUT MOOR
Whittle Pike
BL0
Scout Moor Quarries
Whittle Hill
HAIL STORM HILL
ROSSENDALE
ROCHDALE
Great Lodge
New Gate Brook
Great Ding
HIGHER HILL
Fecit End Delf
Bury
Waterfall
Grain Brook
Naden Brook
Ridge
COAL Lime Leach
Fecit Hill
Kay Close Farm
ROCHDALE
Grain Barn
Rochdale
FECIT ROAD
Fecit Bungalow
Fecit Farm
Cheesden Brook
Top Of Cheesden Pasture
TURF MOOR
Birchen Holts
Ford
FECIT LA.
LANE
Man Road Ditch
Paradise
MOOR SIDE LA.
Cheesden Pasture
Close Nooks Farm
A680
Barn Brook
BAMFORD ROAD
Higher Moss
Gate House
Knowl Hill
Harden Brook
Tom Hill
Red Lumb Brook
KNOWL MOOR
EDGE
Cheesden Bridge
Cheesden Barn
Wham Hill
EDENFIELD
Cheesden
Wham Hill Farm
Cheesden Fold
Gate
Kill
HARDEN MOOR
BL9
CLOSE
Lumb Bridge
Lark Hill
CHEESDEN
OL11
Royds Brook
Higher Red Lumb
Moorlands
CROSTON
Ashworth Moor
Middle Red Lumb Farm
Farther Red Lumb
Throstle Hill
Croston Close Upper Bridge
ASHWORTH MOOR RESERVOIR
26
ROAD
Lower
Higher Knowl

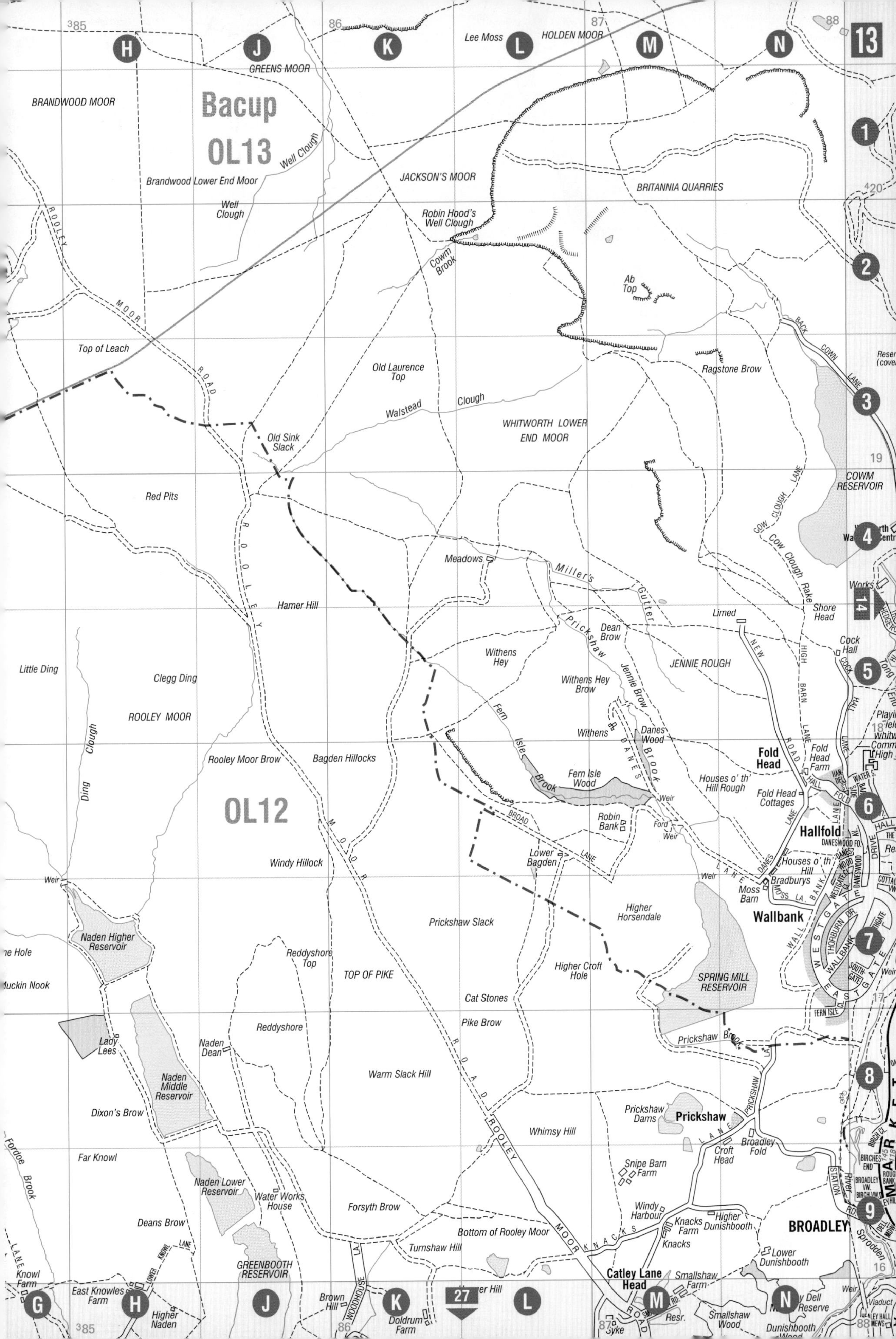
Bacup
OL13
OL12
BRANDWOOD MOOR
GREENS MOOR
Lee Moss
HOLDEN MOOR
Brandwood Lower End Moor
Well Clough
JACKSON'S MOOR
BRITANNIA QUARRIES
Robin Hood's Well Clough
Cowm Brook
Ab Top
Top of Leach
Old Laurence Top
Walstead Clough
Ragstone Brow
WHITWORTH LOWER END MOOR
Old Sink Slack
Red Pits
COWM RESERVOIR
Meadows
Miller's Gutter
Hamer Hill
Limed
Shore Head
Dean Brow
Withens Hey
Withens Hey Brow
JENNIE ROUGH
Jennie Brow
Cock Hall
Little Ding
Clegg Ding
ROOLEY MOOR
Withens
Danes Wood
Fold Head
Fold Head Farm
Rooley Moor Brow
Bagden Hillocks
Fern Isle Wood
Houses o' th' Hill Rough
Fold Head Cottages
Hallfold
Robin Bank
Ford
Weir
Windy Hillock
Lower Bagden
Houses o' th' Hill
Bradburys
Moss Barn
Wallbank
Prickshaw Slack
Higher Horsendale
Naden Higher Reservoir
Reddyshore Top
TOP OF PIKE
Higher Croft Hole
SPRING MILL RESERVOIR
Cat Stones
Pike Brow
Reddyshore
Lady Lees
Naden Dean
Prickshaw Brook
Naden Middle Reservoir
Warm Slack Hill
Dixon's Brow
Prickshaw Dams
Prickshaw
Whimsy Hill
Croft Head
Broadley Fold
Far Knowl
Snipe Barn Farm
Naden Lower Reservoir
Water Works House
Forsyth Brow
Windy Harbour
Knacks Farm
Higher Dunishbooth
BROADLEY
Deans Brow
Bottom of Rooley Moor
Knacks
Turnshaw Hill
Lower Dunishbooth
GREENBOOTH RESERVOIR
Catley Lane Head
Smallshaw Farm
Knowl Farm
East Knowles Farm
Higher Naden
Brown Hill
Doldrum Farm
Smallshaw Wood
Dunishbooth Wood
Resr.
Syke
Fordoe Brook
ROOLEY MOOR ROAD
BACK COWN LANE
COW CLOUGH LANE
Cow Clough Rake
NEW ROAD
HIGH BARN LANE
BROAD LANE
DANES BROOK
DANES LANE
MOSS LA.
WESTGATE
EASTGATE
THORBURN DR.
PRICKSHAW LANE
KNACKS LANE
WOODHOUSE LA.
LOWER KNOWL LANE
STATION RD
Spodden
Viaduct
HEALEY HALL MEWS
27
14
385
86
87
88
H
J
K
L
M
N
G
1
2
3
4
5
6
7
8
9
20
19
18
17
16

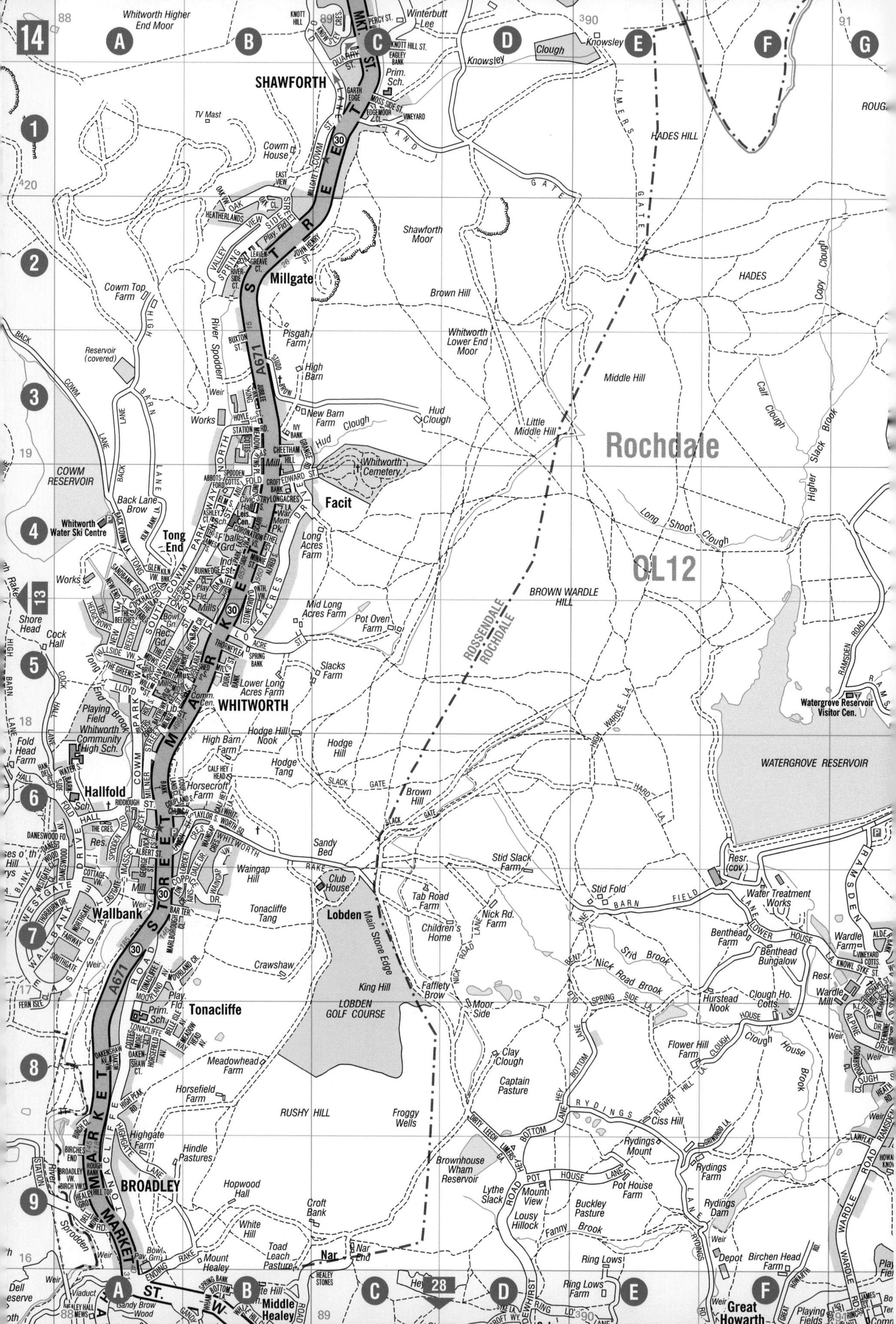
Whitworth Higher End Moor
SHAWFORTH
Winterbutt Lee
Knowsley Clough
Knowsley
HADES HILL
TV Mast
Cowm House
Shawforth Moor
Millgate
Cowm Top Farm
Brown Hill
HADES
Copy Clough
Whitworth Lower End Moor
Reservoir (covered)
Pisgah Farm
High Barn
River Spodden
Middle Hill
Calf Clough
Works
New Barn Farm
Hud Clough
Little Middle Hill
Rochdale
Slack Brook
COWM RESERVOIR
Whitworth Cemetery
Facit
Higher
Back Lane Brow
Whitworth Water Ski Centre
Tong End
Long Acres Farm
Long Shoot Clough
OL12
Works
Shore Head
BROWN WARDLE HILL
Mid Long Acres Farm
Pot Oven Farm
ROSSENDALE
ROCHDALE
Cock Hall
Slacks Farm
Lower Long Acres Farm
WHITWORTH
Watergrove Reservoir Visitor Cen.
Playing Field
Whitworth Community High Sch.
Fold Head Farm
High Barn Farm
Hodge Hill Nook
Hodge Hill
Hodge Tang
WATERGROVE RESERVOIR
Hallfold
Horsecroft Farm
Brown Hill
Sandy Bed
Waingap Hill
Stid Slack Farm
Resr. (cov.)
Club House
Stid Fold
Water Treatment Works
Tab Road Farm
Wallbank
Tonacliffe Tang
Lobden
Main Stone Edge
Children's Home
Nick Rd. Farm
Benthead Farm
Benthead Bungalow
Wardle Farm
Crawshaw
Stid Brook
Nick Road Brook
King Hill
LOBDEN GOLF COURSE
Fafflety Brow
Moor Side
Hurstead Nook
Clough Ho. Cotts.
Wardle Mill
Tonacliffe
Clay Clough
Flower Hill Farm
Meadowhead Farm
Captain Pasture
Clough House Brook
Horsefield Farm
RUSHY HILL
Froggy Wells
Ciss Hill
Highgate Farm
Hindle Pastures
Brownhouse Wham Reservoir
Rydings Mount
Rydings Farm
BROADLEY
Hopwood Hall
Lythe Slack
Mount View
Pot House Farm
Lousy Hillock
Buckley Pasture
Rydings Dam
Croft Bank
White Hill
Fanny Brook
Toad Leach Pasture
Nar
Nar End
Mount Healey
Ring Lows
Depot
Birchen Head Farm
Ring Lows Farm
Dell Reserve
Viaduct
Gandy Brow Wood
Middle Healey
Great Howarth
Playing Fields
A671
MARKET STREET
28
13

Todmorden
OL14
Littleborough
OL15
CALDERDALE
ROCHDALE
Higher Allerscholes
Clunter Clough
Rough Stones
Stone House Bri.
Football Pitches
Cranberry Dam
White Slack
Cranberry Moss
Long Wall
Friezland
Moorhey Wood
Bankhey Wood
Warland Bri.
Warland
Moor Hey Barn
Moor Hey Farm
Moorhey Clough
Moor Bank Clough
Warland Gate End
Horse Pasture Clough
Noon Hill Clough
Noon Hill
Moorhey Flat
Brock Holes Clough
Long Hill
Shore Moor
Birching Brow
Ferny Hill
Reddyshore
Black Clough
Summit Tunnel
Great Hill
Knave Hill Nigher
Knave Hill Farther
Owler Clough Head
Owlet Clough
Crook Moor
Crook Hill
Stubley Cross Hill
Allenden Hill
Calderbrook Moor
Pasture House Plantation
Scout End
Dean Head Fm.
Valley View
Turn Slack Hill
Fox Stones Hill
Old Charles Hill
Blue Pot Brook
Pasture House
Resr. (cov.)
Turn Slack Dam
Turn Slack Clough
Clay Pots Hill
Flight Hill
Cuckoo Hill
Stony Field Farm
Lower Turn Slack Hill
Dearden's Pasture
Slack Farm
Pike Hill
Long Hill
Brook
Wardle
Ringing Pots Hill
Hills Clough
Grimes
CALDERBROOK
Higher Stone Pits
Blackbrow Hill
Pennine Trout Fishery
Stansfield Hill
Far Hey Head
Near Hey Head
Handle Hall
Dobbin Hill
Lower Stone Pits
Long Clough
Stony Brook
Hey Bottom Farm
Hill Top Farm
Whitfield Farm
Whitfield
Higher Lee Slack
Ratcliffe Hill
Long Clough Brook
Higher Newgate
Heights Farm
Clough
Green Hill
Gale
Middle Wood Brook
Higher Shore Wood
Lower Pemmin
Calf Hey
East Hill
High Lea
Higher Shore
Shore Hall
Gorsey Hill Wood
Lower Town Ho.
Wardle Fold
East Top Farm
Higher Shore House
Town House
Playing Fields
New Platt Farm
Sports Cen.
Cricket Grd.
Bent Ho.
Windy Bank Bridge
WARDLE
Middlewood Farm
Shore
Engineering Works
Pedler Brow
Featherstall
Caldermoor
Hare Hill Park
Starring Wood
Higher Starring
Birch Hill
Stubley
Higher Windy Bank Farm
Heathcliffe
Durn
Starring Hill
Middle Starring
Bench Carr
Sports Grd.
Ealees
Ealees Wood
Heritage Cen.
Littleborough
Ben Healey Bri.
Ash Brook
Wardle High Sch.
BIRCH HILL HOSPITAL
Playing Fields
Cemy.
LITTLEBOROUGH
Ealees Brook
Ashbrook Hey
St. Andrew's C of E Prim.
Stubley New Hall
Deanley
Bank Top
Clegg's Wood
Cleggswood Hill
Lane Foot
Weir
ROCHDALE ROAD
A6033
TODMORDEN ROAD
HALIFAX RD.
A58
CHURCH ST.
FEATHERSTALL RD.
NEW RD.
HOLLINGWORTH RD.
B6225
Rochdale Canal
River Roch
HEY HEAD LANE
CALDERBROOK ROAD
SHORE LANE
MIDDLE WOOD LA.
PEDLER LANE
BARN LANE
BANK LANE
HIGHER SHORE ROAD
MOOR GATE LA.
STARRING RD.
CLOUGH ROAD
H
J
K
L
M
N
G
1
2
3
4
5
6
7
8
9
16
29
92
93
94
15

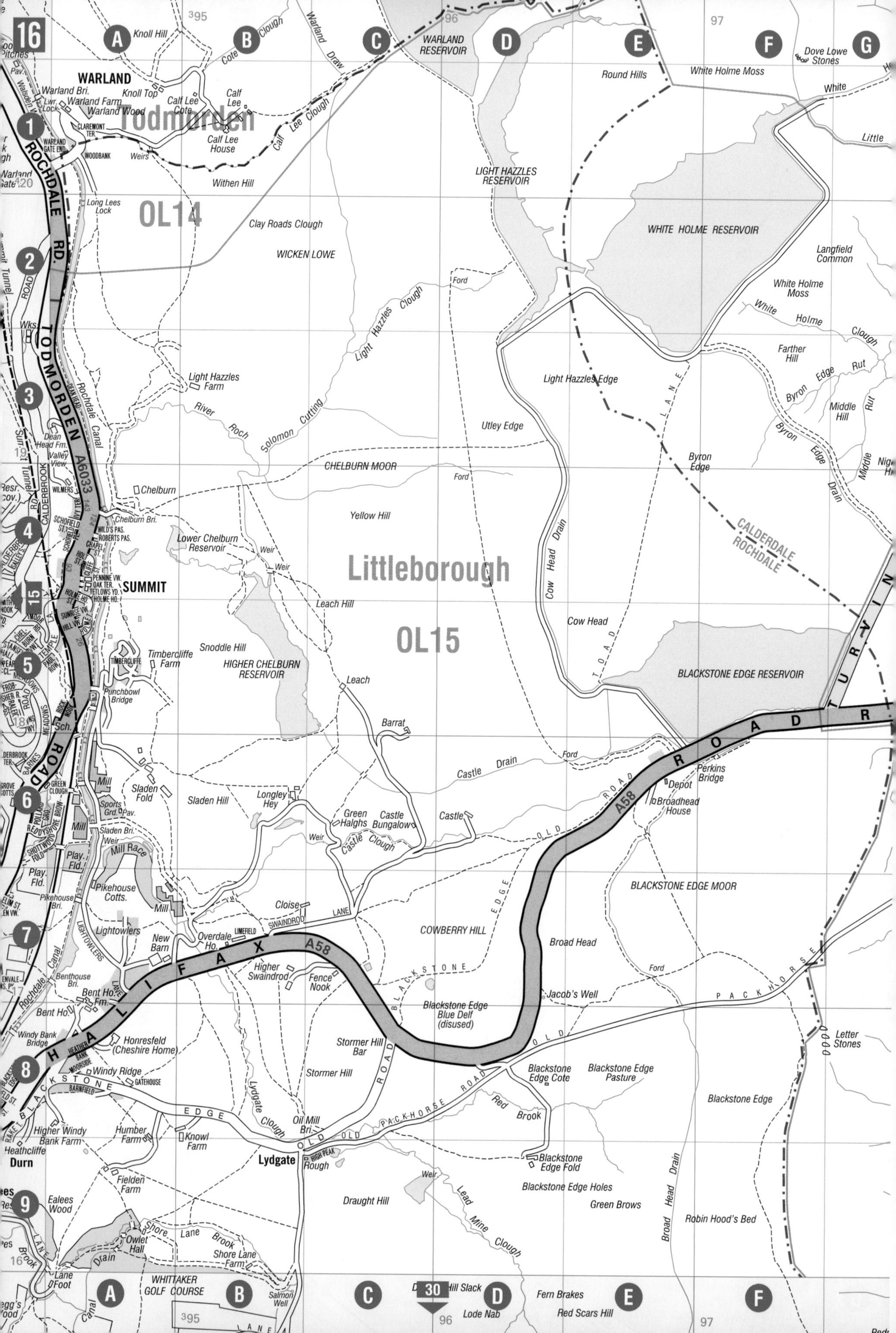

WARLAND
Todmorden
OL14
Littleborough
OL15
SUMMIT
Lydgate
Durn
ROCHDALE RD.
TODMORDEN ROAD
A6033
HALIFAX ROAD
A58
TURVIN ROAD
Knoll Hill
Cote Clough
Warland Draw
WARLAND RESERVOIR
Round Hills
White Holme Moss
Dove Lowe Stones
Warland Bri.
Warland Farm
Warland Wood
Knoll Top
Calf Lee Cote
Calf Lee
Calf Lee Clough
Calf Lee House
Withen Hill
Long Lees Lock
Clay Roads Clough
WICKEN LOWE
LIGHT HAZZLES RESERVOIR
WHITE HOLME RESERVOIR
Langfield Common
White Holme Moss
White Holme Clough
Farther Hill
Byron Edge Rut
Middle Hill
Byron Edge Drain
Byron Edge
Light Hazzles Clough
Light Hazzles Farm
Light Hazzles Edge
River Roch
Solomon Cutting
Utley Edge
CHELBURN MOOR
Chelburn
Chelburn Bri.
Yellow Hill
Lower Chelburn Reservoir
Weir
Leach Hill
Cow Head Drain
Cow Head
CALDERDALE
ROCHDALE
Timbercliffe Farm
Snoddle Hill
HIGHER CHELBURN RESERVOIR
Leach
BLACKSTONE EDGE RESERVOIR
Punchbowl Bridge
Barrat
Castle Drain
Ford
Perkins Bridge
Depot
Broadhead House
Sladen Fold
Sladen Hill
Longley Hey
Green Halghs
Castle Bungalow
Castle
Castle Clough
Mill
Sladen Bri.
Mill Race
Pikehouse Cotts.
Cloise
Swaindrod Lane
BLACKSTONE EDGE MOOR
COWBERRY HILL
Lightowlers
New Barn
Overdale Ho.
Broad Head
Higher Swaindrod
Fence Nook
Blackstone Edge Blue Delf (disused)
Jacob's Well
Packhorse
Letter Stones
Bent Ho. Fm.
Bent Ho.
Windy Bank Bridge
Honresfeld (Cheshire Home)
Windy Ridge
Stormer Hill Bar
Stormer Hill
Blackstone Edge Cote
Blackstone Edge Pasture
Blackstone Edge
Red Brook
Higher Windy Bank Farm
Heathcliffe
Humber Farm
Knowl Farm
Lydgate Clough
Oil Mill Bri.
Old Packhorse Road
Rough
Blackstone Edge Fold
Blackstone Edge Holes
Fielden Farm
Draught Hill
Lead Mine Clough
Green Brows
Broad Head Drain
Robin Hood's Bed
Ealees Wood
Owlet Hall
Shore Lane
Shore Lane Farm
Brook
Lane Foot
WHITTAKER GOLF COURSE
Salmon Well
Hill Slack
Fern Brakes
Red Scars Hill
Lode Nab
Rochdale Canal
Play. Fld.
Sports Grd.

15
30

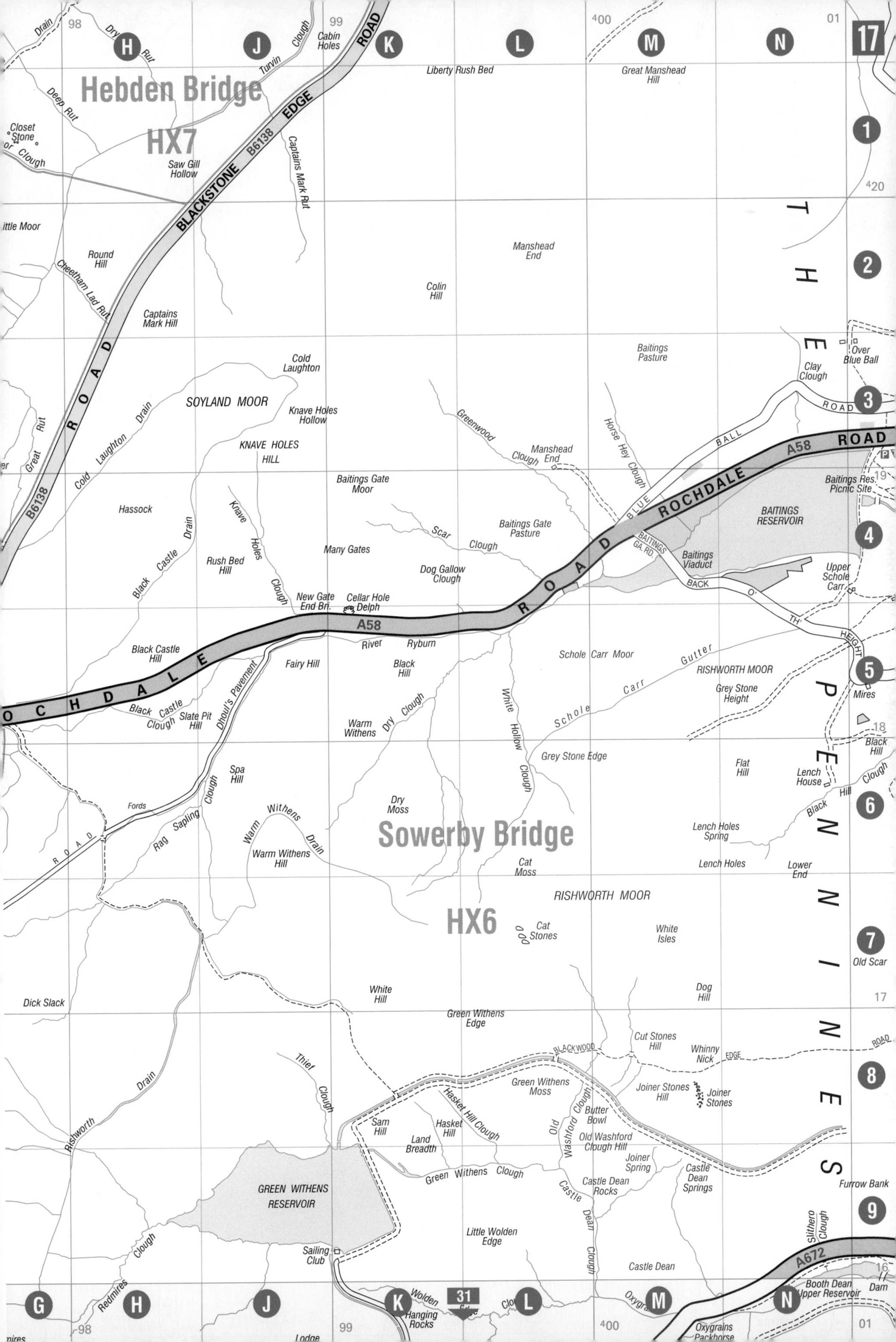

Hebden Bridge
HX7
Sowerby Bridge
HX6
BLACKSTONE EDGE ROAD
B6138
ROCHDALE ROAD
A58
BLUE BALL ROAD
BAITINGS GA. RD.
BACK O' TH' HEIGHT
BLACKWOOD EDGE ROAD
A672
THE PENNINES
Liberty Rush Bed
Great Manshead Hill
Cabin Holes
Turvin Clough
Dry Rut
Deep Rut
Closet Stone
Saw Gill Hollow
Captains Mark Rut
Round Hill
Cheetham Lad Rut
Captains Mark Hill
Manshead End
Colin Hill
Baitings Pasture
Over Blue Ball
Clay Clough
Cold Laughton
SOYLAND MOOR
Knave Holes Hollow
KNAVE HOLES HILL
Cold Laughton Drain
Great Rut
Greenwood Clough
Manshead End
Horse Hey Clough
Baitings Gate Moor
Baitings Res. Picnic Site
BAITINGS RESERVOIR
Hassock
Knave Holes Clough
Black Castle Drain
Scar Clough
Baitings Gate Pasture
Many Gates
Rush Bed Hill
Dog Gallow Clough
Baitings Viaduct
Upper Schole Carr
New Gate End Bri.
Cellar Hole Delph
Black Castle Hill
River Ryburn
Fairy Hill
Black Hill
Schole Carr Moor
Schole Carr Gutter
RISHWORTH MOOR
Grey Stone Height
Mires
Black Castle Clough
Slate Pit Hill
Dhoul's Pavement
Warm Withens
Dry Clough
White Hollow Clough
Grey Stone Edge
Black Hill
Flat Hill
Lench House
Black Hill Clough
Spa Hill
Fords
Rag Sapling Clough
Dry Moss
Warm Withens Drain
Warm Withens Hill
Lench Holes Spring
Lench Holes
Lower End
Cat Moss
RISHWORTH MOOR
Cat Stones
White Isles
Old Scar
Dick Slack
White Hill
Green Withens Edge
Dog Hill
Cut Stones Hill
Whinny Nick
Thief Clough
Green Withens Moss
Joiner Stones Hill
Joiner Stones
Rishworth Drain
Sam Hill
Hasket Hill Clough
Hasket Hill
Land Breadth
Old Washford Clough
Butter Bowl
Old Washford Clough Hill
Joiner Spring
Castle Dean Springs
Green Withens Clough
Castle Dean Rocks
GREEN WITHENS RESERVOIR
Furrow Bank
Castle Dean Clough
Little Wolden Edge
Slithero Clough
Sailing Club
Redmires Clough
Castle Dean
Booth Dean Upper Reservoir
Dam
Wolden Edge
Hanging Rocks
Oxygrains Packhorse
Lodge
31

CHARNOCK RICHARD
Charnock House Farm
Lathom's Farm
Christ Church Charnock Richard C of E Prim. Sch.
Charnock Richard Golf Couse
Football Grd.
White Gates Farm
Haydocks Farm
Cowling's Farm
Darlington's Sidings
White Gates Wood
Fishers Farm
Parker's Wood
Three Arch Bridge
Iddon House Farm
Sharrocks Farm
Willow House
Hill Crest
Wood View
Clancutt House
Plymouth Bridge
Glenbarry
Playing Field
YARROW VALLEY WY.
B5252
MOOR RD.
LOWER BURGH WY.
Plock Wood
Lower Burgh
St. Gregory's Catholic Prim. School
WELD BANK
Holy Cross Catholic High Sch.
MYLES STANDISH WAY
Big Wood
Comm. Cen.
BIRKACRE
Burgh Hall
Birkacre Bridge
Yarrow Valley Vis. Cen.
Big Lodge Water
Burgh Wood
Reservoirs
YARROW VALLEY COUNTRY PARK
Spring Wood
Top Lodge
River Yarrow
Saunders' Wood
Saunders' Bank
Duxbury Hall Farm
Silver Well Wood
DUXBURY PARK BUSINESS CEN.
John Wood
Woodside Cottage
FARNWORTH HOUSE ESTATE
Farnworth House
Burgh Wood
Lowe's Tenement
Drybones Wood
Three Ways
GRUNDY'S LANE
The Firs
Duxbury Sawmills
Eller Brook
NEW ROAD COPPULL
B5251
COPPULL ENTERPRISE CENTRE
Reservoir
Orchard Heyes
Clancut Brook
Tanyard Brook
Barker Bri.
Whittle Bridge Farm
Vicarage
SPENDMORE LANE
Coppull Parish C of E Prim. Sch.
COPPULL
PR7
Yew Tree House
Coppull Old Hall
Coppull Hall Wood
Coppull Hall
Green Lane Farm
Highfield
CHAPEL LANE BUS. PK.
Coppull Comm. Leis. Cen.
Lib.
Prim. Sch.
Blainscough Wood
Blainscough Hall
Depot
Football Grd.
Bernhey House
Elmhurst Farm
PRESTON ROAD A49
Coppull Moor
Coppull Moor Farm
Coppull St. John's C of E Prim. Sch.
Coppull Cross Roads
Fiddler's Nook
Bridge Farm
Troy Fold Farm
Pear Tree Farm
The Nook
Coppull Brow Farm
Moss House Farm
Nursery
COPPULL MOOR LANE
Coppull Hill
White Hill Farm
Moorhouse Farm
Hic-Bibi Local Nature Reserve
Holt Farm
Buckow Brook
Aqueduct
Coppull Mill Bridge
Mill Bridge Farm
CHORLEY
WIGAN
The Grange
Bogburn Hall Farm
Dark Lane Bridge
Old Seven Stars Farm
(SPRINGS BROW)
(STARS BROW)
Stars Brook
Hic-Bibi Brook
WN1
Talbot House Farm
A5106 CHORLEY ROAD
Works
Adlington Hall Farm
Wigan
WN6
Cross Farm
Cross Hey Wood
Gorse Hall
Bores Farm
ADLINGTON PARK
Chadwick Farm
Wrennalls Farm
Black Lawyers
Lodge
Langtree
PLATT LANE
Arley Lodge Nature Reserve

34

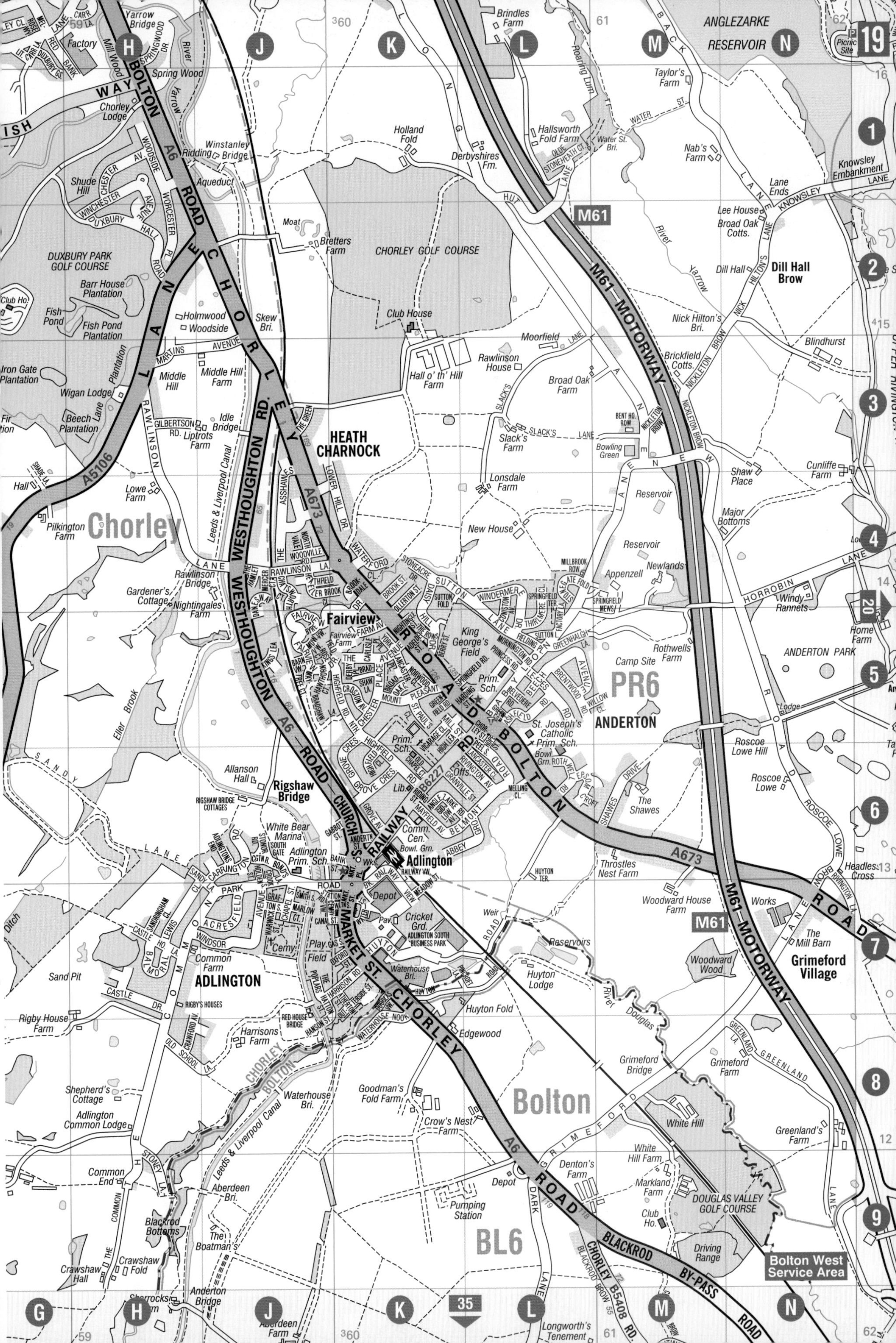
19
Chorley
HEATH CHARNOCK
Fairview
ANDERTON
PR6
Adlington
ADLINGTON
Bolton
BL6
ANGLEZARKE RESERVOIR
CHORLEY GOLF COURSE
DUXBURY PARK GOLF COURSE
DOUGLAS VALLEY GOLF COURSE
ANDERTON PARK
Grimeford Village
Dill Hall Brow
M61 MOTORWAY
Bolton West Service Area
Leeds & Liverpool Canal
20
35

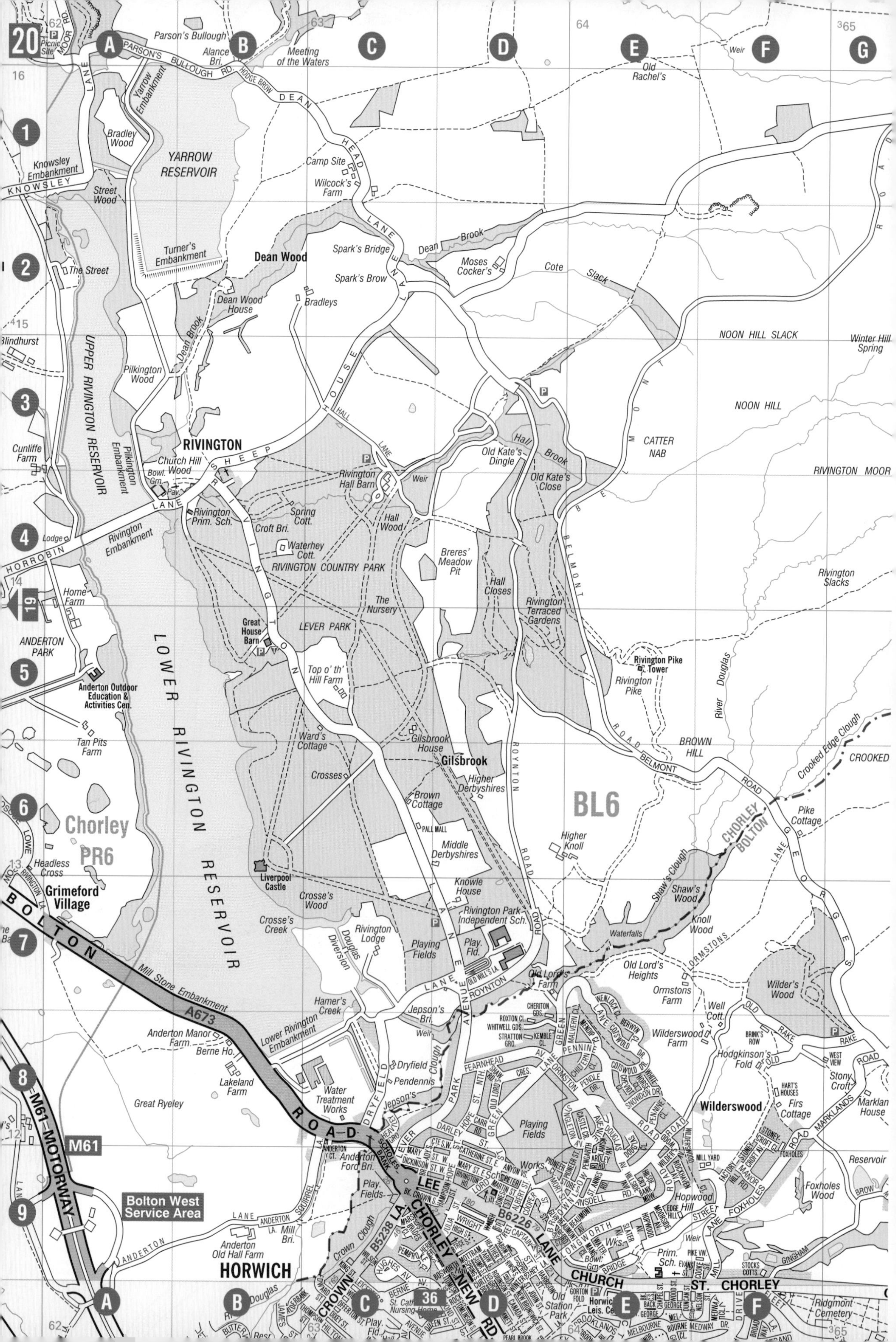
Parson's Bullough
Meeting of the Waters
YARROW RESERVOIR
Bradley Wood
Yarrow Embankment
Knowsley Embankment
Street Wood
Turner's Embankment
Dean Wood
The Street
Camp Site
Wilcock's Farm
Spark's Bridge
Spark's Brow
Dean Brook
Moses Cocker's
Cote Slack
Old Rachel's
Dean Wood House
Bradleys
Blindhurst
UPPER RIVINGTON RESERVOIR
Pilkington Wood
Pilkington Embankment
NOON HILL SLACK
Winter Hill Spring
NOON HILL
CATTER NAB
RIVINGTON MOOR
RIVINGTON
Church Hill Wood
Cunliffe Farm
Rivington Hall Barn
Old Kate's Dingle
Hall Brook
Old Kate's Close
Rivington Prim. Sch.
Spring Cott.
Croft Bri.
Hall Wood
Rivington Embankment
Waterhey Cott.
RIVINGTON COUNTRY PARK
Breres' Meadow Pit
Home Farm
Hall Closes
Rivington Terraced Gardens
Rivington Slacks
ANDERTON PARK
LEVER PARK
The Nursery
Great House Barn
LOWER RIVINGTON RESERVOIR
Top o' th' Hill Farm
Rivington Pike Tower
Rivington Pike
River Douglas
Anderton Outdoor Education & Activities Cen.
Tan Pits Farm
Ward's Cottage
Gilsbrook House
Gilsbrook
Crosses
BROWN HILL
Crooked Edge Clough
CROOKED
Higher Derbyshires
Brown Cottage
BL6
Chorley PR6
Pike Cottage
CHORLEY BOLTON
PALL MALL
Middle Derbyshires
Higher Knoll
Headless Cross
Grimeford Village
Liverpool Castle
Crosse's Wood
Knowle House
Shaw's Clough
Shaw's Wood
Rivington Park Independent Sch.
Knoll Wood
Crosse's Creek
Rivington Lodge
Douglas Diversion
Playing Fields
Play. Fld.
Waterfalls
Old Lord's Farm
Old Lord's Heights
Ormstons Farm
Wilder's Wood
Mill Stone Embankment
Hamer's Creek
Jepson's Bri.
Well Cott.
A673
Lower Rivington Embankment
Anderton Manor Farm
Berne Ho.
Weir
Wilderswood Farm
Hodgkinson's Fold
Stony Croft
Dryfield
Pendennis
Lakeland Farm
Great Ryeley
Jepson's Clough
Water Treatment Works
Firs Cottage
Marklands House
Wilderswood
M61
M61 MOTORWAY
Anderton Ford Bri.
Works
Reservoir
Play. Fields
Foxholes Wood
Bolton West Service Area
Hopwood Hill
Crown Clough
Anderton Old Hall Farm
Mill Bri.
HORWICH
Prim. Sch.
Old Station Park
Horwich Leis. Ce.
Ridgmont Cemetery
Douglas
St. Catherine's Nursing Home
36
19
CHURCH ST.
CHORLEY NEW RD.
B6226
B5238
BOLTON ROAD
BELMONT ROAD
GEORGES LANE
ROYNTON ROAD
RIVINGTON LANE
SHEEP HOUSE LANE
DEAN HEAD LANE
HORROBIN LANE
KNOWSLEY
MOOR RD.
PARSON'S BULLOUGH RD.
HODGE BROW
LEE LANE
PARK AVENUE
GREEN LANE
MARKLANDS ROAD
OLD RAKE
ANDERTON LANE
SQUIRREL LANE
62
63
64
365
16
15
14
13
12

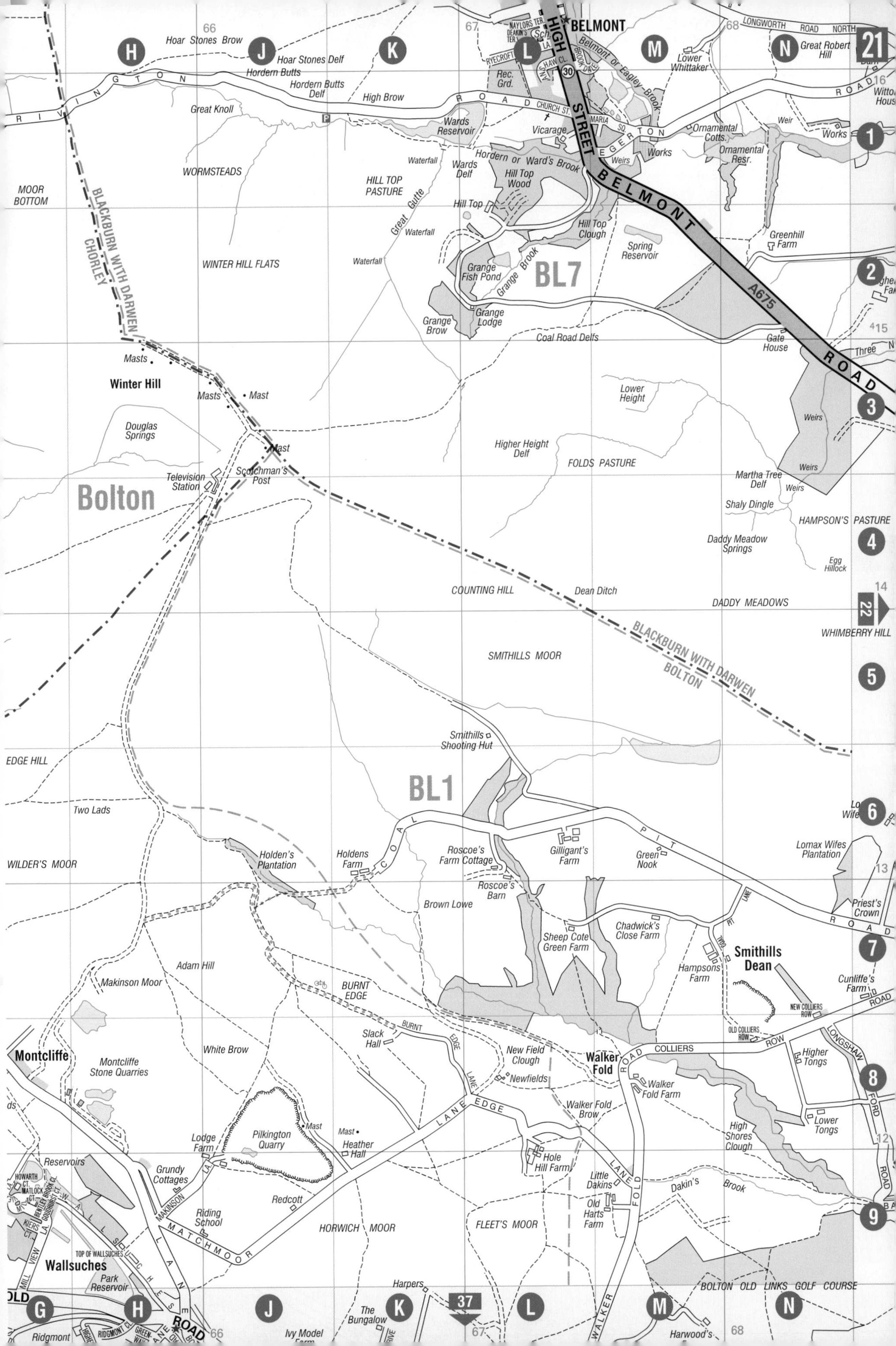

BELMONT
HIGH STREET
BELMONT ROAD
A675
RIVINGTON ROAD
LONGWORTH ROAD NORTH
Great Robert Hill
Lower Whittaker
Belmont or Eagley Brook
Hoar Stones Brow
Hoar Stones Delf
Hordern Butts
Hordern Butts Delf
High Brow
Great Knoll
Wards Reservoir
Rec. Grd.
Vicarage
EGERTON
Ornamental Cotts.
Ornamental Resr.
Works
Weirs
Hordern or Ward's Brook
Wards Delf
Hill Top Wood
Hill Top
Hill Top Clough
Spring Reservoir
WORMSTEADS
MOOR BOTTOM
HILL TOP PASTURE
Waterfall
Great Gutter
Greenhill Farm
WINTER HILL FLATS
Grange Fish Pond
Grange Brook
BL7
Grange Brow
Grange Lodge
Coal Road Delfs
Gate House
BLACKBURN WITH DARWEN
CHORLEY
Masts
Winter Hill
Mast
Douglas Springs
Television Station
Scotchman's Post
Bolton
Lower Height
Higher Height Delf
FOLDS PASTURE
Martha Tree Delf
Shaly Dingle
HAMPSON'S PASTURE
Daddy Meadow Springs
Egg Hillock
COUNTING HILL
Dean Ditch
DADDY MEADOWS
WHIMBERRY HILL
SMITHILLS MOOR
BOLTON
Smithills Shooting Hut
EDGE HILL
BL1
Two Lads
WILDER'S MOOR
Holden's Plantation
Holdens Farm
COAL PIT ROAD
Roscoe's Farm Cottage
Roscoe's Barn
Gilligant's Farm
Green Nook
Lomax Wifes Plantation
Priest's Crown
Brown Lowe
Sheep Cote Green Farm
Chadwick's Close Farm
PIT LANE
Smithills Dean
Hampsons Farm
Cunliffe's Farm
Adam Hill
Makinson Moor
BURNT EDGE
NEW COLLIERS ROW
OLD COLLIERS ROW
COLLIERS ROW
Slack Hall
BURNT EDGE LANE
Montcliffe
Montcliffe Stone Quarries
White Brow
New Field Clough
Newfields
Walker Fold
Higher Tongs
LONGSHAW FORD ROAD
Walker Fold Farm
EDGE LANE
Walker Fold Brow
Lower Tongs
High Shores Clough
Reservoirs
Lodge Farm
Pilkington Quarry
Heather Hall
Hole Hill Farm
Grundy Cottages
Little Dakins
Dakin's Brook
Redcott
Old Harts Farm
Riding School
MATCHMOOR LANE
HORWICH MOOR
FLEET'S MOOR
WALLSUCHES
TOP OF WALLSUCHES
Wallsuches
Park Reservoir
Harpers
The Bungalow
BOLTON OLD LINKS GOLF COURSE
Ridgmont
Ivy Model Farm
Harwood's
WALKER FOLD ROAD
CHURCH ST.
MARIA SQ.
RYECROFT
NAYLORS TER.
DEAKIN'S TER.
BROOK DALE
Three Nooks
Lomax Wifes

22
37

DELPH RESERVOIR
Delph Sailing Club
Dimple
EGERTON
BL7
BL1
Dunscar
Eagley
Sharples
Horrocks Fold
Barrow Bridge
SPRINGS RESERVOIR
DINGLE RESERVOIR
DUNSCAR GOLF COURSE
HORROCKS MOOR
HORROCKS WOODS
SMITHILLS HALL COUNTRY PARK
Smithills Hall
Smithills Sch. & Bolton Sixth Form College (North Campus)
Thornleigh Salesian College
BOLTON OLD LINKS GOLF COURSE
BELMONT ROAD
BLACKBURN ROAD
A666
A675
A58
HAMPSON'S PASTURE
WHIMBERRY HILL
BLACKBURN WITH DARWEN
BOLTON
Longworth Clough Nature Reserve
Shooterslee Wood
Horrocks Scout
Victoria Lake

21
38

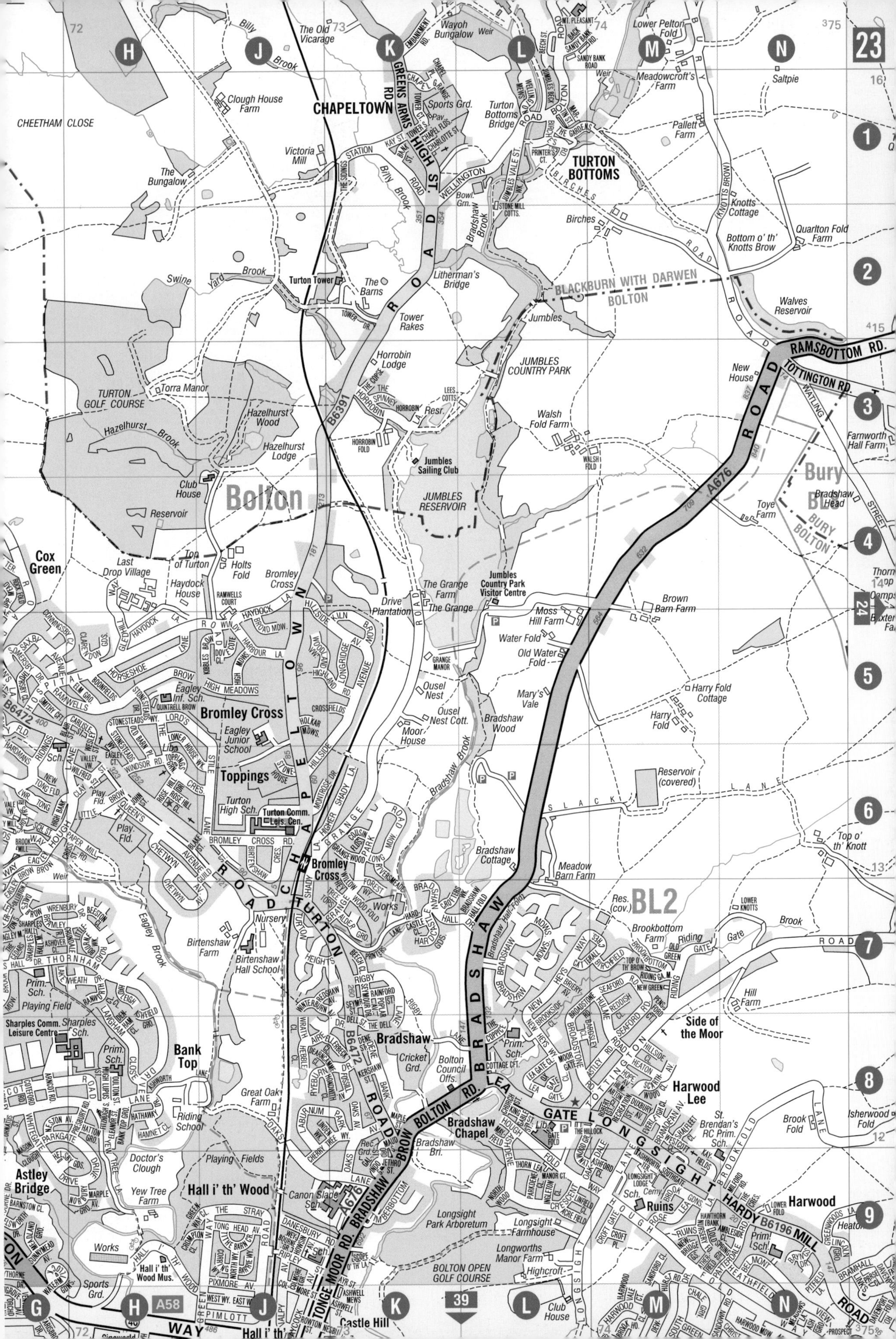
CHAPELTOWN
TURTON BOTTOMS
Turton Tower
Turton Bottoms Bridge
Victoria Mill
The Old Vicarage
Wayoh Bungalow
Clough House Farm
CHEETHAM CLOSE
The Bungalow
Lower Pelton Fold
Meadowcroft's Farm
Saltpie
Pallett Farm
Knotts Cottage
Bottom o' th' Knotts Brow
Quarlton Fold Farm
Walves Reservoir
BLACKBURN WITH DARWEN
BOLTON
Litherman's Bridge
The Barns
Tower Rakes
Horrobin Lodge
Jumbles
JUMBLES COUNTRY PARK
New House
RAMSBOTTOM RD.
TOTTINGTON RD.
Farnworth Hall Farm
Walsh Fold Farm
TURTON GOLF COURSE
Torra Manor
Hazelhurst Wood
Hazelhurst Lodge
Jumbles Sailing Club
JUMBLES RESERVOIR
Bolton
Club House
Reservoir
Bury
Bradshaw Head
Toye Farm
Cox Green
Last Drop Village
Top of Turton
Holts Fold
Bromley Cross
Haydock House
The Grange Farm
The Grange
Jumbles Country Park Visitor Centre
Drive Plantation
Moss Hill Farm
Brown Barn Farm
Water Fold
Old Water Fold
Bromley Cross
Eagley Junior School
Ousel Nest
Ousel Nest Cott.
Mary's Vale
Harry Fold Cottage
Harry Fold
Moor House
Bradshaw Wood
Toppings
Turton High Sch.
Turton Comm. Leis. Cen.
Reservoir (covered)
Top o' th' Knott
Bradshaw Cottage
Meadow Barn Farm
BL2
Brookbottom Farm
Birtenshaw Farm
Birtenshaw Hall School
Nursery
Works
Hill Farm
Side of the Moor
Sharples Comm. Leisure Centre
Playing Field
Bank Top
Bradshaw
Cricket Grd.
Bolton Council Offs.
Harwood Lee
Great Oak Farm
Riding School
Bradshaw Chapel
Brook Fold
Isherwood Fold
Doctor's Clough
Playing Fields
Astley Bridge
Yew Tree Farm
Hall i' th' Wood
Canon Slade Sch.
Longsight Park Arboretum
Longsight Farmhouse
Ruins
Harwood
Works
Hall i' th' Wood Mus.
Longworths Manor Farm
Highcroft
BOLTON OPEN GOLF COURSE
Sports Grd.
Club House
Castle Hill
A676
A58
B6391
B6472
B6196
BRADSHAW ROAD
LONGSIGHT
HARDY MILL ROAD
TURTON ROAD
CHAPELTOWN ROAD
TONGE MOOR RD.
BRADSHAW BROW
BOLTON RD.
24
39

BL7
BL8
BL2
Bolton
HAWKSHAW
Affetside
Holcombe Brook
Greenmount
TOTTINGTON
WALSHAW
Four Lane Ends
Harwood
Bolholt
Pot Green
RAMSBOTTOM RD. BOLTON ROAD BOLTON
A676
TURTON ROAD
B6213
WATLING STREET
HOLCOMBE ROAD
B6215
LONGSIGHT ROAD
BRANDLESHOLME ROAD
MARKET ST
BURY ST
HARWOOD ROAD
BRADSHAW ROAD
BENTLEY ROAD
WALSHAW ROAD
HALL ROAD
TOTTINGTON ROAD
GREENMOUNT GOLF COURSE
HARWOOD GOLF COURSE
BLACKBURN WITH DARWEN
BURY
BOLTON
Redisher Wood
Hawkshaw Wood
Darul Uloom Al-Arabiya Al Islamiya
HIGHBANK PRIORY REHABILITATION CEN. (ELTON UNIT)
Tottington High Sch.
Greenmount Prim. Sch.
Holly Mount RC Prim. Sch.
Old Kays Park
Recreation Grd.
Playing Field
Cricket Grd.
Greenmount Wild Bird Hos
Top of Quarlton
Quarlton Fold Farm
Finny Cote
New Hoyles
Bramley Fold Farm
Tonge Fold Farm
Kenyons Farm
Bleaklow Hall
Brick Kiln Farm
Claremont
Top o' th' Brow
Higher Barn Farm
Farnworth Hall Farm
Fletchers
Whittles
Croichley View
Croichley Fold
Bradshaw Head
Moor Gate
Priory Grange
Three Gates
Sunnybank
Thorn Topp
Campsite
Higher Fold Farm
Birch Hey Farm
Springfield
Baxter Head Farm
Butcher Farm
Tom Nook Farm
Spring Bank Farm
Old Bates
Reynards Bank
Meadow Nook
Buckley Close Farm
Burnt House Farm
Bottoms Hall Farm
Westlinton
Mum's Harris Farm
Meadowcroft Farm
Yeoman's
Windmill Farm
Hillcrest
Leeside
Ralph Moor
Ferns
Brookfield
Stormer Hill House
The Whitehead Gdn.
Stormer Hill Closes
Sheep Hill
Howarth's Farm
Top o' th' Knott
Hoyle's Fold
Old Ned's
Top of Raikes
Four Acre Farm
Bridges Fm.
Huntacres
Gorsey Clough
Riding School
White Paddocks
White Hill
Hey Head
Meadow Head Cott.
Bowstone Hill
Isherwoods
Bowstone Hill Cotts.
Hill End Farm
High Barn
Castle Farm
Asmus Farm
Isherwood Fold
Isherwood Fold Barn
The Height
Height Barn
Bannister's Farm
Birchen Bower Farm
Jackson Fold Farmhouse
Sheep Gate Farm
Walshaw Hall Farm
Resr.
Walshaw Hall
Old Holts
Bentley Hall
High Crompton
Reservoir (covered)
Higher Bury Meadows
Club House
Nab Fold
Heatons
Ashfield
Range House
Higher House Farm
Simons Farm
Hollingrove Farm
Dandy Hall
Higher Redisher Farm
Greystones
Loe Farm
Greenacre
Loe Farm Cottage
Loe Bank
Loe Bri.
The Knoll
Holhouse Farm
Greenhalgh Fold
Club House
Brick Barn
Holly Mount Farm
Brookhouse Farm
Mill
Reservoir
Works
Top o'th' Moor Farm
Hey House Farm
Hey House
Meadow Heys
Hill End Fm.
Dawes Bank Farm
Lumb Carr Farm
Sports Club
Town Meadow
Lib.
Prim. Sch.
Hollingrove Farm
Walves
Mill
Rec. Grd.
Tennis Cts.
Sch.
Weir
Weirs
Middle Ridge
Saplin Wood
Clarke's Tenement Farm
Hawkshaw Farm
Haze
10
23
40
A B C D E F G
1 2 3 4 5 6 7 8 9

25
26
41
11
H
J
K
L
M
N
G
1
2
3
4
5
6
7
8
9
RAMSBOTTOM
BL0
BL9
Bury
SUMMERSEAT
Summerseat
Nuttall
Nuttall Lane
Brooksbottoms
Woodhey
Holcombe Brook
Lower Summerseat
Higher Summerseat
Wood Road
Rowlands
HIGHBANK PRIORY CENTRE
Nangreaves
Junction 1
M66 MOTORWAY
MANCHESTER RD.
WALMERSLEY ROAD
A56
Baldingstone
Carr Bank
Bevis Green
Walmersley
Springside Prim. Sch.
Limefield
LOWES PARK GOLF COURSE
Chesham
Chesham Woods Local Nature Reserve
Freetown
Littlewood
Seedfield
Fernhill
Wood Fields
Burrs
BURRS COUNTRY PARK
Burrs Activity Centre
Castle Steads (Site of Camp)
Higher Woodhill
Woodhill
Brandlesholme
Old Hall Prim. Sch.
Our Lady of Lourdes RC Prim. Sch.
Woolfold
Stables Fitness & Leisure Club
TOTTINGTON ROAD
Beechwood
Reservoirs
EAST LANCASHIRE RAILWAY
River Irwell
Gollinrod Wood
Sunny Clough
Throstle Hill
Far Buckhurst Brow
Ridshaw Farm
Butcher Acre Farm
Mam Hill
Higher Sedger Hey
Snape Hill
High Hope
Whitewall Farm
Gindles Farm
Longcroft House
Pigs Lee Brook
Top o' th' Hill
Club House
Chesham Green
Clarence Rec. Grd.
Refuse Destructor
Nuttall Park
Pike Wood
Park Wood Farm
Grant's Tower (Ruins)
Grant's Wood
Bent House Farm
Hoof Farm
Red Hall
Higher Gollinrod
Bassfield Farm
Bird Hall
Nabbs Farm
Chest Wheel Farm
Springside Farm
Bank Top Farm
Banks Farm
Irwell View Farm
Touch Road Farm
Pigsden Farm
Garside Hey
Kirklees
Owler

Bury
BL9
Ashworth Moor
Ashworth Moor Reservoir
Edenfield Road
A680
Red Lumb
Higher Red Lumb
Middle Red Lumb Farm
Farther Red Lumb
Lower Red Lumb Farm
The Cottage
Bamford Closes Farm
Red Lumb House
The Barn
Hinde Clough Farm
Water Works
Sparrow Row
Wolstenholme Hall Farm
Top o' th' Hill Farm
Meadow Head Lane
Meadow Head Fm.
Meadow Farm
Marcroft Gate Farm
Bird Fields
Wind Hill Farm
Wind Hill
Copped Hill Farm
Copped Hill
Rough Lee Farm
Far Croft Head
Crossgates Farm
Ashworth Moor Ho.
Ashworth Road
Yates Farm
Stand Lees Farm
Greengate Hill
Sandy Ford
Shepherd Hey
Leaches Farm
Cockshouse
Dairy House
Black Dad
Black Dad Lane
Black Dad Wood
Kershaw Bri.
Cheesden Brook
Cleggs Wood
Nab's Wife
Wood Barn
Ashworth Valley
Ashworth Scout
Windy Cliff Bridge
Windy Cliff Wood
Dobb Wood
Heywood's Farm
Thornyhurst Farm
Penn Green Farm
Birtle Green
Marrcroft Farm
Birtle
Fernises Farm
Wrigley Farm
Sunnyside
Higher Tack Lee Fm.
Higher Moorgate Farm
Top o' th' Wood
Lower Tack Lee Farm
Wks.
Bury and Rochdale Old Road
B6222
Gorses
Lower Elbut
Tack Lee Wood
Tack Lee Brook
The Bungalow
Gristlehurst Wood
Gristlehurst
Elbut Wood
River Roch
Lomax Wood
Lower Lomax
Smethurst Wood
Fairfield General Hospital
Broad Oak Wood
Jericho
Woodgate Hill
Boaredge Farm
Gallows Hill
Mawkin Farm
Church Lane
Rochdale Bury
Football Grd.
Birtle Brook Village
Birtle Moor
Higher Moulding
Moulding Moss
White Ash
Delph Ho. Farm
Red Bank
Carr Croft Farm
Mount Pleasant Farm
Moorbank Farm
Old Birtle
Birtle Road
New Birtle Farm
The Rhyddings
Millett Ter.
Resr. (cov.)
Castle Hill Farm
Deneway
Harwood Fields Farm
Castle Road
Birtle Edge House
Walmersley Golf Course
Club House (Garrett's Close)
Scotland Lane
Dunham Farm
Deep Moss
Cheesden Brook
Deeply Vale Lane
Deeply Vale
Deeply Vale Higher Bridge
Deeply Vale Lower Bridge
Deeply Hill
Weir
Rochdale
Rossendale
Croston Close Upper Bridge
Croston Close Bottoms
Croston Close Road
Moorlands
Lumb Bridge
Croston Close
Kirkby's
Far Buckhurst Brow
Buckhurst Brow
Buckhurst Road
Plant Close Farm
Buckhurst Farm
Buckhurst Lodge
Buckhurst Lane
Closes Farm
Closes Barn
Closes Bri.
Throstle Hill
Sales's Farm
Sales's Lane
Whitewall Farm
Lark Mount
Cob House Nab
Gindles Farm
Cob House Farm
Pigs Lee Brook
White Carr Lane
White Carr
Broomses Farm
Nineveh Farm
Bradshaw Hill Farm
Sillinghurst Farm
Castle Hill
Birchen Bower Farm
Cinder Hill
Weir
M66 Motorway
M66
Chesham Green
Chesham Woods Local Nature Reserve
Gorsey Brow Farm
Gipsy Brook
Hercules Farm
Reservoir (covered)
Fern Grove
Riddings Farm
Mast
Cemetery
Fern Grove
Hall
Rochdale Old Road
Fairfield
RC Prim. Sch.
Playing Fields
Club House
Owes Park Golf Course
Prim. Sch.
12
25
42

Deans Brow
Bottom of Rooley Moor
Turnshaw
13
Harbour
Knacks Farm
Higher Dunishbooth
Knacks
Knowl Farm
East Knowles Farm
Higher Naden
Hunger Hill
Brown Hill
Doldrum Farm
Smallshaw Farm
Healey Dell Nature Reserve
Smallshaw Wood
Dunishbooth Wood
Syke Bank
Catley Lane Head
Viaduct
Hungerhill End Farm
Fair View
Hollands Farm
Reservoir
Sidholme
Brown Hill Farm
Rain Shore
Fordoe
Fordoe Brook
Naden Wood
GREENBOOTH RESERVOIR
Hill Top
Harper Road
Fordoe Wood
Works
Rainshore Farm
Royds
Kit Booth
Lower Fold
Top of Nabs
OL12
Fern Hill
Brotherod Wood
Top of Croft Farm
Nabs Plantation
Mill House Farm
The Manor
Birches Farm
Ellis Fold Farm
Shawfield Stones Wood
White Lees
Caldershaw
Redfearn Wood
River Spodden
Rainshore House
Reservoirs
Doctor Dam
Holt Wood
Bank Ho.
Bank Ho. Farm
Shawfield Stones
Shawfield Stones Fm.
Shawfield
Stone Hill Wood
EDENFIELD
A680
Laneside Farm
Laneside Mill
Resr.
Wks.
Mill
Ckt. Grd.
Norden Prim. Sch.
THE CALDERSHAW CENTRE
Passmonds
Fester Clough Wood
Rec. Grd.
Wolstenholme Fold
Mill Croft
Norden
War Meml.
Lib.
The Highwood Cen.
Whittaker Moss Prim. Sch.
Lee Holme
Brook
Caldershaw
Prim. Schs.
Rochdale
Paper House Farm
Coal Bank Lwr. Brk.
Electricity Sub Station
EDEN-FIELD
A680
Club House
Cutgate
Seddons Farm
Clay Lane Wood
Duckworth Farm
Ashworth Wood
Newhouse Fm.
Denehurst Park
Denehurst House
Bagslate Moor
Greave
Resr. (cov.)
Scott House
ROCHDALE GOLF COURSE
Oulder Hill Community Complex
Higher Clough
Lower Clough
OL11
Waterloo Farm
Lower Jowkin Fm.
Playing Fields
Oulder Hill School and Language College
Rugby Grd.
Ashworth Hall Farm
Higher Jowkin Farm
Carr Wood
Bamford
Broadhalgh
Rochdale Crematorium
Rochdale Cemetery
Goose Hill
Play. Flds.
Cricket Grd.
Bamford Prim. Sch.
Comm. Cen.
Carr Wood
Jowkin Wood
Mooredge Farm
Hurst Farm
Bamford Trough
GELDER WOOD COUNTRY PARK
B6222
Ryefield
Gelder Wood
Bamford Wood
Play. Fld.
River Roch
Half Acre Bridge
Butterworth Fold Farm
Bamford Hall
Mills
MARLAND GOLF COURSE
Marland Wood
Heywood
Cobb Wood
Gristlehurst Farm
Simpson Clough
Kenyon Fold
High Trees
Hazelhurst
Springfield Park Track
Mereside House
Marland
Mill
ROCHDALE OLD ROAD
BURY ROAD
Simpson Clough Bri.
St. Michael's C of E Prim. Sch.
Plumpton Hall
The Crimble
Club Ho.
Springfield Park
Plumpton Wood
Crimble Farm
Heywood Cemetery
Ouzle Hall Farm
Hooley Bridge
Crimble
Springfield Park Nursing Home
A58
BOLTON ROAD
OL10
HOOLEY BRI. IND. EST.
Queen's Pk. Bridge
River Roch
Boating Lake
Mill
Primrose Hill Fm.
Matthew Moss High Sch.
Queen's Park
Hooley Brow
Captain Fold
43
Cricket Ground
Chamber House Urban Farm
ROCHDALE RD. EAST
All Souls
28
30

28
A
B
C
D
E
F
G
1
2
3
4
5
6
7
8
9
14
27
30
44
8
Healey
Middle Healey
Lower Healey
Lower Fold
Healey Hall Wood
Reservoir
Healey Bottoms
Brotherod Wood
River Spodden
Shawclough
Thrum Hall
Playing Fields
Hey Wood
Stoney Heys Farm
Lousy Hillock
Buckley Pasture
Ring Lows
Ring Lows Farm
Syke
Reservoir
Cronkeyshaw Common
Buckley Wood
HMP BUCKLEY HALL
Syke Brook
Buckley
Ball Barn Farm
Great Howarth
Birchen Head Farm
Depot
Weir
Playing Fields
Fieldhouse Ind. Est.
Shawclough Trad. Est.
Works
Hollows Wood
Foot Wood
Falinge Fold
Emmanuel Christian Sch.
Falinge Park High Sch.
Falinge Park
Brownhill Sch.
Rochdale Infirmary
Walk In Cen.
Spotland Fold
Meanwood Prim. Sch.
Spotland Bridge
Rochdale FC & Rochdale Hornets RLFC (Spotland)
Denehurst House
Greenbank Prim. Sch.
Heybrook Prim. Sch.
Rochdale
Town Head
Playing Field
Hamer Primary. Sch. & Springside Sch.
Howarth Cross
Mayfield
Stanney
Newbold Brow
Central Leisure Cen.
THE POINT RETAIL PK.
ROCHDALE
Rochdale Exchange Shop. Cen.
Mitchell Hey
Superstore
Colleges
Police HQ
Touchstones
Broadfield Prim. Sch.
War Mem.
Broadfield Park
Castle Hill
Mosque
Oakenrod Mt. East
Cricket Ground
Rochdale Cemetery
Rochdale Crematorium
Sewage Works
Mandale Park
Beech House Sch.
THE HIGHFIELD BMI HOSP
Half Acre Bridge
Marland
Marland Hill Comm. Prim. Sch.
Sudden
Superstore
Works
Junction 4
Strike Ten Bowl & Laser Quest
Odeon Cin.
Fitness First Club
Rochdale Canal
Stoneyfield
Sudden Brook
Offices
Queensway Neighbourhood Cen.
Depots
Kingsway High Sch.
Playing Field
Lowerplace Prim. Sch.
Lower Place
Turf Hill
Kingsway Park Sports Centre
Kingsway Park High Sch.
Oldham Branch Junc.
Scotts Industrial Park
Rochdale Training Assn.
Rochdale Cen. Ret. Cen.
Rochdale
Milkstone
Chichester Bus. Cen.
Rochdale Ind. Cen.
MARKET ST.
WHITWORTH ROAD
SHAWCLOUGH ROAD
FALINGE ROAD
BOLTON ROAD
EDENFIELD RD.
SPOTLAND RD.
MELLOR STREET
ROOLEY MOOR ROAD
SANDY LANE
BURY ROAD
ROCH VALLEY WAY
EDINBURGH WAY
MANCHESTER ROAD
ST MARY'S GATE
DRAKE ST.
OLDHAM ROAD
MOLESWORTH ST.
ENTWISTLE RD.
YORKSHIRE STREET
HALIFAX ROAD
ALBERT ROYDS ST.
QUEENSWAY
KINGSWAY
SIR ISAAC NEWTON WAY
OLDHAM RD.
BROAD LA.
BUCKLEY ROAD
RYDINGS RD.
A58
A640
A664
A671
A680
A6060
B6222
B6223
B6224
B6226
B6266
B6194
B6377
B6452
OL12
88
89
390
91
12
13
16

29
Littleborough
OL15
Hollingworth
HOLLINGWORTH LAKE
Hollingworth Lake Country Park
Hollingworth Lake Nature Reserve
Hollingworth Lake Visitor Cen.
Hollingworth Lake Water Activity Cen.
Hollingworth Lake Sailing Club
Smithy Bridge
Little Clegg
Clegg Hall
Smallbridge
Hurstead
Greengate
Wuerdle
Dearnley
Belfield
Newbold
Firgrove
Clover Hall
MILNROW
OL16
NEWHEY
Lady House
Butterworth Hall
Rakewood
Haugh
Rough Bank
Bentgate
TUNSHILL GOLF COURSE
Soccer Village
Hollingworth High Sch.
Kingsway Business Park (Proposed)
Stanney Brook Park
Ellenroad Steam Engine
Junction 21
M62
M62 MOTORWAY
A640
A6193
B6225
A58
BIRCH HILL HOSPITAL
Wardle High Sch.
15
30
45

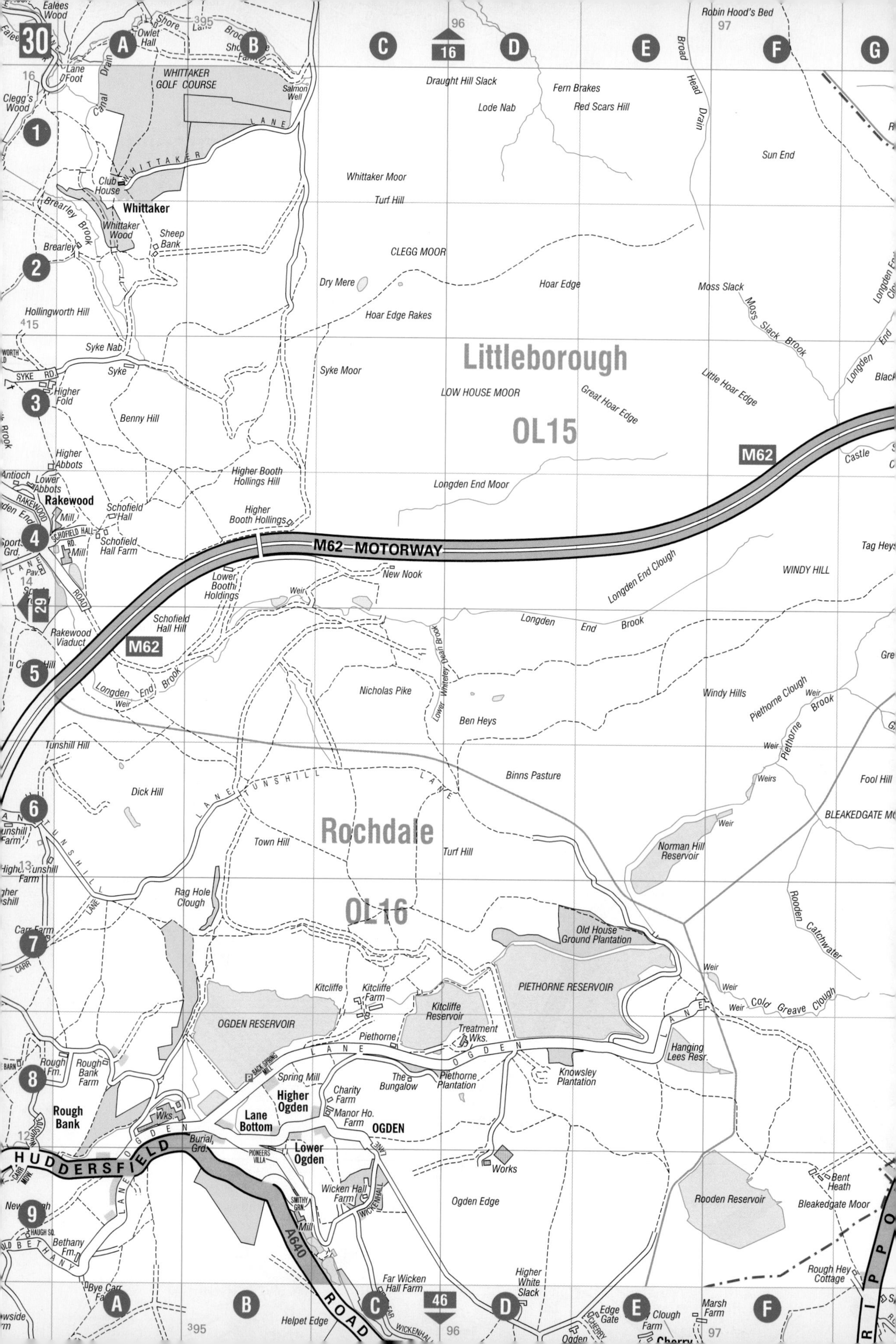
16
46
29
Whittaker
WHITTAKER GOLF COURSE
Whittaker Moor
CLEGG MOOR
Littleborough
OL15
LOW HOUSE MOOR
Longden End Moor
M62 MOTORWAY
M62
Rakewood
Rochdale
OL16
Nicholas Pike
Binns Pasture
Turf Hill
Town Hill
Dick Hill
Tunshill Hill
PIETHORNE RESERVOIR
OGDEN RESERVOIR
Kitcliffe Reservoir
Norman Hill Reservoir
Rooden Reservoir
Hanging Lees Resr.
Higher Ogden
Lower Ogden
Lane Bottom
OGDEN
Rough Bank
HUDDERSFIELD ROAD
A640
Ogden Edge
Helpet Edge
Bleakedgate Moor
WINDY HILL
Windy Hills
Sun End
Moss Slack
Hoar Edge
Hoar Edge Rakes
Dry Mere
Syke Moor
Benny Hill
Fern Brakes
Red Scars Hill
Lode Nab
Draught Hill Slack
Robin Hood's Bed
395
96
97

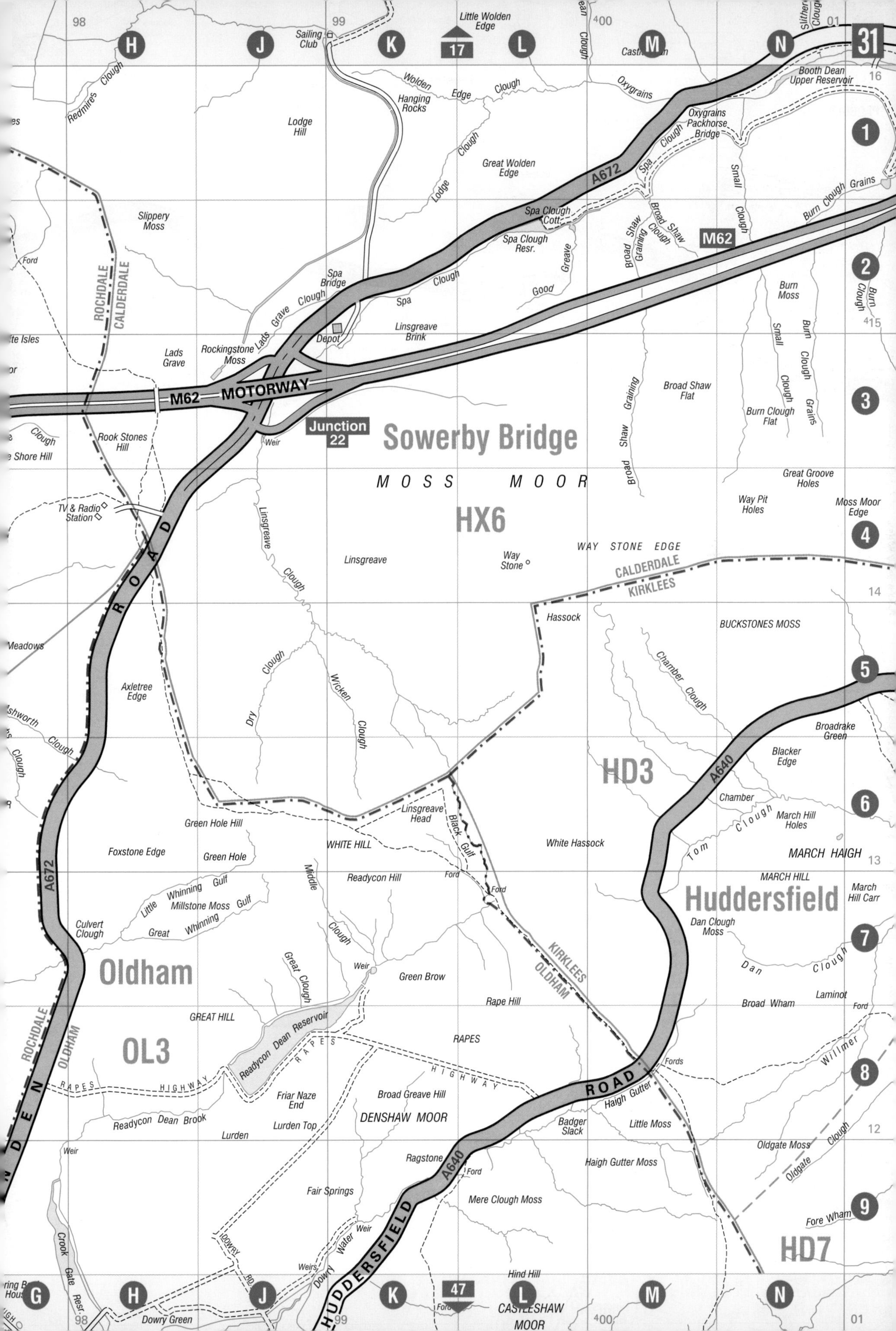
Little Wolden Edge
17
Sailing Club
Booth Dean Upper Reservoir
Oxygrains
Wolden Edge Clough
Hanging Rocks
Lodge Hill
Redmires Clough
Oxygrains Packhorse Bridge
Spa Clough
Great Wolden Edge
A672
Lodge Clough
Small Clough
Burn Clough Grains
Slippery Moss
Spa Clough Cott.
Spa Clough Resr.
Broad Shaw Graining
Broad Shaw Clough
M62
ROCHDALE
CALDERDALE
Ford
Spa Bridge
Lads Grave Clough
Spa Clough
Greave
Good
Burn Moss
Burn Clough
Depot
Linsgreave Brink
Lads Grave
Rockingstone Moss
M62 MOTORWAY
Broad Shaw Flat
Burn Clough Flat
Small Clough
Burn Clough Grains
Rook Stones Hill
Junction 22
Sowerby Bridge
Weir
MOSS MOOR
Broad Shaw Graining
Great Groove Holes
TV & Radio Station
HX6
Way Pit Holes
Moss Moor Edge
ROAD
Linsgreave Clough
Linsgreave
Way Stone
WAY STONE EDGE
CALDERDALE
KIRKLEES
Hassock
BUCKSTONES MOSS
Meadows
Chamber Clough
Axletree Edge
Dry Clough
Wicken Clough
Broadrake Green
Blacker Edge
A640
HD3
Chamber
March Hill Holes
Linsgreave Head
Black Gulf
Tom Clough
Green Hole Hill
Foxstone Edge
Green Hole
WHITE HILL
White Hassock
MARCH HAIGH
A672
Middle Clough
Readycon Hill
Ford
MARCH HILL
Little Whinning Gulf
Millstone Moss
Great Whinning Gulf
Huddersfield
March Hill Carr
Culvert Clough
Dan Clough Moss
Great Clough
KIRKLEES
OLDHAM
Oldham
Weir
Green Brow
Dan Clough
Laminot
ROCHDALE
OLDHAM
GREAT HILL
Readycon Dean Reservoir
Rape Hill
Broad Wham
Ford
OL3
RAPES
Willmer
Fords
RAPES HIGHWAY
ROAD
Haigh Gutter
Friar Naze End
Broad Greave Hill
Readycon Dean Brook
DENSHAW MOOR
Badger Slack
Little Moss
Lurden
Lurden Top
Weir
Ragstone
Oldgate Moss
Oldgate Clough
Haigh Gutter Moss
Fair Springs
A640
Ford
Mere Clough Moss
Crook Gate Resr.
Dowry Water
Weir
Weirs
DOWRY RD.
HUDDERSFIELD
Fore Wham
HD7
Hind Hill
47
Ford
CASTLESHAW MOOR
Dowry Green
G H J K L M N
1 2 3 4 5 6 7 8 9
98 99 400 01
16 15 14 13 12

PARBOLD
Parbold
Robin Hood
Dalton
WN8
Crisp Delf
Forsters Green
Elmers Green
ROBY MILL
Skelmersdale
PARBOLD HILL
SPARROW HILL
HALL LANE
ALDER LANE
A5209
B5246
A577
STANNANOUGHT ROAD
Leeds & Liverpool Canal
River Douglas
Holly House Farm
Bowling Green House Farm
Boggart House
Stony Lane Covert
Boar's Den Farm
Beech Holt
Boar's Den
Coal Gate Cottages
Sprodley Wood
Sprodley Brook
Parbold Douglas C of E Prim. Sch.
Convent
Fairy Green
Parbold Hall
Parbold Hill
Parbold Beacon
Woodvale Farm
Delf House
Playing Field
Alder La. Bri.
Douglas Three Bridges
Douglas Bridge
Douglas Farm
Chapel House Bridge
Chapel Ho.
Whitley Cottage
Gillibrand House
Gillibrand Bri.
Delf House Wood
Finch Farm
Richardson's Farm
Draper's Farm
Worthington's Farm
Pichill Wood
Fish Ponds
Refuse Tip
Hand Lane Bridge
Appley Locks
Factory
Dalton Grange
Grange Farm
Grange Farm Cotts.
Blackbird's Farm
Prior's Wood Farm
Valley Farm
Ram's Clough Wood
Keckle Hey Wood
Oakwood
Mount Farm
Dungeon Wood
Rookery Farm
Holland's House
Lower House
Martin's Farm
Rams Close Wood
Quarry
Cross House Farm
Boydells Farm
Hawksclough
Dalton Lees
Wigan Lane Wood
Halliwell Farm
Douglas Bank Farm
Aspinalls
Whalley's Farm
Dalton St. Michael's C of E Prim. Sch.
Ashurst Hall
Beacon Covert
Bangham's Farm
The Dingle
Catteralls Farm
Ashurst's Hill
Ashurst's Beacon
Atherton's Farm
St. James Catholic Prim. Sch.
Beacon Park
Bradshaws
Beech Tree Farm Riding Centre
Stone Hall
Lees Wood
Lees Brook
Mellings
Stopforths Farm
Chisnall's Farm
Edward Henry Plantation
Cricket Grd.
Stoneacre
Knights Farm
BEACON PARK GOLF COURSE
Don Orione Cen.
Cemetery
Prim. Sch.
Belle Vue Farm
Playing Field
Prim. Sch.
Comm. Cen.
Sports Field
BEACON LANE
LEES LANE
HILLOCK LANE
LONG HEYS LANE
FARLEY LANE
CROW LANE
HIGHER LEES
ROBY MILL
STONEY BROW
SCHOOL LA.
HOUGHTON'S ROAD
APPLEY LANE
LANE WOOD
CHAPEL LANE
DUNGEON LA.
HEYS (BACK LANE)
HALL LANE
STONE
ELMERS GREEN LANE
MILLBANK
LAFFORD
WHITLE
HIGH MOOR LA.
HOOD
ROBIN HOOD LANE
STONEYGATE LA.
GLENSIDE
FINCH LANE
MIRY LA.
BROADHEY LA.
LANCASTER LANE
THE COMMON
TAN HOUSE LANE
STONEY
BRANDRETH
THE DELPH
CROASDALE DR.
PARK CL.
SPRODLEY DR.
GRAHAM
GROVE
THE NORTH
SOUTH
BROADMEAD
EASTSIDE
BURNSIDE
WEST
MILL
BEECH AV.
MILLFIELD
BRADSHAW LA.
BRAMBLE WY.
BROOKFIELD
KESTREL MEWS
KESTREL PK.
PARK
ASHURST
LONG HEY
KINGSBURY CL.
LULWORTH
LOWCROSS
ASHLEY
FAIRSTEAD
FALKLAND
HELMSDALE
HEVERSHAM
FAIRHAVEN
FAIRLIE
BIRCH
BIRCH GREEN RD.
FOXFOLD
FORSTERS GRN. RD.
ELMER'S GREEN
SHERWOOD DR.
PINEWOOD
BEECHWOOD
OAK TREE CT.
PARKLANDS
HARTLAND
Playing Field
Play. Fld.
HEYES
AYREFIELD
ST. GABRIEL CL.
49
350
51
52
09
08
07
410
178

50

APPLEY BRIDGE
Shevington Moor
Langtree
STANDISH
WN6
Wigan
Shevington Vale
SHEVINGTON
Holland Lees
Bank Top
Walthew Green
GATHURST
Crooke
WN5
M6 MOTORWAY
Junction 27
A5209
B5206
B5375
Hunger Hill
TUNLEY MOSS
Wrightington Hospital
Standish Community High Sch.
Shevington High School
GATHURST GOLF COURSE
Leeds & Liverpool Canal
River Douglas
DEAN WOOD
BIRLEY WOOD
STANDISH PARK
34
51

Langtree
STANDISH
Langtree Hall
Saddle Hill Farm
Dam House
Works
Mill
BRADLEY HALL TRADING ESTATE
Depot
Standish Community High Sch.
St. Marie's Catholic Prim. Sch.
Wood Fold Prim. Sch.
Beech Lodge
Cricket Grd.
Strickland House Farm
Beech Walk Plantation
Lime Vale
Standish Hall Farm
STANDISH PARK
Upper Wood Farm
Wood Folds
New Plantation
Lower Wood Farm
Frodsham's Brook
Frodsham's Wood
Frodsham's House
Follient Wood
Christopher Park Playing Fields
Crooke
Standish Lower Ground
Coronation Park
Martland Mill
Marina
Beech Hill
Giant's Hall Farm
Brimelow Farm
Brockhurst Farm
Wakefields
Roundmoor Farm
Boar's Head
WN6
WN1
Gidlow Cemetery
Whitley
Factory
Thorn Hill
Rectory Farm
Barrowcroft Wood
White Bridge Wood
Bradley Brook
Kitchen Carr Wood
Otter Close Wood
STANDISH COURT GOLF COURSE
Club House
Lark Hill
Ashfield House
Playing Fields
Ashfield Park
Black Lawyers
Wrennalls Farm
Lodge
Arley Lodge Nature Reserve
Adlington Reservoir
Worthington Lodge
Worthington Hall
Arly Reservoir
Kilhey Ct.
WORTHINGTON LAKES COUNTRY PARK
Brook's Bank Wood
Lakeside
Worthington Reservoir
WIGAN GOLF COURSE
Worthington Lakes Visitor Centre
Water Works Farm
Red Rock
Red Rock Farm
Wigan
Jolly Mill Wood
Fairclough Wood
Leeds & Liverpool Canal
Pendlebury Bridge
Grimshaws
Samuel's Fold Cottage
Boars Head Farm
Rothwells Farm
Brock Wood
Club House
Brock Mill Farm
Rugby Ground
Wingate Wood
Haigh Cottage
Leyland Mill Farm
Leyland Mill Br.
Marylebone
ROYAL ALBERT EDWARD INFIRMARY
Swinley
Springfield
Sacred Heart Catholic Prim. Sch.
PRESTON ROAD
WIGAN ROAD
CHORLEY ROAD
RECTORY LANE
HIGH ST.
SCHOOL LANE
ALMOND BROOK RD
WOODHOUSE DRIVE
SPENCER RD
WIGAN LANE
MESNES RD
A49
A5106
A5209
B5239
B5375
B5376
18
33
52

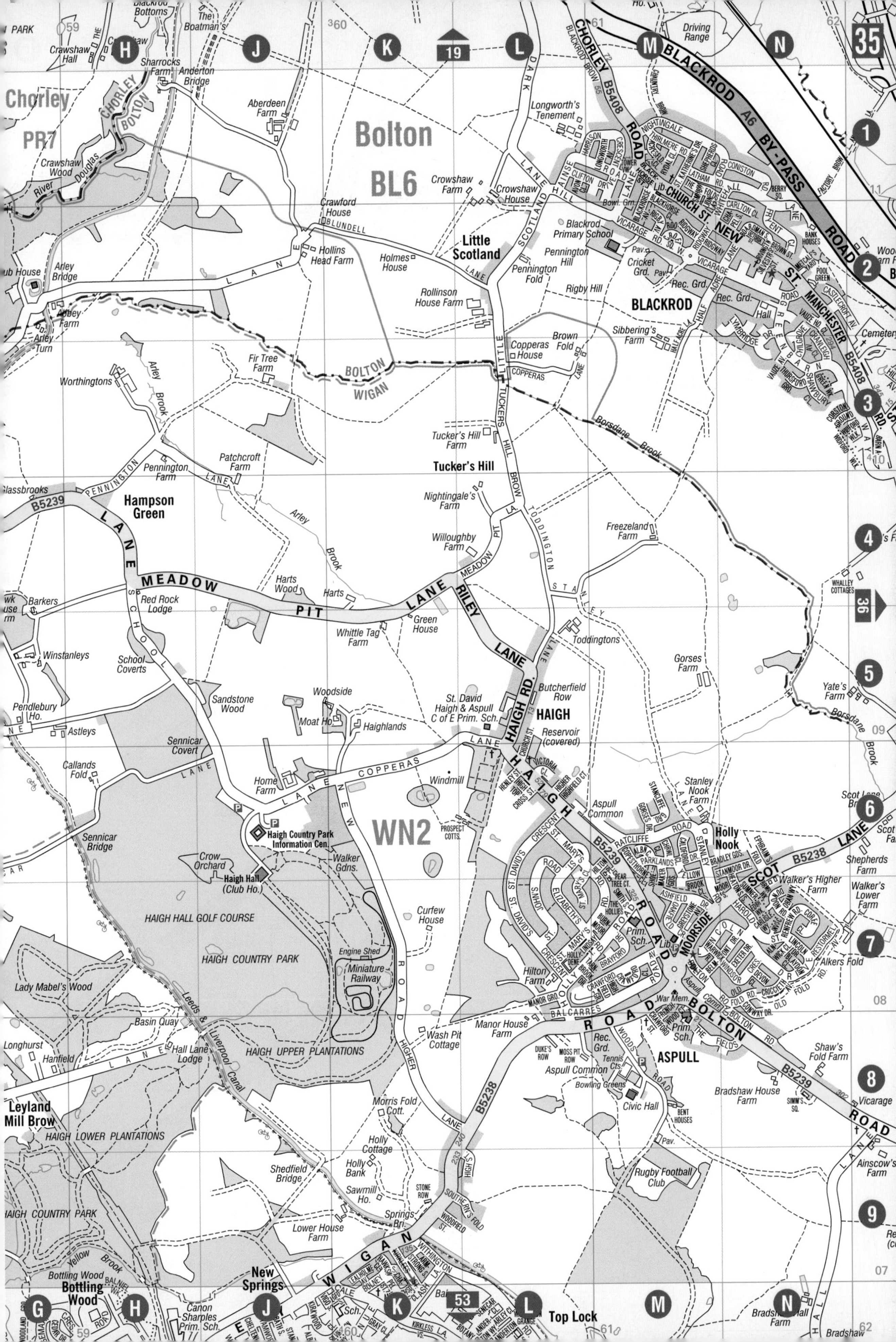
19
53
36
H
J
K
L
M
N
G
1
2
3
4
5
6
7
8
9
Chorley
PR7
Bolton
BL6
WN2
BLACKROD
Little Scotland
Tucker's Hill
Hampson Green
HAIGH
ASPULL
Holly Nook
New Springs
Bottling Wood
Top Lock
Leyland Mill Brow
Blackrod Bottoms
The Boatman's
Crawshaw Hall
Sharrocks Farm
Anderton Bridge
Aberdeen Farm
Crawshaw Wood
River Douglas
Crawford House
Hollins Head Farm
Holmes House
Crowshaw Farm
Crowshaw House
Longworth's Tenement
Driving Range
Arley Bridge
Abbey Farm
Arley Turn
Worthingtons
Fir Tree Farm
Arley Brook
Rollinson House Farm
Copperas House
Brown Fold
Pennington Hill
Pennington Fold
Rigby Hill
Sibbering's Farm
Blackrod Primary School
Cricket Grd.
Rec. Grd.
Borsdane Brook
Tucker's Hill Farm
Nightingale's Farm
Willoughby Farm
Pennington Farm
Patchcroft Farm
Glassbrooks
Freezeland Farm
Harts Wood
Harts
Barkers
Red Rock Lodge
Green House
Whittle Tag Farm
Winstanleys
School Coverts
Toddingtons
Gorses Farm
Yate's Farm
Whalley Cottages
Sandstone Wood
Woodside
Moat Ho.
Haighlands
St. David Haigh & Aspull C of E Prim. Sch.
Butcherfield Row
Reservoir (covered)
Pendlebury Ho.
Astleys
Sennicar Covert
Callands Fold
Home Farm
Windmill
Prospect Cotts.
Aspull Common
Stanley Nook Farm
Scot Lane
Shepherds Farm
Walker's Higher Farm
Walker's Lower Farm
Haigh Country Park Information Cen.
Sennicar Bridge
Crow Orchard
Haigh Hall (Club Ho.)
Walker Gdns.
HAIGH HALL GOLF COURSE
Curfew House
HAIGH COUNTRY PARK
Engine Shed
Miniature Railway
Lady Mabel's Wood
Hilton Farm
Alkers Fold
Basin Quay
Leeds & Liverpool Canal
Manor House Farm
Wash Pit Cottage
War Mem.
Prim. Sch.
Longhurst
Hanfield
Hall Lane Lodge
HAIGH UPPER PLANTATIONS
Rec. Grd.
Tennis Cts.
Aspull Common
Bowling Greens
Civic Hall
Bent Houses
Shaw's Fold Farm
Bradshaw House Farm
Vicarage
Simm's Sq.
Ainscow's Farm
HAIGH LOWER PLANTATIONS
Morris Fold Cott.
Holly Cottage
Holly Bank
Shedfield Bridge
Sawmill Ho.
Stone Row
Springs Bri.
Lower House Farm
Rugby Football Club
Pav.
Yellow Brook
Bottling Wood Farm
Canon Sharples Prim. Sch.
Sch.
Bradshaw Hall Farm
Bradshaw
BLACKROD A6 BY-PASS ROAD
CHORLEY ROAD B5408
MANCHESTER ROAD B5408
CHURCH ST.
NEW ST.
SCOTLAND LANE
LITTLE SCOTLAND
TUCKERS HILL BROW
COPPERAS LANE
BLUNDELL LANE
DARK LANE
MEADOW PIT LANE
PENNINGTON LANE
B5239
SCHOOL LANE
RILEY LANE
HAIGH RD.
TODDINGTON LANE
STANLEY LANE
HAIGH ROAD B5239
RATCLIFFE ROAD
MOORSIDE
LINCOLN
SCOT LANE B5238
BOLTON ROAD B5239
NEW ROAD
HIGHER ROAD
B5238
WIGAN
WOODS ROAD
HALL LANE
59
360
61
62
11
10
09
08
07
460

Bolton West Service Area
HORWICH
BLACKROD
Blackrod
M61
M61-MOTORWAY
BY-PASS
CHORLEY NEW ROAD
A673
BL6
RED MOSS
Middlebrook
MIDDLEBROOK RETAIL & LEISURE PARK
Bolton Wanderers FC (Reebok Stadium)
Bolton Arena
Horwich Parkway
Hollywood Bowl
Vue Cinema
Superstore
A6027
DE HAVILLAND WAY
Junction 6
LOSTOCK INDUSTRIAL ESTATE
LOCOMOTION INDUSTRIAL ESTATE
HORWICH BUSINESS PARK
Bolton College (Horwich Campus)
Club HORWICH GOLF COURSE House
Lever Park Sch.
Horwich Leis. Cen.
CHURCH ST.
CHORLEY ST.
B6226
Ridgmont Cemetery
St. Catherine's C of E Prim. Sch.
St. Joseph's RC Sch.
Reservoir
Sewage Works
Wood's Barn Farm
Gibb Farm
Leigh Tenement Farm
Highfield Farm
Blackrod Prim. Sch.
Edge's Farm
Park Hall Farm
Scot Lane End
Yate's Farm
Shoemaker Fold
Scot Lane Bridge
Scot Lane Farm
Shepherds Farm
ASPULL
Walker's Lower Farm
Alkers Fold
Wigan
WN2
Shaw's Fold Farm
Vicarage
Ainscow's Farm
Reservoir (covered)
Gidlow Hall
Moat
Dodd's Farm
Bank Top Farm
Dicconson Mill Bridge
DICCONSON LANE
B5239
BOLTON ROAD
Landlord's Farm
Cinder Hill
Three Lovers
Radlin's Farm
Lower Leeches Farm
Higher Leeches Farm
Radcliffe Home Farm
Taylor Farm
BORSDANE WOOD
Holden Woods
Carlies
WINGATES INDUSTRIAL ESTATE
Corges
Reeve's House Farm
Cooper Turning
Four Gates
Football Grd.
DODD LANE IND. ESTATE
Blue Bell Farm
Chadwick's Farm
BL5
Brinsop Hall
Brinsop House
Hilton House
Heaton Dene
Heaton's Farm
Irlam's Farm
Dog Holes Farm
Ashcroft Farm
CHORLEY ROAD A6
Barton Bridge
Barton Fold Farm
Stonepit Field Plantation
Middle Brook
Industrial Estate
20
30
40
35
54
A B C D E F G
1 2 3 4 5 6 7 8 9

Bolton
BL1
BL3
Wallsuches
Bottom o' th' Moor
Montserrat
Delph Hill
Markland Hill
Lostock Hall Fold
Lostock
Lostock Junction
CHEW MOOR
WINGATES
Hunger Hill
Knutshaw Bridge
DEANE
BOLTON GOLF COURSE
REGENT PARK GOLF COURSE
BOLTON OLD LINKS GOLF COURSE
High Rid Reservoir
RUMWORTH LODGE RESERVOIR
CHORLEY NEW ROAD
CHORLEY OLD ROAD
M61 MOTORWAY
A673
A58
B6226
B6402
21
55
38

Barrow Bridge
Bolton Old Links Golf Course
Victoria Lake
Lightbounds
Animal World
Open Air Theatre
MOSS BANK PARK
Johnson Fold Prim. Sch.
Johnson Fold
Thornleigh Salesian College
Halliwell
Cemetery
A58
A666
A6099
BANK
HALLIWELL
MOSS
Lower Pools
Cricket Grd.
Doffcocker
Doffcocker Lodge
CHORLEY
B6226
BL1
OLD
Cope Bank
Jubilee Pool
Skagen
Bolton RUFC Club Ho.
Superstore
Bolton Steam Mus.
Victory
Heaton
ROAD
BLACKBURN
HIGHER BRI.
TOPP WAY
MARSDEN RD.
CHORLEY NEW ROAD
A673
Bolton Hospice
David Lloyd Leisure
QUEEN'S PARK
BOLTON
A676
Bolton School
Gilnow Park
Playing Fields
B6202
B6203
AVENUE
GILNOW
Overdale Crematorium
HEATON CEMETERY
Nursery
Atkinson's Farm
Lady Bridge
Ravens Wood
Dover Bank Plantation
Bank Wood
DEANE GOLF COURSE
Deane Church Clough
River Croal
Pocket
Haslam Park
Gilnow
Wellington Yard
Univ. of Bolton
TRINITY
A579
Lecturers Close
Club House
Deane
DEANE
Willows
Rec. Grd.
Ladybridge High Sch.
Rumworth School
Ladybridge Comm. Leisure Centre
St. Mary's C of E Prim. Sch.
WIGAN
BEAUMONT RD.
Knutshaw Bridge
Fernhill Gate
A6145
HULTON LANE
Playing Fields
Pavilion
ST. HELENS
DERBY
STREET
Daubhill
Heywood Park
Lever Edge
PIKE MILL ESTATE
Hermon Bank Farm
A B C D E F G
1 2 3 4 5 6 7 8 9
22
37
56

H
J
K
L
M
N
23
Longsight Park Arboretum
Longsight Farmhouse
Longworths Manor
Heatons
Hall i' th' Wood Mus.
Eagley Brook Bridge
A58
Cineworld Bolton
Virgin Active Health Club
Hall i' th' Wood
Castle Hill
Reservoir
BOLTON OPEN GOLF COURSE
Club House
Firwood Fold
Bottom o' th' Moor
Works
Football Ground
Tonge Moor
Firwood Sch.
Top o' th' Brow
Withins Community Leisure Centre
Withins School
Thicketford Bridge
Thicketford Brow
Back o' th' Bank
Tonge Viaduct
Turner Bri.
SEVEN ACRES COUNTRY PARK
Comm. Cen.
Roscow Fold
Breightmet
Nursing Home
Mecca Bingo
Superstore
BOLTON GATE RETAIL PARK
Mill Hill
A673
A676
A666
A58
A579
A6053
B6207
B6208
B6209
B6196
B6536
Tonge Fold
Tonge Cemetery
Oaken Bottom
LEVERHULME PARK
Powerleague
Leverhulme Park Athletic Stadium
Playing Fields
Playing Field
Bradford Park
St. Stephen & All Martyrs C of E Prim. Sch.
Springfield
BOLTON
CENTRAL RETAIL PK.
TRINITY RETAIL PK.
Rose Hill
BURNDEN PARK
DW Sports Fitness
Burnden Viaduct
Raikes Clough
Darcy Lever
MOSES GATE COUNTRY PARK
Cricket Grd.
Cricket Ground
Sports Field
Reservoirs
Hacken Bri.
River Croal
Bull Hill
Pig Farm
Davenport Farm
Newholme Farm
Five Acre Farm
Dovebank
Dove Bank Bridge
Old Hall Farm
Dove Bank
Bowness Prim. Sch.
Little Lever Leisure Cen.
Little Lever Sch.
CROMPTON LODGE CARAVAN PARK
Farnworth Bridge
Rock Hall
Burnden
Bradford Reservoir
Bus Depot
Great Lever
Great Lever Park
Edge La. Bridge
Industrial Estate
BL2
BL3
BURY ROAD
BRADFORD ST.
ST. PETERS WAY
MANCHESTER ROAD
TONGE MOOR ROAD
CROMPTON WAY
CHURCH ST.
LOXHAM ST.
HALL LANE
HARDY MILL RD.
40
7
50
57
1
2
3
4
5
6
7
8
9
G
H
J
K
L
M
N

24
58
39
BL2
BL3
BL8
M26
Bolton
AINSWORTH
LITTLE LEVER
RADCLIFFE
Bradley Fold
Starling
BURY AND BOLTON ROAD
BURY NEW ROAD
RADCLIFFE MOOR ROAD
BURY OLD RD.
CHURCH ST.
COCKEY MOOR RD.
ARTHUR LANE
AINSWORTH ROAD
STARLING ROAD
HIGHER AINSWORTH RD.
BOLTON RD.
WATER ST.
STOPES ROAD
HIGH ST.
MARKET ST.
COUNTESS LA.
A58
A665
A6053
B6196
B6292
B6209
HARWOOD GOLF COURSE
BREIGHTMET GOLF COURSE
Cockey Moor
Reservoir

BURY
Elton
Woodhill
Fernhill
Freetown
Wood Fields
Woodhill Fold
Bury Ground
Tentersfield
Buckley Wells
Daisyfield
ALPHA HOSPITAL
Pimhole
Fishpool
Lower Hinds
Warth Fold
Gigg
Bury FC (Gigg Lane)
Cemetery
Fletcher Fold
Redvales
Hollins Vale
Hollins
White Brow
BURY GOLF COURSE
Sunny Bank
Blackford Bridge
Barlow Fold
ELTON RESERVOIR
Elton Sailing Club
Old Hall Farm
Doffer Fold
Withins Resr.
Middle Spen Moor
Lower Spen Moor
East Lancashire Crematorium
Crow Trees Farm
Manchester
Radcliffe
Coney Green Sports Cen.
Close Park
M45
SPRINGWATER PARK
Lily Hill
ROCHDALE ROAD
MANCHESTER ROAD
PEEL WAY
ANGOULEME WAY
JUBILEE WAY
BOLTON ROAD
CROSS LANE
DUMERS LANE
SPRING LA.
A56
A58
A6053
B6196
B6222
B6219
River Irwell
River Roch
Manchester, Bolton & Bury Canal
25
7
42
59

Fern Grove
Fairfield
FAIRFIELD GENERAL HOSPITAL
ROCHDALE OLD ROAD
26
Smethurst Wood
River Roch
Broad Oak Wood
Broad Oak Farm
Lower Lomax
Lomax Wood
Elbut Wood
Bottom o' th' Brow
Bridge House
Mills
Summit
Broad Oak Sports Cen.
Broad Oak High Sch.
Junc. 2
ROCHDALE RD.
BURY NEW ROAD
A58
Prettywood
Heady Hill
BURY
Openshaw Park
Pimhole
Primrose Hill
Heap Bridge
Heap Bridge Village Prim. Sch.
Heap Fold Farm
Top of Heap
Broadfield
Darn Hill
Heywood Community High Sch.
EAST LANCASHIRE RAILWAY
Viaduct
Spout Bank Farm
Water Farm
Reservoir
M66 MOTORWAY
M66
ROCHDALE
BURY
Sand Quarry
HEYWOOD INDUSTRIAL PARK
HEYWOOD DISTRIBUTION PARK
Chemical Distribution Centre
MULBERRY
PILSWORTH ROAD
Jackson Fold
Junction 3
Superstore
Megabowl
Bury
BL9
Hill Top
Sewage Works
Brightley Brook
QUEST PARK
Coal Pits Farm
Captain's
Reservoirs
Hollins Vale
Hollins Brook
Brightley Brook
Higher Fields
Higher Barn
BIRCH INDUSTRIAL ESTATE
Birch Service Area
Meadow Croft Fold
Castle House
Broom Hill Farm
Hollins
Thurston Fold
Castle Brook
Whittle Fold
BURY GOLF COURSE
Sunny Bank
Whitegate
Whittle Brook
Whittle Fold Smallholding
Unsworth
Brick House
Playing Fields
M62 MOTORWAY
M62
Castlebrook High Sch.
PIKE FOLD GOLF COURSE
Moss Side
Unsworth Moss
Green Lane End Farm
Sand Field
Club House
Unsworth Prim. Sch.
41
60

43
Hooley Bri.
Hooley Brow
Queen's Park
Cricket Ground
Cycle Track
Captain Fold
27
Primrose Hill Fm.
Matthew Moss High Sch.
Back o' th' Moss
Heywood Sports Village
St. Luke's C of E Prim. Sch.
All Souls C of E Prim. Sch.
Ryecroft Farm
A58
Rochdale
Castleton
Superstore
OL11
Castleton Gabriel's FC Grd.
Harefield Hall
Harefield Hall Farm
ROCHDALE ROAD EAST
Francil
Club Ho.
Driving Range
CASTLE HAWK GOLF COURSE
JUNCTION 19 INDUSTRIAL PARK
Heywood
Hopwood
PHOENIX PARK INDUSTRIAL ESTATE
Depot
Castleton North Junction
Castleton South Junction
HEYWOOD
St. Joseph's RC Prim. Sch.
St. Joseph's RC High Sch.
Higher Broadfield Farm
M62
M62 MOTORWAY
Hope Cottage
Ley Farm
Lane End Farm
Lane End
Sewage Works
44
Playing Field
Heywood
Siddal Moor Sports Coll.
Siddal Moor
Depot
Hares Hill Farm
Collop Gate Farm
MANCHESTER GOLF COURSE
Driving Range
Junction 19
Siddal Moor Farm
OL10
MIDDLETON ROAD
A6046
A6045
MANCHESTER ROAD
Stock Nook Farm
New Gap Farm
Saxon Farm
Yew Tree Farm East
Glade Wood
Round Hill
Hopwood Hall Farm
Club Ho. (Hopwood Cottag
Oakridge Farm
Yew Tree Farm South
Lords Wood
Lower Whittle
Doctor Fold
Siddal Farm
Siddal Fold
Hatters Cottage
Hatters Farm
Oaken Bank Wood
Hopwood Hall
The Butts Resr.
Playing Field
Hopwood Hall College (Middleton Campus)
Top o' th' Hill
Playing Fields
The Queen Elizabeth School
Manchester
Woodside Farm
Hopwood Clough
M24
Graveyard
Dingle Farm
Langley Lane Farm
Close Road Farm
HOLLIN LANE
The Grange
Birch
Grange Farm
Greenhill Farm
Playing Fields
Top of Hebers
Cardinal Langley RC High Sch.
Stanycliffe Bri.
Stanycliffe
Hollins
Hollin & Newlands Prim. Schs.
St. John Fisher RC Prim. Sch.
Boarshaw Prim. Sch.
ROCHDALE ROAD
A664
Playing Fields
Bowlee Community Park
Comm. Cen.
Bowlee Park Prim. Sch.
Bowlee Pk. Sports Cen.
Langley
61
OLD ROAD
G
H
J
K
L
M
N
1
2
3
4
5
6
7
8
9

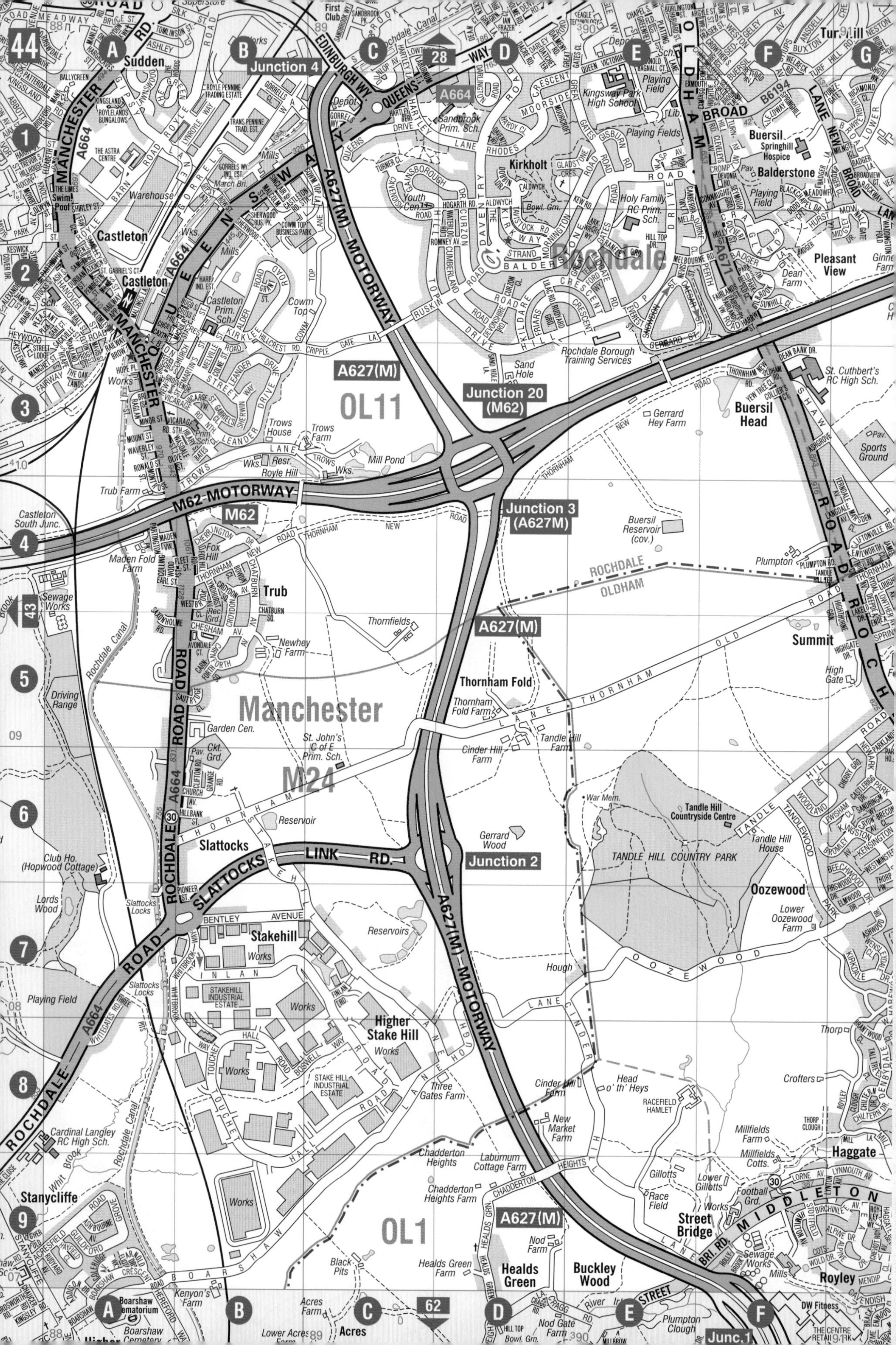
Sudden
Castleton
Junction 4
Junction 20 (M62)
Junction 3 (A627(M))
Junction 2
Kirkholt
Rochdale
Kingsway Park High School
Buersil
Balderstone
Pleasant View
Buersil Head
St. Cuthbert's RC High Sch.
OL11
M62 MOTORWAY
A627(M) MOTORWAY
Trub
Manchester
M24
Slattocks
SLATTOCKS LINK RD.
Stakehill
Higher Stake Hill
STAKEHILL INDUSTRIAL ESTATE
STAKE HILL INDUSTRIAL ESTATE
Thornham Fold
Summit
TANDLE HILL COUNTRY PARK
Tandle Hill Countryside Centre
Oozewood
Thorp
Crofters
Haggate
Royley
Street Bridge
Buckley Wood
Healds Green
OL1
Chadderton Heights
Stanycliffe
Cardinal Langley RC High Sch.
Rochdale Canal
ROCHDALE
OLDHAM
Junc.1
A B C D E F G
1 2 3 4 5 6 7 8 9
28
43
62

M62 MOTORWAY
Junction 21
OL16
Oldham
Green Gate
Burnedge
Green Hill
Higher Rushcroft
Gravel Hole
Hanging Chadder
Narrow Gate Brow
High Crompton
Low Crompton
Bentgate
NEWHEY
Haugh
Jubilee
Whitfield
Wood End
Lower Rushcroft
Goats
Nook
Cowlishaw
OL2
SHAW
Shaw Side
Shaw Edge
New Town
Moss Hey
Fullwood
OL1
SHOLVER
Luzley Brook
Heyside
ROYTON
Thorp
Holden Fold
CROMPTON & ROYTON GOLF COURSE
Crompton House C of E Sch.
New Barn Playing Fields
Royton & Crompton Sch.
Dr. Kershaw's Hospice
Our Lady's RC High School
SHAW ROAD A663
ROCHDALE ROAD
OLDHAM ROAD B6194
MANCHESTER RD.
CROMPTON WAY A663
MILNROW ROAD
BROADWAY

30
Rochdale
OL16
OL2
OL1
OL4
HUDDERSFIELD ROAD A640
ROCHDALE ROAD A640
RIPPONDEN ROAD A672
OLDHAM ROAD A672
DENSHAW ROAD
DELPH ROAD A6052
BUCKSTONES ROAD B6197
GRAINS ROAD
ROCHDALE
OLDHAM
Bethany Fm.
Bye Carr Farm
Helpet Edge
Far Wicken Hall Farm
Wicken Hall Clough
Higher White Slack
Edge Gate
Ogden Edge
Cherry Clough Farm
Cherry Clough
Marsh Farm
Rough Hey Cottage
Haugh Hey
Brimmy Croft
Cherry Top Farm
Cherry Clough Farm
Boothstead
Dumfries Farm
Bone Heys
Ley Wood
Little Rochdale Parish
Stony Hurst
SLENCES HEY
Slences
Whitesides
Boothstead Edge
Wibsey Cotts.
DENSHAW
Far Brownhill Naze Farm
Brownhill Naze Farm
HIGHER PARK
Park Farm
Crow Knowl
Old Brook
CROMPTON MOOR
Top o' th' Meadows
Jordan Brow
Calf Hey Nab
Top o' th' Green
Friarswood
Scout
Woodhouse Farm
Works
Crompton Fold
Brushes
Brushes Clough
Martin Cottages
Brushes Clough Reservoir
Lower Whitehill
WHITE HILL
Way Moss
Shore Edge
Higher Whitehill
Old Tame
Horest Farm
Ashley Ho.
Green Ash
Summer Hill Cottage
Old Field
Model Farm
Nook
Hearthy Hill Farm
Lane Side
Dog Hill
Higher Mantley Gate
Mantley
Hollin Bank
Slackcote
Top o' th' Dog Hill
Burn Farm
Rams Clough
Cricket Grd.
Clough
Roe Gate
Brunchapel Farm
Brookland Lodge
Hillside Bungalow
Dodle Farm
Hanson House
Carchief Nook Farm
Slack Farm
Lower Doghill
Hole Bottom
Fullwood
Besom Hill Reservoir
Grains Bar
Grains Bar Farm
Fullwood Farm
Besom Hill Farm
Besom Hill
Besom Hill End
Cotemans Farm
Tamecroft Farm
Mill Barn
Bishop Park Pitch & Putt Golf Course
Coteman Height Farm
Doorstones Farm
Football Grounds
Wotherhead Hill
May Cottage
Hey Barn Farm
Pearly Bank
Millennium Green
BESOM HILL
Obelisk
Sholver Moor Farm
SHOLVER
Hey Bank
Heys Farm
Prim. Sch.
Strine Dale
Hey Garners Farm
BADGER EDGE
Comm. Cen.
Sholver Grn.
Playing Fld.
HARBOUR HILL
High Lee
Roebuck Low
Green Leach
Jericho
Little End Farm
Cricket Grd.
Heys
Windy Arbour
New Farm
Shiloh Farm
Moorside
Hodge Clough
Count Hill
Strinesdale
Roebuck Low Farm
Valenciennes
Thurston Clough Farm
Hodge Clough Infant School
Higher Barrowshaw
Haven
Strine Dale
Two Acre
Thurston Clough Brook
HIGH MOOR
Thurston House
Higher House
Reservoir
Green Lane Farm
64
395
96
97

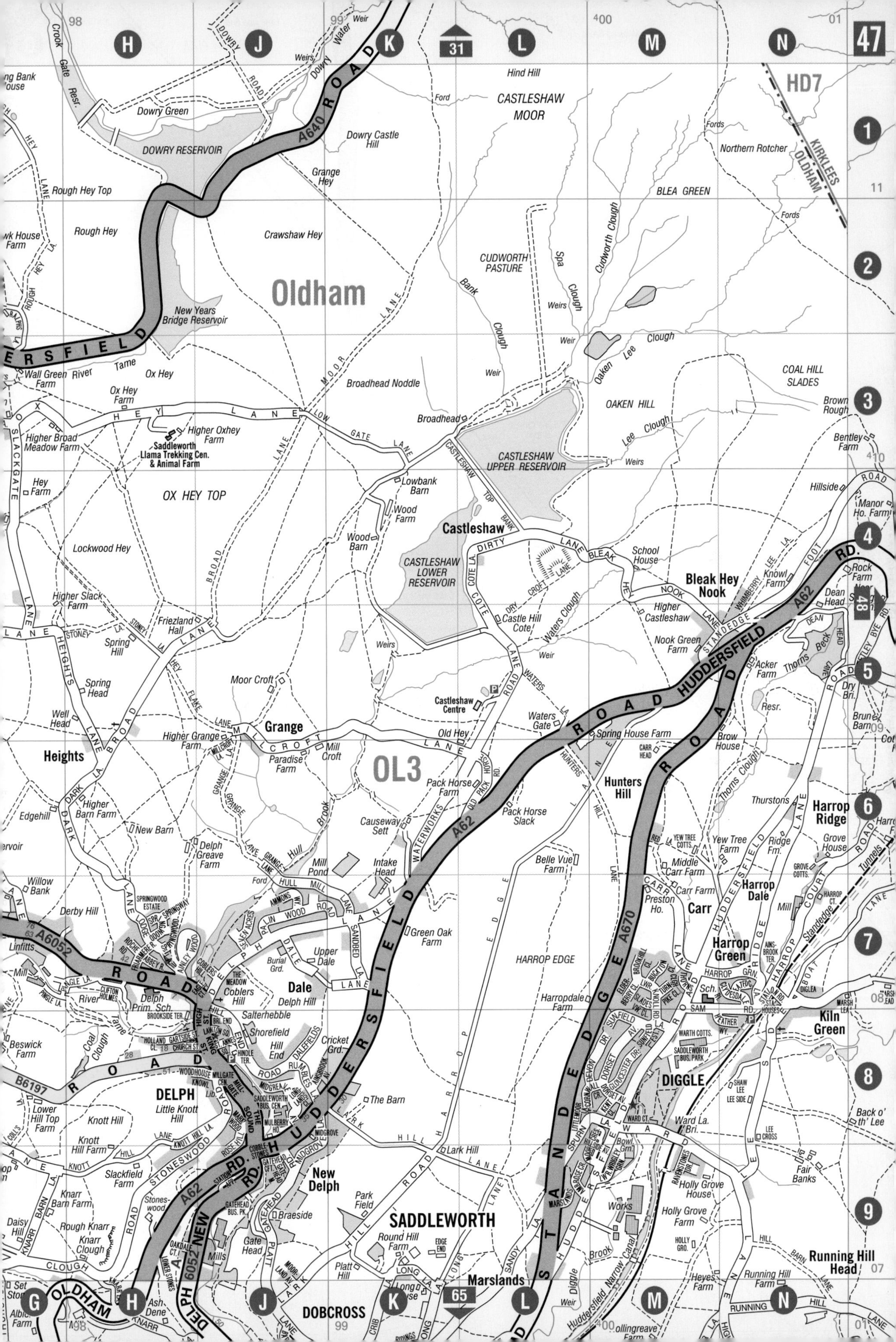

47
HD7
KIRKLEES
OLDHAM
Oldham
OL3
Castleshaw
CASTLESHAW MOOR
Hind Hill
Dowry Green
DOWRY RESERVOIR
Dowry Castle Hill
Grange Hey
Rough Hey Top
Rough Hey
Crawshaw Hey
New Years Bridge Reservoir
CUDWORTH PASTURE
BLEA GREEN
Northern Rotcher
Cudworth Clough
Spa Clough
Bank Clough
Broadhead Noddle
Broadhead
OAKEN HILL
COAL HILL SLADES
Brown Rough
Bentley Farm
Ox Hey
Ox Hey Farm
Higher Oxhey Farm
Saddleworth Llama Trekking Cen. & Animal Farm
Higher Broad Meadow Farm
Hey Farm
OX HEY TOP
CASTLESHAW UPPER RESERVOIR
CASTLESHAW LOWER RESERVOIR
Lowbank Barn
Wood Farm
Wood Barn
Lockwood Hey
Higher Slack Farm
Friezland Hall
Spring Hill
Spring Head
Well Head
Heights
Moor Croft
Castleshaw Centre
Grange
Higher Grange Farm
Paradise Farm
Mill Croft
Old Hey
School House
Bleak Hey Nook
Higher Castleshaw
Nook Green Farm
Castle Hill Cote
Waters Clough
Waters Gate
Spring House Farm
Hunters Hill
Pack Horse Farm
Pack Horse Slack
Acker Farm
Thorns Beck
Brow House
Thorns Clough
Thurstons
Harrop Ridge
Grove House
Ridge Fm.
Yew Tree Farm
Middle Carr Farm
Carr Farm
Preston Ho.
Carr
Harrop Dale
Harrop Green
Edgehill
Higher Barn Farm
New Barn
Delph Greave Farm
Causeway Sett
Mill Pond
Intake Head
Belle Vue Farm
Willow Bank
Derby Hill
Linfitts
Green Oak Farm
Upper Dale
Dale
Delph Hill
Coblers Hill
Salterhebble
Shorefield
Hill End
Cricket Grd.
HARROP EDGE
Harropdale Farm
DIGGLE
Saddleworth Bus. Park
Kiln Green
Beswick Farm
Coal Clough
DELPH
Little Knott Hill
Knott Hill
Knott Hill Farm
Lower Hill Top Farm
The Barn
Lark Hill
Ward La. Bri.
Back o' th' Lee
Fair Banks
Slackfield Farm
Knarr Barn Farm
Daisy Hill
Rough Knarr
Knarr Clough
Stones-wood
New Delph
Braeside
Gate Head
Mills
Park Field
SADDLEWORTH
Round Hill Farm
Platt Hill
Marslands
Holly Grove House
Holly Grove Farm
Works
Running Hill Head
Running Hill Farm
Heyes Farm
Huddersfield Narrow Canal
DOBCROSS
Ash Dene
Albion Farm
A640 ROAD
HUDDERSFIELD ROAD
A62
A670
STANDEDGE
A6052
B6197
DELPH NEW RD.
OLDHAM
31
65
48

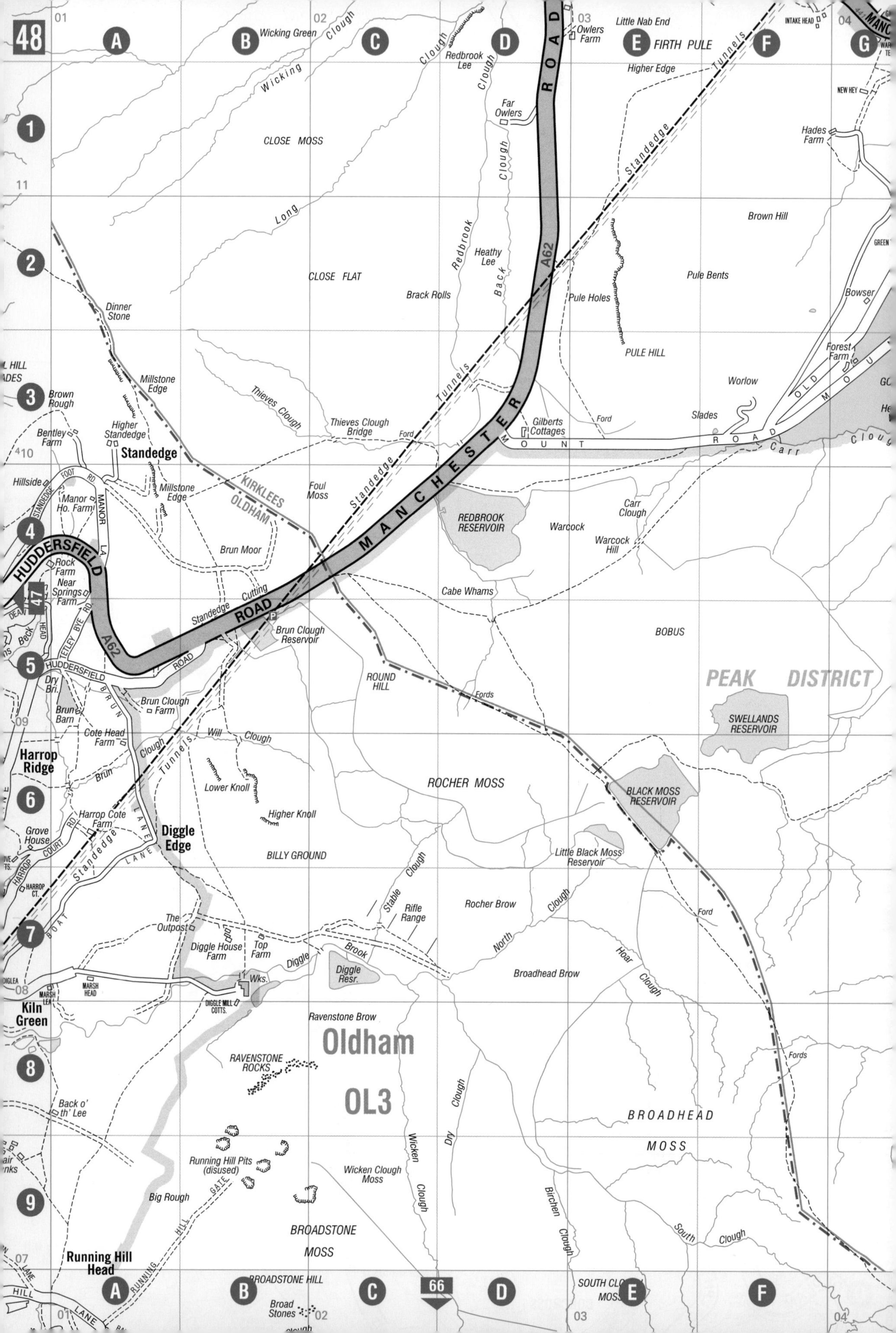
Wicking Green
Wicking Clough
Long Clough
Redbrook Lee
Owlers Farm
Little Nab End
FIRTH PULE
Higher Edge
INTAKE HEAD
NEW HEY
Far Owlers
CLOSE MOSS
Hades Farm
Standedge Tunnels
Brown Hill
Redbrook Clough
Heathy Lee
Back Clough
CLOSE FLAT
Brack Rolls
Pule Holes
Pule Bents
Bowser
Dinner Stone
PULE HILL
Forest Farm
Millstone Edge
Brown Rough
Thieves Clough
Thieves Clough Bridge
Gilberts Cottages
Ford
Worlow
Slades
Bentley Farm
Higher Standedge
Standedge
MOUNT ROAD
Carr Clough
Hillside
STANDEDGE FOOT RD
Manor Ho. Farm
MANOR LA
Millstone Edge
KIRKLEES
OLDHAM
Foul Moss
MANCHESTER ROAD
REDBROOK RESERVOIR
Warcock
Carr Clough
Warcock Hill
HUDDERSFIELD
Rock Farm
Near Springs Farm
Brun Moor
Standedge Cutting
ROAD
A62
Cabe Whams
Brun Clough Reservoir
BOBUS
TETLEY BYE RD
HUDDERSFIELD ROAD
Dry Bri.
Brun Barn
Brun Clough Farm
ROUND HILL
Fords
PEAK DISTRICT
SWELLANDS RESERVOIR
Cote Head Farm
Harrop Ridge
Will Clough
Brun Clough
Lower Knoll
ROCHER MOSS
BLACK MOSS RESERVOIR
Harrop Cote Farm
Higher Knoll
Grove House
Diggle Edge
BILLY GROUND
Little Black Moss Reservoir
HARROP COURT RD
HARROP CT.
Stable Clough
Rifle Range
Rocher Brow
North Clough
Ford
The Outpost
BOAT LANE
Diggle House Farm
Top Farm
Diggle Brook
Diggle Resr.
Hoar Clough
Broadhead Brow
DIGLEA
MARSH LEA
MARSH HEAD
Wks.
DIGGLE MILL COTTS.
Kiln Green
Ravenstone Brow
Oldham
OL3
RAVENSTONE ROCKS
Fords
Back o' th' Lee
Dry Clough
BROADHEAD MOSS
Wicken Clough
Running Hill Pits (disused)
Wicken Clough Moss
Birchen Clough
Big Rough
RUNNING HILL GATE
BROADSTONE MOSS
South Clough
Running Hill Head
BROADSTONE HILL
Broad Stones
SOUTH CLOUGH MOSS
66
47
Old Mount Road
01
02
03
04
11
10
09
08
07
A
B
C
D
E
F
G
1
2
3
4
5
6
7
8
9

MARSDEN
Netherley
Scout
Huddersfield
HD7
NATIONAL PARK
Holmfirth
HD9
BUTTERLEY RESERVOIR
BLAKELEY RESERVOIR
WESSENDEN RESERVOIR
WESSENDEN HEAD RESERVOIR
DEER HILL RESERVOIR
HOLME MOOR
BINN MOOR
WESSENDEN MOOR
DEER HILL MOSS
HORSELEY HEAD MOSS
BLACK MOSS
WHITE MOSS
BUTTERLY
SHOOTERS NAB
DEER HILL
WEST NAB
WESSENDEN HEAD
Deer Hill Conduit
Manor House Farm
Clark Hill Farm
Bank Top Farm
Ox House
Binn Ho.
Ing Lees
Peters Farm
Crowther Cottages
Upper Acre Head
Well Lane Head
Black Edge
Hind Hill
West End
Well Close
Binn Lodge Farm
Hill Top
Naze Wood
Naze Top Wood
Holme Bank Wood
Broadhead Wood
Far New Close
Dry Clough Side
Scar Head
Wham Head
Harrow Hill
Rigg Shaw
Great Clough
Smately Bank
Great Butterly Hill
Little Butterly Hill
Adam Pasture
Small Clough
Blakely Clough
Hey Green
Hey Brinks
Wessenden Lodge
Hey Sike Head Marsh
Sike Clough
Holly Bank Moss
Raven Rocks
Rocking Stone
West Nab Moss
Scope Moss
The Scope
Muddy Brook
Grouse Butts
Waterfalls
Weir
Little Hey Cote Hill
Round Hills
Great Hey Cote Hill
Cradles
Great Dike Springs
Wessenden Brook
Birken Bank
Lower Hills
Leyzing Clough
Winter Clough
Pudding Real Moss
Birk Moss
Long Grain
Short Grain
Jopes Moss
Greystones
Shiny Brook Clough
Shiny Brook
Loadley Clough
Wicken Grain
West Grain
Great Rushbed
Wessenden Head Moss
Upper Hey Heads
Burnt Hill
Piper Stones
Round Hill
Holme Moor Flat
Scout Holes
Top of Scout
Hard Hill
Ellen Clough
Rifle Range
Shooting Box
Crow Hill
Butter Spring
Lower Scout Farm
Scout Farm
Greyston Farm
Carr's Farm
Rec. Grd.
Football Grd.
Cricket Grd.
Club House
Pav.
MARSDEN GOLF COURSE
Mills
Wks.
A62
A635
67

Forsters Green
Birch Green
Elmers Green
Crisp Delf
ROBY MILL
BEACON PARK GOLF COURSE
Beacon Country Pk. Visitor Cen.
Club House
Driving Range
BEACON COUNTRY PARK
Rough Park Wood
Sports Field
Playing Fields
Walthew Park
Carmelite Convent
College Farm
St. Teresa's Catholic Prim. Sch.
Reservoir (covered)
Tanhouse
SKELMERSDALE
Delph Side Prim. Sch.
Skelmersdale Sports Cen.
Tawd Bridge
Holland Moor
Holland Moor Prim. Sch.
Moorside Prim. Sch.
Digmoor
Bishop Martin C of E Prim. Sch.
St. Francis Assisi Prim. Sch.
Little Digmoor Prim. Sch.
Newgate
Garnett Lees Playing Fields
Hall Green
Lower Tower Hill Farm
Higher Tower Hill Farm
UP HOLLAND
Skelmersdale
Chequer
Brick Works
Chequer Lane Playing Fields
Junction 5
Sutche's Farm
WN8
Well Cross Farm
Giant House Farm
Sefton House Farm
M58 MOTORWAY
STANNANOUGHT ROAD
A577
B5312
PIMBO INDUSTRIAL ESTATE
West Pimbo
East Pimbo
PIMBO JUNCTION
Upholland
Moor Side Farm
Barton Ho.
Lower Balcony Farm
Lower Pimbo
Higher Pimbo
Pimbo Bushes
Balcarres Farm
Crawford Village Prim. Sch.
Bounty Farm
Millets Farm
Ambrose Cottage
Captain Leigh's Farm
Crawford
Billinge Bounty Farm
Red House Farm
Birch Wood
WEST LANCASHIRE
ST. HELENS
Black Brook
Sand Brook
BISPHAM HALL BUSINESS PARK
Mountains Farm
Heaton House
Maddock's Wood
Daisy Wood
The Lawns
Tunnel
32
68

Walthew Green
Gathurst
Johnson's Farm
Pearson's Farm
Dean Brook
Dean Wood
Jollies i' th' Dean
Dean Wood Golf Course
West Lancashire Wigan
Dean House
The Paddocks
Orrell House Farm
Rothwell House
Club House
Holland Hall
Strand House
Gathurst Fold
Green Bank
Gathurst Wood
Oakwood
Ackhurst Lane
Chez Nous
Playing Fields
Irvine's Farm
St. John Rigby College
Playing Field
Ackhurst Hall
Porter's Wood
Ackhurst Brook
Warehouse
Martland Mill Industrial Estate
Works
Depot
Factory
Kitt Green
Walthew Lane
Challenge Way
Orrell Hall
Latham House Farm
Wigan
The Bell
Bell House Farm
Kingsdown High Sch.
Norley
Montrose Av.
M6 Motorway
WN5
Orrell Post
Hooton's Farm
Moor Cottage
School La.
Orrell Road
A577
FX Leisure
High School
Dean Brook Bridge
Abbey Lakes
Sand Brook
M58 Motorway
Recreation Grd.
Tontine
Sefton Farm
Orrell
Junction 26
Captain's Clough
Lamberhead Green
Lamberhead Green Primary School
Redwood
Playing Field
Ormskirk Road
Spring Bank
Rose Hill
Pemberton
Duke's Barn Farm
Edge Wood Hall
Smithy Brook
Leopold Street
Up Holland High School
Far Moor
Playing Field
Orrell
Hewitt Business Park
Winstanley Tennis Club
Duke's Wood
Tueson Villas
Little Wood
Wood Cottage
New Covert
Highfield
St. Matthew's Rec. Grd.
Billinge Road
Higher End
Orrell Water Park
Farrar's Farm
Gorsey Hill Wood
Winstanley College
Workshop Wood
Moat Ho.
Garden Wood
Winstanley Park
Winstanley Hall
Birch Tree Farm
Delph Plantation
WN3
Rylance Mill Farm
Lea Wood
Colliery Wood
Winstanley
Mossey Croft Wood
Greenslate Farm
Upholland Road
Moss Road
Upholland Lodges
Gautley Ho.
Oak Wood
Moss Wood
Moss House
The Belt
Camp Hill
New House Fm.
Spring Hall Wood
Pemberton Road
A571
New Houses
Bispham Hall
Bispham House
Longshaw
Long Farm
Cherry Tree

A
B
C
D
E
F
G
1
2
3
4
5
6
7
8
9
34
9
51
70
56
57
58
Martland Mill
Martland Mill Bri.
Martland Mill Farm
Warehouse
Depot
Works
Marsh Green
Laithwaite
Kingsdown High Sch.
Playing Fields
Montrose Sch.
St. Cuthbert's Catholic Prim. Sch.
Spring Bank
Ell Meadow Lock
Sacred Heart Catholic Prim. Sch.
Springfield
Gidlow
River Douglas
Playing Fields
Powerleague Wigan
Sports Grd.
Pagefield Ind. Est.
Robin Park
Wigan Athletic FC & Wigan Warriors RLFC (DW Stadium)
Gala Bingo
Empire Cinema
Robin Park Sports & Tennis Cen.
Robin Park Arena
Robin Park Retail Park
Sports Pitches
Superstore
WIGAN
Leeds & Liverpool Canal
Cricket St. Bus. Pk.
Wigan & Leigh Coll. (Pagefield Bldg.)
Tennis Cts.
Bowling Grns.
Mesnes Park
Thomas Linacre Centre
Bull Hey
Wigan & Leigh Coll. (Wigan Campus)
Deanery High Sch.
Royal Albert Edward Infirmary
Swinley
Bowling Greens
Water Heyes
Grand Arcade
Civic Cen.
Theatre
Wigan Wallgate
Wallgate
AMF Bowl
Wigan Nth. Western
Karting
Courts
Worsley Hall
Playing Fields
Rec. Grd.
Newtown
Parson's Meadow
Bakery
Swan Meadow Ind. Est.
Eckersley Mill
Factory
Recreation Ground
Poolstock
Playing Field
Alexandra Park
Skew Bri.
Lion Bri.
Westwood Hall
Wigan
Westwood Park Gdns.
Westwood Cemetery
Sewage Works
Pearson's Flash
Scotman's Flash
Wigan Sailing Club
Warrington Road Ind. Est.
Oil Depot
Elm Farm
Playing Fields
Worsley Mesnes
Smithy Brook
Football Grd.
Pemberton
Goose Green
Blundell's Wood
Comm. Cen.
Winstanley Shop. Cen.
Hawkley Brook Trading Est.
Warehouses
Tan Pit Cotts.
Tan Pit Slip
Marus Bridge Retail Park
Hope Sch.
Works
Total Fitness
Hawkley
Hawkley Hall High Sch.
Moss Bri.
Rough Wood
Derbyshire
ORMSKIRK RD.
A577
A571
A49
A573
B5375
B5376
B5238
WN5
WN3
ORMSKIRK ROAD
VICTORIA ROAD
WARRINGTON ROAD
POOLSTOCK LANE
WALLGATE
POTTERY RD.
PARK ROAD
PARSON'S WALK
NORTHWAY
RIVERWAY
CENTRAL PARK WAY
WIGAN LANE
MESNES RD.
KENYON RD.
STADIUM WAY
WOODHOUSE DR.
WOODHOUSE LANE
LITTLE LANE
BILLINGE RD.

53
Bottling Wood
New Springs
Canon Sharples Prim. Sch.
Top Lock
Reservoir
Bradshaw Hall Farm
Bradshaw Cottage
Pennington Green
Pennington Hall Farm
Marsh Farm
Withington Barn
WITHINGTON LANE
B5238 WIGAN RD.
Playing Field
Resr. (covered)
Bakery
Works
KIRKLESS INDUSTRIAL ESTATE
Kirkless Hall
Clarrington Brook
Leeds & Liverpool Canal
Whelley
Longshoot
Scholes
Rose Bridge
Rose Bridge Spts. & Comm. Cen.
Peel Hall Bri.
HINDLEY HALL GOLF COURSE
Bank House Farm
Wildfowl Sanctuary
Hindley Hall Farm
Club Ho.
Recycling Centre
Depot
Gidlow House
Superstore
HEMFIELD RD.
MANCHESTER ROAD
DARLINGTON ST. EAST
Higher Ince
Playing Fields
Whalley's Basin
William Foster Playing Field
Britannia Bri.
INCE-IN-MAKERFIELD
WARRINGTON RD.
St. Williams Catholic Prim. Sch.
DOBSON PARK IND. EST.
Amberswood Comn.
Walmesley Park
WN2
Brownlow
MAKERFIELD WAY
Hindley
Ince
Amberswood Common
Low Hall Farm
Ince Farm
Hockery Brook
Playing Field
Recreation Ground
Prim. Sch.
A577
WIGAN ROAD
WIGAN ENTERPRISE PARK
Moss Hall Farm
SEAMAN WAY
Lower Ince
Timber Yard
Ince Cemetery
Wigan Cemetery
Wigan Crematorium
Ince Brook
AMBERSWOOD COMMON
HINDLEY
St. Peter's C of E Prim. Sch.
Wigan & Leigh Hospice
Stoney La. Bri.
CROSS ST.
MARKET ST.
ATHERTON RD.
A577 RD.
Superstore
Depot
Springs Branch Junction
Coal Depot
Liverpool Junction
Bushell's Farm
Spring View
INCE MOSS
Prim. Sch.
Dog Pool Brook
A58
Works
Oakfield High Sch.
A573
WARRINGTON ROAD
Manchester Junction
Newbridge Sch.
Cricket Gdx.
WALTHEW LA.
LIVERPOOL RD.
LOW HALL PARK
SPRINGBANK IND. EST.
Platt Bri. Sch. & Lib.
Leyland Park
Youth Cen.
Caravan Site
Borsdane Brook
PLATT BRIDGE
Playing Field
HMYOI HINDLEY
INCE MOSS
Sewage Works
Brookside Farm
Pear Tree Farm
35
71
9
54
G H J K L M N
59 360 61 62
1 2 3 4 5 6 7 8 9
07 06 05 04 03

A
B
C
D
E
F
G
36
Reservoir (covered)
Dodd's Farm
Bank Top Farm
Home Farm
Moat
Gidlow Hall
Taylor Farm
Holden Woods
Carlies
Wingates Industrial Estate
Industrial Estate
Bradshaw Cottage
Borsdane Wood
Pennington Hall Farm
Bagshaw Lane
Willow Bank
School Farm
Bagshaw Cottage
The Firs Farm
Bordane Wood Bungalow
Borsdane Wood Local Nature Reserve
Westhoughton Golf Course
Pennington Green
Club House
Westhoughton
Wilson's Farm
Borsdane Brook
Borsdane
Cemetery
Aldreds
Old Lane Farm
Hill Crest
America Wood
Bolton
Wigan
Baldwin's Farm
Old Fold Farm
Higher Barn Farm
Crow Nest Farm
Jacks Lane
Dobb Brow
Hart Common
BL5
Hindley
Crow Nest Junction
Hindley Cemetery
Lower Barn Farm
Wigan Road
A58
Playing Field
Seftons Farm
Bolton & Westhoughton Greyhound Stadium
Rayner Park
Castle Hill Road
Lambert Sales Farm
St. George's C of E Prim. Sch.
53
Works
Club House
Eatock Prim. Sch.
Hart Common Golf Course
Bank's Farm
Marsh Brook
Daisy Hill
Wigan
Cunningham Brook
Playing Flds.
WN2
Marshes Farm
Hosker's Nook
Harts i' th' Hole
Chapel Fields
Hindley Pool
Maxwell Farm
The Pungle
Hindley Comm. High Sch.
Alder Farm
Bugle Horn
HINDLEY
Hindley Sports Cen.
The Hollins
Nursery
Thorley Ho.
Playing Field
Land Farm
Land Farm Equestrian Centre
Sewage Works
Greenbank Bus. Park
Hindley Industrial Estate
Atherton Road
A577
Oakfield High Sch.
Training Cen.
Speakman's Farm
Intack Farm
Prim. Sch.
Alder Farm
Close Lane Farm
Close Ho. Farm
Leyland Park
Playing Fields
Scowcroft Farm
Hindley Green Prim. Sch.
Road
Corner La.
Smallbrook
Hall Lane Farm
Haven Lea
Hindley Green
Leigh
Bowker's Bri.
Lower Snipes
HMYOI Hindley
Factories
Barlow's Farm
Works
Dangerous Corner
Hindley Green Bus. Park
WN7
Leigh Road
A578
72
Playing Fields
62
63
64
365
07
06
405
04
03
1
2
3
4
5
6
7
8
9

Westhoughton
Hunger Hill
BL3
Junction 5
M61 MOTORWAY
M61
A6
A58
MANCHESTER ROAD
Water's Nook
Chequerbent
Bolton
Over Hulton
HULTON PARK
Daisy Hill
Hag Fold
Atherton
ATHERTON
A577
A579
B5235
B5215
Old Sirs
Howe Bridge
Hindsford
Howe Bridge Crematorium
Westhoughton High Sch.
Westhoughton Leisure Centre
Snydale Hall Farm
Knowles Bridge Farm
Gorse Wood
Stone Shed Wood
Belgrave Spinney
Rawsthorne Wood
Dog Kennel Wood
New Park Wood
Mill Dam Wood
Park Pits Wood
Cow Wood
Southside Industrial Park
Chowbent Prim. Sch.
Chanters Ind. Est.
37
73
56

Knutshaw Bridge
Lever Edge
Morris Green
BL3
Middle Hulton
Bolton
Over Hulton
Hulton Lane Ends
M61 MOTORWAY
Junction 4
BL5
GREAT LEVER & FARNWORTH GOLF COURSE
ROYAL BOLTON HOSPITAL
BRACKLEY GOLF COURSE
Greenheys
Peel
M46
M29
Shakerley
TYLDESLEY
Cutacre Tip

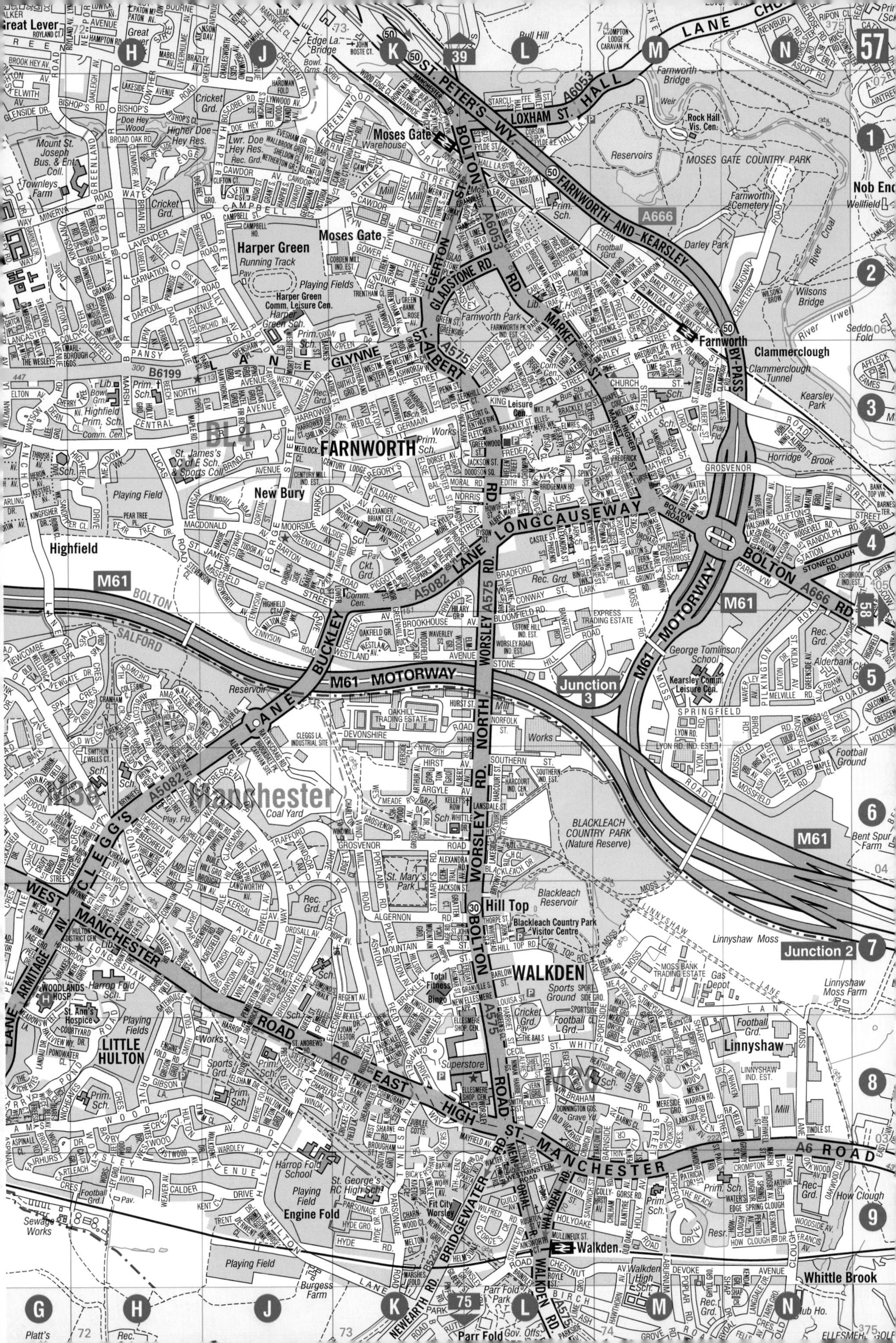
57
Great Lever
H
J
K
L
M
N
39
Bull Hill
Edge La. Bridge
Moses Gate
Farnworth Bridge
Rock Hall Vis. Cen.
Reservoirs
MOSES GATE COUNTRY PARK
Nob End
Mount St. Joseph Bus. & Ent. Coll.
Townleys Farm
Harper Green
Running Track
Harper Green Comm. Leisure Cen.
Farnworth Cemetery
Darley Park
River Croal
Wilsons Bridge
River Irwell
Farnworth Park
Farnworth
Clammerclough
Clammerclough Tunnel
Kearsley Park
FARNWORTH
BL4
Highfield
New Bury
Playing Field
M61
M61 MOTORWAY
Junction 3
George Tomlinson School
Kearsley Comm. Leisure Cen.
Alderbank
OAKHILL TRADING ESTATE
EXPRESS TRADING ESTATE
Manchester
Coal Yard
BLACKLEACH COUNTRY PARK (Nature Reserve)
Bent Spur Farm
St. Mary's Park
Hill Top
Blackleach Reservoir
Blackleach Country Park Visitor Centre
Linnyshaw Moss
Junction 2
WALKDEN
MOSS BANK TRADING ESTATE
Linnyshaw Moss Farm
Linnyshaw
LITTLE HULTON
Harrop Fold Sch.
St. Ann's Hospice
Superstore
Harrop Fold School
Playing Field
Engine Fold
Sewage Works
Walkden
Whittle Brook
How Clough
Burgess Farm
Parr Fold Park
Parr Fold
Platt's
75
58
A6 ROAD
MANCHESTER
LONGCAUSEWAY
BOLTON ROAD
CLEGG'S LANE
WORSLEY RD. NORTH
1
2
3
4
5
6
7
8
9
G

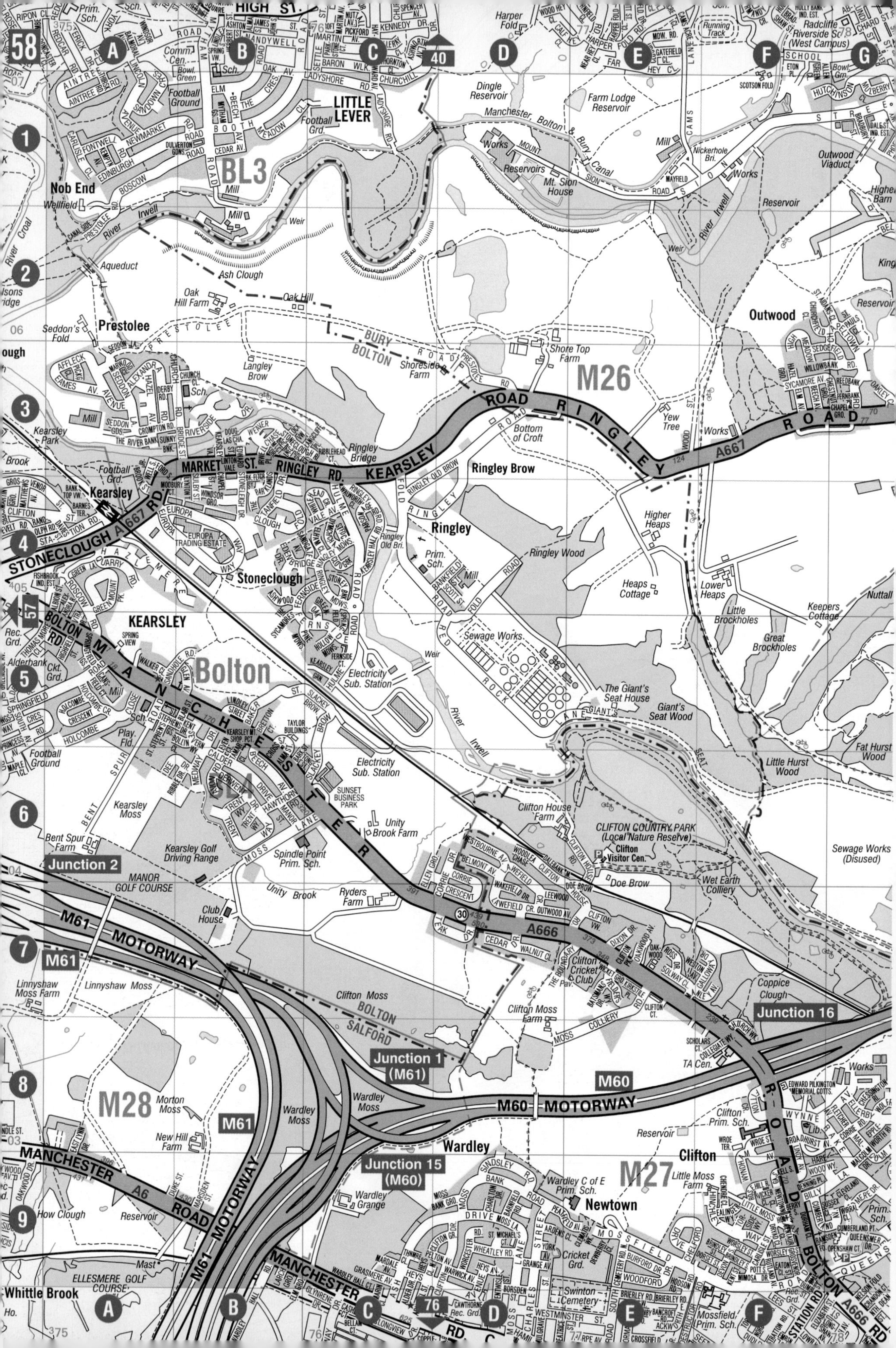

58
A
B
C
D
E
F
G
1
2
3
4
5
6
7
8
9
40
57
76
HIGH ST.
LITTLE LEVER
BL3
Nob End
Wellfield
Prestolee
Seddon's Fold
River Irwell
River Croal
Aqueduct
Ash Clough
Oak Hill Farm
Oak Hill
Dingle Reservoir
Farm Lodge Reservoir
Manchester, Bolton & Bury Canal
Works
Reservoirs
Mt. Sion House
Nickerhole Bri.
Outwood Viaduct
Outwood
Reservoir
Harper Fold
Radcliffe Riverside Sc. (West Campus)
Running Track
Shore Top Farm
Shoreside Farm
BURY
BOLTON
M26
RINGLEY ROAD
A667
Yew Tree
Bottom of Croft
Ringley Brow
Ringley
Ringley Wood
Ringley Bridge
Ringley Old Bri.
Higher Heaps
Heaps Cottage
Lower Heaps
Little Brockholes
Great Brockholes
Keepers Cottage
Nuttall
Kearsley
Kearsley Park
KEARSLEY
Stoneclough
STONECLOUGH RD.
MARKET ST.
RINGLEY RD.
KEARSLEY RD.
Europa Trading Estate
Bolton
BL4
MANCHESTER RD.
BOLTON RD.
Football Ground
Kearsley Moss
Bent Spur Farm
Kearsley Golf Driving Range
Sewage Works
Electricity Sub. Station
Sunset Business Park
Unity Brook Farm
Spindle Point Prim. Sch.
Unity Brook
Ryders Farm
The Giant's Seat House
Giant's Seat Wood
Fat Hurst Wood
Little Hurst Wood
Clifton House Farm
CLIFTON COUNTRY PARK (Local Nature Reserve)
Clifton Visitor Cen.
Doe Brow
Wet Earth Colliery
Sewage Works (Disused)
Junction 2
MANOR GOLF COURSE
Club House
M61 MOTORWAY
M61
A666
Clifton Cricket Club
Clifton Moss Farm
Coppice Clough
Junction 16
Linnyshaw Moss Farm
Linnyshaw Moss
Clifton Moss
BOLTON
SALFORD
Junction 1 (M61)
M60
M60 MOTORWAY
TA Cen.
Wardley Moss
M28
Morton Moss
New Hill Farm
Wardley
Junction 15 (M60)
Wardley Grange
Wardley C of E Prim. Sch.
Newtown
Clifton
Clifton Prim. Sch.
Little Moss Farm
M27
MANCHESTER ROAD
A6
How Clough
Reservoir
Mast
ELLESMERE GOLF COURSE
Whittle Brook
Swinton Cemetery
Cricket Grd.
Mossfield Prim. Sch.
MOSSFIELD ROAD
STATION RD.
BOLTON ROAD
A666 RD.

RADCLIFFE
WHITEFIELD
PRESTWICH
Manchester
Lily Hill
Crow Oak
Chapel Field
Stand
Park Lane
Besses o' th' Barn
Oak Bank
Clifton Green
Clifton Junction
Clifton
Pepper Hill
Hilton Park
Rainsough
STAND GOLF COURSE
WHITEFIELD GOLF COURSE
PRESTWICH FOREST PARK
PHILIPS PARK
M60 MOTORWAY
Junction 17
RADCLIFFE NEW ROAD
RINGLEY ROAD WEST
BURY NEW ROAD
BURY OLD ROAD
HIGHER LANE
A665
A667
A56
A6044
M60
41
60
77

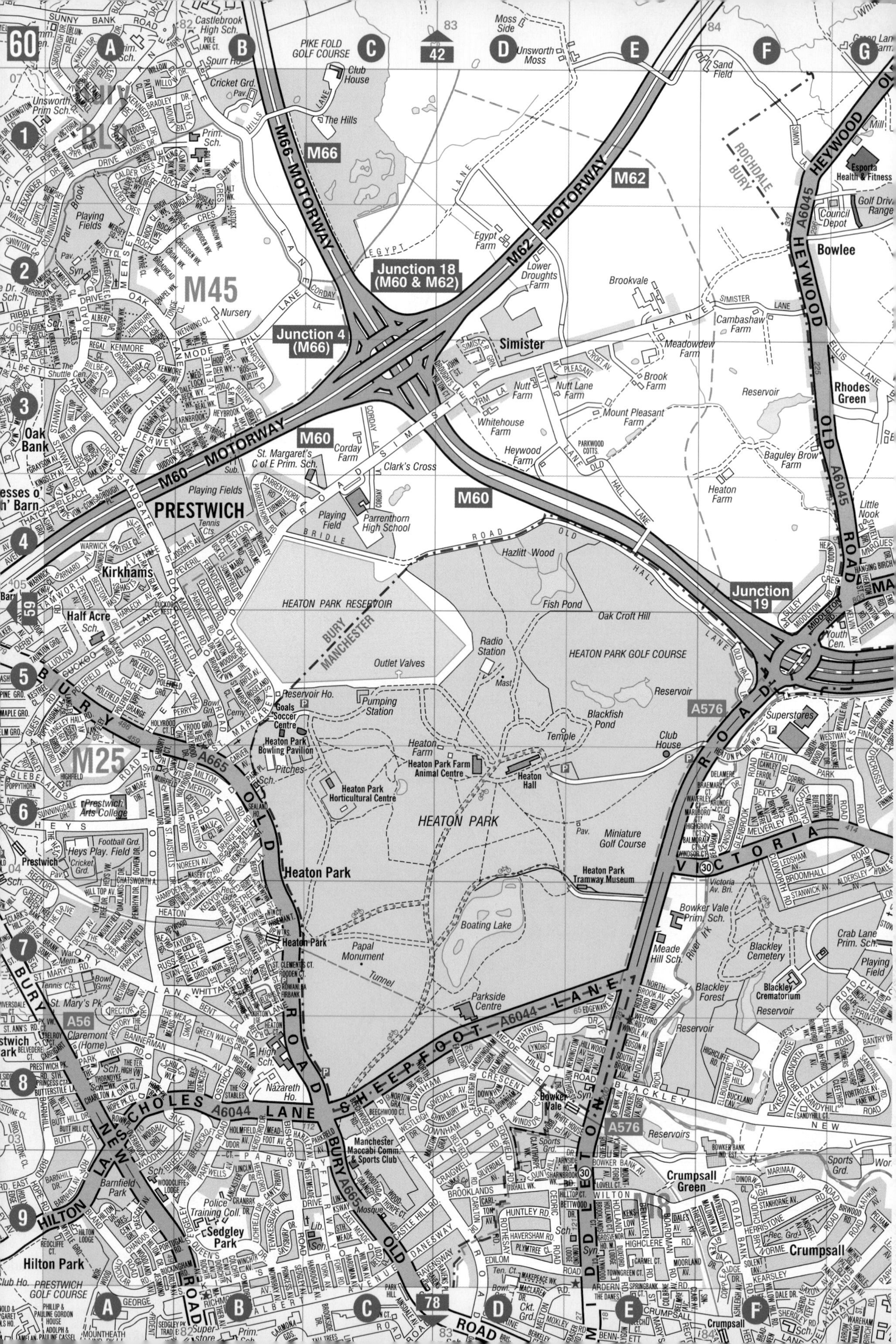

PRESTWICH
Kirkhams
Half Acre
Simister
Bowlee
Rhodes Green
Crumpsall
Crumpsall Green
Sedgley Park
Hilton Park
Heaton Park
HEATON PARK
HEATON PARK RESERVOIR
HEATON PARK GOLF COURSE
Junction 18 (M60 & M62)
Junction 4 (M66)
Junction 19
M60 MOTORWAY
M62 MOTORWAY
M66 MOTORWAY
PIKE FOLD GOLF COURSE
PRESTWICH GOLF COURSE
Blackley Forest
Blackley Cemetery
Boating Lake
Heaton Hall
42
59
78

MIDDLETON
Langley
Bowlee Community Park
Bowlee Park Prim. Sch.
Bowlee Pk. Sports Cen.
St. Mary's RC Prim. Sch.
Langley Children's Project
Council Offs.
Parkside
Truffet Pk. Rec. Grd.
NEW NORTH MANCHESTER GOLF COURSE
Asker Dam
Rhodes Green Farm
Rhodes
Frank's Dam
Reservoirs
Sunny Brow Nursery Sch.
M24
Lime Field
Council Offs.
Parkfield Prim. Sch.
Middleton Parish Church Sch.
Hollin & Newlands Prim. Schs.
John Fisher RC Prim. Sch.
Boarshaw Sch.
Little Green
John Lee Fold
Cromer Industrial Estate
Arena
Superstore
Middleton Shop. Cen.
Bus Sta.
Little Park
Lark Hill
Middleton Technology Sch.
Playing Fields
Ramsden Farm
St. Peter's RC Prim. Sch.
Club Ho. (Rhodes Ho.)
Little Heaton C of E Prim. Sch.
Playing Field
Kitchen Wood
Lever Bridge
Reservoir
Bird Sanctuary
Alkrington Wood
Wood Cottage
M60 MOTORWAY
Manchester
Litchford Hall Cott.
Light Alders
Nursing Home
Convent
Sports College
Playing Fields
Junction 20
Nut Bank
Alkrington Prim. Sch.
Alkrington Garden Village
Comm. Cen.
Youth Cen.
Playing Field
St. Michael's C of E Prim. Sch.
St. Thomas More RC Prim. Sch.
BLACKLEY GOLF COURSE
Warehouse
Club Ho.
Fitness First
Higher Blackley
Plant Hill Arts College
Plant Hill Park
Camberwell Park Special Sch.
Cemetery
Crosslee Prim. Sch.
Prim. Sch.
Charlestown
Charlestown Prim. Sch.
North Manchester High Sch. for Boys
Bailey's Wood
Pike Fold Prim. Sch.
Reservoir
Works
Depot
NORTH MANCHESTER GENERAL HOSPITAL
Pavilion
Oliver Clough
War Memorial
Boggart Hole Clough Track
BOGGART HOLE CLOUGH
Playing Field
Fish Pond
Boating Lake
North Manchester High Sch. for Girls
Tennis Cts.
Playing Field
Moston
Broadhurst Park Playing Fields
Blackley
Bowling Greens
Davis Rec. Grd.
M9
A6104
A664
A576
A669
A6046
B6189
ROCHDALE ROAD
MANCHESTER NEW ROAD
MANCHESTER OLD ROAD
VICTORIA AVENUE
VICTORIA AVENUE EAST
KINGSWAY
OLDHAM ROAD
43
79
62

62
A
B
C
D
E
F
G
1
2
3
4
5
6
7
8
9
44
61
80
Bridge
Buckley Wood
Royley
Black Pits
Healds Green
Nod Farm
Kenyon's Farm
Boarshaw Crematorium
Boarshaw Cemetery
Higher Boarshaw
Acres Farm
Acres
Lower Acres Farm
Healds Green Cricket Grd.
Nod Gate Farm
Plumpton Clough
A627(M)
Junction 1
DW Fitness
THE CENTRE RETAIL PARK
Chadderton Fold
Limefield Field
Chadderton Hall Jun. Sch.
Infant Sch.
Chadderton Hall Park
North Chadderton Upper Sch.
Play. Fld.
Little Green
Playing Field
Snowcroft Farm
River Irk
Rochdale Canal
Mills Hill Bridge
OLDHAM ROAD
A669
HAIGH LANE
CHADDERTON HALL
B6195
Chadderton Park
Mills Hill
Elm Wood Prim. Sch.
Mills Hill Prim. Sch.
MIDDLETON
Nth. Chadderton Lower Sch.
Chadderton Cemetery
A663
Bare Trees Inf. & Jun. Sch.
Football Grd.
Middleton Tech. Sch.
Playing Fields
Moorclose Playing Fld.
St. Gabriel's CE Prim. Sch.
Green Hill
Spring Brook School
Radclyffe Upper School
Radclyffe Athletics Centre
Ferney Field Farm
CHADDERTON
Crossley Bri.
Stock Brook
St. Luke's C of E Prim. Sch.
Crossley Play. Fld.
Cowhill
Alder Root
B6189
Middleton Junction
FOXDENTON LANE
Foxdenton Farm
Matthew Fold
Manchester
BROOKSIDE BUSINESS PARK
Swan Mill
Foxdenton Hall
Albert Taylor Rec. Grd.
Foxdenton Hall Pk.
Radclyffe Lower Sch.
Thatch Leach
Freehold
Comm. Cen.
GREENGATE IND. EST.
CHADDERTON INDUSTRIAL ESTATE
Warehouse
Sludge Beds
Sewage Works
Langwood
Bowling Green
Nimble Nook
The Kingfisher Special Sch.
Ram Mill
Superstore
Recreation Grd.
Butler Green
Refuse Tip
Factory
OLDHAM BROADWAY BUSINESS PARK
Rugby Mill
Gorse Mill
Ace Mill
B6393
M60
Junction 21
BROADGATE
Yew Tree Comm. Sch.
White Gate
Coalshaw Grn. Pk.
South Chadderton
VICTORIA TRADING ESTATE
A62
Fitness First
Chain Bar
Spts. Grd.
VICTORIA AVENUE EAST
HOLLINWOOD
SEMPLE WAY
M60 MOTORWAY
DRURY LA.
White Gate End
South Chadderton Sch.
Moston
A6104
Junction 22
Newspaper Works
Hollinwood
College of Arts & Tech.
Broadway Leis. Cen.
New Moston
Pavilion
Broadhurst Park Playing Fields
JUNCTION 22 BUSINESS PARK
The Edge

Holden Fold
Our Lady's RC High School
Dr. Kershaw's Hospice
Oldham Athletic FC (Boundary Park)
Football Grd.
Long Clough
Woodstock Business Park
Laurel Trading Estate
Higginshaw
Broadbent Moss
Broadbent
Broadbent Farm
Watersheddings
Stoneleigh Prim. Sch.
Stoneleigh Park
Long Sight
Reservoir (cov.)
OLDHAM
Sarah Moor
The Royal Oldham Hospital
Superstore
West Hulme
Westwood Park
Burnley Brow
Coldhurst Hollow
Oldham Edge
Cold Hurst
Frank Hill
Derker
Acre
Greenacres Hill
Greenacres Moor
Lower Moor
North Moor
Mumps
The Blue Coat Sch.
Oldham Sports Cen.
Grange Arts Cen.
The Oldham Coll.
Westwood
Townfield
Yorkshire
Rhodes Bank
Oldham Mumps
Moorhey
Salem
Bank Top
Oldham Werneth
Glodwick Swim. Pool
Alexandra Park
Primrose Bank
Glodwick
New Earth
Roxbury
Roundthorn
Low Side
Werneth
Marian Walker Ho.
Coppice
Hulme Grammar Sch.
Glodwick Brook
Fenny Hill
Lees Rec. Grd.
Snipe Clough
Glodwick Lows
Medlock Valley Junior Sch.
Medlock Valley Infant Sch.
Fitton Hill
Deanshut Clough
Durban Mill
Hollins
Hathershaw
The Hathershaw Tech. Coll.
Hathershaw Sports Cen.
Copster Park
Copster Hill
Hollins Green
Moss Grove
Limeside Park
Medlock Valley Comm. Sch.
St. Martin's C of E Prim. Sch.
New Bridge Sch.
Hathershaw & Fitton Hill Comm. Cen.
Oldham Roughyeds & Oldham Boro (White Bank Stadium)
Werneth Golf Course
Alders Farm
Keverlow Farm
Park Bridge
Dean Ho.
Heritage Cen.
OL6
OLDHAM
TAMESIDE
Alt
A62
A627
A669
A671
A6048
A6104
B6192
B6194
B6477
45
8
81
64

64
Hodge Clough
Hodge Clough Infant Sch.
Count Hill
Higher Barrowshaw
Roebuck Low Farm
46
Strinesdale
Two Acre
Valencienne
Thurston Clough Farm
HIGH MOOR
Thurston House
Higher House
Thurston Clough
High Moor Quarries
OL1
Watersheddings
Counthill School
Lower Count Hill
Near Barrowshaw
Playing Fields
Tennis Cts.
Reservoir
Green Lane Farm
The Bungalow
Strines
Galley Hall
Lower Strinesdale Resr.
Waterhead Water Treatment Works
Reservoir (cov.)
Top o' th' Meadows
Top o' th' Meadows Farm
Brighton
Radio Beacon
Blunder Hall
Daisy Hill Farm
Doctor Lane Head
Doctor Ho.
Doctor House Farm
Upper House Farm
New Inn Farm
Round Hill
Roundhill Farm
Strinesdale Cen.
Waterhead
Spring Hill
Waterhead Park
Pastures Farm
Higher Thorpe Farm
Intake
Herdslow Farm
Lower Houses
Daisy Hollow Farm
Field House
Birks
Mills
Old Nathan's
Scouthead
Saddleworth Prep. Sch.
White Gate
HUDDERSFIELD ROAD
A62
A672
RIPPONDEN ROAD
Cricket Grd.
Quarry (dis.)
Lower Thorpe
Austerlands
The Pastures
Cairo Mills
Top of Moor
Playing Field
Greenacres Fold
Manor Farm
Cross Bank
Cookcroft
Wood Brook
Stone Rake
Platting Farm
Doles Pit
Greenacres Cemetery
War Mem.
Greenacres
Sun Hill
Dowry Park Estates
Jun. Sch.
Load Hill Farm
Oldham
Reservoir
Lower Hills Farm
GRASSCROFT
Hey with Zion Prim. Sch.
St. Edward's RC Prim. Sch.
Cheeky Chimps Activity Cen.
Sheldersclow
Stone Breaks Hill
Stone Breaks
Earnshaw Head Farm
Bank Top
Glen Trading Estate
Walkers
Sports Grd.
Play. Fld.
Grotton Hall
Grotton Head
Springhead
Lydgate
Leesbrook
Salem
HIGH ST. OLDHAM ROAD
A669
OLDHAM ROAD
Leesfield
New Earth
Breeze Hill School
Roundthorn Prim. Sch.
Nether Lees
Youth Cen.
LEES
Ashes Clough
County End
OL4
Grotton
Furberry Court
Lydgate Farm
Thornley
Lees Cemetery
War Meml.
Knowls Lane Farm
Knowls Lane
Thornley Brook Farm
Hopkin Mill Cotts.
Roundthorn
Prim. Sch.
Lower Lydgate Farm
Vicarage
Crown Point Farm
Higher Quick Farm
Quick
Reservoir (disused)
Kiln Farm
High Knowls
Lower Quick Edge Farm
Manor Ho.
Youth Comm. Cen.
Club House
Crow Hill
Butt Farm
Pitses
Golden Spot
Lane Head Farm
St. Hugh's C of E Prim. Sch.
Reservoir (covered)
Quick Farm
Ashton-under-Lyne
A6050
STOCKPORT ROAD
QUICK RD.
A670
Holts
OLDHAM GOLF COURSE
Knowls Farm
Top of Lane
Gorsey Bank Farm
Holly Bank
Hawthorn Farm
Little Haigh Farm
Alt Prim. Sch.
OL8
Alt
Wildmoor Leach Wood
Rowton Clough
Boardmans Edge
Fir Tree Farm
Quick Edge
Brunt Hill Farm
River Medlock
Turner Dingle
Little Lea Farm
Brown Edge
Light Birches
Brook Bottom
Quickwood
Beechwood
Alders Farm
Cockfields Farm
Reservoir (cov.)
Sandbed
LEES NEW ROAD
OL6
Broad Carr
Brown Edge Farm
Stansfield Brow
Millstone Farm
Port Mahon
Yarn Croft
Higher Hartshead
Broadcarr Farm
STAMFORD
STOCKPORT
MANCHESTER
B6177
B6194
HOLTS LANE
Fields Farm
Wyngate
82
63
Wks.

DOBCROSS
SADDLEWORTH
SADDLEWORTH GOLF COURSE
UPPERMILL
Heathfields
Running Hill Head
Pobgreen
Marslands
Tame Water
Wall Hill
Wharmton
Greenfield
GREENFIELD
Frenches
Golburn Clough
OL3
Tunstead
Boarshurst
Road End
Friezland
Dacres
Shaw Hall Bank
Royal George
Sharon
Roaches
Roughtown
Woodend
MOSSLEY
OL5
Lane Head
Greave
Alphin Brow
PEAK DISTRICT NATIONAL PARK
Stalybridge
SK15
OLDHAM
TAMESIDE
HOLMFIRTH ROAD
MANCHESTER ROAD
A635
A669
A670
A6052
B6175
47
83
99

Running Hill Head
Pobgreen
Broadstone Moss
Broadstone Hill
Broad Stones
Broadstone Clough
Wickens Farm
Clough Bottom
Ivy Bank Farm
Slades Barn
Slades
South Clough Moss
Diggle Rake
Hollin Brown Knoll
Near Wain Stones
Far Wain Stones
Boggart Stones
Slades Pits
Rocher Brow
Slades Rocks
Greenfield Hall Quarries (disused)
Great Bank
Upperwood Ho.
Far Deep Clough
Higher Wildeat Lowe
A635
Lower Wildeat Lowe
Great Gruff
Sail Bark Moss
Primrose Hill
Shaw Rocher
Upper Wood
Far Rough Clough
Old Horse Head Pile
Adam's Cross
Little Clough
Shaw Rocks
Pilling Stack
Sugar Loaf
Near Deep Clough
Bill o' Jacks Plantation
Ox Rake Brow
Warmsey Clough
Standing Stones
Pots & Pans
Kinder Stones
DICK HILL
Crane Knoll
GREENFIELD RESERVOIR
SADDLEWORTH
Sail Bark Rocks
Lamb Knoll
MOOR
War Memorial
Upper Wood Edge
Oven Stones
Yeoman Hey Plantation
BOARD HILL
Greenfield Brook
NORTH END
YEOMAN HEY RESERVOIR
Board Hill Brow
Birch Scar
PEAK DISTRICT
Whitebrook Head
Ashway Hey
ASHWAY ROCKS
Little Flat
RAVEN STONES BROW
Raven Stones
Waterfall
Fairy Hole
ALDERMAN'S HILL
Alderman's Brow
Alderman's Rocks
Binn Green
Oak Hole
Wicken Hole
Oldham
Memorial Cross
Low Rocks
Brockley Moor
Weir
Ferny Holes
Birchen Clough
OL3
Dove Stone Clough
Ashway Gap
Weirs
ASHWAY STONE
HOLMFIRTH LANE
Side Bank House
Dean Brow
Ashway Moss
The Rough
DEAN ROCKS
SLATE PIT MOSS
BANK
Nut Bottom
DOVE STONE RESERVOIR
Great Dove Stone Rocks
Green Bri.
Stable Bri.
Little Birchen Clough
Little Dove Stone Rocks
Cairn on Fox Stone
Greenfield Farm
Greenfield Mill
Mill Ponds
Lower Hollins Plantation
Sunny Brow
HEY TOP
BRADBURY'S LANE
New Barn
Bramley's Cot
Dove Stone Sailing Club
Hollins Hill Farm
Dove Stone
DOVE STONE MOSS
Featherbed Moss
Kinder Intake
INTAKE LA.
The Old Lodge
Chew Piece Plantation
Chew Hills
Weir
Ford
Fords
ROAD
Small Clough
Charnel Holes
Wimberry Stones Brow
Wimberry Stones
Rams Clough
Charnel Clough
Ford
LONG RIDGE MOSS
Dish Stone Moss
South Clough
HAWK YARD LA.
WHITE BROOK LA.
LONG LANE
RUNNING HILL GATE
BAKER'S LANE
SLADES LANE
POBGREEN LA.
OLD LA.

48
65
84

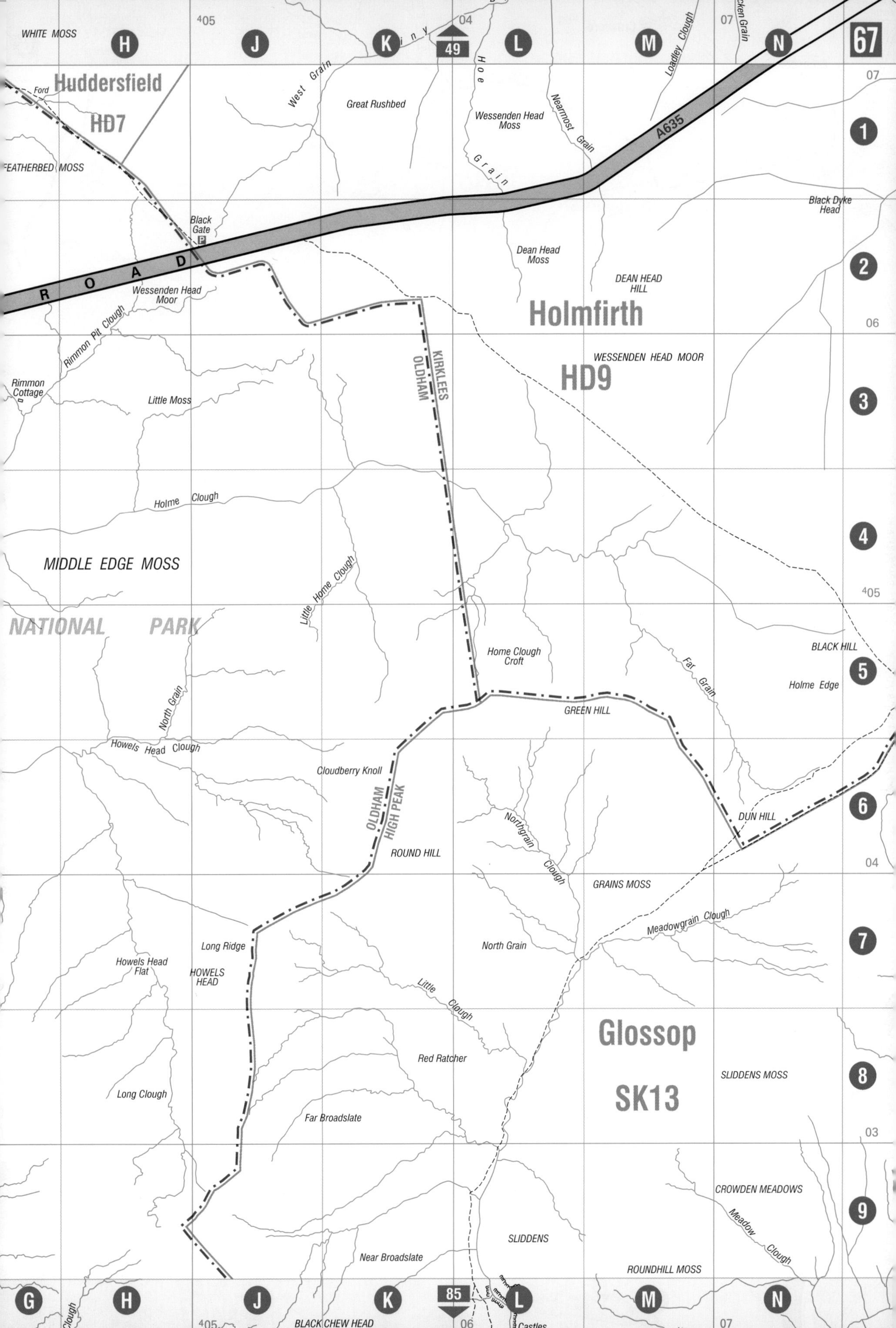
WHITE MOSS
Huddersfield
HD7
Ford
FEATHERBED MOSS
West Grain
Great Rushbed
Hoe Grain
Wessenden Head Moss
Nearmost Grain
Loadley Clough
A635
Black Dyke Head
Black Gate
ROAD
Wessenden Head Moor
Dean Head Moss
DEAN HEAD HILL
Holmfirth
Rimmon Pit Clough
Rimmon Cottage
KIRKLEES
OLDHAM
WESSENDEN HEAD MOOR
HD9
Little Moss
Holme Clough
MIDDLE EDGE MOSS
Little Home Clough
NATIONAL PARK
Home Clough Croft
BLACK HILL
Far Grain
Holme Edge
North Grain
GREEN HILL
Howels Head Clough
Cloudberry Knoll
OLDHAM
HIGH PEAK
DUN HILL
Northgrain Clough
ROUND HILL
GRAINS MOSS
Meadowgrain Clough
Long Ridge
North Grain
Howels Head Flat
HOWELS HEAD
Little Clough
Glossop
Red Ratcher
SLIDDENS MOSS
Long Clough
SK13
Far Broadslate
CROWDEN MEADOWS
Meadow Clough
SLIDDENS
Near Broadslate
ROUNDHILL MOSS
Clough
BLACK CHEW HEAD
Castles
49
85
H J K L M N
G H J K L M N
1 2 3 4 5 6 7 8 9
405 04 07 06 05 03

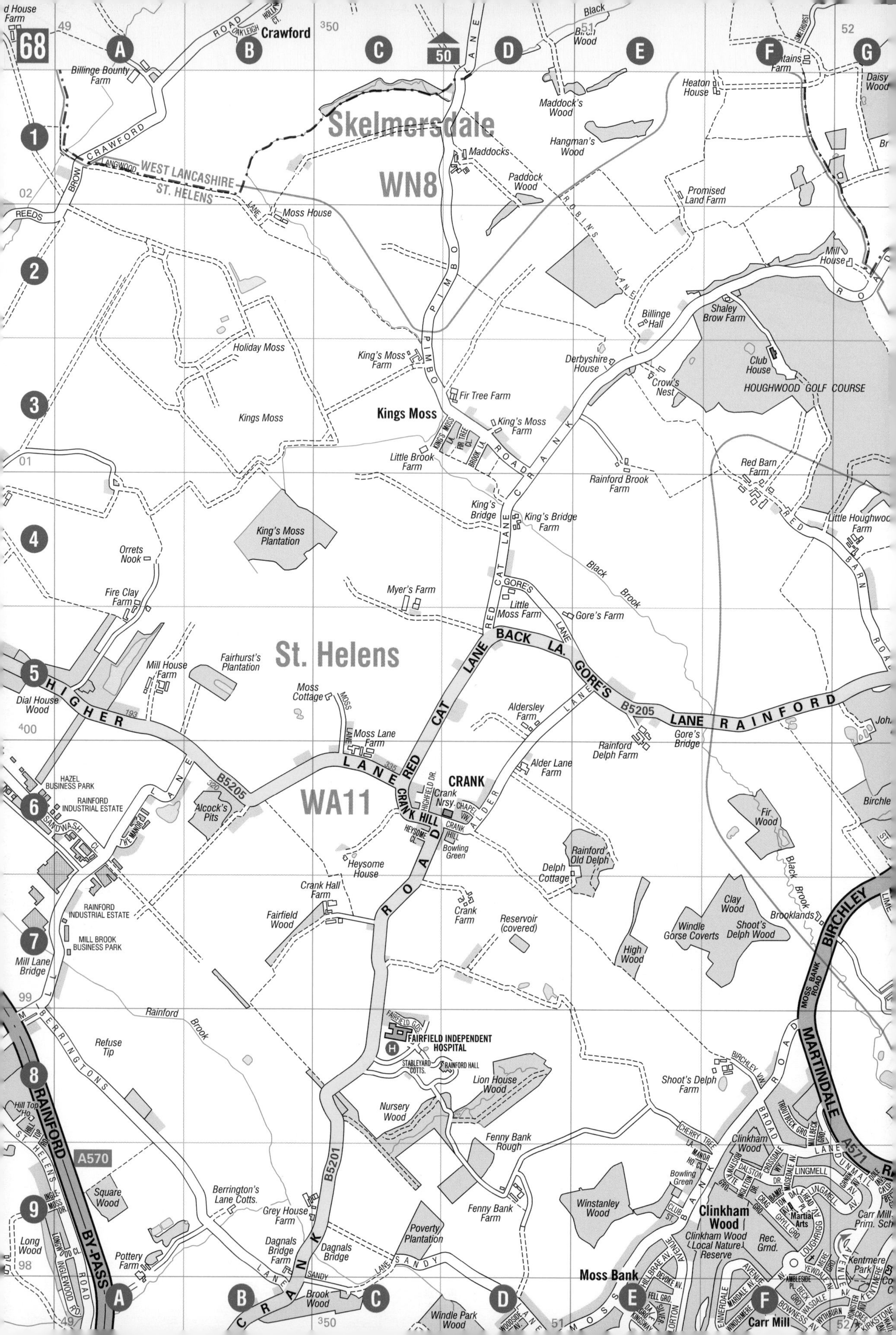
Crawford
Skelmersdale
WN8
WEST LANCASHIRE
ST. HELENS
Moss House
Maddocks
Paddock Wood
Maddock's Wood
Hangman's Wood
Heaton House
Promised Land Farm
Billinge Bounty Farm
Holiday Moss
King's Moss Farm
Fir Tree Farm
Kings Moss
Little Brook Farm
King's Moss Farm
Billinge Hall
Derbyshire House
Crow's Nest
Shaley Brow Farm
Club House
HOUGHWOOD GOLF COURSE
Mill House
Red Barn Farm
Rainford Brook Farm
King's Bridge
King's Bridge Farm
Little Houghwood Farm
King's Moss Plantation
Orrets Nook
Fire Clay Farm
Myer's Farm
Little Moss Farm
Gore's Farm
Black Brook
St. Helens
Mill House Farm
Fairhurst's Plantation
Dial House Wood
HIGHER LANE
B5205
BACK LA.
GORE'S LANE
RAINFORD
Moss Cottage
Moss Lane Farm
Aldersley Farm
Rainford Delph Farm
Gore's Bridge
HAZEL BUSINESS PARK
RAINFORD INDUSTRIAL ESTATE
Alcock's Pits
WA11
CRANK
Crank Nrsy.
Alder Lane Farm
Fir Wood
Bowling Green
Heysome House
Rainford Old Delph
Delph Cottage
Crank Hall Farm
Crank Farm
Reservoir (covered)
Fairfield Wood
MILL BROOK BUSINESS PARK
Mill Lane Bridge
Clay Wood
Windle Gorse Coverts
Shoot's Delph Wood
Brooklands
High Wood
BIRCHLEY
MARTINDALE
Refuse Tip
Rainford Brook
FAIRFIELD INDEPENDENT HOSPITAL
RAINFORD HALL
Lion House Wood
Shoot's Delph Farm
Nursery Wood
Fenny Bank Rough
Clinkham Wood
A570
A571
RAINFORD BY-PASS
Square Wood
Berrington's Lane Cotts.
Grey House Farm
Fenny Bank Farm
Winstanley Wood
Bowling Green
Clinkham Wood
Clinkham Wood Local Nature Reserve
Rec. Grnd.
Martial Arts
Carr Mill Prim. Sch.
Kentmere Park
Long Wood
Pottery Farm
Dagnals Bridge Farm
Dagnals Bridge
Poverty Plantation
Moss Bank
Brook Wood
Windle Park Wood
Carr Mill
CRANK ROAD
B5201
SANDY LANE
MOSS BANK ROAD
50

Bispham Hall
Bispham House
LONGSHAW
Brownlow
Coppice Wood
The Hootons
Plane Tree Farm
Billinge Plants
Mast
Beacon Farm
Billinge Hill
Billinge Beacon
Refuse Tip
Longshaw Farm
Longshaw Bottom
Longshaw Common
Moss Vale Cottages
Wiswall's Farm
Moss Vale Farm
Moss House
Camp Hill
The Belt
Spring Hall Wood
Chair Wood
Windy Arbour
Windy Arbour Farm
New Houses
Cherry Tree Farm
Hill House
WN3
Glead Wood
Cranberry Farm
Sandyforth Farm
Works
Subway
M6 MOTORWAY
M6
PEMBERTON ROAD
A571
WN5
Upper Castle
Mount Pleasant Farm
Maddox House
WIGAN ST. HELENS
B5206
UPHOLLAND ROAD
WIGAN ROAD
Ryecroft Farm
Brocstedes Farm
Gladden Hey Brook
Down Brook
Barton Clough
Tatlock's Hillock
Wigan
Recreation Grd.
Ten. Cts.
Ash Grove Farm
Crookhurst Farm
BILLINGE
B5205
Lower Billinge Lane Farm
NEWTON ROAD
B5207
BILLINGE ROAD
Prim. Sch.
Play Fld.
Football Ground
Pav.
Leyland Green
Downall Green
LEYLAND GREEN ROAD
WINSTANLEY ROAD
Billinge Lane Farm
Simm's Lane End
Playing Field
Basketball Ct.
The Populars
Blackley Hurst Farm
Weathercock Hill Farm
Weathercock Hill
GARSWOOD
Bowling Green
Playing Field
Seneley Green Farm
Chapel End Prim. Sch.
Nugent House School
Barrows Farm
Chadwick Green
Recreation Ground
Sewage Works
Torpen Wood
Montrey Reservoir
WN4
Charity Farm
Works
Montrey House
Arch Lane Farm
Manor House Farm
Garswood
Goyt Hey Wood
Brown Heath Nook
Hollin Hey Plantation
Tithe Barn Farm
TITHEBARN RD.
Caleb's Wood
Caleb's Rough
SANKEY VALLEY COUNTRY PARK
Hollin Hey Farm
Carter's Fold Farm
The Goyt
Higher Colt Shed Wood
Little Oak Meadow Wood
Old Garswood Park
Crock Hey Wood
Deer House Farm
Carr Mill Wood
CARR MILL DAM
Old Garswood Hall Farm
Weir
LIVERPOOL ROAD
A58
Pewfall
Playing Field
70

A
B
C
D
E
F
G
1
2
3
4
5
6
7
8
9
52
Total Fitness
WN3
WN4
WA11
WA12
Depot
Wheatlea Ind. Est.
Derbyshire House Farm
Works
Rough Wood
Park House
Tan Pit Slip
Glead Wood
Cranberry Lea Farm
High Brooks
M6
M6 MOTORWAY
WARRINGTON RD.
WIGAN RD.
A49
Link Farm
Haslemere Industrial Estate
Landgate Industrial Estate
Land Gate
Park Lane Farm
Doe Ridings
Reservoir (covered)
Perry Brook Bri.
Park Brook
Landgate Fm.
Landgate Sch.
Drummersfield Farm
Junction 25
Edmund Collins Park
Rose Hill
BRYN
Ryecroft Farm
Brocstedes
Brocstedes Farm
Football Grd.
Playing Fields
North Ashton
Sougher's Lane End
Booth's Brow Farm
GREEN
B5207
ROAD
Playing Field
Three Sisters Race Circuit
Boating Lake
Warehouse
Kingfisher Ct. Ind. Est.
The Three Sisters Enterprise Park
South Lancashire Industrial Estate
Ashton Grange Ind. Est.
Park Brook Farm
Bryn Hall Farm
LANE
BRYN
Bryn Cross
Bryn
Graveyard
Rectory
C of E Prim. Sch.
Moor Lane Farm
Highfield House
Mill Farm
Nicol Mere Prim. Sch.
Playing Field
Wigan
Stubshaw Cross
Potter's Farm
White Rushes Farm
Ashton Leisure Cen.
Coll.
BILLINGE
ROAD
DOWNALL
Playing Field
Basketball Ct.
ALEXANDRA
BANK
Long Covert
Skitters Grove
Tennis Cts.
Jubilee Parks
King George's Fld.
RL Hughes Prim. Sch.
Millingford
GARSWOOD
Garswood
Depot
Nursery
Saw Mill
Junction 24
Park Industrial Estate
A58
ROAD
A58
Tithebarn
Ashton Cross
Garswood Park
ASHTON-IN-MAKERFIELD GOLF COURSE
Club Ho.
Vista Plantation
New Hall Wood
Haydock Boundary Plantation
LIVERPOOL
ASHTON-IN-MAKERFIELD
Byrchall High Sch.
ASHTON HEATH
Paddock
Stables
Grandstand
Newton-le-Willows
HAYDOCK PARK
Hotel
St. Helens
Millfield Farm
Reservoir (covered)
Playing Field
North Florida
Depot
Haydock Cross
WOOD AVENUE
LODGE LANE
86
69
Fishwicks Ind. Est.
Kilbuck Trad. Est.
Old Boston Trading Estate
HAYDOCK PARK

INCE MOSS
PLATT BRIDGE
Caravan Site
HMYOI HINDLEY
Sewage Works
Platt Br.
Depot
Youth Cen.
53
BICKERSHAW LANE
B5237
Brookside Farm
Pear Tree Farm
Bamfurlong Junction
WARRINGTON LANE
Hey Brook
A58
Bamfurlong Bri.
Lee Lane Pk.
Works
Morris's Farm
Bryn Hall
BAMFURLONG
Bamfurlong Hall Farm
ABRAM
Playing Field
Field Farm Cottage
Abram Brow
Leeds & Liverpool Canal (Leigh Branch)
Rec. Grd.
Prim. Sch.
WN2
LILY LANE
Bryn Gates
Abram Hall Farm
A573
VIRIDOR WOOD
Baldwins
Coffin Lane
Brook
Cheetham's House
Dover
Maypole House Farm
Lee Lane Farm
Dover Bri.
CRANKWOOD
Lily Lane Farm
ROAD
30
72
Chadwick's Farm
Lily Farm
RIDING
AYE BRIDGE ROAD
Aye Bridge Farm
Scotson's Farm
Rose Farm
Aye Bridge
Crankwood
CRANKWOOD ROAD
Locker Lane Farm
Nan Holes Brook
New Bear Hey
Playing Fld.
Balmer's Farm
Windy Bank Brook
Works
Hey Brook
Smith's Bri.
Jameson's Farm
Hillcroft
LIGHTSHAW
Lightshaw Hall
Charity Farm
Windy Bank Farm
Prim. Sch.
B5207
Golborne Road Farm
Sewage Farm
Edge Green Farm
DAM LANE
Wigan Road Farm
Warrington
Town Green
Haydock Branch Junction
Edge Green Common
Edge Green
WA3
Ashton Road Farm
ASHTON ROAD
Factory
Depot
WIGAN ROAD
Stack House Farm
Rothwell's Farm
Playing Field
Golborne High Sch.
WIGAN
ST. HELENS
Millingford Bri.
Superstore
Forsters Farm
GOLBORNE
Play. Fld.
Rec. Grd.
Jun. & Inf. Sch.
Play. Fld.
Bowl. Grn.
Playing Field
RACECOURSE
Park House Farm
Harvey Lane Bri.
Works
Mill
Bank Heath
HIGH ST.
CHURCH ST.
LOWTON ST.
GOLBORNE RD.
87
Lib.
Prim. Sch.
G
H
J
K
L
M
N
1
2
3
4
5
6
7
8
9

BICKERSHAW
Bickershaw
Naylor's Farm
Barlow's Farm
Factories
54
HINDLEY GREEN BUS. PARK
Works
Dangerous Corner
LEIGH A578 RD.
CLOSE LANE
SMITH'S LANE
B5237
Nursery
Bickershaw Hall Farm
Bickershaw C of E Prim. Sch.
Owen's Farm
Rec. Grd.
Park Farm
Tamer Lane End
LEIGH ROAD
WIGAN ROAD
Wigan
WN2
Heron Lodge Farm
ALBERT COLLIERY ESTATE
BOLTON HOUSE RD.
SHUTTLE HILLOCK
Westleigh High Sch.
Parsonage Br.
Hampson's Fold Farm
Westleigh
Westleigh Pk.
Westleigh Brook
Depot
A578
Fir Tree Flash
Bickershaw Development Public Open Space (Proposed)
PARK LANE
Works
Playing Fields
PARSONAGE RETAIL PARK
FIRSDALE IND. EST.
Westleigh Heath Farm
Westleigh Heath (Rec. Grd.)
Firs Park Sch.
Firs Lane
Youth Cen.
TWIST LA.
Cricket Grd.
ATHERLEIGH WAY
A579
Crankwood
Crankwood House
Crank Wood
CRANKWOOD ROAD
New Bear Hey
Old Bear Hey
Works
Smith's Bri.
Gerrard's Bridge
Plank Lane
PLANK LANE
Plank Lane Bridge
Ackers Whitley's Basin
Bickershaw Colliery
Leeds & Liverpool Canal (Leigh Branch)
Westleigh Brook
PENNINGTON GOLF COURSE
Sports Pavilion
Leigh Sports Village
Leigh Centurions RLFC & Leigh Genesis FC
Pennington
Leigh Indoor Sports Cen.
Hotel
Leigh Sixth Form Coll.
Houghton Coat Bridge (North)
LIGHTSHAW LANE
Critchley House
Warrington
Club House
Pennington Flash Visitor Centre
Depot
THE FLASH
Pennington Flash Country Park
Pennington Park
Hey Brook
Mossley Hall
Byrom Hall
BYROM LANE
WA3
Little Byrom Hall
Saddletree Fold Fm.
Elm House Farm
Leigh & Lowton Sailing Club
GREEN LANE
Wilton Cotts.
New Barn Farm
Ballam
Sorrowcow Farm
Rowe Farm
Red House Farm
Laburnum Cottage
Aspull Common
A572 ROAD
LOWTON ST. MARY'S BY-PASS
ST. HELENS ROAD
Garton Common
Small Brook
Liptrot Farm
MOSS INDUSTRIAL ESTATE
LEIGH ROAD
Offs.
Lowton Common
Gilded Hollins Prim. Sch.
Playing Fld.
88
Cheetham Fold
Civic Hall
St. Mary's
Dean's
71

55
Howe Bridge Crematorium
Cemetery
Howe Bridge
Howe Bridge Sports Cen.
Cricket Grd.
Football Grd.
M46
Manchester
Hindsford
Lodge Farm
Sacred Heart Catholic Prim. Sch.
Prim. Sch.
Recreation Ground
Fred Longworth High Sch.
Tyldesley Pool
Pickley Green
A579
B5215
Crab Fold Farm
Atherton Brook
Hindsford Brook
Langley Platt Bri.
Football Grd.
Nuttall's Farm
Old Hall Mill Farm
Atherton Wood
M29
Atherton Hall
Atherton Old Hall Farm
Playing Field
Higher Folds Prim. Sch.
Walmsley Farm
Bedford or Hough Wood
Atherton Lake Brook
Zoological Gardens
LILFORD PARK
Miniature Golf Course
Cemetery Ho.
Leigh Infirmary
Higher Folds
Bates Farm
Lilford
Livesley's Cott.
Rec. Grd.
Comm. Cen.
74
Dawn Farm
Bedford Lodge
Rhyl Fold Farm
Lynndene
Playing Fields
Bedford
Bakery
Cemetery
Playing Field
LEIGH
SPINNING JENNY WAY
CHAPEL ST.
MANCHESTER ROAD
A572
A578
BJ's Bingo
Bedford Basin
Bedford High School
Playing Fields
Bridgewater Canal
Hall House Bri.
Great Fold Bri.
Marsland Green Bri.
Club Common
Hooten Gardens
WARRINGTON RD.
A574
Siddow Common
Leigh Commerce Park
Sewage Works
Leigh WN7
Nursery
Bedford Hall Farm
Crompton House
A580
Grange Farm
Sandy Pool Farm
Sandy Pool Cottage
Bedford Bri.
Magpie's Nest
Hope Carr Nature Reserve
Pennington Brook
Breaston Bri.
Pennington Bri.
Crompton Farm
Warrington
Netherbarrow Farm
The Oaks Farm
Lately Common
EAST LANCASHIRE ROAD
Jennet's Lane Farm
Hawk Hurst Farm
Bridge Farm
Rugby Grds.
Landside Farm
Land Side
Bowland Field
Three Acres
Ward's End
Speakman House
Hawk Hurst Bridge
WA3
Collier's Farm
Arrowsmith's Farm
Collier's Tenement
Old Field Farm
89
Works
Garden Centre

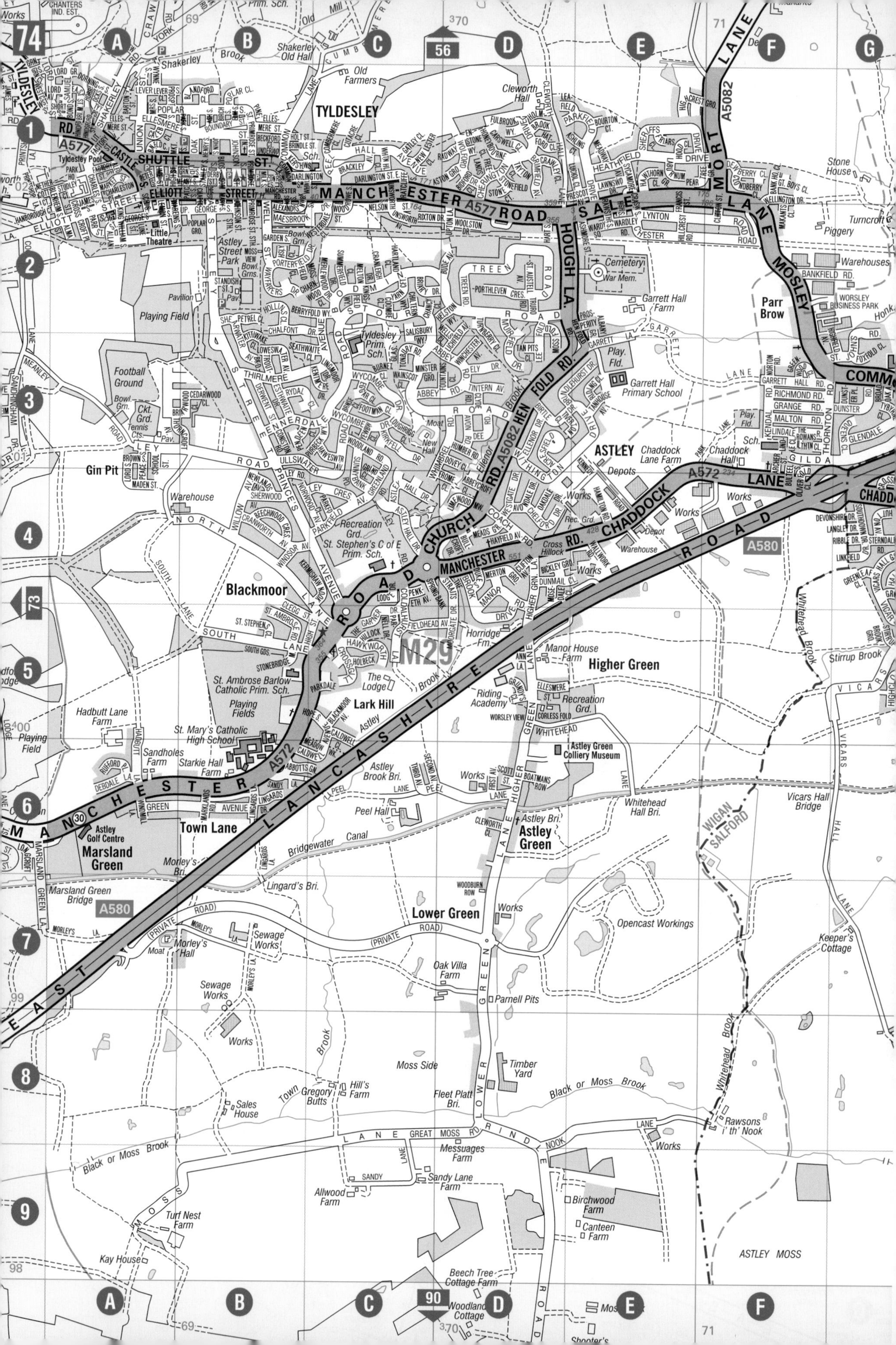
TYLDESLEY
Shakerley
Shakerley Old Hall
Old Farmers
Cleworth Hall
SHUTTLE ST.
CASTLE ST.
ELLIOTT STREET
MANCHESTER A577 ROAD
SALE LANE
MORT LANE A5082
MOSLEY
Tyldesley Pool
Little Theatre
Astley Street Park
Playing Field
Pavilion
Football Ground
Bowl. Grn.
Ckt. Grd.
Tennis Cts.
Gin Pit
Warehouse
Tyldesley Prim. Sch.
Cemetery
War Mem.
Garrett Hall Farm
Garrett Hall Primary School
Play. Fld.
Stone House
Turncroft
Piggery
Warehouses
WORSLEY BUSINESS PARK
Parr Brow
ASTLEY
Chaddock Lane Farm
Chaddock Hall
Depots
Works
A572
CHADDOCK LANE
A580
Recreation Grd.
St. Stephen's C of E Prim. Sch.
CHURCH RD. A5082
HEN FOLD RD.
HOUGH LA.
Blackmoor
Moat
New Hall
Cross Hillock
Warehouse
Depot
Horridge Fm.
M29
Manor House Farm
Higher Green
St. Ambrose Barlow Catholic Prim. Sch.
Playing Fields
St. Mary's Catholic High School
The Lodge
Lark Hill
Riding Academy
Recreation Grd.
Astley Green Colliery Museum
Hadbutt Lane Farm
Playing Field
Sandholes Farm
Starkie Hall Farm
MANCHESTER ROAD
EAST LANCASHIRE ROAD
Astley Golf Centre
Marsland Green
Town Lane
Astley Brook Bri.
Peel Hall
Astley Bri.
Astley Green
Whitehead Hall Bri.
Vicars Hall Bridge
WIGAN
SALFORD
Bridgewater Canal
Morley's Bri.
Lingard's Bri.
Marsland Green Bridge
Lower Green
Works
Opencast Workings
Keeper's Cottage
Morley's Hall
Moat
Sewage Works
Oak Villa Farm
Parnell Pits
Whitehead Brook
Stirrup Brook
Timber Yard
Moss Side
Hill's Farm
Gregory Butts
Sales House
Fleet Platt Bri.
Black or Moss Brook
GREAT MOSS RD
RINDLE
NOOK LANE
Rawsons i' th' Nook
Messuages Farm
Sandy Lane Farm
Allwood Farm
Turf Nest Farm
Birchwood Farm
Canteen Farm
Kay House
ASTLEY MOSS
Beech Tree Cottage Farm
Woodland Cottage
56
73
90
A B C D E F G
1 2 3 4 5 6 7 8 9
69 370 71 02 01 00 99 98

Walkden
Whittle Brook
Burgess Farm
Platt's Fold
Leyland Farm
New Manchester
Parr Fold
Salford Coll.
Inscape Ho.
Playing Fields
ELLESMERE GOLF COURSE
New Manchester Woodland Cemetery
Mosley Common
Ellenbrook
Ellesmere Sports Club
Driving Range
Cricket Grd.
Roe Green
Lady Hill
WORSLEY PARK GOLF COURSE
WORSLEY
Worsley Old Hall
Rands Clough Wood
Kennels
Ellesmere Memorial
St. Mark's C of E Prim. Sch.
Mill Brow
West Lodge
Booth's Bank Farm
Alder Wood
Scout Camp
Middle Wood
Worsley Hall Nurseries
Booth's Bank
Football Ground
Junction 13
Bridgewater Park
Booth's Hall Bridge
BOOTHSTOWN
Boothstown Bridge
Bridgewater Canal
Hollin Wood
Bittern Pits Wood
Moss House Farm
Alder Forest
Manchester
Keepers Cottage
The Grange
BOTANY BAY WOOD
Junction 12 (M60) & (M62)
Malkins Wood Farm
WORSLEY MOSS
Woodside Farm
Salford City Academy
BARTON MOSS
M28
M30
M60
M62
A580
A575
A572
B5232
B5211
EAST LANCASHIRE ROAD
LEIGH ROAD
WALKDEN ROAD
M60-MOTORWAY
M62-MOTORWAY
57
91
76

Hilton Park
PRESTWICH GOLF COURSE
Rainsough
Kersal
Castle Hill
Salford Sports Village
Littleton Road Playing Fields
Lower Kersal
Jubilee Bridge
Charlestown
Salford Coll. (City Campus)
Pendleton
Gala Bingo
Fit City Clarendon
Junc. 3
Manchester
PENDLEBURY
High Bank
Household Waste Site
Rubbish Tip
Sports Ground
DRINKWATER PARK
Reservoir
Synagogues
Burial Ground
River Irwell
BURY
SALFORD
HMP & YOI FOREST BANK
Manchester, Bolton & Bury Canal
Agecroft Bri.
Training Centre
Hall Hill
Agecroft Crematorium
Agecroft Cemetery
Thirlmere Aqueduct
Cemetery
AGECROFT ROAD
A6044
BOLTON ROAD
RAINSOUGH BROW
HILTON LA.
A666
Victoria Park
Albany Ho.
Springwood Sch.
Grosvenor Rd. Prim. Sch.
Sports Field
M27
AGECROFT ENTERPRISE PK.
AGECROFT PARK CIRCLE
AGECROFT COMMERCE PARK
PARK HOUSE BRIDGE ESTATE
Irlams o' th' Height
Oakwood Park
Ingleside Bowl. Grn.
MANCHESTER ROAD
A6
Beis Yaakov High Sch.
Lightoaks Park
Duncan Mathieson Playing Fields
Bowling Greens
Bolton Road Playing Fields
Refuse Treatment Plant
Brindle Heath
BROAD STREET
M6
Salford
Pendleton Coll.
Buile Hill High School
Buile Hill Park
Hope High Sch.
Oaklands Hospital
Sports Ground
LANCASTER ROAD
A5185
CLAREMONT ROAD
B5228
OLD ROAD
A576
WEASTE LANE
LANGWORTHY ROAD
A5186
Seedley
Seedley Park
Langworthy Park
ECCLES OLD ROAD
STOTT LANE
SALFORD ROYAL HOSPITAL
Junction 2
Playing Field
M602 MOTORWAY
ECCLES NEW ROAD
A57
Ladywell
ECCLES
Little Bolton
Turnpike Ho.
M50
Sewage Works
Filter Beds
Pumping Station
Weaste
Weaste Cemetery
All Souls RC Prim. Sch.
Langworthy
RSPCA HQ
CENTENARY WAY
SALFORD
TRAFFORD
M17
REGENT RD.
BROUGHTON RD.
CROMWELL RD.
H
J
K
L
M
N
G
1
2
3
4
5
6
7
8
9
59
93
78

78
Hilton Park
Sedgley Park
Crumpsall
Prestwich Golf Course
M25
BURY
SALFORD
Heathlands Village
Kersal Moor Recreation Ground
Football Grd.
Castle Hill Viewpoint
Kersal Dale
Kersal Vale
Castle Hill
Higher Broughton
Playing Fields
The Cliff
Lower Kersal
Sports Ground
River Irwell
Lower Kersal Primary Sch.
Littleton Bridge
Charlestown
Broughton Park
Clowes Park
Higher Crumpsall
Crumpsall Park
Abraham Moss
Abraham Moss Leisure Cen.
Hightown
Cheetham Hill
Mandley Park
Woodlands Road
Smedle Fields
Manchester Fort Shopping Park
Strangeways
HMP Manchester
Fairholm Caravan Site
Newtown
Albert Park
Fit City
Lower Broughton
Salford Coll (City Campus)
Lissadel Science Park
David Lewis Recreation Ground
Wallness
Pavilions
Tom Husband Leisure Complex
Robert Powell Theatre, Uni. of Salford
Salford Cres.
University of Salford
Peel Park
Salford Mus. & Art Gallery
Maxwell Bldg.
Sports Ground
Univ. of Salford (Adelphi Ho.)
University of Salford (Irwell Pl.)
New Windsor
Gasholder Sta.
M5
SALFORD
Red Rose Retail Centre
Regent Retail Park
Salford Central
Mancentral Trading Centre
Granada TV Cen.
Mus. of Science & Industry
MEN Arena
VICTORIA
Cath.
Arndale Shopping Centre
The Printworks
Shudehill
Market St.
Piccadilly Gdns.
St. Peter's Sq.
Royal Exchange Thr.
A56
A576
A665
A6010
A6041
A6042
A5066
A5063
A6
A59
B6180
B6186
B5461
B5225
A5103
BURY NEW ROAD
GT. CHEETHAM ST. WEST
GT. DUCIE ST.
CHEETHAM HILL ROAD
LEICESTER ROAD
MIDDLETON ROAD
QUEENS ROAD
WATERLOO ROAD
ELIZABETH ST.
CROMWELL ROAD
BROAD ST.
FREDERICK ROAD
THE CRESCENT
CHAPEL ST.
TRINITY WAY
OLDFIELD RD.
DEANSGATE
CORPORATION ST.
MILLER ST.
ROCHDALE RD.
PICCADILLY
PORTLAND ST.
QUAY ST.
PETER ST.
BRIDGE ST.
REGENT RD.
LIVERPOOL ST.
ALBION WAY
CAMP ST.
BROUGHTON RD.
GREAT CLOWES ST.
BLACKFRIARS ST.
SILK ST.
ADELPHI ST.
77
60
4
5
94
A B C D E F G
1 2 3 4 5 6 7 8 9

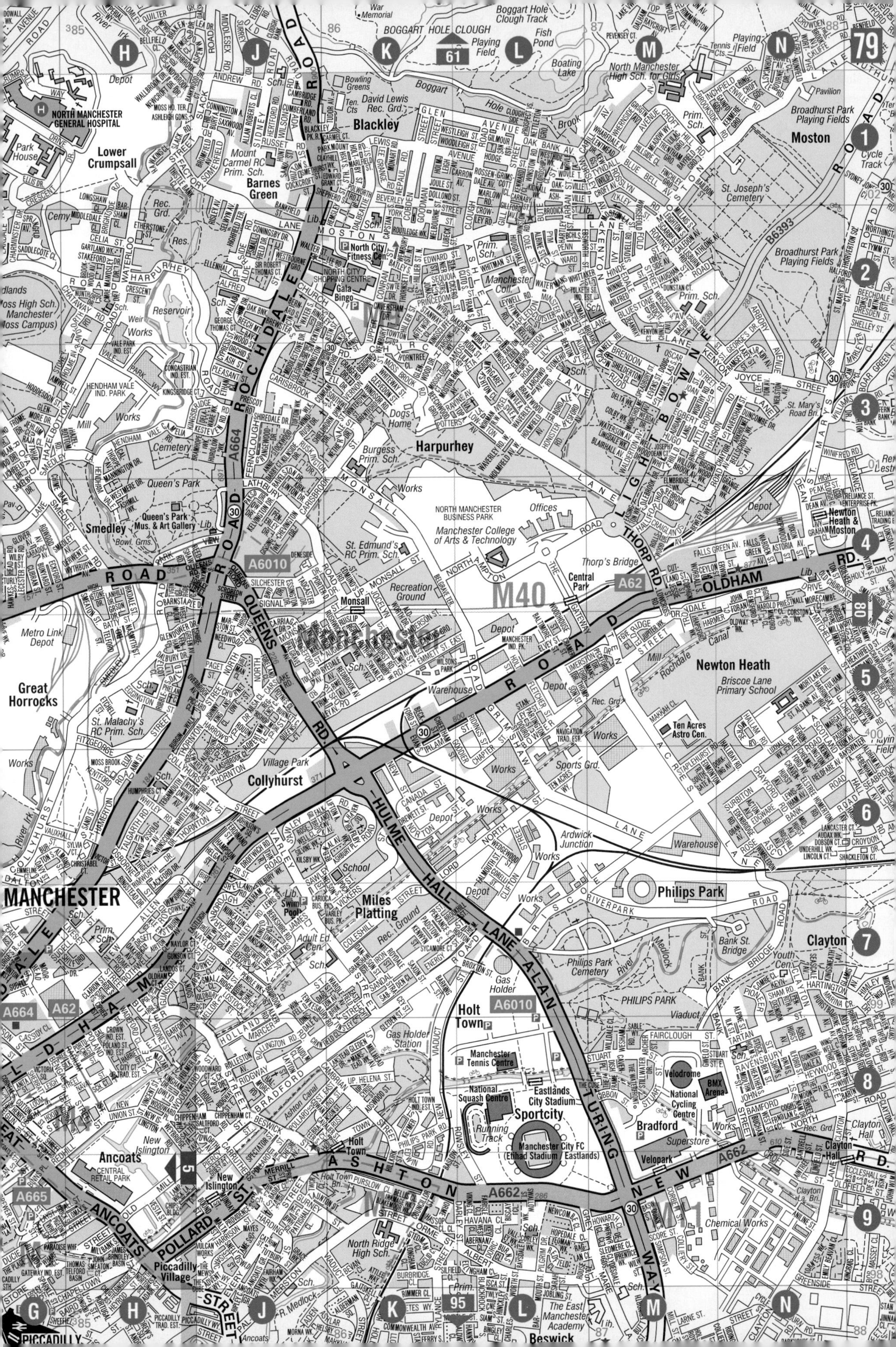
Blackley
Moston
Lower Crumpsall
Barnes Green
Harpurhey
Smedley
Great Horrocks
Collyhurst
Miles Platting
Newton Heath
Philips Park
Clayton
Holt Town
Bradford
Ancoats
New Islington
Piccadilly Village
Beswick
MANCHESTER
NORTH MANCHESTER GENERAL HOSPITAL
BOGGART HOLE CLOUGH
Broadhurst Park Playing Fields
St. Joseph's Cemetery
Queen's Park
Reservoir
NORTH MANCHESTER BUSINESS PARK
Manchester College of Arts & Technology
Recreation Ground
Village Park
Philips Park Cemetery
Velodrome
National Cycling Centre
Manchester Tennis Centre
National Squash Centre
Sportcity
Manchester City FC (Etihad Stadium Eastlands)
ROCHDALE ROAD
OLDHAM ROAD
ASHTON NEW ROAD
HULME HALL LANE
ALAN TURING WAY
QUEENS RD.
A664
A6010
A62
A662
A665
M40
M11
61
80
95
5

80
Moston
Broadhurst Park Playing Fields
New Moston
Failsworth
FAILSWORTH
Manchester
Hollinwood
Cutler Hill
Holt Lane End
Woodhouses
Street End
Culcheth
Clayton
Clayton Bridge
CLAYTON VALE
Greenside
DROYLSDEN
Medlock Vale
Bottom of Woodhouses
Newton Heath & Moston
Moston Fairway Nature Reserve
Lower Memorial Park
Brookdale Park
BROOKDALE GOLF COURSE
Kaskenmoor School
Failsworth Sch. (Upper)
Failsworth Cemetery
Rochdale Canal
MANCHESTER
OLDHAM
TAMESIDE
River Medlock
BROADWAY
OLDHAM ROAD
ASHTON NEW ROAD
MANCHESTER ROAD
ASHTON ROAD
DROYLSDEN RD.
LIGHTBOWNE B6393
M60 MOTORWAY
Junc. 22
A62
A663
A662
A6104
M35
M40
M43
M11
62
79
96
Medlock Leisure Cen.
Sewage Works
Police Training Unit
Droylsden Academy
St. Willibrord's RC Prim. Sch.
Broadhurst Prim. Sch.
Greenside Prim. Sch.

Moss Grove
Hollins Green
Lime Side
Oldham Crematorium
Oldham Roughyeds RLFC & Oldham Boro FC (White Bank Stadium)
WERNETH GOLF COURSE
A627
63
St. Martin's C of E Prim. Sch.
Hathershaw & Fitton Hill Comm.Cen.
Keverlow Farm
Park Bridge
Heritage Cen.
Dean Ho.
Rabbit Clough
Alt Hill
Higher Alt Hill Farm
Alt Hill Farm
Briaracre Terrace
Belsfield
Lower Fold
Bankfield Clough
Little Bankfield Clough
Bank Top Farm
Fairbottom
Tanpit House
Fernlea
Bardsley
Cricket Ground
Fenny Field Bri.
River Medlock
Oldham
OL8
Brooks Farm
Wood Park
Wood Park Clough
Oldham RUFC (Manor Pk.)
Manor House Farm
Bardsley Fold Farm
Bardsley Park Golf Centre
Sports Grd.
Bowling Green
Slaters Farm
Riversvale Farm
Knott Lanes
Green Fold Farm
Crime Lake
Crime View
Crime Farm
Woodhouse Green
Croft End Farm
Valley Farm
Valley Bri.
Riversvale Arboretum
Fairbottom Branch Canal
Bardsley Vale Mills
Holden Clough
Limehurst Farm
Holden Clough Prim. Sch.
Sports Ground
New Charter Academy
Crime Bridge Farm
Pinch Fm.
Sammy's Basin
Boodle Wood
Tree Ho. Bank
Medlock Vale
DAISY NOOK COUNTRY PARK
Limehurst
Downshaw Clough
Timperley Clough
Daisy Nook Farm
Oakhill Farm House
Daisy Nook
John Howarth Countryside Cen.
Taunton
Canon Burrows C of E Prim. Sch.
Waterloo Prim. Sch.
Waterloo
Broadoak Prim. Sch.
Smallshaw
Hurst Knoll
Hurst Knoll St. James C of E Prim. Sch.
Wellstyle Farm
Ashton-under-Lyne Canal
Nook View Farm
Meadow View Farm
Willow Bank Farm
Gravel Hill Farm
Cinderland Hall Farm
Littlemoss
The Willows
Buckley Hill Farm
Hope Fold Farm
Jaum Farm
Curzon Ashton FC (Tameside Stadium)
Crowhill
Richmond Park Athletic Stadium
King George V Play. Flds.
Hurst Brook
Ashton Moss North Junction
Superstore
Ashton-under-Lyne
M60 MOTORWAY
M60
A6140
SHELDON WAY
WELLINGTON RD.
Cineworld
Hollywood Bowl
ASHTON-UNDER-LYNE
Moss Side Farm
OL7
ASHTON MOSS
Depot
Junction 23
Garden Centre
Police HQ
A635
Factory
Aldwyn Prim. Sch.
MANCHESTER ROAD
West End Prim. Sch.
West End Park
PARK PARADE
Superstore
Depot
DUKINFIELD
Dukinfield Cemetery
Dukinfield Crematorium
Dukinfield Junction
B6445
MILL ROAD
Guide Bridge
Plantation Farm
Oxford Park Sports Cen.
97
FOUNDRY
G
H
J
K
L
M
N
1
2
3
4
5
6
7
8
9
82
92
93
94

Higher Hartshead
Hartshead Pike Tower
Broad Carr
Brown Edge Farm
Millstone Farm
Broadcarr Farm
Port Mahon
Yarn Croft
Fields Farm
Colts Hey Farm
Rabbit Clough
Alt Hill
Alt Hill Farm
Twirl Hill Farm
Lily Lanes
Lily Lanes Farm No.1
Lily Lanes Farm No.2
Hartshead Green
Crossleys Farm
Lane End Farm
Willow Cottage
Mossley Cross
Fox Platt
Mossley Brow
Mossley
Heritage Cen.
Bottoms
Ashton-under-Lyne
OL6
Reservoir (covered)
New Covert
St. Damian's RC Science College
Holden Clough Prim. Sch.
Greenhurst Clough
Knott Hill Farm
Knott Hill Local Nature Reserve
Broadoak Clough
Luzley Brows
Luzley Hall
Luzley
Smithy Farm
Springfield Farm
Hilltop Farm
Scout Farm
Scout
Scout Tunnel
Dirk Farm
Club Ho.
ASHTON-UNDER-LYNE GOLF COURSE
Samuel Laycock School
New Charter Academy
Hurst Nook
Higher Hurst
Hurst Cemetery
Hazelhurst
Ashton United FC
Smallshaw
Hurst
Luzley End Farm
Oak Wood View
Whitehall House
Hopkins Farm
Greenhollin
Windy Harbour Farm
Standrick Hill
Heyrod
Sewage Works
Arlies Prim. Sch.
Staley House
TAMESIDE GENERAL HOSPITAL
Ashton-under-Lyne Sixth Form College
Willow Wood Hospice
Boating Lake
Playing Fields
Ridge Hill
Ridge Hill Prim. Sch.
Clay Leaches
Staveleigh
Souracre
Woodfield
Primrose Wood
Higher Glent Quarry
Cocker Hill
Cockbrook
Tameside College
Stamford Park
West Hill Sch.
STALYBRIDGE
Stalybridge
Copley
The Copley Centre
Copley High Sch.
Wild Bank Prim. Sch.
Fern Bank
DUKINFIELD
Dukinfield Cemetery
Dukinfield Crematorium
Tame Valley
River Tame
Huddersfield Narrow Canal
Trinity Christian Sch.
Castle Hall
Industrial Estate
Eastwood Educational Nature Reserve
SK16
STAMFORD ST.
STAMFORD SQ.
MOSSLEY RD.
QUEEN'S ROAD
MANCHESTER ROAD
HUDDERSFIELD ROAD
MOTTRAM ROAD
WAKEFIELD ROAD
A670
A635
A6018
B6194
B6175
B6431
B6445
81
64
98
96
395
97

MOSSLEY
Mossley Hollins High School
Howard's Farm
Top o' th' Green
ABRAHAM'S CHAIR
Warlow Pike
Tamyon Brook
Slack Head Brow
ALPIN PIKE
OLDHAM
TAMESIDE
Greentop
Green Hollow
Water Works
Overgreen
Micklehurst
Intake Cott.
Micklehurst Brook
BUCKTON MOOR
BROKEN GROUND
B6175
HARE HILL
Far Harehill Clough
Buckton Castle
Buckton Vale Quarry
Castle Clough
Staly Brook
Castle Farm
Heyheads
Near Harehill Clough
Reservoir
Iron Tongue
Carr
STALYBRIDGE COUNTRY PARK
Moorgate
Cowbury Dale
Carr Brook
Buckton Vale
Buckton Grange
Reservoirs
Oakfield Ho. (Club Ho.)
STAMFORD GOLF COURSE
Carrbrook
Shire Clough Farm
SLATEPIT MOOR
IRONTONGUE HILL
Crows o' th' Wood
Fold Farm
Lwr. Little Bank Farm
Winterhill Farm
Higher Littlebank Farm
Wicken Spring
Wicken Spring Clough
SWINESHAW MOOR
Stalybridge
TURF PITS
Hill Top
Harridge Hall
Millbrook Prim. Sch.
Higher Hydegreen
St. Raphael's Catholic Prim. Sch.
Harridge Pike
Lwr. Hyde Green Fm.
Heritage House
Cooper Farm
HARRIDGE
Dry Clough
Higher Swineshaw Reservoir
Swineshaw Brook
Oakwood
SK15
Cote Farm
Millbrook
BRUSHES
BRUSHES ROAD
Brushes
Brushes Reservoir
Lower Swineshaw Reservoir
LEES HILL
Walkerwood Reservoir
STALYBRIDGE COUNTRY PARK
Swineshaw Brook
Cock Wood
COCK KNARR
PACK SADDLE
Middle Bank
Range Ho.
Reservoir
WILD BANK
Flaxfield
Devil's Bri.
Lower Bank
HOLLINGWORTHHALL MOOR
Hyde
SK14
TAMESIDE
HIGH PEAK
Sidebottom Fold
Cockers
Ford
Swallows Wood Nature Reserve
65
84
99

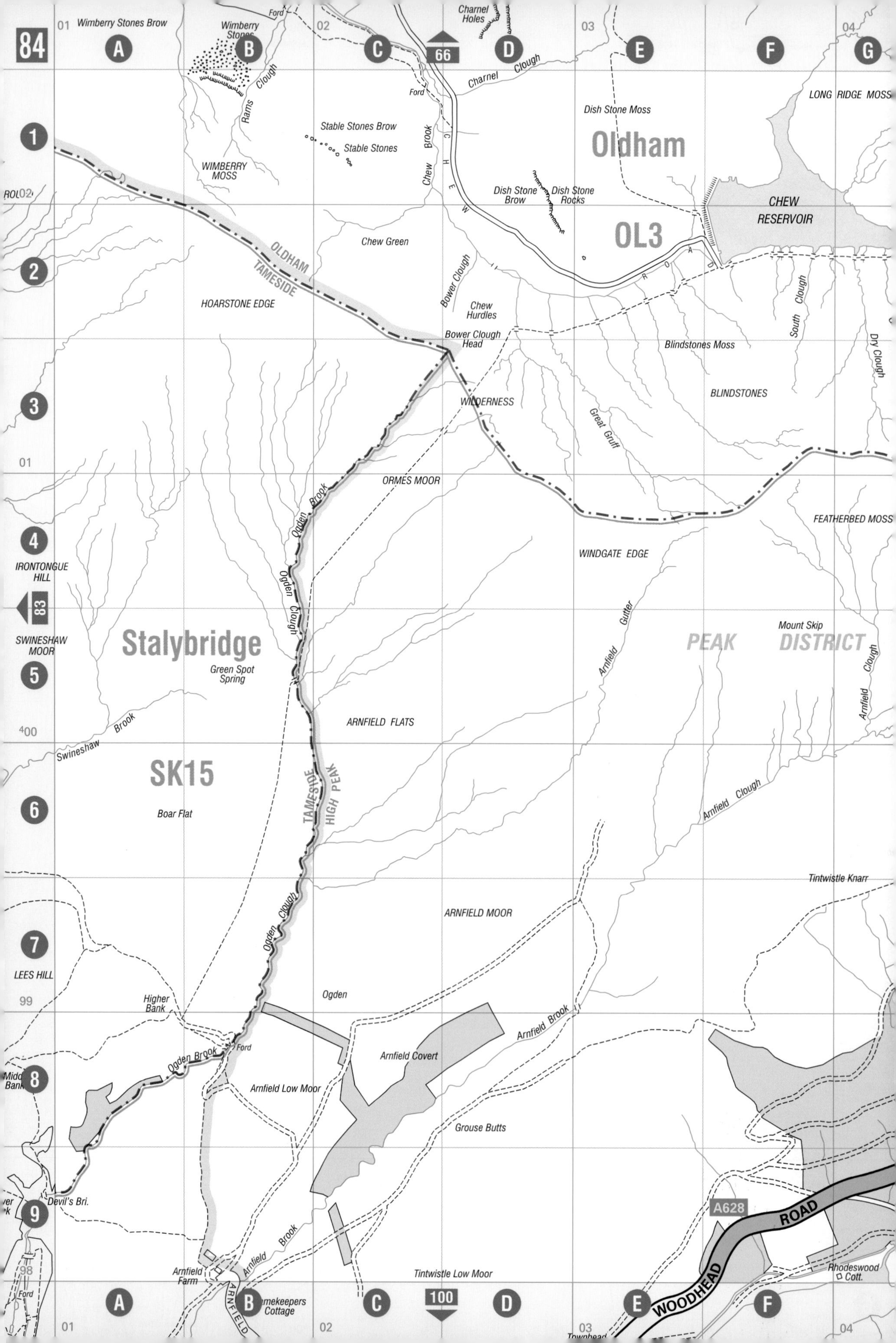
Wimberry Stones Brow
Wimberry Stones
Ford
Charnel Holes
66
Charnel Clough
Rams Clough
Ford
Dish Stone Moss
LONG RIDGE MOSS
Stable Stones Brow
Stable Stones
Chew Brook
CHEW ROAD
Oldham
WIMBERRY MOSS
Dish Stone Brow
Dish Stone Rocks
CHEW RESERVOIR
OL3
Chew Green
OLDHAM
TAMESIDE
HOARSTONE EDGE
Bower Clough
Chew Hurdles
South Clough
Bower Clough Head
Blindstones Moss
Dry Clough
WILDERNESS
BLINDSTONES
Great Gruff
ORMES MOOR
FEATHERBED MOSS
Ogden Brook
WINDGATE EDGE
IRONTONGUE HILL
Ogden Clough
83
Arnfield Gutter
Mount Skip
SWINESHAW MOOR
Stalybridge
PEAK DISTRICT
Green Spot Spring
Arnfield Clough
ARNFIELD FLATS
Swineshaw Brook
SK15
TAMESIDE
HIGH PEAK
Arnfield Clough
Boar Flat
Tintwistle Knarr
ARNFIELD MOOR
Ogden Clough
LEES HILL
Ogden
Higher Bank
Arnfield Brook
Ford
Ogden Brook
Arnfield Covert
Arnfield Low Moor
Grouse Butts
A628
ROAD
Devil's Bri.
WOODHEAD
Arnfield Brook
Rhodeswood Cott.
Arnfield Farm
Tintwistle Low Moor
Ford
ARNFIELD
Gamekeepers Cottage
100
Townhead
A B C D E F G
1 2 3 4 5 6 7 8 9
01 02 03 04
01 400 99 98

Near Broadslate
67
SLIDDENS
Meadow
ROUNDHILL MOSS
Castles
BLACK CHEW HEAD
North Clough
Wiggin Clough
Ford
Black Chew Grain
Clough
Chew
Fords
Chew Bird Grain
Brook
Fords
CHEW ROAD
CROWDEN LITTLE MOOR
Laddow Moss
Laddow Rocks
Oakenclough Grains
Fords
OLDHAM
HIGH PEAK
Oaken Clough
Crowden
BAREHOLME MOSS
Oakenclough Brook
Great Brook
Crowden Little Brook
RAKES MOSS
Hollins Clough
Rakes Rocks
NATIONAL PARK
ROBINSON'S MOSS
SPAN
Black Tor
Glossop
Lad's Leap
Span Gutter
Brockholes Quarry (disused)
Brockholes Wood Nature Reserve
Robinson's Spring
Millstone Rocks
Coombes Clough
Crowden Outdoor Education Centre & Youth Hostel
Highstone Rocks
CROWDEN CAMP SITE
SK13
Ford
Hollins Clough
CROWDEN
A628
Didsbury Intake
Highstones
Rawkins Brook
Pasture Wood
ROAD
A628
Quiet Shepherd Farm
Highstones Lodge
Glossop & District Sailing Club
Wildboar Clough
TORSIDE RESERVOIR
B6105
RHODESWOOD RESERVOIR
WOODHEAD
Torside Bridge
Long Gutter Edge
101
Reaps
White Mare

North Florida
Haydock Industrial Estate
Millfield Bus. Pk.
Depot
Haydock Cross
Fishwicks Ind. Est.
Kilbuck Trad. Est.
Old Boston Trading Estate
Yew Tree Trading Estate
Haydock Park
Hotel
East Lancashire Road
A580
A599
A49
Junction 23
Warehouse
Haydock
Cricket Ground
Haydock English Martyrs Catholic Prim. Sch.
King George V Playing Field
St. James' Prim. Sch.
Playing Field
Old Boston
Factory
Wicken Hedge
Haydock Park Farm
Cowhey Dam
M6 Motorway
King's Coppice
Ellam's Rough
Newton Haydock Bri.
New Boston
Wood Pit Covert
St. Helens
Clipsley La.
Church Road
Penny Vista Road
Superstore
Lyme House
Grange Valley Prim. Sch.
WA11
Slag Heap (disused)
B5209
Lawson's Farm
M6
Selwyn Jones Sports Cen.
Grange Farm
Fox Covert
Woodside Farm
Rough Hey Wood
Hall House Farm
Lyme Primary Sch.
Swan Road
Crow Lane
West Crow Lane
A572
Newton Common
Earlestown
Newton-Le-Willows Primary School
Wargrave
Sankey Valley Country Park
King George V Field
Penkford Bri.
Penkford School
Deacon Trading Estate
Earlestown
Newton-Le-Willows
Works
Sports Grd.
Red Brow Wood
Newton Community Hospital
Sankey Valley Industrial Estate
Pennington Lane
Common Lane
Nine Arches Farm
Sankey Viaduct
Collins Green Farm
Rose Villa
Collins Green
Park Brow Plantation
Vulcan Gym
WA5
Moss Hall Farm
Hillside
Bradlegh Hall Farm
New Bradlegh Hall Farm
Old Hey Wood
White House Farm
Higher Farm
Bradlegh Old Hall
Vulcan Village
Burtonwood Brewery
Yew Tree Farm
Hall Lane Farm
Sankey Brook
Sankey Canal
Bank House Cottages
Burtonwood Prim. Sch.
Derby Farm
Mill Farm Cottage
Boarded Barn Farm
Winwick Junction
B5204
Penkford Lane
Penny Lane
Lumber Lane
Bold

WA3
Bank Heath
GOLBORNE
LOWTON
HAYDOCK PARK
Lady Hill Plantation
White Door Covert
White Door Dam
Harvey Lane Bri.
Park House Farm
Barn La. Bri.
War Mem. Rec. Grd.
Millfield Farm
Stone Cross Park
Recreation Ground
Little Lowes Fold
Stirrups Farm
Thompson's Farm
LANCASHIRE ROAD
A580
A573
A572
A579
A49
B5207
M6
Dean Dam
Dean Dam Farm
Dean Dam House
Ellam's Rough
Dean Moor Wood
Hollows Wood
Newton Hollows
Willow Cott.
Dean Sch. House
Hollows Bridge
Park Plantation
Colonel's Wood
HAYDOCK PARK GOLF COURSE
Club Ho.
Golborne Park Wood
Millingford Brook
Lodge
Golborne Dale
Golborne Junction
Golborne Dale Bridge
Castle Hill
Lowton Heath
Grange Farm
Lowton House Farm
Byrom's Farm
Marsh Farm
Rawlinson Farm
Highfield Farm
Town of Lowton
Sandup Farm
Warrington
Sandfield Hall
Parkside Manchester Junction
Lowton Junc.
Garden Centre
Huskisson Memorial
Highfield Moss
Parkside Liverpool Junc.
WIGAN
ST. HELENS
Newton Lake
Willow Park
Newton-le-Willows
Stones Crossing
St. Aelred's Catholic Tech. Coll.
Moss Pits
Parkside Farm
Newton Park Farm
Bloody Stone
Kenyon Hall
Cemetery
Football Ground
Red Bank Community Home
M6 MOTORWAY
Oven Back Cottage
Oven Back Farm
Wood Head
Red Bank
New Hey Farm
Hermitage Farm
The Orchard
Reeves House
Rough Farm
Hill Crest
Mains Pits
Junction 22
Cop Holt Wood
Cop Holt Farm
Hermitage Green
WA2
ALDER ROOT GOLF COURSE
Alder Root Wood
Highfields
Southworth Hall
WARRINGTON ROAD
GOLBORNE DALE RD.
NEWTON ROAD
PARKSIDE ROAD
SOUTHWORTH ROAD
WINWICK LANE
WINWICK ROAD
NEWTON ROAD
WINWICK LINK RD.
GREEN LANE
HIGHFIELD LANE
BARROW LANE
STONE CROSS LANE
HIGH ST.
CHURCH ST.
MILL LANE
88
71

Lowton Common
72
Moss Industrial Estate
Gilded Hollins Prim. Sch.
Leigh
WN7
A579
Dean's Farm
Old Carr House
Yates' Farm
Playing Fld.
Cheetham Fold
Civic Hall
St. Mary's C of E Prim. Sch.
Lowton Community Sports Coll.
Wash End
Fair House
Pocket Nook
Pocket Nook Farm
Lowton Bus. Park
Carr Farm
Carr
Brook
LOWTON
Prim. Sch.
Play. Fld.
FX Leisure
Lowton Jun. & Inf. Sch.
Lowton St. Mary's
NEWTON ROAD
A572
ST. HELENS RD.
LOWTON ST. MARY'S BY-PASS
LANCASHIRE
WIGAN
WARRINGTON
EAST LANCASHIRE ROAD
A580
Culcheth
Lane Head
KENYON LANE
B5207
Dickinson's Farm
Hayes Farm
Johnson's Farm
Five Acres
Locking Stoop Farm
Diggle Green Farm
Layland's Farm
Hall Farm
Pumping Station
Broseley Bridge
BROSELEY LANE
LEIGH GOLF COURSE
Broseley Hall Farm
Jibcroft
Birchall's Farm
Tunnel Top
WILTON LANE
The Covert
Little Covert
Highfield
Wilton Grange
Mole End
Dolly's Bridge
Beard's Battery
Pagoda Wood
Club House
COMMON LANE
Kenyon
Peak's Farm
Barrow Farm
Morris's Farm
MAIN LANE
A579
WINWICK LANE
CULCHETH LINEAR COUNTRY PARK
Kinknall Hall Farm
HOB HEY LANE
Lowe's Farm
Heath House
New Lane End
Kenyon Hall
Green Bank
Kenylo Bridge
Sandy Bank Farm
STONE PIT LANE
SANDY BROW
Turret Hall
Rock House
Beech Farm
Kenyon Farm
Hill Top
Blakeley Farm
Claremont
Wigshaw
Glaziers Lane Farm
Phillips Farm
WIGSHAW LANE
Water Works
Oven Back Cottage
South View
INGHAM'S RD.
St. Lewis Catholic Primary Sch.
Beech Trees Farm
Little Town
Highcroft Farm
Yew Tree Farm
Brook
Cockshot
Sirocco
Oaklands Farm
Gresley House
Mount Pleasant
Croft Heath
Croft Primary School
Brook House Farm
Mains Pits
Island Plantation
Hope Farm
Clare's Farm
Laneside
LADY LANE
MUSTARD LANE
Oak Tree Farm
Southworth Hall
Cockshot Farm
Smithy Brow
Playing Field
CROFT
Rectory
Eaves Fm.
Cockshot Bridge
A574
WARRINGTON
87

Warrington
WA3
GLAZEBURY
CULCHETH
Fowley Common
Twiss Green
Land Side
Leigh End
BEDFORD MOSS
LITTLE WOOLDEN MOSS
Windy Bank Wood
Hitchfield Wood
Old Woods
Wellfield Wood
Crow Wood
Hollin Wood
Knowle's Wood
WARRINGTON ROAD
A574
A580
HOLCROFT LANE
B5212
M62 MOTORWAY
M62
Junction 11
Glaze Brook
Carr Brook
WIGAN
SALFORD
WARRINGTON
HMP RISLEY
Culcheth High Sch.
Culcheth Prim. Sch.
Culcheth Sports Club
Glazebury C of E Prim. Sch.
Newchurch Prim. Sch.
Twiss Grn. Prim. Sch.
Sewage Works
TAYLOR BUSINESS PARK
Playing Field
73
90

Turf Nest Farm
Canteen Farm
ASTLEY MOSS
Beech Tree Cottage Farm
Woodlands Cottage
Moss Bank
Shooter's Grove
M28
Rindle Farm
BEDFORD MOSS
M29
RINDLE ROAD
ASTLEY MOSS
Station Cotts.
Red House
Whitegates
Moss Side Farm
Sunny Bowers
Home-Stead
Westleigh
Silver Birch
Ash Cott.
Rose Farm
Hill Crest
Fern Cottage
Light Oaks Moss Farm
OLD MOSS LANE
Four Winds Farm
Showclough Farm
Birch Farm
CHAT MOSS
WIGAN
SALFORD
Red Chalis Farm
Knowle's Wood
Olive Mount Cottage
Olive Mount Farm
Railway View Farm
CHAT MOSS
White Gate Farm
Moss Farm
Red House Farm
Platt House Farm
Mosslands Farm
Woodbarn Farm
Warrington
New Farm
Moss Lodge Farm
Birch View Farm
Oakfield
IRLAM MOSS
TWELVE YARDS ROAD
WA3
Larkhill
IRLAM MOSS
Manchester
Four Lane Ends Farm
Larkhill House
Landhill Farm
LITTLE WOOLDEN MOSS
Ebeneezer Farm
Hope Cottage Farm
Westholme
Hephzibah
Boundary Drain
Hollin Wood
Pigeon Wood
IRLAM MOSS
Little Woolden Moss Drain
Woodstock Farm
Birch Covert
Ringing Pits Farm
Plant Cottage Farm
MOSS ROAD
Gable End Farm
SPRINGFIELD LA.
Mosshall Farm
M62
Birch Tree Farm
Little Woolden Hall
Worsley View
Mast
Brackley Farm
Boundary Drain
Glaze Brook
Woodland Farm
ROSCOE
GREAT WOOLDEN MOSS
M62 MOTORWAY
Prospect Grange
ASTLEY RD.
Keeper's Cottage
Great Woolden Wood
CADISHEAD MOSS
HOLCROFT LANE
Woolden View Farm
Rose Farm
Nook Farm
Sports Ground
ROAD
Tudor Rose Cottage
Rose Bank Farm
Great Woolden Hall Farm
Lower Irlam
HOLCROFT LA.
B5212 GLAZEBROOK
WOOLDEN
Ryefield Farm
CHAT MOSS
Astley Road Farm
LIVERPOOL
Lower Stanley Bank Farm
Irlam & Cadishead Community High School
CADISHEAD MOSS
ASTLEY ROAD

74
89
102

91
H
J
K
L
M
N
75
103
WORSLEY MOSS
Woodside Farm
BARTON MOSS
Playing Fields
Salford City Academy
Prim. Sch.
Sports Ground
Peel Green Cemetery & Crematorium
Eccles Cemetery
Barton
Brighton Grange
Moss Lane Farm
Moss View Farm
Manor Farm
Birch Farm
Tunnel Farm
TWELVE YARDS RD.
CITY AIRPORT MANCHESTER
Control Tower
Hangars
Barton Aerodrome Visitor Centre
Foxhill Glen
Park House
Research Lab.
Marriots Farm
Boyle Brook
Salford City Reds RLFC
(City of Salford Community Stadium)
Black Wood
Bartonmoss Farm
M62 MOTORWAY
M62
M30
A57
River Irwell (Old Course)
Barton Locks
Wharf
Parkhall
Storage Depot
Driving Range
Club Ho.
BOYSNOPE PARK GOLF COURSE
SALFORD
TRAFFORD
DAVYHULME MILLENNIUM PARK
Barton Grange
RASPBERRY LANE
Mast
Oxcheek Cottage
Gladwyn Farm
Fallows Farm
Hulme Brt. Ferry
BOYSNOPE WHARF
River Irwell
Bent Lanes Brook
Calder Bank
DAVYHULME RD.
Woods End
Club House
DAVYHULME PARK GOLF COURSE
Rec. Grd.
Sports Ground
Primary Schools
Flixton FC
LIVERPOOL ROAD
Woods End Centre
MANCHESTER SHIP CANAL
MOORSIDE ROAD
Ckt. Grd.
Pav.
Comm. Cen.
Woodsend Park
Acre Hall Prim. Sch.
Flixton Inf. & Jun. Schs.
M44
B5320
Lib.
Sch.
IRLAM
Jenny Green
Towns Gate
Towngate Farm
Big Three Farm
IRLAM ROAD
Wellacre Tech. College
Delamere School
St. Monica's RC Prim. Sch.
FLIXTON
B5158
Sports Ground
Flixton House
Flixton Park & Gardens
WILLIAM WROE GOLF COURSE
Club
Flixton
Sch.
THE GROVE
CHURCH RD.
B5213
The Village
Shawe Hey Farm
Woodlands
M41
CADISHEAD WAY
Grave Yd.
Irlam Prim. Sch.
Fit City Irlam
Prince's Park
River Irwell (Old Course)
FAIRHILLS ROAD
B5311
Works
Superstore
Linear Park
Flixton Sewage Works
Irlam Locks
Jack Lane Nature Reserve
Jack Lane Farm
River Mersey
Storage Depot
M31
Weir
Abbey Cross Farm
Flixton Bri.
FLIXTON RD.
CARRINGTON RD.
Blakeswell Meadow
FLIXTON GOLF COURSE
Depot
NORTHBANK INDUSTRIAL PARK

92
A
B
C
D
E
F
G
1
2
3
4
5
6
7
8
9
76
104
91
Peel Green
Barton
Barton upon Irwell
Dumplington
Davyhulme
Crofts Bank
Manchester
FLIXTON
URMSTON
Urmston
Sale
Junction 11
Junction 10
Junction 9
Junction 8
M30
M60
M41
M33
A57
A5081
A6144
B5211
B5214
B5158
B5213
B5230
LIVERPOOL RD.
M60 MOTORWAY
MANCHESTER SHIP CANAL
SALFORD
TRAFFORD
Barton Aqueduct
Bridgewater Canal
Irwell Park Wharf
Barton Locks
Eccles Sewage Works
Sewage Works
Salford City Reds RLFC (City of Salford Community Stadium)
DW Fitness
Powerleague
David Lloyd Leisure
Chill Factore
Playgolf Manchester
THE TRAFFORD CENTRE
Laser Quest & The Rock
Odeon Cinema
TRAFFORD RETAIL PARK
BARTON SQUARE
Coach Park
TRAFFORD GENERAL HOSPITAL
DAVYHULME PARK GOLF COURSE
Davyhulme Park
Davyhulme Jun. & Inf. Sch.
Recreation Ground
Urmston Leisure Cen.
Flixton Girls High Sch.
Urmston Grammar Sch.
Golden Hill Pk.
St. Antony's Cath. College
Egerton High Sch.
George H Carnall Leisure Centre
Barton Clough Prim. Sch.
Lostock Park
Lostock College
Miniature Railway
Abbotsfield Park
Trafford FC
Chassen Rd.
Shawe House
Club House
WILLIAM WROE GOLF COURSE
FLIXTON GOLF COURSE
Shawe Hey Farm
Barrowfield Farm
Magmare Farm
Big Ras Farm
New Croft Farm
Meadowgate Farm
Cemetery
Sports Ground
River Mersey
Old Eea Brook
Salteye Brook
Ousel Brook
CARRINGTON SPUR
ASHBURTON RD.
BARTON DOCK ROAD
REDCLYFFE RD.
TRAFFORD BOULEVARD
KINGSWAY PARK
LOSTOCK ROAD
MOORSIDE ROAD
BOWFELL RD.
FLIXTON RD.
CHURCH RD.
STRETFORD ROAD
MOSS VALE ROAD
GUINNESS ROAD
BARTON RD.

Salford Quays
Pacific Quays
Salford
M50
MediaCityUk
Harbour City
Broadway
Anchorage
Ordsall
Pomona
The Lowry
Imperial War Museum North
Manchester Docks
Manchester Ship Canal
Huron Basin
Erie Basin
Ontario Basin
South Bay
North Bay
Exchange Quay
Weaste Cemetery
Trafford Park
Trafford Ecology Park
M17
Manchester Utd. Museum
Manchester United FC (Old Trafford)
United Trading Estate
Freightliner Terminal
Euroterminal
Bridgewater Canal
Gorse Hill
Stretford
Stretford Mall
Stretford Cemetery
Victoria Park
Longford Park
Trafford Athletics Stadium
Lancashire County Cricket Club (Old Trafford)
Old Trafford
Firswood
M16
M21
M32
Urmston
Humphrey Pk.
Chorlton-cum-Hardy
Turn Moss
Playing Fields
M60 Motorway
Junction 7
Eye Platt New Bridge
Mosley Acre Farm
Cut Hole Bridge
White City Retail Park
Talbot Road
Chester Road
Barton Road
Mosley Road
Park Road
Village Way
Wharfside Way
Trafford Road
Broadway
Westinghouse Road
Kingsway
Edge Lane
Wilbraham Road
Manchester Road
A5081
A5181
A56
A5063
A5186
A5145
A5067
A576
B5211
B5213
B5214
H
J
K
L
M
N
G
1
2
3
4
5
6
7
8
9
77
94
105

SALFORD
REGENT RD.
Ordsall
Ordsall Park
Ordsall Hall Mus.
Exchange Quay
ORDSALL LA.
Pomona
Pomona Docks
No.3 Dock
BRIDGEWATER WAY
Old Trafford
TALBOT RD.
CHESTER RD.
Trafford Bar
SEYMOUR GROVE
Seymour Park
Firswood
Darley Park
Whalley Range
Chorlton
Manley Park
Cricket Grd.
Football Grd.
St. Bede's Coll. Playing Field
Alexandra Park
ALEXANDRA PARK
Moss Side
Hulme
Greenheys
Castlefield
Cornbrook
St. Georges
Knott Mill
Gaythorn
Oxford Rd.
Deansgate
Granada TV Cen.
Mus. of Science & Industry
Manchester Central
Palace Theatre
Universities
University of Manchester
Manchester Science Pk.
Royal Brewery
Manchester Academy
BRIDGEWATER HOSPITAL
Loreto Coll.
William Hulme's Gram. Sch. Academy
Whalley Range High Sch. & College
Range Stadium & Powerleague Soccer Cen.
Islamic Sch.
Hindu Temple
Football Ground
Sports Grd.
St. Werburgh's Rd.
Thirlmere Aqueduct
Red Lion Brook
HOUGH END PLAYING FIELDS
MANCUNIAN WAY
PRINCESS RD.
MOSS LANE WEST
UPPER CHORLTON RD.
CHORLTON RD.
WILBRAHAM RD.
STRETFORD RD.
CHESTER RD.
NORTHUMBERLAND RD.
BARLOW MOOR RD.
MAULDETH RD. WEST
LIVERPOOL RD.
A57 A6042 A56 A5067 A5014 A5066 A5103 A6010 A5145 A57(M) B5217 B5218 B5219 B5222 B6469
M15 M16 M21 M14
A B C D E F G
1 2 3 4 5 6 7 8 9
78 4 93 106 5

95
MANCHESTER
PICCADILLY
Piccadilly Village
ANCOATS
Ardwick
Beswick
The East Manchester Academy
Ashburys
West Gorton
Openshaw
Manchester College of Arts & Tech. (Openshaw Campus)
City Coll. Manchester (Universal Sq.)
Apollo Manch.
Brunswick
University of Manchester
The Pankhurst Cen.
ROYAL INFIRMARY
EYE HOSPITAL
ST. MARY'S HOSP.
CHILDREN'S HOSPITAL
Whitworth Art Gallery
Whitworth Park
Chorlton upon Medlock
Victoria Baths
Manchester Met. Univ.
Rusholme
Ardwick Sports Hall
Longsight
Belle Vue
Showcase Cinema
Gala Bingo
Rileys Snooker Club
Belle Vue Greyhound Stadium
Belle Vue Leisure Cen.
St. Peter's RC High Sch.
Mecca Bingo
Car Auction
Gorton Park
Recreation Ground
Nutsford Vale
Cricket Grd.
Crowcroft Park
Gorton Mount Primary Sch.
Levenshulme
Green Bank Fields
Levenshulme Swim. Pools
Rushford Park
Coston Park
Birchfields Park
Manchester Grammar Sch.
Manchester Metropolitan University (Hollings Campus)
Manchester High Sch. for Girls
Platt Hall (The Gallery of Costume)
Platt Lane Complex
PLATT FIELDS PARK
Fallowfield
Playing Fields
Armitage Sports Cen.
Manchester University Athletics Ground
Withington Girls' Sch.
Ladybarn
Burnage Park
Alma Park
Levenshulme Sch.
Cringle Fields
ASHTON OLD ROAD
HYDE ROAD
STOCKPORT ROAD
PLYMOUTH GROVE
OXFORD ROAD
WILMSLOW ROAD
MOSELEY ROAD
KINGSWAY
BIRCHFIELDS ROAD
DICKENSON ROAD
ANSON ROAD
ALAN TURING WAY
POTTERY LANE
SLADE LANE
ALBERT ROAD
DEVONSHIRE ST. N.
A6010
A635
A665
A57
A6
A34
A5184
A5079
B5093
B6469
B6178
B5117
M11
M12
M19
79
96
107
G
H
J
K
L
M
N
1
2
3
4
5
6
7
8
9

A
B
C
D
E
F
G
1
2
3
4
5
6
7
8
9
80
95
108
Openshaw
Droylsden
DROYLSDEN
Fairfield
Gorton
Higher Openshaw
Abbey Hey
Belle Vue
Debdale
Ryder Brow
Brook Green
Levenshulme
North Reddish
REDDISH
Reddish Green
Mid Reddish
Dane Bank
Crowcroft Park
Manchester
ASHTON OLD ROAD
MANCHESTER ROAD
HYDE ROAD
GORTON LANE
REDDISH LANE
KINGS ROAD
A635
A662
A57
M60
M60-MOTORWAY
B6178
B6167
Junction 24
New Smithfield Market
Openshaw Complex
Karting 2000
King George V Play. Fld.
Wright Robinson Sports College
Abbey Hey Playing Fields
Fairfield Golf Course
Denton Golf Course
Gorton Upper Reservoir
Gorton Lower Reservoir
Debdale Park
Debdale Outdoor Centre
Fitness First
Gorton House
Melland Sports Centre
Melland Playing Field
Gorton Education Village (Cedar Mount High Sch. & Melland SEN)
Gorton Mount Primary Sch.
Houldsworth Golf Course
Highfield Country Park
St. Andrew's C of E Prim. Sch.
Reddish Vale Sports Centre (NW Regional Basketball Centre)
Reddish Vale Technology College
Reddish Vale Nature Reserve
Reddish Vale Visitor Cen.
Reddish Vale Country
Denton Wood
Holt Wood
Reddish Nth.
Reddish Sth.
Fairfield High Sch.
Denton West End Prim. Sch.
Dane Bank Prim. Sch.
Crown Industrial Estate
Aspinal Prim. Sch.
Fir Tree Nursy. Sch.
North Reddish Park
Recreation Ground
Audenshaw Lodge
Lodge Farm
The Barn
Edge Lane Business Park
Higher Openshaw Community Sch.
Police Training Unit
Stonebridge House
Ashton Canal
MANCHESTER TAMESIDE
AUDENS
No.3

Aldwyn Prim. Sch.
H
J
K
L
M
N
81
93
94
92
Junc. 23
SNIPE RETAIL PARK
Ryecroft Hall
Playing Fields
Depot
MOSS
ROAD
WAY
A6140
STOCKPORT
A6017
GUIDE
LANE
Guide Bridge
Oxford Park Sports Cen.
Ashton Canal
Brookside Sidings
Plantation Farm
River Tame
Dukinfield Junction
Swing Bri.
Dukinfield Cemetery
FOUNDRY ST.
Dukinfield Park
Playing Fields
Cricket Ground
TAMESIDE PARK INDUSTRIAL ESTATE
KING STREET
A627
B6169
ASTLEY ST.
Astley St. Bri.
Dukinfield Hall
Warehouse
DUKINFIELD
Sewage Works
Hooley Hill
King George's Playing Field
Audenshaw
Poplar St. Prim. Sch.
SHEPLEY
ASHTON RD.
Shepley Bri.
SHEPLEY IND. EST. NORTH
SHEPLEY IND. EST. SOUTH
Globe La. School
Peak Forest Canal
VICTORIA RD.
Newton Wood
NEWTON WOOD IND. EST.
BROADWAY IND. EST.
Hyde Junc.
Hyde Nth.
B6390
No.1
Audenshaw Sch.
Audenshaw Cemy.
War Memi.
Rec. Grd.
Jet Amber Fields
Hawthorns Sch.
ARROW TRADING ESTATE
DENTON
ASHTON
Sports Grd.
Factory
Depot
Dunkirk Farm
Dunkirk Wood
Newton Hall
HYDE POINT
Flowery Field
Hyde Sch.
No.2
SHAW RESERVOIRS
Denton College (North)
Russell Scott Prim. Sch.
Cricket Grd.
Picnic Area
Rec. Grd.
Broomstair Farm
Junc. 1a
Junction 2
M67
HYDE
Kingston Nursery
Football Grd.
Reservoir (covered)
Denton
M67 MOTORWAY
MANCHESTER ROAD
HYDE RD.
A57
Junc. 1
Superstore
Esporta Health & Fitness
Denton Pools
CROWN POINT SOUTH INDUSTRIAL PARK
Playing Fields
Playing Field
DENTON
M34
Linden Rd. Prim. Sch.
Nursery
Sewage Works
Clarke's Bridge
Hyde Central
Works
The City
St. Thomas More RC College
Play. Fld.
Greswell Prim. Sch.
Comm. Cen.
FIELDING INDUSTRIAL CENTRE
Denton College (South)
Playing Field
Dan Wood
Woodend Farm
Gower Hey Wood
Hyde Hall
Horse Close Wood
M60
M60-MOTORWAY
Corrie Prim. Sch.
Sports Grd.
Ckt. Grd.
Prim. Sch.
Haughton Green
Manor Gn. Prim. Sch.
Gibraltar Wood
Gibraltar Bridge
Sewage Works
Nursery
Hulme's Wood
Denton Cemetery
Hardy Wood
Beight Bridge
Arden Hall
109
Apethorn Fold
Clough Fold Fm.
G
1
2
3
4
5
6
7
8
9

Tame Valley
Dukinfield Cemetery
Dukinfield Crematorium
FOUNDRY ST.
OXFORD RD.
HIGH ST.
SANDY LA.
B6431
Superstore
Dukinfield
Castle Hall
Eastwood Educational Nature Reserve
Cheetham Park
A6018
Stalybridge Celtic FC (Bower Fold)
Bower Fold
FX Leisure
MOTTRAM
Early Bank Wood
Hough Hill
Reservoir (covered)
Woodlands
Bardsley Fold Farm
Yew Tree
DUKINFIELD
Dukinfield Pool
Blocksages Playing Fields
All Saints Catholic Coll.
B6170
B6175
CHEETHAM HILL ROAD
Broadbent Fold Prim. Sch.
SK16
Newton Wood
Cromwell High School
Astley High Sch.
Oakdale School & Acorn Nursery
Club House
DUKINFIELD GOLF COURSE
Playing Field
St. Mary's Catholic Prim. Sch.
Johnson Brook
Bradley Green Prim. Sch.
Matley Moor Cottage
Pott House Farm
Wrigley Fold Farm
Matley
Oak Farm
Taylor Fold Farm
EAST TAME BUSINESS PARK
ST. MARYS INDUSTRIAL PARK
NEWTON BUSINESS PARK
Hyde North
Hyde Junc.
Oakfield Prim. Sch.
Shawhall
TALBOT ROAD
BENNETT ST.
Flowery Field
Flowery Field Prim. Sch.
NEWTON MOOR IND. EST.
Hyde
Lower Matley Hall
Higher Matley Hall
Newton
Newton Sports Ground
Rec. Grd.
Hyde Sch.
Bayley Hall
Hyde Park
Tennis Cts.
Woodside Farm
Woodside
SK14
Westwood Clough
M67
M67 MOTORWAY
Newton for Hyde
Water Works
Tetlowfold Farm
Longlands
HYDE
Mills
CLARENDON RD.
Junc. 3
A627
Godley Reservoir
Longlands Farm
Westwood
Godley
Godley Works
Bonemill Dam
A57
MANCHESTER RD.
CLARK WAY
MARKET ST.
Theatre
Hyde United FC (Ewen Fields)
Hyde Leisure Pool
MOTTRAM RD.
Godley Hill
The Lawn
Reservoir (cov.)
The Thorns
HATTERSLEY ROAD WEST
Brookfold Farm
Brookfold Wood
Hattersley
Backbower
Glendarach
Albert Farm
Godley Green Farm
Greenfield
Godley Green
The Villa
Rushafield
Cemetery
Werneth Grange
STOCKPORT RD.
Clough Fold Fm.
DOWSON ROAD
Gower Hey Wood
Dowson Prim. Sch.
B6458
Alder Comm. High Sch.
Football Ground
A560
OLD ROAD
Greenside
Shangrila
High Bank
Greenacres
Little Acre Farm
Oak Tree Farm
Higham Prim. Sch.
Lower Higham Visitor Cen.
WERNETH LOW COUNTRY PARK
War Meml.
HIGHAM COTTAGES
Lowend
Gee Cross
Pear Tree
Apethorn
Pipers Clough
82
110
97
A B C D E F G
1 2 3 4 5 6 7 8 9

HOLLINGWORTHHALL MOOR
83
Stalybridge
SK15
Mottram Rise
Stalyhill Jun. Sch.
Stalyhill Inf. Sch.
Cockers Farm
Reservoir (covered)
Ashtonhill Cross
Shawmoor
Ivy Cottage
Shaw Moor
Gallows Clough
Hobson Moor
Hollingworth Farm
Hall Farm
Moorside Farm
Landslow Green Farm
Landslow Green
Higher Landslow Green Farm
Hardtimes Farm
Nailors
Gallowsclough Farm
Swallows Wood Nature Reserve
Widowscroft Farm
Filter Beds
Millbrook House
Meadowbank Farm
Thorncliffe Farm
Thorncliffe
Thorncliffe Hall
Hollingworth Manor Farm
Playing Field
Longdendale Community Language College
Ckt. Grd.
Burial Grd.
Ingledene
Hollingworth Prim. Sch.
Albion Mill
Vale Farm
Resr.
HOLLINGWORTH
Lumb Farm
Roe Cross
Dewsnap Farm
Bardsley Gate
Golden Springs Farm
Lower Roe Cross
A6018
Reservoir (covered)
Harrop Edge
Old Mill Farm
Mottram Old Hall
Nettle Hall Farm
Paddock Farm
Silver Springs Farm
Winter Bottom
Raglans
Bates
Cheetham Fold Farm
Mainsgrass
Grange Farm
Miniature Castle
(Proposed)
A57
MOTTRAM
MOTTRAM IN LONGDENDALE
Mottram Moor Farm
Robin Hood Farm
Woolley Bridge
Tara Brook Farm
Carr House
Cemetery
Tameside Gymnastics Centre (Longdendale)
Playing Fields
Arundale Prim. Sch.
Mottram C of E Prim. Sch.
Warhill
Targeton Hill
Parsonage Farm
Mudd
Lower Mudd Farm
Marl Villa
HATTERSLEY
ASHWORTH
Hollow Cottage
Pinfold Prim. Sch.
The Ken Ward Sports Centre
Pear Tree Farm
The Hague
GAMESLEY
Melandra Castle
Melandra Cottage
Melandra
Refuse Tip
River Etherow
TAMESIDE HIGH PEAK
The Golf Pavilion
Sewage Works
Parsonage Fields Farm
Home Farm
Robin Wood
Poultry Houses
Brown Road Farm
Hague
Resr. (cov.)
Bankwood Mill
Bankwood
Bankwood Cottage
Glossop
Robinwood Farm
Higher Gamesley
St. Margaret's Catholic Prim. Sch.
SK13
Sandy Oak Farm
Hurstclough
Clough End
Great Wood
BROADBOTTOM
Broadbottom C of E Prim. Sch.
Broadbottom
Hodge House
Warrastfold Bridge
Hodge Cottage
Lymefield
Lymefield Visitor Cen.
Great Wood Local Nature Reserve
Hodgefold
Leylands Farm
Sylvandale Farm
111
Bankwood Gate
Rugby Ground
Slack Edge
A560
STOCKPORT ROAD
A626
GLOSSOP ROAD
A628
WOOLLEY BRIDGE
100

84
99
A
B
C
D
E
F
G
1
2
3
4
5
6
7
8
9
Arnfield Farm
Tintwistle Low Moor
A628
(Proposed)
Gamekeepers Cottage
Townhead Farm
Valehouse Wood
VALEHOUSE RESERVOIR
Deepclough
Greenclough
Valehouse Farm
Rhodes Cott.
ARNFIELD RESERVOIR
Crossgates Farm
TINTWISTLE
Cockerhill
WOODHEAD ROAD
CHURCH ST.
MANCHESTER ROAD
Filter Beds
Water Treatment Plant
Tintwistle C of E Prim. Sch.
Sewage Works
Gauge Basin
Tintwistle Bri.
BOTTOMS RESERVOIR
Owls Nest Farm
Weirs
Millbrook House
Millbrook Bridge
Hollingworth Manor Farm
Etherow Lodge
HIGH PEAK
TAMESIDE
River Etherow
Football Grds.
HADFIELD IND. EST.
WATERSIDE BUSINESS PK.
ROSSINGTON PARK
HADFIELD
HOLLINGWORTH
Hadfield
PADFIELD MAIN ROAD
Football Ground
Reservoir
Reservoirs
Higher Cross Farm
Water Works
Cross Farm
Padfield Prim. Sch.
Padfield
Little Padfield Farm
HOLLINS IND. PK.
Hadfield Mills
Top o' Th' Hill Farm
Allman's Heath
Upper Swineshaw Reservoir
Cemetery House
Arundel Ho.
Cemetery
Lanehead House
Cat Wood
B6105
Bankswood Park
Banks Wood
Castlehill Wood
Playing Fields
St. Andrew's C of E Jun. Sch.
Hadfield Inf. Sch.
Glossopdale Comm. Coll. (Upper)
Brookfield
Playing Field
Mouselow Cottage
Mouselow Quarry
Laneside Farm
SHIRE HILL HOSPITAL
Wimberry Hill Farm
Heath Fm.
Beeley Clough
WOOD'S HOSP.
Howard Pk.
Glossop Swim. Pool
Glossopdale Comm. Coll. (Talbot Ho.)
All Saints Catholic Prim. School
DINTING LODGE INDUSTRIAL ESTATE
DINTING VALE BUSINESS PARK
Gamesley Comm. & Sports Cen.
GAMESLEY
Reservoirs
Dinting
Higher Dinting Farm
Higher Dinting
Ashes Fm.
Glossopdale Comm. Coll. (Lwr.)
GLOSSOP
Miniature Railway
Manor Park
Boating Lake
A57
A626
GLOSSOP RD.
Dinting Vale
DINTING LANE IND. ESTATE
Lower Dinting
GLOSSOP BROOK BUSINESS PARK
St. Luke's Prim. Sch.
Football Grd.
Glossop
Duke of Norfolk's Prim. Sch.
Warehouse
HIGH ST. WEST
HIGH ST. EAST
Glossop Leis. Cen.
Simmondley
St. Margaret's Catholic Prim. Sch.
Hargate Hill Equestrian Centre
Rugby Ground
Hargate Hill Farm
Hargate Hill
Slack Edge
A6016
PRIMROSE LANE
VICTORIA ST.
A624
St. Mary's Catholic Prim. Sch.
Whitfield
Whitfield Barn Farm
Bank House
Simmondley Village
TURNLEE RD.

WOODHEAD ROAD
B6105
Torside Bridge
Long Gutter Edge
White Mare
Reaps
Ford
Higher Deepclough
BRAMAH EDGE
Reaps Bent
Torside Clough
Long Gutter Edge
Torside Naze
Devil's Elbow
Nell's Pike
PEAKNAZE MOOR
Clough Edge
Torside Grain
Ogden Clough
Clough Head
Glossop
Peak Naze
Torside Castle
GLOSSOP LOW
SK13
Cock Hill
BLAKE MOOR
Blackshaw Clough
Blackshaw Farm
HARROP MOSS
PEAK DISTRICT NATIONAL PARK
Reservoir
Dog Rock
Blakemoor Plantation
Small Clough
Yellow Slacks
Broom Hill
Cote Lodge
Dowstone Clough
Wigan Clough
Lightside
Yellowslacks Brook
Shittern Clough
Mill
Moorside
Edge Plantation
FERNY HOLE
Mill Pond
The Tanyard
Shelf Benches
Shelf Brook
Mdw. Mills
Old Glossop
Hall Fold Farm
Mossy Lea Farm
Lower Shelf
Shire Hill
Football Ground
Rec. Grd.
Little Clough
SHEFFIELD ROAD
A57
WOODCOCK RD.
SNAKE PASS
Shelf Brook
Wash Brow
Doctor's Gate
Fords
Woodcock Farm
GLOSSOP & DISTRICT GOLF COURSE
Hey Clough
Lordship Hill
Club House
Reservoir Houses
SNAKE
Old Dike
Hurst Reservoir
Lower Ridge
Shirebrook Park
White Cottage
COLDHARBOUR MOOR
Carr House
Span Clough
Hurst Brook
SNAKE ROAD
HURST MOOR
Higher Ridge

HOLCROFT MOSS
GLAZEBROOK MOSS
Great Woolden Hall Farm
Nursery
CADISHEAD MOSS
NEW MOSS WOOD
Ash Farm
Tudor Rose Cottage
Rose Bank Farm
Ryefield Farm
CHAT MOSS
Lower Stanley Bank Farm
Higher Stanley Bank Farm
Ellesmere Farm
Bridge House Farm
Lower Irlam
Astley Road Farm
Irlam & Cadishead Community High School
Irlam
EXCALIBUR
NORTHBANK INDUSTRIAL PARK
Works
BRINELL
CADISHEAD
Glazebrook East Junction
Glazebrook
Brush Farm
Rose Cottage
School
Rec. Grd.
M44
Fit City Cadishead
Sewage Works
Birchley
Depot
Ivy Cottage
Bridge Farm
Townley Brow Farm
Hollingreave Farm
Warrington
WA3
Lea Brook Farm
Mount Pleasant Farm
Grave Yard
HOLLINFARE
Vicarage
Hollins Green
Prim. Sch.
Works
RIXTON PARK HOMES
Cleveland's Farm
Rixton
Wks.
Rixton Claypits Local Nature Reserve
Brook Farm
HOLLY BANK CARAVAN PARK
Water Works
Millbank Farm
Sewage Works
Recreation Ground
Coroners Wood
Partington Leisure Cen
Broadoak School
Playing Fields
Pear Tree Cottage
Birch Cottage
MANCHESTER SHIP CANAL
A57
Lane End
Rye Park House
Warburton High Level Bridge
Warburton Park
Lymm
Lighthouse Farm
Heathlands Farm
West Cottage
Park Cottages
Jack Hey Gate Farm
WA13
Rixton New Hall
Rixton & Warburton Bridge (Toll)
Toll Gate
WARBURTON
Paddocklane Farm
Wigsey Farm
Paddocklake Farm
Overtown Farm
Newton Bank Cottages
The Bent
Roughlands Cottage
Villa Farm
Mossbrow
Yewtree Farm
Moss Brow Farm
School House
Warburton Nurseries
Moss Cottage
Rixton Old Hall
Lane End Cottage
Carr Green
MANCHESTER ROAD
CADISHEAD ROAD
LIVERPOOL ROAD
GLAZEBROOK LANE
WARBURTON LANE
PADDOCK LA.
DUNHAM
TOWNFIELD
B5212
B5320
B5159
B5160
A6144
B5471
90
112

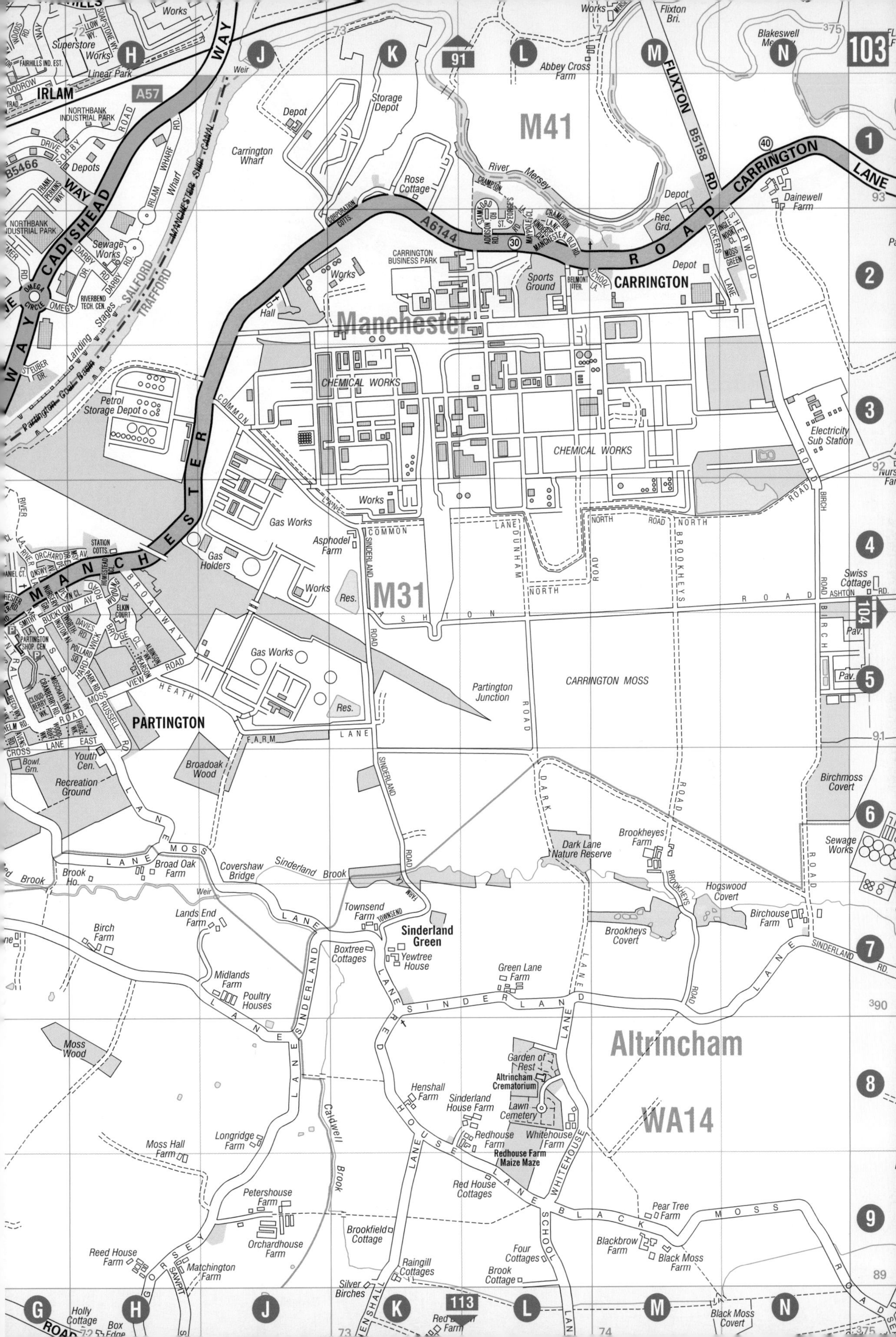

IRLAM
NORTHBANK INDUSTRIAL PARK
CADISHEAD WAY
A57
MANCHESTER SHIP CANAL
Carrington Wharf
Depot
Storage Depot
Rose Cottage
M41
River Mersey
Abbey Cross Farm
FLIXTON B5158 RD.
Flixton Bri.
Blakeswell
CARRINGTON LANE
CARRINGTON ROAD
A6144
Dainewell Farm
CARRINGTON BUSINESS PARK
Sports Ground
CARRINGTON
Manchester
CHEMICAL WORKS
Petrol Storage Depot
Partington Coal Basin
Gas Works
Gas Holders
Asphodel Farm
M31
ASHTON ROAD
Electricity Sub Station
Swiss Cottage
CARRINGTON MOSS
Partington Junction
PARTINGTON
Broadoak Wood
Recreation Ground
Youth Cen.
Birchmoss Covert
Sewage Works
Dark Lane Nature Reserve
Brookheyes Farm
Hogswood Covert
Birchouse Farm
Brookheys Covert
Covershaw Bridge
Sinderland Brook
Broad Oak Farm
Brook Ho.
Lands End Farm
Birch Farm
Townsend Farm
Sinderland Green
Boxtree Cottages
Yewtree House
Green Lane Farm
SINDERLAND LANE
Midlands Farm
Poultry Houses
Moss Wood
Altrincham
Garden of Rest
Altrincham Crematorium
Lawn Cemetery
Henshall Farm
Sinderland House Farm
WA14
Redhouse Farm
Whitehouse Farm
Redhouse Farm Maize Maze
Longridge Farm
Moss Hall Farm
Red House Cottages
Pear Tree Farm
BLACK MOSS ROAD
Petershouse Farm
Orchardhouse Farm
Brookfield Cottage
Blackbrow Farm
Black Moss Farm
Four Cottages
Brook Cottage
Reed House Farm
Matchington Farm
Raingill Cottages
Silver Birches
Holly Cottage
Box Edge
Black Moss Covert
91
104
113

A
B
C
D
E
F
G
1
2
3
4
5
6
7
8
9
92
103
114
FLIXTON GOLF COURSE
River Mersey
Magmare Farm
Big Ras Farm
Sports Ground
Old Eea Brook
New Croft Farm
Ckt. Grd.
Pav.
ASHTON-ON-MERSEY GOLF COURSE
Club House
Stables
Dunbar Farm
Sports Ground
SPUR
A6144
Stretford Brook
Sewage Works
Banky Meadow
Willow Farm
M41
Broadoak Cottage
CARRINGTON
A6144
Training Ground
Training Ground
CARRINGTON LANE
Ashton Old Hall Farm
War Memorial
Ashton Park
Ashton upon Mersey
Wellfield Jun. & Inf. Schs.
Manchester
Electricity Sub Station
Carrington Riding Centre
Nursery Farm
CARRINGTON MOSS
M31
Swiss Cottage
ASHTON
Training Ground
Birchmoss Covert
Sewage Works
Woodhouses
Woodcote Farm
Sinderland Brook
Malljurs Covert
Ash Farm
Firs Plantation
High Sch.
Firs Prim. Sch.
Brook Wood
HARBORO ROAD
ASHTON LANE
B5166
Sale
M33
Ashton-on-Mersey Sch.
Fitness Cen.
CECIL AVENUE
Recreation Ground
Comm. Cen.
A56
Walton Park Leis. Cen.
Miniature Railway
Walton Rd. Park
Prim. Schs.
Woodheys Prim. Sch.
Woodheys Park
WASHWAY ROAD
Woodheys Clough
Baguley Brook
Newton Park
Trafford College
West Timperley
Timperley
B5165
Altrincham
Smith's Bri.
St. Hugh's Cath. Prim. Sch.
Bowl. Grn.
WA14
ALTRINCHAM RETAIL PARK
Broadheath
Dairyhouse Farm
Higher House
Sports Ground
Timperley Brook
Bridgewater Canal
Rileys Snooker Club
LYON IND. ESTATE
Navigation Rec. Grd.
Navigation
Rec. Grd.
Willows Prim. Sch.
MANCHESTER ROAD
GEORGE STREET
RICHARDS STREET
DAIRYHOUSE ROAD
SINDERLAND ROAD
WOODCOTE ROAD
MOSS LANE
PARK ROAD

Junction 7
Manchester
M32
M60
M60-MOTORWAY
SALE WATER PARK
Broad Ees Dole Local Nature Reserve
Crossford Bridge Sports Ground
Trafford Water Sports Cen.
CHORLTON-CUM-HARDY
Chorlton Ees Nature Reserve
M21
Chorltonville
University of Manchester Hardy Farm Sports Ground
Jackson's Bridge
Barrow Nature Reserve
Mersey Valley Visitor Cen.
CHORLTON-CUM-HARDY GOLF COURSE
Junction 6
SALE
SALE GOLF COURSE
Worthington Park
Recreation Ground
Moorlands Jun. Sch.
NORTHENDEN
Sale Grammar Sch.
Walkden Gdns.
Brooklands
Brooklands Sports Club
Sale High School
Sale Football Club
Brooklands Prim. Sch.
Button Lane Prim. Sch.
Rack Ho. Prim. Sch.
Northern Moor
Wythenshawe Park Running Track
Miniature Golf Course
Wythenshawe Hall
WYTHENSHAWE PARK
The Horticultural Centre in Wythenshawe Park
Wythenshawe Community Farm
M23
Baguley
Baguley Recreation Ground
Brookway Sch. & Sports College
Royal Oak Rec. Grd.
Sandilands Prim. Sch.
WA15
Timperley
Pictor Sch.
ROUNDTHORN INDUSTRIAL ESTATE
SOUTHMOOR BUSINESS PARK
Princes Spinney
ALTRINCHAM ROAD
WYTHENSHAWE ROAD
A6144
A560
B5166
B5397
B5167
B5165
A56
93
115
106

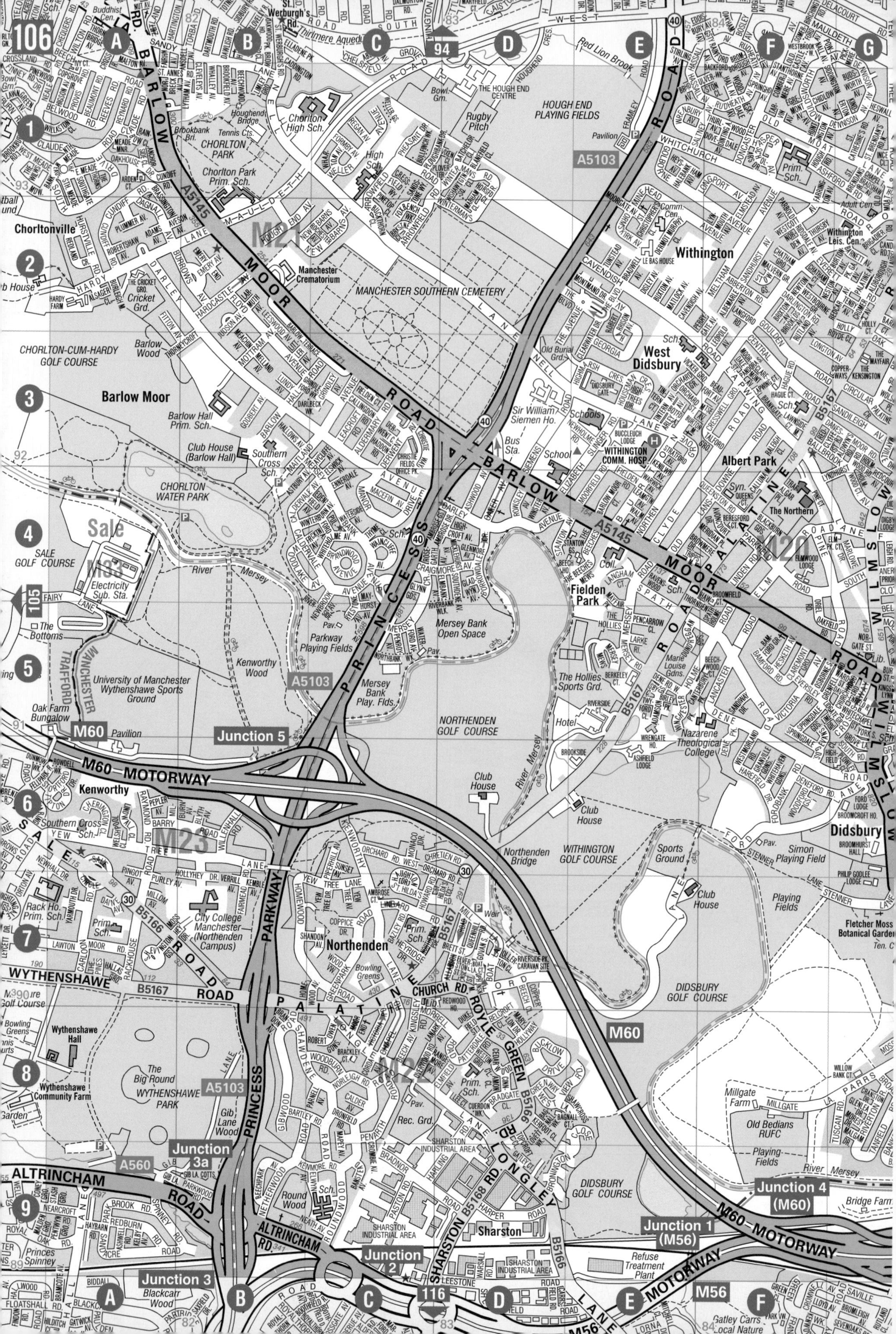
94
Thirlmere Aqueduct
St. Werburgh's Rd.
Red Lion Brook
Chorlton High Sch.
THE HOUGH END CENTRE
HOUGH END PLAYING FIELDS
Rugby Pitch
Pavilion
A5103
CHORLTON PARK
Chorlton Park Prim. Sch.
Houghend Bridge
Brookbank Bri.
Tennis Cts.
High Sch.
Chorltonville
M21
Manchester Crematorium
MANCHESTER SOUTHERN CEMETERY
Withington
Comm. Cen.
LE BAS HOUSE
Prim. Sch.
Withington Leis. Cen.
Adult Cen.
Cricket Grd.
HARDY FARM
CHORLTON-CUM-HARDY GOLF COURSE
Barlow Wood
Barlow Moor
Barlow Hall Prim. Sch.
Club House (Barlow Hall)
Southern Cross Sch.
CHORLTON WATER PARK
BARLOW MOOR ROAD
A5145
West Didsbury
Old Burial Grd.
Sir William Siemen Ho.
Bus Sta.
Schools
School
BUCCLEUCH LODGE
WITHINGTON COMM. HOSP.
Albert Park
The Northern
M20
Sale
SALE GOLF COURSE
M33
Electricity Sub. Sta.
105
FAIRY LANE
The Bottoms
River Mersey
Kenworthy Wood
Parkway Playing Fields
Mersey Bank Open Space
Mersey Bank Play. Flds.
PRINCESS PARKWAY
A5103
Fielden Park
Coll.
The Hollies Sports Grd.
Marie Louise Gdns.
Hotel
Nazarene Theological College
PALATINE ROAD
B5167
WILMSLOW ROAD
TRAFFORD MANCHESTER
University of Manchester Wythenshawe Sports Ground
Oak Farm Bungalow
M60
Pavilion
Junction 5
NORTHENDEN GOLF COURSE
Club House
River Mersey
M60 MOTORWAY
Kenworthy
Southern Cross Sch.
M23
SALE ROAD
Rack Ho. Prim. Sch.
Prim. Sch.
City College Manchester (Northenden Campus)
B5166
Northenden Bridge
WITHINGTON GOLF COURSE
Sports Ground
Club House
Simon Playing Field
Didsbury
Playing Fields
Fletcher Moss Botanical Garden
Northenden
Bowling Greens
Weir
RIVERSIDE PK. CARAVAN SITE
WYTHENSHAWE ROAD
B5167
PALATINE ROAD
CHURCH RD.
ROYLE GREEN RD.
DIDSBURY GOLF COURSE
M60
Wythenshawe Hall
Wythenshawe Community Farm
The Big Round
WYTHENSHAWE PARK
A5103
Gib Lane Wood
Junction 3a
A560
M22
Prim. Sch.
Rec. Grd.
SHARSTON INDUSTRIAL AREA
LONGLEY LANE
Millgate Farm
Old Bedians RUFC
Playing Fields
River Mersey
DIDSBURY GOLF COURSE
Junction 4 (M60)
Bridge Farm
ALTRINCHAM ROAD
Round Wood
Sch.
Sharston
SHARSTON B5168 RD.
Junction 1 (M56)
M60 MOTORWAY
Refuse Treatment Plant
Princes Spinney
ALTRINCHAM RD.
Junction 2
Junction 3
Blackcarr Wood
116
M56 MOTORWAY
M56
Gatley Carrs Local Nature
A B C D E F G
1 2 3 4 5 6 7 8 9

107
95
108
117
Burnage Park
Alma Park
Manchester
Ladybarn
Mauldeth Rd.
Burnage
Green End
Levenshulme High Sch.
Cringle Fields Park
Peel Moat
Peel Moat Sports Centre
Heaton Moor Golf Course
Heaton Moor
Stockport
Heaton Mersey
Heaton Mersey Common
Heaton Mersey Pk.
Norris Hill
Norris Bank
Fog Lane Park
Didsbury Park
East Didsbury
Christie Hospital
Manchester Met. Univ. (Didsbury Campus)
The Barlow RC High Sch.
Parrs Wood High School
Parrs Wood Sports Centre
Parrs Wood Entertainment Cen.
Cheadle
Cheadle Heath
Edgeley
Abney Hall
Abney Hall Park
Sewage Works
River Mersey
The Bungalow Reservoir
Vale Road Farm
Powerleague Soccer Cen.
Avondale Rec. Cen.
Stockport Trading Estate
Junction 2
Junction 3
M60 Motorway
A34
A5145
A6
A560
B5093
B5095
B5169
B5465
Kingsway
Didsbury Road
Stockport Road
Wilmslow Road
Manchester Road
Parrs Wood La.
The Alexandra BMI Hospital
M14
M19
M20
SK4
SK3
SK8
1
2
3
4
5
6
7
8
9
G
H
J
K
L
M
N
385
86
87
88
89
90
91
92
93

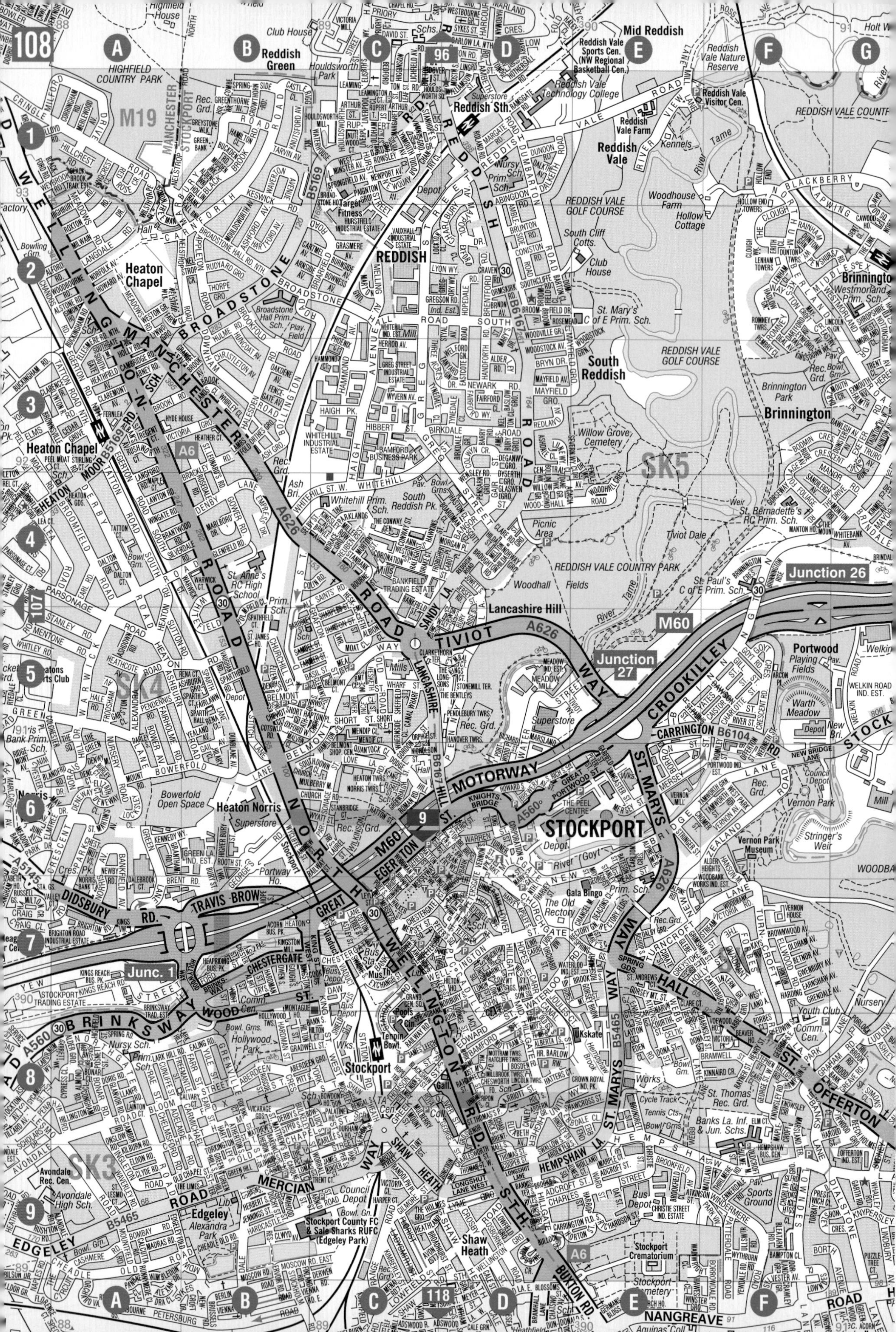

Reddish Green
Reddish Vale Country Park
Reddish Vale Golf Course
Heaton Chapel
Reddish
South Reddish
Brinnington
Heaton Norris
Stockport
Edgeley
Shaw Heath
Junction 26
Junction 27
Junc. 1
M60
SK3
SK4
SK5
M19

Castle Hill
Haughton Dale
Woodley
Bredbury
BREDBURY
ROMILEY
Lower Bredbury
Barrack Hill
Bredbury Green
Hatherlow
Tang
Stockport
Stockport Little Moor
Chadkirk
CHADKIRK COUNTRY ESTATE
Bunkers Hill
Foggbrook
Offerton Green
SK2
SK6
SK14
M60 MOTORWAY
Junction 25
STOCKPORT ROAD WEST
STOCKPORT RD. WEST
ASHTON ROAD
GEORGE LANE
OTTERSPOOL ROAD
DOOLEY LANE
COMPSTALL RD.
MARPLE ROAD
Peak Forest Canal
River Tame
River Goyt
Sports Ground
Recreation Ground
Woodbank Park Athletics Track
Offerton High School
Marple Hall School
Target Life (Werneth)
Harrytown Catholic High Sch.
Werneth School

Hyde
SK14
Gee Cross
A560
A627
Stockport Rd.
Dowson Rd.
Apethorn Fold
Pear Tree Farm
Pole Bank Hall
Tameside College (Hyde Centre)
Bamford Hall
Bowlacre Farm
Lower Higham Visitor Cen.
Higher Higham
Werneth Low Country Park
Pipers Clough
Hartley Fold Cottage
Idle Hill
Windy Harbour
Green Mdws.
Rhodes Fold Cott.
Lumn
Lower Cliff
Lowend
Little Acre Farm
Oak Tree Farm
Higham Cottages
War Meml.
Lofty Top
Club House
Werneth Low Golf Course
Reservoir (covered)
Hythe Ckt. Grd.
Hare & Hounds Farm
Wicken Cottage
Werneth Low
Ash Tree
Birches
Needham's Farm
Tameside
Stockport
Tor Wood
Back o' th' Hill
Cowlishaw Brow
Top-o'th'-Low Cottage
Wood Lane Farm
Lowtop Plantation
Lowtop
Werneth Hall Farm
Werneth Hall Cottages
Near Cloughside
Far Cloughside Farm
Beacon Houses
Ridd Wood
Long Alders Wood
Hillside Farm
Greave Prim. Sch.
Lowbank Ho.
Lowbank Cottage
Rose Cottage
Cowlishaw Farm
Spring Wood
Clough Wood
Hyde's Farm
Beacom Wood
Keg Pool
Greavefold
Springwood Farm
Near Benfield
Far Benfield
Gigg Brook
Campville Farm
John Hirst Cottage
Whitebottom
Lane Ends
Higher Mossacre
Romiley Golf Course
Club House
Barlowfold
Mossacre
Stockport
Mortin Farm
Mortin Clough
Etherow Country Park Local Nature Reserve
Benfield Clough
Brakanes
Greenways
Compstall Brow
Bardsley Knoll
School Lane Farm
Yew Tree Cottages
Weir Cotts.
Rydeacre House
Gothic Farm
SK6
Compstall
The Mount
Ernocroft Wood
Rabbit Warren
Etherow Country Park
Compstall Brow
Compstall Hall
Vicarage
War Meml.
Visitor Cen.
Priory Cottage
Cowhey Farm
Romiley Prim. Sch.
Compstall Rd.
B6104
Fordsdale
Redbrow Wood
River Etherow
Reservoir
Rec. Ground
Cherry Tree
Tangshutt Fields
Romiley
Bowl. Grn.
Ten. Cts.
Mills
Sewage Works
Lower Ernocroft Farm
Compstall Bri.
Cricket Grd.
Cherry Tree Estate
Mast
Lower Watermeetings Farm
Hyde Bank Farm
Hydebank Tunnel
Watermeetings Cottage
River Goyt
Upper Watermeetings Farm
Hillside Farm
Cote Green
Lane Ends
The Lodes
Glossop Rd.
River Wood
Peak Forest Canal
Oakwood Hall
Lower Dale Farm
Marple Dale Farm
Aqueduct
Aqueduct House
Bottomlocks House
Brabyns Park
Iron Bridge
Play. Field
Broadst.
Marple Dale
Marple Wharf Junction
Brabyns Pk. Rec. Cen.
Rec. Grd.
Turncliff Wood
Marple
Marple Dale Hall
Brabyns Wood
Marple Locks
Ludworth Prim. Sch.
Lower Fold A626
Ley Hey Park
Ley Hey Wood
St. Martins Cott.
Marple Bridge
Mill Pond
Heathy Bank
Towncliffe Farm
The Dale Prim. Sch.
Rose Hill Prim. Sch.
Ckt. Grd.
Brabyns Brow
Marple Bri.
Prim. Sch.
Prep. Sch.
Burial Grd.
Brabyn's Sch.
Memorial Park
Coun. Offs.
Mills
Goyt House
Cataract Bridge
Station Rd.
Stockport Rd.
A626
Longhurst
Townscliffe Lane
Clement Rd.

98
109
120

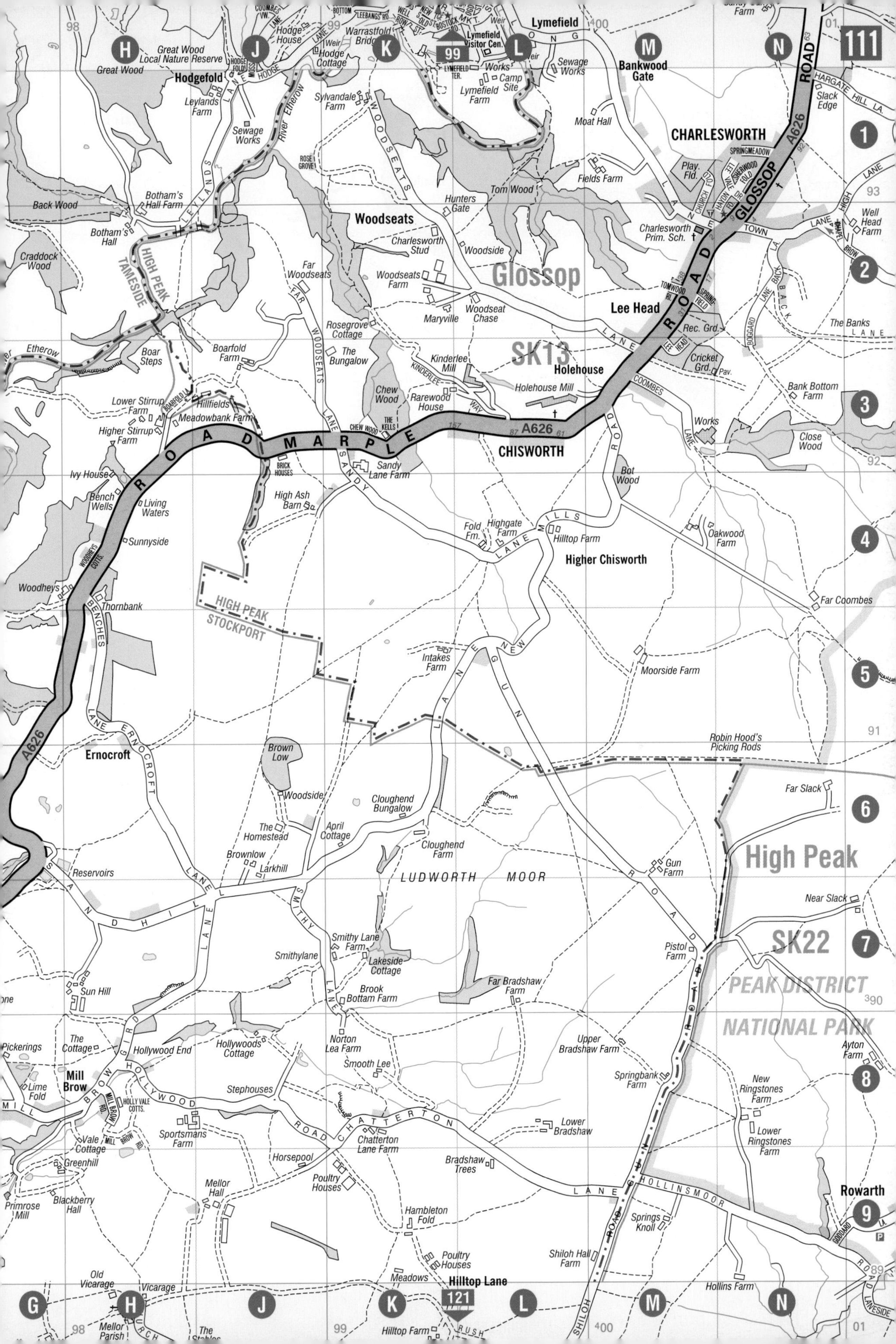
Lymefield
Lymefield Visitor Cen.
99
Great Wood Local Nature Reserve
Great Wood
Hodgefold
Hodge House
Hodge Cottage
Warrastfold Bridge
Leylands Farm
Sewage Works
Bankwood Gate
Moat Hall
CHARLESWORTH
Lymefield Farm
Camp Site
Sylvandale Farm
River Etherow
Botham's Hall Farm
Back Wood
Botham's Hall
Craddock Wood
Woodseats
Hunters Gate
Tom Wood
Fields Farm
Charlesworth Prim. Sch.
Charlesworth Stud
Woodside
Glossop
Well Head Farm
Far Woodseats
Woodseats Farm
Maryville
Woodseat Chase
Lee Head
Rec. Grd.
The Banks
Etherow
Boar Steps
Boarfold Farm
Rosegrove Cottage
The Bungalow
Kinderlee Mill
SK13
Holehouse
Cricket Grd.
Bank Bottom Farm
HIGH PEAK
TAMESIDE
Lower Stirrup Farm
Hillfields
Meadowbank Farm
Higher Stirrup Farm
Chew Wood
Rarewood House
Holehouse Mill
Works
Close Wood
MARPLE ROAD
A626
CHISWORTH
GLOSSOP ROAD
Ivy House
Bench Wells
Living Waters
Sunnyside
Sandy Lane Farm
High Ash Barn
Bot Wood
Fold Fm.
Highgate Farm
Hilltop Farm
Oakwood Farm
Higher Chisworth
Woodheys
Thornbank
Far Coombes
HIGH PEAK
STOCKPORT
Intakes Farm
Moorside Farm
Ernocroft
Brown Low
Robin Hood's Picking Rods
Woodside
Cloughend Bungalow
Far Slack
The Homestead
April Cottage
Cloughend Farm
High Peak
Reservoirs
Brownlow
Larkhill
LUDWORTH MOOR
Gun Farm
Near Slack
Smithy Lane Farm
Smithylane
Lakeside Cottage
Pistol Farm
SK22
Sun Hill
Brook Bottam Farm
Far Bradshaw Farm
PEAK DISTRICT NATIONAL PARK
Pickerings
The Cottage
Hollywood End
Hollywoods Cottage
Norton Lea Farm
Upper Bradshaw Farm
Ayton Farm
Mill Brow
Lime Fold
Smooth Lee
Springbank Farm
Stephouses
New Ringstones Farm
Sportsmans Farm
Chatterton Lane Farm
Lower Bradshaw
Lower Ringstones Farm
Vale Cottage
Greenhill
Horsepool
Bradshaw Trees
Poultry Houses
Mellor Hall
Rowarth
Primrose Mill
Blackberry Hall
Springs Knoll
Hambleton Fold
Shiloh Hall Farm
Poultry Houses
Old Vicarage
Vicarage
Meadows
Hilltop Lane
121
Hollins Farm
Mellor Parish
Hilltop Farm
The Stables

102
MANCHESTER SHIP CANAL
River Bollin
Reddish Hall
Reddish
Heatley
Warburton Bridge
Old Bollin
Fox Covert
Carr Green
Lane End Cottage
Higher Carr Green Farm
Carr Green House
Lower Carr Green Farm
Boarded Barn Farm
Platt Farm
Moss Brow Farm
The Bent
Wet Gate Lane Farm
Wet Gate Farm
TRAFFORD
WARRINGTON
Little Heatley
Heatley Heath Farm
Gailey Wood
New Farm
Sewage Works
Reddish Crossing
Play. Fld.
RUSHGREEN
Rushgreen
OUGHTRINGTON
Oughtrington Prim. Sch.
Lymm
Nursery
Bridgewater Canal
Lloyd Bri.
Grantham's Bridge
WA13
Spring Farm
Rose Cottages
Lower Helsdale Wood
Ravenbank Prim. Sch.
LYMM
Helsdale Wood
Sports Ground
Pav. Ckt. Grd.
Cotebrook
Lymm Leisure Cen.
Lymm High School
Newhay's Plantation
Agden Bridge Farm
Agden Bridge
Burford Lane Farm
Water Tower
Rugby Ground
Broomedge Nurseries
Agdenlane Farm
Hollybank House
Crouchley Hall Farm
Wildersmoor Farm
Model Farm
Ashlea Farm
Willow Pool Nurseries
BROOMEDGE
Broomedge Farm
Wildersmoor Hall Farm
Agden Brow
Agden Park
Crouchley Cottage
Yewtree Farm
Field House
Top Farm
Hall
Kaylane Brook
Nurseries
Dorkensville
Brook Cottage
Kaylane Farm
Deansgreen Hall
WARRINGTON
MACCLESFIELD
Silent Valley Cottages
Willow Bed
Cornheys Cottage
Cornheys
Deansgreen
Hawthorn Cottage
Agden Hall
Agden Hall Farm
Agden Ho.
The Howlers
Old Farm
Woodiers Farm
Redoak
Great Oak Farm
M56-MOTORWAY
Beech Tree Farm
Depot
Diamond Cottages
Abbey Leys Farm
Endfield Farm
Lime Tree Cott.
Agden Cottage Thatch
Crackling Farm
Mowpenbrow Farm
Heywood Court
Limetree Farm
Moss Lane Farm
Knutsford
Hey Wood
Moss's Strip
Sewage Works
Walnut Farm
Westlane Farm
Crossroads Farm
Peacock Lodge
Broad Oak Farm
Whyte Cottage
Mowpen Farm
Abbey Cotts.
Boundary Farm
Little Oaks
WA16
Peter's Covert
HIGH LEGH PARK GOLF COURSE
Little Moss Farm
HIGH LEGH
A50

103
114
Altrincham
WA14
Dunham Massey
Oldfield Brow
DUNHAM WOODHOUSES
Dunham Town
Little Bollington
Arthill
Booth Bank
Castle Hill
B5160
A56
A556
B5161
M56
M56 MOTORWAY
Junction 8
Junc. 7
Bridgewater Canal
River Bollin
Agden Brook
TRAFFORD
MACCLESFIELD
DUNHAM PARK (Deer Park)
DUNHAM FOREST GOLF COURSE
DUNHAM NEW PARK
Dunham Massey Sawmill
North Park
Fish Pond
Old Man Pool
New Covert
Headsman's Covert
Pitstead Covert
Redmoor Covert
Scout Camp
Dunham Massey Lodge
Home Farm
Stamford Cottage
Tipping's Bank
Watlingford
Paddock Covert
Sutt's Hollow
The Paddocks
Grey's Gorse
Rushy-pits Covert
Yarwoodheath Covert
Mere Covert
Gale Bog
Harpers Bank Wood
ROSTHERNE MERE
Whiteoaks Wood
Brickkiln Nursery Wood
Sewage Works
Aqueduct
Woolstencroft Farm
Agden Bridge
Agden Brook Farm
The Smithy
Little Bollington C of E Prim. Sch.
Black Moss Covert
Playing Field
Oldfield Brow Prim. Sch.
Club House
Forest Edge
Levenot
Parklands
Red Beech Farm
Grovehouse Farm
Little Heath Farm
Big Tree Cottages
Dunham Sch. Bri.
Dunhamtown Bridge
Dunham Underbridge
Station House
Warburton Bridge
Holly Cottage
Box Edge
Gatehouse Farm
Boundary Farm
Smithy Cottage
Park View
Bridge Farm
Reed House Farm
Matchington Farm
Orchardhouse Farm
Brookfield Cottage
Silver Birches
Raingill Cottages
Four Cottages
Brook Cottage
Cinderland
Moss Bridge
Holly Bank
The Hollies
Ash Farm
Barns Lane Farm
Manor House Farm
Yewtree Farm
Bollin Cottages
Agden View
Sewage Works Cottage
Bollington Hall Farm
Hillcroft
Ivy Lodge
Stamford Farm
Yewtree Farm
Four Winds
Model Farm
The Gables
Strathyre
New Cotts.
New Farm
Ivy Bank
The Meadows
The Old House
Spodegreen Farm
Brook Farm
The Dell
The Pastures
Brook Cottage
Bowdon View
Arthill Farm
Reddy Lane Cottage
Old Chapel House
The Paddock
Arthill Heath Farm
Booth Bank Farm
Booth Bank Cotts.
Booth Bank Farm
Booth Bank House
Booth Bank Cottage
Stonedelph Farm
Thowlerlane Farm
Ivyhouse Farm
Moss House Farm
Five Acres
Millington Hall
Keldan
Newhall Farm
Three Oaks
Newhall Cottages
Mereside Farm
Mereside Cottage
Cherrytree Farm
Yarwood Heath Farm
Hope Cottage
Covert Cottage
Mere Covert
Bowden View Farm
Hanging Bank Covert
Langham Grove
ROAD
WOODHOUSE
STATION ROAD
PADDOCK LA.
BACK LANE
SMITHY LA.
CHARCOAL LANE
OLDFIELD LANE
SCHOOL LANE
MAIN DRIVE
FARM WALK
BOW GREEN LA.
DUNHAM ROAD
A56 ROAD
CHESTER ROAD
YARWOODHEATH LANE
TOM LANE
CHERRY TREE LANE
MILLINGTON LANE
MILLINGTON HALL LA.
THOWLER LANE
BOOTHBANK LANE
REDDY LANE
SPODE GREEN LANE
COE LANE
PARK LANE
BRICKKILN LANE
PARK VW.
ARTHILL LA.
HENSHALL STREET
GORSEY LANE
SAWPIT LANE
BLACK MOSS RD.
SEAMONS RD.
WEST AVE.
TAYLOR RD.
STANHOPE RD.
BLUEBERRY RD.
EYEBROOK RD.
MARLOW DR.
72
73
74
375
89
88
87
86
385
A
B
C
D
E
F
G
H
J
K
L
M
N
1
2
3
4
5
6
7
8
9

ALTRINCHAM
Altrincham
BOWDON
HALE
Hale Moss
Rosehill
Bowgreen
Ashley Heath
Oldfield Brow
Castle Hill
Ashley
WA14
DUNHAM FOREST GOLF COURSE
DUNHAM NEW PARK
ALTRINCHAM GOLF COURSE
Navigation Rd.
Stamford Park
Altrincham Grammar School for Girls
Altrincham Grammar Sch. for Boys
Bowdon Cricket, Hockey & Squash Club
Timperley Cricket, Hockey, Tennis & Lacrosse Club
Wellington School
Blessed Thomas Holford Catholic College
St. Vincent Catholic Jun. & Inf. Schs.
Altrincham Leisure Cen
Altrincham FC (Moss Lane Ground)
John Leigh Park
Century Park Industrial Estate
Bridgewater Canal
Dunham Road
Stockport Rd.
Woodlands Rd.
Manchester Rd.
Ashley Rd.
Park Road
Hale Road
Langham Road
South Downs Road
Junction 7
M56
M56 MOTORWAY
River Bollin
Sewage Works
Hancock's Banks
Ryecroft Farm
Ashley Hall
The Rookery
Dairyhouse Farm
Jackson's Bank
Tanyard Farm
Bankhall Farm
Cemetery
A56
A560
A538
B5160
B5161
B5162
B5357
B5164
104
113
6
30
50
A B C D E F G
1 2 3 4 5 6 7 8 9
375
76
77
78
385
86
87
88
89

H
J
K
L
M
N
105
Pictor Sch.
B5165
THORLEY
STOCKPORT
SHAFTESBURY
A560
Broomwood Prim. Sch.
Cloverlea Prim. Sch.
RIDGEWAY
Manor Farm
Sports Ground
Rugby Ground
Fairywell Wood
Roundthorn Industrial Estate
Mill Brook Industrial Estate
Southmoor Ind. Estate
Millbrook Business Centre
Works
Manchester
Wythenshawe Hospital
Baguley Park
Rodger's Park
Newall Green Prim. Sch.
Newall Green
St. Paul's Catholic High Sch.
Junc. 4
Roundthorn
M23
The Dobbinetts
Holly Tree Cottage
Holly Tree Farm
Duncalf Farm
Clay House
Latham Hall Farm
Ash Farm
Well Green
Timperley Brook
Delaheys Farm
Altrincham College of Arts
Wood La. Nurseries
Clay Lane Nursery
A5144
Playing Field
Manch. Coll. Newall Green High Sch.
Roaring Gate Farm
Chapel House Farm
Fairywell Brook
Well Green Prim. Sch.
WA15
Davenport Green
Davenport Green Hall
M56
Junction 5
RINGWAY GOLF COURSE
Humphrey's Wood
Davenportgreen Wood
Airport Long Term Car Park
Oaklands Court
St. Ambrose College
St. Ambrose Prep. Sch.
Club House
A538
Halebarns
Elmridge Prim. Sch.
Graythwaite
Tomfield Bank
Flaxhigh Covert
Cricket Ground
M56 MOTORWAY
Manchester
M90
TERMINAL 2
MANCHESTER INTERNATIONAL AIRPORT
World Freight Centre
TERMINAL 1
Hotel
Warburton Green
Junction 6
Oak Farm
WILMSLOW ROAD
Ringway
Aircraft Hangars
Keepers Cottage
Oak Cottages
Jackson's Bank
HALE GOLF COURSE
ALTRINCHAM PRIORY HOSPITAL
Halebank Farm
Lower Thornsgreen Farm
Halebank Cottage
The Runway Visitor Park
Painswick Park
1
2
3
4
5
6
7
8
9
116
G

Sharston
Sharston Industrial Area
Altrincham Rd
Longley
M60
Junction 3
Junc. 2
Junction 1 (M56)
106
M56 Motorway
Gatley Carrs Local Nature Reserve
Sharston Green Business Park
A560
Park Road
Gatley
Benchill Prim. Sch.
Gymnastic Cen.
Youth Cen.
Hollyhedge Park
Manchester
Benchill
Rodger's Park
Newall Green Prim. Sch.
Haveley Hey Prim. Sch.
Crossacres Prim. Sch.
Gatley Prim. Sch.
Gatley Hill
Scholes Park Track (Athletics Ground)
Scholes Park
St. Paul's Catholic High Sch.
Junction 4
Wythenshawe
Parklands Sports Cen.
Parklands High Sch.
Peter's Spinney
Ashgate Sch.
Park Wood
Gatley Golf Course
The Forum Cen.
Market Place
Gala Bingo
Adult Learning Cen.
Peel Hall Prim. Sch.
Peel Hall
Peel Hall Play Park
Lumhead Wood
Kirkup Gdns.
The Willows Prim. Sch.
Ash Wood
Hatchetts Wood
Rose Vale Park
Little Wood
Big Wood
Chamber Hall
Woodhouse Park
Painswick Park
Ringway Prim. Sch.
Concord Bus. Park
Atlas Business Park
Sports Ground
Daisy Bank Farm
Heald Green
Airport Long Term Car Park
Moss Nook Industrial Area
Ringway Trading Estate
Recreation Ground
Manchester Airport
Terminal 2
Hotel
Hotels
Moss Nook
Greencourts Bus. Cen.
Manchester International Business Centre
Shadow Moss Farm
Wood Farm
Terminal 1
Pier C
Olympic Ho.
Terminal 3
Pier B
Pier A
M90
Manchester
Macclesfield
Wilmslow SK9
Boundary Farm
Outwood Farm
Stockport
Beech Farm
Hollin La.
Styal
Manchester International Airport
Styal Golf Course
Driving Range
Club House
Moss Lane Farm
122
115
B5166

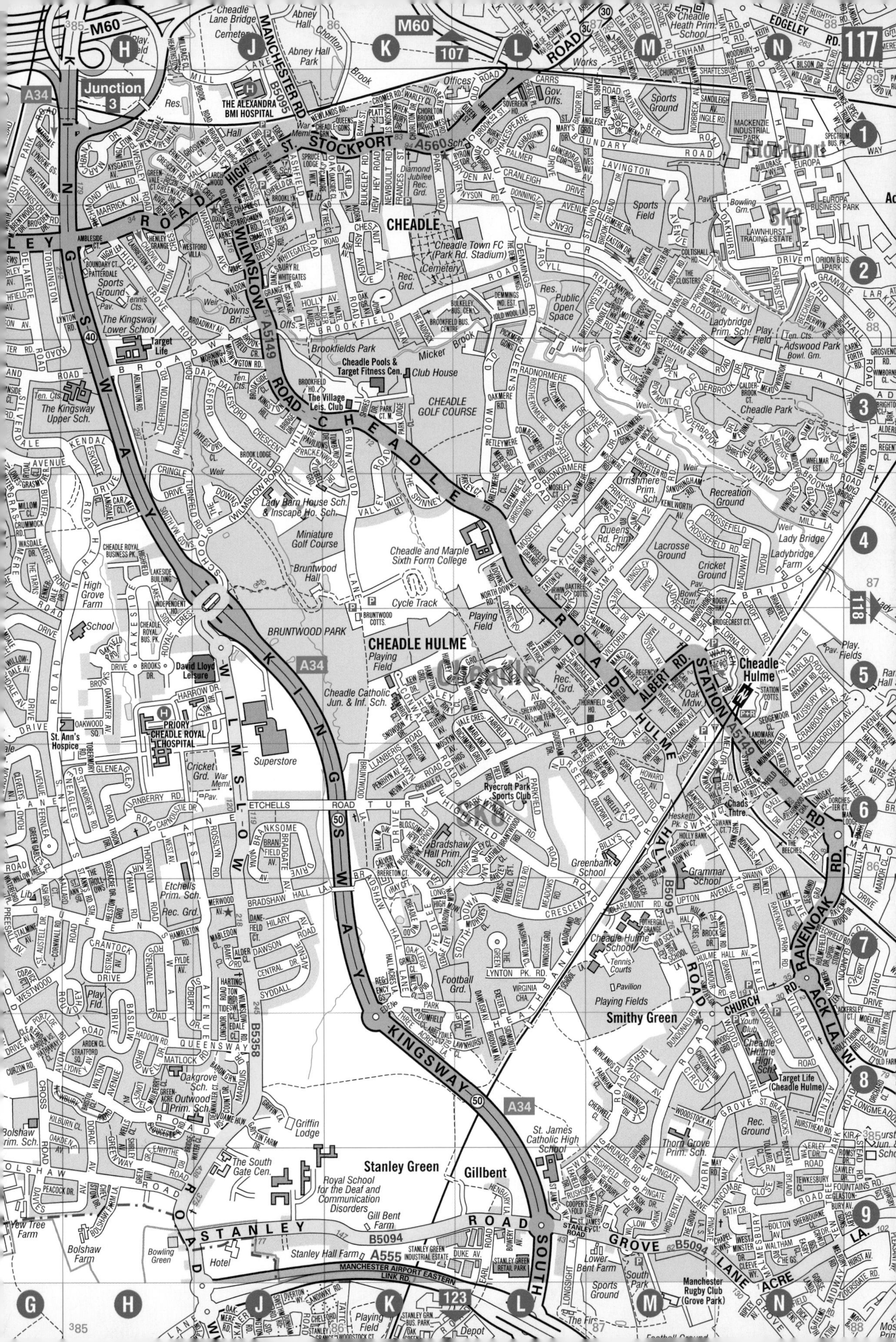

M60
Junction 3
A34
THE ALEXANDRA BMI HOSPITAL
MANCHESTER RD
B5095
Abney Hall
Abney Hall Park
Cheadle Lane Bridge
Cemetery
107
STOCKPORT ROAD
A560
EDGELEY RD.
Cheadle Heath Prim. School
MACKENZIE INDUSTRIAL PARK
Stockport
EUROPA BUSINESS PARK
LAWNHURST TRADING ESTATE
ORION BUS. PARK
SK3
CHEADLE
Cheadle Town FC (Park Rd. Stadium)
Cemetery
Diamond Jubilee Rec. Grd.
Sports Ground
Sports Field
Public Open Space
Ladybridge Prim. Sch.
Adswood Park Bowl. Grn.
Cheadle Park
HIGH ST.
WILMSLOW ROAD
A5149
BROADWAY
The Kingsway Lower School
The Kingsway Upper Sch.
Target Life
Cheadle Pools & Target Fitness Cen.
Brookfields Park
Micker Brook
The Village Leis. Club
CHEADLE GOLF COURSE
CHEADLE ROAD
Lady Barn House Sch. & Inscape Ho. Sch.
Miniature Golf Course
Bruntwood Hall
Cheadle and Marple Sixth Form College
Cycle Track
BRUNTWOOD PARK
CHEADLE HULME
Playing Field
Orrishmere Prim. Sch.
Queens Rd. Prim. Sch.
Recreation Ground
Lacrosse Ground
Cricket Ground
Lady Bridge
Ladybridge Farm
118
KINGSWAY
A34
David Lloyd Leisure
PRIORY CHEADLE ROYAL HOSPITAL
St. Ann's Hospice
Superstore
CHEADLE ROYAL BUSINESS PK.
High Grove Farm
Cheadle Catholic Jun. & Inf. Sch.
Cheadle Hulme
ALBERT RD.
STATION RD.
HULME HALL ROAD
B5095
ETCHELLS ROAD
Ryecroft Park Sports Club
SK8
Bradshaw Hall Prim. Sch.
Greenbank School
Grammar School
Etchells Prim. Sch.
Rec. Grd.
Cheadle Hulme School
Playing Fields
Smithy Green
RAVENOAK RD.
CHURCH RD.
Cheadle Hulme High Sch.
Target Life (Cheadle Hulme)
Football Grd.
Oakgrove Sch.
Outwood Prim. Sch.
B5358
QUEENSWAY
Griffin Lodge
The South Gate Cen.
Stanley Green
Royal School for the Deaf and Communication Disorders
Gillbent
St. James Catholic High School
Thorn Grove Prim. Sch.
Rec. Ground
STANLEY ROAD
B5094
A555
MANCHESTER AIRPORT EASTERN LINK RD.
Stanley Hall Farm
STANLEY GREEN INDUSTRIAL ESTATE
STANLEY GREEN RETAIL PARK
Gill Bent Farm
Bolshaw Farm
Yew Tree Farm
Bowling Green
Hotel
Lower Bent Farm
Sports Ground
South Park
Manchester Rugby Club (Grove Park)
GROVE LANE
ACRE LA.
123
Playing Field
Depot
The Firs
1 2 3 4 5 6 7 8 9
G H J K L M N

118
A
B
C
D
E
F
G
1
2
3
4
5
6
7
8
9
108
117
124
EDGELEY RD.
Alexandra Park
Stockport County FC & Sharks RUFC (Edgeley Park)
Shaw Heath
Stockport Crematorium
Stockport Cemetery
NANGREAVE
B6171
ROAD
Aquinas Coll.
Mile End
Stockport Great Moor
Sports Grd.
Heaviley
PETERSBURG
Bridge Hall Prim. Sch.
Adswood
Hospice
ADSWOOD INDUSTRIAL ESTATE
Sports Ground
Cale Green
Hillcrest Gram. Sch.
War Meml. Cricket Grd.
Heathfield Ho.
BRAMHALL
BUXTON
Davenport
Stockport School
Stockport Grammar Sch.
Davenport Park
A6
30
EUROPA BUSINESS PARK
ORION BUSINESS PARK
SPECTRUM BUS. PK.
Cheadle
SK3
SK8
Fish Ponds
Adswood Brick & Tile Works
Depot
Playing Fields
A5102
Woodsmoor
Woods Moor
Gt. Moor Park
STEPPING HILL HOSPITAL
Sports Ground
Cricket Grd.
Works
MIRRLEES DRIVE
STATION
Lady Brook
Play. Field
Nevill Road Jun. & Inf. Schs.
Playing Field
Ramillies Hall School
Lane End Prim. Sch.
Bramhall Pk. Lawn Tennis Club
Bramhall Park
Bramall Hall
Bramhall Green
Bramhall Bri.
Lodge
Ten. Cts.
Bowl. Grn.
BRIDGE
A5143
LANE
JACKSONS
Womanscroft Bridge
Pool & Fit. Cen.
BRAMHALL MOOR INDUSTRIAL ESTATE
Davenport Rugby Club & Ground
Buddhist Cen.
The White House
Wall Bank Farm
Dingle Farm
SK7
Norbury House Farm
Hazel Grove High School
Football Grd.
Club House
Bramhall Park
BRAMALL PARK GOLF COURSE
Carr Wood Park
Bramhall High School
Target Life (Bramhall)
Great Reddish Wood
Further Dairyground
Ladybrook Nursery
Bramhall Lane Lawn Tennis Club
Prim. Sch.
Pownall Green
Dairyground
STOCKPORT
MACCLESFIELD
Mill Hill Farm
Kitt's Moss
Hursthead Jun. & Inf. Schools
A5149
WEST
ACK
LANE
EAST
Bramhall
BRAMHALL
BRAMHALL GOLF COURSE
Kennels
Birch Hall
Hill Green Farm
Club House
B5094
ACRE LANE
MOSS
Moss Hey Prim. Sch.
Village Hall
SOUTH
LANE
RAVENOAK RD.
385
390
89
91
86
88
87

109
125
120
H
J
K
L
M
N
G
1
2
3
4
5
6
7
8
9
SK2
SK6
SK12
Stockport
MARPLE ROAD
A626
STOCKPORT ROAD
DOOLEY LA.
A627
OFFERTON ROAD
TORKINGTON ROAD
LONDON ROAD
A6
BUXTON ROAD
MACCLESFIELD ROAD
A523
LONDON ROAD NORTH
DEAN LANE
A5143
MILL LANE
THREAPHURST LANE
MIDDLEWOOD ROAD
Offerton
Offerton Green
Foggbrook
Halliday Farm
Foggbrook Bri.
The Meadows Hosp.
Valley Cottage
Sewage Works
The Lodge
Marple Hall School
Lower Danbank Farm
Bongs
Nabwood
Nab Wood
Nab Wood Farm
Warren Lodge
Warren Wood
Marple Brook
Higher Danbank Farm
Danbank Bri.
High Trees
Yew Tree Farm
Marple Wood
Torkington Brook
Wood Farm
Target Life (Dialstone)
Library
The Dialstone Centre
Playing Field
Lisburne Sch.
Dial Park Primary Sch.
Offerton Hall Nursy. Sch.
Offerton Hall Rec. Grd.
Warren Wood Prim. Sch.
Brooklands Farm
Poise Brook
Canberra
Club House
Brook Vale Farm
Brook House
The Hollow
STOCKPORT GOLF COURSE
Torkington Wood
Stepping Hill
Superstore
Reservoir
Moat
Broadoak
Hazel Knoll Farm
Poise Bridge
HAZEL GROVE
Prim. Sch.
Rec. Ground
Bramhall Moor
Civic Hall
Library
Manor Cottages
White House
The Willows
Holly Farm
Springfield Farm
Torkington Manor
Brookside Farm
Ochreley Brook
Greenclough Farm
Holly Cottages
Higher Farm
Torkington Prim. Sch.
Torkington
Hazel Grove
Cricket Grd.
Offices.
The Secret Garden
Torkington Park
Playing Field
School Street Industrial Estate
Clough House Farm
The Ash
HAZEL GROVE GOLF COURSE
Club House
Golf Course Cotts.
Dean Fold
Cricket Ground
Playing Field
Prim. Sch.
Marcliffe Ind. Est.
Norbury Hall Prim. Sch.
Threaphurst Farm
Oakfield Farm
Disley Tunnel
Ox Hey
Oxhey Farm
Oak Tree Farm
Reservoir (covered)
Shores Farm
Station Farm
Denbigh Farm
Norbury Moor
Norbury Hall
Norbury Bri.
Brookside Miniature Railway & Museum
Garden Cen.
Norbury Brook
Sewage Works
Millbank
Millhill Bri.
Norbury Hollow
Parkgate Farm
Shady Nook
Long Plantation
Towers Farm
Serpentine Wood
Barlowfold
Barlowfold Farm
Poynton Lake
Poynton Brook
Park House Farm
Park Pit Plantation
Park Pit Cottages
Correction Farm
New House Farm
Norbury Hollow Caravan Site
Poynton Park
Phillip's Bridge
Prince's
Middlewood

120
A
B
C
D
E
F
G
1
2
3
4
5
6
7
8
9
110
119
STOCKPORT ROAD
A626
ROAD STATION
STOCKPORT RD.
BRABYNS RD.
Rose Hill Marple
MARPLE
The Dale Prim. Sch.
Rose Hill Prim. Sch.
Ckt. Grd.
Brabyn's Sch.
Lib.
Memorial Park
Coun. Offs.
Cin.
Target Life
Thtre.
Rec. Grd.
Peacefield Prim. Sch.
Sixth Form College
All Saints C of E Prim. Sch.
Brick Bridge
STRINES ROAD
Tanpit Cottage
Goyt House
Cataract Bridge
Mills
Knowle House
Mellor Prim. Sch.
Sports Ground
Mellor Sports Cl
Heathy Bank
Townscliffe Farm
CLEMENT
TOWNSCLIFFE
LONGHURST LANE
Bottom's Bri.
Bottom's Hall
Res.
Linnet Clough
River Goyt
ROMAN LAKES LEISURE PARK
LAKES ROAD
OLD ROAD
Mill Lade
Weir
MELLOR & TOWN GOLF COURSE
Windybottom Wood
Barlow Wood
Floodgates Cottage
Marple Packhorse Bri.
Strawberry Hill
Windybottom Farm
The Station
Lum Ho.
Pav.
Wood Fm
Playing Field
War Memorial
MARPLE GOLF COURSE
Eccles Bridge
SK6
B6101
Peak Forest Canal
Hazelbank
Hawk Green
Rope Race
Club House
Hill Top Farm
Macclesfield Canal
Hazel Knoll Farm
SK7
Marple Wood
Barnsfold
Rec. Grd.
Lower Ridge Farm
Brae Side
TORKINGTON ROAD
TORKINGTON LANE
Oak Cott.
Higher Farm
Windlehurst School
Victoria Cottage
Lower-ridge
The Grange
Sewage Works
Greenclough Farm
Broadhurst's Bridge
Stockport
Doodfield Farm
Doodfield Works
Moult Wood
Higherfold Farm
Beeston Park Farm
Ridge End Fold Farm
Turf Lea
Whitecroft House
Strines
Carrington Barn
Hunters Park Farm
Windlehurst Hall
Lea Cote Farm
Turf Lea Farm
Slack Hall Farm
Swingbridge
Brook Farm
Windlehurst
Oakfield Farm
Peeres Cotts
Whitecroft Farm
Disley Tunnel
Lomber Hey House
Lomber Hey Farm
Aqueduct
Greenhills
Littlewoodend
Oak Tree Farm
Grange Farm
Reservoir (covered)
Stanleyhall Wood
Wooden
Woodend House
HIGH LANE
Wybersley Water Treatment Works
Dove House Farm
Station Farm
A6
BUXTON ROAD
Playing Fields
High La. Prim. Sch.
Haycroft
Res. (cov.)
Wybersley Hall
STOCKPORT
MACCLESFIELD
DISLEY GOLF COURSE
SK12
Widowhurst
Stanley Hall
Club House
Lib.
War Meml.
30
Marsden House
Cricket Ground
Jacksonsedge Quarry (disused)
JACKSONS EDGE
Hagg Bank Farm
Middlewood House
Middle Wood
Resr. (cov.)
Disleybank Wood
Ten. Cts.
Sports Field
DISLEY
Middlewood
Woodside Tennis Club
Brookside Prim. Sch.
Homestead Farm
WEST MARKET ST.
Bollinhurst Brook
Coppiceside Farm
The Homestead
Jacksons' Brickworks Local Nature Reserve
Brookside Farm
High Jinx
Lyme Gate Cott.
Main Lodge
Disley
Pool House Farm
395
96
97

MELLOR
Mellor Parish Centre
Old Vicarage
Knowle Farm
Knowle Wood
Tarden
Moorend
Hilltop Lane
Cheetham Hill
Melkin Farm
How Green Farm
Shiloh Hall Farm
Hollins Farm
Thornsett Fields Farm
Larkhill Cottage
Longshaw Clough
Damsteads Farm
Reservoir (cov.)
Briergrove Farm
Carr Noor Farm
Blake Hall
Lydiate Farm
Holly Farm
Birchenough
Shirdfields
Whitehouse Farm
Cannon Hill
Cold Wall
Whetmorhurst
Cobden Farm
Cobdenedge Farm
Cobden Edge
MELLOR MOOR
STOCKPORT
HIGH PEAK
Broadhurst Edge Wood Nature Reserve
Broadhurstedge Plantation
Golden Spring
Playing Fields
Snape Hey
Paradise
Napkin Piece Farm
Windy Ridge
Bull Hill Farm
Cross Gates
Higher Banks
Three Chimneys
Castle Edge Farm
Woodhouse Home
Broadhurst House
Highwood Farm
Reservoir
Greenclough Cottage
Capstone
Higher Capstone
Stony Piece Farm
Redishaw Farm
SK22
Sunnyside Farm
Tanpits Farm
Bate Mill
Thornsett
Lower Cliffe
The Cottage
Primrose Bank
Higher Cliffe Poultry Farm
Shaw Farm
NEW MILLS GOLF COURSE
Whitle
Watford House
Watford Lodge Nature Reserve
Strines
Brook Bottom
Clough Bank Farm
Shaw Marsh
Club House
Beardhough Farm
Eaves Knoll
NEW MILLS
High Peak
Knightwake Farm
Mill Ponds
Woodend
Woodend Fold
Hague Fold Farm
Hague Bar
Hague Bar Prim. Sch.
Lower Haguefold
Roach-hey Wood
Hidebank
St. George's C of E Prim. Sch.
Football Ground
New Mills Leis. Cen.
New Mills Sch. & Sixth Form Cen.
Hague Bridge
Brow Farm
High Lee
High Lea Hall
High Lea Pk.
Higgin's Clough
Disley Paper Mill
The Torrs Riverside Park
New Mills Central
Heritage Cen.
Mousley Bottom
Upper Waterside
Grove Mill
Knathole Wood
Cloughside Farm
Cheshire Mills
Newtown
Sports Ground
Laneside Farm
Low Leighton
Marsh Lane Trad. Est.
Works
New Mills Newtown
Goytside Farm
Beard Hall Farm
Danebank
Greenshall Farm
Mill Pond
Recreation Ground
Ellibancke Farm
The Old Farmhouse
Bankend Farm
SK23
BUXTON ROAD
A6
A6015
B6101
HAGUE BAR ROAD
LOW LEIGHTON RD.
CHURCH ROAD
HAYFIELD RD.

MANCHESTER INTERNATIONAL AIRPORT
Manchester
M90
MANCHESTER MACCLESFIELD
116
126
Moss Lane Farm
Moss Farm
The Old Cottage
Oversley Lodge Farm
Lode Hill Farm
Styal House
Lode Hill
Norcliffe Farm
Oak Farm
Styal Prim. Sch.
Giant's Castle
Norcliffe Hall
STYAL COUNTRY PARK
Football Grd.
Cricket Grd.
STYAL
Styal
Highfield
Driving Range
Club House
STYAL GOLF COURSE
Woodend
Kent House
Cross Fm.
Styal Green
Sports Ground
Linney's Bridge
Viaduct
Oakwood Farm
Norcliffe Farm
Quarry Bank Mill
Weirs
Res.
Bank House Farm
Holly Bank Farm
Hotel
Oversleyford Bridge
A538
ALTRINCHAM ROAD
Morley
Chelsea Cottage
Shadygrove House
Oak Farm
Nansmoss Farm
The Coach House
Wood Farm
Moss Grove Farm
Morley Green
Brybour Lodge
Stamford Lodge
Transmitting Station
HMP STYAL
Sewage Works
Deadman's Clough
Lacey Green Prim. Sch.
Lacey Green
Wilmslow
B5166
Willow Ground Wood
Burned Hey Wood
Twinnies Bri.
Rugby Grd.
Jim Evison Playing Field
Nurseries
Heald House Farm
Pownall Hall Sch.
Pownall Hall Farm
Carr Wood
River Bollin
SK9
THE CARRS
Mossways Park
LINDOW MOSS
Platt Cottage
Pownall Park
Ten. Cts.
Miniature Golf Course
Play. Flds.
WILMSLOW
Burleyhurst Farm
Cedar Lodge Farm
Bowers Folly
Sandy Lea Poultry Farm
Refuse Tip (Public)
Gorsey Bank Prim. Sch.
Carnival Field
Lindow Common Local Nature Reserve
Black Lake
Hawthorn Hall
Rossmere
Lindow Poultry Farm
Saltersley Hall Farm
Lindow Moss
WATER LA.
Superstore
Hollingee
MOBBERLEY GOLF COURSE
Knutsford
Maple Farm
Lime Cottage Farm
Paddock Chase
Garden Centre
Yew Tree Farm
Coppock House Farm
WA16
LINDOW COURT FARM CARAVAN PARK
Sugar Brook
Lindow Manor Farm
Barlow House Farm
Green Hedges
Hetlee Farm
Rec. Grd.
Prim. Sch.
Ashdene Prim. Sch.
B5086
KNUTSFORD ROAD
Fulshaw Hall
Fulshaw Park
Harefield Farm
Royal London House
Harefield Ho.
The Yews
A B C D E F G
1 2 3 4 5 6 7 8 9

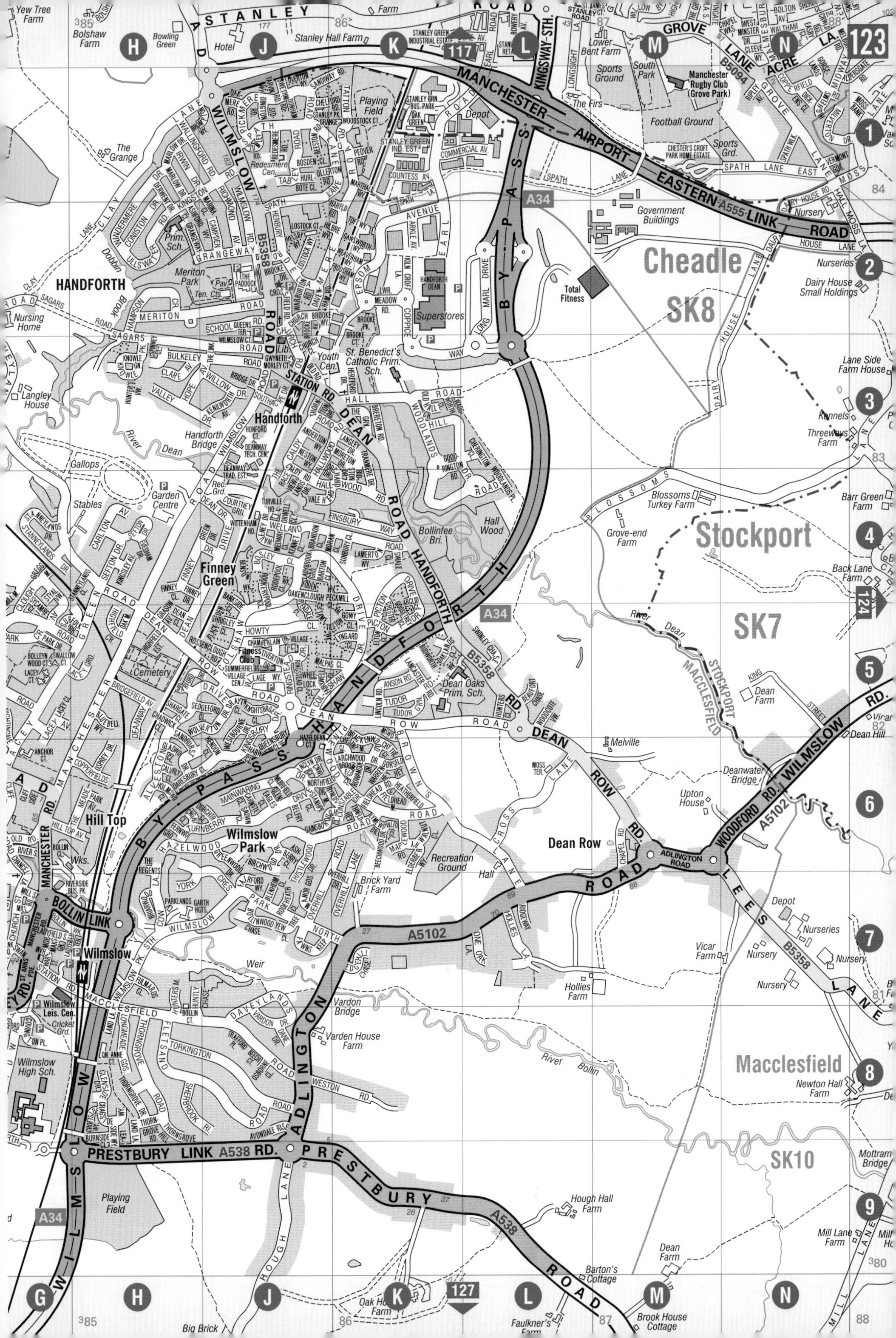
HANDFORTH
Handforth
Finney Green
Wilmslow Park
Hill Top
Wilmslow
Dean Row
Cheadle
SK8
Stockport
SK7
Macclesfield
SK10
MANCHESTER AIRPORT EASTERN LINK ROAD
A555
HANDFORTH BY-PASS
A34
WILMSLOW ROAD
B5358
STATION RD.
DEAN ROAD
DEAN ROW ROAD
ADLINGTON ROAD
A5102
WOODFORD RD.
WILMSLOW RD.
LEES LANE
PRESTBURY LINK A538 RD.
PRESTBURY ROAD
A538
ADLINGTON ROAD
BOLLIN LINK
WILMSLOW BY-PASS
SPATH LANE EAST
MOSS LANE
HALL MOSS LA.
DAIRY HOUSE LANE
BLOSSOMS LANE
KING STREET
CROSS LANE
HOUGH LANE
MILL LANE
GROVE LANE
B5094
Government Buildings
Total Fitness
Handforth Dean Superstores
St. Benedict's Catholic Prim. Sch.
Dean Oaks Prim. Sch.
Fitness Club
Cemetery
Garden Centre
Recreation Ground
Wilmslow Leis. Cen.
Wilmslow High Sch.
Playing Field
Manchester Rugby Club (Grove Park)
Football Ground
Sports Ground
South Park
Lower Bent Farm
The Firs
Stanley Hall Farm
Stanley Green Industrial Estate
Bolshaw Farm
Yew Tree Farm
Bowling Green
Hotel
The Grange
Nursing Home
Langley House
Handforth Bridge
River Dean
Gallops
Stables
Hall Wood
Bollinfee Bri.
Blossoms Turkey Farm
Grove-end Farm
Lane Side Farm House
Kennels
Threeways Farm
Barr Green Farm
Back Lane Farm
Dairy House Small Holdings
Nurseries
Dean Farm
Dean Hill
Melville
Deanwater Bridge
Upton House
Vicar Farm
Nursery
Depot
Hollies Farm
Brick Yard Farm
Vardon Bridge
Varden House Farm
River Bollin
Weir
Newton Hall Farm
Mottram Bridge
Hough Hall Farm
Mill Lane Farm
Dean Farm
Barton's Cottage
Brook House Cottage
Faulkner's Farm
Oak House Farm
Big Brick
Chester's Croft Park Home Estate
H J K L M N G
1 2 3 4 5 6 7 8 9
117
124
127
385 86 87 88
84 83 82 81 80

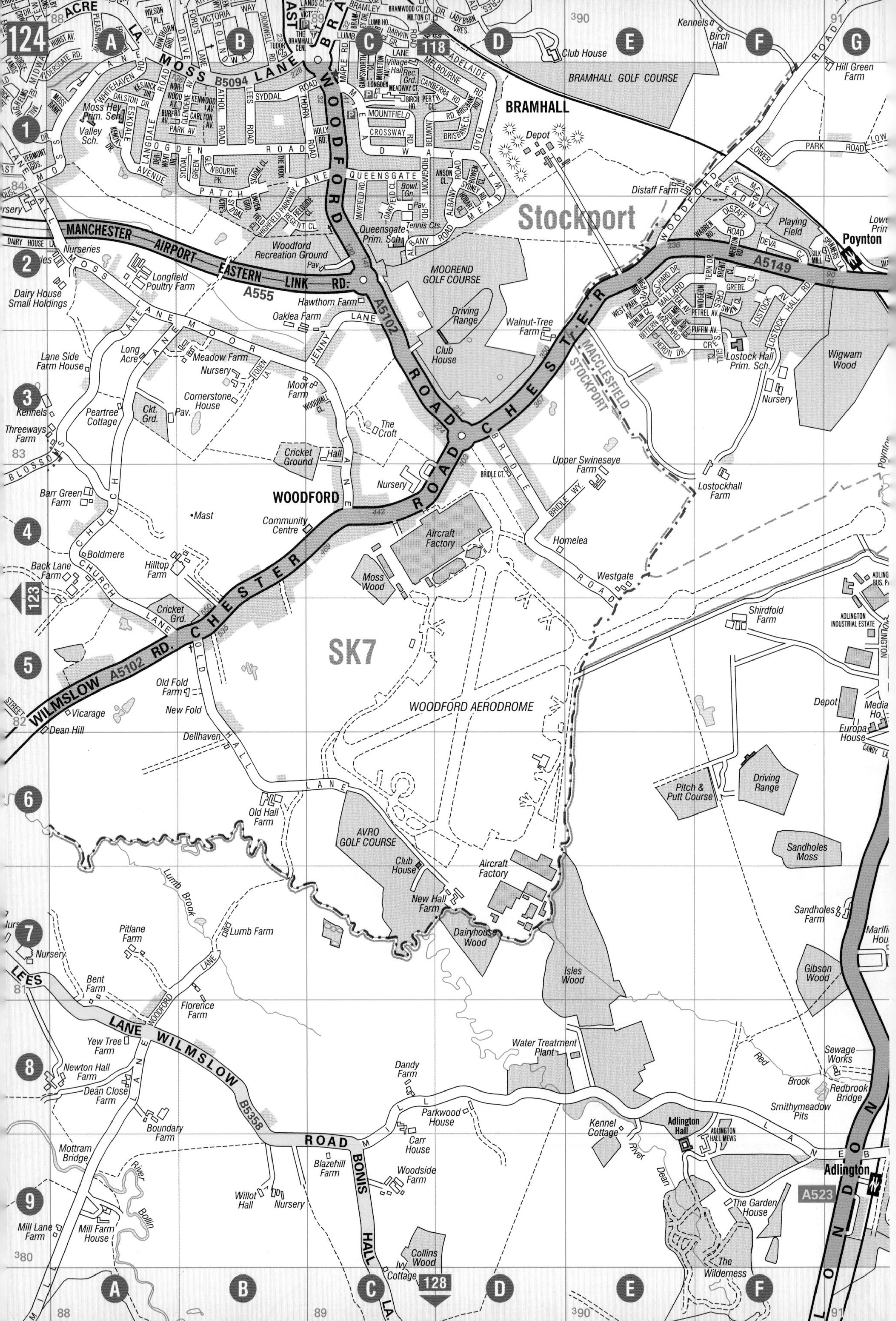

Moss Lane
B5094
Bramhall
Bramhall Golf Course
Club House
Stockport
Woodford Road
Manchester Airport Eastern Link Rd.
A555
A5102
A5149
Woodford Recreation Ground
Queensgate Prim. Sch.
Moorend Golf Course
Driving Range
Club House
Walnut-Tree Farm
Distaff Farm
Playing Field
Poynton
Lostock Hall Prim. Sch.
Wigwam Wood
Macclesfield
Stockport
Longfield Poultry Farm
Dairy House Small Holdings
Hawthorn Farm
Oaklea Farm
Meadow Farm
Cornerstone House
Moor Farm
Cricket Ground
The Croft
Upper Swineseye Farm
Lostockhall Farm
Woodford
Community Centre
Aircraft Factory
Moss Wood
Homelea
Westgate
Chester Road
Wilmslow Rd.
SK7
Woodford Aerodrome
Old Fold Farm
New Fold
Vicarage
Dean Hill
Dellhaven
Old Hall Farm
Avro Golf Course
Club House
Aircraft Factory
New Hall Farm
Dairyhouse Wood
Lumb Farm
Pitlane Farm
Isles Wood
Pitch & Putt Course
Driving Range
Sandholes Moss
Sandholes Farm
Gibson Wood
Shirdfold Farm
Adlington Industrial Estate
Depot
Europa House
Bent Farm
Florence Farm
Yew Tree Farm
Newton Hall Farm
Dean Close Farm
Wilmslow Lane
B5358
Road
Boundary Farm
Mottram Bridge
River Bollin
Mill Lane Farm
Mill Farm House
Willot Hall
Nursery
Blazehill Farm
Bonis Hall La.
Dandy Farm
Parkwood House
Carr House
Woodside Farm
Collins Wood
Ivy Cottage
Water Treatment Plant
Kennel Cottage
River Dean
Adlington Hall
Adlington Hall Mews
Mill Lane
Red Brook
Redbrook Bridge
Smithymeadow Pits
Sewage Works
The Garden House
The Wilderness
Adlington
A523
London Road
Kennels
Birch Hall
Hill Green Farm
Park Road
118
123
128

POYNTON
Poynton Park
Poynton Lake
Poynton Brook
Park House Farm
Phillip's Bridge
Middlewood
Prince's Wood
DAVENPORT GOLF COURSE
Club House
Rabbit Burrow Farm
Towers Yard Barns
Beechfield
SK12
Lady's Wood
Poynton Sports Club
Civic Hall
Petre Bank
Woodlands
Works
Newtown
Potters Clough
The Anson Engine Museum
The Gables Farm
Marine Ville Mooring
Nelson Pit Visitor Cen.
Red Legg Farm
Vernon Primary Sch.
Hockley
Worth Prim. Sch.
Midway
St. Paul's Catholic Prim. Sch.
Poynton Leisure Centre
Poynton High Sch. & Performing Arts Coll.
Playing Field
Lynden
Alma Cottages
Coppice Farm
HIGHER POYNTON
Springbank Farm
Elm Wood
Kennels
High Lodge
Poynton Coppice
Garden Cen.
Res. (cov.)
ELM BEDS CARAVAN PARK
Sprink Farm
Wardsend Bridge
Works
POYNTON INDUSTRIAL ESTATE
Wardsend Old Farm
Wardsend
Yewtree Farm
Wood Lane End
Wood Lane End Farm
Brook Bank Farm
Hagg Farm
Macclesfield Canal
Hope Green Farm
Hope Green
A523
Hope Lane Cottage
The Oaks
Clayton Greaves Farm
Holly Bank Farm
Woodhouse Farm
Rams Clough
Welfield
Well Farm
Brookside Farm
Adlington Manor
Oak Farm
Skellorngreen Farm
Noggin Farm
Mitchell Fold
Nelson Farm
Streetlane Farm
Ash Tree Farm
Woodlands
Lyme View Marina
Skellorn Green
Fourlane Ends
Adlington Basin
Gorsewood Farm
Trugs i' th' Hole Farm
Redacre Hall Farm
Simpson Lane Cott.
Macclesfield
Booth Green Farm
Pedleyhill Farm
Eastwood End
Schoolfold
Pedley House
Woodend Farm
Lockgate Farm
SK10
Boothgreen Farm
Booth Green
Eastwood End House
EASTWOOD END CARAVAN PARK
Marlfields Hall
Walnut Tree Cottage
Jepson Clough
East Woodend Farm
Roundy House
Jepsonclough Farm
Highbarn Farm
Newfold Farm
Harrop Brow
The Hole
Roundylane Farm
Springbank Farm
Blakehey Wood
Hill View
Redbrook Farm
Pine Tree Cottage
Brookledge
Gibhill Wood
ADLINGTON
Dingle Hey
Adlington Prim. Sch.
Hibbert Brow Wood
Hibbertbrow Farm
Ryles Wood
Brookledge Farm
Maubern Hall
Norman's Hall Farm
The Oakridge
Gibhill Farm
Wych Wood
Wych Cottage
Harropgreen Farm
Barton's Clough
Styperson Quarries (disused)
SHRIGLEY HALL GOLF COURSE
Club House
Park Pit Plantation
Park Pit Cottages
Correction Farm
Bank Farm Riding Sch.
119
129

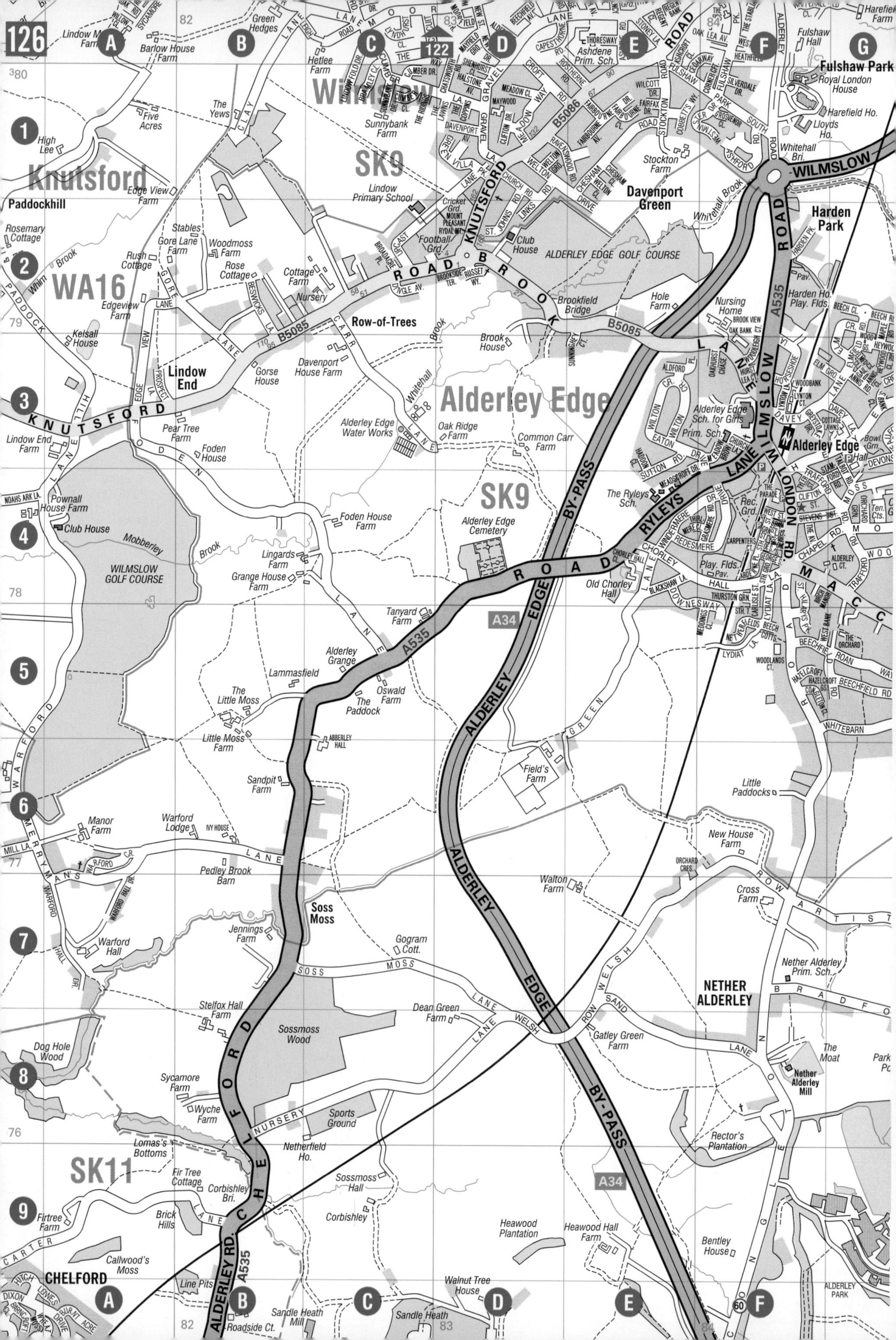
122
Wilmslow
SK9
Knutsford
Paddockhill
WA16
Lindow End
Row-of-Trees
Alderley Edge
Davenport Green
Harden Park
Fulshaw Park
Royal London House
Harefield Ho.
Lloyds Ho.
Whitehall Bri.
Lindow Primary School
Alderley Edge Golf Course
Club House
Brookfield Bridge
Hole Farm
Nursing Home
Alderley Edge Sch. for Girls
Alderley Edge Prim. Sch.
The Ryleys Sch.
Old Chorley Hall
Alderley Edge Cemetery
Alderley Edge Water Works
Oak Ridge Farm
Common Carr Farm
Foden House Farm
Lingards Farm
Grange House Farm
Tanyard Farm
Alderley Grange
Lammasfield
Oswald Farm
The Paddock
The Little Moss
Little Moss Farm
Sandpit Farm
Wilmslow Golf Course
Mobberley Brook
Lindow End Farm
Pownall House Farm
Manor Farm
Warford Lodge
Pedley Brook Barn
Soss Moss
Jennings Farm
Gogram Cott.
Warford Hall
Stelfox Hall Farm
Sossmoss Wood
Dean Green Farm
Gatley Green Farm
Dog Hole Wood
Sycamore Farm
Wyche Farm
Sports Ground
Netherfield Ho.
Lomas's Bottoms
SK11
Fir Tree Cottage
Corbishley Bri.
Sossmoss Hall
Corbishley
Brick Hills
Firtree Farm
Callwood's Moss
CHELFORD
Line Pits
Roadside Ct.
Sandle Heath Mill
Sandle Heath
Walnut Tree House
Heawood Plantation
Heawood Hall Farm
Bentley House
ALDERLEY PARK
Rector's Plantation
Nether Alderley Mill
The Moat
NETHER ALDERLEY
Nether Alderley Prim. Sch.
Cross Farm
New House Farm
Walton Farm
Little Paddocks
Field's Farm
A34
A535
B5085
B5086
KNUTSFORD ROAD
ALDERLEY EDGE BY-PASS
RYLEYS LANE
WILMSLOW ROAD
LONDON RD
CHELFORD RD.
ALDERLEY RD.
SOSS MOSS LANE
WELSH ROW
CONGLETON RD
A B C D E F G
1 2 3 4 5 6 7 8 9
80 82 83 84 79 78 77 76

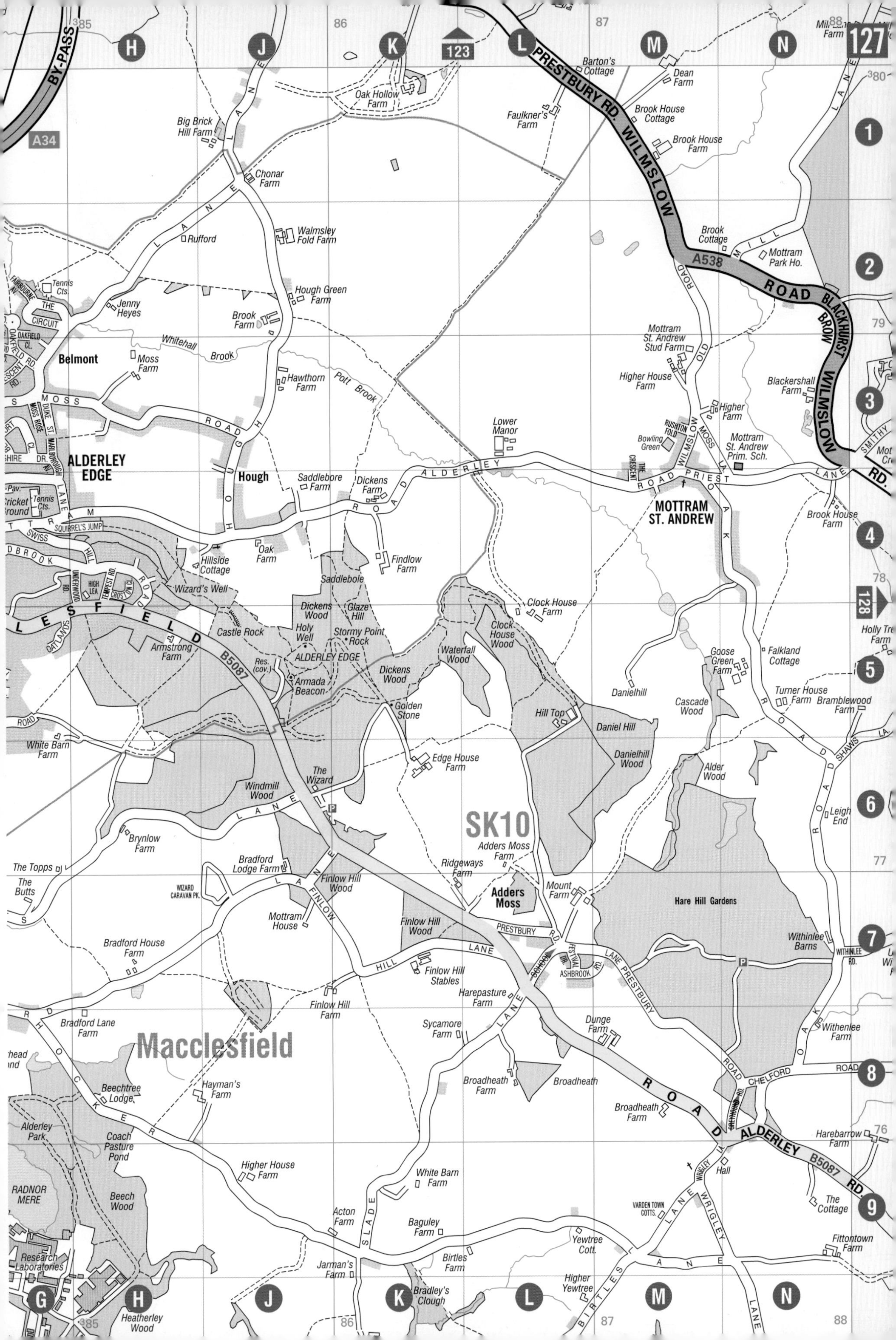

Macclesfield
SK10
ALDERLEY EDGE
Belmont
Hough
MOTTRAM ST. ANDREW
PRESTBURY RD.
WILMSLOW ROAD
A538
BLACKHURST BROW
WILMSLOW RD.
BY-PASS
A34
B5087
ALDERLEY ROAD
LESFIELD
Oak Hollow Farm
Big Brick Hill Farm
Chonar Farm
Walmsley Fold Farm
Rufford
Jenny Heyes
Hough Green Farm
Brook Farm
Whitehall Brook
Moss Farm
Hawthorn Farm
Pott Brook
Barton's Cottage
Dean Farm
Faulkner's Farm
Brook House Cottage
Brook House Farm
Brook Cottage
Mottram Park Ho.
Mottram St. Andrew Stud Farm
Higher House Farm
Blackershall Farm
Higher Farm
Lower Manor
Bowling Green
Mottram St. Andrew Prim. Sch.
Saddlebore Farm
Dickens Farm
Oak Farm
Findlow Farm
Hillside Cottage
Wizard's Well
Saddlebole
Dickens Wood
Glaze Hill
Castle Rock
Holy Well
Stormy Point Rock
Armstrong Farm
Armada Beacon
Golden Stone
Waterfall Wood
Clock House Wood
Clock House Farm
Daniel Hill
Danielhill
Danielhill Wood
Hill Top
Goose Green Farm
Cascade Wood
Falkland Cottage
Turner House Farm
Bramblewood Farm
Holly Tree Farm
White Barn Farm
Edge House Farm
The Wizard
Windmill Wood
Alder Wood
Leigh End
Brynlow Farm
The Topps
The Butts
Bradford Lodge Farm
Wizard Caravan Pk.
Finlow Hill Wood
Mottram House
Ridgeways Farm
Adders Moss Farm
Adders Moss
Mount Farm
Hare Hill Gardens
Withinlee Barns
Bradford House Farm
Finlow Hill Stables
Finlow Hill Farm
Harepasture Farm
Dunge Farm
Withenlee Farm
Bradford Lane Farm
Sycamore Farm
Broadheath Farm
Broadheath
Beechtree Lodge
Hayman's Farm
Alderley Park
Coach Pasture Pond
Radnor Mere
Beech Wood
Higher House Farm
White Barn Farm
Harebarrow Farm
Hall
The Cottage
Varden Town Cotts.
Acton Farm
Baguley Farm
Yewtree Cott.
Fittontown Farm
Research Laboratories
Jarman's Farm
Birtles Farm
Higher Yewtree
Bradley's Clough
Heatherley Wood
Moss Road
Hough Lane
Mottram Road
Swiss Hill
Squirrel's Jump
Priest Lane
Old Road
Oak Road
Moss La.
Shaws La.
Prestbury Rd.
Prestbury Lane
Chelford Road
Withinlee Rd.
Finlow Hill Lane
Hocker Lane
Slade Lane
Wrigley Lane
Birtles Lane
Harden Lane
Underwood Rd.
High Lea
Tempest Rd.
Croston Cl.
Oatlands
Fairbourne Av.
The Circuit
Oakfield Cl.
Oakfield Rd.
Crescent Rd.
Duke St.
Moss Rose
Marlborough Av.
Cricket Ground
Tennis Cts.
Rushton Fold
The Crescent
School La.
Festival Dr.
Ashbrook Rd.
H J K L M N G
1 2 3 4 5 6 7 8 9
85 86 87 88
76 77 78 79 80
123
128

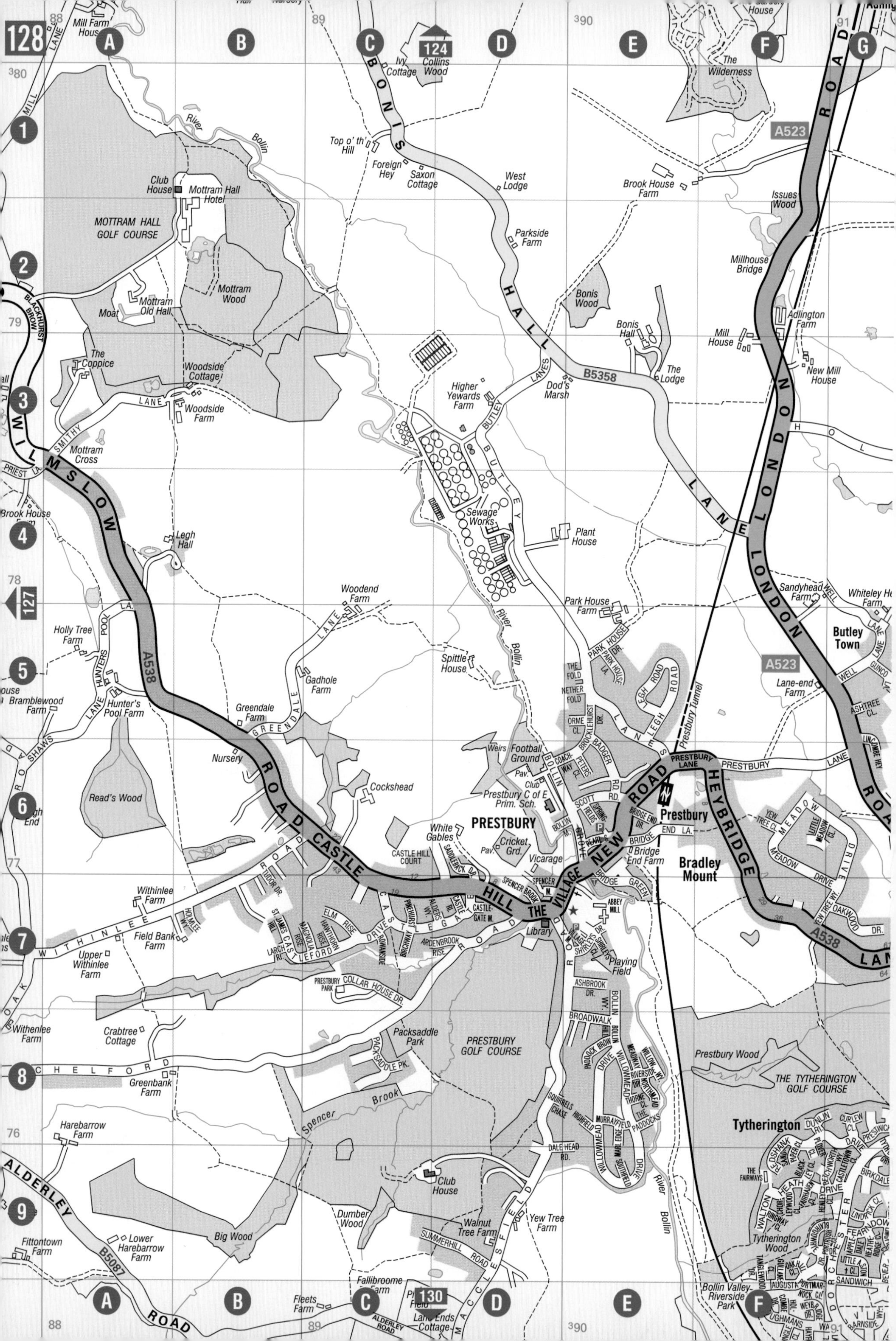
Mill Farm House
Ivy Cottage
Collins Wood
The Wilderness
Top o' th' Hill
Foreign Hey
Saxon Cottage
West Lodge
Brook House Farm
Issues Wood
Club House
Mottram Hall Hotel
MOTTRAM HALL GOLF COURSE
Parkside Farm
Millhouse Bridge
Mottram Old Hall
Moat
Mottram Wood
Bonis Wood
Bonis Hall
Adlington Farm
Mill House
The Lodge
New Mill House
The Coppice
Woodside Cottage
Woodside Farm
Higher Yewards Farm
Dod's Marsh
Mottram Cross
Sewage Works
Plant House
Legh Hall
Woodend Farm
Park House Farm
Sandyhead Farm
Holly Tree Farm
Butley Town
Spittle House
Gadhole Farm
Lane-end Farm
Bramblewood Farm
Hunter's Pool Farm
Greendale Farm
Nursery
Football Ground
Cockshead
Read's Wood
Prestbury C of E Prim. Sch.
PRESTBURY
White Gables
Cricket Grd.
Prestbury
Bradley Mount
Vicarage
Bridge End Farm
Withinlee Farm
Field Bank Farm
Upper Withinlee Farm
Library
Playing Field
Withenlee Farm
Crabtree Cottage
Packsaddle Park
PRESTBURY GOLF COURSE
Prestbury Wood
THE TYTHERINGTON GOLF COURSE
Greenbank Farm
Harebarrow Farm
Tytherington
Club House
Dumber Wood
Yew Tree Farm
Walnut Tree Farm
Big Wood
Lower Harebarrow Farm
Fittontown Farm
Tytherington Wood
Fallibroome Farm
Fleets Farm
Lane Ends Cottage
Bollin Valley Riverside Park
River Bollin
Spencer Brook
A538
A523
B5358
B5087
WILMSLOW ROAD
CASTLE HILL
NEW ROAD
HEYBRIDGE
LONDON ROAD
BONIS HALL LANE
PRESTBURY LANE
CHELFORD ROAD
WITHINLEE ROAD
ALDERLEY ROAD
MACCLESFIELD ROAD
SUMMERHILL ROAD
124
127
130

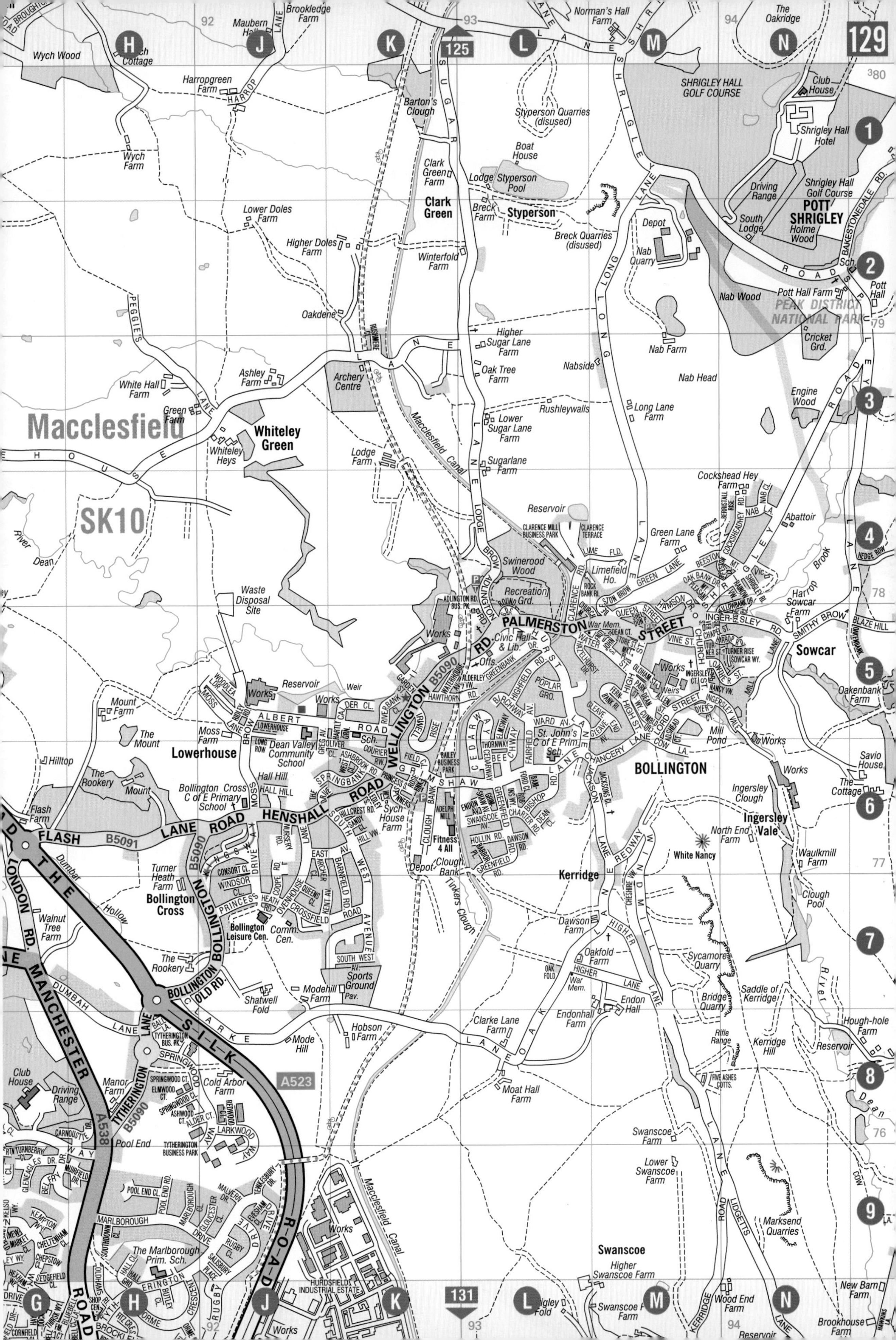

Macclesfield
SK10
Bollington
Pott Shrigley
Whiteley Green
Clark Green
Styperson
Lowerhouse
Bollington Cross
Kerridge
Sowcar
Ingersley Vale
Swanscoe
White Nancy
Shrigley Hall Golf Course
Peak District National Park
Macclesfield Canal
Palmerston Street
Wellington Rd.
Henshall Road
Flash Lane
Silk Road
A523
A538
B5090
B5091
125
131

A
B
C
D
E
F
G
1
2
3
4
5
6
7
8
9
88
89
390
375
74
73
72
71
128
Lower Harebarrow Farm
Big Wood
Walnut Tree Farm
Fallibroome Farm
Fleets Farm
Playing Field
Lane Ends Cottage
ALDERLEY ROAD
B5087
PRESTBURY ROAD
Whirley Grove
SANDY LANE
Playing Fields
Upton Wood
Upton Hall
Weir
Tytherington Wood
Bollin Valley Riverside Park
Macclesfield Riverside Park
Upton Priory Sch.
Backlane Farm
Cricket Grd.
Whirleymere
The Fallibroome Academy
Running Track
Macclesfield Leisure Centre
SK10
Prim. Sch.
Cemetery
Macclesfield Crematorium
WHIRLEY ROAD
Damson Cottage
Whirleybarn
Roewoods
Lower Roewood
BIRTLES ROAD
Whirley Primary School
Priors Hill
Hospice
Playing Field
Sch.
West Park
Mus.
Bowling Green
Moss Cottages
Longmoss
VICTORIA ROAD
PAVILION WAY
Cricket Grd.
MACCLESFIELD DISTRICT GENERAL HOSPITAL
Millbrook Unit
REGENCY SPIRE HOSP.
CUMBERLAND STREET
Henbury
Broken Cross
CHELFORD ROAD
A537
BROKEN CROSS
CHESTER ROAD
The Old School House
Ruewood House
Gorseyknoll
Hill Top Farm
Cock Wood
Lib.
Broken Cross Comm. Sch.
Macclesfield
Playing Fields
All Hallows Catholic Coll.
B5088
Primary Sch.
Weston
Weston Rec. Grd.
Broomfield Farm
Brickbank Farm
Shayes Farm
Hopedale Farm
New Farm
B5392
PEXHILL ROAD
OXFORD ROAD
PARK LANE
A536
Council Offs.
Macclesfield College
Macclesfield High Sch.
Park La. Sch.
ECAT
Lifestyle Fitness Centre
SK11
Ivy Bank Pri. Sch.
West Wynds
Tansy Moss Farm
Little Bailey Riddings Farm
Big Bailey Riddings Farm
PENNINGTONS LANE
Overbank Farm
Highbirch Wood
Weston Park Nursing Home
Moss Lane
Depot
Ash Grove Prim. Sch.
Underbank Farm
Dalehouse Farm
Brownhills Farm
Playing Field
Playing Fields
Pav.
North Gate
Moss Ho. Farm
Greenacres
Limetree House
Gardens Cottage
Lagoon
GAWSWORTH ROAD
Deans Farm
CONGLETON ROAD
DARK LANE
Danes Moss Farm
Whitegate Farm
Lowes Farm
Beaumont Farm
Moss Cott.
LOWES LANE
Danes Moss Nature Reserve

129
Swanscoe
Higher Swanscoe Farm
Marksend Quarries
Brookhouse
Brookhouse Farm
New Barn Farm
Kerridge-end
Plungebrook
Calrofold
Higher Hurdsfield
CLIFF HILL
Hurdsfield
MACCLESFIELD
Macclesfield
Commonside
Higherfence
MACCLESFIELD COMMON
MACCLESFIELD GOLF COURSE
Tegg's Nose Country Park
Bradley Smithy
Gurnett
SUTTON LANE ENDS
LANGLEY
Lyme Green
Hollinhey Wood
Macclesfield Canal
River Bollin
SOUTH PARK
Macclesfield Town FC (Moss Rose Stadium)
Tytherington High School
Victoria Park
Knight's Pool
King George's Field
Birch Knoll
Ward's Knob
Teggsnose Wood
Teggsnose Reservoir
Bottoms Reservoir
Ridgehill
Rossendale Hall
Backridges Farm
Hockley
A523
A537
A538
B5470
B5181
SILK ROAD
BUXTON ROAD
RAINOW ROAD
NEW ROAD
LONDON ROAD
MANCHESTER ROAD

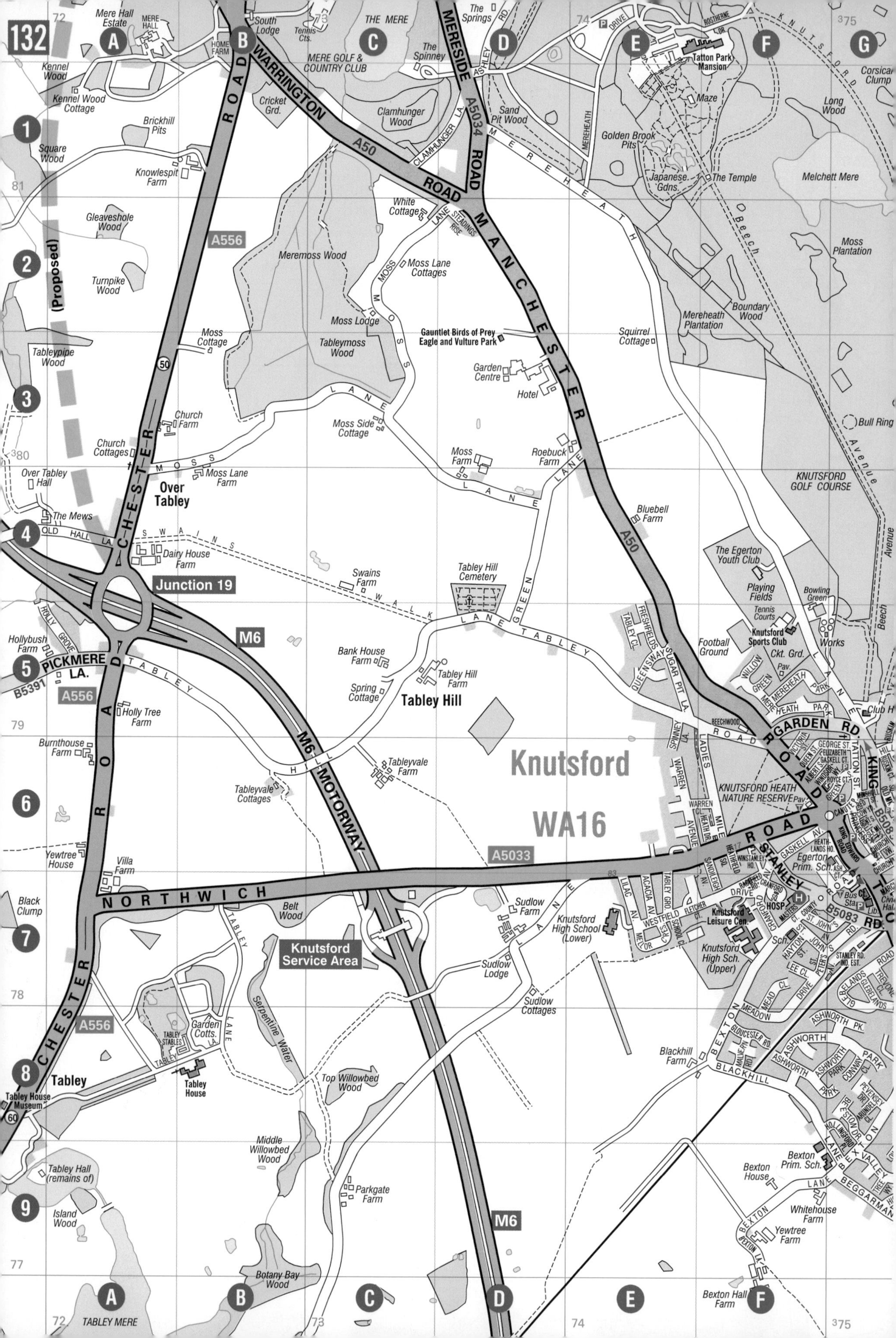

Mere Hall Estate
Mere Hall
Home Farm
South Lodge
Tennis Cts.
THE MERE
MERE GOLF & COUNTRY CLUB
The Springs
The Spinney
Tatton Park Mansion
Kennel Wood
Kennel Wood Cottage
Cricket Grd.
WARRINGTON ROAD
Clamhunger Wood
Sand Pit Wood
Maze
Long Wood
Corsican Clump
Brickhill Pits
Square Wood
Knowlespit Farm
A50
CLAMHUNGER LA.
MERESIDE
A5034
MEREHEATH
Golden Brook Pits
Japanese Gdns.
The Temple
Melchett Mere
White Cottage
Gleaveshole Wood
A556
Meremoss Wood
Moss Lane Cottages
STEADINGS RISE
MANCHESTER ROAD
Beech Avenue
Moss Plantation
(Proposed)
Turnpike Wood
Moss Lodge
Tableymoss Wood
Gauntlet Birds of Prey Eagle and Vulture Park
Squirrel Cottage
Mereheath Plantation
Boundary Wood
Tableypipe Wood
Moss Cottage
Garden Centre
Hotel
Church Farm
Moss Side Cottage
Bull Ring
Church Cottages
Moss Farm
Roebuck Farm
KNUTSFORD GOLF COURSE
Over Tabley Hall
Moss Lane Farm
Over Tabley
The Mews
OLD HALL LA.
CHESTER ROAD
SWAINS WALK
Dairy House Farm
Bluebell Farm
Junction 19
Swains Farm
Tabley Hill Cemetery
The Egerton Youth Club
Playing Fields
Bowling Green
Tennis Courts
Knutsford Sports Club
Hollybush Farm
HOLLY GROVE
M6
FRESHFIELDS
TABLEY CL.
Football Ground
Ckt. Grd.
Works
PICKMERE LA.
B5391
Bank House Farm
Tabley Hill Farm
QUEENSWAY
SUGAR PIT LA.
WILLOW GREEN
MEREHEATH PARK
Club H.
Holly Tree Farm
Spring Cottage
Tabley Hill
TABLEY HILL
TABLEY LANE
GREEN LANE
BEECHWOOD
GARDEN RD.
TATTON ST.
Burnthouse Farm
Tableyvale Farm
Knutsford
SPINNEY LA.
LADIES MILE
WARREN AV.
GEORGE ST.
QUEEN ST.
KING ST.
M6 MOTORWAY
Tableyvale Cottages
KNUTSFORD HEATH NATURE RESERVE
Pav.
WA16
B5085
Yewtree House
Villa Farm
A5033
NORTHWICH ROAD
STANLEY ROAD
GASKELL AV.
Egerton Prim. Sch.
Black Clump
Belt Wood
Sudlow Farm
Knutsford High School (Lower)
WESTFIELD DR.
LILAC AV.
ACACIA AV.
TABLEY GRO.
Knutsford Leisure Cen.
HOSP.
Bus Sta.
B5083 RD.
Knutsford Service Area
SUDLOW LANE
Knutsford High Sch. (Upper)
HAYTON ST.
ST. JOHN'S AV.
STANLEY RD. IND. EST.
Sudlow Lodge
LEE CL.
MEAD CL.
DRIVE
Serpentine Water
Garden Cotts.
Tabley Stables
Sudlow Cottages
MEADOW DR.
ASHWORTH PK.
ASHWORTH PARK
TABLEY LANE
Tabley House
Tabley
Tabley House Museum
Top Willowbed Wood
Blackhill Farm
BEXTON RD.
BLACKHILL LA.
GLOUCESTER RD.
MALVERN RD.
CONWAY CL.
PEVENSEY DR.
Middle Willowbed Wood
Bexton Prim. Sch.
VALLEY
Tabley Hall (remains of)
Parkgate Farm
Bexton House
BEGGARMAN LANE
Island Wood
Whitehouse Farm
Yewtree Farm
BEXTON LA.
Botany Bay Wood
Bexton Hall Farm
TABLEY MERE

TATTON PARK
Old Hall
Swan Clump
Mobberley Bottoms
Raleigh Wood
Park Farm
Owen House Farm
Mobberley
Station Rd.
Hobcroft Lane
Small Lane
Barnfield
Bowl. Grn.
Key House Farm
Leycester Dr.
Greenbank
Hobcroft House
Hobcroft Farm
Holly House
Wee Bridge Farm
Slade Lane
Tatton Mere Brook
Mobberley Spinney
Old Hall Covert
Crow Wood
Hanging Bank
Square Wood
Broad Oak Lane
Boathouse Plantation
Shawheath Covert
Cotton Relief Wood
Witchcote Wood
Jetty
Beech Av.
Broad Oak Farm
Smithlane Farm
Valewood Farm
Shawheath Coverts
Works
Mobberley Brook
Sewage Works
Tatton Mere
Shawheath Plantation
Drive
Summerfield Rd.
Sports Grd.
Smith Lane
MOBBERLEY
Tatton Mere Covert
Parkgate Farm
Parkgate Trading Estate
Oak Tree Farm
Town Lane
B5085
Mayfield Rd.
Springfield Rd.
Grove Ho.
Ryecroft
Knutsford Bus. Pk.
Rooks Wood
Dukenfield Hall
Town Lane Farm
Approach Clump
Haig Ct.
Pavement Lane
Boothmill Bridge
Longridge Trading Estate
Bucklow Av.
Bernisdale Rd.
Meadow-sweet Rd.
Edenfield Cl.
Badgers Cft.
Field Side Cl.
Higmere Plantation
Waste Disposal Site
Shaw Heath
Pavement Lane Farm
Dog Wood
Parkgate
Knutsford Road
Mobberley Road
Longridge
Birkin
Knutsford Moor Nature Reserve
KNUTSFORD
Cross Town
St. John's Wood
St. John's Wood Sch.
Gleavehouse Farm
Brook
Manor Pk. Sch.
Pedley Brook
Springwood Farm
Prim. Sch.
Play. Fld.
Booths Mere
Knutsford
Adams Hill
Brook St.
Chelford Road
Springwood Cottage
The Belt
Spring Wood
Boat House
Over Knutsford
Hallside
Booths Hall Farm
Booths Hall
Moat
Woodvale Rd.
Carrwood
Sanctuary Moor
Bowling Green
Cricket Ground
Marthall Brook
A50
Parkfield Road
The Hill
Brickhill Wood
Booths Park
A537
Leycester Road
Rutherford Dr.
Oak Leigh
Oak Wood
Moseley Hall Farm
Moseley Hall
Ollerton Grange
Brackenwood
Kerfield House
Meadowland Farm
Sandfield Wood
Ollerton
Goughs Lane
Windmill Wood
Marthall Lane
G
H
J
K
L
M
N
1
2
3
4
5
6
7
8
9
76
77
78
79
80
81

POSTCODE MAP

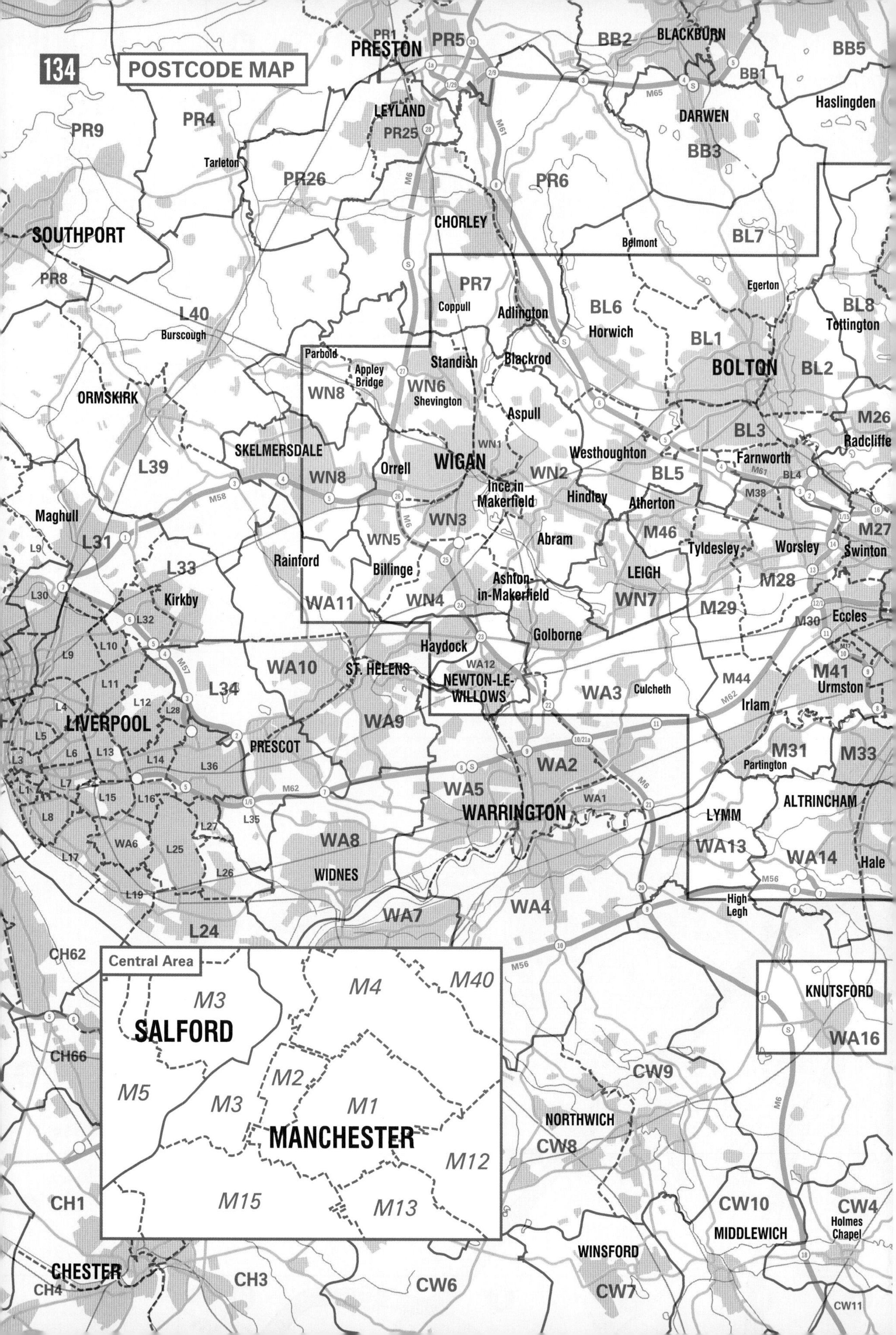
PRESTON
BLACKBURN
LEYLAND
DARWEN
Haslingden
Tarleton
SOUTHPORT
CHORLEY
Belmont
Coppull
Adlington
Horwich
Egerton
Tottington
Burscough
Parbold
Appley Bridge
Standish
Blackrod
BOLTON
ORMSKIRK
Shevington
Aspull
Radcliffe
SKELMERSDALE
Orrell
WIGAN
Westhoughton
Farnworth
Ince in Makerfield
Hindley
Atherton
Maghull
Tyldesley
Worsley
Swinton
Abram
Rainford
Billinge
LEIGH
Kirkby
Ashton-in-Makerfield
Eccles
Golborne
Haydock
ST. HELENS
NEWTON-LE-WILLOWS
Culcheth
Urmston
Irlam
LIVERPOOL
PRESCOT
Partington
ALTRINCHAM
WARRINGTON
LYMM
WIDNES
Hale
High Legh
Central Area
SALFORD
MANCHESTER
KNUTSFORD
NORTHWICH
MIDDLEWICH
Holmes Chapel
WINSFORD
CHESTER
PR1
PR5
BB2
BB5
BB1
PR4
PR9
PR25
BB3
PR26
PR6
BL7
PR8
PR7
BL6
BL8
L40
BL1
BL2
WN8
WN6
M26
L39
WN1
BL3
WN2
BL5
BL4
M38
L31
L9
WN3
M46
M27
WN5
L33
L30
M28
WA11
WN4
WN7
M29
L32
M30
L10
WA10
WA12
M17
L11
L34
WA3
M44
M41
L12
L4
L28
WA9
L5
M31
M33
L6
L13
L14
L36
L3
WA2
L7
WA5
L1
L15
L16
WA1
L8
L35
WA6
L27
WA8
WA13
WA14
L25
L17
L26
L19
WA4
WA7
L24
CH62
M40
M4
M3
CH66
M2
M5
M1
CW9
M12
CW8
M15
M13
CH1
CW10
CW4
CH3
CW6
CW7
CH4
CW11
WA16
M65
M61
M6
M58
M57
M62
M56

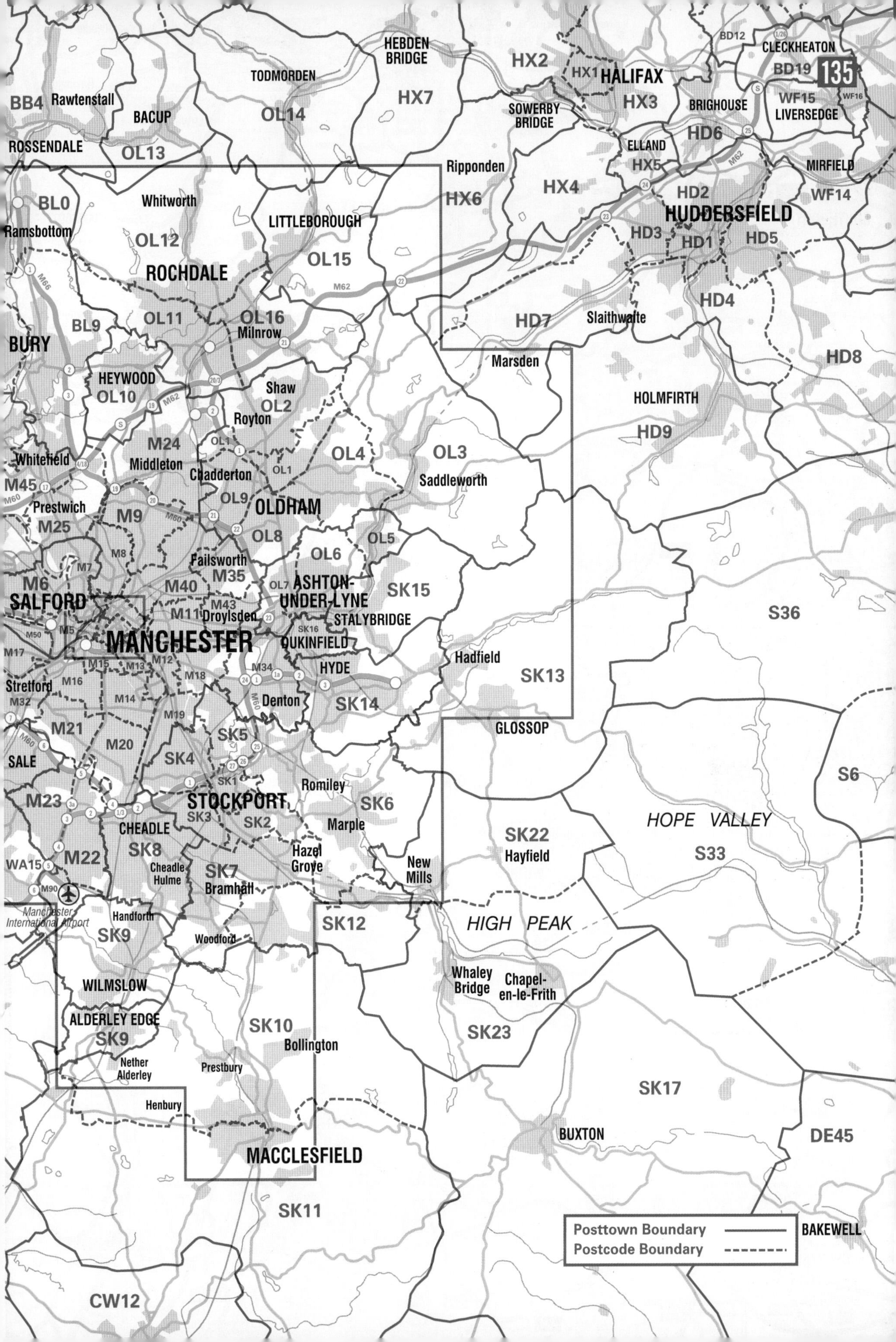
135
HEBDEN BRIDGE
TODMORDEN
HX2
HX1
HALIFAX
HX3
BD12
CLECKHEATON
BD19
WF15
LIVERSEDGE
WF16
BRIGHOUSE
HD6
SOWERBY BRIDGE
HX7
OL14
BB4
Rawtenstall
BACUP
ROSSENDALE
OL13
ELLAND
HX5
MIRFIELD
WF14
Ripponden
HX6
HX4
HD2
HUDDERSFIELD
HD3
HD1
HD5
BL0
Ramsbottom
Whitworth
OL12
LITTLEBOROUGH
OL15
ROCHDALE
HD4
HD7
Slaithwaite
OL11
OL16
Milnrow
BL9
BURY
HEYWOOD
OL10
Shaw
OL2
Royton
Marsden
HD8
HOLMFIRTH
HD9
M24
Middleton
OL4
OL3
Saddleworth
Whitefield
M45
Prestwich
M25
Chadderton
OL9
OLDHAM
M9
OL8
OL6
OL5
M8
M7
Failsworth
M35
M6
SALFORD
M40
M43
ASHTON-UNDER-LYNE
SK15
M11
Droylsden
STALYBRIDGE
S36
MANCHESTER
DUKINFIELD
SK16
M17
M15
M13
M12
M18
M34
HYDE
Hadfield
SK13
Stretford
M16
M32
M14
Denton
SK14
M19
M21
M20
SK5
SK4
GLOSSOP
SALE
S6
M23
STOCKPORT
SK1
SK3
SK2
Romiley
SK6
Marple
CHEADLE
SK22
Hayfield
HOPE VALLEY
S33
M22
SK8
Hazel Grove
WA15
Cheadle Hulme
SK7
Bramhall
New Mills
Manchester International Airport
Handforth
SK9
SK12
HIGH PEAK
Woodford
Whaley Bridge
Chapel-en-le-Frith
WILMSLOW
ALDERLEY EDGE
SK9
SK10
Bollington
SK23
Nether Alderley
Prestbury
SK17
Henbury
BUXTON
DE45
MACCLESFIELD
SK11
Posttown Boundary
Postcode Boundary
BAKEWELL
CW12

SOUTHPORT
ORMSKIRK
SKELMERSDALE
KIRKBY
LIVERPOOL
ST. HELENS
PRESCOT
HUYTON
WIDNES
RUNCORN
WARRINGTON
WIGAN
CHORLEY
LEYLAND
BOLTON
HORWICH
DARWEN
LEIGH
ATHERTON
FARNWORTH
WESTHOUGHTON
HAYDOCK
GOLBORNE
NEWTON-LE-WILLOWS
ELLESMERE PORT
CHESTER
FRODSHAM
NORTHWICH
KNUTSFORD
WINSFORD
Middlewich
ECCLES
SWINTON
URMSTON
SALE
ALTRINCHAM
RAMSBOTTOM
MAGHULL
STANDISH
ORRELL
HINDLEY
TYLDESLEY
WORSLEY

HALIFAX
HUDDERSFIELD
BRIGHOUSE
CLECKHEATON
LIVERSEDGE
Heckmondwike
DEWSBURY
MIRFIELD
Hebden Bridge
Mytholmroyd
Todmorden
Bacup
SOWERBY BRIDGE
Elland
Ripponden
Whitworth
LITTLEBOROUGH
ROCHDALE
Milnrow
HEYWOOD
MIDDLETON
ROYTON
SHAW
CHADDERTON
OLDHAM
FAILSWORTH
ASHTON-UNDER-LYNE
MANCHESTER
DROYLSDEN
STALYBRIDGE
DUKINFIELD
DENTON
HYDE
GLOSSOP
STRETFORD
STOCKPORT
Romiley
CHEADLE
Cheadle Hulme
Bramhall
Marple
New Mills
Whaley Bridge
Chapel-en-le-Frith
WILMSLOW
Alderley Edge
BOLLINGTON
MACCLESFIELD
BUXTON
CONGLETON
Slaithwaite
Marsden
Meltham
Holmfirth
Kirkburton
Skelmanthorpe
Denby Dale
Penistone
Mossley
Hadfield
Tintwistle
Hayfield
Bamford
Hathersage
Castleton
Hope
Tideswell
Bakewell
PEAK DISTRICT
HIGH PEAK
Kinder Scout
PEAK DISTRICT NATIONAL PARK
M62
M60
M66
M67
A6
A57
A628
SCALE
0 1 2 3 Miles
1: 250,000
0 1 2 3 4 5 Kilometres

INDEX

Including Streets, Places & Areas, Industrial Estates, Selected Flats & Walkways, Junction Names & Service Areas, Stations and Selected Places of Interest.

HOW TO USE THIS INDEX

1. Each street name is followed by its Postcode District, then by its Locality abbreviation(s) and then by its map reference; e.g. **Abbey Hey La.** M11: Man . . . .2C **96** is in the M11 Postcode District and the Manchester Locality and is to be found in square 2C on page **96**. The page number is shown in bold type.
2. A strict alphabetical order is followed in which Av., Rd., St., etc. (though abbreviated) are read in full and as part of the street name; e.g. **Ash Lodge** appears after **Ashling Ct.** but before **Ashlor St.**
3. Streets and a selection of flats and walkways that cannot be shown on the mapping, appear in the index with the thoroughfare to which they are connected shown in brackets; e.g. **Abbey Cl.** *BL3: Bolt . . . .1C **56** (off Zetland Av. Nth.)*
4. Addresses that are in more than one part are referred to as not continuous.
5. Places and areas are shown in the index in **BLUE TYPE** and the map reference is to the actual map square in which the town centre or area is located and not to the place name shown on the map; e.g. **ASHTON-IN-MAKERFIELD 7E 70**
6. An example of a selected place of interest is **Anson Engine Museum, The 2N 125**
7. An example of a station is **Alderley Edge Station (Rail) . . . .3F 126**. Included are Rail **(Rail)**, Metro **(Metro)** & **Park & Ride**. e.g. **Broadbottom (Park & Ride) 9K 99**
8. Junction names and Service Areas are shown in the index in **BOLD CAPITAL TYPE**; e.g. **BIRCH SERVICE AREA 7G 42**
9. Map references for entries that appear on large scale pages **4-9** are shown first, with small scale map references shown in brackets; e.g. **Aberdeen Cres.** SK3: Stoc 5G **9** (8B **108**)

GENERAL ABBREVIATIONS

All. : Alley
App. : Approach
Arc. : Arcade
Av. : Avenue
Bk. : Back
Blvd. : Boulevard
Bri. : Bridge
B'way. : Broadway
Bldg. : Building
Bldgs. : Buildings
Bungs. : Bungalows
Bus. : Business
Cen. : Centre
Chyd. : Churchyard
Circ. : Circle
Cl. : Close
Comn. : Common
Cnr. : Corner
Cott. : Cottage
Cotts. : Cottages
Ct. : Court
Cres. : Crescent
Cft. : Croft
Dr. : Drive
E. : East
Emb. : Embankment
Ent. : Enterprise
Est. : Estate
Ests. : Estates
Fld. : Field
Flds. : Fields
Gdn. : Garden
Gdns. : Gardens
Gth. : Garth
Ga. : Gate
Gt. : Great
Grn. : Green
Gro. : Grove
Hgts. : Heights
Ho. : House
Ho's. : Houses
Ind. : Industrial
Info. : Information
Intl. : International
Junc. : Junction
La. : Lane
Lit. : Little
Lwr. : Lower
Mnr. : Manor
Mans. : Mansions
Mkt. : Market
Mdw. : Meadow
Mdws. : Meadows
M. : Mews
Mt. : Mount
Mus. : Museum
Nth. : North
No. : Number
Pde. : Parade
Pk. : Park
Pas. : Passage
Pl. : Place
Pct. : Precinct
Ri. : Rise
Rd. : Road
Rdbt. : Roundabout
Shop. : Shopping
Sth. : South
Sq. : Square
Sta. : Station
St. : Street
Ter. : Terrace
Twr. : Tower
Trad. : Trading
Up. : Upper
Va. : Vale
Vw. : View
Vs. : Villas
Vis. : Visitors
Wlk. : Walk
W. : West
Yd. : Yard

POSTTOWN AND POSTAL LOCALITY ABBREVIATIONS

Abr : **Abram**
Adl : **Adlington**
Aff : **Affetside**
Ain : **Ainsworth**
A Edg : **Alderley Edge**
Alt : **Altrincham**
And : **Anderton**
App B : **Appley Bridge**
Ash : **Ashley**
A Mak : **Ashton-in-Makerfield**
A Lyne : **Ashton-under-Lyne**
Asp : **Aspull**
Ast : **Astley**
Ath : **Atherton**
Aud : **Audenshaw**
Aus : **Austerlands**
Bac : **Bacup**
Bam : **Bamfurlong**
Bel : **Belmont**
B'haw : **Bickershaw**
Bil : **Billinge**
Bir V : **Birch Vale**
Bla : **Blackrod**
Boll : **Bollington**
Bolt : **Bolton**
Bow : **Bowdon**
Bram : **Bramhall**
Bred : **Bredbury**
B'tom : **Broadbottom**
B'ath : **Broadheath**
Bro X : **Bromley Cross**
Burt : **Burtonwood**
Bury : **Bury**
Cad : **Cadishead**
C'ook : **Carrbrook**
C'ton : **Carrington**
Chad : **Chadderton**
Char : **Charlesworth**
Char R : **Charnock Richard**
Chea : **Cheadle**
Chea H : **Cheadle Hulme**
Chel : **Chelford**
Chis : **Chisworth**
Chor : **Chorley**
Cho H : **Chorlton-cum-Hardy**
Clif : **Clifton**
Coll G : **Collins Green**
Comp : **Compstall**
Cop : **Coppull**
Cra : **Crank**
Cro : **Croft**
Crow : **Crowden**
Cul : **Culcheth**
Dal : **Dalton**
Del : **Delph**
Dens : **Denshaw**
Dent : **Denton**
Dig : **Diggle**
Dis : **Disley**
Dob : **Dobcross**
Droy : **Droylsden**
Duk : **Dukinfield**
D Mas : **Dunham Massey**
Ecc : **Eccles**
Eden : **Edenfield**
Edg : **Edgworth**
Eger : **Egerton**
Fail : **Failsworth**
Farn : **Farnworth**
Fur V : **Furness Vale**
Gam : **Gamesley**
Gars : **Garswood**
Gat : **Gatley**
Gaws : **Gawsworth**
G'ook : **Glazebrook**
G'ury : **Glazebury**
Glos : **Glossop**
Gol : **Golborne**
Gras : **Grasscroft**
G'fld : **Greenfield**
G'mount : **Greenmount**
Grot : **Grotton**
Had : **Hadfield**
Hai : **Haigh**
Hale : **Hale**
Haleb : **Halebarns**
Hand : **Handforth**
Has : **Haslingden**
Hat : **Hattersley**
Haw : **Hawkshaw**
Hay : **Haydock**
H Gro : **Hazel Grove**
H Grn : **Heald Green**
H Char : **Heath Charnock**
Hen : **Henbury**
H'rod : **Heyrod**
H'ood : **Heywood**
H Lan : **High Lane**
H Leg : **High Legh**
Hin : **Hindley**
Holc : **Holcombe**
Holl : **Hollingworth**
Holme : **Holme**
Hor : **Horwich**
Hyde : **Hyde**
I Mak : **Ince-in-Makerfield**
Irl : **Irlam**
Kea : **Kearsley**
Kerr : **Kerridge**
K Mos : **Kings Moss**
Knut : **Knutsford**
Lang : **Langley**
Lees : **Lees**
Lei : **Leigh**
Lit B : **Little Bollington**
Lit : **Littleborough**
Lit H : **Little Hulton**
Lit L : **Little Lever**
Los : **Lostock**
Low : **Lowton**
Lyd : **Lydgate**
Lym G : **Lyme Green**
Lym : **Lymm**
Macc : **Macclesfield**
Man : **Manchester**
Man A : **Manchester Airport**
Mar : **Marple**
Mar B : **Marple Bridge**
Mars : **Marsden**
Mart : **Marthall**
Mat : **Matley**
Mel : **Mellor**
Melt : **Meltham**
Mere : **Mere**
Mid : **Middleton**
Mill : **Millbrook**
M'ton : **Millington**
Miln : **Milnrow**
Mob : **Mobberley**
Mos : **Mossley**
Mot : **Mottram**
Mot S A : **Mottram St Andrew**
N Ald : **Nether Alderley**
N Mil : **New Mills**
N Wil : **Newton-le-Willows**
Nor : **Northenden**
O'ham : **Oldham**
Old T : **Old Trafford**
Olle : **Ollerton**
Orr : **Orrell**
O Ald : **Over Alderley**
O Hul : **Over Hulton**
O Tab : **Over Tabley**
Par : **Parbold**
Part : **Partington**
Pen : **Pendlebury**
P Bri : **Platt Bridge**
P Shr : **Pott Shrigley**
Poy : **Poynton**
P'bury : **Prestbury**
Pres : **Prestwich**
Rad : **Radcliffe**
R'ford : **Rainford**
Rain : **Rainow**
Ram : **Ramsbottom**
Rawt : **Rawtenstall**
Ring : **Ringway**
Ripp : **Ripponden**
Rish : **Rishworth**
Ris : **Risley**
R'ton : **Rivington**
Rix : **Rixton**
Roby M : **Roby Mill**
Roch : **Rochdale**
Rom : **Romiley**
Rost : **Rostherne**
Row : **Rowarth**
St H : **St Helens**
Sale : **Sale**
Sal : **Salford**
Scout : **Scouthead**
Shar : **Sharston**
Shaw : **Shaw**
She : **Shevington**
Skel : **Skelmersdale**
Spri : **Springhead**
Stal : **Stalybridge**
Stan : **Standish**
Stoc : **Stockport**
Stre : **Stretford**
Stri : **Strines**
Sty : **Styal**
Sum : **Summerseat**
Sut E : **Sutton Lane Ends**
Swin : **Swinton**
Tab : **Tabley**
Tim : **Timperley**
Tin : **Tintwistle**
Tot : **Tottington**
T Pk : **Trafford Park**
Tur : **Turton**
Tyld : **Tyldesley**
Uph : **Upholland**
Upp : **Uppermill**
Urm : **Urmston**
Walk : **Walkden**
Wals : **Walsden**
Warb : **Warburton**
W'le : **Wardle**
Ward : **Wardley**
Water : **Waterfoot**
Wat : **Waterhead**
W Tim : **West Timperley**
W'ton : **Westhoughton**
Whall R : **Whalley Range**
Whitef : **Whitefield**
White G : **Whiteley Green**
Whitw : **Whitworth**
Wig : **Wigan**
Wilm : **Wilmslow**
Wind : **Windle**
Wins : **Winstanley**
Win : **Winwick**
W'ford : **Woodford**
Wood : **Woodley**
Wors : **Worsley**
Wrig : **Wrightington**
Wyth : **Wythenshawe**

A

Abberley Dr. M40: Man 9B **62**
Abberley Hall SK9: A Edg 5C **126**
Abberley Way WN3: Wig 7M **51**
Abberton Rd. M20: Man 2F **106**
Abbey Cl. *BL3: Bolt 1C **56***
(off Zetland Av. Nth.)
M26: Rad 7E **40**
M32: Stre 6F **92**
SK14: Mot 6J **99**
WA3: Cro 9C **88**
WA14: Bow 6B **114**
WN8: Uph 4G **50**
Abbey Ct. M18: Man 3C **96**
M26: Rad 8E **40**
*M30: Ecc 8E **76***
(off Abbey Gro.)
*SK1: Stoc 8F **108***
(off Abbey Gro.)
SK12: Poy 3H **125**
WN6: Wig 1B **52**
Abbey Cres. OL10: H'ood 9G **27**
Abbeycroft Cl. M29: Ast 4D **74**
Abbey Dale WN6: App B 5H **33**
Abbeydale OL12: Roch 5B **8** (5C **28**)
Abbeydale Cl. OL6: A Lyne 4B **82**
SK8: Chea H 8K **117**
Abbeydale Gdns. M28: Walk 8K **57**
Abbeydale Rd. M40: Man 2A **80**
Abbey Dr. BL8: Bury 3G **40**
M27: Swin 2E **76**
OL15: Lit 2K **29**
WN5: Orr 5J **51**
Abbeyfield Cl. SK3: Stoc 1C **118**
Abbeyfield Ho. *M28: Walk 7K **57***
(off Mountain St.)
Abbeyfields WN6: Wig 1B **52**
Abbeyfield Sq. *M11: Man 1N **95***
(off Herne St.)
Abbey Gdns. SK14: Mot 6J **99**
Abbey Gro. M30: Ecc 8E **76**
OL9: Chad 6E **62**
PR6: Adl 6K **19**
SK1: Stoc 8F **108**
SK14: Mot 6J **99**
ABBEY HEY 3D 96
Abbey Hey La. M11: Man 2C **96**
M18: Man 4C **96**
Abbey Hills Rd. OL4: O'ham 6M **63**
OL8: O'ham 6M **63**
Abbey La. WN7: Lei 1F **72**
Abbey Lawn M16: Old T 6A **94**
Abbeylea Cres. BL5: W'ton 1J **55**
Abbeylea Dr. BL5: W'ton 1J **55**
Abbey Mill SK10: P'bury 7E **128**
Abbey Rd. M24: Mid 8L **43**
M29: Ast 3D **74**
M33: Sale 2G **104**
M35: Fail 2F **80**
M43: Droy 7D **80**
OL3: Del 7H **47**
SK8: Chea 2M **117**
SK10: Macc 2F **130**
WA3: Low 1E **88**
WA11: Hay 2B **86**
Abbey Sq. WN7: Lei 1F **72**
Abbeystead WN8: Skel 4A **50**
Abbeystead Av. M21: Cho H 9C **94**
Abbey St. WN7: Lei 4H **73**
Abbeyville Wlk. *M15: Man 4D **94***
(off Wilberforce Cl.)
Abbey Way M26: Rad 9G **40**
Abbeyway Nth. WA11: Hay 2D **86**
Abbeyway Sth. WA11: Hay 3D **86**
Abbeywood WN8: Skel 5A **50**
Abbeywood Av. M18: Man 5C **96**
Abbingdon Way WN7: Lei 1F **72**
Abbot Cft. BL5: W'ton 5H **55**
Abbotsbury Cl. M12: Man 3M **95**
SK12: Poy 1H **125**
Abbots Cl. M33: Sale 3K **105**
SK10: Macc 2F **130**
Abbots Ct. M33: Sale 3K **105**
Abbotsfield Cl. M41: Urm 6L **91**
Abbotsfield Ct. M8: Man 3F **78**
Abbot's Fold Rd. M28: Wors 3J **75**
Abbotsford OL12: Whitw 4B **14**
Abbotsford Cl. WA3: Low 9N **71**
Abbotsford Dr. M24: Mid 8J **43**
Abbotsford Gro. WA14: Tim 8E **104**
Abbotsford Pk. Miniature Railway 7B 92
Abbotsford Rd. BL1: Bolt 3B **38**
M21: Cho H 7A **94**
OL1: O'ham 2M **63**
OL9: Chad 3C **62**
Abbotside Cl. M16: Whall R 6C **94**
Abbotsleigh Av. M23: Wyth 8M **105**
Abbotsleigh Dr. SK7: Bram 5D **118**
Abbots Way WN5: Bil 7H **69**
Abbotts Grn. M29: Ast 6B **74**
Abbott St. BL3: Bolt 7F **38**
BL6: Hor 9D **20**
OL11: Roch 1N **43**
WN2: Hin 5M **53**
Abden St. M26: Rad 9G **40**
Abels La. OL3: Upp 3M **65**
Aber Av. SK2: Stoc 3G **119**
Abercarn Cl. M8: Man 3F **78**
Abercorn Rd. BL1: Bolt 1C **38**
Abercorn St. OL4: O'ham 5A **64**
Abercrombie Ct. M33: Sale 3K **105**
Aberdare Wlk. *M9: Man 6K **61***
(off Crossmead Dr.)
Aberdaron Wlk. M13: Man 9L **5**
Aberdeen *M30: Ecc 8E **76***
(off Monton La.)
Aberdeen Cres.
SK3: Stoc 5G **9** (8B **108**)
Aberdeen Gdns. OL12: Roch 1B **28**
Aberdeen Gro.
SK3: Stoc 4H **9** (8B **108**)
Aberdeen Ho. M15: Man 4G **95**

Aberdeen St. M15: Man 4G 95
Aberdeen Wlk. SK10: Macc 1D 130
(off Berwick Cl.)
Aberford Rd. M23: Wyth 2N 115
Abergele Rd. M14: Man 9K 95
Abergele St. SK2: Stoc 2E 118
Aberley Fold OL15: Lit 7K 15
Abernant Cl. M11: Man 9L 79
Abernethy St. BL6: Hor 2F 36
Aber Rd. SK8: Chea 1M 117
Abersoch Av. M14: Man 9K 95
Abingdon Av. M45: Whitef 1M 59
Abingdon Cl. M45: Whitef 1M 59
OL9: Chad 7F 62
OL11: Roch 8C 28
SK11: Macc 4D 130
Abingdon Dr. WN2: P Bri 1K 71
Abingdon Rd. BL2: Bolt 4K 39
M41: Urm 6E 92
SK5: Stoc 1D 108
SK7: Bram 5C 118
Abingdon St. M1: Man 6H 5 (1F 94)
OL6: A Lyne 8A 82
Abinger Rd. WN4: Gars 6A 70
Abinger Wlk. M40: Man 6B 80
(off Eastmoor Dr.)
Abington Rd. M33: Sale 5J 105
Abito M3: Sal 2F 4 (8E 78)
Abney Grange OL5: Mos 2H 83
Abney Pl. SK8: Chea 2J 117
Abney Rd. OL5: Mos 2F 82
SK4: Stoc 3A 108
Abney Steps OL5: Mos 2F 82
(off Manchester Rd.)
Aboukir St. OL16: Roch 6G 8 (5F 28)
Abraham Moss Cen. 2G 78
Abraham Moss Leisure Cen. 2F 78
Abraham Moss Theatre 2F 78
Abraham St. BL6: Hor 9D 20
ABRAM 2L 71
ABRAM BROW 3M 71
Abram Cl. M14: Man 8F 94
Abram Moss Stop (Metro) 2F 78
Abram St. M6: Sal 4M 77
Absalom Dr. M8: Man 2E 78
Abson St. OL1: Chad 2G 63
Acacia Av. M27: Swin 4E 76
M34: Dent 6L 97
SK8: Chea H 5M 117
SK9: Wilm 9E 122
WA15: Hale 4F 114
WA16: Knut 7E 132
Acacia Cres. WN6: Wig 9C 34
Acacia Dr. M6: Sal 7H 77
WA15: Hale 4F 114
Acacia Gro. SK5: Stoc 4D 108
Acacia Rd. OL8: O'ham 1H 81
Acacias M41: Urm 6E 92
(off Granville Rd.)
Acacia St. WA12: N Wil 5C 86
Academy Wlk. M15: Man 4D 94
(off Wilberforce Cl.)
Acer Cl. OL11: Roch 4J 27
SK14: Hyde 7D 98
Acer Gro. M7: Sal 3C 78
(off Wellington St. W.)
Acheson St. M18: Man 4B 96
Acheson Way M17: T Pk 2J 93
Ackers Barn Courtyard
M31: C'ton 2A 104
Ackers La. M31: C'ton 2M 103
Ackersley Ct. SK8: Chea H 7A 118
Ackers St. M13: Man 4G 95
Acker St. OL16: Roch 6D 8 (5D 28)
Ackhurst La. WN5: Orr 9L 33
Ack La. E. SK7: Bram 8A 118
Ack La. W. SK8: Chea H 7N 117
Ackroyd Av. M18: Man 3D 96
Ackroyd St. M11: Man 2C 96
Ackworth Dr. M23: Wyth 1N 115
Ackworth Rd. M27: Swin 1E 76
Acme Dr. M27: Pen 2H 77
Acomb Ho. M15: Man 4G 94
(off Dilworth St.)
Acomb St. M14: Man 6G 94
M15: Man 4G 94
Acorn Av. SK8: Chea 2K 117
SK14: Hyde 9B 98
(not continuous)
Acorn Bus. Cen. WN7: Lei 6K 73
Acorn Bus. Pk.
SK4: Stoc 2H 9 (7B 108)
Acorn Cen., The OL1: O'ham 3M 63
Acorn Cl. M19: Man 9L 95
M45: Whitef 5M 59
WN7: Lei 7H 73
Acorn Ct. WN7: Lei 7K 73
Acorn Ho. M22: Shar 1D 116
(off Altrincham Rd.)
Acorn Ho., The SK15: Mill 6G 83
(off Bramble Ct.)
Acorn M. SK2: Stoc 1G 118
Acorn St. OL4: Lees 5B 64
WA12: N Wil 6F 86
Acorn Ter. SK22: N Mil 9L 121
Acorn Way OL1: O'ham 1C 8 (4J 63)
A Court WN4: A Mak 8E 70
ACRE 3M 63
Acre Barn OL2: Shaw 4J 45
Acre Cl. BL0: Eden 3K 11
Acre Ct. SK13: Glos 9E 100
(off Whitfield Av.)
Acre Fld. BL2: Bolt 9L 23
Acrefield M33: Sale 5G 105
Acrefield Av. M41: Urm 8F 92
SK4: Stoc 4N 107
Acregate M41: Urm 7A 92
(off Penny Bri. La.)
WN8: Skel 4A 50
Acre La. OL1: O'ham 2L 63
SK8: Chea H 1N 123
ACRES 1C 62
Acresbrook SK15: Stal 2F 98
Acresbrook Wlk. BL8: Tot 8F 24
Acres Ct. M22: Wyth 3C 116
Acresdale BL6: Los 5L 37
Acresfield M29: Ast 3D 74
PR7: Adl 7J 19
Acresfield Av. M34: Aud 9G 80
Acresfield Cl. BL6: Bla 1M 35
M27: Swin 4G 76
Acresfield Rd. M6: Sal 5K 77
M24: Mid 9N 43
M38: Lit H 7J 57
SK14: Hyde 4C 98
WA15: Tim 8G 104
Acres Fold Av. M22: Wyth 4D 116
Acres La. SK15: Stal 9E 82
Acres Pass M21: Cho H 9N 93
Acres Rd. M21: Cho H 9N 93
SK8: Gat 2F 116
Acres St. BL8: Tot 8F 24
Acre St. M26: Rad 9E 40
M34: Dent 6J 97
OL9: Chad 9F 62
OL12: Whitw 5B 14
SK13: Glos 9E 100
Acreswood Av. WN2: Hin 7C 54
Acreswood Cl. PR7: Cop 5B 18
Acre Top Rd. M9: Man 6G 61
Acre Vw. BL0: Ram 4K 11
Acreville Gro. WA3: G'ury 2L 89
Acre Wood BL6: Los 9K 37
Acton Av. M40: Man 6N 79
Acton Ho. WN1: Wig 8M 9 (3G 52)
Acton Pl. SK11: Macc 4D 130
Acton Sq. M5: Sal 8A 78
Acton St. OL1: O'ham 3M 63
OL12: Roch 4E 28
WN1: Wig 6K 9 (2F 52)
Acton's Wlk. WN3: Wig 4F 52
Acton's Wlk. Trad. Cen.
WN3: Wig 4F 52
Acton Ter. WN1: Wig 5K 9 (2F 52)
Actonville Av. M22: Wyth 4C 116
Adair St. M1: Man 6M 5 (1H 95)
OL11: Roch 2N 43
Adam Cl. SK8: Chea H 3N 117
Adams Av. M21: Cho H 2A 106
Adams Cl. SK12: Poy 4J 125
WA12: N Wil 7G 86
Adams Dr. WN3: Wig 6D 52
Adams Hill WA16: Knut 7G 133
Adamson Circ. M17: Urm 2C 92
Adamson Gdns. M20: Man 5E 106
Adamson Ho. M5: Sal 3N 93
(off Elmira Way)
M16: Old T 3A 94
Adamson Rd. M30: Ecc 1C 92
Adamson St. SK16: Duk 3N 97
WN4: A Mak 7D 70
Adamson Wlk. M14: Man 6G 95
(off Walmer St.)
Adam St. BL3: Bolt 7H 39
OL6: A Lyne 7F 6 (7N 81)
OL8: O'ham 9K 63
Adastral Ho. M21: Cho H 9B 94
Ada St. BL0: Ram 9H 11
M9: Man 1J 79
OL12: Roch 3E 28
Adbaston Rd. M32: Stre 4G 93
Adcroft St. SK1: Stoc 9D 108
(not continuous)
Addenbrook Rd. M8: Man 5D 78
Adderley Pl. SK13: Glos 8B 100
Adderley Rd. SK13: Glos 8B 100
ADDERS MOSS 7L 127
Addingham Cl. M9: Man 7G 61
Addington Cl. WN2: Hin 7N 53
Addington Rd. BL3: Bolt 9A 38
Addington St. M4: Man 2K 5 (8G 78)
Addison Av. OL6: A Lyne 7A 82
Addison Cl. M13: Man 3H 95
Addison Cres. M16: Old T 5A 94
Addison Dr. M24: Mid 1A 62
Addison Grange M33: Sale 5J 105
(off Princes Rd.)
Addison Rd. M31: C'ton 2L 103
M32: Stre 6H 93
M41: Urm 8D 92
M44: Irl 5K 91
WA15: Hale 5E 114
Addison St. WN3: Wig 9H 9 (4E 52)
Adelaide Rd. SK3: Stoc 8A 108
SK7: Bram 9D 118
Adelaide St. BL0: Ram 1G 24
BL3: Bolt 8E 38
M8: Man 5E 78
M24: Mid 3M 61
M27: Swin 3D 76
M30: Ecc 9D 76
OL10: H'ood 2J 43
PR6: Adl 5K 19
SK10: Macc 3J 131
Adelaide St. E.
OL10: H'ood 2K 43
Adelphi Ct. M3: Sal 1B 4 (7C 78)
Adelphi Dr. M38: Lit H 6J 57
Adelphi Gro. M38: Lit H 6J 57
Adelphi Mill SK10: Boll 6K 129
Adelphi St. M3: Sal 3B 4 (8C 78)
M26: Rad 7F 40
WN6: Stan 2B 34
Aden Cl. M12: Man 1J 95
Aden St. OL4: O'ham 6A 64
OL12: Roch 4E 28
Adey Rd. WA13: Lym 2B 112
Adisham Dr. BL1: Bolt 3G 38
ADLINGTON
PR7 6K 19
SK10 9G 125
Adlington Bus. Pk. SK10: Adl 4G 124
Adlington Cl. BL8: Bury 3G 40
SK12: Poy 4K 125
WA15: Tim 1K 115
Adlington Dr. M32: Stre 5M 93
Adlington Hall 8E 124
Adlington Hall M. SK10: Adl 8F 124
Adlington Ind. Est. SK10: Adl 5G 124
Adlington Pk. SK10: Adl 5G 124
Adlington Rd. SK9: Wilm 8J 123
SK10: Boll 4L 129
Adlington Rd. Bus. Pk.
SK10: Boll 4K 129
Adlington Sth. Bus. Pk.
PR7: Adl 7K 19
Adlington Station (Rail)
Cheshire 9G 124
Lancashire 6K 19
Adlington St. BL3: Bolt 8E 38
M12: Man 1J 95
OL4: O'ham 2A 64
SK10: Macc 4G 130
Adlington Wlk.
SK1: Stoc 1K 9 (7C 108)
Adlington Way M34: Dent 8L 97
(off Two Trees La.)
Admel Sq. M15: Man 3E 94
(off Eden Cl.)
Admiral Way SK14: Hyde 3A 98
Adolph & Pauline Cassel Ho.
M25: Pres 1A 78
Adrian Rd. BL1: Bolt 2D 38
Adrian St. M40: Man 3M 79
Adrian Ter. OL16: Roch 7G 29
Adria Rd. M20: Man 5H 107
Adscombe St. M16: Whall R 5D 94
Adshall Rd. SK8: Chea 2M 117
Adshead Cl. M22: Wyth 4A 116
Adshead Ct. SK10: Boll 5M 129
Adstock Wlk. M40: Man 1N 5
Adstone Cl. M4: Man 9J 79
ADSWOOD 1B 118
Adswood Cl. OL4: O'ham 2A 64
Adswood Gro. SK3: Stoc 1B 118
Adswood Ind. Est. SK3: Stoc 1B 118
Adswood La. E. SK2: Stoc 1D 118
Adswood La. W. SK3: Stoc 1D 118
Adswood Old Hall Rd.
SK8: Chea H 3B 118
Adswood Old Rd. SK3: Stoc 1C 118
Adswood Rd. SK3: Stoc 2B 118
SK8: Chea H 3A 118
Adswood St. M40: Man 8K 79
Adswood Ter. SK3: Stoc 1C 118
Advent Ho. M4: Man 5N 5
Advent Way M4: Man 5N 5 (9J 79)
Adwell Cl. WA3: Low 1C 88
Aegean Gdns. M7: Sal 5B 78
Aegean Rd. WA14: B'ath 1A 114
AFFETSIDE 5B 24
Affetside Dr. BL8: Bury 2F 40
Affleck Av. M26: Rad 3A 58
Afghan St. OL1: O'ham 3M 63
Agate M. M5: Sal 2A 94
AGDEN BROW 6F 112
Agden Brow WA13: Lym 7E 112
Agden Brow Pk. WA13: Lym 6E 112
Agden La. WA13: Lym 7E 112
WA14: M'ton 7E 112
Agden Pk. La. WA13: Lym 7E 112
Age Cft. OL8: O'ham 8N 63
Agecroft Commerce Pk.
M27: Pen 4L 77
Agecroft Crematorium
M27: Pen 2M 77
Agecroft Ent. Pk. M27: Pen 3K 77
Agecroft Pk. Circ. M27: Pen 3K 77
Agecroft Rd. M27: Pen 3J 77
SK6: Rom 7L 109
Agecroft Rd. E. M25: Pres 9N 59
Agecroft Rd. W. M25: Pres 9M 59
Agecroft Trad. Est. M6: Sal 3L 77
Agincourt St. OL10: H'ood 2G 43
Agnes Cl. OL9: O'ham 7C 62
Agnes Ct. M14: Man 1H 107
Agnes St. M7: Sal 3E 78
M19: Man 7M 95
OL9: Chad 6F 62
Agnew Pl. M6: Sal 6N 77
Agnew Rd. M18: Man 4A 96
Aigburth Gro. SK5: Stoc 7C 96
Ailsa Cl. M40: Man 5J 79
Ailsa Ho. M6: Sal 9M 77
(off Langworthy Rd.)
Aimson Pl. WA15: Tim 1J 115
Aimson Rd. E. WA15: Tim 1J 115
Aimson Rd. W. WA15: Tim 9J 105
Aines St. M12: Man 2M 95
Ainley Rd. M22: Wyth 4C 116
Ainley Wood OL3: Del 7H 47
SK16: Duk 2A 98
Ainsbrook Av. M9: Man 8N 61
OL3: Del 8J 47
Ainsbrook Ter. OL3: Dig 7N 47
Ainscoughs Ct. WN7: Lei 6G 73
Ainscow Av. BL6: Los 4H 37
Ainsdale Av. BL8: Bury 2H 41
M7: Sal 1C 78
M46: Ath 7L 55
Ainsdale Cl. OL8: O'ham 7H 63
SK7: Bram 8E 118
Ainsdale Ct. BL3: Bolt 9G 38
Ainsdale Cres. OL2: O'ham 1J 63
Ainsdale Dr. M33: Sale 6E 104
OL12: Whitw 7B 14
SK8: H Grn 6G 116
Ainsdale Gro. SK5: Stoc 9D 96
Ainsdale Rd. BL3: Bolt 1F 56
(not continuous)
Ainsdale St. M12: Man 3L 95
Ainse Rd. BL6: Bla 1L 35
Ainsford Rd. M20: Man 3J 107
Ainsley Gro. M28: Walk 9K 57
Ainsley St. M40: Man 5A 80
Ainslie Rd. BL1: Bolt 3B 38
Ainsty Rd. M14: Man 5F 94
AINSWORTH 3C 40
Ainsworth Av. BL6: Hor 3G 36
Ainsworth Cl. M34: Dent 6F 96
Ainsworth Ct. BL2: Bolt 5K 39
M28: Walk 9L 57
Ainsworth Hall Rd.
BL2: Ain, Bolt 5B 40
Ainsworth La. BL2: Bolt 3J 39
Ainsworth Rd. BL3: Lit L 9A 40
BL8: Bury 3F 40
M26: Rad 6F 40
Ainsworth Sq. BL1: Bolt 1E 38
(off Ainsworth St.)
Ainsworth St. BL1: Bolt 2D 38
OL16: Roch 9E 8 (7E 28)
Ainthorpe Wlk. M40: Man 5B 80
(off Droyden Rd.)
Aintree Av. M33: Sale 5C 104
Aintree Cl. SK7: H Gro 5K 119
Aintree Dr. OL11: Roch 5K 27
Aintree Gro. SK3: Stoc 1C 118
Aintree Rd. BL3: Lit L 1A 58
Aintree St. M11: Man 9N 79
Aintree Wlk. OL9: Chad 4G 62
(off Bentley St.)
Airedale Cl. SK8: Chea 1H 117
Airedale Ct. WA14: Alt 1E 6
Aire Dr. BL2: Bolt 8J 23
Aireworth St. BL5: W'ton 9H 37
Air Hill Ter. OL12: Roch 4A 28
Airton Cl. M40: Man 7H 79
Airton Pl. WN3: Wig 8E 52
Aitken Cl. BL0: Ram 9H 11
Aitken St. BL0: Ram 1J 11
M19: Man 8A 96
Ajax Dr. BL9: Bury 9M 41
Ajax St. BL0: Ram 9H 11
OL11: Roch 1N 43
Aked Cl. M12: Man 3J 95
Akesmoor Dr. SK2: Stoc 1G 118
Alamein Dr. SK6: Rom 6B 110
Alan Av. M35: Fail 5D 80
Alanbrooke Wlk. M15: Man 4D 94
(off Rankin Cl.)
Alandale Av. M34: Aud 2J 97
Alandale Dr. OL2: O'ham 7G 45
Alandale Rd. SK3: Stoc 9A 108
Alan Dr. SK6: Mar 1B 120
WA15: Hale 7G 114
Alan Rd. M20: Man 2H 107
SK4: Stoc 5M 107
Alan St. BL1: Bolt 1E 38
(off Newry St.)
Alan Turing Way M11: Man 7L 79
Alasdair Cl. OL9: Chad 3D 62
Alba Cl. M30: Ecc 9C 76
Alban Ct. BL5: W'ton 4G 55
OL6: A Lyne 3A 82
Alban St. M7: Sal 5C 78
Albanvale Cl. WA14: Bow 6B 114
Albany Av. M11: Man 2D 96
Albany Cl. M38: Lit H 5J 57
Albany Ct. M20: Man 2G 106
(off Redcar Av.)
M33: Sale 3J 105
M41: Urm 6B 92
Albany Dr. BL9: Bury 5M 41
Albany Fold BL5: W'ton 3H 55
Albany Gro. M29: Ast 2E 74
Albany Rd. M21: Cho H 8A 94
M30: Ecc 7B 76
SK7: Bram 2C 124
SK9: Wilm 9E 122
Albany St. M24: Mid 4N 61
OL4: O'ham 2A 64
OL11: Roch 8E 28
Albany Trad. Est. M21: Cho H 8A 94
Albany Way M6: Sal 7N 77
(off Salford Shop. City)
SK14: Hat 7H 99
Alba St. BL8: Holc 8G 10
Alba Way M32: Stre 4G 92
Albemarle Av. M20: Man 2F 106
Albemarle Pl. BL8: Tot 6F 24
Albemarle Rd. M21: Cho H 9N 93
M27: Swin 3E 76
Albemarle St. M14: Man 5F 94
Albemarle Ter.
OL6: A Lyne 6E 6 (7N 81)
Alberbury Av. WA15: Tim 9K 105
Albermarle St.
OL6: A Lyne 6E 6 (7N 81)
(not continuous)
Alberta St. BL3: Bolt 7D 38
SK1: Stoc 4M 9 (8D 108)
Albert Av. M18: Man 5D 96
M25: Pres 1B 78
M28: Walk 6K 57
M41: Urm 7E 92
OL2: Shaw 7L 45
OL8: O'ham 7K 63
Albert Bri. Ho. M3: Sal 4E 4 (9D 78)
Albert Cl. M45: Whitef 3N 59
SK8: Chea H 5M 117
Albert Cl. Trad. Est.
M45: Whitef 3N 59
Albert Colliery Est.
WN2: B'haw 3B 72
Albert Ct. WA14: Alt 4C 6 (3D 114)
Albert Dr. M45: Whitef 2A 60
Albert Fildes Wlk. M8: Man 3E 78
(off Greenland St.)
Albert Gdns. M40: Man 5B 80
Albert Gro. BL4: Farn 3L 57
M12: Man 5M 95
(not continuous)
Albert Hill St. M20: Man 5G 107
Albert M. BL5: W'ton 2H 55
Albert Mt. OL1: O'ham 2M 63
Alberton Cl. WN2: Asp 6M 35
ALBERT PARK 3F 106
Albert Pk. Rd. M7: Sal 5B 78
Albert Pl. M13: Man 6L 95
M45: Whitef 2A 60
OL4: Lees 6B 64
SK11: Macc 4H 131
WA14: Alt 2C 6 (2D 114)
Albert Rd. BL1: Bolt 4B 38
BL4: Farn 3K 57
M19: Man 8L 95
M30: Ecc 8F 76
M33: Sale 4J 105
M45: Whitef 3N 59
SK4: Stoc 5M 107
SK8: Chea H 5M 117
SK9: Wilm 8F 122
SK10: Boll 5J 129
Albert Rd. SK14: Hyde 7A 98
WA14: Alt 4C 6 (3D 114)
WA15: Hale 4E 114
Albert Rd. E. WA15: Hale 4E 114
Albert Rd. W. BL1: Bolt 3A 38
Albert Royds St. OL16: Roch 3F 28
Albert Sq. M2: Man 5G 4 (9E 78)
SK15: Stal 9C 82
WA14: Bow 4C 114
Albert St. BL0: Ram 8H 11
BL3: Lit L 9B 40
BL4: Farn 4L 57
BL4: Kea 3M 57
BL6: Hor 9D 20
BL7: Eger 2E 22
BL9: Bury 2N 41
M11: Man 9L 79
M24: Mid 3M 61
M25: Pres 7B 60
M30: Ecc 8F 76
M34: Dent 6K 97
M43: Droy 9F 80
M44: Cad 2F 102
OL2: O'ham 8H 45
OL2: Shaw 5L 45
OL4: Lees 6B 64
OL8: O'ham 1F 80
OL9: Chad 8F 62
OL10: H'ood 2G 42
OL12: Whitw 6A 14
OL15: Lit 9M 15
OL16: Miln 8L 29
SK3: Stoc 3H 9 (7B 108)
SK7: H Gro 4H 119
SK11: Macc 4G 130
SK13: Had 4C 100
SK14: Hyde 6C 98
WA16: Knut 6F 132
WN2: Hin 6N 53
WN4: A Mak 7E 70
WN5: Wig 5C 52
Albert St. W. M35: Fail 4B 80
Albert Ter. SK1: Stoc 2L 9
WA5: Coll G 8B 86
Albert Wlk. OL7: A Lyne 9A 6 (9L 81)
Albine St. M40: Man 2L 79
Albinson Wlk. M31: Part 5H 103
Albion Cl. M46: Ath 9J 55
SK4: Stoc 5C 108
Albion Ct. BL8: Bury 2K 41
Albion Dr. M43: Droy 8E 80
WN2: Asp 1L 53
Albion Fold M43: Droy 8E 80
Albion Gdns. SK15: Stal 8E 82
Albion Gdns. Cl. OL2: O'ham 8K 45
Albion Gro. M33: Sale 4G 105
Albion Ho. SK15: Stal 8E 82
Albion M. SK22: N Mil 8M 121
Albion Pk. WA3: G'ury 3L 89
Albion Pl. M5: Sal 8B 78
M7: Sal 5B 78
M25: Pres 7N 59
SK7: H Gro 4H 119
Albion Rd. M14: Man 8H 95
OL11: Roch 9A 8 (7B 28)
SK22: N Mil 9K 121
Albion Rd. Ind. Est. OL11: Roch 7B 28
Albion St. BL3: Bolt 7G 38
BL4: Kea 4A 58
BL5: W'ton 9H 37
BL8: Bury 7G 7 (2K 41)
M1: Man 8F 4 (2E 94)
M16: Old T 5C 94
M26: Rad 2H 59
M27: Pen 2G 77
M33: Sale 4H 105
M35: Fail 3C 80
OL1: O'ham 2C 8 (4K 63)
(not continuous)
OL6: A Lyne 7E 6 (7N 81)
OL9: Chad 4E 62
OL11: Roch 3A 44
OL15: Lit 9L 15
SK15: Stal 8E 82
WN2: Asp 1L 53
WN2: P Bri 9K 53
WN7: Lei 5H 73
Albion Ter. BL1: Bolt 1C 38
Albion Towers M5: Sal 8A 78
Albion Trad. Est. M6: Sal 6N 77
OL6: A Lyne 7A 82
Albion Way M5: Sal 9A 78
Albury Cl. WA11: Hay 2A 86
Albury Dr. M19: Man 6J 107
OL12: Roch 3L 27
Albury Way WN2: Wig 1J 53
Albyns Av. M8: Man 3F 78
Alcester Av. SK3: Stoc 9L 107
Alcester Cl. BL8: Bury 1H 41
M24: Mid 5N 61
Alcester Rd. M33: Sale 6H 105
SK8: Gat 3G 117
Alcester St. OL9: Chad 8E 62
Alcester Wlk. M9: Man 6H 61
Alconbury Ct. M43: Droy 1F 96
(off Florence St.)
Alconbury Wlk. M9: Man 5G 61
Aldborough Cl. M20: Man 2G 106
Aldbourne Cl. M40: Man 6J 79
Aldbury Ter. BL1: Bolt 3E 38
(off Eskrick St.)
Aldcliffe WA3: Low 1B 88
Aldcroft St. M18: Man 3D 96
Alden Cl. BB4: Has 1G 10
M45: Whitef 3N 59
WN1: Stan 3E 34
Alden Rd. BB4: Has 2E 10
Alden Wlk. SK4: Stoc 1B 108
Alder Av. BL9: Bury 1B 42
SK12: Poy 3K 125
WN4: A Mak 5C 70
WN5: Bil 5H 69
WN5: Wig 5A 52
Alderbank BL6: Hor 1B 36
OL12: W'le 7G 14
Alderbank Cl. BL4: Kea 5N 57

Alderbrook Dr. WN8: Par 2A 32
Alderbrook Rd. M38: Lit H 8G 56
Alder Cl. BL8: Bury 2J 41
OL6: A Lyne 3M 81
SK8: H Grn 7J 117
SK13: Had 5B 100
SK16: Duk 1D 98
WN7: Lei 8H 73
Alder Ct. M8: Man 1E 78
SK10: Boll 8H 129
Aldercroft Av. BL2: Bolt 3L 39
M22: Wyth 5B 116
Alderdale Cl. SK4: Stoc 4M 107
Alderdale Dr. M43: Droy 8B 80
SK4: Stoc 3M 107
SK6: H Lan 8B 120
Alderdale Gro. SK9: Wilm 9D 122
Alderdale Rd.
SK8: Chea H 3A 118
Alder Dr. M27: Ward 1C 76
PR7: Char R 2A 18
SK15: Stal 7F 82
WA15: Tim 3K 115
Alder Edge M21: Cho H 8M 93
(off Alderford Rd.)
Alderfield Ho. M21: Cho H 8M 93
Alderfield Rd. M21: Cho H 8M 93
Alderfold St. M46: Ath 8M 55
Alderford Pde. M8: Man 4E 78
ALDER FOREST 6A 76
Alder Forest Av. M30: Ecc 6A 76
Aldergate Ct. M27: Swin 3C 76
Aldergate Gro. OL6: A Lyne 5C 82
Alderglen Rd. M8: Man 4E 78
Alder Gro. BL7: Bro X 7K 23
M32: Stre 7L 93
M34: Dent 6L 97
PR7: Cop 4C 18
SK3: Stoc 8A 108
Alder Hgts. SK1: Stoc 6F 108
Alder Ho. M46: Ath 8N 55
Alder La. OL8: O'ham 9H 63
WA11: Cra 6D 68
WN2: Hin 6C 54
WN8: Par 3A 32
Alder Lee Cl. WN3: Wins 9A 52
Alderley WN8: Skel 5A 50
Alderley Av. BL1: Bolt 8F 22
WA3: Low 2N 87
Alderley Cl. SK7: H Gro 7K 119
SK12: Poy 4K 125
WN5: Bil 5J 69
Alderley Ct. SK2: Stoc 3G 119
SK9: A Edg 4G 126
Alderley Dr. SK6: Bred 5J 109
ALDERLEY EDGE 4F 126
Alderley Edge 5J 127
Alderley Edge By-Pass
SK9: A Edg 5D 126
SK10: N Ald 6D 126
Alderley Edge Golf Course 2D 126
Alderley Edge Station (Rail) 3F 126
Alderley La. WN7: Lei 7K 73
Alderley Lodge SK9: Wilm 9F 122
Alderley Pk. SK10: N Ald 9G 126
Alderley Rd. M33: Sale 6L 105
M41: Urm 7A 92
SK5: Stoc 3D 108
SK9: A Edg 4K 127
SK9: Wilm 8F 122
SK10: Mot S A 4K 127
SK10: O Ald, P'bury 8N 127
SK11: Chel 9B 126
WN2: Hin 6C 54
Alderley St. OL6: A Lyne 5A 82
Alderley Ter. SK16: Duk 9M 81
Alderley Vw. SK10: Boll 5L 129
Alderley Wlk. SK11: Macc 5J 131
(off Bank St.)
Alderley Way SK3: Stoc 3C 118
Alderman Foley Dr. OL12: Roch 3M 27
Alderman Sq. M12: Man 1K 95
Aldermary Rd. M21: Cho H 3C 106
Aldermaston Gro. M9: Man 5G 60
Aldermere Cres. M41: Urm 6N 91
Alderminster Av. M38: Lit H 6H 57
Aldermoor Cl. M11: Man 1A 96
Alderney Cl. SK11: Macc 4D 130
Alderney Dr. WN3: Wig 8D 52
Alder Rd. M24: Mid 1A 62
M35: Fail 5D 80
OL11: Roch 2B 44
SK8: Chea 2K 117
WA3: Low 1B 88
ALDER ROOT 5F 62
Alder Root Golf Course 9G 87
Alder Root La. WA2: Win 9G 87
Alders, The WN6: Stan 8A 34
Alders Ct. OL8: O'ham 2L 81
Aldersgate SK22: N Mil 7L 121
Aldersgate Rd. SK2: Stoc 1F 118
SK8: Chea H 1A 124
Alders Grn. Av. SK6: H Lan 8C 120
Alders Grn. Rd. WN2: Hin 6C 54
Aldershot Wlk. M11: Man 9L 79
(off Newcombe Cl.)
Alderside Rd. M9: Man 2J 79
Aldersley Av. M9: Man 6G 60
Alderson St. M6: Sal 6N 77
OL9: O'ham 1B 8 (4J 63)
Alders Rd. M22: Wyth 2B 116
SK12: Dis 8D 120
Alder St. BL3: Bolt 9G 38
M6: Sal 8M 77
M30: Ecc 6A 76
M46: Ath 8M 55
WA12: N Wil 7F 86
Alders Way SK10: P'bury 7D 128
Aldersyde St. BL3: Bolt 9E 38
Alderton Dr. BL5: W'ton 5G 54
WN4: A Mak 7C 70
Alderue Av. M22: Wyth 1C 116
Alderway BL0: Ram 5J 11
Alderwood Av. SK4: Stoc 7M 107
Alderwood Fold OL4: O'ham 6C 64
Alderwood Gro. BL0: Eden 2K 11

Alderwood Wlk. M8: Man 4E 78
(off Ermington Dr.)
Aldfield Rd. M23: Wyth 7M 105
Aldford Cl. M20: Man 5H 107
(off Whitehall Rd.)
Aldford Dr. M46: Ath 6N 55
Aldford Gro. BL2: Bolt 7B 40
Aldford Pl. SK9: A Edg 3E 126
Aldford Way WN6: Stan 4B 34
Aldham Av. M40: Man 6A 80
Aldow Ind. Pk. M12: Man 6N 5 (1H 95)
Aldred Cl. M8: Man 4G 78
Aldred St. BL3: Bolt 9C 38
M5: Sal 8A 78
M30: Ecc 9C 76
M35: Fail 3C 80
WN2: Hin 7N 53
WN7: Lei 2G 72
Aldridge Cl. WN3: Wig 8E 52
Aldsworth Dr. BL3: Bolt 8F 38
Aldwick Av. M20: Man 5H 107
Aldwinians Cl. M34: Aud 4J 97
Aldworth Dr. M40: Man 4K 79
Aldworth Gro. M33: Sale 5D 104
Aldwych OL11: Roch 1D 44
(not continuous)
Aldwych Av. M14: Man 6G 95
Aldwyn Cl. M26: Rad 2H 59
M34: Aud 4J 97
WN3: Wins 1A 70
Aldwyn Cres. SK7: H Gro 5G 118
Aldwyn Pk. Rd. M34: Aud 1G 96
Alexander Av. M35: Fail 2E 80
Alexander Briant Ct. BL4: Farn 4K 57
Alexander Ct. M5: Sal 1N 93
(off Rowland St.)
Alexander Dr. BL9: Bury 2N 59
OL16: Miln 7J 29
WA15: Tim 1G 114
Alexander Gdns. M7: Sal 6C 78
Alexander Ho. M16: Old T 5N 93
Alexander Pk. OL6: A Lyne 8A 82
Alexander Rd. BL2: Bolt 3K 39
Alexander St. M6: Sal 8L 77
M29: Tyld 2B 74
OL11: Roch 2N 43
Alexandra, The M14: Man 9J 95
M50: Sal 2M 93
Alexandra Av. M14: Man 7E 94
M45: Whitef 3N 59
SK14: Hyde 7N 97
Alexandra Cen. Retail Pk.
OL4: O'ham 4E 8 (5K 63)
Alexandra Cl. SK3: Stoc 1A 118
Alexandra Ct. M31: Part 5G 102
(off Bailey La.)
M41: Urm 8M 91
Alexandra Cres. OL1: O'ham 3M 63
WN5: Wig 5B 52
Alexandra Dr. M19: Man 1L 107
Alexandra Gro. M44: Irl 9G 90
Alexandra Ho. M30: Ecc 9C 76
(off Liverpool Rd.)
OL1: O'ham 3M 63
Alexandra Ind. Est. M34: Dent 5L 97
(off Alexandra Rd.)
Alexandra M. OL8: O'ham 6L 63
Alexandra Mill OL3: Upp 4L 65
ALEXANDRA PARK 7D 94
Alexandra Pk.
Alexandra Rd. Sth. 6E 94
Queens Rd. 6L 63
Alexandra Pk. Ho. M16: Whall R 7D 94
Alexandra Rd. BL4: Kea 5A 58
BL6: Los 4G 37
M16: Whall R 6D 94
M26: Rad 3A 58
M28: Walk 6K 57
M30: Ecc 9B 76
M33: Sale 4J 105
M34: Dent 5L 97
OL6: A Lyne 6D 6 (7M 81)
OL8: O'ham 7L 63
SK4: Stoc 5A 108
WN4: A Mak 6E 70
Alexandra Rd. Sth. M16: Whall R 6D 94
M21: Cho H 6D 94
Alexandra St. BL3: Bolt 8E 38
BL4: Farn 4L 57
M7: Sal 7C 78
OL6: A Lyne 6A 82
OL8: O'ham 6L 63
OL10: H'ood 4K 43
SK14: Hyde 8N 97
WN2: Abr 2L 71
WN5: Wig 4C 52
Alexandra Ter. M19: Man 8M 95
OL4: O'ham 9A 46
Alexandria Dr. BL5: W'ton 3K 55
OL7: A Lyne 8J 81
Alford Av. M20: Man 9F 94
Alford Cl. BL2: Bolt 6N 39
Alford Rd. SK4: Stoc 2N 107
Alford St. OL9: O'ham 9F 62
Alfred Av. M28: Wors 3A 76
Alfred Ct. OL9: O'ham 5G 63
Alfred James Cl.
M40: Man 1N 5 (7H 79)
Alfred Morris Ct. M23: Wyth 6N 105
(off Fellpark Rd.)
Alfred Rd. WA3: Low 1C 88
WA11: Hay 2C 86
Alfred St. BL0: Ram 9H 11
BL3: Bolt 8J 39
BL4: Farn 1L 57
BL4: Kea 3N 57
BL7: Eger 2E 22
BL9: Bury 9N 7 (4N 41)
M9: Man 2J 79
M28: Walk 8L 57
M29: Tyld 1A 74
M30: Ecc 7D 76
M35: Fail 2D 80
M44: Cad 2F 102
(off Dean Rd.)
OL2: Shaw 5L 45

Alfred St. OL6: A Lyne 6A 82
OL9: O'ham 5G 63
(not continuous)
OL12: Whitw 4B 14
OL15: Lit 8L 15
SK14: Hyde 6N 97
WA12: N Wil 6H 87
WN1: Wig 1E 52
WN2: P Bri 8K 53
WN3: I Mak 5G 53
Alfreton Av. M34: Dent 9L 97
Alfreton Rd. SK2: Stoc 1H 119
Alfreton Wlk. M40: Man 4M 79
(off Halliford Rd.)
Alfriston Dr. M23: Wyth 6N 105
Alger M. OL6: A Lyne 6A 82
Algernon Rd. M28: Walk 7K 57
Algernon St. M27: Swin 2D 76
M30: Ecc 7D 76
WN2: Hin 6N 53
WN3: Wig 7D 52
Alger St. OL6: A Lyne 6A 82
Algreave Rd. SK3: Stoc 8M 107
Alice Ingham Ct. OL12: Roch 4A 28
Alice St. BL3: Bolt 7D 38
M27: Pen 2H 77
M33: Sale 4K 105
OL12: Roch 4F 28
SK14: Hyde 1B 110
Alicia Ct. OL12: Roch 4C 28
Alicia Dr. OL12: Roch 4C 28
Alick's Fold BL5: W'ton 2G 55
Alison Ct. SK4: Stoc 4N 107
Alison Dr. SK10: Macc 3K 131
Alison Kelly Cl. M9: Man 2L 79
Alison St. M14: Man 6E 94
OL2: Shaw 4L 45
(not continuous)
Alker Rd. M40: Man 7J 79
Alker St. WN5: Wig 5C 52
Alkrington Cl. BL9: Bury 1N 59
Alkrington Ct. M24: Mid 6N 61
ALKRINGTON GARDEN VILLAGE
5M 61
Alkrington Grn. M24: Mid 5L 61
Alkrington Hall M24: Mid 4L 61
Alkrington Hall Rd. Nth.
M24: Mid 4L 61
Alkrington Hall Rd. Sth.
M24: Mid 5K 61
Alkrington Pk. Rd. M24: Mid 4K 61
Allama Iqbal Rd. OL4: O'ham 6N 63
Allanadale Ct. M7: Sal 1D 78
Allan Ct. M21: Cho H 1N 105
Allandale WA14: Alt 3B 114
Allandale Rd. M19: Man 8L 95
Allan Roberts Cl. M9: Man 1J 79
Allanson Rd. M22: Nor 7D 106
Allan St. M29: Tyld 2A 74
Alldis Cl. M12: Man 4K 95
(off Kingfisher Cl.)
Alldis St. SK2: Stoc 2F 118
Allen Av. SK14: Hyde 9C 98
WA3: Cul 5L 89
Allenby Gro. BL5: W'ton 4F 54
Allenby Rd. M27: Swin 4C 76
M44: Cad 4E 102
Allenby St. M46: Ath 9K 55
OL2: Shaw 5L 45
Allenby Wlk. M40: Man 5H 79
(off Dalbury Dr.)
Allen Cl. OL2: Shaw 6L 45
Allendale Dr. BL9: Bury 9N 41
Allendale Gdns. BL1: Bolt 2F 38
(off Jennaby Wlk.)
Allendale Wlk. M3: Sal 2B 4 (8C 78)
Allen Grn. Cl. M26: Rad 9F 40
Allen Hall M14: Man 7J 95
Allen Rd. M41: Urm 7F 92
Allen St. BL3: Lit L 9A 40
BL8: Bury 1J 41
M26: Rad 9E 40
(not continuous)
OL8: O'ham 4A 8 (6H 63)
OL16: Roch 7E 28
SK10: Boll 5M 129
SK11: Macc 5J 131
Allerby Way WA3: Low 1A 88
Allerdean Wlk. SK4: Stoc 5L 107
Allerford St. M16: Whall R 5D 94
Allerton Cl. BL5: W'ton 2J 55
Allerton Ct. BL1: Bolt 4F 38
(off School Hill)
Allerton Ho. OL2: O'ham 8J 45
(off Royton Hall Pk.)
Allerton Wlk. M13: Man 3G 95
(off Glenbarry Cl.)
Allescholes Rd. OL14: Wals 1M 15
Allesley Cl. BL5: W'ton 2J 55
Allesley Dr. M7: Sal 5D 78
Allgreave Cl. M33: Sale 7K 105
Alliance Ind. Est. M34: Dent 6H 97
Alliance St. WN1: Wig 7L 9 (3G 52)
Alligin Cl. OL9: Chad 3E 62
Allingham St. M13: Man 5K 95
Allington OL11: Roch 7C 28
(off Tweedale St.)
Allington Dr. M30: Ecc 6E 76
Alliott Wlk. M15: Man 4D 94
(off Elverdon Cl.)
Allison Gro. M30: Ecc 9B 76
Allison St. M8: Man 5E 78
Allonby Cl. WN3: Wins 1A 70
Allonby Wlk. M24: Mid 1H 61
Allotment Rd. M44: Cad 2E 102
Alloway Wlk. M40: Man 4M 79
(off Halliford Rd.)
All Saints BL8: Bury 1J 41
All Saints Cl. OL2: O'ham 7H 45
All Saints Ct. M32: Stre 7H 93
(off Manor Rd.)
All Saints Gro. WN2: Hin 6A 54
All Saints Pl. BL8: Bury 1J 41
All Saints' Rd. SK4: Stoc 4B 108
All Saints St. BL1: Bolt 1K 7 (4G 39)
M40: Man 5A 80

All Saints Ter. OL12: Roch 3F 28
Allscott Way WN4: A Mak 7F 70
Allsopp St. BL3: Bolt 5L 7 (6G 38)
Alma Cl. SK11: Macc 5E 130
WN8: Uph 4G 50
Alma Ct. M15: Man 5D 94
(off Moss La. W.)
WN8: Uph 4G 50
Alma Dr. PR7: Char R 1B 18
Alma Grn. WN8: Uph 4F 50
Alma Gro. WN3: Wig 9B 52
Alma Hill WN8: Uph 4F 50
Alma Ind. Est. OL12: Roch 4D 28
Alma La. SK9: Wilm 8F 122
Alma Pde. WN8: Uph 4G 50
ALMA PARK 9N 95
Alma Rd. BL5: W'ton 3H 55
M19: Man 9M 95
M33: Sale 6E 104
SK4: Stoc 3N 107
SK7: H Gro 7L 119
WN8: Uph 4G 50
Alma St. BL3: Bolt 8D 38
BL3: Lit L 9B 40
BL4: Kea 6B 58
M26: Rad 7F 40
M29: Tyld 2A 74
M30: Ecc 9F 76
M46: Ath 8L 55
OL12: Roch 4D 28
SK15: Stal 8E 82
WA12: N Wil 6E 86
WN7: Lei 2G 72
Alma Wlk. WN8: Uph 4G 50
Alma Works SK16: Duk 9C 6 (9M 81)
Alminstone Cl. M40: Man 6B 80
Almond Av. BL9: Bury 1B 42
ALMOND BROOK 2M 33
Almond Brook Rd.
WN6: She, Stan 2M 33
Almond Cl. M6: Sal 8N 77
M35: Fail 4D 80
OL15: Lit 8K 15
SK3: Stoc 8A 108
Almond Ct. SK16: Duk 9N 81
(off Combermere St.)
Almond Cres. WN6: Stan 5C 34
Almond Dr. M33: Sale 2F 104
Almond Gro. BL1: Bolt 1G 38
WN5: Wig 5B 52
Almond Rd. OL4: O'ham 2A 64
Almond St. BL1: Bolt 9G 22
BL4: Farn 3K 57
M40: Man 6G 79
Almond Tree Rd. SK8: Chea H 6M 117
Almond Wlk. M31: Part 5E 102
(off Wood La.)
Almond Way SK14: Hyde 7D 98
Alms Hill Rd. M8: Man 3F 78
Almshouses M33: Sale 4L 105
Alness Rd. M16: Whall R 6D 94
Alnwick Cl. WN2: Asp 7N 35
Alnwick Dr. BL9: Bury 7M 41
Alnwick Rd. M9: Man 6J 61
Alperton Wlk. M40: Man 6B 80
(off Thaxmead Dr.)
Alpha Ct. M34: Dent 6G 97
Alpha Ct. Ind. Est. M34: Dent 6G 97
Alphagate Dr. M34: Dent 6G 96
Alpha Pl. M15: Man 8E 4
Alpha Rd. M32: Stre 7J 93
Alpha St. M6: Sal 7M 77
M11: Man 2C 96
M26: Rad 8F 40
Alpha St. W. M6: Sal 7L 77
Alphin Cl. OL3: G'fld 6L 65
OL5: Mos 8H 65
Alphingate Cl. SK15: C'ook 6G 82
Alphin Sq. OL5: Mos 1G 83
Alphonsus St. M16: Old T 5B 94
Alpine Dr. OL2: O'ham 9G 44
OL12: W'le 8G 14
OL16: Miln 6L 29
WN7: Lei 2E 72
Alpine Rd. SK1: Stoc 1N 9 (6E 108)
(not continuous)
Alpine St. M11: Man 7N 79
WA12: N Wil 6D 86
Alpington Wlk. M40: Man 9A 62
(off Ogmore Wlk.)
Alport Av. M16: Whall R 7B 94
Alport Gro. SK13: Gam 7A 100
(off Melandra Castle Rd.)
Alport Lea SK13: Gam 7A 100
(off Hathersage Cres.)
Alport Way SK13: Gam 7A 100
(off Melandra Castle Rd.)
Alresford Rd. M6: Sal 5K 77
M24: Mid 6L 61
Alric Wlk. M22: Wyth 7D 116
Alsager Cl. M21: Cho H 2A 106
Alsfeld Way SK22: N Mil 7K 121
Alsham Wlk. M8: Man 4E 78
(off Heatherdale Dr.)
Alsop Av. M7: Sal 3A 78
Alstead Av. WA15: Hale 4G 115
Alston Av. M32: Stre 6H 93
M33: Sale 5F 104
OL2: Shaw 4M 45
Alston Cl. SK7: H Gro 6E 118
Alstone Dr. WA14: Alt 1A 114
Alstone Rd. SK4: Stoc 2A 108
Alston Gdns. M19: Man 3L 107
Alston Lea M46: Ath 7N 55
Alston Rd. M18: Man 4C 96
WN2: Wig 1J 53
Alston St. BL3: Bolt 9F 38
BL8: Bury 1J 41
Alston Wlk. M24: Mid 1H 61
ALT 8N 63
Altair Av. M22: Wyth 6C 116
Altair Pl. M7: Sal 6B 78
Altcar Gro. SK5: Stoc 7C 96
Altcar Wlk. M22: Wyth 5B 116
Alt Cl. WN7: Lei 4F 72
Alt Fold Dr. OL8: O'ham 8N 63

Alt Gro. OL6: A Lyne 4M 81
Altham Cl. BL9: Bury 5K 41
Altham Wlk. M40: Man 4M 79
(off Craiglands Av.)
ALT HILL 1N 81
Alt Hill La. OL6: A Lyne 2M 81
Alt Hill Rd. OL6: A Lyne 1N 81
Althorn Wlk. M23: Wyth 2N 115
Althorpe Wlk. M40: Man 6B 80
(off Eastmoor Dr.)
Alt La. OL6: O'ham 9N 63
OL8: O'ham 9N 63
Alton Av. M41: Urm 7L 91
Alton Cl. BL9: Bury 7N 41
OL6: A Lyne 3N 81
WN4: A Mak 6D 70
Alton Dr. SK10: Macc 2K 131
Alton Rd. SK9: Wilm 6E 122
Alton Sq. M11: Man 2C 96
Alton St. OL8: O'ham 8K 63
Alton Towers M16: Whall R 8C 94
ALTRINCHAM 3D 6 (3D 114)
Altrincham Crematorium
WA14: D Mas 8L 103
Altrincham FC 3F 114
Altrincham Garrick Playhouse
1D 6 (1D 114)
Altrincham Golf Course 2F 6 (2F 114)
Altrincham Leisure Cen.
3E 6 (3E 114)
Altrincham Retail Pk.
WA14: B'ath 9C 104
Altrincham Rd. M22: Shar 9B 106
(not continuous)
M23: Wyth 9K 105
SK8: Gat 1C 116
SK9: Sty 2C 122
SK9: Sty, Wilm 3A 122
Altrincham Station (Rail & Metro)
3E 6 (3E 114)
Altrincham St. M1: Man 7K 5 (1G 94)
Alt Rd. OL6: A Lyne 4M 81
Alt Wlk. M45: Whitef 1B 60
Alum Cres. BL9: Bury 9N 41
Alvanley Cl. M33: Sale 7H 105
WN5: Wig 2N 51
Alvanley Cres. SK3: Stoc 1A 118
Alvanley Ind. Est.
SK6: Bred 4K 109
Alvan Sq. M11: Man 2C 96
Alva Rd. OL4: O'ham 1A 64
Alvaston Av. SK4: Stoc 5N 107
Alvaston Rd. M18: Man 5C 96
Alveley Av. M20: Man 3H 107
Alverstone Rd. M20: Man 2H 107
Alverton Ct. WN3: I Mak 6H 53
Alveston Cl. SK10: Macc 3D 130
Alveston Dr. SK9: Wilm 6H 123
Alvington Gro. SK7: H Gro 6E 118
Alvingham Av. OL8: O'ham 7J 63
Alvon Ct. SK14: Hyde 7D 98
Alwin Rd. OL2: Shaw 4L 45
Alwinton Av. SK4: Stoc 5K 107
Alworth Rd. M9: Man 6J 61
Alwyn Cl. WN7: Lei 9H 73
Alwyn Dr. M13: Man 5K 95
Alwyn St. WN1: Wig 2G 53
Alwyn Ter. WN1: Wig 5M 9 (2G 53)
Amani St. M14: Man 6F 94
Amar St. WN2: I Mak 4J 53
Ambassador Pl.
WA15: Alt 1E 6 (2E 114)
Amber Ct. WN5: Wig 2M 51
Amber Gdns. SK16: Duk 1M 97
(off Railway St.)
WN2: Hin 7A 54
Ambergate M46: Ath 9M 55
WN8: Skel 4A 50
Amber Gro. BL5: W'ton 1H 55
Amberhill Way M28: Wors 5G 75
Amberley Cl. BL3: Bolt 7A 38
WN2: Wig 1J 53
Amberley Dr. M23: Wyth 3N 115
M44: Irl 8H 91
WA15: Haleb 7H 115
Amberley Rd. M33: Sale 3E 104
SK11: Macc 6E 130
Amberley Wlk. OL9: Chad 4G 62
Amberswood WN2: Hin 5N 53
Amberswood Cl. WN2: I Mak 4L 53
AMBERSWOOD COMMON 5M 53
Amberwood OL9: Chad 3C 62
Amberwood Dr. M23: Wyth 1K 115
Amblecote Dr. E. M38: Lit H 5H 57
Amblecote Dr. W. M38: Lit H 5H 57
Ambleside SK15: Stal 7D 82
WN2: I Mak 3L 53
WN5: Wig 4N 51
Ambleside Av. OL7: A Lyne 6K 81
WA15: Tim 2J 115
Ambleside Cl. BL2: Bolt 9N 23
M24: Mid 2K 61
SK11: Macc 6D 130
Ambleside Ct. SK8: Chea 2H 117
SK15: Stal 7D 82
Ambleside Pl. WA11: St H 9F 68
Ambleside Rd. M41: Urm 8M 91
SK5: Stoc 2D 108
Ambleside Wlk. M9: Man 9M 61
Amblethorn Dr. BL1: Bolt 8E 22
Ambrose Av. WN7: Lei 1G 72
Ambrose Ct. M22: Nor 7C 106
Ambrose Cres. OL3: Dig 9L 47
Ambrose Dr. M20: Man 4D 106
Ambrose Fold WN7: Lei 1G 72
Ambrose Gdns. M20: Man 4C 106
Ambrose St. M12: Man 2M 95
OL11: Roch 8D 28
SK14: Hyde 1B 110
Ambuscade Ct. M41: Urm 7M 91
Ambush St. M11: Man 2D 96
Amelan Ho. M25: Pres 1N 77
Amelia St. SK14: Hyde 7B 98
(off Lumn Hollow)
Amelia St. W. M34: Dent 5K 97
Amersham WN8: Skel 4A 50

Amersham Cl. M41: Urm 4B **92**
SK10: Macc 1G **131**
Amersham Pl. M19: Man 2M **107**
Amersham St. M5: Sal 9M **77**
Amesbury Dr. WN3: Wins 9N **51**
Amesbury Gro. SK5: Stoc 3D **108**
Amesbury Rd. M9: Man 7K **61**
Amethyst Cl. WN2: Asp 1K **53**
AMF Bowling
Macclesfield 9H **131**
Wigan 9H **9** (4E **52**)
Amherst Rd. M14: Man 1H **107**
M20: Man 1H **107**
Amis Gro. WA3: Low 1A **88**
Amlwch Av. SK2: Stoc 1H **119**
Ammons Way OL3: Del 7J **47**
Ammon Wrigley Cl.
OL1: O'ham 1D **8** (4K **63**)
Amory St. M12: Man 7M **5** (1H **95**)
Amos Av. M40: Man 6A **80**
Amos St. M6: Sal 8L **77**
M9: Man 3L **79**
Ampleforth Gdns. M26: Rad 7E **40**
Ampney Cl. M30: Ecc 9B **76**
Amport Wlk. M40: Man 9A **62**
Amwell St. M8: Man 3G **79**
Amy St. M24: Mid 2N **61**
OL12: Roch 4N **27**
Anaconda Dr. M3: Sal 1D **4** (7D **78**)
Ancaster Wlk. M40: Man 9A **62**
Anchorage Quay M50: Sal 1N **93**
Anchorage Rd. M41: Urm 8G **93**
Anchorage Stop (Metro) 1N **93**
Anchorage Wlk. *M18: Man* *3A* **96**
(off Briercliffe Cl.)
Anchor Cl. M19: Man 8A **96**
Anchor Ct. M8: Man 1E **78**
SK9: Wilm 6G **123**
Anchor La. BL4: Farn, Walk 3G **57**
Anchorside Cl. M21: Cho H 1A **106**
Anchor St. OL1: O'ham 3K **63**
ANCOATS 9J **79**
Ancoats Gro. M4: Man 1J **95**
Ancoats Gro. Nth. M4: Man 9J **79**
Ancoats St. OL4: Lees 5B **64**
Ancroft Dr. WN2: Hin 8N **53**
Ancroft Gdns. *BL3: Bolt* *1D* **56**
(off Maltby Dr.)
Ancroft St. M15: Man 3D **94**
Anderby Wlk. BL5: W'ton 1G **54**
Anderson St. SK10: Macc 4G **130**
ANDERTON 5L **19**
Anderton Cl. BL8: Bury 3F **40**
Anderton Ct. BL6: Hor 9C **20**
Anderton Gro. OL6: A Lyne 5B **82**
Anderton La. BL6: Hor 1A **36**
Anderton Outdoor Education &
Activities Cen. 5A **20**
Andertons La. SK10: Hen 3A **130**
SK11: Hen 3A **130**
Anderton St. PR7: Adl 6K **19**
WN2: I Mak 4J **53**
Anderton Way SK9: Hand 3J **123**
WN2: Asp 1L **53**
(not continuous)
Andoc Av. M30: Ecc 9G **76**
Andover Av. M24: Mid 6N **61**
Andover Cres. WN3: Wins 9N **51**
Andover Rd. WA11: Hay 1B **86**
Andover St. M30: Ecc 9C **76**
Andover Wlk. M8: Man 2F **78**
Andre St. M11: Man 8A **80**
Andrew Av. WN5: Bil 5K **69**
Andrew Cl. BL8: G'mount 4F **24**
M26: Rad 2J **59**
Andrew Ct. *M20: Man* *2G* **106**
(off Aldborough Cl.)
Andrew Gro. SK10: Macc 5L **131**
SK16: Duk 1A **98**
Andrew Ho. SK4: Stoc 4N **107**
Andrew La. BL1: Bolt 7G **22**
SK6: H Lan 6B **120**
Andrew Rd. M9: Man 1J **79**
Andrews Av. M41: Urm 6M **91**
Andrews Bldgs. *OL5: Mos* *1H* **83**
(off Bk. Micklehurst Rd.)
Andrews Cl. M34: Dent 8M **97**
Andrew's Ter. *BL5: W'ton* *2G* **55**
(off Church St.)
Andrew St. BL9: Bury 8N **7** (2N **41**)
M24: Mid 4A **62**
M35: Fail 2C **80**
M43: Droy 6G **81**
OL5: Mos 2F **82**
OL6: A Lyne 5A **82**
OL9: Chad 3F **62**
SK4: Stoc 1H **9** (6B **108**)
SK6: Comp 6D **110**
SK14: Hyde 6C **98**
Andy Nicholson Wlk. *M9: Man* *2L* **79**
(off Amos St.)
Anerley Rd. M20: Man 4G **106**
Anfield Cl. BL9: Bury 9A **42**
Anfield Rd. BL3: Bolt 9F **38**
M33: Sale 3J **105**
M40: Man 1B **80**
SK8: Chea H 4L **117**
Angela Av. OL2: O'ham 1J **63**
Angela St. M15: Man 9C **4** (2C **94**)
Angelbank BL6: Hor 2B **36**
Angel Cl. SK16: Duk 1M **97**
Angelico Ri. OL1: O'ham 9A **46**
Angelo St. BL1: Bolt 1E **38**
Angel St. M4: Man 1J **5** (7F **78**)
M34: Dent 5L **97**
SK7: H Gro 4H **119**
Angel Trad. Est. M4: Man 1J **5**
Angier Gro. M34: Dent 6K **97**
Anglers Rest M44: Cad 3F **102**
Anglesea Av. SK2: Stoc 1D **118**
Anglesey Cl. OL7: A Lyne 4L **81**
Anglesey Dr. SK12: Poy 9J **119**
Anglesey Gro. SK8: Chea 1M **117**
Anglesey Rd. OL7: A Lyne 4K **81**
Anglesey Water SK12: Poy 9J **119**
Angleside Av. M19: Man 4K **107**
Angle St. BL2: Bolt 3J **39**
Anglezarke Rd. PR6: Adl 6K **19**
WA12: N Wil 7D **86**
Anglia Gro. BL3: Bolt 8D **38**
Angora Dr. M3: Sal 1B **4** (7C **78**)
Angouleme Pl. BL9: Bury . . .7L **7** (2M **41**)
Angouleme Retail Pk.
BL9: Bury 8M **7** (2M **41**)
Angouleme Way
BL9: Bury 8J **7** (3L **41**)
Angus Av. OL10: H'ood 3F **42**
WN7: Lei 3E **72**
Angus Wlk. SK10: Macc 2D **130**
Aniline St. M11: Man 9N **79**
(Croft St.)
M11: Man 1D **96**
(Wells Cl.)
Animal World 1B **38**
Anita St. M4: Man 2L **5** (8G **79**)
Anjou Blvd. WN5: Wig 3B **52**
Annable Rd. M18: Man 3C **96**
M43: Droy 9F **80**
M44: Irl 9G **91**
SK6: Bred 5H **109**
Annald Sq. M43: Droy 1E **96**
Annandale Gdns. WN8: Uph 4E **50**
Annan Gro. WN4: A Mak 5H **71**
Annan St. M34: Dent 5K **97**
Anne Cl. OL7: A Lyne 4L **81**
Annecy Cl. BL8: Bury 9H **25**
Anne Line Cl. *OL11: Roch* *8E* **28**
(off Wellfield St.)
Anne Nuttall Rd.
M15: Man 9C **4** (2C **94**)
Annersley Av. OL2: Shaw 6L **45**
Annesley Ct. M30: Ecc 8E **76**
Annesley Cres. WN3: Wig 8C **52**
Annesley Gdns. *M18: Man* *3B* **96**
(off Keary Cl.)
Annesley Rd. M40: Man 1C **80**
Anne St. SK16: Duk 1A **98**
Annette Av. WA12: N Wil 4D **86**
Annie Darby Ct. M9: Man 3J **79**
Annie St. BL0: Ram 1G **25**
M6: Sal 8L **77**
Annis Cl. SK9: A Edg 3G **126**
Annisdale Cl. M30: Ecc 8B **76**
Annisfield Av. OL3: G'fld 6L **65**
Annis Rd. BL3: Bolt 8C **38**
SK9: A Edg 3G **126**
Annis St. M9: Man 3K **79**
Ann La. M29: Ast 5D **74**
Ann Sq. OL4: O'ham 3A **64**
Ann St. BL4: Kea 4M **57**
M34: Dent 6J **97**
OL7: A Lyne 1K **97**
OL10: H'ood 1J **43**
OL11: Roch 9C **8** (7D **28**)
OL12: Roch *2H* **29**
(off Oakcliffe Rd.)
OL16: Roch 9C **8** (7D **28**)
SK5: Stoc 4C **108**
SK14: Hyde 6N **97**
WN7: Lei 2G **72**
Anscombe Cl. M40: Man 7J **79**
Ansdell Av. M21: Cho H 9B **94**
Ansdell Dr. M43: Droy 8C **80**
Ansdell Rd. BL6: Hor 9E **20**
OL16: Roch 9F **28**
SK5: Stoc 8E **96**
WN5: Wig 6A **52**
Ansdell St. M8: Man 3F **78**
Ansell Cl. M18: Man 3B **96**
Anselms Ct. OL8: O'ham 7G **63**
Ansford Av. WN2: Abr 2L **71**
Ansford Wlk. *M9: Man* *4H* **79**
(off Hendham Va.)
Anshaw Cl. BL7: Bel 1L **21**
Ansleigh Av. M8: Man 1F **78**
Ansley Gro. SK4: Stoc 5N **107**
Anslow Cl. M40: Man 5J **79**
Anson Av. M27: Swin 4E **76**
Anson Cl. SK7: Bram 1D **124**
Anson Engine Museum, The 2N **125**
Anson Pl. WN5: Wig 3N **51**
Anson Rd. M14: Man 5J **95**
M27: Swin 4E **76**
M34: Dent 7E **96**
SK9: Wilm 5K **123**
SK12: Poy 2M **125**
Anson St. BL1: Bolt 1G **38**
M30: Ecc 7B **76**
WN5: Wig 4C **52**
Answell Av. M8: Man 9F **60**
Antares Av. M7: Sal 7C **78**
Anthistle Ct. *M5: Sal* *8K* **77**
(off Sheader Dr.)
Anthony Cl. M12: Man 2K **95**
Anthony St. OL5: Mos 1E **82**
Anthorn Rd. WN3: Wig 8B **52**
Antilles Cl. M12: Man 5M **95**
Antler Ct. WN4: A Mak 4E **70**
Anton Wlk. *M9: Man* *3J* **79**
(off Shiredale Dr.)
Antrim Cl. M19: Man 6J **107**
WN3: Wins 9N **51**
Anvil Cl. WN5: Orr 6H **51**
Anvil St. M1: Man 8G **5**
Anvil Way OL1: O'ham 1C **8** (4J **63**)
Anyon Vs. BL6: Hor 9D **20**
Apethorn La. SK14: Hyde 9N **97**
Apfel La. OL9: Chad 4F **62**
Apollo Av. BL9: Bury 9M **41**
Apollo Cinema
Altrincham 4D **6** (3D **114**)
Apollo Wlk. *M12: Man* *3M* **95**
(off Bridgend Cl.)
Apperley Grange M30: Ecc 6E **76**
Appian Way M7: Sal 4D **78**
Apple Blossom Gro. M44: Cad 4E **102**
Appleby Av. M12: Man 6M **95**
SK14: Hyde 4N **97**
WA15: Tim 2J **115**
Appleby Cl. BL8: Bury 2F **40**
SK3: Stoc 2B **118**
SK11: Macc 7D **130**
Appleby Cres. WA16: Mob 4N **133**
Appleby Gdns. BL2: Bolt 3H **39**
BL9: Bury 9M **41**
Appleby Lodge M14: Man 7J **95**
Appleby Rd. SK8: Gat 3G **116**
Appleby Wlk. *OL2: O'ham* *8J* **45**
(off Shaw St.)
Apple Cl. OL8: O'ham 8N **63**
Applecross Wlk. *M11: Man* *1A* **96**
(off Bill Williams Cl.)
Appledale SK10: Macc 9G **128**
Apple Dell Av. WA3: Gol 9M **71**
Appledore Dr. BL2: Bolt 2N **39**
M23: Wyth 9K **105**
Appledore Wlk. OL9: Chad 5F **62**
Appleford Av. M23: Wyth 3N **115**
Appleford Dr. M8: Man 4G **78**
Apple Hey WN6: App B 4G **33**
Applemint Cl. WA14: W Tim 8B **104**
Apple St. SK14: Hyde 1F **110**
WN7: Lei 6K **73**
Applethwaite WN2: I Mak 3L **53**
Appleton Ct. M33: Sale 4H **105**
Appleton Dr. SK13: Glos 9H **101**
Appleton Gro. M33: Sale 6E **104**
WN3: Wig 7B **52**
Appleton La. BL5: W'ton 2H **55**
Appleton Rd. SK4: Stoc 2B **108**
WA15: Hale 6E **114**
Appleton St. M8: Man 3G **78**
WN3: Wig 8H **9** (3E **52**)
Appleton Wlk. *SK9: Wilm* *5J* **123**
(off Colshaw Dr.)
Apple Tree Ct. M5: Sal 8N **77**
Apple Tree Rd. SK22: N Mil 6L **121**
Apple Tree Wlk. M33: Sale 3C **104**
Apple Way M24: Mid 5N **61**
Applewood OL9: Chad 4B **62**
Appleyard Cl. M27: Pen 2K **77**
APPLEY BRIDGE 4G **33**
Appley Bridge Station (Rail) 5G **33**
Appley Cl. WN6: App B 2G **32**
Appley La. Nth. WN6: App B 2G **32**
Appley La. Sth. WN6: App B 6G **32**
WN8: Roby M 6G **32**
Apprentice Ct. *M9: Man* *2K* **79**
(off Caversham Dr.)
Apprentice La. SK9: Sty 3E **122**
April Cl. M13: Man 4J **95**
OL8: O'ham 7N **63**
April Ri. SK10: Macc 3E **130**
Apsley Cl. WA14: Bow 6B **114**
Apsley Gro. M12: Man 9N **5** (3H **95**)
WA14: Bow 6B **114**
Apsley Pl. OL6: A Lyne 8A **6** (8L **81**)
Apsley Rd. M34: Dent 5K **97**
Apsley Side *OL5: Mos* *2F* **82**
(off Abney Rd.)
Apsley St. SK1: Stoc 2M **9** (7D **108**)
Aquarius La. *M6: Sal* *6B* **78**
(off Gemini Rd.)
Aquarius St. M15: Man 4F **94**
Aqueduct Bus. Pk. SK6: Mar 8C **110**
Aqueduct Rd. BL3: Bolt 8K **39**
Aragon Dr. OL10: H'ood 2H **43**
Aragon Way SK6: Mar 1B **120**
Arbor Av. M19: Man 1L **107**
Arbor Dr. M19: Man 1L **107**
Arbor Gro. M38: Lit H 7F **56**
M43: Droy 7D **80**
Arbory Av. M40: Man 2N **79**
Arbory Cl. WN7: Lei 5L **73**
Arbour Cl. BL9: Bury 7L **25**
M6: Sal 7M **77**
SK10: Macc 1H **131**
Arbour Ct. SK6: Mar 2B **120**
Arbour Cres. SK10: Macc 1H **131**
Arbour La. WN6: Stan 3M **33**
Arbour M. SK10: Macc 1H **131**
Arbournay St. SK10: Macc 3J **131**
Arbour Rd. OL4: O'ham 7B **64**
Arbroath St. M11: Man 9C **80**
Arbury Av. OL11: Roch 8C **28**
SK3: Stoc 9M **107**
Arcade, The SK15: Stal 1C **98**
Arcades, The
OL6: A Lyne 7C **6** (7M **81**)
Arcade St. WN1: Wig 8K **9** (3F **52**)
Arcadia Av. M33: Sale 7G **105**
Arcadia Sports Cen. 8M **95**
Archer Av. BL2: Bolt 4K **39**
Archer Cl. SK10: Boll 6J **129**
Archer Gro. BL2: Bolt 4K **39**
Archer Pk. M24: Mid 3K **61**
Archer Pl. M32: Stre 6F **92**
Archer St. M11: Man 8M **79**
M28: Wors 3F **74**
OL5: Mos 9F **64**
SK2: Stoc 2G **118**
WN7: Lei 8K **73**
Arches, The BL1: Bolt 3L **7**
Archie St. M5: Sal 2N **93**
Arch La. WN4: Gars 7L **69**
Arch St. BL1: Bolt 3H **39**
Archway M15: Man 3E **94**
Archway Wlk. WA12: N Wil 6H **87**
Arclid Cl. SK9: Wilm 4K **123**
Arcon Cl. OL16: Roch 7J **29**
Arcon Dr. M16: Whall R 6D **94**
Arcon Pl. SK1: Stoc 5F **108**
WA14: Alt 1A **114**
Arcon Rd. PR7: Cop 4B **18**
Ardale Av. M40: Man 9A **62**
Ardcombe Av. M9: Man 6H **61**
Ardeen Wlk. M13: Man 9M **5**
Arden Av. M24: Mid 6N **61**
Ardenbrook Ri. SK10: P'bury 7C **128**
Arden Bldgs. SK3: Stoc 4K **9**
Arden Bus. Cen. SK6: Bred 2J **109**
Arden Cl. BL9: Bury 4L **41**
OL6: A Lyne 4C **82**
SK8: H Grn 8H **117**
SK13: Glos 9C **100**
Arden Ct. M21: Cho H 1A **106**
SK7: Bram 6B **118**
Arden St. SK22: N Mil 8N **121**
Ardenfield M34: Dent 1L **109**
Ardenfield Cl. M26: Rad 2H **59**
Ardenfield Dr. M22: Wyth 4D **116**
Arden Gro. M40: Man 1A **80**
Arden Ho. OL2: O'ham 8J **45**
Arden Lodge Rd. M23: Wyth 9L **105**
ARDEN PARK 5H **109**
Arden Rd. SK6: Bred 1J **109**
Ardens Cl. M27: Swin 9D **58**
Arden St. OL9: Chad 8E **62**
SK22: N Mil 8M **121**
Ardent Way M25: Pres 1A **78**
Arden Wlk. M33: Sale 3C **104**
Arderne Pl. SK9: A Edg 4F **126**
Arderne Rd. WA15: Tim 8D **104**
Ardern Fld. St. SK1: Stoc 9D **108**
Ardern Gro. SK1: Stoc 8D **108**
Ardern Rd. M8: Man 9E **60**
Ardern Wlk. SK1: Stoc 2K **9**
Ardingley Wlk. M23: Wyth 8K **105**
Ardley Rd. BL6: Hor 9E **20**
Ardmore Wlk. M22: Wyth 5D **116**
ARDWICK 9M **5** (2H **95**)
Ardwick Grn. Nth.
M12: Man 8M **5** (2H **95**)
Ardwick Grn. Sth.
M13: Man 8M **5** (2H **95**)
Ardwick Sports Hall 4K **95**
Ardwick Station (Rail) 2K **95**
Ardwick Ter. *M12: Man* *3J* **95**
(off Aked Cl.)
Arena App. BL6: Hor 5E **36**
Argo St. BL3: Bolt 8E **38**
Argosy Dr. M30: Ecc 2N **91**
M90: Man A 8M **115**
Argus St. OL8: O'ham 9G **62**
Argyle Av. M14: Man 5K **95**
M28: Walk 6K **57**
M45: Whitef 3N **59**
Argyle Cres. OL10: H'ood 3G **43**
Argyle Pde. OL10: H'ood 3F **42**
Argyle St. BL9: Bury 9M **25**
HD7: Mars 1H **49**
M18: Man 4B **96**
M27: Swin 3E **76**
M43: Droy 9E **80**
M46: Ath 9L **55**
OL1: O'ham 3M **63**
OL5: Mos 1F **82**
OL10: H'ood 3E **42**
OL16: Roch 3G **29**
SK7: H Gro 5J **119**
WN2: Hin 6A **54**
Argyll Av. M32: Stre 7H **93**
Argyll Cl. M35: Fail 3F **80**
SK10: Macc 3E **130**
WN4: Gars 6N **69**
Argyll Pk. Rd. M35: Fail 3F **80**
Argyll Rd. OL9: Chad 8D **62**
SK8: Chea 2L **117**
Argyll St. OL6: A Lyne 7B **82**
WN5: Wig 5C **52**
Ariel Gdns. WA3: Cul 7J **89**
Ariel Wlk. WA3: Low 1B **88**
Arkendale Cl. M35: Fail 3G **80**
Arkenshaw Rd. WA3: Cro 9C **88**
Arkholme M28: Wors 2H **75**
Arkholme Wlk. M40: Man 3N **79**
Arkle Av. SK9: Hand 2K **123**
Arkle Dr. OL9: Chad 3D **62**
Arkley Wlk. *M13: Man* *3H* **95**
(off Sefton Cl.)
Ark St. M19: Man 7M **95**
Arkwright Cl. BL1: Bolt 3D **38**
Arkwright Dr. SK6: Mar 1D **120**
Arkwright Rd. SK6: Mar 9D **110**
Arkwright St. BL6: Hor 2E **36**
OL9: O'ham 5G **62**
Arkwright Way OL11: Roch 2E **44**
Arlen Ct. BL2: Bolt 7J **39**
Arlen Rd. BL2: Bolt 7J **39**
Arlen Way OL10: H'ood 2G **43**
Arley Av. BL9: Bury 7L **25**
M20: Man 3E **106**
Arley Cl. SK11: Macc 5E **130**
SK16: Duk 3A **98**
WA14: W Tim 8D **104**
WN2: Asp 1L **53**
Arley Dr. M33: Sale 6G **105**
OL2: Shaw 4N **45**
Arley Gro. SK3: Stoc 3B **118**
WA13: Lym 5B **112**
Arley Ho. M23: Wyth 3N **115**
Arley La. WN1: Hai 3G **34**
Arley Lodge Nature Reserve 1F **34**
Arleymere Cl. SK8: Chea H 4L **117**
Arley Moss Wlk. M13: Man 9L **5**
Arley St. M26: Rad 2H **59**
WN3: I Mak 7H **53**
Arley Way *M34: Dent* *8L* **97**
(off Two Trees La.)
M46: Ath 9N **55**
Arlies Cl. SK15: Stal 6D **82**
Arlies La. SK15: Stal 6E **82**
Arlies St. OL6: A Lyne 6A **82**
Arlington Av. M25: Pres 9A **60**
M27: Swin 4D **76**
M34: Dent 7L **97**
Arlington Cl. BL9: Sum 3J **25**
OL2: O'ham 1J **63**
Arlington Cres. SK9: Wilm 9D **122**
Arlington Dr. SK2: Stoc 4E **118**
SK11: Macc 5E **130**
SK12: Poy 3H **125**
WN7: Lei 1E **88**
Arlington M. SK3: Stoc 3C **118**
Arlington Rd. M32: Stre 7H **93**
SK8: Chea 3H **117**
Arlington St. BL3: Bolt 9G **39**
M3: Sal 2C **4** (8C **78**)
M8: Man 2E **78**
OL6: A Lyne 7F **6** (7N **81**)
Arlington Way SK9: Wilm 9D **122**
Arliss Av. M19: Man 9M **95**
Armadale Av. M9: Man 7M **61**
Armadale Cl. SK3: Stoc 2C **118**
Armadale Ct. BL3: Bolt 7N **37**
Armadale Rd. BL3: Bolt 6N **37**
SK16: Duk 1N **97**
Armdale Ri. OL4: O'ham 2B **64**
Armentieres Sq. SK15: Stal 9D **82**
Armentieres Way *SK15: Stal* *9D* **82**
(off Melbourne St.)
Armitage Av. M38: Lit H 7G **57**
Armitage Cl. M24: Mid 4J **61**
OL8: O'ham 8G **63**
SK14: Hyde 9B **98**
Armitage Gro. M38: Lit H 7G **57**
Armitage Ho. *M6: Sal* *7J* **77**
(off Edgehill Rd.)
Armitage Owen Wlk. *M40: Man* . . .*3M* **79**
(off Brendon Av.)
Armitage Rd. WA14: Alt . . .4D **6** (4D **114**)
Armitage Sports Cen. 8K **95**
Armitage St. M30: Ecc 9C **76**
Armit Rd. OL3: G'fld 7H **65**
Armitstead St. WN2: Hin 7N **53**
Armitt St. SK11: Macc 5G **131**
Armour Pl. *M9: Man* *9H* **61**
(off Oakworth St.)
Armoury Bank WN4: A Mak 7E **70**
Armoury Ct. M. *SK11: Macc* *6G* **130**
(off Crompton Rd.)
Armoury St. SK3: Stoc 5K **9** (8C **108**)
Armoury Towers *SK11: Macc* *6F* **130**
(off Barracks Sq.)
Arm Rd. OL15: Lit 9J **15**
Armstrong Hurst Cl. OL12: Roch . . .2F **28**
Armstrong St. BL6: Hor 2E **36**
WN2: Asp 9K **35**
Arncliffe Cl. *BL4: Farn* *2L* **57**
(off Spring St.)
BL9: Bury 5N **41**
WN2: Hin 7M **53**
Arncliffe Ct. WN2: Hin 6M **53**
Arncliffe Dr. M23: Wyth 4N **115**
Arncliffe Ri. OL4: O'ham 8D **46**
Arncot Rd. BL1: Bolt 8G **23**
Arncott Cl. OL2: O'ham 8L **45**
Arndale Shop. Cen.
M4: Man 3H **5** (8F **78**)
Arne Cl. SK2: Stoc 2L **119**
Arnesby Av. M33: Sale 3L **105**
Arnesby Gro. BL2: Bolt 4J **39**
Arne St. OL9: Chad 6E **62**
Arnfield Dr. M28: Wors 4J **75**
Arnfield La. SK13: Tin 1B **100**
Arnfield Rd. M20: Man 2G **107**
SK3: Stoc 2B **118**
Arnold & Margaret Wills Ho.
M25: Pres 1N **77**
Arnold Av. OL10: H'ood 5K **43**
SK14: Hyde 1C **110**
Arnold Bagnall Ct. OL11: Roch 9E **28**
Arnold Cl. SK16: Duk 2D **98**
Arnold Ct. *M16: Whall R* *8D* **94**
(off Wilbraham Rd.)
Arnold Dr. M24: Mid 9A **44**
M43: Droy 9E **80**
Arnold Pl. PR7: Chor 1D **18**
Arnold Rd. BL7: Eger 5G **22**
M16: Whall R 8D **94**
SK14: Hyde 1C **110**
Arnold St. BL1: Bolt 2D **38**
OL1: O'ham 3L **63**
OL6: A Lyne 5F **6** (6N **81**)
SK3: Stoc 9C **108**
Arnolds Yd. WA14: Alt 2D **6** (2D **114**)
Arnold Wlk. *M34: Dent* *1L* **109**
(off Wordsworth Rd.)
Arnott Cres. M15: Man 4E **94**
Arnside Av. OL9: Chad 6E **62**
SK4: Stoc 2B **108**
SK7: H Gro 5G **119**
WN2: I Mak 4K **53**
Arnside Cl. OL2: Shaw 5A **46**
SK6: H Lan 7B **120**
SK8: Gat 3G **117**
Arnside Dr. M6: Sal 7H **77**
OL11: Roch 8K **27**
SK14: Hyde 5N **97**
Arnside Gro. BL2: Bolt 4N **39**
M33: Sale 2H **105**
Arnside Rd. WN2: Hin 6C **54**
WN5: Orr 3M **51**
Arnside St. M14: Man 7G **94**
Arosa Ct. M20: Man 1H **107**
Arran Av. M32: Stre 7G **93**
M33: Sale 5J **105**
OL8: O'ham 8K **63**
Arran Cl. BL3: Bolt 6N **37**
Arran Ct. *SK8: Chea H* *5M* **117**
(off Vaudrey Dr.)
Arrandale Ct. M41: Urm 6D **92**
Arran Gdns. M41: Urm 4C **92**
(not continuous)
Arran Gro. M26: Rad 7E **40**
Arran Rd. SK16: Duk 2N **97**
Arran St. M7: Sal 4C **78**
M40: Man 2L **79**
Arran Wlk. OL10: H'ood 3F **42**
Arras Gro. M34: Dent 6D **96**
Arreton Sq. *M14: Man* *6J* **95**
(off Rusholme Gro.)
Arrivals Way M90: Man A 8A **116**
Arrowfield Rd. M21: Cho H 2C **106**
Arrowhill Rd. M26: Rad 4F **40**
Arrowscroft Way
SK14: Holl 4N **99**
Arrowsmith Ct. BL6: Hor 3G **36**
Arrowsmith Rd. WA11: Hay 2C **86**
Arrowsmith Wlk. *M11: Man* *9L* **79**
(off Redfield Cl.)
Arrow St. BL1: Bolt 1H **7** (4F **38**)
M7: Sal 5C **78**
WN7: Lei 7K **73**
Arrow Trad. Est. M34: Aud 4H **97**
ARTHILL 7J **113**
Arthill La. WA14: Lit B 7J **113**
Arthington St.
OL16: Roch 6G **8** (5F **28**)
Arthog Dr. WA15: Hale 7F **114**

Arthog Rd. M20: Man 5H 107
WA15: Hale 7F 114
Arthur Av. M28: Walk 6K 57
Arthur La. BL2: Ain, Bolt 1A 40
Arthur Millwood Ct. M3: Sal 4C 4
Arthur Pits OL11: Roch 6L 27
Arthur Rd. M16: Old T 6B 94
Arthurs La. OL3: G'fld 5L 65
Arthur St. BL3: Lit L 9B 40
BL4: Farn 3L 57
(off Ellesmere St.)
BL8: Bury 2J 41
M25: Pres 7M 59
M27: Swin 3D 76
M28: Walk 9N 57
(Crosby Av.)
M28: Walk 1M 75
(Park Ct.)
M30: Ecc 9C 76
OL2: Shaw 5M 45
OL10: H'ood 2J 43
OL12: Roch 6A 8 (5B 28)
SK5: Stoc 1C 108
(not continuous)
SK14: Hyde 8N 97
WN2: Hin 6A 54
WN7: Lei 6G 73
Arthur Ter. SK5: Stoc 1C 108
(off Arthur St.)
Artillery Ct. M13: Man 9M 5
Artillery Pl. M22: Wyth 3E 116
Artillery St. BL3: Bolt 7G 39
M3: Man 6E 4 (1D 94)
Artists La. SK10: N Ald 7F 126
ArTzu Gallery 3K 5
Arundale BL5: W'ton 1H 55
Arundale Av. M16: Whall R 8D 94
Arundale Cl. SK14: Mot 6J 99
Arundale Ct. M16: Whall R 8D 94
(off Arundale Av.)
Arundale Gro. SK14: Mot 6J 99
Arundel Av. M41: Urm 8K 91
M45: Whitef 4A 60
OL11: Roch 9C 28
SK7: H Gro 7H 119
Arundel Cl. BL8: Bury 7J 25
SK10: Macc 2K 131
SK15: C'ook 4J 83
WA15: Hale 6J 115
WA16: Knut 8G 132
Arundel Ct. M9: Man 6F 60
Arundel Dr. WN7: Lei 4H 73
Arundel Grange SK13: Glos 8C 100
Arundel Gro. SK2: Stoc 3F 118
Arundel Rd. SK8: Chea H 9M 117
Arundel St. BL1: Bolt 8F 22
M15: Man 8C 4 (2C 94)
M27: Ward 1C 76
OL4: O'ham 4N 63
OL5: Mos 1E 82
OL6: A Lyne 8B 82
OL11: Roch 9C 28
SK13: Glos 8E 100
WN2: Hin 6A 54
WN5: Wig 5C 52
Arundel Wlk. OL9: Chad 5E 62
Asbury Ct. M30: Ecc 7C 76
Asby Cl. M24: Mid 1J 61
Ascot Av. M32: Stre 6M 93
M33: Sale 5C 104
Ascot Cl. OL9: Chad 4G 62
OL11: Roch 5K 27
SK10: Macc 1G 130
Ascot Ct. M7: Sal 4C 78
Ascot Dr. M41: Urm 7K 91
M46: Ath 7N 55
SK7: H Gro 5L 119
Ascot Mdw. BL9: Bury 4L 41
Ascot Pde. M19: Man 2L 107
Ascot Rd. BL3: Lit L 9N 39
M40: Man 6N 79
Ascot Wlk. M6: Sal 5N 77
Ascroft Av. WN6: Wig 9B 34
Ascroft Ct. OL1: O'ham 3D 8
Ascroft St. OL1: O'ham 3D 8 (5K 63)
OL9: Chad 6E 62
WN1: Wig 9N 9 (4H 53)
Asgard Dr. M5: Sal 7A 4 (1B 94)
Asgard Gro. M5: Sal 7A 4
Ash Av. M44: Cad 3E 102
SK8: Chea 2K 117
WA12: N Wil 7F 86
WA14: Alt 2A 114
Ashawe Cl. M38: Lit H 8F 56
Ashawe Gro. M38: Lit H 8F 56
Ashawe Ter. M38: Lit H 8F 56
Ashbank Av. BL3: Bolt 6N 37
Ashbee St. BL1: Bolt 1F 38
Ashberry Cl. SK9: Wilm 6J 123
Ashborne Dr. BL9: Bury 3K 25
Ashbourne Av. BL2: Bolt 6J 39
M24: Mid 9A 44
M41: Urm 7M 91
SK8: Chea 1L 117
WN2: Hin 6B 54
WN2: Wig 1J 53
Ashbourne Cl. OL12: W'le 8H 15
WN7: Lei 1F 72
Ashbourne Ct. SK13: Glos 9H 101
(off Hebden Dr.)
Ashbourne Cres. M33: Sale 6K 105
Ashbourne Dr. OL6: A Lyne 4C 82
SK6: H Lan 9B 120
Ashbourne Gdns. WN2: Hin 6B 54
Ashbourne Gro. M7: Sal 3D 78
M28: Wors 2M 75
M45: Whitef 2K 59
Ashbourne M. SK10: Macc 3D 130
Ashbourne Rd. M6: Sal 5J 77
M30: Ecc 9E 76
M32: Stre 5G 93
M34: Dent 7J 97
SK7: H Gro 7K 119
Ashbourne Sq. OL8: O'ham 6J 63
Ashbourne St. OL11: Roch 4K 27
Ashbridge M17: T Pk 3H 93
Ashbridge Rd. M35: Fail 4F 80
Ashbrook Av. M34: Dent 6F 96
Ashbrook Cl. M34: Dent 6F 96
M45: Whitef 2A 60
SK8: H Grn 6G 116
Ashbrook Cres. OL12: Roch 1G 29
Ashbrook Dr. SK10: P'bury 7E 128
Ashbrook Farm Cl. SK5: Stoc 7D 96
ASHBROOK HEY 1G 28
Ashbrook Hey La. OL12: Roch 1G 29
Ashbrook La. SK5: Stoc 7D 96
Ashbrook Office Pk. M22: Wyth 7F 116
Ashbrook Rd. OL4: Spri 6C 64
SK10: Boll 6K 129
SK10: O Ald 7L 127
Ashbrook St. M11: Man 2E 96
Ashburn Av. M19: Man 3L 107
Ashburn Cl. BL6: Hor 3F 36
Ashburne Hall M14: Man 8J 95
Ashburne Ho. M14: Man 5J 95
(off Conyngham Rd.)
Ashburner St. BL1: Bolt 4J 7 (6F 38)
(not continuous)
Ashburn Flats OL10: H'ood 2H 43
(off School St.)
Ashburn Gro. SK4: Stoc 5B 108
Ashburn Rd. SK4: Stoc 5A 108
Ashburton Cl. SK14: Hat 7H 99
Ashburton Rd. SK3: Stoc 3C 118
Ashburton Rd. W. M17: T Pk 2D 92
M41: Urm 2D 92
Ashbury Cl. BL3: Bolt 7F 38
Ashbury Dr. WA11: Hay 2A 86
Ashbury Pl. M40: Man 6K 79
Ashburys Station (Rail) 2M 95
Ashby Av. M19: Man 4K 107
Ashby Cl. BL4: Farn 1K 57
Ashby Gdns. SK14: Hat 7F 98
Ashby Gro. M45: Whitef 4A 60
WN7: Lei 2E 72
Ashby Rd. WN3: Wig 8E 52
Ash Cl. OL6: A Lyne 5A 82
OL12: Roch 1G 29
SK2: Stoc 2G 118
SK14: Mot 5K 99
WN6: App B 5H 33
Ashcombe Dr. BL2: Bolt 6A 40
M26: Rad 7D 40
Ashcombe Wlk. M11: Man 9L 79
(off Newcombe Cl.)
Ash Cotts. BL8: Bury 8J 25
Ashcott Av. M22: Wyth 3C 116
Ashcott Cl. BL6: Los 7N 37
Ash Ct. M16: Whall R 7D 94
SK4: Stoc 5N 107
SK6: Wood 3L 109
WA16: Knut 6G 132
Ashcroft OL12: Roch 1H 29
Ashcroft Av. M6: Sal 6L 77
Ashcroft Cl. SK9: Wilm 9E 122
Ashcroft Ho. WA14: Alt 3D 6
Ashcroft Rd. WA13: Lym 3C 112
Ashcroft St. WN2: Hin 7A 54
Ashdale Av. BL3: Bolt 7N 37
Ashdale Cl. PR7: Cop 5A 18
SK5: Stoc 3D 108
Ashdale Cres. M43: Droy 9D 80
Ashdale Dr. M20: Man 3J 107
SK8: H Grn 5G 116
Ashdale Rd. WN2: Hin 6B 54
WN3: Wig 9D 52
Ashdene OL6: A Lyne 8G 6 (8A 82)
OL12: Roch 1G 29
Ashdene Cl. OL1: Chad 2G 62
OL4: Spri 4C 64
Ashdene Cres. BL2: Bolt 8L 23
Ashdene Ri. OL1: O'ham 8A 46
Ashdene Rd. M20: Man 2J 107
SK4: Stoc 6J 107
SK9: Wilm 9E 122
Ashdown Av. M9: Man 7J 61
SK6: Wood 3N 109
Ashdown Cl. SK8: Chea H 9M 117
Ashdown Dr. BL2: Bolt 1K 39
M27: Swin 4G 77
M28: Wors 3H 75
Ashdowne Lawns SK15: Stal 7G 82
Ashdown Gro. M9: Man 7J 61
Ashdown Rd. SK4: Stoc 5A 108
WA16: Olle 9M 133
Ashdown Ter. M9: Man 7J 61
Ashdown Way OL2: Shaw 4J 45
Ash Dr. M27: Ward 9C 58
Ashen Bottom BB4: Has 1K 11
Asher St. BL3: Bolt 1D 56
Ashes Cl. SK15: Stal 1F 98
Ashes Dr. BL2: Bolt 4N 39
Ashes La. OL4: Spri 5C 64
OL16: Miln 6J 29
SK13: Glos 7D 100
SK15: Stal 1F 98
Ashfell Ct. M21: Cho H 9M 93
Ashfield M34: Dent 4L 97
Ashfield Av. M46: Ath 7L 55
WN2: Hin 7B 54
Ashfield Cl. M6: Sal 7L 77
WA13: Lym 3C 112
Ashfield Ct. PR6: And 5L 19
(off Ashfield Rd.)
Ashfield Cres. OL4: Spri 5C 64
SK8: Chea 1J 117
WN5: Bil 5J 69
Ashfield Dr. M40: Man 6B 80
SK10: Macc 2E 130
WN2: Asp 7M 35
Ashfield Gro. BL1: Bolt 7H 23
M18: Man 5D 96
M44: Irl 2F 102
SK3: Stoc 3D 118
SK6: Mar B 7E 110
Ashfield Ho. OL11: Roch 8D 28
Ashfield Ho. Gdns. WN6: Stan 4C 34
Ashfield La. OL16: Miln 9K 29
Ashfield Lodge M20: Man 6E 106
SK3: Stoc 3D 118
Ashfield Pk. Dr. WN6: Stan 4C 34
Ashfield Rd. M13: Man 6K 95
M33: Sale 3H 105
M41: Urm 7D 92
OL11: Roch 9C 28
PR6: And 5L 19
SK3: Stoc 3D 118
SK8: Chea 1J 117
(not continuous)
SK13: Had 6B 100
WA15: Alt 5E 6 (4E 114)
Ashfield Sq. M43: Droy 8D 80
Ashfield St. OL8: O'ham 8G 62
Ashfield Ter.
WN6: App B 4G 33
Ashford M33: Sale 4C 104
Ashford Av. M27: Swin 4C 76
M28: Wors 4G 75
M30: Ecc 1C 92
SK5: Stoc 7D 96
Ashford Cl. BL2: Bolt 9M 23
BL8: Bury 3H 41
SK9: Hand 2H 123
Ashford Ct. OL4: O'ham 2A 64
SK5: Stoc 7D 96
(off Ashford Av.)
Ashford Grn. SK13: Gam 8A 100
(off Youlgreave Cres.)
Ashford Gro. M28: Wors 2N 75
Ashford M. SK13: Gam 8N 99
Ashford Ri. WN1: Wig 8E 34
Ashford Rd. M20: Man 1F 106
SK4: Stoc 2B 108
SK9: Wilm 1F 126
Ashford St. OL10: H'ood 2E 42
Ashford Wlk. BL1: Bolt 3F 38
OL9: Chad 5F 62
Ashgate Av. M22: Wyth 3D 116
Ashgill Wlk. M9: Man 3K 79
(off Osborne Rd.)
Ash Gro. BL0: Ram 2F 24
BL1: Bolt 4C 38
BL2: Bolt 1N 39
BL5: W'ton 4G 55
BL6: Hor 4G 37
BL8: Tot 8G 24
M14: Man 5K 95
M25: Pres 5N 59
M27: Swin 5D 76
M28: Walk 1L 75
M32: Stre 9J 93
M43: Droy 1E 96
OL2: O'ham 6H 45
OL4: Spri 4D 64
(not continuous)
OL15: Lit 9K 15
OL16: Miln 1L 45
OL16: Roch 3F 44
SK4: Stoc 3B 108
SK6: Mar 2B 120
SK8: H Grn 7G 117
SK9: Hand 3H 123
(off Sagars Rd.)
SK11: Macc 8G 130
SK14: Holl 4N 99
SK15: Stal 7C 82
WA3: Gol 1L 87
WA14: Bow 6C 114
WA15: Tim 9F 104
WA16: Knut 7K 133
WN5: Orr 5K 51
WN6: Stan 4C 34
Ash Gro. Cres. WN5: Bil 4H 69
Ash Hill OL5: Mos 3H 83
(off Staley Rd.)
Ash Hill Dr. OL5: Mos 2H 83
Ash Ho. WA12: N Wil 5D 86
Ashia Cl. OL16: Roch 9G 8 (7E 28)
Ashill Wlk. M3: Man 6E 4
Ashington Cl. BL1: Bolt 1C 38
WN5: Wig 2M 51
Ashington Dr. BL8: Bury 3F 40
Ashkirk St. M18: Man 4B 96
Ashland Av. WN1: Wig 1F 52
WN4: A Mak 6D 70
Ashlands M33: Sale 3G 104
Ashlands Av. M27: Swin 4C 76
M28: Wors 3H 75
M40: Man 1A 80
Ashlands Cl. BL0: Ram 4K 11
(off Bolton Rd.)
Ashlands Dr. M34: Aud 3J 97
Ashlands Rd. WA15: Tim 7G 104
Ash La. WA15: Hale 5J 115
WN2: Asp 1K 53
Ashlar Dr. M12: Man 1J 95
Ash Lawns BL1: Bolt 5C 38
Ash Lea SK15: Stal 7C 82
Ash-Lea Ct. M25: Pres 7N 59
(off Greengate La.)
Ash Lea Grange M30: Ecc 7F 76
Ashlea Gro. OL4: Grot 5E 64
Ashleigh Apartments
SK7: H Gro 4H 119
(off London Rd.)
Ashleigh Av. SK13: Glos 7D 100
Ashleigh Cl. OL2: O'ham 1J 63
Ashleigh Dr. BL1: Bolt 4N 37
Ashleigh Gdns. M9: Man 1H 79
Ashleigh Rd. WA15: Tim 8H 105
ASHLEY 9F 114
Ashley Av. BL2: Bolt 4L 39
M16: Old T 5C 94
M27: Swin 4D 76
M41: Urm 7M 91
Ashley Cl. OL11: Roch 9A 28
Ashley Ct. M27: Pen 9F 58
(off Hall St.)
M40: Man 1D 80
M44: Cad 3E 102
OL12: Whitw 4B 14
SK4: Stoc 4N 107
(off Heaton Moor Rd.)
WA15: Hale 6E 114
Ashley Ct. Dr. M40: Man 1D 80
Ashley Cres. M27: Swin 3D 76
Ashley Dearnley Ct. OL15: Lit 1K 29
Ashley Dr. M27: Swin 3D 76
M33: Sale 6E 104
SK7: Bram 9A 118
WN7: Lei 2E 72
Ashley Gdns. SK6: H Lan 7A 120
SK14: Hyde 8B 98
Ashley Gro. BL4: Farn 3K 57
(off Westminster St.)
ASHLEY HEATH 7D 114
Ashley La. M9: Man 2L 79
Ashley M. M45: Whitef 4A 60
OL9: O'ham 4G 63
SK14: Hyde 8B 98
Ashley Mill La. WA14: Ash 7D 114
Ashley Mill La. Nth.
WA14: Hale 7D 114
Ashley Rd. M43: Droy 8C 80
SK2: Stoc 8G 108
SK9: Wilm 5G 122
WA14: Alt, Bow, Hale
5C 6 (4D 114)
WA15: Ash 8E 114
WA15: Hale 5D 114
WA16: Mere 1D 132 & 9D 114
WN2: Hin 8D 54
WN8: Skel 9A 32
Ashleys, The SK4: Stoc 5N 107
Ashley Station (Rail) 9F 114
Ashley St. M4: Man 1K 5 (7G 78)
M6: Sal 8L 77
OL9: O'ham 3G 63
SK14: Hyde 5B 98
Ashling Ct. M29: Tyld 1D 74
Ash Lodge SK12: Poy 2H 125
Ashlor St. BL9: Bury 9J 7 (3L 41)
Ashlyn Gro. M14: Man 9J 95
Ashlynne OL6: A Lyne 7F 6 (7N 81)
Ashmeade WA15: Hale 6H 115
Ashmill Wlk. M9: Man 4H 79
Ashmond OL4: Spri 6C 64
Ashmond Rd. OL4: Spri 5C 64
Ashmoor Rd. M22: Wyth 6D 116
Ashmoor Wlk. M22: Wyth 6D 116
Ashmore Av. SK3: Stoc 9L 107
Ashmore St. M29: Tyld 2E 74
Ash Mt. Ct. SK4: Stoc 6L 107
Ashmount Dr. OL12: Roch 3D 28
Ashness Cl. BL6: Hor 1B 36
Ashness Dr. BL2: Bolt 3M 39
M24: Mid 9J 43
SK7: Bram 7C 118
Ashness Gro. BL2: Bolt 3M 39
Ashness Pl. BL2: Bolt 3M 39
Ashover Av. M12: Man 3L 95
Ashover Cl. BL1: Bolt 7G 23
Ashover St. M32: Stre 6L 93
Ashridge Cl. BL6: Los 6L 37
Ashridge Dr. M30: Ecc 1C 92
SK16: Duk 2M 97
Ashridge Way WN5: Orr 2M 51
Ash Rd. BL4: Kea 6N 57
M31: Part 5E 102
M34: Dent 6D 96
M43: Droy 8D 80
PR7: Cop 5B 18
SK12: Poy 3K 125
WA3: Rix 6B 102
WA11: Hay 2B 86
Ash Sq. OL4: O'ham 3A 64
Ashstead Rd. M33: Sale 7J 105
Ash St. BL2: Bolt 4M 7 (6H 39)
BL9: Bury 2N 41
M6: Sal 8M 77
M9: Man 3J 79
M24: Mid 2A 62
M29: Tyld 1B 74
M34: Aud 2H 97
M35: Fail 2C 80
OL4: O'ham 5M 63
OL10: H'ood 1G 43
OL11: Roch 2A 44
SK3: Stoc 8N 107
SK7: H Gro 4H 119
WA3: Gol 8L 71
Ash Ter. SK11: Macc 8G 131
Ashton Av. SK10: Macc 3B 130
WA14: Alt 1E 6 (1E 114)
Ashton Ct. M33: Sale 4E 104
M34: Aud 3K 97
Ashton Cres. OL9: Chad 8E 62
ASHTON CROSS 8A 70
Ashton Fld. Dr. M28: Walk 7K 57
Ashton Gallery WN1: Wig 7J 9
(off The Galleries)
Ashton Gdns. OL11: Roch 8C 28
Ashton Grange Ind. Est.
WN4: A Mak 4E 70
Ashton Heath WN4: A Mak 8F 70
Ashton Hill La. M43: Droy 1E 96
Ashton Ho. M4: Man 1H 5
M15: Man 7C 4
M43: Droy 1E 96
(off Old Mill Wharf)
ASHTON-IN-MAKERFIELD 7E 70
Ashton-in-Makerfield Golf Course
8B 70
Ashton La. M24: Mid 3M 61
M33: Sale 3F 104
Ashton Leisure Cen. 6D 70
Ashton Lodge BL0: Ram 7J 11
Ashton New Rd. M11: Man 9K 79
M12: Man 9K 79
Ashton Old Rd. M11: Man 1J 95
M12: Man 1J 95
Ashton-on-Mersey Golf Course 1E 104
Ashton on Mersey Health & Fitness Cen.
5E 104
Ashton Pl. SK7: H Gro 6K 119
Ashton Pools 7C 6 (7M 81)
Ashton Retail Pk.
OL6: A Lyne 6C 6 (7M 81)
Ashton Rd. M9: Man 6J 61
M31: C'ton 5K 103
(not continuous)
M33: Sale 4A 104
M34: Dent 4J 97
Ashton Rd. M35: Fail 4G 80
M43: Droy 9F 80
OL8: O'ham 5C 8 (6J 63)
SK6: Bred 3J 109
SK14: Hyde 3A 98
WA3: Gol 8J 71
WA12: N Wil 3F 86
WN5: Bil 2M 69
Ashton Rd. E. M35: Fail 2D 80
Ashton Rd. W. M35: Fail 3C 80
Ashton St. BL3: Bolt 8C 38
BL3: Lit L 9B 40
OL9: Chad 8E 62
OL10: H'ood 2H 43
OL11: Roch 8C 28
SK6: Wood 2N 109
SK13: Glos 9E 100
SK16: Duk 3L 97
WN1: I Mak 3J 53
ASHTON-UNDER-LYNE 6D 6 (7M 81)
Ashton-under-Lyne Golf Course 3B 82
Ashton-under-Lyne Station (Rail)
6D 6 (7M 81)
ASHTON UPON MERSEY 2E 104
Ash Tree Av. M43: Droy 8D 80
Ashtree Cl. SK10: P'bury 5G 128
Ash Tree Dr. SK16: Duk 2C 98
Ash Tree Rd. M8: Man 1F 78
SK14: Hyde 4E 98
ASHURST 8A 32
Ashurst Av. M11: Man 8N 79
Ashurst Cl. BL2: Bolt 1N 39
SK14: Hyde 8D 98
Ashurst Dr. SK3: Stoc 2N 117
Ashurst Gdns. OL6: A Lyne 5M 81
Ashurst Gro. M26: Rad 2H 59
Ashurst Rd. M22: Wyth 3E 116
WN6: Stan 2M 33
WN8: Skel 8A 32
Ash Vw. OL6: A Lyne 6N 81
Ashville Ter. M40: Man 1L 79
Ash Wlk. M24: Mid 5L 61
M33: Sale 3D 104
OL9: Chad 3F 62
Ashway OL6: A Lyne 7A 6 (7L 81)
Ashway Clough SK2: Stoc 2H 119
(not continuous)
Ashwell Av. WA3: Low 9N 71
Ashwell M. BL2: Bolt 1K 39
Ashwell Rd. M23: Wyth 9A 106
Ashwell St. BL2: Bolt 1K 39
Ashwin Wlk. M8: Man 4E 78
(off Ermington Dr.)
Ashwood M26: Rad 4B 58
OL9: Chad 4C 62
SK13: Glos 9B 100
WA14: Bow 7B 114
WN8: Skel 9A 32
(off Forest Dr.)
Ashwood Av. BL0: Ram 7K 11
M20: Man 4D 106
M28: Walk 6K 57
M33: Sale 5E 104
M34: Dent 6E 96
WA3: Low 1N 87
WN2: Abr 3M 71
WN4: A Mak 8D 70
Ashwood Ct. SK10: Boll 8H 129
WA3: Low 2N 87
Ashwood Cres. SK6: Mar 9C 110
Ashwood Dr. BL8: Bury 7H 25
OL2: O'ham 7G 44
OL15: Lit 9K 15
Ashwood Rd. SK12: Dis 8G 121
Ashworth Av. BL3: Lit L 9C 40
M34: Aud 2J 97
M41: Urm 7M 91
Ashworth Cl. OL2: O'ham 8K 45
OL9: Chad 7G 62
OL15: Lit 7L 15
WA14: Bow 6B 114
Ashworth Ct. M26: Rad 8J 41
OL2: Shaw 6M 45
(off Ashworth St.)
Ashworth Gdns. OL3: G'fld 6L 65
Ashworth La. BL1: Bolt 8G 22
SK14: Mot 7J 99
Ashworth Pk. WA16: Knut 8F 132
Ashworth Rd. OL10: H'ood 5G 27
OL11: Roch 2D 26
Ashworth St. BL4: Farn 3K 57
BL8: Bury 1J 41
(not continuous)
M26: Rad 8K 41
M34: Dent 5J 97
M35: Fail 4B 80
OL1: O'ham 3E 8 (5K 63)
OL2: Shaw 6M 45
OL10: H'ood 4J 43
OL12: Roch 6A 8 (5B 28)
WN2: Asp 9A 36
Ashworth Ter. BL2: Bolt 9M 23
Ashworth Way SK14: Mot 6J 99
Asia Ho. M1: Man 7J 5 (1F 94)
Asia St. BL3: Bolt 9H 39
Askern Av. M22: Wyth 4C 116
Askett Cl. M40: Man 4B 80
WA11: Hay 2A 86
Askrigg Cl. M46: Ath 2J 73
Askrigg Wlk. M13: Man 5L 95
(off Bates St.)
Askwith Rd. WN2: Hin 8A 54
Aspell Cl. M24: Mid 3L 61
Aspen Cl. BL5: W'ton 1H 55
SK4: Stoc 7M 107
WA15: Tim 2L 115
Aspen Gdns. OL12: Roch 4M 27
Aspen Grn. M34: Dent 7L 97
Aspens, The SK8: Gat 1F 116
Aspenshaw Rd.
SK22: Bir V 3N 121
Aspen Wlk. WN6: Wig 8D 34
Aspen Way SK6: H Lan 8D 120
Aspen Wood SK14: Hyde 6C 98
Aspenwood WN4: A Mak 8D 70
Aspenwood Cl. SK6: Mar 9B 110

Aspenwood Dr. M9: Man 9J 61
M33: Sale 4C 104
OL9: Chad 4C 62
Aspinall Cl. BL6: Hor 3E 36
M28: Walk 8G 57
Aspinall Ct. BL6: Hor 2E 36
Aspinall Cres. M28: Walk 8G 57
Aspinall Gdns. M24: Mid 4B 62
Aspinall Gro. M28: Walk 8G 56
Aspinall Rd. WN6: Stan 3M 33
Aspinall St. BL6: Hor 3F 36
M14: Man 6H 95
M24: Mid 4A 62
OL10: H'ood 2K 43
WN2: P Bri 9K 53
Aspinall Way BL6: Hor 4E 36
Aspin La. M4: Man 1H 5 (7F 78)
Aspland Rd. SK14: Hyde 1C 110
ASPULL 7M 35
ASPULL COMMON 9E 72
Aspull Comn. WN7: Lei 9E 72
Aspull Ct. WN7: Lei 9E 72
Aspull St. OL4: O'ham 6N 63
Aspull Wlk. M13: Man 3H 95
Asquith Av. SK16: Duk 3N 97
Asquith Rd. M19: Man 2L 107
Asquith St. SK5: Stoc 8D 96
Asshawes, The PR6: H Char 4J 19
Assheton Av. M34: Aud 9G 81
Assheton Cl. OL6: A Lyne 6C 6 (7M 81)
WA12: N Wil 5E 86
Assheton Cres. M40: Man 6B 80
Assheton Ho. OL6: A Lyne 6C 6
Assheton Rd. M40: Man 6B 80
OL2: Shaw 5K 45
Assheton St. M24: Mid 1M 61
Assheton Way M24: Mid 3M 61
Assisi Gdns. M12: Man 3N 95
Assumption Rd. M24: Mid 9J 43
Astan Av. M43: Droy 7B 80
Astbury Av. M21: Cho H 4B 106
M34: Aud 9H 81
Astbury Cl. BL9: Bury 4N 41
OL4: Spri 5C 64
WA3: Low 1D 88
WA15: Alt 1E 114
Astbury Cres. SK3: Stoc 1B 118
Astbury St. M26: Rad 2H 59
Astbury Wlk. SK8: Chea 2M 117
Asten Fold M6: Sal 4K 77
Aster Av. BL4: Farn 2H 57
Aster Ho. OL1: O'ham 2J 63
Aster Rd. WA11: Hay 2C 86
Aster St. OL1: O'ham 2J 63
Aster Wlk. *M31: Part 6G 102*
(off Cross La. W.)
ASTLEY 3D 74
ASTLEY BRIDGE 9G 23
Astley Brook Cl. BL1: Bolt 1H 39
Astley Cheetham Art Gallery *8D 82*
(off Trinity St.)
Astley Cl. OL2: Shaw 5K 45
WA16: Knut 9J 133
Astley Ct. M44: Irl 9F 90
WN4: A Mak 5F 70
Astley Gdns. SK16: Duk 1M 97
Astley Golf Cen. 6A 74
ASTLEY GREEN 6D 74
Astley Green Colliery Mus. 6E 74
Astley Gro. SK15: Stal 7C 82
Astley Hall Dr. BL0: Ram 1J 25
M29: Ast 4C 74
Astley La. BL1: Bolt 1F 38
Astley Rd. BL2: Bolt 8M 23
M44: Irl 4D 90
SK15: Stal 8C 82
Astley St. BL1: Bolt 2F 38
M11: Man 9A 80
M29: Ast, Tyld 2B 74
SK4: Stoc 2J 9 (7C 108)
SK15: Stal 1D 98
SK16: Duk 2L 97
WN7: Lei 6K 73
Astley Ter. *SK16: Duk 9N 81*
(off Peel St.)
Aston Av. M14: Man 7E 94
Aston Cl. SK3: Stoc 1A 118
Aston Ct. *OL1: O'ham 3J 63*
(off Mold St.)
Aston Gdns. *BL4: Farn 2L 57*
(off Spring St.)
Aston Gro. M29: Tyld 1C 74
Aston Ho. BL1: Bolt 5D 38
Aston Way *SK9: Hand 1J 123*
(off Spath La.)
Astoria Av. M40: Man 4N 79
Astor Rd. M19: Man 1K 107
M50: Sal 9J 77
Astra Bus. Pk. M17: T Pk 1F 92
Astra Cen., The OL11: Roch 1A 44
Astral M. M14: Man 7J 95
Astra Rd. M17: T Pk 1F 92
Astule Dr. SK11: Macc 5F 130
Atcham Gro. M9: Man 5G 60
Athenian Gdns. M7: Sal 5B 78
Athens Dr. M28: Walk 9K 57
Athens St. SK1: Stoc 3N 9 (7E 108)
Athens Way OL4: Lees 5B 64
Atherfield BL2: Bolt 9M 23
Atherfield Cl. M18: Man 3D 96
Atherleigh Bus. Pk. M46: Ath 7J 55
Atherleigh Gro. WN7: Lei 3H 73
Atherleigh Way M46: Ath 8F 72
WN7: Lei 8F 72
Atherley Gro. M40: Man 9D 62
OL9: Chad 9D 62
Atherstone OL12: Roch 5C 8
Atherstone Av. M8: Man 9F 60
Atherstone Cl. BL8: Bury 9J 25
ATHERTON 8M 55
Atherton Av. SK14: Mot 5K 99
Atherton Cl. M35: Fail 5F 80
Atherton Gro. SK14: Mot 5K 99
Atherton Ho. M46: Ath 7M 55
Atherton Ind. Cen. M46: Ath 7M 55
Atherton La. M44: Cad 3F 102
Atherton Rd. WN2: Hin 6N 53
Atherton Sq. WN1: Wig 7J 9
Atherton Station (Rail) 7N 55
Atherton St. M3: Man 5D 4 (9D 78)
M30: Ecc 9B 76
OL4: Lees 6B 64
OL4: Spri 5C 64
PR7: Adl 7K 19
SK3: Stoc 8B 108
WN2: B'haw 2A 72
WN5: Wig 5C 52
Atherton Way M30: Ecc 9B 76
Athey St. SK11: Macc 5G 130
Athletes Way M11: Man 1K 95
Athlone Av. BL1: Bolt 8D 22
BL9: Bury 9M 25
M40: Man 2M 79
SK8: Chea H 2A 118
Athol Cl. WA12: N Wil 5C 86
Athol Cres. WN2: Hin 7D 54
Athole St. M5: Sal 9M 77
Atholl Av. M32: Stre 7G 93
Atholl Cl. BL3: Bolt 6A 38
SK10: Macc 3E 130
Atholl Dr. OL10: H'ood 3F 42
Atholl Gro. WN3: Wig 8D 52
Athol Rd. M16: Whall R 8D 94
SK7: Bram 1B 124
Athol St. BL0: Ram 7J 11
M18: Man 6C 96
M30: Ecc 9B 76
OL6: A Lyne 7F 6 (7N 81)
OL12: Roch 4F 28
(not continuous)
SK4: Stoc 5B 108
Athos Wlk. M40: Man 9A 62
Atkinson Av. BL3: Bolt 9J 39
Atkinson Ho. *M33: Sale 3H 105*
(off Atkinson Rd.)
Atkinson Rd. M33: Sale 2G 105
M41: Urm 7D 92
Atkinson St. M3: Man 5E 4 (9D 78)
OL11: Roch 2A 44
SK1: Stoc 9E 108
WN2: Abr 2L 71
Atkin St. M28: Walk 9L 57
Atlanta Av. M90: Man A 7N 115
Atlantic Bus. Cen.
WA14: B'ath 9C 104
Atlantic St. WA14: B'ath 1A 114
Atlantic Wlk. *M11: Man 9L 79*
(off Yeoman Wlk.)
Atlas Bus. Pk. M22: Wyth 6E 116
Atlas Fold BL8: Bury 1J 41
Atlas Ho. BL1: Bolt 1L 7
Atlas St. OL7: A Lyne 5L 81
OL8: O'ham 4C 8
SK16: Duk 1A 98
Atlow Dr. M23: Wyth 2A 116
Atrium, The M45: Whitef 4M 59
Attenburys La. WA14: Tim 8E 104
Attenbury's Pk. Est. WA14: Tim 8E 104
Attercliffe Rd. M21: Cho H 1N 105
Attewell St. M11: Man 1M 95
Attingham Wlk. M34: Dent 8J 97
WN3: Wig 6D 52
Attleboro Rd. M40: Man 3M 79
(not continuous)
Attlee Av. WA3: Cul 5K 89
Attlee Way M12: Man 9K 79
Attock Cl. OL9: Chad 6F 62
Attwood Rd. WA15: Tim 2H 115
Attwood St. M12: Man 6M 95
Atwood Rd. M20: Man 5H 107
Atwood St. M1: Man 7H 5 (1F 94)
Auberge Ho. SK2: Stoc 1F 118
Auberson Rd. BL3: Bolt 9E 38
Aubrey Rd. M14: Man 1K 107
Aubrey St. M50: Sal 1N 93
OL11: Roch 8D 28
Auburn Av. SK6: Bred 4K 109
SK14: Hyde 8B 98
Auburn Dr. M41: Urm 8E 92
Auburn Rd. M16: Old T 5A 94
M34: Dent 7J 97
Auburn St. BL3: Bolt 8E 38
M1: Man 6K 5 (9G 78)
(not continuous)
Auckland Dr. M6: Sal 5N 77
Auckland Rd. M19: Man 9L 95
Audax Wlk. M40: Man 6N 79
Auden Cl. M11: Man 9B 80
Auden Ct. *M11: Man 9B 80*
(off Auden Cl.)
AUDENSHAW 3K 97
Audenshaw Ct. M34: Aud 3J 97
Audenshaw Hall Gro. M34: Aud 2F 96
Audenshaw Rd. M34: Aud 2F 96
(not continuous)
Audlem Cl. M40: Man 8J 79
Audlem Wlk. SK8: Chea 2M 117
Audley Av. M32: Stre 5F 92
Audley Rd. M19: Man 7N 95
Audley St. OL5: Mos 1G 82
(not continuous)
OL6: A Lyne 8B 82
Audlum Ct. BL9: Bury 2N 41
Audrey Av. M18: Man 4C 96
Audrey St. M9: Man 3L 79
Aughton Cl. WN5: Bil 6J 69
Aughton St. WN2: Hin 7N 53
Augusta Cl. OL12: Roch 3C 28
Augusta Dr. SK10: Macc 1F 130
Augusta St. OL12: Roch 4C 28
Augustine Webster Cl. M9: Man 2K 79
Augustus St. BL3: Bolt 8H 39
M3: Man 6F 78
Augustus Way M15: Man 5D 94
Auriga Wlk. *M7: Sal 7B 78*
(off Tucana Av.)
Austell Rd. M22: Wyth 7C 116
Austen Av. BL9: Bury 6M 41
Austen Ho. *SK10: Macc 3D 130*
(off Priory Ct.)
Austen Rd. M30: Ecc 9D 76
Austen Wlk. OL1: O'ham 7B 46
Auster Cl. *M14: Man 9F 94*
(off Bethnall Dr.)
AUSTERLANDS 3D 64
Austin Av. WN4: Gars 6B 70
Austin Ct. *M20: Man 4H 107*
(off Milden Cl.)
Austin Dr. M20: Man 4H 107
Austin Gro. M19: Man 9L 95
Austin's La. BL6: Los 4H 37
Austin St. WN7: Lei 5F 72
Autumn Av. WA16: Knut 6J 133
Autumn St. M13: Man 5H 95
Avallon Cl. BL8: Tot 6F 24
Avalon Dr. M20: Man 8H 107
Avebury Cl. BL6: Hor 3H 37
M7: Sal 4E 78
WA3: Low 1A 88
Avebury Rd. M23: Wyth 2N 115
Aveley Gdns. WN3: Wig 7N 51
Avenham Cl. M15: Man 4D 94
Avening Wlk. M22: Wyth 5B 116
Avensbeck
WA14: W Tim 7B 104
Avens Rd. M31: Part 5G 103
Avenue, The BL2: Bolt 5J 39
BL5: W'ton 2H 55
BL9: Bury 8M 25
M7: Sal 5B 78
M20: Man 3D 106
M28: Wors 3M 75
(Delaford Av.)
M28: Wors 7H 75
(Rock Rd.)
M30: Ecc 9D 76
M33: Sale 5D 104
M41: Urm 7M 91
OL2: Shaw 6L 45
PR6: Adl 5K 19
SK6: Bred 5H 109
SK8: H Grn 6F 116
SK9: A Edg 4F 126
SK13: Had 5C 100
WA12: N Wil 5G 86
WA15: Hale 7F 114
WN1: Wig 1G 52
WN5: Bil 8H 51
WN6: Stan 8B 34
WN7: Lei 5H 73
Avenue St. BL1: Bolt 4E 38
SK1: Stoc 1M 9 (6D 108)
Averham Cl. WN4: A Mak 9E 70
Averhill M28: Wors 2J 75
Averill St. M40: Man 5B 80
Averon Ri. OL1: O'ham 8A 46
Aveson Av. M21: Cho H 2A 106
Avian Cl. M30: Ecc 2N 91
Avian Dr. M14: Man 9G 94
Aviary Rd. M28: Wors 4N 75
Aviation Rd. BL9: Bury 7B 42
Aviator Way M22: Wyth 7B 116
Aviemore Cl. BL0: Ram 3G 25
WN4: Gars 6A 70
Avis St. OL2: Shaw 5M 45
Avocet Cl. WA12: N Wil 5F 86
WN7: Lei 4J 73
Avocet Dr. M44: Irl 6H 91
WA14: B'ath 8B 104
Avon Bank SK6: Bred 5K 109
Avonbrook Dr. M40: Man 9D 62
Avoncliff Cl. BL1: Bolt 1E 38
Avon Cl. M28: Walk 9H 57
OL16: Miln 7L 29
SK6: Mar 2B 120
SK10: Macc 2E 130
Avon Cotts. M25: Pres 6L 59
Avon Ct. *M15: Man 3C 94*
(off Eastnor Cl.)
Avoncourt Dr. M20: Man 4F 106
Avondale M27: Clif 9G 59
Avondale Av. BL9: Bury 9L 25
SK7: H Gro 5K 119
Avondale Ct. OL11: Roch 5B 44
Avondale Cres.
M41: Urm 6C 92
Avondale Dr. BL0: Ram 3F 24
M6: Sal 5H 77
M29: Ast 4D 74
Avondale Ind. Est.
SK3: Stoc 9N 107
Avondale Lodge *M33: Sale 5H 105*
(off Whitehill Rd.)
Avondale Recreation Cen. 9N 107
Avondale Ri. SK9: Wilm 8J 123
Avondale Rd. BL4: Farn 3G 56
M32: Stre 5L 93
M45: Whitef 2L 59
SK3: Stoc 9N 107
SK7: H Gro 5K 119
WN1: Wig 2F 52
Avondale St. BL1: Bolt 3D 38
M8: Man 2E 78
OL8: O'ham 7J 63
WN6: Stan 3B 34
Avon Dr. BL9: Bury 5M 25
Avon Flats *OL10: H'ood 2H 43*
(off Kay St.)
Avon Gdns. M19: Man 2M 107
Avonhead Cl. BL6: Hor 1B 36
Avonlea Dr. M19: Man 2K 107
Avonlea Rd. M33: Sale 7D 104
M43: Droy 8C 80
Avonleigh Gdns. *OL1: O'ham 2N 63*
(off Clyde St.)
Avon Rd. BL4: Kea 6B 58
M19: Man 2L 107
M29: Ast 3D 74
OL2: Shaw 4M 45
OL9: Chad 3D 62
OL10: H'ood 2F 42
SK8: H Grn 8G 117
WA3: Cul 7J 89
WA15: Hale 7E 114
WN4: A Mak 5H 71
WN5: Bil 7G 69
WN5: Wig 4N 51
Avonside Way SK11: Macc 7G 131
Avon St. BL1: Bolt 3C 38
OL8: O'ham 7K 63
SK3: Stoc 9C 108
WN7: Lei 6K 73
Avril Cl. SK5: Stoc 9D 96
Avril Ct. WN3: I Mak 7H 53
Avro Cl. M14: Man 8G 94
Avro Ct. M24: Mid 3B 62
Avroe Rd. M30: Ecc 2N 91
Avro Golf Course 6C 124
Avro Way M90: Man A 8M 115
Awburn Rd. SK14: Hat 8H 99
Axbridge Wlk. *M40: Man 8J 79*
(off Ridgway St.)
Axford Cl. M7: Sal 4E 78
Axholme Ct. BL6: Hor 1B 36
Axminster Wlk. SK7: Bram 8C 118
Axon Sq. M16: Whall R 5E 94
Aycliffe Av. M21: Cho H 3C 106
Aye Bri. Rd. WN2: Abr 5L 71
Aylcliffe Gro. M13: Man 6K 95
Aylesbury Av. M34: Dent 8K 97
M41: Urm 5E 92
Aylesbury Cl. M5: Sal 9N 77
SK10: Macc 1H 131
Aylesbury Cres. WN2: Hin 9E 54
Aylesbury Gro. M24: Mid 1A 62
Aylesby Av. M18: Man 5N 95
Aylesby Cl. WA16: Knut 7H 133
Aylesby Ct. M21: Cho H 8B 94
Aylesford Rd. M14: Man 6J 95
Aylesford Wlk. *BL1: Bolt 3F 38*
(off Blackburn Rd.)
Aylestone Wlk. *M40: Man 3M 79*
(off Hugo St.)
Aylsham Cl. SK6: Bred 3K 109
Aylsham M. M27: Swin 5D 76
Aylwin Dr. M33: Sale 5J 105
Ayr Av. OL8: O'ham 8K 63
Ayr Cl. SK7: H Gro 5L 119
Ayrefield Gro. WN6: She 6H 33
Ayrefield Rd. WN8: Roby M 8G 32
Ayres Rd. M16: Old T 5N 93
Ayr Gro. OL10: H'ood 3F 42
Ayrshire Rd. M7: Sal 4A 78
Ayr St. BL2: Bolt 9K 23
Ayrton Gro. M38: Lit H 6H 57
Aysgarth OL16: Roch 4F 28
Aysgarth Av. M18: Man 3C 96
SK6: Rom 4A 110
SK8: Chea 1H 117
Aysgarth Cl. M33: Sale 5D 104
Ayshford Cl. WA14: Alt 1B 114
Ayton Ct. *M16: Old T 5C 94*
(off Ayres Rd.)
Ayton Gro. M14: Man 5K 95
Aytoun St. M1: Man 5J 5 (9F 78)
Azalea Av. M18: Man 3B 96

B

Babbacombe Gro. M9: Man 6G 61
Babbacombe Rd. SK2: Stoc 1G 119
Baber Wlk. *BL1: Bolt 9F 22*
(off Warwick St.)
Babylon La. PR6: Adl, And 5L 19
Bk. Acton St. M1: Man 6K 5
Bk. Adcroft St. *SK1: Stoc 9D 108*
(off Adcroft St.)
Bk. Ainscow St. *BL1: Bolt 4F 38*
(off Vernon St.)
Bk. Albion Pl. *BL9: Bury 9M 25*
(off Hanson St.)
Bk. Alfred St. *BL0: Ram 9H 11*
(off Mary St.)
Bk. Andrew St. BL9: Bury 8N 7
OL5: Mos 2F 82
(off Fox Platt Ter.)
Bk. Andrew St. Nth. BL9: Bury 8N 7
Bk. Apple Ter. BL1: Bolt 2E 38
Bk. Ashford Wlk. *BL1: Bolt 3F 38*
(off Vernon St.)
Bk. Ashley St. M4: Man 1K 5
Bk. Bark St. BL1: Bolt 2J 7
Bk. Bell La. BL9: Bury 6N 7
Bk. Benson St. BL9: Bury 9N 7
Bk. Birch St. *BL9: Bury 1M 41*
(off Hornby St.)
Bk. Blackburn Rd. BL1: Bolt 3G 38
BL7: Eger 2E 22
(off Blackburn Rd.)
Bk. Blackburn Rd. E. *BL7: Eger 2E 22*
(off Albert St.)
Bk. Blackburn Rd. W. *BL1: Bolt 1F 38*
(off Viola St.)
Bk. Bolton St. Sth. BL9: Bury 7J 7
Bk. Bond St. W. *BL9: Bury 2N 41*
(off Croft St.)
BACKBOWER 8B 98
Bk. Bower Fold *SK15: Stal 1F 98*
(off Bower Fold)
Bk. Bower La. SK14: Hyde 9C 98
Bk. Bradford St. W. BL2: Bolt 4N 7
(not continuous)
Bk. Bradshaw Brow *BL2: Bolt 9K 23*
(off Bradshaw Brow)
Bk. Bradshaw Brow E. *BL2: Bolt 9K 23*
(off Bradshaw Brow)
Bk. Bradshaw Chapel *BL2: Bolt 8L 23*
(off Cottage Cft.)
Bk. Bradshaw Rd. *BL2: Bolt 8L 23*
(off Bradshaw Rd.)
Bk. Bradshaw St. OL16: Roch 5E 28
Bk. Bridge St. M3: Man 4F 4
SK22: N Mil 6M 121
WA12: N Wil 6E 86
Bk. Broad St. BL9: Bury 7K 7 (2L 41)
Bk. Broom St. BL2: Bolt 2N 7 (5H 39)
OL16: Miln 9M 29
(off Broomfield Ter.)
Back Brow WN8: Uph 4G 50
Bk. Caledonia St. *BL3: Bolt 7D 38*
(off Hibernia St.)
Bk. Caley St. *BL1: Bolt 2A 38*
(off Caley St.)
Bk. Cambridge St. *OL7: A Lyne 9K 81*
(off Bennett St.)
Bk. Camp St. M7: Sal 5C 78
Bk. Canning St. *BL9: Bury 9M 25*
(off Hornby St.)
Bk. Cateaton St. *BL9: Bury 1M 41*
(off Hornby St., not continuous)
Bk. Cecil St. *OL5: Mos 2F 82*
(off Park Ter.)
Bk. Chapel St. BL6: Hor 1E 36
BL8: Tot 6F 24
M19: Man 8M 95
(off Bankley St.)
M30: Ecc 8F 76
(off Church St.)
OL12: W'le 8G 14
SK7: H Gro 4J 119
Back Cheapside BL1: Bolt 3K 7
Bk. China La. M1: Man 5K 5 (9G 78)
Bk. Chorley New Rd. *BL6: Hor 1D 36*
(off Chorley New Rd.)
Bk. Church St. BL1: Bolt 1J 7
(not continuous)
Bk. Cobden St. BL9: Bury 5N 7
Bk. College Land M3: Man 3F 4
Bk. Cowm La. OL12: Whitw 2N 13
Bk. Crescent Av. BL1: Bolt 1G 7
Bk. Cross La. WA12: N Wil 5E 86
Bk. Crostons Rd.
BL8: Bury 6G 7 (1K 41)
Bk. Crown St. BL6: Hor 9C 20
Bk. Dale St. *OL16: Miln 8K 29*
(off Dale St.)
Bk. Darwen Rd. *BL7: Bro X 6H 23*
(off Darwen Rd.)
Bk. Darwin St. *BL1: Bolt 2E 38*
(off Darwin St.)
Bk. Deacon's Dr. M6: Sal 4K 77
Bk. Deane Church La. *BL3: Bolt 8C 38*
(off Deane Church La.)
Bk. Drake St. OL16: Roch 9D 8 (7D 28)
Bk. Duncan St. M7: Sal 3B 78
Bk. Durham St. OL11: Roch 8E 28
Bk. East St. BL9: Bury 9M 7
Bk. Eddisbury Rd. SK11: Macc 5N 131
Bk. Elsworth St. *M4: Man 6F 78*
(off Chatley St.)
Bk. Emmett St. *BL6: Hor 1D 36*
(off Winter Hey La.)
Bk. Eskrick St. *BL1: Bolt 2E 38*
(off Dobson St.)
Bk. Ewart St. *BL1: Bolt 2F 38*
(off Ewart St.)
Bk. Fletcher St. BL9: Bury 7N 7
M26: Rad 4B 58
Backford Wlk. M20: Man 1F 106
Bk. Foundry St. BL9: Bury 8M 7
Bk. Frank St. BL9: Bury 9M 7
Bk. George St. BL6: Hor 1E 36
M1: Man 6H 5 (1F 94)
(not continuous)
Bk. Gladstone St. OL4: O'ham 5M 63
Bk. Grafton St. WA14: Alt 4D 6
Bk. Greaves St. OL1: O'ham 2E 8
Bk. Grosvenor St. SK15: Stal 9D 82
Bk. Hadwin St. *BL1: Bolt 3G 38*
(off Higher Bri. St.)
Bk. Halliwell Rd. Sth. BL1: Bolt 2E 38
Bk. Hamel St. *SK14: Hyde 4C 98*
(off Hamel St.)
Bk. Hamilton St. M7: Sal 3C 78
Bk. Hampson St. *M40: Man 6J 79*
(off Hampson St.)
Bk. Haslam St. BL9: Bury 9N 25
Bk. Heywood St. E. BL9: Bury 8N 7
Bk. Heywood St. W. BL9: Bury 9N 7
Bk. High St. *BL3: Bolt 8E 38*
(off High St.)
Bk. Hilton St. M7: Sal 3C 78
Bk. Hope St. M7: Sal 3C 78
Bk. Horbury St. *BL8: Bury 2J 41*
(off Horbury Dr.)
Bk. Hornby St. E. BL9: Bury 5L 7
Bk. Hornby St. W. BL9: Bury 5L 7
Bk. Hotel St. BL1: Bolt 2K 7
Bk. Howe St. M7: Sal 3B 78
Bk. Hulme St. M5: Sal 4A 4 (9B 78)
Bk. Hurst St. BL9: Bury 9N 7
Bk. Ingham St. BL9: Bury 9N 7
Bk. Ingham St. E. BL9: Bury 9N 7
Bk. James St. *OL15: Lit 9K 15*
(off James St.)
Bk. Jodrell St. SK22: N Mil 8L 121
Bk. Kershaw St. BL9: Bury 8N 7
Bk. King St. OL1: O'ham 3C 8 (5J 63)
Bk. Knowl St. SK15: Stal 8E 82
Bk. Knowsley St. BL9: Bury 8K 7
Back La. BL1: Bolt 1H 7 (4F 38)
BL5: O Hul 5C 56
OL4: O'ham 8D 64
OL4: Scout 2F 64
OL6: A Lyne 9D 64
OL7: A Lyne 5J 81
(not continuous)
OL12: Roch 2L 27
OL12: Whitw 4A 14
PR6: H Char 1M 19
SK13: Char 2N 111
SK14: Mot 6K 99
WA5: Coll G 9A 86
WA11: Cra 5D 68
WA14: D Mas 2J 113
WA14: M'ton 9G 113
WN6: App B, Stan 4H 33
WN8: Dal 7D 32
WN8: Skel 4C 50
(Barnfield Dr.)
WN8: Skel 5B 50
(Beavers La.)
Bk. Lee St. OL3: Upp 3L 65
Bk. Legh St. WA12: N Wil 6D 86
Bk. Longworth Rd. *BL6: Hor 9E 20*
(off Longworth Rd.)
Bk. Lord St. BL9: Bury 9M 7
Bk. Louise St. *OL12: Roch 2G 28*
(off Kitter St.)

Bk. Manchester Old Rd.
BL9: Bury 3L 41
(off Manchester Old Rd.)
Bk. Manchester Rd. BL9: Bury 8J 7
Bk. Manor St. BL9: Bury 7N 7 (2N 41)
Bk. Market St. BL9: Bury 8K 7
WA12: N Wil 5D 86
WN2: Hin 6N 53
WN7: Lei 5H 73
Bk. Market St. W. BL9: Bury 7K 7
Bk. Mason St. BL9: Bury 8N 7
Bk. Massie St. SK8: Chea 1J 117
Bk. Mawdsley St. BL1: Bolt 3K 7
Bk. Melbourne St. SK15: Stal 8D 82
Bk. Mellor Rd. SK22: N Mil 6M 121
Bk. Merton St. BL8: Bury 5G 7
Bk. Micklehurst Rd. OL5: Mos 1H 83
Bk. Millett St. BL9: Bury 8H 7
Bk. Mill La. OL5: Mos 9F 64
Back Moor SK14: Mot 5K 99
Bk. Moorgate W. BL9: Bury 6M 7
Bk. Moss Ter. BL1: Bolt 1K 7
Bk. Oldham Rd.
OL16: Roch 9E 8 (7E 28)
Bk. Olga St. *BL1: Bolt 2E 38*
(off Wordsworth St.)
Bk. Olive Bank *BL8: Bury 9H 25*
(off Elson St.)
Bk. Ormrod St. *BL9: Bury 2N 41*
(off Ormrod St.)
BACK O' TH' BANK 3G 39
Bk. o' th' Height HX6: Rish 4M 17
BACK O' TH' HILL 3A 110
Bk. o' th' Low Rd. OL4: Wat 3C 64
BACK O' TH' MOSS 1H 43
Back o' th' Moss La.
OL10: H'ood 1H 43
Bk. Oxford St. BL9: Bury 9N 7
Bk. Paradise St. SK11: Macc 5G 131
Bk. Parkhills Rd. Sth. BL9: Bury 4L 41
Bk. Parsons La. BL9: Bury 6L 7
Bk. Patience St. *OL12: Roch 4A 28*
(off Patience St.)
Bk. Peter St. BL9: Bury 5N 7
Bk. Phoenix St. BL9: Bury 8J 7
Back Piccadilly M1: Man 4J 5 (9F 78)
Bk. Pine St. *OL16: Miln 1M 45*
(off Pine St.)
Bk. Pool Fold M2: Man 4G 5 (9E 78)
Bk. Portland St.
OL6: A Lyne 8B 6 (8L 81)
Bk. Quay St. M3: Man 5D 4
Bk. Queen St. BL1: Bolt 3J 7
WN7: Lei 5J 73
(off Brown St. Nth.)
Bk. Railway Vw. PR7: Adl 7K 19
Bk. Red Bank M4: Man 1J 5 (7F 78)
Bk. Redhill Gro. *BL1: Bolt 4F 38*
(off Vernon St.)
Bk. Richard Burch St. *BL9: Bury 1M 41*
(off Richard Burch St.)
Bk. Rochdale Rd. BL9: Bury 7N 7
Bk. Rochdale Rd. Sth. BL9: Bury 7N 7
Bk. Roman Rd. *M7: Sal 4D 78*
(off Appian Way)
Back St George's Rd. BL1: Bolt 1J 7
M4: Man 1L 5 (7G 78)
Back St George's Rd. Nth.
BL1: Bolt 1H 7
Back St Helens Rd. Sth.
BL3: Bolt 1B 56
(off Reginald St.)
Back St James St. OL1: O'ham 4M 63
Back St Marks' La. *M8: Man 2E 78*
(off Cheetham Hill Rd.)
Back St Mary's Pl. BL9: Bury 8J 7
Back Salford WN7: Lei 5H 73
Bk. Salford St. BL9: Bury 9N 25
Bk. Sandy Bank Rd. BL7: Edg 1L 23
Bk. Sankey St. BL9: Bury 7H 7
Bk. School La. WN8: Uph 4G 51
Bk. Scott St. *OL8: O'ham 6K 63*
(off Scott St.)
Bk. Shakerley Rd. *M29: Tyld 1A 74*
(off Tydlesley Pas.)
Bk. Shed St. *OL12: Whitw 5B 14*
(off Clara St.)
Bk. Shepherd St. BL9: Bury 8M 7
Bk. Short St. *M46: Ath 1A 74*
(off Short St.)
Bk. Silver St. BL9: Bury 7K 7
Bk. Skull Ho. La. WN6: App B 4H 33
Bk. South Cross St. E. BL9: Bury 8M 7
Bk. South Pde. M3: Man 4F 4 (9E 78)
Back Spa Rd. Nth. *BL1: Bolt 6E 38*
(off Tavistock Rd.)
Bk. Spear St. M1: Man 3K 5
Bk. Spring Gdns.
BL1: Bolt 4K 7 (6G 38)
Bk. Spring Mill OL16: Miln 8B 30
Bk. Spring St. E. BL9: Bury 9M 7
Bk. Spring St. W. BL9: Bury 9M 7
Bk. Square St. BL0: Ram 8J 11
Bk. Stanley St. *M46: Ath 8L 55*
(off Stanley St.)
Bk. Teak St. BL9: Bury 2A 42
Bk. Tenterden St. BL9: Bury 8H 7
(not continuous)
Bk. Thomas St. M4: Man 3J 5
Bk. Tinline St. BL9: Bury 8N 7
Bk. Tonge Moor Rd. *BL2: Bolt 1J 39*
(off Tonge Moor Rd.)
Backton Pl. *M40: Man 6J 79*
(off Sawley Rd.)
Bk. Tootal Rd. *M5: Sal 8K 77*
(off Tootal Rd.)
Bk. Turner St. M4: Man 3J 5 (8F 78)
Bk. Union Rd. SK22: N Mil 8M 121
Bk. Vernon St. *BL1: Bolt 4F 38*
(off Merehall Dr.)
BL9: Bury 9M 25
(off Hornby St.)
SK14: Hyde 7B 98
(off Vernon St.)
Bk. Viola St. BL1: Bolt 1F 38
Bk. Wall Ga. SK11: Macc 4H 131
Bk. Walmersley Rd. E.
BL9: Bury 9M 25
(off Taylor St.)
Bk. Walmersley Rd. W.
BL9: Bury 9M 25
(off Eldon St.)
Bk. Water St. *BL7: Eger 3E 22*
(off Water St.)
OL6: A Lyne 5E 6 (6N 81)
SK1: Stoc 6D 108
(off Gt. Portwood St.)
Bk. Wellington Rd. Sth.
BL9: Bury 4M 41
(off Wellington Rd.)
Bk. Wells St. *BL9: Bury 3L 41*
(off Wells St.)
Back Whitegate *OL15: Lit 1J 29*
(off Whitegate)
Bk. Willows La. BL3: Bolt 8D 38
Bk. Wright St. *BL6: Hor 9D 20*
(off Walsh St.)
Bk. Young St. BL4: Farn 4M 57
Baclaw Cl. WN1: Wig 2J 53
Bacon Av. M34: Dent 1L 109
Bacup St. M40: Man 2M 79
Badbury Cl. WA11: Hay 2A 86
Badby Cl. M4: Man 9J 79
Baddeley Cl. SK3: Stoc 2B 118
Badder St. BL1: Bolt 1K 7 (4G 38)
Bader Dr. OL10: H'ood 5J 43
Badger Cl. OL16: Roch 1G 44
SK6: Mar 4C 120
SK14: Hyde 5B 98
Badger Edge La. OL4: O'ham 9F 46
Badger Ho. SK10: Macc 2H 131
Badger La. OL16: Roch 2F 44
(not continuous)
Badger Rd. SK10: Macc 2H 131
SK10: P'bury 6E 128
WA14: W Tim 8C 104
Badgers Cft. WA16: Mob 4N 133
Badger St. BL9: Bury 5M 7 (1M 41)
Badgers Wlk. M22: Wyth 6D 116
Badgers Way SK13: Glos 9D 100
Badminton Rd. M21: Cho H 8B 94
Bag La. M46: Ath 7K 55
Bag La. Ent. Cen. M46: Ath 7K 55
Bagnall Cl. OL3: Upp 2M 65
OL12: Roch 3L 27
Bagnall Ct. M22: Nor 8D 106
Bagnall Wlk. M22: Nor 8D 106
Bagot St. M11: Man 8A 80
M27: Ward 1C 76
Bagshaw La. WN2: Asp 1A 54
Bagshaw Rd. M18: Man 7B 96
Bagshaw St. SK14: Hyde 4B 98
BAGSLATE MOOR 5L 27
Bagslate Moor La. OL11: Roch 5L 27
Bagslate Moor Rd. OL11: Roch 6L 27
Bagstock Av. SK12: Poy 4J 125
BAGULEY 9M 105
Baguley Cres. M24: Mid 5F 60
SK3: Stoc 1B 118
Baguley Dr. BL9: Bury 1N 59
Baguley La. M33: Sale 5L 105
(not continuous)
Baguley Rd. M33: Sale 4L 105
Baguley St. M43: Droy 9F 80
Bahama Cl. WA11: Hay 1A 86
Bahama Rd. WA11: Hay 1A 86
Baildon Rd. OL12: Roch 4N 27
Baildon St. M40: Man 1M 79
Bailey Bus. Pk. SK10: Boll 6K 129
Bailey Fold BL5: W'ton 3K 55
Bailey La. BL2: Bolt 3M 39
M31: Part 5G 102
M90: Man A 6A 116
Bailey Rd. M17: T Pk 2G 92
Bailey's Ct. WN1: Wig 7J 9
Bailey St. M11: Man 9C 80
M25: Pres 7B 60
OL1: O'ham 2F 8 (4L 63)
Bailey Wlk. WA14: Bow 7C 114
Baillie St. M26: Rad 7L 41
OL16: Roch 6D 8 (5D 28)
(Milton St.)
OL16: Roch 7C 8 (6D 28)
(Yorkshire St.)
Baillie St. E. OL16: Roch 6E 8 (5E 28)
Bails, The M7: Sal 4B 78
M28: Walk 8L 57
Bainbridge Av. WA3: Low 1B 88
Bainbridge Cl. M12: Man 3J 95
Bainbridge Rd. OL4: O'ham 2A 64
Bainburgh Clough OL8: O'ham 7N 63
Baines Av. M44: Irl 9G 91
Baines St. BL1: Bolt 4C 38
Bain St. M27: Swin 3F 76
Bainton Wlk. *M9: Man 6H 61*
(off Munn Rd.)
Baird St. M1: Man 6L 5 (1G 95)
Baitings Cl. OL12: Roch 3H 27
Baitings Ga. Rd. HX6: Rish 4M 17
Baitings Row OL12: Roch 3H 27
Bakehurst Cl. SK22: N Mil 8M 121
Baker Ho. *OL2: O'ham 8J 45*
(off Royton Hall Pk.)
Bakersfield Pl. M33: Sale 4J 105
Baker's La. OL3: Upp 1A 66
Baker St. BL0: Ram 9H 11
BL4: Kea 5B 58
M24: Mid 3N 61
OL10: H'ood 4K 43
PR7: Cop 4B 18
SK4: Stoc 5C 108
SK11: Macc 5G 130
SK15: Stal 9E 82
WA15: Tim 9J 105
WN3: Wig 5E 52
Bakery Ct. OL6: A Lyne 5A 82
Bakestonedale Rd.
SK10: P Shr 2N 129
Bakewell Av. M34: Dent 9L 97
OL6: A Lyne 4C 82
Bakewell Bank *SK13: Gam 8N 99*
(off Melandra Castle Rd.)
Bakewell Cl. *SK13: Gam 8N 99*
(off Youlgreave Cres.)
Bakewell Dr. WN6: Wig 8D 34
Bakewell Fold *SK13: Gam 8N 99*
(off Youlgreave Cres.)
Bakewell Gdns. *SK13: Gam 8N 99*
(off Youlgreave Cres.)
Bakewell Grn. *SK13: Gam 8N 99*
(off Bakewell M.)
Bakewell Gro. SK13: Gam 8N 99
Bakewell Lea *SK13: Gam 8N 99*
(off Youlgreave Cres.)
Bakewell M. SK13: Gam 8N 99
Bakewell Rd. M30: Ecc 1C 92
M32: Stre 6G 93
M43: Droy 8C 80
SK7: H Gro 7J 119
Bakewell St. M18: Man 5A 96
SK3: Stoc 8B 108
Bakewell Wlk. *SK13: Gam 8N 99*
(off Totley M.)
Bala Cl. M5: Sal 8N 77
Balcarres Av. WN1: Wig 1H 53
Balcarres Rd. WN2: Asp 8L 35
Balcary Gro. BL1: Bolt 4C 38
Balcombe Cl. BL8: Bury 6H 25
BALDERSTONE 1F 44
Balderstone Rd. OL11: Roch 2D 44
BALDINGSTONE 4M 25
Baldock Rd. M20: Man 5J 107
Baldrine Dr. WN2: Hin 6D 54
Baldwin Rd. M19: Man 2L 107
Baldwins Cl. OL2: O'ham 9H 45
Baldwin St. BL3: Bolt 7F 38
WN1: Wig 7M 9 (3G 53)
WN2: Hin 8D 54
WN3: I Mak 4G 53
WN5: Orr 5M 51
Bale St. M2: Man 6G 5 (1E 94)
Balfern Fold BL5: W'ton 2G 55
Balfour Gro. SK5: Stoc 9D 96
Balfour Rd. M41: Urm 6B 92
OL12: Roch 4A 28
WA14: B'ath 9D 104
Balfour St. BL3: Bolt 6E 38
M6: Sal 4N 77
M8: Man 2F 78
OL2: Shaw 5M 45
OL4: O'ham 4N 63
Balham Wlk. *M12: Man 3L 95*
(off Pollitt Cl.)
Balharry Av. WA11: Hay 2C 86
Ballantine St. M40: Man 6A 80
Ballantyne Way WA3: Low 1A 88
Ballard Cl. OL15: Lit 7M 15
Ballard Way OL2: Shaw 4N 45
Ballater Av. M41: Urm 8A 92
Ballater Cl. OL10: H'ood 3F 42
Ballater Wlk. *M8: Man 3E 78*
(off Heath St.)
Ballbrook Av. M20: Man 3F 106
Ballbrook Ct. M20: Man 4G 107
Ballerat St. M19: Man 8N 95
Ball Grn. M32: Stre 4H 93
Ballgrove OL3: Upp 4M 65
Balliol Cl. SK6: Wood 4N 109
SK11: Sut E 9K 131
Balliol Ct. M33: Sale 3C 104
Balliol St. M8: Man 2F 78
M27: Swin 2E 76
Balliol Way WN4: A Mak 6C 70
Ball La. SK10: Boll 8H 129
Balloon La. M4: Man 2H 5
Balloon St. M4: Man 2H 5 (8F 78)
Balls Cotts. WN3: I Mak 3K 53
Ball St. OL16: Roch 6E 8 (5E 28)
WN6: Wig 1B 52
Ball Wlk. SK14: Hat 8J 99
Ballycreen OL11: Roch 1A 44
Balmain Av. M18: Man 6A 96
Balmain Rd. M41: Urm 6B 92
Balmer Dr. M23: Wyth 3A 116
Balmfield St. M8: Man 5F 78
Balmforth St. M15: Man 8C 4
Balmoral PR7: Adl 7H 19
Balmoral Av. BL3: Lit L 9A 40
M32: Stre 6K 93
M34: Aud 2H 97
M41: Urm 8B 92
M45: Whitef 4N 59
OL2: O'ham 8K 45
OL11: Roch 5N 27
SK8: Chea H 5M 117
SK14: Hyde 9B 98
WA3: Low 9N 71
Balmoral Cl. BL6: Hor 2G 36
BL8: G'mount 4G 24
BL9: Bury 7N 41
OL16: Miln 7L 29
WA16: Knut 7H 133
Balmoral Ct. M9: Man 6F 60
OL7: A Lyne 9L 81
(off Victoria St.)
Balmoral Cres. SK10: Macc 2K 131
Balmoral Dr. M34: Dent 5E 96
OL10: H'ood 3F 42
SK6: H Lan 8B 120
SK12: Poy 3H 125
SK15: Stal 7D 82
WA14: Tim 8F 104
WN2: Hin 7M 53
WN7: Lei 4M 73
Balmoral Grange M25: Pres 8D 60
Balmoral Gro. SK7: H Gro 4K 119
Balmoral Ho. *M30: Ecc 8C 76*
(off Queen Victoria St.)
Balmoral Rd. BL4: Farn 4K 57
M14: Man 9J 95
M27: Clif 9G 59
M41: Urm 8A 92
SK4: Stoc 5M 107
WA15: Alt 3E 6 (3E 114)
WN4: A Mak 6D 70
WN5: Wig 5B 52
Balmoral St. M18: Man 5A 96
Balmoral Way SK9: Wilm 8F 122
Balmore Cl. BL3: Bolt 9B 38
Balm St. BL0: Ram 1G 25
Balniel Wlk. WN1: Wig 9H 35
Balsam Cl. M13: Man 9M 5 (2H 95)
Balshaw Av. M44: Irl 7G 91
Balshaw Cl. BL3: Bolt 7D 38
Balshaw Ct. M44: Irl 7H 91
Baltic Rd. WA14: B'ath, D Mas 1A 114
Baltic St. M5: Sal 8L 77
Baltimore St. M40: Man 5L 79
Bamber Av. M33: Sale 5L 105
Bamber Cft. BL5: W'ton 9G 36
Bamber's Bldgs. *WN2: Hin 6A 54*
(off Durham Rd.)
Bamber Wlk. *BL3: Bolt 7E 38*
(off Derby St.)
Bamburgh Cl. M26: Rad 7C 40
Bamburgh Dr. OL7: A Lyne 5J 81
Bamburgh Pl. WN4: A Mak 5D 70
Bambury St. BL9: Bury 6M 7 (1M 41)
BAMFORD 7K 27
Bamford Av. M24: Mid 1M 61
M34: Dent 9K 97
Bamford Bus. Pk. SK4: Stoc 3C 108
Bamford Cl. BL9: Bury 9D 26
SK8: H Grn 7J 117
SK10: Boll 6L 129
Bamford Ct. OL11: Roch 7N 27
Bamford Dr. WN2: Wig 2J 53
Bamford Fold *SK13: Gam 8A 100*
(off Castleton Cres.)
Bamford Gdns. WA15: Tim 1K 115
Bamford Grn. *SK13: Gam 8A 100*
(off Castleton Cres.)
Bamford Gro. M20: Man 5F 106
OL6: A Lyne 4C 82
Bamford La. SK13: Gam 8A 100
Bamford M. OL11: Roch 6K 27
SK13: Gam 8A 100
Bamford Pl. OL12: Roch 4C 28
Bamford Pct. OL11: Roch 6K 27
Bamford Rd. BL0: Ram 6L 11
M9: Man 6J 61
M20: Man 5F 106
OL10: H'ood 9H 27
Bamfords Pas. OL15: Lit 8M 15
Bamford St. M11: Man 8N 79
OL2: O'ham 9J 45
OL9: Chad 3G 62
OL15: Lit 8K 15
(Cote La.)
OL15: Lit 9K 15
(Featherstall Rd.)
SK1: Stoc 4L 9 (8D 108)
SK10: Macc 3J 131
Bamford Way OL11: Roch 7K 27
BAMFURLONG 2J 71
Bampton Av. WA11: St H 9F 68
Bampton Cl. BL5: W'ton 1G 55
SK2: Stoc 9F 108
Bampton Rd. M22: Wyth 6C 116
Bampton Wlk. M24: Mid 1K 61
Banastre Dr. WA12: N Wil 6J 87
Banbury Cl. SK10: Macc 2J 131
WN7: Lei 9G 73
Banbury Dr. WA14: Tim 8E 104
Banbury M. M27: Ward 1D 76
Banbury Rd. M23: Wyth 2M 115
M24: Mid 6L 61
M35: Fail 6C 80
WN5: Bil 9H 51
Banbury St. BL2: Bolt 3K 39
SK1: Stoc 3L 9 (7D 108)
Bancroft Av. SK8: Chea H 6M 117
Bancroft Cl. SK6: Bred 5J 109
Bancroft Ct. *WA15: Hale 4G 114*
(off Bancroft Rd.)
Bancroft Fold SK14: Hyde 4E 98
Bancroft Rd. M27: Swin 1E 76
WA15: Hale 4G 114
Bandy Flds. Pl. M7: Sal 5C 78
Banff Gro. OL10: H'ood 3F 42
Banff Rd. M14: Man 5H 95
Bangor Fold WN7: Lei 6L 73
Bangor Rd. SK8: Chea 1L 117
Bangor St. BL1: Bolt 4F 38
M15: Man 4C 94
OL6: A Lyne 8B 82
OL16: Roch 7F 28
SK5: Stoc 4D 108
Banham Av. WN3: Wins 8N 51
Bank OL12: W'le 7G 15
Bank, The OL16: Roch 6C 8 (5D 28)
SK13: Glos 9F 100
Bank Av. WN5: Orr 6H 51
Bank Barn OL12: W'le 7H 15
Bank Barn La. OL12: W'le 7H 15
Bankbottom SK13: Had 4C 100
Bank Bottom Cotts. HD7: Mars 1H 49
Bank Bri. Rd. M11: Man 7N 79
Bankbrook WN6: Stan 8A 34
Bank Brow WN8: Roby M 8G 32
Bank Cl. OL15: Lit 2L 29
SK11: Macc 5J 131
Bank End Cotts. SK23: Fur V 9L 121
Banker St. BL3: Bolt 7K 39
Bankes Av. WN5: Orr 5L 51
Bank Fld. BL5: W'ton 4J 55
Bankfield BL2: Ain 4C 40
HD7: Mars 1J 49
(off Manchester Rd.)
SK14: Hyde 4A 98
WN8: Skel 4A 50
Bankfield Av. M13: Man 6K 95
M43: Droy 8E 80
M44: Cad 3E 102
SK4: Stoc 6A 108
Bankfield Cl. BL2: Ain 3C 40
Bankfield Cotts. OL3: Dob 1J 65
SK6: Wood 3M 109
(off Woodlands Dr.)
Bankfield Dr. M28: Wors 3J 75
OL8: O'ham 9M 63
Bankfield Ho. SK6: Wood 3M 109
Bankfield La. OL11: Roch 5K 27
Bankfield M. BL9: Bury 5M 41
Bankfield Rd. BL4: Farn 5L 57
M29: Tyld 2F 74
M33: Sale 2E 104
SK6: Wood 3M 109
SK8: Chea H 6L 117
Bankfield St. BL3: Bolt 8D 38
(Anglia Gro.)
BL3: Bolt 7D 38
(Deane Rd.)
M9: Man 2J 79
M26: Rad 4D 58
SK5: Stoc 4C 108
Bankfield Trad. Est. SK5: Stoc 4C 108
Bankfoot Wlk. *M8: Man 5F 78*
(off Barnsdale Dr.)
Bank Gate SK14: B'tom 9K 99
Bank Gro. M38: Lit H 6G 57
Bankhall Cl. BL8: Bury 2G 40
WN2: Hin 1D 72
Bankhall La. WA15: Hale 7E 114
Bankhall Rd. SK4: Stoc 5M 107
Bankhall Wlk. *M9: Man 3K 79*
(off Craigend Dr.)
BANK HEATH 1K 87
Bank Hey BL5: W'ton 3H 55
Bank Hill St. OL4: O'ham 4N 63
Bankhirst Cl. M8: Man 1F 78
Bank Ho. BL9: Bury 5L 41
Bank Ho. Cl. M29: Tyld 1F 74
Bank Ho. Rd. M9: Man 7G 61
Bankhouse Rd.
BL8: Bury 8J 25
Bank Ho's. BL6: Bla 2N 35
Banklands Cl. M44: Cad 3E 102
BANK LANE 7L 11
Bank La. M6: Sal 5K 77
M27: Pen 4K 77
M38: Lit H 5G 57
OL3: G'fld 7N 65
OL12: W'le 7H 15
SK13: Tin 2C 100
Bankley St. M19: Man 8M 95
Bank Mdw. BL6: Hor 9E 20
Bankmill Cl. M13: Man 9L 5
Bank Pl. BL8: Bury 1J 41
M3: Sal 3B 4
WA3: Gol 9K 71
Bank Pl. Apartments
SK9: Wilm 7G 123
(off Green La.)
Bankquay Ct. M44: Irl 8J 91
Bank Rd. BL1: Bolt 8F 22
M8: Man 9F 60
SK6: Bred 5L 109
SK15: C'ook 5H 83
WN8: Roby M 7G 33
Bank Row *SK13: Tin 2C 100*
(off Stocks Brow)
Banksbarn WN8: Skel 4A 50
Banks Ct. WA15: Tim 2K 115
WN7: Lei 5F 72
Banks Cft. OL10: H'ood 5J 43
Bank Side BL5: W'ton 4H 55
OL5: Mos 2F 82
Bankside SK14: Hat 8G 98
SK22: N Mil 7M 121
WA15: Haleb 9K 115
WN8: Par 2A 32
(off Burnside)
Bankside Av. M26: Rad 8K 41
OL3: Upp 4M 65
WN4: A Mak 2D 70
Bankside Cl. OL3: Upp 3M 65
OL9: O'ham 3A 8 (5H 63)
SK6: Mar B 7F 110
SK9: Wilm 4J 123
Bankside Ct. M12: Man 5M 95
SK4: Stoc 6M 107
Bankside Rd. M20: Man 9G 106
Bankside Wlk.
SK14: Hat 7G 98
Banks La. SK1: Stoc 8F 108
Banksman Way M27: Pen 2K 77
Bank Sq. SK9: Wilm 7G 123
Bank St. BL0: Ram 7L 11
BL1: Bolt 2L 7 (5G 39)
BL4: Farn 3L 57
BL7: Tur 1K 23
BL8: Bury 9F 24
BL9: Bury 8K 7 (2L 41)
M3: Sal 3B 4 (8C 78)
M7: Sal 2E 78
M11: Man 7M 79
M26: Rad 1H 59
M33: Sale 3J 105
M34: Aud 3K 97
M34: Dent 9M 97
M43: Droy 1D 96
M45: Whitef 2L 59
OL2: Shaw 5L 45
OL4: O'ham 5A 64
OL7: A Lyne 9C 6 (8M 81)
OL10: H'ood 2G 42
(not continuous)
OL11: Roch 9E 28
PR7: Adl 6K 19
SK6: Wood 3M 109
SK8: Chea 1K 117
SK11: Macc 5J 131
SK13: Glos 9F 100
SK13: Had 4C 100
SK13: B'tom 9K 99
SK14: Hyde 6A 98
WA3: Gol 9K 71
WA3: G'ook 3B 102
WA12: N Wil 6C 86
WN2: P Bri 8K 53
WN5: Wig 5B 52
Bankswood Cl. SK13: Had 5B 100
Bank Ter. OL12: Whitw 6A 14
SK13: Had 4C 100
BANK TOP
BL1 8H 23
OL4 5A 64
OL8 3B 8 (5J 63)
WN8 8G 32

Bank Top BL9: Bury .4M 25
M24: Mid .3M 61
M26: Bury, Rad .6H 41
OL6: A Lyne .8F 6 (8N 81)
OL10: H'ood .1G 43
Bank Top Gro. BL1: Bolt .8H 23
Bank Top Pk. OL4: O'ham .5A 64
Bank Top St. OL10: H'ood .1G 43
Bank Top Vw. BL4: Kea .4A 58
Bankwell St. M15: Man .4D 94
BANKWOOD .8M 99
Bank Wood BL1: Bolt .5A 38
Bankwood WN6: She .6J 33
Bankwood Ct. M9: Man .1J 79
BANKWOOD GATE .9M 99
Banky La. M33: Sale .2C 104
Bannach Dr. OL9: Chad .2E 62
Bannatyne Cl. M40: Man .1C 80
Bannatyne's Health Club
Manchester, Quay St. .5E 4
Manchester, Whitworth St. .6J 5
Bannerdale Cl. M13: Man .5L 95
(off Bowscale Cl.)
Bannerman Av. M25: Pres .8A 60
Bannerman Rd. M43: Droy .9F 80
Banner St. WN2: Hin .6A 54
WN3: I Mak .6H 53
Banner Wlk. M11: Man .9L 79
(off Pilgrim Dr.)
Bannister Dr. SK8: Chea H .5L 117
Bannister St. BL2: Bolt .4M 39
SK1: Stoc .9D 108
Bannister Way WN3: Wins .9B 52
Bann St. SK3: Stoc .4J 9 (8C 108)
Banstead Av. M22: Nor .9C 106
Bantry Dr. M9: Man .8G 60
Bantry St. BL3: Bolt .7F 38
OL12: Roch .3E 28
Baptist St. M4: Man .1K 5 (7G 78)
Barathea Cl. OL11: Roch .1M 43
Barbara Castle Sq. M13: Man .3J 95
Barbara Rd. BL3: Bolt .1B 56
Barbara St. BL3: Bolt .8E 38
Barbeck Cl. M40: Man .7K 79
Barberry Bank BL7: Eger .3E 22
Barberry Cl. WA14: B'ath .8B 104
Barberry Wlk. M31: Part .5G 102
(off Wychelm Rd.)
Barber St. M11: Man .2C 96
SK11: Macc .6J 131
SK13: Had .4D 100
Barbican St. M20: Man .1G 107
(not continuous)
Barbirolli Sq. M2: Man .7G 4
Barbrook Cl. WN6: Stan .2M 33
Barbury Cl. WN7: Lei .3H 73
Barbury Ct. BL4: Farn .4M 57
Barchester Av. BL2: Bolt .3M 39
Barcheston Rd. SK8: Chea .3H 117
Barcicroft Rd. M19: Man .4K 107
SK4: Stoc .4K 107
Barcicroft Wlk. M19: Man .4K 107
Barclay Dr. M30: Ecc .7E 76
Barclay Rd. SK12: Poy .4J 125
Barclays Av. M6: Sal .4K 77
Barcliffe Av. M40: Man .9A 62
Barclyde St. OL11: Roch .8C 28
Barcombe Cl. M32: Stre .6F 92
OL4: O'ham .1A 64
Barcombe Wlk. M9: Man .3J 79
(off Fernclough Rd., not continuous)
Barcroft Rd. BL1: Bolt .2C 38
Barcroft St. BL9: Bury .5L 7 (1M 41)
Bardale Gro. WN4: A Mak .7D 70
Bardell Cres. SK12: Poy .4H 125
Bardney Av. WA3: Gol .8J 71
Bardon Cl. BL1: Bolt .3E 38
(off Kirkhope Dr.)
Bardon Rd. M23: Wyth .1M 115
Bardsea Av. M22: Wyth .6C 116
BARDSLEY .2L 81
Bardsley Av. M35: Fail .3D 80
Bardsley Cl. BL2: Bolt .8L 23
SK14: Hat .7H 99
WN8: Uph .4E 50
BARDSLEY GATE .3H 99
Bardsley Ga. Av. SK15: Stal .3H 99
Bardsley Pk. Golf Cen. .3K 81
Bardsley St. M24: Mid .2M 61
M40: Man .5B 80
OL4: Lees .3B 64
OL4: O'ham .3B 64
OL9: Chad .8D 62
SK4: Stoc .5B 108
Bardsley Va. Av. OL8: O'ham .2L 81
Bardwell Av. BL5: W'ton .3F 54
Barehill St. OL15: Lit .8M 15
Bare St. BL1: Bolt .1N 7 (5H 39)
Barff Rd. M5: Sal .8J 77
Barfold Cl. SK2: Stoc .2L 119
Barford Cl. WN8: Uph .4E 50
Barford Dr. SK9: Wilm .5H 123
WA3: Low .1C 88
Barford Gro. BL6: Los .3H 37
Barford Wlk. M23: Wyth .3A 116
Bar Gap Rd. OL1: O'ham .3K 63
Baric Cl. M30: Ecc .9F 76
(off Lane End)
Baring St. M1: Man .7L 5 (1G 95)
Baring St. Ind. Est.
M1: Man .7M 5 (1H 95)
Barkan Way M27: Pen .2H 77
Barker De Lane BL6: Bla .6A 36
Barker Rd. SK6: Bred .6K 109
Barkers La. M33: Sale .3F 104
Barker St. BL9: Bury .3L 41
M3: Man .7E 78
OL1: O'ham .1C 8 (4J 63)
OL10: H'ood .3G 43
WN7: Lei .5E 72
Barke St. OL15: Lit .2K 29
Barking St. M40: Man .7K 79
Bark St. BL1: Bolt .2H 7 (5F 38)
BL4: Kea .6B 58
Bark St. E. BL1: Bolt .1K 7 (4G 38)
Bark Wlk. M15: Man .9G 5

Barkway Rd. M32: Stre .7G 93
Barkwell La. OL5: Mos .1E 82
Barkworth Wlk. M40: Man .4N 79
(off Harold Priestnall Cl.)
Bar La. BL1: Bolt .8F 22
Barlborough Rd. WN5: Wig .6A 52
Barlby Wlk. M40: Man .4N 79
(off Harold Priestnall Cl.)
Barlea Av. M40: Man .1B 80
Barley Brook Mdw. BL1: Bolt .7G 22
Barley Brook St. WN6: Wig .2D 52
Barleycorn Cl. M33: Sale .5N 105
Barley Cft. SK8: Chea H .6L 117
Barleycroft SK13: Had .5B 100
Barley Cft. Rd. SK14: Hyde .3B 98
Barleycroft St. M16: Whall R .5E 94
Barley Dr. SK7: Bram .8C 118
Barleyfield Wlk. M24: Mid .2L 61
Barley Hall St. OL10: H'ood .1K 43
Barley Mere Cl. WA12: N Wil .7F 86
Barleywood Dr. M11: Man .1L 95
Barleywood Wlk. SK15: Stal .1G 99
Barlow Cl. BL9: Bury .8M 25
Barlow Ct. M28: Walk .8M 57
Barlow Cres. SK6: Mar .3C 120
BARLOW FOLD .7M 41
BARLOWFOLD .5B 110
Barlow Fold BL9: Bury .7M 41
SK6: Rom .5A 110
Barlow Fold Cl. BL9: Bury .7L 41
Barlow Fold Rd. SK5: Stoc .9D 96
SK6: Rom .5A 110
Barlow Hall Rd. M21: Cho H .3B 106
Barlow Ho. BL1: Bolt .2C 38
OL8: O'ham .5D 8 (6J 63)
Barlow La. M30: Ecc .8C 76
Barlow La. Nth. SK5: Stoc .9D 96
BARLOW MOOR .3B 106
Barlow Moor Cl. OL12: Roch .3K 27
Barlow Moor Ct. M20: Man .4E 106
Barlow Moor Rd. M20: Man .3D 106
M21: Cho H .8A 94
Barlow Pk. Av. BL1: Bolt .8E 22
Barlow Rd. M5: Sal .5A 4 (9B 78)
M19: Man .8M 95
M32: Stre .5M 93
SK9: Wilm .5G 122
SK16: Duk .1A 98
WA14: B'ath .8B 104
Barlow's Cft. M3: Sal .3E 4 (8D 78)
Barlow's La. Sth. SK7: H Gro .4G 118
Barlow St. BL6: Hor .2E 36
M26: Rad .9H 41
M28: Walk .7L 57
M30: Ecc .9D 76
OL4: O'ham .4G 8 (5L 63)
OL10: H'ood .1H 43
OL16: Roch .7E 8 (6E 28)
Barlow Ter. M21: Cho H .2B 106
Barlow Wlk. SK5: Stoc .9D 96
(off Barlow La. Nth.)
Barlow Wood Dr. SK6: Mar .4E 120
Barmeadow OL3: Dob .1J 65
Barmhouse Cl. SK14: Hyde .6D 98
Barmhouse La. SK14: Hyde .6D 98
(Carlton Rd.)
SK14: Hyde .6D 98
(Mt. Pleasant)
Barmhouse M. SK14: Hyde .6D 98
Barmouth Ct. OL8: O'ham .9F 62
Barmouth St. M11: Man .1L 95
Barmouth Wlk. OL8: O'ham .9F 62
Barnaby Rd. SK12: Poy .4H 125
Barnabys Rd. BL5: W'ton .9F 36
Barn Acre BL6: Bla .3A 36
Barnacre Av. BL2: Bolt .5N 39
M23: Wyth .4M 115
Barnard Av. M45: Whitef .4A 60
SK4: Stoc .6N 107
Barnard Cl. OL7: A Lyne .5K 81
SK11: Macc .6D 130
Barnard Rd. M18: Man .6N 95
Barnard St. BL2: Bolt .4K 39
Barnbrook St.
BL9: Bury .6N 7 (1N 41)
Barnby St. M12: Man .6M 95
Barn Cl. M41: Urm .7K 91
Barnclose Rd. M22: Wyth .6B 116
Barn Ct. BL2: Bolt .2K 39
Barncroft Cl. SK11: Chel .9A 126
Barncroft Dr. BL6: Hor .1H 37
Barncroft Gdns.
M22: Wyth .2B 116
Barncroft Rd. BL4: Farn .3L 57
Barnes Av. SK4: Stoc .6M 107
Barnes Cl. BL0: Ram .2G 25
BL4: Farn .3L 57
Barnes Dr. BL4: Farn .2G 57
BARNES GREEN .1J 79
Barnes Ho. BL4: Farn .3L 57
(off Hesketh Wlk.)
Barnes Mdws. OL15: Lit .5N 15
Barnes Pas. M46: Ath .8N 55
Barnes St. BL4: Farn .3J 57
Barnes Ter. BL4: Kea .4A 58
Barneswell St. M40: Man .5A 80
Barnet Rd. BL1: Bolt .2D 38
Barnett Av. M20: Man .2G 106
WA12: N Wil .6B 86
Barnett Cl. OL10: H'ood .3H 43
Barnett Dr. M3: Sal .2C 4 (8C 78)
Barnett St. SK11: Macc .5F 130
Barnfield M41: Urm .8B 92
OL15: Lit .8A 16
Barnfield Av. SK6: Rom .5A 110
Barnfield Cl. BL7: Eger .3F 22
M5: Sal .9M 77
M26: Rad .9E 40
M29: Tyld .1A 74
Barnfield Cres. M33: Sale .3F 104
Barnfield Dr. BL5: W'ton .2J 55
M28: Wors .4J 75
WN8: Skel .4C 50
Barnfield Ho. M3: Sal .3F 4
Barn Fld. La. OL12: W'le .7E 14
Barnfield Ri. OL2: Shaw .3L 45

Barnfield Rd. M19: Man .4K 107
M27: Ward .9D 58
SK10: Boll .6K 129
SK14: Hyde .4E 98
Barnfield Rd. E. SK3: Stoc .3D 118
Barnfield Rd. W. SK3: Stoc .3B 118
Barnfield St. M34: Dent .5H 97
OL10: H'ood .2K 43
OL12: Roch .3D 28
Barnfield Wlk. WA15: Tim .2J 115
(off Merefield Rd.)
Barn Fold OL4: Lees .6B 64
Barngate Dr. OL5: Mos .2F 82
Barngate Rd. SK8: Gat .1F 116
Barngill Gro. WN3: Wig .8B 52
Barn Gro. M34: Aud .2J 97
Barnham Cl. WA3: Gol .1K 87
Barnham Wlk. M23: Wyth .8L 105
Barn Hill BL5: W'ton .2G 55
Barnhill Av. M25: Pres .9A 60
Barnhill Dr. M25: Pres .9A 60
Barnhill Rd. M25: Pres .8A 60
Barnhill St. M14: Man .5E 94
Barn Hill Ter. BL5: W'ton .2G 55
(off Tithebarn St.)
Barn La. WA3: Gol .2J 87
Barnley Cl. M44: Irl .6J 91
Barnsdale Cl. BL2: Ain .3C 40
Barnsdale Dr. M8: Man .4F 78
Barnsfold Av. M14: Man .9H 95
Barnsfold Rd. SK6: Mar .4C 120
Barnside OL12: Whitw .6A 14
Barnside Av. M28: Walk .9M 57
Barnside Cl. BL9: Bury .5L 25
Barnside Way M35: Fail .4G 80
SK10: Macc .1G 130
Barns La. WA13: Warb .1H 113
WA14: D Mas, Warb .2H 113
Barnsley St. SK1: Stoc .8F 108
WN6: Wig .9D 34
Barns Pl. WA15: Haleb .7J 115
Barnstaple Dr. M40: Man .4H 79
Barnstead Av. M20: Man .3J 107
Barnston Av. M14: Man .7G 94
Barnston Cl. BL1: Bolt .9G 23
Barn St. BL1: Bolt .3J 7 (5F 38)
M45: Whitef .4M 59
OL1: O'ham .3C 8 (5J 63)
Barnton Cl. WA3: Low .2N 87
Barn Vw. PR6: H Char .5J 19
Barnview Dr. M44: Irl .8G 91
Barn Wlk. M11: Man .2C 96
Barn Way WA12: N Wil .6E 86
Barnway Wlk. M40: Man .9A 62
Barnwell Av. WA3: Cul .5F 88
Barnwell Cl. M34: Aud .4J 97
Barnwood Cl. BL1: Bolt .3F 38
(off Barnwood Dr.)
Barnwood Dr. BL1: Bolt .3F 38
Barnwood Rd. M23: Wyth .4N 115
Barnwood Ter. BL1: Bolt .3F 38
(off Faraday Dr.)
Baroness Rd. M34: Aud .2G 96
Baronet Wlk. M7: Sal .6C 78
Baron Fold M38: Lit H .6H 57
Baron Fold Cres. M38: Lit H .6G 56
Baron Fold Gro. M38: Lit H .6G 57
Baron Fold Rd. M38: Lit H .6G 57
(off Manchester Rd. W.)
Baron Grn. SK8: H Grn .8J 117
Baron Rd. SK14: Hyde .1C 110
Barons Ct. M35: Fail .4B 80
SK9: Wilm .7G 123
(off Swan St.)
Baron St. BL9: Bury .9H 7 (3K 41)
(not continuous)
OL4: O'ham .6M 63
OL16: Roch .8D 8 (6D 28)
Baron Wlk. BL3: Lit L .9C 40
BARRACK HILL .6L 109
Barrack Hill SK6: Rom .6L 109
Barrack Hill Cl. SK6: Bred .5L 109
Barracks SK13: Dens .3F 46
Barracks La. M33: Sale .2D 104
(off Banky La.)
SK10: Macc .4K 131
Barracks Rd. WN2: B'haw .1N 71
Barracks Sq. SK11: Macc .6F 130
WN1: Wig .8K 9
Barrack St. M15: Man .9B 4 (2C 94)
Barracks Yd. WN1: Wig .8J 9
Barra Dr. M41: Urm .4D 92
Barrass St. M11: Man .2B 96
Barratt Gdns. M24: Mid .9J 43
Barrett Av. BL4: Kea .4N 57
Barrett Ct. BL9: Bury .2N 41
Barrett St. OL4: O'ham .6M 63
Barrfield Rd. M6: Sal .6L 77
Barr Hill Av. M6: Sal .5L 77
Barrhill Cl. M15: Man .3D 94
Barrie St. WN7: Lei .2F 72
Barrie Way BL1: Bolt .9J 23
Barrington Av. M43: Droy .9D 80
SK8: Chea H .6M 117
Barrington Cl. WA14: Alt .1D 114
WN3: Wins .9A 52
Barrington Rd.
WA14: Alt .1D 6 (1D 114)
Barrington St. M11: Man .8A 80
Barrisdale Cl. BL3: Bolt .7A 38
Barron Mdw. WN7: Lei .3F 72
BARROW BRIDGE .9A 22
Barrow Bri. Rd. BL1: Bolt .9A 22
Barrowcroft Cl. WN1: Stan .3E 34
Barrowdale Rd. WA3: Gol .1L 87
Barrowdene Ho. BL1: Bolt .9A 22
(off Bazley St.)
Barrowfield Rd. M22: Wyth .5N 115
Barrowfields M24: Mid .1M 61
Barrowfield Wlk. M24: Mid .2M 61
Barrow Hill Rd. M8: Man .5E 78
Barrow La. WA2: Cro, Win .7L 87
WA3: Cro .7L 87
WA15: Hale .8H 115
Barrow Mdw. SK8: Chea H .7K 117
Barrows Ct. BL1: Bolt .4K 7 (6G 38)

Barrowshaw Cl. M28: Walk .9K 57
Barrow St. M3: Sal .4B 4 (9C 78)
WN4: A Mak .5G 71
Barrs Fold Cl. BL5: W'ton .9F 36
Barrs Fold Rd. BL5: W'ton .1F 54
Barrule Av. SK7: H Gro .6J 119
Barry Ct. M20: Man .2G 106
Barry Cres. M28: Walk .8H 57
Barry Lawson Cl. M8: Man .3E 78
Barry Ri. WA14: Bow .5A 114
Barry Rd. M23: Wyth .6A 106
SK5: Stoc .3D 108
Barry St. OL1: O'ham .3M 63
Barsham Cl. M8: Man .1H 79
Barsham Dr. BL3: Bolt .7E 38
Bar St. WN2: P Bri .1K 71
Bar Ter. OL12: Whitw .7A 14
Bartlam Pl. OL1: O'ham .2E 8
Bartlemore St. OL1: O'ham .2L 63
Bartlett Rd. OL2: Shaw .6L 45
Bartlett St. M11: Man .2N 95
Bartley Rd. M22: Nor .8B 106
BARTON .8F 76
Barton Aerodrome Vis. Cen. .2M 91
Barton Arc. M3: Man .4G 4
Barton Av. M41: Urm .7B 92
WN1: Wig .1E 52
Barton Bri. M30: Ecc .1D 92
Barton Bus. Pk. M30: Ecc .9C 76
Barton Cl. SK9: Wilm .4J 123
Barton Clough WN5: Bil .5J 69
Barton Ct. M30: Ecc .1D 92
(off Barton La.)
Barton Dock Rd. M32: Stre .4G 92
M41: Stre, Urm .3D 92
Barton Emb. M17: Urm .2C 92
Barton Fold SK14: Hyde .8A 98
Barton Hall Av. M30: Ecc .9A 76
Barton Ho. M6: Sal .6J 77
(off Moss Mdw. Rd.)
Barton La. M30: Ecc .1D 92
Barton Moss Rd. M30: Ecc .1K 91
Barton Pl. M4: Man .1H 5
Barton Rd. BL4: Farn .4J 57
M24: Mid .3L 61
M27: Swin .3G 77
M28: Wors .5N 75
M30: Ecc .9C 76
M32: Stre .5F 92
M41: Urm .5C 92
SK4: Stoc .7K 107
SK16: Duk .3N 97
Barton Sq. M2: Man .4F 4 (9E 78)
M41: Urm .3E 92
Barton St. BL4: Farn .4M 57
M3: Man .7E 4 (1D 94)
M29: Tyld .1A 74
OL1: O'ham .3H 63
SK11: Macc .6G 131
WA3: Gol .9K 71
WN2: P Bri .8L 53
WN5: Wig .6M 51
Barton Ter. M44: Irl .6K 91
BARTON UPON IRWELL .1D 92
Barton Wlk. BL4: Farn .4J 57
Barway Rd. M21: Cho H .8M 93
Barwell Cl. SK5: Stoc .9D 96
WA3: Gol .9M 71
Barwell Rd. M33: Sale .3E 104
Barwell Sq. BL4: Farn .1J 57
Barwick Pl. M33: Sale .4G 104
Barwood Lea BL0: Ram .9J 11
Barwood Lea Mill BL0: Ram .8H 11
Basechurch Wlk. M12: Man .3L 95
(off Skarratt Cl.)
Basford Rd. M16: Old T .6A 94
Bashall St. BL1: Bolt .4D 38
Basil Ct. OL16: Roch .7F 28
Basildon Rd. M13: Man .4J 95
Basil St. BL3: Bolt .7F 38
M14: Man .6H 95
OL16: Roch .7F 28
SK4: Stoc .5C 108
Basle Cl. SK7: Bram .3C 118
Baslow Av. M19: Man .7B 96
WN2: Hin .8A 54
Baslow Cl. SK13: Gam .8A 100
Baslow Dr. SK7: H Gro .7K 119
SK8: H Grn .8H 117
Baslow Fold SK13: Gam .8A 100
(off Castleton Cres.)
Baslow Grn. SK13: Gam .8A 100
(off Castleton Cres.)
Baslow Gro. SK5: Stoc .3D 108
Baslow M. SK13: Gam .8A 100
Baslow Rd. M32: Stre .6G 93
M34: Dent .9K 97
M43: Droy .7C 80
Baslow St. M11: Man .9K 79
Baslow Way SK13: Gam .8A 100
(off Castleton Cres.)
Bassenthwaite Cl. M24: Mid .9J 43
Basset Av. M6: Sal .5B 78
Bassett Cl. OL12: Roch .2C 28
Bassett Gdns. OL12: Roch .2C 28
Bassett Gro. WN3: Wins .9N 51
Bassett Way OL12: Roch .3C 28
Bass La. BL9: Sum .2K 25
Bass St. BL2: Bolt .5K 39
(off Dunstan St.)
SK16: Duk .1M 97
Basswood Grn. WN2: Hin .8C 54
Basten Dr. M7: Sal .4E 78
Batchelor Cl. M21: Cho H .1D 106
Bateman St. BL6: Hor .2F 36
Batemill Cl. SK10: Macc .3D 130
Batemill Rd. SK22: N Mil .5N 121
Bates Cl. OL11: Roch .3B 44
Bateson Dr. OL4: Spri .5C 64
Bateson St. SK1: Stoc .1N 9 (6E 108)
Bateson Way OL8: O'ham .6K 63
Bates St. M13: Man .5L 95
SK16: Duk .1N 97
Bath Cl. SK7: H Gro .5L 119
Bath Cres. M16: Old T .2B 94
SK8: Chea H .9N 117

Batheaston Gro. WN7: Lei .2F 72
Bath Pl. WA14: Alt .5D 114
Bath St. BL1: Bolt .1K 7 (4G 38)
M46: Ath .8J 55
OL9: Chad .4F 62
OL9: O'ham .6G 63
OL12: Roch .4E 28
WA14: Alt .5D 114
WN2: Wig .1J 53
Batley St. M9: Man .2K 79
OL5: Mos .1E 82
(off Seel St.)
Batsmans Dr. M27: Clif .7E 58
Battenberg Rd. BL1: Bolt .4D 38
Battersbay Gro. SK7: H Gro .5J 119
Battersby Ct. SK2: Stoc .1J 119
Battersby St. BL9: Bury .1C 42
M11: Man .2C 96
OL11: Roch .7N 27
WN2: I Mak .3L 53
WN7: Lei .6K 73
Battersea Rd. SK4: Stoc .7K 107
Battery La. SK9: Wilm .8C 122
Batty St. M8: Man .5H 79
Baucher Rd. WN3: Wig .6C 52
Baum, The OL16: Roch .6C 8 (5D 28)
Baverstock Cl. WN3: I Mak .5G 53
Baxendale St. BL1: Bolt .9F 22
Baxter Gdns. M23: Wyth .9N 105
Baxter Rd. M33: Sale .4H 105
Baxter's Row WN2: Hin .9D 54
Baxter St. OL8: O'ham .9F 62
WN6: Stan .3C 34
Baybutt St. M26: Rad .9J 41
Baycliff Cl. WN2: Hin .8B 54
Baycliffe Wlk. M8: Man .4E 78
(off Felthorpe Dr.)
Baycroft Gro. M23: Wyth .7N 105
Baydon Av. M7: Sal .4E 78
Bayfield Gro. M40: Man .1M 79
Bayley Cl. SK14: Hyde .4B 98
Bayley Ct. BL1: Bolt .4E 38
Bayleyfield SK14: Hyde .5A 98
Bayley Ind. Est. SK15: Stal .9C 82
Bayley St. SK15: Stal .8B 82
Baynard Wlk. M9: Man .7G 61
(off Crab La.)
Baysdale Av. BL3: Bolt .8A 38
Baysdale Dr. OL2: O'ham .7G 45
Baysdale Wlk. M11: Man .9L 79
Bayston Wlk. M12: Man .3L 95
(off Kempley Cl.)
Bay St. OL9: O'ham .2A 8 (4H 63)
OL10: H'ood .1G 43
OL12: Roch .4E 28
Bayswater Av. M40: Man .6A 80
Bayswater St. BL3: Bolt .1D 56
Baythorpe St. BL1: Bolt .3F 38
Bay Tree Av. M28: Wors .5A 76
Baytree Av. M34: Dent .5L 97
OL9: Chad .3C 62
Baytree Dr. SK6: Bred .4K 109
Baytree Gro. BL0: Ram .3H 25
Baytree La. M24: Mid .3B 62
Baytree M. M24: Mid .2B 62
(off Baytree La.)
Baytree Rd. WN6: Wig .1C 52
Baytree Wlk. OL12: Whitw .5A 14
Baywood St. M9: Man .2J 79
Bazaar St. M6: Sal .6N 77
Bazley Rd. M22: Nor .7C 106
Bazley St. BL1: Bolt .9A 22
BBC Broadcasting House
Manchester .8J 5 (2F 94)
Beacomfold SK6: Comp .5E 110
Beacon Cl. M46: Ath .9J 55
Beacon Country Pk. .2D 50
Beacon Country Pk. Vis. Cen. .1C 50
Beacon Crossing WN8: Par .2A 32
Beacon Dr. M23: Wyth .5N 115
Beaconfield Av. SK14: Hyde .7B 98
Beacon Grn. WN8: Skel .3C 50
Beacon Gro. OL8: O'ham .7N 63
Beacon Hgts. WN8: Uph .3E 50
Beacon La. WN8: Dal .7A 32
Beacon Park Golf Course .1D 50
Beacon Rd. M17: T Pk .2E 92
SK6: Rom .7L 109
WN2: B'haw .2C 72
WN5: Bil .3H 69
WN6: Stan .2M 33
Beacons, The WN6: She .5H 33
Beaconsfield M14: Man .1H 107
Beaconsfield Rd. WA14: B'ath .9D 104
Beaconsfield St. BL3: Bolt .6E 38
Beaconsfield Ter.
SK15: C'ook .3J 83
Beacon Vw. SK6: Mar .8C 110
WN6: App B .4G 33
WN6: Stan .3N 33
Beacon Vw. Dr. WN8: Uph .4F 50
Beadham Dr. M9: Man .6F 60
Beadle Av. OL12: Roch .9H 15
Beaford Cl. WN5: Wig .6M 51
Beaford Rd. M22: Wyth .7C 116
Beagle Wlk. M22: Wyth .7D 116
Bealbank Cl. OL16: Miln .1L 45
Beal Cl. SK4: Stoc .5J 107
Beal Cres. OL16: Roch .4G 29
(not continuous)
Bealcroft Cl. OL16: Miln .6J 29
Bealcroft Wlk. OL16: Miln .6J 29
Beal Dr. WN2: P Bri .9K 53
Beale Gro. M21: Cho H .9A 94
Bealey Av. M26: Rad .7L 41
Bealey Cl. M18: Man .4N 95
M26: Rad .8K 41
Bealey Dr. BL9: Bury .5K 41
Bealey Ind. Est. M26: Rad .7K 41
Bealey Row M26: Rad .8J 41
Beal La. OL2: Shaw .6M 45
Beal Ter. OL16: Miln .7K 29
Beal Vw. OL2: Shaw .5A 46
Beal Wlk. M45: Whitef .3B 60
Beaminster Av. SK4: Stoc .5L 107
Beaminster Cl. SK4: Stoc .5L 107

Beaminster Ct. *SK4: Stoc 5L 107*
(off Priestnall Rd.)
Beaminster Rd. SK4: Stoc 5L 107
Beaminster Wlk. *M13: Man 4H 95*
(off Lauderdale Cres.)
Beamish Cl. M13: Man 9M 5 (3H 95)
Beamsley Dr. M22: Wyth 5A 116
Beamsmoor Cl. SK6: Mar 3C 120
Beanfields M28: Wors 5N 75
Beanfield Ter. M28: Wors 5N 75
Bean Leach Av. SK2: Stoc 1K 119
Bean Leach Dr. SK2: Stoc 1K 119
Bean Leach Rd. SK2: Stoc 3J 119
SK7: H Gro 3J 119
Beard Cres. SK22: N Mil 7N 121
Beard Rd. M18: Man 5A 96
Beardsmore Dr. WA3: Low 1A 88
Beard St. M43: Droy 9D 80
OL2: O'ham 9J 45
Beardwood Rd. M9: Man 7J 61
Bearncroft WN8: Skel 5A 50
Bearswood Cl. SK14: Hyde 8C 98
Beathwaite Dr. SK7: Bram 6A 118
Beatrice Av. M18: Man 5D 96
SK8: Chea H 5L 117
Beatrice M. *BL6: Hor 9D 20*
(off Beatrice St.)
Beatrice Rd. BL1: Bolt 4D 38
M28: Wors 3B 76
Beatrice St. BL4: Farn 3K 57
BL6: Hor 9D 20
M27: Swin 1D 76
M34: Dent 6J 97
OL11: Roch 6B 28
Beatrice Wignall St. M43: Droy 1E 96
Beatrix Dr. SK13: Had 6A 100
Beatrix Ho. SK16: Duk 2C 98
Beattock Cl. M15: Man 9C 4 (2C 94)
Beatty Dr. BL5: W'ton 2G 54
Beauchamp St.
OL6: A Lyne 6E 6 (6N 81)
Beaufont Dr. OL4: O'ham 6N 63
Beaufort Av. M20: Man 3F 106
M27: Swin 3D 76
M33: Sale 5J 105
Beaufort Chase SK9: Wilm 5L 123
Beaufort Cl. SK9: A Edg 3G 127
SK14: Hat 7H 99
Beaufort Rd. M33: Sale 5J 105
OL6: A Lyne 6G 6 (7A 82)
SK2: Stoc 3H 119
SK14: Hat 7H 99
Beaufort St. M3: Man 7D 4 (1D 94)
M25: Pres 7B 60
M30: Ecc 7B 76
OL12: Roch 4A 28
WN2: Hin 6N 53
WN5: Wig 5B 52
Beaufort Way *SK14: Hat 8H 99*
(off Beaufort Rd.)
Beaulieu WA15: Hale 5F 114
Beauly Cl. BL0: Ram 3G 25
Beaumaris Cl. M12: Man 3L 95
WN7: Lei 5E 72
Beaumaris Cres. SK7: H Gro 7G 119
Beaumaris Rd. WN2: Hin 8C 54
Beaumonds Way OL11: Roch 7M 27
Beaumont Av. BL6: Hor 9E 20
Beaumont Chase BL3: Bolt 9A 38
Beaumont Cl. OL15: Lit 9K 15
Beaumont Ct. BL1: Bolt 4M 37
SK9: Hand 1H 123
(off Clay La.)
Beaumont Dr. BL3: Bolt 7N 37
Beaumont Gro. WN5: Orr 3M 51
Beaumont Pl. SK15: Stal 6C 82
Beaumont Rd. BL1: Bolt 5M 37
BL3: Bolt 5M 37
BL6: Hor 9E 20
BL6: Los 5M 37
M21: Cho H 1A 106
Beaumont St.
OL6: A Lyne 6F 6 (7N 81)
Beauvale Av. SK2: Stoc 9G 109
Beaverbrook Av. WA3: Cul 5K 89
Beaver Ct. WN4: A Mak 4F 70
Beaver Dr. BL9: Bury 8A 42
Beaver Ho. SK1: Stoc 8F 108
Beaver Rd. M20: Man 5G 107
Beavers La. WN8: Skel 5B 50
Beaver St. M1: Man 7H 5 (1F 94)
Beavers Way WN8: Skel 5B 50
Beaver Wlk. SK14: Hat 8G 99
Bebbington Cl. M33: Sale 5M 105
Bebbington St. M11: Man 9A 80
Beccles Rd. M33: Sale 7H 105
Beckenham Cl. BL8: Bury 3H 41
Beckenham Rd. M8: Man 3F 78
Becket Av. M7: Sal 4D 78
Becket Mdws. OL4: O'ham 5M 63
Becket Mdw. St.
OL4: O'ham 5M 63
Beckett Dr. WA13: Warb 8D 102
Beckett St. M18: Man 5A 96
OL4: Lees 4B 64
Beckfield Rd. M23: Wyth 2N 115
Beckfoot Dr. M13: Man 6K 95
Beckford Ct. M29: Tyld 1B 74
Beckford St. M40: Man 5K 79
Beck Gro. M28: Walk 1M 75
OL2: Shaw 4A 46
WA11: St H 9F 68
Beckhampton Cl. M13: Man 4H 95
Beck Ho. SK14: Hat 8G 98
Beckley Av. M25: Pres 9N 59
Beckley Cl. OL2: O'ham 7M 45
Beckside M29: Tyld 2N 73
SK5: Stoc 8E 96
Becks La. SK10: Macc 2C 130
Beck St. M11: Man 2C 96
Beckton Gdns. M22: Wyth 4B 116
Beckwith WN2: P Bri 8L 53
Becontree Av. M34: Dent 5L 97
Becontree Dr. M23: Wyth 9K 105
Bedale Cl. WA12: N Wil 8G 86
Bedells La. SK9: Wilm 8F 122
Bede St. BL1: Bolt 2D 38
Bedfont Wlk. *M9: Man 1K 79*
(off Hemsley St. Sth.)
BEDFORD 6L 73
Bedford Av. M16: Whall R 7C 94
M27: Swin 3E 76
M28: Wors 1K 75
M33: Sale 6K 105
OL2: Shaw 5K 45
SK14: Hyde 6B 98
Bedford Ct. M7: Sal 1C 78
WA15: Tim 1J 115
WN7: Lei 6J 73
(off Duke St.)
Bedford Dr. M46: Ath 1J 73
WA15: Tim 9J 105
Bedford Gdns. WN2: Hin 5B 54
Bedford Gro. M44: Cad 2C 102
Bedford Pl.
WN4: A Mak 5D 70
Bedford Rd. M16: Old T 6N 93
M30: Ecc 7E 76
M41: Urm 5C 92
SK11: Macc 5F 130
Bedfordshire Cl. OL9: Chad 6F 62
Bedford Sq. WN7: Lei 6J 73
Bedford St. BL1: Bolt 4E 38
BL7: Eger 3E 22
BL9: Bury 9N 25
M25: Pres 6B 60
OL6: A Lyne 8F 6 (8N 81)
OL10: H'ood 2K 43
SK5: Stoc 9C 96
(not continuous)
WN1: Wig 6N 9 (2H 53)
WN5: Wig 6N 51
WN7: Lei 5J 73
Bedford Wlk. M34: Dent 7K 97
Bedlington Cl. M23: Wyth 1L 115
Bednal Av. M40: Man 6K 79
Bedwell St. M16: Whall R 6E 94
Bedworth Cl. BL2: Bolt 7J 39
Beechacre BL0: Ram 9K 11
Beecham Ct. WN3: Wig 7B 52
Beech Av. BL3: Lit L 1B 58
BL4: Farn 3H 57
BL4: Kea 6B 58
BL6: Hor 3G 36
M6: Sal 6L 77
M22: Nor 8C 106
M26: Rad 3F 58
M28: Wors 4H 75
M32: Stre 8L 93
M34: Dent 5H 97
M41: Urm 7C 92
M43: Droy 9D 80
M44: Irl 6K 91
M45: Whitef 4M 59
M46: Ath 8N 55
OL1: Chad 1E 62
OL3: G'fld 5L 65
OL4: O'ham 3A 64
PR6: And 5L 19
SK3: Stoc 1D 118
SK6: Mar 1A 120
SK7: H Gro 5J 119
SK8: Gat 3G 116
SK13: Glos 9C 100
SK22: N Mil 6N 121
WA3: Cul 6J 89
WA3: Low 2B 88
WA11: Hay 2C 86
WA15: Tim 8H 105
WA16: Mob 2L 133
WN8: Par 3A 32
Beech Bank SK10: Macc 2G 131
Beech Cl. BL2: Bolt 7K 23
M25: Pres 8B 60
M31: Part 5G 103
OL12: Whitw 5A 14
SK9: A Edg 2G 126
WA12: N Wil 7F 86
WA16: Olle 9N 133
(off Marthall La.)
Beech Cotts. SK9: A Edg 5F 126
Beech Ct. M6: Sal 7N 77
M8: Man 1E 78
M14: Man 9H 95
M21: Cho H 8M 93
M33: Sale 4F 104
SK9: Wilm 8J 123
WA3: Ris 8H 89
Beech Cres. SK12: Poy 2J 125
WN6: Stan 4B 34
WN7: Lei 7G 73
Beechcroft M25: Pres 8B 60
Beechcroft Av. BL2: Bolt 6M 39
Beechcroft Cl.
M40: Man 1N 5 (7J 79)
Beechcroft Gro. BL2: Bolt 6M 39
Beechdale Cl. M40: Man 2A 80
Beech Dr. WA16: Knut 6J 133
WN7: Lei 8H 73
Beecher Wlk. *M9: Man 4J 79*
(off Kelvington Dr.)
Beeches, The BL1: Bolt 7E 22
M20: Man 4E 106
M30: Ecc 7F 76
M46: Ath 8M 55
(off George St.)
OL5: Mos 1H 83
OL6: A Lyne 8A 82
(off Crawford M.)
OL10: H'ood 2H 43
OL12: Whitw 5A 14
SK6: Rom 6M 109
SK8: Chea H 6N 117
WA14: Bow 5C 114
Beeches Ct. SK14: Hyde 3D 98
Beeches M., The M20: Man 4E 106
Beech Farm Dr. SK10: Macc 2H 131
Beechfield OL4: Gras 6G 64
OL11: Roch 7K 27
SK9: Wilm 8F 122
(off Albert Rd.)
WA14: Alt 4C 114
Beechfield Av. M26: Rad 2J 59
M38: Lit H 6H 57
M41: Urm 6A 92
SK9: Wilm 9D 122
WN2: Hin 7C 54
Beechfield Cl. M33: Sale 6F 104
OL4: Spri 5C 64
OL11: Roch 7K 27
Beechfield Ct. BL9: Bury 5L 41
Beechfield Dr. BL9: Bury 5L 41
WN7: Lei 7H 73
Beechfield M. SK14: Hyde 6D 98
Beechfield Rd. BL1: Bolt 2C 38
M27: Swin 5E 76
OL16: Miln 8J 29
SK3: Stoc 3D 118
SK8: Chea H 7N 117
SK9: A Edg 5F 126
SK13: Had 6A 100
Beechfield St. M8: Man 4F 78
Beech Gro. BL8: G'mount 4G 24
M6: Sal 6L 77
M14: Man 1J 107
M33: Sale 4F 104
M38: Lit H 6F 56
OL7: A Lyne 9K 81
SK9: Wilm 8F 122
SK11: Macc 7J 131
SK15: Stal 1C 98
WN2: Abr 3M 71
WN6: Wig 9B 34
WN7: Lei 8G 73
Beech Gro. Cl. BL9: Bury 9A 26
Beech Hall Dr. SK10: Macc 2G 131
Beech Hall St. WN6: Wig 1D 52
BEECH HILL 9D 34
Beech Hill Av. WN6: Wig 9B 34
Beech Hill La. WN6: Wig 9B 34
Beech Hill Rd. OL4: Gras 5G 64
Beech Holme Gro. SK2: Stoc 8G 108
Beech Ho. BL5: W'ton 9H 37
M20: Man 4D 106
M22: Shar 1D 116
(off Lauriston Cl.)
M30: Ecc 9B 76
(off New La.)
OL2: Shaw 7M 45
Beech Ho. Gdns. WA15: Tim 8G 104
Beech Hurst Cl. M16: Whall R 7C 94
Beechlands WA14: Alt 4B 114
Beech La. OL4: Gras 6G 65
SK6: Rom 6N 109
SK9: Wilm 8F 122
SK10: Macc 3H 131
Beech Lawn WA14: Alt 3A 6 (3C 114)
Beech M. M21: Cho H 9N 93
SK2: Stoc 2E 118
Beechmill Dr. WA3: Cul 6G 88
Beech Mt. M9: Man 2J 79
OL7: A Lyne 4L 81
Beechpark Av. M22: Nor 9B 106
Beech Range M19: Man 8M 95
Beech Rd. M21: Cho H 9N 93
M33: Sale 4K 105
SK2: Stoc 1D 118
SK3: Stoc 1C 118
SK6: H Lan 8C 120
SK8: Chea H 6N 117
SK9: A Edg 2G 126
WA3: Gol 9K 71
WA15: Hale 5F 6 (4E 114)
WA16: Mob 9A 122
Beech St. BL1: Bolt 2G 39
BL7: Edg 1L 23
BL9: Bury 2A 42
BL9: Sum 2J 25
M24: Mid 3L 61
M26: Rad 2J 59
M27: Swin 3F 76
M30: Ecc 9B 76
M35: Fail 2C 80
M46: Ath 8N 55
OL1: O'ham 1F 8 (4L 63)
OL11: Roch 9A 8 (7B 28)
OL16: Miln 9M 29
SK14: Hyde 6A 98
(off John St.)
WN4: A Mak 4D 70
Beech Tree Av. WN6: App B 4H 33
Beech Tree Bank M25: Pres 7N 59
Beechtree Farm Cl.
WA16: H Leg 8C 112
Beech Tree Ho's.
WN2: Bam 4H 71
Beechtree La. WA13: Lym 8B 112
Beechtrees WN8: Skel 4A 50
Beechurst Rd. SK8: Chea H 2N 117
Beech Vw. SK14: Hyde 7D 98
Beech Vs. *M33: Sale 4K 105*
(off Carlyn Av.)
Beechville BL6: Los 5J 37
Beech Wlk. M24: Mid 5L 61
M32: Stre 8J 93
WN3: Wins 9N 51
WN6: Stan 4A 34
WN7: Lei 8G 73
Beechway SK6: H Lan 8C 120
SK9: Wilm 9F 122
SK10: Boll 6L 129
Beechwood BL9: Bury 6N 41
OL2: Shaw 4A 46
SK13: Glos 9B 100
WA14: Bow 6B 114
WA16: Knut 5F 132
(Garden Rd.)
WA16: Knut 6J 133
(Higher Downs)
WN8: Skel 9A 32
Beechwood Av. BL0: Ram 8K 11
M21: Cho H 1B 106
M41: Urm 6M 91
OL15: Lit 1L 29
SK5: Stoc 4D 108
SK6: Rom 6N 109
SK15: H'rod 6F 82
WA12: N Wil 5G 86
Beechwood Av. WN4: A Mak 8D 70
WN6: She 7K 33
Beechwood Ct. BL8: Tot 8G 25
M20: Man 5F 106
M25: Pres 8C 60
PR7: Cop 5C 18
SK10: Boll 8J 129
(off Alder Ct.)
WN8: Skel 5B 50
Beechwood Cres. M29: Ast 4B 74
WN5: Orr 5J 51
Beechwood Dr. M28: Wors 4B 76
M33: Sale 4C 104
OL2: O'ham 6G 44
OL5: Mos 9F 64
SK6: Mar 1D 120
SK9: Wilm 6K 123
SK14: Hyde 8C 98
Beechwood Gdns. *M14: Man 9J 95*
(off Ladybarn La.)
Beechwood Gro. M9: Man 3K 79
SK8: Chea H 7M 117
Beechwood La. SK15: H'rod 6F 82
WA3: Cul 5F 88
Beechwood M. SK10: Macc 2G 131
Beechwood Rd. M25: Pres 8C 60
OL8: O'ham 9K 63
Beechwood St. BL3: Bolt 9G 38
Beechy Sq. OL1: O'ham 1F 8
Beede St. M11: Man 1N 95
Beedon Av. BL3: Lit L 8A 40
Bee Fold La. M46: Ath 9K 55
(not continuous)
Beeford Dr. WN5: Orr 6J 51
Beehive Grn. BL5: W'ton 2K 55
Bee Hive Ind. Est. BL6: Los 4H 37
Beehive St. OL8: O'ham 8K 63
Beeley St. M6: Sal 5A 78
SK14: Hyde 7B 98
Beenham Cl. M33: Sale 5C 104
Beesley Grn. M28: Wors 2N 75
Beeston Av. M7: Sal 4A 78
WA15: Tim 1F 114
Beeston Brow SK10: Boll 5M 129
Beeston Cl. BL1: Bolt 7H 23
SK10: Boll 4N 129
Beeston Dr. WA16: Knut 8G 132
Beeston Gro. M45: Whitef 4A 60
SK3: Stoc 2C 118
WN7: Lei 3M 73
Beeston Mt. SK10: Boll 4M 129
Beeston Rd. M33: Sale 4E 104
SK9: Hand 1J 123
Beeston St. M9: Man 2K 79
Beeston Ter. SK11: Macc 6C 130
Beetham Twr. M3: Man 7E 4
Beeth St. M11: Man 2B 96
Beeton Gro. M13: Man 5K 95
Beever St. M16: Old T 4B 94
OL1: O'ham 2F 8 (4L 63)
Beggarman's La.
WA16: Knut 9G 132
Beggars Wlk. WN1: Wig 9E 34
WN6: Wig 9E 34
Begley Cl. SK6: Rom 7K 109
Begonia Av. BL4: Farn 2J 57
Begonia Wlk. *M12: Man 3L 95*
(off Clowes St.)
Beightons Wlk. OL12: Roch 1B 28
Beilby Rd. WA11: Hay 2C 86
Belayse Cl. BL1: Bolt 1C 38
Belbeck St. BL8: Bury 2J 41
Belbeck St. Sth. BL8: Bury 2J 41
Belcroft Cl. M22: Nor 8D 106
Belcroft Dr. M38: Lit H 5F 56
Belcroft Gro. M38: Lit H 6F 56
Belding Av. M40: Man 1D 80
Beldon Rd. M9: Man 7G 61
Belfairs Cl. OL7: A Lyne 3M 81
BELFIELD 5G 29
Belfield WN8: Skel 5B 50
Belfield Cl. OL16: Roch 5G 29
Belfield Ho. WA14: Bow 5C 114
Belfield La. OL16: Roch 6H 29
(East St.)
OL16: Roch 6G 29
(Newbold Hall Dr.)
Belfield Lawn OL16: Roch 5H 29
Belfield Mill La.
OL16: Roch 5H 29
Belfield Old Rd.
OL16: Roch 5G 28
Belfield Rd. M20: Man 5G 106
M25: Pres 8D 60
OL16: Roch 5F 28
SK5: Stoc 6D 96
Belford Av. M34: Dent 6E 96
Belford Dr. BL3: Bolt 8F 38
Belford Rd. M32: Stre 6K 93
Belford Wlk. M23: Wyth 1N 115
Belfort Dr. M5: Sal 1A 94
Belfry Cl. SK9: Wilm 6J 123
Belfry Cres. WN6: Stan 2C 34
Belfry Dr. SK10: Macc 9G 129
Belgate Cl. M12: Man 5M 95
Belgian Ter. OL2: O'ham 8K 45
Belgium St. OL11: Roch 6K 27
Belgrave Av. M14: Man 6K 95
M35: Fail 2F 80
M41: Urm 6M 91
OL8: O'ham 7L 63
SK6: Mar 1C 120
Belgrave Bungs. M26: Rad 8F 40
Belgrave Cl. M26: Rad 8G 40
WN3: Wins 8N 51
WN7: Lei 1E 88
Belgrave Ct. *M34: Dent 5H 97*
(off Belgrave St.)
OL8: O'ham 6K 63
Belgrave Cres. BL6: Hor 1F 36
M30: Ecc 7F 76
SK2: Stoc 3F 118
Belgrave Dr. M26: Rad 8G 40
Belgrave Gdns. *BL1: Bolt 2F 38*
(off Gladstone St.)
Belgrave Ind. Est. OL8: O'ham 8L 63
Belgrave Rd. M33: Sale 4G 104
M40: Man 1C 80
M44: Cad 3E 102
OL8: O'ham 7K 63
SK11: Macc 8G 131
WA14: Bow 4C 114
Belgrave St. *BL1: Bolt 2F 38*
(off Gladstone St.)
M26: Rad 8F 40
M34: Dent 5H 97
M46: Ath 9J 55
OL10: H'ood 3H 43
(not continuous)
OL12: Roch 4B 28
Belgrave St. Sth. BL1: Bolt 3F 38
Belgrave Ter. M40: Man 4K 79
Belgravia Gdns. M21: Cho H 9N 93
WA15: Hale 7E 114
Belgravia Ho. *WA14: Alt 4D 114*
(off Brown St.)
Belgravia M. OL2: Shaw 5N 45
Belhaven Rd. M8: Man 9E 60
Belhill Gdns. M6: Sal 7M 77
BELL, THE 3M 51
Bellairs St. BL3: Bolt 9D 38
Bellam Ct. M27: Ward 1C 76
Bellamy Dr. WN7: Lei 5K 73
Bella St. BL3: Bolt 8D 38
Bell Av. SK11: Sut E 9K 131
Bell Clough Rd. M43: Droy 7F 80
Bell Cres. M11: Man 1K 95
(not continuous)
Belldale Cl. SK4: Stoc 6M 107
Belldean WN2: I Mak 3L 53
Belle Grn. Ind. Est. WN2: I Mak 3K 53
Belle Grn. La. WN2: I Mak 4K 53
Belle Isle Av. OL12: Whitw 8A 14
Bellerby Cl. M45: Whitef 3L 59
Bellerophon Way WA11: Hay 3B 86
Belleville Av. M22: Wyth 7D 116
BELLE VUE 4M 95
Belle-Vue WA3: Low 8B 72
Belle Vue Av. M12: Man 4L 95
Belle Vue Greyhound Stadium 4N 95
Belle Vue Leisure Cen. 5M 95
Belle Vue Station (Rail) 4A 96
Belle Vue St. M12: Man 3M 95
WN5: Wig 6A 52
Belle Vue Ter. BL9: Bury 9J 7 (3L 41)
Bellew St. M11: Man 1K 95
Bell Farm Ct. SK10: Macc 1G 131
Bellfield Av. OL8: O'ham 9K 63
SK8: Chea H 6N 117
Bellfield Cl. M9: Man 9H 61
Bellfield Vw. BL1: Bolt 1H 39
Bellingham Av. WN1: Wig 1G 52
Bellingham Cl. BL8: Bury 2F 40
OL2: Shaw 4M 45
WA16: Knut 6J 133
Bellingham Dr. WN1: Wig 1G 52
Bellingham Mt. WN1: Wig 9F 34
Bellis Cl. M12: Man 9K 79
Bell La. BL9: Bury 6N 7 (1N 41)
OL16: Miln 6M 29
WN5: Orr 3M 51
Bell Mdw. Dr. OL11: Roch 8L 27
Bellott St. M8: Man 4F 78
Bellott Wlk. *OL1: O'ham 3J 63*
(off Crompton St.)
Bellpit Cl. M28: Wors 3K 75
Bellscroft Av. M40: Man 3N 79
Bellsfield Cl. WA13: Lym 5A 112
Bellshill Cres. OL16: Roch 4G 29
(not continuous)
Bell St. M43: Droy 8F 80
OL1: O'ham 1G 8 (4L 63)
OL16: Roch 6C 8 (5D 28)
WN2: Hin 5A 54
WN7: Lei 1F 72
Bell Ter. M30: Ecc 1C 92
Bellwood BL5: W'ton 5E 54
BELMONT
BL7 1L 21
SK9 3H 127
Belmont Av. M6: Sal 7G 77
M27: Clif 6D 58
M34: Dent 5H 97
M46: Ath 7A 56
OL4: Spri 4C 64
SK10: Macc 3A 130
WA3: Gol 9M 71
WN2: B'haw 1B 72
WN5: Bil 8H 51
Belmont Cl. SK4: Stoc 5C 108
Belmont Ct. SK4: Stoc 5C 108
Belmont Dr. BL8: Bury 3G 40
SK6: Mar B 7E 110
WN2: Asp 7M 35
Belmont Pl. PR7: Cop 7A 18
Belmont Ri. WN6: Stan 4C 34
Belmont Rd. BL1: Bolt 1M 21
BL6: R'ton 4E 20
BL7: Bel 1M 21
M26: Rad 2G 58
M33: Sale 2G 104
PR6: Adl 6K 19
SK7: Bram 1C 124
SK8: Gat 1G 116
WA15: Hale 5E 114
WN2: Hin 6B 54
Belmont Shop. Cen.
SK4: Stoc 6C 108
Belmont St. *M5: Sal 9K 77*
(off Foster St.)
M16: Old T 4C 94
M30: Ecc 7D 76
OL1: O'ham 1B 8 (3J 63)
OL4: Lees 6B 64
SK4: Stoc 5B 108
Belmont Ter. M31: C'ton 2L 103
Belmont Vw. BL2: Bolt 9N 23
Belmont Wlk. M13: Man 9M 5
Belmont Way OL9: Chad 3G 63
OL12: Roch 3C 28
SK4: Stoc 6B 108
Belmore Av. M8: Man 1E 78

Belper Rd. M30: Ecc 1B 92
SK4: Stoc 7L 107
Belper St. OL6: A Lyne 6M 81
Belper Wlk. M18: Man 3A 96
(off Peacock Cl.)
Belper Way M34: Dent 9L 97
(off Heanor Av.)
Belroy Ct. M25: Pres 8A 60
Belsay Cl. OL7: A Lyne 5K 81
Belsay Dr. M23: Wyth 3N 115
Belstone Av. M23: Wyth 4N 115
Belstone Cl. SK7: Bram 5D 118
Belsyde Wlk. M9: Man 3K 79
(off Craigend Dr.)
Belthorne Av. M9: Man 9M 61
Belton Av. OL16: Roch 4G 29
Belton Cl. WA3: Gol 2K 87
Beltone Cl. M32: Stre 8H 93
Belton Wlk. M8: Man 4F 78
(off Cranlington Dr.)
OL9: O'ham 3A 8 (5H 63)
Belvedere Av. BL8: G'mount 4G 24
M46: Ath 7A 56
SK5: Stoc 7D 96
Belvedere Cl. WN7: Lei 3M 73
Belvedere Ct. M25: Pres 8N 59
Belvedere Dr. SK6: Bred 5G 109
SK16: Duk 1B 98
Belvedere Gdns. SK4: Stoc 4N 107
(off Heaton Moor Rd.)
Belvedere Hgts. BL1: Bolt 5N 37
(off The Rowans)
Belvedere Pl. WN3: Wig 6C 52
Belvedere Ri. OL1: O'ham 9A 46
Belvedere Rd. M6: Sal 7N 77
M14: Man 9K 95
PR6: And 5L 19
WA12: N Wil 5E 86
WN4: A Mak 7F 70
Belvedere Sq. M22: Wyth 4E 116
Belvoir Av. M19: Man 7M 95
SK7: H Gro 7J 119
Belvoir Mdws. OL16: Roch 1J 29
Belvoir St. BL2: Bolt 5K 39
OL12: Roch 4A 28
WN1: Wig 8M 9 (3H 53)
Belvor Av. M34: Aud 2J 97
Belwood Rd. M21: Cho H 1A 106
Bembridge Cl. M14: Man 7H 95
Bembridge Ct. WN3: Wins 9B 52
Bembridge Dr. BL3: Bolt 7L 39
Bembridge Rd. M34: Dent 9M 97
Bempton Cl. SK2: Stoc 2L 119
Bemrose Av. WA14: Alt 1C 114
Bemsley Pl. M5: Sal 1N 93
Benbecula Way M41: Urm 4C 92
Benbow Av. M12: Man 4L 95
Benbow St. M33: Sale 3H 105
Ben Brierley Wharf M35: Fail 2D 80
Benbrook Gro. SK9: Wilm 4J 123
(off Barton Cl.)
Bench Carr OL12: Roch 4C 28
Benches La. SK6: Mar B 5H 111
BENCHILL 2C 116
Benchill Av. M22: Wyth 2C 116
Benchill Ct. M22: Wyth 3D 116
Benchill Ct. Rd. M22: Wyth 3D 116
Benchill Cres. M22: Wyth 2B 116
Benchill Dr. M22: Wyth 2C 116
Benchill Rd. M22: Wyth 1B 116
Bendall St. M11: Man 1C 96
Ben Davies Ct. SK6: Rom 5N 109
Bendemeer M41: Urm 6C 92
Bendix Ct. SK14: Hyde 7B 98
(off Mottram Rd.)
Bendix St. M4: Man 2K 5 (8G 78)
(not continuous)
Benedict Cl. M7: Sal 5B 78
(off Cromwell Gro.)
Benedict Dr. SK16: Duk 3A 98
Benfield Av. M40: Man 9A 62
Benfield St. OL10: H'ood 2J 43
Benfleet Cl. M12: Man 3M 95
Benfold Wlk. M24: Mid 9J 43
Bengain M7: Sal 4C 78
Bengairn Cl. WN1: Wig 2J 53
Bengal La. OL6: A Lyne 6N 81
(not continuous)
Bengal Sq. OL6: A Lyne 6N 81
Bengal St. M4: Man 2L 5 (8G 79)
SK3: Stoc 5J 9 (8C 108)
WN7: Lei 5H 73
Benhale Wlk. M8: Man 4F 78
(off Tamerton Dr.)
Benham Cl. M20: Man 5H 107
Benin Wlk. M40: Man 5A 80
(off Marlinford Dr.)
Benja Fold SK7: Bram 9B 118
Benjamin Ct. BL1: Bolt 3F 38
(off Skagen Ct.)
Benjamin Fold WN4: A Mak 5E 70
Benjamin St. OL7: A Lyne 9A 6 (9L 81)
(not continuous)
Benjamin Wilson Ct. M7: Sal 6C 78
(off Sussex St.)
Benmore Cl. OL10: H'ood 2F 42
Benmore Rd. M9: Man 7L 61
Bennett Cl. SK3: Stoc 8A 108
Bennett Dr. M7: Sal 4D 78
WN5: Orr 7H 51
Bennett M. SK14: Hyde 4A 98
(off Harding St.)
Bennett Rd. M8: Man 1E 78
Bennett's La. BL1: Bolt 2D 38
Bennett St. M12: Man 3K 95
M26: Rad 8D 40
M32: Stre 7J 93
OL7: A Lyne 9K 81
(not continuous)
SK3: Stoc 8A 108
SK14: Holl 4N 99
SK14: Hyde 4N 97
SK15: Stal 9D 82
Benny La. M43: Droy 7G 81
Bensey Ri. BL6: Hor 1A 36
Benson Cl. M7: Sal 5D 78
Benson St. BL9: Bury 9N 7 (3N 41)
Benson Wlk. SK9: Wilm 4J 123
Ben St. M11: Man 8N 79
Bentcliffe Way M30: Ecc 9F 76
Bentfield Cres. OL16: Miln 9L 29
Bentfield Ind. Units OL9: Chad 5F 62
Bent Fold Dr. BL9: Bury 2N 57
BENTGATE 1L 45
Bentgate Cl. OL16: Miln 9L 29
Bentgate St. OL16: Miln 1L 45
Benthall Wlk. M34: Dent 9J 97
Bentham Cl. BL4: Farn 2L 57
(off Bentley St.)
BL8: Bury 1E 40
Bentham Pl. WN6: Stan 2C 34
Bentham Rd. WA3: Cul 7J 89
WN6: Stan 3B 34
Bentham St. PR7: Cop 4B 18
Bent Hill Sth. BL3: Bolt 8B 38
Bent Ho Row PR6: H Char 3M 19
Bent Ho's. WN2: Asp 8M 35
Bentinck Bus. Cen. OL6: A Lyne 8B 6
Bentinck Cl. WA14: Alt 4B 6 (3C 114)
Bentinck Ho. OL6: A Lyne 8B 6 (8L 81)
Bentinck Ind. Est. M15: Man 9B 4
Bentinck Rd. WA14: Alt 4A 6 (3C 114)
Bentinck St. BL1: Bolt 3C 38
BL4: Farn 2K 57
M15: Man 9B 4 (2C 94)
OL6: A Lyne 7B 6 (7L 81)
(not continuous)
OL7: A Lyne 9C 6 (8M 81)
OL12: Roch 4A 28
WN3: Wig 7B 52
Bentinck Ter. OL6: A Lyne 8B 6
Bent La. M8: Man 3E 78
M25: Pres 7B 60
WA3: Cul 7J 89
WA13: Warb 1D 112
Bent Lanes M41: Urm 4N 91
(not continuous)
Bentley Av. M24: Mid 7B 44
Bentley Brook Cl. BL6: Hor 9G 21
Bentley Cl. M26: Rad 8K 41
Bentley Ct. BL4: Farn 2L 57
BL5: W'ton 3H 55
(off Victoria St.)
M7: Sal 2D 78
Bentley Fold BL8: Bury 9F 24
Bentley Hall Rd. BL8: Bury 9E 24
Bentley La. BL9: Bury 4M 25
Bentley Mdws. BL8: Bury 9E 24
Bentley M. OL12: Roch 3C 28
Bentley Rd. M7: Sal 2C 78
M21: Cho H 8N 93
M34: Dent 6K 97
Bentleys, The SK5: Stoc 5D 108
Bentley St. BL2: Bolt 7K 39
BL4: Farn 2L 57
OL1: O'ham 3M 63
OL9: Chad 4F 62
OL12: Roch 3B 28
Bentmeadows OL12: Roch 4C 28
Benton Dr. SK6: Mar B 8F 110
Benton St. M9: Man 3L 79
Bents Av. M41: Urm 8N 91
SK6: Bred 5K 109
Bents Farm Cl. OL15: Lit 9K 15
Bentside Rd. SK12: Dis 9G 120
Bent Spur Rd. BL4: Kea 6A 58
Bent St. BL4: Kea 4M 57
M8: Man 6F 78
Bent Ter. M41: Urm 5C 92
Bentworth Cl. BL5: W'ton 5N 55
Bentworth Wlk. M9: Man 3K 79
(off Broadwell Dr.)
Benville Wlk. M40: Man 4N 79
(off Harold Priestnall Cl.)
Benwick Ter. BL1: Bolt 2F 38
(off Boardman St.)
Benyon St. OL4: Lees 5B 64
Berberis Wlk. M33: Sale 2C 104
Beresford Av. BL3: Bolt 5C 38
Beresford Ct. M20: Man 4F 106
SK9: A Edg 4F 126
(off Brown St.)
Beresford Cres. OL4: O'ham 3A 64
SK5: Stoc 6C 96
Beresford Rd. M13: Man 6L 95
M32: Stre 5L 93
Beresford St. M14: Man 6E 94
M35: Fail 3C 80
OL4: O'ham 3A 64
OL16: Miln 9M 29
WN6: Wig 2D 52
Bergman Wlk. M40: Man 4N 79
(off Harmer Cl.)
Berigan Cl. M12: Man 4K 95
Berisford Cl. WA15: Tim 9E 104
Berkeley Av. M14: Man 5K 95
M32: Stre 5G 92
OL9: Chad 8D 62
WN3: Wins 9A 52
Berkeley Bus. Pk. OL6: A Lyne 6M 81
Berkeley Cl. PR7: Chor 1G 18
SK2: Stoc 8G 109
SK14: Hyde 8A 98
WN7: Lei 1E 88
Berkeley Ct. M7: Sal 1D 78
M20: Man 5E 106
WA12: N Wil 5C 86
Berkeley Cres. M26: Rad 7C 40
SK14: Hyde 8A 98
Berkeley Dr. OL2: O'ham 1H 63
OL16: Roch 9F 28
Berkeley Ho. BL1: Bolt 5D 38
(off Westgate Av.)
Berkeley Rd. BL1: Bolt 9F 22
SK7: H Gro 4K 119
Berkeley St. OL2: O'ham 7H 45
OL6: A Lyne 7B 6 (7L 81)
Berkley Av. M19: Man 8M 95
Berkley Wlk. OL15: Lit 9K 15
Berkshire Cl. OL9: Chad 6F 62
SK10: Macc 2C 130
Berkshire Ct. BL9: Bury 5M 41
Berkshire Dr. M44: Cad 3D 102
Berkshire Pl. OL9: O'ham 6G 62
Berkshire Rd. M40: Man 7J 79
Berlin Rd. SK3: Stoc 1B 118
Berlin St. BL3: Bolt 6D 38
Bermondsay St. M5: Sal 1A 94
(off St Joseph's Dr)
Bermside Cl. WN6: Wig 1B 52
Bernard Gro. BL1: Bolt 2D 38
Bernard St. M9: Man 2J 79
OL12: Roch 2C 28
SK13: Glos 8E 100
Bernard Walker Ct. SK6: Comp 6E 110
Bernard Wood Ct. WN5: Bil 6G 69
Berne Av. BL6: Hor 1C 36
Berne Cl. OL9: Chad 5G 62
SK7: Bram 3C 118
Bernice Av. OL9: Chad 5F 62
Bernice St. BL1: Bolt 2D 38
Bernisdale Rd. WA16: Mob 4M 133
Berriedale Cl. M16: Whall R 7C 94
Berrie Gro. M19: Man 9N 95
(off Henderson St.)
Berrington Gro. WN4: A Mak 7D 70
Berringtons La. WA11: R'ford 8A 68
Berrington Wlk. BL2: Bolt 3H 39
Berristall Ri. SK10: Boll 4N 129
Berry Brow M40: Man 6B 80
OL3: G'fld 6L 65
Berry Cl. SK9: Wilm 9F 122
Berrycroft La. SK6: Rom 5L 109
Berryfield Gdns. WA14: W Tim 8D 104
Berryfold Way M29: Ast 2B 74
Berry Sq. BL6: Bla 1N 35
Berry St. M1: Man 7L 5 (1G 95)
M27: Pen 9F 58
M30: Ecc 1B 92
OL3: G'fld 6L 65
PR6: Adl 5K 19
SK15: Stal 1F 98
Bertha Rd. OL16: Roch 6G 28
Bertha St. BL1: Bolt 2E 38
M11: Man 2N 95
OL2: Shaw 7M 45
Bertie St. OL11: Roch 9B 28
Bertram St. M12: Man 3M 95
M33: Sale 4L 105
WA12: N Wil 6D 86
Bertrand Rd. BL1: Bolt 5D 38
Bert St. BL3: Bolt 9C 38
(not continuous)
Berwick Av. M41: Urm 7G 92
M45: Whitef 4N 59
SK4: Stoc 5J 107
Berwick Cl. M28: Wors 3G 75
OL10: H'ood 3F 42
SK10: Macc 2D 130
Berwick Pde. SK5: Stoc 3G 108
Berwick Pl. WN1: Wig 2H 53
Berwick St. OL16: Roch 9G 8 (7F 28)
Berwyn Av. M9: Man 6H 61
M24: Mid 3A 62
SK8: Chea H 2N 117
Berwyn Cl. BL6: Hor 8E 20
OL8: O'ham 8J 63
Beryl Av. BL8: Tot 6F 24
Beryl St. BL1: Bolt 1G 38
BESOM HILL 7C 46
Besom La. SK15: Mill 7G 83
Bessemer Rd. M44: Irl 2G 102
Bessemer St. M11: Man 2A 96
Bessemer Way
OL1: O'ham 1C 8 (4J 63)
BESSES O' TH' BARN 4N 59
Besses o' th' Barn Stop (Metro)
4N 59
Bessie's Well Pl. WN6: Stan 4C 34
Bessybrook Cl. BL6: Los 6L 37
Besthill Cotts. SK13: Char 9L 99
BESWICK 1L 95
Beswick Dr. M35: Fail 4E 80
Beswicke Royds St. OL16: Roch 4G 28
Beswicke St. OL12: Roch 5A 8 (5C 28)
OL15: Lit 9N 15
Beswick Row M4: Man 1H 5 (7F 78)
Beswicks La. SK9: A Edg 2B 126
Beswick St. M4: Man 8J 79
M43: Droy 9F 80
OL2: O'ham 1J 63
SK11: Macc 5F 130
Beta Av. M32: Stre 9J 93
Beta St. BL1: Bolt 1J 7 (4F 38)
Betchworth Way SK10: Macc 9G 128
Bethany La. OL16: Miln 9N 29
Bethany M. WN2: Hin 7D 54
Bethel Av. M35: Fail 3C 80
Bethel Grn. OL15: Lit 5N 15
Bethel St. OL10: H'ood 2H 43
Bethersden Rd. WN1: Wig 7E 34
Bethesda Ho. M7: Sal 2D 78
Bethesda St. OL8: O'ham 7K 63
Bethnall Dr. M14: Man 8F 94
Betjeman Pl. OL2: Shaw 5A 46
Betleymere Rd. SK8: Chea H 3L 117
Betley Rd. SK5: Stoc 8D 96
Betley St. M1: Man 6M 5 (1H 95)
M26: Rad 8J 41
OL10: H'ood 3H 43
Betnor Av. SK1: Stoc 7F 108
Betony Cl. OL12: Roch 2B 28
Betsham St. M15: Man 4E 94
Betsyfield Dr. WA3: Cro 9C 88
Bettison Av. WN7: Lei 7L 73
Bettwood Dr. M8: Man 2D 78
Betula Gro. M7: Sal 3C 78
(off Bk. Hilton St.)
Betula M. OL11: Roch 4J 27
Beulah Av. WN5: Bil 6H 69
Beulah St. M11: Man 2A 96
Bevan Cl. M12: Man 9K 79
Bevendon Sq. M7: Sal 4D 78
Beveridge St. M14: Man 6E 94
Beverley Av. M34: Dent 7L 97
M41: Urm 6E 92
WN5: Bil 1J 69
WN7: Lei 4J 73
Beverley Cl. M45: Whitef 2A 60
OL6: A Lyne 4M 81
Beverley Flats OL10: H'ood 2H 43
(off Wilton St.)
Beverley Pl. OL16: Roch 6F 8 (5E 28)
Beverley Rd. BL1: Bolt 4C 38
BL3: Lit L 9N 39
M27: Pen 3J 77
SK2: Stoc 8G 109
WN5: Wig 3M 51
Beverley St. M9: Man 1K 79
Beverley Wlk. OL8: O'ham 6J 63
SK6: Rom 7L 109
Beverley Way SK10: Macc 9G 128
Beverly Rd. M14: Man 1J 107
Beverston OL11: Roch 7C 28
Beverston Dr. M7: Sal 4C 78
Bevill Sq. M3: Sal 2D 4 (8D 78)
Bevin Av. WA3: Cul 5K 89
Bevington St. WN4: A Mak 5C 70
BEVIS GREEN 5M 25
Bevis Grn. BL9: Bury 5M 25
Bewerley Cl. WN3: Wig 5E 52
Bewick St. BL2: Bolt 1J 39
Bewick Wlk. WA16: Knut 5H 133
(off Mobberley Rd.)
Bewley Gro. WN7: Lei 4J 73
Bewley St. OL8: O'ham 9H 63
Bewley Wlk. M40: Man 4M 79
Bexhill Av. WA15: Tim 1G 6 (1F 114)
Bexhill Cl. BL3: Lit L 9C 40
Bexhill Dr. M13: Man 6K 95
WN7: Lei 9E 54
Bexhill Rd. SK3: Stoc 3C 118
Bexhill Wlk. OL9: Chad 5F 62
Bexington Rd. M16: Whall R 6D 94
Bexley Cl. M41: Urm 5B 92
SK13: Glos 6E 100
Bexley Dr. BL8: Bury 3H 41
M38: Lit H 7K 57
Bexley Ho. BL1: Bolt 3F 38
(off Kenton Cl.)
Bexley Sq. M3: Sal 3C 4 (8C 78)
Bexley St. OL9: O'ham 6G 63
WN2: Hin 8D 54
Bexley Wlk. M40: Man 4N 79
(off John Foran Cl.)
Bexton La. WA16: Knut 9F 132
Bexton Rd. WA16: Knut 8F 132
Beyer Cl. M18: Man 4A 96
Bibby La. M19: Man 2L 107
(not continuous)
Bibby's La. SK10: Macc 3L 131
Bibby St. BL9: Bury 7M 41
SK14: Hyde 4A 98
Bibury Av. M22: Wyth 4A 116
Bickerdike Av. M12: Man 6N 95
Bickerdike Ct. M12: Man 6N 95
BICKERSHAW 1A 72
Bickershaw Dr. M28: Walk 9K 57
(not continuous)
Bickershaw La. WN2: Abr, B'haw 1L 71
WN7: Lei 6C 72
Bickerstaffe Cl. OL2: Shaw 6L 45
Bickerton Ct. OL9: Chad 7F 62
Bickerton Dr. SK7: H Gro 6E 118
Bickerton Rd. WA14: Alt 2B 114
Bickley Gro. M29: Ast 4D 74
Biddall Dr. M23: Wyth 1A 116
Biddisham Wlk. M40: Man 5J 79
(off Thornton St. Nth.)
Biddulph Av. SK2: Stoc 2G 119
Bideford Dr. BL2: Bolt 6A 40
M23: Wyth 9M 105
Bideford Rd. M23: Wyth 8M 105
OL11: Roch 1N 43
SK2: Stoc 7G 109
Bidford Cl. M29: Tyld 1D 74
Bidston Av. M14: Man 7G 94
Bidston Cl. BL8: Bury 2G 40
OL2: Shaw 6A 46
Bidston Dr. SK9: Hand 4K 123
Bidworth La. SK13: Gam 8N 99
Big Fold BL6: Bla 2N 35
(off Victoria St.)
Biggin Gdns. OL10: H'ood 5K 43
Bigginwood Wlk. M40: Man 3M 79
Bignor St. M8: Man 4F 78
Bilbao St. BL1: Bolt 4D 38
Bilberry St. OL16: Roch 9F 8 (7E 28)
(not continuous)
Bilbrook St. M4: Man 1K 5 (7G 78)
Billberry Cl. M45: Whitef 3A 60
Billing Av. M12: Man 8N 5 (2H 95)
BILLINGE 5J 69
Billinge Arc. WN1: Wig 7J 9
(off The Galleries)
Billinge Cl. BL1: Bolt 1K 7 (4G 38)
Billinge Rd. WN3: Wig 7N 51
WN4: Gars 5M 69
WN5: Bil 5M 69
WN5: Wig 5B 52
Billington Av. WA12: N Wil 3E 86
Billington Rd. M27: Pen 2L 77
Bill La. M45: Whitef 3M 59
Bill Williams Cl. M11: Man 1A 96
Billy La. M27: Clif 9F 58
Billy Meredith Cl. M14: Man 6F 94
Billy's La. SK8: Chea H 6M 117
Billy Whelan Wlk. M40: Man 5A 80
(off Tommy Taylor Cl.)
Bilsborrow Rd. M14: Man 6F 94
Bilsland Wlk. M40: Man 5A 80
(off Orford Rd.)
Bilson Dr. SK3: Stoc 9N 107
Bilson Sq. OL16: Miln 8L 29
(off Newhey St.)
Bilton Wlk. M8: Man 2H 79
(off Nunthorpe Dr.)
Binbrook Wlk. BL3: Bolt 8A 38
(off Lever St.)
Bincombe Wlk. M13: Man 4H 95
(off Carmoor Rd.)
Bindloss Av. M30: Ecc 7F 76
Bindon Wlk. M9: Man 3J 79
(off Carisbrook St.)
Bingham Dr. M23: Wyth 1M 115
Bingham St. M27: Swin 2F 76
Bingley Cl. M11: Man 1L 95
Bingley Dr. M41: Urm 5N 91
Bingley Rd. OL16: Roch 6G 29
Bingley Sq. OL16: Roch 6G 29
Bingley Ter. OL16: Roch 6G 29
Bingley Wlk. BL4: Farn 4L 57
M7: Sal 2M 77
Binn La. HD7: Mars 2J 49
Binn Rd. HD7: Mars 1H 49
Binns Nook Rd. OL12: Roch 3E 28
Binns Pl. M4: Man 4L 5 (9G 79)
Binns St. SK15: Stal 9B 82
Binn's Ter. OL15: Lit 8M 15
(off Lodge St.)
Binsley Cl. M44: Irl 8H 91
Binstead Cl. M14: Man 6K 95
Birbeck Cl. WN3: Wins 1B 70
Birbeck St. OL5: Mos 9F 64
SK15: Stal 9C 82
BIRCH 8H 43
Birchacre Gro. M14: Man 1J 107
Birchall Av. WA3: Cul 5F 88
Birchall Cl. SK16: Duk 2A 98
Birchall Grn. SK6: Wood 3K 109
Birchall Way M15: Man 3E 94
Birch Av. BL5: W'ton 4H 55
BL8: Tot 8G 24
M6: Sal 6L 77
M16: Old T 5N 93
M24: Mid 4M 61
M33: Sale 5H 105
(off Hazel Av.)
M35: Fail 4D 80
M44: Cad 3E 102
M45: Whitef 5M 59
OL1: Chad 1E 62
OL8: O'ham 9H 63
OL12: Roch 1H 29
SK4: Stoc 4N 107
SK6: Rom 6A 110
SK9: Wilm 8E 122
SK10: Macc 3E 130
WN6: Stan 4C 34
Birchbrook Rd. WA13: Lym 2C 112
Birch Cl. OL12: Whitw 8A 14
Birch Ct. M13: Man 6K 95
OL10: H'ood 3K 43
(off Twin St.)
SK6: Mar 2B 120
SK16: Duk 1A 98
(off Birch La.)
Birch Cres. OL16: Miln 1L 45
WA12: N Wil 5C 86
Birchdale WA14: Bow 5C 114
Birchdale Av. SK8: H Grn 5G 117
Birch Dr. M27: Pen 2H 77
OL4: Lees 6B 64
SK7: H Gro 5G 118
Birchenall St. M40: Man 2L 79
Birchen Bower Wlk. BL8: Tot 8F 24
Birchenlea St. OL9: Chad 8E 62
Birchenlee SK14: Hat 6F 98
Birches, The M33: Sale 3E 104
OL5: Mos 1E 82
Birches Cft. Dr. SK10: Macc 3D 130
Birches End OL12: Whitw 9A 14
Birches Rd. BL7: Tur 1L 23
Birchfield BL2: Bolt 7M 23
OL7: A Lyne 1K 97
Birchfield Av. BL9: Bury 3D 42
M46: Ath 7K 55
Birchfield Dr. M28: Wors 3H 75
OL11: Roch 8A 28
Birchfield Gro. BL3: Bolt 8N 37
Birchfield Ho. SK1: Stoc 3M 9
Birchfield M. SK14: Hyde 7A 98
Birchfield Rd. SK3: Stoc 9M 107
WA13: Lym 3C 112
Birchfields OL4: O'ham 7C 64
WA15: Hale 6F 114
Birchfields Av. M13: Man 6K 95
Birchfields Rd. M13: Man 6K 95
M14: Man 6K 95
Birchfold M38: Lit H 7J 57
Birchfold Cl. M38: Lit H 7J 57
Birchgate Cl. SK10: Macc 3C 130
Birchgate Wlk. BL3: Bolt 7G 38
BIRCH GREEN 1A 50
Birch Grn. SK13: Glos 8G 101
Birch Grn. Rd. WN8: Skel 1A 50
Birch Gro. BL0: Ram 2G 25
M14: Man 6J 95
M25: Pres 5N 59
M34: Aud 3K 97
M34: Dent 6J 97
WA15: Tim 2L 115
WA16: Knut 6K 133
WN4: Gars 5N 69
Birchgrove Cl. BL3: Bolt 1B 56
Birch Hall Cl. OL4: O'ham 7B 64
Birch Hall La. M13: Man 7K 95
Birch Hey Cl. OL12: Roch 1G 29
Birch Hill Cres. OL12: Roch 1J 29
Birch Hill La. OL12: W'le 8H 15
Birch Hill Wlk. OL15: Lit 9K 15
Birch Ho. BL5: W'ton 4H 55
SK7: Bram 1C 124
Birchinall Cl. SK11: Macc 6E 130
Birch Ind. Est. OL10: H'ood 7F 42
Birchington Rd. M14: Man 9F 94
Birchin La. M4: Man 4J 5 (9F 78)
Birchinlee Av. OL2: O'ham 9F 44
Birchin Pl. M4: Man 4J 5
Birch La. M13: Man 6K 95
SK16: Duk 1A 98
(not continuous)
Birchlea WA15: Alt 3F 114
Birch Lea Cl. BL9: Bury 5M 41
Birchleaf Gro. M5: Sal 8J 77
Birchley Av. WN5: Bil 7G 69
Birchley Rd. WN5: Bil 7G 68
Birchley Vw. WA11: St H 8F 68
Birch Mill Bus. Cen.
OL10: H'ood 7H 43

Birch Mt. OL12: Roch 1J 29
Birch Polygon M14: Man 6J 95
Birch Rd. BL4: Kea 5N 57
M8: Man 1G 78
M24: Mid 1A 62
M27: Swin 5D 76
M28: Walk 1L 75
M31: C'ton 4N 103
M31: Part 5E 102
M46: Ath 8N 55
OL3: Upp 4M 65
OL12: Roch, W'le 8G 15
PR7: Cop 4B 18
SK8: Gat 2F 116
SK12: Poy 4K 125
WA3: Rix 5C 102
WA11: Hay 2B 86
WA14: D Mas 4N 103
WN2: Abr 3L 71
WN7: Lei 3H 73
BIRCH SERVICE AREA 7G 42
Birchside Av. SK13: Glos 7D 100
Birch St. BL2: Bolt 5N 7 (6J 39)
BL9: Bury 9M 25
M12: Man 3M 95
M26: Rad 7L 41
M29: Tyld 1B 74
M43: Droy 1F 96
OL7: A Lyne 9J 81
OL10: H'ood 3J 43
OL12: W'le 8G 15
SK15: H'rod 5F 82
WN2: Hin 6N 53
WN6: Wig 2D 52
Birch Ter. SK14: Hyde 7N 97
Birch Tree Av. SK7: H Gro 6L 119
Birchtree Cl. WA14: Bow 6C 114
Birch Tree Cl. M22: Wyth 4C 116
Birch Tree Dr. M22: Wyth 4C 116
Birch Tree Rd. WA3: Low 1B 88
Birch Tree Way BL6: Hor 3G 37
(off Claypool Rd.)
Birchvale Cl. M15: Man 9E 4 (3D 94)
SK12: Poy 3J 125
Birchvale Dr. SK6: Rom 5A 110
Birch Vw. OL12: Roch 1H 29
Birch Vs. OL12: Whitw 9A 14
Birchway SK6: H Lan 8C 120
SK7: Bram 8B 118
SK10: Boll 5L 129
SK10: P'bury 7C 128
Birchwood M43: Droy 7F 80
OL9: Chad 4C 62
Birchwood Cl. SK4: Stoc 7M 107
WN3: Wins 1A 70
WN7: Lei 7H 73
Birchwood Cres. SK14: Hyde 3D 98
Birchwood Dr. M40: Man 4J 79
PR7: Cop 3B 18
SK9: Wilm 6J 123
Birchwood Rd. M24: Mid 3A 62
Birchwood Way SK16: Duk 3A 98
Bird Hall Av. SK8: Chea H 3A 118
Birdhall Gro. M19: Man 9M 95
Bird Hall La. SK3: Stoc 9N 107
Bird Hall Rd. SK8: Chea H 2N 117
Birdlip Dr. M23: Wyth 4N 115
Bird St. WN2: I Mak 4J 53
BIRKACRE 2D 18
Birkacre Brow PR7: Cop 3C 18
Birkacre Rd. PR7: Chor 1C 18
Birkby Dr. M24: Mid 1K 61
Birkdale Av. M45: Whitef 5K 59
M46: Ath 6L 55
OL2: O'ham 1J 63
Birkdale Cl. OL10: H'ood 4J 43
SK7: Bram 8E 118
SK10: Macc 9G 128
SK14: Hyde 4B 98
Birkdale Dr. BL8: Bury 2H 41
M33: Sale 6E 104
Birkdale Gdns. BL3: Bolt 7E 38
Birkdale Gro. M30: Ecc 8F 76
SK5: Stoc 3D 108
Birkdale Pl. M33: Sale 2F 104
Birkdale Rd. OL16: Roch 9G 28
SK5: Stoc 3C 108
Birkdale St. M8: Man 3F 78
Birkenhills Dr. BL3: Bolt 7N 37
Birkett Bank WN1: Wig 8N 9 (3H 53)
Birkett Cl. BL1: Bolt 7E 22
Birkett Dr. BL1: Bolt 7E 22
Birkett St. WN1: Wig 3H 53
Birkinbrook Cl. M45: Whitef 2N 59
Birkin Cl. WA16: Knut 4K 133
Birkleigh Wlk. BL2: Bolt 6M 39
Birkrig WN8: Skel 5B 50
BIRKS 3C 64
Birks Av. OL4: Lees 3C 64
Birks Dr. BL8: Bury 7H 25
Birkside Cl. WN3: Wig 1D 70
Birkworth Ct. SK2: Stoc 1H 119
Birley Cl. WA15: Tim 9F 104
WN6: App B 4K 33
Birley Ct. M5: Sal 8M 77
Birley Flds. M15: Man 4E 94
Birley Pk. M20: Man 5E 106
Birley St. BL1: Bolt 9F 22
BL9: Bury 8M 25
OL12: Roch 4E 28
WA12: N Wil 5G 86
WN7: Lei 4J 73
Birleywood WN8: Skel 5B 50
Birling Dr. M23: Wyth 3A 116
Birnam Gro. OL10: H'ood 3F 42
Birshaw Cl. OL2: Shaw 7M 45
Birstall Wlk. M23: Wyth 1N 115
Birtenshaw Cres. BL7: Bro X 6J 23
BIRTLE 7E 26
Birtle Brook Vw. W. BL9: Bury 8E 26
(off Birtle Rd.)
Birtle Brook Village E. BL9: Bury 8E 26
Birtle Brook Village W.
BL9: Bury 8D 26
Birtle Brook W. BL9: Bury 8D 26
Birtle Dr. M29: Ast 3D 74
BIRTLE GREEN 7D 26
Birtle Moor BL9: Bury 8D 26
Birtle Rd. BL9: Bury 6D 26
Birtles, The M22: Wyth 4C 116
Birtles Av. SK5: Stoc 6D 96
Birtles Cl. SK8: Chea 2M 117
SK16: Duk 3N 97
Birtles La. SK10: O Ald 9L 127
Birtlespool Rd. SK8: Chea H 3L 117
Birtles Rd. SK10: Macc 3A 130
Birtles Way SK9: Hand 1J 123
(off Sandiway Rd.)
Birt St. M40: Man 6J 79
Birwood Rd. M8: Man 9G 60
Biscay Cl. M11: Man 9L 79
Bishop Cl. OL7: A Lyne 5L 81
Bishopdale Cl. OL2: O'ham 7H 45
Bishopgate WN1: Wig 8J 9 (3F 52)
Bishopgate St. OL9: Chad 5E 62
Bishop Marshall Cl. M40: Man 5J 79
Bishop Marshall Way M24: Mid 8J 43
Bishop Reeves Rd. WA11: Hay 2B 86
Bishop Rd. M6: Sal 6H 77
M41: Urm 7L 91
SK10: Boll 6L 129
Bishopsbridge Cl. BL3: Bolt 8G 38
Bishops Cl. BL3: Bolt 1H 57
SK8: Chea 2M 117
WA14: Bow 6B 114
Bishops Cnr. M15: Man 3E 94
(off Stretford Rd.)
Bishopscourt M7: Sal 2B 78
Bishopsgate M2: Man 6G 4 (1E 94)
Bishopsgate Wlk. OL16: Roch 9G 28
Bishops Mdw. M24: Mid 9J 43
Bishops M. M33: Sale 2E 104
Bishops Rd. BL3: Bolt 1H 57
M25: Pres 8B 60
Bishop St. M24: Mid 4B 62
OL16: Roch 4F 28
SK1: Stoc 2N 9 (7E 108)
Bishops Wlk. OL7: A Lyne 9L 81
(off Hertford St.)
Bishopton Cl. M19: Man 8A 96
Bishopton Dr. SK11: Macc 4D 130
Bisley Av. M23: Wyth 1M 115
Bisley St. OL8: O'ham 4A 8 (5H 63)
Bismarck St. OL4: O'ham 6L 63
Bispham Av. BL2: Bolt 5N 39
SK5: Stoc 7D 96
Bispham Cl. BL8: Bury 3F 40
Bispham Ct. WN5: Bil 9H 51
Bispham Dr. WN4: A Mak 5C 70
Bispham Gro. M7: Sal 3D 78
Bispham Hall Bus. Pk. WN5: Bil 9G 50
Bispham St. BL2: Bolt 4K 39
Bittern Cl. OL11: Roch 6L 27
SK12: Poy 3E 124
Bittern Dr. M43: Droy 7G 80
Bittern Gro. SK10: Macc 3E 130
BJ's Bingo 6H 73
Blackbank St. BL1: Bolt 2G 38
(not continuous)
Blackberry Cl. WA14: B'ath 8B 104
Blackberry Dr. WN2: Hin 7M 53
Blackberry La. SK5: Stoc 1F 108
Black Brook Rd. SK4: Stoc 1B 108
Blackbrook Trad. Est.
M19: Man 1A 108
Blackburn Cl. WA3: Low 1A 88
Blackburne Dr. WA12: N Wil 5D 86
Blackburn Gdns. M20: Man 4F 106
Blackburn Pl. M5: Sal 9B 78
Blackburn Rd. BL0: Eden 1K 11
BL1: Bolt 9F 22
BL7: Bel, Eger 1D 22
BL7: Eger 8F 22
Blackburn St. M3: Sal 1B 4 (7C 78)
M16: Old T 4B 94
M25: Pres 7B 60
M26: Rad 9G 41
Blackcap Cl. M28: Wors 3J 75
Blackcarr Rd. M23: Wyth 1A 116
Blackchapel Dr. OL16: Roch 1F 44
Black Clough OL2: Shaw 5A 46
Blackcroft Cl. M27: Swin 2E 76
Black Dad La. OL11: Roch 5F 26
Blackden Wlk. SK9: Wilm 5J 123
Blackdown Gro. OL8: O'ham 8J 63
Blackett St. M12: Man 7N 5 (1J 95)
Blackfield La. M7: Sal 2B 78
Blackfields M7: Sal 2C 78
(off Bury New Rd.)
Blackford Av. BL9: Bury 8M 41
BLACKFORD BRIDGE 8L 41
Blackford Rd. M19: Man 1N 107
Blackford Wlk. M40: Man 7J 79
(off Denver Av.)
Black Friar Ct. M3: Sal 1C 4
Blackfriars Rd. M3: Sal 1C 4 (7C 78)
Blackfriars St. M3: Sal 3F 4 (8E 78)
Blackhill Cl. M13: Man 9L 5 (2G 95)
Blackhill La. WA16: Knut 8F 132
Blackhorse Av. BL6: Bla 2M 35
Blackhorse Cl. BL6: Bla 1M 35
Black Horse St. BL4: Farn 4M 57
Blackhorse St. BL1: Bolt 3J 7 (5F 38)
BL6: Bla 1M 35
Blackhurst Brow
SK10: Mot S A 2N 127
BLACK LANE 6F 40
Black La. BL0: Ram 6N 11
SK6: Mel 4J 121
SK10: Macc 3J 131
WN7: Lei 5M 73
Blackleach Country Pk. (Nature Reserve)
6L 57
Blackleach Country Pk. Vis. Cen.
7L 57
Blackleach Dr. M28: Walk 6L 57
Blackledge Cl. WN5: Orr 6J 51
Blackledge St. BL3: Bolt 8D 38
BLACKLEY 1K 79
Blackley Cl. BL9: Bury 1N 25
SK10: Macc 9F 128
Blackley Crematorium M9: Man 7F 60
Blackley Golf Course 7N 61
Blackleyhurst Av. WN5: Bil 8D 4
Blackley New Rd. M9: Man 8E 60
Blackley Pk. Rd. M9: Man 1J 79
Blackley St. M16: Old T 4B 94
M24: Mid 4G 61
Black Lion Pas. SK1: Stoc 4M 9
Blacklock St. M8: Man 6E 78
BLACKMOOR 5C 74
Blackmoor Av. M29: Ast 5C 74
Blackmore Rd. M32: Stre 4H 93
Black Moss Cl. M26: Rad 9D 40
Black Moss Ct. M26: Rad 8D 40
Black Moss Rd. WA14: D Mas 9L 103
Blackpits Rd. OL11: Roch 4J 27
Blackpool St. M11: Man 8A 80
Black Rd. SK11: Macc 6J 131
Blackrock OL5: Mos 4F 82
Blackrock St. M11: Man 9L 79
BLACKROD 2N 35
Blackrod Brow BL6: Bla 9L 19
Blackrod By-Pass Rd. BL6: Bla 9M 19
Blackrod Dr. BL8: Bury 3F 40
Blackrod Station (Rail) 2A 36
Blacksail Wlk. OL1: O'ham 2L 63
Blackshaw Clough SK13: Glos 6G 101
Blackshaw Ho. BL3: Bolt 6D 38
Blackshaw La. BL3: Bolt 6D 38
OL2: O'ham 8K 45
SK9: A Edg 4E 126
Blackshaw Rd. SK13: Glos 7G 100
Blackshaw Row BL3: Bolt 7D 38
(off Blackshaw La.)
Blackshaw St. SK3: Stoc 4K 9 (8C 108)
SK11: Macc 5G 131
Blacksmith La. OL11: Roch 9N 27
Blacksmiths Fold M46: Ath 8N 55
Blackstock St. M13: Man 5H 95
Blackstone Av. OL16: Roch 5G 29
Blackstone Edge Ct. OL15: Lit 8N 15
Blackstone Edge Old Rd.
OL15: Lit 8N 15
Blackstone Edge Rd. HX6: Ripp 2H 17
Blackstone Ho. SK2: Stoc 2H 119
Blackstone Rd. SK2: Stoc 2H 119
Blackstone Wlk. M9: Man 4J 79
(off Carisbrook St.)
Black St. SK11: Macc 6J 131
Blackthorn Av. M19: Man 1M 107
WN6: Wig 9C 34
Blackthorn Cl. OL12: Roch 3C 28
Blackthorne Cl. BL1: Bolt 3B 38
Blackthorne Dr. M33: Sale 6D 104
Blackthorne Rd. SK14: Hyde 2B 110
Blackthorn M. OL12: Roch 3C 28
Blackthorn Rd. OL8: O'ham 2H 81
Blackthorn Wlk. M31: Part 6F 102
(off Wood La.)
Blackwin St. M12: Man 3M 95
Blackwood Dr. M23: Wyth 8K 105
Blackwood Edge Rd. HX6: Rish 8L 17
Blackwood St. BL3: Bolt 8H 39
Bladen Cl. SK8: Chea H 3M 117
Blainscough La. PR7: Cop 5A 18
Blainscough Rd. PR7: Cop 5B 18
Blair Av. M38: Lit H 7J 57
M41: Urm 7M 91
WN2: Hin 8D 54
Blair Cl. M33: Sale 7C 104
OL2: Shaw 5M 45
SK7: H Gro 7G 119
Blairgowrie Dr. SK10: Macc 9F 128
Blairhall Av. M40: Man 3M 79
Blair La. BL2: Bolt 3L 39
Blairmore Dr. BL3: Bolt 7N 37
Blair Rd. M16: Whall R 8D 94
Blair St. BL4: Kea 5B 58
BL7: Bro X 5G 23
M16: Old T 4C 94
OL12: Roch 4B 28
Blake Av. M46: Ath 6M 55
Blakeborough Ho. M46: Ath 8M 55
(off Elizabeth St.)
Blake Cl. WN3: Wig 6D 52
Blakedown Wlk. M12: Man 4K 95
(off Cochrane Av.)
Blake Dr. SK2: Stoc 9J 109
Blakefield Dr. M28: Walk 1M 75
Blake Gdns. BL1: Bolt 2D 38
Blakehall WN8: Skel 4B 50
(not continuous)
Blakelock St. OL2: Shaw 5M 45
Blakelow Bank SK11: Macc 6K 131
Blakelow Gdns. SK11: Macc 6K 131
Blakelow Rd. SK11: Macc 6K 131
Blakemere Av. M33: Sale 5L 105
Blakemore Pk. M46: Ath 7K 55
Blakemore Wlk. M12: Man 9K 79
Blake St. BL1: Bolt 2E 38
BL7: Bro X 6H 23
OL16: Roch 6F 8 (5E 28)
Blakeswell Cl. M41: Urm 6L 91
Blakey Cl. BL3: Bolt 8A 38
Blakey St. M12: Man 5M 95
Blanchard St. M15: Man 4D 94
Blanche St. OL12: Roch 3E 28
Blanche Wlk. OL1: O'ham 1F 8 (4L 63)
Bland Cl. M35: Fail 3C 80
Blandford Av. M28: Wors 2N 75
Blandford Cl. BL8: Bury 8K 25
M29: Tyld 1B 74
Blandford Ct. OL6: A Lyne 7A 6 (7L 81)
SK15: Stal 8D 82
Blandford Dr. M40: Man 9B 62
SK11: Macc 4D 130
Blandford Ho. SK15: Stal 8D 82
Blandford Ri. BL6: Los 3H 37
Blandford Rd. M6: Sal 5A 78
M30: Ecc 8B 76
SK4: Stoc 6N 107
Blandford St. OL6: A Lyne 8A 6 (7L 81)
SK15: Stal 8D 82
Bland Rd. M25: Pres 9A 60
Bland St. BL9: Bury 6L 7 (1M 41)
M16: Whall R 5D 94
Blanefield Cl. M21: Cho H 1D 106
Blantyre Av. M28: Walk 9M 57
Blantyre Ho. M15: Man 8D 4
Blantyre Rd. M27: Swin 4H 77
Blantyre St. M15: Man 8C 4 (2C 94)
M27: Swin 2D 76
M30: Ecc 7A 76
WN2: Hin 5A 54
Blanwood Dr. M8: Man 3G 79
Blaven Cl. SK3: Stoc 2D 118
Blaydon Cl. WN2: Asp 7N 35
Blaydon Pk. WN8: Skel 4B 50
Blaze Hill SK10: Rain 5N 129
Blaze Moss Bank SK2: Stoc 2H 119
Bleach St. WN2: Hin 6M 53
Bleackley St. BL8: Bury 9J 25
Bleadale Cl. SK9: Wilm 5J 123
BLEAK HEY NOOK 4M 47
Bleak Hey Nook La. OL3: Del 4M 47
Bleak Hey Rd. M22: Wyth 5E 116
Bleakholt Rd. BL0: Ram 5M 11
Bleakledge Gro. WN2: Hin 5A 54
Bleakley St. M45: Whitef 2L 59
Bleaklow Cl. WN3: Wig 9E 52
Bleaklow Wlk. SK13: Gam 8A 100
(off Castleton Cres.)
Bleak St. BL2: Bolt 2J 39
Bleasby St. OL4: O'ham 4N 63
Bleasdale Cl. BL6: Los 4H 37
BL9: Bury 9N 41
Bleasdale Rd. BL1: Bolt 2A 38
M22: Wyth 5N 115
WA12: N Wil 5E 86
WN2: Hin 6C 54
Bleasdale St. OL2: O'ham 7H 45
Bleasefell Chase M28: Wors 5H 75
Bleatarn Rd. SK1: Stoc 9F 108
Bledlow Cl. M30: Ecc 7E 76
Blencarn Wlk. M9: Man 4J 79
(off Ravelston Dr.)
Blendworth Cl. M8: Man 3E 78
(off Broomfield Dr.)
Blenheim Av. M16: Whall R 7C 94
OL1: O'ham 9A 46
Blenheim Cl. BL9: Bury 7M 41
OL10: H'ood 2K 43
SK9: Wilm 7J 123
SK12: Poy 2K 125
SK13: Had 4C 100
WA14: Bow 5D 114
Blenheim Ct. M9: Man 6F 60
(off Deanswood Dr.)
Blenheim Dr. WN7: Lei 3N 73
Blenheim Rd. BL2: Bolt 5L 39
M16: Old T 5N 93
SK8: Chea H 5N 117
WN4: A Mak 8G 70
WN5: Wig 2N 51
Blenheim St. M29: Tyld 1A 74
OL4: O'ham 2A 64
OL12: Roch 4A 28
Blenheim Way OL6: A Lyne 6B 82
SK10: Macc 3E 130
Blenmar Cl. M26: Rad 7J 41
Bleriot St. BL3: Bolt 9E 38
Bletchley Rd. SK4: Stoc 7K 107
Blethyn St. BL3: Bolt 1C 56
Blewbury Cl. WN7: Lei 3H 73
Bligh Rd. BL5: W'ton 2G 55
Blinco Rd. M41: Urm 8F 92
Blind La. M12: Man 2J 95
Blindsill Rd. BL4: Farn 4J 57
Blissford Cl. WN2: Hin 7N 53
Blisworth Av. M30: Ecc 1E 92
Blisworth Cl. M4: Man 9J 79
Blithfield Wlk. M34: Dent 7J 97
Block A M4: Man 5N 5
(off Pollard St.)
Block B M4: Man 5N 5
(off Pollard St.)
Block C M4: Man 5N 5
(off Pollard St.)
Block D M4: Man 5N 5
(off Pollard St.)
Block E M4: Man 5N 5
(off Pollard St.)
Block La. OL9: Chad 7F 62
Blocksage St. SK16: Duk 2A 98
Blodwell St. M6: Sal 8M 77
Blofield Ct. BL4: Farn 4L 57
(off Mary St.)
Blomley St. OL11: Roch 2A 44
Bloomfield Cl. SK8: Chea H 8K 117
Bloomfield Dr. BL9: Bury 9A 42
M8: Sal 5D 78
M28: Wors 3H 75
Bloomfield Rd. BL4: Farn 5L 57
Bloomfield St. BL1: Bolt 1F 38
Bloomsbury Gro. WA15: Tim 1G 114
Bloomsbury La. WA15: Tim 1G 114
Bloom St. BL0: Ram 1G 24
M1: Man 7H 5 (1F 94)
M3: Sal 3D 4 (8D 78)
OL9: O'ham 3B 8 (5J 63)
SK3: Stoc 5G 9 (8A 108)
Blossom Pl. OL16: Roch 6D 8 (5D 28)
Blossom Rd. M31: Part 6F 102
Blossoms Hey SK8: Chea H 6K 117
Blossoms Hey Wlk.
SK8: Chea H 6K 117
Blossoms La. SK7: W'ford 4M 123
Blossoms St. SK2: Stoc 1D 118
Blossom St. M3: Sal 2E 4
M4: Man 3L 5 (8G 79)
M29: Tyld 1B 74
Bloxham Wlk. M9: Man 8L 61
Blucher St. M5: Sal 9B 78
M12: Man 3K 95
OL7: A Lyne 4L 81
Blue Ball Rd. HX6: Ripp 4M 17
Blue Bell Av. M40: Man 1M 79
Bluebell Av. WA11: Hay 2B 86
WN6: Wig 9C 34
Blue Bell Cl. SK14: Hyde 4C 98
Bluebell Cl. SK10: Macc 1H 131
Bluebell Dr. OL11: Roch 1N 43
Bluebell Gro. SK8: Chea 3J 117
Bluebell La. SK10: Macc 1G 131
Bluebell M. SK10: Macc 1H 131
(off Cavendish Cl.)
Bluebell Way SK9: Wilm 5H 123
Blueberry Av. M40: Man 9A 62
Blueberry Bus. Pk. OL16: Roch 6H 29
Blueberry Dr. OL2: Shaw 5A 46
Blueberry Rd. WA14: Bow 5A 114
Blue Chip Bus. Pk.
WA14: B'ath 9C 104
Bluefields OL2: Shaw 4A 46
Blue Moon Way M14: Man 7F 94
Blue Ribbon Wlk. M27: Swin 1G 76
Bluestone Dr. SK4: Stoc 5K 107
Bluestone Rd. M34: Dent 7E 96
M40: Man 2M 79
Bluestone Ter. M34: Dent 7E 96
Blundell Cl. BL9: Bury 9A 42
Blundell La. BL6: Bla 2K 35
Blundell M. WN3: Wig 7A 52
Blundells Ct. WN3: Wig 7A 52
Blundell St. BL1: Bolt 2J 7 (5F 38)
Blundering La. SK15: Stal 3G 99
Blunn St. OL8: O'ham 7K 63
Blyborough Cl. M6: Sal 6L 77
Blyth Av. M23: Wyth 6B 106
OL15: Lit 2K 29
Blyth Cl. SK10: Macc 3C 130
WA15: Tim 1K 115
Blythe Av. SK7: Bram 9A 118
Blythewood WN8: Skel 4A 50
Blyton La. M7: Sal 2N 77
Blyton St. M15: Man 4G 94
Blyton Way M34: Dent 9K 97
Boad St. M1: Man 6L 5 (1G 95)
Boardale Dr. M24: Mid 2K 61
Boardman Cl. BL1: Bolt 2F 38
SK5: Stoc 4D 108
Boardman Fold Cl. M24: Mid 6M 61
Boardman Fold Rd. M24: Mid 6L 61
Boardman La. M24: Mid 3G 61
Boardman Rd. M8: Man 9E 60
Boardman St. BL1: Bolt 2F 38
BL6: Bla 2N 35
M30: Ecc 9E 76
Board St. BL3: Bolt 6E 38
OL6: A Lyne 6A 82
Boarfold La. SK13: Chis 3H 111
Boar Grn. Cl. M40: Man 3A 80
Boarhurst Farm OL3: G'fld 6M 65
(off Boarhurst La.)
BOARSGREAVE 1F 12
Boarshaw Clough M24: Mid 1N 61
Boarshaw Clough Way M24: Mid 1N 61
Boarshaw Crematorium
M24: Mid 1A 62
Boarshaw Cres. M24: Mid 1A 62
Boarshaw La. M24: Mid 9B 44
Boarshaw Rd. M24: Mid 2M 61
BOAR'S HEAD 5D 34
Boars Head Av. WN6: Stan 5D 34
BOARSHURST 6M 65
Boarshurst Bus. Pk. OL3: G'fld 5L 65
Boarshurst La. OL3: G'fld 6L 65
Boat La. M22: Nor 7D 106
M44: Irl 7J 91
OL3: Dig 7N 47
Boat La. Ct. M22: Nor 7D 106
Boatmans Row M29: Ast 6D 74
Boatman's Wlk.
OL7: A Lyne 9B 6 (9L 81)
Boatyard, The M32: Stre 7L 93
Bobbin Wlk. OL4: O'ham 4G 8 (5L 63)
Bob Massey Cl. M11: Man 9A 80
Bob's La. M44: Cad 4E 102
Boddens Hill Rd. SK4: Stoc 7M 107
Bodden St. WA3: Low 9C 72
Boddington Rd. M30: Ecc 9N 75
Boden St. SK11: Macc 4H 131
Bodiam Rd. BL8: G'mount 4F 24
Bodley St. M11: Man 8A 80
Bodmin Av. SK10: Macc 3C 130
Bodmin Cl. OL2: O'ham 9L 45
Bodmin Cres. SK5: Stoc 3F 108
Bodmin Dr. SK7: Bram 8C 118
WN2: P Bri 1K 71
Bodmin Rd. M29: Ast 2C 74
M33: Sale 3D 104
Bodmin Wlk. M23: Wyth 2N 115
Bodney Wlk. M9: Man 8G 61
Body Matrix, The 9J 61
(off Old Market St.)
Body Work Gymnasium 9F 40
Bogart Ct. M6: Sal 6L 77
(off Monroe Cl.)
Bogburn La. PR7: Cop 7A 18
Boggard La. SK13: Char 2N 111
Boggart Hole Clough 9K 61
Bogguard Rd. SK6: Mel 3J 121
Bohemia Cotts. SK15: Stal 8E 82
(off Cocker Hill)
Bolam Cl. M23: Wyth 7M 105
Boland Dr. M14: Man 9J 95
Bolbury Cres. M27: Pen 2K 77
Bolderod Pl. OL1: O'ham 3L 63
Bolderstone Pl. SK2: Stoc 3J 119
Bolderwood Dr. WN2: Hin 7N 53
Bold La. WA5: Coll G 9A 86
Bold St. BL1: Bolt 4K 7 (5G 38)
BL9: Bury 6N 7 (1N 41)
M15: Man 4D 94
M16: Whall R 5D 94
WA14: Alt 4D 114
WN5: Wig 6A 52
WN7: Lei 4H 73
(not continuous)
Bolesworth Cl. M21: Cho H 9M 93
Boleyn Ct. OL10: H'ood 3H 43
BOLHOLT 9G 24
Bolholt Ind. Est. BL8: Bury 9H 25
Bolholt Ind. Pk. BL8: Bury 9G 25
Bolholt Ter. BL8: Bury 9H 25
Bolivia St. M5: Sal 8J 77
Bolleyn Wood Ct. SK9: Wilm 5G 123
Bollin Av. WA14: Bow 7B 114
Bollinbarn SK10: Macc 2F 130

Bollinbarn Dr. SK10: Macc 2E 130
Bollinbrook Rd. SK10: Macc 3E 130
Bollin Cl. BL4: Kea 5B 58
SK9: Wilm 6G 123
WA3: Cul 7J 89
WA13: Lym 3B 112
Bollin Ct. M15: Man 3C 94
(off Johnson St.)
M33: Sale 6H 105
(off Bollin Dr.)
SK9: Wilm 8H 123
WA14: Bow 6B 114
Bollin Dr. M33: Sale 6H 105
WA13: Lym 3B 112
WA14: Tim 8E 104
Bollin Gro. SK10: P'bury 6D 128
Bollings Yd. BL1: Bolt 4L 7 (6G 39)
BOLLINGTON 5M 129
BOLLINGTON CROSS 7J 129
Bollington Leisure Cen. 7J 129
Bollington Mill WA14: Lit B 4K 113
Bollington Old Rd. SK10: Boll 7H 129
Bollington Rd. M40: Man 8J 79
SK4: Stoc 3B 108
SK10: Boll 7J 129
Bollington St.
OL7: A Lyne 9A 6 (9L 81)
Bollin Hill SK9: Wilm 6F 122
SK10: P'bury 8E 128
Bollin Ho. M7: Sal 5B 78
(off Victoria Lodge)
Bollin Link SK9: Wilm 7G 123
Bollin M. SK10: P'bury 6D 128
Bollin Sq. WA14: Bow 6B 114
Bollin Wlk. M45: Whitef 1B 60
SK5: Stoc 3D 108
SK9: Wilm 7G 123
Bollin Way M45: Whitef 1B 60
SK10: P'bury 7E 128
Bollinway WA15: Hale 7G 115
Bollinwood Chase SK9: Wilm 7J 123
Bolney St. WN2: Asp 1K 53
Bolney Wlk. M40: Man 6J 79
(off Collyhurst St.)
Bolshaw Farm La. SK8: H Grn 9H 117
Bolshaw Rd. SK8: H Grn 9G 117
Bolt Mdw. OL3: G'fld 7K 65
BOLTON 3K 7 (5G 38)
Bolton & Westhoughton Greyhound Stadium 4C 54
Bolton Arena 5E 36
Bolton Av. M19: Man 6J 107
SK8: Chea H 9N 117
Bolton Cl. M25: Pres 9M 59
SK12: Poy 2H 125
WA3: Low 1D 88
Bolton Ent. Cen. BL3: Bolt 6D 38
Bolton Ga. Retail Pk. BL1: Bolt 3H 39
Bolton Golf Course 4J 37
Bolton Ho. Rd. WN2: B'haw 3B 72
Bolton Lads & Girls Club 3H 7
Bolton Little Theatre 3H 7 (5F 38)
Bolton Museum, Art Gallery & Aquarium 3K 7 (5G 38)
Bolton Old Links Golf Course 2N 37
Bolton Old Rd. M46: Ath 8M 55
Bolton Open Golf Course 1L 39
Bolton Retail Pk.
BL3: Bolt 5K 7 (6G 38)
Bolton Rd. BL2: Bolt 8K 23
BL3: Bolt 1L 57
(Fylde St.)
BL3: Bolt 1M 55
(Snydale Way)
BL4: Farn 1L 57
BL4: Kea 4M 57
BL5: W'ton 3H 55
BL6: Hor 6L 19
BL7: Edg, Tur 1L 23
BL8: Bury 7G 7 (4G 41)
BL8: Haw 2B 24
BL9: Bury 7G 7 (4G 41)
M6: Sal 4J 77
M26: Rad 8D 40
M27: Pen 9F 58
M28: Walk 7L 57
M46: Ath 8M 55
OL11: Roch 9M 27
PR6: Adl, And 6L 19
PR7: Chor 1H 19
WN2: Asp 7M 35
WN2: Bam 7E 70
WN4: A Mak 7E 70
Bolton Rd. Ind. Est. BL5: W'ton 2H 55
M46: Ath 7N 55
Bolton Rd. Nth. BL0: Ram 6J 11
Bolton Rd. W. BL0: Ram 2F 24
BL8: Haw 2F 24
Bolton Sq. WN1: Wig 6N 9 (2H 53)
Bolton Station (Rail) 5L 7 (6G 39)
Bolton Steam Mus. 4D 38
Bolton St. BL0: Ram 9H 11
BL9: Bury 7J 7 (2L 41)
M26: Rad 9F 40
OL4: O'ham 5M 63
(not continuous)
SK5: Stoc 1C 108
WN4: Gars 5A 70
Boltons Yd. OL3: Upp 3L 65
Bolton Technology Exchange
BL1: Bolt 3H 7 (5F 38)
Bolton Wanderers FC 5F 36
Bolton Wanderers FC Visitor & Tour Cen. 5F 36
(within Reebok Stadium)
BOLTON WEST SERVICE AREA 9A 20
Bombay Ho. M1: Man 1F 94
(off Whitworth St.)
Bombay Rd. SK3: Stoc 9A 108
WN5: Wig 3N 51
Bombay Sq. M1: Man 7J 5
Bombay St. M1: Man 7J 5 (1F 94)
(not continuous)
OL6: A Lyne 6A 82
Bonar Cl. SK3: Stoc 8A 108
Bonar Rd. SK3: Stoc 8A 108
Boncarn Dr. M23: Wyth 3N 115
Bonchurch Wlk. M18: Man 3N 95
Bond Cl. BL6: Hor 1E 36
Bondmark Rd. M18: Man 3A 96
Bond's La. PR7: Adl 6J 19
Bond St. BL0: Eden 4L 11
BL9: Bury 7N 7 (2N 41)
M12: Man 7M 5 (1H 95)
M34: Dent 6K 97
M46: Ath 1A 74
OL12: Roch 3E 28
SK11: Macc 6G 130
SK15: Stal 7D 82
WN7: Lei 5H 73
Bond St. Ind. Est.
M12: Man 7M 5 (1H 95)
Bongs Rd. SK2: Stoc 1K 119
Bonhill Wlk. M11: Man 8N 79
(off Coghlan Cl.)
Bonington Ri. SK6: Mar B 8E 110
Bonis Cres. SK2: Stoc 3G 119
Bonis Hall La. SK10: P'bury 9C 124
Bonny Brow St. M24: Mid 4G 61
Bonnyfields SK6: Rom 6M 109
Bonnywell Rd. WN7: Lei 7G 73
Bonsall Bank SK13: Gam 7A 100
(off Melandra Castle Rd.)
Bonsall Cl. SK13: Gam 7A 100
(off Melandra Castle Rd.)
Bonsall Fold SK13: Gam 7A 100
(off Rowsley Cl.)
Bonsall St. M15: Man 3E 94
Bonscale Cres. M24: Mid 9K 43
Bonville Chase WA14: Alt 3A 114
Bonville Rd. WA14: Alt 2A 114
Boodle St. OL6: A Lyne 6C 6 (7M 81)
Bookham Wlk. M9: Man 2K 79
(off Swainsthorpe Dr.)
Boond St. M3: Sal 2E 4 (8D 78)
M4: Man 4N 5 (9J 79)
Boonfields BL7: Bro X 5H 23
Booth Av. M14: Man 1J 107
BOOTH BANK 8H 113
Boothbank La. WA14: M'ton 9H 113
Booth Bri. Cl. M24: Mid 4H 61
Boothby Ct. M27: Swin 1D 76
(off Boothby Rd.)
Boothby Rd. M27: Swin 1E 76
Boothby St. SK2: Stoc 3G 119
SK10: Macc 4G 130
Booth Clibborn Ct. M7: Sal 2C 78
(off Park La.)
Booth Cl. BL8: Tot 8G 24
SK15: Stal 9C 82
Boothcote M34: Aud 3H 97
Boothdale Dr. M34: Aud 2E 96
Booth Dr. M41: Urm 4N 91
Boothfield M30: Ecc 7A 76
Boothfield Av. M22: Wyth 1C 116
Boothfield Dr. M22: Wyth 1C 116
Boothfield Rd. M22: Wyth 1B 116
Boothfields BL8: Bury 1J 41
WA16: Knut 6J 133
BOOTH GREEN 7K 125
Booth Hall Dr. BL8: Tot 8F 24
Booth Hall Rd. M9: Man 8M 61
Booth Hill La. OL1: O'ham 2J 63
Booth Ho. Trad. Est. OL9: O'ham 5G 63
Boothman Ct. M30: Ecc 7F 76
Booth Rd. BL3: Lit L 1B 58
M16: Old T 6B 94
M33: Sale 2H 105
M34: Aud 2E 96
SK9: Wilm 5F 122
WA14: Alt 3A 6 (3C 114)
Boothroyden Cl. M24: Mid 4H 61
Boothroyden Rd. M9: Man 5H 61
M24: Mid 4H 61
Boothroyden Ter. M9: Man 5H 61
BOOTH'S BANK 4J 75
Boothsbank Av. M28: Wors 4J 75
Booth's Brow Rd. WN4: A Mak 4A 70
Booth's Ct. SK13: Glos 8F 100
(off Ellison St.)
Booths Hall WA16: Knut 7K 133
Booth's Hall Gro. M28: Wors 4J 75
Booths Hall Paddock M28: Wors 5J 75
Booth's Hall Rd. M28: Wors 4J 75
Boothshall Way M28: Wors 4J 75
BOOTHSTOWN 5G 75
Boothstown Dr. M28: Wors 5H 75
Booth St. BL1: Bolt 1D 38
BL8: Tot 7F 24
M2: Man 5G 5 (9F 78)
M3: Sal 3F 4 (8E 78)
M24: Mid 5B 62
M34: Dent 4K 97
M35: Fail 3C 80
OL4: Lees 3C 64
OL6: A Lyne 8C 6 (8M 81)
OL9: O'ham 2B 8 (5J 63)
SK3: Stoc 9C 108
SK14: Holl 4M 99
SK14: Hyde 8B 98
SK15: Stal 1C 98
Booth St. E. M13: Man 9K 5 (3G 94)
Booth St. W. M15: Man 3F 94
Booth Way BL8: Tot 8F 24
Boothway M30: Ecc 8F 76
Boothwood Stile BL8: Holc 2F 24
Boot La. BL1: Bolt 3M 37
Bootle St. M2: Man 5F 4 (9E 78)
Bor Av. WN3: Wig 7E 52
Bordale Av. M9: Man 3L 79
Borden Cl. WN2: Wig 1J 53
Borden Way BL9: Bury 6N 41
Border Brook La. M28: Wors 4H 75
Border Mill Fold OL5: Mos 1G 82
Bordesley Av. M38: Lit H 5H 57
Bordley Wlk. M23: Wyth 7L 105
Bordon Rd. SK3: Stoc 9N 107
Bores Hill WN1: Stan 9F 18
Boringdon Cl. M40: Man 4N 79
Borland Av. M40: Man 1B 80
Bornmore Ind. Cen. BL8: Bury 1J 41
Borough Arc. SK14: Hyde 6A 98
Borough Av. M26: Rad 7K 41
M27: Pen 1G 76
Borough Rd. M50: Sal 9K 77
WA15: Alt 4E 6 (3E 114)
Borough St. SK15: Stal 9D 82
Borrans, The M28: Wors 5G 75
Borron Ho. WA12: N Wil 5E 86
Borron Rd. WA12: N Wil 4E 86
Borron Rd. Ind. Est.
WA12: N Wil 5E 86
(off Borron Rd.)
Borron St. SK1: Stoc 6E 108
Borrowbeck Cl. WN2: P Bri 9J 53
Borrowdale Av. BL1: Bolt 4B 38
SK8: Gat 3G 116
Borrowdale Cl. OL2: O'ham 6H 45
Borrowdale Cres.
M20: Man 4D 106
OL7: A Lyne 5K 81
Borrowdale Dr. BL9: Bury 9N 41
OL11: Roch 9N 27
Borrowdale Rd. M24: Mid 1J 61
SK2: Stoc 9F 108
WN5: Wig 4M 51
Borrowdale Ter. SK15: Stal 6D 82
(off Springs La.)
Borsdane Av. WN2: Hin 7A 54
Borsdane Wood Local Nature Reserve 2B 54
Borsden St. M27: Ward 9D 58
Borth Av. SK2: Stoc 9F 108
Borth Wlk. M23: Wyth 1M 115
Borwell St. M18: Man 3B 96
Boscobel Rd. BL3: Bolt 1J 57
Boscombe Av. M30: Ecc 1C 92
Boscombe Dr. SK7: H Gro 5G 118
Boscombe Pl. WN2: Hin 7A 54
Boscombe St. M14: Man 7G 95
SK5: Stoc 7D 96
Boscow Rd. BL3: Lit L 1A 58
Bosden Av. SK7: H Gro 4J 119
Bosden Cl. SK1: Stoc 4M 9
SK9: Hand 1J 123
Bosden Fold SK1: Stoc 4M 9 (8D 108)
Bosden Fold Rd.
SK7: H Gro 3J 119
Bosden Hall Rd. SK7: H Gro 4J 119
Bosdin Rd. E. M41: Urm 8M 91
Bosdin Rd. W. M41: Urm 8M 91
Boslam Wlk. M4: Man 3N 5
Bosley Av. M20: Man 9F 94
Bosley Cl. SK9: Wilm 4J 123
Bosley Dr. SK12: Poy 3L 125
Bosley Rd. SK3: Stoc 8M 107
Bossall Av. M9: Man 7K 61
Bossington Cl. SK2: Stoc 8G 109
Bostock Rd. SK11: Macc 5C 130
SK14: B'tom 9K 99
Bostock Wlk. M13: Man 9L 5
Boston Cl. M35: Fail 1D 80
SK7: Bram 8B 118
WA3: Cul 5H 89
Boston Ct. M50: Sal 1L 93
Boston Gro. WN7: Lei 2G 72
Boston St. BL1: Bolt 3F 38
M15: Man 4E 94
OL8: O'ham 7K 63
SK14: Hyde 7B 98
Boston Wlk. M34: Dent 8L 97
Boswell Av. M34: Aud 9H 81
Boswell Pl. WN3: Wig 7C 52
Boswell Way M24: Mid 8B 44
Bosworth Cl. M45: Whitef 3B 60
Bosworth Sq. OL11: Roch 9B 28
(off Bosworth St.)
Bosworth St. BL6: Hor 9D 20
M11: Man 1M 95
OL11: Roch 9B 28
Botanical Av. M16: Old T 4N 93
Botanical Ho. M16: Old T 4N 93
Botanic Ct. WN1: Wig 8F 34
WN5: Wig 2N 51
Botany Cl. OL10: H'ood 1G 42
WN2: Asp 1L 53
Botany La. OL6: A Lyne 5F 6 (6N 81)
Botany Rd. M30: Ecc 6A 76
SK6: Wood 2L 109
Botesworth Cl. WN2: Hin 6C 54
Botesworth Gro. OL16: Miln 8L 29
Botha Cl. M11: Man 2B 96
Botham Cl. M15: Man 4E 94
Botham Ct. M30: Ecc 7B 76
(off Worsley Rd.)
Bothwell Rd. M40: Man 1M 5 (7H 79)
Bottesford Av. M20: Man 3E 106
BOTTLING WOOD 1G 53
Bottomfield Cl. OL1: O'ham 2L 63
Bottomley Side M9: Man 9H 61
BOTTOM OF WOODHOUSES 5E 80
BOTTOM O' TH' BROW 1G 42
BOTTOM O 'TH' MOOR
BL2 .... 1M 39
BL6 .... 1H 37
Bottom o' th' Moor BL2: Ain 3B 40
BL2: Bolt 2L 39
BL6: Hor 1H 37
OL1: O'ham 4L 63
OL4: O'ham 4L 63
BOTTOMS 2G 82
Bottoms Fold OL5: Mos 2G 82
Bottoms Hall Cotts. BL8: Tot 4D 24
Bottoms Mill Rd. SK6: Mar B 2E 120
Bottom's Row BB4: Water 1E 12
Bottom St. SK14: Hyde 6C 98
Boughey St. WN7: Lei 5G 73
Boulden Dr. BL8: Bury 8J 25
Boulder Dr. M23: Wyth 5N 115
Boulderstone Rd. SK15: Stal 5D 82
Boulevard, The M20: Man 2D 106
(not continuous)
SK7: H Gro 5J 119
SK14: Holl 4N 99
Bouley Wlk. M12: Man 3M 95
(off Conquest Cl.)
Boulters Cl. M24: Mid 9L 43
Boundary, The M27: Clif 7D 58
Boundary Cl. OL5: Mos 4F 82
(not continuous)
SK6: Wood 3N 109
Boundary Cotts. SK15: C'ook 3H 83
Boundary Ct. M28: Wors 2J 75
(off Morston Cl.)
SK4: Stoc 1M 107
SK8: Chea 2H 117
Boundary Dr. BL2: Bolt 7A 40
Boundary Edge BL0: Eden 3L 11
Boundary Gdns. BL1: Bolt 2F 38
(off Portland St.)
OL1: O'ham 3J 63
Boundary Grn. M34: Dent 4J 97
Boundary Gro. M33: Sale 5M 105
Boundary Ind. Est. BL2: Bolt 5A 40
Boundary La. M15: Man 3F 94
WN6: Wrig 1L 33
Boundary Pk. 1H 63
Boundary Pk. Rd. OL1: O'ham 2G 63
Boundary Rd. M23: Wyth 3M 115
M27: Swin 1F 76
M44: Irl 6J 91
SK8: Chea 1L 117
Boundary St. BL1: Bolt 2E 38
M12: Man 4M 95
M29: Tyld 1B 74
OL11: Roch 7C 28
OL15: Lit 8L 15
WN1: Wig 9M 9 (4G 53)
WN7: Lei 6K 73
Boundary St. E. M13: Man 9J 5 (2F 94)
Boundary St. W.
M15: Man 9H 5 (3F 94)
Boundary Trad. Est. M44: Irl 6K 91
Boundary Wlk. OL11: Roch 8C 28
Bourdon St. M40: Man 7J 79
Bourget St. M7: Sal 2E 78
Bournbrook Av. M38: Lit H 5H 57
Bourne Av. M27: Swin 3F 76
WA3: Low 1N 87
Bourne Dr. M40: Man 1N 79
Bourne Ho. M5: Sal 8M 77
(off Amersham St.)
Bournelea Av. M19: Man 2L 107
Bourne Rd. OL2: Shaw 4L 45
Bourne St. OL9: Chad 9F 62
SK4: Stoc 4C 108
SK9: Wilm 8E 122
Bourne Wlk. BL1: Bolt 3F 38
(off Charnock Dr.)
Bournville Av. SK4: Stoc 4C 108
Bournville Dr. BL8: Bury 2G 40
Bournville Gro. M19: Man 8A 96
Bourton Cl. BL8: Bury 1H 41
Bourton Ct. M29: Tyld 1E 74
Bourton Dr. M18: Man 5N 95
Bowden Cl. OL11: Roch 4B 44
SK14: Hat 8H 99
WA3: Cul 5H 89
WN7: Lei 8K 73
Bowden Cres. SK22: N Mil 7N 121
Bowden Downs La.
SK11: Macc 5N 131
Bowden La. SK6: Mar 9B 110
Bowden Rd. M27: Swin 3G 77
SK13: Glos 6E 100
Bowden St. M34: Dent 6J 97
SK7: H Gro 4J 119
BOWDON 5B 114
Bowdon Av. M14: Man 8E 94
Bowdon Ct. M16: Old T 4N 93
Bowdon Cricket, Hockey & Squash Club 6C 114
Bowdon Ho. SK3: Stoc 5J 9 (8C 108)
Bowdon Ri. WA14: Bow 5D 114
Bowdon Rd. WA14: Alt 5A 6 (4C 114)
Bowdon St. SK3: Stoc 5J 9 (8C 108)
(not continuous)
Bowen Cl. SK7: Bram 1D 124
Bowen St. BL1: Bolt 3C 38
Bower Av. OL12: Roch 1H 29
SK4: Stoc 5A 108
SK7: H Gro 6H 119
Bower Ct. SK14: Hyde 4D 98
Bowercup Fold SK15: C'ook 6H 83
Bowerfield Av. SK7: H Gro 7H 119
Bowerfield Cres. SK7: H Gro 7H 119
BOWER FOLD 1E 98
Bower Fold 1F 98
Bower Fold SK15: Stal 1F 98
Bowerfold La. SK4: Stoc 6A 108
(not continuous)
Bower Gdns. SK15: Stal 1G 99
Bower Gro. SK15: Stal 8F 82
Bower Rd. WA15: Hale 6E 114
Bowers, The PR7: Chor 1G 18
Bowers Av. M41: Urm 5B 92
Bowers St. M14: Man 1K 107
Bower St. BL9: Bury 1B 42
M7: Sal 3D 78
M40: Man 5L 79
OL1: O'ham 4M 63
SK5: Stoc 7D 96
Bower Ter. M43: Droy 7G 80
Bowery Av. SK8: Chea H 9L 117
Bowes Cl. BL8: Bury 8H 25
Bowes St. M14: Man 6E 94
Bowfell Circ. M41: Urm 6B 92
Bowfell Dr. SK6: H Lan 7B 120
Bowfell Gro. M9: Man 7G 61
Bowfell Rd. M41: Urm 7A 92
Bowfield Wlk. M40: Man 5A 80
(off Langcroft Dr.)
Bowgreave Av. BL2: Bolt 5N 39
BOWGREEN 6A 114
Bow Grn. M. WA14: Bow 5B 114
Bow Grn. Rd. WA14: Bow 6N 113
Bowgreen Wlk. M15: Man 3C 94
(off Shawheath Cl.)
Bowker Av. M34: Dent 9M 97
Bowker Bank Av. M8: Man 9E 60
Bowker Bank Ind. Est. M8: Man 8F 60
Bowker Cl. OL11: Roch 4K 27
Bowker Ct. M7: Sal 4C 78
Bowkers Row BL1: Bolt 3L 7 (5G 39)
Bowker St. BL0: Ram 1J 11
M7: Sal 4C 78
M26: Rad 9G 40
M28: Walk 8J 57
SK14: Hyde 6B 98
Bowker Va. Gdns. M9: Man 8E 60
Bowker Vale Stop (Metro) 8E 60
Bowlacre Rd. SK14: Hyde 2A 110
Bowland Av. M18: Man 5E 96
WA3: Gol 9M 71
WN4: A Mak 6E 70
Bowland Cl. BL8: Bury 1E 40
OL2: Shaw 5J 45
OL6: A Lyne 3N 81
SK2: Stoc 2J 119
Bowland Ct. M33: Sale 4H 105
Bowland Dr. BL1: Bolt 2N 37
Bowland Gro. OL16: Miln 9K 29
Bowland Rd. M23: Wyth 1M 115
M34: Dent 6F 96
SK6: Wood 3M 109
SK13: Glos 9C 100
Bowland's Hey BL5: W'ton 3G 54
Bow La. M2: Man 5G 4 (9E 78)
OL10: H'ood 2J 43
WA14: Bow 6A 114
BOWLEE 2H 61
Bowlee Cl. BL9: Bury 2N 59
Bowlee Pk. Sports Cen. 1H 61
Bowler St. M19: Man 9N 95
OL2: Shaw 5M 45
Bowlers Wlk. OL12: Roch 3D 28
Bowler Way OL3: G'fld 6L 65
Bowley Av. M22: Wyth 5N 115
Bowling Ct. BL1: Bolt 8F 22
Bowling Grn. BL0: Eden 3K 11
Bowling Grn., The M32: Stre 6J 93
Bowling Grn. Cl. OL9: Chad 7E 62
Bowling Grn. Ct. M16: Whall R 5C 94
Bowling Grn. Row M46: Ath 9K 55
Bowling Grn. St. OL10: H'ood 2J 43
SK14: Hyde 7A 98
Bowling Grn. Way OL11: Roch 6L 27
Bowling Rd. M18: Man 6C 96
Bowlings, The WN6: Wig 1D 52
Bowling St. OL9: Chad 9F 62
Bowling Wood WN2: Hin 7D 54
Bowman Cres. OL6: A Lyne 7A 82
Bowmans, The SK10: Macc 3F 130
Bowmeadow Grange M12: Man 5L 95
Bowmead Wlk. M8: Man 4E 78
(off Ermington Dr.)
Bowmont Cl. SK8: Chea H 3M 117
Bowness Av. M44: Cad 4E 102
OL12: Roch 4A 28
SK4: Stoc 2C 108
SK8: Chea H 6N 117
WA11: St H 9F 68
Bowness Ct. M24: Mid 1J 61
Bowness Dr. M33: Sale 3F 104
Bowness Pl. WN2: I Mak 3L 53
Bowness Rd. BL3: Bolt 8E 38
BL3: Lit L 8N 39
M24: Mid 2H 61
OL7: A Lyne 6K 81
WA15: Tim 2K 115
Bowness St. M11: Man 2D 96
M32: Stre 6K 93
Bowness Wlk. OL2: O'ham 8J 45
(off Shaw St.)
Bowring St. M7: Sal 5B 78
(off Croft St.)
Bow Rd. WN7: Lei 7K 73
Bowscale Cl. M13: Man 5L 95
Bowstone Hill Rd. BL2: Bolt 8B 24
Bow St. BL1: Bolt 2L 7 (5G 39)
M2: Man 4F 4 (9E 78)
OL1: O'ham 2E 8 (4K 63)
OL6: A Lyne 7D 6 (7M 81)
OL11: Roch 1B 44
SK3: Stoc 8A 108
SK16: Duk 9E 6 (8N 81)
Bow Vs. WA14: Bow 5B 114
Bowyer Gdns. BL3: Bolt 9A 38
Boxgrove Rd. M33: Sale 3F 104
Boxgrove Wlk. M8: Man 4F 78
(off Brentfield Av.)
Boxhill Dr. M23: Wyth 7N 105
Box St. BL0: Ram 8K 11
OL15: Lit 9L 15
Boxtree Av. M18: Man 5B 96
Box Tree M. SK11: Macc 5E 130
Box Wlk. M31: Part 5F 102
Box Works, The
M15: Man 8C 4 (2C 94)
Boyd Cl. WN6: Stan 3C 34
Boydell St. WN7: Lei 4H 73
Boyd St. M12: Man 2M 95
Boyd's Wlk. SK16: Duk 2N 97
Boyer St. M16: Old T 4A 94
Boyle St. BL1: Bolt 3B 38
M8: Man 4G 78
Boysnope Cres. M30: Ecc 5K 91
Boysnope Pk. Golf Course 4L 91
Boysnope Wharf M30: Ecc 5L 91
Boyswell Ho. WN1: Wig 7M 9 (3G 53)
Brabant Rd. SK8: Chea H 5N 117
Brabazon Pl. WN5: Wig 3N 51
Brabham Cl. M21: Cho H 9A 94
Brabham M. M27: Swin 3C 76
Brabyns Av. SK6: Rom 5A 110
Brabyns Brow SK6: Mar 9D 110
Brabyns Pk. Recreation Cen. 8D 110
Brabyns Rd. SK14: Hyde 1B 110
Bracadale Dr. SK3: Stoc 2C 118
Bracewell Cl. M12: Man 4M 95
Bracken Av. M28: Walk 8M 57
Bracken Cl. BL1: Bolt 7E 22
M33: Sale 3C 104
M43: Droy 8G 81
OL4: Spri 5C 64
OL10: H'ood 4J 43
SK6: Mar B 9F 110
SK10: Macc 3D 130
SK14: Holl 3N 99
Bracken Dr. M23: Wyth 2A 116

Brackenfield Wlk. *WA15: Tim* 1K **115**
(off Aimson Rd. E.)
Brackenhall Ct. *OL10: H'ood* 2F **42**
(off Todd St.)
Brackenhill Ter. *M34: Dent* 1L **109**
(off Wordsworth Rd.)
Brackenhurst Av. OL5: Mos 1H **83**
Bracken Lea BL5: W'ton 6H **55**
Brackenlea Fold OL12: Roch 3N **27**
Brackenlea Pl. SK3: Stoc 2B **118**
Bracken Lodge OL2: O'ham 2J **63**
Bracken Rd. M46: Ath 9M **55**
WA14: W Tim 7C **104**
WN7: Lei 5D **72**
Brackenside SK5: Stoc 9E **96**
Bracken Trade Pk. BL9: Bury 7L **41**
Bracken Way SK13: Glos 9H **101**
WA16: Knut 8G **133**
Brackenwood Cl. OL2: O'ham 1G **62**
Brackenwood Dr. SK8: Chea 3J **117**
Brackenwood M. SK9: Wilm 6K **123**
Brackley Av. M15: Man 9B **4** (2C **94**)
M29: Tyld 1C **74**
M44: Cad 2E **102**
Brackley Ct. M22: Nor 8C **106**
Brackley Dr. M24: Mid 6M **61**
Brackley Golf Course 5G **56**
Brackley Lodge M30: Ecc 7F **76**
Brackley Rd. BL5: O Hul 3B **56**
M30: Ecc 6D **76**
SK4: Stoc 4B **108**
Brackley Sq. *OL1: O'ham* 3L **63**
(off St Stephens St.)
Brackley St. BL4: Farn 3L **57**
(not continuous)
M28: Walk 7K **57**
OL1: O'ham 1F **8** (3L **63**)
Bracondale Av. BL1: Bolt 2C **38**
Bradbourne Cl. BL3: Bolt 7G **38**
Bradburn Av. M30: Ecc 9D **76**
Bradburn Cl. M30: Ecc 9D **76**
Bradburn Gro. M30: Ecc 9D **76**
Bradburn Rd. M44: Irl 1F **102**
Bradburn St. M30: Ecc 9D **76**
Bradburn Wlk. *M8: Man* 4G **79**
(off Moordown Cl.)
Bradbury Av. WA14: Alt 2A **114**
Bradbury's La. OL3: G'fld 7M **65**
Bradbury St. M26: Rad 1G **58**
OL7: A Lyne 6L **81**
SK14: Hyde 8B **98**
Bradbury Wlk. *OL2: O'ham* 8J **45**
(off Shaw St.)
Bradda Mt. SK7: Bram 5E **118**
Braddan Av. M33: Sale 5J **105**
Bradden Cl. M5: Sal 9N **77**
Braddocks Cl. OL12: Roch 1H **29**
Braddon Av. M41: Urm 7D **92**
Braddon Rd. SK6: Wood 3L **109**
Braddon St. M11: Man 9A **80**
Braddyll Rd. BL5: O Hul 3A **56**
Brade Cl. M11: Man 1A **96**
Bradfield Av. M6: Sal 8J **77**
Bradfield Cl. SK5: Stoc 7C **96**
Bradfield Rd. M32: Stre 7G **93**
M41: Urm 7F **92**
BRADFORD 8M **79**
Bradford Av. BL3: Bolt 9J **39**
PR7: Chor 2E **18**
Bradford Ct. M40: Man 1A **96**
Bradford Cres. BL3: Bolt 8H **39**
Bradford La. SK10: N Ald 7F **126**
Bradford Pk. Dr. BL2: Bolt 6J **39**
Bradford Pl. WN3: Wig 4F **52**
Bradford Rd. BL3: Bolt 2H **57**
BL4: Bolt, Farn 2H **57**
M30: Ecc 5E **76**
M40: Man 8J **79**
Bradford St. BL2: Bolt 4N **7** (6H **39**)
BL4: Farn 4L **57**
(not continuous)
OL1: O'ham 3J **63**
WN3: Wig 4F **52**
Bradford Ter. BL9: Bury 3K **41**
Bradgate Av. SK8: H Grn 6J **117**
Bradgate Cl. M22: Nor 8D **106**
Bradgate Rd. M33: Sale 6H **105**
WA14: Alt 2A **114**
Bradgate St. OL7: A Lyne 9L **81**
Bradgreen Rd. M30: Ecc 7C **76**
Brading Wlk. M22: Wyth 7D **116**
Bradlegh Rd. WA12: N Wil 7E **86**
Bradley Av. M7: Sal 3A **78**
Bradley Cl. M34: Aud 2J **97**
WA15: Tim 9E **104**
Bradley Dr. BL9: Bury 1A **60**
BRADLEY FOLD 6B **40**
Bradley Fold OL4: Lees 5B **64**
SK15: Stal 8E **82**
Bradley Fold Cotts. BL2: Bolt 6B **40**
Bradley Fold Rd. BL2: Ain, Bolt 4C **40**
Bradley Fold Trad. Est. BL2: Bolt 6C **40**
Bradley Gdns. WN2: Asp 6M **35**
Bradley Grn. Rd. SK14: Hyde 3C **98**
Bradley Hall Trad. Est.
WN6: Stan 2D **34**
Bradley Ho. OL8: O'ham 6K **63**
Bradley La. BL2: Bolt 7B **40**
M32: Stre 1G **105**
OL16: Miln 9M **29**
WA5: Burt 7C **86**
WA12: N Wil 7C **86**
WN1: Stan 2B **34**
WN6: Stan 2B **34**
(Ormsby Cl.)
WN6: Stan 3B **34**
(Smalley St.)
BRADLEY MOUNT 6F **128**
Bradley's Ct. M1: Man 4K **5**
BRADLEY SMITHY 8K **131**
Bradley Smithy Cl. OL12: Roch 3C **28**
Bradley St. M1: Man 3K **5**
OL16: Miln 9M **29**
SK11: Macc 6J **131**
Bradney Cl. M9: Man 7G **61**
Bradnor Rd. M22: Shar 9C **106**
Bradshaigh Ho. WN1: Wig 5K **9**
BRADSHAW 8K **23**
Bradshaw Av. M20: Man 1G **106**
M35: Fail 5C **80**
M45: Whitef 1L **59**
Bradshaw Brow BL2: Bolt 9K **23**
BRADSHAW CHAPEL 8L **23**
Bradshaw Cl. WN6: Stan 3A **34**
Bradshaw Cres. SK6: Mar 9D **110**
Bradshaw Fold Av. M40: Man 8B **62**
Bradshawgate BL1: Bolt 3L **7** (5G **39**)
BL2: Bolt 3L **7** (5G **39**)
WN1: Wig 8M **9** (3G **53**)
WN7: Lei 5H **73**
Bradshawgate Shopping Arc.
WN7: Lei 5H **73**
(off Bradshawgate)
Bradshaw Hall Dr. BL2: Bolt 7K **23**
Bradshaw Hall Fold BL2: Bolt 7L **23**
Bradshaw Hall La.
SK8: Chea H, H Grn 7J **117**
(not continuous)
Bradshaw La. M32: Stre 9K **93**
PR6: Adl 5K **19**
(Derby Pl.)
PR6: Adl 5J **19**
(Maytree Ct.)
WA13: Lym 4E **112**
WN8: Par 3A **32**
Bradshaw Mdws. BL2: Bolt 7L **23**
Bradshaw Mill *BL2: Bolt* 8K **23**
(off Maple St.)
Bradshaw Rd. BL2: Bolt 8L **23**
BL7: Tur 8L **23**
BL8: Tot 7C **24**
SK6: Mar 9C **110**
Bradshaw St. *BL4: Farn* 4L **57**
(off Longcauseway)
M7: Sal 4D **78**
M24: Mid 4A **62**
(off Shawbury St.)
M26: Rad 9F **40**
M46: Ath 8M **55**
OL1: O'ham 2E **8** (4K **63**)
OL10: H'ood 2K **43**
(not continuous)
OL16: Roch 5F **8** (5E **28**)
WN1: Wig 1G **53**
WN5: Orr 5L **51**
Bradstock Rd. M16: Whall R 6D **94**
Bradstone Rd. M8: Man 5E **78**
Bradwell Av. M20: Man 2E **106**
M32: Stre 5G **93**
Bradwell Dr. SK8: H Grn 8H **117**
Bradwell Fold *SK13: Gam* 8A **100**
(off Buxton M.)
Bradwell Lea *SK13: Gam* 8A **100**
(off Buxton M.)
Bradwell Pl. BL2: Bolt 3J **39**
Bradwell Rd. SK7: H Gro 7J **119**
WA3: Low 2A **88**
Bradwell Ter. *SK13: Gam* 8A **100**
(off Buxton M.)
Bradwell Wlk. *M41: Urm* 6L **91**
(off Padbury Cl.)
Bradwen Av. M8: Man 1F **78**
Bradwen Cl. M34: Dent 8L **97**
Brady St. BL6: Hor 9C **20**
Braeburn Ct. WN7: Lei 5F **72**
Braemar Av. M32: Stre 7G **93**
M41: Urm 8A **92**
Braemar Ct. M9: Man 6F **60**
Braemar Dr. BL9: Bury 2C **42**
M33: Sale 6C **104**
Braemar Gdns. BL3: Bolt 7N **37**
Braemar Gro. OL10: H'ood 3F **42**
Braemar La. M28: Wors 4J **75**
Braemar Rd. M14: Man 9K **95**
SK7: H Gro 4K **119**
Braemar Wlk. WN2: Asp 7N **35**
Braemore Cl. OL2: Shaw 4J **45**
WN3: Wins 9A **52**
Braemore Dr. SK14: B'tom 8J **99**
Braes, The WN2: Hin 7B **54**
Brae Side OL8: O'ham 9J **63**
Braeside *M32: Stre* 8G **93**
(off Urmston La.)
Braeside Cl. SK2: Stoc 1K **119**
SK11: Macc 6K **131**
Braeside Cres. WN5: Bil 5H **69**
Braeside Gro. BL3: Bolt 7N **37**
Braewood Cl. BL9: Bury 1B **42**
Bragenham St. M18: Man 4A **96**
Braidhaven WN6: She 5J **33**
Braidwood Av. WA16: Knut 5J **133**
Brailsford Av. SK13: Gam 7A **100**
Brailsford Cl. *SK13: Gam* 7A **100**
(off Hathersage Cres.)
Brailsford Gdns. *SK13: Gam* 7A **100**
(off Hathersage Cres.)
Brailsford Grn. *SK13: Gam* 7A **100**
(off Melandra Castle Rd.)
Brailsford M. SK13: Gam 7A **100**
Brailsford Rd. BL2: Bolt 1K **39**
M14: Man 9K **95**
Braintree Rd. M22: Wyth 7C **116**
Braithwaite WN6: She 6L **33**
Braithwaite Rd. M18: Man 7B **96**
M24: Mid 8J **43**
WA3: Low 9N **71**
Brakehouse Cl. OL16: Miln 7J **29**
Brakenhurst Dr. M7: Sal 4E **78**
Brakenlea Dr. M9: Man 9H **61**
Brakesmere Gro. M28: Walk 7G **57**
Braley St. M12: Man 8L **5** (2G **95**)
Bramah Edge Ct. SK13: Tin 3B **100**
Bramall Cl. BL9: Bury 1A **60**
Bramall Ct. M3: Sal 1C **4** (7C **78**)
Bramall Hall 6B **118**
Bramall Pk. Golf Course 6A **118**
Bramall St. SK14: Hyde 5A **98**
Bramber Way *OL9: Chad* 5F **62**
(off Petworth Rd.)
Bramble Av. M5: Sal 2B **94**
OL4: O'ham 2A **64**
Bramble Bank SK13: Glos 9G **100**
Bramble Cl. OL15: Lit 9K **15**
SK10: Macc 2F **130**
Bramble Ct. SK15: Mill 6G **83**
Bramble Cft. BL6: Los 9J **37**
Bramble Gro. WN5: Wig 5B **52**
Brambles, The PR7: Cop 3C **18**
WA5: Burt 9C **86**
WN4: Gars 5A **70**
Bramble Wlk. M22: Wyth 5B **116**
M33: Sale 3C **104**
Bramble Way WN8: Par 3A **32**
Bramblewood OL9: Chad 4B **62**
WN2: Hin 4B **54**
Brambling Cl. M34: Aud 8G **81**
SK2: Stoc 2L **119**
Brambling Dr. BL5: W'ton 5F **54**
Brambling Way WA3: Low 2A **88**
Bramcote Av. BL2: Bolt 7J **39**
M23: Wyth 1A **116**
Bramdean Av. BL2: Bolt 8M **23**
Bramfield Wlk. M15: Man 9C **4**
Bramford Cl. BL5: W'ton 5G **54**
BRAMHALL 1C **124**
Bramhall Av. BL2: Bolt 9N **23**
Bramhall Cen., The SK7: Bram 9B **118**
Bramhall Cl. M33: Sale 5L **105**
OL16: Miln 7J **29**
SK16: Duk 3A **98**
WA15: Tim 1K **115**
Bramhall Golf Course 9D **118**
BRAMHALL GREEN 5D **118**
Bramhall La. SK2: Stoc 1D **118**
SK3: Stoc 1D **118**
Bramhall Lane Lawn Tennis Club
. . . .7B **118**
Bramhall La. Sth. SK7: Bram 9C **118**
BRAMHALL MOOR 4G **119**
Bramhall Moor Ind. Est.
SK7: H Gro 5F **118**
Bramhall Moor La. SK7: H Gro 6E **118**
Bramhall Mt. SK2: Stoc 2D **118**
BRAMHALL PARK 6A **118**
Bramhall Pk. Gro. SK7: Bram 6A **118**
Bramhall Pk. Lawn Tennis Club
. . . .5B **118**
Bramhall Pk. Rd. SK7: Bram 6A **118**
Bramhall Station (Rail) 9C **118**
Bramhall St. BL3: Bolt 9J **39**
M18: Man 4C **96**
Bramhall Wlk. M34: Dent 8K **97**
Bramhall Way SK10: Macc 4E **130**
Bramham Rd. SK6: Mar 3D **120**
Bramhope Wlk. M9: Man 3J **79**
Bramley Av. M19: Man 9M **95**
M32: Stre 7H **93**
Bramley Cl. M27: Swin 4C **76**
SK7: Bram 9C **118**
SK9: Wilm 1C **126**
Bramley Ct. WN6: Stan 3B **34**
Bramley Cres. SK4: Stoc 7N **107**
Bramley Dr. BL8: Bury 7J **25**
SK7: Bram 9C **118**
Bramley Meade M7: Sal 3D **78**
Bramley Rd. BL1: Bolt 7G **23**
OL11: Roch 5K **27**
SK7: Bram 9C **118**
Bramley St. M7: Sal 6D **78**
Brammay Dr. BL8: Tot 8E **24**
Brampton Av. SK10: Macc 2E **130**
Brampton Cl. WN2: P Bri 1J **71**
Brampton Rd. BL3: Bolt 1B **56**
SK7: Bram 5D **118**
Brampton St. M46: Ath 8M **55**
Brampton Wlk. *M40: Man* 4N **79**
(off Harold Priestnall Cl.)
Bramway SK6: H Lan 8C **120**
SK7: Bram 8A **118**
Bramwell Dr. M13: Man 9M **5** (3H **95**)
Bramwell St. SK1: Stoc 8F **108**
Bramwood Ct. SK7: Bram 9C **118**
Bramworth Av. BL0: Ram 8H **11**
Brancaster Dr. WA3: Low 2C **88**
Brancaster Rd. M1: Man 8J **5** (2F **94**)
Branch Cl. BL8: Bury 1K **41**
Branch Rd. OL15: Lit 3J **29**
Branch St. WN2: I Mak 4K **53**
Branchway WA11: Hay 3A **86**
Brancker St. BL5: W'ton 2L **55**
PR7: Chor 1D **18**
Branden Dr. WA16: Knut 7H **133**
Brandforth Gdns. BL5: W'ton 9J **37**
Brandforth Rd. M8: Man 2H **79**
Brandish Cl. M13: Man 4J **95**
Brandle Av. BL8: Bury 9J **25**
Brandlehow Dr. M24: Mid 1H **61**
BRANDLESHOLME 7J **25**
Brandlesholme Cl.
BL8: Bury 9K **25**
Brandlesholme Rd.
BL8: Bury, G'mount 5G **7** (4F **24**)
Brandon Av. M22: Nor 8B **106**
M30: Ecc 5G **76**
M34: Dent 6D **96**
SK8: H Grn 6G **117**
Brandon Brow *OL1: O'ham* 3J **63**
(off Sunfield Rd.)
Brandon Cl. BL8: Bury 8K **25**
SK9: Wilm 4J **123**
WN8: Uph 4E **50**
Brandon Cres. OL2: Shaw 4L **45**
Brandon Rd. M6: Sal 6H **77**
Brandon St. BL3: Bolt 8E **38**
OL16: Miln 7J **29**
Brandram Rd. M25: Pres 7B **60**
Brandreth Delph WN8: Par 1A **32**
Brandreth Dr. WN8: Par 2A **32**
Brandreth Pk. WN8: Par 1A **32**
Brandreth Pl. WN6: Stan 3C **34**
Brandsby Gdns. M5: Sal 1N **93**
Brandwood OL1: Chad 2C **62**
Brandwood Av. M21: Cho H 4C **106**
Brandwood Cl. M28: Wors 2H **75**
Brandwood St. BL3: Bolt 8D **38**
Branfield Av. SK8: H Grn 6J **117**
Brangate Ct. M20: Man 3F **106**
Branksome Av. M25: Pres 7N **59**
Branksome Dr. M6: Sal 5G **77**
M9: Man 6G **60**
SK8: H Grn 6J **117**
Branksome Rd. SK4: Stoc 7N **107**
Bransby Av. M9: Man 7K **61**
Branscombe Dr. M33: Sale 3C **104**
Branscombe Gdns. *BL3: Bolt* 7L **39**
(off Bembridge Dr.)
Bransdale Av. OL2: O'ham 8G **45**
Bransdale Cl. BL3: Bolt 8A **38**
Bransdale Dr. WN4: A Mak 7G **70**
Bransdale Way SK11: Macc 5D **130**
Bransfield Cl. WN3: Wig 8D **52**
Bransfield Rd. M12: Man 3L **95**
Bransford Cl. WN4: A Mak 8F **70**
Bransford Rd. M11: Man 1C **96**
M41: Urm 6C **92**
Branson Cl. WA3: Gol 8K **71**
Branson St. M40: Man 8J **79**
Branson Wlk. WA15: Tim 1K **115**
Branston Rd. M40: Man 9B **62**
Brantfell Gro. BL2: Bolt 4N **39**
Branthwaite WN2: I Mak 2L **53**
Brantingham Ct. M16: Whall R 8D **94**
Brantingham Rd. M16: Whall R 8A **94**
M21: Cho H 8A **94**
Brantwood Cl. OL2: O'ham 8G **44**
Brantwood Ct. M7: Sal 2C **78**
Brantwood Dr. BL2: Bolt 4N **39**
Brantwood Rd. M7: Sal 2C **78**
SK4: Stoc 4A **108**
SK8: Chea H 6L **117**
Brantwood Ter. M9: Man 3L **79**
Brassey St. M24: Mid 2M **61**
OL6: A Lyne 6M **81**
Brassica Cl. M30: Ecc 6A **76**
Brassington Av. M5: Sal 1A **94**
M21: Cho H 1A **106**
Brassington Cres. SK13: Gam 7N **99**
Brassington Rd. SK4: Stoc 4K **107**
Brathay Cl. BL2: Bolt 2N **39**
M45: Whitef 3B **60**
Brathey Pl. *M26: Rad* 3B **58**
(off Weaver Chase)
Brattice Dr. M27: Pen 2J **77**
Bratton Cl. WN3: Wins 1N **69**
Brattray Dr. M24: Mid 9K **43**
Braunston Cl. M30: Ecc 1E **92**
Braxton Wlk. *M9: Man* 2K **79**
(off Hillier St.)
Bray Av. M30: Ecc 7B **76**
Braybrook Dr. BL1: Bolt 5M **37**
Bray Cl. SK8: Chea H 5K **117**
Brayford Dr. WN2: Asp 7M **35**
Brayford Rd. M22: Wyth 6C **116**
Brayshaw Cl. OL10: H'ood 3G **43**
Brayside Rd. M19: Man 4J **107**
M20: Man 4J **107**
Braystan Gdns. SK8: Gat 1G **117**
Braystones Cl. WA15: Tim 1K **115**
Brayston Fold M24: Mid 3H **61**
Brayton Av. M20: Man 6H **107**
M33: Sale 3D **104**
Brayton Ct. WN2: Hin 5N **53**
Brazennose St. M2: Man 5F **4** (9E **78**)
Brazil St. M1: Man 6J **5** (1F **94**)
Brazley Av. BL3: Bolt 9J **39**
BL6: Hor 3G **36**
Bread St. M18: Man 3C **96**
SK11: Macc 5G **130**
Breaktemper BL5: W'ton 2G **54**
Brean Wlk. M22: Wyth 6B **116**
Breaston Av. WN7: Lei 7L **73**
Brechin Wlk. *M11: Man* 9A **80**
(off Bob Massey Cl.)
Brechin Way OL10: H'ood 3F **42**
Breckland Cl. SK15: Stal 8G **82**
Breckland Dr. BL1: Bolt 4M **37**
Breckles Pl. *BL3: Bolt* 7E **38**
(off Emblem St.)
Breck Rd. M30: Ecc 8B **76**
Brecon Av. M19: Man 1L **107**
M34: Dent 8K **97**
M41: Urm 6L **91**
SK8: Chea H 6K **117**
Brecon Cl. OL2: O'ham 6G **44**
SK12: Poy 2K **125**
WN2: P Bri 9L **53**
Brecon Cres. OL6: A Lyne 4M **81**
Brecon Dr. BL9: Bury 5L **41**
WN2: Hin 8C **54**
Brecon Towers SK5: Stoc 1G **108**
BREDBURY 5L **109**
Bredbury Ct. SK6: Bred 3H **109**
Bredbury Dr. BL4: Farn 3M **57**
BREDBURY GREEN 6L **109**
Bredbury Grn. SK6: Rom 6L **109**
Bredbury Pk. Ind. Est.
SK6: Bred 2H **109**
(not continuous)
Bredbury Pk. Way SK6: Bred 3J **109**
Bredbury Rd. M14: Man 7G **94**
Bredbury Station (Rail) 4K **109**
Bredbury St. OL9: Chad 5F **62**
SK14: Hyde 4A **98**
Brede Wlk. M23: Wyth 7K **105**
Bredon Way OL8: O'ham 8J **63**
Breeze Hill WN6: Stan 5E **34**
Breezehill Cotts. *OL5: Mos* 1H **83**
(off Duke St.)
Breeze Hill Rd. M46: Ath 6A **56**
OL4: O'ham 6A **64**
Breeze Mt. M25: Pres 9A **60**
BREIGHTMET 5N **39**
Breightmet Dr. BL2: Bolt 5M **39**
Breightmet Fold BL2: Bolt 4N **39**
Breightmet Fold La. BL2: Bolt 4N **39**
Breightmet Golf Course 3A **40**
Breightmet Hill BL2: Bolt 3M **39**
Breightmet Ind. Est. BL2: Bolt 5N **39**
Breightmet St. BL2: Bolt 4L **7** (6G **39**)
Brellafield Dr. OL2: Shaw 4K **45**
Brenbar Cres. OL12: Whitw 5B **14**
Brenchley Dr. M23: Wyth 6N **105**
Brencon Av. M23: Wyth 7J **105**
Brendall Cl. SK2: Stoc 2L **119**
Brendon Av. M40: Man 3M **79**
SK5: Stoc 2D **108**
Brendon Cl. SK13: Glos 9C **100**
Brendon Dr. M34: Aud 9H **81**
Brendon Hills OL2: O'ham 9H **45**
Brenley Wlk. *M9: Man* 2J **79**
(off Alfred St.)
Brennan Cl. M15: Man 4F **94**
Brennan Ct. OL8: O'ham 9G **62**
Brennock Cl. M11: Man 1L **95**
Brentbridge Rd. M14: Man 9G **95**
Brent Cl. BL2: Bolt 7B **40**
SK12: Poy 2F **124**
Brentfield Av. M8: Man 4E **78**
Brentford Av. BL1: Bolt 2C **38**
Brentford Rd. SK5: Stoc 2D **108**
Brentford St. M9: Man 3K **79**
Brent Ho. *BL1: Bolt* 3F **38**
(off Enfield Cl.)
Brent Moor Rd. SK7: Bram 4E **118**
Brentnall St. SK1: Stoc 8D **108**
Brentnor Rd. M40: Man 9A **62**
Brenton Av. M33: Sale 4G **104**
Brenton Bus. Complex BL9: Bury 7N **7**
Brent Rd. M23: Wyth 6N **105**
SK4: Stoc 7A **108**
Brentwood M6: Sal 7L **77**
M33: Sale 4G **104**
M41: Urm 8M **91**
WN5: Wig 6A **52**
Brentwood Av. M28: Wors 4B **76**
M41: Urm 7D **92**
M44: Cad 2E **102**
WA14: Tim 9E **104**
Brentwood Cl. OL15: Lit 2K **29**
SK5: Stoc 3G **109**
SK15: Stal 8F **82**
Brentwood Ct. M25: Pres 8M **59**
M30: Ecc 7F **76**
Brentwood Cres. WA14: Alt 1E **114**
Brentwood Dr. BL4: Farn 1K **57**
M30: Ecc 6D **76**
SK8: Gat 2G **117**
Brentwood Gro. WN7: Lei 3H **73**
Brentwood Rd. M27: Swin 4D **76**
PR6: And 5L **19**
Brentwood St. M16: Whall R 5E **94**
Brereton Cl. WA14: Bow 6C **114**
Brereton Ct. SK8: Chea H 6K **117**
Brereton Dr. M28: Wors 3N **75**
Brereton Gro. M44: Cad 2F **102**
Brereton Rd. M30: Ecc 9N **75**
SK9: Hand 3K **123**
Breslyn St. M3: Man 1G **4**
Bretherton Row WN1: Wig 8J **9**
Bretherton St. WN2: Hin 5M **53**
Brethren St. M43: Droy 1E **96**
Bretland Gdns. SK14: Hat 8H **99**
Bretland Wlk. M22: Wyth 4E **116**
Breton Ho. *SK2: Stoc* 1E **118**
(off Canada St.)
Brettargh St. M6: Sal 6N **77**
Bretton Ct. BL4: Kea 5B **58**
Bretton Wlk. M22: Wyth 7C **116**
Brett Rd. M28: Wors 4H **75**
Brett St. M22: Nor 7D **106**
(not continuous)
Brewers Grn. SK7: H Gro 4H **119**
Brewer St. M1: Man 4K **5** (9G **78**)
Brewerton Rd. OL4: O'ham 6N **63**
Brewery La. WN7: Lei 6J **73**
Brewery St. SK1: Stoc 1M **9** (6D **108**)
(not continuous)
WA14: Alt 3D **6** (3D **114**)
Brewery Yd. M3: Sal 3E **4** (8D **78**)
WN1: Wig 8J **9**
Brewster St. M9: Man 2J **79**
M24: Mid 1M **61**
Brian Av. M43: Droy 7G **80**
Brian Farrell Dr. SK16: Duk 3B **98**
Brian Redhead Ct.
M15: Man 9D **4** (2D **94**)
Brian Rd. BL4: Farn 1H **57**
Brian Statham Way M16: Old T 5N **93**
Brian St. OL11: Roch 2N **43**
Briar Av. OL4: O'ham 2A **64**
SK7: H Gro 5K **119**
WA3: Rix 6C **102**
Briar Cl. M33: Sale 4C **104**
M41: Urm 6A **92**
OL12: Roch 4M **27**
WA16: Knut 5G **133**
WN2: Hin 7D **54**
WN4: A Mak 6D **70**
Briar Cres. M22: Shar 2D **116**
Briarcroft Dr. M46: Ath 1J **73**
Briardale Wlk. WA14: W Tim 7C **104**
Briardene M34: Dent 5L **97**
Briardene Gdns. M22: Wyth 3D **116**
Briarfield BL7: Eger 3E **22**
Briarfield Rd. BL4: Farn 2H **57**
M19: Man 2J **107**
M20: Man 2J **107**
M28: Wors 3N **75**
OL3: Dob 1K **65**
SK4: Stoc 2C **108**
SK8: Chea H 4N **117**
WA15: Tim 2J **115**
Briarfields Hall *M15: Man* 3F **94**
(off Boundary La.)
Briar Gro. OL9: Chad 2F **62**
SK6: Wood 3L **109**
WN7: Lei 2G **73**
Briargrove Rd. SK22: Bir V 2L **121**
Briar Hill Av. M38: Lit H 7F **56**
Briar Hill Cl. M38: Lit H 7F **56**
Briar Hill Ct. M6: Sal 7N **77**
Briar Hill Gro. M38: Lit H 7F **56**
Briar Hill Way *M6: Sal* 7N **77**
(off Salford Shop. City)
Briar Hollow SK4: Stoc 7N **107**
Briarlands Av. M33: Sale 6F **104**
Briarlands Cl. SK7: Bram 9C **118**
Briar Lea Cl. *BL3: Bolt* 8F **38**
(off Aldsworth Dr.)
Briarlea Gdns. M19: Man 3K **107**

Briarley Gdns. SK6: Wood 2N 109
Briarly WN6: Stan 5D 34
Briarmere Wlk. OL9: Chad 4G 62
Briar Rd. WA3: Gol 1L 87
WN5: Wig 4A 52
Briarrose M. WA14: W Tim 7B 104
Briars Mt. SK4: Stoc 6M 107
Briarstead Cl. SK7: Bram 8B 118
Briar St. BL2: Bolt 5L 39
OL11: Roch 9A 8 (7B 28)
Briarthorn Cl. SK6: Mar 4C 120
Briar Wlk. WA3: Gol 1L 87
Briarwood SK9: Wilm 7H 123
Briarwood Av. M23: Wyth 8L 105
M43: Droy 7C 80
SK11: Macc 7H 131
Briarwood Chase SK8: Chea H 6N 117
Briarwood Cl. M29: Ast 3A 74
Briarwood Cres. SK6: Mar 4D 120
Briary Dr. M29: Ast 2C 74
Brice St. SK16: Duk 1M 97
Brickbridge Rd. SK6: Mar 2D 120
Brickbridge Rd. Nth. SK6: Mar 2D 120
Brickcroft WN5: Wig 5M 51
Brickfield St. OL16: Roch 3F 28
SK13: Had 4D 100
Brickground OL12: Roch 3H 27
Brick Ho's. SK13: Chis 3J 111
Brick Kiln La. WN1: Wig 6K 9 (2F 52)
Brickkiln La. WA14: Lit B 4J 113
Brick Kiln Row WA14: Bow 6C 114
Brickley St. M3: Man 7F 78
Bricknell Wlk. M22: Wyth 4E 116
Brick St. BL9: Bury 6N 7 (1N 41)
M4: Man 3J 5
WA12: N Wil 6C 86
Bridcam St. M8: Man 5F 78
Briddon St. M3: Man 7E 78
Brideoake St. WN7: Lei 6K 73
Brideoak St. M8: Man 4F 78
OL4: O'ham 3B 64
Bridestowe Av. SK14: Hat 6F 98
Bridestowe Wlk. SK14: Hat 6F 98
Bride St. BL1: Bolt 2F 38
Bridge Apartments, The
M3: Sal 3E 4 (9D 78)
Bridge Av. SK6: Wood 3L 109
Bridge Bank Cl. WA3: Gol 2L 87
Bridgebank Ind. Est. BL6: Hor 1D 36
(off Taylor St.)
Bridge Bank Rd. OL15: Lit 2K 29
Bridge Cl. M26: Rad 1H 59
M31: Part 5H 103
WA13: Lym 4C 112
Bridgecrest Ct. SK8: Chea H 5N 117
Bridge Dr. SK8: Chea 3J 117
SK9: Hand 3J 123
Bridge End OL3: Del 8J 47
WN6: Wig 3E 52
Bridge End Dr. SK10: P'bury 6E 128
Bridge End La. SK10: P'bury 6E 128
Bridgefield SK13: Glos 9D 100
Bridgefield Av. SK9: Wilm 5H 123
Bridgefield Cl. SK6: H Lan 8B 120
Bridgefield Cres. OL4: Spri 5C 64
Bridgefield Dr. BL9: Bury 2B 42
Bridgefield St. M26: Rad 9H 41
OL11: Roch 8A 8 (6B 28)
SK1: Stoc 2K 9 (7C 108)
Bridgefield Wlk. M26: Rad 9H 41
Bridgefold Rd. OL11: Roch 6A 28
Bridgefoot Cl. M28: Wors 5H 75
Bridgeford Ct. M32: Stre 9K 93
(off Highfield Rd.)
Bridgeford St. M15: Man 3F 94
Bridge Grn. SK10: P'bury 7E 128
Bridge Gro. WA15: Tim 9F 104
Bridge Hall Dr. BL9: Bury 2B 42
Bridgehall Dr. WN8: Uph 4F 50
Bridge Hall Fold BL9: Bury 2B 42
Bridge Hall Ind. Est. BL9: Bury 2B 42
Bridge Hall La. BL9: Bury 2B 42
Bridge Ho. M1: Man 5L 5
Bridge La. SK7: Bram 6D 118
Bridgelea Rd. M20: Man 2G 106
Bridgeman Ho. BL4: Farn 4L 57
Bridgeman Pl. BL2: Bolt 4M 7 (6H 39)
Bridgeman St. BL3: Bolt 8E 38
BL4: Farn 2L 57
Bridgeman Ter. WN1: Wig 5J 9 (2F 52)
Bridge Mdw. WA13: Lym 3C 112
Bridgemere Cl. M26: Rad 7F 40
Bridge Mills BL0: Eden 3L 11
Bridge Mills Bus. Pk. M6: Sal 5M 77
Bridgend Cl. M12: Man 3M 95
SK8: Chea H 3A 118
Bridgenorth Av. M41: Urm 7F 92
Bridgenorth Dr. OL15: Lit 2K 29
Bridge Rd. BL9: Bury 9H 7 (3K 41)
M23: Wyth 9J 105
Bridges Av. BL9: Bury 6M 41
Bridges Ct. BL3: Bolt 4K 7
Bridgeside Bus. Cen.
SK6: Bred 2H 109
Bridge's St. M46: Ath 9K 55
Bridge St. BL0: Ram 8J 11
BL1: Bolt 1K 7 (4G 38)
BL4: Farn 2M 57
BL6: Hor 9E 20
(not continuous)
BL9: Bury 6N 7 (1N 41)
M3: Man, Sal 4E 4 (9D 78)
M24: Mid 3M 61
M26: Rad 3B 58
M27: Pen 2G 77
M34: Aud 2K 97
M43: Droy 1C 96
OL1: O'ham 3F 8 (5L 63)
OL2: Shaw 4N 45
OL3: Upp 4L 65
OL4: Spri 5C 64
OL10: H'ood 2G 43
OL11: Roch 3A 44
OL12: Roch 2G 28
OL12: Whitw 5A 14
OL16: Miln 7K 29
Bridge St. SK1: Stoc 1L 9 (6D 108)
SK11: Macc 5G 131
SK15: Stal 9C 82
SK16: Duk 3L 97
SK22: N Mil 6M 121
WA3: Gol 2K 87
WA12: N Wil 6E 86
WN2: Hin 5N 53
WN3: I Mak 5G 53
WN3: Wig 4E 52
Bridge St. Brow
SK1: Stoc 1L 9 (6D 108)
Bridge St. W. M3: Sal 4E 4 (9D 78)
Bridges Way M34: Dent 1K 109
Bridge Ter. BL9: Bury 2B 42
Bridge Trad. Est.
BL8: Bury 7G 7 (2K 41)
Bridgewater Cen., The
M41: Urm 2E 92
Bridgewater Circ. M17: Urm 3D 92
Bridgewater Cl. SK8: H Grn 8H 117
Bridgewater Ct. M32: Stre 6L 93
Bridgewater Embankment
WA14: Alt 1D 114
Bridgewater Gdns. M28: Walk 7L 57
(off Fereday St.)
Bridgewater Hall, The 7G 4 (1E 94)
Bridgewater Ho. M1: Man 7H 5
M15: Man 7C 4
M43: Droy 1E 96
(off Bridgewater Wharf)
Bridgewater Pl. M4: Man 4H 5 (9F 78)
Bridgewater Rd. M27: Swin 3H 77
M28: Walk 9K 57
M28: Wors 3G 75
WA14: Alt 9D 104
Bridgewater St. BL1: Bolt 6E 38
BL4: Farn 3L 57
M3: Man 7D 4 (1D 94)
(not continuous)
M3: Sal 1D 4 (7D 78)
M30: Ecc 8B 76
M32: Stre 7K 93
M33: Sale 3H 105
M38: Lit H 7J 57
OL1: O'ham 1F 8 (3L 63)
WN2: Hin 6A 54
WN3: Wig 9H 9 (4E 52)
WN5: Wig 5C 52
Bridgewater Viaduct
M3: Man 8E 4 (2D 94)
Bridgewater Vw. M30: Ecc 6C 76
(off Anson St.)
Bridgewater Wlk. M28: Walk 8L 57
(off Ellesmere Shop. Cen.)
Bridgewater Way
M16: Old T 9A 4 (4N 93)
Bridgewater Wharf M43: Droy 9E 80
Bridgeway SK6: Mar 1B 120
Bridgewood Lodge OL10: H'ood 2G 43
Bridgnorth Rd. M9: Man 8F 60
Bridle Cl. M41: Urm 7M 91
M43: Droy 7G 81
Bridle Ct. SK7: W'ford 4D 124
Bridle Dell BL7: Eger 3E 22
Bridle Fold M26: Rad 8G 41
Bridle Rd. M25: Pres 4C 60
SK7: W'ford 3D 124
Bridle Way SK7: W'ford 4D 124
Bridleway SK22: N Mil 6N 121
Bridlington Av. M6: Sal 7J 77
Bridlington Cl. M40: Man 4A 80
Bridport Av. M40: Man 2B 80
Bridson La. BL2: Bolt 3L 39
Bridson St. M5: Sal 9L 77
OL4: O'ham 4N 63
Brief St. BL2: Bolt 3K 39
Brien Av. WA14: Alt 9D 104
Briercliffe Cl. M18: Man 3A 96
Briercliffe Rd. BL3: Bolt 7D 38
Brierfield WN8: Skel 5B 50
Brierfield Av. M46: Ath 7L 55
Brierfield Dr. BL9: Bury 5L 25
Brierfields M35: Fail 3E 80
Brierholme Av. BL7: Eger 4F 22
Brierley Av. M35: Fail 3D 80
M45: Whitef 1L 59
Brierley Cl. M34: Dent 8J 97
OL6: A Lyne 4D 82
Brierley Dr. M24: Mid 4M 61
Brierley Rd. E. M27: Swin 1E 76
Brierley Rd. W. M27: Swin 1E 76
Brierleys Pl. OL15: Lit 8L 15
Brierley St. BL9: Bury 4L 41
OL8: O'ham 8K 63
OL9: Chad 3G 63
OL10: H'ood 2J 43
SK15: Stal 9E 82
SK16: Duk 9A 82
Brierley Wlk. OL9: Chad 3G 63
Brierwood BL2: Bolt 3J 39
Brierwood Cl. OL2: O'ham 2J 63
Briery Av. BL2: Bolt 7L 23
Brigade Dr. M32: Stre 6J 93
Brigade St. BL1: Bolt 5D 38
Brigadier Cl. M20: Man 2G 106
Brigantine Cl. M5: Sal 1N 93
(off Jennings Av.)
Briggs Cl. M33: Sale 7C 104
Briggs Fold BL7: Eger 3F 22
Briggs Fold Cl. BL7: Eger 3F 22
Briggs Fold Rd. BL7: Eger 3F 22
Briggs Rd. M32: Stre 5M 93
Briggs St. M3: Sal 1C 4 (7C 78)
WN7: Lei 3G 72
Brigham St. M11: Man 1A 96
Bright Circ. M41: Urm 3E 92
Brightgate Way M32: Stre 4G 93
Brightman St. M18: Man 3C 96
Brighton Av. BL1: Bolt 3B 38
M7: Sal 4D 78
M19: Man 1L 107
M41: Urm 6M 91
SK5: Stoc 7D 96
Brighton Cl. SK8: Chea H 3A 118
Brighton Ct. M5: Sal 2A 94
Brighton Cres. SK11: Lang 9M 131
Brighton Gro. M14: Man 7J 95
M33: Sale 3G 105
M41: Urm 7M 91
SK14: Hyde 8B 98
Brighton Pl. M13: Man 4G 94
Brighton Range M18: Man 5D 96
Brighton Rd. OL4: Scout 2D 64
SK4: Stoc 7A 108
Brighton Rd. Ind. Est.
SK4: Stoc 7A 108
Brighton St. BL9: Bury 1A 42
M4: Man 7F 78
Bright Rd. M30: Ecc 8E 76
Brightside Rd. M8: Man 2H 79
Brightstone Wlk. M13: Man 5K 95
(off Clarence Rd.)
Bright St. BL7: Eger 3E 22
BL9: Bury 5N 7 (1N 41)
M26: Rad 8J 41
M43: Droy 9F 80
OL6: A Lyne 8G 6 (8A 82)
OL8: O'ham 6H 63
OL9: Chad 7E 62
OL16: Roch 7E 28
WN7: Lei 3G 73
(not continuous)
Brightwater BL6: Hor 2B 36
Brightwater Cl. M45: Whitef 3N 59
Brightwell Wlk. M4: Man 3K 5
(off Oak St.)
Brignall Gro. WA3: Low 9N 71
Brigsteer Wlk. M40: Man 5J 79
(off Bishop Marshall Cl.)
Brigstock Av. M18: Man 4A 96
Briksdal Way BL6: Los 5L 37
Brimelows Bldgs. M29: Ast 5D 74
(off Higher Grn. La.)
Brimelow St. SK6: Bred 5G 109
Brimfield Av. M29: Tyld 1D 74
Brimfield Wlk. M40: Man 4A 80
(off Bridlington Cl.)
Brimmy Cft. La. OL3: Dens 1F 46
Brimpton Wlk. M8: Man 4E 78
(off Kilmington Dr.)
Brimrod La. OL11: Roch 8B 28
Brimscombe Av. M22: Wyth 5B 116
Brindale Ho. SK5: Stoc 4G 108
Brindale Rd. SK5: Stoc 4G 108
Brindle Cl. M6: Sal 6M 77
BRINDLE HEATH 6M 77
Brindle Heath Ind. Est. M6: Sal 6N 77
Brindle Heath Rd. M6: Sal 6M 77
Brindlehurst Dr. M29: Ast 3D 74
Brindle Pl. M15: Man 3E 94
Brindle St. M29: Tyld 1B 74
WN2: Hin 4B 54
Brindle Way OL2: Shaw 5A 46
Brindley Av. M9: Man 6G 60
M33: Sale 2J 105
SK6: Mar 1C 120
Brindley Cl. BL4: Farn 3J 57
M30: Ecc 1D 92
M46: Ath 9J 55
Brindley Dr. M28: Wors 4H 75
Brindley Gro. SK9: Wilm 4K 123
(off Picton Dr.)
Brindley Lodge M27: Swin 4E 76
(off Worsley Rd.)
Brindley Rd. M16: Old T 4A 94
Brindley St. BL1: Bolt 9G 22
BL6: Hor 2E 36
M27: Pen 9F 58
(not continuous)
M28: Walk 9L 57
M28: Wors 4G 75
M30: Ecc 7B 76
WN5: Wig 6N 51
Brindley Way SK11: Lym G 9G 131
Brindley Wharf M43: Droy 1E 96
Brinell Dr. M44: Irl 2F 102
Brinkburn Rd. SK7: H Gro 4L 119
Brinklow Cl. M11: Man 2C 96
Brinkshaw Av. M22: Wyth 4D 116
Brinks La. BL2: Bolt 5A 40
Brink's Row BL6: Hor 8F 20
Brinksway BL1: Bolt 5L 37
SK3: Stoc 3G 9 (8A 108)
Brinksway Trad. Est. SK4: Stoc 7A 108
Brinksworth Cl. BL2: Bolt 4A 40
BRINNINGTON 2G 108
Brinnington Cres. SK5: Stoc 4F 108
Brinnington Ri. SK5: Stoc 4F 108
Brinnington Rd. SK1: Stoc 5E 108
SK5: Stoc 5E 108
Brinnington Station (Rail) 2G 108
Brinsop Hall La. BL5: W'ton 7C 36
Brinsop Sq. M12: Man 3N 95
Brinston Wlk. M40: Man 3M 79
(off Whitehill Dr.)
Brinsworth Dr. M8: Man 4F 78
Briony Av. WA15: Hale 5J 115
Briony Cl. OL2: O'ham 1J 63
Brisbane Cl. SK7: Bram 1D 124
Brisbane Rd. SK7: Bram 1D 124
Brisbane St. M15: Man 4G 94
Briscoe La. M40: Man 7L 79
Briscoe M. BL3: Bolt 8H 39
Briscoe St. OL1: O'ham 3K 63
Briscoe Wlk. M24: Mid 1H 61
Bristle Hall Way BL5: W'ton 1H 55
Bristol Av. BL2: Bolt 3K 39
M19: Man 9N 95
OL6: A Lyne 4M 81
Bristol Cl. SK8: H Grn 8H 117
Bristol Ct. M7: Sal 1D 78
Bristol St. M7: Sal 3D 78
Bristowe St. M11: Man 7B 80
Britain St. BL9: Bury 6L 41
Britannia Av. OL2: Shaw 6N 45
Britannia Bus. Pk. BL2: Bolt 2H 39
Britannia Cl. M26: Rad 9G 40
Britannia Ind. Est. OL10: H'ood 2H 43
Britannia Mills M15: Man 8B 4 (2C 94)
Britannia Rd. M33: Sale 3H 105
WN5: Wig 3N 51
Britannia St. M6: Sal 4N 77
OL1: O'ham 1G 8 (4L 63)
OL10: H'ood 2G 43
Britannia Way BL2: Bolt 2H 39
Brite Ct. SK8: Gat 2F 116
Britnall Av. M12: Man 4K 95
Briton St. OL2: O'ham 1J 63
OL16: Roch 5E 28
Britton Ho. M4: Man 7F 78
(off Lord St.)
Britwell Wlk. M8: Man 2H 79
(off Mawdsley Dr.)
Brixham Av. SK8: Chea H 8L 117
Brixham Dr. M33: Sale 2D 104
Brixham Rd. M16: Old T 5A 94
Brixham Wlk. SK7: Bram 8C 118
Brixton Av. M20: Man 2F 106
Brixworth Wlk. M9: Man 8K 61
(off Greendale Dr.)
Broach St. BL3: Bolt 8F 38
Broad Acre OL12: Roch 3K 27
Broadacre SK15: Stal 3H 99
WN6: Stan 2L 33
WN8: Uph 5E 50
Broadacre Pl. SK9: A Edg 2C 126
Broadacre Rd. M18: Man 6C 96
BROADBENT 1M 63
Broadbent Av. OL6: A Lyne 4N 81
SK16: Duk 1A 98
Broadbent Cl. OL2: O'ham 7K 45
SK15: C'ook 4H 83
Broadbent Dr. BL9: Bury 9D 26
Broadbent Gro. SK14: Hat 8H 99
Broadbent Rd. OL1: O'ham 1N 63
Broadbent St. M27: Swin 3D 76
SK14: Hyde 5A 98
BROADBOTTOM 9K 99
Broadbottom (Park & Ride) 9K 99
Broadbottom Rd. SK14: Mot 8J 99
Broadbottom Station (Rail) 9K 99
BROAD CARR 9D 64
Broadcarr La. OL4: O'ham 9D 64
OL5: Mos 9D 64
Broadcar Rd. SK11: Macc 6N 131
Broad Ees Dole Local Nature Reserve
1K 105
BROADFIELD 3F 42
Broadfield Cl. M34: Dent 7L 97
Broadfield Distribution Cen.
OL10: H'ood 3G 43
Broadfield Dr. OL15: Lit 2K 29
Broadfield Gro. SK5: Stoc 6C 96
Broadfield Rd. M14: Man 7F 94
SK5: Stoc 6C 96
Broadfield Stile
OL16: Roch 9B 8 (7C 28)
Broadfield St. OL10: H'ood 3G 43
OL16: Roch 9C 8 (7D 28)
Broadford Rd. BL3: Bolt 7A 38
Broadgate BL3: Bolt 7A 38
M24: Mid 5B 62
OL3: Dob 2H 65
OL9: Chad 5B 62
Broadgate Ho. BL3: Bolt 7A 38
Broadgate Mdw. M27: Swin 4F 76
Broadgate Wlk. M9: Man 2K 79
(off Augustine Webster Cl.)
Broadgreen Gdns. BL4: Farn 1L 57
BROADHALGH 6M 27
Broadhalgh Av. OL11: Roch 6M 27
Broadhalgh Rd. OL11: Roch 7M 27
Broadhaven Rd. M40: Man 7J 79
(off Farnborough Rd.)
Broadhead Wlk. M45: Whitef 2A 60
BROADHEATH 9B 104
Broadheath Cl. BL5: W'ton 2J 55
Broad Hey SK6: Rom 5A 110
Broadhey La. WN6: Wrig 1D 32
Broadhey Vw. SK22: N Mil 6L 121
Broadhill Cl. SK7: Bram 5E 118
Broadhill Rd. M19: Man 2K 107
SK15: Stal 6D 82
Broadhurst M34: Dent 4L 97
Broadhurst Av. M27: Clif 8F 58
OL1: Chad 2F 62
WA3: Cul 7H 89
Broadhurst Ct. BL3: Bolt 8E 38
Broadhurst Edge Wood Nature Reserve
3L 121
Broadhurst Gro. OL6: A Lyne 4N 81
Broadhurst St. BL3: Bolt 8E 38
M26: Rad 7F 40
SK3: Stoc 9C 108
Broad Ing OL12: Roch 4A 28
Broadlands OL10: H'ood 4D 42
WN6: She 6M 33
Broadlands Av. OL10: H'ood 4D 42
Broadlands Cres. OL10: H'ood 4D 42
Broadlands Rd. M28: Wors 4C 76
Broadlands Wlk. M40: Man 4M 79
(off Halliford Rd.)
Broadlands Way OL10: H'ood 4D 42
Broad La. OL3: Del 6L 47
OL12: Whitw 6L 13
OL16: Roch 1F 44
(not continuous)
WA5: Burt, Coll G 8A 86
WA11: St H 8F 68
WA15: Hale 7H 115
Broadlea M41: Urm 6C 92
Broadlea Gro. OL12: Roch 3A 28
Broadlea Rd. M19: Man 3K 107
BROADLEY 9A 14
Broadley Av. M22: Wyth 3C 116
WA3: Low 2M 87
Broadley Vw. OL12: Whitw 9A 14
Broadlink M24: Mid 5B 62
Broadmead WN8: Par 2A 32
Broad Mdw. BL7: Bro X 5J 23
Broadmeadow Av. M16: Whall R 8E 94
Broadmoss Dr. M9: Man 8M 61
Broadmount Ter. OL9: O'ham 7F 62
(off Devon St.)
BROAD OAK 4B 76
Broadoak Av. M22: Wyth 2B 116
M28: Wors 3G 74
Broadoak Bus. Pk. M17: T Pk 2F 92
Broad Oak Cl. PR6: Adl 5K 19
Broadoak Ct. M8: Man 4G 78
Broad Oak Cres. OL8: O'ham 9L 63
Broadoak Cres. OL6: A Lyne 5M 81
Broadoak Dr. M22: Wyth 2C 116
Broad Oak La. BL9: Bury 1B 42
M20: Man 8H 107
(Laneside Rd.)
M20: Man 8G 106
(Maywood Av.)
WA16: Mob 1L 133
Broadoak La. WA16: H Leg 9E 112
BROADOAK PARK 4C 76
Broad Oak Pk. M30: Ecc 6D 76
Broad Oak Rd. BL3: Bolt 1H 57
M28: Wors 4B 76
Broadoak Rd. M22: Wyth 3B 116
OL6: A Lyne 5M 81
OL11: Roch 7K 27
SK7: Bram 5C 118
Broadoaks BL9: Bury 1C 42
Broad Oak Sports Cen. 2B 42
Broadoaks Rd. M33: Sale 4G 105
M41: Urm 8B 92
Broad Oak Ter. BL9: Bury 1D 42
Broad o' th' La. BL1: Bolt 9F 22
(not continuous)
WN6: She 6L 33
Broadriding Rd. WN6: She 6J 33
Broad Rd. M33: Sale 3J 105
Broad Shaw La. OL16: Roch 2H 45
(not continuous)
Broadstone Av. OL4: O'ham 8C 46
Broadstone Cl. M25: Pres 8N 59
OL12: Roch 4M 27
Broadstone Hall Rd. Nth.
SK4: Stoc 2B 108
Broadstone Hall Rd. Sth.
SK4: Stoc 2B 108
SK5: Stoc 2B 108
Broadstone Ho. SK5: Stoc 1C 108
Broadstone Rd. BL2: Bolt 8L 23
SK4: Stoc 2B 108
SK5: Stoc 2B 108
Broad St. BL9: Bury 8K 7 (2L 41)
M6: Sal 4K 77
(not continuous)
M24: Mid 4H 61
Broadview Ct. OL16: Roch 1G 44
Broad Wlk. BL5: W'ton 4G 54
SK9: Wilm 6D 122
Broadwalk M6: Sal 7N 77
SK10: P'bury 8E 128
Broadway BL4: Farn 2H 57
BL6: Hor 1F 36
M28: Walk, Wors 1K 75
M31: Part 4H 103
M33: Sale 3G 104
M35: Fail 3B 80
M40: Man 3B 80
M41: Urm 5A 92
M43: Droy 2E 96
M44: Irl 8H 91
M46: Ath 6A 56
M50: Sal 1K 93
OL2: O'ham 1G 62
OL9: Chad 3B 80
SK2: Stoc 9G 109
SK7: Bram 5D 118
SK8: Chea 3H 117
SK9: Wilm 8G 122
SK14: Hyde 4M 97
SK16: Duk, Hyde 3M 97
WA15: Hale 7G 115
WN2: Hin 6B 54
Broadway, The SK6: Bred 4J 109
Broadway Av. SK8: Chea 2J 117
Broadway Cl. M41: Urm 4C 92
Broadway Ind. Est. M50: Sal 1N 93
SK14: Hyde 3M 97
Broadway Leisure Cen. 9C 62
Broadway M. WA15: Hale 6H 115
Broadway Nth. M43: Droy 1E 96
Broadway Stop (Metro) 1M 93
Broadway St. OL8: O'ham 7K 63
Broadwell Dr. M9: Man 3K 79
WN7: Lei 9G 72
Broadwood BL6: Los 5L 37
Broadwood Cl. SK12: Dis 2E 126
Brocade Cl. M3: Sal 1B 4 (7C 78)
Broche Cl. OL11: Roch 1N 43
Brock, The OL2: Shaw 4K 45
Brock Av. BL2: Bolt 5N 39
Brock Cl. M11: Man 2B 96
Brock Dr. SK8: Chea H 7M 117
Brockenhurst Dr. BL2: Bolt 1N 39
Brockford Dr. M9: Man 6K 61
Brockholes SK13: Glos 9B 100
Brockholes Wood Nature Reserve
6N 85
Brockhurst Wlk. WN3: Wig 6D 52
Brocklebank Rd. M14: Man 9H 95
OL16: Roch 6H 29
Brocklehurst Av. BL9: Bury 3M 41
SK10: Macc 2J 131
Brocklehurst Ct. SK10: Macc 1H 131
(off Brocklehurst Way)
Brocklehurst Dr. SK10: P'bury 6E 128
Brocklehurst Mnr. SK10: Macc 3J 131
(off Brocklehurst Av.)
Brocklehurst M. SK10: Macc 1H 131
Brocklehurst St. M9: Man 2M 79
Brocklehurst Way SK10: Macc 1H 131
Brockley Av. M14: Man 7G 94
Brock Mill La. WN1: Wig 7F 34
Brock Pl. WN2: P Bri 9J 53
Brocksby Chase BL1: Bolt 3F 38
Brock St. M1: Man 4L 5 (9G 79)
SK10: Macc 4H 131
(Cumberland St.)
SK10: Macc 3H 131
(Pearle St.)
WN1: I Mak 3H 53
Brockton Wlk. M8: Man 2F 78
Brockway OL16: Roch 1G 44

Brocstedes Av. WN4: A Mak 4B 70
Brocstedes Rd. WN4: A Mak 2A 70
(not continuous)
Brocton Ct. M7: Sal 1C 78
Brodick Dr. BL2: Bolt 6N 39
Brodick St. M40: Man 2L 79
Brodie Cl. M30: Ecc 8B 76
Brogan St. M18: Man 4B 96
Brogden Av. WA3: Cul 5G 88
Brogden Dr. SK8: Gat 2G 117
Brogden Gro. M33: Sale 5G 104
Brogden Ter. M33: Sale 4G 104
Broken Banks *SK11: Macc* *5H 131*
(off Lowe St.)
BROKEN CROSS 4C 130
Broken Cross SK11: Macc 4C 130
Bromborough Av. M20: Man 2J 107
Bromfield OL12: Roch 5C 8 (5D 28)
Bromfield Av. M9: Man 1J 79
Bromleigh Av. SK8: Gat 1G 116
Bromley Av. M41: Urm 8M 91
OL2: O'ham 6G 44
WA3: Low 2N 87
Bromley Cl. WN2: Wig 1K 53
Bromley Cres. OL6: A Lyne 4M 81
BROMLEY CROSS 6H 23
Bromley Cross Rd. BL7: Bro X 6J 23
Bromley Cross Station (Rail) 6J 23
Bromley Dr. WN7: Lei 2F 72
Bromley Rd. M33: Sale 6J 105
SK10: Macc 4C 130
Bromley St. M4: Man 1K 5 (7G 78)
M34: Dent 5K 97
OL9: Chad 8E 62
Bromlow St. M11: Man 9A 80
Brompton Av. M35: Fail 2F 80
Brompton Rd. M14: Man 7G 94
M32: Stre 6F 92
SK4: Stoc 6M 107
Brompton St. OL4: O'ham 6L 63
Brompton Ter. *SK16: Duk* . . . . *.9M 81*
(off Queen St.)
Brompton Way SK9: Hand 1J 123
Bromsgrove Av. M30: Ecc 8C 76
Bromshill Dr. M7: Sal 4D 78
Bromwich Dr. M9: Man 3J 79
Bromwich St. BL2: Bolt 4N 7 (6H 39)
Bronington Cl. M22: Nor 9D 106
Bronte Av. BL9: Bury 6M 41
Bronte Cl. BL1: Bolt 3E 38
OL1: O'ham 8A 46
OL12: Roch 3M 27
WN3: Wig 6D 52
Bronte St. M15: Man 4F 94
Bronville Cl. OL1: Chad 2G 62
Brook, The OL15: Lit 5N 15
Brookash Rd. M22: Wyth 7F 116
Brook Av. M19: Man 7N 95
M27: Swin 3F 76
M43: Droy 9D 80
OL2: Shaw 4M 45
OL3: Upp 3M 65
SK4: Stoc 3B 108
WA15: Tim 1E 114
Brook Bank BL2: Bolt 1L 39
Brookbank Cl. M24: Mid 4N 61
BROOK BOTTOM
OL5 . . . . .9E 64
SK22 .6H 121
Brookbottom BL2: Bolt 7M 23
Brookbottom Rd. M26: Rad 6F 40
SK22: N Mil 6J 121
Brook Bldg., The BL7: Eger 3E 22
Brookburn Rd. M21: Cho H 1N 105
Brook Bus. Complex M12: Man 2L 95
Brook Cl. M29: Tyld 9B 56
M45: Whitef 3A 60
WA15: Tim 1E 114
Brookcot Rd. M23: Wyth 9M 105
Brook Cotts. OL16: Roch 6G 29
Brook Ct. M7: Sal 1B 78
Brookcroft Av. M22: Wyth 2C 116
Brookcroft Rd. M22: Wyth 2C 116
Brookdale BL7: Bel 1L 21
M46: Ath 5A 56
OL12: Roch 2C 28
PR6: H Char 4K 19
Brookdale Av. M34: Aud 2H 97
M34: Dent 7M 97
M40: Man 6B 80
SK6: Mar 3D 120
WA16: Knut 6J 133
Brookdale Cl. BL1: Bolt 2G 38
SK6: Bred 5K 109
Brookdale Cotts. SK2: Stoc 9K 109
Brookdale Ct. M33: Sale 7J 105
WN7: Lei 7H 73
Brookdale Golf Course 5F 80
Brookdale Pk. Caravan Site
M38: Lit H 6J 57
Brookdale Ri. SK7: Bram 6D 118
Brookdale Rd. SK7: Bram 6D 118
SK8: Gat 2E 116
WN2: Hin 6B 54
Brookdale St. M35: Fail 3C 80
Brookdean Cl. BL1: Bolt 1D 38
Brookdene Rd. BL9: Bury 2N 59
M19: Man 2K 107
Brook Dr. M29: Ast 4D 74
M45: Whitef 3A 60
SK6: Mar 3C 120
Brooke Av. SK9: Hand 2J 123
Brooke Ct. SK9: Hand 2K 123
Brooke Dr. SK9: Hand 2J 123
Brooke Ho. *SK10: Macc* *3D 130*
(off Priory Ct.)
Brooke Pk. SK9: Hand 2K 123
Brookes St. M24: Mid 1N 61
Brooke Way SK9: Hand 2J 123
Brook Farm Cl. M31: Part 7F 102
BROOKFIELD 6B 100
Brookfield M25: Pres 7A 60
OL2: Shaw 3L 45
SK13: Gam, Had 6A 100
WN5: Wig 3B 52
WN8: Par 2A 32
Brookfield Apartments M46: Ath . . .9K 55
Brookfield Av. BL2: Ain 3C 40
M6: Sal 7J 77
M21: Cho H 1B 106
M41: Urm 7A 92
OL2: O'ham 9H 45
SK1: Stoc 9E 108
SK6: Bred 4L 109
SK12: Poy 2G 125
WA15: Tim 8F 104
Brookfield Bus. Cen.
SK8: Chea 2K 117
Brookfield Cl. M25: Pres 7A 60
SK1: Stoc 9E 108
Brookfield Ct. M18: Man 5B 96
M19: Man 9L 95
Brookfield Cres. SK8: Chea 3J 117
Brookfield Dr. M27: Swin 1E 76
M28: Wors 4G 75
OL15: Lit 8J 15
WA15: Tim 9G 105
Brookfield Gdns. M22: Wyth 1B 116
Brookfield Gro. M18: Man 5B 96
OL6: A Lyne 8A 82
Brookfield Ho. SK8: Chea 3J 117
Brookfield Ind. Est. SK13: Had . . .6A 100
Brookfield La. SK11: Macc 5K 131
Brookfield Rd. BL9: Bury 5L 25
M8: Man 1F 78
M30: Ecc 6B 76
SK8: Chea 2K 117
WA3: Cul 6F 88
WN6: Stan 2M 33
WN8: Uph 4F 50
Brookfields OL5: Mos 9F 64
Brookfield St. BL2: Bolt 5J 39
OL8: O'ham 5D 8 (6K 63)
WA12: N Wil 6E 86
WN7: Lei 4J 73
Brookfield Ter. SK7: H Gro 4K 119
Brook Fold M46: Ath 9K 55
Brookfold M35: Fail 2C 80
Brookfold La. BL2: Bolt 9N 23
SK14: Hyde 7E 98
Brookfold Rd. SK4: Stoc 2B 108
Brook Gdns. BL2: Bolt 9M 23
OL10: H'ood 2H 43
BROOK GREEN 5C 96
Brook Grn. La. M18: Man 6D 96
Brook Gro. M44: Irl 7H 91
Brookhead Av. M20: Man 1E 106
Brookhead Dr. SK8: Chea 2M 117
Brookhey SK14: Hyde 6M 97
Brook Hey Av. BL3: Bolt 9G 39
Brook Hey Cl. OL12: Roch 1H 29
Brookheys Rd WA14: D Mas 6M 103
Brookheys Rd. M31: C'ton 4M 103
Brookhill Cl. OL3: Dig 7M 47
Brookhill St. M40: Man 7K 79
BROOKHOUSE 1N 131
Brook Ho. M15: Man 9B 4
M23: Wyth . . . . *.9J 105*
(off Bridge Rd.)
WN1: Wig 9L 9 (4G 52)
Brookhouse Av. BL4: Farn 5K 57
M30: Ecc 9A 76
Brook Ho. Cl. BL2: Bolt 1M 39
Brookhouse Cl. BL8: G'mount 5E 24
SK10: Macc 3D 130
Brookhouse Mill La.
BL8: G'mount 5F 24
Brookhouse St.
WN1: Wig 9L 9 (4G 52)
Brookhouse Ter.
WN1: Wig 9L 9 (4G 52)
Brookhurst La. M38: Lit H 5F 56
Brookhurst Rd. M18: Man 5B 96
Brookland Av. BL4: Farn 4K 57
WN2: Hin 6N 53
Brookland Cl. M44: Irl 7G 91
Brookland Gro. BL1: Bolt 2B 38
Brookland Rd. WN1: Wig 9E 34
BROOKLANDS 6H 105
Brooklands BL6: Hor 1E 36
OL12: W'le 7G 15
WN8: Uph 3F 50
Brooklands, The OL10: H'ood 2H 43
Brooklands (Park & Ride) 5G 105
Brooklands Av. M20: Man 2F 106
M34: Dent 7H 97
M46: Ath 7M 55
OL9: Chad 6F 62
SK11: Macc 5F 130
WN4: A Mak 8G 70
WN7: Lei 7G 73
Brooklands Cl. M34: Dent 5H 97
OL5: Mos 9E 64
SK4: Stoc 3B 108
Brooklands Ct. M8: Man 9E 60
M33: Sale 6H 105
OL11: Roch 7A 28
Brooklands Cres. M33: Sale 5H 105
Brooklands Dr. M43: Droy 7G 80
OL4: Grot 5E 64
SK13: Glos 9D 100
WN5: Orr 6H 51
Brooklands Ho. *M33: Sale* . . . . . . *.5H 105*
(off Brooklands Rd.)
Brooklands M. SK11: Macc 5F 130
Brooklands Pde. OL4: Grot 5E 64
Brooklands Pl. M33: Sale 5G 105
Brooklands Rd. BL0: Ram 3G 24
M8: Man 9D 60
M23: Wyth 5H 105
M25: Pres 9D 60
M27: Swin 4D 76
M33: Sale 5H 105
SK5: Stoc 7C 96
SK7: H Gro 6J 119
WN8: Uph 4G 51
Brooklands Sports Club 6H 105
Brooklands Sta. App.
M33: Sale 5G 105
Brooklands Stop (Metro) 5G 105
Brooklands St. M24: Mid 2M 61
OL2: O'ham 7H 45
Brookland St. OL16: Roch 1F 44
Brooklands Va. SK14: Hyde 6B 98
Brook La. BL9: Bury 8N 41
OL3: Dob 1J 65
OL4: Lees 5B 64
OL8: O'ham 7L 63
(not continuous)
OL16: Roch 1F 44
SK7: H Gro 5L 119
SK9: A Edg 2D 126
WA11: K Mos 3D 68
WA15: Tim 1E 114
WA16: Knut 7H 133
WN5: Orr 6L 51
Brooklawn Dr. M20: Man 4G 107
M25: Pres 5B 60
Brookledge La. SK10: Adl 9G 125
Brookleigh Rd. M20: Man 2J 107
Brooklet Cl. OL4: Spri 6C 64
Brook Lodge SK8: Chea 3J 117
Brooklyn Av. M16: Whall R 7B 94
M41: Urm 7M 91
OL15: Lit 7L 15
OL16: Roch 1H 29
Brooklyn Ct. M20: Man 1H 107
Brooklyn Cres. SK8: Chea 2J 117
Brook Lynn Av. WA3: Low 9B 72
Brooklyn Pl. SK8: Chea 1J 117
Brooklyn Rd. SK2: Stoc 1G 118
SK8: Chea 2J 117
Brooklyn St. BL1: Bolt 3F 38
OL1: O'ham 2N 63
Brook Mdw. BL5: W'ton 2J 55
SK13: Glos 8G 101
Brook Mill BL7: Bolt 6G 23
Brook Rd. M14: Man 1H 107
M41: Urm 6A 92
SK4: Stoc 3A 108
SK8: Chea 1J 117
Brooks Av. M26: Rad 6F 40
SK7: H Gro 4H 119
SK14: Hyde 8B 98
BROOKSBOTTOMS 2J 25
Brooksbottoms Cl. BL0: Ram 1J 25
Brooks Dr. M35: Fail 4C 80
SK8: Chea 5H 117
WA15: Hale, Tim 3K 115
WA15: Haleb 7K 115
WA15: Tim 9K 105
Brooks End OL11: Roch 4K 27
Brook Shaw St. BL9: Bury 9N 25
Brookshaw St. BL9: Bury 9M 25
(not continuous)
M11: Man 9M 79
Brooks Ho's. WN7: Lei 2G 72
Brook Side OL4: O'ham 5A 64
Brookside M20: Man 6E 106
OL5: Mos 1E 82
PR7: Cop 4C 18
SK13: Glos 9D 100
WN3: Wig 6D 52
Brookside Av. BL4: Farn 4K 57
M43: Droy 7G 81
OL4: Grot 5E 64
SK2: Stoc 9J 109
SK11: Sut E 9K 131
SK12: Poy 3J 125
WN4: A Mak 2C 70
Brookside Bus. Pk. M24: Mid 5B 62
Brookside Cl. BL0: Ram 2G 25
BL2: Bolt 8L 23
M46: Ath 7N 55
SK8: Chea 3J 117
SK13: Had 5B 100
SK14: Hyde 6D 98
WN5: Bil 5J 69
Brookside Ct. M19: Man 7M 95
SK10: Macc 3E 130
Brookside Cres. BL8: G'mount 4E 24
M24: Mid 5A 62
M28: Walk 8M 57
Brookside Dr. M7: Sal 1C 78
SK14: Hyde 6D 98
Brookside La. SK6: H Lan 8B 120
Brookside Mill *SK11: Macc* . . . . . . *.5J 131*
(off Brook St.)
Brookside Miniature Railway . . .8K 119
Brookside Pl. WN2: Hin 5A 54
Brookside Railway Mus. 8K 119
Brookside Rd. BL2: Bolt 4L 39
M33: Sale 6G 105
M40: Man 1M 79
SK8: Gat 1F 116
WN1: Stan 3E 34
Brookside Ter. OL3: Del 8H 47
SK9: A Edg 2D 126
Brookside Vs. *SK8: Gat* . . . . *.1F 116*
(off Pendlebury Rd.)
Brookside Wlk. M26: Rad 5F 40
Brooksmouth BL8: Bury 2K 41
Brook's Pl. OL12: Roch 5A 8 (5C 28)
Brook's Rd. M16: Old T 6B 94
Brooks St. SK1: Stoc 9D 108
Brookstone Cl. M21: Cho H 1B 106
Brook St. BL1: Bolt 2K 7 (5G 38)
BL4: Farn 2M 57
BL5: W'ton 2J 55
BL9: Bury 6N 7 (9N 25)
(not continuous)
M1: Man 8J 5 (2G 94)
M26: Rad 9H 41
(Glebe St.)
M26: Rad 4A 58
(Irwell St.)
M27: Swin 2D 76
M33: Sale 3J 105
M35: Fail 4B 80
M46: Ath 8K 55
OL1: O'ham 4L 63
OL2: O'ham 9H 45
OL9: Chad 3F 62
OL12: W'le 8G 14
OL15: Lit 9N 15
PR6: Adl 4K 19
SK7: H Gro 5J 119
SK8: Chea 1L 117
Brook St. SK11: Macc 5H 131
SK13: Glos 8E 100
SK14: Hyde 6B 98
WA3: Gol 1K 87
WA3: Low 9C 72
WA16: Knut 7H 133
WN2: I Mak 4K 53
WN3: Wig 7C 52
WN4: A Mak 8F 70
WN5: Wig 6M 51
Brook St. E. OL6: A Lyne 8B 6 (8L 81)
Brook St. Ind. Est.
SK1: Stoc . . . . *.9D 108*
(off Brook St.)
Brook St. W. OL6: A Lyne . . .8A 6 (8L 81)
Brook Ter. M12: Man 6L 95
M41: Urm 5C 92
OL16: Miln 9N 29
Brookthorn Cl. SK2: Stoc 2K 119
Brookthorpe Av. M19: Man 2K 107
Brookthorpe Mdws. BL8: Bury 1G 40
Brookthorpe Rd. BL8: Bury 1G 40
Brookvale WN6: Wig 2D 52
Brook Vw. SK9: A Edg 2F 126
Brookview WN2: Hin 7N 53
Brook Vs. WN7: Lei 5H 73
Brookville Flats
OL12: Whitw 5A 14
Brook Wlk. BL8: Bury 7G 25
M34: Dent 9K 97
Brookwater Cl. BL8: Tot 7F 24
Brook Way WA15: Tim 9F 104
Brookway OL4: Gras 5H 65
OL4: Lees 6B 64
OL15: Lit 1L 29
Brookway Cl. M19: Man 4K 107
Brookway Ct. M23: Wyth 9M 105
Brookway Retail Pk.
M23: Wyth 8L 105
Brookwood Av. M8: Man 2H 79
M33: Sale 5E 104
Brookwood Cl. M34: Dent 1L 109
Broom Av. M7: Sal 2D 78
M19: Man 9N 95
SK5: Stoc 2D 108
WN7: Lei 3G 73
Broom Cres. M6: Sal 7J 77
Broomcroft Ho. M20: Man 6G 106
BROOMEDGE 6D 112
Broomedge M7: Sal 2C 78
Broome Gro. M35: Fail 4D 80
Broomehouse Av. M44: Irl 9F 90
Broomes Pk. OL9: Chad 4E 62
Broome St. OL9: O'ham 3A 8 (5H 63)
Broomfield M27: Pen 4K 77
Broomfield Cl. BL2: Ain 3C 40
SK5: Stoc 2D 108
SK9: Wilm 6K 123
Broomfield Ct. M20: Man 4F 106
WA15: Hale . . . . *.4E 114*
(off Broomfield La.)
Broomfield Cres. M24: Mid 2J 61
SK2: Stoc 3E 118
Broomfield Dr. M8: Man 3E 78
SK5: Stoc 2D 108
Broomfield Ho. WN6: Stan 2B 34
Broomfield La. WA15: Hale 5E 114
Broomfield Pk. M24: Mid 3K 61
Broomfield Pl. WN6: Stan 3B 34
Broomfield Rd. BL3: Bolt 8D 38
SK4: Stoc 4A 108
WN6: Stan 3B 34
Broomfields M34: Dent 4L 97
Broomfield Sq. OL11: Roch 8D 28
Broomfield Ter. OL16: Miln 9M 29
WN1: I Mak 4H 53
Broomflat Cl. WN6: Stan 3B 34
Broomgrove La. M34: Dent 5L 97
Broomhall Rd. M9: Man 6F 60
M27: Pen 4K 77
Broomhey Av. WN1: Wig 7F 34
Broomhey Ter. WN1: I Mak 4H 53
Broomhill Dr. SK7: Bram 6B 118
Broomholme WN6: Stan 5H 33
Broomhurst Av. OL8: O'ham 7H 63
Broomhurst Hall M20: Man 6G 106
Broom La. M7: Sal 3C 78
M19: Man 9N 95
Broomleigh WA14: Alt 2A 6 (2C 114)
Broom Rd. M31: Part 6G 102
WA15: Hale 4E 114
WN5: Wig 5A 52
Broomstair Rd. M34: Aud 3K 97
Broom St. BL8: Bury 2K 41
M27: Swin 3F 76
OL16: Miln 9M 29
Broomville Av. M33: Sale 4H 105
Broom Way BL5: W'ton 1J 55
Broomwood Gdns. WA15: Tim 2J 115
Broomwood Rd. WA15: Tim 2J 115
Broomwood Wlk. *M15: Man* *9H 5*
(off Chevril Cl.)
Broseley Av. M20: Man 5J 107
WA3: Cul 5F 88
Broseley La. WA3: Cul 4F 88
Broseley Pl. WA3: Cul 4F 88
Broseley Rd. M16: Old T 7N 93
Brosscroft SK13: Had 3C 100
Brosscroft Cl. SK13: Had 3C 100
Brosscroft Village SK13: Had 3C 100
Brotherdale Cl. OL2: O'ham 7H 45
Brotherod Hall Rd. OL12: Roch 3A 28
Brotherton Cl. M15: Man . . .9B 4 (3C 94)
Brotherton Ct. *M14: Man* *5J 95*
(off Hope Rd.)
Brotherton Dr. M3: Sal 2C 4 (8C 78)
Brotherton Way WA12: N Wil 5E 86
Brougham Rd. HD7: Mars 1H 49
Brougham St. M28: Walk 8K 57
Brough Cl. WN2: Hin 8A 54
Brough St. M11: Man 2C 96
Brough St. W. SK11: Macc 5F 130
Broughton Av. M38: Lit H 6J 57
WA3: Low 2N 87
Broughton Cl. M24: Mid 1J 61
Broughton Grn. Sq. M7: Sal 3C 78
Broughton La. M7: Sal 5C 78
(not continuous)
M8: Man 5C 78
Broughton M. M33: Sale 5J 105
BROUGHTON PARK 2C 78
Broughton Rd. M6: Sal 6N 77
SK5: Stoc 4D 108
SK10: Adl 9G 125
Broughton Rd. E. M6: Sal 6A 78
Broughton St. BL1: Bolt 1E 38
M8: Man 5E 78
Broughton Trade Cen. M7: Sal 6C 78
Broughton Vw. M6: Sal 7A 78
Broughville Dr. M20: Man 8H 107
Brow, The M9: Man 9J 61
Brow Av. M24: Mid 5N 61
Browbeck OL1: O'ham 1C 8 (4J 63)
Browfield Av. M5: Sal 2A 94
Browfield Way OL2: O'ham 2J 63
Browmere WN6: Wig 1C 52
Browmere Dr. M20: Man 4E 106
WA3: Cro 9C 88
Brownacre St. M20: Man 2G 107
Brown Bank Rd. OL15: Lit 2K 29
Brownbank Wlk. *M15: Man* *4E 94*
(off Arnott Cres.)
Brown Ct. WN5: Wig 6A 52
Browncross St. M3: Sal 4E 4 (9D 78)
Brown Edge Rd. OL4: O'ham 7B 64
Brown Heath Av. WN5: Bil 7H 69
Brownhill Countryside Cen. 2K 65
Brownhill Dr. OL4: Aus 4D 64
Brownhill La. OL3: Upp 2L 65
Brownhills Cl. BL8: Tot 8G 25
Brownhill Vw. OL12: Roch 4C 28
Browning Av. M43: Droy 9E 80
M46: Ath 6M 55
WN3: Wig 7C 52
Browning Cl. BL1: Bolt 3E 38
Browning Gro. WN6: Stan 9B 34
Browning Rd. M24: Mid 1N 61
M27: Swin 2E 76
OL1: O'ham 2M 63
SK5: Stoc 8B 96
Browning St. M3: Sal 3C 4 (8C 78)
M15: Man 3C 94
WN7: Lei 4F 72
Browning Wlk. M46: Ath 6M 55
Brown La. SK8: H Grn 6F 116
Brownlea Av. SK16: Duk 2N 97
Brownley Ct. M22: Wyth 2D 116
Brownley Ct. Rd. M22: Wyth 2C 116
Brownley Rd. M22: Shar, Wyth . . .1D 116
Brown Lodge Dr. OL15: Lit 2K 29
Brown Lodge St. OL15: Lit 2K 29
BROWNLOW 1H 69
Brownlow Av. OL2: O'ham 9L 45
WN2: I Mak 4L 53
Brownlow Cen. *BL1: Bolt* . . . . *.3F 38*
(off Brownlow Way)
Brownlow Cl. SK12: Poy 4J 125
BROWNLOW FOLD 2C 38
Brownlow La. WN5: Bil 1G 69
Brownlow Rd. BL6: Hor 9D 20
Brownlow Way BL1: Bolt 3F 38
Brownrigg Cl. M24: Mid 2H 61
Brown's La. SK9: Wilm 6K 123
(not continuous)
Brownslow Wlk. M13: Man 9L 5
Brownson Wlk. *M9: Man* . . . . *.2K 79*
(off Sequoia St.)
Browns Rd. BL2: Bolt 6B 40
Brown St. BL0: Ram 9H 11
BL1: Bolt 2L 7 (5G 39)
BL6: Bla 2N 35
M2: Man 5G 5 (9E 78)
M6: Sal 9M 77
M24: Mid 1M 61
M26: Rad 6F 40
M29: Ast 3A 74
M34: Aud . . . . *.4J 97*
(off Denton Rd.)
M35: Fail 3C 80
OL1: O'ham 1G 8 (4L 63)
OL9: Chad 3E 62
OL10: H'ood 1J 43
OL15: Lit 9M 15
SK1: Stoc 1K 9 (7C 108)
SK9: A Edg 4F 126
SK11: Macc 5G 131
WA14: Alt 4D 114
WN2: B'haw 1A 72
WN2: I Mak 4K 53
WN3: Wig 9H 9 (4E 52)
Brown St. Nth. WN7: Lei 5J 73
Brown St. Sth. WN7: Lei 6J 73
(not continuous)
Brownsville Rd. SK4: Stoc 3N 107
Brownville Gro. SK16: Duk 2B 98
Brownwood Av. SK1: Stoc 7F 108
Brownwood Cl. M33: Sale 7J 105
Brows Av. M23: Wyth 6N 105
Browsholme Ct. *BL5: W'ton* . . . . *.1J 55*
(off Abbeylea Dr.)
Browsholme Ho. BL1: Bolt 5D 38
Browside Cl. OL16: Roch 2H 29
Brow St. OL11: Roch 9E 28
Brow Wlk. M9: Man 8J 61
Broxton Av. BL3: Bolt 9C 38
WN5: Orr 4K 51
Broxton St. M40: Man 7L 79
Broxwood Cl. *M18: Man* . . . . *.4B 96*
(off Kirk St.)
Broyne Cl. M11: Man 1L 95
Bruce St. OL11: Roch 9A 28
Bruce Wlk. *M11: Man* *2B 96*
(off Brock Cl.)
Brundage Rd. M22: Wyth 5C 116
Brundrett Pl. M33: Sale 4F 104
Brundrett's Rd. M21: Cho H 9A 94
Brundrett St. SK1: Stoc 8E 108
Brunel Av. M5: Sal 9A 78
Brunel Cl. M32: Stre 7L 93
Brunel Rd. SK11: Lym G 9G 131
Brunel St. BL1: Bolt 1E 38
BL6: Hor 2E 36

Brunet Wlk. M12: Man . . . 3L 95
(off Skarratt Cl.)
Brun La. OL3: Dig . . . 5A 48
Bruno St. M9: Man . . . 7G 61
Brunstead Cl. M23: Wyth . . . 1K 115
BRUNSWICK . . . 3H 95
Brunswick Av. BL6: Hor . . . 2F 36
Brunswick Ct. BL1: Bolt . . . 1J 7 (4F 38)
SK11: Macc . . . 6H 131
(off Chapel St.)
Brunswick Hill SK10: Macc . . . 4H 131
Brunswick Rd. M20: Man . . . 2H 107
WA12: N Wil . . . 5C 86
WA14: Alt . . . 9D 104
Brunswick Sq. OL1: O'ham . . . 3D 8
Brunswick St. BL9: Bury . . . 5L 7 (1M 41)
M13: Man . . . 9M 5 (3G 94)
M32: Stre . . . 9K 93
OL1: O'ham . . . 3C 8 (5J 63)
OL2: Shaw . . . 5M 45
OL5: Mos . . . 2G 83
OL10: H'ood . . . 2H 43
(not continuous)
OL16: Roch . . . 5F 8 (5E 28)
SK10: Macc . . . 4H 131
SK16: Duk . . . 9N 81
WN7: Lei . . . 6J 73
Brunswick Ter. SK10: Macc . . . 4H 131
(off Brunswick St.)
Brunton Rd. SK5: Stoc . . . 2D 108
Brunt St. M14: Man . . . 6G 95
Bruntwood Av. SK8: H Grn . . . 6F 116
Bruntwood Cotts. SK8: Chea . . . 5K 117
Bruntwood La. SK8: Chea . . . 3K 117
SK8: H Grn . . . 6K 117
Bruntwood Pk. . . . 5J 117
BRUSHES . . . 7G 83
Brushes SK15: Stal . . . 7K 83
Brushes Av. SK15: Stal . . . 7G 82
Brushes Rd. SK15: Stal . . . 7G 82
Brussels Rd. SK3: Stoc . . . 1B 118
Bruton Av. M32: Stre . . . 8H 93
Brutus Wlk. M7: Sal . . . 4D 78
(off Bradshaw St.)
Bryan Rd. M21: Cho H . . . 7A 94
Bryan St. OL4: O'ham . . . 2N 63
Bryant Cl. M13: Man . . . 4H 95
Bryant's Acre BL1: Bolt . . . 5M 37
Bryantsfield BL1: Bolt . . . 6M 37
Bryceland Cl. M12: Man . . . 1K 95
Bryce St. BL3: Bolt . . . 7F 38
SK14: Hyde . . . 5A 98
Brydges Rd. SK6: Mar . . . 2B 120
Brydon Av. M12: Man . . . 8N 5 (2H 95)
Brydon Cl. M6: Sal . . . 8M 77
Bryham St. WN1: Wig . . . 8M 9 (3G 53)
BRYN . . . 4D 70
Bryndale Gro. M33: Sale . . . 7F 104
Brynden Av. M20: Man . . . 3H 107
Bryn Dr. SK5: Stoc . . . 3D 108
Brynford Av. M9: Man . . . 6F 60
BRYN GATES . . . 3H 71
Bryn Gates La. WN2: Bam . . . 2F 70
Bryngs Dr. BL2: Bolt . . . 9N 23
Brynhall Cl. M26: Rad . . . 7E 40
Bryheys M38: Lit H . . . 6H 57
Brynheys Cl. M38: Lit H . . . 6H 57
Bryn Lea Ter. BL1: Bolt . . . 9A 22
Brynmoor BL1: Bolt . . . 1C 38
Brynmore Dr. SK11: Macc . . . 5K 131
Brynorme Rd. M8: Man . . . 9F 60
Bryn Rd. WN4: A Mak . . . 4D 70
Bryn Rd. Sth. WN4: A Mak . . . 6F 70
Bryn Station (Rail) . . . 5D 70
Bryn St. WN2: Bam . . . 3J 71
WN3: I Mak . . . 5H 53
WN4: A Mak . . . 7E 70
Brynton Cl. SK10: Macc . . . 3G 131
Brynton Rd. M13: Man . . . 6K 95
(not continuous)
SK10: Macc . . . 3G 131
Bryn Wlk. BL1: Bolt . . . 1K 7
Bryone Dr. SK2: Stoc . . . 2F 118
Bryony Cl. M22: Wyth . . . 6B 116
M28: Walk . . . 7L 57
WN5: Orr . . . 6H 51
Bryson Wlk. M18: Man . . . 4A 96
Buccleuch Lodge M20: Man . . . 3E 106
Buchanan Dr. WN2: Hin . . . 8D 54
Buchanan Rd. WN5: Wig . . . 4B 52
Buchanan St. BL0: Ram . . . 8H 11
M27: Pen . . . 1F 76
WN7: Lei . . . 5G 73
Buchan St. M11: Man . . . 8N 79
Buckden Rd. SK4: Stoc . . . 1B 108
Buckden Wlk. M23: Wyth . . . 6M 105
Buckden Way SK10: Macc . . . 4G 130
(off Longacre St.)
Buckfast Av. OL8: O'ham . . . 7N 63
WA11: Hay . . . 2D 86
Buckfast Cl. M21: Cho H . . . 8A 94
SK8: Chea H . . . 9N 117
SK10: Macc . . . 2F 130
SK12: Poy . . . 1H 125
WA15: Hale . . . 5N 115
Buckfast Rd. M24: Mid . . . 9L 43
M33: Sale . . . 2D 104
Buckfast Wlk. M7: Sal . . . 4D 78
Buckfield Av. M5: Sal . . . 2A 94
Buckhurst Rd. BL9: Bury . . . 1N 25
M19: Man . . . 8M 95
Buckingham Av. BL6: Hor . . . 2G 36
M6: Sal . . . 8K 77
M34: Dent . . . 7M 97
M45: Whitef . . . 4N 59
Buckingham Bingo
Middleton . . . 3L 61
Old Trafford . . . 4A 94
Walkden . . . 7K 57
Buckingham Cl. WN5: Wig . . . 6B 52
Buckingham Dr. BL8: Bury . . . 4H 41
SK11: Macc . . . 7F 130
SK16: Duk . . . 2C 98
WA16: Knut . . . 7H 133
Buckingham Gro. WA14: Tim . . . 7F 104
Buckingham Pl. M29: Tyld . . . 8A 56
Buckingham Ri. SK11: Macc . . . 8F 130
Buckingham Rd. M21: Cho H . . . 7A 94
M25: Pres . . . 9A 60
M27: Clif . . . 9G 59
M32: Stre . . . 5M 93
M43: Droy . . . 9C 80
M44: Cad . . . 2D 102
SK4: Stoc . . . 3N 107
(not continuous)
SK8: Chea H . . . 5M 117
SK9: Wilm . . . 8E 122
SK12: Poy . . . 3H 125
SK15: Stal . . . 7D 82
Buckingham Rd. W. SK4: Stoc . . . 4M 107
Buckingham Row WN1: Wig . . . 6K 9
Buckinghamshire Pk. Cl.
OL2: Shaw . . . 4M 45
Buckingham St. M5: Sal . . . 9M 77
OL16: Roch . . . 5F 8 (5E 28)
SK2: Stoc . . . 1E 118
Buckingham Way SK2: Stoc . . . 1D 118
(off Windsor St.)
WA15: Tim . . . 9G 105
Buckland Av. M9: Man . . . 8F 60
Buckland Dr. WN5: Wig . . . 2M 51
Buckland Gro. SK14: Hyde . . . 9D 98
Buckland Rd. M6: Sal . . . 6K 77
Buck La. M33: Sale . . . 2E 104
Buckle M30: Ecc . . . 8E 76
BUCKLEY . . . 2F 28
Buckley Av. M18: Man . . . 5A 96
Buckley Barn Ct. OL11: Roch . . . 3A 44
(off Heape St.)
Buckley Brook St. OL12: Roch . . . 3F 28
Buckley Bldgs. OL5: Mos . . . 1H 83
Buckley Chase OL16: Miln . . . 8J 29
Buckley Cl. SK14: Hyde . . . 1B 110
Buckley Dr. OL3: Dens . . . 3F 46
SK6: Rom . . . 7L 109
Buckley Farm La. OL12: Roch . . . 2F 28
Buckley Flds. OL12: Roch . . . 3E 28
Buckley Hall Ind. Est.
OL12: Roch . . . 2F 28
Buckley Hill La. OL16: Miln . . . 8J 29
Buckley La. BL4: Farn . . . 5J 57
M45: Whitef . . . 8L 59
OL12: Roch . . . 2F 28
Buckley Mill OL3: Upp . . . 3L 65
(off Mortimer St.)
Buckley Rd. M18: Man . . . 5N 95
OL4: O'ham . . . 3A 64
OL12: Roch . . . 3F 28
Buckley Rd. Ind. Est.
OL12: Roch . . . 3E 28
Buckley Sq. BL4: Farn . . . 5K 57
Buckley St. BL9: Bury . . . 5L 7 (1M 41)
M11: Man . . . 1B 96
M26: Rad . . . 9G 40
M34: Aud . . . 2H 97
M43: Droy . . . 1E 96
OL2: Shaw . . . 5N 45
OL3: Upp . . . 3L 65
OL4: Lees . . . 6B 64
OL9: Chad . . . 4E 62
OL10: H'ood . . . 1K 43
OL16: Roch . . . 5E 8 (5E 28)
SK5: Stoc . . . 7C 96
SK11: Macc . . . 5H 131
SK15: Stal . . . 1C 98
WN6: Wig . . . 1D 52
Buckley St. W. WN6: Wig . . . 1D 52
Buckley Ter. OL12: Roch . . . 2F 28
Buckley Vw. OL12: Roch . . . 2F 28
BUCKLEY WELLS . . . 9H 7 (3K 41)
BUCKLEY WOOD . . . 9E 44
Bucklow Av. M14: Man . . . 7G 94
M31: Part . . . 5G 103
WA16: Mob . . . 4N 133
Bucklow Cl. OL4: O'ham . . . 9B 46
SK14: Mot . . . 8J 99
Bucklow Dr. M22: Nor . . . 8D 106
Bucklow Gdns. WA13: Lym . . . 3B 112
Bucklow Vw. WA14: Bow . . . 4A 114
Bucklow Wlk. SK11: Macc . . . 5J 131
(off Bank St.)
Buckstones Rd. OL1: O'ham . . . 3N 45
OL2: Shaw . . . 3N 45
Buck St. WN7: Lei . . . 6H 73
Buckthorn Cl. BL5: W'ton . . . 1H 55
M21: Cho H . . . 2C 106
WA15: Tim . . . 2L 115
Buckthorn La. M30: Ecc . . . 9N 75
Buckton Cl. OL3: Dig . . . 7M 47
Buckton Dr. SK15: C'ook . . . 5H 83
BUCKTON VALE . . . 4K 83
Buckton Va. M. SK15: C'ook . . . 3J 83
Buckton Va. Rd. SK15: C'ook . . . 4H 83
SK15: Mill . . . 6G 82
Buckton Vw. SK15: C'ook . . . 3J 83
Buckwood Cl. SK7: H Gro . . . 4L 119
Budding Vw. M4: Man . . . 1H 5
Buddleia Gro. M7: Sal . . . 4C 78
(off Bk. Hilton St.)
Bude Av. M29: Ast . . . 2D 74
M41: Urm . . . 9B 92
SK5: Stoc . . . 3F 108
Bude Cl. SK7: Bram . . . 8D 118
Bude Ter. SK16: Duk . . . 9M 81
Bude Wlk. M23: Wyth . . . 2A 116
Budsworth Av. M20: Man . . . 1G 106
Budworth Gdns. M43: Droy . . . 9F 80
Budworth Rd. M33: Sale . . . 5L 105
Budworth Wlk. SK9: Wilm . . . 5K 123
Buer Av. WN3: Wig . . . 7C 52
BUERSIL . . . 1F 44
Buersil Av. OL16: Roch . . . 9F 28
BUERSIL HEAD . . . 3F 44
Buersil St. OL16: Roch . . . 1F 44
Buerton Av. M9: Man . . . 6F 60
Buffalo Ct. M50: Sal . . . 1L 93
Buffoline Trad. Est. M19: Man . . . 8N 95
Bugle St. M1: Man . . . 7E 4 (1D 94)
Buildbase Way SK3: Stoc . . . 1N 117
Buile Dr. M9: Man . . . 7L 61
Buile Hill Av. M38: Lit H . . . 7J 57
Buile Hill Dr. M5: Sal . . . 7K 77
Buile Hill Gro. M38: Lit H . . . 6J 57
Buile Ho. M6: Sal . . . 7L 77
Buile St. M7: Sal . . . 3D 78
Bulford Av. M22: Wyth . . . 5A 116
Bulkeley Bus. Cen. SK8: Chea . . . 2L 117
Bulkeley Rd. SK8: Chea . . . 1K 117
SK9: Hand . . . 3H 123
SK12: Poy . . . 3J 125
Bulkeley St. SK3: Stoc . . . 5H 9 (8B 108)
Bullcote Grn. OL2: O'ham . . . 8K 45
Bullcote La. OL1: O'ham . . . 8L 45
Bullcroft Dr. M29: Ast . . . 4D 74
Buller M. BL8: Bury . . . 4H 41
Buller Rd. M13: Man . . . 7L 95
Buller St. BL3: Bolt . . . 1K 57
BL8: Bury . . . 3H 41
M43: Droy . . . 1F 96
OL4: O'ham . . . 3A 64
Bullfinch Dr. BL9: Bury . . . 8B 26
Bullfinch Wlk. M21: Cho H . . . 1C 106
BULL HEY . . . 6G 9 (2E 52)
Bull Hill Cres. M26: Rad . . . 3H 59
Bull Hill La. SK11: Macc . . . 3N 131
Bullock's La. SK11: Sut E . . . 9J 131
Bullock St. SK1: Stoc . . . 9D 108
Bullough St. M46: Ath . . . 8L 55
(not continuous)
Bullows Rd. M38: Lit H . . . 5G 56
Bulrush Cl. M28: Walk . . . 6L 57
Bulteel St. BL3: Bolt . . . 1D 56
M28: Wors . . . 4F 74
M30: Ecc . . . 7B 76
WN5: Wig . . . 5A 52
Bulwer St. OL16: Roch . . . 5F 8 (5E 28)
Bungalow Rd. WA12: N Wil . . . 8H 87
Bungalows, The
SK7: H Gro . . . 3K 119
SK22: N Mil . . . 6N 121
WN4: A Mak . . . 3C 70
BUNKERS HILL . . . 8L 109
Bunkers Hill M45: Whitef . . . 8K 59
SK6: Rom . . . 7M 109
Bunkers Hill Rd. SK14: Hat . . . 8H 99
Bunsen St. M1: Man . . . 4K 5 (9G 78)
Bunting Cl. WA3: Low . . . 1A 88
Bunting M. M28: Wors . . . 2J 75
Bunyan Cl. OL1: O'ham . . . 8B 46
Bunyan St. OL12: Roch . . . 4D 28
(not continuous)
Bunyard St. M8: Man . . . 4G 79
Burbage Bank SK13: Gam . . . 7A 100
(off Edale Cres.)
Burbage Gro. SK13: Gam . . . 7A 100
(off Edale Cres.)
Burbage Rd. M23: Wyth . . . 5N 115
Burbage Way SK13: Gam . . . 7A 100
(off Edale Cres.)
Burbank Cl. WN3: Wins . . . 1B 70
Burbridge Cl. M11: Man . . . 9K 79
Burchall Fld. OL16: Roch . . . 6F 28
Burdale Dr. M6: Sal . . . 6H 77
Burdale Wlk. M23: Wyth . . . 7M 105
Burder St. OL8: O'ham . . . 9G 62
Burdett Av. OL12: Roch . . . 4L 27
Burdett Way M12: Man . . . 4K 95
(off Chipstead Av.)
Burdith Av. M14: Man . . . 7F 94
Burdon Av. M22: Wyth . . . 4D 116
Burford Av. M16: Whall R . . . 7C 94
M41: Urm . . . 5E 92
SK7: Bram . . . 1A 124
Burford Cl. SK9: Wilm . . . 9D 122
Burford Cres. SK9: Wilm . . . 9D 122
Burford Dr. BL3: Bolt . . . 7F 38
M16: Whall R . . . 7C 94
M27: Swin . . . 9E 58
Burford Gro. M33: Sale . . . 7E 104
Burford La. WA13: Lym . . . 4D 112
Burford Rd. M16: Whall R . . . 7C 94
Burford Wlk. M16: Whall R . . . 7C 94
(off Burford Rd.)
Burgess Av. OL6: A Lyne . . . 5N 81
Burgess Dr. M35: Fail . . . 4D 80
Burgess St. SK10: Macc . . . 4K 131
WN3: I Mak . . . 6H 53
Burgh Hall Rd. PR7: Chor . . . 2D 18
Burgh La. PR7: Chor . . . 1F 18
(not continuous)
Burgh La. Sth. PR7: Chor . . . 3E 18
Burghley Av. OL4: O'ham . . . 5A 64
Burghley Cl. M26: Rad . . . 7B 40
SK15: Stal . . . 8D 82
Burghley Dr. M26: Rad . . . 7B 40
Burghley Way WN3: I Mak . . . 6J 53
Burgh Mdws. PR7: Chor . . . 1F 18
Burgin Wlk. M40: Man . . . 5H 79
Burgundy Dr. BL8: Tot . . . 6F 24
Burke St. BL1: Bolt . . . 2E 38
Burkhardt Dr. WA12: N Wil . . . 6H 87
Burkitt St. SK14: Hyde . . . 7B 98
Burland Cl. M7: Sal . . . 5D 78
Burland St. WN5: Wig . . . 4C 52
Burleigh Cl. SK7: H Gro . . . 6E 118
Burleigh Ct. M32: Stre . . . 5L 93
Burleigh Ho. M15: Man . . . 4G 94
(off Dilworth St.)
Burleigh M. M21: Cho H . . . 2A 106
Burleigh Rd. M32: Stre . . . 6L 93
Burleigh St. M15: Man . . . 4G 94
Burlescombe Cl. WA14: Alt . . . 1B 114
Burley Av. WA3: Low . . . 9N 71
Burley Ct. SK4: Stoc . . . 6A 108
Burley Cres. WN3: Wins . . . 9N 51
Burleyhurst La. SK9: Wilm . . . 7A 122
Burlin Ct. M16: Whall R . . . 6C 94
Burlington Av. OL8: O'ham . . . 7J 63
Burlington Cl. SK4: Stoc . . . 6K 107
Burlington Ct.
WA14: Alt . . . 1D 6 (2D 114)
Burlington Dr. SK3: Stoc . . . 3D 118
Burlington Gdns. SK3: Stoc . . . 3D 118
Burlington Ho. OL6: A Lyne . . . 7B 6
Burlington M. SK3: Stoc . . . 3D 118
Burlington Rd. M20: Man . . . 1H 107
M30: Ecc . . . 6E 76
WA14: Alt . . . 1D 6 (2D 114)
Burlington St. M15: Man . . . 4F 94
OL6: A Lyne . . . 8A 6 (8K 81)
OL7: A Lyne . . . 8A 6 (8K 81)
OL11: Roch . . . 9E 28
WN2: Hin . . . 6N 53
(not continuous)
Burlington St. E. M15: Man . . . 4F 94
Burlton Gro. WN2: Asp . . . 1K 53
Burman St. M11: Man . . . 2D 96
M43: Droy . . . 2D 96
Burnaby St. BL3: Bolt . . . 7E 38
OL8: O'ham . . . 6G 63
OL11: Roch . . . 9A 28
BURNAGE . . . 3K 107
Burnage Av. M19: Man . . . 9L 95
Burnage Hall Rd. M19: Man . . . 1K 107
Burnage La. M19: Man . . . 6J 107
BURNAGE PARK . . . 9L 95
Burnage Range M19: Man . . . 8M 95
Burnage Station (Rail) . . . 4J 107
Burnaston Gro. WN5: Wig . . . 6A 52
Burn Bank OL3: G'fld . . . 6H 65
Burnbray Av. M19: Man . . . 2K 107
Burnby Wlk. M23: Wyth . . . 7M 105
Burndale Dr. BL9: Bury . . . 9N 41
BURNDEN . . . 8J 39
Burnden Ind. Est. BL3: Bolt . . . 8J 39
Burnden Pk. BL3: Bolt . . . 7H 39
Burnden Rd. BL3: Bolt . . . 7J 39
Burnden Way BL6: Hor . . . 4E 36
BURNEDGE . . . 2H 45
Burnedge Cl. OL12: Whitw . . . 4B 14
Burnedge Fold Rd. OL4: Gras . . . 5G 64
Burnedge La. OL4: Gras . . . 5F 64
Burnedge M. OL4: Gras . . . 5G 64
Burnell Cl. M40: Man . . . 1N 5 (7J 79)
Burnell Ct. OL10: H'ood . . . 5J 43
Burnet Cl. M29: Ast . . . 3C 74
OL16: Roch . . . 9G 28
Burnett Av. M5: Sal . . . 1A 94
Burnett Cl. M40: Man . . . 5J 79
Burnfell WA3: Low . . . 2A 88
Burnfield Rd. M18: Man . . . 6B 96
SK5: Stoc . . . 6D 96
Burnham Av. BL1: Bolt . . . 3B 38
SK5: Stoc . . . 8D 96
Burnham Cl. SK8: Chea H . . . 5L 117
WA3: Cul . . . 5G 89
Burnham Dr. M19: Man . . . 9L 95
M41: Urm . . . 6C 92
Burnham Gro. WN2: Wig . . . 1J 53
Burnham Rd. M34: Dent . . . 6E 96
Burnham Wlk. BL4: Farn . . . 2L 57
(off Bentley St.)
Burnhill Ct. WN6: Stan . . . 4B 34
Burnleigh Ct. BL5: O Hul . . . 3A 56
BURNLEY BROW . . . 3H 63
Burnley La. OL1: Chad . . . 1E 62
(not continuous)
OL9: Chad . . . 1E 62
(not continuous)
Burnley Rd. BL0: Eden . . . 1K 11
BL9: Bury . . . 5L 25
(not continuous)
Burnley St. M35: Fail . . . 2E 80
OL9: Chad . . . 4F 62
Burnmoor WN2: Asp . . . 7M 35
Burnmoor Rd. BL2: Bolt . . . 4N 39
Burnsall Av. M45: Whitef . . . 3K 59
WA3: Low . . . 1B 88
Burnsall Gro. OL2: O'ham . . . 8H 45
Burnsall Wlk. M22: Wyth . . . 5N 115
Burns Av. BL9: Bury . . . 6M 41
M27: Swin . . . 1D 76
M46: Ath . . . 6M 55
SK8: Chea . . . 1L 117
WN7: Lei . . . 2E 72
Burns Cl. M11: Man . . . 9L 79
OL1: O'ham . . . 7B 46
WN3: Wig . . . 7D 52
WN4: A Mak . . . 4C 70
WN5: Bil . . . 1H 69
Burns Ct. OL11: Roch . . . 7K 27
Burns Cres. SK2: Stoc . . . 9J 109
Burns Fold SK16: Duk . . . 2D 98
Burns Gdns. M25: Pres . . . 8M 59
Burns Gro. M43: Droy . . . 8E 80
Burnside BL0: Ram . . . 4K 11
OL2: Shaw . . . 4A 46
SK13: Had . . . 5B 100
SK15: Stal . . . 2G 99
WA15: Haleb . . . 8K 115
WN8: Par . . . 2A 32
Burnside Av. M6: Sal . . . 5H 77
SK4: Stoc . . . 2C 108
Burnside Cl. M26: Rad . . . 5F 40
M29: Ast . . . 3C 74
OL10: H'ood . . . 3J 43
SK6: Bred . . . 5K 109
SK9: Wilm . . . 8H 123
SK15: Stal . . . 2G 99
Burnside Cres. M24: Mid . . . 9K 43
Burnside Dr. M19: Man . . . 2K 107
Burnside Rd. BL1: Bolt . . . 2C 38
OL16: Roch . . . 7G 29
SK8: Gat . . . 2F 116
Burns Rd. M34: Dent . . . 1L 109
M38: Lit H . . . 6J 57
M90: Man A . . . 1L 71
Burns St. BL3: Bolt . . . 6G 39
OL10: H'ood . . . 3J 43
Burnt Acre SK11: Chel . . . 9A 126
Burnt Edge La. BL6: Hor . . . 8K 21
Burnthorp Av. M9: Man . . . 8G 60
Burnthorpe Cl. OL11: Roch . . . 7K 27
Burntwood Wlk. M9: Man . . . 2K 79
(off Princedom St.)
Burnvale WN3: Wins . . . 9A 52
Burran Rd. M22: Wyth . . . 7C 116
Burrington Dr. WN7: Lei . . . 3F 72
Burrows Av. M21: Cho H . . . 2A 106
Burrows Yd. WN1: Wig . . . 8K 9
BURRS . . . 7K 25
Burrs Activity Cen. . . . 7K 25
Burrs Cl. BL8: Bury . . . 7J 25
Burrs Country Pk. . . . 7K 25
Burrs Country Pk. Caravan Club Site
BL8: Bury . . . 7K 25
Burrs Lea Cl. BL9: Bury . . . 7L 25
Burrswood Av. BL9: Bury . . . 7L 25
Burrwood Dr. SK3: Stoc . . . 2B 118
Bursar Cl. WA12: N Wil . . . 5G 86
Burslem Av. M20: Man . . . 9F 94
Burstead St. M18: Man . . . 2C 96
Burstock St. M4: Man . . . 1K 5 (7G 79)
Burston St. M18: Man . . . 3A 96
Burtinshaw St. M18: Man . . . 4B 96
Burton Av. BL8: Bury . . . 9F 24
M20: Man . . . 2G 106
WA15: Tim . . . 7G 104
Burton Bldg. M1: Man . . . 3K 5
Burton Cl. WA3: Cul . . . 6H 89
Burton Dr. SK12: Poy . . . 2H 125
Burton Gro. M28: Wors . . . 3C 76
Burton M. M20: Man . . . 3E 106
Burton Pl. M15: Man . . . 8B 4 (2C 94)
Burton Rd. M20: Man . . . 4E 106
Burton St. M24: Mid . . . 3L 61
(not continuous)
M40: Man . . . 6G 79
OL4: Lees . . . 6B 64
SK4: Stoc . . . 5C 108
Burton Wlk. M3: Sal . . . 2C 4 (8C 78)
SK4: Stoc . . . 5C 108
(off Heskith St.)
Burtonwood Ct. M24: Mid . . . 2L 61
Burtree St. M12: Man . . . 3M 95
Burwell Av. PR7: Cop . . . 5A 18
Burwell Cl. BL3: Bolt . . . 8E 38
OL12: Roch . . . 2B 28
SK13: Glos . . . 9C 100
WN7: Lei . . . 6K 73
Burwell Gro. M23: Wyth . . . 9M 105
BURY . . . 8K 7 (2L 41)
Bury & Bolton Rd.
M26: Ain, Bury, Rad . . . 5C 40
Bury & Rochdale Old Rd.
BL9: Bury . . . 9E 26
OL10: H'ood . . . 9E 26
Bury Art Gallery, Mus. & Archives
. . . 8K 7 (2L 41)
Bury Av. M16: Whall R . . . 7B 94
Bury Bolton Street Station
East Lancashire Railway
. . . 8J 7 (2L 41)
Bury Bus. Cen. BL9: Bury . . . 1N 41
Bury FC . . . 5M 41
Bury Golf Course . . . 8M 41
BURY GROUND . . . 6H 7 (1K 41)
Bury Ind. Est. BL2: Bolt . . . 5N 39
Bury New Rd. BL0: Ram . . . 8K 11
BL1: Bolt . . . 1M 7 (4H 39)
BL2: Ain, Bolt . . . 5A 40
BL2: Bolt . . . 1M 7 (4H 39)
BL9: Bury, H'ood . . . 2B 42
M7: Sal . . . 3C 78
M8: Man . . . 3C 78
M25: Pres . . . 6N 59
M45: Whitef . . . 2L 59
OL10: H'ood . . . 2B 42
Bury Old Rd. BL0: Ram . . . 4M 11
BL2: Ain, Bolt . . . 3A 40
BL2: Bolt . . . 2N 7 (5H 39)
(not continuous)
BL9: Bury . . . 3C 42
(Heap Brow)
BL9: Bury . . . 9M 11
(Whitelow Rd.)
M7: Sal . . . 9C 60
M8: Man . . . 9C 60
M25: Pres . . . 9C 60
M45: Pres, Whitef . . . 4M 59
OL10: H'ood . . . 3C 42
Bury Pl. M11: Man . . . 8A 80
Bury Rd. BB4: Rawt . . . 1K 11
BL0: Eden . . . 3K 11
BL2: Bolt . . . 5J 39
BL7: Edg . . . 1M 23
BL8: Tot . . . 7F 24
BL9: Bury . . . 8H 41
M26: Rad . . . 8H 41
OL11: Roch . . . 8K 27
Bury Sports for All Centre . . . 3L 59
Bury Stop (Metro) . . . 8K 7 (2L 41)
Bury St. M3: Sal . . . 2E 4 (8D 78)
M26: Rad . . . 8J 41
OL5: Mos . . . 2F 82
OL10: H'ood . . . 2G 42
SK5: Stoc . . . 5D 108
Bury Transport Mus. . . . 7J 7 (2L 41)
Bushell St. BL3: Bolt . . . 8C 38
Bushey Dr. M23: Wyth . . . 2N 115
Busheyfield Cl. SK14: Hyde . . . 4A 98
Bushfield Wlk. M23: Wyth . . . 9L 105
(off Sandy La.)
Bushgrove Wlk. M9: Man . . . 6J 61
(off Claygate Dr.)
Bushmoor Wlk. M13: Man . . . 4J 95
Bushnell Wlk. M9: Man . . . 6K 61
(off Claygate Dr.)
Bush St. M40: Man . . . 5K 79
Bushton Wlk. M40: Man . . . 5H 79
(off Ribblesdale Dr.)
Bushway Wlk. M8: Man . . . 4G 78
(off Appleford Dr.)
Business & Technology Cen.
M30: Ecc . . . 8C 76
BUSK . . . 3G 63
Busk Rd. OL9: Chad . . . 3G 62
Busk Wlk. OL9: Chad . . . 3G 63
Butcher La. M23: Wyth . . . 9K 105
(not continuous)
OL2: O'ham . . . 7G 45
Butchers La. WN4: A Mak . . . 8E 70
Bute Av. OL8: O'ham . . . 8K 63
Bute St. BL1: Bolt . . . 3C 38
M40: Man . . . 2L 79
M50: Sal . . . 9K 77
SK13: Glos . . . 7G 100
Butler Ct. M32: Stre . . . 8K 93
M40: Man . . . 1N 5
BUTLER GREEN . . . 7E 62

Butler Grn. OL9: Chad 7E 62
Butler La. M4: Man 1N 5 (7H 79)
Butler St. BL0: Ram 1G 25
M4: Man 1N 5 (7H 79)
WN1: Wig 8L 9 (3G 52)
Butley Cl. SK10: Macc 1H 131
Butley Lanes SK10: P'bury 3D 128
Butley St. SK7: H Gro 3J 119
BUTLEY TOWN 5G 128
Butman St. M18: Man 3D 96
Buttercup Av. M38: Lit H 8G 56
Buttercup Cl. M46: Ath 6M 55
SK13: Glos 9G 101
Buttercup Dr. OL4: O'ham 1A 64
OL11: Roch 1N 43
SK3: Stoc 2B 118
Butterfield Cl. SK8: Chea H 6N 117
Butterfield Hall Farm BL5: O Hul 2C 56
Butterfield Rd. BL5: O Hul 3A 56
Butterhouse La. OL3: Dob 1M 65
Butter La. M3: Man 4F 4
Butterley Cl. SK16: Duk 2C 98
Buttermere Av. M22: Wyth 5A 116
M27: Swin 4F 76
OL10: H'ood 4J 43
WN4: A Mak 5E 70
Buttermere Cl. BL3: Lit L 8N 39
M32: Stre 6J 93
Buttermere Dr. BL0: Ram 7H 11
M24: Mid 1K 61
WA15: Haleb 9K 115
Buttermere Gro. OL2: O'ham 5H 45
Buttermere Rd. BL4: Farn 3F 56
M31: Part 5F 102
OL4: O'ham 3A 64
OL7: A Lyne 5A 6 (6K 81)
SK8: Gat 4G 117
WN5: Wig 4N 51
Buttermere Ter. SK15: Stal 7D 82
(off Springs La.)
Buttermill Cl. M44: Irl 6J 91
Butterstile Av. M25: Pres 9M 59
Butterstile Cl. M25: Pres 1M 77
Butterstile La. M25: Pres 1M 77
Butterton Dr. M18: Man 3C 96
Butterwick Cl. M12: Man 6N 95
Butterwick Flds. BL6: Hor 1B 36
Butterworth Brow PR7: Chor 1C 18
(not continuous)
Butterworth Cl. OL16: Miln 8L 29
BUTTERWORTH HALL 8L 29
Butterworth Hall OL16: Miln 8L 29
Butterworth La. OL9: Chad 8C 62
Butterworth Pl. OL15: Lit 8L 15
Butterworth St. M11: Man 1M 95
M24: Mid 4A 62
M26: Rad 8H 41
OL4: O'ham 4N 63
OL9: Chad 3F 62
OL15: Lit 9L 15
Butterworth Way OL3: G'fld 6L 65
Buttery Ho. La. WA15: Haleb 5L 115
Butt Hill Av. M25: Pres 8A 60
Butt Hill Ct. M25: Pres 8A 60
Butt Hill Dr. M25: Pres 8A 60
Butt Hill Rd. M25: Pres 8A 60
Butt La. OL5: Mos 7E 64
Button Hole OL2: Shaw 5A 46
Button La. M23: Wyth 6N 105
Buttress St. M18: Man 3A 96
Butts, The OL16: Roch 7C 8 (6D 28)
Butts Av. WN7: Lei 7L 73
Butts Avenue, The OL16: Roch 7C 8
Butts Ct. WN7: Lei 6J 73
Butts La. OL3: Del 8G 46
Butts St. WN7: Lei 7J 73
Buxted Rd. OL1: O'ham 2M 63
Buxton Av. M20: Man 2E 106
OL6: A Lyne 4C 82
Buxton Cl. M46: Ath 7N 55
SK13: Gam 7A 100
(off Buxton M.)
Buxton Ct. SK2: Stoc 1E 118
Buxton Cres. M33: Sale 7K 105
OL16: Roch 9F 28
Buxton La. M43: Droy 1C 96
SK6: Mar 2B 120
Buxton M. SK13: Gam 7A 100
Buxton New Rd. SK11: Macc 4M 131
Buxton Old Rd. SK11: Macc 5L 131
SK12: Dis 9G 120
Buxton Pl. OL8: O'ham 6J 63
Buxton Rd. M32: Stre 6G 93
SK1: Stoc 1E 118
SK2: Stoc 1E 118
SK6: H Lan 6K 119
SK7: H Gro 6K 119
SK10: Macc 4J 131
SK11: Macc 4J 131
SK12: Dis 9G 121
(Greenhill Wlk.)
SK12: Dis 6K 119
(Melford Rd.)
SK22: Fur V, N Mil 9G 121
SK23: Fur V 9G 120
Buxton Rd. W. SK12: Dis 9D 120
Buxton St. BL8: Bury 2J 41
M1: Man 7L 5 (1G 95)
OL10: H'ood 3J 43
OL12: Whitw 3B 14
SK7: H Gro 4H 119
SK8: Gat 2F 116
Buxton Ter. SK14: Holl 3N 99
Buxton Wlk. SK13: Gam 8A 100
(off Buxton M.)
Buxton Way M34: Dent 9K 97
Buxworth Rd. WA14: W Tim 7C 104
Bycroft Wlk. M40: Man 6B 80
(off Eastmoor Dr.)
Bye Rd. BL0: Ram 7L 11
Bye St. M34: Aud 2K 97
Byfield Rd. M22: Wyth 3B 116
Byfleet Cl. WN3: Wins 1N 69
Byland Av. OL4: O'ham 7A 64
SK8: Chea H 9N 117
Byland Cl. BL1: Bolt 2F 38
Byland Gdns. M26: Rad 8E 40
Bylands Cl. SK12: Poy 2H 125
Bylands Fold SK16: Duk 3A 98
Byland Wlk. M22: Wyth 6C 116
Byley Ri. WN6: Stan 4B 34
Byng Av. M44: Cad 4E 102
Byng St. BL4: Farn 5L 57
BL5: W'ton 4D 54
OL10: H'ood 4K 43
Byre Cl. M33: Sale 5N 105
Byre Vw. PR6: H Char 5J 19
Byrness Cl. M46: Ath 7N 55
Byroe Ct. WA14: Alt 1D 6 (1D 114)
Byrom Av. M19: Man 8A 96
Byrom Ct. M43: Droy 9D 80
Byrom La. WA3: Low 8B 72
Byrom Pde. M19: Man 8A 96
Byrom Pl. M3: Man 5E 4
Byrom St. BL8: Bury 9H 25
M3: Man 6E 4 (1D 94)
M5: Sal 1N 93
M16: Old T 5C 94
WA14: Alt 4D 114
Byron Av. M25: Pres 8M 59
M26: Rad 8D 40
M27: Swin 2E 76
M43: Droy 8E 80
WN2: Hin 6N 53
Byron Cl. WN2: Abr 1L 71
WN5: Orr 4K 51
WN6: Stan 9B 34
Byron Cres. PR7: Cop 4B 18
Byron Dr. SK8: Chea 1L 117
Byron Gro. M46: Ath 6M 55
OL11: Roch 7N 27
SK5: Stoc 8C 96
WN7: Lei 3H 73
Byron Ho. OL8: O'ham 9F 62
(off Grammar School Rd.)
Byron Rd. BL8: G'mount 3F 24
M24: Mid 1N 61
M32: Stre 6L 93
M34: Dent 9K 97
Byrons Dr. WA15: Tim 1G 114
Byron's La. SK11: Macc, Sut E 6J 131
Byrons St. SK11: Macc 6H 131
Byron St. M30: Ecc 8D 76
OL2: O'ham 8J 45
OL8: O'ham 9F 62
WN7: Lei 4H 73
Byron Wlk. BL4: Farn 5J 57
OL2: O'ham 8J 45
(off Shaw St.)
Byrth Rd. OL8: O'ham 2K 81
Bywell Wlk. M8: Man 3E 78
(off Levenhurst Rd.)

C

Cabin La. OL4: O'ham 9D 46
Cable St. BL1: Bolt 1L 7 (4G 39)
M3: Sal 2E 4 (8D 78)
M4: Man 2K 5 (8G 78)
Cabot Pl. SK5: Stoc 4D 108
Cabot St. M13: Man 3G 95
Caddington Rd. M21: Cho H 1B 106
CADISHEAD 3F 102
Cadishead Way M30: Ecc 8J 91
M44: Cad, Irl 5E 102
Cadishead Way Circ. M44: Cad 5D 102
Cadleigh Wlk. M40: Man 3M 79
(off Shelderton Cl.)
Cadman Gro. WN2: Hin 7N 53
Cadmium Wlk. M18: Man 5A 96
Cadnam Dr. M22: Wyth 4E 116
Cadogan Dr. WN3: Wins 9A 52
Cadogan Pl. M7: Sal 1D 78
Cadogan St. M14: Man 5F 94
Cadum Wlk. M13: Man 3H 95
(off Bramwell Dr.)
Caen Av. M40: Man 8A 62
Caernarvon Cl. BL8: G'mount 4F 24
Caernarvon Dr. SK7: H Gro 6G 119
Caernarvon Rd. WN2: Hin 8C 54
Caernarvon Way M34: Dent 8K 97
Caesar St. OL11: Roch 2E 44
Cairn Brae WA12: N Wil 5F 86
Cairn Dr. M6: Sal 5B 78
OL11: Roch 7K 27
Cairngorm Dr. BL3: Bolt 8N 37
Cairns Pl. OL6: A Lyne 5A 82
Cairn Wlk. M11: Man 9L 79
(off Raglan Cl.)
Cairnwell Rd. OL9: Chad 3D 62
Caister Av. M45: Whitef 4N 59
Caister Cl. M41: Urm 8K 91
WN8: Skel 3B 50
Caistor Cl. M16: Whall R 9D 94
Caistor St. SK1: Stoc 5F 108
Caistor Wlk. OL1: O'ham 1D 8
Caithness Cl. M23: Wyth 3N 115
Caithness Dr. BL3: Bolt 6N 37
Caithness Rd. OL11: Roch 8K 27
Cajetan Ho. M24: Mid 6L 61
Cakebread St. M12: Man 8M 5 (2H 95)
Calamanco Way M44: Irl 9H 91
Calamine St. SK11: Macc 6J 131
Calbourne Cres. M12: Man 6N 95
Calcot Wlk. M23: Wyth 1M 115
Calcutta Rd. SK3: Stoc 9A 108
Caldbeck Av. BL1: Bolt 3A 38
M33: Sale 3L 105
Caldbeck Cl. WN4: A Mak 6E 70
Caldbeck Dr. BL4: Farn 4F 56
M24: Mid 2K 61
Caldbeck Gro. WA11: St H 9G 68
Caldecott Rd. M9: Man 6F 60
Calder Av. M22: Nor 8C 106
M44: Irl 8G 91
OL15: Lit 7L 15
PR7: Chor 1E 18
WN2: Hin 8E 54
CALDER BANK 5M 91
Calderbank WN5: Orr 5L 51
Calderbank Av. M41: Urm 5M 91
Calderbank St. WN5: Wig 6B 52
Calderbeck Way M22: Shar 1D 116
CALDERBROOK 5N 15
Calderbrook Ct. SK8: Chea H 3N 117
Calderbrook Dr. SK8: Chea H 3M 117
Calderbrook Rd. OL15: Lit 8L 15
Calderbrook Ter. OL15: Lit 6N 15
Calderbrook Wlk. M9: Man 3J 79
(off Grangewood Dr.)
Calderbrook Way OL4: O'ham 6M 63
Calderburn Cl. BL6: Hor 4F 36
Calder Cl. BL9: Bury 5N 25
SK5: Stoc 3E 108
SK10: Boll 5K 129
SK12: Poy 4H 125
Calder Ct. M41: Urm 5M 91
Calder Cres. M45: Whitef 1A 60
Calderdale Ct. OL2: O'ham 7G 45
(off Denbydale Way)
Calder Dr. BL4: Kea 6B 58
M27: Swin 1E 76
M28: Walk 9H 57
WN2: P Bri 9K 53
Calder Flats OL10: H'ood 2H 43
(off Wilton St.)
Calder Gdns. OL15: Lit 8L 15
Calder Gro. OL2: Shaw 4L 45
Calder Ho. M7: Sal 5B 78
M43: Droy 1E 96
(off Old Mill Wharf)
CALDERMOOR 8L 15
Calder Pl. WN5: Wig 4N 51
Calder Rd. BL3: Bolt 9F 38
CALDERSHAW 3N 27
Caldershaw Bus. Cen.
OL12: Roch 3N 27
Caldershaw Cen., The
OL12: Roch 3N 27
Caldershaw La. OL12: Roch 3M 27
Caldershaw Rd. OL12: Roch 4M 27
Calder St. OL16: Roch 3F 28
Caldervale Av. M21: Cho H 4B 106
Calder Wlk. M24: Mid 1H 61
M45: Whitef 1A 60
Calder Way M45: Whitef 1A 60
Calderwood Cl. BL8: Tot 7F 24
Caldew Cl. WN2: Hin 7A 54
Caldey Rd. M23: Wyth 2L 115
Caldford Cl. WN2: Asp 6M 35
Caldon Cl. M30: Ecc 1D 92
Caldwell Av. M29: Ast 6B 74
Caldwell Cl. M29: Ast 5C 74
Caldwell St. BL5: W'ton 6H 55
SK5: Stoc 8D 96
Caldy Dr. BL0: Ram 2G 25
Caldy Rd. M6: Sal 6K 77
SK9: Hand 3J 123
Caleb Cl. M29: Tyld 1A 74
Caledon Av. M40: Man 2M 79
Caledonian Dr. M30: Ecc 1E 92
Caledonia St. BL3: Bolt 7D 38
M26: Rad 8J 41
(not continuous)
Caledonia Way M32: Stre 4G 92
CALE GREEN 1D 118
Cale Grn. SK2: Stoc 1D 118
Cale Grn. Ct. SK2: Stoc 1D 118
Cale La. WN2: Asp 1K 53
Cale Rd. SK22: N Mil 7N 121
Cale St. SK2: Stoc 9D 108
Caley St. BL1: Bolt 2A 38
M1: Man 7H 5
Calf Hey OL15: Lit 8K 15
Calf Hey Cl. M26: Rad 9D 40
Calf Hey Head OL12: Whitw 6B 14
Calf Hey La. OL12: Whitw 6B 14
Calf Hey Nth. OL11: Roch 9E 28
Calf Hey Rd. OL2: Shaw 4A 46
Calf Hey Sth. OL11: Roch 9E 28
Calf La. OL5: Mos 7H 65
Calgarth Dr. M24: Mid 9J 43
Calgary St. M18: Man 4A 96
Calico Cl. M3: Sal 1B 4 (7C 78)
Calico Cres. SK15: C'ook 4J 83
Calico Dr. SK6: Stri 5F 120
Calico Wood Av. WN6: She 6K 33
Callaghan Wlk. OL10: H'ood 3H 43
Calland Av. SK14: Hyde 6C 98
Callander Ct. WN5: Wig 4B 52
Callander Sq. OL10: H'ood 3E 42
Callender St. BL0: Ram 8H 11
Calliards La. OL15: Lit 1K 29
Calliard's Rd. OL16: Roch 1J 29
Callingdon Rd. M21: Cho H 3C 106
Callington Cl. SK14: Hat 7H 99
Callington Dr. SK14: Hat 7H 99
Callington Wlk. SK14: Hat 7H 99
(off Callington Dr.)
Callis Rd. BL3: Bolt 6D 38
Callthorpe Cl. BL1: Bolt 3F 38
Callum Wlk. M13: Man 3H 95
(off Watkin Cl.)
Calluna M. M20: Man 4F 106
Calne Wlk. M23: Wyth 2N 115
Calow Cl. SK13: Gam 8A 100
Calow Dr. WN7: Lei 7L 73
Calow Grn. SK13: Gam 8A 100
CALROFOLD 2N 131
Calrofold La. SK11: Macc 3M 131
Caltha St. BL0: Ram 8H 11
Calthorpe Av. M9: Man 3H 79
Calton Av. M7: Sal 3N 77
Calton Cl. WN3: Wig 7A 52
Calvary Ct. SK3: Stoc 8B 108
Calve Cft. Rd. M22: Wyth 5D 116
Calveley Rd. SK10: Macc 3D 130
Calveley Wlk. WN6: Stan 4B 34
Calver Av. M30: Ecc 1C 92
Calver Bank SK13: Gam 7A 100
(off Eyam La.)
Calver Cl. M41: Urm 6L 91
SK13: Gam 7A 100
(off Hathersage Cres.)
Calver Fold SK13: Gam 7N 99
(off Calver M.)
Calverhall Way WN4: A Mak 7D 70
Calver Hey Cl. BL5: W'ton 1L 55
Calverleigh Cl. BL3: Bolt 1B 56
Calverley Av. M19: Man 1L 107
Calverley Cl. SK9: Wilm 6H 123
Calverley Rd. SK8: Chea 2M 117
Calverley Way OL12: Roch 1C 28
Calver M. SK13: Gam 7N 99
Calver Pl. SK13: Gam 7A 100
(off Hathersage Cres.)
Calverton Dr. M40: Man 3A 80
Calvert Rd. BL3: Bolt 9F 38
Calvert St. M5: Sal 8K 77
Calver Wlk. M34: Dent 9L 97
SK8: Chea H 6K 117
Calvine Wlk. M40: Man 1N 5
Calvin St. BL1: Bolt 3G 39
Cambeck Cl. M45: Whitef 2A 60
Cambeck Wlk. M45: Whitef 2N 59
Cambell Rd. M30: Ecc 8B 76
Camberley Cl. BL8: Tot 8G 24
SK7: Bram 8E 118
Camberley Dr. OL11: Roch 7L 27
Cambert La. M18: Man 4A 96
(Garratt Way)
M18: Man 4B 96
(Wellington St.)
Camberwell Cres. WN2: Wig 1J 53
Camberwell Dr. OL7: A Lyne 4L 81
Camberwell St. M8: Man 6F 78
OL8: O'ham 7J 63
Camberwell Way OL2: O'ham 8G 45
Camble St. WN7: Lei 5J 73
Camborne Av. SK10: Macc 4C 130
Camborne St. M14: Man 7G 95
Cambourne Dr. BL3: Bolt 7B 38
WN2: Hin 9E 54
Cambourne Rd. SK14: Hat 6H 99
Cambo Wlk. SK4: Stoc 5L 107
Cambrai Cres. M30: Ecc 6A 76
Cambrian Bus. Pk. BL3: Bolt 7F 38
Cambrian Cres. WN3: Wins 9N 51
Cambrian Dr. OL2: O'ham 9G 45
OL16: Miln 7L 29
Cambrian Rd. SK3: Stoc 8A 108
Cambrian St. M11: Man 8K 79
M40: Man 8K 79
Cambria Sq. BL3: Bolt 7D 38
(off Cambria St.)
Cambria St. BL3: Bolt 7D 38
OL4: O'ham 4A 64
Cambridge Av. M16: Whall R 7B 94
OL11: Roch 7M 27
SK9: Wilm 7E 122
SK11: Macc 5F 130
Cambridge Cl. BL4: Farn 2G 57
M33: Sale 5D 104
Cambridge Dr. BL3: Lit L 8B 40
M34: Dent 6E 96
SK6: Wood 3N 109
Cambridge Gro. M30: Ecc 8F 76
M45: Whitef 3N 59
Cambridge Hall M13: Man 3G 95
(off Rudcroft Cl.)
M15: Man 9H 5
Cambridge Ho. M15: Man 9H 5
Cambridge Ind. Est. M7: Sal 6D 78
(not continuous)
Cambridge Rd. BL6: Los 4H 37
M9: Man 1J 79
M35: Fail 5D 80
M41: Urm 8B 92
M43: Droy 7F 80
SK4: Stoc 3A 108
SK8: Gat 1G 116
SK11: Macc 6F 130
WA15: Hale 5E 114
WN5: Orr 3K 51
Cambridge St. M1: Man 8G 4 (2E 94)
(not continuous)
M7: Sal 6D 78
M15: Man 9H 5 (2F 94)
M46: Ath 9L 55
OL7: A Lyne 9K 81
OL9: O'ham 6F 62
SK2: Stoc 1E 118
SK15: Stal 8D 82
SK16: Duk 9N 81
WN1: Wig 9N 9 (4H 53)
Cambridge Ter. SK2: Stoc 1E 118
(off Russell St.)
SK15: Mill 6G 83
Cambridge Way
WN1: Wig 8M 9 (3G 53)
Camdale Wlk. M8: Man 4E 78
(off Felthorpe Dr.)
Camden Av. M40: Man 6A 80
Camden Cl. BL2: Ain 3C 40
Camden Ho. BL1: Bolt 3F 38
(off Kenton Cl.)
Camden St. OL5: Mos 8G 65
Camelford Cl. M15: Man 3F 94
Camelia Rd. M9: Man 3H 79
Camellia Cl. BL1: Bolt 5C 38
Camelot Cl. WA12: N Wil 5C 86
Cameron Ct. OL2: O'ham 6H 45
Cameron Ho. BL8: Bury 2J 41
M38: Lit H 6F 56
Cameron Pl. WN5: Wig 3B 52
Cameron St. BL1: Bolt 8E 22
BL8: Bury 2J 41
M1: Man 7F 4 (1E 94)
WN7: Lei 3F 72
Caminada Ho. M15: Man 3C 94
(off St Lawrence St.)
Camley Wlk. M8: Man 4G 78
(off Appleford Dr.)
Camm St. WN2: Abr 2L 71
Camomile Wlk. M31: Part 5G 103
(off Wychelm Rd.)
Campania St. OL2: O'ham 1J 63
Campanula Wlk. M8: Man 4F 78
(off Magnolia Dr.)
Campbell Cl. BL8: Bury 9E 24
SK10: Macc 3D 130
Campbell Ct. BL4: Farn 1K 57
Campbell Ho. BL4: Farn 2J 57
Campbell Rd. BL3: Bolt 1B 56
M13: Man 7L 95
M27: Swin 4E 76
M33: Sale 5F 104
Campbell St. BL4: Farn 1J 57
OL12: Roch 3C 28
SK5: Stoc 8D 96
WN5: Wig 6A 52
Campbell Wlk. BL4: Farn 1K 57
(off Campbell Ct.)
Campbell Way M28: Walk 8K 57
Campden Way SK9: Hand 2J 123
Campfield Av. M3: Man 7E 4
Campion Gro. WN4: A Mak 6C 70
Campion Way M34: Dent 9L 97
OL12: Roch 2A 28
Camponia Gdns. M7: Sal 5C 78
Camp Rd. WN4: Gars 7B 70
Camp St. BL8: Bury 1J 41
M3: Man 6E 4 (1D 94)
M7: Sal 6B 78
OL6: A Lyne 6D 6 (7M 81)
Camrose Gdns. BL1: Bolt 3F 38
(off Woking Ter.)
Camrose Wlk. M13: Man 4J 95
(off Winterford Av.)
Cams Acre Cl. M26: Rad 9E 40
Cams La. M26: Rad 1E 58
(not continuous)
Canaan WA3: Low 1E 88
WN7: Low 1E 88
Canada St. BL1: Bolt 2D 38
BL6: Hor 1D 36
M40: Man 6K 79
SK2: Stoc 1E 118
Canal Bank M30: Ecc 7C 76
WA13: Lym 4A 112
WN6: App B 5G 32
Canal Circ. M30: Ecc 9G 76
Canal Cotts. WN3: Wig 9H 9 (4E 52)
Canal Rd. WA14: Tim 9E 104
Canal Row WN2: Hai 4G 34
Canal Side BL3: Lit L 2A 58
M30: Ecc 7C 76
SK11: Macc 5K 131
Canalside M26: Rad 9F 40
SK15: Stal 9D 82
(off Melbourne St.)
Canalside Cl. OL5: Mos 7H 65
Canalside Ind. Est. OL16: Roch 8F 28
Canalside Nth. M17: T Pk 4L 93
Canal Side Wlk.
OL7: A Lyne 9C 6 (9M 81)
Canalside Warehouse OL15: Lit 3J 29
Canal St. M1: Man 6J 5 (1F 94)
M5: Sal 4A 4 (9B 78)
M43: Droy 1E 96
OL9: Chad 8F 62
OL10: H'ood 4K 43
OL11: Roch 8E 28
OL15: Lit 9M 15
PR7: Adl 7J 19
SK1: Stoc 3M 9 (7D 108)
SK6: Mar 1D 120
SK10: Macc 5J 131
SK14: Hyde 6N 97
SK15: Stal 9D 82
WA12: N Wil 6C 86
WN2: Asp 1L 53
WN2: I Mak 5J 53
WN6: Wig 2C 52
WN7: Lei 6H 73
Canal Ter. WN1: I Mak 4H 53
Canal Vw. SK15: Stal 8E 82
(off Bk. Knowl St.)
Canal Wharf SK4: Stoc 5C 108
Canary Way M27: Pen 3L 77
Canberra Rd. SK7: Bram 1C 124
WN5: Wig 3N 51
Canberra St. M11: Man 9A 80
Canberra Way OL11: Roch 1E 44
Candahar St. BL3: Bolt 9H 39
Candleberry Cl. WA14: W Tim 7B 104
Candleford Pl. SK2: Stoc 3J 119
Candleford Rd. M20: Man 2G 106
Candlestick Pk. BL9: Bury 9C 26
Candy La. SK10: Adl 6G 124
Canisp Cl. OL9: Chad 3D 62
Canley Cl. SK1: Stoc 8D 108
Canmore Cl. BL3: Bolt 9B 38
Cannel Ct. M28: Wors 3J 75
Canning Cl. WN2: Hin 7M 53
Canning Dr. BL1: Bolt 2F 38
Canning St. BL1: Bolt 2G 38
BL9: Bury 9M 25
SK4: Stoc 6C 108
Cannock Dr. SK4: Stoc 6M 107
Cannon Ct. M3: Man 3G 4
(off Cateaton St.)
Cannon Gro. BL3: Bolt 6E 38
Cannon St. BL0: Ram 1G 25
BL3: Bolt 6E 38
M3: Sal 2B 4 (8C 78)
M26: Rad 7F 40
M30: Ecc 8E 76
M46: Ath 8M 55
OL9: O'ham 2B 8
SK14: Holl 4M 99
Cannon St. Nth. BL3: Bolt 6E 38
Cannon Wlk. M34: Dent 7J 97
Cann St. BL8: Tot 5D 24
Canon Cl. WN6: Stan 2C 34
Canon Dr. WA14: Bow 6B 114
Canon Flynn Ct. OL16: Roch 6G 29
Canon Grn. Ct. M3: Sal 2D 4
Canon Grn. Dr. M3: Sal 1D 4 (7D 78)
Canon Hussey Ct. M3: Sal 4B 4
Canons Cl. BL1: Bolt 2C 38
Canons Gro. M40: Man 5K 79
Canonsleigh Cl. M8: Man 5D 78
Canon St. BL9: Bury 9N 25
OL16: Roch 3F 28
Canonsway M27: Swin 2E 76
Canon Tighe Ct. OL9: Chad 4E 62
Canon Wilson Cl. WA11: Hay 3A 86
Cansfield Ct. BL4: Kea 5A 58

Cansfield Gro. WN4: A Mak 6D 70
Canterbury Av. WA3: Low 9N 71
Canterbury Cl. M46: Ath 7N 55
OL11: Roch 6M 27
SK16: Duk 3A 98
Canterbury Cres. M24: Mid 1B 62
Canterbury Dr. BL8: Bury 9K 25
M25: Pres 9B 60
Canterbury Gdns. M5: Sal 8G 77
Canterbury Grange SK9: Wilm 7G 122
Canterbury Gro. BL3: Bolt 9E 38
Canterbury Pk. M20: Man 5E 106
Canterbury Rd. M41: Urm 6B 92
SK1: Stoc 7F 108
WA15: Hale 4J 115
Canterbury St.
OL6: A Lyne 5E 6 (6N 81)
Canterfield Cl. M43: Droy 8H 81
Cantley Wlk. M8: Man 4F 78
(off Dinnington Dr.)
Canton St. SK11: Macc 6H 131
Canton Walks SK11: Macc 6H 131
Cantrell St. M11: Man 9N 79
Canute Ct. M32: Stre 6L 93
Canute Pl. WA16: Knut 6G 132
Canute Rd. M32: Stre 6L 93
Canute Sq. WA16: Knut 6G 132
(off Canute Pl.)
Canute St. BL2: Bolt 3K 39
M26: Rad 9E 40
Cape Gdns. OL2: Shaw 6M 45
Capella Dr. M11: Man 1L 95
Capella Wlk. M7: Sal 6B 78
Capenhurst Cl. M23: Wyth 3M 115
SK12: Poy 2K 125
Capesthorne Cl. SK7: H Gro 7K 119
Capesthorne Dr. OL2: Shaw 5K 45
PR7: Chor 2E 18
Capesthorne Rd. SK6: H Lan 8B 120
SK7: H Gro 7K 119
SK9: Wilm 9D 122
SK16: Duk 3A 98
WA15: Tim 1K 115
Capesthorne Wlk. M34: Dent 7J 97
Capesthorne Way SK11: Macc 5K 131
Cape St. M20: Man 1H 107
Capital Ho. M50: Sal 2N 93
Capital Quay M50: Sal 2N 93
Capital Rd. M11: Man 2D 96
Capitol Cl. BL1: Bolt 1B 38
Cappadocia Way BL5: W'ton 4F 54
Capps St. WN2: P Bri 8L 53
Capricorn Rd. M9: Man 8N 61
Capricorn Way M6: Sal 6B 78
(off Gemini Rd.)
Capstan St. M9: Man 2K 79
Capstone Dr. SK6: Mar 1B 120
Captain Clarke Rd. SK14: Hyde 4M 97
CAPTAIN FOLD 1K 43
Captain Fold OL10: H'ood 1K 43
Captain Fold Rd. M38: Lit H 6F 56
Captain Lees Gdns. BL5: W'ton 3J 55
Captain Lees Rd. BL5: W'ton 2J 55
Captain's Clough Rd. BL1: Bolt 2B 38
Captain's La. WN4: A Mak 7F 70
Captain St. BL6: Hor 9D 20
Captain Wlk. M5: Sal 1A 94
(off Robert Hall St.)
Capton Cl. SK7: Bram 5E 118
Caradoc Av. M8: Man 4G 79
Carawood Cl. WN6: She 5H 33
Car Bank Av. M46: Ath 7M 55
Car Bank Cres. M46: Ath 7M 55
Car Bank Sq. M46: Ath 7M 55
Car Bank St. M46: Ath 7K 55
(not continuous)
Carberry Ct. SK8: Chea H 5M 117
Carberry Rd. M18: Man 4B 96
Cardale Wlk. M9: Man 3J 79
(off Conran St.)
Carden Av. M27: Swin 3D 76
M41: Urm 7M 91
Cardenbrook Gro. SK9: Wilm 4J 123
(off Rookerypool Cl.)
Carder Cl. M27: Swin 3F 76
Carders Cl. WN7: Lei 6G 73
Carders Ct. OL11: Roch 1N 43
Cardew Av. M22: Wyth 3E 116
Cardiff Cl. OL8: O'ham 9F 62
Cardiff St. M7: Sal 3D 78
Cardiff Wlk. M34: Dent 8K 97
Cardigan Cl. SK11: Macc 4E 130
Cardigan Dr. BL9: Bury 5L 41
Cardigan Rd. OL8: O'ham 9F 62
Cardigan St. M6: Sal 9L 77
M26: Rad 6F 40
OL2: O'ham 8J 45
OL12: Roch 2C 28
Cardigan Ter. M14: Man 5E 94
Cardinal M. M24: Mid 1J 61
Cardinal St. M8: Man 4G 78
OL1: O'ham 2F 8 (4L 63)
Cardinal Vaughan Ct.
OL11: Roch 9C 8 (7D 28)
Carding Gro. M3: Sal 1D 4 (7D 78)
Cardrona St. M18: Man 6B 96
Cardus St. M19: Man 8M 95
Cardwell Gdns. BL1: Bolt 2F 38
(off Canning Dr.)
Cardwell Rd. M30: Ecc 9A 76
Cardwell St. OL8: O'ham 8K 63
Careless La. WN2: I Mak 3J 53
(not continuous)
Caremine Av. M19: Man 7N 95
Carey Cl. M7: Sal 6C 78
WN3: Wins 9A 52
Carey Wlk. M15: Man 4E 94
(off Wellhead Cl.)
Carfax Fold OL12: Roch 3N 27
Carfax St. M18: Man 4B 96
Carfield WN8: Skel 5C 50
Cargate Wlk. M8: Man 4E 78
Carib St. M15: Man 4E 94
Carill Av. M9: Man 1L 79
M40: Man 1L 79
Carill Dr. M14: Man 9J 95
Carina Pl. M7: Sal 6B 78
Cariocca Bus. Pk. M12: Man 3J 95
M40: Man 7J 79
Carisbrook Av. M41: Urm 8C 92
M45: Whitef 5N 59
SK10: Macc 2J 131
Carisbrook Dr. M27: Swin 4G 77
Carisbrooke Av.
SK7: H Gro 6H 119
Carisbrooke Dr. BL1: Bolt 1G 39
Carisbrooke Rd. WN7: Lei 4M 73
Carisbrook St. M9: Man 3J 79
Carlburn St. M11: Man 8B 80
Carleton Rd. SK12: Poy 2N 125
Carley Fold BL3: Bolt 8A 38
Carley Gro. M9: Man 7H 61
Carlford Gro. M25: Pres 8M 59
Carlile St. SK3: Stoc 8C 108
Carlin Ga. WA15: Tim 1G 115
Carling Dr. M22: Wyth 5D 116
Carlingford Cl.
SK3: Stoc 2C 118
Carlisle Cl. BL3: Lit L 1A 58
M45: Whitef 4A 60
SK6: Rom 7L 109
SK11: Macc 7D 130
WA16: Mob 4N 133
Carlisle Cres. OL6: A Lyne 3N 81
Carlisle Dr. M44: Irl 7H 91
WA14: Tim 8E 104
Carlisle Pl. PR6: Adl 5K 19
Carlisle St. BL7: Bro X 5H 23
M27: Pen 9F 58
OL9: O'ham 6G 63
(Derby Ct.)
OL9: O'ham 7G 62
(Durham St.)
OL12: Roch 2D 28
SK9: A Edg 4F 126
WN2: Hin 5A 54
WN5: Wig 5A 52
Carlisle Way M34: Dent 8K 97
WN2: Asp 7N 35
Carloon Rd. M23: Wyth 7A 106
Carlow Dr. M22: Wyth 5D 116
Carl St. BL1: Bolt 2E 38
Carlton Av. BL3: Bolt 8B 38
M14: Man 6G 94
M16: Old T 5A 94
M25: Pres 9D 60
M45: Whitef 2K 59
OL4: O'ham 2A 64
SK6: Rom 5A 110
SK7: Bram 1B 124
SK8: Chea H 4L 117
SK9: Wilm 4H 123
WN8: Uph 4E 50
Carlton Cl. BL2: Bolt 1M 39
BL6: Bla 2N 35
M28: Wors 1K 75
WN4: A Mak 6D 70
Carlton Ct. M25: Pres 1N 77
WA15: Hale 6H 115
Carlton Cres. M41: Urm 8D 92
SK1: Stoc 1N 9 (6E 108)
Carlton Dr. M25: Pres 9D 60
SK8: Gat 1F 116
Carlton Flats OL10: H'ood 2H 43
(off St James St.)
Carlton Gdns. BL4: Farn 2L 57
Carlton Gro. BL6: Hor 3F 36
WN2: Hin 7B 54
Carlton Ho. M16: Whall R 6B 94
Carlton Mans. M16: Whall R 6C 94
Carlton Pl. BL4: Farn 2L 57
M45: Whitef 4J 59
SK7: H Gro 6L 119
Carlton Range M18: Man 5D 96
Carlton Rd. BL1: Bolt 4B 38
M6: Sal 6L 77
M16: Whall R 6C 94
M28: Wors 1K 75
M33: Sale 2G 104
M41: Urm 8C 92
OL6: A Lyne 5N 81
SK4: Stoc 6M 107
SK14: Hyde 6D 98
WA3: Low 9N 71
WA13: Lym 2C 112
(not continuous)
WA15: Hale 6H 115
Carlton Springs OL6: A Lyne 5D 6
Carlton St. BL2: Bolt 4M 7 (6H 39)
BL4: Farn 2L 57
BL9: Bury 4M 41
M16: Old T 5B 94
M30: Ecc 7D 76
WN3: Wig 5E 52
Carlton Way OL2: O'ham 1H 63
WA3: G'ook 3D 102
Carlyle Cl. M8: Man 4F 78
Carlyle Gro. WN7: Lei 2E 72
Carlyn Av. M33: Sale 4K 105
Carmel Av. M5: Sal 1B 94
Carmel Cl. M5: Sal 1B 94
Carmel Ct. M8: Man 9E 60
M9: Man 1K 79
Carmenna Dr. SK7: Bram 8D 118
Carmichael Cl. M31: Part 5F 102
Carmichael St. SK3: Stoc 8B 108
Carmine Fold M24: Mid 1L 61
Carmona Dr. M25: Pres 7N 59
Carmona Gdns. M7: Sal 1B 78
Carmoor Rd. M13: Man 4H 95
Carnaby St. M9: Man 1L 79
Carna Rd. SK5: Stoc 7C 96
Carnarvon St. M3: Man 7E 78
M7: Sal 3D 78
OL8: O'ham 9F 62
SK1: Stoc 4N 9 (8E 108)
Carnation Rd. BL4: Farn 2H 57
OL4: O'ham 7B 64
Carnegie Av. M19: Man 8N 95
Carnegie Cl. M33: Sale 5D 104
SK10: Macc 3D 130
Carnegie Dr. WN4: A Mak 5D 70
Carnforth Av. OL9: Chad 5E 62
OL11: Roch 5B 44
WN2: Hin 6C 54
Carnforth Dr. BL8: G'mount 3G 24
M33: Sale 5G 104
Carnforth Rd. SK4: Stoc 2A 108
SK8: Chea H 3A 118
Carnforth Sq. OL11: Roch 5B 44
Carnforth St. M14: Man 6G 94
Carnival Pl. M14: Man 7F 94
Carnoustie BL3: Bolt 9B 38
Carnoustie Cl. M40: Man 3A 80
SK9: Wilm 6J 123
Carnoustie Dr. BL0: Ram 9G 11
SK8: H Grn 6H 117
SK10: Macc 8G 129
Carnwood Cl. M40: Man 6B 80
Carolina Way M50: Sal 9L 77
Caroline St. BL3: Bolt 8E 38
M7: Sal 6D 78
M44: Irl 9G 90
OL6: A Lyne 6F 6 (7N 81)
SK3: Stoc 9B 108
(not continuous)
SK15: Stal 9D 82
WN1: I Mak 3J 53
WN3: Wig 9J 9 (4F 52)
Carpenters Ct. SK9: A Edg 4F 126
Carpenters La.
M4: Man 3J 5 (8F 78)
Carpenters Wlk. M43: Droy 9D 80
Carpenters Way OL16: Roch 9F 28
CARR
BL0 7H 11
OL3 7M 47
SK15 3J 83
Carradale Dr. M33: Sale 3C 104
Carradale Wlk. M40: Man 4M 79
(off Halliford Rd.)
Carradon Dr. WN6: Stan 3B 34
Carr Av. M25: Pres 9M 59
CARR BANK 5M 25
Carr Bank BL0: Ram 7H 11
SK13: Glos 9G 100
Carr Bank Av. BL0: Ram 7H 11
M9: Man 8E 60
Carr Bank Dr. BL0: Ram 7H 11
Carr Bank Rd. BL0: Ram 7H 11
CARRBROOK 4H 83
Carrbrook Cl. SK15: C'ook 4H 83
Carrbrook Cres. SK15: C'ook 4H 83
Carr Brook Dr. M46: Ath 7N 55
Carrbrook Dr. OL2: O'ham 2J 63
Carrbrook Rd. SK15: C'ook 3J 83
(not continuous)
Carrbrook Ter. M26: Rad 8J 41
Carr Brow SK6: H Lan 8D 120
Carr Cl. OL16: Roch 7G 29
SK1: Stoc 8F 108
Carr Comn. Rd. WN2: Hin 8F 54
Carr Farm Cl. SK13: Glos 9G 101
Carrfield SK14: Hyde 5A 98
Carrfield Av. M38: Lit H 7F 56
SK3: Stoc 3E 118
WA15: Tim 1K 115
Carrfield Cl. M38: Lit H 7F 56
Carrfield Gro. M38: Lit H 7F 56
Carr Fold BL0: Ram 7H 11
Carrgate Rd. M34: Dent 8M 97
CARR GREEN 1F 112
Carrgreen Cl. M19: Man 3L 107
Carrgreen La. WA13: Warb 1F 112
Carr Gro. OL16: Miln 7L 29
Carr Head OL3: Dig 6M 47
Carrhill Quarry Cl. OL5: Mos 9F 64
Carrhill Rd. OL5: Mos 9F 64
Carrhouse La. SK14: Gam, Holl 5M 99
(not continuous)
Carr Ho. Rd. OL4: Spri 4C 64
Carriage Dr. M40: Man 5J 79
OL15: Lit 7N 15
Carriage Dr., The SK13: Had 5B 100
Carriages, The
WA14: Alt 3A 6 (3C 114)
Carriage St. M16: Old T 4C 94
Carrick Cl. WN1: Wig 1F 52
Carrick Gdns. M22: Wyth 3C 116
M24: Mid 8L 43
Carrie St. BL1: Bolt 4C 38
Carrigart M25: Pres 8A 60
Carrill Gro. M19: Man 8M 95
Carrill Gro. E. M19: Man 8M 95
CARRINGTON 2M 103
Carrington Barn SK6: Mar 6C 120
Carrington Bus. Pk. M31: C'ton 2K 103
Carrington Cl. OL16: Roch 2H 29
Carrington Dr. BL3: Bolt 8G 38
Carrington Fld. St. SK1: Stoc 9D 108
Carrington Gro. WN7: Lei 3H 73
Carrington Ho. M6: Sal 6J 77
(off Moss Mdw. Rd.)
Carrington La. M31: C'ton 1N 103
M33: Sale 2C 104
Carrington Rd. M14: Man 9H 95
M41: Urm 9M 91
PR7: Adl 6J 19
(not continuous)
SK1: Stoc 5E 108
Carrington Spur M33: Sale 2C 104
M41: Urm 2C 104
Carrington St. M27: Pen 1H 77
OL9: Chad 8F 62
WN7: Lei 3H 73
Carrington Ter. M27: Pen 1H 77
(off Carrington St.)
Carr La. OL3: Dig 7M 47
OL3: G'fld 5L 65
OL16: Miln 7N 29
PR7: Chor 1F 18
SK9: A Edg 2C 126
SK15: C'ook 3J 83
WA3: Low 2C 88
WN3: Wig 8D 52
WN7: Lei 1G 88
Carr Lea OL4: Lyd 5F 64
Carr Mdw. OL16: Miln 9N 29
Carrmel Ct. OL3: Del 9J 47
(off Oldham Rd.)
CARR MILL 9G 68
Carr Mill Cres. WN5: Bil 6J 69
Carr Mill M. SK9: Wilm 5G 122
Carr Mill Rd. WA11: St H 9G 69
WN5: Bil 7H 69
Carrock Wlk. M24: Mid 2G 61
Carron Av. M9: Man 1L 79
Carron Gro. BL2: Bolt 5N 39
Carr Ri. SK15: C'ook 3J 83
Carr Rd. BL6: Hor 8D 20
M44: Irl 7J 91
WA15: Hale 5H 115
Carrs Av. SK8: Chea 1M 117
Carrs Ct. SK9: Wilm 7G 122
Carrsdale Dr. M9: Man 9H 61
Carrsfield Rd. M22: Shar 1D 116
Carrslea Cl. M26: Rad 7E 40
Carrs Rd. HD7: Mars 1H 49
SK8: Chea 1L 117
Carrs Side St. No. 2 HD7: Mars 1J 49
Carrs St. HD7: Mars 1J 49
Carr St. BL0: Ram 7H 11
M27: Swin 3D 76
OL6: A Lyne 5A 82
WN2: Hin 5N 53
WN7: Lei 5E 72
Carrsvale Av. M41: Urm 6B 92
Carrswood Rd. M23: Wyth 8J 105
Carruthers Cl. OL10: H'ood 1L 43
Carruthers St. M4: Man 8J 79
Carr Vw. SK22: N Mil 9N 121
CARR WOOD 6J 27
Carrwood WA15: Haleb 8H 115
WA16: Knut 8J 133
Carr Wood Av. SK7: Bram 7C 118
Carrwood Hey BL0: Ram 1G 24
Carrwood Rd. SK7: Bram 6B 118
SK9: Wilm 5E 122
Carsdale Rd. M22: Wyth 7D 116
Carslake Av. BL1: Bolt 4D 38
Carslake Rd. M40: Man 5J 79
Carson Rd. M19: Man 9M 95
Carstairs Av. SK2: Stoc 3E 118
Carstairs Cl. M8: Man 8E 60
Car St. OL1: O'ham 2G 8 (4L 63)
WN2: P Bri 1K 71
Carswell Cl. M29: Tyld 1D 74
Carter Cl. M34: Dent 7K 97
Carter La. SK11: Chel 9A 126
Carter Pl. SK14: Hyde 4A 98
Carter St. BL3: Bolt 8H 39
BL4: Kea 4M 57
M7: Sal 5C 78
OL5: Mos 2F 82
SK14: Hyde 4A 98
SK15: Stal 8E 82
WN3: I Mak 5H 53
Carthage St. OL8: O'ham 7K 63
Carthorpe Arch M5: Sal 9M 77
Cartleach Gro. M28: Walk 9H 57
Cartleach La. M28: Walk 9G 57
Cartmel OL12: Roch 5C 8
Cartmel Av. OL16: Miln 9K 29
SK4: Stoc 2B 108
WN1: Wig 9E 34
Cartmel Cl. BL3: Bolt 1M 55
BL9: Bury 9N 41
OL7: A Lyne 6K 81
OL8: O'ham 8H 63
SK7: H Gro 4G 119
SK8: Gat 4H 117
SK10: Macc 2F 130
Cartmel Cres. BL2: Bolt 2K 39
OL9: Chad 9D 62
Cartmel Dr. WA15: Tim 1K 115
Cartmel Gro. M28: Wors 3B 76
Cartmell Ct. M9: Man 7M 61
Cartmel Wlk. M9: Man 3J 79
(off Shiredale Dr., not continuous)
M24: Mid 1K 61
Cartridge Cl. M22: Wyth 4E 116
Cartridge St. OL10: H'ood 2H 43
Cartwright Gro. WN7: Lei 1F 72
Cartwright Rd. M21: Cho H 9M 93
Cartwright St. M34: Aud 3K 97
SK14: Hyde 4D 98
Carver Av. M25: Pres 6B 60
Carver Cl. M16: Old T 4A 94
Carver Dr. SK6: Mar 2B 120
Carver Rd. SK6: Mar 2B 120
WA15: Hale 5E 114
Carver St. M16: Old T 4A 94
Carver Theatre 2C 120
Carver Wlk. M15: Man 4E 94
(off Wellhead Cl.)
Carville Gro. WN2: Hin 7D 54
Carville Rd. M9: Man 8N 61
Carwood Gro. BL6: Hor 3F 36
Casablanca Health and Fitness Cen.
9D 82
(off Armentieres Sq.)
Cascade Dr. M7: Sal 5D 78
Case Rd. WA11: Hay 3A 86
Cashel Ct. M27: Ward 1C 76
Cashgate Ct. OL8: O'ham 8H 63
Cashmere Rd. SK3: Stoc 9A 108
Cashmoor Wlk. M12: Man 3K 95
(off Langport Av.)
Cashmore Dr. WN2: Hin 7N 53
Caspian Rd. M9: Man 8N 61
WA14: B'ath 1A 114
Cassandra Ct. M5: Sal 7A 4 (1B 94)
Cass Av. M5: Sal 1N 93
Cassidy Cl. M4: Man 2L 5 (8G 79)
Cassidy Ct. M50: Sal 1L 93
Cassidy Gdns. M24: Mid 8J 43
Casson Ga. OL12: Roch 4C 28
Casson St. M35: Fail 3D 80
Casterton Way M28: Wors 5H 75
Castle Av. M34: Dent 7J 97
OL11: Roch 9A 8 (7C 28)
Castlebrook Cl. BL9: Bury 8A 42
Castle Cl. M43: Droy 8F 80
Castle Cotts. SK15: C'ook 2J 83
Castle Ct. BL2: Bolt 2N 7
OL6: A Lyne 3M 81
Castle Courts M5: Sal 9A 78
Castle Cres. BL6: Hor 8E 20
Castle Cft. BL2: Bolt 1L 39
(not continuous)
Castlecroft Av. BL6: Bla 2N 35
Castlecroft Ct. BL9: Bury 7J 7
Castlecroft M. BL9: Bury 7J 7 (2L 41)
Castlecroft Rd. BL9: Bury 7J 7 (2L 41)
Castledene Av. M6: Sal 7L 77
Castle Dr. PR7: Adl 7H 19
Castle Edge Rd. SK22: N Mil 5K 121
Castle Farm Dr. SK2: Stoc 2F 118
Castle Farm La. SK2: Stoc 1F 118
CASTLEFIELD 7D 4 (1D 94)
Castlefield Av. M7: Sal 2D 78
Castlefield Gallery 8E 4
Castleford Cl. BL1: Bolt 4E 38
(off Gaskell St.)
Castleford Dr. SK10: P'bury 7B 128
Castleford St. OL1: Chad 2G 63
Castleford Wlk. M21: Cho H 1C 106
(off Arrowfield Rd.)
Castlegate M15: Man 8D 4 (2D 94)
SK10: P'bury 7C 128
Castlegate M. SK10: P'bury 7D 128
Castle Gro. BL0: Ram 3G 24
WN7: Lei 4M 73
CASTLE HALL 9E 82
Castle Hall Cl. SK15: Stal 9E 82
Castle Hall Ct. SK15: Stal 9D 82
Castle Hall Vw. SK15: Stal 9D 82
Castle Hawk Golf Course 3M 43
Castlehey WN8: Skel 5C 50
Castle Hey Cl. BL9: Bury 9B 42
CASTLE HILL
BL2 1K 39
SK6 1J 109
WA14 7N 113
Castle Hill SK6: Bred 1J 109
SK10: P'bury 6C 128
SK13: Glos 6G 100
WA12: N Wil 5H 87
Castle Hill Ct. SK10: P'bury 6C 128
Castle Hill Cres.
OL11: Roch 9A 8 (7C 28)
Castle Hill Dr. M9: Man 9H 61
(off Marshbrook Dr.)
Castlehill Ind. Pk. SK6: Bred 3K 109
Castle Hill Pk. SK6: Wood 2K 109
WN2: Hin 4B 54
Castle Hill Rd. BL9: Bury 5B 26
(not continuous)
M25: Pres 9C 60
WN2: Hin 5A 54
Castle Hill St. BL2: Bolt 2J 39
Castle Ho. La. PR7: Adl 7H 19
Castle Irwell Student Village
M6: Sal 5A 78
Castle La. OL5: Mos, Stal 2H 83
SK15: C'ook, Mos 2H 83
Castle Leisure Cen. 7J 7 (2L 41)
Castlemere Cl. WN3: Wins 1A 70
Castlemere Dr. OL2: Shaw 4A 46
Castlemere Rd. M9: Man 8H 61
Castlemere St.
OL11: Roch 9B 8 (7C 28)
Castlemere Ter.
OL11: Roch 9B 8 (7D 28)
Castle M. BL4: Farn 4L 57
(off Castle St.)
Castle Mill La. WA15: Ash 9F 114
Castlemill St. OL1: O'ham 4M 63
Castlemoor Av. M7: Sal 2A 78
Castle Pk. Ind. Est. OL1: O'ham 4M 63
Castle Quay M15: Man 8D 4 (2D 94)
Castlerea Cl. M30: Ecc 1D 92
Castlerigg Cl. SK4: Stoc 1B 108
Castlerigg Dr. M24: Mid 9H 43
OL2: O'ham 6G 44
Castle Ri. SK10: P'bury 7D 128
WN2: Hin 6A 54
(not continuous)
Castle Rd. BL9: Bury 9B 42
CASTLESHAW 4L 47
Castleshaw Cen. 5K 47
Castle Shaw Rd. SK2: Stoc 2H 119
Castleshaw Top Bank OL3: Del 3K 47
Castle St. BL2: Bolt 3N 7 (5H 39)
BL4: Farn 4L 57
BL9: Bury 7K 7 (2L 41)
BL9: Sum 3K 25
M3: Man 7D 4 (1D 94)
M24: Mid 4B 62
M29: Tyld 1A 74
M30: Ecc 8F 76
SK3: Stoc 9B 108
SK11: Macc 4H 131
SK13: Had 5C 100
SK14: Hyde 6C 98
SK15: Stal 9D 82
WN2: Hin 5A 54
Castle St. Mall SK11: Macc 4H 131
(off Grosvenor Cen.)
Castle Ter. SK15: C'ook 3J 83
CASTLETON 3A 44
Castleton Av. M32: Stre 5H 93
Castleton Bank SK13: Gam 8A 100
(off Castleton Cres.)
Castleton Ct. M29: Tyld 1A 74
(off Elliott St.)
M34: Dent 9L 97
Castleton Cres. SK13: Gam 8A 100
Castleton Dr. SK6: H Lan 9C 120
Castleton Grn. SK13: Gam 8A 100
(off Castleton Cres.)
Castleton Gro. OL6: A Lyne 4C 82
SK13: Gam 8A 100
(off Castleton Cres.)
Castleton Rd. M7: Sal 1D 78
OL2: O'ham 4G 45
SK7: H Gro 6J 119
Castleton Rd. Sth.
OL11: Roch 1B 44
Castleton Station (Rail) 2A 44

Castleton St. BL2: Bolt ... 2J 39
OL9: O'ham ... 5G 62
WA14: B'ath ... 9C 104
Castleton Swimming Pool ... 1A 44
Castleton Ter. SK13: Gam ... 8A 100
Castleton Wlk. *M11: Man* ... *9L 79*
(off Burns Cl.)
Castleton Water Activity Cen. ... *2A 44*
(off Maltings La.)
Castleton Way M34: Dent ... 9L 97
WN3: Wins ... 9N 51
Castletown Cl. SK10: Macc ... 9G 128
Castle Wlk. OL6: A Lyne ... 3M 81
SK15: Stal ... *9D 82*
(off Crossfield Cl.)
Castle Way M27: Clif ... 9G 59
Castleway M6: Sal ... 6L 77
OL11: Roch ... 3N 43
WA15: Haleb ... 8J 115
WN2: Hin ... 6B 54
Castlewood Gdns. SK2: Stoc ... 2G 118
Castlewood Rd. M7: Sal ... 2N 77
Castlewood Sq. BL2: Bolt ... 3K 39
Castle Yd. SK1: Stoc ... 1L 9
Catalan Sq. M3: Man ... 7D 4
Catchdale Cl. M9: Man ... 6H 61
Catches Cl. OL11: Roch ... 5N 27
Catches La. OL11: Roch ... 4N 27
Cateaton St. BL9: Bury ... 1M 41
M3: Man ... 3G 4 (8E 78)
Caterham Av. BL3: Bolt ... 1A 56
Caterham St. M4: Man ... 9J 79
Catesby Rd. M16: Whall R ... 6C 94
Catfield Wlk. M15: Man ... 9C 4
Catford Rd. M23: Wyth ... 2M 115
Cathedral App. M3: Sal ... 2G 4 (8E 78)
Cathedral Cl. SK16: Duk ... 3A 98
Cathedral Gates M3: Man ... 3G 5
Cathedral Rd. OL9: Chad ... 2D 62
Cathedral St. M4: Man ... 3G 5 (8E 78)
Cathedral Yd. M3: Man ... 3G 4
Catherine Ho. SK4: Stoc ... 6L 107
Catherine Rd. M8: Man ... 1D 78
M27: Swin ... 3C 76
SK6: Rom ... 7K 109
WA14: Bow ... 4C 114
Catherine St. BL3: Bolt ... 1C 56
BL9: Bury ... 6L 41
M11: Man ... 2C 96
M30: Ecc ... 7A 76
OL4: Lees ... 5B 64
SK7: H Gro ... 3J 119
SK11: Macc ... 4G 131
SK14: Hyde ... 6A 98
WN1: Wig ... 8N 9 (3H 53)
WN7: Lei ... 4H 73
Catherine St. E. BL6: Hor ... 9D 20
M34: Dent ... 6H 97
Catherine St. W. BL6: Hor ... 8D 20
M34: Dent ... 6H 97
Catherine Ter.
WN1: Wig ... 8N 9 (3H 53)
Catherine Way WA12: N Wil ... 7E 86
Catherston Rd. M16: Whall R ... 6D 94
CATLEY LANE HEAD ... 1M 27
Catlow La. M4: Man ... 3J 5
Catlow St. M7: Sal ... 6D 78
Caton Cl. BL9: Bury ... 4L 41
Caton Dr. M46: Ath ... 2J 73
Caton St. OL16: Roch ... 9D 8 (7D 28)
Cato St. BL0: Ram ... 1G 24
Catskowl Cl. M18: Man ... 6B 96
Catterall Cres. BL2: Bolt ... 7L 23
Catterick Av. M20: Man ... 5H 107
M33: Sale ... 6C 104
Catterick Dr. BL3: Lit L ... 9A 40
Catterick Rd. M20: Man ... 5H 107
Catterwood Dr. SK6: Comp ... 6E 110
Catterwood Rd. SK6: Comp ... 6E 110
Cattlin Way OL8: O'ham ... 9G 62
Cauldale Cl. M24: Mid ... 9J 43
Caunce Av. WA3: Gol ... 2K 87
WA12: N Wil ... 8F 86
Caunce Rd. WN1: Wig ... 7N 9 (3H 53)
Caunce St.
WN1: Wig ... 8N 9 (3H 53)
Causeway, The OL9: Chad ... 6B 62
WA14: Alt ... 3D 6 (3D 114)
Causewood Cl. OL4: O'ham ... 8B 46
Causey Dr. M24: Mid ... 9J 43
Cavalier St. M40: Man ... 8J 79
Cavanagh Cl. M13: Man ... 3J 95
Cavan Cl. SK3: Stoc ... 9L 107
Cavan Dr. WA11: Hay ... 2A 86
Cavannah Ct. *OL1: O'ham* ... *9B 46*
(off Northgate La.)
Cavell St. M1: Man ... 4K 5
Cavell Way M5: Sal ... 9N 77
M6: Sal ... 8N 77
Cavendish Av. M20: Man ... 2E 106
M27: Clif ... 8J 59
Cavendish Cl. SK10: Macc ... 1G 131
Cavendish Ct. M7: Sal ... 1C 78
M9: Man ... *6F 60*
(off Deanswood Dr.)
M32: Stre ... *5L 93*
(off Nansen Cl.)
M41: Urm ... *7E 92*
(off Cavendish Rd.)
SK4: Stoc ... 6L 107
WN3: I Mak ... 6H 53
Cavendish Dr. WN3: Wins ... 9A 52
Cavendish Gdns. BL3: Bolt ... 9D 38
Cavendish Gro. M30: Ecc ... 7E 76
Cavendish Hall M15: Man ... 9H 5
Cavendish Ho. M30: Ecc ... 7E 76
(not continuous)
OL6: A Lyne ... *9C 6*
(off Cavendish St.)
Cavendish Ind. Est. OL6: A Lyne ... 7B 6
Cavendish M. SK9: Wilm ... 9F 122
Cavendish Mill
OL6: A Lyne ... 9C 6 (8M 81)
Cavendish Pl. M11: Man ... 8M 79
M27: Pen ... *2G 77*
(off Bridge St.)
Cavendish Rd. M7: Sal ... 1B 78
M20: Man ... 2E 106
M28: Wors ... 4B 76
M30: Ecc ... 7E 76
M32: Stre ... 5L 93
M41: Urm ... 7E 92
OL11: Roch ... 1C 44
SK4: Stoc ... 6L 107
SK7: H Gro ... 6H 119
WA14: Bow ... 4C 114
Cavendish St. M15: Man ... 9H 5 (3F 94)
OL6: A Lyne ... 7B 6 (7L 81)
OL8: O'ham ... 4C 8 (5J 63)
WN7: Lei ... 3H 73
Cavendish Ter. *M21: Cho H* ... *9A 94*
(off Wilbraham Rd.)
Cavendish Way OL2: O'ham ... 1G 62
Cavenham Gro. BL1: Bolt ... 4D 38
Cavenham Wlk. *M9: Man* ... *3H 79*
(off Mannington Dr.)
Caversham Dr. M9: Man ... 2K 79
Cawdor Av. BL4: Farn ... 1J 57
Cawdor Ct. BL4: Farn ... 1K 57
Cawdor Ho. *M30: Ecc* ... *1D 92*
(off Enfield Cl.)
Cawdor Pl. WA15: Tim ... 1J 115
Cawdor Rd. M14: Man ... 8H 95
Cawdor St. BL4: Farn ... 1J 57
M15: Man ... 9B 4 (2C 94)
M27: Swin ... 2D 76
M28: Walk ... 9M 57
M30: Ecc ... 9C 76
WN2: Hin ... 6A 54
WN5: Wig ... 5C 52
WN7: Lei ... 6H 73
Cawdor Wlk. *BL4: Farn* ... *1K 57*
(off Cawdor St.)
Cawley Av. M25: Pres ... 9M 59
WA3: Cul ... 5G 88
Cawley La. SK10: Adl ... 6J 125
Cawley Ter. M9: Man ... 6F 60
Cawood Ho. SK5: Stoc ... 2G 108
Cawood Sq. SK5: Stoc ... 1G 108
Cawston Wlk. *M8: Man* ... *4F 78*
(off Cranlington Dr.)
Cawthorne Ct. M27: Ward ... 1D 76
Caxton Cl. WN3: Wig ... 9C 52
Caxton Ho. WN1: Wig ... 8H 9
Caxton Rd. M14: Man ... 8G 95
Caxton St. M3: Sal ... 3E 4 (8D 78)
OL10: H'ood ... 2J 43
OL11: Roch ... 2A 44
Caygill St. M3: Sal ... 2E 4 (8D 78)
Cayley St. OL16: Roch ... 6F 28
Caythorpe St. M14: Man ... 6F 94
Cayton St. M12: Man ... 6M 95
C Court WN4: A Mak ... 8E 70
Ceal, The SK6: Comp ... 6E 110
Cecil Av. M33: Sale ... 5E 104
WN6: Wig ... 1D 52
Cecil Ct. SK3: Stoc ... 8N 107
WA15: Hale ... 5E 114
Cecil Dr. M41: Urm ... 7M 91
Cecil Gro. M18: Man ... 4B 96
Cecilia Ct. Nth. *BL3: Bolt* ... *8H 39*
(off Cecilia St.)
Cecilia Ct. Sth. *BL3: Bolt* ... *8H 39*
(off Cecilia St.)
Cecilia St. BL3: Bolt ... 8H 39
Cecil Rd. M9: Man ... 6J 61
M30: Ecc ... 9E 76
M32: Stre ... 8J 93
WA15: Hale ... 5E 114
Cecil St. BL2: Bolt ... 3N 7 (5J 39)
BL9: Bury ... 9L 7 (3M 41)
M15: Man ... 4G 94
M28: Walk ... 8L 57
OL2: O'ham ... 8G 45
OL5: Mos ... 2F 82
OL7: A Lyne ... 9L 81
OL8: O'ham ... 6J 63
OL11: Roch ... 8D 28
OL15: Lit ... 9K 15
SK3: Stoc ... *9C 108*
(off James St.)
SK15: Stal ... 9E 82
SK16: Duk ... 1M 97
WN1: Wig ... 3H 53
WN3: I Mak ... 7H 53
WN7: Lei ... 6J 73
Cecil Wlk. *OL7: A Lyne* ... *9L 81*
(off Cecil St.)
Cedar Av. BL3: Lit L ... 1B 58
BL6: Hor ... 3G 36
M45: Whitef ... 5M 59
M46: Ath ... 7K 55
OL6: A Lyne ... 5A 82
OL10: H'ood ... 1H 43
SK7: H Gro ... 5J 119
SK15: Stal ... 7F 82
WA3: Low ... 2B 88
WA14: Alt ... 4B 6 (3C 114)
WN2: Hin ... 8B 54
WN6: Stan ... 4C 34
Cedar Bank Cl. OL16: Roch ... 6H 29
Cedar Cl. SK12: Poy ... 3J 125
SK13: Glos ... 7D 100
Cedar Ct. M14: Man ... 8H 95
M25: Pres ... *6N 59*
(off Longfield Cen.)
SK8: Chea H ... *5M 117*
(off Vaudrey Dr.)
WA3: Ris ... 7H 89
WA15: Tim ... *2H 115*
(off Edenhurst Dr.)
Cedar Cres. BL0: Ram ... 7J 11
OL9: Chad ... 3F 62
Cedar Dr. M27: Clif ... 7D 58
M41: Urm ... 8C 92
M43: Droy ... 8G 80
WN1: Wig ... 1G 53
Cedarfield Rd. WA13: Lym ... 2C 112
Cedar Gro. BL4: Farn ... 3J 57
BL5: W'ton ... 4G 55
M14: Man ... 9J 95
M25: Pres ... 5N 59
Cedar Gro. M34: Dent ... 6J 97
OL2: O'ham ... 6H 45
OL2: Shaw ... 6M 45
SK4: Stoc ... 3A 108
SK11: Macc ... 7H 131
SK16: Duk ... 1C 98
WA11: Hay ... 2B 86
WN4: Gars ... 5A 70
WN5: Orr ... 5K 51
Cedar Ho., The *SK15: Mill* ... *6G 83*
(off Bramble Ct.)
Cedar La. OL4: Gras ... 5G 64
OL16: Miln ... 1L 45
Cedar Lawn *SK8: Chea H* ... *5M 117*
(off Vaudrey Dr.)
Cedar Lodge SK7: Bram ... 8D 118
Cedar M. OL7: A Lyne ... 5M 81
Cedar Pl. M7: Sal ... 6B 78
Cedar Rd. M24: Mid ... 3A 62
M31: Part ... 5F 102
M33: Sale ... 2D 104
M35: Fail ... 4D 80
SK2: Stoc ... 3F 118
SK6: Mar ... 3B 120
SK8: Gat ... 2F 116
WA15: Hale ... 4E 114
WN7: Lei ... 2G 73
Cedars, The BL1: Bolt ... 7G 23
PR7: Chor ... 1E 18
Cedars Rd. M22: Wyth ... 4C 116
Cedar St. BL9: Bury ... 1N 41
(not continuous)
OL4: O'ham ... 4N 63
OL6: A Lyne ... 6A 82
OL12: Roch ... 4D 28
SK14: Hyde ... 4B 98
WA12: N Wil ... 7F 86
Cedar Technology Cen.
WA14: B'ath ... 9B 104
Cedar Vw. *OL6: A Lyne* ... *6A 82*
(off Cedar St.)
Cedarway SK9: Wilm ... 1E 126
SK10: Boll ... 6L 129
Cedarwood SK12: Poy ... 2J 125
Cedarwood Av. SK4: Stoc ... 7M 107
Cedarwood Cl. M22: Nor ... 8D 106
M29: Ast ... 3B 74
Cedar Wood Ct. BL1: Bolt ... 5B 38
Cedric Rd. M8: Man ... 9D 60
OL4: O'ham ... 4N 63
Cedric St. M5: Sal ... 8L 77
Celandine Cl. OL15: Lit ... 8K 15
Celandine Wlk. WN3: Wig ... 7M 51
Celia St. M8: Man ... 2H 79
Cellini Sq. BL1: Bolt ... 3E 38
Celtic St. SK1: Stoc ... 8E 108
Cemetery La. BL9: Bury ... 4N 41
Cemetery Rd. BL0: Ram ... 1G 25
BL2: Bolt ... 5J 39
BL4: Farn, Kea ... 2N 57
M5: Sal ... 9L 77
M26: Rad ... 8F 40
(not continuous)
M34: Aud ... 3K 97
M34: Dent ... 8K 97
M35: Fail ... 4D 80
M43: Droy ... 9D 80
OL2: O'ham ... 7G 45
OL5: Mos ... 3G 83
SK13: Glos ... 5E 100
WN3: I Mak ... 7H 53
Cemetery Rd. Nth. M27: Swin ... 9E 58
Cemetery Rd. Sth. M27: Swin ... 1E 76
Cemetery Road Stop (Metro) ... 9D 80
Cemetery St. BL5: W'ton ... 2G 54
M24: Mid ... 2M 61
Cemetery Vw. PR7: Adl ... 7J 19
Cenacle Ho. *M16: Whall R* ... *7D 94*
(off Alexandra Rd. Sth.)
Cennick Cl. OL4: O'ham ... 5A 64
Centaur Cl. M27: Clif ... 9F 58
Centaur Way *M8: Man* ... *3E 78*
(off Narbuth Dr.)
Centenary Circ. M50: Ecc ... 9G 77
Centenary Ct. BL3: Bolt ... 8G 39
Centenary Way M17: T Pk ... 9H 77
M50: Ecc ... 9G 77
Central Art Gallery ... 8C 6
Central Av. BL0: Ram ... 4K 11
BL4: Farn ... 3H 57
BL9: Bury ... 5K 41
M6: Sal ... 4L 77
M19: Man ... 7M 95
M27: Clif ... 9K 59
M28: Walk ... 6K 57
M33: Sale ... 7D 104
M46: Ath ... 7N 55
OL3: G'fld ... 6L 65
OL15: Lit ... 8M 15
WN7: Lei ... 7L 73
Central Ct. Apartments
M3: Sal ... 3C 4
Central Dr. BL5: W'ton ... 2G 55
BL9: Bury ... 5M 25
M8: Man ... 1G 79
M27: Swin ... 3H 77
M41: Urm ... 7D 92
SK5: Stoc ... 3D 108
SK6: Rom ... 5N 109
SK7: Bram ... 5B 118
SK8: H Grn ... 7J 117
WN6: She ... 6M 33
Central Ho. M9: Man ... 6K 61
Central Leisure Cen. ... 7E 8 (6E 28)
Central Pk. Est. M17: T Pk ... 3H 93
Central Park Stop (Metro) ... 4L 79
Central Pk. Way
WN1: Wig ... 7L 9 (2G 52)
Central Pl. *SK9: Wilm* ... *7G 123*
(off Station Rd.)
Central Retail Pk.
BL2: Bolt ... 5L 7 (6G 39)
M4: Man ... 4M 5 (9H 79)
Central Rd. M20: Man ... 3F 106
M23: Wyth ... 3M 115
M31: Part ... 5G 103
Central St. BL0: Ram ... 8H 11
BL1: Bolt ... 2J 7 (5F 38)
BL9: Bury ... 7L 7 (2M 41)
M2: Man ... 5G 4 (9E 78)
Central Way WA12: N Wil ... 7H 87
WA14: Alt ... 3C 6 (3D 114)
Centre, The WN7: Lei ... 4N 73
Centre Ct. WN7: Lei ... 9D 72
Centre Gdns. BL1: Bolt ... 3E 38
Centre Pk. Rd. BL1: Bolt ... 3E 38
Centrepoint M17: T Pk ... 4G 93
Centre Retail Pk., The
OL2: O'ham ... 1F 62
Centre Va. OL15: Lit ... 7N 15
Centre Va. Cl. OL15: Lit ... 7N 15
Centurion Gro. M7: Sal ... 4D 78
Century Gdns.
OL12: Roch ... 5C 8 (5D 28)
Century Lodge BL4: Farn ... 3K 57
Century Mill Ind. Est. BL4: Farn ... 3J 57
Century Pk. Ind. Est.
WA14: B'ath ... 1A 114
Century St. M3: Man ... 7E 4 (1D 94)
Century Way SK10: Macc ... 2K 131
Ceres Ct. *BL4: Farn* ... *4M 57*
(off Corn Mill Dr.)
Cestrian St. BL3: Bolt ... 9G 39
Ceylon St. M40: Man ... 4M 79
OL4: O'ham ... 6A 64
Chadbury Cl. BL6: Los ... 9L 37
CHADDERTON ... 4F 62
Chadderton Dr. BL9: Bury ... 1N 59
CHADDERTON FOLD ... 1D 62
Chadderton Fold OL1: Chad ... 1D 62
(not continuous)
Chadderton Hall Rd. OL1: Chad ... 2C 62
OL9: Chad ... 2C 62
Chadderton Hgts. OL1: Chad ... 9D 44
Chadderton Ind. Est. M24: Mid ... 6A 62
CHADDERTON PARK ... 2D 62
Chadderton Pk. Rd. OL9: Chad ... 2D 62
Chadderton Pct. OL9: Chad ... 4F 62
Chadderton St. M4: Man ... 2K 5 (8G 78)
Chadderton Way OL1: O'ham ... 1G 62
OL9: O'ham ... 1A 8 (3H 63)
Chadderton Wellbeing Cen. ... 3F 62
Chaddock La. M28: Wors ... 4G 74
M29: Ast ... 4E 74
Chaddock Level, The M28: Wors ... 5H 75
CHADKIRK ... 8M 109
Chadkirk Chapel ... 7N 109
Chadkirk Country Estate ... 7M 109
Chadkirk Ind. Est. SK6: Rom ... 8M 109
Chadkirk M. SK6: Rom ... 6N 109
Chadkirk Rd. SK6: Rom ... 7M 109
Chads Theatre ... 6N 117
Chadvil Rd. SK8: Chea ... 2H 117
Chadwell Rd. SK2: Stoc ... 9J 109
Chadwick Av. WA3: Cro ... 9D 88
Chadwick Cl. *M14: Man* ... *6G 95*
(off Union Pl.)
OL16: Miln ... 8L 29
SK9: Wilm ... 5H 123
Chadwick Fold BL9: Bury ... 6M 25
OL10: H'ood ... 2L 43
CHADWICK GREEN ... 7H 69
Chadwick Hall Rd. OL11: Roch ... 7N 27
Chadwick La. OL10: H'ood ... 2L 43
OL11: Roch ... 2N 43
OL16: Roch ... 2G 45
Chadwick Rd. M30: Ecc ... 8E 76
M41: Urm ... 7F 92
Chadwicks Cl. SK15: Stal ... 7C 82
Chadwick St. BL2: Bolt ... 4N 7 (6H 39)
BL3: Lit L ... 9B 40
BL9: Bury ... 9D 26
M27: Swin ... 2F 76
OL6: A Lyne ... 8B 82
OL11: Roch ... 6B 28
OL16: Roch ... 6J 29
SK1: Stoc ... 8D 108
SK6: Mar ... 2C 120
SK13: Glos ... 9D 100
WN2: Hin ... 5A 54
WN3: Wig ... 5E 52
WN7: Lei ... 4H 73
Chadwick Ter. OL12: Roch ... 1B 28
SK10: Macc ... 3J 131
Chadwick Wlk. *M27: Swin* ... *2F 76*
(off Chadwick St.)
Chaffinch Cl. M22: Shar ... 2E 116
M43: Droy ... 7G 81
OL4: O'ham ... 7A 64
Chaffinch Dr. BL9: Bury ... 9B 26
CHAIN BAR ... 8A 62
Chain Bar La. SK14: Mot ... 7J 99
Chain Bar Way SK14: Mot ... 7J 99
Chainhurst Wlk. *M13: Man* ... *3H 95*
(off Weald Cl.)
Chain Rd. M9: Man ... 5J 61
Chain St. M1: Man ... 5H 5 (9F 78)
Chain Wlk. M9: Man ... 6K 61
Chaise Mdw. WA13: Lym ... 2C 112
Chalbury Cl. WN2: Hin ... 7N 53
Chalcombe Grange M12: Man ... 5L 95
Chale Cl. M40: Man ... 7J 79
Chale Dr. M24: Mid ... 5A 62
Chale Grn. BL2: Bolt ... 1M 39
Chalfont Av. *M41: Urm* ... *7E 92*
(off Gladstone Rd.)
Chalfont Cl. OL8: O'ham ... 7M 63
Chalfont Ct. WA16: Knut ... 5J 133
Chalfont Dr. M8: Man ... 3F 78
M28: Walk ... 2M 75
M29: Ast ... 2B 74
Chalfont Ho. *M5: Sal* ... *8M 77*
(off Amersham St.)
Chalfont St. BL1: Bolt ... 2G 38
(not continuous)
Chalford Rd. M23: Wyth ... 3N 115
Challenge Way WN5: Wig ... 1N 51
Challenor Sq. *M12: Man* ... *3M 95*
(off Polesworth Cl.)
Challinor St. BL1: Bolt ... 4C 38
Challum Dr. OL9: Chad ... 3E 62
Chamber Hall Cl. OL8: O'ham ... 7H 63
Chamberhall St.
BL9: Bury ... 5K 7 (1L 41)
Chamber Ho. Dr. OL11: Roch ... 1N 43
Chamberlain Dr. SK9: Wilm ... 5J 123
Chamberlain Gdns. SK6: Bred ... 4K 109
Chamberlain Rd. SK15: H'rod ... 5F 82
Chamberlain St.
BL3: Bolt ... 5G 7 (6E 38)
Chamber Rd. OL2: Shaw ... 5L 45
OL8: O'ham ... 8G 62
Chambers, The *M33: Sale* ... *3G 105*
(off York Rd.)
Chambers Ct. SK14: Mot ... 6K 99
Chambersfield Ct. M5: Sal ... 9N 77
Champagnole Ct. *SK16: Duk* ... *9M 81*
(off Hill St.)
Champness Hall OL16: Roch ... 8D 8
Champneys Wlk. *M9: Man* ... *4J 79*
(off Penerley Dr.)
Chancel Av. M5: Sal ... 1B 94
Chancel Cl. SK16: Duk ... 3N 97
Chancel La. SK9: Wilm ... 6G 123
Chancellor La. M12: Man ... 1J 95
Chancel M. SK1: Stoc ... 2N 9 (7E 108)
Chancel Pl. M1: Man ... 5M 5
OL16: Roch ... 8C 8 (6D 28)
Chancery Cl. M29: Ast ... 2C 74
PR7: Cop ... 4C 18
Chancery La. BL1: Bolt ... 3L 7 (5G 39)
(not continuous)
M2: Man ... 5G 5 (9F 78)
OL2: Shaw ... 5N 45
OL3: Dob ... 1K 65
SK10: Boll ... 6M 129
Chancery Pl. M2: Man ... 5G 5
Chancery St. OL4: O'ham ... 5N 63
OL9: Chad ... 3G 63
Chancery Wlk. OL9: Chad ... 3G 63
Chandlers Point M50: Sal ... 1N 93
Chandlers Row M28: Wors ... 5A 76
Chandler Way WA3: Low ... 1A 88
Chandlery, The M32: Stre ... 6K 93
Chandley Ct. *SK1: Stoc* ... *9E 108*
(off Ward St.)
Chandley St. SK8: Chea ... 1J 117
Chandos Gro. M5: Sal ... 8K 77
Chandos Hall M1: Man ... 7K 5
Chandos Rd. M21: Cho H ... 8B 94
M25: Pres ... 9A 60
SK4: Stoc ... 2N 107
Chandos Rd. Sth. M21: Cho H ... 9B 94
Chandos St. OL2: Shaw ... 5N 45
Change Way M3: Sal ... 1D 4 (7D 78)
Channing Ct. OL16: Roch ... 7F 28
Channing Sq. OL16: Roch ... 7F 28
Channing St. OL16: Roch ... 7F 28
Chanters, The M28: Wors ... 3K 75
Chanters Av. M46: Ath ... 9N 55
Chanters Cl. M9: Man ... 7H 61
Chanters Ind. Est. M46: Ath ... 9A 56
Chantler's Av. BL8: Bury ... 2G 41
Chantry Cl. BL5: W'ton ... 6H 55
SK5: Stoc ... 1C 108
SK12: Dis ... 9H 121
Chantry Ct. SK11: Macc ... 7H 131
Chantry Fold SK12: Dis ... 9H 121
Chantry Rd. SK12: Dis ... 9G 120
Chantry Wlk. *M8: Man* ... *3E 78*
(off Lanfield Dr.)
WN4: A Mak ... 5C 70
Chapel All. BL1: Bolt ... 2K 7 (5G 38)
Chapel Brow SK13: Char ... 2N 111
SK13: Tin ... 2C 100
Chapel Cl. BL9: Bury ... 8A 42
SK16: Duk ... 1N 97
WN3: I Mak ... 5G 53
Chapel Cotts. SK9: Wilm ... 5B 122
Chapel Ct. *M26: Rad* ... *8F 40*
(off Ainsworth Rd.)
M33: Sale ... *2E 104*
(off Green La.)
SK6: Mar ... *2C 120*
(off Chadwick St.)
SK9: Wilm ... 8F 122
SK11: Macc ... *6H 131*
(off Chapel St.)
SK14: Hyde ... 8N 97
WA14: Alt ... 4C 6 (3D 114)
Chapel Cft. OL2: O'ham ... 8H 45
Chapel Dr. OL6: A Lyne ... 5B 82
WA15: Haleb ... 8J 115
CHAPEL FIELD ... 2J 59
Chapelfield M26: Rad ... 2J 59
Chapelfield Cl. SK15: Mill ... 6G 83
Chapelfield Dr. M28: Walk ... 8J 57
Chapel Fld. Rd. M34: Dent ... 6K 97
Chapelfield Rd.
M12: Man ... 7N 5 (1H 95)
CHAPEL FIELDS ... 6A 54
Chapel Flds. BL7: Tur ... 1K 23
SK6: Mar ... *2C 120*
(off Church La.)
Chapel Fields La. WN2: Hin ... 6A 54
Chapelfield St. BL1: Bolt ... 1F 38
Chapel Gdns. BL8: G'mount ... 4D 24
M34: Aud ... *3K 97*
(off Guide La.)
Chapel Ga. OL16: Miln ... 7K 29
Chapel Grange BL7: Tur ... 1K 23
Chapel Grn. M34: Dent ... 6K 97
Chapel Grn. Rd. WN2: Hin ... 5A 54
Chapel Gro. M26: Rad ... 3G 58
M41: Urm ... 7E 92
Chapel Hill OL15: Lit ... 8M 15
SK16: Duk ... 1N 97
Chapelhill Dr. M9: Man ... 8H 61
Chapel Ho. SK5: Stoc ... 9C 96
Chapel Ho. M. WA3: Low ... 1M 87
Chapel Ho's. *OL12: Whitw* ... *2B 14*
(off Oak St.)
SK2: H Gro ... 3G 119
SK6: Mar ... 2D 120
Chapel La. BL8: Holc ... 8G 11
M9: Man ... 7G 60
M31: Part ... 5G 102
M32: Stre ... 8J 93

Chapel La. M33: Sale 2E 104
OL2: O'ham 8H 45
OL11: Roch 5G 27
PR7: Cop 3C 18
SK9: Wilm 8E 122
SK13: Had 4B 100
WA3: Rix 7A 102
WA13: Warb 5G 102
WA15: Haleb 7H 115
WN1: Wig 9K 9 (5F 52)
WN3: Wig 9K 9 (5F 52)
WN8: Par 3B 32
Chapel La. Bus. Pk. PR7: Cop 4C 18
Chapel Mdw. M28: Wors 3J 75
Chapel Pl. BL2: Bolt 7K 39
BL3: Bolt 7K 39
M41: Urm 1D 92
WN4: A Mak 7E 70
Chapel Rd. M22: Nor 8C 106
M25: Pres 1M 77
M27: Swin 3C 76
M33: Sale 3H 105
M44: Irl 7H 91
OL3: G'fld 5K 65
OL8: O'ham 8G 62
SK9: A Edg 4F 126
SK9: Wilm 6M 123
WA16: Olle 9N 133
(off Marthall La.)
Chapelside Cl. WN2: Asp 1K 53
Chapelstead BL5: W'ton 6H 55
Chapel St. BL1: Bolt 1L 7
BL3: Lit L 9B 40
BL4: Farn 3M 57
BL6: Bla 2N 35
BL6: Hor 1E 36
BL7: Eger 2E 22
BL8: Tot 6F 24
M3: Sal 3B 4 (8C 78)
M19: Man 8M 95
M24: Mid 3L 61
(Wood St., not continuous)
M24: Mid 4H 61
(Yates St.)
M25: Pres 7N 59
M26: Rad 4B 58
M27: Pen 1G 77
M28: Wors 4G 75
M29: Tyld 1B 74
M30: Ecc 9C 76
M34: Aud 3K 97
M43: Droy 9F 80
M46: Ath 8M 55
OL2: O'ham 8H 45
OL2: Shaw 5M 45
OL3: Upp 3L 65
(not continuous)
OL4: Lees 5B 64
OL5: Mos 1F 82
OL6: A Lyne 7E 6 (7N 81)
OL10: H'ood 2J 43
OL11: Roch 9E 28
OL12: Whitw 6A 14
OL12: W'le 7G 14
OL15: Lit 4A 16
PR7: Adl 7J 19
PR7: Cop 4B 18
SK4: Stoc 6J 107
SK6: Wood 3M 109
SK7: H Gro 4J 119
SK8: Chea 2J 117
SK9: A Edg 4F 126
SK10: Boll 5M 129
SK11: Macc 6H 131
SK13: Glos 8E 100
SK14: Hyde 7A 98
SK15: Stal 8D 82
SK16: Duk 1M 97
SK22: N Mil 9L 121
WA11: Hay 3A 86
(not continuous)
WA12: N Wil 6E 86
WN2: Asp 1K 53
WN2: B'haw 1A 72
WN2: Hin 6N 53
WN2: P Bri 9K 53
WN3: I Mak 5G 53
WN3: Wig 9J 9 (4F 52)
WN4: A Mak 7E 70
WN5: Orr 5M 51
WN5: Wig 6M 51
WN7: Lei 6J 73
(not continuous)
Chapel Ter. BL0: Ram 1J 11
M20: Man 1G 106
WA3: Low 9D 72
CHAPELTOWN 1K 23
Chapeltown Rd. BL7: Bro X 6J 23
M26: Rad 2G 58
Chapeltown St. M1: Man 6L 5 (1G 95)
Chapel Vw. SK16: Duk 1N 97
WA11: Cra 6D 68
Chapelview Cl. SK14: Hyde 1B 110
Chapel Wlk. M24: Mid 4H 61
(off Chapel St.)
M25: Pres 1N 77
M30: Ecc 8F 76
(off Cambridge Gro.)
M45: Whitef 2A 60
PR7: Cop 4B 18
SK6: Mar 1C 120
SK13: Had 4B 100
SK15: Stal 9E 82
WA3: Low 9D 72
Chapel Walks M2: Man 4G 5 (9E 78)
M33: Sale 3H 105
SK8: Chea H 9N 117
WA13: Lym 6E 112
Chapel Way PR7: Cop 5C 18
Chapelway Gdns. OL2: O'ham 6H 45
Chapel Yd. PR7: Cop 4C 18
Chaplin Cl. M6: Sal 6L 77
Chapman Ct. SK14: Hat 7G 98
Chapman Gallery 8A 78
Chapman M. M18: Man 4B 96
Chapman Rd. SK14: Hat 8H 99
Chapman St. BL1: Bolt 3C 38
M18: Man 3B 96
Chappell Rd. M43: Droy 8E 80
Chapter St. M40: Man 6L 79
Charcoal La. WA14: Bow 4M 113
Charcoal Rd. WA14: Bow 3M 113
Charcoal Woods WA14: Bow 4A 114
Charcon Wlk. OL2: O'ham 8J 45
Chard Dr. M22: Wyth 6C 116
Chardin Av. SK6: Mar B 8F 110
Chard St. M26: Rad 9G 40
Charges St. OL7: A Lyne 9K 81
Chariot St. M11: Man 1B 96
Charity St. WN7: Lei 5E 72
Charlbury Av. M25: Pres 8D 60
SK5: Stoc 2D 108
Charlbury Way OL2: O'ham 7L 45
Charlecote Rd. SK12: Poy 2K 125
Charles Av. M34: Aud 2E 96
SK6: Mar 9N 109
Charles Babbage Av.
OL16: Roch 9H 29
Charles Ct. BL1: Bolt 1L 7 (4G 39)
WA15: Tim 1H 115
(off Thorley La.)
Charles Halle Rd. M15: Man 4F 94
Charles Holden St. BL1: Bolt 6E 38
Charles La. OL16: Miln 8L 29
SK13: Glos 6G 101
Charles M. OL16: Miln 8L 29
Charles Morris Cl. M35: Fail 2F 80
Charles Morris Ho. M35: Fail 3E 80
Charles Shaw Cl. OL4: O'ham 2A 64
Charles St. BL1: Bolt 1L 7 (4G 39)
BL4: Farn 2M 57
BL4: Kea 4M 57
BL7: Eger 2E 22
BL9: Bury 5M 7 (1M 41)
M1: Man 8H 5 (2F 94)
M6: Sal 6M 77
(not continuous)
M27: Swin 1D 76
M29: Tyld 1A 74
M34: Dent 4K 97
M43: Droy 9C 80
M44: Cad 2F 102
M45: Whitef 4M 59
OL2: O'ham 8H 45
OL7: A Lyne 9C 6 (8M 81)
OL9: O'ham 5G 63
OL10: H'ood 4K 43
OL15: Lit 9L 15
SK1: Stoc 9D 108
SK7: H Gro 4H 119
SK13: Glos 8E 100
SK16: Duk 1M 97
WA3: Gol 9K 71
WN1: Wig 2F 52
WN2: Hin 4A 54
WN2: I Mak 4K 53
WN7: Lei 7H 73
(not continuous)
Charleston Cl. M33: Sale 6D 104
Charleston Ct. M29: Tyld 1A 74
Charleston Sq. M41: Urm 6B 92
Charleston St. OL8: O'ham 7K 63
CHARLESTOWN
M6 5A 78
M9 8M 61
Charlestown Ct. OL6: A Lyne 6M 81
Charlestown Ind. Est.
OL6: A Lyne 6M 81
Charlestown Rd. M9: Man 9J 61
SK13: Glos 9E 100
Charlestown Rd. E. SK2: Stoc 4E 118
Charlestown Rd. W. SK3: Stoc 4D 118
Charlestown Way
OL6: A Lyne 6B 6 (7L 81)
Charles Wlk. M45: Whitef 4M 59
Charles Whittaker St.
OL12: Roch 4L 27
CHARLESWORTH 2N 111
Charlesworth Av. BL3: Bolt 9J 39
M34: Dent 9K 97
WN2: Hin 7B 54
Charlesworth St. M11: Man 1L 95
SK1: Stoc 9D 108
Charlock Av. BL5: W'ton 5G 54
Charlock Cl. WN7: Lei 7H 73
Charlock Sq. WA14: B'ath 8B 104
Charlock Wlk. M31: Part 5G 103
(off Central Rd.)
Charlotte Dr. WN3: Wig 7A 52
Charlotte La. OL4: Gras 6H 65
Charlotte Pl. WA15: Hale 4F 114
Charlotte St. BL0: Ram 9H 11
BL1: Bolt 2F 38
BL7: Tur 1K 23
M1: Man 5H 5 (9F 78)
OL16: Roch 9E 28
SK1: Stoc 5F 108
SK8: Chea 2J 117
SK11: Macc 5H 131
Charlotte St. W. SK11: Macc 4G 131
Charlton Av. M25: Pres 8A 60
M30: Ecc 9D 76
SK14: Hyde 5D 98
Charlton Ct. M25: Pres 8A 60
Charlton Dr. M27: Ward 9D 58
M33: Sale 4J 105
Charlton Fold M28: Walk 6K 57
Charlton Pl. M12: Man 8L 5 (2G 95)
Charlton Rd. M19: Man 8N 95
Charlton St. SK11: Macc 4F 130
Charminster Dr. M8: Man 2G 79
Charminster M. M27: Swin 4F 76
Charmouth Cl. WA12: N Wil 5E 86
Charmouth Wlk. M22: Wyth 4E 116
Charnley Cl. M33: Sale 4G 105
M40: Man 7K 79
Charnley Grange BL6: Los 5K 37
Charnley St. M45: Whitef 3M 59
Charnock WN8: Skel 5C 50
Charnock Av. WA12: N Wil 6C 86
Charnock Dr. BL1: Bolt 3F 38
CHARNOCK RICHARD 1A 18
Charnock Rd. WA3: Cul 6H 89
Charnock St. WN2: Abr 1L 71
Charnock's Yd. WN5: Wig 6M 51
Charnville Rd. SK8: Gat 2E 116
Charnwood SK6: H Lan 8C 120
Charnwood Av. M34: Dent 6F 96
Charnwood Cl. M28: Walk 9K 57
M29: Ast 2B 74
OL2: Shaw 4J 45
OL6: A Lyne 3N 81
SK10: Macc 3E 130
Charnwood Cres. SK7: H Gro 7H 119
Charnwood Rd. M9: Man 6J 61
SK6: Wood 3N 109
Charter Av. M26: Rad 1J 59
Charter Cl. M33: Sale 5D 104
Charter Fold PR7: Char R 2A 18
Charter Ho. M30: Ecc 9F 76
Charterhouse Rd. WN3: I Mak 5G 53
Charter La. PR7: Char R 1A 18
Charter Rd. SK10: Boll 6L 129
WA15: Alt 5E 6 (3E 114)
Charter St. M3: Man 7E 78
OL1: O'ham 3L 63
OL16: Roch 9E 28
Charter Way SK10: Macc 1J 131
Chartist Ho. SK14: Hyde 7B 98
Chartwell Cl. M5: Sal 8M 77
Chartwell Dr. M23: Wyth 9L 105
Chase, The BL1: Bolt 5B 38
M28: Wors 5A 76
Chasefield WA14: Bow 5A 114
Chaseley Fld. Mans. M6: Sal 6L 77
Chaseley Rd. M6: Sal 6L 77
OL12: Roch 5A 8 (5C 28)
Chase St. M4: Man 7F 78
Chasetown Cl. M23: Wyth 1K 115
Chasewood M19: Man 8M 95
(off Motherwell Av.)
Chassen Av. M41: Urm 7A 92
Chassen Ct. M41: Urm 8B 92
Chassen Rd. BL1: Bolt 5C 38
M41: Urm 7B 92
Chassen Road Station (Rail) 8B 92
Chataway Rd. M8: Man 2H 79
Chatburn Av. OL11: Roch 4B 44
WA3: Gol 9M 71
Chatburn Ct. OL2: Shaw 4M 45
WA3: Cul 7H 89
Chatburn Gdns. OL10: H'ood 2E 42
Chatburn Rd. BL1: Bolt 1A 38
M21: Cho H 9B 94
Chatburn Sq. OL11: Roch 4B 44
Chatcombe Rd. M22: Wyth 5N 115
Chatfield Rd. M21: Cho H 9A 94
Chatford Cl. M7: Sal 6D 78
Chatham Ct. M20: Man 2F 106
Chatham Gdns. BL3: Bolt 7E 38
Chatham Gro. M20: Man 2F 106
Chatham Ho. SK3: Stoc 5J 9
Chatham Pl. BL3: Bolt 7E 38
Chatham Rd. M16: Old T 6B 94
M18: Man 6C 96
Chatham St. M1: Man 5K 5 (9G 78)
SK3: Stoc 5H 9 (8B 108)
SK11: Macc 4H 131
SK14: Hyde 1B 110
WN1: Wig 9N 9 (4H 53)
WN2: I Mak 3K 53
WN7: Lei 3H 73
Chatley Rd. M30: Ecc 9N 75
Chatley St. M3: Man 6E 78
Chatswood Av. SK2: Stoc 1D 118
Chatsworth Av. M25: Pres 7A 60
SK11: Macc 6C 130
WA3: Cul 5H 89
WN3: I Mak 7J 53
Chatsworth Cl. BL9: Bury 7N 41
M41: Urm 7E 92
M43: Droy 7B 80
OL2: Shaw 4A 46
WA15: Tim 2J 115
WN4: A Mak 6C 70
Chatsworth Ct. M9: Man 6F 60
(off Deanswood Dr.)
PR6: H Char 4J 19
SK2: Stoc 2E 118
Chatsworth Cres. M32: Stre 6F 92
(off Chatsworth Rd.)
Chatsworth Dr. WN7: Lei 3M 73
(not continuous)
Chatsworth Fold WN3: I Mak 6H 53
Chatsworth Gdns. WN3: I Mak 6H 53
Chatsworth Gro. BL3: Lit L 8A 40
M16: Whall R 7C 94
Chatsworth M. SK7: Bram 5B 118
Chatsworth Rd. M18: Man 4A 96
M26: Rad 7D 40
M28: Wors 4B 76
M30: Ecc 6F 76
M32: Stre 6F 92
M43: Droy 8C 80
SK6: H Lan 9C 120
SK7: H Gro 6K 119
SK8: Chea H 2N 117
SK9: Wilm 1D 126
Chatsworth St. OL4: O'ham 6N 63
OL12: Roch 2C 28
WN5: Wig 6N 51
Chatteris Cl. WN2: Hin 7A 54
CHATTERTON 4J 11
Chatterton BL0: Ram 4J 11
Chatterton Cl. M20: Man 2H 107
Chatterton La. SK6: Mel 8K 111
Chatterton Old La. BL0: Ram 4J 11
Chatterton Rd. BL0: Ram 4J 11
Chattock St. M16: Whall R 6D 94
Chatton Cl. BL8: Bury 2F 40
Chatwell Ct. OL16: Miln 9N 29
Chatwood Rd. M40: Man 9B 62
Chaucer Av. M26: Rad 8E 40
M34: Dent 1L 109
M43: Droy 9E 80
SK5: Stoc 9B 96
Chaucer Gro. M46: Ath 6M 55
WN7: Lei 2E 72
Chaucer M. SK1: Stoc 7F 108
Chaucer Pl. WN1: Wig 9F 34
WN2: Abr 1L 71
Chaucer Ri. SK16: Duk 2D 98
Chaucer Rd. M24: Mid 1N 61
Chaucer St. BL1: Bolt 2E 38
OL1: O'ham 3C 8 (5J 63)
OL2: O'ham 7J 45
OL11: Roch 2A 44
Chaumont Way
OL6: A Lyne 7D 6 (7M 81)
Chauncy Rd. M40: Man 2C 80
Chauntry Brow BL6: Bla 1M 35
Chaytor Av. M40: Man 3N 79
CHEADLE 1J 117
Cheadle Av. M7: Sal 3N 77
Cheadle Ct. SK8: Chea H 6K 117
Cheadle Golf Course 3K 117
Cheadle Grn. SK8: Chea 1K 117
CHEADLE HEATH 9M 107
CHEADLE HULME 5M 117
Cheadle Hulme Station (Rail) 5N 117
Cheadle Old Rd. SK3: Stoc 9A 108
Cheadle Pl. SK8: Chea 1L 117
Cheadle Pools & Target Fitness Cen.
3K 117
Cheadle Rd. SK8: Chea, Chea H 3K 117
Cheadle Royal Bus. Pk.
SK8: Chea 4H 117
(not continuous)
Cheadle Sq. BL1: Bolt 3J 7 (5F 38)
Cheadle St. M11: Man 1B 96
Cheadle Wood SK8: Chea H 7K 117
Chealdle Hulme (Park & Ride) 5N 117
Cheam Cl. M11: Man 2N 95
Cheam Rd. WA15: Tim 8F 104
Cheapside M2: Man 4G 5 (9E 78)
M24: Mid 1M 61
OL1: O'ham 2C 8 (4J 63)
SK14: Hyde 6B 98
Cheapside Sq. BL1: Bolt 3K 7 (5G 38)
Cheddar St. M18: Man 4B 96
Cheddington Cl. SK8: Chea H 8M 117
Cheddleton Rd. WA14: W Tim 8C 104
Chedlee Dr. SK8: Chea H 7K 117
Chedlin Dr. M23: Wyth 3N 115
Chedworth Cres. M38: Lit H 5H 57
Chedworth Dr. M23: Wyth 1A 116
Chedworth Gro. BL3: Bolt 7F 38
(off Parrot St.)
Cheeky Chimps Activity Cen. 5B 64
Cheeryble St. M11: Man 2D 96
(not continuous)
M43: Droy 1D 96
CHEESDEN 9C 12
Cheesden Edge OL12: Roch 9D 12
Cheesden Wlk. M45: Whitef 2B 60
Cheetham Av. M24: Mid 2N 61
Cheetham Fold Rd. SK14: Hyde 9A 98
Cheetham Gdns. SK15: Stal 9E 82
Cheetham Gro. WN3: Wig 6C 52
CHEETHAM HILL
M8 3E 78
SK6 2L 121
Cheetham Hill OL2: Shaw 6M 45
OL12: Whitw 3B 14
Cheetham Hill Rd.
M4: Man 1H 5 (7F 78)
M8: Man 2E 78
SK15: Stal 3A 98
SK16: Duk 3A 98
Cheetham Hill Shop. Cen.
M8: Man 2E 78
Cheetham Pde. M8: Man 2E 78
Cheetham Pk. Cen. M8: Man 5E 78
Cheetham Pl. SK6: Bred 4K 109
Cheetham Rd. M27: Swin 3G 76
Cheethams, The BL6: Bla 5A 36
Cheethams Cres. OL2: O'ham 8L 45
Cheethams Fold SK16: Duk 2B 98
Cheetham St. M24: Mid 3L 61
M26: Rad 9J 41
M35: Fail 2E 80
(not continuous)
M40: Man 5K 79
OL1: O'ham 4M 63
OL2: Shaw 6N 45
OL16: Roch 6C 8 (5D 28)
Cheetham Wlk. SK14: Hyde 6B 98
Cheetwood Rd. M8: Man 6E 78
Cheetwood St. M8: Man 6D 78
Chelbourne Dr. OL8: O'ham 9F 62
Chelburn Cl. SK2: Stoc 2H 119
WN2: B'haw 1A 72
Chelburn Ct. SK3: Stoc 1C 118
Chell Vw. OL15: Lit 5N 15
Cheldon Wlk. M40: Man 4A 80
(off Bridlington Cl.)
CHELFORD 9A 126
Chelford Av. BL1: Bolt 8F 22
WA3: Low 2N 87
Chelford Cl. M13: Man 4J 95
M24: Mid 1A 62
WA15: Alt 1E 114
WN3: Wig 9C 52
Chelford Dr. M27: Swin 9E 58
M29: Ast 4D 74
Chelford Gro. SK3: Stoc 2A 118
Chelford Ho. SK2: Stoc 2M 119
Chelford Rd. M16: Old T 6B 94
M33: Sale 6L 105
SK9: A Edg, N Ald 9B 126
SK9: Hand 1J 123
SK10: Macc 4A 130
SK10: N Ald 9B 126
SK10: P'bury 8N 127
SK11: Chel 9B 126
SK11: Hen 4A 130
WA16: Knut, Olle 7H 133
Chellow Ct. OL5: Mos 1E 82
Chellow Dene OL5: Mos 1E 82
Chell St. M12: Man 5L 95
Chelmarsh Av. WN4: A Mak 7F 70
Chelmer Cl. BL5: W'ton 2J 55
Chelmer Gro. OL10: H'ood 1F 42
Chelmorton Gro. WN3: Wins 9N 51
Chelmsford Av. M40: Man 6N 79
Chelmsford Dr. WN3: Wig 7D 52
Chelmsford M. WN1: Wig 1F 52
Chelmsford Rd. SK3: Stoc 8A 108
Chelmsford St. OL8: O'ham 6J 63
Chelmsford Wlk. M34: Dent 8L 97
(off Kendal Av.)
Chelsea Av. M26: Rad 8D 40
Chelsea Cl. BL5: W'ton 4G 55
OL2: Shaw 5M 45
Chelsea Rd. BL3: Bolt 9E 38
M40: Man 5A 80
M41: Urm 8K 91
Chelsea St. BL9: Bury 7M 41
OL11: Roch 8B 28
Chelsfield Gro. M21: Cho H 9C 94
Chelston Av. M40: Man 9B 62
Chelston Dr. SK8: H Grn 9H 117
Cheltenham Av. WN3: I Mak 5G 53
Cheltenham Cl. SK10: Macc 9G 129
Cheltenham Cres. M7: Sal 2D 78
Cheltenham Dr. M33: Sale 4J 105
WA12: N Wil 4F 86
WN5: Bil 9H 51
Cheltenham Grn. M24: Mid 5M 61
Cheltenham Rd. M21: Cho H 7A 94
M24: Mid 5M 61
SK3: Stoc 9M 107
Cheltenham St. M6: Sal 6N 77
OL1: O'ham 2M 63
OL11: Roch 9B 28
WN2: Wig 1J 53
Chelt Wlk. M22: Wyth 5A 116
Chelwood Cl. BL1: Bolt 6E 22
Chelwood Dr. M43: Droy 8D 80
Chelwood M. BL6: Los 5K 37
Chelwood Pk. WN4: A Mak 9E 70
Chelworth Mnr. SK7: Bram 6A 118
Chemical St. WA12: N Wil 6E 86
Chendre Cl. M27: Pen 9F 58
Chendre Rd. M9: Man 8N 61
Cheney Cl. M11: Man 2B 96
Chepstow Av. M33: Sale 5C 104
Chepstow Cl. OL11: Roch 5L 27
SK10: Macc 9G 129
Chepstow Dr. OL1: O'ham 2M 63
SK7: H Gro 5L 119
Chepstow Gro. WN7: Lei 3N 73
Chepstow Ho. M1: Man 7G 4
Chepstow Rd. M21: Cho H 8N 93
M27: Clif 9G 59
Chepstow St. M1: Man 7G 4 (1E 94)
(not continuous)
Chepstow St. Sth.
M1: Man 7G 5 (1E 94)
CHEQUER 5D 50
CHEQUERBENT 3K 55
Chequer Cl. WN8: Uph 6D 50
Chequer La. WN8: Uph 4D 50
Chequers, The WA15: Hale 4F 114
Chequers Rd. M21: Cho H 9A 94
Chequers St. WN1: Wig 8H 9 (3E 52)
Cherington Cl. M23: Wyth 6A 106
SK9: Hand 3L 123
Cherington Cres. SK11: Macc 5F 130
Cherington Dr. M29: Tyld 1D 74
Cherington Rd. SK8: Chea 3H 117
Cheriton Av. M33: Sale 3J 105
Cheriton Cl. SK14: Hat 7G 99
Cheriton Dr. BL2: Bolt 5M 39
Cheriton Gdns. BL6: Hor 7D 20
Cheriton Ri. SK2: Stoc 1L 119
Cheriton Rd. M41: Urm 6L 91
Cherrington Dr. OL11: Roch 4B 44
Cherry Av. BL9: Bury 1B 42
M11: Man 2B 96
OL6: A Lyne 4M 81
OL8: O'ham 8N 63
Cherrybrook Dr. WN3: Wins 1A 70
Cherry Cl. BL9: Bury 5N 41
SK2: Stoc 9J 109
WA12: N Wil 5C 86
CHERRY CLOUGH 1E 46
Cherry Ct. M33: Sale 4G 105
WA15: Tim 9J 105
(off Whitley Pl.)
Cherry Cft. SK6: Rom 7B 110
Cherrycroft WN8: Skel 4C 50
Cherry Dr. M27: Swin 2G 76
Cherryfields Rd. SK11: Macc 5D 130
Cherry Gdns. BL1: Bolt 4A 38
Cherry Gro. OL2: O'ham 6G 44
OL11: Roch 5M 27
SK15: Stal 1D 98
WN6: Wig 9C 34
WN7: Lei 2H 73
Cherry Hall Dr. OL2: Shaw 5J 45
Cherry Hinton OL1: O'ham 3H 63
(off Cottam St.)
Cherry Holt Av. SK4: Stoc 4L 107
Cherry La. M33: Sale 6C 104
OL3: Dens 1E 46
Cherry Orchard Cl.
SK7: Bram 6B 118
Cherry St. M25: Pres 6B 60
Cherryton Wlk. M13: Man 3H 95
CHERRY TREE 6B 110
Cherry Tree Av. BL4: Farn 3G 57
SK12: Poy 3K 125
Cherry Tree Cl. SK6: Rom 6B 110
SK9: Wilm 6K 123
WA15: Tim 2H 115
Cherry Tree Ct. M6: Sal 8N 77
M29: Tyld 2E 74
(off Ashmore St.)
SK2: Stoc 3G 118
WN6: Stan 2A 34
Cherry Tree Dr. SK7: H Gro 7K 119
Cherry Tree Est. SK6: Rom 7C 110
Cherry Tree Gro. M46: Ath 7L 55
WN7: Lei 4F 72
Cherry Tree La. BL8: Bury 3J 41
SK2: Stoc 2G 118
SK6: Rom 6B 110
WA11: St H 8E 68
WA14: Ash, Rost 9L 113

Cherry Tree Rd. M23: Wyth 7M 105
SK8: Chea H 6M 117
WA3: Low 1B 88
Cherry Tree Wlk. M32: Stre 8J 93
OL5: Mos 1E 82
Cherry Tree Way BL2: Bolt 9J 23
BL6: Hor 3G 37
(off Claypool Rd.)
Cherry Wlk. M31: Part 6E 102
SK8: Chea H 7A 118
Cherrywood OL9: Chad 4B 62
Cherrywood Av. BL5: O Hul 4B 56
Cherrywood Cl. M28: Wors 1J 75
Chertsey Cl. M18: Man 4C 96
OL2: Shaw 4M 45
Chervil Cl. M14: Man 9H 95
Chervil Wlk. WN3: Wig 7N 51
Cherwell Av. OL10: H'ood 1F 42
Cherwell Cl. M45: Whitef 3N 59
OL8: O'ham 1G 80
SK8: Chea H 8M 117
WN2: Asp 6M 35
Cherwell Ct. *OL10: H'ood 1G 43*
(off Peel La.)
Cherwell Rd. BL5: W'ton 2H 55
Cheryls Bank SK13: Glos 9D 100
CHESHAM 9M 25
Chesham Av. BL1: Bolt 2F 38
M22: Wyth 3B 116
M41: Urm 6M 91
OL11: Roch 5B 44
Chesham Cl. SK9: Wilm 1E 126
SK13: Had 4D 100
Chesham Cres. BL9: Bury 1N 41
Chesham Fold Rd. BL9: Bury 1A 42
Chesham Ho. *M5: Sal 9M 77*
(off Amersham St.)
Chesham Ind. Est. BL9: Bury 9N 25
Chesham Pl. WA14: Bow 5C 114
Chesham Rd. BL9: Bury 9M 25
M30: Ecc 1C 92
OL4: O'ham 5N 63
SK9: Wilm 1E 126
Chesham St. BL3: Bolt 1C 56
Chesham Woods Local Nature Reserve 8N 25
Cheshill Ct. M7: Sal 4E 78
Cheshire Cl. M32: Stre 8H 93
WA12: N Wil 6H 87
Cheshire Ct. BL0: Ram 8K 11
Cheshire Gdns. M14: Man 8F 94
Cheshire Rd. M31: Part 6E 102
SK15: C'ook 5H 83
Cheshires, The OL5: Mos 1G 83
Cheshire Sq. SK15: C'ook 5H 83
Cheshire St. OL5: Mos 2G 82
Cheshire Vw. SK10: Kerr 7M 129
Chesney Av. OL9: Chad 9C 62
Chesshyre Av. M4: Man 8J 79
Chessington Ri. M27: Clif 8G 58
Chester Av. BL3: Lit L 8B 40
M33: Sale 7B 104
M41: Urm 6E 92
M45: Whitef 4N 59
OL11: Roch 7M 27
PR7: Chor 1H 19
SK15: Stal 7G 82
SK16: Duk 2B 98
WA3: Low 1N 87
WA15: Hale 5F 114
Chester Cl. BL3: Lit L 8B 40
M44: Cad 3E 102
SK9: Wilm 5K 123
WN3: I Mak 7J 53
Chester Ct. SK16: Duk 2B 98
Chester Dr. BL0: Ram 1G 25
WN4: A Mak 8G 70
Chesterfield Gro. OL6: A Lyne 7A 82
Chesterfield St. OL4: O'ham 5M 63
Chesterfield Way M34: Dent 9L 97
Chestergate SK1: Stoc 2K 9 (7C 108)
SK3: Stoc 3H 9 (7B 108)
(not continuous)
SK11: Macc 4G 131
Chestergate Mall *SK11: Macc 4H 131*
(off Grosvenor Cen.)
Chester Pl. OL2: O'ham 8H 45
PR6: Adl 5K 19
Chester Rd. M15: Man 2C 94
M16: Old T 9A 4 (4A 94)
M29: Tyld 2E 74
M32: Stre 9J 93
SK7: H Gro 8H 119
SK7: W'ford 5B 124
SK11: Macc 4D 130
SK12: Poy 3D 124
WA14: M'ton, Rost 9L 113
WA16: Mere, O Tab, Tab 8A 132
Chester Row WA12: N Wil 9G 86
Chester's Cft. Pk. Home Est.
SK8: Chea H 1M 123
Chester Sq. OL6: A Lyne 9A 6 (8L 81)
Chester St. BL9: Bury 9N 25
M1: Man 9G 4 (2F 94)
M15: Man 9G 4 (2E 94)
M25: Pres 6N 59
M27: Swin 3E 76
M34: Dent 7K 97
M46: Ath 9M 55
OL9: O'ham 6G 62
SK3: Stoc 3G 9 (7B 108)
WN2: Hin 9D 54
WN7: Lei 5H 73
Chesterton Cl. WN3: Wig 6D 52
Chesterton Dr. BL3: Bolt 7N 37
Chesterton Gro. M43: Droy 8E 80
Chesterton Rd. M23: Wyth 8K 105
OL1: O'ham 1M 63
Chester Wlk. *BL1: Bolt 2F 38*
(off Halliwell Rd.)
Chester Walks SK6: Rom 7L 109
Chestnut Av. BL8: Tot 8G 24
BL9: Bury 2A 42
M21: Cho H 9A 94
M28: Walk 9L 57
M43: Droy 7C 80
Chestnut Av. M44: Cad 3E 102
M45: Whitef 4M 59
M46: Ath 7L 55
SK8: Chea 2K 117
SK10: Macc 2J 131
WN7: Lei 7G 73
Chestnut Cl. BL3: Bolt 8C 38
OL4: O'ham 3A 64
SK9: Wilm 6K 123
SK15: Stal 1D 98
SK22: N Mil 6N 121
Chestnut Ct. BL9: Bury 7M 25
SK7: Bram 5B 118
Chestnut Cres. OL8: O'ham 9L 63
Chestnut Dr. BL5: W'ton 4H 55
BL9: Bury 6M 25
M33: Sale 7D 104
SK12: Poy 3K 125
WN7: Lei 7H 73
Chestnut Dr. Sth. WN7: Lei 8H 73
Chestnut Fold M26: Rad 8G 41
Chestnut Gdns. M34: Dent 7J 97
OL10: H'ood 3H 43
Chestnut Gro. M26: Rad 3G 58
M35: Fail 4D 80
SK14: Hyde 3D 98
WA3: Low 1B 88
WN2: Hin 7C 54
WN4: A Mak 6G 71
Chestnut La. WN7: Lei 8H 73
Chestnut Pl. OL16: Roch 5G 8 (5F 28)
Chestnut Rd. M30: Ecc 6A 76
WN1: Wig 1G 53
Chestnuts, The PR7: Cop 3C 18
Chestnut St. OL9: Chad 8D 62
Chestnut Vs. SK4: Stoc 6A 108
Chestnut Wlk. M31: Part 6E 102
Chestnut Way OL15: Lit 9J 15
Chesworth Cl. SK1: Stoc 5L 9
Chesworth Ct. M43: Droy 9D 80
Chesworth Fold
SK1: Stoc 5L 9 (8D 108)
Chetwode Av. WN4: A Mak 9E 70
Chetwood Cl. WA12: N Wil 4E 86
Chetwood Dr. BL1: Bolt 3F 38
Chetwyn Av. BL7: Bro X 6H 23
OL2: O'ham 8G 45
Chetwynd Av. M41: Urm 7C 92
Chetwynd Cl. M33: Sale 2E 104
Chevassut St. M15: Man 3D 94
Cheveley Cl. SK10: Macc 2G 131
Chevin Gdns. SK7: Bram 8E 118
Chevington Dr. M9: Man 4J 79
SK4: Stoc 5J 107
Chevington Gdns. *BL1: Bolt 1F 38*
(off Walley St.)
Cheviot Av. OL2: O'ham 9G 44
OL8: O'ham 8J 63
SK8: Chea H 5L 117
Cheviot Cl. BL0: Ram 1J 25
BL1: Bolt 8E 22
BL6: Hor 8E 20
BL8: Bury 1G 41
M6: Sal 7L 77
M24: Mid 3B 62
OL9: Chad 6E 62
OL16: Miln 6L 29
SK4: Stoc 5B 108
WN3: Wins 9N 51
Cheviot Ct. OL8: O'ham 7J 63
Cheviot Rd. SK7: H Gro 6F 118
Cheviots Rd. OL2: Shaw 4L 45
Cheviot St. M3: Man 7E 78
Cheviot Wlk. WN2: P Bri 9L 53
Chevithorne Cl. WA14: Alt 1B 114
Chevril Cl. M15: Man 9H 5 (3F 94)
Chevron Cl. M6: Sal 8A 78
OL11: Roch 1N 43
Chevron Pl. WA14: Alt 9D 104
Chew Brook Dr. OL3: G'fld 6L 65
CHEW MOOR 8K 37
Chew Moor La. BL5: Bolt, W'ton 1J 55
BL6: Los 1J 55
Chew Rd. OL3: G'fld 8A 66
Chew Va. OL3: G'fld 6L 65
SK16: Duk 2C 98
Chew Valley Rd. OL3: G'fld 5K 65
Chew Wood SK13: Chis 3K 111
Chicago Av. M90: Man A 8A 116
Chichester Av. M46: Ath 9J 55
Chichester Bus. Cen.
OL16: Roch 8F 8 (6E 28)
Chichester Cl. M33: Sale 5D 104
OL15: Lit 2K 29
Chichester Cres. OL9: Chad 2E 62
Chichester Rd. M15: Man 3E 94
(Old Birley St.)
M15: Man 4D 94
(Weir St.)
SK6: Rom 6N 109
Chichester Rd. Sth. M15: Man 4D 94
Chichester St.
OL16: Roch 8F 8 (6E 28)
Chichester Way *M34: Dent 8L 97*
(off Trowbridge Rd.)
Chicken La. SK5: Stoc 7D 96
Chidlow Av. M20: Man 1F 106
Chidwall Rd. M22: Wyth 5A 116
Chief St. OL4: O'ham 4G 8 (5L 63)
Chiffon Way M3: Sal 1B 4 (7C 78)
Chigwell Cl. M22: Wyth 2D 116
Chilcombe Wlk. *M9: Man 6K 61*
(off Crossmead Dr.)
Chilcote Av. M33: Sale 4E 104
Childwall Cl. BL3: Bolt 1F 56
Chilgrove Av. BL6: Bla 3N 35
Chilham Pl. SK11: Macc 6D 130
Chilham Rd. M28: Walk 9M 57
M30: Ecc 6F 76
Chilham St. BL3: Bolt 9C 38
M27: Swin 4E 76
WN5: Orr 5L 51
Chill Factore 3C 92
Chillingham Dr. WN7: Lei 6K 73
Chillington Wlk. M34: Dent 8J 97
Chilmark Dr. M23: Wyth 1N 115
Chiltern Av. M41: Urm 6M 91
M46: Ath 6A 56
SK8: Chea H 5L 117
SK11: Macc 5E 130
Chiltern Cl. BL0: Ram 1J 25
BL6: Hor 8E 20
M28: Walk 2M 75
OL2: Shaw 4K 45
SK7: H Gro 6F 118
WN4: A Mak 8F 70
Chiltern Dr. BL2: Bolt 5K 39
BL8: Bury 9H 25
M27: Swin 4F 76
OL2: O'ham 8G 44
SK2: Stoc 3E 118
WA15: Hale 5F 114
WN3: Wins 9A 52
Chiltern Gdns. M33: Sale 7J 105
Chiltern M. PR7: Chor 2E 18
Chiltern Rd. BL0: Ram 1J 25
WA3: Cul 5G 89
Chiltern Way M29: Ast 2C 74
Chilton Av. OL9: Chad 5E 62
Chilton Cl. WN7: Lei 3H 73
Chilton Dr. M24: Mid 4A 62
Chilworth St. M14: Man 7G 94
Chime Bank M8: Man 4G 79
Chimes Ct. OL4: Grot 6E 64
Chimes Rd. WN4: A Mak 4C 70
China La. M1: Man 5K 5 (9G 78)
Chinese Arts Cen. 3J 5
Chingford Wlk. *M13: Man 5L 95*
(off Bates St.)
Chinley Av. M32: Stre 5G 93
M40: Man 2M 79
Chinley Cl. M33: Sale 5K 105
SK4: Stoc 5N 107
SK7: Bram 4C 118
Chinley St. M6: Sal 5A 78
OL1: O'ham 3M 63
Chinnor Cl. WN7: Lei 3H 73
Chinwell Vw. *M19: Man 8M 95*
(off Carrill Gro. E.)
Chip Hill Rd. BL3: Bolt 8A 38
Chippendale Pl. OL6: A Lyne 5B 82
Chippenham Av. SK2: Stoc 9H 109
Chippenham Ct. M4: Man 8J 79
Chippenham Rd.
M4: Man 3N 5 (8H 79)
Chipping Fold OL16: Miln 8K 29
Chipping Rd. BL1: Bolt 2A 38
Chipping Sq. M12: Man 5L 95
Chips Bldg. M4: Man 4N 5 (9H 79)
Chipstead Av. M12: Man 4K 95
Chirmside St. BL8: Bury 3H 41
Chirton Cl. WA11: Hay 2A 86
Chirton Wlk. *M40: Man 3M 79*
(off Webdale Dr.)
Chisacre Dr. WN6: She 5H 33
Chiseldon Av. M22: Wyth 5D 116
Chiselhurst St. M8: Man 3F 78
Chisholm Cl. WN6: Stan 1M 33
Chisholm Ct. *M24: Mid 2L 61*
(off Cross St.)
Chisholme Cl. BL8: G'mount 3E 24
Chisholm St. M11: Man 2B 96
Chisledon Av. M7: Sal 4E 78
Chisledon Cl. *BL3: Bolt 7F 38*
(off Bantry St.)
WA11: Hay 2A 86
Chislehurst Av. M41: Urm 6D 92
Chislehurst Cl. BL8: Bury 3H 41
Chisnall La. PR7: Cop, Wrig 7A 18
Chiswell St. WN5: Wig 6N 51
Chiswick Dr. M26: Rad 7B 40
Chiswick Rd. M20: Man 5H 107
CHISWORTH 3L 111
Chisworth Cl. SK7: Bram 4C 118
WN7: Lei 3G 72
Chisworth St. BL2: Bolt 1J 39
Chisworth Wlk. *M34: Dent 9L 97*
(off Matlock Av.)
Choir St. M7: Sal 6D 78
Chokeberry Cl. WA14: B'ath 8B 104
Cholmley Dr. WA12: N Wil 7H 87
Cholmondeley Av. WA14: Tim 7E 104
Cholmondeley Rd. M6: Sal 6H 77
Cholmondeley St. SK11: Macc 6H 131
Chomlea WA14: Alt 3B 114
Chomlea Mnr. M6: Sal 6J 77
Choral Gro. M7: Sal 5D 78
Chorlegh Grange *SK9: A Edg 4F 126*
(off Chapel Rd.)
Chorley Cl. BL8: Bury 3F 40
Chorley Golf Course 2K 19
Chorley Hall Cl. SK9: A Edg 4E 126
Chorley Hall La. SK9: A Edg 4E 126
Chorley La. PR7: Char R 3A 18
Chorley New Rd.
BL1: Bolt 1G 7 (4H 37)
BL6: Hor, Los 9C 20
Chorley Old Rd. BL1: Bolt 1G 7 (2A 38)
BL6: Hor 1F 36
Chorley Rd. BL5: W'ton 6C 36
BL6: Bla 7K 19
M27: Swin, Ward 1D 76
M33: Sale 6L 105
PR6: Adl, H Char 2J 19
PR7: H Char 2J 19
WN1: Stan 3E 34
WN6: Stan 3E 34
WN8: Par 1A 32
Chorley St. BL1: Bolt 1H 7 (4F 38)
M32: Stre 5M 93
PR6: Adl 5L 19
WN3: I Mak 5H 53
Chorley Wood Av. M19: Man 2L 107
Chorleywood Cl. SK10: Macc 9F 128
Chorlton Brook M30: Ecc 5D 76
Chorlton Brook Ho. SK8: Chea 1K 117
Chorlton Ct. *M16: Old T 6B 94*
(off Up. Chorlton Rd.)
CHORLTON-CUM-HARDY 9N 93
Chorlton-cum-Hardy Golf Course
3B 106
Chorlton Dr. SK8: Chea 1K 117
Chorlton Ees Nature Reserve 1M 105
CHORLTON FOLD 5D 76
Chorlton Fold M30: Ecc 5D 76
SK6: Wood 3N 109
Chorlton Grn. M21: Cho H 9N 93
Chorlton Gro. SK1: Stoc 9F 108
Chorlton Leisure Cen. 8A 94
Chorlton Mill M1: Man 8G 5
Chorlton Pk. 1B 106
Chorlton Pl. M21: Cho H 8A 94
Chorlton Point *M21: Cho H 9N 93*
(off Wilbraham Rd.)
Chorlton Rd. M15: Man 5C 94
M16: Old T 5C 94
Chorlton Stop (Metro) 8A 94
Chorlton St. M1: Man 6J 5 (1F 94)
M16: Old T 4B 94
CHORLTON UPON MEDLOCK 5J 95
Chorlton Vw. *M21: Cho H 9N 93*
(off Whitelow Rd.)
CHORLTONVILLE 2B 106
Chorlton Water Pk. 4A 106
Chowbent Cl. M46: Ath 8N 55
Chretien Rd. M22: Nor 6C 106
Christabel Ct. M40: Man 6H 79
Christchurch Av. M5: Sal 8A 78
Christchurch Cl. BL2: Bolt 1N 39
Christchurch Ct. OL9: O'ham 6G 62
Christ Church La. BL2: Bolt 1N 39
Christchurch Rd. M33: Sale 3C 104
Christie Flds. Office Pk.
M21: Cho H 3C 106
Christie La. M7: Sal 2N 77
Christie Rd. M32: Stre 6L 93
Christie St. SK1: Stoc 9E 108
Christie St. Ind. Est. SK1: Stoc 9E 108
Christie Way M21: Cho H 3C 106
Christine St. OL2: Shaw 5M 45
(not continuous)
Christleton WN6: She 6M 33
Christleton Av. SK4: Stoc 3B 108
Christleton Way *SK9: Hand 1J 123*
(off Spath La.)
Christopher Acre OL11: Roch 4K 27
Christopher St. M5: Sal 9N 77
M40: Man 6B 80
WN3: I Mak 5J 53
Christy Cl. SK14: Hyde 6N 97
Christy Ho. *M43: Droy 9E 80*
(off Christy Wharf)
Christy Wharf M43: Droy 9E 80
Chronnell Dr. BL2: Bolt 4M 39
Chudleigh Cl. SK7: Bram 4E 118
WA14: Alt 1B 114
Chudleigh Rd. M8: Man 9F 60
Chulsey Ga. La. BL6: Los 8J 37
Chulsey St. BL3: Bolt 8C 38
Church Av. BL3: Bolt 8D 38
M6: Sal 8K 77
M24: Mid 6B 44
M34: Dent 9L 97
M40: Man 5A 80
SK9: Sty 4F 122
SK14: Hyde 9C 98
WN2: B'haw 2B 72
Church Bank BL1: Bolt 2M 7 (5H 39)
WA14: Bow 5B 114
Churchbank SK15: Stal 8G 82
Churchbeck Chase *M26: Rad 3B 58*
(off Weaver Chase)
Church Brow M24: Mid 2M 61
SK14: Hyde 8A 98
SK14: Mot 6K 99
WA14: Bow 5B 114
Church Cl. BL0: Ram 9H 11
M26: Rad 3B 58
M34: Aud 2K 97
(off Ashworth Av.)
SK9: Hand 3J 123
SK13: Glos 7G 100
Church Coppice WA15: Hale 5F 114
Church Ct. BL0: Eden 2K 11
BL9: Bury 6N 7 (1N 41)
M46: Ath 9N 55
SK16: Duk 9M 81
WA15: Hale 6E 114
Church Cft. BL9: Bury 8A 42
Churchdale Rd. M9: Man 7G 61
Church Dr. M25: Pres 7N 59
WA12: N Wil 8F 86
WN5: Orr 6H 51
Churches, The
OL6: A Lyne 8F 6 (8N 81)
Churchfield M21: Cho H 9N 93
WN6: She 6L 33
Churchfield Cl. M26: Rad 2F 58
Churchfield Rd. M6: Sal 5K 77
Church Flds. OL3: Dob 1K 65
Churchfields M33: Sale 2D 104
M34: Aud 2J 97
WA3: Cro 9D 88
WA14: Bow 6B 114
WA16: Knut 6J 133
Churchfield Wlk. *M11: Man 1M 95*
(off Pitman Cl.)
Church Fold PR7: Char R 1B 18
PR7: Cop 5C 18
SK13: Char 2M 111
Churchgate BL1: Bolt 2L 7 (5G 39)
M41: Urm 8E 92
SK1: Stoc 2M 9 (7D 108)
Churchgate Bldgs.
M1: Man 6M 5 (1H 95)
Church Gates WN1: Wig 8J 9
Church Grn. M6: Sal 7M 77
M26: Rad 8K 41
WA13: Warb 8C 102
Church Grn. Gdns WA3: Gol 9L 71
Church Gro. M30: Ecc 9E 76
SK7: H Gro 5J 119
WN1: Wig 8N 9
Church Hill WA16: Knut 6G 132
Churchill Av. BL2: Bolt 3D 40
M16: Whall R 7C 94
WA3: Cul 5K 89
Churchill Cl. OL10: H'ood 4K 43
Churchill Ct. M6: Sal 8M 77
Churchill Cres. SK5: Stoc 8C 96
SK6: Mar 9A 110
Churchill Dr. BL3: Lit L 9C 40
BL4: Farn 2F 56
Churchill Pl. M30: Ecc 6C 76
Churchill Point M17: T Pk 2J 93
Churchill Rd. WA14: B'ath 9D 104
Churchill St. BL2: Bolt 5K 39
OL4: O'ham 4F 8 (5L 63)
OL11: Roch 5A 28
OL12: Roch 4A 28
SK4: Stoc 5B 108
Churchill St. E.
OL4: O'ham 4F 8 (5L 63)
Churchill Way M6: Sal 8N 77
M17: T Pk 2J 93
SK11: Macc 4H 131
Churchlands La. WN6: Stan 3C 34
Church La. BL0: Eden 2K 11
BL5: W'ton 9G 36
BL9: Bury 8C 26
HD7: Mars 1H 49
M7: Sal 1A 78
M9: Man 2J 79
(not continuous)
M19: Man 2L 107
M25: Pres 7N 59
M33: Sale 2E 104
M45: Whitef 3L 59
OL1: O'ham 2D 8 (4K 63)
OL3: Upp 2N 65
OL5: Mos 1G 83
OL16: Roch 8C 8 (6D 28)
PR7: Char R 1A 18
SK6: Mar 1C 120
SK6: Rom 6N 109
SK7: W'ford 4A 124
SK9: A Edg 3F 126
SK11: Hen 4A 130
SK11: Sut E 9K 131
SK22: N Mil 7M 121
WA3: Cul 6H 89
WA3: Low 1N 87
WN6: She 6L 33
Churchley Cl. SK3: Stoc 1M 117
Churchley Rd. SK3: Stoc 9M 107
Church Lodge SK4: Stoc 6K 107
Church Mnr. SK4: Stoc 4N 107
Church Mdw. BL9: Bury 7A 42
OL3: G'fld 6H 65
SK14: Hyde 6N 97
Church Mdw. Gdns. SK14: Hyde 6N 97
Church Mdws. BL2: Bolt 1N 39
Church M. BL8: Bury 3J 41
M26: Rad 2J 59
M34: Dent 6J 97
SK10: Boll 5L 129
WA16: Knut 6H 133
Church Pas. OL1: O'ham 2D 8 (4K 63)
Church Pl. OL10: H'ood 2J 43
Church Ri. *BL2: Bolt 5K 39*
(off Tonge Old Rd.)
Church Rd. BL0: Ram 6L 11
BL1: Bolt 2A 38
BL4: Farn, Kea 3M 57
M22: Nor 7C 106
M24: Mid 4B 62
M26: Rad 3A 58
M28: Walk 8L 57
M29: Ast 4C 74
M30: Ecc 8F 76
M33: Sale 4K 105
M41: Urm 8N 91
OL2: Shaw 6M 45
OL3: G'fld 6H 65
OL3: Upp 3L 65
OL16: Roch 7F 28
SK4: Stoc 1H 9 (6B 108)
SK6: Mel 1H 121
SK8: Chea H 7N 117
SK8: Gat 2F 116
SK9: Hand 2J 123
SK9: Wilm 1D 126
SK14: Holl 5N 99
SK22: N Mil 8M 121
WA11: Hay 3B 86
WN2: P Bri 8L 53
Church Rd. E. M33: Sale 4K 105
Church Rd. W. M33: Sale 4K 105
Churchside BL4: Farn 4J 57
SK10: Macc 4H 131
Churchside Cl. M9: Man 9J 61
Church Sq. SK16: Duk 9M 81
Church Stile OL16: Roch 8C 8 (6D 28)
Churchstoke Wlk. M23: Wyth 9L 105
Churchston Av. SK7: Bram 5E 118
Church St. BL0: Ram 8J 11
BL2: Ain 3C 40
BL2: Bolt 8L 23
BL3: Lit L 9N 39
BL4: Farn 3M 57
BL4: Kea 4M 57
BL5: W'ton 2G 55
BL6: Bla 1M 35
BL6: Hor 9E 20
BL7: Bel 1L 21
BL8: Bury 9F 24
BL9: Bury 6N 7 (1N 41)
M4: Man 3J 5 (8F 78)
M24: Mid 1M 61
M27: Pen 2H 77
M27: Swin 2E 76
M30: Ecc 8E 76
(not continuous)
M32: Stre 8J 93
M34: Aud 2J 97
(off Ryecroft La.)
M35: Fail 2D 80
M43: Droy 9E 80
M46: Ath 8M 55
OL1: O'ham 2D 8 (4K 63)
OL2: O'ham 8H 45
OL3: Del 8H 47
OL4: Lees 6B 64
OL6: A Lyne 8D 6 (8M 81)

Church St. OL10: H'ood 2J 43
OL11: Roch 8A 8 (7C 28)
OL12: Whitw 6A 14
OL15: Lit 9L 15
OL16: Miln 9M 29
OL16: Roch 2H 29
(off Laycock St.)
PR7: Adl 6K 19
SK4: Stoc 5C 108
(not continuous)
SK6: Bred 3L 109
SK6: Mar 1C 120
SK8: Chea 1J 117
SK9: Wilm 7G 123
SK10: Boll 5M 129
SK11: Macc 4H 131
SK13: Glos 7F 100
SK13: Had 5C 100
SK13: Tin 2C 100
SK14: Hyde 8A 98
SK15: Stal 8D 82
SK16: Duk 9M 81
WA3: Gol 9L 71
WA12: N Wil 5H 87
WA14: Alt 1C 6 (2D 114)
WN1: Wig 7K 9 (3F 52)
WN2: Asp 6L 35
WN2: Hin 6N 53
WN3: I Mak 5J 53
WN5: Orr 6H 51
WN5: Wig 5M 51
WN6: Stan 3B 34
WN7: Lei 5H 73
WN8: Uph 4G 51
Church St. E. M26: Rad 9J 41
(not continuous)
OL4: O'ham 3B 64
Church St. Ind. Est. M24: Mid 1M 61
Church St. Sth. SK13: Glos 7G 100
Church St. W. M26: Rad 9H 41
SK11: Macc 4G 131
Church Ter. M33: Sale 2G 105
(off Stamford St.)
OL1: O'ham 2D 8 (4K 63)
OL12: W'le 7G 15
OL16: Miln 8L 29
SK4: Stoc 6B 108
SK9: Hand 2J 123
SK13: Glos 7F 100
WN4: A Mak 8E 70
Churchtown Av. BL2: Bolt 5N 39
Church Vw. M35: Fail 2D 80
M44: Irl 7H 91
OL12: Roch 3K 27
SK9: Sty 4F 122
SK14: Hyde 8A 98
SK14: Mot 6K 99
SK22: N Mil 7M 121
WA13: Lym 3C 112
WA14: Bow 6B 114
WA16: Knut 6G 132
Church Vw. Ter. SK11: Sut E 9K 131
Church Wlk. BL4: Farn 3K 57
BL8: G'mount 4D 24
M27: Clif 8F 58
OL2: O'ham 8H 45
SK9: Wilm 8E 122
SK13: Glos 7G 100
SK15: Stal 7D 82
WA14: Alt 2C 6 (2D 114)
WA16: Knut 7G 133
Church Walks BL5: W'ton 2G 54
Churchward Sq. BL6: Hor 2E 36
(off Barlow St.)
Churchway SK10: Macc 2D 130
Churchwood Rd. M20: Man 5G 106
Churchwood Vw.
WA13: Lym 4A 112
Churnet Cl. BL5: W'ton 1H 55
Churnet St. M40: Man 5J 79
Churning Ter. M44: Irl 6J 91
Churston Av. M9: Man 7K 61
Churton Av. M14: Man 7G 94
M33: Sale 5E 104
Churton Gro. WN6: Stan 2M 33
Churton Rd. M18: Man 6A 96
Churwell Av. SK4: Stoc 4L 107
Cicero St. M9: Man 2K 79
OL1: O'ham 2L 63
Cinder Hill BL9: Bury 7A 26
Cinder Hill La. M24: Mid 8E 44
OL1: Chad 8E 44
Cinder La. BL1: Bolt 1A 38
Cinder St. M4: Man 2M 5 (8H 79)
Cinemac 5H 131
Cineworld Cinema
Ashton-under-Lyne 7K 81
Bolton 1H 39
East Didsbury 7J 107
Stockport 4K 9
Cinnabar Dr. M24: Mid 1L 61
Cinnamon Av. WN2: Hin 7C 54
Cinnamon Brow WN8: Uph 5G 51
Cinnamon Cl. M22: Nor 8D 106
OL12: Roch 5B 28
(off Spotland Rd.)
Cinnamon St.
OL12: Roch 5B 28
Cipher St. M4: Man 1M 5 (7H 79)
Circle, The M32: Stre 5F 92
Circle Ct. M32: Stre 5F 92
Circle Sth. M17: T Pk 3L 93
Circuit, The M20: Man 3G 107
SK3: Stoc 1A 118
SK8: Chea H 8M 117
SK9: A Edg 2G 127
SK9: Wilm 9C 122
Circular Rd. M20: Man 3G 106
M25: Pres 9A 60
M34: Dent 7J 97
Cirencester Cl. M38: Lit H 5H 57
Ciss La. M41: Urm 7C 92
Citadel, The SK1: Stoc 4L 9
Citrus Way M6: Sal 8N 77
CITY, THE 7H 97
City Av. M34: Dent 7J 97
City Course Trad. Est.
M11: Man 2M 95
(off Whitworth St.)
City Ct. Trad. Est.
M4: Man 2M 5 (8H 79)
City Gdns. M34: Dent 7H 97
City Lofts Salford Quays
M50: Sal 2M 93
CITY MANCHESTER AIRPORT 2M 91
City of Salford Community Stadium
2A 92
City Pk. M16: Old T 4A 94
City Point M3: Sal 3D 4 (8D 78)
M32: Stre 4M 93
City Rd. M15: Man 3B 94
M28: Wors 2H 75
WN5: Wig 3M 51
City Rd. E. M15: Man 8F 4 (2E 94)
City Sth. M15: Man 8F 4 (2E 94)
City Tower M1: Man 5J 5
City Wlk. M27: Pen 2H 77
City Works, The M11: Man 2N 95
Civic Cen.
Middleton 3M 61
(within Middleton Arena)
Civic Sq. WN7: Lei 5H 73
(off Market Pl.)
Civic Wlk. OL10: H'ood 2J 43
Clack Rd. M9: Man 1J 79
Clacton Wlk. M13: Man 3H 95
(off Kirkstall Sq.)
Claife Av. M40: Man 9N 61
Clamhunger La. WA16: Mere 1C 132
CLAMMERCLOUGH 3N 57
Clammerclough Rd. BL4: Kea 3M 57
Clanbrook Av. WA13: Lym 5B 112
Clancutt La. PR7: Cop 2B 18
Clandon Av. M30: Ecc 9B 76
Clanwood Cl. WN3: Wins 9B 52
Clapgate SK6: Rom 7K 109
Clap Ga. La. WN3: Wig 8B 52
Clapgate Rd. OL11: Roch 4K 27
Clapham St. M40: Man 2A 80
Clara Gorton Ct. OL16: Roch 7F 28
(off Ethel St.)
Clara St. OL9: O'ham 7G 62
OL11: Roch 8D 28
OL12: Whitw 5B 14
Clare Av. SK9: Hand 3H 123
Clarebank BL1: Bolt 5A 38
Clare Cl. BL8: Bury 8K 25
Clare Ct. BL4: Farn 2G 56
SK1: Stoc 7E 108
Clare Dr. SK10: Macc 1G 130
Claremont Av. M20: Man 3F 106
SK4: Stoc 3A 108
SK6: Mar 1N 119
WA14: W Tim 8D 104
WN2: Hin 6N 53
Claremont Ct. BL1: Bolt 3F 38
(off Faraday Dr.)
Claremont Dr. M38: Lit H 6J 57
WA14: W Tim 8D 104
Claremont Gdns. OL6: A Lyne 5B 82
Claremont Gro. M20: Man 5F 106
WA15: Hale 4E 114
Claremont Range M18: Man 5D 96
Claremont Rd. M6: Sal 5K 77
M14: Man 6E 94
M16: Whall R 6D 94
M33: Sale 3H 105
OL11: Roch 6A 28
OL16: Miln 8J 29
SK2: Stoc 2F 118
SK8: Chea H 7M 117
WA3: Cul 5F 88
WN5: Bil 5J 69
Claremont St. M35: Fail 2D 80
OL6: A Lyne 6A 82
OL8: O'ham 9K 63
OL9: Chad 2G 62
Claremont Ter. OL14: Wals 1A 16
Clarence Arc.
OL6: A Lyne 8D 6 (8M 81)
Clarence Av. M17: T Pk 2F 92
M45: Whitef 4N 59
OL8: O'ham 7H 63
Clarence Cl. BL9: Bury 9N 25
Clarence Ct. BL1: Bolt 1H 7
SK9: Wilm 8F 122
Clarence Ho. SK15: Stal 1B 98
(off High St.)
Clarence Mill Bus. Pk.
SK10: Boll 4L 129
Clarence Rd. M13: Man 6K 95
M27: Swin 3C 76
OL6: A Lyne 6N 81
SK4: Stoc 3N 107
SK10: Boll 5L 129
WA15: Hale 4F 114
Clarence St. BL1: Bolt 1K 7 (4G 38)
(not continuous)
BL4: Farn 2M 57
M2: Man 5G 5 (9E 78)
M7: Sal 6B 78
M46: Ath 1N 73
OL2: O'ham 9L 45
OL12: Roch 3B 28
SK14: Hyde 5B 98
SK15: Stal 9B 82
WA3: Gol 9K 71
WA12: N Wil 5C 86
WN2: I Mak 4K 53
WN4: A Mak 5C 70
WN7: Lei 6K 73
Clarence Ter. SK10: Boll 4L 129
Clarence Yd. WN1: Wig 8J 9 (3F 52)
Clarendon Av. SK4: Stoc 5N 107
WA15: Alt 1E 6 (2E 114)
Clarendon Cotts. SK9: Sty 3F 122
Clarendon Cres. M30: Ecc 7F 76
M33: Sale 3K 105
Clarendon Dr. SK10: Macc 3L 131
Clarendon Gdns. BL7: Bro X 5H 23
Clarendon Gro. BL2: Bolt 6J 39
Clarendon Ind. Est. SK14: Hyde 6B 98
Clarendon Pl. M30: Ecc 8F 76
(off Wellington Rd.)
SK14: Hyde 7A 98
Clarendon Rd. BL2: Bolt 5K 39
M16: Whall R 7B 94
M27: Swin 2F 76
M30: Ecc 7F 76
M33: Sale 4K 105
M34: Aud 2E 96
M34: Dent 7M 97
M41: Urm 6M 91
M44: Irl 1F 102
SK7: H Gro 4K 119
SK14: Hyde 6A 98
Clarendon Rd. W. M21: Cho H 7A 94
Clarendon St. BL3: Bolt 7F 38
BL9: Bury 9N 25
M15: Man 9F 4 (3E 94)
(not continuous)
M45: Whitef 3M 59
OL5: Mos 2G 83
OL16: Roch 9F 28
SK5: Stoc 5D 108
SK14: Hyde 6A 98
(Grafton St., not continuous)
SK14: Hyde 7A 98
(The Square)
SK16: Duk 1L 97
(not continuous)
Clarendon Wlk. M5: Sal 8N 77
(off Cavell Way)
Clare Rd. M19: Man 9M 95
SK5: Stoc 4D 108
Clare St. M1: Man 8L 5 (2G 95)
M34: Dent 5J 97
Claribel St. M11: Man 1K 95
Claridge Rd. M21: Cho H 7N 93
Clarington Gro.
WN1: Wig 9N 9 (4H 53)
Clarington Pl. WN2: I Mak 4J 53
Clarion St. M4: Man 1M 5 (7H 79)
Clark Av. M18: Man 4C 96
Clarke Av. M5: Sal 2A 94
WA3: Cul 5H 89
Clarke Brow M24: Mid 2M 61
Clarke Cres. M38: Lit H 5E 56
WA15: Hale 4H 115
Clarke Ind. Est. M32: Stre 4F 92
Clarke La. SK10: Boll 3J 129
SK11: Lang 8N 131
Clarkes Cft. BL9: Bury 1B 42
Clarke's Hill M45: Whitef 4H 59
Clarke's La. OL12: Roch 5A 8 (5B 28)
Clarke St. BL1: Bolt 4D 38
BL4: Farn 4M 57
OL7: A Lyne 1K 97
OL10: H'ood 2J 43
OL16: Roch 3F 28
WA14: B'ath 9D 104
WN7: Lei 6G 72
Clarke Ter. SK11: Macc 6H 131
Clarkethorn Ter. SK5: Stoc 5C 108
CLARK GREEN 2K 129
Clarksfield Rd. OL4: O'ham 5N 63
Clarksfield St. OL4: O'ham 5N 63
Clark's Hill M25: Pres 7N 59
Clarkson Cl. M24: Mid 4H 61
M34: Dent 7H 97
Clark Way SK14: Hyde 6A 98
Clarkwell Cl. OL1: O'ham 1B 8
Clatford Wlk. M9: Man 3J 79
(off Carisbrook St.)
Claude Av. M27: Swin 2D 76
Claude Rd. M21: Cho H 1N 105
Claude St. M8: Man 1F 78
M27: Swin 2D 76
M30: Ecc 7B 76
WN5: Wig 5A 52
Claudia Sq. SK15: C'ook 5H 83
Claughton Av. BL2: Bolt 5N 39
M28: Wors 2K 75
Claughton Rd. BL8: Bury, Tot 8F 24
Claverham Wlk. M23: Wyth 9L 105
(off Sandy La.)
Claverton Rd. M23: Wyth 2L 115
Claxton Av. M9: Man 8J 61
Clay Bank M43: Droy 9D 80
Claybank BL8: Tot 5D 24
Claybank Dr. BL8: Tot 6D 24
Claybank St. OL10: H'ood 1H 43
Claybank Ter. OL5: Mos 7H 65
Claybarn M. M44: Irl 7J 91
Clayborne Cl. M46: Ath 8K 55
Claybridge Cl. WN5: Wig 2M 51
Claybrook Cl. M46: Ath 9J 55
Claybrook Wlk. M11: Man 9M 79
(off Sledmere Cl.)
Clay Brow Rd. WN8: Skel 5C 50
Clayburn St. M15: Man 3D 94
Claycourt Av. M30: Ecc 6B 76
Claycroft Bungs. WN7: Lei 7J 73
Clay Cft. Ter. OL15: Lit 7L 15
Claydon Dr. M26: Rad 7B 40
WN3: I Mak 6J 53
Claydon Gdns. WA3: Rix 7A 102
Clayfield Dr. OL11: Roch 5L 27
Claygate Dr. M9: Man 6J 61
Clayhill Gro. WA3: Low 1D 88
Clayhill Wlk. M9: Man 1K 79
Clayland Cl. SK14: Holl 5N 99
Clayland St. SK14: Holl 5N 99
Clay La. M23: Wyth 3M 115
OL11: Roch 5J 27
SK9: Hand, Sty 2G 123
SK9: Wilm 1B 126
WA15: Hale, Tim 3J 115
Claymere Av. OL11: Roch 5K 27
Claymoor OL1: O'ham 1C 8
Claymore St. BL3: Bolt 9G 39
M18: Man 3C 96
Claypool Rd. BL6: Hor 2G 37
Clay St. BL7: Bro X 6H 23
(not continuous)
OL8: O'ham 7J 63
OL15: Lit 9K 15
Claythorpe Wlk. M8: Man 8D 60
CLAYTON 9A 80
Clayton Av. BL2: Bolt 7K 39
M20: Man 4G 107
WA3: Low 1A 88
CLAYTON BRIDGE 6B 80
Claytonbrook Rd. M11: Man 9A 80
Clayton Cl. BL8: Bury 3F 40
M15: Man 4D 94
Clayton Ct. M11: Man 2A 96
WN3: Wig 9H 9 (4E 52)
Claytongate PR7: Cop 3C 18
Clayton Hall Rd. M11: Man 8A 80
Clayton Hall Stop (Metro) 9N 79
Clayton Ho. WN7: Lei 5E 72
Clayton Ind. Est. M11: Man 9B 80
Clayton La. M11: Man 1N 95
Clayton La. Sth. M11: Man 2M 95
Claytons Cl. OL4: Spri 4C 64
Clayton St. BL2: Bolt 7J 39
M11: Man 7N 79
M34: Dent 7K 97
M35: Fail 3D 80
OL9: Chad 8E 62
OL12: Roch 3F 28
SK16: Duk 1A 98
WN3: Wig 8G 9 (3E 52)
Clayton Vale 7A 80
Cleabarrow Dr. M28: Wors 5H 75
Cleadon Av. M18: Man 5A 96
Cleadon Dr. Sth. BL8: Bury 8J 25
Clearwater Dr. M20: Man 3E 106
Cleaver M. SK11: Macc 7G 130
Cleavley St. M30: Ecc 8B 76
Clee Av. M13: Man 7L 95
Cleethorpes Av. M9: Man 8G 60
Cleeve Rd. M23: Wyth 6N 105
OL4: O'ham 5N 63
Cleeve Way SK8: Chea H 9N 117
CLEGG HALL 3J 29
Clegg Hall Rd. OL15: Lit 3J 29
OL16: Roch 3H 29
Clegg Pl. OL6: A Lyne 6A 82
Clegg's Av. OL12: Whitw 4A 14
(off Tong La.)
Clegg's Bldgs. BL1: Bolt 1H 7 (4F 38)
Clegg's La. M38: Lit H 6H 57
Cleggs La. Ind. Site M38: Lit H 5J 57
Clegg St. BL2: Bolt 5K 39
M29: Ast 5B 74
M43: Droy 9D 80
M45: Whitef 4M 59
OL1: O'ham 3D 8 (5K 63)
(not continuous)
OL4: O'ham 4E 8 (5K 63)
OL4: Spri 5D 64
OL12: Whitw 4A 14
OL15: Lit 8K 15
OL16: Miln 8L 29
SK6: Bred 5K 109
Cleggswood Av. OL15: Lit 2L 29
Cleggs Yd. OL15: Lit 9K 15
Clelland St. BL4: Farn 4M 57
Clematis Wlk. M27: Ward 9E 58
Clement Av. M46: Ath 9J 55
Clement Ct. M11: Man 2D 96
(off Toxteth St.)
OL16: Roch 7F 28
Clementina St. OL12: Roch 4D 28
(not continuous)
Clementine Cl. M6: Sal 8A 78
(off Coconut Gro.)
Clement Pl. OL12: Roch 6A 8
(off Clement Royds St.)
OL15: Lit 9N 15
(off Halifax Rd.)
Clement Rd. SK6: Mar B 9E 110
Clement Royds St.
OL12: Roch 6A 8 (5C 28)
(not continuous)
Clement Stott Cl. M9: Man 7L 61
Clement St. OL9: O'ham 8F 62
SK4: Stoc 5C 108
Cleminson St. M3: Sal 3B 4 (8C 78)
Clemshaw Cl. OL10: H'ood 3H 43
Clerewood Av. SK8: H Grn 8G 117
Clerke St. BL9: Bury 7L 7 (2M 41)
Clerk's Ct. M5: Sal 8H 77
Clevedon Av. M41: Urm 7G 92
Clevedon Cl. SK11: Macc 5E 130
Clevedon Dr. WN3: Wig 7N 51
Clevedon Rd. OL9: Chad 2E 62
Clevedon St. M9: Man 3K 79
Cleveland Av. M6: Sal 7J 77
M19: Man 7N 95
SK14: Hyde 7N 97
WN3: Wins 9N 51
Cleveland Cl. BL0: Ram 2J 25
M27: Clif 9G 58
Cleveland Dr. OL16: Miln 7L 29
WA3: Low 1N 87
WN4: A Mak 6F 70
Cleveland Gdns. BL3: Bolt 8C 38
(off Cleveland St.)
WN4: A Mak 6F 70
Cleveland Gro. OL2: O'ham 9G 45
Cleveland Rd. M8: Man 1G 78
SK4: Stoc 4M 107
WA15: Hale 4F 114
Clevelands Cl. OL2: Shaw 4L 45
Clevelands Dr. BL1: Bolt 5B 38
Cleveland St. BL3: Bolt 8C 38
PR7: Cop 4B 18
Cleveleys Av. BL2: Bolt 4K 39
BL9: Bury 4L 41
M21: Cho H 1B 106
OL16: Roch 1F 44
SK8: H Grn 6G 117
Cleveleys Gro. M7: Sal 3D 78
Cleves Ct. OL10: H'ood 3H 43
Cleworth Cl. M29: Ast 6D 74
Cleworth Hall La. M29: Tyld 1D 74
Cleworth Rd. M24: Mid 1L 61
Cleworth St. M15: Man 9B 4 (2C 94)
Cleworth Wlk. M15: Man 9B 4
Clibran St. M8: Man 4G 79
Clifden Dr. M22: Wyth 5D 116
CLIFF, THE 3C 78
Cliff Av. BL9: Sum 3J 25
M7: Sal 4B 78
Cliffbrook Gro. SK9: Wilm 4J 123
(off Bosley Cl.)
Cliff Cres. M7: Sal 3C 78
Cliff Dale SK15: Stal 1C 98
Cliffdale Dr. M8: Man 1F 78
Cliffe Rd. SK13: Glos 9F 100
Cliffe St. OL15: Lit 4A 16
Cliff Grange M7: Sal 3C 78
Cliff Gro. SK4: Stoc 4N 107
Cliff Hill OL2: Shaw 3A 46
Cliff Hill Rd. OL2: Shaw 3N 45
Cliff La. SK10: Macc 2L 131
SK11: Macc 3M 131
Cliffmere Cl. SK8: Chea H 4L 117
Cliff Mt. BL0: Ram 7H 11
Clifford Av. M34: Dent 4J 97
WA15: Tim 1H 115
Clifford Ct. M15: Man 4D 94
(off Chorlton Rd.)
SK2: Stoc 2F 118
Clifford Lamb Ct. M9: Man 9N 61
Clifford Rd. BL3: Bolt 1B 56
SK9: Wilm 8E 122
SK11: Macc 4E 130
SK12: Poy 2G 125
Clifford St. M13: Man 3G 94
M27: Pen 2H 77
M30: Ecc 1B 92
OL11: Roch 8D 28
WN7: Lei 6K 73
Cliff Rd. BL9: Bury 7M 41
SK9: Wilm 6G 123
Cliff Side SK9: Wilm 6G 123
Cliff St. OL16: Roch 4F 28
CLIFTON 8F 58
Clifton Av. M14: Man 9J 95
M29: Ast 4D 74
M30: Ecc 7D 76
OL4: O'ham 6M 63
SK8: H Grn 5F 116
WA3: Cul 6F 88
WA15: Alt 1E 6 (2E 114)
Clifton Cl. M16: Old T 4C 94
OL4: O'ham 6M 63
OL10: H'ood 3H 43
Clifton Country Pk.
(Local Nature Reserve) 6E 58
Clifton Ct. BL4: Farn 1J 57
M27: Clif 7E 58
SK4: Stoc 4M 107
Clifton Cres. OL2: O'ham 9L 45
WN1: Wig 1F 52
Clifton Dr. BL6: Bla 1L 35
M27: Clif 9J 59
M27: Ward 1D 76
SK6: Mar 9B 110
SK8: Gat 2E 116
SK8: H Grn 5F 116
SK9: Wilm 1D 126
CLIFTON GREEN 8G 59
Clifton Gro. M16: Old T 4C 94
(off Hamilton St.)
M27: Ward 9D 58
Clifton Holmes OL3: Del 7H 47
Clifton Ho. M30: Ecc 7D 76
(off Clifton Rd.)
WN3: Wig 6E 52
Clifton Ho. Rd. M27: Clif 6D 58
(not continuous)
Clifton Ind. Est. M27: Clif 8H 59
CLIFTON JUNCTION 8J 59
Clifton Lodge SK2: Stoc 2E 118
Cliftonmill Mdws.
WA3: Gol 1J 87
Clifton Pk. M27: Clif 7E 58
Clifton Pk. Rd. SK2: Stoc 2E 118
Clifton Pl. M25: Pres 6N 59
Clifton Rd. M21: Cho H 9B 94
M24: Mid 6B 44
M25: Pres 7L 59
M30: Ecc 7D 76
M33: Sale 5H 105
M41: Urm 7A 92
SK4: Stoc 5M 107
WN4: A Mak 4C 70
WN5: Bil 6H 69
WN7: Lei 8G 72
Clifton Station (Rail) 9J 59
Clifton St. BL1: Bolt 1H 7 (4F 38)
BL4: Farn 1J 57
BL4: Kea 4N 57
BL9: Bury 9M 25
M16: Old T 4C 94
(not continuous)
M29: Tyld 2F 74
M35: Fail 1E 80
M40: Man 7L 79
OL3: G'fld 6L 65
OL6: A Lyne 7A 6 (7L 81)
OL11: Roch 8E 28
(off Well St.)
OL16: Miln 7K 29
SK9: A Edg 4F 126
WN1: Wig 2F 52
WN3: Wig 7D 52
WN7: Lei 5F 72
Clifton Vw. M27: Clif 7E 58
Clifton Vs. M35: Fail 1E 80
WN3: I Mak 7H 53
(off Marlborough Av.)
Cliftonville Dr. M6: Sal 4H 77
M27: Swin 4G 77
Cliftonville Rd. OL16: Roch 4G 44
Clifton Vis. Cen. 6E 58
Clifton Wlk. M24: Mid 9J 43
Climax Works SK5: Stoc 7C 96
Climb Rochdale 8D 8
CLINKHAM WOOD 9F 68
Clinkham Wood Local Nature Reserve
9E 68
Clinton Av. M14: Man 7E 94
Clinton Gdns. M14: Man 7F 94

Clinton Ho. M5: Sal 9M 77
(off Amersham St.)
Clinton St. OL6: A Lyne 6A 82
Clinton Wlk. OL4: O'ham 4F 8 (5L 63)
Clippers Quay M50: Sal 3N 93
Clipsley Cres. OL4: O'ham 8C 46
Clipsley La. WA11: Hay 3A 86
Cliston Wlk. SK7: H Gro 5E 118
Clitheroe Cl. OL10: H'ood 1J 43
Clitheroe Dr. BL8: Bury 2F 40
Clitheroe Rd. M13: Man 6L 95
Clito St. M9: Man 2L 79
Clive Av. M45: Whitef 2L 59
Clivedale Pl. BL1: Bolt 3L 7 (5G 39)
Cliveley Wlk. M27: Pen 2H 77
Clive Lloyd Ct. M32: Stre 6L 93
Clively Av. M27: Clif 1H 77
Clive Rd. BL5: W'ton 5G 55
M35: Fail 3C 80
Clive St. BL1: Bolt 3L 7 (5G 39)
M4: Man 1K 5 (7G 78)
OL7: A Lyne 5L 81
OL8: O'ham 9H 63
(not continuous)
Clivewood Wlk. M12: Man 3K 95
(off Bennett St.)
Clivia Gro. M7: Sal 4C 78
(off Bk. Hilton St.)
Cloak St. M1: Man 8J 5 (2F 94)
Clockhouse Av.
M43: Droy 7C 80
Clockhouse M. M43: Droy 7C 80
Clock St. OL9: Chad 9F 62
Clock Twr. Cl. M28: Walk 8G 57
SK14: Hyde 8B 98
Clock Twr. Ct. OL16: Miln 8L 29
Cloister Av. WN7: Lei 1F 72
Cloister Cl. SK16: Duk 3N 97
Cloister Rd. SK4: Stoc 6J 107
Cloisters, The BL5: W'ton 7G 55
M33: Sale 4K 105
OL16: Roch 4F 28
SK8: Chea 2M 117
Cloister St. BL1: Bolt 2D 38
M9: Man 2L 79
Clondberry Cl. M29: Tyld 1F 74
Clopton Wlk. M15: Man 9E 4 (3D 94)
(Birchvale Cl.)
M15: Man 3D 94
(off Ellis St.)
Close, The BL2: Bolt 1J 39
BL8: Bury 7J 25
M24: Mid 9N 43
M34: Dent 5H 97
M46: Ath 6A 56
SK6: Mar B 7E 110
SK15: Stal 6C 82
(not continuous)
WA12: N Wil 8H 87
WA14: Alt 1A 6 (2C 114)
Closebrook Rd. WN5: Wig 5A 52
Close La. WN2: Hin 1C 72
(Belmont Av.)
WN2: Hin 7A 54
(Glossop Way)
Closes Farm BL3: Bolt 1C 56
Close St. WN2: Hin 5B 54
Clothorn Rd. M20: Man 4G 106
Cloudberry Wlk. M31: Part 5G 103
Cloudstock Gro. M38: Lit H 6F 56
CLOUGH
OL2 6A 46
OL15 7L 15
Clough OL2: Shaw 6A 46
Clough, The BL1: Bolt 5N 37
OL7: A Lyne 4M 81
SK5: Stoc 2F 108
WN4: Gars 6A 70
Clough Av. BL5: W'ton 3H 55
M33: Sale 7D 104
SK6: Mar B 1F 120
SK9: Wilm 4G 123
Clough Bank M9: Man 9J 61
OL15: Lit 6L 15
SK10: Boll 6K 129
Cloughbank M26: Rad 4C 58
Clough Cl. OL4: Gras 5H 65
Clough Ct. M24: Mid 1N 61
Clough Dr. M25: Pres 7M 59
Clough End Rd. SK14: Hat 8H 99
Cloughfield Av. M5: Sal 1A 94
Clough Flats OL10: H'ood 2H 43
(off St James St.)
Clough Fold BL5: W'ton 3H 55
M26: Rad 4B 58
Clough Fold Rd.
SK14: Hyde 8N 97
Clough Ga. OL8: O'ham 9H 63
SK14: Hyde 9B 98
Cloughgate Ho. OL8: O'ham 9H 63
(off Hollins Rd.)
Clough Gro. M45: Whitef 1K 59
WN4: A Mak 5C 70
Clough Head OL15: Lit 4N 15
(off Higher Calderbrook Rd.)
Clough Hey HD7: Mars 1H 49
Clough Ho. Dr. WN7: Lei 5K 73
Clough Ho. La. OL12: W'le 8F 14
Clough La. M25: Pres 7M 59
OL4: Gras 5G 65
OL10: H'ood 9H 27
Clough Lea HD7: Mars 1H 49
Clough Mdw. BL1: Bolt 6M 37
SK6: Wood 3N 109
Clough Mdw. Rd. M26: Rad 9E 40
Clough Pk. Av. OL4: Gras 5H 65
Clough Rd. M9: Man 2L 79
M24: Mid 1M 61
M35: Fail 3E 80
M43: Droy 8E 80
OL2: Shaw 6A 46
OL15: Lit 6L 15
Cloughs Av. OL9: Chad 3B 62
Clough Side M9: Man 1L 79
Cloughside SK6: Mar B 9F 110
SK12: Dis 9H 121
Clough St. BL4: Kea 4N 57
M24: Mid 1N 61
M26: Rad 2J 59
M40: Man 6A 80
OL12: W'le 8G 14
Clough Ter. OL15: Lit 7L 15
Cloughton Wlk. M40: Man 5B 80
(off Terence St.)
Clough Top Rd. M9: Man 9M 61
Clough Wlk. SK5: Stoc 2F 108
Cloughwood Cres. WN6: She 6H 33
Clovelly Av. OL8: O'ham 9G 63
WN7: Lei 2H 73
Clovelly Rd. M21: Cho H 9B 94
M27: Swin 3C 76
SK2: Stoc 8G 109
Clovelly St. M40: Man 5B 80
OL11: Roch 1N 43
Clover Av. SK3: Stoc 2B 118
Cloverbank Av. M19: Man 4J 107
Clover Cres. OL8: O'ham 8A 64
Clover Cft. M33: Sale 7K 105
Cloverdale Dr. WN4: A Mak 8F 70
Cloverdale Rd. SK11: Macc 7E 130
Cloverdale Sq. BL1: Bolt 3B 38
Cloverfield WA13: Lym 3A 112
Cloverfield Wlk. M28: Walk 8L 57
(off Malvern Gro.)
Clovergreen Gdns.
WA14: W Tim 8B 104
CLOVER HALL 4G 29
Clover Hall Cres. OL16: Roch 4G 29
Cloverley M33: Sale 6H 105
Cloverley Dr. WA15: Tim 3G 115
Clover Rd. PR7: Chor 1D 18
SK6: Rom 5B 110
WA15: Tim 2G 115
Clover St. OL12: Roch 6B 8 (5C 28)
WN6: Wig 1D 52
Clover Vw. OL16: Roch 6G 28
Clowes St. M3: Sal 3E 4 (8D 78)
M12: Man 3L 95
(not continuous)
OL9: Chad 9F 62
SK11: Macc 5F 130
(not continuous)
Clubhouse Cl. OL2: Shaw 6M 45
OL11: Roch 6M 27
Club St. M11: Man 2D 96
WA11: St H 9E 68
Club Theatre 5D 6 (4D 114)
Clumber Cl. SK12: Poy 3J 125
Clumber Rd. M18: Man 5D 96
SK12: Poy 3J 125
Clunton Av. BL3: Bolt 8C 38
Clutha Rd. SK3: Stoc 3D 118
Clwyd Av. SK3: Stoc 9B 108
Clyde Av. M45: Whitef 5M 59
Clyde Ct. OL16: Roch 7F 28
Clyde Rd. M20: Man 4E 106
M26: Rad 7F 40
M29: Ast 3D 74
SK3: Stoc 9A 108
Clydesdale Gdns. M11: Man 9M 79
Clydesdale Ri. OL3: Dig 7N 47
Clydesdale St. OL8: O'ham 7J 63
Clyde St. BL1: Bolt 2F 38
OL1: O'ham 2N 63
OL7: A Lyne 1K 97
WN7: Lei 6K 73
Clyde Ter. M26: Rad 7F 40
Clyne Ct. M32: Stre 5M 93
(off Adlington Dr.)
Clyne St. M32: Stre 4M 93
Clysbarton Ct. SK7: Bram 6B 118
Coach Ho. Dr. WN6: She 6M 33
Coach La. OL11: Roch 8K 27
Coach Rd. M29: Ast 4D 74
SK14: Holl 4K 99
Coach St. M46: Ath 8M 55
Coachway SK10: P'bury 6E 128
Coal Bank Fold OL11: Roch 4J 27
Coalbrook Wlk. M12: Man 1K 95
(off Aden Cl.)
Coalburn St. M12: Man 3M 95
Coal Pit La. BL1: Bolt 7M 21
M46: Ath 8K 55
(not continuous)
OL8: O'ham 3G 81
WN2: Hin 1D 72
WN7: Lei 2G 72
Coalpit La. SK11: Lang 8N 131
Coal Pit Rd. BL1: Bolt 6K 21
Coal Rd. BL0: Ram 6N 11
Coalshaw Grn. Rd. OL9: Chad 8E 62
Coare St. SK10: Macc 3G 131
Coatbridge St. M11: Man 9A 80
Cobal Ct. SK2: Stoc 2E 118
Cobalt Av. M41: Urm 3F 92
Cobalt Way M24: Mid 5B 62
Cobb Cl. M8: Man 8D 60
Cobbett's Way SK9: Wilm 1E 126
Cobble Bank M9: Man 8J 61
Cobblestones OL3: Del 9J 47
Cobden Cen., The M50: Sal 9M 77
(off Vere St.)
Cobden Edge SK6: Mel 4J 121
Cobden Lodge OL11: Roch 2A 44
(off Tudor Hall St.)
Cobden Mill Ind. Est. BL4: Farn 2K 57
Cobden St. BL1: Bolt 1E 38
BL7: Eger 3E 22
BL9: Bury 5N 7 (1N 41)
M6: Sal 6M 77
M9: Man 2K 79
M26: Rad 6F 40
M29: Tyld 1B 74
OL4: O'ham 2A 64
OL6: A Lyne 8G 6 (8A 82)
OL9: Chad 4F 62
OL10: H'ood 3J 43
WA12: N Wil 5G 87
Coberley Av. M41: Urm 5N 91
Cob Hall Rd. M32: Stre 8J 93
Cobham Av. BL3: Bolt 9E 38
M40: Man 9A 62
Cob Kiln La. M41: Urm 8D 92
Coblers Hill OL3: Del 7J 47
Cob Moor Av. WN5: Bil 1H 69
Cob Moor Rd. WN5: Bil 1H 69
Cobourg St. M1: Man 6K 5 (1G 94)
Coburg Av. M7: Sal 6C 78
Cochrane Av. M12: Man 4K 95
Cochrane St. BL3: Bolt 7G 39
COCKBROOK 7A 82
Cock Brow SK14: Hyde 1F 110
Cock Clod St. M26: Rad 9J 41
Cockcroft Rd. M5: Sal 8A 78
Cockcroft St. M9: Man 1J 79
Cockerell Springs BL2: Bolt 4M 7
COCKER HILL 7D 82
COCKERHILL 2C 100
Cocker Hill SK15: Stal 8D 82
Cocker Mill La. OL2: O'ham 7K 45
Cockers La. SK15: Stal 1G 99
Cocker St. M38: Lit H 7H 57
Cockey Moor Rd. BL2: Ain 3D 40
BL8: Bury 3D 40
Cock Hall La. OL12: Whitw 5A 14
SK11: Lang, Sut E 9N 131
Cocklinstones BL8: Bury 1H 41
Cocksfoot Dr. OL5: Mos 2H 83
Cocksheadhey Rd. SK10: Boll 4N 129
Coconut Gro. M6: Sal 8A 78
Codale Dr. BL2: Bolt 3N 39
Coddington Av. M11: Man 1C 96
Code La. BL5: W'ton 8D 36
Cody Av. M9: Man 9H 61
Cody Ct. M50: Sal 1L 93
Coe La. WA14: M'ton 8K 113
Coe St. BL3: Bolt 7G 38
Coffin La. WN2: Bam 4G 71
Coghlan Cl. M11: Man 8N 79
Coin St. OL2: O'ham 8J 45
Coke St. M7: Sal 2E 78
Coke St. W. M7: Sal 2E 78
Colborne Av. M30: Ecc 8B 76
SK5: Stoc 6D 96
SK6: Rom 6N 109
Colbourne Av. M8: Man 1E 78
Colbourne Gro. SK14: Hat 6H 99
Colbourne Way SK14: Hat 6H 99
Colburn Cl. WN3: Wig 9D 52
Colby Rd. WN3: Wig 8E 52
Colby Wlk. M40: Man 3M 79
Colchester Av. BL2: Bolt 4M 39
M25: Pres 9B 60
Colchester Cl. M23: Wyth 7L 105
Colchester Dr. BL4: Farn 2H 57
Colchester Pl. SK4: Stoc 5N 107
Colchester Wlk. OL1: O'ham 1D 8
Colclough Cl. M40: Man 4N 79
Coldalhurst La. M29: Ast 4C 74
Coldfield Dr. M23: Wyth 1M 115
Cold Greave Cl. OL16: Miln 9N 29
COLD HURST 3J 63
COLDHURST HOLLOW 3K 63
Coldhurst Hollow Est.
OL1: O'ham 2K 63
Coldhurst St. OL1: O'ham 1C 8 (3J 63)
Coldhurst St. W. OL1: O'ham 3J 63
(off Trafalgar St.)
Coldstone Dr. WN4: Gars 7A 70
Coldstream Av. M9: Man 7J 61
Coldwall Ind. Est. OL12: Roch 5B 28
Cole Av. WA12: N Wil 5F 86
Colebrook Dr. M40: Man 4M 79
Colebrook Rd. WA15: Tim 1G 115
Coleby Av. M16: Old T 5B 94
M22: Wyth 6E 116
Colecleugh Pl. WA3: Cul 5H 89
Coledale Dr. M24: Mid 1H 61
Coleford Gro. BL1: Bolt 4H 7 (6F 38)
Colemore Av. M20: Man 5J 107
Colenso Ct. BL2: Bolt 5K 39
Colenso Gro. SK4: Stoc 5N 107
Colenso Rd. BL2: Bolt 5L 39
Colenso St. OL8: O'ham 8H 63
Colenso Way M4: Man 1H 5 (7F 78)
Coleport Cl. SK8: Chea H 6M 117
Coleridge Av. M24: Mid 9A 44
M26: Rad 9E 40
WN5: Orr 5L 51
Coleridge Cl. SK5: Stoc 8C 96
Coleridge Pl. WN3: Wig 8C 52
Coleridge Rd. BL8: G'mount 3F 24
M16: Old T 6B 94
OL1: O'ham 8B 46
OL15: Lit 3K 29
SK5: Stoc 8C 96
WN5: Bil 1H 69
Coleridge St. M40: Man 6A 80
Coleridge Way SK5: Stoc 8C 96
Colerne Way WN3: Wins 9A 52
Colesbourne Cl.
M38: Lit H 5H 57
Coleshill Ri. WN3: Wins 9N 51
Coleshill St. M40: Man 7K 79
Colesmere Wlk. M40: Man 1B 80
Cole St. M40: Man 2L 79
Colgate Cres. M14: Man 9G 95
Colgate La. M5: Sal 3N 93
Colgrove Av. M40: Man 9A 62
Colina Dr. M7: Sal 5D 78
M8: Man 5D 78
Colindale Av. M9: Man 7K 61
Colindale Cl. BL3: Bolt 7D 38
(off Langshaw Wlk.)
Colin Murphy Rd.
M15: Man 9D 4 (3D 94)
Colin Rd. SK4: Stoc 4C 108
Colin St. WN1: Wig 5L 9 (2G 52)
Colinton WN8: Skel 4C 50
Colinton Cl. BL1: Bolt 3E 38
Colinwood Cl. BL9: Bury 9M 41
Collard St. M46: Ath 7K 55
Collar Ho. Dr. SK10: P'bury 7C 128
Coll Dr. M41: Urm 4D 92
College Av. M43: Droy 1D 96
OL8: O'ham 2K 81
WN1: Wig 9K 9 (4F 52)
College Bank Way
OL12: Roch 7A 8 (6C 28)
College Cl. SK2: Stoc 1E 118
SK9: Wilm 6E 122
College Ct. OL12: Roch 6B 28
SK4: Stoc 5M 107
SK11: Macc 7F 130
College Cft. M30: Ecc 8F 76
College Dr. M16: Whall R 7B 94
College Ho. SK4: Stoc 4N 107
WA14: Bow 6C 114
College Land M3: Man 4F 4 (9E 78)
College Rd. M16: Whall R 6B 94
M30: Ecc 8G 76
(off St Mary's Rd.)
OL8: O'ham 7H 63
OL12: Roch 7A 8 (6B 28)
WN8: Uph 2F 50
College St. WN7: Lei 5J 73
College Vw. M14: Man 5G 94
College Way BL3: Bolt 4G 7 (6E 38)
Collegiate Way M27: Clif 8F 58
Collen Cres. BL8: Bury 7J 25
Collett Cl. WN1: Wig 8N 9 (3H 53)
Collett St. OL1: O'ham 3N 63
Colley St. M32: Stre 4M 93
OL16: Roch 4F 28
Collie Av. M6: Sal 5B 78
Collier Av. OL16: Miln 6K 29
Collier Brook Ind. Cen. M46: Ath 8L 55
Collier Cl. SK14: Hat 8H 99
Collier Hill OL8: O'ham 8H 63
Collier Hill Av. OL8: O'ham 8G 63
Colliers Cl. WN7: Lei 7G 73
Collier's Ct. OL11: Roch 3F 44
Colliers Gro. M46: Ath 8J 55
Colliers Row Rd. BL1: Bolt 8M 21
Collier St. M3: Man 2E 4 (1D 94)
M3: Sal 2E 4 (8D 78)
M6: Sal 4M 77
M26: Rad 9H 41
M27: Swin 3E 76
SK13: Glos 9F 100
WN2: Hin 5N 53
Collier Wlk. SK14: Hat 8H 99
Colliery La. M46: Ath 7J 55
Colliery St. M11: Man 9M 79
(not continuous)
Collin Av. M18: Man 5A 96
Collingburn Av. M5: Sal 2A 94
Colling Cl. M44: Irl 8H 91
Collinge Av. M24: Mid 3A 62
Collinge St. BL8: Bury 9H 25
M24: Mid 4B 62
OL2: Shaw 5M 45
OL10: H'ood 2H 43
WN2: P Bri 9K 53
Collingham Rd. WA14: W Tim 7C 104
Collingham St. M8: Man 6G 78
Colling St. BL0: Ram 9H 11
Collington Cl. M12: Man 4M 95
Collingwood Av. M43: Droy 7C 80
Collingwood Cl. SK7: H Gro 3K 119
SK10: Macc 2F 130
SK12: Poy 3L 125
Collingwood Dr. M27: Swin 3H 77
Collingwood Rd. M19: Man 8L 95
WA12: N Wil 6E 86
Collingwood St. OL11: Roch 4A 44
WN6: Stan 3B 34
Collingwood Way BL5: W'ton 2G 54
OL1: O'ham 3K 63
Collins Ct. SK5: Stoc 9D 96
COLLINS GREEN 8A 86
Collins Grn. La. WA5: Coll G 8B 86
Collins La. BL5: W'ton 5H 55
Collins St. BL8: Bury 9F 24
Collins Way OL9: Chad 8G 62
Collisdene Rd. WN5: Orr 5H 51
Collop Dr. OL10: H'ood 5K 43
Coll's La. OL3: Del 8G 47
COLLYHURST 5J 79
Collyhurst Av. M28: Walk 9M 57
Collyhurst Rd. M40: Man 6G 79
Collyhurst St. M40: Man 6H 79
Colman Gdns. M5: Sal 2A 94
Colmore Dr. M9: Man 7M 61
Colmore Gro. BL2: Bolt 9J 23
Colmore St. BL2: Bolt 9J 23
Colnbrook WN6: Stan 2M 33
Colne St. OL11: Roch 3B 44
Colonial Rd. SK2: Stoc 1E 118
Colshaw Cl. E. M26: Rad 8F 40
Colshaw Cl. Sth.
M26: Rad 8F 40
Colshaw Dr. SK9: Wilm 5J 123
Colshaw Rd. M23: Wyth 2N 115
Colshaw Wlk. SK9: Wilm 5J 123
(off Howty Cl.)
Colson Dr. M24: Mid 4L 61
Colsterdale Cl. OL2: O'ham 7J 45
Colt Hill La. OL3: Upp 3J 65
(not continuous)
Coltishall Ho. SK8: Chea 2M 117
Coltness Wlk. M40: Man 5A 80
(off Marlinford Dr.)
Coltsfoot Cl. WN7: Lei 5K 73
Coltsfoot Dr. WA14: B'ath 8B 104
Columbia Av. M18: Man 5D 96
Columbia Rd. BL1: Bolt 4D 38
Columbia St. OL8: O'ham 7K 63
Columbine Cl. OL12: Roch 2A 28
Columbine St. M11: Man 2B 96
Columbine Wlk. M31: Part 5G 103
(off Central Rd.)
Columbus St. WN4: A Mak 5C 70
Columbus Way M50: Sal 1K 93
Colville Dr. BL8: Bury 3H 41
Colville Gro. M33: Sale 7E 104
WA15: Tim 1G 114
Colville Rd. OL1: O'ham 2H 63
SK11: Macc 4D 130
Colwell Av. M32: Stre 7H 93
Colwell Wlk. M9: Man 6G 61
Colwick Av. WA14: Alt 1E 6 (1E 114)
Colwith Av. BL2: Bolt 3M 39
Colwood Wlk. M8: Man 4E 78
(off Kilmington Dr.)
Colwyn Av. M14: Man 9K 95
M24: Mid 5M 61
Colwyn Cres. SK5: Stoc 3D 108
Colwyn Dr. WN2: Hin 9E 54
Colwyn Gro. BL1: Bolt 3E 38
M46: Ath 6L 55
Colwyn Rd. M27: Swin 4C 76
SK7: Bram 7C 118
SK8: Chea H 6K 117
Colwyn St. M6: Sal 7M 77
OL7: A Lyne 4L 81
OL9: O'ham 2A 8 (4H 63)
OL11: Roch 2N 43
Colwyn Ter. OL7: A Lyne 4L 81
(off Colwyn St.)
Colyton Wlk. M22: Wyth 4E 116
Combe Cl. M11: Man 7N 79
Combermere Av. M20: Man 1F 106
Combermere Cl. M29: Tyld 1C 74
SK8: Chea H 3L 117
Combermere St. SK16: Duk 9N 81
Comber Way WA16: Knut 8G 133
Combined Court Cen.
Bolton 3J 7 (5F 38)
Combs Bank SK13: Gam 7N 99
(off Brassington Cres.)
Combs Cl. SK22: N Mil 7K 121
Combs Fold SK13: Gam 7N 99
(off Brassington Cres.)
Combs Gdns. SK13: Gam 8N 99
(off Brassington Cres.)
Combs Gro. SK13: Gam 7N 99
(off Brassington Cres.)
Combs Lea SK13: Gam 8N 99
(off Brassington Cres.)
Combs M. SK13: Gam 8N 99
Combs Ter. SK13: Gam 8N 99
(off Brassington Cres.)
Combs Way SK13: Gam 7N 99
(off Brassington Cres.)
Comer Ter. M33: Sale 4G 104
Comet Rd. WN5: Wig 3N 51
Commerce Way M17: T Pk 5J 93
Commercial Av. SK8: Chea H 1K 123
Commercial Brow SK14: Hyde 5B 98
Commercial Rd. SK7: H Gro 4H 119
SK10: Macc 4J 131
Commercial St.
M15: Man 8E 4 (2D 94)
SK14: Hyde 6B 98
Commodore Pl. WN5: Wig 2B 52
Common, The PR7: Adl 9H 19
WN8: Par 1A 32
Commongate SK10: Macc 4J 131
Common La. M29: Tyld 1B 74
M31: C'ton 3J 103
(not continuous)
WA3: Cul 5F 88
WN7: Lei 6D 72
Common Nook WN2: I Mak 5K 53
Common Rd. WA12: N Wil 6B 86
COMMONSIDE 4L 131
Common Side Rd. M28: Wors 3G 75
Common St. BL5: W'ton 4D 54
WA12: N Wil 6B 86
Commonwealth Av. M11: Man 1K 95
Commonwealth Cl. WN7: Lei 7K 73
Community St. OL7: A Lyne 9K 81
Como St. BL3: Bolt 8D 38
(off Randal St.)
Como Wlk. M18: Man 3N 95
Compass St. M11: Man 2A 96
COMPSTALL 6E 110
Compstall Av. M14: Man 7G 94
COMPSTALL BROW 5D 110
Compstall Gro. M18: Man 3C 96
Compstall Mills Est.
SK6: Comp 6E 110
Compstall Rd.
SK6: Comp, Rom 6N 109
SK6: Mar B 6D 110
Compton Cl. M41: Urm 8K 91
WN2: Hin 7N 53
Compton Dr. M23: Wyth 5N 115
Compton Fold OL2: Shaw 4N 45
Compton St. SK15: Stal 9E 82
Compton Way M24: Mid 4A 62
Comrie Wlk. M23: Wyth 2N 115
Comus St. M5: Sal 1B 94
Concastrian Ind. Est. M9: Man 3H 79
Concert La. M2: Man 5H 5 (9F 78)
Concord Bus. Pk. M22: Wyth 6D 116
Concorde Av. WN3: Wig 8E 52
Concord Pl. M6: Sal 5N 77
Concord Way SK16: Duk 1N 97
Concourse Shop. Cen.
WN8: Skel 2A 50
Condor Cl. M43: Droy 7G 81
Condor Pl. M6: Sal 5N 77
Condor Wlk. M13: Man 3G 95
(off Glenbarry Cl.)
Conduit St. OL1: O'ham 9A 46
OL6: A Lyne 9E 6 (8N 81)
SK13: Tin 2B 100
Coney Grn. M26: Rad 7G 41
Coney Green Sports Cen. 8H 41
Coney Gro. M23: Wyth 9N 105
Coneymead SK15: Stal 6D 82
Congham Rd. SK3: Stoc 8A 108
Congleton Av. M14: Man 7F 94
Congleton Cl. SK9: A Edg 5F 126
Congleton Rd.
SK9: A Edg, N Ald 9F 126
SK10: N Ald 9F 126
SK11: Gaws, Macc 5D 130
Congou St. M1: Man 6M 5 (1H 95)
Congreave St. OL1: O'ham 3J 63
Congresbury Rd. WN7: Lei 3F 72
Conifer Wlk. M31: Part 5F 102
WN7: Lei 5D 72
Coningsby Dr. M9: Man 2J 79
Coningsby Gdns. WA3: Low 1A 88
Conisber Cl. BL7: Eger 4F 22
Conisborough OL11: Roch 7C 28

Conisborough Pl. M45: Whitef 4A 60
Coniston Av. BL4: Farn 4F 56
M9: Man 2J 79
M33: Sale 6J 105
M38: Lit H 6H 57
M45: Whitef 3M 59
M46: Ath 6M 55
OL8: O'ham 8H 63
PR6: Adl 5L 19
SK14: Hyde 5N 97
WN1: Wig 9E 34
WN2: I Mak 4L 53
WN4: A Mak 6E 70
WN5: Orr 4K 51
Coniston Cl. BL0: Ram 6J 11
BL3: Lit L 8A 40
M34: Dent 7F 96
OL9: Chad 4E 62
Coniston Ct. M22: Shar 1D 116
(off Downes Way)
Coniston Dr. BL9: Bury 5L 41
M24: Mid 1K 61
SK9: Hand 2H 123
SK15: Stal 7D 82
WN2: Abr 2L 71
Coniston Gro. M38: Lit H 7H 57
OL2: O'ham 6H 45
OL7: A Lyne 5A 6 (6L 81)
OL10: H'ood 3J 43
Coniston Hall M13: Man 5J 95
(off Hathersage Rd.)
Coniston Ho. M28: Walk 9M 57
(off Holyoake Rd.)
Coniston Pk. Dr. WN6: Stan 6D 34
Coniston Rd. BL6: Bla 1N 35
M27: Swin 3F 77
M29: Ast 3B 74
M31: Part 4F 102
M32: Stre 6J 93
M41: Urm 9M 91
SK5: Stoc 2D 108
SK6: H Lan 7A 120
SK8: Gat 1G 117
WN2: Hin 7A 54
Coniston St. BL1: Bolt 1G 38
M6: Sal 6A 78
M40: Man 5A 80
WN7: Lei 5G 73
Coniston Wlk. WA15: Tim 2K 115
Coniston Way SK11: Macc 7D 130
Conival Way OL9: Chad 2E 62
Conmere Sq. M15: Man 9G 5 (2E 94)
Connaught Av. M19: Man 1L 107
M45: Whitef 4N 59
OL16: Roch 1F 44
Connaught Cl. SK9: Wilm 6H 123
Connaught Dr. WA12: N Wil 7F 86
Connaught Sq. BL2: Bolt 2J 39
Connaught St. BL8: Bury 3H 41
OL8: O'ham 4C 8 (5J 63)
Connel Cl. BL2: Bolt 6N 39
Connell Rd. M23: Wyth 1N 115
Connell Way OL10: H'ood 1L 43
Connery Cres. OL6: A Lyne 4A 82
Connie St. M11: Man 1A 96
Conningsby Cl. BL7: Bro X 5G 23
Connington Av. M9: Man 1J 79
Connington Cl. OL2: O'ham 8G 45
Connor Way SK8: Gat 3E 116
Conquest Cl. M12: Man 3M 95
Conrad Cl. OL1: O'ham 8B 46
WN3: Wig 6D 52
Conran St. M9: Man 3J 79
Conroy Way WA12: N Wil 8F 86
Consett Av. M23: Wyth 1N 115
Consort Av. OL2: O'ham 6G 45
Consort Cl. SK10: Boll 6J 129
SK16: Duk 3N 97
Consort Pl. WA14: Bow 5B 114
Consort Way M34: Aud 2F 96
Constable Cl. BL1: Bolt 3E 38
Constable Dr. SK6: Mar B 8E 110
SK9: Wilm 6K 123
Constable Ho. M34: Dent 6K 97
Constable St. M18: Man 3C 96
Constable Wlk. M34: Dent 1L 109
OL1: O'ham 9A 46
Constance Gdns. M5: Sal 9M 77
Constance Rd. BL3: Bolt 7D 38
M31: Part 5G 102
Constance St. M15: Man 8E 4 (2D 94)
Constantia St. WN3: I Mak 8J 53
Constantine Ct. M5: Sal 7A 78
Constantine Rd.
OL16: Roch 7C 8 (6D 28)
Constantine St. OL4: O'ham 5A 64
Constellation Trad. Est.
M26: Rad 6F 40
Consul St. M22: Nor 7D 106
Contact Theatre 4G 94
Convamore Rd. SK7: Bram 8B 118
Convent, The WN7: Lei 3J 73
Convent Gro. OL11: Roch 8B 28
Convent St. OL4: O'ham 7N 63
Conway Av. BL1: Bolt 3B 38
M27: Clif 8H 59
M44: Irl 9G 90
M45: Whitef 4M 59
Conway Cen., The SK5: Stoc 4C 108
Conway Cl. BL0: Ram 8H 11
M16: Old T 6N 93
M24: Mid 4M 61
M45: Whitef 4M 59
OL10: H'ood 1F 42
WA16: Knut 8G 132
WN7: Lei 3N 73
Conway Cres. BL8: G'mount 3F 24
SK10: Macc 3K 131
WN5: Bil 4J 69
Conway Dr. BL9: Bury 2C 42
SK7: H Gro 6G 119
SK15: Stal 7D 82
WA12: N Wil 6H 87
WA15: Tim 1J 115
WN2: Asp 7N 35
WN5: Bil 5K 69
Conway Gro. OL9: Chad 2D 62
Conway Rd. M33: Sale 5K 105
M41: Urm 5D 92
SK8: Chea H 5K 117
WN2: Hin 7B 54
WN4: A Mak 5H 71
Conway St. BL4: Farn 4L 57
SK5: Stoc 4C 108
WN5: Wig 6N 51
Conway Towers SK5: Stoc 1G 109
Conyngham Rd. M14: Man 5J 95
Cook Av. WA11: Hay 2B 86
COOKCROFT 4C 64
Cooke Pl. M5: Sal 2A 94
Cooke St. BL4: Farn 4M 57
BL6: Hor 9F 20
M34: Dent 6J 97
M35: Fail 2D 80
SK7: H Gro 4H 119
WN4: A Mak 4C 70
Cook Rd. OL16: Roch 8G 28
Cook St. BL9: Bury 8M 7 (2M 41)
M3: Sal 3E 4 (8D 78)
M30: Ecc 8C 76
M34: Aud 3K 97
OL4: O'ham 4N 63
OL16: Roch 4F 28
SK3: Stoc 3J 9 (7C 108)
SK14: Hyde 4C 98
WN2: Abr 1K 71
WN7: Lei 5H 73
Cook Ter. OL16: Roch 4F 28
SK16: Duk 9M 81
(off Hill St.)
Cooling La. M29: Tyld 2N 73
Coomassie St. M6: Sal 7M 77
M26: Rad 9G 40
OL10: H'ood 2H 43
Coombe Cl. M29: Ast 2C 74
Coombes Av. SK6: Mar 2C 120
SK14: Hyde 6E 98
Coombes La. SK13: Char 3M 111
Coombes St. SK2: Stoc 2F 118
Coombes Vw. SK14: B'tom 9J 99
Co-operation St. M35: Fail 1D 80
Co-operative St. M6: Sal 8M 77
M26: Rad 8G 40
M38: Lit H 5F 56
OL2: Shaw 5M 45
OL3: Upp 3L 65
OL4: Spri 5C 64
SK7: H Gro 4J 119
SK12: Dis 9G 120
WN7: Lei 5F 72
Cooper Av. WA12: N Wil 6C 86
Cooper Fold M24: Mid 8M 43
Cooper Ho. M15: Man 3F 94
(off Camelford Cl.)
Cooper La. M9: Man 6J 61
M24: Mid 9L 43
Coope Rd. SK10: Boll 7J 129
Coopers Brow SK1: Stoc 2L 9
Cooper's Fold SK8: Chea H 9L 117
Coopers Glen WN2: I Mak 3K 53
Coopers Row WN1: Wig 8K 9
Cooper St. BL6: Hor 9D 20
BL9: Bury 7K 7 (2L 41)
M2: Man 5G 5 (9E 78)
(not continuous)
M32: Stre 8K 93
M43: Droy 9C 80
OL4: Spri 4D 64
OL12: Roch 1H 29
SK1: Stoc 9D 108
SK7: H Gro 4K 119
SK13: Glos 8D 100
SK16: Duk 9D 6 (9M 81)
Coopers Wlk. OL16: Roch 3G 28
COOPER TURNING 7D 36
Coops Bus. Cen. WN1: Wig 8H 9
Coops Foyer WN1: Wig 8H 9
Coop St. BL1: Bolt 9F 22
M4: Man 2K 5 (8G 78)
WN1: Wig 6M 9 (2G 53)
Co-op's Yd. BL5: W'ton 2G 55
(off Church St.)
Copage Dr. SK6: Bred 4L 109
COPE BANK 2D 38
Cope Bank BL1: Bolt 3D 38
(not continuous)
Cope Bank E. BL1: Bolt 3D 38
(off Valletts La.)
Cope Bank W. BL1: Bolt 2C 38
Cope Cl. M11: Man 2C 96
Copeland Av. M27: Clif 1J 77
Copeland Cl. M24: Mid 2H 61
Copeland Dr. WN6: Stan 2C 34
Copeland M. BL1: Bolt 5B 38
Copeland St. SK14: Hyde 4A 98
Copeman Cl. M13: Man 3H 95
Copenhagen Sq.
OL16: Roch 6F 8 (5E 28)
Copenhagen St. M40: Man 4M 79
OL16: Roch 6F 8 (5E 28)
(not continuous)
Copesthorne Cl. WN2: Asp 6M 35
Cope St. BL1: Bolt 3D 38
Copgrove Rd. M21: Cho H 1A 106
Copgrove Wlk. M22: Wyth 8D 116
COPLEY 8F 82
Copley Av. SK15: Stal 8F 82
Copley Centre, The 8F 82
Copley Pk. M. SK15: Stal 8F 82
Copley Rd. M21: Cho H 7N 93
Copley St. OL2: Shaw 4N 45
Coplow Dale WN2: Hin 8A 54
Cop Mdw. SK11: Sut E 9K 131
Copperas Cl. WN6: She 5M 33
Copperas La. M43: Droy 1C 96
(not continuous)
WN2: Hai 3L 35
(Little Scotland)
WN2: Hai 6K 35
(New Rd.)
Copperas St. M4: Man 3J 5 (8F 78)
Copperbeech Cl. M22: Nor 7D 106
Copper Beech Dr. SK13: Gam 8A 100
SK15: Stal 7G 82
Copperbeech Dr. WN6: Stan 5E 34
Copper Beech Mnr. SK13: Gam . . .8A 100
(off Orchard Dr.)
Copperfield WN1: Wig 1F 52
Copperfield Ct.
WA14: Alt 5B 6 (4C 114)
Copperfield Rd. SK8: Chea H 1N 123
SK12: Poy 4H 125
Copperfields BL6: Los 9K 37
SK9: Wilm 6H 123
SK12: Poy 4H 125
(off Weller Av.)
Copper La. M45: Whitef 4H 59
Copper Pl. M14: Man 8F 94
Copper St. SK11: Macc 6J 131
Copperways M20: Man 3G 106
COPPICE 7J 63
Coppice, The BL0: Ram 1G 24
BL2: Bolt 8L 23
M9: Man 9M 61
M24: Mid 6N 61
M25: Pres 7N 59
M28: Wors 5C 76
(Hollowgate)
M28: Wors 2N 75
(Old Clough La.)
SK7: Bram 9C 118
SK12: Poy 4L 125
WA15: Haleb 7H 115
Coppice Av. M33: Sale 6D 104
SK12: Dis 9D 120
Coppice Cl. BL6: Los 9J 37
SK6: Wood 4M 109
SK12: Dis 9D 120
Coppice Ct. SK8: H Grn 7G 117
Coppice Dr. M22: Nor 7C 106
OL12: Whitw 7A 14
WN3: Wig 8C 52
WN5: Bil 9H 51
Coppice Gro. WA16: Knut 5G 133
Coppice Ho. SK12: Poy 4G 125
Coppice Ind. Est. OL8: O'ham 6H 63
(off Windsor Rd.)
Coppice La. SK12: Dis 9D 120
Coppice Ri. SK11: Macc 7H 131
Coppice Rd. SK12: Poy 3L 125
Coppice St. BL9: Bury 1A 42
OL8: O'ham 6H 63
Coppice Wlk. M34: Dent 7H 97
Coppice Way SK9: Hand 2K 123
Coppicewood Cl. M31: Part 6F 102
Coppingford Cl. OL12: Roch 3M 27
Coppins Cl. M12: Man 3L 95
Coppins, The SK9: Wilm 1D 126
Coppleridge Dr. M8: Man 1F 78
Copplestone Ct. M27: Ward 1C 76
Copplestone Dr. M33: Sale 3C 104
COPPULL 4C 18
Coppull Community Leisure Cen.
. . . . .5B 18
Coppull Ent. Cen. PR7: Cop 3B 18
Coppull Hall La. PR7: Cop 4D 18
Coppull La. WN1: Wig 1G 52
COPPULL MOOR 7A 18
Coppull Moor La. PR7: Cop 7A 18
Coppull Rd. PR7: Char R, Chor 2C 18
Coppy Bri. Dr. OL16: Roch 5H 29
Cop Rd. OL1: O'ham 8N 45
Copse, The BL7: Tur 3K 23
PR7: Chor 1E 18
SK6: Mar B 8F 110
WA12: N Wil 5D 86
WA15: Haleb 8K 115
WN5: Orr 5L 51
Copse Av. M22: Wyth 4D 116
Copse Dr. BL9: Bury 7M 25
Copse Wlk. OL15: Lit 9K 15
Copson St. M20: Man 1G 107
Copster Av. OL8: O'ham 8J 63
COPSTER HILL 8J 63
Copster Hill Rd. OL8: O'ham 8J 63
Copster Pl. OL8: O'ham 8J 63
Copthall La. M8: Man 2E 78
(not continuous)
Copthorne Cl. OL10: H'ood 4J 43
Copthorne Cres. M13: Man 7K 95
Copthorne Dr. BL2: Bolt 6M 39
Copthorne Wlk. BL8: Tot 8F 24
Coptic Rd. OL9: Chad 3D 62
Coptrod Head Cl. OL12: Roch 1C 28
Coptrod Rd. OL11: Roch 5B 28
Coral Av. SK8: Chea H 6M 117
Coral Gro. WN7: Lei 6G 73
Coralin Way WN4: A Mak 3C 70
Coral M. OL2: O'ham 9J 45
Coral Rd. SK8: Chea H 6M 117
Coral St. M13: Man 9M 5 (2H 95)
WN6: Wig 9D 34
Coram St. M18: Man 3D 96
Corbar Rd. SK2: Stoc 2E 118
Corbel Ho. M30: Ecc 7D 76
(off Clifton Rd.)
Corbel Way M30: Ecc 7D 76
Corbett Ct. WN2: Hin 6A 54
(off Banner St.)
Corbett St. M11: Man 9M 79
OL16: Roch 5G 8 (5F 28)
Corbett Way OL3: Dens 3F 46
Corbridge Wlk. M8: Man 4G 78
(off Appleford Dr.)
Corbrook Rd. OL9: Chad 2C 62
Corby Cl. BL1: Bolt 3F 38
Corby St. M12: Man 3M 95
Corcoran Cl. OL10: H'ood 1H 43
Corcoran Dr. SK6: Rom 6C 110
Corda Av. M22: Nor 8C 106
Corday La. M25: Pres 3C 60
M45: Bury 2C 60
Cordingley Av. M43: Droy 1D 96
Cordova Av. M34: Dent 6D 96
Corelli St. M40: Man 6L 79
Corfe Cl. M41: Urm 8K 91
WN2: Asp 7N 35
Corfe Cres. SK7: H Gro 6G 119
Corhampton Cres. M46: Ath 6N 55
Corinthian Av. M7: Sal 5B 78
Corinth Wlk. M28: Walk 9L 57
(off Bridgewater Rd.)
Corkland Cl. OL6: A Lyne 8B 82
Corkland Rd. M21: Cho H 9A 94
Corkland St. OL6: A Lyne 8B 82
Cork St. BL9: Bury 7N 7 (2N 41)
M12: Man 1J 95
OL6: A Lyne 7E 6 (7N 81)
Corless Fold M29: Ast 5D 74
Corley Av. SK3: Stoc 9L 107
Corley Wlk. M11: Man 9L 79
Cormallen Gro. M35: Fail 3E 80
Cormorant Cl. M28: Walk 8K 57
Cormorant Wlk. M12: Man 3M 95
(off Flamingo Cl.)
Cornall St. BL8: Bury 1J 41
CORNBROOK 8B 4 (2C 94)
Cornbrook WN8: Skel 4C 50
Cornbrook Arches
M15: Man 9A 4 (2B 94)
Cornbrook Cl. BL5: W'ton 5F 54
OL12: W'le 8G 14
Cornbrook Ct. M15: Man 3C 94
Cornbrook Gro. M16: Old T 4C 94
Cornbrook Pk. Rd.
M15: Man 9A 4 (3B 94)
(not continuous)
Cornbrook Rd.
M16: Old T 9A 4 (2B 94)
SK11: Macc 8G 131
Cornbrook Stop (Metro) 9A 4 (2B 94)
Cornbrook St. M16: Old T 4C 94
(not continuous)
Cornbrook Way M16: Old T 4C 94
Corn Cl. M13: Man 4H 95
Cornelian Gro. WN4: A Mak 5C 70
Cornell St. M4: Man 2L 5 (8G 79)
Corner Brook BL6: Los 9J 37
Corner Cft. SK9: Wilm 1F 126
Cornergate BL5: W'ton 6G 54
Cornerhouse Art Gallery . . .7H 5 (1F 94)
Corner La. WN7: Lei 8F 54
Corner St. OL6: A Lyne 9F 6 (8N 81)
Cornet St. M7: Sal 4C 78
Cornfield SK15: Stal 2H 99
Cornfield Cl. BL9: Bury 6N 25
M33: Sale 5M 105
(off Pimmcroft Way)
SK10: Macc 1G 131
Cornfield Dr. M22: Wyth 4B 116
Cornfield Rd. SK6: Rom 5B 110
Cornfield St. OL16: Miln 8K 29
Cornford Av. M18: Man 6N 95
Cornhey Rd. M33: Sale 6C 104
Cornhill Av. M41: Urm 6B 92
Corn Hill La. M34: Aud 4E 96
Cornhill Rd. M41: Urm 5B 92
Cornhill St. OL1: O'ham 1A 64
Cornish Cl. M22: Wyth 7C 116
Cornish Way OL2: O'ham 9K 45
Cornishway M22: Wyth 6B 116
Cornishway Ind. Est.
M22: Wyth 7C 116
(off Cornishway)
Cornlea Dr. M28: Wors 3K 75
Corn Mill Cl. OL12: Roch 1G 29
WN4: Gars 6A 70
Cornmill Ct. WA3: Cro 9C 88
Corn Mill Dr. BL4: Farn 4M 57
Corn Mill La. SK15: Stal 9E 82
Corn St. M35: Fail 4A 80
OL4: O'ham 4L 63
(off Lees Rd.)
SK13: Glos 8F 100
WN7: Lei 5F 72
Cornwall Av. BL5: O Hul 3A 56
M19: Man 9N 95
M29: Tyld 8B 56
Cornwall Cl. SK6: H Lan 8B 120
SK10: Macc 3C 130
Cornwall Ct. M18: Man 3B 96
Cornwall Cres. OL3: Dig 8L 47
SK5: Stoc 2G 108
WN1: Stan 3E 34
Cornwall Dr. BL9: Bury 4M 41
WN2: Hin 5B 54
Cornwall Ho. M3: Sal 4C 4
Cornwallis Rd. WN3: Wig 6C 52
Cornwall Pl. WN5: Wig 5N 51
Cornwall Rd. M43: Droy 7E 80
M44: Cad 3E 102
SK8: H Grn 7G 117
Cornwall St. M11: Man 2B 96
M30: Ecc 9C 76
OL9: O'ham 6F 62
Cornwall St. Ind. Est.
M11: Man 2B 96
(off Cornwall St.)
Cornwell Cl. SK9: Wilm 6J 123
Cornwood Cl. M8: Man 3E 78
(off Narbuth Dr.)
Corona Av. OL8: O'ham 8H 63
SK14: Hyde 6B 98
Coronation Av. M46: Ath 6L 55
OL10: H'ood 4K 43
SK14: Hyde 8B 98
SK16: Duk 2C 98
WA3: G'ury 2L 89
Coronation Bldgs.
SK10: Boll 5L 129
(off Wellington Rd.)
Coronation Dr. WA11: Hay 2D 86
WN7: Lei 4M 73
Coronation Gdns. M26: Rad 8E 40
(not continuous)
Coronation Rd. M26: Rad 7E 40
M35: Fail 4C 80
M43: Droy 7D 80
OL6: A Lyne 4N 81
WN6: Stan 9A 34
Coronation Sq. BL3: Lit L 9B 40
M12: Man 7N 5 (1H 95)
M34: Aud 2H 97
WA16: Knut 6G 133
Coronation St. BL1: Bolt 3K 7 (5G 38)
M3: Man 6D 4 (1D 94)
M5: Sal 1A 94
M11: Man 1A 96
M27: Pen 1F 76
M34: Dent 6H 97
OL1: O'ham 2F 8 (4L 63)
SK5: Stoc 4C 108
SK11: Macc 6H 131
WN3: I Mak 8J 53
WN3: Wig 5E 52
WN4: A Mak 4A 70
WN5: Bil 6H 69
Coronation Vs. OL12: Whitw 4B 14
Coronation Wlk. M26: Rad 7E 40
Coroners Court
Manchester City 5E 4 (9D 78)
Coronet Cl. WN6: App B 5G 33
Coronet Way M50: Sal 9H 77
Corporation Cotts. M31: C'ton 2K 103
Corporation Rd. M30: Ecc 8F 76
M34: Aud, Dent 4H 97
OL11: Roch 7B 28
(not continuous)
Corporation St. BL1: Bolt . . .2K 7 (5G 38)
M3: Man 3G 5 (8E 78)
M4: Man 3G 5 (8E 78)
M24: Mid 3M 61
SK1: Stoc 1M 9 (6D 108)
SK14: Hyde 7A 98
SK15: Stal 9D 82
WN3: Wig 5E 52
Corporation Yd. SK5: Stoc 9D 96
Corran Cl. M30: Ecc 8B 76
Corranstone Cl. BL6: Hor 1D 36
Corrie Cl. M34: Dent 8K 97
Corrie Cres. BL4: Kea 6D 58
Corrie Dr. BL4: Kea 7D 58
Corrie Rd. M27: Clif 8G 58
Corrie St. M38: Lit H 7H 57
Corrie Way SK6: Bred 3J 109
Corrigan St. M18: Man 3C 96
Corringham Rd. M19: Man 1A 108
Corring Way BL1: Bolt 9J 23
Corrin Rd. BL2: Bolt 7J 39
Corris Av. M9: Man 6F 60
Corry St. OL10: H'ood 2K 43
Corsey Rd. WN2: Hin 7A 54
Corsock Dr. WN1: Wig 2H 53
Corson St. BL3: Bolt 1L 57
Corston Gro. BL6: Bla 3N 35
Corston Wlk. M40: Man 5N 79
Corwen Cl. OL8: O'ham 9F 62
Cosgate Cl. WN5: Orr 6J 51
Cosgrove Cres. M35: Fail 5C 80
Cosgrove Rd. M35: Fail 5C 80
Cosgroves Physio & Fitness Cen.
. . . . .7N 55
Cosham Rd. M22: Wyth 4E 116
Cosmo Bingo 9C 76
Costabeck Wlk. M40: Man 6B 80
(off Stansfield St.)
Costessey Way WN3: Wins 8N 51
Costobadie Cl. SK14: Mot 6J 99
Costobadie Way SK14: Mot 6J 99
(off Ashworth La.)
COSTON PARK 7M 95
Cosworth Cl. WN7: Lei 6K 73
Cotaline Cl. OL11: Roch 1N 43
Cotefield Av. BL3: Bolt 9G 39
Cotefield Cl. SK6: Mar 2C 120
Cotefield Rd. M22: Wyth 5A 116
COTE GREEN 7E 110
Cote Grn. La. SK6: Mar B 7E 110
Cote Grn. Rd. SK6: Mar B 7E 110
Cote La. OL3: Del 4L 47
OL5: Mos 8H 65
OL15: Lit 8K 15
Cote Royd OL6: A Lyne 6G 6
Cotford Rd. BL1: Bolt 8G 23
Cotham St. M3: Man 6E 78
Cotman Dr. SK6: Mar B 8F 110
Cotswold Av. M41: Urm 6N 91
OL2: Shaw 4K 45
OL9: Chad 6E 62
SK7: H Gro 6F 118
WA3: Low 3N 87
WN5: Wig 6M 51
Cotswold Cl. BL0: Ram 1J 25
M25: Pres 6B 60
SK10: Macc 3C 130
SK13: Glos 9C 100
Cotswold Cres. BL8: Bury 1G 41
OL16: Miln 6L 29
Cotswold Dr. BL6: Hor 8E 20
M6: Sal 7M 77
OL2: O'ham 9F 44
Cotswold Gdns. WA3: Low 3A 88
Cotswold Rd. SK4: Stoc 5B 108
Cottage Cft. BL2: Bolt 8L 23
Cottage Flds. PR7: Chor 1E 18
Cottage Gdns. OL4: O'ham 7N 63
SK6: Bred 5H 109
Cottage Gro. SK9: Wilm 9D 122
Cottage La. SK10: Macc 5K 131
SK13: Gam 7A 100
Cottage Lawns SK9: A Edg 3G 126
Cottages, The OL4: Scout 2E 64
Cottage St. SK11: Macc 4F 130
Cottage Vw. OL12: Whitw 7A 14
Cottage Wlk. M43: Droy 7D 80
OL12: Roch 1A 28
Cottam Cres. SK6: Mar B 9E 110
Cottam Gro. M27: Swin 3G 76
Cottam St. BL8: Bury 1J 41
OL1: O'ham 3H 63
Cottenham La. M3: Sal 7D 78
M7: Sal 6D 78
Cottenham St. M13: Man 3G 95
Cotterdale Cl. M16: Whall R 7C 94
Cotterill Cl. M23: Wyth 7J 105
Cotterill St. M6: Sal 8N 77
Cotter St. M12: Man 8M 5 (2H 95)
Cottesmore Cl. OL12: Whitw 8A 14
Cottesmore Dr. M8: Man 2H 79
Cottesmore Gdns. WA15: Haleb . . .7J 115

Cottesmore Way WA3: Gol 9L 71
Cottingham Dr.
OL6: A Lyne 5F 6 (6N 81)
Cottingham Rd. M12: Man 3K 95
Cottingley Cl. BL1: Bolt 8E 22
Cotton Bldg., The BL7: Eger 3E 22
(off Deakins Mill Way)
Cotton Cl. SK14: Hyde 8B 98
Cottonfield Rd. M20: Man 2H 107
Cottonfields BL7: Bolt 6G 22
Cotton Fold OL16: Roch 7G 28
Cotton Hill M20: Man 3H 107
Cotton La. M20: Man 2H 107
OL11: Roch 9A 28
Cotton Lodge Cl. BL3: Bolt 9H 39
Cotton Mill, The SK13: Glos 9F 100
Cotton Mill Cres. OL9: O'ham 7F 62
Cotton Mills Dr. SK14: Hyde 3B 98
Cotton Shop Yd. WA16: Knut 6G 133
Cottonside WN3: Wig 9H 9
Cotton Sq. M14: Man 6G 94
Cotton St. BL1: Bolt 2E 38
M4: Man 3L 5 (8G 79)
WN7: Lei 5F 72
Cotton St. E. OL6: A Lyne . . .8B 6 (8L 81)
Cotton St. W. OL6: A Lyne . .8A 6 (8L 81)
Cotton Tree Cl. OL4: O'ham 3A 64
Cotton Tree Ct. SK14: Hyde 7A 98
(off Reynold St.)
Cotton Tree St.
SK4: Stoc 2J 9 (7C 108)
Cottonwood Dr. M33: Sale 3C 104
Cottonworks, The BL1: Bolt 8G 22
Cottrell Rd. WA15: Haleb 8K 115
Coucill Sq. BL4: Farn 3M 57
Coulsden Dr. M9: Man 8J 61
Coulthart St.
OL6: A Lyne 7D 6 (7M 81)
Coulthurst St. BL0: Ram 8H 11
Coulton Cl. OL1: O'ham 3L 63
Coulton Wlk. M5: Sal 8M 77
Coultshead Av. WN5: Bil 4J 69
Council Av. WN4: A Mak 7E 70
Councillor La.
SK8: Chea, Chea H 1L 117
Councillor St. M12: Man 9K 79
Countess Av. SK8: Chea H 1K 123
Countess Cl. SK11: Macc 5D 130
Countess La. M26: Rad 7D 40
Countess Pl. M25: Pres 7B 60
Countess Rd. M20: Man 5G 107
SK11: Macc 5D 130
Countess St. OL6: A Lyne 8A 82
SK2: Stoc 2E 118
Counthill Dr. M8: Man 9D 60
Counthill Rd. OL4: O'ham 2A 64
Count St. OL16: Roch 8E 28
County Av. OL6: A Lyne 6B 82
County Court
Altrincham 3G 105
Bury 8H 7 (2K 41)
Macclesfield 5H 131
Manchester 4E 4 (9D 78)
Oldham 2C 8 (4J 63)
Stockport 4L 9 (8D 108)
Tameside 8B 6 (8L 81)
Wigan 9L 9 (4G 52)
COUNTY END 6C 64
County End Bus. Pk. OL4: Lees 5C 64
County End Ter. OL4: Spri 5C 64
(off Oldham Rd.)
County Police St. WN2: I Mak 4J 53
County Rd. M28: Walk 7H 57
County St. M2: Man 5G 4
OL8: O'ham 9G 62
County Ter. WA16: Knut 7F 132
Coupes Grn. BL5: W'ton 5G 55
Coupland Cl. OL4: O'ham 8C 46
OL12: Whitw 6E 14
Coupland Rd. WN2: Hin 7E 54
Couplands, The PR7: Cop 5B 18
Coupland St. M15: Man 4F 94
OL12: Whitw 6A 14
Coupland St. E. M15: Man 3F 94
Courier Pl. WN5: Wig 2B 52
Courier Row SK10: Boll 6K 129
Courier St. M18: Man 3C 96
Course Vw. OL4: O'ham 8B 64
Court, The M25: Pres 8A 60
Court Dr. M40: Man 6C 80
Courteney Pl. WA14: Bow 6A 114
Courtfield Av. M9: Man 7J 61
Courthill St. SK1: Stoc 8E 108
Courthouse Way OL10: H'ood 2J 43
(off Woodland St.)
Courtney Grn. SK9: Wilm 4J 123
Court St. BL2: Bolt 3N 7 (5H 39)
OL3: Upp 3L 65
Courts Vw. M33: Sale 3J 105
Courtyard, The BL1: Bolt 3G 39
M7: Sal .2B 78
OL10: H'ood 3K 43
SK6: Bred 3L 109
(off Rodney Dr.)
SK14: Holl 4N 99
WA12: N Wil 5H 87
(off Golborne St.)
Courtyard Dr. M28: Walk 8H 57
Cousin Flds. BL7: Bro X 6K 23
Covall Wlk. M8: Man 4G 79
(off Hawkeshead Rd.)
Cove, The WA15: Hale 4F 114
Covell Rd. SK12: Poy 1H 125
Covent Gdns. SK1: Stoc . . .3L 9 (7D 108)
Coventry Av. SK3: Stoc 9L 107
Coventry Gro. OL9: Chad 2E 62
Coventry Rd. M26: Rad 7F 40
Coverdale Av. BL1: Bolt 4B 38
OL2: O'ham 7G 45
Coverdale Cl. OL10: H'ood 3H 43
WN2: P Bri 9J 53
Coverdale Cres. M12: Man 3J 95
Coverdale Rd. BL5: W'ton 3F 54
Cover Dr. OL11: Roch 2N 43
Coverham Av. OL4: O'ham 7A 64
Coverhill Rd. OL4: Grot 6E 64
Covert Rd. M22: Shar 2D 116
OL4: O'ham 8A 64
Coverts, The WN6: Wig 1C 52
Covington Pl. SK9: Wilm 8G 123
Cowan St. M40: Man 8J 79
Cowbrook Av. SK13: Glos 8H 101
Cowbrook Ct. SK13: Glos 8H 101
Cowburn Dr. SK22: N Mil 6M 121
Cowburn St. M3: Man 1G 5 (7E 78)
OL10: H'ood 3K 43
WN2: Hin 5B 54
WN7: Lei 5F 72
Cow Clough La. OL12: Whitw 4N 13
Cowdals Rd. BL6: Los 8K 37
Cowesby St. M14: Man 6F 94
COWHILL 5F 62
Cowhill La. OL6: A Lyne 6E 6 (7N 81)
Cowhill Trad. Est. OL6: A Lyne 5E 6
Cowie St. OL2: Shaw 4M 45
Cow La. BL3: Bolt 1C 56
M5: Sal 5A 4 (9B 78)
M33: Sale 2L 105
(not continuous)
M35: Fail 3C 80
OL4: O'ham 4N 63
SK2: Stoc 3H 119
SK7: Stoc 3H 119
SK9: Wilm 7H 123
SK10: Boll 6M 129
SK10: Rain 9N 129
SK11: Macc 6H 131
WA14: D Mas 2M 113
WA15: Ash 9F 114
Cow Lees BL5: W'ton 2J 55
Cowley Rd. BL1: Bolt 8B 22
Cowley St. M40: Man 4A 80
Cowling Cotts. PR7: Char R 2A 18
Cowling St. M7: Sal 2M 77
OL8: O'ham 7K 63
WN3: Wig 5E 52
COWLISHAW 6L 45
Cowlishaw OL2: Shaw 7L 45
COWLISHAW BROW 3C 110
Cowlishaw La. OL2: Shaw 7L 45
Cowlishaw Rd. SK6: Rom 3C 110
SK14: Hyde, Stoc 3C 110
Cowm Pk. Way Nth.
OL12: Whitw 4A 14
Cowm Pk. Way Sth.
OL12: Whitw 6A 14
Cowm St. OL12: Whitw 1C 14
Cowm Top Bus. Pk. OL11: Roch 2B 44
Cowm Top La. OL11: Roch 1C 44
Cowper Av. M46: Ath 6M 55
Cowpe Rd. BB4: Water 1E 12
Cowper St. M24: Mid 3B 62
OL6: A Lyne 6E 6 (7N 81)
WN7: Lei 5F 72
Cowper Wlk. M11: Man 9L 79
(off Newcombe Cl.)
Coxfield Gro. WN6: She 5H 33
COX GREEN 4G 23
Cox Grn. Cl. BL7: Eger 2E 22
Cox Grn. Rd. BL7: Eger 1E 22
Coxton Rd. M22: Wyth 6D 116
Cox Way M46: Ath 8M 55
Coxwold Gro. BL3: Bolt 1D 56
(off Maltby Dr.)
Crabbe St. M4: Man 7F 78
Crab Brow M46: Ath 8K 55
Crab La. M9: Man 7G 61
Crabtree Av. WA15: Haleb 8K 115
Crabtree Cl. WA12: N Wil 6H 87
Crabtree Ct. SK12: Dis 9G 120
(off Buxton Old Rd.)
Crab Tree La. M46: Ath 8M 55
Crabtree La. M11: Man 1B 96
(not continuous)
WA13: Lym 8B 112
WA16: H Leg 9B 112
Crabtree Rd. OL1: O'ham 3M 63
WN5: Wig 4A 52
Craddock Rd. M33: Sale 6J 105
Craddock St. OL5: Mos 1F 82
Cradley Av. M11: Man 1B 96
Crag Av. BL9: Sum 3K 25
Cragg Fold BL9: Sum 3K 25
Cragg Pl. OL15: Lit 9M 15
Cragg Rd. OL1: Chad 1D 62
(not continuous)
Crag Gro. WA11: St H 9F 68
Crag La. BL9: Sum 3K 25
Cragside Way SK9: Wilm 8H 123
Craig Av. BL8: Bury 3H 41
M41: Urm 6A 92
Craig Cl. SK4: Stoc 7N 107
SK11: Macc 7F 130
Craigend Dr. M9: Man 3K 79
Craig Hall M44: Irl 1G 102
Craighall Av. M19: Man 9L 95
Craighall Rd. BL1: Bolt 7F 22
Craigie St. M8: Man 5E 78
Craiglands OL16: Roch 2F 44
Craiglands Av. M40: Man 4M 79
Craigmore Av. M20: Man 4C 106
Craignair Ct. M27: Pen 3H 77
Craig Rd. M18: Man 5A 96
SK4: Stoc 7L 107
SK11: Macc 7F 130
Craigweil Av. M20: Man 5J 107
Craigwell Rd. M25: Pres 9D 60
Craigwell Wlk. M13: Man 9K 5
Crail Pl. OL10: H'ood 3E 42
Cramer St. M40: Man 5L 79
Crammond Cl. M40: Man 4B 80
Cramond Cl. BL1: Bolt 3E 38
WN3: Wig 7A 52
Cramond Wlk. BL1: Bolt 3E 38
(off Cramond Cl.)
Crampton Dr. WA15: Haleb 7J 115
Crampton La. M31: C'ton 1L 103
Cranage Av. SK9: Hand 1J 123
(off Spath La.)
Cranage Rd. M19: Man 9N 95
Cranark Cl. BL1: Bolt 5B 38
Cranberry Av. WN6: Wig 9C 34
Cranberry Cl. WA14: B'ath 8B 104
Cranberry Dr. BL3: Bolt 8A 38
M34: Dent 6H 97
Cranberry Rd. M31: Part 5G 103
Cranberry St. OL4: O'ham 5M 63
Cranborne Cl. BL6: Los 3H 37
WN6: Stan 3N 33
Cranbourne Av. SK8: Chea H 5N 117
Cranbourne Cl. OL7: A Lyne 6L 81
WA15: Tim 1G 114
Cranbourne Ct. SK4: Stoc 4N 107
Cranbourne Rd. M16: Old T 5B 94
M21: Cho H 9A 94
OL6: A Lyne 6L 81
OL7: A Lyne 6L 81
OL11: Roch 7K 27
SK4: Stoc 4N 107
Cranbourne St. M5: Sal 9A 78
Cranbourne Ter. OL6: A Lyne 5M 81
Cranbrook Av. WN4: A Mak 6D 70
Cranbrook Cl. BL1: Bolt 3G 38
(off Lindfield Dr.)
Cranbrook Dr. M25: Pres 9B 60
Cranbrook Gdns. OL7: A Lyne 6M 81
Cranbrook Pl. OL4: O'ham 5N 63
Cranbrook Rd. M18: Man 6C 96
M30: Ecc 6A 76
Cranbrook St. M26: Rad 7J 41
OL4: O'ham 5M 63
OL7: A Lyne 5B 6 (6L 81)
Cranbrook Wlk. OL9: Chad 5E 62
Cranbrook Way WN1: Wig 8F 34
Cranby Nook WN2: Hin 6C 54
Cranby St. WN2: Hin 6N 53
Crandon Ct. M27: Pen 1G 76
Crandon Dr. M20: Man 8H 107
Cranesbill Cl. M22: Wyth 6B 116
Crane St. BL3: Bolt 9C 38
M12: Man 7N 5 (1H 95)
PR7: Cop 7A 18
Cranfield Cl. M40: Man 8J 79
Cranfield Rd. BL6: Los 5F 36
WN3: Wig 8D 52
Cranford Av. M20: Man 4J 107
M32: Stre 6M 93
M33: Sale 2J 105
M45: Whitef 1L 59
SK11: Macc 5K 131
WA16: Knut 7F 132
Cranford Cl. M27: Swin 4H 77
M45: Whitef 1L 59
Cranford Dr. M44: Irl 6G 91
WA16: Knut 4K 133
Cranford Gdns. M41: Urm 6M 91
SK6: Mar 8C 110
Cranford Golf Range 6K 107
Cranford Ho. M30: Ecc 7F 76
(off Half Edge La.)
Cranford Rd. M41: Urm 6M 91
SK9: Wilm 5F 122
Cranford Sq. WA16: Knut 7F 132
Cranford St. BL3: Bolt 1D 56
Cranham Av. WA3: Low 2A 88
Cranham Cl. BL8: Bury 1H 41
M38: Lit H 5H 57
Cranham Rd. M22: Wyth 5N 115
CRANK 6C 68
Crank Hill WA11: Cra 6C 68
Crank Rd. WA11: Cra, St H 9B 68
WA11: K Mos 4D 68
WN5: Bil 4D 68
CRANKWOOD 6A 72
Crankwood Rd. WN2: Abr 4L 71
WN7: Lei 4L 71
Cranleigh WN6: Stan 4C 34
Cranleigh Av. SK4: Stoc 4L 107
Cranleigh Cl. BL6: Bla 3N 35
OL4: O'ham 2A 64
Cranleigh Dr. M28: Walk 2M 75
M29: Ast 2C 74
M33: Sale 7J 105
(Ashstead Rd.)
M33: Sale 3G 105
(Oaklands Dr.)
SK7: H Gro 7L 119
SK8: Chea 1L 117
Cranlington Dr. M8: Man 4E 78
Cranmer Ct. OL10: H'ood 3H 43
Cranmere Av. M19: Man 7A 96
Cranmere Dr. M33: Sale 6D 104
Cranmer Rd. M20: Man 4G 107
Cranshaw St. M29: Tyld 1E 74
Cranstal Dr. WN2: Hin 4C 54
Cranston Dr. M20: Man 8G 106
M33: Sale 5L 105
Cranston Gro. SK8: Gat 2E 116
Cranswick St. M14: Man 6F 94
Crantock Dr. SK8: H Grn 7H 117
SK15: Stal 7G 82
Crantock Rd. WN5: Wig 6N 51
Crantock St. M12: Man 6H 95
Cranwell Av. WA3: Cul 5N 89
Cranwell Ct. M43: Droy 1F 96
(off Williamson La.)
Cranwell Dr. M19: Man 4K 107
Cranworth Av. M29: Ast 4B 74
Cranworth St. SK15: Stal 9E 82
Craston Rd. M13: Man 7K 95
Crathie Ct. BL1: Bolt 3C 38
Craunton Ho. M30: Ecc 8F 76
Craven Av. M5: Sal 1A 94
WA3: Low 2A 88
Craven Ct. BL6: Hor 2F 36
Craven Dr. M5: Sal 3N 93
WA14: B'ath 8C 104
Craven Gdns. OL11: Roch 8C 28
Cravenhurst Av. M40: Man 6N 79
Craven Pl. BL1: Bolt 2N 37
M11: Man 8A 80
Craven Rd. SK5: Stoc 2D 108
WA14: B'ath 9C 104
(not continuous)
Craven St. BL9: Bury 1A 42
M5: Sal 5A 4 (9B 78)
OL1: O'ham 2J 63
OL6: A Lyne 5A 82
Craven St. E. BL6: Hor 2F 36
Craven Ter. M33: Sale 4J 105
Cravenwood OL6: A Lyne 4C 82
Cravenwood Ri. BL5: W'ton 1J 55
(off Abbeylea Dr.)
Cravenwood Rd. M8: Man 2F 78
SK5: Stoc 7C 96
CRAWFORD 9B 50
Crawford Av. BL2: Bolt 6J 39
M28: Wors 2N 75
M29: Tyld 9A 56
PR7: Adl 8H 19
WN2: Asp 7M 35
Crawford Cl. WN2: Asp 7M 35
Crawford M. OL6: A Lyne 8A 82
Crawford Pl. WN1: Wig 1G 52
(off Wigan La.)
Crawford Rd. WN8: Skel 1A 68
Crawford Sq. OL10: H'ood 3F 42
Crawford St. BL2: Bolt 4N 7 (6J 39)
M30: Ecc 7D 76
M40: Man 5A 80
OL6: A Lyne 8A 82
OL16: Roch 8E 28
WN1: Wig 8J 9 (3F 52)
WN2: Asp 8M 35
Crawley Av. M22: Wyth 4C 116
M30: Ecc 7G 76
Crawley Cl. M29: Tyld 1D 74
Crawley Gro. SK2: Stoc 1F 118
Crawley Way OL9: Chad 5E 62
Cray, The OL16: Miln 7J 29
Craydon St. M11: Man 1A 96
Crayfield Rd. M19: Man 9N 95
Crayford Rd. M40: Man 6N 79
Cray Wlk. M13: Man 9K 5
Creaton Way M24: Mid 8H 43
Creden Av. M22: Wyth 4E 116
Crediton Cl. M15: Man 4E 94
WA14: Alt 1B 114
Crediton Dr. BL2: Bolt 5A 40
WN2: P Bri 1K 71
Crediton Ho. M6: Sal 7G 77
Creel Cl. M9: Man 7G 61
Cremer Ho. M30: Ecc 8F 76
Cresbury St. M12: Man 2J 95
Crescent, The BL2: Bolt 9N 23
BL3: Lit L 1B 58
BL5: W'ton 4G 55
BL6: Hor 3G 36
BL7: Bro X 5H 23
BL9: Bury 6N 7 (1N 41)
M5: Sal 3A 4 (8A 78)
M19: Man 8M 95
M24: Mid 3K 61
M25: Pres 7A 60
M26: Rad 7D 40
M28: Wors 5A 76
M41: Urm 6N 91
M43: Droy 9D 80
M44: Irl 6J 91
OL2: Shaw 6L 45
OL5: Mos 1E 82
OL12: Whitw 6A 14
SK3: Stoc 2D 118
SK6: Bred 4H 109
SK8: Chea 1J 117
SK10: Macc 3J 131
(not continuous)
SK10: Mot S A 4M 127
SK15: Stal 3G 99
SK22: N Mil 7L 121
WA13: Lym 5A 112
WA14: Alt 2A 114
WA15: Tim 9F 104
WN2: I Mak 4L 53
WN5: Wig 5A 52
Crescent Av. BL1: Bolt 1G 7 (4E 38)
BL4: Farn 5K 57
BL5: O Hul 3B 56
M8: Man 2F 78
M25: Pres 9A 60
M27: Pen 2J 77
WN4: A Mak 6D 70
Crescent Cl. SK3: Stoc 2E 118
SK16: Duk 9N 81
Crescent Ct. M21: Cho H 8M 93
(off Alderfield Rd.)
M33: Sale 5H 105
Crescent Dr. M8: Man 1G 79
M38: Lit H 6J 57
Crescent Gro. M19: Man 8M 95
M25: Pres 9A 60
SK8: Chea 1H 117
Crescent Pk. SK4: Stoc 6A 108
Crescent Range M14: Man 6H 95
Crescent Rd. BL3: Bolt 8H 39
BL4: Kea 5N 57
BL6: Los 4G 37
M8: Man 2E 78
OL9: Chad 9C 62
OL11: Roch 9N 27
SK1: Stoc 5F 108
SK8: Chea 1H 117
SK9: A Edg 3G 126
SK16: Duk 9E 6 (9N 81)
WA14: Alt 1A 114
WA15: Hale 5E 114
Crescent St. M8: Man 2H 79
Crescent Vw. SK16: Duk 9N 81
(off Peel St.)
Crescent Way SK3: Stoc 2E 118
Cresgarth Ho. SK3: Stoc 3E 118
Cressell Pk. WN6: Stan 2L 33
Cressfield Way M21: Cho H 1C 106
Cressingham Rd. BL3: Bolt 8A 38
M32: Stre 8H 93
Cressington Cl. M5: Sal 8L 77
(off Cedric St.)
Cresswell Av. SK22: N Mil 7M 121
Cresswell Gro. M20: Man 3F 106
Cresswell St. SK22: N Mil 7M 121
Crest, The M43: Droy 2E 96
Crestfield Gro. WN6: Wig 1C 52
Crestfold M38: Walk 7H 57
Crest Lodge SK7: Bram 5D 118
Crest St. M3: Man 1H 5 (7E 78)
Crestwood Av. WN3: Wig 8B 52
Crestwood Wlk. M40: Man 4H 79
(off Barnstaple Dr.)
Creswick Cl. WN2: Hin 7M 53
Crete St. OL8: O'ham 7K 63
Crew Av. SK10: Macc 3J 131
Crewe Rd. M23: Wyth 8L 105
Crib Fold OL3: Dob 1K 65
Crib La. OL3: Dob 1K 65
Criccieth Av. WN2: Asp 7N 35
Criccieth Rd. SK3: Stoc 9M 107
Criccieth St. M16: Whall R 5E 94
Cricketers Way BL5: W'ton 3G 55
Cricketfield La. M28: Walk 8K 57
Cricket Gro., The
M21: Cho H 2A 106
Crickets La. OL6: A Lyne 7F 6 (7N 81)
(not continuous)
Crickets La. Nth.
OL6: A Lyne 7E 6 (7N 81)
Cricket St. BL3: Bolt 7E 38
M34: Dent 5L 97
WN6: Wig 3E 52
Cricket St. Bus. Cen.
WN6: Wig 3E 52
Cricket St. Bus. Pk. WN6: Wig 3D 52
Cricket Vw. OL16: Miln 8K 29
Cricklewood Rd. M22: Wyth 5B 116
CRIMBLE 9K 27
Crimble La. OL10: H'ood, Roch 9K 27
OL11: Roch 8K 27
Crimble St. OL12: Roch 6A 8 (5B 28)
Crime La. M35: O'ham 3H 81
OL8: O'ham 3H 81
CRIME VIEW 3H 81
Crimsworth Av. M16: Old T 7A 94
Crinan Sq. OL10: H'ood 3E 42
Crinan Wlk. M40: Man 7J 79
(off Nuneaton Dr.)
Crinan Way BL2: Bolt 6N 39
Cringlebarrow Cl. M28: Wors 5G 75
Cringle Cl. BL3: Bolt 8N 37
Cringle Dr. SK8: Chea 3H 117
Cringleford Cl. M12: Man 4L 95
Cringle Hall Rd. M19: Man 9L 95
Cringle Rd. M19: Man 1N 107
Crippen St. M46: Ath 1J 73
Cripplegate WN6: Stan 2K 33
Cripple Ga. La. OL11: Roch 3C 44
CRISP DELF 9D 32
Crispin Rd. M22: Wyth 7D 116
Critchley Cl. SK14: Hyde 8C 98
Criterion St. SK5: Stoc 7D 96
Croal Av. WN2: P Bri 9K 53
Croal St. BL1: Bolt 6E 38
Croal Wlk. M45: Whitef 2A 60
Croasdale Av. M14: Man 9G 95
Croasdale Cl. OL2: O'ham 7J 45
Croasdale Dr. WN8: Par 1A 32
Croasdale St. BL1: Bolt 3G 38
(not continuous)
Crocker Wlk. M9: Man 2K 79
(off Kingscliffe St.)
Crocus Dr. OL2: O'ham 7L 45
Crocus St. BL1: Bolt 9G 22
Crocus Wlk. M7: Sal 4C 78
(off Hilton St. Nth.)
CROFT 9C 88
Croft, The BL1: Bolt 1K 7
BL5: W'ton 9G 36
BL9: Bury 6N 41
OL8: O'ham 9J 63
SK2: Stoc 1F 118
SK13: Had 3C 100
SK14: Mot 5K 99
WN5: Bil 7H 51
Croft Acres BL0: Ram 4K 11
Croft Av. M25: Pres 3E 60
M46: Ath 9M 55
WA3: Gol 8J 71
WN5: Orr 6H 51
Croft Bank M7: Sal 5B 78
M18: Man 4C 96
OL12: Whitw 3A 14
SK15: Mill 6G 82
Croft Brow OL8: O'ham 9J 63
Croft Cl. WA15: Haleb 9J 115
Croft Ct. WN7: Lei 9E 72
Croft Dell BL1: Bolt 1B 38
Croft Dr. BL8: Tot 7E 24
Croft Edge OL3: G'fld 6K 65
Crofters, The M33: Sale 5M 105
Crofters Brook M26: Rad 8J 41
Crofters Grn. SK9: Wilm 8E 122
Crofters Hall Wlk. M40: Man 3N 79
(off Duncombe Dr.)
Crofters Wlk. BL2: Bolt 7K 23
Crofters Yd. WN1: Wig 7J 9
Croft Ga. BL2: Bolt 9M 23
Croft Gates Rd. M24: Mid 4J 61
Croft Gro. M38: Lit H 6G 57
Crofthead OL15: Lit 7M 15
Croft Head Dr. OL16: Miln 6K 29
CROFT HEATH 9C 88
Croft Heath Gdns. WA3: Cro 9C 88
Croft Hey BL0: Ram 4K 11
Crofthill Ct. OL12: Roch 1H 29
Croft Hill Rd. M40: Man 1M 79
Croft Ind. Est. BL9: Bury 7N 41
Croftlands BL0: Ram 2G 24
WN5: Orr 7H 51
Croftlands Rd. M22: Wyth 3D 116
Croft La. BL3: Bolt 7J 39
BL9: Bury 7N 41
M26: Rad 8J 41
WA16: Knut 8H 133
Croftleigh Cl. M45: Whitef 1L 59
Croft Mnr. SK13: Glos 8G 100
Crofton Av. WA15: Tim 7G 105
Crofton Gdns. WA3: Cul 6G 89
Crofton St. M14: Man 6G 94
M16: Old T 5C 94
OL8: O'ham 8J 63
(not continuous)
Croft Pl. M29: Tyld 2A 74

Croft Rd. M33: Sale 6K 105
SK8: Chea H 5N 117
SK9: Wilm 1D 126
Croft Row OL5: Mos 1G 82
Crofts OL2: Shaw 4B 46
CROFTS BANK 5C 92
Crofts Bank Rd. M41: Urm 5C 92
Croft Side BL3: Bolt 7M 39
Croftside Av. M28: Walk 8M 57
Croftside Cl. M28: Walk 8M 57
Croftside Gro. M28: Walk 8M 57
Croftside Way SK9: Wilm 8H 123
Croft Sq. OL12: Roch 2G 29
Croft St. BL3: Bolt 8J 39
BL5: W'ton 9G 37
BL9: Bury 7N 7 (2N 41)
M7: Sal 5B 78
M11: Man 9N 79
M35: Fail 1E 80
M38: Lit H 6G 57
OL12: Roch 2G 29
SK14: Hyde 7N 97
SK15: Stal 8E 82
WA3: Gol 1K 87
Croftwood Sq. WN5: Wig 1N 51
Croich Bank BL8: Haw 3B 24
Croich Grn. BL8: Haw 3B 24
Cromar Rd. SK7: H Gro 4K 119
Cromarty Av. OL9: Chad 8D 62
Cromarty Sq. OL10: H'ood 3F 42
Cromarty Wlk. *M11: Man 9L 79*
(off Biscay Cl.)
Crombie Av. M22: Nor 9C 106
Crombouke Dr. WN7: Lei 1G 72
Crombouke Fold M28: Wors 3J 75
Cromdale Av. BL1: Bolt 4C 38
SK7: H Gro 4K 119
Cromedale Cres.
WN6: Stan 5D 34
Cromer Av. BL2: Bolt 3K 39
M20: Man 2G 106
M34: Dent 6E 96
Cromer Dr. M46: Ath 9J 55
Cromer Ind. Est. M24: Mid 2N 61
Cromer Rd. BL8: Bury 8K 25
M33: Sale 5J 105
SK8: Chea 1K 117
WN3: Wig 8B 52
Cromer St. M11: Man 9B 80
M24: Mid 2N 61
OL2: Shaw 5M 45
OL12: Roch 4C 28
SK1: Stoc 6F 108
Cromford Av. M32: Stre 6H 93
Cromford Bank *SK13: Gam 7N 99*
(off Grassmoor Cres.)
Cromford Bus. Cen. OL1: O'ham 3L 63
Cromford Cl. BL1: Bolt 3F 38
SK13: Gam 7N 99
(off Grassmoor Cres.)
Cromford Dr. WN5: Wig 6M 51
Cromford Fold *SK13: Gam 7N 99*
(off Grassmoor Cres.)
Cromford Gdns. BL1: Bolt 2G 38
Cromford Grn. *SK13: Gam 7N 99*
(off Grassmoor Cres.)
Cromford Gro. *SK13: Gam 7N 99*
(off Grassmoor Cres.)
Cromford Lea *SK13: Gam 7N 99*
(off Grassmoor Cres.)
Cromford Pl. *SK13: Gam 7N 99*
(off Grassmoor Cres.)
Cromford St. OL1: O'ham 3L 63
Cromford Way SK13: Gam 7N 99
Cromhall Wlk. *M8: Man 4F 78*
(off Starmoor Dr.)
Cromhurst St. M8: Man 2F 78
Cromley Dr. SK6: H Lan 9B 120
Cromley Rd. SK2: Stoc 4E 118
SK6: H Lan 8B 120
Crompton & Royton Golf Course 7K 45
Crompton Av. BL2: Bolt 4M 39
M7: Sal 2N 77
OL16: Roch 1F 44
Crompton Cl. BL1: Bolt 9H 23
M26: Rad 2H 59
SK6: Mar 9C 110
Crompton Ct. BL3: Lit L 9C 40
WN4: A Mak 8E 70
CROMPTON FOLD 4A 46
Crompton Fold *BL8: Bury 9H 25*
(off Dorning St.)
Crompton Ga. OL2: Shaw 4L 45
Crompton Ho. M27: Swin 2E 76
WN1: Wig 8L 9 (3G 52)
Crompton Lodge Caravan Pk.
BL4: Bolt 9M 39
Crompton Mews BL4: Farn 3L 57
Crompton Pl. BL1: Bolt 3K 7 (5G 38)
M26: Rad 9H 41
Crompton Pool 6M 45
Crompton Rd. BL6: Los 4H 37
M19: Man 1M 107
M26: Rad 3A 58
SK11: Macc 4G 130
Crompton St. BL1: Bolt 1M 7 (4H 39)
BL4: Farn 4M 57
BL9: Bury 7K 7 (2L 41)
M27: Swin 2E 76
M28: Walk 9N 57
M38: Lit H 6E 56
OL1: O'ham 3J 63
OL2: O'ham 9J 45
OL2: Shaw 5M 45
OL6: A Lyne 6B 82
OL9: Chad 4G 62
(not continuous)
WN1: Wig 7K 9 (3F 52)
WN2: P Bri 8L 53
WN3: I Mak 8J 53
Crompton Va. BL2: Bolt 4L 39
Crompton Way BL1: Bolt 9G 22
BL2: Bolt 9G 22
OL2: Shaw 6M 45
WA3: Low 1D 88

Cromwell Av. M16: Whall R 7B 94
SK5: Dent 7E 96
SK6: Mar 9A 110
SK8: Gat 1F 116
Cromwell Bri. M6: Sal 5B 78
Cromwell Cl. WA12: N Wil 5D 86
Cromwell Ct. *M6: Sal 6A 78*
(off Cromwell Rd.)
M44: Irl 1F 102
OL1: O'ham 4D 8
Cromwell Gro. M7: Sal 5B 78
M19: Man 8M 95
Cromwell Range M14: Man 7J 95
Cromwell Rd. M6: Sal 6N 77
M25: Pres 7B 60
M27: Swin 1E 76
M30: Ecc 8C 76
M32: Stre 8L 93
M44: Irl 1F 102
M45: Whitef 1K 59
OL2: O'ham 6G 45
SK6: Bred 2H 109
SK7: Bram 9B 118
Cromwell St. BL1: Bolt 4H 7 (6E 38)
OL1: O'ham 4D 8 (5K 63)
OL10: H'ood 3J 43
SK4: Stoc 5B 108
Crondale Wlk. *M13: Man 3H 95*
(off Watkin Cl.)
Crondall St. M14: Man 6F 94
Cronkeyshaw Av. OL12: Roch 3C 28
Cronkeyshaw Rd. OL12: Roch 4C 28
Cronshaw Ind. Est. *OL11: Roch 7E 28*
(off Durham St.)
Cronshaw St. M19: Man 9N 95
Crookall St. WN4: A Mak 6F 70
CROOKE 9N 33
Crooke Rd. WN6: Stan 9N 33
Crookhill Dr. M8: Man 3E 78
Crookhurst Av. WN5: Bil 4H 69
Crookilley Way SK1: Stoc 5E 108
SK6: Bred 3H 109
Crook St. BL3: Bolt 5K 7 (6G 38)
M26: Rad 9H 41
OL16: Roch 6E 8 (5E 28)
PR7: Adl 6J 19
SK14: Hyde 7A 98
WN1: Wig 7H 9 (3E 52)
WN2: Hin 7N 53
Croom Wlk. *M40: Man 8J 79*
(off Marcer Rd.)
Cropton Way WN2: Hin 8B 54
Crosby Av. M28: Walk 9N 57
Crosby Gro. M46: Ath 7N 55
Crosby Rd. BL1: Bolt 4C 38
M6: Sal 5K 77
M26: Rad 5E 40
M40: Man 5B 80
Crosby St. M46: Ath 7N 55
OL12: Roch 3D 28
SK2: Stoc 9D 108
Crosfield Av. BL9: Sum 3J 25
Crosfield Gro. M18: Man 5B 96
Crosland Ind. Est. SK6: Bred 4J 109
Cross, The BL8: Bury 9F 24
SK13: Had 4C 100
Crossacres Rd. M22: Wyth 4C 116
Crossall St. SK11: Macc 5G 131
Cross Av. M25: Pres 5N 59
CROSS BANK 3C 64
Crossbank Av. OL4: Lees 4C 64
Crossbank Cl. M13: Man 4J 95
Crossbank Ho. OL9: O'ham 3A 8
Crossbank St.
OL8: O'ham 4B 8 (5J 63)
(not continuous)
Crossbank Way M24: Mid 2L 61
Crossbill Brow WA14: W Tim 7C 104
Crossbridge Rd. SK14: Hyde 7D 98
Crossbrook Way OL16: Miln 8L 29
Crossby Cl. M24: Mid 6L 61
Cross Cliffe SK13: Glos 9F 100
SK14: Hyde 9N 97
Crosscliffe St. M16: Whall R 5E 94
Crossdale Rd. BL2: Bolt 4M 39
M9: Man 7L 61
WN2: Hin 6B 54
(not continuous)
Crossdale Way WA11: St H 9F 68
Crossefield Rd. SK8: Chea H 4M 117
Crossen St. BL3: Bolt 7K 39
Crossfell Av. M9: Man 6G 61
Crossfield Av. WA3: Cul 7H 89
WA13: Lym 4A 112
Crossfield Cl. M34: Dent 7L 97
OL2: Shaw 3N 45
OL12: W'le 7G 15
SK15: Stal 9D 82
Cross Fld. Dr. M26: Rad 9E 40
Crossfield Dr. M27: Swin 1E 76
M28: Wors 3N 75
WN2: Hin 8E 54
Crossfield Gro. SK2: Stoc 3F 118
SK6: Mar B 7E 110
Crossfield Pl. OL11: Roch 8E 28
Crossfield Rd. M30: Ecc 5K 91
OL12: W'le 8G 15
SK9: Hand 2J 123
SK10: Boll 7J 129
WA15: Hale 5H 115
WN8: Skel 3A 50
Crossfields BL7: Bro X 5J 23
Crossfield St. BL9: Bury 8M 41
Crossford Cl. WN3: Wig 7A 52
Crossford Ct. M33: Sale 2H 105
Crossford Dr. BL3: Bolt 7N 37
Crossford St. M32: Stre 8K 93
Crossgate Av. M22: Wyth 1C 116
Crossgate La. SK13: Tin 2B 100
Crossgate M. SK4: Stoc 6K 107
Crossgates Rd. OL16: Miln 6K 29
Crossgill M29: Ast 5C 74
Cross Glebe St.
OL6: A Lyne 7E 6 (7N 81)
Cross Gro. WA15: Tim 8F 104
Crosshill St. M16: Whall R 5E 94

Crosshill Wlk. BL3: Bolt 7N 37
Cross Hope St. OL6: A Lyne 6A 82
Crossings, The WA12: N Wil 6F 86
Cross Keys St. M4: Man 2K 5 (8G 78)
Cross Knowle Vw. M41: Urm 5N 91
Crossland Rd. M21: Cho H 9N 93
M43: Droy 8F 80
Crosslands M25: Pres 8N 59
Crosslands Cl. SK13: Glos 9F 100
Crosslands Rd. M28: Wors 4G 74
Cross La. BL8: Holc 9G 10
M5: Sal 9N 77
M18: Man 4B 96
M26: Rad 8J 41
M43: Droy 6H 81
SK6: Mar 2B 120
SK9: Wilm 6L 123
WA12: N Wil 6E 86
WN5: Bil 8H 51
Cross La. E. M31: Part 6G 103
Cross La. W. M31: Part 6G 102
Crosslee Rd. M9: Man 7L 61
Cross Lees OL12: Roch 2E 28
Crossley Ct. *M4: Man 9J 79*
(off Pollard St.)
Crossley Cres. OL6: A Lyne 4A 82
Crossley Est. OL9: Chad 5F 62
Crossley Pk. SK4: Stoc 1N 107
Crossley Rd. M19: Man 1L 107
M33: Sale 2G 104
SK4: Stoc 1L 107
Crossley St. BL3: Lit L 8A 40
M18: Man 3N 95
OL2: O'ham 1J 63
OL2: Shaw 5N 45
OL16: Miln 7J 29
SK15: Stal 8C 82
SK16: Duk 9A 82
Crossmead Dr. M9: Man 6K 61
Crossmeadow Cl. OL11: Roch 5M 27
Crossmoor Cres. SK6: Rom 6N 109
Crossmoor Dr. BL2: Bolt 4J 39
Crossmoor Gro. SK6: Rom 6N 109
Cross Ormrod St. BL3: Bolt 6E 38
Cross Ri. SK13: Glos 9G 100
Cross Rd. M21: Cho H 9A 94
SK8: H Grn 8G 117
Cross St. BL0: Ram 8J 11
BL1: Bolt 1L 7 (4G 39)
BL3: Lit L 9B 40
BL4: Farn 2L 57
BL4: Kea 6B 58
BL7: Bro X 6H 23
BL9: Bury 7L 7 (2M 41)
(not continuous)
M2: Man 5G 4 (9E 78)
M3: Sal 2E 4 (8D 78)
M16: Old T 4C 94
M24: Mid 3L 61
(not continuous)
M26: Rad 9H 41
M27: Clif 9K 59
M28: Wors 3C 76
M29: Tyld 2A 74
M32: Stre 7K 93
M33: Sale 3H 105
M34: Dent 4J 97
M41: Urm 8C 92
M45: Whitef 2L 59
M46: Ath 7K 55
OL4: Lees 5B 64
OL4: O'ham 4M 63
OL4: Spri 5D 64
OL5: Mos 8G 64
OL6: A Lyne 8B 6 (8L 81)
OL10: H'ood 3K 43
OL11: Roch 2B 44
OL16: Roch 6H 29
SK11: Macc 6J 131
SK13: Glos 8E 100
SK13: Had 4C 100
SK14: B'tom 9K 99
(off Gorsey Brow)
SK14: Holl 5N 99
SK14: Hyde 7A 98
SK15: Mill 6G 83
SK22: N Mil 7M 121
WA3: Gol 2K 87
WA14: Alt 3D 6 (3D 114)
WN2: Asp 6L 35
WN2: Hin 6N 53
WN3: I Mak 7H 53
WN3: Wig 4F 52
WN5: Orr 5M 51
WN5: Wig 5M 51
WN6: Stan 3B 34
WN7: Lei 6J 73
Cross Swords Cl. PR7: Chor 1E 18
CROSS TOWN 6H 133
Crosswaite Rd. SK2: Stoc 1H 119
Crossway M20: Man 5G 106
M43: Droy 2E 96
SK2: Stoc 3E 118
SK7: Bram 1C 124
Crossway Cl. WN4: A Mak 5H 71
Crossway Rd. M33: Sale 7F 104
Crossways OL8: O'ham 1L 81
SK7: Bram 6A 118
Cross Yd. WN1: Wig 6K 9
Croston Av. PR6: Adl 5K 19
Croston Cl. SK9: A Edg 4H 127
Croston Cl. Rd. BL0: Ram 3A 26
BL9: Bury 3A 26
Crostons Ct. *BL8: Bury 1K 41*
(off Crostons Rd.)
Crostons Rd.
BL8: Bury 6G 7 & 7G 7 (1K 41)
Croston St. BL3: Bolt 8D 38
WN2: Hin 5M 53
Croston Wlk. M11: Man 9K 79
Crote St. SK4: Stoc 6K 107
Crouchley Hall M. WA13: Lym 6A 112
Crouchley La. WA13: Lym 5A 112
Croughton Cl. M11: Man 2B 96
Crowbank Wlk. *M40: Man 5M 79*
(off Bower St.)

Crowborough Cl. BL6: Los 3H 37
Crowborough Wlk.
M15: Man 4E 94
(off Arnott Cres.)
Crowbrook Gro. *SK9: Wilm 5J 123*
(off Colshaw Dr.)
CROWCROFT PARK 7N 95
Crowcroft Rd. M12: Man 6M 95
M13: Man 6M 95
CROWDEN 7N 85
Crowden Camp Site
SK13: Crow 7N 85
Crowden Dr. SK13: Had 4C 100
Crowden Outdoor Education Centre & Youth Hostel 6M 85
Crowden Rd. M40: Man 9N 61
CROWHILL 5K 81
Crow Hill SK15: C'ook 5H 83
Crowhill Cotts. OL7: A Lyne 6L 81
Crow Hill Nth. M24: Mid 5L 61
Crowhill Rd. OL7: A Lyne 6K 81
Crow Hill Sth. M24: Mid 5L 61
Crow Hill Vw. OL4: O'ham 7C 64
Crowhurst Dr. WN1: Wig 9E 34
Crowhurst Wlk. *M23: Wyth 9L 105*
(off Sandy La.)
Crowland Gdns. SK8: Chea H 9N 117
Crowland Rd. BL2: Bolt 2K 39
M23: Wyth 4M 115
Crow La. BL0: Ram 8J 11
WN8: Dal 9D 32
Crow La. E. WA12: N Wil 5E 86
Crow La. W. WA12: N Wil 5C 86
Crowley La. OL4: O'ham 2A 64
Crowley Rd. M9: Man 2L 79
WA15: Tim 1H 115
Crown Bus. Cen. M35: Fail 2D 80
Crown Cen., The SK11: Macc 4G 130
Crown Court
Knutsford 7G 132
Manchester, Crown Sq. 5E 4 (9D 78)
Manchester, Minshull St. 5K 5 (9F 78)
Crown Ct. SK7: H Gro 4H 119
Crowneast St. OL11: Roch 6A 28
Crown Flds. Cl. WA12: N Wil 4E 86
Crown Gdns. OL16: Roch 8F 28
WA12: N Wil 5E 86
Crown Grn. WA13: Lym 4C 112
Crowngreen Rd. M30: Ecc 9E 76
Crown Gro. WN7: Lei 4M 73
Crown Hill OL5: Mos 2G 83
Crownhill Ct. M43: Droy 8E 80
Crownhill Dr. M43: Droy 8E 80
Crown Ho. *M22: Shar 1D 116*
(off Lauriston Cl.)
Crown Ind. Est. M4: Man 2M 5 (8H 79)
SK5: Stoc 6C 96
WA14: Tim 9E 104
Crown La. BL6: Hor 2B 36
M4: Man 1J 5 (7F 78)
Crown M. BL8: Haw 2C 24
SK2: Stoc 3G 118
Crown Pk. Dr. WA12: N Wil 4E 86
Crown Passages WA15: Hale 5E 114
CROWN POINT *6K 97*
(Junction of A57 with A6017)
Crown Point Av. M40: Man 5A 80
Crown Point Nth. Shop. Pk.
M34: Dent 5J 97
Crown Point Sth. Ind. Pk.
M34: Dent 6K 97
Crown Rd. OL10: H'ood 2G 42
Crown Royal Ind. Pk.
SK1: Stoc 5M 9 (8E 108)
Crown Sq. M3: Man 5E 4 (9D 78)
Crown St. BL1: Bolt 2L 7 (5G 39)
M3: Sal 2D 4 (8D 78)
M15: Man 8D 4 (2D 94)
M34: Dent 5J 97
M35: Fail 2D 80
M40: Man 5A 80
M46: Ath 8L 55
OL2: Shaw 5L 45
OL6: A Lyne 8C 6 (8M 81)
OL16: Roch 8F 28
SK6: Bred 4K 109
SK6: Mar 4C 120
SK10: Macc 4H 131
(off Market Pl.)
WA12: N Wil 6D 86
WN2: Hin 5M 53
WN3: Wig 5E 52
Crown St. W. SK11: Macc 5G 130
Crown Wood Ct. *WN2: Bam 3J 71*
(off Fourth St.)
CROW OAK 2J 59
Crow Orchard Rd. WN6: Stan 2L 33
WN6: Wrig 2K 33
(not continuous)
Crowsdale Pl. SK2: Stoc 3J 119
Crowshaw Dr. OL12: Roch 2C 28
Crows Nest BL3: Bolt 7N 39
Crowswood Dr. SK15: C'ook 5G 82
Crowther Av. M5: Sal 1N 93
Crowther Ct. OL15: Lit 1J 29
Crowther Dr. WN3: Wins 1B 70
Crowther St. M18: Man 4C 96
OL15: Lit 9J 15
OL16: Roch 9F 28
SK1: Stoc 3L 9 (7D 108)
Crowthorn Dr. M23: Wyth 5N 115
Crowthorn Rd. BL7: Edg 5A 10
OL7: A Lyne 9K 81
SK4: Stoc 1B 108
Crowton Av. M33: Sale 6E 104
Crow Wood Rd. BL0: Eden 1K 11
WA3: Low 9N 71
Crow Woods BL0: Eden 1K 11
Croxdale Cl. OL7: A Lyne 5J 81
Croxdale Wlk. *M9: Man 6J 61*
(off Claygate Dr.)
Croxton Av. OL16: Roch 5F 28
Croxton Cl. M33: Sale 6D 104
SK6: Mar 2B 120

Croxton Wlk. *BL6: Hor 9D 20*
(off Beatrice St.)
M13: Man 3H 95
(off Sefton Cl.)
Croyde Cl. BL2: Bolt 1N 39
M22: Wyth 8E 116
WN2: Hin 8F 54
Croydon Av. OL2: O'ham 6G 44
OL11: Roch 5B 44
WN7: Lei 2H 73
Croydon Ct. M5: Sal 1A 94
Croydon Dr. M40: Man 6A 80
Croydon Ho. *BL1: Bolt 3F 38*
(off Kenton Cl.)
Croydon Sq. OL11: Roch 4B 44
Crummock Cl. BL3: Lit L 9N 39
Crummock Dr. M24: Mid 9K 43
WN3: Wig 8C 52
Crummock Gro. BL4: Farn 4F 56
Crummock Rd. SK8: Gat 4G 117
CRUMPSALL 9E 60
CRUMPSALL GREEN 9F 60
Crumpsall La. M8: Man 1E 78
Crumpsall Stop (Metro) 1F 78
Crumpsall St. BL1: Bolt 2F 38
Crumpsall Va. M9: Man 9H 61
Crumpsall Way M8: Man 1G 79
Crundale Rd. BL1: Bolt 7H 23
Cruttenden Rd. SK2: Stoc 3G 119
Cryer St. M43: Droy 6G 81
Crystal Cl. WN2: P Bri 8K 53
Crystal Ho. M16: Whall R 6C 94
Cuba Ind. Est. BL0: Ram 6J 11
Cube 6H 5
Cube, The M4: Man 5N 5 (9J 79)
M11: Man 8L 79
Cubley Rd. M7: Sal 2D 78
Cuckoo Gro. M25: Pres 5A 60
Cuckoo La. BL9: Bury 2B 42
(Bridge Hall La.)
BL9: Bury 1B 42
(Clarkes Cft.)
M25: Pres 5A 60
M45: Whitef 5A 60
Cuckoo Nest M25: Pres 4A 60
Cuckstoolpit Hill SK10: Macc 4J 131
Cuddington Av. M20: Man 9F 94
Cuddington Cres. SK3: Stoc 1B 118
Cuddington Way *SK9: Hand 1J 123*
(off Pickmere Rd.)
Cudworth Rd. M9: Man 6F 60
Cuerdon Wlk. M22: Nor 8D 106
Culand St. M12: Man 3K 95
Culbert Av. M20: Man 5H 107
CULCHETH
M40 5A 80
WA3 7J 89
Culcheth Av. SK6: Mar 1C 120
WN2: Abr 1L 71
Culcheth Hall Dr. WA3: Cul 5H 89
Culcheth Hall Farm WA3: Cul 5J 89
Culcheth La. M40: Man 5A 80
Culcheth Linear Country Pk. 5D 88
Culcheth Rd. WA14: Alt 4D 114
Culcheth Sports Club 6H 89
Culcombe Wlk. *M13: Man 4H 95*
(off Corn Cl.)
Culcross Av. WN3: Wig 7N 51
Culford Cl. M12: Man 4K 95
Culgaith Wlk. *M9: Man 3J 79*
(off Ruskington Dr.)
Culham Cl. *BL1: Bolt 2E 38*
(off Raglan St.)
Cullen Cl. WN2: I Mak 3K 53
Cullen Gro. M9: Man 8L 61
Cullercoats Wlk. M12: Man 6N 95
Culmere Rd. M22: Wyth 6C 116
Culmington Cl. M15: Man 4D 94
Culross Av. BL3: Bolt 6N 37
M40: Man 1C 80
Culvercliff Wlk. M3: Man 6E 4
Culverden Wlk. M6: Sal 4M 77
Culver Rd. SK3: Stoc 2B 118
Culvert St. OL4: O'ham 2B 64
OL16: Roch 2F 44
WN6: Wig 9D 34
Culverwell Dr. M5: Sal 8A 78
Culzean Cl. WN7: Lei 6K 73
Cumberbatch Pl. WN3: I Mak 7J 53
Cumber Cl. SK9: Wilm 1C 126
Cumber Dr. SK9: Wilm 1C 126
Cumberland Av. M27: Clif 9F 58
M29: Tyld 9A 56
M44: Cad 4D 102
OL10: H'ood 2F 42
SK5: Stoc 4G 108
SK16: Duk 1B 98
Cumberland Cl. BL9: Bury 6L 41
Cumberland Dr. OL1: O'ham 2H 63
OL2: O'ham 2H 63
SK10: Boll 5M 129
WA14: Bow 7A 114
Cumberland Gro. OL7: A Lyne 6M 81
Cumberland Point M27: Clif 9G 58
Cumberland Rd. M9: Man 1J 79
M31: Part 6F 102
M33: Sale 6J 105
M41: Urm 8C 92
M46: Ath 7N 55
OL11: Roch 2D 44
Cumberland St. M7: Sal 6C 78
SK10: Macc 4F 130
(not continuous)
SK15: Stal 8C 82
WN1: Wig 5N 9 (2H 53)
Cumber La. SK9: Wilm 9C 122
Cumbermere La. M29: Tyld 9C 56
Cumbrae Gdns. M5: Sal 9K 77
Cumbrae Rd. M19: Man 8A 96
Cumbria Ct. M25: Pres 1N 77
Cumbrian Cl. M13: Man 3H 95
OL2: Shaw 4K 45
WN2: P Bri 9L 53
Cumbria Wlk. M6: Sal 6A 78
Cummings St. OL8: O'ham 9G 63
Cunard Cl. M13: Man 3H 95

Cundall Wlk. M23: Wyth 7M 105
Cundey St. BL1: Bolt 3D 38
Cundiff Cl. SK11: Macc 6J 131
Cundiff Ct. M19: Man 8A 96
Cundiff Rd. M21: Cho H 2A 106
(not continuous)
Cundy St. SK14: Hyde 5B 98
Cunliffe Av. BL0: Ram 1G 25
WA12: N Wil 4E 86
Cunliffe Brow BL1: Bolt 2C 38
Cunliffe Ct. WN7: Lei 6C 72
Cunliffe Dr. M33: Sale 5J 105
OL2: Shaw 5A 46
Cunliffe St. BL0: Ram 7J 11
M26: Rad 9J 41
SK3: Stoc 8A 108
SK14: Hyde 5N 97
WN7: Lei 5E 72
Cunningham Dr. BL9: Bury 2A 26
M22: Wyth 7F 116
Cunningham Rd. BL5: W'ton 4F 54
Cunningham Way OL1: O'ham 3K 63
Curate Ct. *SK1: Stoc 7E 108*
(off Curate St.)
Curate St. SK1: Stoc 7E 108
Curlew Cl. OL11: Roch 6L 27
SK10: Macc 8G 128
WA3: Low 1N 87
Curlew Dr. M44: Irl 5H 91
Curlew Rd. OL4: O'ham 7B 64
Curlew Wlk. M12: Man 4K 95
Curlew Way SK13: Glos 8B 100
Currier La. OL6: A Lyne 8F 6 (8N 81)
Curtain Theatre 9C 8 (7D 28)
Curtels St. BL6: Hor 9D 20
Curtels Cl. M28: Wors 3C 76
Curtis Gro. SK13: Had 4C 100
Curtis Rd. SK4: Stoc 6M 107
Curtis St. BL3: Bolt 1D 56
M19: Man 8A 96
WN5: Wig 5A 52
Curzon Ashton FC 6J 81
Curzon Av. M14: Man 5K 95
Curzon Cl. OL11: Roch 2D 44
Curzon Dr. WA15: Tim 1H 115
Curzon Grn. SK2: Stoc 8H 109
Curzon M. SK9: Wilm 9F 122
Curzon Pl. *WA12: N Wil 6E 86*
(off King St.)
Curzon Rd. BL1: Bolt 5D 38
M7: Sal 3C 78
M32: Stre 6G 92
M33: Sale 3H 105
OL6: A Lyne 6A 82
OL11: Roch 2D 44
SK2: Stoc 9H 109
SK8: H Grn 8G 117
SK12: Poy 4J 125
Curzon St. OL1: O'ham 2D 8 (4K 63)
OL5: Mos 1F 82
Cutacre Cl. M29: Tyld 1C 74
Cutacre La. BL5: O Hul 5E 56
CUTGATE 5M 27
Cutgate Cl. M23: Wyth 7L 105
Cutgate Rd. OL12: Roch 4N 27
Cutgate Shop. Pct. OL11: Roch 5N 27
Cuthbert Av. M19: Man 7N 95
Cuthbert Bus. Cen. *M11: Man 2A 96*
(off Ashton Old Rd.)
Cuthbert Mayne Ct.
OL16: Roch 9B 8 (7C 28)
Cuthbert Rd. SK8: Chea 1K 117
Cuthbert St. BL3: Bolt 1C 56
WN5: Wig 5A 52
Cuthill Wlk. *M40: Man 6B 80*
(off Eastmoor Dr.)
Cutland St. M40: Man 4M 79
Cutland Way OL15: Lit 1L 29
Cut La. OL12: Roch 4L 27
CUTLER HILL 3F 80
Cutler Hill Rd. M35: Fail 3F 80
OL8: Fail 3F 80
Cutler St. OL9: Chad 4G 63
Cutnook La. M44: Irl 4G 90
Cutter Cl. M5: Sal 1N 93
Cycle St. M11: Man 1N 95
Cyclone St. M11: Man 1L 95
Cygnet St. WN3: Wig 5E 52
Cygnus Av. M7: Sal 1A 4 (7B 78)
Cymbal Ct. SK5: Stoc 5D 108
Cynthia Dr. SK6: Mar 2C 120
Cypress Av. OL9: Chad 3F 62
Cypress Cl. SK3: Stoc 8A 108
Cypress Gdns. OL16: Roch 6H 29
Cypress Gro. BL4: Kea 4N 57
M34: Dent 6L 97
Cypress Oaks SK15: Mill, Stal 7G 82
Cypress Pl. M4: Man 1H 5 (7F 78)
Cypress Rd. M30: Ecc 6A 76
M43: Droy 7E 80
OL4: O'ham 3A 64
WN5: Wig 5B 52
Cypress St. M9: Man 3J 79
M24: Mid 3A 62
Cypress Wlk. M33: Sale 2C 104
Cypress Way SK6: H Lan 8D 120
Cyprus Cl. M5: Sal 9M 77
OL4: O'ham 6A 64
Cyprus St. M32: Stre 7K 93
Cyril Bell Cl. WA13: Lym 4A 112
Cyril St. BL3: Bolt 7H 39
M14: Man 6G 94
OL2: Shaw 5N 45
Cyrus St. M40: Man 8J 79

D

Daccamill Dr. M27: Swin 4F 76
Dacre Av. M16: Whall R 7A 94
Dacre Cl. M24: Mid 2G 61
Dacre Rd. OL11: Roch 9D 28
DACRES 7J 65
Dacres Av. OL3: G'fld 7J 65
Dacres Dr. OL3: G'fld 7J 65
Dacres Rd. OL3: G'fld 7J 65
Daffodil Cl. OL12: Roch 2C 28
Daffodil Rd. BL4: Farn 2H 57
Daffodil St. BL1: Bolt 8G 22
Dagenham Rd. M14: Man 5H 95
Dagenham Rd. Ind. Est.
M14: Man 6H 95
(off Dagenham Rd.)
Dagmar St. M28: Walk 7K 57
Dagnall Av. M21: Cho H 2A 106
Dahlia Cl. M19: Man 2L 107
OL12: Roch 2B 28
Dailton Rd. WN8: Uph 4E 50
Daimler St. M8: Man 4F 78
Dain Cl. SK16: Duk 1A 98
Daine Av. M23: Wyth 7A 106
Dainton St. M12: Man 2J 95
Daintry Cl. M15: Man 3E 94
Daintry Rd. OL9: O'ham 4G 63
Daintry St. SK11: Macc 5J 131
Daintry Ter. SK10: Macc 5J 131
Dairybrook Gro. *SK9: Wilm 5K 123*
(off Lyngard Cl.)
Dairydale Cl. M44: Irl 6J 91
Dairy Farm Cl. WA13: Lym 4A 112
Dairyground Rd.
SK7: Bram 8C 118
Dairy Ho. La.
SK7: Bram, Chea H 3M 123
Dairyhouse La.
WA14: B'ath, D Mas 1A 114
Dairy Ho. Rd. SK7: Bram 2N 123
Dairy St. OL9: Chad 4F 62
Daisy Av. BL4: Farn 2H 57
M13: Man 5K 95
WA12: N Wil 7F 86
Daisy Bank M40: Man 5A 80
Daisy Bank Av. M6: Sal 4J 77
M27: Pen 4J 77
Daisybank Cl. WN2: Hin 6N 53
Daisy Bank Hall M14: Man 5J 95
Daisy Bank La. SK8: H Grn 6F 116
Daisy Bank Mill Cl. WA3: Cul 6G 88
Daisy Bank Rd. M14: Man 5J 95
Daisy Bank Vs. *M14: Man 5J 95*
(off Hope Rd.)
DAISYFIELD 3J 41
Daisyfield *BL6: Hor 3F 36*
(off Chorley New Rd.)
BL8: Bury 4J 41
Daisyfield Cl. M22: Wyth 6B 116
Daisyfield Ct. BL8: Bury 3J 41
Daisyfield Wlk. *M28: Walk 8L 57*
(off Cecil St.)
Daisygate Dr. WA14: W Tim 8B 104
Daisy Hall Dr. BL5: W'ton 5G 54
DAISY HILL 6G 55
Daisy Hill Cl. M33: Sale 4L 105
Daisy Hill Ct. *OL4: O'ham 3B 64*
(off Howard St.)
Daisyhill Ct. BL5: W'ton 6H 55
Daisy Hill Dr. PR6: Adl 4K 19
Daisy Hill Rd. OL5: Mos 1G 83
Daisy Hill Station (Rail) 5H 55
Daisy M. SK3: Stoc 3B 118
DAISY NOOK 4H 81
Daisy Nook Country Pk. 4H 81
Daisy Rd. WN5: Wig 5B 52
Daisy St. BL3: Bolt 8D 38
BL8: Bury 2J 41
OL9: Chad 3E 62
OL9: O'ham 4H 63
OL12: Roch 6A 8 (5C 28)
SK1: Stoc 9D 108
Daisy Way SK6: H Lan 8C 120
Dakerwood Cl. M40: Man 5A 80
Dakin's Lea WN7: Lei 7K 73
Dakins Rd. WN7: Lei 8K 73
Dakota Av. M50: Sal 4N 93
Dakota Sth. M50: Sal 1M 93
Dalbeattie Ri. WN1: Wig 2J 53
Dalbeattie St. M9: Man 2K 79
Dalberg St. M12: Man 9N 5 (2J 95)
Dalbury Dr. M40: Man 5H 79
Dalby Av. M27: Swin 3E 76
Dalby Gro. SK1: Stoc 2N 9 (7E 108)
Dalby Rd. WN2: Hin 6D 54
DALE 7J 47
Dale Av. M30: Ecc 7C 76
OL5: Mos 8H 65
SK7: Bram 7D 118
Dalebank M46: Ath 6L 55
Dalebank M. M27: Clif 6D 58
Dalebeck Cl. M45: Whitef 3A 60
Dalebeck Wlk. M45: Whitef 3B 60
Dale Brook Av. SK16: Duk 3A 98
Dalebrook Cl. BL3: Lit L 8A 40
Dalebrook Ct. SK4: Stoc 7A 108
Dalebrook Rd. M33: Sale 7J 105
Dale Cl. *WN8: Par 2A 32*
(off Fairhurst Dr.)
Dale Ct. M34: Dent 7K 97
Dalecrest WN5: Bil 1H 69
Dale End OL8: O'ham 9L 63
Dalefields OL3: Del 8J 47
Daleford Sq. M13: Man 9M 5
Dalegarth Av. BL1: Bolt 5L 37
Dale Gro. M44: Cad 2F 102
OL7: A Lyne 5L 81
WA15: Tim 9F 104
WN7: Lei 6E 72
Dalehead Cl. M18: Man 3D 96
Dalehead Dr. OL2: Shaw 5A 46
Dalehead Gro. WN7: Lei 6E 72
Dalehead Pl. WA11: St H 9F 68
Dale Head Rd. SK10: P'bury 9D 128
Dale Ho. M24: Mid 2A 62
OL2: Shaw 6M 45
SK1: Stoc 1L 9
Dale Ho. Fold SK12: Poy 2L 125
Dale La. OL3: Del 7J 47
Dale Lee BL5: W'ton 3J 55
Dale Rd. M24: Mid 1N 61
SK6: Mar 8B 110
SK22: N Mil 8M 121
WA3: Gol 2K 87
Dales Av. M8: Man 9E 60
M45: Whitef 2K 59
DALES BROW 4D 76
Dales Brow BL1: Bolt 7G 23
M27: Swin 4E 76
Dales Brow Av. OL7: A Lyne 5L 81
Dalesfield Cres. OL5: Mos 1H 83
Dalesford Cl. WN7: Lei 1E 88
Dalesford Cres. SK10: Macc 4C 130
Dales Gro. M28: Walk 1N 75
Daleside Av. WN4: A Mak 2D 70
Dales La. M45: Whitef 2L 59
Dalesman Cl. M9: Man 2L 79
Dalesman Dr. OL1: O'ham 9A 46
Dalesman Wlk. *M15: Man 3F 94*
(off Cavendish St.)
Dales Pk. Dr. M27: Swin 4D 76
Dales Pl. SK11: Macc 6J 131
Dale Sq. OL2: O'ham 8K 45
Dale St. BL0: Ram 6J 11
BL4: Farn 2M 57
BL5: W'ton 6H 55
BL8: Bury 9J 25
M1: Man 4J 5 (9F 78)
M24: Mid 4N 61
M26: Rad 1G 59
M27: Swin 4E 76
M45: Whitef 2L 59
OL2: Shaw 6M 45
OL6: A Lyne 4D 82
OL16: Miln 7K 29
OL16: Roch 6G 28
SK3: Stoc 1B 118
SK10: Macc 4J 131
SK15: Stal 9C 82
WN3: I Mak 8J 53
WN7: Lei 5E 72
Dale St. E. BL6: Hor 3F 36
OL6: A Lyne 8B 6 (8L 81)
Dale St. Ind. Est. M26: Rad 1G 58
Dale St. W. BL6: Hor 2F 36
OL6: A Lyne 9A 6 (8L 81)
Daleswood Av. M45: Whitef 2K 59
Dale Vw. M34: Dent 1L 109
OL15: Lit 3K 29
PR7: Chor 1F 18
SK14: Hyde 9A 98
SK14: Mot 6K 99
WA12: N Wil 5H 87
Dalham Av. M9: Man 9M 61
Dalkeith Av. SK5: Stoc 1D 108
Dalkeith Gro. BL3: Bolt 7A 38
Dalkeith Rd. SK5: Stoc 1D 108
WN2: Hin 6C 54
Dalkeith Sq. OL10: H'ood 3F 42
Dalkeith St. M18: Man 3N 95
Dallas Ct. M50: Sal 1L 93
Dalley Av. M7: Sal 6C 78
Dallimore Rd. M23: Wyth 1L 115
Dalmahoy Cl. M40: Man 2A 80
Dalmain Cl. M8: Man 4E 78
Dalmeny Ter. OL11: Roch 9D 28
Dalmorton Rd. M21: Cho H 9C 94
Dalny St. M19: Man 8N 95
Dalry Wlk. M23: Wyth 1N 115
Dalston Av. M35: Fail 2F 80
Dalston Dr. M20: Man 6H 107
SK7: Bram 1A 124
WA11: St H 9F 68
Dalston Gdns. *BL1: Bolt 2F 38*
(off Gladstone St.)
Dalston Gro. WN3: Wins 8A 52
DALTON 6A 32
Dalton Av. M14: Man 7F 94
M27: Clif 8J 59
M32: Stre 5F 92
M45: Whitef 4N 59
OL16: Roch 6H 29
Dalton Bldgs. OL5: Mos 9G 65
Dalton Cl. BL0: Ram 1G 24
OL16: Roch 6H 29
WN5: Orr 4M 51
Dalton Ct. SK4: Stoc 4A 108
Dalton Dr. M27: Pen 3K 77
WN3: Wins 9B 52
Dalton Ellis Hall *M14: Man 5J 95*
(off Conyngham Rd.)
Dalton Fold BL5: W'ton 3H 55
Dalton Gdns. M41: Urm 6B 92
Dalton Gro. SK4: Stoc 4A 108
WN4: A Mak 6D 70
Dalton Rd. M9: Man 6J 61
M24: Mid 4G 61
Dalton St. BL8: Bury 2H 41
(not continuous)
M4: Man 6G 79
M30: Ecc 7D 76
M33: Sale 2J 105
M35: Fail 2C 80
M40: Man 6G 79
OL9: Chad 4F 62
Daltry St. OL1: O'ham 3L 63
Dalveen Av. M41: Urm 5C 92
Dalveen Dr. WA15: Tim 9F 104
Dalwood Cl. WN2: Hin 7B 54
Dalymount Cl. BL2: Bolt 2J 39
Damask Av. M3: Sal 2B 4 (8C 78)
Dame Hollow SK8: H Grn 8J 117
Dameral Cl. M8: Man 4F 78
Damery Ct. SK7: Bram 7C 118
Damery Rd. SK7: Bram 7C 118
Dam Head Dr. M9: Man 8K 61
Dam Head La. WA3: G'ook, Rix 4A 102
Damian Dr. WA12: N Wil 4D 86
Damien St. M12: Man 7N 95
Dam La. WA3: Cro 9B 88
WA3: Rix 3A 102
WN4: A Mak 7J 71
Dams Head Fold BL5: W'ton 2H 55
Damside SK13: Had 3C 100
Damson Grn. M24: Mid 3B 62
Damson Wlk. *M31: Part 5E 102*
(off Wood La.)
Dan Bank SK6: Mar 1N 119
Danbers WN8: Uph 5D 50
Danbury Wlk. M23: Wyth 8K 105
Danby Cl. SK14: Hyde 5C 98
Danby Ct. *OL1: O'ham 3J 63*
(off Bradford St.)
Danby Pl. SK14: Hyde 5C 98
Danby Rd. BL3: Bolt 9F 38
SK14: Hyde 5C 98
Danby Wlk. *M9: Man 1K 79*
(off Polworth Rd.)
Dancehouse, The 8H 5
Dane Av. M31: Part 4G 103
SK3: Stoc 8M 107
DANE BANK 7F 96
DANEBANK 9H 121
Dane Bank M24: Mid 3N 61
Dane Bank Dr. SK12: Dis 9G 120
Danebank M. M34: Dent 7F 96
Dane Bank Rd. E. WA13: Lym 3A 112
Danebank Wlk. M13: Man 9L 5
Danebridge Cl. *BL4: Farn 3M 57*
(off Peel St.)
Danebury Cl. WN2: Hin 7N 53
Dane Cl. SK7: Bram 4B 118
Danecroft BL3: Lit L 9C 40
Dane Dr. SK9: Wilm 8J 123
Danefield Ct. SK8: H Grn 7J 117
Danefield Rd. M33: Sale 2J 105
Dane Hill Cl. SK12: Dis 9G 120
Daneholme Rd. M19: Man 3K 107
Dane Ho. *M33: Sale 4J 105*
(off Northenden Rd.)
Dane M. M33: Sale 2H 105
Dane Rd. M33: Sale 2J 105
M34: Dent 7E 96
Dane Rd. Ind. Est. M33: Sale 2J 105
Dane Road Stop (Metro) 2J 105
Danes, The M8: Man 1E 78
Danes Av. WN2: Hin 5A 54
Danesbrook Cl. WN2: Hin 5A 54
Danesbury Cl. WN5: Bil 6J 69
Danesbury Ri. SK8: Chea 2J 117
Danesbury Rd. BL2: Bolt 9J 23
Danes Grn. WN2: Hin 4A 54
Daneshill M25: Pres 5A 60
Daneshill Dr. *M23: Wyth 3N 115*
(off Chedlin Dr.)
Danes La. OL12: Whitw 6M 13
Danesmoor Dr. BL9: Bury 9N 25
Danesmoor Rd. M20: Man 3F 106
Danes Moss Nature Reserve 9F 130
Danes Rd. M14: Man 7J 95
Danes Sq. SK11: Macc 7H 131
Dane St. BL3: Bolt 8D 38
M11: Man 2C 96
OL4: O'ham 4N 63
OL5: Mos 8G 64
OL11: Roch 8A 8 (6C 28)
OL12: Roch 8A 8 (6C 28)
Danesway M25: Pres 9C 60
M27: Pen 3J 77
PR7: H Char 4J 19
WN1: Wig 9E 34
Danesway Ct. BL1: Bolt 2E 38
Daneswood Av. M9: Man 7L 61
OL12: Whitw 7A 14
Daneswood Cl. OL12: Whitw 6N 13
Daneswood Fold OL12: Whitw 6N 13
Danett Cl. M12: Man 3N 95
Dane Wlk. SK5: Stoc 4D 108
Danforth Gro. M19: Man 9N 95
DANGEROUS CORNER
WN6 2G 32
WN7 9F 54
Daniel Adamson Av. M31: Part 5E 102
Daniel Adamson Rd. M50: Sal 1K 93
Daniel Ct. M31: Part 4G 103
Daniel Fold OL12: Roch 2N 27
Daniels La. SK1: Stoc 1L 9
WN8: Skel 4A 50
Daniel St. OL1: O'ham 3M 63
OL2: O'ham 9L 45
OL10: H'ood 2G 42
OL12: Whitw 4B 14
SK7: H Gro 5J 119
Daniel St. Ind. Est. *OL12: Whitw 4B 14*
(off Daniel St.)
Danisher La. OL8: O'ham 2K 81
Dannywood Cl. SK14: Hyde 9N 97
Danson St. M40: Man 7K 79
Dantall Av. M9: Man 8M 61
Dante Cl. M30: Ecc 6G 77
Danty St. SK16: Duk 9M 81
Dantzic St. M4: Man 3H 5 (8F 78)
Danube, The M15: Man 8E 4
Danwood Cl. M34: Dent 7N 97
Darbishire St. BL1: Bolt 3H 39
Darby La. WN2: Hin 5M 53
Darby Rd. M44: Irl 2H 103
Darbyshire Cl. BL1: Bolt 4D 38
Darbyshire Ho. *WA15: Tim 9J 105*
(off Oakleigh Ct.)
Darbyshire St. M26: Rad 9G 41
Darbyshire Wlk. M26: Rad 9H 41
DARCY LEVER 7L 39
Darcy Wlk. M14: Man 5F 94
Darden Cl. SK4: Stoc 5K 107
Daresbury Av. M41: Urm 5L 91
WA15: Alt 1E 6 (2E 114)
Daresbury Cl. M33: Sale 5M 105
SK3: Stoc 2B 118
SK9: Wilm 6H 123
Daresbury Rd. M21: Cho H 8M 93
Daresbury St. M8: Man 2F 78
(not continuous)
Darfield WN8: Uph 4D 50
Darfield Wlk. *M40: Man 7J 79*
(off Burnell Cl.)
Dargai St. M11: Man 9B 80
Dargle Rd. M33: Sale 2H 105
Darian Av. M22: Wyth 7C 116
Daric Cl. WN7: Lei 9E 72
Dark La. BL6: Bla 9L 19
M12: Man 7N 5 (1J 95)
OL3: Del 6H 47
OL3: Upp 3K 65
OL5: Mos 9G 64
(not continuous)
Dark La. SK6: Bred 5H 109
SK11: Gaws 9A 130
WA14: D Mas 6L 103
Dark Lane Nature Reserve 6L 103
Darlbeck Wlk. M21: Cho H 3B 106
Darley Av. BL4: Farn 2M 57
M20: Man 4D 106
M21: Cho H 2A 106
(not continuous)
M30: Ecc 1C 92
SK8: Gat 2G 117
Darley Ct. BL1: Bolt 2D 38
Darley Gro. BL4: Farn 2M 57
DARLEY PARK 5B 94
Darley Rd. M16: Old T 6B 94
OL11: Roch 9D 28
SK7: H Gro 8K 119
WN3: Wig 8E 52
Darley St. BL1: Bolt 3E 38
BL4: Farn 3M 57
BL6: Hor 8D 20
M11: Man 9L 79
M32: Stre 5K 93
M33: Sale 4H 105
SK4: Stoc 5A 108
Darley Ter. *BL1: Bolt 3E 38*
(off Peterhead Cl.)
Darlington Cl. BL8: Bury 8H 25
Darlington Rd. M20: Man 2F 106
OL11: Roch 1D 44
Darlington St. M29: Tyld 1B 74
PR7: Cop 4A 18
WN1: Wig 9K 9 (4G 52)
WN2: I Mak 4K 53
Darlington St. E. M29: Tyld 1C 74
WN1: Wig 9M 9 (4G 53)
Darliston Av. M9: Man 6F 60
Darlton Wlk. *M9: Man 2K 79*
(off Sequoia St.)
Darnall Av. M20: Man 9F 94
Darncombe Cl.
M16: Whall R 5E 94
Darnhall St. WN3: I Mak 7J 53
DARN HILL 3E 42
Darnley Av. M28: Wors 1J 75
Darnley St. M16: Old T 5C 94
Darnton Gdns. OL6: A Lyne 7B 82
Darnton Rd. OL6: A Lyne 6B 82
SK15: Stal 6B 82
Darran Av. WN3: Wig 8C 52
Darras Rd. M18: Man 6A 96
Darrell Wlk. M8: Man 4G 78
Dart Cl. OL9: Chad 3D 62
Dartford Av. M30: Ecc 8B 76
SK5: Stoc 2F 108
Dartford Cl. M12: Man 3J 95
Dartford Rd. M41: Urm 8C 92
Dartington Cl. M23: Wyth 1K 115
SK7: Bram 4D 118
Dartington Rd. WN2: P Bri 9J 53
Dartmouth Cl. OL8: O'ham 7K 63
Dartmouth Cres. SK5: Stoc 3G 108
Dartmouth Rd.
M21: Cho H 9B 94
M45: Whitef 4N 59
Dartnall Cl. SK12: Dis 9D 120
Darton Av. M40: Man 7J 79
Darvel Av. WN4: Gars 6N 69
Darvel Cl. BL2: Bolt 6N 39
Darwell Av. M30: Ecc 1C 92
Darwen Dr. WN2: P Bri 9K 53
Darwen Rd. BL7: Bro X, Eger 4F 22
Darwen St. M16: Old T 4B 94
Darwin Gro. SK7: Bram 9C 118
Darwin St. BL1: Bolt 2E 38
OL4: O'ham 6N 63
OL7: A Lyne 9A 6 (8L 81)
SK14: Hyde 4D 98
Dashwood Rd. M25: Pres 6N 59
Dashwood Wlk. *M12: Man 3M 95*
(off Radbourne Cl.)
Datchet Ter. OL11: Roch 9D 28
DAUBHILL 9D 38
Dauntesy Av. M27: Pen 3K 77
Davehall Av. SK9: Wilm 7F 122
Davenfield Gro. *M20: Man 5G 106*
(off Davenfield Rd.)
Davenfield Rd. M20: Man 5G 106
Davenham Rd. M33: Sale 2E 104
SK5: Stoc 7D 96
SK9: Hand 2J 123
Davenhill Rd. M19: Man 9M 95
DAVENPORT 2D 118
Davenport (Park & Ride) 2D 118
Davenport Av. M20: Man 1G 107
M26: Rad 6F 40
SK9: Wilm 1D 126
Davenport Dr. SK6: Wood 2M 109
Davenport Fold BL2: Bolt 1A 40
Davenport Fold Rd. BL2: Bolt 9A 24
Davenport Gdns. BL1: Bolt 1J 7
Davenport Golf Course 2M 125
DAVENPORT GREEN
SK9 1D 126
WA15 6L 115
Davenport La. WA14: B'ath 9C 104
Davenport Lodge SK3: Stoc 2D 118
DAVENPORT PARK 2E 118
Davenport Pk. Rd. SK2: Stoc 2E 118
SK7: H Gro 4H 119
Davenport Station (Rail) 2D 118
Davenport St. BL1: Bolt 1H 7 (4F 38)
M34: Aud 1J 97
M43: Droy 9C 80
SK10: Macc 4J 131
Davenport Ter. M9: Man 2K 79
Daventry Rd. M21: Cho H 9C 94
OL11: Roch 9D 28
Daventry Way OL11: Roch 1D 44
Daveylands SK9: Wilm 8J 123
Davey La. SK9: A Edg 3F 126
David Brow BL3: Bolt 1B 56
David Cl. M34: Dent 8L 97
David Cuthbert Ct. *M11: Man 2A 96*
(off Greenside St.)
David Lewis Cl. OL16: Roch 7G 28

David Lloyd Leisure
Bolton 2G 7 (5E 38)
Cheadle 5H 117
Urmston 2C 92
David M. M14: Man 1H 107
David Pegg Wlk. M40: Man 5N 79
(off Roger Byrne Cl.)
David's Farm Cl. M24: Mid 4N 61
Davids La. OL4: Spri 4C 64
Davidson Dr. M24: Mid 5N 61
Davidson Wlk. WN5: Wig 4B 52
David's Rd. M43: Droy 8C 80
David St. BL8: Bury 1J 41
(not continuous)
M34: Dent 7L 97
OL1: O'ham 3C 8 (5J 63)
OL12: Roch 4D 28
SK5: Stoc 9C 96
David St. Nth. OL12: Roch 4D 28
Davies Av. SK8: H Grn 9G 117
WA12: N Wil 4F 86
Davies Ct. M32: Stre 8K 93
(off Cyprus St.)
SK6: Rom 6M 109
(off Metcalfe Dr.)
Davies Rd. M31: Part 5H 103
SK6: Bred 5H 109
Davies Sq. M14: Man 5F 94
Davies St. BL4: Kea 4A 58
OL1: O'ham 3H 63
OL7: A Lyne 9K 81
SK10: Macc 4J 131
WN2: P Bri 9K 53
Davis Hall M14: Man 5J 95
(off Daisy Bank Hall)
Davis St. M30: Ecc 9E 76
Davy Av. M27: Clif 9K 59
DAVYHULME 6C 92
Davyhulme Circ. M41: Urm 5C 92
Davyhulme Millennium Pk. 4M 91
Davyhulme Pk. Golf Course 5N 91
Davyhulme Rd. M32: Stre 6J 93
M41: Urm 5M 91
Davyhulme Rd. E. M32: Stre 6K 93
Davyhulme St. OL12: Roch 4F 28
Davylands M41: Urm 4N 91
Davy Rd. WN2: Abr 3M 71
Davy St. M40: Man 6G 79
Daw Bank SK3: Stoc 3J 9 (7C 108)
Dawber Delf Ind. Area
WN6: App B 4H 33
Dawber Delph WN6: App B 4H 33
Dawbers Ter. WN3: Wig 3E 52
Dawber St. WN1: Wig 7G 9
WN4: A Mak 6G 71
Dawes St. BL3: Bolt 4K 7 (6G 38)
Dawley Cl. BL3: Bolt 6D 38
(off Blackshaw La.)
WN4: A Mak 7D 70
Dawley Flats OL10: H'ood 2H 43
(off St James St.)
Dawlish Av. M43: Droy 8C 80
OL9: Chad 2D 62
SK5: Stoc 3G 108
SK8: Chea H 7L 117
Dawlish Cl. SK7: Bram 8C 118
SK14: Hat 6H 99
WA3: Rix 5C 102
Dawlish Rd. M21: Cho H 9B 94
M33: Sale 3E 104
Dawlish Way WA3: Gol 9J 71
Dawnay St. M11: Man 2N 95
Dawn St. OL2: Shaw 6M 45
Dawnwood Sq. WN5: Wig 1N 51
Dawson Av. WN6: Wig 9D 34
Dawson Cl. SK11: Macc 6D 130
Dawson La. BL1: Bolt 2H 7 (5F 38)
Dawson Rd. SK8: H Grn 7J 117
SK10: Boll 6L 129
SK11: Macc 5D 130
WA14: B'ath 9D 104
Dawson St. BL9: Bury 9N 25
M3: Man 7B 4 (1C 94)
M3: Sal 2F 4 (8E 78)
M27: Pen 2G 77
M46: Ath 8L 55
OL4: Lees 6B 64
OL4: O'ham 5A 64
OL10: H'ood 2H 43
OL12: Roch 5C 8 (5D 28)
SK1: Stoc 5F 108
SK14: Hyde 8B 98
Daybrook WN8: Uph 4D 50
Daybrook Wlk. SK10: Macc 4J 131
Day Dr. M35: Fail 4D 80
Dayfield WN8: Uph 4E 50
Day Gro. SK14: Mot 6K 99
Daylesford Cl. SK8: Chea 3J 117
Daylesford Cres. SK8: Chea 3J 117
Daylesford Rd. SK8: Chea 3J 117
Daytona Karting 3L 93
Deacon Av. M27: Swin 1E 76
Deacon Cl. WA14: Bow 6B 114
Deacons Cl. SK1: Stoc 2N 9 (7E 108)
WA3: Cro 9C 88
Deacons Cres. BL8: Tot 8G 25
Deacon's Dr. M6: Sal 4K 77
Deacon St. OL16: Roch 4F 28
Deacon Trad. Est. WA12: N Wil 7C 86
Deakins Bus. Pk. BL7: Eger 4E 22
Deakins Mill Way BL7: Eger 3E 22
Deakin's Ter. BL7: Bel 1L 21
Deakin St. WN3: I Mak 6H 53
Deal Av. SK5: Stoc 3F 108
Deal Cl. M40: Man 5B 80
Dealey Rd. BL3: Bolt 8B 38
Deal Sq. SK14: Hyde 7B 98
Deal St. BL3: Bolt 9G 38
BL9: Bury 2A 42
(not continuous)
SK14: Hyde 7B 98
Deal Wlk. OL9: Chad 5E 62
Dean Av. M16: Old T 6A 94
M40: Man 4N 79
Dean Bank Av. M19: Man 9L 95
Dean Bank Dr. OL16: Roch 3F 44
Dean Brook Cl. M40: Man 3A 80
Dean Cl. BL0: Eden 3K 11
BL4: Farn 3G 57
M15: Man 3C 94
M31: Part 4G 103
SK9: Wilm 5H 123
SK10: Boll 6L 129
WN5: Bil 7H 69
WN8: Uph 4G 50
Dean Ct. BL1: Bolt 1L 7 (4G 39)
M15: Man 3C 94
(off Lucy St.)
OL11: Roch 9D 28
SK10: Boll 5M 129
SK16: Duk 9M 81
(off Hill St.)
WA3: Gol 2K 87
WN5: Orr 2M 51
Dean Cres. WN5: Orr 3M 51
Dean Dr. SK9: Wilm 4J 123
WA14: Bow 6B 114
DEANE 8B 38
Deane Av. BL3: Bolt 7C 38
SK8: Chea 2L 117
WA15: Tim 2G 115
Deane Church Clough
BL3: Bolt 7B 38
Deane Church La. BL3: Bolt 8C 38
Deane Cl. M45: Whitef 4K 59
Deane Golf Course 7B 38
Deane Rd. BL3: Bolt 5H 7 (7D 38)
Deanery Ct. M8: Man 3F 78
WN1: Wig 7H 9
Deanery Gdns. M7: Sal 2C 78
Deanery Way SK1: Stoc . . . 1K 9 (6D 108)
Deane Wlk. BL3: Bolt 5H 7 (6F 38)
Dean Hall M14: Man 5J 95
(off Daisy Bank Hall)
Dean Head OL15: Lit 3A 16
Dean Head La. BL6: R'ton 1B 20
OL3: Del, Dig 5N 47
Dean La. M40: Man 4N 79
SK7: H Gro 7H 119
Dean Mdw. WA12: N Wil 5F 86
Dean Moor Rd. SK7: H Gro 5E 118
Dean Rd. M3: Sal 1E 4 (7D 78)
M18: Man 5C 96
M44: Cad 2F 102
SK9: Hand 3K 123
WA3: Gol 2K 87
DEAN ROW 6L 123
Dean Row Rd. SK9: Wilm 5H 123
DEANS 3E 76
Deanscourt Av. M27: Swin 3E 76
Deansgate BL1: Bolt 3J 7 (5F 38)
M3: Man 8E 4 (2D 94)
(not continuous)
M26: Rad 9H 41
WN2: Hin 5A 54
Deansgate, The M14: Man 9J 95
Deansgate - Castlefield Stop (Metro)
. . . . . 7E 4 (1E 94)
Deansgate La. WA14: Tim 9E 104
WA15: Tim 9E 104
Deansgate M. M3: Man 7E 4
Deansgate Quay M3: Man 8E 4
Deansgate Station (Rail) . . . 7E 4 (1D 94)
DEANSGREEN 8C 112
Deanshut Rd. OL8: O'ham 9L 63
Deans Rd. M27: Swin 3E 76
Deans Rd. Ind. Est. M27: Swin 3E 76
Dean St. M1: Man 4K 5 (9G 79)
M26: Rad 9F 40
M35: Fail 3B 80
OL5: Mos 1E 82
OL6: A Lyne 7A 6 (7L 81)
OL16: Roch 4F 28
SK15: Stal 9D 82
Deansway M27: Swin 2E 76
Deanswood Dr. M9: Man 6F 60
Dean Ter. OL6: A Lyne 9N 63
Dean Wlk. M24: Mid 1J 61
Deanwater Cl. M13: Man . . . 9L 5 (2G 95)
Deanwater Ct. M32: Stre 9J 93
SK8: H Grn 8J 117
Dean Way SK10: Boll 5M 129
Deanway M40: Man 2M 79
M41: Urm 7L 91
SK9: Wilm 5H 123
Deanway Technology Cen.
SK9: Hand 3J 123
Deanway Trad. Est. SK9: Hand . . . 3J 123
DEAN WOOD 2B 20
Dean Wood Av. WN5: Orr 3J 51
Dean Wood Golf Course 3G 51
Dearden Av. M38: Lit H 6H 57
Dearden Clough BL0: Eden 4L 11
Dearden Fold BL0: Eden 4L 11
BL8: Bury 3J 41
Deardens St. BL8: Bury 3J 41
Dearden St. BL3: Lit L 8A 40
M15: Man 3D 94
OL15: Lit 8M 15
SK15: Stal 8D 82
Dearden Way WN8: Uph 4E 50
Dearman's Pl. M3: Sal 3E 4 (8D 78)
Dearnalay Way OL9: Chad 7F 62
Dearncamme Cl. BL2: Bolt 8J 23
Dearne Dr. M32: Stre 7L 93
DEARNLEY 1J 29
Dearnley Cl. OL15: Lit 1J 29
Dearnley Pas. OL15: Lit 1J 29
DEBDALE 5D 96
Debdale Av. M18: Man 5D 96
Debdale La. M18: Man 5D 96
M29: Ast 6A 74
Debdale Outdoor Cen. 5C 96
Debdale Pk. 5D 96
Deben Cl. WN6: Stan 3A 34
Debenham Av. M40: Man 6A 80
Debenham Ct. BL4: Farn 4L 57
Debenham Rd. M32: Stre 7G 93
De Brook Cl. M41: Urm 8M 91
Dee Av. WA15: Tim 2K 115
Dee Dr. BL4: Kea 6A 58
Deepcar St. M19: Man 7M 95
Deepdale OL4: O'ham 5A 64
WN7: Lei 7L 73
Deepdale Av. M20: Man 9F 94
OL2: O'ham 4G 44
OL16: Roch 7G 29
WA11: St H 9G 68
Deepdale Cl. SK5: Stoc 8D 96
Deepdale Ct. M9: Man 8N 61
Deepdale Dr. M27: Pen 3K 77
Deepdale Rd. BL2: Bolt 3N 39
Deepdene St. M12: Man 3L 95
Deeping Av. M16: Whall R 7C 94
Deep La. OL15: Lit 4N 29
OL16: Miln 6M 29
Deeplish Cotts. OL11: Roch 8D 28
(off Clifford St.)
Deeplish Rd. OL11: Roch 8D 28
Deeplish St. OL11: Roch 8D 28
Deeply Va. La. BL9: Bury 3B 26
Deeracre Av. SK2: Stoc 1G 119
Deerfold Cl. M18: Man 4B 96
Deer Hill Cl. HD7: Mars 1H 49
Deer Hill Cft. HD7: Mars 1H 49
(off Deer Hill Dr.)
Deer Hill Dr. HD7: Mars 1H 49
Deerhurst Dr. M8: Man 4E 78
Dee Rd. M29: Ast 3D 74
Deeroak Cl. M18: Man 3N 95
Deerpark Rd. M16: Whall R 6D 94
Deerwood Cl. SK10: Macc 3D 130
Deerwood Gdns. WN1: Stan 5E 34
Deerwood Va. SK14: Hat 8H 99
Defence St. BL3: Bolt 6E 38
Defiance St. M46: Ath 8L 55
Deganwy Gro. SK5: Stoc 3D 108
Degas Cl. M7: Sal 2A 78
De-Haviland Way WN8: Skel 3C 50
De Havilland Way
BL5: W'ton 6E 36
BL6: Hor 6E 36
Deighton Av. M20: Man 9F 94
Deighton Cl. WN5: Orr 5J 51
Delacourt Rd. M14: Man 9F 94
Delafield Av. M12: Man 7M 95
Delaford Av. M28: Wors 3M 75
Delaford Cl. SK3: Stoc 3C 118
Delaford Wlk. M40: Man 6B 80
(off Eastmoor Dr.)
Delahays Dr. WA15: Hale 5H 115
Delahays Range M18: Man 5D 96
Delahays Rd. WA15: Hale 5G 115
Delaheyes Lodge WA15: Tim 2H 115
Delaine Rd. M20: Man 2H 107
Delamere Av. M6: Sal 4J 77
M27: Clif 9H 59
M32: Stre 7K 93
(not continuous)
M33: Sale 5L 105
M45: Whitef 3K 59
OL2: Shaw 4A 46
WA3: Low 3A 88
Delamere Cl. SK6: Wood 3N 109
SK7: H Gro 4L 119
SK15: C'ook 4H 83
Delamere Ct. M9: Man 6F 60
Delamere Dr. SK10: Macc 2K 131
Delamere Gdns. BL1: Bolt 1E 38
(off Harvey St.)
Delamere Lodge SK7: H Gro 5H 119
Delamere Rd. M19: Man 9N 95
M34: Dent 7F 96
M41: Urm 7N 91
OL16: Roch 9G 28
SK2: Stoc 3F 118
SK7: H Gro 4L 119
SK8: Gat 2G 117
SK9: Hand 2J 123
Delamere St. BL9: Bury 8N 25
M11: Man 2D 96
OL6: A Lyne 7D 6 (8M 81)
OL8: O'ham 6M 63
Delamere Way WN8: Uph 4E 50
Delamer Rd.
WA14: Alt, Bow 5B 6 (4C 114)
Delaunays Rd. M8: Man 1F 78
M9: Man 1F 78
M33: Sale 4F 104
Delaware Wlk. M9: Man 3J 79
Delbooth Av. M41: Urm 5M 91
Delegarte St. WN3: I Mak 5H 53
Delfhaven Ct. WN6: Stan 5D 34
Delf Ho. WN8: Skel 2A 50
Delft Wlk. M6: Sal 5N 77
Delfur Rd. SK7: Bram 8D 118
Delhi Rd. M44: Irl 9G 90
Dell, The BL2: Bolt 8K 23
WA14: Hale 7E 114
WN6: App B 5H 33
WN8: Uph 4F 50
Dellar St. OL12: Roch 4A 28
Dell Av. M27: Pen 3K 77
WN6: Wig 9B 34
Dell Cl. OL4: Spri 6C 64
Dellcot Cl. M6: Sal 5H 77
M25: Pres 9C 60
Dellcot La. M28: Wors 5N 75
Dell Gdns. OL12: Roch 3N 27
Dellhide Cl. OL4: Spri 5D 64
Dell Mdw. OL12: Whitw 9A 14
Dell Rd. OL12: Roch 1N 27
Dell Side SK6: Bred 5J 109
Dellside Cl. WN4: A Mak 4A 70
Dellside Gro. M28: Walk 8M 57
Dell Side Way OL12: Roch 3A 28
Dell St. BL2: Bolt 8K 23
Delmar Rd. WA16: Knut 7J 133
DELPH 8J 47
Delph, The WN8: Par 1A 32
Delph Av. BL7: Eger 2E 22
Delph Brook Way BL7: Eger 3E 22
Delph Cotts. BL8: Haw 2A 24
Delph Gro. WN7: Lei 1F 72
DELPH HILL 2N 37
Delph Hill BL1: Bolt 2N 37
Delph Hill Cl. BL1: Bolt 2N 37
Delphi Av. M28: Walk 9L 57
Delph La. BL2: Ain 3C 40
OL3: Del 7J 47
PR7: Char R 1A 18
(not continuous)
Delph Mdw. Gdns. WN5: Bil 6G 69
Delph New Rd. OL3: Del, Dob 1H 65
Delph Rd. OL3: Dens 5F 46
Delph Sailing Club 2C 22
Delphside Cl. WN5: Orr 6H 51
Delphside Rd. WN5: Orr 6H 51
Delph St. BL3: Bolt 7E 38
OL16: Miln 7K 29
WN6: Wig 2E 52
Delside Av. M40: Man 2M 79
Delta Cl. OL2: O'ham 1H 63
Delta Point M34: Aud 2J 97
Delta Rd. M34: Aud 2J 97
Delta Wlk. M40: Man 3M 79
Delves Rd. WA14: W Tim 7D 104
Delvino Wlk. M14: Man 5F 94
Delwood Gdns. M22: Wyth 3C 116
De Massey Cl. SK6: Wood 2M 109
Demesne Cl. SK15: Stal 9F 82
Demesne Cres. SK15: Stal 9F 82
Demesne Dr. SK15: Stal 8F 82
Demesne Rd. M16: Whall R 7D 94
Demmings, The SK8: Chea 2L 117
Demmings Ind. Est.
SK8: Chea 2L 117
Demmings Rd. SK8: Chea 2L 117
Dempsey Dr. BL9: Bury 1A 60
Denbigh Cl. SK7: H Gro 7G 119
Denbigh Dr. OL2: Shaw 6K 45
Denbigh Gro. M46: Ath 6L 55
Denbigh Pl. M5: Sal 8N 77
Denbigh Rd. BL2: Bolt 7J 23
M27: Clif 9G 59
M34: Dent 8K 97
Denbigh St. OL5: Mos 2G 83
OL8: O'ham 8K 63
SK4: Stoc 5B 108
Denbigh Wlk. M15: Man 4D 94
(off Shearsby Cl.)
Denbury Dr. WA14: Alt 2B 114
Denbury Grn. SK7: H Gro 6E 118
Denbury Wlk. M9: Man 4H 79
(off Mannington Dr.)
Denbydale Way OL2: O'ham 8G 44
Denby La. SK4: Stoc 4B 108
Denby Rd. SK16: Duk 2N 97
Dencombe St. M13: Man 5L 95
Dene Av. WA12: N Wil 5C 86
Dene Bank BL2: Bolt 8K 23
Dene Brow M34: Dent 9M 97
Dene Ct. SK4: Stoc 6A 108
Dene Dr. M24: Mid 4L 61
Denefield Cl. SK6: Mar B 7E 110
Denefield Pl. M30: Ecc 7F 76
Deneford Rd. M20: Man 6F 106
Dene Gro. WN7: Lei 6D 72
Dene Hollow SK5: Stoc 8E 96
Dene Ho. SK4: Stoc 7K 107
Denehurst Rd. OL11: Roch 5N 27
Dene Pk. M20: Man 6F 106
Dene Rd. M20: Man 6F 106
Dene Rd. W. M20: Man 5E 106
Denes, The SK5: Stoc 8D 96
Deneside M40: Man 4J 79
Deneside Cres. SK7: H Gro 4K 119
Deneside Wlk. M9: Man 1K 79
(off Dalbeattie St.)
Dene St. BL2: Bolt 8K 23
WN7: Lei 6D 72
Denesway M33: Sale 5E 104
(not continuous)
Deneway SK4: Stoc 6A 108
SK6: H Lan 7C 120
SK7: Bram 8A 118
Deneway Cl. SK4: Stoc 6A 108
Deneway M. SK4: Stoc 6A 108
Denewell Av. M13: Man 3J 95
Denewood Ct. SK9: Wilm 8F 122
Denford Cl. WN3: Wig 8C 52
Denham Cl. BL1: Bolt 8H 23
Denham Dr. M44: Irl 8H 91
SK7: Bram 8B 118
WN3: Wig 8D 52
Denham St. M13: Man 5J 95
M26: Rad 7F 40
Den Hill Dr. OL4: Spri 5C 64
Denhill Rd. M15: Man 5E 94
Denholme WN8: Uph 4D 50
(not continuous)
Denholme Rd. OL11: Roch 9D 28
Denholm Rd. M20: Man 8H 107
Denhurst Rd. OL15: Lit 8M 15
Denis Av. M16: Whall R 7D 94
Denison Rd. M14: Man 6H 95
SK7: H Gro 7J 119
Denison St. M14: Man 6H 95
Deniston Rd. SK4: Stoc 3N 107
Den La. OL3: Upp 2L 65
OL4: Spri 4C 64
Denman Wlk. M8: Man 4E 78
(off Ermington Dr.)
Denmark Rd. M15: Man 4F 94
M33: Sale 2H 105
Denmark St. OL4: O'ham 4M 63
OL9: Chad 3G 63
OL16: Roch 5E 28
WA14: Alt 4D 6 (3D 114)
Denmark Way OL9: Chad 3G 63
Denmore Rd. M40: Man 8A 62
Denning Pl. M27: Clif 9F 58
Dennington Dr. M41: Urm 5C 92
Dennis Ho. SK4: Stoc 4N 107
Dennison Av. M20: Man 1G 106
Dennison Rd. SK8: Chea H 7N 117
DENSHAW 3G 46
Denshaw WN8: Uph 4D 50
Denshaw Av. M34: Dent 8H 97
Denshaw Cl. M19: Man 5K 107
Denshaw Fold OL3: Dens 2G 46
Denshaw Rd. OL3: Del 5F 46
Densmore St. M35: Fail 3D 80
Denson Rd. WA15: Tim 8H 105
Denstone Av. M30: Ecc 7E 76
M33: Sale 5E 104
M41: Urm 6C 92
Denstone Cres. BL2: Bolt 2L 39
Denstone Rd. M6: Sal 5K 77
M41: Urm 6C 92
SK5: Stoc 8D 96
Denstone Wlk. M9: Man 8K 61
(off Woodmere Dr.)
Dent Cl. SK5: Stoc 2G 108
Dentdale Cl. BL1: Bolt 6M 37
Dentdale Wlk. M22: Wyth 7B 116
DENTON 6K 97
Denton Bus. Pk. M34: Dent 6H 97
Denton Community College Sports Hall
. . . . . 5H 97
(off Taylor La.)
Denton Ct. M34: Dent 4J 97
Denton Ent. Cen. M34: Dent 6K 97
(off Pitt St.)
Denton Golf Course 5F 96
Denton Gro. WN5: Orr 3M 51
Denton Hall Farm Rd.
M34: Dent 7G 97
Denton La. OL9: Chad 6E 62
Denton Pools 6J 97
Denton Rd. BL2: Bolt 6B 40
M34: Aud 4J 97
Denton St Lawrence's Church . . . 6K 97
Denton Station (Rail) 5G 97
Denton St. BL9: Bury 9M 25
OL10: H'ood 3H 43
OL12: Roch 4D 28
Denton Ter. M34: Aud 3J 97
Denver Av. M40: Man 7J 79
Denver Dr. WA15: Tim 1G 115
Denver Rd. OL11: Roch 9D 28
Denville Cres. M22: Wyth 4D 116
Denyer Ter. SK16: Duk 9M 81
(off Hill St.)
Denzell Gdns. 4A 114
Depleach Rd. SK8: Chea 2J 117
(not continuous)
Deptford Av. M23: Wyth 4N 115
De Quincey Cl. WA14: W Tim 7D 104
De Quincey Rd. WA14: W Tim 7D 104
Deramore Cl. OL6: A Lyne 7B 82
Deramore St. M14: Man 6G 94
Derby Av. M6: Sal 8L 77
Derby Cl. M44: Cad 3D 102
WA12: N Wil 6E 86
Derby Ct. BL9: Bury 8M 25
M33: Sale 5J 105
OL9: O'ham 6G 62
Derby Gro. M19: Man 8N 95
Derby Ho. M15: Man 4G 94
(off Dilworth St.)
WN1: Wig 8L 9 (3G 52)
Derby Pl. PR6: Adl 5K 19
Derby Range SK4: Stoc 4N 107
Derby Rd. M5: Sal 9L 77
M6: Sal 9L 77
M14: Man 1H 107
M26: Rad 3A 58
M33: Sale 2E 104
M41: Urm 6D 92
M45: Whitef 5N 59
OL6: A Lyne 7A 82
SK4: Stoc 4A 108
SK14: Hyde 5B 98
SK22: N Mil 6N 121
WA3: Gol 9M 71
Derby Row WA12: N Wil 9G 86
Derbyshire Av. M32: Stre 6G 93
Derbyshire Cres. M32: Stre 6H 93
Derbyshire Grn. M32: Stre 7K 93
Derbyshire Gro. M32: Stre 6H 93
Derbyshire La. M32: Stre 7J 93
Derbyshire La. W. M32: Stre 6G 93
Derbyshire Level SK13: Glos 9J 101
Derbyshire Rd. M31: Part 6E 102
M33: Sale 4J 105
M40: Man 6B 80
SK12: Poy 1N 125
WN3: Wins 1A 70
Derbyshire Rd. Sth. M33: Sale . . . 5K 105
Derbyshire Row BL1: Bolt 1F 38
Derbyshire St. M11: Man 1A 96
Derby Shop. Cen. BL3: Bolt 7E 38
(off Cannon St.)
Derby St. BL0: Ram 8K 11
BL3: Bolt 5J 7 (8E 38)
BL5: W'ton 2H 55
BL6: Hor 3F 36
M8: Man 5D 78
M25: Pres 7N 59
M29: Tyld 1B 74
M34: Dent 6H 97
(not continuous)
M35: Fail 1D 80
M46: Ath 7L 55
OL5: Mos 2G 83
OL7: A Lyne 5L 81
OL9: Chad 8F 62
OL9: O'ham 6G 62
OL10: H'ood 2G 42
OL11: Roch 8E 28
SK3: Stoc 8B 108
SK6: Mar 1C 120
SK13: Glos 9E 100
WA12: N Wil 6E 86
WA14: Alt 1D 6 (2E 114)
WN3: I Mak 7J 53
WN7: Lei 6H 73
Derby Ter. HD7: Mars 1H 49
M34: Aud 1H 97
Derby Way BL9: Bury 6M 7 (1M 41)
SK6: Mar 1C 120
Dereham Cl. BL8: Bury 8K 25
Dereham Way WN3: Wins 8A 52
Derg St. M6: Sal 8M 77
Derker Stop (Metro) 3L 63
Derker St. OL1: O'ham 3L 63
Dermot Murphy Cl. M20: Man . . . 2E 106
Dernford Av. M19: Man 3L 107
Derngate Dr. WN6: Stan 5D 34

Derrick Walker Ct. OL11: Roch 8B 28
Derry Av. M22: Wyth 3D 116
Derry St. OL1: O'ham 3D 8 (5K 63)
Derville Wlk. *M9: Man* 2J 79
(off Alderside Rd.)
Derwen Rd. SK3: Stoc 9C 108
Derwent Av. M21: Cho H 3C 106
M43: Droy 9C 80
M45: Whitef 3A 60
OL7: A Lyne 6L 81
OL10: H'ood 3J 43
OL16: Miln 7M 29
WA3: Gol 9M 71
WA15: Tim 2K 115
WN2: I Mak 4L 53
Derwent Cl. BL3: Lit L 9N 39
BL6: Hor 2E 36
M21: Cho H 3C 106
M28: Walk 9J 57
M31: Part 4G 102
M34: Dent 7F 96
M45: Whitef 3A 60
SK11: Macc 6E 130
SK13: Glos 9H 101
WA3: Cul 7J 89
WN7: Lei 7G 73
Derwent Dr. BL4: Kea 6B 58
BL9: Bury 5K 41
M33: Sale 6G 105
OL2: Shaw 4L 45
OL9: Chad 4E 62
OL15: Lit 3K 29
SK7: Bram 1A 124
SK9: Hand 1H 123
Derwent Pl. WN5: Wig 4N 51
Derwent Rd. BL4: Farn 4G 56
M24: Mid 9K 43
M32: Stre 6K 93
M41: Urm 7M 91
SK6: H Lan 7B 120
WN2: Hin 6A 54
WN4: A Mak 5H 71
WN5: Orr 3K 51
Derwent St. M5: Sal 7A 4 (1B 94)
M8: Man 4H 79
M29: Ast 3B 74
M43: Droy 9B 80
OL12: Roch 4D 28
WN7: Lei 7G 73
Derwent St. Trad. Est.
M5: Sal 7A 4 (2B 94)
Derwent Ter. SK15: Stal 6D 82
Derwent Wlk. M45: Whitef 3A 60
OL4: O'ham 4A 64
Derwent Way WN7: Lei 9D 72
Desford Av. M21: Cho H 8B 94
Design St. BL3: Bolt 8C 38
Desmond Rd. M22: Wyth 3D 116
Desmond St. M46: Ath 9J 55
(not continuous)
Destructor Rd. M27: Swin 1E 76
De Trafford Dr. WN2: I Mak 3L 53
De Trafford Ho. *M30: Ecc* 9D 76
(off Fintry Gro.)
De Trafford M. *SK9: Wilm* 4J 123
(off Colshaw Dr.)
De Traffords, The M44: Irl 6J 91
Dettingen St. M6: Sal 4K 77
Deva Cen. M3: Sal 3D 4 (8D 78)
Deva Cl. SK7: H Gro 6H 119
SK12: Poy 2F 124
Deva Ct. M16: Old T 4B 94
Devaney Wlk. M34: Dent 8J 97
Deva Sq. OL9: O'ham 6G 62
Devas St. M15: Man 4G 94
(not continuous)
Devell Ho. M14: Man 5H 95
Deverill Av. M18: Man 5D 96
Devine Cl. M3: Sal 2B 4 (8C 78)
OL2: O'ham 6H 45
Devisdale Ct. WA14: Alt 4B 114
Devisdale Grange
WA14: Bow 5A 6 (4B 114)
Devisdale Rd.
WA14: Alt 3A 6 (3B 114)
Devoke Av. M28: Walk 9M 57
WA11: St H 9E 68
Devoke Gro. BL4: Farn 3F 56
Devoke Rd. M22: Wyth 5A 116
Devon Av. M19: Man 9L 95
M45: Whitef 2L 59
WN8: Uph 5F 50
Devon Cl. BL3: Lit L 8B 40
M6: Sal 7G 77
OL2: Shaw 5K 45
SK5: Stoc 4G 108
SK10: Macc 2D 130
WN2: Asp 7N 35
WN5: Wig 5N 51
Devon Dr. BL2: Ain 3C 40
OL3: Dig 8L 47
WN1: Stan 3E 34
Devonia Ho. OL16: Roch 1F 44
Devon M. M45: Whitef 2L 59
Devonport Cres. OL2: O'ham 8K 45
Devon Rd. M29: Tyld 9A 56
M31: Part 6F 102
M35: Fail 4C 80
M41: Urm 8M 91
M43: Droy 7E 80
M44: Cad 3E 102
Devonshire Cl. M41: Urm 7E 92
OL10: H'ood 2F 42
WN3: I Mak 6H 53
Devonshire Ct. BL1: Bolt 4C 38
M7: Sal 2C 78
M33: Sale 5K 105
(off Derbyshire Rd. Sth.)
SK2: Stoc 2E 118
Devonshire Dr. M28: Wors 4G 74
SK9: A Edg 3G 126
Devonshire Gdns. WA12: N Wil 7F 86
Devonshire Pk. Rd. SK2: Stoc 2E 118
Devonshire Pl. M25: Pres 6N 59
M46: Ath 7M 55
Devonshire Point M30: Ecc 8E 76
Devonshire Rd. BL1: Bolt 3B 38
M6: Sal 7G 77
M21: Cho H 9B 94
M28: Walk 5K 57
M30: Ecc 8E 76
M46: Ath 6L 55
OL11: Roch 2D 44
SK4: Stoc 6N 107
SK7: H Gro 7K 119
WA14: Alt 1D 114
Devonshire St. M7: Sal 4C 78
M12: Man 3J 95
Devonshire St. E. M35: Fail 5B 80
Devonshire St. Ind. Est.
M12: Man 3J 95
(off Devonshire St.)
Devonshire St. Nth. M12: Man 2J 95
Devonshire St. Sth. M13: Man 4J 95
Devon St. BL2: Bolt 3N 7 (5J 39)
BL4: Farn 1L 57
BL9: Bury 4M 41
M27: Pen 9F 58
OL9: O'ham 7F 62
(not continuous)
OL11: Roch 9C 8 (7D 28)
WN2: Hin 6A 54
WN7: Lei 6N 73
Devon Way OL8: O'ham 9G 62
Dewar Cl. M11: Man 9M 79
Dewberry Cl. M27: Swin 9E 58
M29: Tyld 1F 74
Dewberry Flds. WN8: Uph 4F 50
Dewes Av. M27: Clif 9H 59
Dewey St. M11: Man 2B 96
Dewham Cl. BL5: W'ton 2H 55
Dewhirst Rd. OL12: Roch, W'le 1D 28
Dewhirst Way OL12: Roch 1D 28
Dewhurst Clough Rd. BL7: Eger 3E 22
Dewhurst Ct. BL7: Eger 2E 22
Dewhurst Rd. BL2: Bolt 1M 39
Dewhurst St. M8: Man 6E 78
OL10: H'ood 2K 43
De Wint Av. SK6: Mar B 8E 110
Dew Mdw. Cl. OL12: Roch 3C 28
Dewsnap Bri. SK16: Duk 3N 97
Dewsnap Cl. SK16: Duk 3N 97
Dewsnap La. SK14: Mot 3J 99
SK16: Duk 3N 97
Dewsnap Way *SK14: Hat* 7H 99
(off Stockport Rd.)
Dew Way OL9: O'ham 4H 63
Dexter Rd. M9: Man 6F 60
Dexter Way WN8: Uph 5F 50
Deyne Av. M14: Man 5H 95
M25: Pres 7A 60
Deyne St. M6: Sal 8L 77
Dial Ct. BL4: Farn 3L 57
Dial Pk. Rd. SK2: Stoc 3H 119
Dial Rd. SK2: Stoc 2G 119
WA15: Haleb 7J 115
Dialstone La. SK2: Stoc 9G 108
Diamond Cl. OL6: A Lyne 6A 82
Diamond St. OL6: A Lyne 6A 82
SK2: Stoc 1E 118
WN6: Wig 9D 34
WN7: Lei 6G 73
Diamond Ter. SK6: Mar 3C 120
Diane Rd. WN4: A Mak 5G 71
Dibden Wlk. M23: Wyth 2N 115
Dicconson Cres.
WN1: Wig 6K 9 (2F 52)
Dicconson La. BL5: W'ton 8B 36
WN2: W'ton 8B 36
Dicconson St. WN1: Wig 5J 9 (2F 52)
Dicconson Ter. WN1: Wig 5J 9 (2F 52)
Dicken Grn. OL11: Roch 9D 28
Dicken Grn. La. OL11: Roch 9D 28
Dickens Cl. SK8: Chea H 1N 123
Dickens Dr. WN2: Abr 2M 71
Dickens La. SK12: Poy 3H 125
Dickenson Rd. M13: Man 6H 95
M14: Man 6H 95
Dickenson St. WN2: Hin 7A 54
Dickens Pl. WN3: Wig 7C 52
Dickens Rd. M30: Ecc 9D 76
PR7: Cop 5B 18
Dickens St. OL1: O'ham 8B 46
Dickinson Cl. *BL1: Bolt* 3F 38
(off Dickinson St.)
Dickinson Ct. *BL6: Hor* 9D 20
(off Hope St.)
Dickinson St. BL1: Bolt 3F 38
M1: Man 6G 5 (1F 94)
M3: Sal 6D 78
OL4: O'ham 4M 63
Dickinson St. W. BL6: Hor 9C 20
Dickinson Ter. *BL1: Bolt* 3F 38
(off Dickinson St.)
Dickins St. OL10: H'ood 2G 43
Didcot Rd. M22: Wyth 6B 116
Didley Sq. M12: Man 2M 95
DIDSBURY 5G 107
Didsbury Ct. M20: Man 4G 106
Didsbury Ga. M20: Man 3E 106
Didsbury Golf Course 7F 106
Didsbury Gro. WN2: Hin 6N 53
Didsbury Pk. M20: Man 6G 107
Didsbury Rd. SK4: Stoc 6J 107
Didsbury Sports Cen. & Swimming Pool 6G 107
Digby Rd. OL11: Roch 9D 28
Digby Wlk. *M11: Man* 9L 79
(off Albert St.)
Dig Gate La. OL16: Miln 1H 45
DIGGLE 8M 47
DIGGLE EDGE 6A 48
Diggle Mill Cotts. OL3: Dig 8B 48
Diggles La. OL11: Roch 7K 27
(Hawthorn Rd.)
OL11: Roch 6L 27
(Swift Rd.)
Diggle St. OL2: Shaw 6M 45
WN6: Wig 2D 52
(not continuous)
Diggle Wlk. *SK15: C'ook* 4H 83
(off Friezland Cl.)
Diglands Av. SK22: N Mil 6N 121
Diglands Cl. SK22: N Mil 6N 121
Diglea OL3: Dig 7N 47
DIGMOOR 5B 50
Digmoor Dr. WN8: Skel 4A 50
Digmoor Rd. WN8: Skel 4A 50
Digsby Ct. M20: Man 4G 106
Dijon St. BL3: Bolt 8D 38
Dilham Ct. BL1: Bolt 4D 38
DILL HALL BROW 2N 19
Dillicar Wlk. *M9: Man* 3J 79
(off Ravelston Dr.)
Dillmoss Wlk. *M15: Man* 3C 94
(off Shawgreen Cl.)
Dillon Dr. M12: Man 4K 95
Dilworth Cl. OL10: H'ood 2E 42
Dilworth Ct. SK2: Stoc 2J 119
Dilworth Ho. *M15: Man* 4G 94
(off Dilworth St.)
Dilworth St. M15: Man 4G 94
Dimora Dr. M27: Pen 4K 77
DIMPLE 1E 22
Dimple Pk. BL7: Eger 2E 22
Dimple Rd. BL7: Eger 1D 22
Dingle, The SK7: Bram 6A 118
SK14: Hyde 2B 110
Dingle Av. M34: Dent 7M 97
OL2: Shaw 3N 45
SK9: A Edg 2C 126
WA12: N Wil 7C 86
WN6: App B 4J 33
WN8: Uph 3F 50
Dingle Bank Rd. SK7: Bram 5B 118
Dinglebrook Gro. *SK9: Wilm* 5K 123
(off Malpas Cl.)
Dingle Cl. M26: Rad 2H 59
SK6: Rom 6A 110
SK10: Macc 1F 130
SK13: Glos 9C 100
Dingle Dr. M43: Droy 7F 80
Dingle Gro. SK8: Gat 1E 116
Dingle Hollow SK6: Rom 6B 110
Dingle Rd. M24: Mid 5K 61
WN8: Uph 3F 50
Dingle Ter. OL6: A Lyne 9M 63
Dingle Wlk. BL1: Bolt 1K 7
WN6: Stan 8A 34
Dinglewood SK7: Bram 6A 118
Dinmore Ct. *SK2: Stoc* 2H 119
(off Lisburne La.)
Dinmor Rd. M22: Wyth 6B 116
Dinnington Dr. M8: Man 4E 78
Dinorwic Cl. M8: Man 9F 60
Dinsdale Cl. M40: Man 8J 79
Dinsdale Dr. BL3: Bolt 7E 38
Dinslow Wlk. *M8: Man* 3E 78
(off Winterford Rd.)
Dinting Av. M20: Man 1F 106
Dinting La. SK13: Glos 8C 100
Dinting La. Ind. Est.
SK13: Glos 8C 100
Dinting Lodge Ind. Est.
SK13: Had 7B 100
Dinting Rd. SK13: Glos, Had 7B 100
Dinting Station (Rail) 7C 100
DINTING VALE 8B 100
Dinting Va.
SK13: Gam, Glos, Had 7A 100
Dinting Va. Bus. Pk.
SK13: Gam 7A 100
Dinton Ho. *M5: Sal* 9M 77
(off Buckingham St.)
Dinton St. M15: Man 9A 4 (2B 94)
Dipper Dr. WA14: W Tim 7C 104
Dipton Wlk. *M8: Man* 4H 79
(off Lanhill Dr.)
Dirty La. OL3: Del 4L 47
OL4: Scout 2E 64
Dirty Leech OL12: W'le 8D 14
Discovery Pk. SK4: Stoc 2N 107
DISLEY 9G 120
Disley Av. M20: Man 2E 106
Disley Golf Course 8F 120
Disley Ho. *SK3: Stoc* 9C 108
(off James St.)
Disley Station (Rail) 9F 120
Disley St. OL11: Roch 9A 28
Disley Wlk. M34: Dent 8L 97
Distaff Rd. SK12: Poy 2F 124
District Probate Registry
Manchester 4E 4
(within Manchester County Court)
Ditton Brook BL5: W'ton 2H 55
Ditton Mead Cl. OL12: Roch 3F 28
Ditton Wlk. M23: Wyth 1M 115
Division St. BL3: Bolt 8G 38
OL12: Roch 3F 28
Dixey St. BL6: Hor 1C 36
Dixon Av. M7: Sal 4D 78
WA12: N Wil 4F 86
WN6: She 7L 33
Dixon Cl. M33: Sale 6K 105
WA11: Hay 1D 86
Dixon Closes OL11: Roch 6K 27
Dixon Ct. SK8: Chea 2J 117
Dixon Dr. M27: Clif 7E 58
SK11: Chel 9A 126
WN6: She 7L 33
Dixon Fold M45: Whitef 2L 59
OL11: Roch 7K 27
Dixon Grn. Dr. BL4: Farn 2J 57
Dixon Pl. WN2: Abr 1L 71
Dixon Rd. M34: Dent 8M 97
Dixon St. BL5: W'ton 9G 37
BL6: Hor 1D 36
M6: Sal 4M 77
M24: Mid 1M 61
M40: Man 4N 79
M44: Irl 9G 90
OL1: O'ham 3J 63
OL4: Lees 3B 64
OL6: A Lyne 6A 82
OL11: Roch 9B 28
WN2: P Bri 8K 53
DOBB BROW 4E 54
Dobb Brow Rd. BL5: W'ton 4F 54
Dobb Hedge Cl. WA15: Haleb 9J 115
Dobbin Dr. OL11: Roch 1D 44
Dobbinetts La. M23: Wyth 3K 115
WA15: Hale 3K 115
Dob Brook Cl. M40: Man 4A 80
Dob Brow PR7: Char R 1B 18
Dob Brow Cl. PR7: Char R 1B 18
DOBCROSS 1K 65
Dobcross Cl. M13: Man 7M 95
Dobcross New Rd. OL3: Dob 2K 65
Dobfield Rd. OL16: Roch 5H 29
Dobhill St. BL4: Farn 3L 57
Dobroyd Ho. *OL4: O'ham* 3B 64
(off Huddersfield Rd.)
Dobroyd St. M8: Man 2F 78
Dobson Cl. WN6: App B 2J 33
Dobson Ct. M40: Man 6N 79
Dobson Pk. Ind. Est.
WN2: I Mak 4K 53
Dobson Pk. Way WN2: I Mak 5J 53
Dobson Rd. BL1: Bolt 5D 38
Dobson St. BL1: Bolt 2E 38
Dock Office M50: Sal 2N 93
Doctor Dam Cotts. OL12: Roch 2H 27
Doctor Fold La. OL10: H'ood 6G 43
Doctor La. OL4: Scout 2F 64
DOCTOR LANE HEAD 2F 64
Doctor La. Head Cotts.
OL4: Scout 2F 64
Doctors La. BL9: Bury 7H 7 (2K 41)
Doctor's Nook WN7: Lei 5H 73
Dodd Cft. OL16: Roch 1F 44
Doddington La. M5: Sal 1N 93
Doddington Wlk. M34: Dent 8K 97
Dodd La. BL5: W'ton 9C 36
Dodd La. Ind. Est. BL5: W'ton 8D 36
Dodds Farm La. WN2: Asp 9A 36
Dodd St. M5: Sal 8K 77
Dodge Fold SK2: Stoc 1J 119
Dodge Hill SK4: Stoc 1K 9 (6C 108)
Dodgson St. OL16: Roch 7E 28
Dodhurst Rd. WN2: Hin 5B 54
Dodson Cl. WN4: A Mak 7F 70
Doe Brow M27: Clif 7E 58
Doefield Av. M28: Wors 2K 75
Doeford Cl. WA3: Cul 4F 88
Doe Hey Gro. BL4: Farn 1J 57
Doe Hey Rd. BL3: Bolt 1J 57
DOFFCOCKER 3B 38
Doffcocker La. BL1: Bolt 3A 38
Doffcocker Lodge Local Nature Reserve 3N 37
Dogford Rd. OL2: O'ham 7H 45
DOG HILL 5B 46
Dog Hill La. OL2: Shaw 5B 46
Dolbey St. M5: Sal 9L 77
Dolefield M3: Man 4E 4 (9D 78)
D'Oliveira Ct. M24: Mid 1K 61
Dollond St. M9: Man 1K 79
Dolman Wlk. *M8: Man* 4E 78
(off Felthorpe Dr.)
Dolphin Pl. M12: Man 9N 5 (2H 95)
Dolphin St. M12: Man 9N 5 (2H 95)
Dolwen Wlk. *M40: Man* 4N 79
(off Harold Priestnall Cl.)
Dombey Rd. SK12: Poy 4H 125
Dome, The *M17: Urm* 3D 92
(within The Trafford Cen.)
Domestic App. M90: Man A 8B 116
Domett St. M9: Man 9H 61
Dominic Cl. M23: Wyth 7L 105
Domville Cl. WA13: Lym 4A 112
Donagh Cl. SK10: Macc 2D 130
Donald Av. SK14: Hyde 8C 98
Donald St. M1: Man 7J 5 (1F 94)
Dona St. SK1: Stoc 8E 108
(not continuous)
Don Av. M6: Sal 9J 77
Doncaster Av. M20: Man 1F 106
Doncaster Cl. BL3: Lit L 9N 39
Doncasters Cl. OL1: O'ham 9A 46
Doncaster Wlk. OL1: O'ham 1D 8
Donhead Wlk. *M13: Man* 3H 95
(off Lauderdale Cres.)
Donkey La. SK9: Wilm 9F 122
Donleigh St. M40: Man 4B 80
Donnington OL11: Roch 7C 28
Donnington Av. SK8: Chea 1L 117
Donnington Cl. WN7: Lei 9F 72
Donnington Gdns. M28: Walk 8L 57
Donnington Rd. M18: Man 4C 96
M26: Rad 7C 40
Donnison St. M12: Man 3L 95
Donovan Av. M40: Man 2B 80
Don St. BL3: Bolt 9E 38
M24: Mid 2A 62
Doodson Av. M44: Irl 7H 91
Doodson Sq. BL4: Farn 3L 57
Dooley La. SK6: Mar 9M 109
Dooley's La. SK9: Wilm 4B 122
Dootson St. WN2: Abr 1L 71
WN2: Hin 5C 54
Dorac Av. SK8: H Grn 8H 117
Dora St. BL0: Ram 1G 25
Dorchester Av. BL2: Bolt 3M 39
M25: Pres 9B 60
M34: Dent 8K 97
M41: Urm 6F 92
Dorchester Cl. SK9: Wilm 6J 123
WA15: Hale 4J 115
Dorchester Ct. M33: Sale 6H 105
SK8: Chea H 6N 117
Dorchester Dr. M23: Wyth 7L 105
OL2: O'ham 1H 63
Dorchester Gro. OL10: H'ood 4H 43
Dorchester Pde. *SK7: H Gro* 6F 118
(off Jackson's La.)
Dorchester Rd. M27: Swin 4F 76
SK7: H Gro 6F 118
WN8: Uph 4E 50
Dorchester Way SK10: Macc 9G 128
Dorclyn Av. M41: Urm 7D 92
Dorfield Cl. SK6: Bred 5J 109
Doric Av. SK6: Bred 5H 109
Doric Cl. M11: Man 9L 79
Doric Grn. WN5: Bil 8H 51
Doris Av. BL2: Bolt 5L 39
Doris Rd. SK3: Stoc 8A 108
Doris St. M24: Mid 1M 61
Dorket Gro. BL5: W'ton 5F 54
Dorking Av. M40: Man 6N 79
Dorking Cl. BL1: Bolt 2G 39
SK1: Stoc 9F 108
Dorlan Av. M18: Man 5D 96
Dorland Gro. SK2: Stoc 9F 108
Dorman St. *M11: Man* 2B 96
(off Lees St.)
Dormer St. BL1: Bolt 1G 38
Dorning Rd. M27: Swin 3G 76
Dorning St. BL4: Kea 3N 57
BL6: Bla 5B 36
BL8: Bury 9H 25
M29: Tyld 1A 74
M30: Ecc 9D 76
WN1: Wig 7H 9 (3E 52)
WN7: Lei 5G 73
Dornton Wlk. *M8: Man* 4E 78
(off Dudley St.)
Dorothy Gro. WN7: Lei 6G 73
Dorothy Rd. SK7: H Gro 4K 119
Dorothy St. BL0: Ram 9H 11
M7: Sal 3E 78
Dorothy Wlk. WN2: Bam 2J 71
Dorrian M. BL1: Bolt 5A 38
Dorrington Rd. M33: Sale 4D 104
SK3: Stoc 9M 107
Dorris St. BL3: Bolt 9D 38
M19: Man 9N 95
Dorrit Cl. SK12: Poy 4J 125
Dorset Av. BL4: Farn 3K 57
M14: Man 7F 94
M29: Tyld 8A 56
M34: Aud 1G 96
OL2: Shaw 5K 45
OL3: Dig 8M 47
SK5: Stoc 3G 109
SK7: Bram 5B 118
SK8: Chea H 2A 118
Dorset Cl. BL4: Farn 3K 57
OL10: H'ood 3F 42
WN5: Wig 5N 51
Dorset Dr. BL9: Bury 4N 41
Dorset Rd. M19: Man 8A 96
M35: Fail 4D 80
M43: Droy 7D 80
M44: Cad 3E 102
M46: Ath 7L 55
WA14: Alt 2B 114
WN1: Stan 3E 34
Dorset Rd. Ent. Cen. M46: Ath 6L 55
Dorset St. BL2: Bolt 3N 7 (5H 39)
M27: Pen 9F 58
M32: Stre 8K 93
OL6: A Lyne 7A 82
OL9: O'ham 6G 62
OL11: Roch 7D 28
WN2: Hin 5A 54
WN7: Lei 6M 73
Dorset Wlk. *SK10: Macc* 2D 130
(off Kennedy Av.)
Dorsey St. M4: Man 3K 5 (8G 78)
Dorstone Cl. M40: Man 6B 80
WN2: Hin 6D 54
Dorwood Av. M9: Man 6H 61
Dotterel Cl. WN7: Lei 4J 73
Double Cop WN7: Lei 9F 72
Dougall Wlk. *M12: Man* 3M 95
(off Bridgend Cl.)
Dougals Way WN7: Lei 9D 72
Doughty Av. M30: Ecc 7F 76
Dougill St. BL1: Bolt 3C 38
Douglas Av. BL6: Hor 8E 20
BL8: Bury 2H 41
M32: Stre 6K 93
WN5: Bil 7H 69
WN8: Uph 4F 50
Douglas Bank Dr. WN6: Wig 1C 52
Douglas Chase M26: Rad 3B 58
Douglas Cl. BL6: Hor 9E 20
M45: Whitef 1B 60
Douglas Dr. WN5: Orr 4K 51
WN6: She 7K 33
Douglas Grn. M6: Sal 5N 77
Douglas Ho. WN1: Wig 9L 9 (4G 52)
Douglas Pk. M46: Ath 8N 55
Douglas Rd. M28: Wors 3C 76
M46: Ath 9N 55
SK3: Stoc 3C 118
SK7: H Gro 4J 119
WN1: Wig 2G 52
WN6: Stan 2M 33
WN7: Lei 3E 72
Douglas Sq. *OL10: H'ood* 3E 42
(off Sutherland Rd.)
Douglas St. BL0: Ram 8H 11
BL1: Bolt 8F 22
M7: Sal 4C 78
M27: Swin 3G 76
M35: Fail 3E 80
M40: Man 3M 79
M46: Ath 8N 55
OL1: O'ham 3L 63
OL6: A Lyne 7A 82
SK14: Hyde 7B 98
WN1: Wig 9L 9
WN2: Hin 7M 53
WN5: Wig 4D 52
Douglas Valley Golf Course 9M 19
Douglas Vw. BL6: Bla 7K 19
WN1: Stan 6E 34
Douglas Wlk. M33: Sale 3C 104
M45: Whitef 1B 60
Douglas Way M45: Whitef 2B 60
Doulton Cl. WN2: P Bri 8J 53
Doulton St. M40: Man 2A 80
Dounby Av. M30: Ecc 7B 76
Douro St. M40: Man 5L 79
Douthwaite Dr. SK6: Rom 7B 110
DOVE BANK 8A 40
Dove Bank SK6: Mel 1J 121
Dove Bank Rd. BL3: Lit L 8A 40
Dovebrook Cl. SK15: C'ook 3H 83

Dovecote M43: Droy 7H 81
Dovecote Bus. & Technology Pk.
M33: Sale 4M 105
Dovecote Cl. BL7: Bro X 5J 23
Dovecote La. M38: Lit H 8F 56
OL4: Lees 4C 64
Dovecote M. M21: Cho H 9N 93
Dovecote Rd. SK6: Stri 5G 120
Dovedale Av. M20: Man 1F 106
M25: Pres 8D 60
M30: Ecc 7E 76
M41: Urm 7D 92
M43: Droy 8C 80
Dovedale Cl. SK6: H Lan 8B 120
Dovedale Ct. M24: Mid 1K 61
SK13: Glos 8H 101
Dovedale Cres. WN4: A Mak 2D 70
Dovedale Dr. OL12: W'le 8H 15
WN6: Stan 2B 34
Dovedale Rd. BL2: Bolt 3N 39
SK2: Stoc 9H 109
WN4: A Mak 3D 70
Dovedale St. M35: Fail 3C 80
Dove Dr. BL9: Bury 9A 26
M44: Irl 6H 91
Dovehouse Cl. M45: Whitef 3K 59
Doveleys Rd. M6: Sal 6K 77
Dovenby Fold WN2: I Mak 4K 53
DOVER 4L 71
Dover Cl. BL8: G'mount 4G 24
Dovercourt Av. SK4: Stoc 5L 107
Dover Gro. BL3: Bolt 7E 38
Doveridge Gdns. M6: Sal 7M 77
Dove Rd. BL3: Bolt 8C 38
Dover Pk. M41: Urm 5D 92
Dover Rd. M27: Clif 9G 59
SK10: Macc 2K 131
Dover St. BL4: Farn 1K 57
M13: Man 3G 94
M30: Ecc 8B 76
OL9: O'ham 6G 63
OL16: Roch 3F 28
SK5: Stoc 1C 108
DOVE STONE 8A 66
Dovestone Cres. SK16: Duk 2C 98
Dove Stone Sailing Club 8A 66
Dovestone Wlk. M40: Man 1C 80
Doveston Gro. M33: Sale 2H 105
Doveston Rd. M33: Sale 2H 105
Dove St. BL1: Bolt 9G 22
OL4: O'ham 6N 63
OL11: Roch 6B 28
WA3: Gol 8K 71
Dove Wlk. BL4: Farn 3G 57
M8: Man 5G 79
Dovey Cl. M29: Ast 3D 74
Dower St. WN2: P Bri 8K 53
Dow Fold BL8: Bury 1F 40
Dowland Cl. M23: Wyth 6M 105
Dow La. BL8: Bury 1F 40
Dowling Cl. WN6: Stan 9A 34
Dowling St. OL11: Roch 9D 8 (7D 28)
DOWNALL GREEN 6A 70
Downall Grn. Rd. WN4: A Mak 5B 70
Downbrook Way *WN4: A Mak* 5C 70
(off North St.)
Downcast Way *M27: Pen* 2K 77
(off Shearer Way)
Downes Cl. SK10: Macc 3E 130
Downes Way M22: Shar 1D 116
Downesway SK9: A Edg 4E 126
Downfield Cl. BL0: Ram 8G 11
Downfields SK5: Stoc 8E 96
Downgate Wlk. *M8: Man* 4F 78
(off Tamerton Dr.)
Down Grn. Rd. BL2: Bolt 1M 39
Downhall Grn. BL1: Bolt 1K 7 (4G 38)
Downham Av. BL2: Bolt 4K 39
WA3: Cul 7H 89
Downham Chase WA15: Tim 1H 115
Downham Cl. OL2: O'ham 1G 63
Downham Cres. M25: Pres 8C 60
Downham Gdns. M25: Pres 8D 60
Downham Gro. M25: Pres 8D 60
Downham Rd. OL10: H'ood 2F 42
SK4: Stoc 3B 108
Downham Wlk. M23: Wyth 8L 105
WN5: Bil 1H 69
Downhill Cl. OL1: O'ham 2J 63
Downing Cl. OL7: A Lyne 4K 81
SK11: Sut E 9K 131
WN2: P Bri 9K 53
Downing St. M1: Man 8L 5 (2G 95)
M13: Man 9M 5
OL7: A Lyne 4K 81
WN7: Lei 5H 73
Downing St. Ind. Est.
M12: Man 8L 5 (2G 95)
Downley Cl. OL12: Roch 3N 27
Downley Dr. M4: Man 3N 5 (8H 79)
Downs, The M24: Mid 5N 61
M25: Pres 9N 59
SK8: Chea 4J 117
WA14: Alt 5B 6 (4C 114)
WN3: Wig 7N 51
Downs Dr. WA14: Tim 8E 104
Downs End WA16: Knut 7J 133
Downshaw Rd. OL7: A Lyne 4L 81
Downton Av. WN2: Hin 7N 53
Dowry Pk. Ests. OL4: Lees 4B 64
Dowry Rd. OL3: Dens 9J 31
OL4: Lees 4B 64
Dowry St. OL8: O'ham 8K 63
Dowson Rd. SK14: Hyde 1A 110
Dowson St. BL2: Bolt 3N 7 (5H 39)
Dow St. SK14: Hyde 4A 98
Doyle Av. SK6: Bred 5H 109
Doyle Cl. OL1: O'ham 8B 46
Doyle Rd. BL3: Bolt 9N 37
Dragon Cl. WN8: Skel 3C 50
Drake Av. BL4: Farn 4L 57
M22: Wyth 5A 116
M44: Cad 2F 102
Drake Cl. OL1: O'ham 3K 63
Drake Ct. SK5: Stoc 4C 108
Drake Hall BL5: W'ton 6G 54
Drake Rd. OL15: Lit 5N 15
WA14: B'ath 8B 104
Drake St. M46: Ath 9L 55
OL11: Roch 9B 8 (7C 28)
OL16: Roch 7D 8 (6D 28)
Draperfield PR7: Chor 1D 18
Drapers Ct. WA3: Low 2B 88
Draxford Ct. SK9: Wilm 8G 122
Draybank Rd. WA14: W Tim 8B 104
Draycott Cl. WN2: Hin 8B 54
Draycott St. BL1: Bolt 2F 38
Draycott St. E. BL1: Bolt 2G 38
Drayfields M43: Droy 8H 81
Drayford Cl. M23: Wyth 6M 105
Drayton Cl. BL1: Bolt 2E 38
M33: Sale 6D 104
SK9: Wilm 5J 123
Drayton Dr. SK8: H Grn 8G 116
Drayton Gro. WA15: Tim 3G 115
Drayton Mnr. M20: Man 8G 107
Drayton St. M15: Man 4D 94
Drayton Wlk. *M16: Old T* 4C 94
(off Fernleigh Dr.)
Drefus Av. M11: Man 8A 80
Dresden St. M40: Man 2A 80
Dresser Cen., The M11: Man 2N 95
Drew Av. OL11: Roch 5B 28
Drewett St. M40: Man 6K 79
Driffield St. M14: Man 6F 94
M30: Ecc 1C 92
Drinkwater La. BL6: Hor 1D 36
Drinkwater Rd. M25: Pres 1M 77
Driscoll St. M13: Man 6L 95
Drive, The BL0: Eden 3K 11
BL9: Bury 8M 25
M7: Sal 1B 78
M20: Man 5H 107
M25: Pres 7A 60
M33: Sale 7E 104
SK5: Stoc 4F 108
SK6: Bred 5H 109
SK6: Mar 1B 120
SK8: Chea H 3A 118
SK10: Boll 6J 129
WA13: Lym 6E 112
WA15: Haleb 7K 115
WN7: Lei 7H 73
Droitwich Rd. M40: Man 6J 79
Dronfield Rd. M6: Sal 6K 77
M22: Nor 8C 106
Droughts La. M25: Pres 3D 60
Drovers Wlk. SK13: Glos 8F 100
Droxford Gro. M46: Ath 6N 55
DROYLSDEN 9E 80
Droylsden FC (Butchers Arms Ground)
9E 80
Droylsden Little Theatre *8F 80*
(off Market St.)
Droylsden Rd. M34: Aud 9F 80
M40: Man 4A 80
Droylsden Stop (Metro) 9E 80
Droylsden Wharf Rd. M43: Droy 1E 96
Druids Cl. BL7: Eger 2E 22
Druid St. WN4: A Mak 8F 70
Drumcroon Gallery 6J 9 (2E 52)
Drummer's La. WN4: A Mak 3A 70
Drummond Sq. WN5: Wig 4B 52
Drummond St. BL1: Bolt 9F 22
Drummond Way SK10: Macc 3C 130
Drury Cl. WN1: Lei 5K 73
Drury La. OL9: Chad 8E 62
WA16: Knut 6G 133
Drury St. M19: Man 8M 95
Dryad Cl. M27: Pen 9F 58
Drybrook Cl. M13: Man 4K 95
Dryburgh Av. BL1: Bolt 1E 38
Dry Clough La. OL3: Upp 4K 65
Dryclough Wlk. OL2: O'ham 9J 45
Dry Cft. La. OL3: Del 5L 47
Dryden Av. M27: Swin 3D 76
SK8: Chea 1L 117
WN4: A Mak 3C 70
Dryden Cl. SK6: Mar 3C 120
SK16: Duk 2E 98
WN3: Wig 6D 52
Dryden Rd. M16: Old T 6B 94
Dryden St. M13: Man 3H 95
Dryden Way *M34: Dent* 9L 97
(off Spenser Av.)
Drydock Mill *OL15: Lit* 9K 15
(off James St.)
Dryfield La. BL6: Hor, R'ton 8C 20
Drygate Wlk. *M9: Man* 3K 79
(off Craigend Dr.)
Dryhurst Dr. SK12: Dis 8G 121
Dryhurst La. SK12: Dis 9G 121
Dryhurst Wlk. M15: Man 3F 94
Drymoss OL8: O'ham 1L 81
Drysdale Vw. BL1: Bolt 9F 22
Dryton Wlk. WN2: Asp 1K 53
Drywood Av. M28: Wors 5A 76
Drywood Cotts. OL10: H'ood 8H 43
Ducal St. M4: Man 7G 78
Ducess Dr. M34: Aud 2F 96
Duchess Grn. SK14: Hyde 4C 98
Duchess Pk. Cl. OL2: Shaw 4M 45
Duchess Rd. M8: Man 2G 78
Duchess St. OL2: Shaw 4L 45
Duchess St. Ind. Est.
OL2: Shaw 4M 45
Duchess Wlk. BL3: Bolt 8C 38
Duchy Av. BL5: O Hul 3B 56
M28: Walk 2L 75
Duchy Caravan Pk. M6: Sal 5M 77
Duchy Rd. M6: Sal 2F 46
Duchy St. M6: Sal 7M 77
SK3: Stoc 9B 108
Ducie Av. BL1: Bolt 5D 38
Ducie Ct. M15: Man 4G 94
Ducie St. BL0: Ram 7H 11
M1: Man 5K 5 (9G 78)
M26: Rad 7F 40
M45: Whitef 3M 59
OL8: O'ham 9K 63
Duckshaw La. BL4: Farn 3L 57
Duckworth Rd. M25: Pres 8M 59
Duckworth St. BL3: Bolt 8D 38
BL9: Bury 9N 25
(not continuous)
OL2: Shaw 5N 45
Duddon Av. BL2: Bolt 3N 39
Duddon Cl. M45: Whitef 3A 60
WN6: Stan 5C 34
Duddon Wlk. M24: Mid 1K 61
Dudley Av. BL2: Bolt 3K 39
M45: Whitef 3M 59
Dudley Cl. M15: Man 4D 94
Dudley Ct. M16: Whall R 6C 94
Dudley Rd. M16: Whall R 7C 94
M27: Pen 1F 76
M33: Sale 2J 105
M44: Cad 4E 102
WA15: Tim 9H 105
Dudley St. M7: Sal 3D 78
M8: Man 4E 78
M30: Ecc 9C 76
OL4: O'ham 5A 64
WN4: A Mak 5D 70
Dudley Wlk. SK11: Macc 5D 130
Dudlow Wlk. *M15: Man* 3C 94
(off Shawgreen Cl.)
Dudwell Cl. BL1: Bolt 2D 38
Duerden St. BL3: Bolt 1B 56
Duffield Ct. *M15: Man* 4F 94
(off Brennan Cl.)
M24: Mid 6L 61
Duffield Gdns. M24: Mid 6L 61
Duffield Rd. M6: Sal 5K 77
M24: Mid 6L 61
Duffins Cl. OL12: Roch 2B 28
Dufton Wlk. M22: Wyth 6D 116
M24: Mid 1K 61
Dugdale Av. M9: Man 7K 61
Duke Av. SK8: Chea H 9L 117
WA3: G'ury 2L 89
Duke Ct. M16: Old T 4C 94
Dukefield St. M22: Nor 8D 106
Duke Pl. M3: Man 7D 4 (1D 94)
Duke Rd. BL2: Ain 3C 40
SK14: Hyde 4C 98
Duke's Av. BL3: Lit L 8A 40
Dukesbridge Ct. *WA13: Lym* 4E 112
(off New Rd.)
Dukes Ct. *M30: Ecc* 8E 76
(off Wellington Rd.)
Dukes Platting OL6: A Lyne 5C 82
Duke's Row WN2: Asp 8L 35
Duke's Ter. SK16: Duk 9M 81
Duke St. BL0: Ram 1G 25
BL1: Bolt 1J 7 (4F 38)
(not continuous)
BL9: Bury 9K 7 (3L 41)
M3: Man 7D 4 (1D 94)
M3: Sal 2F 4 (8E 78)
M7: Sal 5C 78
M26: Rad 1H 59
M28: Walk 9B 58
M29: Ast 4D 74
M30: Ecc 6C 76
M34: Dent 6J 97
M35: Fail 2E 80
M38: Lit H 6H 57
OL2: Shaw 6M 45
OL5: Mos 1H 83
OL6: A Lyne 7D 6 (7M 81)
OL10: H'ood 2G 42
OL12: Roch 4D 28
(not continuous)
OL15: Lit 9L 15
SK1: Stoc 3K 9 (7D 108)
SK9: A Edg 3G 127
SK11: Macc 5H 131
SK13: Glos 9E 100
SK15: Stal 9C 82
WA3: Gol 9K 71
WA12: N Wil 6E 86
WN1: Wig 1F 52
WN2: P Bri 8K 53
WN3: Wig 7C 52
WN4: A Mak 7F 70
WN7: Lei 6J 73
Duke St. Nth. BL1: Bolt 4F 38
Dukes Wlk. WA15: Hale 4F 114
Dukes Wharf M28: Wors 5N 75
M43: Droy 1E 96
Duke's Wood La. WN8: Skel 8B 50
DUKINFIELD 1A 98
Dukinfield Crematorium
SK16: Duk 9A 82
Dukinfield Golf Course 3D 98
DUKINFIELD HALL 2L 97
Dukinfield Pool 2A 98
Dukinfield Rd. SK14: Hyde 4N 97
Dulford Wlk. *M13: Man* 4H 95
(off Plymouth Gro.)
Dulgar St. M11: Man 1M 95
Dulverton Gdns. BL3: Lit L 1A 58
Dulverton St. M40: Man 4N 79
Dulwich Cl. M33: Sale 5D 104
Dulwich St. M4: Man 7G 78
Dumbah La. SK10: Boll 7G 129
Dumbarton Cl. SK5: Stoc 2D 108
Dumbarton Dr. OL10: H'ood 3F 42
Dumbarton Grn. WN6: Wig 1B 52
Dumbarton Rd. SK5: Stoc 1D 108
Dumbell St. M27: Pen 9F 58
Dumber La. M33: Sale 2F 104
Dumers Cl. M26: Rad 8K 41
Dumers La. BL9: Bury 8K 41
M26: Rad 8K 41
Dumfries Av. OL3: Dens 2F 46
Dumfries Dr. OL3: Dens 2F 46
Dumfries Hollow OL10: H'ood 1L 43
Dumfries Wlk. OL10: H'ood 3F 42
DUMPLINGTON 2C 92
Dumvilles Brow SK1: Stoc 2L 9
Dunbar Dr. M23: Wyth 4N 115
Dunbar St. BL3: Bolt 9F 38
Dunbar Gro. OL10: H'ood 4E 42
Dunbar St. OL1: O'ham 3J 63
Dunblane Av. BL3: Bolt 7N 37
SK4: Stoc 6B 108
Dunblane Cl. WN4: Gars 6N 69
Dunblane Gro. OL10: H'ood 4F 42
Duncan Av. WA12: N Wil 4F 86
Duncan Edwards Ct. *M40: Man* 5N 79
(off Eddie Colman Cl.)
Duncan Edwards Ho. *M6: Sal* 7M 77
(off Florin Gdns.)
Duncan Edwards Ter. *M6: Sal* 7M 77
(off Doveridge Gdns.)
Duncan Pl. WN5: Wig 3B 52
Duncan Rd. M13: Man 6L 95
(not continuous)
Duncan St. BL6: Hor 1E 36
M5: Sal 6A 4 (1B 94)
M7: Sal 4B 78
SK16: Duk 3N 97
Dunchurch Cl. BL6: Los 6M 37
Dunchurch Rd. M33: Sale 4E 104
Dun Cl. M3: Sal 2B 4 (8C 78)
Duncombe Cl. SK7: Bram 4E 118
Duncombe Dr. M40: Man 3N 79
Duncombe Rd. BL3: Bolt 9F 38
Duncombe St. M7: Sal 4D 78
Duncote Gro. OL2: O'ham 7L 45
Dundee *M30: Ecc* 8E 76
(off Monton La.)
Dundee Cl. OL10: H'ood 3E 42
Dundee La. BL0: Ram 8H 11
Dundonald Rd. M20: Man 5H 107
SK8: Chea H 8M 117
Dundonald St. SK2: Stoc 1D 118
Dundraw Cl. M24: Mid 2G 61
Dundreggan Gdns. M20: Man 5E 106
Dundrennan Cl. SK12: Poy 1H 125
Dunecroft M34: Dent 5L 97
Dunedin Dr. M6: Sal 5M 77
Dunedin Rd. BL8: G'mount 3F 24
Dunelm Dr. M33: Sale 7K 105
Dungeon La. WN8: Dal 5A 32
Dungeon Wlk. SK9: Wilm 7G 122
Dunham Av. WA3: Gol 9J 71
Dunham Cl. BL5: W'ton 6F 54
Dunham Forest Golf Course 3N 113
Dunham Gro. WN7: Lei 8L 73
Dunham Ho. WA14: Bow 4N 113
Dunham Lawn WA14: Alt 3B 114
DUNHAM MASSEY 2L 113
Dunham Massey 4L 113
Dunham Massey Sawmill 4K 113
Dunham M. WA14: Bow 6N 113
Dunham Ri. WA14: Alt 3B 6 (3C 114)
Dunham Rd. M31: C'ton 4L 103
SK9: Hand 1J 123
SK16: Duk 3A 98
WA13: Warb 9F 102
WA14: Alt, Bow 3A 6 (6N 113)
Dunham St. M15: Man 3D 94
OL4: Lees 3B 64
DUNHAM TOWN 3L 113
DUNHAM WOODHOUSES 3J 113
Dunkeld Gdns. M23: Wyth 1N 115
Dunkeld Rd. M23: Wyth 1M 115
Dunkerley Av. M35: Fail 3D 80
Dunkerleys Cl. *M8: Man* 2E 78
(off Grangeforth Rd.)
Dunkerley St. OL2: O'ham 8H 45
OL4: O'ham 3N 63
OL7: A Lyne 5L 81
Dunkery Rd. M22: Wyth 6C 116
Dunkirk Cl. M34: Dent 7E 96
Dunkirk La. SK14: Hyde 4M 97
Dunkirk Ri. OL12: Roch 7A 8 (5C 28)
Dunkirk Rd. M45: Whitef 2M 59
Dunkirk St. M43: Droy 9F 80
Dunley Cl. M12: Man 4M 95
Dunlin Av. WA12: N Wil 5F 86
Dunlin Cl. BL2: Bolt 7H 39
OL11: Roch 6L 27
SK2: Stoc 2L 119
SK12: Poy 2E 124
Dunlin Dr. M44: Irl 6H 91
Dunlin Gro. WN7: Lei 5K 73
Dunlin Rd. SK10: Macc 8F 128
Dunlin Wlk. *WA14: B'ath* 8B 104
(off Barlow Rd.)
Dunlop Av. OL11: Roch 1C 44
Dunlop St. M3: Man 4F 4 (9E 78)
Dunmail Av. WA11: St H 9G 68
Dunmail Cl. M29: Ast 4D 74
Dunmail Dr. M24: Mid 9K 43
Dunmaston Av. WA15: Tim 9K 105
Dunmere Wlk. *M9: Man* 4H 79
(off Hendham Va.)
Dunmore Rd. SK8: Gat 1G 116
Dunmow Ct. SK2: Stoc 2J 119
Dunmow Wlk. M23: Wyth 6N 105
Dunne La. SK13: Glos 7G 100
Dunnerdale Wlk. *M18: Man* 4A 96
(off Beyer Cl.)
Dunnisher Rd. M23: Wyth 3A 116
Dunnock Cl. SK2: Stoc 2K 119
Dunollie Rd. M33: Sale 5L 105
Dunoon Cl. OL10: H'ood 3F 42
Dunoon Dr. BL1: Bolt 8D 22
Dunoon Rd. SK5: Stoc 1D 108
WN2: Asp 7N 35
Dunoon Wlk. *M9: Man* 3J 79
(off Kingsbridge Rd.)
Dunrobin Cl. OL10: H'ood 4F 42
DUNSCAR 5F 22
Dunscar Bri. BL7: Eger 5F 22
Dunscar Cl. M45: Whitef 4K 59
Dunscar Fold BL7: Eger 5F 22
Dunscar Golf Course 5E 22
Dunscar Grange BL7: Bro X 5G 22
Dunscar Ind. Est. BL7: Eger 5F 22
Dunscar Sq. BL7: Eger 5F 22
Dunscore Rd. WN3: Wins 8B 52
Dunsdale Dr. WN4: A Mak 7F 70
Dunsfold Dr. M23: Wyth 8K 105
Dunsford Ct. *OL4: Spri* 5C 64
(off Lauren Cl.)
Dunsley Av. M40: Man 9B 62
Dunsmore Cl. M16: Whall R 5C 94
WA11: Hay 2A 86
Dunsop Dr. BL1: Bolt 1A 38
Dunstable OL12: Roch 5B 8
Dunstable St. M19: Man 8N 95
Dunstall Rd. M22: Shar 2D 116
Dunstan Ct. M40: Man 2M 79
Dunstan St. BL2: Bolt 5K 39
Dunstar Av. M34: Aud 2J 97
Dunster Av. M9: Man 7K 61
M27: Clif 9H 59
OL11: Roch 8C 28
SK5: Stoc 3G 108
Dunster Cl. OL9: Chad 7E 62
SK7: H Gro 6G 119
WN2: P Bri 1K 71
Dunster Dr. M41: Urm 8K 91
Dunster Pl. M28: Wors 3G 74
Dunster Rd. BL9: Bury 6J 7 (1L 41)
M28: Wors 3G 74
SK10: Macc 3K 131
Dunsters Av. BL8: Bury 8J 25
Dunsters Ct. BL8: Bury 8J 25
Dunsterville Ter. *OL11: Roch* 8C 28
(off New Barn La.)
Dunston St. M11: Man 1A 96
Dunton Grn. SK5: Stoc 2F 108
Dunton Towers SK5: Stoc 2F 108
Dunvegan Rd. SK7: H Gro 6K 119
Dunwood Av. OL2: Shaw 4N 45
Dunwood Pk. Courts OL2: Shaw 3N 45
Dunworth St. M14: Man 6G 94
Dura Bank OL12: Whitw 5B 14
Durant St. M4: Man 1K 5 (7G 78)
Durban Cl. OL2: Shaw 6L 45
Durban Rd. BL1: Bolt 8F 22
Durban St. M46: Ath 9J 55
OL7: A Lyne 9J 81
OL8: O'ham 8G 63
OL11: Roch 2A 44
WN7: Lei 6A 72
Durden M. OL2: Shaw 6M 45
Durham Av. M41: Urm 6E 92
Durham Cl. BL3: Lit L 8B 40
M27: Clif 9F 58
M29: Tyld 8B 56
SK6: Rom 7L 109
SK10: Macc 2D 130
SK16: Duk 2B 98
Durham Cres. M35: Fail 4E 80
Durham Dr. BL0: Ram 2G 25
BL9: Bury 4N 41
OL6: A Lyne 2A 82
Durham Gro. M44: Cad 2D 102
Durham Ho. SK3: Stoc 8C 108
Durham Rd. M6: Sal 6J 77
WN2: Hin 6A 54
Durhams Pas. OL15: Lit 9L 15
Durham St. BL1: Bolt 2G 38
M9: Man 3K 79
M26: Rad 7J 41
OL9: O'ham 7G 62
(not continuous)
OL11: Roch 7D 28
SK5: Stoc 7C 96
WN1: Wig 2H 53
Durham St. Bri. OL11: Roch 8E 28
Durham Wlk. *M34: Dent* 8K 97
(off Lancaster Rd.)
OL10: H'ood 2F 42
Durley Av. M8: Man 3G 78
WA15: Tim 9H 105
Durling St. M12: Man 9N 5 (2H 95)
DURN 9N 15
Durnford Av. M41: Urm 7G 92
Durnford Cl. OL12: Roch 3J 27
Durnford St. M24: Mid 2L 61
Durnford Wlk. M22: Wyth 4A 116
Durn Ind. Est. OL15: Lit 8N 15
Durnlaw Cl. OL15: Lit 9N 15
Durn St. OL15: Lit 9N 15
Durrell Way WA3: Low 1A 88
Durrington Pl. BL5: W'ton 5C 54
Durrington Wlk. *M40: Man* 8A 62
(off Moston La.)
Dursley Dr. WN4: A Mak 6G 70
Dutton Gro. WN7: Lei 8L 73
Dutton St. M3: Man 1G 5 (7E 78)
Duty St. BL1: Bolt 1F 38
Duxbury Av. BL2: Bolt 8M 23
BL3: Lit L 7A 40
Duxbury Dr. BL9: Bury 2B 42
Duxbury Gdns. PR7: Chor 1G 19
Duxbury Hall Rd. PR7: Chor 2H 19
Duxbury Pk. Bus. Cen.
PR7: Chor 2G 18
Duxbury Pk. Golf Course 2G 19
Duxbury St. *BL1: Bolt* 1E 38
(off Winter St.)
Duxford Lodge M8: Man 9E 60
Duxford Wlk. *M40: Man* 8A 62
(off Moston La.)
DW Sports Fitness
Bolton 7H 39
Bury 8L 7 (2M 41)
Macclesfield 4H 131
Oldham 1F 62
Trafford 2B 92
DW Stadium 3C 52
Dyche St. M4: Man 2J 5 (7G 78)
Dyche St. Trad. Est.
M4: Man 1K 5
Dye Ho. La. OL16: Roch 2G 29
Dyehouse La. SK22: N Mil 7M 121
Dye La. SK6: Rom 6M 109
Dyers Cl. WA13: Lym 3B 112
Dyers Ct. OL15: Lit 8L 15
SK10: Boll 5M 129
Dyers La. WA13: Lym 3B 112
Dyer St. M5: Sal 8A 4 (2B 94)
WA3: Gol 9J 71
Dymchurch Av. M26: Rad 4C 58
Dymchurch St. M40: Man 6A 80
Dysarts Cl. OL5: Mos 8H 65
Dysart St. OL6: A Lyne 8A 82
SK2: Stoc 2F 118
Dyserth Gro. SK5: Stoc 4D 108
Dyson Cl. BL4: Farn 3L 57
Dyson Gro. OL4: Lees 3C 64

Dyson Ho. BL4: Farn 3L 57
(off Hesketh Wlk.)
Dyson St. BL4: Farn 4L 57
OL5: Mos 1F 82
Dystelegh Rd. SK12: Dis 9G 121

E

Eades St. M6: Sal 7N 77
Eadington St. M8: Man 1F 78
Eafield Av. OL16: Miln 6K 29
Eafield Cl. OL16: Miln 6K 29
Eafield Rd. OL15: Lit 2J 29
OL16: Roch 4G 28
Eagar St. M40: Man 4A 80
Eaglais Way SK10: Macc 2D 130
Eagle Ct. M15: Man 4D 94
(off Dudley Cl.)
OL3: Del 7J 47
Eagle Dr. M6: Sal 5N 77
Eagle Fold SK14: Hyde 3D 98
Eagles Nest M25: Pres 8N 59
Eagle St. BL2: Bolt 2N 7 (5H 39)
M4: Man 2J 5 (8F 78)
OL9: O'ham 3B 8 (5J 63)
OL16: Roch 9E 8 (7E 28)
Eagle Technology Pk.
OL11: Roch 9E 28
Eagle Way OL11: Roch 9E 28
EAGLEY 6G 22
Eagley Bank BL1: Bolt 7G 22
OL12: Whitw 1C 14
Eagley Brook Way BL1: Bolt 1G 39
Eagley Brow BL1: Bolt 7G 23
(not continuous)
Eagley Ct. BL7: Bro X 6H 23
Eagley Dr. BL8: Bury 3G 41
Eagley Vw. BL8: Bury 3G 41
Eagley Way BL1: Bolt 6G 22
Ealand Chase BL6: Hor 1B 36
EALEES 9N 15
Ealees Rd. OL15: Lit 9N 15
Ealing Av. M14: Man 7H 95
Ealinger Way M27: Pen 9F 58
Ealing Ho. BL1: Bolt 3F 38
(off Enfield Cl.)
Ealing Pl. M19: Man 2M 107
Ealing Rd. SK3: Stoc 8B 108
Eames Av. M26: Rad 3A 58
Eamont Wlk. M9: Man 3J 79
(off Ruskington Dr.)
Earby Gro. M9: Man 8L 61
Earhart Cl. WN8: Skel 3C 50
Earle Cl. WA12: N Wil 6C 86
Earle Ct. OL7: A Lyne 9K 81
(off Graham St.)
Earle Rd. SK7: Bram 5C 118
Earlesdon Cres. M38: Lit H 6H 57
Earlesfield Cl. M33: Sale 6D 104
EARLESTOWN 6E 86
Earlestown Station (Rail) 6E 86
Earle St. OL7: A Lyne 8K 81
WA12: N Wil 7C 86
(not continuous)
Earl Rd. BL0: Ram 8H 11
SK4: Stoc 4A 108
SK8: Chea H 9L 117
SK9: Hand 2K 123
Earlscliffe Ct. WA14: Alt 3B 114
Earls Ct. SK11: Macc 5D 130
(off Earlsway)
Earl's Lodge M35: Fail 4B 80
Earlston Av. M34: Dent 6E 96
Earl St. BL0: Ram 8K 11
M25: Pres 7B 60
M34: Dent 5E 96
M46: Ath 9K 55
OL5: Mos 1E 82
OL10: H'ood 2H 43
OL11: Roch 4A 44
SK3: Stoc 8B 108
WN1: Wig 1F 52
WN2: I Mak 4K 53
WN7: Lei 5J 73
Earls Way M35: Fail 4B 80
SK13: Glos 9D 100
Earlsway SK11: Macc 6C 130
Earlswood WN8: Skel 2C 50
Earlswood Rd. OL8: O'ham 8J 63
Earlswood Wlk. BL3: Bolt 8G 39
M18: Man 3A 96
(off Briercliffe Cl.)
Earl Ter. SK16: Duk 9M 81
Earl Wlk. M12: Man 4L 95
Early Bank SK15: Stal 1F 98
Early Bank Rd. SK14: Hyde 3E 98
SK15: Hyde, Stal 1E 98
Earnshaw Av. OL12: Roch 2C 28
SK1: Stoc 7F 108
Earnshaw Cl. OL7: A Lyne 5K 81
Earnshaw Clough OL5: Mos 2H 83
Earnshaw St. BL3: Bolt 9C 38
SK14: Holl 5N 99
Easby Cl. SK8: Chea H 9N 117
SK12: Poy 1H 125
Easby Rd. M24: Mid 9L 43
Easedale Cl. M41: Urm 6N 91
Easedale Rd. BL1: Bolt 4B 38
M40: Man 2A 80
Easington Wlk. M40: Man 4M 79
Easingwold WA14: Alt 3B 6
East Av. M19: Man 1L 107
M45: Whitef 1L 59
SK8: H Grn 6H 117
SK10: Macc 6J 129
SK15: Stal 7D 82
(not continuous)
WA3: Gol 9M 71
WN7: Lei 7L 73
Eastbank St. BL1: Bolt 2G 38
E. Bond St. WN7: Lei 5J 73
Eastbourne Gro. BL1: Bolt 4B 38
Eastbourne St. OL8: O'ham 6M 63
OL11: Roch 8D 28
E. Bridgewater St. WN7: Lei 6J 73
Eastbrook Av. M26: Rad 8J 41
Eastburn Av.
M40: Man 1N 5 (7H 79)
E. Central Dr. M27: Swin 3H 77
Eastchurch Cl. BL4: Farn 4L 57
E. Church Way OL10: H'ood 5L 43
Eastcombe Av. M7: Sal 3A 78
Eastcote Av. M11: Man 1C 96
Eastcote Rd. SK5: Stoc 3D 108
Eastcote Wlk. BL4: Farn 2M 57
(off Darley St.)
East Ct. Wlk. M13: Man 3H 95
East Cres. M24: Mid 4L 61
Eastdale Pl. WA14: B'ath 9D 104
Eastdene WN8: Par 2A 32
EAST DIDSBURY 7H 107
East Didsbury Station (Rail) 7H 107
E. Downs Rd. SK8: Chea H 5L 117
WA14: Bow 5C 114
East Dr. BL9: Bury 8A 42
M6: Sal 5L 77
M21: Cho H 8M 93
M27: Swin 3H 77
SK6: Mar 4C 120
Easterdale OL4: O'ham 5N 63
Eastern Av. M27: Clif 8K 59
(not continuous)
Eastern By-Pass M11: Man 1B 96
(Crabtree La.)
M11: Man 8A 80
(Stanton St.)
Eastern Circ. M19: Man 2M 107
Eastfield M6: Sal 6L 77
Eastfield Av. M24: Mid 4M 61
M40: Man 7K 79
Eastfields M26: Rad 7E 40
Eastford Sq. M40: Man 6H 79
(off Sand St.)
Eastgarth WN2: P Bri 9L 53
Eastgarth Wlk. M9: Man 8K 61
(off Greendale Dr.)
Eastgate OL12: Whitw 7N 13
SK10: Macc 4J 131
Eastgate App. BL6: Hor 5F 36
Eastgate St. OL7: A Lyne 9B 6 (9L 81)
OL16: Roch 6D 8 (5D 28)
E. Grange Av. M11: Man 7A 80
East Gro. M13: Man 4H 95
Eastgrove Av. BL1: Bolt 7F 22
Eastham Av. BL9: Bury 7L 25
M14: Man 8G 94
Eastham Way M38: Lit H 6J 57
SK9: Hand 1J 123
(off Redesmere Rd.)
Easthaven Av. M11: Man 8A 80
East Hill St.
OL4: O'ham 4G 8 (5L 63)
Eastholme Dr. M19: Man 1N 107
Easthope Cl. M20: Man 1G 107
E. Lancashire Crematorium
M26: Rad 6G 41
East Lancashire Railway
Bury Bolton Street Station
8J 7 (2L 41)
Heywood Station 3K 43
Irwell Vale Station 1J 11
Ramsbottom Station 8J 11
Summerseat Station 3J 25
E. Lancashire Rd.
M27: Pen, Sal, Swin 3H 75
M28: Swin, Walk, Wors 3H 75
M29: Ast 3H 75
WA3: Gol, Low 2F 86
WA11: Hay, St H 1A 86
WA12: N Wil 2F 86
WN7: Lei 2F 86
Eastlands City Stadium Stop (Metro)
8L 79
East Lea M34: Dent 6L 97
Eastleigh WN8: Skel 2B 50
Eastleigh Av. M7: Sal 2D 78
Eastleigh Cres. WN7: Lei 7K 73
Eastleigh Dr. M40: Man 7J 79
Eastleigh Gro.
BL1: Bolt 4F 38
(off Vernon St.)
Eastleigh Rd. M25: Pres 8D 60
SK8: H Grn 6G 116
E. Lynn Dr. M28: Walk 8A 58
East Meade BL3: Bolt 1F 56
M21: Cho H 1A 106
M25: Pres 9C 60
M27: Swin 4E 76
East Moor M28: Wors 3H 75
Eastmoor Dr. M40: Man 6B 80
Eastmoor Gro. BL3: Bolt 1C 56
East Mt. WN5: Orr 5K 51
E. Newton St. M4: Man 1N 5
Eastnor Cl. M15: Man 3C 94
Easton Cl. M24: Mid 4A 62
WN3: Wig 9D 52
Easton Dr. SK8: Chea 2M 117
Easton Rd. M43: Droy 8C 80
E. Ordsall La.
M3: Sal 4B 4 (9C 78)
M5: Sal 5B 4 (9C 78)
Eastover SK6: Rom 8L 109
Eastpark Cl. M13: Man 3H 95
East Pk. Rd.
SK11: Macc 7F 130
E. Philip St. M3: Sal 1E 4 (7D 78)
EAST PIMBO 7D 50
East Rd. M12: Man 6M 95
M18: Man 6N 95
SK15: C'ook 4H 83
Eastry Av. SK5: Stoc 2F 108
Eastside Valley M4: Man 9J 79
(off Isaac Way)
East St. BL0: Eden 2K 11
BL9: Bury 9M 7 (3M 41)
M26: Rad 9H 41
M34: Aud 2K 97
M46: Ath 1A 74
OL6: A Lyne 6A 82
OL12: W'le 8G 15
OL15: Lit 9N 15
East St. OL16: Roch 5E 8 (5E 28)
(Buckley St.)
OL16: Roch 6H 29
(Hartley St., not continuous)
WN2: Hin 8D 54
WN4: A Mak 6G 70
E. Tame Bus. Pk. SK14: Hyde 3D 98
E. Union St. M16: Old T 3B 94
East Va. SK6: Mar 2D 120
East Vw. BL0: Ram 5H 11
BL9: Sum 2J 25
M24: Mid 3L 61
M33: Sale 5H 105
OL12: Whitw 1B 14
Eastville Gdns. M19: Man 3K 107
East Wlk. BL7: Eger 3E 22
Eastward Av. SK9: Wilm 8E 122
East Way BL1: Bolt 1J 39
Eastway M24: Mid 2L 61
M33: Sale 6E 104
M41: Urm 6M 91
OL2: Shaw 6M 45
Eastwell Rd. WN4: A Mak 7D 70
WN6: Wig 9C 34
Eastwood M14: Man 8H 95
Eastwood Av. M28: Walk 8H 57
M40: Man 1D 80
M41: Urm 7D 92
M43: Droy 9C 80
WA12: N Wil 6J 87
Eastwood Cl. BL3: Bolt 9B 38
BL9: Bury 2A 42
Eastwood Ct. BL9: Bury 2A 42
Eastwood Dr. SK3: Stoc 2B 118
SK6: Mar 2A 120
Eastwood Educational Nature Reserve
1E 98
EASTWOOD END 7M 125
Eastwood End Caravan Pk.
SK10: Adl 8M 125
Eastwood Gro. WN7: Lei 5E 72
Eastwood Rd. M40: Man 1C 80
Eastwood St. M34: Aud 2H 97
OL15: Lit 9M 15
Eastwood Ter. BL1: Bolt 4A 38
Eastwood Vw. SK15: Stal 9E 82
Eatock St. WN2: P Bri 8L 53
Eatock Way BL5: W'ton 5F 54
Eaton Cl. M27: Pen 9F 58
SK8: Chea H 4L 117
SK12: Poy 3L 125
SK16: Duk 3N 97
Eaton Ct. WA14: Bow 6C 114
Eaton Dr. OL7: A Lyne 6K 81
SK9: A Edg 3E 126
WA15: Tim 8G 104
Eaton La. SK11: Macc 7H 131
Eaton Rd. M8: Man 1E 78
M33: Sale 4G 104
WA14: Bow 6C 114
Eaton St. WN2: Hin 5A 54
Eaves Brow Rd. WA3: Cro 9D 88
Eavesdale WN8: Skel 3C 50
Eaves Grn. Rd. PR7: Chor 1E 18
EAVES KNOLL 6L 121
Eaves Knoll Rd.
SK22: N Mil 6K 121
Eaves La. OL9: Chad 6E 62
Ebbdale Cl. SK1: Stoc 8D 108
Ebberstone St. M14: Man 7F 94
Ebden St. M1: Man 7K 5
Ebenezer St. M15: Man 9G 4 (2E 94)
SK13: Glos 9F 100
Ebnall Wlk. M14: Man 1J 107
Ebor Cl. OL2: Shaw 4L 45
Ebor Ho. M32: Stre 8M 93
Ebor Rd. M22: Wyth 3D 116
Ebor St. OL15: Lit 9M 15
Ebsworth St. M40: Man 2L 79
Ebury St. M26: Rad 8F 40
ECCLES 8F 76
Ecclesbridge Rd. SK6: Mar 2C 120
Eccles Cl. M11: Man 1A 96
Eccles Dr. M27: Swin 4F 76
Eccles Fold M30: Ecc 8E 76
Eccleshall St. M11: Man 9N 79
(not continuous)
Eccles New Rd.
M5: Ecc, Sal 8G 77
M50: Ecc, Sal 8G 77
Eccles Old Rd. M6: Sal 7H 77
Eccles Rd. M27: Swin 4F 76
WN5: Orr 2M 51
Eccles Station (Rail) 8F 76
Eccles Stop (Metro) 8F 76
Eccles St. BL0: Ram 8H 11
Eccleston Av. BL2: Bolt 3J 39
M14: Man 8G 94
M27: Swin 3D 76
Eccleston Cl. BL8: Bury 3G 40
Eccleston Pl. M7: Sal 2D 78
Eccleston Rd. SK3: Stoc 3C 118
Eccleston St. M35: Fail 2E 80
WN1: Wig 6J 9 (2F 52)
Eccleston Way SK9: Hand 2J 123
(off Henbury Rd.)
Eccups La. SK9: Wilm 6B 122
Echo St. M1: Man 7K 5 (1G 94)
Eckersley Cl. M23: Wyth 1M 115
Eckersley Fold La.
M46: Ath 2J 73
Eckersley Mill WN3: Wig 5E 52
Eckersley Pct. M46: Ath 8M 55
(off Alma St.)
Eckersley Rd. BL1: Bolt 1F 38
Eckersley St. BL3: Bolt 8L 39
WN1: Wig 5N 9 (2H 53)
Eckford St. M8: Man 4G 79
Eclipse Cl. OL16: Roch 6G 28
Ecton Av. SK10: Macc 5L 131
Edale Av. M34: Aud 2H 97
M34: Dent 9K 97
M40: Man 2M 79
M41: Urm 8B 92
SK5: Stoc 8E 96
Edale Bank SK13: Gam 7A 100
Edale Cl. M44: Irl 8H 91
M46: Ath 8L 55
SK7: H Gro 6J 119
SK8: H Grn 8J 117
SK13: Gam 7A 100
WA14: Bow 6C 114
Edale Cres. SK13: Gam 7A 100
Edale Dr. WN6: Stan 2B 34
Edale Fold SK13: Gam 7A 100
(off Edale Cl.)
Edale Gro. M33: Sale 6E 104
OL6: A Lyne 4D 82
Edale Rd. BL3: Bolt 8B 38
BL4: Farn 4K 57
M32: Stre 6H 93
WN7: Lei 6K 73
Edale St. M6: Sal 5A 78
Edbrook Wlk. M13: Man 4J 95
Edburton Ct. WA3: Gol 1K 87
Eddie Colman Cl. M40: Man 5N 79
Eddie Colman Ct. M6: Sal 7N 77
(off Belvedere Rd.)
Eddisbury Av. M20: Man 9E 94
M41: Urm 5L 91
Eddisbury Cl. SK11: Macc 5K 131
Eddisbury Ter. SK11: Macc 5K 131
Eddisford Dr. WA3: Cul 4F 88
Edditch Gro. BL2: Bolt 5K 39
Eddleston St. WN4: A Mak 4C 70
Eddystone Cl. M5: Sal 9N 77
Eden Av. BL0: Eden 3K 11
BL1: Bolt 1F 38
SK6: H Lan 8B 120
WA3: Cul 5L 89
Eden Bank WN7: Lei 4K 73
Edenbridge Dr. M26: Rad 4B 58
Edenbridge Rd. M40: Man 6N 79
SK8: Chea H 3N 117
Eden Cl. M15: Man 3F 94
OL10: H'ood 1F 42
SK1: Stoc 4N 9 (8E 108)
SK9: Wilm 9D 122
Eden Ct. BL0: Eden 4K 11
M19: Man 9M 95
Edendale Dr. M22: Wyth 6C 116
Eden Dr. SK10: Macc 3K 131
EDENFIELD 3L 11
Edenfield Av. M21: Cho H 4C 106
Edenfield Cl. WA16: Mob 5N 133
Edenfield Ct. SK14: Hyde 8B 98
Edenfield La. M28: Wors 6N 75
Edenfield Rd. M25: Pres 8D 60
OL11: Roch 4M 27
OL12: Roch 9B 12
WA16: Mob 5N 133
Edenfield St. OL12: Roch 4A 28
Eden Gro. BL1: Bolt 1F 38
WN7: Lei 5E 72
Edenhall Av. M19: Man 9L 95
Edenhall Gro. WN2: Hin 8B 54
Edenham Wlk. M40: Man 9B 62
(off Enstone Dr.)
Edenhurst WN8: Skel 3C 50
Edenhurst Dr. WA15: Tim 2H 115
Edenhurst Rd. SK2: Stoc 1F 118
Eden La. BL0: Ram 4K 11
Eden Lodge BL1: Bolt 1F 38
(off Eden St.)
Eden Pk. Rd. SK8: Chea H 7K 117
Eden Pl. M33: Sale 3H 105
SK8: Chea 1J 117
Edensor Cl. WN6: Wig 8D 34
Edensor Dr. WA15: Hale 4J 115
Eden Sq. Shop. Cen. M41: Urm 7D 92
Eden St. BL0: Eden 4K 11
BL1: Bolt 1F 38
BL9: Bury 7L 7 (2M 41)
OL1: O'ham 1C 8 (4J 63)
OL12: Roch 6A 8 (5B 28)
Eden Va. M28: Wors 3H 75
Eden Way OL2: Shaw 4L 45
Edenwood Rd. BL0: Ram 5K 11
Edgar Ct. SK11: Macc 4G 131
(off Bridge St.)
Edgar St. BL0: Ram 9H 11
BL3: Bolt 6F 38
OL16: Roch 3G 28
Edgar St. W. BL0: Ram 9H 11
Edgbaston Dr. M16: Old T 6N 93
EDGE, THE 9F 62
Edge, The M3: Sal 3F 4 (8D 78)
Edgecote Cl. M22: Shar 1E 116
Edgedale Av. M19: Man 3K 107
Edge End OL3: Dob 9K 47
Edgefield Av. M9: Man 7K 61
Edge Fold BL4: Farn 3D 56
Edge Fold Cres. M28: Walk 2L 75
Edgefold Ind. Est. BL4: Farn 2D 56
Edge Fold Rd. M28: Walk, Wors 1L 75
EDGE GREEN 8J 71
Edge Grn. M28: Wors 2K 75
Edge Grn. La. WA3: Gol 8J 71
Edge Grn. Rd. WN4: A Mak 7J 71
Edge Grn. St. WN4: A Mak 6G 70
Edge Hall Rd. WN5: Orr 7J 51
(not continuous)
Edge Hill BL6: Hor 9E 20
Edge Hill Av. OL2: O'ham 9J 45
Edgehill Chase SK9: Wilm 7K 123
Edgehill Cl. M5: Sal 8M 77
Edgehill Ct. M32: Stre 8L 93
Edge Hill Rd. BL3: Bolt 9C 38
OL2: O'ham 9J 45
Edgehill Rd. M6: Sal 7J 77
Edgehill St. M4: Man 3J 5
Edge La. BL1: Hor 8L 21
BL6: Hor 8L 21
M21: Cho H 8K 93
M32: Stre 8K 93
M43: Droy 8B 80
SK14: Mot 5H 99
(not continuous)
Edge La. Bus. Pk. M11: Man 1C 96
Edge La. Rd. OL1: O'ham 3L 63
Edge Lane Stop (Metro) 9C 80
Edge La. St. OL2: O'ham 8J 45
EDGELEY 9A 108
Edgeley Fold SK3: Stoc 9A 108
Edgeley Pk. 9C 108
Edgeley Rd. M41: Urm 9A 92
SK3: Stoc 9M 107
Edgemoor WA14: Bow 5A 114
Edgemoor Cl. M26: Rad 7E 40
OL4: O'ham 2A 64
OL12: Whitw 1C 14
Edgemoor Dr. OL11: Roch 8L 27
Edgerley Pl. WN4: A Mak 7D 70
Edgerton Rd. WA3: Low 1B 88
Edge St. M4: Man 3J 5 (8F 78)
Edge Vw. OL1: Chad 2C 62
Edge Vw. La. SK9: A Edg 3A 126
Edgeview Wlk. M13: Man 9L 5
Edge Wlk. SK15: Stal 9E 82
Edgeware Av. M25: Pres 7E 60
Edgeware Gro. WN3: Wins 8A 52
Edgeware Rd. M30: Ecc 6A 76
OL9: Chad 8C 62
Edgewater M5: Sal 8K 77
Edgeway SK9: Wilm 9G 122
SK11: Hen 4A 130
Edgeway Rd. WN3: Wig 1D 70
Edgewood WN6: She 7L 33
Edgeworth Av. BL2: Ain 3D 40
Edgeworth Dr. M14: Man 1K 107
Edgeworth Rd. WA3: Gol 9J 71
WN2: Hin 8C 54
Edgmont Av. BL3: Bolt 8E 38
Edgware Rd. M40: Man 6N 79
Edgworth Cl. OL10: H'ood 2F 42
Edgworth Dr. BL8: Bury 3G 41
Edilom Rd. M8: Man 9D 60
Edinburgh M30: Ecc 8E 76
(off Monton St.)
Edinburgh Cl. M33: Sale 5D 104
SK8: Chea 1L 117
WN2: I Mak 3K 53
Edinburgh Dr. SK6: Wood 4N 109
SK10: Macc 3E 130
WN2: Hin 8D 54
WN5: Wig 6A 52
Edinburgh Ho. M3: Sal 4C 4
(off Rocket St.)
Edinburgh Rd. BL3: Lit L 1A 58
Edinburgh Sq. M40: Man 6K 79
(off Giltbrook Av.)
Edinburgh Wlk. WN2: Asp 7N 35
Edinburgh Way OL11: Roch 9B 28
Edington OL12: Roch 5C 8
Edison Rd. M30: Ecc 9C 76
Edison St. M11: Man 2C 96
Edith Av. M14: Man 6F 94
Edith Cavell Cl. M11: Man 9A 80
Edith Cliff Wlk. M40: Man 1D 80
Edith St. BL0: Ram 6L 11
BL1: Bolt 6D 38
BL4: Farn 4L 57
OL8: O'ham 8K 63
WN3: Wig 4E 52
Edith Ter. SK6: Comp 6E 110
Edleston Gro. SK9: Wilm 5K 123
(off Picton Dr.)
Edlin Cl. M12: Man 4K 95
Edlingham OL11: Roch 7C 28
Edlington Wlk. M40: Man 4A 80
Edmonds St. M24: Mid 2N 61
Edmonton Ct. SK2: Stoc 3E 118
Edmonton Rd. M40: Man 6M 79
SK2: Stoc 3E 118
Edmund Cl. SK4: Stoc 5C 108
Edmund Dr. WN7: Lei 5E 72
Edmunds Ct. BL3: Bolt 6E 38
Edmunds Fold OL15: Lit 8K 15
Edmunds Pas. OL15: Lit 7L 15
Edmund St. M6: Sal 7L 77
M26: Rad 8J 41
M35: Fail 2D 80
M43: Droy 9E 80
OL2: Shaw 5N 45
OL12: Roch 5A 8 (5B 28)
OL16: Miln 7K 29
Edna Rd. WN7: Lei 3E 72
Edna St. SK14: Hyde 8A 98
Edridge Way WN2: Hin 7M 53
Edson Rd. M8: Man 8E 60
Edstone Cl. BL3: Bolt 8A 38
Edward Av. M6: Sal 7J 77
M21: Cho H 1M 105
OL15: Lit 2K 29
SK6: Bred 5J 109
Edward Charlton Rd. M16: Old T 7A 94
Edward Ct. WA14: B'ath 9B 104
Edward Dr. WN4: A Mak 6E 70
Edward Grant Ct. M9: Man 1K 79
Edward M. OL9: O'ham 6G 63
Edward Onyon Ct. M6: Sal 8L 77
Edward Pilkington Memorial Cotts.
M27: Clif 8F 58
Edward Rd. M9: Man 6J 61
OL2: Shaw 6L 45
WN1: Wig 1F 52
Edwards Cl. SK6: Mar 2B 120
Edwards Ct. M22: Wyth 4C 116
SK7: H Gro 7K 119
Edwards Dr. M45: Whitef 3A 60
Edward St. BL3: Bolt 7E 38
BL4: Farn 1J 57
BL5: W'ton 3G 55
BL6: Hor 1E 36
BL9: Bury 9M 7 (3M 41)
M7: Sal 6D 78
M9: Man 2K 79
M24: Mid 1M 61
M25: Pres 6N 59
M26: Rad 1H 59
(Fir St.)
M26: Rad 3B 58
(Linton Va.)
M33: Sale 4L 105
M34: Aud 2H 97
M34: Dent 5K 97
M43: Droy 1E 96
OL6: A Lyne 8B 82

Edward St. OL9: Chad 3E 62
OL9: O'ham 5G 62
OL12: Roch 1H 29
OL12: Whitw 4B 14
OL16: Roch 5F 8 (5E 28)
SK1: Stoc 4L 9 (8D 108)
SK6: Mar B 7D 110
SK11: Macc 5F 130
SK13: Glos 8E 100
SK14: Hyde 6N 97
(not continuous)
SK16: Duk 3N 97
WN1: I Mak 3J 53
WN7: Lei 6J 73
Edward Sutcliffe Cl. M14: Man 7F 94
Edwards Way SK6: Mar 2B 120
Edwin Rd. M11: Man 9K 79
Edwin St. BL9: Bury 8K 7 (2L 41)
SK1: Stoc 8F 108
WN1: Wig 9N 9 (4H 53)
Edwin Waugh Gdns. OL12: Roch 2B 28
Edzell Wlk. M11: Man 9A 80
(off Kincraig Cl.)
Eeasbrook M41: Urm 8D 92
Egbert St. M40: Man 3M 79
EGERTON 3E 22
Egerton WN8: Skel 3B 50
Egerton Av. WA13: Warb 8D 102
Egerton Cl. OL10: H'ood 3J 43
Egerton Ct. M14: Man 5H 95
(off Up. Park Rd.)
M21: Cho H 9M 93
M28: Wors 2A 76
M34: Dent 5L 97
(off Margaret Rd.)
SK3: Stoc 3E 118
WN2: Hin 6A 54
Egerton Cres. M20: Man 1G 107
OL10: H'ood 3H 43
Egerton Dr. M33: Sale 3H 105
WA15: Hale 5G 114
Egerton Gro. M28: Walk 8L 57
Egerton Ho. M5: Sal 2N 93
(off Elmira Way)
M15: Man 8C 4
SK4: Stoc 4M 107
Egerton Lodge BL7: Eger 4F 22
M34: Dent 5L 97
(off Margaret Rd.)
Egerton M. M43: Droy 1E 96
EGERTON PARK 3B 76
Egerton Pk. M28: Wors 3B 76
Egerton Pl. OL2: Shaw 6L 45
Egerton Rd. BL7: Bel 1M 21
M14: Man 9J 95
M28: Walk 8L 57
M30: Ecc 6D 76
M45: Whitef 4M 59
SK3: Stoc 2E 118
SK9: Wilm 5G 122
WA15: Hale 4G 114
Egerton Rd. Nth. M16: Whall R 7B 94
M21: Cho H 7B 94
SK4: Stoc 3A 108
Egerton Rd. Sth. M21: Cho H 9B 94
SK4: Stoc 3A 108
Egerton Sq. WA16: Knut 6G 133
Egerton St. BL4: Farn 2K 57
M3: Sal 4C 4 (9C 78)
M15: Man 8C 4 (2C 94)
M24: Mid 4H 61
M25: Pres 7B 60
M30: Ecc 8B 76
M34: Dent 4H 97
M43: Droy 9F 80
OL1: O'ham 2E 8 (4K 63)
OL5: Mos 9F 64
OL6: A Lyne 6F 6 (7N 81)
OL10: H'ood 3H 43
OL15: Lit 9N 15
WN2: Abr 3L 71
Egerton Ter. M14: Man 1J 107
Egerton Va. BL7: Eger 3E 22
Egerton Wlk. M28: Walk 8L 57
(off Ellesmere Shop. Cen.)
Eggar Cl. M29: Ast 3C 74
Eggington St. M40: Man 5H 79
Egham Ct. BL2: Bolt 3J 39
(off Horsa St.)
Egham Ho. BL3: Bolt 1C 56
Egmont St. M6: Sal 4L 77
M8: Man 2F 78
OL5: Mos 2F 82
Egmont Ter. SK15: Stal 1E 98
(off Spring Bank)
Egremont Av. M20: Man 1F 106
Egremont Cl. M45: Whitef 2N 59
Egremont Ct. M7: Sal 2B 78
(off Bury New Rd.)
Egremont Gro. SK3: Stoc 8N 107
Egremont Rd. OL16: Miln 9J 29
Egret Dr. M44: Irl 6H 91
Egyptian St. BL1: Bolt 3G 38
Egypt La. M25: Pres 2C 60
Ehlinger Av. SK13: Had 4C 100
Eida Way M17: T Pk 1J 93
Eight Acre M45: Whitef 4J 59
Eighth Av. OL8: O'ham 1H 81
Eighth St. M17: T Pk 3K 93
(not continuous)
Eighth St. W. M17: T Pk 3J 93
Eileen Gro. M14: Man 7H 95
Eileen Gro. W. M14: Man 7G 95
Elaine Av. M9: Man 9N 61
Elaine Cl. WN4: A Mak 5G 71
Elbain Wlk. M40: Man 5A 80
(off Orford Rd.)
Elberton Wlk. M8: Man 3E 78
(off Highshore Dr.)
Elbe St. M12: Man 7N 5 (1H 95)
Elbow St. M19: Man 8M 95
Elbut La. BL9: Bury 8E 26
Elcho Ct. WA14: Bow 5B 114
Elcho Rd. WA14: Bow 4B 114
Elcombe Av. WA3: Low 2A 88
Elcot Cl. M40: Man 5H 79
Elderberry Cl. OL3: Dig 7M 47
WN1: Wig 8E 34
Elderberry Wlk. M31: Part 5F 102
(off Wood La.)
Elderberry Way SK9: Wilm 6K 123
Elder Cl. BL8: Tot 8F 24
SK2: Stoc 8H 109
Eldercot Gro. BL3: Bolt 8B 38
Eldercot Rd. BL3: Bolt 8B 38
Elder Ct. SK4: Stoc 5N 107
Eldercroft Rd. WA15: Tim 2J 115
Elder Dr. BL3: Bolt 7M 39
Elderfield Dr. SK6: Bred 4K 109
Elder Gro. M40: Man 9D 62
Elder Mt. Rd. M9: Man 9J 61
Elder Rd. OL4: Lees 5B 64
Elder St. OL16: Roch 8F 28
Elderwood OL9: Chad 4C 62
Eldon Cl. M34: Aud 2J 97
Eldon Gdns. WN4: A Mak 4D 70
Eldon Pl. M30: Ecc 9C 76
Eldon Pct. OL8: O'ham 5C 8
Eldon Rd. M44: Irl 7H 91
SK3: Stoc 9A 108
SK10: Macc 4D 130
Eldon St. BL2: Bolt 3J 39
BL9: Bury 9M 25
OL8: O'ham 5D 8 (6K 63)
WN7: Lei 4F 72
Eldon St. Est. OL8: O'ham 5D 8
Eldridge Dr. M40: Man 5M 79
Eldroth Av. M22: Wyth 4C 116
Eleanor Rd. M21: Cho H 9N 93
OL2: O'ham 9J 45
Eleanor St. BL1: Bolt 8H 23
OL1: O'ham 3H 63
WN3: Wig 4D 52
Electo St. M11: Man 2C 96
Electric Pk. M17: T Pk 4J 93
Elevator Rd. M17: T Pk 3L 93
Eleventh St. M17: T Pk 3J 93
Elf Mill Cl. SK3: Stoc 1C 118
Elf Mill Ter. SK3: Stoc 1C 118
Elford Gro. M18: Man 5E 96
Elgar St. M12: Man 5M 95
Elgin Av. M20: Man 5J 107
SK10: Macc 2E 130
WN4: Gars 6A 70
Elgin Cl. WN2: I Mak 3K 53
Elgin Dr. M33: Sale 5L 105
Elgin Rd. OL4: O'ham 6N 63
SK16: Duk 3N 97
Elgin St. BL1: Bolt 2D 38
OL7: A Lyne 6L 81
(not continuous)
SK15: Stal 9E 82
Elgol Cl. SK3: Stoc 2D 118
Elgol Ct. OL10: H'ood 3F 42
Elgol Dr. BL3: Bolt 6N 37
Elham Cl. M26: Rad 4C 58
Elim St. OL15: Lit 7N 15
Elim Ter. OL15: Lit 7N 15
Eliot Dr. WN3: Wig 6D 52
(not continuous)
Eliot Gdns. WN3: Wig 6D 52
Eliot Rd. M30: Ecc 9D 76
Eliot Wlk. M24: Mid 9A 44
Elishaw Row M5: Sal 9M 77
Eli St. OL9: Chad 8E 62
Elite Cl. M8: Man 2E 78
Elite Karting 9K 9 (4F 52)
Elitex Ho. M7: Sal 6D 78
Eliza Ann St. M30: Ecc 9C 76
M40: Man 6H 79
Elizabeth Ct. M29: Tyld 1A 74
(off Market St.)
Elizabethan Dr. WN3: I Mak 7H 53
Elizabethan Wlk. WN2: P Bri 9K 53
Elizabethan Way OL16: Miln 7K 29
Elizabeth Av. M34: Dent 4J 97
OL2: O'ham 9H 45
OL9: Chad 8E 62
SK1: Stoc 8D 108
SK15: Stal 8D 82
WN2: B'haw 1A 72
Elizabeth Cl. M32: Stre 7K 93
Elizabeth Ct. M14: Man 1J 107
M18: Man 6D 96
(off Reddish La.)
SK4: Stoc 6A 108
Elizabeth Gaskell Ct.
WA16: Knut 6F 132
Elizabeth Gro. OL2: Shaw 5M 45
Elizabeth Ho. SK4: Stoc 7N 107
SK11: Macc 5J 131
(off Swettenham St.)
Elizabeth Rd. M31: Part 4G 102
WA11: Hay 2B 86
Elizabeth Slinger Rd.
M20: Man 4D 106
Elizabeth St. BL0: Eden 3K 11
M8: Man 4E 78
M25: Pres 7B 60
M26: Rad 9G 41
M27: Pen 1F 76
M34: Dent 6H 97
M45: Whitef 4M 59
M46: Ath 8M 55
(not continuous)
OL6: A Lyne 6M 81
OL10: H'ood 2H 43
OL11: Roch 1A 44
SK11: Macc 5H 131
SK14: Hyde 6A 98
WN2: I Mak 3K 53
WN7: Lei 7K 73
Elizabeth St. Ind. Est.
M34: Dent 6H 97
(off Grey St.)
Elizabeth Yarwood Ct.
M13: Man 3G 95
Eliza St. BL0: Ram 8K 11
M15: Man 3D 94
Elkanagh Gdns. M6: Sal 7M 77
Elkin Ct. M31: Part 4H 103
Elkstone Av. M38: Lit H 5H 57
Elkstone Cl. WN3: Wins 9N 51
Elkwood Cl. WN1: Wig 8E 34
Elladene Pk. M21: Cho H 9B 94
Ella Gro. WA16: Knut 6H 133
Ellanby Cl. M14: Man 6G 95
Elland Cl. BL5: W'ton 9F 36
Ellaston Dr. M41: Urm 7D 92
Ellastone Rd. M6: Sal 6J 77
Ella Vw. Lodge M46: Ath 7J 55
Ellbourne Rd. M9: Man 8F 60
ELLENBROOK 2K 75
Ellenbrook Cl. M12: Man 3N 95
Ellenbrook Rd. M22: Wyth 7C 116
M28: Wors 2J 75
(not continuous)
Ellenbrook St. M12: Man 3N 95
Ellendale Grange M28: Wors 2J 75
Ellen Gro. BL4: Kea 6C 58
Ellenhall Cl. M9: Man 2J 79
Ellenor Dr. M29: Ast 3D 74
Ellenroad App. OL16: Miln 9L 29
Ellenroad St. OL16: Miln 9L 29
Ellenroad
The World's Largest Working
Steam Mill Engine 9L 29
Ellenrod Dr. OL12: Roch 3M 27
Ellenrod La. OL12: Roch 3M 27
Ellenshaw Cl. OL12: Roch 3M 27
Ellens Pl. OL15: Lit 2K 29
Ellen St. BL1: Bolt 1D 38
(not continuous)
M43: Droy 1F 96
OL9: O'ham 3H 63
SK4: Stoc 5B 108
WN1: Wig 9L 9 (4G 52)
WN2: I Mak 4K 53
Ellen Wilkinson Cres.
M12: Man 4M 95
Elleray Cl. BL3: Lit L 9C 40
Elleray Rd. M6: Sal 5K 77
M24: Mid 6L 61
Ellerbeck Cl. BL2: Bolt 8K 23
WN6: Stan 5C 34
Ellerbeck Cres. M28: Wors 2K 75
Eller Brook Cl. PR6: H Char 4J 19
Ellerby Av. M27: Clif 8G 58
Ellergreen Rd. WN2: Hin 8E 54
Ellerscroft SK22: N Mil 6N 121
Ellerslie Ct. M14: Man 6H 95
Ellesmere Av. M28: Walk 8K 57
M30: Ecc 7E 76
OL6: A Lyne 3N 81
SK6: Mar 1C 120
Ellesmere Circ. M41: Urm 2D 92
Ellesmere Cl. M38: Lit H 7J 57
SK16: Duk 2B 98
Ellesmere Dr. SK8: Chea 2M 117
Ellesmere Gdns. BL3: Bolt 9E 38
Ellesmere Golf Course 1N 75
Ellesmere Grn. M30: Ecc 7E 76
Ellesmere Ho. M30: Ecc 7F 76
(off Sandwich Rd.)
ELLESMERE PARK 6E 76
Ellesmere Pk. M30: Ecc 6G 77
(off Park Rd.)
Ellesmere Rd. BL3: Bolt 9D 38
M21: Cho H 8B 94
M30: Ecc 6E 76
SK3: Stoc 9M 107
WA3: Cul 5G 89
WA14: Alt 1D 114
WN4: A Mak 5C 70
WN5: Wig 5A 52
Ellesmere Rd. Nth. SK4: Stoc 3A 108
Ellesmere Rd. Sth. M21: Cho H 9B 94
Ellesmere Shop. Cen.
M28: Walk 8K 57
(not continuous)
Ellesmere Sports Club 2L 75
Ellesmere St. BL3: Bolt 6E 38
BL4: Farn 2K 57
M15: Man 9B 4 (2C 94)
M27: Pen 1G 77
M27: Swin 3D 76
M29: Ast 5D 74
M29: Tyld 1A 74
(not continuous)
M30: Ecc 9D 76
(not continuous)
M35: Fail 2D 80
M38: Lit H 8J 57
OL11: Roch 2D 44
WN7: Lei 6H 73
(not continuous)
Ellesmere Ter. M14: Man 1J 107
Ellesmere Wlk. BL4: Farn 3L 57
Ellingham Cl. M11: Man 9L 79
Elliot Dr. WN2: Hin 4N 53
Elliot Sq. OL1: O'ham 1G 8 (3L 63)
Elliott Av. SK14: Hyde 4A 98
WA3: Gol 9L 71
Elliott Dr. M33: Sale 4E 104
Elliott Gdns. WN6: App B 5J 33
Elliott St. BL1: Bolt 1D 38
BL4: Farn 4K 57
M29: Tyld 2N 73
OL4: Lees 5B 64
OL12: Roch 5E 28
Ellisbank Wlk. M13: Man 9L 5
(off Deanwater Cl.)
Ellis Cres. M28: Walk 8J 57
Ellis Dr. M8: Man 1G 79
Ellis Fold OL12: Roch 2K 27
Ellisland Wlk. M40: Man 4M 79
(off Colebrook Dr.)
Ellis La. M24: Mid 3G 60
Ellison Cl. SK14: Holl 4N 99
Ellison Ho. OL7: A Lyne 9A 6
Ellison St. SK13: Glos 8F 100
Ellis Rd. WN5: Bil 6H 69
Ellis St. BL0: Ram 9H 11
(off Silvermere Cl.)
BL3: Bolt 7E 38
BL8: Bury 2H 41
M7: Sal 6D 78
Ellis St. M15: Man 3D 94
SK14: Hyde 6C 98
WN1: Wig 5N 9 (2H 53)
Elliston Sq. M12: Man 3M 95
(off Bridgend Cl.)
Ellonby Ri. BL6: Los 7L 37
Ellon Wlk. M11: Man 9A 80
(off Edith Cavell Cl.)
Ellor St. M6: Sal 7M 77
Ellwood Rd. SK1: Stoc 7F 108
Elly Clough OL2: O'ham 9G 45
Elm Av. M26: Rad 9K 41
WA3: Gol 9K 71
WA12: N Wil 7F 86
WN4: Gars 5A 70
WN5: Wig 5B 52
WN6: Stan 4C 34
Elmbank Av. M20: Man 4D 106
Elmbank Rd. M24: Mid 3A 62
Elm Beds Caravan Pk.
SK12: Poy 4N 125
Elm Beds Rd. SK12: Poy 4N 125
Elmbridge Ct. WA3: Low 1B 88
Elmbridge Wlk. BL3: Bolt 7E 38
M40: Man 4M 79
Elm Cl. M31: Part 5G 103
SK12: Poy 3K 125
SK14: Mot 5K 99
Elm Ct. SK1: Stoc 8F 108
Elm Cres. M28: Wors 3A 76
SK9: A Edg 3G 126
Elm Cft. WN1: Wig 8E 34
Elmdale Av. SK8: H Grn 5G 117
Elmdale Wlk. M15: Man 9H 5
Elm Dr. M32: Stre 8H 93
SK10: Macc 2J 131
WN5: Bil 5H 69
ELMERS GREEN 1B 50
Elmers Grn. WN8: Skel 1B 50
(not continuous)
Elmer's Grn. La. WN8: Dal, Skel 7A 32
(not continuous)
Elmers Wood Rd. WN8: Skel 2B 50
Elmfield WN6: She 6M 33
Elmfield Av. M22: Nor 8D 106
M46: Ath 7N 55
Elmfield Cl. SK9: A Edg 3G 126
Elmfield Ct. SK3: Stoc 2D 118
(off Elmfield Rd.)
Elmfield Dr. SK6: Mar 1B 120
Elmfield Ho. SK3: Stoc 2D 118
(off Plumley Cl.)
Elmfield Rd. M34: Aud 1G 97
SK3: Stoc 2D 118
SK9: A Edg 3G 126
WN1: Wig 7E 34
Elmfield St. BL1: Bolt 2G 39
(Walnut St.)
BL1: Bolt 1G 38
(Waters Meeting Rd.)
M8: Man 4F 78
Elmgate Gro. M19: Man 8M 95
Elm Gro. BL4: Farn 3J 57
BL6: Hor 3G 37
BL7: Bro X 5H 23
M20: Man 5G 106
M25: Pres 5N 59
M27: Ward 1B 76
M33: Sale 2H 105
M34: Dent 4H 97
M41: Urm 7E 92
M43: Droy 8B 80
OL4: Grot 5E 64
OL6: A Lyne 5N 81
OL11: Roch 8C 28
OL12: W'le 9G 15
OL16: Miln 1L 45
SK9: A Edg 3F 126
SK9: Hand 3H 123
(off Sagars Rd.)
SK13: Glos 7D 100
SK14: Hyde 7C 98
Elmham Wlk. M40: Man 6H 79
(off Rimworth Dr.)
Elmhow Gro. WN3: Wig 9D 52
Elmhurst Dr. M19: Man 3L 107
Elmira Way M5: Sal 2N 93
Elmlea WA15: Alt 3F 114
Elmley Cl. SK2: Stoc 2L 119
Elmore Wood OL15: Lit 8J 15
Elm Pk. Ct. M20: Man 4G 106
Elmpark Ga. OL12: Roch 2N 27
Elmpark Gro. OL12: Roch 2N 27
Elmpark Va. OL12: Roch 2N 27
Elmpark Vw. OL12: Roch 2N 27
Elmpark Way OL12: Roch 2N 27
Elmridge WN7: Lei 4K 73
WN8: Skel 2B 50
Elmridge Dr. WA15: Haleb 7J 115
Elm Ri. SK10: P'bury 7C 128
Elm Rd. BL3: Lit L 1B 58
BL4: Kea 6N 57
BL5: W'ton 4G 55
M20: Man 4F 106
OL8: O'ham 1H 81
SK6: H Lan 9C 120
SK8: Gat 2F 116
WA3: Rix 6B 102
WA11: Hay 2B 86
WA15: Hale 4E 114
WN2: Abr 3M 71
Elm Rd. Sth. SK3: Stoc 9M 107
Elms, The M45: Whitef 1M 59
OL5: Mos 1E 82
OL15: Lit 1K 29
WA3: Low 2B 88
Elmsbury St. WN4: A Mak 5C 70
Elms Cl. M45: Whitef 1M 59
Elmscott Wlk. M13: Man 4J 95
(off Bletchley Cl.)
Elmsdale Av. M9: Man 6J 61
Elms Farm M45: Whitef 1M 59
Elmsfield Av. OL11: Roch 4K 27
Elmsleigh Ct. M30: Ecc 2F 76
Elmsleigh Rd. SK8: H Grn 5F 116
Elmsmere Rd. M20: Man 5J 107
Elms Rd. M45: Whitef 2M 59
SK4: Stoc 3N 107
SK15: Stal 7G 83
Elms Sq. M45: Whitef 2L 59
Elms St. M45: Whitef 2L 59
Elmstead WN8: Skel 2B 50
Elmstead Av.
M20: Man 2F 106
Elmstead Ho. M27: Swin 3F 76
Elmsted Cl. SK8: Chea H 4N 117
Elmstone Cl. M9: Man 9H 61
Elmstone Dr. OL2: O'ham 7H 45
Elmstone Gro. BL1: Bolt 3G 38
(off Kentford Rd.)
Elm St. BL0: Eden 3L 11
BL0: Ram 8K 11
BL4: Farn 2L 57
BL9: Bury 2A 42
M24: Mid 2A 62
M27: Swin 1E 76
M29: Tyld 1B 74
M30: Ecc 9D 76
M35: Fail 2D 80
OL10: H'ood 2J 43
OL12: Roch 4D 28
OL12: Whitw 4B 14
OL15: Lit 3K 29
SK6: Bred 4K 109
WN2: P Bri 9K 53
WN7: Lei 7H 73
Elmsway SK6: H Lan 9B 120
SK7: Bram 8A 118
SK10: Boll 5L 129
WA15: Haleb 7H 115
Elmswood Av. M14: Man 7E 94
Elmswood Dr. SK14: Hyde 6D 98
Elmsworth Av. M19: Man 8N 95
Elmton Rd. M9: Man 8K 61
Elm Tree Cl. M35: Fail 3F 80
SK15: Stal 1D 98
Elm Tree Dr. SK16: Duk 2C 98
Elmtree Dr. SK4: Stoc 6N 107
Elm Tree Rd. SK6: Bred 5G 109
WA3: Low 1B 88
Elmwood M28: Wors 5A 76
M33: Sale 4C 104
WN8: Skel 9A 32
Elmwood Av.
WN4: A Mak 8D 70
Elmwood Cl. BL5: O Hul 5B 56
Elmwood Ct. M32: Stre 9J 93
SK10: Boll 8H 129
Elmwood Dr. OL2: O'ham 7G 44
Elmwood Gro. BL1: Bolt 4D 38
BL4: Farn 5L 57
M9: Man 3L 79
Elmwood Lodge
M20: Man 4F 106
Elmwood Pk. SK15: Stal 7G 82
Elnup Av. WN6: She 6M 33
Elrick Wlk. M11: Man 9N 79
(off Emily Beavan Cl.)
Elsa Rd. M19: Man 8A 96
Elsdon Dr. M18: Man 3B 96
M46: Ath 7N 55
Elsdon Gdns. BL2: Bolt 3J 39
Elsdon Rd. M13: Man 7L 95
Elsfield Cl. BL1: Bolt 2E 38
(off Raglan St.)
Elsham Cl. BL1: Bolt 8F 22
Elsham Dr. M28: Walk 8J 57
Elsham Gdns. M18: Man 5N 95
Elsie St. BL0: Ram 1G 25
BL4: Farn 3K 57
M9: Man 2K 79
Elsinore Av. M44: Irl 8G 91
Elsinore Cl. M35: Fail 3F 80
Elsinore Rd. M16: Old T 5N 93
Elsinore St. BL2: Bolt 1J 39
Elsma Rd. M40: Man 6C 80
Elsmore Rd. M14: Man 8F 94
Elson Dr. SK14: Hyde 1A 110
Elson St. BL8: Bury 9H 25
Elstead Gro. WN4: Gars 6A 70
Elstead Wlk. M9: Man 8G 60
Elsted Rd. OL3: G'fld 6H 65
Elston Av. WA12: N Wil 4E 86
Elstree Av. M40: Man 6N 79
Elstree Ct. M41: Urm 7D 92
Elswick WN8: Skel 3A 50
Elswick Av. BL3: Bolt 7C 38
M21: Cho H 3C 106
SK7: Bram 8C 118
Elsworth Cl. M26: Rad 2H 59
Elsworth Dr. BL1: Bolt 9G 23
Elsworth St. M3: Man 7F 78
Elterwater Cl. BL8: Bury 9H 25
M24: Mid 9J 43
Elterwater Rd. BL4: Farn 4F 56
Eltham Av. SK2: Stoc 2G 118
Eltham Cl. WN4: A Mak 7G 70
Eltham Dr. M41: Urm 4C 92
Eltham St. M19: Man 7M 95
ELTON 2J 41
Elton Av. BL4: Farn 3G 57
M19: Man 9M 95
Elton Bank SK13: Gam 8N 99
(off Brassington Cres.)
Elton Brook Cl. BL8: Bury 1H 41
Elton Cl. M45: Whitef 3N 59
SK9: Wilm 5K 123
SK13: Gam 8N 99
(off Brassington Cres.)
WA3: Low 2A 88
Elton Dr. SK7: H Gro 7H 119
Elton Ho. BL8: Bury 2H 41
WN5: Wig 4N 51
Elton Lea SK13: Gam 8N 99
(off Brassington Cres.)
Elton Lofts BL8: Bury 2J 41
(off Fairy St.)
Elton Pl. SK13: Gam 8N 99
(off Brassington Cres.)
Elton Rd. M33: Sale 6E 104
Elton Sailing Club 4J 41
Elton Sq. Ho. BL8: Bury 3J 41

Elton St. BL2: Bolt 2N 7 (5H 39)
M7: Sal 7C 78
M32: Stre 4M 93
OL11: Roch 3A 44
Elton's Yd. M7: Sal 7C 78
Elton Va. Rd. BL8: Bury 2H 41
Elton Vale Sports Club 2G 41
Elvate Cres. M8: Man 5D 78
Elverdon Cl. M15: Man 4D 94
Elverston St. M22: Nor 7D 106
Elverston Way OL9: Chad 3G 62
Elvey St. M40: Man 5L 79
Elvington Cl. WN5: Wig 2M 51
Elvington Cres. M28: Wors 2K 75
Elvira Cl. M35: Fail 3F 80
Elway Rd. WN4: A Mak 6F 70
Elwick Cl. M16: Whall R 6E 94
Elworth Way SK9: Hand 2J 123
(off Delamere Rd.)
Elworthy Gro. WN1: Wig 1H 53
Elwyn Av. M22: Nor 9C 106
Ely Av. M32: Stre 6F 92
Ely Cl. M28: Wors 2J 75
Ely Cres. M35: Fail 5D 80
Ely Dr. BL8: Bury 9K 25
M29: Ast 3D 74
Ely Gdns. M41: Urm 7E 92
Ely Gro. BL1: Bolt 3F 38
(off Kentford Rd.)
Elysian Flds. M6: Sal 7H 77
Elysian St. M11: Man 1A 96
Ely St. OL9: O'ham 6F 62
Embankment Bus. Pk., The
SK4: Stoc 7L 107
Embankment Rd. BL7: Tur 1K 23
Embassy Wlk. M18: Man 5B 96
Ember St. M11: Man 8B 80
Embla Wlk. BL3: Bolt 8H 39
Emblem St. BL3: Bolt 7E 38
Embleton Cl. BL2: Bolt 3M 39
Embleton Wlk. M18: Man 3A 96
(off Peacock Cl.)
Embsay Cl. BL1: Bolt 8E 22
Emerald Av. WN7: Lei 6G 73
Emerald Cotts. BL8: Holc 2F 24
Emerald Dr. OL1: O'ham 9B 46
Emerald Rd. M22: Wyth 8E 116
Emerald St. BL1: Bolt 1G 38
M34: Dent 6J 97
WN6: Wig 9D 34
Emerson Av. M30: Ecc 7G 76
Emerson Dr. M24: Mid 2L 61
Emerson Ho. M30: Ecc 8F 76
Emerson St. M5: Sal 8K 77
Emery Av. M21: Cho H 2B 106
Emery Cl. SK4: Stoc 4M 107
WA14: Alt 9D 104
Emery Ct. SK4: Stoc 7L 107
Emily Beavan Cl. M11: Man 9N 79
Emily Cl. M35: Fail 1E 80
Emily Pl. M43: Droy 9D 80
Emlea Gdns. WN2: I Mak 4L 53
Emley St. M19: Man 8N 95
Emlyn Gro. SK8: Chea 1M 117
Emlyn St. BL4: Farn 2K 57
M27: Swin 2D 76
M28: Walk 8L 57
WN2: Hin 6M 53
Emmanuel Cl. BL3: Bolt 7E 38
(off Emblem St.)
Emmanuel Ct. OL6: A Lyne 6M 81
Emmanuel Pl. BL3: Bolt 7E 38
(off Emblem St.)
Emma St. OL8: O'ham 8K 63
OL12: Roch 6A 8 (5C 28)
Emmaus Wlk. M6: Sal 7M 77
Emmeline Ct. M40: Man 6G 79
Emmeline Grange M6: Sal 8L 77
Emmerson St. M27: Pen 1F 76
Emmett St. BL6: Hor 1D 36
Emmett St. E. M40: Man 5K 79
Emmott Cl. OL10: H'ood 2H 43
Emmott Way OL1: O'ham 4D 8 (5K 63)
Empire Cinema
Robin Park 3C 52
Empire Rd. BL2: Bolt 5M 39
SK16: Duk 3N 97
Empire St. M3: Man 6E 78
Empress Av. SK6: Mar 2C 120
Empress Bus. Cen. M16: Old T 3B 94
Empress Ct. M15: Man 3B 94
Empress Dr. SK4: Stoc 4B 108
WN7: Lei 4N 73
Empress Ind. Est. WN2: I Mak 4J 53
Empress St. BL1: Bolt 3C 38
M8: Man 2E 78
M16: Old T 3B 94
Emsworth Cl. BL2: Bolt 3H 39
Emsworth Dr. M33: Sale 7J 105
Ena Cres. WN7: Lei 3E 72
Ena St. BL3: Bolt 9H 39
OL1: O'ham 2N 63
Enbridge St. M5: Sal 1N 93
Encombe Pl. M3: Sal 3B 4 (8C 78)
Endcott Cl. M18: Man 3N 95
Enderby Rd. M40: Man 1A 80
Endfield Farm Caravan Pk.
WA16: H Leg 9E 112
Ending Rake OL12: Whitw 1A 28
Endon Av. SK10: Boll 6L 129
Endon Dr. M21: Cho H 9E 94
Endon St. BL1: Bolt 3C 38
Endsleigh Gdns. WN7: Lei 5H 73
Endsleigh Rd. M20: Man 2H 107
Endsley Av. M28: Wors 1K 75
Energie Fitness Club
Wilmslow 5J 123
Energy St. M40: Man 7K 79
Enfield Av. M19: Man 2M 107
OL8: O'ham 8J 63
Enfield Cl. BL1: Bolt 3F 38
BL9: Bury 7M 41
M30: Ecc 1D 92
OL11: Roch 5K 27
Enfield Dr. M11: Man 8A 80
Enfield Gro. WN7: Lei 4J 73
Enfield Ho. M30: Ecc 1D 92
(off Enfield Cl.)
Enfield Rd. M27: Swin 4E 76
M30: Ecc 6D 76
Enfield St. M28: Walk 6L 57
(off Worsley Rd. Nth.)
SK14: Hyde 1B 110
WN5: Wig 6N 51
Enford Av. M22: Wyth 5N 115
Engal Cl. BL0: Ram 9G 11
Engell Cl. M18: Man 4B 96
Engels Ho. M30: Ecc 1D 92
(off Trafford Rd.)
Engineer St. WN2: I Mak 4K 53
ENGINE FOLD 8J 57
Engine Fold WN5: Wig 5M 51
Engine Fold Rd. M28: Walk 8H 57
Engine La. M29: Tyld 7A 56
Engine St. OL9: Chad 7F 62
England St. OL6: A Lyne 8E 6 (7N 81)
Engledene BL1: Bolt 7E 22
Englefield Gro. M18: Man 5B 96
(off Milkwood Gro.)
English St. WN7: Lei 6J 73
Enid Cl. M7: Sal 5C 78
Enid Pl. WN2: Bam 2J 71
Ennerdale SK11: Macc 7D 130
WN8: Skel 3B 50
Ennerdale Av. BL2: Bolt 3N 39
(not continuous)
M21: Cho H 4C 106
M27: Swin 4F 76
OL2: O'ham 5H 45
WA11: St H 9F 68
WN4: A Mak 5E 70
Ennerdale Cl. BL3: Lit L 9N 39
Ennerdale Dr. BL9: Bury 1N 59
M33: Sale 3E 104
SK8: Gat 4G 117
WA15: Tim 8G 104
Ennerdale Gdns. BL2: Bolt 3M 39
Ennerdale Gro. BL4: Farn 3F 56
OL7: A Lyne 5K 81
Ennerdale Pl. WN2: I Mak 3L 53
Ennerdale Rd. M24: Mid 1L 61
M29: Ast 3B 74
M31: Part 5F 102
M32: Stre 6J 93
OL11: Roch 9N 27
SK1: Stoc 9F 108
SK6: Wood 4M 109
WN2: Hin 6A 54
WN7: Lei 5K 73
Ennerdale Ter. SK15: Stal 7D 82
Ennis Cl. M23: Wyth 2L 115
Ennismore Av. M30: Ecc 8G 76
Ensor Way SK22: N Mil 8M 121
(Church Rd.)
SK22: N Mil 6N 121
(High Hill Rd.)
Enstone WN8: Skel 2B 50
Enstone Dr. M40: Man 1B 80
Enstone Way M29: Tyld 1D 74
Enterprise Cen. Two SK3: Stoc 3G 9
Enterprise Ho. M50: Sal 2N 93
Enterprise Pk. BL6: Hor 4E 36
Enterprise Trad. Est. M17: T Pk 1G 93
Enterprise Way WA3: Low 2C 88
Enticott Rd. M44: Cad 3D 102
Entron Ho. OL2: Shaw 5K 45
Entwisle Av. M41: Urm 5B 92
Entwisle Rd. OL16: Roch 6E 8 (6E 28)
Entwisle Row BL4: Farn 3L 57
Entwisle St. BL4: Farn 2L 57
M27: Ward 1C 76
OL16: Miln 7J 29
Entwistle Gro. WN7: Lei 7L 73
Entwistle St. BL2: Bolt 4J 39
Enver Rd. M8: Man 2G 78
Enville Rd. M6: Sal 4L 77
M40: Man 1N 79
WA14: Bow 4C 114
Enville St. M9: Man 8J 61
M34: Aud 2K 97
OL6: A Lyne 6E 6
Envoy Cl. WN5: Wig 2B 52
Enys Wlk. M6: Sal 5N 77
Ephraim's Fold WN2: Asp 6N 35
Epping Cl. OL6: A Lyne 3N 81
OL9: Chad 3C 62
Epping Dr. M33: Sale 3C 104
Epping Rd. M34: Dent 7F 96
Epping St. M15: Man 3E 94
Eppleworth Ri. M27: Clif 8G 58
Epsley Cl. M15: Man 3F 94
Epsom Av. M19: Man 2L 107
M33: Sale 6C 104
SK9: Hand 2K 123
Epsom Cl. OL11: Roch 5L 27
SK7: H Gro 5K 119
Epsom Cft. PR6: And 6L 19
Epsom Dr. WN2: Bam 3J 71
Epsom M. M7: Sal 4C 78
(off Rigby St.)
Epsom Wlk. OL9: Chad 4G 62
(off Garforth St.)
Epworth Ct. SK4: Stoc 5N 107
Epworth Gro. BL3: Bolt 9D 38
(off Maltby Dr.)
Epworth St. M1: Man 5N 5 (9H 79)
Equitable St. OL4: O'ham 3A 64
OL11: Roch 7E 28
OL16: Miln 8K 29
Era St. BL2: Bolt 5M 39
M33: Sale 4H 105
Ercall Av. M12: Man 3K 95
Erica Av. OL4: O'ham 8C 46
Erica Cl. SK5: Stoc 9E 96
Erica Dr. M19: Man 4K 107
Erica Wlk. WN7: Lei 5D 72
Eric Brook Cl. M14: Man 6F 94
Eric Bullows Cl. M22: Wyth 6B 116
Eric St. M5: Sal 9M 77
OL4: O'ham 4N 63
OL15: Lit 8L 15
Erin Cl. OL9: Chad 6F 62
Erindale Wlk. M40: Man 4J 79
(off Barnstaple Dr.)
Erin St. M11: Man 2C 96
Erith Cl. SK5: Stoc 2F 108
Erith Rd. OL4: O'ham 5N 63
Erlesdene WA14: Bow 4B 114
Erlesmere Av. M34: Dent 5L 97
Erlesmere Cl. OL4: O'ham 8C 46
Erlington Av. M16: Old T 7A 94
Ermen Rd. M30: Ecc 1C 92
Ermington Ct. OL10: H'ood 3H 43
Ermington Dr. M8: Man 4E 78
Erneley Cl. M12: Man 6N 95
Ernest St. BL1: Bolt 6E 38
(not continuous)
M25: Pres 7M 59
SK2: Stoc 1E 118
SK8: Chea 1H 117
Ernest Ter. OL12: Roch 4F 28
Ernlouen Av. BL1: Bolt 4B 38
ERNOCROFT 6H 111
Ernocroft Gro. M18: Man 3C 96
Ernocroft La. SK6: Mar B 5H 111
Ernocroft Rd. SK6: Mar B 7E 110
Erradale Cres. WN3: Wins 9A 52
Erringdon Cl. SK2: Stoc 1H 119
Errington Cl. BL3: Bolt 7A 38
Errington Dr. M7: Sal 6C 78
Errol Av. M9: Man 6F 60
M22: Wyth 3B 116
Errwood Cres. M19: Man 9M 95
Errwood Pk. Works
SK4: Stoc 2N 107
Errwood Rd. M19: Man 3L 107
Erskine Cl. BL3: Bolt 7N 37
Erskine Pl. WN2: Abr 1L 71
Erskine Rd. M9: Man 6K 61
M31: Part 6G 102
Erskine St. M15: Man 3C 94
SK6: Comp 5E 110
Erwin St. M40: Man 4N 79
Eryngo St. SK1: Stoc 7E 108
Escott St. M16: Whall R 6E 94
Esher Dr. M33: Sale 7J 105
Esk Av. BL0: Eden 1K 11
Eskbank WN8: Skel 3A 50
Eskbrook WN8: Skel 2A 50
Esk Cl. M41: Urm 5A 92
Eskdale SK8: Gat 3H 117
WN8: Skel 3A 50
Eskdale Av. BL2: Bolt 2N 39
BL6: Bla 5A 36
M20: Man 1F 106
OL2: O'ham 5H 45
OL3: G'fld 6L 65
OL8: O'ham 7H 63
OL11: Roch 9N 27
SK6: Wood 3M 109
SK7: Bram 1A 124
WN1: Wig 9E 34
Eskdale Cl. BL9: Bury 9N 41
Eskdale Dr. M24: Mid 9L 43
WA15: Tim 9J 105
Eskdale Gro. BL4: Farn 3G 56
Eskdale Ho. M13: Man 5K 95
Eskdale M. OL3: G'fld 6L 65
Eskdale Rd. WN2: Hin 6A 54
WN4: A Mak 5E 70
Eskdale Ter. SK15: Stal 6D 82
Eskrick St. BL1: Bolt 3E 38
Eskrigge Cl. M7: Sal 2E 78
Esmond Rd. M8: Man 3F 78
Esmont Dr. M24: Mid 9K 43
Esplanade, The
OL16: Roch 8B 8 (6C 28)
Esporta Health & Fitness
Denton 6G 97
Middleton 1G 60
Salford Quays 2M 93
Essex Av. BL9: Bury 3D 42
M20: Man 4G 107
M43: Droy 7E 80
SK3: Stoc 8N 107
Essex Cl. M35: Fail 5D 80
OL2: Shaw 5K 45
Essex Dr. BL9: Bury 4N 41
Essex Gdns. M44: Cad 4D 102
Essex Pl. M27: Clif 9F 58
(off Cumberland Av.)
M29: Tyld 8A 56
Essex Rd. M18: Man 5D 96
SK5: Stoc 3G 109
WN1: Stan 3E 34
Essex St. BL6: Hor 3F 36
M2: Man 5G 5 (9E 78)
OL11: Roch 9C 8 (7D 28)
WN1: Wig 6N 9 (2H 53)
Essex Wlk. SK10: Macc 3D 130
Essex Way M16: Old T 4C 94
Essingdon St. BL3: Bolt 8E 38
(not continuous)
Essington Dr. M40: Man 4J 79
Essington Wlk. M34: Dent 8J 97
Essoldo Cl. M18: Man 4A 96
Estate St. OL8: O'ham 7K 63
Estate St. Sth. OL8: O'ham 7K 63
Est Bank Rd. BL0: Ram 2G 24
(not continuous)
Esther Fold BL5: W'ton 3G 54
Esther St. OL4: O'ham 4A 64
OL15: Lit 9K 15
(off Bamford St.)
Esthwaite Av.
WA11: St H 9G 68
Esthwaite Dr. M29: Ast 3B 74
Estonfield Dr. M41: Urm 7F 92
Eston St. M13: Man 5J 95
Eswick St. M11: Man 9A 80
Etchells Rd. SK8: H Grn 6J 117
WA14: W Tim 8D 104
Etchells St. SK1: Stoc 2L 9 (7D 108)
Etchell St. M40: Man 5H 79
Ethan Cl. M9: Man 3J 79
Ethel Av. M9: Man 6J 61
M27: Pen 2H 77
Ethel Ct. OL16: Roch 7F 28
Ethel St. BL3: Bolt 6E 38
OL8: O'ham 8K 63
OL12: Whitw 4B 14
OL16: Roch 7F 28
Ethel Ter. M19: Man 8M 95
Etherley Cl. M44: Irl 7H 91
Etherley Dr. WA12: N Wil 8G 86
Etherow Av. M40: Man 9D 62
SK6: Rom 6B 110
Etherow Bowling & Activity Cen.
9K 99
Etherow Brow SK14: B'tom 9L 99
Etherow Country Pk. 6F 110
Etherow Country Pk.
Local Nature Reserve 5F 110
Etherow Country Pk. Vis. Cen. 6E 110
Etherow Ct. SK14: Hyde 7B 98
(off Ridling La.)
Etherow Ind. Est. SK13: Had 5N 99
(not continuous)
Etherow Way SK13: Had 4A 100
Etherstone St. M8: Man 2H 79
WN7: Lei 6G 72
Etihad Stadium / Eastlands 9L 79
Eton Av. OL8: O'ham 8J 63
Eton Cl. M16: Old T 4C 94
OL11: Roch 7N 27
Eton Ct. M16: Old T 4C 94
(off Eton Cl.)
Eton Dr. SK8: Chea 5J 117
Eton Hill Ind. Est.
M26: Rad 7K 41
Eton Hill Rd. M26: Rad 7J 41
Eton Pl. M26: Rad 9F 40
Eton St. WN7: Lei 7H 73
Eton Ter. WN3: I Mak 6H 53
Eton Way WN5: Orr 3K 51
Eton Way Nth. M26: Rad 7J 41
Eton Way Sth. M26: Rad 7J 41
Etrop Ct. M22: Wyth 4C 116
Etruria Cl. M13: Man 4K 95
Ettington Cl. BL8: Bury 1G 41
Ettrick Cl. M11: Man 2B 96
Euan Pl. M33: Sale 4J 105
(off Montague Rd.)
Euclid Cl. M11: Man 9K 79
Europa Bus. Pk. SK3: Stoc 1N 117
Europa Circ. M17: T Pk 4K 93
Europa Ga. M17: T Pk 4K 93
Europa Rd. BL9: Bury 5L 7 (1M 41)
Europa Trad. Est. M26: Rad 4B 58
Europa Way M17: T Pk 4K 93
M26: Rad 4A 58
SK3: Stoc 1N 117
Eustace St. BL3: Bolt 9H 39
OL9: Chad 2F 62
Euston Av. M9: Man 8M 61
Euxton Cl. BL8: Bury 3G 40
Evan Cl. WN6: Stan 8A 34
Evans Bus. Cen. OL11: Roch 8A 8
Evans Cl. M20: Man 5F 106
WA11: Hay 2C 86
Evans Rd. M30: Ecc 9A 76
Evans St. BL6: Hor 9E 20
M3: Sal 1E 4 (7D 78)
M24: Mid 3N 61
OL1: O'ham 1D 8 (3K 63)
OL6: A Lyne 6A 82
WN7: Lei 5H 73
Evanstone Cl. BL6: Hor 1D 36
Evan St. M40: Man 5K 79
Evanton Wlk. M9: Man 3K 79
(off Nethervale Dr.)
Eva Rd. SK3: Stoc 9M 107
Eva St. M14: Man 6H 95
OL12: Roch 3E 28
WN7: Lei 3E 72
Evelyn St. M14: Man 9J 95
OL1: O'ham 2M 63
Evenholme Flats WA14: Bow 5B 114
Evening St. M35: Fail 2D 80
Evenley Cl. M11: Man 3C 96
Eventhall Ho. M25: Pres 1N 77
Evenwood WN8: Skel 2B 50
Evenwood Ct. WN8: Skel 2A 50
Everard Cl. M28: Wors 1K 75
Everard St.
M5: Sal 8A 4 (2B 94)
Everbrom Rd. BL3: Bolt 1B 56
Everdingen Wlk.
OL1: O'ham 9A 46
Everest Av. OL7: A Lyne 5M 81
Everest Cl. SK14: Hyde 5D 98
SK16: Duk 9M 81
Everest Pl. WN1: Wig 1F 52
Everest Rd. M46: Ath 5L 55
SK14: Hyde 5D 98
Everest St. OL11: Roch 2E 44
Everett Ct. M20: Man 2G 106
(off Aldborough Cl.)
Everett Rd. M20: Man 2F 106
Everglade OL8: O'ham 1L 81
Everglade Cl. SK11: Macc 7F 130
Evergreen Av. BL6: Hor 1D 36
Evergreen M. M7: Sal 3C 78
Evergreens, The BL6: Hor 3G 37
Evergreen Wlk. M33: Sale 2C 104
(off Epping Dr.)
Everleigh Cl. BL2: Bolt 8M 23
Everleigh Dr. M7: Sal 4E 78
Eversden Ct. M7: Sal 6D 78
Everside Cl. M28: Walk 6K 57
Everside Dr. M8: Sal 5D 78
Eversley WN8: Skel 2B 50
Eversley Ct. M33: Sale 6H 105
Eversley Rd. M20: Man 5F 106
Everton Rd. OL8: O'ham 8H 63
SK5: Stoc 7D 96
Everton St. M27: Swin 2E 76
WN4: Gars 5A 70
Every St. BL0: Ram 8K 11
BL9: Bury 9M 25
M4: Man 9J 79
Evesham Av. M23: Wyth 9K 105
SK4: Stoc 5N 107
SK13: Had 4C 100
Evesham Cl. BL3: Bolt 6E 38
(off Punch St.)
M24: Mid 6N 61
SK10: Macc 9J 129
WN7: Lei 9F 72
Evesham Dr. BL4: Farn 1J 57
SK9: Wilm 4H 123
Evesham Gdns. M24: Mid 6M 61
Evesham Gro. M33: Sale 4L 105
OL6: A Lyne 3N 81
Evesham Rd. M9: Man 9M 61
M24: Mid 6M 61
SK8: Chea 3M 117
Evesham Wlk. BL3: Bolt 7E 38
(off Stanway Cl.)
M24: Mid 6N 61
OL8: O'ham 6J 63
Eveside Cl. SK8: Chea H 3N 117
Eve St. OL8: O'ham 9K 63
Evington WN8: Skel 2B 50
Evington Av. M11: Man 2E 96
Ewan St. M18: Man 3B 96
Ewart Av. M5: Sal 9N 77
Ewart Ct. SK13: Had 4C 100
(off Wesley St.)
Ewart St. BL1: Bolt 2F 38
Ewen Fields 7C 98
Ewhurst Av. M27: Swin 4D 76
Ewing Cl. M8: Man 1F 78
Ewood OL8: O'ham 2L 81
Ewood Dr. BL8: Bury 4G 40
Ewood Ho. M30: Ecc 8F 76
Exbourne Rd.
M22: Wyth 6B 116
Exbridge Wlk. M40: Man 6B 80
(off Stansfield St.)
Exbury OL12: Roch 5B 8
Exbury St. M14: Man 1J 107
Excalibur Way M44: Irl 1F 102
Excelsior Gdns. OL10: H'ood 4L 43
Excelsior Ter. OL15: Lit 2K 29
(off Barke St.)
Exchange Cl. SK11: Macc 4H 131
Exchange Ct. M4: Man 3H 5
Exchange Quay M5: Sal 3N 93
Exchange Quay Stop (Metro) 3N 93
Exchange Sq. M3: Man 3G 5 (8E 78)
Exchange St. BL0: Eden 3K 11
BL1: Bolt 3K 7 (5G 38)
M2: Man 4G 4 (9E 78)
OL4: O'ham 4M 63
(off Gravel Walks)
SK1: Stoc 3K 9 (7C 108)
SK3: Stoc 3J 9 (7C 108)
SK11: Macc 4H 131
Exeter Av. BL2: Bolt 2J 39
BL4: Farn 2G 56
M26: Rad 7E 40
M30: Ecc 6G 76
M34: Dent 8K 97
Exeter Cl. SK8: Chea H 7L 117
SK16: Duk 3A 98
Exeter Ct. M14: Man 1H 107
(off Wilmslow Rd.)
M24: Mid 2L 61
Exeter Dr. M44: Irl 7J 91
OL6: A Lyne 3A 82
WN2: Asp 7N 35
Exeter Gro. OL11: Roch 8D 28
(off Exeter St.)
Exeter Rd. M41: Urm 5D 92
SK5: Stoc 3G 108
WN2: Hin 6A 54
Exeter St. M6: Sal 8L 77
(off Langton St.)
OL11: Roch 8D 28
Exeter Wlk. SK7: Bram 8D 118
Exford Av. WN3: Wig 7E 52
Exford Cl. M40: Man 7J 79
SK5: Stoc 2D 108
Exford Dr. BL2: Bolt 6A 40
Exhall Cl. M38: Lit H 5H 57
Exmoor Cl. OL6: A Lyne 3N 81
Exmoor Wlk. M23: Wyth 4N 115
Exmouth Av. SK5: Stoc 3G 108
Exmouth Pl. OL16: Roch 1F 44
Exmouth Rd. M33: Sale 3D 104
Exmouth Sq. OL16: Roch 1E 44
Exmouth St. OL16: Roch 1E 44
Express Trad. Est. BL4: Farn 5M 57
Eyam Cl. SK13: Gam 7N 99
(off Eyam M.)
Eyam Fold SK13: Gam 7N 99
(off Haddon M.)
Eyam Gdns. SK13: Gam 7N 99
(off Eyam M.)
Eyam Grn. SK13: Gam 7N 99
(off Grassmoor Cres.)
Eyam Gro. SK2: Stoc 2H 119
SK13: Gam 7N 99
(off Grassmoor Cres.)
Eyam La. SK13: Gam 7N 99
Eyam Lea SK13: Gam 7A 100
(off Eyam M.)
Eyam M. SK13: Gam 7A 100
Eyam Rd. SK7: H Gro 7J 119
Eycott Dr. M24: Mid 2J 61
Eyebrook Rd. WA14: Bow 5N 113
Eyes La. WN8: Par 1A 32
Eyet St. WN7: Lei 5G 73
Eynford Av. SK5: Stoc 2F 108
Eyre St. M15: Man 4F 94

F

Faber St. M4: Man 1J 5 (7F 78)
FACIT 4B 14
Factory Brow BL6: Bla 1N 35
M24: Mid 4H 61
Factory Hill BL6: Hor 9F 20
Factory La. M5: Sal 4B 4
M9: Man 1H 79
PR6: H Char 5L 19
Factory St. BL0: Ram 7J 11
M24: Mid 3L 61

Factory St. M26: Rad 9H **41**
M29: Tyld 1A **74**
Factory St. E. M46: Ath 8L **55**
Factory St. W. M46: Ath 8L **55**
Faggy La. WN3: Wig 9K **9** (4F **52**)
FAILSWORTH 3D 80
Failsworth Ind. Est. M35: Fail 4A **80**
Failsworth Pct. M35: Fail 3D **80**
Failsworth Rd. M35: Fail 3F **80**
Failsworth Sports Cen. 3E 80
Failsworth Stop (Metro) 2C 80
Fairacres BL2: Bolt 1M **39**
WN6: Stan 3M **33**
Fairacres Rd. SK6: H Lan 7B **120**
Fairbairn Apartments M4: Man 3L **5**
Fairbairn St. BL6: Hor 2D **36**
Fairbank M43: Droy 1D **96**
Fairbank Av. M14: Man 5G **94**
Fairbank Dr. M24: Mid 1J **61**
Fairbottom St.
OL1: O'ham 2E **8** (4K **63**)
Fairbottom Wlk. *M43: Droy* *1E* ***96***
(off Wood Sq.)
Fairbourne Av. SK9: A Edg 2G **127**
SK9: Wilm 1E **126**
WN3: Wig 7D **52**
Fairbourne Cl. SK9: Wilm 1E **126**
Fairbourne Dr. SK9: Wilm 1E **126**
WA15: Tim 7H **105**
Fairbourne Rd. M19: Man 8A **96**
M34: Dent 7J **97**
Fairbourne Wlk. OL1: O'ham 2N **63**
Fairbrook Dr. M6: Sal 8L **77**
Fairbrother St. M5: Sal 2B **94**
Fairburn Cl. M41: Urm 5A **92**
Fairclough St. BL3: Bolt 8G **39**
M11: Man 8M **79**
WA12: N Wil 6E **86**
WN1: Wig 9L **9** (4G **52**)
WN2: Hin 5N **53**
Fairfax Av. M20: Man 4G **107**
WA15: Tim 1G **115**
Fairfax Cl. SK6: Mar 9A **110**
Fairfax Dr. OL15: Lit 2K **29**
SK9: Wilm 1E **126**
Fairfax Rd. M25: Pres 6N **59**
FAIRFIELD
BL9 1C 42
M43 1E 96
Fairfield Av. M43: Droy 2E **96**
SK6: Bred 4L **109**
SK8: Chea H 5L **117**
SK10: Boll 6L **129**
WN2: P Bri 8K **53**
WN5: Wig 6A **52**
Fairfield Ct. M14: Man 5J **95**
M43: Droy 1D **96**
Fairfield Dr. BL9: Bury 1C **42**
Fairfield Gdns. WA11: Cra 8C **68**
Fairfield Golf Course 2E 96
Fairfield Ho. M43: Droy 9E **80**
Fairfield Rd. BL4: Farn 4K **57**
M11: Man 2C **96**
M24: Mid 2K **61**
M43: Droy 1C **96**
M44: Cad 3D **102**
WA13: Lym 4A **112**
WA15: Tim 2J **115**
Fairfields BL7: Eger 5G **22**
OL8: O'ham 9J **63**
Fairfields High School Sports Hall
1E 96
(off Fairfield Av.)
Fairfield Sq. M43: Droy 1E **96**
(not continuous)
Fairfield Station (Rail) 2E 96
Fairfield St. M1: Man 6K **5** (1G **94**)
M6: Sal 5K **77**
M12: Man 6L **5** (1J **95**)
WN5: Wig 6N **51**
Fairfield Vw. M34: Aud 2E **96**
Fairford Cl. SK5: Stoc 3D **108**
Fairford Dr. BL3: Bolt 7F **38**
Fairford Way SK5: Stoc 3D **108**
SK9: Wilm 7J **123**
Fairham Wlk. M4: Man 9J **79**
Fairhaven WN8: Skel 9A **32**
Fairhaven Av. BL5: W'ton 3K **55**
M21: Cho H 9A **94**
M45: Whitef 4K **59**
Fairhaven Caravan Pk.
SK14: Hyde 7N **97**
Fairhaven Cl. SK7: Bram 7D **118**
SK10: Macc 9F **128**
Fairhaven Rd. BL1: Bolt 1G **39**
Fairhaven St. M12: Man 3L **95**
Fairhills Ind. Est. M44: Irl 9G **91**
Fairhills Rd. M44: Irl 9G **91**
Fairholme Av. M41: Urm 8C **92**
WN4: A Mak 6E **70**
Fairholme Caravan Site
M8: Man 6G **78**
Fairholme Rd. M20: Man 2H **107**
SK4: Stoc 5A **108**
Fairhope Av. M6: Sal 6H **77**
Fairhope Ct. *M6: Sal* *7J* ***77***
(off Fairhope Av.)
Fairhurst Av. WN6: Stan 1A **34**
Fairhurst Dr. M28: Walk 9G **57**
WN8: Par 2A **32**
Fairhurst La. WN1: Stan 4D **34**
WN6: Stan 4D **34**
Fairhurst St. WN3: Wig 8G **9** (3E **52**)
WN7: Lei 5G **72**
Fairisle Cl. M11: Man 9L **79**
Fairlands Pl. OL11: Roch 2F **44**
Fairlands Rd. BL9: Bury 6M **25**
M33: Sale 6F **104**
Fairlands St. OL11: Roch 2F **44**
Fairlands Vw. OL11: Roch 2F **44**
Fairlawn SK4: Stoc 5B **108**
Fairlawn Cl. M14: Man 5F **94**
Fairlea M34: Dent 7L **97**
Fairlea Av. M20: Man 6H **107**
Fairlee Av. M34: Aud 9G **80**
Fairleigh Av. M6: Sal 7J **77**
Fairless Rd. M30: Ecc 9D **76**
Fairlie WN8: Skel 9A **32**
Fairlie Av. BL3: Bolt 7A **38**
Fairlie Dr. WA15: Tim 8H **105**
Fairlyn Cl. BL5: O Hul 4B **56**
Fairlyn Dr. BL5: O Hul 4B **56**
Fairman Dr. WN2: Hin 4A **54**
Fairman St. M16: Whall R 6E **94**
Fairmead WA16: Knut 8H **133**
Fairmead Rd. M23: Wyth 7B **106**
Fairmile Dr. M20: Man 8H **107**
Fairmount Av. BL2: Bolt 4M **39**
Fairmount Rd. M27: Swin 4B **76**
Fairoak Ct. BL3: Bolt 7E **38**
Fair Oak Rd. M19: Man 3L **107**
Fairstead WN8: Skel 9A **32**
Fairstead Cl. BL5: W'ton 3F **54**
Fairstead Wlk. M11: Man 2D **96**
Fair St. BL3: Bolt 1D **56**
M27: Pen 1G **76**
Fairthorne Grange
OL7: A Lyne *9K* ***81***
(off Bennett St.)
FAIRVIEW 5J 19
Fair Vw. WN5: Bil 5H **69**
Fair Vw. Av. WN5: Bil 5H **69**
Fairview Av. M19: Man 7L **95**
M34: Dent 8E **96**
Fairview Caravan Pk. M46: Ath 7K **55**
Fairview Cl. OL9: Chad 3C **62**
OL12: Roch 3H **27**
SK6: Mar 9C **110**
WN4: A Mak 6E **70**
Fairview Dr. PR6: H Char 5J **19**
SK6: Mar 9C **110**
Fairview Rd. M34: Dent 7E **96**
SK11: Macc 6E **130**
WA15: Tim 2J **115**
Fair Vw. Ter. OL15: Lit 6N **15**
Fairway M25: Pres 9C **60**
M27: Pen 3J **77**
M43: Droy 1E **96**
OL11: Roch 3N **43**
OL12: Whitw 7A **14**
OL16: Miln 7L **29**
SK7: Bram 9B **118**
SK8: Gat 3G **116**
Fairway, The M40: Man 3A **80**
SK2: Stoc 9H **109**
Fairway Av. BL2: Bolt 9A **24**
M23: Wyth 9K **105**
Fairway Ct. M34: Dent 5F **96**
Fairway Cres. OL2: O'ham 6H **45**
Fairway Dr. M33: Sale 6E **104**
Fairway Ho. SK4: Stoc 4M **107**
Fairway Rd. BL9: Bury 9N **41**
OL4: O'ham 7B **64**
Fairways BL6: Hor 1E **36**
Fairways, The BL5: W'ton 3J **54**
M45: Whitef 5M **59**
OL2: O'ham 7H **45**
SK10: Macc 9F **128**
SK16: Duk 2C **98**
WN4: A Mak 8B **70**
WN8: Skel 9B **32**
Fairways Cl. SK13: Glos 8H **101**
Fairwood Rd. M23: Wyth 9K **105**
Fairy La. M8: Man 5D **78**
M33: Sale 4M **105**
Fairy St. BL8: Bury 2J **41**
Fairywell Cl. SK9: Wilm 5J **123**
Fairywell Dr. M33: Sale 7G **105**
Fairywell Rd. WA15: Tim 8H **105**
Faith St. BL1: Bolt 3B **38**
WN7: Lei 5E **72**
Falcon Av. M41: Urm 7E **92**
Falcon Bus. Cen. OL9: Chad 3G **62**
Falcon Cl. BL9: Bury 9A **26**
M50: Sal 9J **77**
OL12: Roch 3J **27**
SK22: N Mil 7N **121**
WN7: Lei 5L **73**
Falcon Ct. M7: Sal 1C **78**
M15: Man 4D **94**
M50: Sal 1K **93**
Falcon Cres. M27: Clif 9H **59**
Falcon Dr. M24: Mid 9K **43**
M38: Lit H 6H **57**
M44: Irl 5J **91**
OL9: Chad 3G **62**
Falconers Grn. WN3: Wig 6E **52**
Falcon Ho. BL9: Bury 9N **25**
Falcon St. BL1: Bolt 1K **7** (4G **38**)
OL8: O'ham 6J **63**
Falcon's Vw. OL8: O'ham 8J **63**
Falconwood Chase M28: Wors 4J **75**
Falconwood Cl. WN6: Wig 2D **52**
Falconwood Way M11: Man 1L **95**
Falfield Dr. M8: Man 5G **78**
Falinge Fold OL12: Roch 4B **28**
Falinge Mnr. M. OL12: Roch 4C **28**
Falinge M. OL12: Roch 6A **8** (5C **28**)
Falinge Rd. OL12: Roch 5B **8** (4B **28**)
Falkirk Dr. BL2: Bolt 6N **39**
WN2: I Mak 3K **53**
Falkirk Gro. WN5: Wig 3N **51**
Falkirk St. OL4: O'ham 4N **63**
Falkirk Wlk. M23: Wyth 5N **115**
Falkland WN8: Skel 9A **32**
Falkland Av. M40: Man 6J **79**
OL11: Roch 5A **28**
Falkland Cl. OL4: O'ham 8B **46**
Falkland Dr. WN4: Gars 6N **69**
Falkland Ho. M14: Man 8H **95**
Falkland Rd. BL2: Bolt 5A **40**
Fall Bank SK4: Stoc 2B **108**
Fall Birch Rd. BL6: Los 4H **37**
Fallibroome Cl. SK10: Macc 4C **130**
Fallibroome Rd. SK10: Macc 4C **130**
Fall La. HD7: Mars 1H **49**
Fallons Rd. M28: Ward 1C **76**
Fallow Av. M18: Man 7B **96**
Fallow Cl. BL5: W'ton 1G **55**
FALLOWFIELD 9H 95
Fallowfield Ct. OL12: Roch 3B **28**
Fallow Flds. Dr. SK5: Stoc 8E **96**
Fallowfield Shop. Cen.
M14: Man 8K **95**
Fallowfield Way M46: Ath 1N **73**
Fallows, The OL9: Chad 6E **62**
Falls Grn. Av. M40: Man 4M **79**
(not continuous)
Falls Gro. SK8: H Grn 4F **116**
Falmer Cl. BL8: Bury 7J **25**
M18: Man 3D **96**
Falmer Dr. M22: Wyth 6B **116**
Falmouth Av. M33: Sale 3D **104**
M41: Urm 6M **91**
Falmouth Cl. SK10: Macc 4C **130**
Falmouth Cres. SK5: Stoc 3G **108**
Falmouth Rd. M44: Irl 7J **91**
Falmouth St. M40: Man 6L **79**
OL8: O'ham 7K **63**
OL11: Roch 8E **28**
Falsgrave Cl. M40: Man 5M **79**
Falshaw Dr. BL9: Bury 4L **25**
Falshaw Way M18: Man 6B **96**
Falside Wlk. M40: Man 5A **80**
Falstaff M. *SK6: Bred* *5L* ***109***
(off Thomas St.)
Falston Av. M40: Man 9B **62**
Falstone Av. BL0: Ram 1J **25**
Falstone Cl. WN3: Wins 9A **52**
Falterley Rd. M23: Wyth 8M **105**
Fancroft Rd. M22: Wyth 2B **116**
Fane Wlk. M9: Man 8G **60**
Faraday Av. M8: Man 4F **78**
M27: Clif 9K **59**
Faraday Cl. WN6: Wig 3D **52**
Faraday Dr. BL1: Bolt 3F **38**
Faraday Ri. OL12: Roch 4N **27**
Faraday St. M1: Man 3K **5** (9G **78**)
Farcroft Av. M26: Rad 6J **41**
Farcroft Cl. M23: Wyth 8M **105**
SK2: Stoc 9J **109**
WA13: Lym 2D **112**
Far Cromwell Rd. SK6: Bred 1H **109**
Fardale OL2: Shaw 6M **45**
Farden Dr. M23: Wyth 8K **105**
Fardon Cl. WN3: Wig 8C **52**
Farefield Av. WA3: Gol 8J **71**
Farewell Cl. OL11: Roch 2A **44**
Far Hey Cl. M26: Rad 9E **40**
Farholme OL2: O'ham 1G **62**
Faringdon OL11: Roch 7C **28**
Faringdon Wlk. BL3: Bolt 7F **38**
Farland Pl. BL3: Bolt 5J **39**
Farlands Dr. M20: Man 9G **107**
Farlands Ri. OL16: Roch 1G **45**
Far La. M18: Man 5B **96**
Farleigh Cl. BL5: W'ton 1J **55**
Farley Av. M18: Man 5E **96**
Farley Ct. SK8: Chea H 4L **117**
Farley La. WN8: Roby M 9E **32**
Farley Rd. M33: Sale 6J **105**
Farley Way SK5: Stoc 8C **96**
Farman St. BL3: Bolt 9E **38**
Farm Av. M32: Stre 5G **92**
PR6: Adl 5K **19**
Farm Cl. BL8: Tot 7F **24**
SK4: Stoc 2A **108**
Farm Cotts. BL0: Ram 5H **11**
Farmers Cl. M33: Sale 5N **105**
Farmer St. SK4: Stoc 5B **108**
Farmfield M33: Sale 2E **104**
Farmfield Dr. SK10: Macc 1F **130**
Farmfold SK9: Sty 2E **122**
Farm Hill M25: Pres 6L **59**
Farmlands Wlk. OL1: O'ham 8N **45**
Farm La. M25: Pres 3D **60**
M28: Wors 5N **75**
SK12: Dis 9D **120**
SK14: Hyde 9A **98**
WN2: Asp 2K **53**
Farm Mdw. Rd. WN5: Orr 6J **51**
FAR MOOR 7H 51
Farm Rd. OL8: O'ham 2G **81**
Farmside Av. M44: Irl 6H **91**
Farmside Pl. M19: Man 8M **95**
Farmstead Cl. M35: Fail 4G **80**
Farm St. M35: Fail 4B **80**
OL1: Chad 2F **62**
OL10: H'ood 4K **43**
Farm Wlk. OL15: Lit 9K **15**
OL16: Roch 4G **29**
WA14: Bow, D Mas 4L **113**
Farm Way WA12: N Wil 8H **87**
Farmway M24: Mid 4M **61**
Farm Yd. M19: Man 8M **95**
Farn Av. SK5: Stoc 7C **96**
Farnborough Av. OL4: O'ham 5A **64**
Farnborough Rd. BL1: Bolt 7F **22**
M40: Man 7J **79**
Farncombe Cl. *M23: Wyth* *9K* ***105***
(off Petersfield Dr.)
Farndale Gro. WN4: A Mak 8F **70**
Farndale Sq. M28: Walk 8K **57**
Farndale Wlk. *M9: Man* *2K* ***79***
(off Caversham Dr.)
SK11: Macc *6H* ***131***
(off White St.)
Farndon Av. SK7: H Gro 3K **119**
Farndon Cl. M33: Sale 1G **105**
Farndon Dr. WA15: Tim 1G **115**
Farndon Rd. SK5: Stoc 7C **96**
Farnham Av. M9: Man 6J **61**
SK11: Macc 6E **130**
Farnham Cl. *BL1: Bolt* *3F* ***38***
(off Bk. Ashford Wlk.)
SK8: Chea H 8M **117**
WN7: Lei 4H **73**
Farnham Dr. M44: Irl 8H **91**
Farnhill Wlk. M23: Wyth 7L **105**
Farnley Cl. OL12: Roch 3L **27**
Farnsfield WN1: Wig 2J **53**
Farnsworth Av. OL7: A Lyne 5M **81**
Farnsworth Cl. OL7: A Lyne 5M **81**
FARNWORTH 3L 57
Farnworth & Kearsley By-Pass
BL4: Farn, Kea 1L **57**
Farnworth Dr. M14: Man 7H **95**
Farnworth Ho. Est. PR7: Chor 3F **18**
Farnworth Leisure Cen. 3L 57
Farnworth Pk. Ind. Est.
BL4: Farn 2L **57**
Farnworth Station (Rail) 2M 57
Farnworth St. BL3: Bolt 8D **38**
OL10: H'ood 2H **43**
WN7: Lei 6K **73**
(not continuous)
Farrand Rd. OL8: O'ham 9F **62**
Farrant Ho. M12: Man 5M **95**
Farrant Rd. M12: Man 5M **95**
Farrar Rd. M43: Droy 1D **96**
Farr Cl. WN3: Wig 6C **52**
Farrell St. M7: Sal 7D **78**
WN5: Wig 6N **51**
Farrer Rd. M13: Man 6L **95**
Far Ridings SK6: Rom 5A **110**
Farrier Cl. M33: Sale 5M **105**
Farriers Cft. WN6: Wig 9B **34**
Farriers La. OL11: Roch 9N **27**
Farrier Way WN6: App B 5G **33**
Farringdon Dr. M26: Rad 8E **40**
Farringdon St. M6: Sal 7L **77**
Farrington Av. M20: Man 1F **106**
Farrowdale Av. OL2: Shaw 6M **45**
Farrow St. OL2: Shaw 6M **45**
(not continuous)
Farrow St. E. OL2: Shaw 6M **45**
Farr St. SK3: Stoc 8B **108**
Farsley Pk. BL5: W'ton 9F **36**
Far Wickenhall La. OL16: Miln 1C **46**
Farwood Cl. *M16: Old T* *4B* ***94***
(off Stanley Rd.)
SK10: Macc 2D **130**
Far Woodseats La. SK13: Chis 2J **111**
Fastnet St. M11: Man 1M **95**
Fatherford Cl. OL3: Dig 7N **47**
Faulkenhurst M. OL1: Chad 2G **62**
Faulkenhurst St. OL1: Chad 2G **62**
Faulkner Dr. WA15: Tim 3H **115**
Faulkner Rd. M32: Stre 7L **93**
Faulkner St. BL3: Bolt 7F **38**
M1: Man 6H **5** (1F **94**)
OL16: Roch 7D **8** (6D **28**)
Fauvel Rd. SK13: Glos 8E **100**
Faversham Brow *OL1: O'ham* *3J* ***63***
(off Sunfield Rd.)
Faversham St. M40: Man 3N **79**
Fawborough Rd. M23: Wyth 7M **105**
Fawcetts Fold BL5: W'ton 8G **37**
Fawcett St. BL2: Bolt 5J **39**
Fawley Av. SK14: Hyde 8A **98**
Fawley Gro. M22: Wyth 3C **116**
Fawns Keep SK9: Wilm 7J **123**
SK15: Stal 3H **99**
Fay Av. M9: Man 8N **61**
Fay Gdns. SK13: Had 5A **100**
Faywood Dr. SK6: Mar 1D **120**
Fearn Dene OL12: Roch 3N **27**
Fearndown Way SK10: Macc 9G **128**
Fearneyside BL3: Lit L 9N **39**
Fearnham Cl. WN7: Lei 9G **72**
Fearnhead Av. BL6: Hor 8D **20**
Fearnhead Cl. BL4: Farn 3M **57**
Fearnhead St. BL3: Bolt 8D **38**
Fearnley Way WA12: N Wil 8F **86**
Fearn St. OL10: H'ood 2H **43**
Featherstall Brook Vw. *OL15: Lit* *9L* ***15***
(off William St.)
Featherstall Ho. *OL9: O'ham* *6G* ***63***
(off Featherstall Rd. Sth.)
Featherstall Rd. OL15: Lit 9K **15**
Featherstall Rd. Nth.
OL1: O'ham 4H **63**
OL9: O'ham 4H **63**
Featherstall Rd. Nth. Rdbt.
OL9: O'ham *3H* ***63***
(off Featherstall Rd. Nth.)
Featherstall Rd. Sth.
OL9: O'ham 6G **63**
Featherstall Sq. OL15: Lit 9L **15**
Fecit La. BL0: Ram 6A **12**
OL12: Ram 6A **12**
Federation St. M4: Man 2H **5** (8F **78**)
M25: Pres 6M **59**
Feldom Rd. M23: Wyth 6M **105**
Fellbridge Cl. BL5: W'ton 2J **55**
Fellbrigg Cl. M18: Man 6A **96**
Fellfoot Cl. M28: Wors 5G **75**
Fellfoot Mdw. BL5: W'ton 1J **55**
Fell Gro. WA11: St H 9E **68**
Felling Wlk. *M14: Man* *6G* ***95***
(off Gt. Western St.)
Fellpark Rd. M23: Wyth 6N **105**
Fells Gro. M28: Walk 1N **75**
Fellside BL2: Bolt 1A **40**
OL1: O'ham 1C **8** (4J **63**)
WN1: Wig 1G **53**
Fellside Cl. BL8: G'mount 4F **24**
Fellside Gdns. OL15: Lit 7K **15**
Fellside Grn. SK15: Stal 7D **82**
Fell St. BL8: Bury 2J **41**
WN7: Lei 6D **72**
Felltop Ct. OL4: Lyd 6F **64**
Felltop Dr. SK5: Stoc 9E **96**
Felsham Cl. BL4: Farn 2K **57**
Felskirk Rd. M22: Wyth 7B **116**
Felstead WN8: Skel 1A **50**
Felsted BL1: Bolt 4N **37**
Felt Ct. M34: Dent 7G **96**
Feltham St. M12: Man 3M **95**
Felthorpe Dr. M8: Man 4E **78**
Felton Av. M22: Wyth 4C **116**
Felton Cl. BL9: Bury 7N **41**
Felton Wlk. BL1: Bolt 2F **38**
Fence Av. SK10: Macc 3J **131**
Fence Av. Ind. Est. SK10: Macc 4J **131**
Fencegate Av. SK4: Stoc 3B **108**
Fence St. SK2: Stoc 3H **119**
Fenchurch Av. M40: Man 6A **80**
Fencot Dr. M12: Man 5M **95**
Fenella St. M13: Man 5K **95**
Fenham Cl. M40: Man 5H **79**
Fenmore Av. M18: Man 6N **95**
Fennel St. M4: Man 2G **5** (8E **78**)
Fenners Cl. BL3: Bolt 9E **38**
Fenney Ct. WN8: Skel 2A **50**
Fenney St. M7: Sal 5C **78**
Fenney St. E. M7: Sal 4D **78**
Fenn St. M15: Man 3D **94**
FENNY HILL 7M 63
Fenside Rd. M22: Shar 2D **116**
Fenstock Wlk. *M40: Man* *6B* ***80***
(off Assheton Rd.)
Fentewan Wlk. SK14: Hat 6H **99**
Fenton Av. SK7: H Gro 3G **119**
Fenton M. OL11: Roch 8C **28**
Fenton St. BL8: Bury 1J **41**
M12: Man 4M **95**
OL2: Shaw 7M **45**
OL4: O'ham 5M **63**
OL11: Roch 8C **28**
Fenton Way WN2: Hin 7B **54**
Fenwick Cl. BL5: W'ton 5H **55**
Fenwick Dr. M24: Mid 2J **61**
SK4: Stoc 5K **107**
Fenwick St. M15: Man 3F **94**
OL12: Roch 8A **8** (6C **28**)
Ferdinand St. M40: Man 6J **79**
Fereday St. M28: Walk 7L **57**
Ferguson Ct. M19: Man 9L **95**
Ferguson Gdns. OL12: Roch 2D **28**
Ferguson Ri. WN5: Wig 3B **52**
Ferguson Way OL4: O'ham 2A **64**
Fernacre M33: Sale 3J **105**
Fernally St. SK14: Hyde 7B **98**
Fern Av. M41: Urm 7A **92**
FERN BANK 9F 82
Fern Bank M40: Man 3A **80**
SK15: Stal 1F **98**
Fernbank M26: Rad 3G **58**
Fern Bank Cl. SK15: Stal 1F **98**
Fern Bank Ct. *SK14: Hyde* *9B* ***98***
(off Fern Bank St.)
Fern Bank Dr. M23: Wyth 8L **105**
Fernbank Gdns. BL3: Lit L 8N **39**
Fernbank Ri. SK10: Boll 5M **129**
Fern Bank St. SK14: Hyde 9B **98**
Fernbeck Cl. BL4: Kea 4M **57**
Fernbray Av. M19: Man 4J **107**
Fernbray Rd. WN2: Hin 6C **54**
Fernbrook Wlk. *M8: Man* *3E* ***78***
(off Highshore Dr.)
Fern Cl. M24: Mid 3B **62**
M46: Ath 9M **55**
OL4: Spri 5C **64**
SK6: Mar 1C **120**
WN6: She 6L **33**
Fern Clough BL1: Bolt 5A **38**
Fernclough Rd. M9: Man 3J **79**
Fern Comn. OL2: Shaw 5M **45**
Fern Cott. OL4: Grot 6D **64**
Fern Cres. SK15: Stal 1F **98**
Ferndale *SK9: Hand* *3J* ***123***
(off Station Rd.)
SK14: Hyde 3D **98**
WN8: Skel 1A **50**
Ferndale Av. M45: Whitef 4J **59**
OL16: Roch 4G **44**
SK2: Stoc 3F **118**
Ferndale Cl. OL4: O'ham 7A **64**
Ferndale Cres. SK11: Macc 5C **130**
Ferndale Dr. WN6: App B 5H **33**
Ferndale Gdns. M19: Man 2K **107**
Ferndale Rd. M33: Sale 6H **105**
Ferndale Wlk. WN7: Lei 5D **72**
Ferndene Gdns. M20: Man 3G **107**
Ferndene Rd. M20: Man 3G **107**
M25: Pres 4B **60**
M45: Whitef 4B **60**
Ferndown Av. OL9: Chad 6F **62**
SK7: H Gro 6G **118**
Ferndown Dr. M44: Irl 6H **91**
Ferndown Rd. BL2: Bolt 1M **39**
M23: Wyth 8K **105**
Ferney Fld. Rd. OL9: Chad 4D **62**
Ferngate Dr. M20: Man 2G **107**
FERN GROVE 9B 26
Ferngrove BL9: Bury 8A **26**
Ferngrove East BL9: Bury 1B **42**
FERNHILL 9L 25
Fernhill OL4: Gras 5H **65**
OL4: O'ham 7A **64**
SK6: Mel 1E **120**
Fernhill Av. BL3: Bolt 8B **38**
Fernhill Caravan Pk. BL9: Bury 9L **25**
Fernhill Cl. SK13: Glos 6F **100**
Fernhill Dr. M18: Man 5N **95**
FERNHILL GATE 9B 38
Fern Hill La. OL12: Roch 2M **27**
Fernhills BL7: Eger 3F **22**
Fernhill St. BL9: Bury 1M **41**
Fernholme Ct. OL8: O'ham 7G **63**
Fern Ho. M23: Wyth 3N **115**
Fernhurst Cl. WN3: I Mak 5J **53**
Fernhurst Gro. *BL1: Bolt* *3F* ***38***
(off Lindfield Dr.)
Fernhurst Rd. M20: Man 3H **107**
Fernhurst St. OL1: Chad 2G **62**
Fernie St. M4: Man 7F **78**
Fernilee Cl. *SK22: N Mil* *6M* ***121***
(off Winhill Rd.)
Fern Isle Cl. OL12: Whitw 8N **13**
Fern Lea SK14: Holl 3N **99**
Fernlea SK4: Stoc 3A **108**
SK8: H Grn 6G **117**
WA15: Hale 6F **114**
Fernlea Av. OL1: Chad 2G **62**
Fernlea Cl. OL12: Roch 3N **27**
SK13: Had 5A **100**
Fernlea Cres. M27: Swin 3E **76**
Fern Lea Dr. SK11: Macc 4E **130**
Fernleaf St. M14: Man 5F **94**
Fern Lea Gro. M38: Lit H 7G **56**
Fernlea Gro. WN4: Gars 5A **70**
Fernlea Lodge *BL4: Farn* *4M* ***57***
(off Longcauseway)
Fernleigh *BL6: Hor* *3F* ***36***
(off Chorley New Rd.)
Fernleigh Av. M19: Man 8A **96**
Fernleigh Dr. M16: Old T 4B **94**
Fernley Av. M34: Dent 7L **97**

Fernley Rd. SK2: Stoc 1F 118
Fern Lodge Dr. OL6: A Lyne 5A 82
Ferns, The SK14: Hyde 4D 98
Ferns Gro. BL1: Bolt 5C 38
Fernside M26: Rad 4B 58
Fernside Av. M20: Man 3J 107
Fernside Ct. M26: Rad 5C 58
Fernside Gro. M28: Walk 7M 57
WN3: Wins 1A 70
Fernside Way OL12: Roch 3M 27
Fernstead BL3: Bolt 6D 38
Fernstone Cl. BL6: Hor 1C 36
Fern St. BL0: Ram 7K 11
(not continuous)
BL3: Bolt 6D 38
BL4: Farn 2M 57
BL9: Bury 1M 41
M4: Man 6F 78
OL8: O'ham 6H 63
OL9: Chad 3E 62
OL11: Roch 9A 8 (7B 28)
OL12: W'le 8G 15
Fernthorpe Av. OL3: Upp 2M 65
Fern Vw. WA15: Tim 2L 115
Fernview Dr. BL0: Ram 4G 25
Fernwood SK6: Mar B 9E 110
Fernwood Av. M18: Man 6B 96
Fernwood Gro. SK9: Wilm 6H 123
Ferrand Lodge OL15: Lit 7N 15
Ferrand Rd. OL15: Lit 8M 15
Ferrer St. WN4: A Mak 4C 70
Ferring Wlk. OL9: Chad 5F 62
Ferris St. M11: Man 1B 96
Ferrous Way M44: Irl 2G 102
Ferryhill Rd. M44: Irl 7H 91
Ferrymasters Way M44: Irl 8H 91
Ferry Rd. M44: Irl 7H 91
(not continuous)
Ferry St. M11: Man 1K 95
Festival Dr. SK10: O Ald 7L 127
Festival Village *M17: Urm* *3E 92*
(within The Trafford Cen.)
Fettler Cl. M27: Swin 4F 76
Feversham Cl. M30: Ecc 6F 76
Fewston Cl. BL1: Bolt 8F 22
Fiddick Ct. *M6: Sal* *8M 77*
(off Newport St.)
Fiddlers La. M44: Irl 6J 91
Field Bank Gro. M19: Man 8A 96
Fieldbank Rd. SK11: Macc 4F 130
Fieldbrook Wlk. BL5: W'ton 2J 55
Field Cl. SK6: Mar 2A 120
SK7: Bram 2B 124
SK10: Boll 6K 129
Fieldcroft OL11: Roch 6N 27
Fielden Av. M21: Cho H 8A 94
Fielden Ct. M21: Cho H 3C 106
FIELDEN PARK 4E 106
Fielden Rd. M20: Man 4E 106
Fielden St. OL15: Lit 3J 29
(Lit. Clegg Rd.)
OL15: Lit *5A 16*
(off Todmorden Rd.)
Fielders Way M27: Clif 7E 58
Fieldfare Av. M40: Man 6N 79
Fieldfare Cl. WA3: Low 1N 87
Fieldfare Way OL7: A Lyne 3L 81
Fieldhead Av. BL8: Bury 2G 40
M29: Ast 5C 74
OL11: Roch 6M 27
Fieldhead M. SK9: Wilm 6K 123
Fieldhead Rd. SK9: Wilm 6K 123
Fieldhouse Ind. Est. OL12: Roch 3D 28
Fieldhouse La. SK6: Mar 1D 120
Fieldhouse Rd. OL12: Roch 3D 28
Fielding Av. SK12: Poy 4J 125
Fielding Ind. Est. M34: Dent 7G 97
Fielding Pl. PR6: Adl 5L 19
Fieldings Cl. WN5: Wig 6A 52
Fielding St. M24: Mid 1M 61
(not continuous)
M30: Ecc 9C 76
Fieldings Wharf *M43: Droy* *1E 96*
(off Market St.)
Field La. OL6: A Lyne 5A 82
Field Pl. *M20: Man* *5G 106*
(off Crossway)
Field Rd. M33: Sale 2E 104
OL16: Roch 6H 29
Field Rose Ct. PR6: Adl 5J 19
Fields, The SK6: Rom 7L 109
WN2: Asp 8M 35
WN6: Stan 4C 34
Fields Cres. SK14: Holl 3N 99
Fieldsend Cl. SK15: Stal 1G 99
Fieldsend Dr. WN7: Lei 1E 88
Fields End Fold M30: Ecc 5K 91
Fields Farm Cl. SK14: Hat 7G 98
Fields Farm Rd. SK14: Hat 8F 98
Fields Farm Wlk. *SK14: Hat* *7G 98*
(off Fields Farm Rd.)
Fields Gro. SK14: Holl 4N 99
Field Side Cl. WA16: Mob 4N 133
Fieldside Cl. SK7: Bram 2B 124
Fields New Rd. OL9: Chad 7E 62
Field St. M6: Sal 8M 77
M18: Man 3C 96
M35: Fail 3C 80
M43: Droy 1D 96
OL11: Roch 9E 28
SK6: Bred 5K 109
SK14: Hyde 4A 98
WN2: Hin 7A 54
WN3: I Mak 7J 53
WN6: Wig 3E 52
Fieldsway OL8: O'ham 9J 63
Field Va. Dr. SK5: Stoc 8E 96
Fieldvale Rd. M33: Sale 7E 104
Fieldview WN8: Uph 4E 50
Field Vw. Dr. SK11: Macc 7J 131
Field Vw. Wlk. M16: Man 7E 94
Field Wlk. M31: Part 5F 102
WA15: Hale 4H 115
Fieldway OL16: Roch 1F 44
WN2: P Bri 9L 53
Fife Av. OL9: Chad 7D 62
Fifield Cl. OL8: O'ham 8L 63
Fifth Av. BL1: Bolt 5C 38
BL3: Lit L 8N 39
BL9: Bury 9C 26
M11: Man 8A 80
M17: T Pk 4J 93
OL8: O'ham 9G 63
SK16: Duk 1L 97
Fifth St. BL1: Bolt 9A 22
M17: T Pk 4J 93
Filbert St. OL1: O'ham 2N 63
Filby Wlk. M40: Man 6K 79
Fildes St. M24: Mid 4B 62
Filey Av. M16: Whall R 7C 94
M41: Urm 5A 92
Filey Dr. M6: Sal 4K 77
Filey Rd. M14: Man 9J 95
SK2: Stoc 9G 109
Filey St. OL16: Roch 2G 28
Filleigh WA14: Bow 5A 114
Filton Av. BL3: Bolt 7E 38
Filton Wlk. *M9: Man* *4H 79*
(off Westmere Dr.)
Finance St. OL15: Lit 9J 15
Finborough Cl. M16: Whall R 5D 94
Finchale Dr. WA15: Hale 6H 115
Finch Av. BL4: Farn 4G 57
Finchcroft OL1: O'ham 1B 8 (4J 63)
Finchdale Gdns. WA3: Low 1D 88
Finch La. WN6: App B 3F 32
Finchley Av. M40: Man 6A 80
Finchley Cl. BL8: Bury 3H 41
Finchley Cres. WN2: Wig 1K 53
Finchley Gro. M40: Man 1M 79
Finchley Rd. M14: Man 9G 95
WA15: Hale 5E 6 (4E 114)
Finch Mill Av. WN6: App B 5H 33
Finchwood Rd. M22: Shar 2D 116
Findlay Cl. WA12: N Wil 7E 86
(not continuous)
Findlay St. WN7: Lei 5G 72
Findon WN8: Skel 2A 50
Findon Rd. M23: Wyth 1N 115
Finger Post BL3: Lit L 8A 40
Finghall Rd. M41: Urm 7B 92
Finland Rd. SK3: Stoc 9B 108
Finlan Rd. M24: Mid 7B 44
Finlay Ct. WN5: Wig 3B 52
Finlay St. BL4: Farn 3L 57
Finlow Hill La.
SK10: N Ald, O Ald 7J 127
Finney Cl. SK9: Wilm 4H 123
Finney Dr. M21: Cho H 1N 105
SK9: Wilm 4H 123
FINNEY GREEN 5J 123
Finney Gro. WA11: Hay 3B 86
Finney La. SK8: H Grn 7F 116
Finney St. BL3: Bolt 8G 38
Finningley Rd. M9: Man 5G 60
Finny Bank Rd. M33: Sale 2G 104
Finsbury Av. M40: Man 6A 80
Finsbury Cl. OL8: O'ham 7M 63
Finsbury Ct. BL1: Bolt 1J 39
Finsbury Rd. SK5: Stoc 9C 96
Finsbury St. OL11: Roch 8B 28
Finsbury Way SK9: Hand 4K 123
Finstock Cl. M30: Ecc 9B 76
Fintry Gro. M30: Ecc 9D 76
Fir Av. SK7: Bram 7C 118
Firbank M25: Pres 7B 60
Firbank Cl. OL7: A Lyne 8K 81
Firbank Rd. M23: Wyth 2N 115
OL2: O'ham 6H 45
WN3: Wig 8E 52
Firbarn Cl. OL16: Roch 6H 29
Firbeck WN8: Skel 2A 50
Firbeck Dr. M4: Man 8J 79
Fir Cl. SK7: H Gro 4J 119
SK12: Poy 3J 125
Fir Ct. SK10: Macc 3D 130
Fircroft WN6: Stan 2L 33
Fircroft Ct. SK3: Stoc 3D 118
Fircroft Rd. OL8: O'ham 9L 63
Firdale Av. M40: Man 1C 80
Firdale Wlk. OL9: Chad 4G 62
Firdon Wlk. *M9: Man* *3K 79*
(off Nethervale Dr.)
Firecrest Cl. M28: Wors 2J 75
Firefly Cl. M3: Sal 4B 4
Fire Station Sq. M5: Sal 8B 78
Fire Station Yd.
OL11: Roch 9D 8 (7D 28)
Firethorn Av. M19: Man 2L 107
Firethorn Cl. BL5: W'ton 1H 55
Firethorn Dr. SK14: Hyde 7D 98
Firethorn Wlk. *M33: Sale* *3C 104*
(off Lavender Cl.)
Firfield Gro. M28: Walk 8N 57
FIRGROVE 6H 29
Fir Gro. M19: Man 8M 95
OL9: Chad 3F 62
SK11: Macc 7G 131
WN6: Wig 9D 34
Firgrove Av. OL16: Roch 5H 29
Firgrove Bus. Pk. OL16: Roch 4H 29
Firgrove Gdns. OL16: Roch 5H 29
Fir La. OL2: O'ham 6H 45
Fir Rd. BL4: Farn 3J 57
M27: Swin 4E 76
M34: Dent 6L 97
SK6: Mar 2B 120
SK7: Bram 6D 118
Firs, The SK9: Wilm 9F 122
WA14: Bow 5B 114
Firs Av. M16: Old T 7A 94
M35: Fail 3C 80
OL6: A Lyne 5M 81
Firsby Av. SK6: Bred 4K 109
Firsby St. *M19: Man* *8M 95*
(off Barlow Rd.)
Firs Cl. SK8: Gat 4F 116
Firs Cotts. WN2: Asp 2A 54
Firsdale Ind. Est. WN7: Lei 4E 72
Firs Gro. SK8: Gat 3F 116
FIRS LANE 5F 72
Firs La. WN7: Lei 5E 72
Firs Pk. Cres. WN2: Asp 2N 53
Firs Rd. BL5: O Hul 5A 56
M33: Sale 4D 104
SK8: Gat 4F 116
First Av. BL3: Lit L 8A 40
BL8: Tot 7F 24
M11: Man 8B 80
M17: T Pk 4K 93
M27: Swin 5D 76
M29: Ast 6D 74
M46: Ath 7M 55
OL8: O'ham 9H 63
SK12: Poy 5H 125
SK15: C'ook 5H 83
WN2: Hin 6N 53
WN6: Wig 1D 52
Fir St. BL0: Ram 7K 11
BL1: Bolt 2G 38
BL9: Bury 2N 41
M6: Sal 8M 77
M16: Old T *5B 94*
(off Worthington St.)
M26: Rad 1H 59
M30: Ecc 9D 76
M35: Fail 3C 80
M40: Man 6J 79
M44: Cad 2D 102
OL2: O'ham 6H 45
OL10: H'ood 3K 43
SK4: Stoc 1J 9 (6C 108)
First St. BL1: Bolt 9A 22
M15: Man 8F 4 (2E 94)
WN2: Bam 3H 71
Firsway M33: Sale 5C 104
WN7: Lei 5D 72
FIRSWOOD 6N 93
Firswood Dr. M27: Swin 4E 76
OL2: O'ham 6G 44
SK14: Hyde 6D 98
Firswood Mt. SK8: Gat 3F 116
Firswood Stop (Metro) 7A 94
Firth Cl. M7: Sal 4C 78
Firth Rd. M20: Man 3H 107
Firth St. OL1: O'ham 3D 8 (5K 63)
Fir Tree Av. M28: Wors 5J 75
OL8: O'ham 9K 63
WA3: Low 1B 88
WA16: Knut 8J 133
Firtree Av. M33: Sale 4C 104
Fir Tree Cl. SK16: Duk 1C 98
WA11: K Mos 3D 68
WN8: Skel 4B 50
Firtree Cl. PR7: Chor 2F 18
Fir Tree Cres. SK16: Duk 1C 98
WN3: I Mak 8J 53
Fir Tree Dr. SK14: Hyde 4B 98
WN3: I Mak 8J 53
Fir Tree La. SK16: Duk 2C 98
WA5: Burt 9D 86
Fir Tree St. WN3: I Mak 7J 53
Fir Tree Wlk. WA3: Low 1B 88
Fir Tree Way *BL6: Hor* *3G 37*
(off Claypool Rd.)
Firvale Av. SK8: H Grn 6G 116
Firvale Cl. WN7: Lei 5E 72
Firwood WN8: Skel 9B 32
Firwood Av. BL4: Farn 4K 57
M41: Urm 7G 93
(not continuous)
Firwood Cl. SK2: Stoc 8G 108
Firwood Ct. M30: Ecc 7E 76
Firwood Cres. M26: Rad 2H 59
FIRWOOD FOLD 1K 39
Firwood Fold BL2: Bolt 1K 39
Firwood Gro. BL2: Bolt 2J 39
WN4: A Mak 8D 70
Firwood Ind. Est. BL2: Bolt 1K 39
Firwood La. BL2: Bolt 1J 39
(not continuous)
Firwood Pk. OL9: Chad 3C 62
Firwood Stables *BL2: Bolt* *1K 39*
(off Ashdown Dr.)
Fiscal Way M35: Fail 3C 80
Fishbourne Sq. *M14: Man* *6H 95*
(off Claremont Rd.)
Fishbrook Ind. Est. BL4: Kea 4N 57
Fisher Av. WN2: Abr 3M 71
Fisher Cl. WN3: Wig 5C 52
Fisher Dr. WN5: Orr 5J 51
Fisherfield OL12: Roch 4L 27
Fishermans Wharf BL3: Bolt 7G 38
Fishermore Rd. M41: Urm 7M 91
Fisher St. OL1: O'ham 3K 63
FISHPOOL 4M 41
Fish Rake La. BB4: Rawt 1K 11
Fishwicks Ind. Est. WA11: Hay 1C 86
Fishwick St. OL16: Roch 9F 8 (7E 28)
Fistral Av. SK8: H Grn 7H 117
Fistral Cres. SK15: Stal 7G 82
Fitchfield Wlk. *M28: Walk* *8L 57*
(off Malvern Gro.)
Fit City
Broughton Cen. 5C 78
Broughton Pool 4C 78
Cadishead 3E 102
Clarendon 8N 77
Eccles *9F 76*
(off Barton La.)
Irlam 8H 91
Ordsall 2N 93
Pendlebury 1E 76
Worsley 9K 57
Fitness 4 All 6K 129
Fitness First
Manchester Central 6G 4
Manchester, Victoria Av. E.
8A 62
Manchester, Wall Way 5C 96
Rochdale 9C 28
Whitefield 2N 59
Fitton Av. M21: Cho H 2A 106
Fitton Cres. M27: Clif 8F 58
FITTON HILL 8L 63
Fitton Hill Rd. OL8: O'ham 7L 63
Fitton Hill Shop. Pct.
OL8: O'ham 9L 63
Fitton St. OL2: O'ham 8K 45
OL2: Shaw 5K 45
OL16: Roch 5F 8 (5E 28)
Fitzadam St. WN1: Wig 7H 9 (3E 52)
Fitzalan St. SK13: Glos 8E 100
Fitz Cl. SK10: Macc 1H 131
Fitz Cres. SK10: Macc 1H 131
Fitzgeorge St. M40: Man 5H 79
Fitzgerald Cl. M25: Pres 9M 59
Fitzgerald Ct. M34: Dent 9L 97
Fitzgerald Way *M6: Sal* *7M 77*
(off Salford Shop. City)
Fitzhugh St. BL1: Bolt 8H 23
Fitzroy St. M43: Droy 1F 96
OL7: A Lyne 1K 97
SK15: Mill 6G 83
Fitzwarren Ct. M6: Sal 8M 77
Fitzwarren St. M6: Sal 7M 77
Fitzwilliam Av. SK11: Sut E 9K 131
Fitzwilliam Ct. M14: Man 5J 95
Fitzwilliam St. M7: Sal 6C 78
Five Ashes Cotts. SK10: Kerr 8M 129
Five Fold Ind. Pk.
OL9: O'ham 4A 8 (5H 63)
Five Quarters M26: Rad 7E 40
Fiveways M43: Droy 8D 80
Fiveways Pde. SK7: H Gro 7J 119
Flagcroft Dr. M23: Wyth 2A 116
Flaggwood Av. SK6: Mar 9A 110
Flagship Av. *M5: Sal* *1A 94*
(off St Joseph's Dr.)
Flake La. OL2: O'ham 7H 45
Flamborough Wlk. *M14: Man* *5G 95*
(off Gateshead Cl.)
Flamingo Cl. M12: Man 3M 95
Flamingo Vs. *M44: Irl* *6H 91*
(off Robin Dr.)
Flamstead WN8: Skel 2A 50
Flamstead Av. M23: Wyth 1L 115
Flannel St. OL12: Roch 5E 28
Flapper Fold La. M46: Ath 7L 55
Flash *SK15: C'ook* *3J 83*
(off Carisbrook Rd.)
Flash Cotts. OL4: O'ham 6D 64
Flashfields M25: Pres 1M 77
Flash La. SK10: Boll 6G 129
Flash St. M40: Man 4A 80
Flatley Cl. M15: Man 3F 94
Flavian Wlk. *M11: Man* *1N 95*
(off Herne St.)
Flaxcroft Rd. M22: Wyth 4A 116
Flaxfield Av. SK15: Stal 8G 83
Flaxman Ri. OL1: O'ham 8N 45
Flaxpool Cl. M16: Whall R 5D 94
(not continuous)
Flax St. BL0: Ram 1G 25
M3: Sal 1C 4 (7C 78)
Flaxton WN8: Skel 2A 50
Flaxwood Wlk. M22: Wyth 4A 116
Fleece St. *OL4: O'ham* *4M 63*
(off Honduras St.)
OL16: Roch 7C 8 (6D 28)
Fleeson St. M14: Man 6H 95
Fleet St. BL6: Hor 1F 36
M18: Man 3D 96
OL4: O'ham 4N 63
OL6: A Lyne 9B 6 (8L 81)
(not continuous)
OL11: Roch 4B 44
SK14: Hyde 5B 98
WN5: Wig 5M 51
Fleetwood Dr. WA12: N Wil 5E 86
Fleetwood Rd. M28: Walk 8H 57
Fleming Cl. OL12: Roch 9H 15
Fleming Dr. WN4: A Mak 6G 70
Fleming Pl. OL9: O'ham 3A 8 (5H 63)
Fleming Rd. M22: Wyth 5C 116
Flemish Rd. M34: Dent 7M 97
Fletcher Av. M27: Clif 8G 58
M46: Ath 6M 55
FLETCHER BANK 8J 11
Fletcher Cl. OL9: O'ham 3A 8 (5H 63)
OL10: H'ood 2J 43
Fletcher Ct. *M26: Rad* *1H 59*
(off New Rd.)
M26: Rad 3B 58
(Stoneclough Ri.)
WA16: Knut 7E 132
Fletcher Dr. SK12: Dis 9C 120
WA14: Bow 6C 114
FLETCHER FOLD 6M 41
Fletcher Fold BL9: Bury 6M 41
Fletcher Fold Rd. BL9: Bury 6M 41
Fletcher Moss Botanical Gdns.
7G 106
Fletchers La. WA13: Lym 3A 112
Fletchers Pas. OL15: Lit 8L 15
Fletcher's Rd. OL15: Lit 2J 29
Fletchers Sq. *OL15: Lit* *8M 15*
(off Sutcliffe St.)
Fletcher St. BL3: Bolt 7F 38
BL3: Lit L 9B 40
BL4: Farn 3L 57
BL9: Bury 7N 7 (2N 41)
M26: Rad 8J 41
M40: Man 5L 79
M46: Ath 8L 55
OL6: A Lyne 7E 6 (7N 81)
OL11: Roch 8E 28
OL15: Lit 8L 15
SK1: Stoc 2L 9 (7D 108)
Fletsand Rd. SK9: Wilm 8H 123
Fletton Cl. OL12: Roch 3C 28
Fletton M. OL12: Roch 3C 28
Flexbury Wlk. *M40: Man* *6B 80*
(off Eastmoor Dr.)
Flimby WN8: Skel 1B 50
Flint Cl. M11: Man 8N 79
SK7: H Gro 6G 119
Flint Gro. M44: Cad 2D 102
Flint Hill Way OL8: O'ham 7J 63
Flint St. M43: Droy 8F 80
OL1: O'ham 3N 63
SK3: Stoc 8C 108
SK10: Macc 4J 131
Flitcroft Ct. BL3: Bolt 8G 38
Flitcroft St. OL4: O'ham 7N 63
FLIXTON 8N 91
Flixton Golf Course 9A 92
Flixton Park & Gardens 8N 91
Flixton Rd. M13: Man 4J 95
M31: C'ton 9M 91
M41: Urm 8N 91
(not continuous)
Flixton Station (Rail) 8N 91
Floatshall Rd. M23: Wyth 1M 115
Floats Rd. M23: Wyth 1L 115
Flockton Av. WN6: Stan 8A 34
Flockton Ct. *BL6: Hor* *9D 20*
(off High St.)
Flora Dr. M7: Sal 6C 78
Floral Ct. M7: Sal 4C 78
Flora St. BL3: Bolt 8E 38
M9: Man 8H 61
OL1: O'ham 1C 8 (4J 63)
WN4: A Mak 8E 70
Flordon WN8: Skel 1B 50
Florence Av. BL1: Bolt 9G 22
Florence Ct. SK3: Stoc 1N 117
Florence Pk. Ct. M20: Man 4H 107
Florence St. BL3: Bolt 8E 38
M30: Ecc 9B 76
M33: Sale 2H 105
M35: Fail 2D 80
M43: Droy 1F 96
OL16: Roch 7F 28
SK4: Stoc 1K 9 (6C 108)
WN1: Wig 3H 53
Florence Way SK14: Holl 4N 99
Florian Ho. OL1: O'ham 1D 8
Florida St. OL8: O'ham 6J 63
Florin Gdns. M6: Sal 7M 77
Florist St. SK3: Stoc 9C 108
Flower Hill La. OL12: W'le 8E 14
Flowery Bank OL8: O'ham 7M 63
FLOWERY FIELD 4A 98
Flowery Fld. SK14: Hyde 3E 98
Flowery Fld. Grn. SK14: Hyde 5N 97
Flowery Fld. Ind. Pk.
SK14: Hyde 4A 98
Flowery Field Station (Rail) 4A 98
Floyd Av. M21: Cho H 2B 106
Floyer Rd. M9: Man 7K 61
Flying Flds. Dr. SK11: Macc 7E 130
Flynn Ct. *M6: Sal* *6L 77*
(off Monroe Cl.)
Foden La. SK7: W'ford 3B 124
SK9: A Edg 3A 126
Foden St. SK10: Macc 3H 131
Foden Wlk. SK9: Wilm 4J 123
FOGGBROOK 1K 119
Foggbrook Cl. SK2: Stoc 1K 119
Fogg La. BL3: Bolt 8L 39
Fog La. M19: Man 4J 107
M20: Man 4G 106
Fog Lane Pk. 4H 107
Fold, The M9: Man 8J 61
M41: Urm 6A 92
OL2: O'ham 8L 45
SK10: P'bury 5E 128
SK15: C'ook 4J 83
Fold Av. M43: Droy 8F 80
Fold Cres. SK15: C'ook 4J 83
Fold Gdns. OL12: Roch 2N 27
Fold Grn. OL9: Chad 6E 62
FOLD HEAD 6N 13
Fold M. BL9: Bury 7M 25
SK7: H Gro 4J 119
Fold Rd. M26: Rad 4C 58
Folds, The BL6: Bla 1M 35
Folds Point BL1: Bolt 1L 7
Folds Rd. BL1: Bolt 1L 7 (4G 39)
Fold St. BL1: Bolt 3L 7 (5G 39)
BL9: Bury 7H 7 (2K 41)
M40: Man 2M 79
OL10: H'ood 1K 43
WA3: Gol 9K 71
Fold Vw. BL7: Eger 4F 22
OL8: O'ham 9L 63
Fold Way OL7: A Lyne 7K 81
Foleshill Av. M9: Man 3J 79
Foley Gdns. OL10: H'ood 5K 43
Foley St. WN2: Hin 6N 53
Foley Wlk. M22: Wyth 7D 116
Foliage Cres. SK5: Stoc 4F 108
Foliage Gdns. SK5: Stoc 3G 108
Foliage Rd. SK5: Stoc 4F 108
Folkestone Cl. SK10: Macc 2F 130
Folkestone Rd. M11: Man 8B 80
Folkestone Rd. E. M11: Man 8B 80
Folkestone Rd. W. M11: Man 8A 80
Follows St. M18: Man 3B 96
Folly La. M27: Swin 5D 76
Folly Vw. M27: Swin 4D 76
Folly Wlk. OL12: Roch 4D 28
Fonthill Gro. M33: Sale 7F 104
Fontwell Cl. M16: Old T 6B 94
WN6: Stan 3C 34
Fontwell La. OL1: O'ham 2L 63
Fontwell Rd. BL3: Lit L 1A 58
Fontwell Wlk. M40: Man 9B 62
Footman Cl. M29: Ast 3C 74
Foot Mill Cres. OL12: Roch 3B 28
Foot O' Th' Rake *BL0: Ram* *8H 11*
(off Milton St.)
Foot Wood Cres. OL12: Roch 3B 28
Forber Cres. M18: Man 6B 96
Forbes Cl. M33: Sale 6K 105
SK1: Stoc 8F 108
WN2: Hin 4A 54
Forbes Pk. SK7: Bram 8B 118
Forbes Rd. SK1: Stoc 7F 108
Forbes St. SK6: Bred 4K 109
Fordbank Rd. M20: Man 6F 106
Forde Cl. M24: Mid 1M 61
Ford Gdns. OL11: Roch 7N 27
Ford Gro. SK14: Mot 5K 99
Fordham Gro. BL1: Bolt 4D 38
Fordland Cl. WA3: Low 9A 72
Ford La. M6: Sal 6N 77
M20: Man 6F 106
M22: Nor 7D 106

Ford Lodge M20: Man ... 6G 106
Fordoe La. OL12: Roch ... 1H 27
Ford's La. SK7: Bram ... 9B 118
Ford St. M3: Sal ... 3C 4 (8C 78)
M12: Man ... 2J 95
M26: Rad ... 3A 58
SK3: Stoc ... 3G 9 (7B 108)
SK16: Duk ... 3N 97
Ford Way SK14: Mot ... 5K 99
(off Hyde Rd.)
Fordyce Way WN2: I Mak ... 3K 53
Forebay Dr. M44: Irl ... 8J 91
Foreland Cl. M40: Man ... 5J 79
Forest Av. WN6: Wig ... 9B 34
Forest Cl. SK16: Duk ... 3N 97
Forest Ct. M41: Urm ... 6L 91
Forest Dr. BL5: W'ton ... 3J 55
M33: Sale ... 6E 104
SK11: Lang ... 8N 131
WA15: Tim ... 1F 114
WN6: Stan ... 2L 33
WN8: Skel ... 9A 32
Forester Av. WA16: Knut ... 6J 133
Forester Dr. SK15: Stal ... 9D 82
Forester Hill Av. BL3: Bolt ... 9G 38
(Meredith St.)
BL3: Bolt ... 9H 39
(Smedley Av.)
Forester Hill Cl. BL3: Bolt ... 9G 39
Foresters Grn. M17: T Pk ... 3L 93
(off Wharfside Way)
Forest Fold WN6: She ... 6J 33
Forest Gdns. M31: Part ... 5E 102
Forest Ho. SK10: Macc ... 2K 131
Forest Range M19: Man ... 8M 95
Forest Rd. BL1: Bolt ... 1C 38
Forest St. M30: Ecc ... 6A 76
OL6: A Lyne ... 5F 6 (6N 81)
OL8: O'ham ... 9K 63
Forest Vw. OL12: Roch ... 3B 28
Forest Way BL7: Bro X ... 7K 23
Forfar St. BL1: Bolt ... 8F 22
Forge Ind. Est.
OL4: O'ham ... 4M 63
Forge St. OL4: O'ham ... 4M 63
WN1: I Mak ... 4H 53
Formby Av. M21: Cho H ... 1C 106
M46: Ath ... 7M 55
Formby Dr. SK8: H Grn ... 7G 116
Formby Rd. M6: Sal ... 5L 77
Forres Gro. WN4: Gars ... 6A 70
Forrester Dr. OL2: Shaw ... 4A 46
Forrester Ho. M12: Man ... 3M 95
(off Blackwin St.)
Forresters Cl. WN2: B'haw ... 2A 72
Forrester St. M28: Wors ... 2A 76
Forrest Rd. M34: Dent ... 8M 97
Forshaw Av. M18: Man ... 3D 96
Forshaw's La. WA5: Burt ... 9B 86
Forshaw St. M34: Dent ... 5H 97
FORSTERS GREEN ... 9B 32
Forsters Grn. Rd.
WN8: Skel ... 9B 32
Forster St. WA3: Gol ... 9K 71
Forston Wlk. M8: Man ... 4G 78
Forsythia Wlk. M31: Part ... 6F 102
(off Blossom Rd.)
Forsyth St. OL12: Roch ... 3K 27
Fortescue Rd. SK2: Stoc ... 9H 109
Forth Pl. M26: Rad ... 7F 40
Forth Rd. M26: Rad ... 7F 40
Forth St. WN7: Lei ... 6L 73
Forton Av. BL2: Bolt ... 5M 39
Forton Rd. WN3: Wig ... 9C 52
Fortran Cl. M5: Sal ... 9N 77
Fort Rd. M25: Pres ... 9C 60
Fortrose Av. M9: Man ... 8G 60
Fortuna Gro. M19: Man ... 9L 95
Fortune St. BL3: Bolt ... 7J 39
Fortyacre Dr. SK6: Bred ... 5J 109
Forum Centre, The ... 4B 116
Forum Gro. M7: Sal ... 5D 78
Forum Sq. M22: Wyth ... 4C 116
(off Ainley Rd.)
Fosbrook Av. M20: Man ... 4H 107
Foscarn Dr. M23: Wyth ... 2A 116
Fossgill Av. BL2: Bolt ... 8K 23
Foster Av. WN3: I Mak ... 5H 53
Foster Ct. BL9: Bury ... 9C 26
Foster La. BL2: Bolt ... 3N 39
(not continuous)
Fosters Bldgs. WN6: Wig ... 3E 52
Fosters Island WN8: Skel ... 9A 32
Foster St. M5: Sal ... 9K 77
M26: Rad ... 9F 40
M34: Dent ... 6K 97
OL4: O'ham ... 4N 63
WN6: Wig ... 2D 52
Foster Ter. BL1: Bolt ... 3F 38
(off Barnwood Dr.)
Fotherby Dr. M9: Man ... 8J 61
Fotherby Pl. WN3: Wig ... 8D 52
Fothergill Grange SK8: Chea H ... 7M 117
Foulds Av. BL8: Bury ... 2H 41
Foundry, The M1: Man ... 8G 5
Foundry Ct. SK11: Macc ... 4G 131
(off Pinfold St.)
SK22: N Mil ... 8M 121
(off Torr Top St.)
Foundry La. M4: Man ... 3K 5 (8G 78)
WN3: Wig ... 7A 52
Foundry St. BL3: Bolt ... 7G 39
BL3: Lit L ... 9A 40
BL9: Bury ... 8M 7 (2M 41)
M26: Rad ... 9G 41
OL8: O'ham ... 4B 8 (5J 63)
OL10: H'ood ... 2H 43
SK10: Boll ... 5M 129
SK16: Duk ... 1N 97
(not continuous)
WA12: N Wil ... 6E 86
WN2: Hin ... 6N 53
WN7: Lei ... 6K 73
Fountain Av. WA15: Hale ... 5H 115
Fountain Cl. SK12: Poy ... 2H 125
Fountain Pk. BL5: W'ton ... 6F 54
Fountain Pl. M45: Whitef ... 4M 59
SK12: Poy ... 2H 125
(off Chester Rd.)
Fountains Av. BL2: Bolt ... 3K 39
WA11: Hay ... 2C 86
Fountains Cl. M29: Ast ... 3D 74
Fountain Sq. M27: Swin ... 2F 76
(off Swinton Shop. Cen.)
SK12: Dis ... 9G 120
(off Market St.)
Fountains Rd. M32: Stre ... 6F 92
SK7: Bram ... 9N 117
SK8: Chea H ... 9N 117
Fountain St. BL8: Bury ... 3J 41
BL9: Bury ... 2N 41
M2: Man ... 5H 5 (9F 78)
M24: Mid ... 3L 61
M30: Ecc ... 1D 92
OL1: O'ham ... 2C 8 (4J 63)
OL6: A Lyne ... 6B 82
SK10: Macc ... 4J 131
SK14: Hyde ... 6C 98
Fountain St. Nth.
BL9: Bury ... 7N 7 (2N 41)
Fountains Wlk. OL9: Chad ... 6E 62
SK16: Duk ... 3N 97
WA3: Low ... 1D 88
Fouracres Rd. M23: Wyth ... 2M 115
FOUR GATES ... 7E 36
FOUR LANE ENDS ... 8D 24
FOURLANE ENDS ... 6M 125
Four Lanes SK14: Mot ... 5K 99
Four Lanes Way OL11: Roch ... 3H 27
Fourmarts Rd. WN5: Wig ... 1N 51
Four Stalls End OL15: Lit ... 1L 29
Fourteen Mdws. Rd. WN3: Wig ... 5E 52
Fourth Av. BL1: Bolt ... 5C 38
BL3: Lit L ... 8N 39
BL9: Bury ... 9B 26
M11: Man ... 7A 80
M17: T Pk ... 4J 93
M27: Swin ... 5D 76
OL8: O'ham ... 1G 81
OL9: Chad ... 6E 62
SK15: C'ook ... 4H 83
Fourth St. BL1: Bolt ... 9A 22
WN2: Bam ... 3J 71
Fourways M17: T Pk ... 3G 93
Fourways Wlk. M40: Man ... 9N 61
Four Yards M2: Man ... 5G 4 (9E 78)
Fovant Cres. SK5: Stoc ... 8C 96
Fowey Cl. SK10: Macc ... 3B 130
Fowey Wlk. M23: Wyth ... 2N 115
SK14: Hat ... 6H 99
Fowler Av. M18: Man ... 2D 96
Fowler Cl. WN1: Wig ... 8N 9 (3H 53)
Fowler Ind. Est. BL6: Hor ... 2E 36
Fowler St. OL8: O'ham ... 8G 62
SK10: Macc ... 3H 131
FOWLEY COMMON ... 5K 89
Fowley Comn. La. WA3: Cul ... 4K 89
Fownhope Av. M33: Sale ... 5F 104
Fownhope Rd. M33: Sale ... 5F 104
Foxall Cl. M24: Mid ... 4H 61
Foxall St. M24: Mid ... 4H 61
Fox Bank Ct. SK3: Stoc ... 5G 9 (8B 108)
Foxbank St. M13: Man ... 5K 95
Foxbench Cl. SK7: Bram ... 9A 118
Foxbench Wlk. M21: Cho H ... 2C 106
Fox Cl. WA15: Tim ... 1F 114
Foxcroft St. OL15: Lit ... 9K 15
Foxdale St. M11: Man ... 9A 80
Foxdene Gro. WN3: Wins ... 9B 52
Foxdenton Dr. M32: Stre ... 6F 92
Foxdenton La. M24: Mid ... 5C 62
OL9: Chad ... 5C 62
Foxdenton Wlk. M34: Dent ... 8J 97
Foxendale Wlk. BL3: Bolt ... 7G 38
(off Fletcher St.)
Foxfield Cl. BL8: Bury ... 8H 25
Foxfield Dr. OL8: O'ham ... 1G 80
Foxfield Gro. WN6: She ... 6M 33
Foxfield Rd. M23: Wyth ... 4M 115
Foxfold WN8: Skel ... 9A 32
Foxford Wlk. M22: Wyth ... 5D 116
Foxglove Cl. SK10: Boll ... 5N 129
WA3: Low ... 1N 87
WN6: Stan ... 2A 34
Foxglove Ct. OL12: Roch ... 2B 28
Foxglove Dr. BL9: Bury ... 1C 42
WA14: B'ath ... 8C 104
Foxglove La. SK15: Stal ... 7D 82
Foxglove Wlk. M31: Part ... 6G 102
(off Cross La. W.)
Fox Gro. WA16: Knut ... 7J 133
Foxhall Rd. M34: Dent ... 5H 97
WA15: Tim ... 1E 114
Foxham Dr. M7: Sal ... 4D 78
Foxhill OL2: Shaw ... 4J 45
WA14: Alt ... 2A 114
Foxhill Chase SK2: Stoc ... 2L 119
Fox Hill Ct. SK4: Stoc ... 6M 107
Fox Hill Dr. SK15: Stal ... 1F 98
Foxhill Pk. SK15: Stal ... 1F 98
Fox Hill Rd. OL11: Roch ... 4B 44
Foxhill Rd. M30: Ecc ... 9N 75
Foxholes BL6: Hor ... 9F 20
Foxholes Cl. OL12: Roch ... 4E 28
Foxholes Rd. BL6: Hor ... 9F 20
OL12: Roch ... 4E 28
SK14: Hyde ... 9N 97
Foxlair Ct. M22: Wyth ... 4A 116
Foxlair Rd. M22: Wyth ... 4A 116
Foxland Rd. SK8: Gat ... 3G 116
Foxlea SK13: Glos ... 9B 100
Foxley Cl. M43: Droy ... 1C 96
WA13: Lym ... 5B 112
Foxley Gro.
BL3: Bolt ... 4G 7 (6E 38)
Foxley Hall M. WA13: Lym ... 6B 112
Foxley Wlk. M12: Man ... 4M 95
Fox Pk. Rd. OL8: O'ham ... 9G 62
FOX PLATT ... 1E 82
Fox Platt Rd. OL5: Mos ... 1E 82
Fox Platt Ter. OL5: Mos ... 2F 82
Fox St. BL6: Hor ... 2E 36
BL9: Bury ... 5M 7 (1M 41)
M30: Ecc ... 8F 76
OL8: O'ham ... 9G 63
OL10: H'ood ... 2H 43
OL16: Miln ... 7J 29
OL16: Roch ... 2F 28
SK3: Stoc ... 5G 9 (8B 108)
Foxton St. M24: Mid ... 4H 61
Foxton Wlk. M23: Wyth ... 4N 115
Foxwell Wlk. M8: Man ... 4G 78
(off Moordown Cl.)
Foxwood Cl. WN5: Orr ... 6J 51
Foxwood Dr. OL5: Mos ... 9G 64
SK14: Hyde ... 5B 98
Foxwood Gdns. M19: Man ... 3K 107
Foynes Cl. M40: Man ... 5J 79
Foy St. WN4: A Mak ... 7E 70
Frame, The M11: Man ... 8M 79
Framingham Rd.
M33: Sale ... 5G 105
Framley Rd. M21: Cho H ... 1E 106
Frampton Cl. M24: Mid ... 4N 61
Fram St. M6: Sal ... 8L 77
M9: Man ... 2L 79
Frances Av. SK8: Gat ... 1F 116
Francesca Wlk. M18: Man ... 3B 96
(off Briercliffe Cl.)
Frances Pl. M46: Ath ... 9J 55
Frances St. BL1: Bolt ... 2E 38
M13: Man ... 3G 95
(off Cabot St.)
OL1: O'ham ... 2L 63
OL16: Roch ... 2H 29
SK3: Stoc ... 4K 9 (8C 108)
SK8: Chea ... 1K 117
SK11: Macc ... 4F 130
SK14: Hyde ... 6N 97
Frances St. W. SK14: Hyde ... 6N 97
France St. BL5: W'ton ... 5G 54
WN2: Hin ... 5N 53
WN5: Wig ... 4C 52
Francis Av. M28: Walk ... 9N 57
M30: Ecc ... 8E 76
Francis Rd. M20: Man ... 3H 107
M44: Irl ... 9G 91
Francis St. BL4: Farn ... 2L 57
M3: Man ... 1F 4 (7E 78)
M29: Tyld ... 2E 74
M30: Ecc ... 7D 76
M34: Dent ... 9M 97
M35: Fail ... 3D 80
M44: Cad ... 3F 102
WN2: Hin ... 6N 53
WN7: Lei ... 3G 72
Francis Ter. SK16: Duk ... 9N 81
(off Astley St.)
Francis Thompson Dr.
OL6: A Lyne ... 6C 6
Frandley Wlk. M13: Man ... 8L 5
Frankby Cl. M27: Pen ... 3J 77
Frank Cowin Ct. M7: Sal ... 6C 78
(off Fitzwilliam St.)
Frank Fold OL10: H'ood ... 2F 42
Frankford Av. BL1: Bolt ... 2D 38
Frankford Sq. BL1: Bolt ... 2D 38
FRANK HILL ... 1C 8 (3J 63)
Frank Hulme Ho. M32: Stre ... 8L 93
Frankland Cl. M11: Man ... 8N 79
Franklin Cl. OL1: O'ham ... 1C 8 (3J 63)
SK11: Macc ... 7F 130
Franklin St. M30: Ecc ... 8D 76
OL1: O'ham ... 1C 8 (3J 63)
OL16: Roch ... 8F 28
Franklyn Av. M41: Urm ... 7M 91
Franklyn Cl. M34: Dent ... 7E 96
Franklyn Dr. WA12: N Wil ... 8G 87
Franklyn Rd. M18: Man ... 3C 96
M43: Droy ... 9E 80
Franklyn Ter. OL15: Lit ... 9L 15
(off Church Rd.)
Frank Perkins Way M44: Irl ... 1G 103
Frank Price Ct. M22: Wyth ... 4B 116
Frank St. BL1: Bolt ... 2E 38
BL9: Bury ... 9M 7 (3M 41)
M1: Man ... 8H 5
M6: Sal ... 6N 77
M35: Fail ... 3C 80
SK14: Hyde ... 7B 98
Frank Swift Wlk. M14: Man ... 6F 94
(off Fred Tilson Cl.)
Frankton Rd. M45: Whitef ... 4M 59
Franton Rd. M11: Man ... 8L 79
Fraser Av. M33: Sale ... 5L 105
Fraser Ho. BL1: Bolt ... 3E 38
(off Kirkhope Dr.)
Fraser Pl. M17: T Pk ... 5J 93
Fraser Rd. M8: Man ... 1E 78
WN5: Wig ... 4B 52
Fraser St. M27: Pen ... 1G 76
OL2: Shaw ... 4L 45
OL6: A Lyne ... 7F 6 (7N 81)
OL16: Roch ... 9F 28
Fraternitas Ter. M43: Droy ... 7C 80
Frawley Av. WA12: N Wil ... 4F 86
Frecheville Ct. BL9: Bury ... 9J 7 (3L 41)
Frecheville Pl. BL9: Bury ... 9J 7 (3L 41)
Freckleton Av. M21: Cho H ... 4C 106
Freckleton Dr. BL8: Bury ... 3F 40
Freckleton St. WN1: Wig ... 1F 52
Freda Wlk. M11: Man ... 9N 79
(off Doric Cl.)
Frederica Gdns. WN2: P Bri ... 8K 53
Frederick Av. OL2: Shaw ... 7M 45
Frederick Ct. BL4: Farn ... 3M 57
SK15: A Lyne ... 8B 82
(off Clarence St.)
Frederick Rd. M6: Sal ... 7A 78
M7: Sal ... 7A 78
Frederick St. BL0: Ram ... 9H 11
BL4: Farn ... 3L 57
M3: Sal ... 3D 4 (8D 78)
M34: Dent ... 4J 97
OL6: A Lyne ... 8B 82
OL8: O'ham ... 6G 63
OL9: Chad ... 3F 62
Frederick St. OL15: Lit ... 8L 15
WN2: Hin ... 6N 53
WN3: I Mak ... 5G 53
WN4: A Mak ... 5D 70
Frederick Ter. M9: Man ... 1J 79
(off Slack Rd.)
Frederic St. WN1: Wig ... 3H 53
Fred Tilson Cl. M14: Man ... 6F 94
Freehold Stop (Metro) ... 5F 62
Freehold St. OL11: Roch ... 8C 28
Freelands M29: Tyld ... 1D 74
Freeland Wlk. M11: Man ... 2A 96
(off Eccles Cl.)
Free La. BB4: Has ... 1G 10
Freeman Av. OL6: A Lyne ... 7A 82
Freeman Rd. SK16: Duk ... 3N 97
Freeman's La. PR7: Char R ... 2B 18
Freeman Sq. M15: Man ... 3F 94
Freemantle St. SK3: Stoc ... 8A 108
Freesia Av. M38: Lit H ... 8G 57
Freestone Cl. BL8: Bury ... 1K 41
FREETOWN ... 9N 25
Freetown SK13: Glos ... 9E 100
(not continuous)
Freetown Bus. Pk. BL9: Bury ... 9N 25
Freetown Cl. M14: Man ... 5F 94
Freetrade St. OL11: Roch ... 8C 28
Fremantle Av. M18: Man ... 6B 96
French Av. OL1: O'ham ... 2N 63
SK15: Stal ... 9F 82
French Barn La. M9: Man ... 8H 61
FRENCHES ... 5L 65
Frenches Ct. OL3: G'fld ... 5K 65
French Gro. BL3: Bolt ... 7L 39
French St. OL6: A Lyne ... 6A 82
SK15: Stal ... 9F 82
Frenchwood Ct. WN2: Asp ... 8M 35
Frensham Wlk. M23: Wyth ... 3M 115
Fresca Rd. OL1: O'ham ... 8A 46
Fresh Ct. SK13: Glos ... 9B 100
Freshfield M9: Man ... 7M 61
SK8: H Grn ... 6G 116
Freshfield Av. BL3: Bolt ... 1E 56
(not continuous)
M25: Pres ... 5B 60
M46: Ath ... 7L 55
SK14: Hyde ... 8A 98
Freshfield Cl. M35: Fail ... 4E 80
SK6: Mar B ... 7E 110
Freshfield Dr. SK10: Macc ... 1G 130
Freshfield Gro. BL3: Bolt ... 1G 56
Freshfield Rd. SK4: Stoc ... 6L 107
WN2: Hin ... 6B 54
WN3: Wig ... 8B 52
Freshfields M26: Rad ... 7D 40
WA16: Knut ... 5E 132
Freshfield Wlk. M11: Man ... 8A 80
Freshford Wlk. M22: Wyth ... 6A 116
Freshpool Way M22: Shar ... 1D 116
Freshwater Dr. M34: Dent ... 9M 97
OL6: A Lyne ... 6B 82
Freshwater St. M18: Man ... 3C 96
Freshwinds Ct. OL4: O'ham ... 7A 64
Fresnel Cl. SK14: Hyde ... 3E 98
Frew Ho. M40: Man ... 9N 61
Frewland Av. SK3: Stoc ... 3D 118
Freya Gro. M5: Sal ... 7A 4
Friarmere Rd. OL3: Del ... 7H 47
Friars Cl. M29: Tyld ... 1E 74
SK9: Wilm ... 6D 122
WA14: Bow ... 6B 114
Friar's Ct. M5: Sal ... 8H 77
Friars Cres. OL11: Roch ... 2D 44
Friar's Rd. M33: Sale ... 4H 105
Friars Way SK10: Macc ... 2D 130
Friendship Av. M18: Man ... 5C 96
Friendship Sq. SK14: Holl ... 4N 99
Frieston OL12: Roch ... 5B 8
Frieston Rd. WA14: Tim ... 8E 104
FRIEZLAND ... 6K 65
Friezland Cl. SK15: C'ook ... 4H 83
Friezland La. OL3: G'fld ... 7K 65
Frimley Gdns. M22: Wyth ... 4C 116
Frinton Av. M40: Man ... 8B 62
Frinton Cl. M33: Sale ... 7F 104
Frinton Rd. BL3: Bolt ... 9C 38
Frith St. WN5: Wig ... 4D 52
Frith Ter. SK11: Macc ... 8H 131
Frobisher Cl. M13: Man ... 4J 95
Frobisher Pl. SK5: Stoc ... 4C 108
Frobisher Rd. OL15: Lit ... 5N 15
Frodsham Av. SK4: Stoc ... 5A 108
Frodsham Cl. WN6: Stan ... 9A 34
Frodsham Rd. M33: Sale ... 6L 105
Frodsham St. M14: Man ... 6G 95
Frodsham Way SK9: Hand ... 2K 123
Frodsley Wlk. M12: Man ... 3L 95
(off Wenlock Way)
Froghall La. WA13: Lym ... 7E 112
(not continuous)
WA16: H Leg ... 7E 112
Frog La. WN1: Wig ... 7G 9 (2D 52)
WN6: Wig ... 7G 9 (2D 52)
Frogley St. BL2: Bolt ... 1J 39
Frogmore Av. SK14: Hyde ... 1B 110
Frome Av. M41: Urm ... 8B 92
SK2: Stoc ... 2G 118
Frome Cl. M29: Ast ... 4D 74
Frome Dr. M8: Man ... 3G 79
Frome St. OL4: O'ham ... 5N 63
Frostlands St. M16: Whall R ... 6D 94
Frost St. OL8: O'ham ... 7J 63
Froxmer St. M18: Man ... 3A 96
Froxmer St. Ind. Est. M18: Man ... 3A 96
(off Froxmer St.)
Fryent Cl. BL6: Bla ... 2N 35
Fuchsia Gro. M7: Sal ... 4C 78
(off Hilton St. Nth.)
Fulbeck Av. WN3: Wig ... 9C 52
Fulbeck Wlk. M7: Sal ... 5D 78
Fulbeck Way OL8: O'ham ... 7K 63
Fulbrook Dr. SK8: Chea H ... 9M 117
Fulbrook Way M29: Tyld ... 1D 74
Fulford St. M16: Old T ... 5B 94
Fulham Av. M40: Man ... 5N 79
Fulham St. OL4: O'ham ... 5N 63
Fullerton Rd. SK4: Stoc ... 6N 107
Full Pot La. OL11: Roch ... 5K 27
FULLWOOD ... 6N 45
Fulmar Cl. BL5: W'ton ... 5F 54
SK12: Poy ... 2E 124
Fulmar Dr. M33: Sale ... 6C 104
SK2: Stoc ... 2K 119
Fulmards Cl. SK9: Wilm ... 7H 123
Fulmar Gdns. OL11: Roch ... 6L 27
Fulmead Wlk. M8: Man ... 4E 78
(off Kilmington Dr.)
Fulmer Dr. M4: Man ... 2N 5 (8H 79)
Fulmere Ct. M27: Swin ... 4D 76
Fulneck Sq. M43: Droy ... 1E 96
Fulshaw Av. SK9: Wilm ... 8F 122
Fulshaw Ct. SK9: Wilm ... 9F 122
FULSHAW PARK ... 9F 122
Fulshaw Pk. SK9: Wilm ... 1F 126
Fulshaw Pk. Sth. SK9: Wilm ... 1E 126
Fulshaw Wlk. M13: Man ... 9L 5
Fulstone M. SK2: Stoc ... 1F 118
Fulton Ct. M15: Man ... 4F 94
(off Boundary La.)
Fulwell Av. M29: Tyld ... 2N 73
Fulwood Av. M9: Man ... 7L 61
Fulwood Cl. BL8: Bury ... 3F 40
Fulwood Rd. WA3: Low ... 2A 88
Furbarn La. OL11: Roch ... 5J 27
Furbarn Rd. OL11: Roch ... 6J 27
Furberry Ct. OL4: Grot ... 6E 64
FUR LANE ... 5M 65
Furlong Cl. WN2: Bam ... 3J 71
Furlong Rd. M22: Wyth ... 4A 116
Furnace St. SK14: Hyde ... 5N 97
SK16: Duk ... 9D 6 (9M 81)
Furness Av. BL2: Bolt ... 2J 39
M45: Whitef ... 3N 59
OL7: A Lyne ... 6K 81
OL8: O'ham ... 8N 63
OL10: H'ood ... 1H 43
OL15: Lit ... 8L 15
Furness Cl. OL16: Miln ... 7J 29
SK12: Poy ... 2G 125
SK13: Glos ... 9H 101
(off Hillwood Dr.)
Furness Cres. WN7: Lei ... 1F 72
Furness Fld. SK14: Hyde ... 2D 110
Furness Gro. SK4: Stoc ... 7N 107
Furness Quay M50: Sal ... 2N 93
Furness Rd. BL1: Bolt ... 5C 38
M14: Man ... 8H 95
M24: Mid ... 9L 43
M41: Urm ... 6D 92
SK8: Chea H ... 9A 118
Furness Sq. BL2: Bolt ... 2J 39
Furnival Cl. M34: Dent ... 7E 96
Furnival Rd. M18: Man ... 3A 96
Furnival St. SK5: Stoc ... 7D 96
WN7: Lei ... 3H 73
Furrow Dr. M30: Ecc ... 6B 76
Furrows, The M32: Stre ... 5H 93
Further Fld. OL11: Roch ... 4J 27
Further Hgts. Rd. OL12: Roch ... 3D 28
Further Hey Cl. OL4: Lees ... 4B 64
Further La. SK14: Hat ... 6H 99
Further Pits OL11: Roch ... 6A 28
Furtherwood Rd. OL1: O'ham ... 2G 63
Furze Av. BL5: W'ton ... 4H 55
Furzegate OL16: Roch ... 1F 44
Furze La. OL4: O'ham ... 2A 64
Furze Wlk. M31: Part ... 5H 103
Fusilier Museum, The ... 8K 7 (2L 41)
Fusion (1-9) M5: Sal ... 5A 4 (9B 78)
Fustian Av. OL10: H'ood ... 4F 42
Futura Pk. BL6: Hor ... 3E 36
FX Leisure
Lowton ... 2C 88
Orrell ... 4H 51
Stalybridge ... 1F 98
Fyfield Wlk. M8: Man ... 4G 79
(off Moordown Cl.)
Fylde Av. BL2: Bolt ... 5M 39
SK8: H Grn ... 7H 117
Fylde Ct. M32: Stre ... 9J 93
(off Highfield Rd.)
Fylde La. M18: Man ... 6B 96
Fylde Rd. SK4: Stoc ... 6M 107
Fylde St. BL3: Bolt ... 1L 57
Fylde St. E. BL3: Bolt ... 1L 57

G

Gabbot St. PR7: Adl ... 6K 19
Gable Av. SK9: Wilm ... 7F 122
Gable Ct. M34: Dent ... 6K 97
Gable Dr. M24: Mid ... 2K 61
Gables, The M33: Sale ... 5H 105
(Brooklands Rd.)
M33: Sale ... 3J 105
(Irlam Rd.)
Gable St. BL2: Bolt ... 8L 23
M11: Man ... 1L 95
WA12: N Wil ... 6D 86
Gabriels, The OL2: Shaw ... 5K 45
Gabriels Ter. M24: Mid ... 4A 62
Gadbrook Gro. M46: Ath ... 9J 55
Gadbury Av. M46: Ath ... 8K 55
Gadbury Ct. M46: Ath ... 9J 55
Gadbury Fold M46: Ath ... 8J 55
Gaddum Rd. M20: Man ... 5H 107
WA14: Bow ... 6A 114
Gadfield Ct. M46: Ath ... 8K 55
Gadfield Gro. M46: Ath ... 8J 55
Gadwall Cl. M28: Wors ... 2L 75
Gail Av. SK4: Stoc ... 6B 108
Gail Cl. M35: Fail ... 5C 80
SK9: A Edg ... 3G 126
Gainford Av. SK8: Gat ... 3G 116
Gainford Gdns. M40: Man ... 1N 79
Gainford Rd. SK5: Stoc ... 8D 96
Gainford Wlk. BL3: Bolt ... 8F 38
Gainsboro Rd. M34: Aud ... 9H 81
Gainsborough Av. BL3: Bolt ... 9D 38
M20: Man ... 3H 107
M32: Stre ... 6M 93

Gainsborough Av. OL8: O'ham 7J 63
SK6: Mar B 8E 110
Gainsborough Cl. SK9: Wilm 6J 123
WN3: Wins 8A 52
Gainsborough Dr. OL11: Roch 1C 44
SK8: Chea 1L 117
Gainsborough Ho. M33: Sale 5F 104
Gainsborough Rd. BL0: Ram 4H 25
OL9: Chad 2C 62
Gainsborough St. M7: Sal 3D 78
Gainsborough Wlk. M34: Dent 8J 97
(not continuous)
SK14: Hyde 4B 98
Gairloch Av. M32: Stre 7H 93
Gair Rd. SK5: Stoc 4D 108
Gair St. SK14: Hyde 5A 98
Gaitskell Cl. M12: Man 9K 79
Gala Bingo
Ashton-under-Lyne ...6C 6 (7M 81)
Belle Vue 4N 95
Manchester 2K 79
Robin Park 3C 52
Salford 7N 77
Stockport 2N 9 (7E 108)
Wigan 7K 9 (3F 52)
Wythenshawe 5C 116
Galbraith Rd. M20: Man 5H 107
Galbraith Way OL11: Roch 5K 27
GALE 7N 15
Gale Cl. OL15: Lit 7N 15
Gale Ct. OL12: Roch 2C 28
(off Whitworth Rd.)
Gale Dr. M24: Mid 1J 61
Gale Rd. M25: Pres 8M 59
Gales Ter. OL11: Roch 8C 28
Gale St. OL10: H'ood 2G 42
OL12: Roch 2D 28
Galgate Cl. BL8: Bury 3F 40
M15: Man 9D 4 (2D 94)
Galindo St. BL2: Bolt 9K 23
Galland St. OL4: O'ham 3L 63
Galleries, The WN1: Wig 7J 9 (3F 52)
Gallery, The M3: Sal 3F 4
M16: Whall R 6D 94
Gallery Oldham 3E 8 (5K 63)
Galloway Cl. BL3: Bolt 7N 37
OL10: H'ood 4E 42
Galloway Dr. M27: Clif 7F 58
WN8: Uph 5F 50
Galloway Rd. M27: Swin 4D 76
Gallowsclough Rd. SK15: Mat 3H 99
Galsworthy Av. M8: Man 4F 78
Galvin Rd. M9: Man 8G 61
Galway Cres. WA11: Hay 2A 86
Galway St. OL1: O'ham 3D 8 (5K 63)
Galway Wlk. M23: Wyth 5M 115
Galwey Gro. WN1: Wig 8F 34
Gambleside Cl. M28: Wors 2J 75
Gambrel Bank Rd. OL6: A Lyne 4M 81
Gambrel Gro. OL6: A Lyne 4M 81
GAMESLEY 7A 100
Gamesley Community & Sports Cen.
.......................7A 100
Gamesley Fold SK13: Char 9N 99
Game St. OL4: O'ham 6N 63
Games Wlk. M22: Wyth 6A 116
Gamma Wlk. M11: Man 8N 79
(off John Heywood St.)
Gandy La. OL12: Roch 1B 28
Gan Eden M7: Sal 2D 78
Gantley Av. WN5: Bil 7H 51
Gantley Cres. WN5: Bil 8H 51
Gantley Rd. WN5: Bil 7H 51
Gantock Wlk. M14: Man 6H 95
(off Stenbury Cl.)
Ganton Av. M45: Whitef 4K 59
Garbo Ct. M6: Sal 6L 77
(off Monroe Cl.)
Garbrook Av. M9: Man 6H 61
Garden Av. M32: Stre 6K 93
M43: Droy 8F 80
Garden City BL0: Ram 3G 24
Garden Cl. OL15: Lit 2K 29
SK10: Macc 3J 131
Garden Ct. BL0: Ram 7J 11
(off Garden St.)
OL16: Roch 5H 29
Gardeners Way OL7: A Lyne 8J 81
Gardenfold Ho. M43: Droy 8F 80
Gardenfold Way
M43: Droy 8F 80
Garden La. M3: Man 4F 4 (9E 78)
M3: Sal 2E 4 (8D 78)
M28: Wors 4H 75
OL16: Roch 6E 8 (5E 28)
WA14: Alt 2D 6 (2D 114)
Garden M. OL15: Lit 9M 15
(off Industry St.)
Garden Rd. WA16: Knut 5F 132
Garden Row OL10: H'ood 9G 27
OL12: Roch 3B 28
Gardens, The BL1: Bolt 7G 22
BL7: Tur 1L 23
M30: Ecc 6G 76
Garden St. BL0: Ram 8J 11
BL4: Kea 3M 57
BL8: Tot 6F 24
BL9: Sum 2J 25
M4: Man 3H 5 (8F 78)
M29: Tyld 2B 74
M30: Ecc 9E 76
M34: Aud 3K 97
OL1: O'ham 1G 8 (4L 63)
OL4: Spri 6C 64
OL10: H'ood 1H 43
OL16: Miln 9M 29
SK2: Stoc 2G 118
SK10: Boll 5K 129
SK10: Macc 3J 131
SK14: B'tom 9K 99
(off Gorsey Brow)
SK14: Hyde 5B 98
Garden Ter. OL2: O'ham 5G 45
SK6: Mar 6E 120
Garden Va. WN7: Lei 2E 72
Garden Vs. SK8: H Grn 8G 117
Garden Wlk. M31: Part 5F 102
M34: Dent 6L 97
OL6: A Lyne 5F 6 (6N 81)
Garden Wall Cl. M5: Sal 1B 94
Garden Way OL15: Lit 3K 29
Gardinar Cl. WN1: Stan 3F 34
Gardner Grange SK5: Stoc 4G 109
Gardner Ho. M30: Ecc 8E 76
(off Church St.)
Gardner Rd. M25: Pres 7M 59
Gardner St. M6: Sal 7N 77
M12: Man 3N 95
Garfield Av. M19: Man 8N 95
Garfield Cl. OL11: Roch 5K 27
Garfield Gro. BL3: Bolt 7E 38
Garfield Pl. HD7: Mars 1H 49
Garfield St. BL3: Bolt 9D 38
SK1: Stoc 6E 108
Garforth Av. M4: Man 2N 5 (8H 79)
Garforth Cres. M43: Droy 7F 80
Garforth Ri. BL1: Bolt 5B 38
Garforth St. OL9: Chad 4G 62
Gargrave Av. BL1: Bolt 2A 38
Gargrave St. M7: Sal 2M 77
OL4: O'ham 5M 63
Garland Rd. M22: Wyth 4D 116
Garlick St. M18: Man 4B 96
OL9: O'ham 3B 8
SK14: Hyde 6C 98
Garnant Cl. M9: Man 2L 79
(off Gillford Av.)
Garner Av. WA15: Tim 7G 104
Garner Cl. WA14: Bow 5D 114
Garner Dr. M5: Sal 7K 77
M29: Ast 5C 74
M30: Ecc 7C 76
Garners La. SK3: Stoc 2B 118
Garnett St. BL0: Ram 8J 11
BL1: Bolt 1F 38
OL1: O'ham 3M 63
SK1: Stoc 3L 9 (7D 108)
Garratt Way M18: Man 4A 96
Garrett Gro. OL2: Shaw 5N 45
Garrett Hall Rd. M28: Wors 3F 74
Garrett La. M29: Ast 3E 74
Garrett Wlk. SK3: Stoc 8A 108
Garrick Cl. WA14: Alt 1D 114
Garron Wlk. M22: Wyth 5N 115
Garrowmore Wlk. M9: Man 8K 61
(off Greendale Dr.)
Garsdale Cl. BL9: Bury 5N 41
Garsdale La. BL1: Bolt 5M 37
Garsden Wlk. M23: Wyth 3M 115
Garside Av. WA3: Low 2B 87
Garside Gro. BL1: Bolt 2D 38
WN3: Wig 9B 52
Garside Hey Rd. BL8: Bury 7H 25
Garside St. BL1: Bolt 3H 7 (5F 38)
M34: Dent 7K 97
SK14: Hyde 8B 98
Garstang Av. BL2: Bolt 6M 39
Garstang Dr. BL8: Bury 3F 40
Garstang Ho. M15: Man 4G 95
Garston Av. M46: Ath 6K 55
Garston Cl. SK4: Stoc 5A 108
WN7: Lei 1G 72
Garston St. BL9: Bury 5N 41
GARSWOOD 7N 69
Garswood Cres. WN5: Bil 6J 69
Garswood Dr. BL8: Bury 7H 25
Garswood Old Rd. WA11: St H 9H 69
WN4: Gars 9K 69
Garswood Rd. BL3: Bolt 1F 56
M14: Man 7E 94
WA11: Hay 9M 69
WN4: Gars 5M 69
WN5: Bil 6J 69
Garswood Station (Rail) 7A 70
Garswood St. WN4: A Mak 7E 70
Garth, The M5: Sal 8K 77
Garth Av. WA15: Tim 1E 114
Garth Edge OL12: Whitw 1C 14
Garth Hgts. SK9: Wilm 7H 123
Garthland Rd. SK7: H Gro 4K 119
Garthmere Rd. M46: Ath 6A 56
Garthorne Cl. M16: Whall R 5C 94
Garthorp Rd. M23: Wyth 7L 105
Garth Rd. M22: Wyth 3C 116
SK2: Stoc 9G 108
SK6: Mar 1D 120
Garthwaite Av. OL8: O'ham 8J 63
Gartland Wlk. M8: Man 2H 79
Garton Dr. WA3: Low 9A 72
Gartside St. M3: Man 5E 4 (9D 78)
(not continuous)
OL3: Del 8H 47
OL4: O'ham 6M 63
OL7: A Lyne 9J 81
Garwick Rd. BL1: Bolt 1C 38
Garwood St. M15: Man 9F 4 (2D 94)
Gascoyne St. M14: Man 6G 94
Gaskell Av. WA16: Knut 6F 132
Gaskell Cl. OL15: Lit 8L 15
Gaskell Ri. OL1: O'ham 7B 46
Gaskell Rd. M30: Ecc 9E 76
WA14: Alt 1D 6 (1D 114)
Gaskell's Brow WN4: A Mak 5B 70
Gaskell St. BL1: Bolt 1G 7 (4E 38)
M27: Pen 9F 58
M40: Man 4B 80
SK16: Duk 1M 97
WN1: Wig 7M 9 (3H 53)
WN2: Hin 4A 54
Gaskill St. OL10: H'ood 2F 42
Gas Rd. SK11: Macc 4H 131
Gas St. BL1: Bolt 3H 7 (5F 38)
(not continuous)
BL4: Farn 3L 57
OL6: A Lyne 7C 6 (7M 81)
OL10: H'ood 2J 43
OL11: Roch 8A 8 (6C 28)
PR7: Adl 7K 19
SK4: Stoc 2J 9 (7C 108)
SK14: Holl 4N 99
WN2: P Bri 9L 53
WN7: Lei 5H 73
Gaston Wlk. M9: Man 6J 61
(off Claygate Dr.)
Gatcombe M. M26: Rad 7F 40
SK9: Wilm 8F 122
Gatcombe Sq. M14: Man 6J 95
(off Rusholme Gro.)
Gateacre Wlk. M23: Wyth 8L 105
Gate Cen., The SK6: Bred 2J 109
Gatefield Cl. M26: Rad 9E 40
Gate Fold BL2: Bolt 8L 23
Gategill Gro. WN5: Bil 8H 51
Gatehead Bus. Pk.
OL3: Del 9J 47
Gatehead Cft. OL3: Del 9J 47
Gatehead M. OL3: Del 9J 47
Gatehead Rd. OL3: Del 9J 47
Gatehouse OL15: Lit 8A 16
Gatehouse Ct. BL9: Bury 2B 42
(off Bridgefield Dr.)
Gatehouse Rd. M28: Walk 7H 57
Gate Keeper Fold OL7: A Lyne 3L 81
Gatemere Cl. M28: Wors 2J 75
Gates, The BL2: Bolt 1A 40
Gatesgarth Rd. M24: Mid 1H 61
Gateshead Cl. M14: Man 5G 95
Gateside Wlk. M9: Man 6K 61
(off Crossmead Dr.)
Gates Shop. Cen., The
BL1: Bolt 2L 7 (5G 39)
Gate St. M11: Man 1A 96
OL11: Roch 8D 28
SK16: Duk 3L 97
Gateway, The M6: Sal 6N 77
(off Broughton Rd.)
M40: Man 4L 79
OL10: H'ood 2J 43
(off Manchester St.)
Gateway Cres. OL9: Chad 6B 62
Gateway Ho. M1: Man 5L 5
Gateway Ind. Est.
M1: Man 5L 5 (9G 79)
Gateway Rd. M18: Man 3A 96
Gateways, The M27: Pen 1F 76
Gathill Cl. SK8: Chea H 6L 117
GATHURST 9L 33
Gathurst Golf Course 7K 33
Gathurst Hall WN6: She 9K 33
Gathurst La. WN6: She 9L 33
Gathurst Rd. WN5: Orr 4J 51
WN6: She 9K 33
Gathurst Station (Rail) 9L 33
Gathurst St. M18: Man 3C 96
GATLEY 2G 116
Gatley Av. M14: Man 8F 94
Gatley Brow OL1: O'ham 3J 63
(off Sunfield Rd.)
Gatley Carrs Local Nature Reserve
.............................1F 116
Gatley Cl. M29: Tyld 1C 74
Gatley Ct. M22: Nor 9D 106
Gatley Golf Course 4F 116
Gatley Grn. SK8: Gat 2F 116
Gatley Rd. M33: Sale 5L 105
SK8: Chea, Gat 2G 116
Gatley Station (Rail) 1G 116
Gatling Av. M12: Man 7N 95
Gatwick Av. M23: Wyth 1A 116
Gauntlet Birds of Prey
Eagle and Vulture Pk. 2C 132
Gavel Wlk. M24: Mid 2K 61
Gavin Av. M5: Sal 9N 77
Gaw End La. SK11: Lym G 9G 130
Gawsworth Av. M20: Man 7H 107
Gawsworth Cl. OL2: Shaw 5K 45
SK3: Stoc 2B 118
SK7: Bram 1C 124
SK12: Poy 4K 125
SK13: Had 4C 100
WA15: Tim 1K 115
Gawsworth Ct. M9: Man 6F 60
(off Deanswood Dr.)
Gawsworth M. SK8: Gat 2G 117
Gawsworth Pl. M22: Wyth 6E 116
Gawsworth Rd. M33: Sale 7L 105
SK11: Gaws, Macc 9B 130
WA3: Gol 9J 71
Gawsworth Way M34: Dent 8L 97
SK9: Hand 2K 123
Gawthorne Cl. SK7: H Gro 5G 119
Gawthorpe Cl. BL9: Bury 7N 41
Gaydon Rd. M33: Sale 4D 104
Gaynor Av. WA11: Hay 2C 86
GAYTHORN 8F 4 (2E 94)
Gaythorne St. BL1: Bolt 1G 38
Gaythorn St. M5: Sal 4A 4 (9B 78)
Gayton Cl. WN3: Wins 8A 52
Gayton Wlk. M40: Man 9B 62
Gaywood Wlk. M40: Man 4H 79
(off Westmount Cl.)
Geddington Rd. WA14: W Tim 7C 104
GEE CROSS 1B 110
Gee Cross Fold SK14: Hyde 1B 110
Gee La. M30: Ecc 7B 76
OL8: O'ham 9F 62
Gee St. SK3: Stoc 9B 108
Gelder Clough Pk. OL11: Roch 8H 27
Gelder Wood Country Pk.
OL11: Roch 7H 27
Gellert Pl. BL5: W'ton 5G 55
Gellert Rd. BL5: W'ton 5G 55
Gellfield La. OL3: Upp 2N 65
Gemini Rd. M6: Sal 6B 78
Gendre Rd. BL7: Eger 5F 22
Geneva Rd. SK7: Bram 4B 118
Geneva Ter. OL11: Roch 5A 28
Geneva Wlk. M8: Man 4G 79
(off Moordown Cl.)
OL9: Chad 5G 62
Genista Gro. M7: Sal 4C 78
(off Hilton St. Nth.)
Geoff Bent Wlk. M40: Man 5N 79
(off Roger Byrne Cl.)
Geoffrey St. BL0: Ram 1G 25
BL5: W'ton 3B 56
BL9: Bury 9N 25
George Barton St. BL2: Bolt 3J 39
George Ct. SK16: Duk 9M 81
(off Hill St.)
George Halstead Ct. M8: Man 1F 78
(off Station Rd.)
George H Carnall Leisure Cen. ...5E 92
George Kenyon Bldg. M13: Man ...3G 94
George La. SK6: Bred 4L 109
George Leigh St.
M4: Man 3L 5 (8G 79)
George Mann Cl. M22: Wyth 6B 116
George Parr Rd. M15: Man 3E 94
George Richards Way
WA14: B'ath 9B 104
George Rd. BL0: Ram 9H 11
George Sq. OL1: O'ham 3C 8 (5J 63)
George's Cl. SK12: Poy 3J 125
George's Ct. SK11: Macc 4G 131
(off Chestergate)
Georges La. BL6: Hor 6F 20
WN1: I Mak 3J 53
George's Rd. M33: Sale 5H 105
SK4: Stoc 2G 9 (7B 108)
George's Rd. E. SK12: Poy 3J 125
George's Rd. W. SK12: Poy 3H 125
George St. BL4: Farn 4J 57
BL5: W'ton 3H 55
BL6: Hor 1E 36
(not continuous)
BL9: Bury 8M 7 (2M 41)
M1: Man 6G 5 (1E 94)
M25: Pres 1A 78
M26: Rad 9F 40
M30: Ecc 9C 76
M34: Dent 6L 97
M35: Fail 2D 80
M41: Urm 7E 92
M44: Irl 6J 91
M45: Whitef 2M 59
M46: Ath 8M 55
OL1: O'ham 3C 8 (5J 63)
OL2: Shaw 3N 45
OL5: Mos 1F 82
OL6: A Lyne 7E 6 (7N 81)
OL9: Chad 4E 62
OL10: H'ood 1G 43
OL12: Whitw 7A 14
OL15: Lit 8M 15
OL16: Roch 6E 8 (5E 28)
(Ball St.)
OL16: Roch 2H 29
(Greenfield La.)
OL16: Roch 6J 29
(Rochdale Rd.)
SK1: Stoc 2N 9 (7E 108)
SK6: Comp 6E 110
SK9: A Edg 4F 126
SK11: Macc 5H 131
SK13: Glos 9E 100
SK15: Stal 8D 82
WA12: N Wil 5D 86
WA14: Alt 4C 6 (3D 114)
WA16: Knut 6F 132
WN2: Hin 6A 54
WN2: I Mak 4J 53
WN4: A Mak 6F 70
George St. E. SK1: Stoc 8F 108
George St. Nth. M7: Sal 2E 78
George St. Sth. M7: Sal 2D 78
George St. West SK1: Stoc 8F 108
SK11: Macc 4G 131
George Ter. M30: Ecc 8D 76
(off Byron St.)
WN5: Orr 6H 51
George Thomas Ct. M9: Man 2J 79
Georgette Dr. M3: Sal 1E 4 (7D 78)
Georgia Av. M20: Man 3E 106
Georgiana St. BL4: Farn 1J 57
Georgian Ct. M29: Tyld 1A 74
(off Market St.)
SK6: Rom 6M 109
(off Stockport Rd.)
WN7: Lei 6K 73
Georgian Sq. WN2: P Bri 9K 53
Georgina Ct. BL3: Bolt 9C 38
Georgina St. BL3: Bolt 1C 56
Gerald Av. M8: Man 2F 78
Gerald Rd. M6: Sal 5N 77
Gerard Cen., The WN4: A Mak 7E 70
Gerard St. WN4: A Mak 7E 70
Germain Cl. M9: Man 6H 61
German La. PR7: Cop 4B 18
Germans Bldgs. SK2: Stoc 1E 118
Gerosa Av. WA2: Win 9L 87
Gerrard Av. WA15: Tim 8G 105
Gerrard Cl. OL7: A Lyne 9K 81
WN2: Asp 1N 53
Gerrard Rd. WA3: Cro 9C 88
WN5: Bil 5J 69
Gerrards, The SK14: Hyde 1A 110
Gerrards Cl. M44: Irl 7H 91
Gerrards Gdns. SK14: Hyde 1B 110
Gerrards Hollow SK14: Hyde 1A 110
Gerrard St. BL4: Kea 3M 57
BL5: W'ton 2G 54
M6: Sal 7A 78
OL11: Roch 2E 44
SK15: Stal 9E 82
WN7: Lei 5H 73
Gerrardswood SK14: Hyde 1A 110
Gerry Wheale Sq. M14: Man 6F 94
Gertrude Cl. M5: Sal 1N 93
Gervis Cl. M40: Man 5J 79
Ghyll Gro. M28: Walk 1M 75
WA11: St H 9F 68
Giants Hall Rd. WN6: Stan 9B 34
Giant's Seat M26: Rad 5E 58
Giants Seat Gro. M27: Pen 2K 77
Gibb La. SK6: Mel 3G 121
Gibble Gabble SK14: B'tom 9K 99
(off King St.)
Gibbon Av. M22: Wyth 5C 116
Gibbon's Rd. WN4: Gars 8A 70
Gibbon St. BL3: Bolt 7E 38
M11: Man 8M 79
Gibb Rd. M28: Wors 3B 76
Gibbs Cl. OL3: G'fld 6H 65
Gibbs St. M3: Sal 4B 4 (9C 78)
Gib Fld. M46: Ath 8K 55
Gibfield Bus. Pk. M46: Ath 7K 55
Gibfield Dr. M46: Ath 9J 55
Gibfield Pk. Av. M46: Ath 7J 55
Gib Fold M46: Ath 7M 55
Gib La. M23: Wyth 9A 106
Gib La. Cotts. M23: Wyth 9B 106
Gibraltar La. M34: Dent 9M 97
Gibraltar St. BL3: Bolt 5G 7 (6E 38)
OL4: O'ham 6A 64
Gibsmere Cl. WA15: Tim 1K 115
Gibson Av. M18: Man 2D 96
Gibson Gro. M28: Walk 8H 57
Gibson La. M28: Walk 8H 57
Gibson Pl. M3: Man 7F 78
Gibson Sq. WA3: Gol 1K 87
(off Turton St.)
Gibsons Rd. SK4: Stoc 4N 107
Gibson St. BL2: Bolt 3K 39
OL4: O'ham 5N 63
OL16: Roch 5G 29
WN2: B'haw 1N 71
Gibson Ter. OL7: A Lyne 1L 97
Gibson Way WA14: B'ath 8C 104
Gibstone Cl. M46: Ath 9J 55
Gibwood Rd. M22: Nor 8B 106
GIDLOW 1D 52
Gidlow Av. PR6: Adl 6K 19
WN6: Wig 1D 52
Gidlow Ho's. WN6: Wig 8D 34
Gidlow La. WN6: Wig 7D 34
Gidlow St. M18: Man 3C 96
WN2: Hin 5N 53
WN2: I Mak 3K 53
Giffard Wlk. SK7: Bram 5E 118
Gifford Av. M9: Man 7L 61
Gifford Pl. WN2: Hin 7B 54
GIGG 5N 41
Gigg Lane 5M 41
Gigg La. BL9: Bury 5L 41
Gilbert Bank SK6: Bred 4M 109
Gilbert Ct. WA3: Cul 6H 89
Gilbert Ho. M5: Sal 2N 93
(off Elmira Way)
Gilbert Rd. WA15: Hale 6E 114
Gilbertson Rd. PR7: H Char 3H 19
Gilbert St. BL0: Ram 5J 11
M6: Sal 9M 77
(off Hodge La.)
M15: Man 8E 4
M28: Walk 9K 57
M30: Ecc 1B 92
WN2: Hin 6M 53
Gilbrook Way OL16: Roch 2F 44
Gilchrist Av. SK11: Macc 5C 130
Gilchrist Rd. M44: Irl 2F 102
Gilda Brook Rd. M30: Ecc, Sal 9G 76
Gilda Brook Rdbt. M30: Ecc 8G 76
Gilda Cres. Rd. M30: Ecc 7G 76
Gilda Rd. M28: Wors 3F 74
Gildenhall M35: Fail 3E 80
Gilderdale Cl. OL2: Shaw 4M 45
Gilderdale St. BL3: Bolt 8H 39
Gildersdale Dr. M9: Man 5G 61
Gilder's Villa OL4: Grot 7E 64
Gildridge Rd. M16: Whall R 8D 94
Gilesgate M14: Man 6H 95
(off Viscount St.)
Giles St. M12: Man 5M 95
Gillan Rd. WN6: Wig 1E 52
Gill Av. WN6: She 6M 33
GILLBENT 9L 117
Gillbent Rd. SK8: Chea H 9M 117
Gillbrook Rd. M20: Man 5G 107
Gillbrow Cres. WN1: Wig 2J 53
Gillemere Gro. OL2: Shaw 5M 45
Gillers Grn. M28: Walk 8K 57
Gillford Av. M9: Man 2L 79
Gillibrands Rd. WN8: Skel 4A 50
Gilliburns Fold M28: Wors 3G 75
Gilliburns Wlk. BL5: W'ton 6H 55
Gillingham Rd. M30: Ecc 8B 76
Gill St. M9: Man 2L 79
SK1: Stoc 5F 108
Gillwood Dr. SK6: Rom 7K 109
Gilman Cl. M9: Man 9H 61
Gilman St. M9: Man 9H 61
Gilmerton Dr. M40: Man 5A 80
Gilmore Dr. M25: Pres 9A 60
Gilmore St. SK3: Stoc 9C 108
Gilmour St. M24: Mid 3M 61
Gilmour Ter. M9: Man 1L 79
(not continuous)
GILNOW 6E 38
Gilnow Gdns. BL1: Bolt 6D 38
Gilnow Gro. BL1: Bolt 6E 38
Gilnow La. BL3: Bolt 6D 38
Gilnow Mill Ind. Est. BL1: Bolt 6D 38
GILNOW PARK 5C 38
Gilnow Rd. BL1: Bolt 6D 38
Gilpin Rd. M41: Urm 8F 92
Gilpin Wlk. M24: Mid 2K 61
Gilroy St. WN1: Wig 8M 9 (3G 53)
GILSBROOK 6D 20
Giltbrook Av. M40: Man 6J 79
Gilwell Dr. M23: Wyth 3M 115
Gilwood Gro. M24: Mid 8L 43
Gincroft La. BL0: Eden 1L 11
Gingham Brow BL6: Hor 9F 20
Gingham Ct. M26: Rad 8J 41
(off Butterworth St.)
Gingham Pk. M26: Rad 7E 40
GIN PIT 3A 74
Gipsey Moth Cl. WA15: Tim 2K 115
Gipsy La. OL11: Roch 1A 44
(not continuous)
Gird La. SK6: Mar B 8H 111
Girton Av. WN4: A Mak 6C 70
Girton St. BL2: Bolt 5L 39
M7: Sal 1D 78
Girton Wlk. M40: Man 1B 80
Girvan Av. M40: Man 9B 62
Girvan Cl. BL3: Bolt 9D 38
Girvan Cres. WN4: Gars 6A 70
Girvan Wlk. OL10: H'ood 3E 42

Gisborne Dr. M6: Sal 5N 77
Gisburn Av. BL1: Bolt 2N 37
WA3: Gol 8J 71
Gisburn Dr. BL8: Bury 1E 40
OL11: Roch 1E 44
Gisburne Av. M40: Man 9B 62
Gissing Wlk. M9: Man 4J 79
Givendale Dr. M8: Man 9F 60
Givvons Fold OL4: O'ham 2A 64
Glabyn Av. BL6: Los 4H 37
Gladden Hey Dr. WN3: Wins 1A 70
Glade, The BL1: Bolt 3E 38
SK4: Stoc 7M 107
WN6: She 6M 33
Glade Brow OL4: Grot 5D 64
Gladeside Ct. M22: Wyth 3B 116
Gladeside Rd. M22: Wyth 3B 116
Glade St. BL1: Bolt 5D 38
Gladewood Cl. SK9: Wilm 6H 123
Glade Wood Dr. M35: Fail 2F 80
Gladstone Bus. Pk. OL4: O'ham 5M 63
Gladstone Cl. BL1: Bolt 2F 38
(off Gladstone St.)
M15: Man 5D 94
SK13: Glos 9F 100
Gladstone Ct. BL4: Farn 2K 57
(off Gladstone Pl.)
OL7: A Lyne 9A 6
SK4: Stoc 5M 107
Gladstone Cres. OL11: Roch 1D 44
Gladstone Gro. SK4: Stoc 5M 107
Gladstone Ho. OL12: W'le 8G 14
(off Old School Pl.)
Gladstone M. SK4: Stoc 5C 108
(off Short St.)
Gladstone Mill SK15: Stal 8E 82
(off Warrington St.)
Gladstone Pl. BL4: Farn 2K 57
Gladstone Rd. BL4: Farn 2K 57
M30: Ecc 8E 76
M41: Urm 7E 92
WA14: Alt 1D 114
Gladstone St. BL1: Bolt 2F 38
BL5: W'ton 2G 55
BL9: Bury 1A 42
M27: Pen 2G 77
OL4: O'ham 5M 63
SK2: Stoc 3G 118
SK13: Glos 9E 100
SK13: Had 5C 100
Gladstone Ter. Rd. OL3: G'fld 7K 65
Gladstone Way WA12: N Wil 5D 86
Gladville Dr. SK8: Chea 1M 117
Gladwyn Av. M20: Man 4D 106
Gladys St. BL3: Bolt 1L 57
M16: Old T 5B 94
Glaisdale OL4: O'ham 5A 64
Glaisdale Cl. BL2: Bolt 2J 39
WN4: A Mak 7F 70
Glaisdale Ct. BL2: Bolt 2J 39
Glaisdale St. BL2: Bolt 2J 39
Glaister La. BL2: Bolt 3L 39
Glamis Av. M11: Man 7N 79
M32: Stre 7G 93
OL10: H'ood 4K 43
Glamis Cl. WN7: Lei 4M 73
Glamorgan Pl. OL9: O'ham 6G 62
Glandon Dr. SK8: Chea H 7A 118
Glanford Av. M9: Man 8F 60
Glanton Wlk. M40: Man 1B 80
(off Enstone Dr.)
Glanvor Rd. SK3: Stoc 8A 108
Glassbrook St. WN6: Wig 2D 52
Glasshouse St. M4: Man 1M 5 (7H 79)
Glasson Wlk. OL9: Chad 5E 62
Glass St. BL4: Farn 4M 57
Glastonbury OL12: Roch 5B 8
Glastonbury Av. SK8: Chea H 9N 117
WA3: Low 1E 88
WA15: Hale 5H 115
Glastonbury Dr. SK12: Poy 2H 125
Glastonbury Gdns. M26: Rad 7E 40
Glastonbury Rd. M29: Ast 3C 74
M32: Stre 6F 92
Glaswen Gro. SK5: Stoc 4D 108
GLAZEBROOK 3B 102
Glazebrook Cl. OL10: H'ood 3H 43
Glazebrook La. WA3: G'ook 1B 102
Glazebrook Station (Rail) 3B 102
GLAZEBURY 2L 89
Glazebury Dr. BL5: W'ton 1H 55
M23: Wyth 2A 116
Glazedale Av. OL2: O'ham 8G 45
Glaze Wlk. M45: Whitef 1B 60
Glaziers La. WA3: Cul 7F 88
Gleave Av. SK10: Boll 5M 129
Gleave Cl. WA15: Alt 4E 6 (3E 114)
Gleaves Av. BL2: Bolt 9A 24
Gleaves Rd. M30: Ecc 9E 76
Gleave St. BL1: Bolt 1L 7 (4G 39)
M33: Sale 2H 105
Glebe Av. WN4: A Mak 8F 70
Glebe Cl. WN6: Stan 3B 34
Glebe End St. WN6: Wig 7G 9 (3E 52)
Glebe Ho. M24: Mid 1M 61
(off Rochdale Rd.)
Glebeland WA3: Cul 6G 88
Glebeland Rd. BL3: Bolt 7C 38
Glebelands Rd. M23: Wyth 1M 115
M25: Pres 6N 59
M33: Sale 2E 104
WA16: Knut 7G 132
Glebe La. OL1: O'ham 8B 46
Glebe Rd. M41: Urm 7D 92
WN6: Stan 3C 34
Glebe St. BL2: Bolt 4M 7 (6H 39)
BL5: W'ton 2G 55
M26: Rad 9H 41
M34: Dent 5L 97
OL2: Shaw 5M 45
OL6: A Lyne 7E 6 (7N 81)
OL9: Chad 8E 62
SK1: Stoc 7E 108
WN2: Hin 9E 54
WN7: Lei 4H 73
Gleden St. M40: Man 8K 79
(not continuous)
Gledhall St. SK15: Stal 8D 82
Gledhill Av. M5: Sal 2N 93
Gledhill Cl. OL2: Shaw 3L 45
Gledhill St. M20: Man 1G 107
Gledhill Way BL7: Bro X 5H 23
Glegg St. SK11: Macc 5J 131
WN2: I Mak 3J 53
Glemsford Cl. M40: Man 4N 79
WN3: Wig 8E 52
Glen, The BL1: Bolt 5N 37
M24: Mid 5N 61
Glenacre Gdns. M18: Man 5C 96
Glenarm Wlk. M22: Wyth 5D 116
Glenart M30: Ecc 7E 76
Glen Av. BL3: Bolt 7C 38
BL4: Kea 5B 58
M9: Man 1K 79
M27: Swin 2D 76
M28: Wors 2A 76
M33: Sale 2G 104
Glenavon Dr. OL2: Shaw 4K 45
OL12: Roch 2B 28
Glenbarry Cl. M13: Man 3G 95
Glenbarry St. M12: Man 1J 95
Glenbeck Cl. BL6: Hor 3F 36
Glenbeck Rd. M45: Whitef 2L 59
Glenboro Av. BL8: Bury 2H 41
Glenboro Ct. BL8: Bury 3J 41
(off Glenboro Av.)
Glen Bott St. BL1: Bolt 2E 38
Glenbourne Pk. SK7: Bram 1B 124
Glenbranter Av. WN2: I Mak 3K 53
Glenbrook Gdns. BL4: Farn 1L 57
Glenbrook Hill SK13: Glos 7E 100
Glenbrook Rd. M9: Man 6F 60
Glenburn St. BL3: Bolt 9E 38
Glenby Av. M22: Wyth 4E 116
Glenby Est. OL9: Chad 5G 62
Glencar BL4: W'ton 4F 54
Glencar Dr. M40: Man 9B 62
Glencastle Rd. M18: Man 4A 96
(not continuous)
Glen Cl. WA3: Rix 6C 102
Glencoe BL2: Bolt 5J 39
Glencoe Cl. OL10: H'ood 3E 42
Glencoe Dr. BL2: Bolt 6N 39
M33: Sale 6C 104
Glencoe Pl. OL11: Roch 6B 28
Glencoe St. OL8: O'ham 9G 63
Glen Cotts. BL1: Bolt 2N 37
Glencoyne Dr. BL1: Bolt 7E 22
Glencross Av. M21: Cho H 7N 93
Glendale M27: Clif 9H 59
Glendale Av. BL9: Bury 9M 41
M19: Man 2L 107
WN4: A Mak 6F 70
Glendale Cl. M28: Wors 3G 75
OL10: H'ood 2J 43
(off Prince St.)
Glendale Ct. OL8: O'ham 7K 63
Glendale Dr. BL3: Bolt 6A 38
Glendale Rd. M28: Wors 3G 74
M30: Ecc 7G 76
Glendene Av. M43: Droy 7G 81
SK7: Bram 1B 124
Glenden Foot OL12: Roch 3B 28
Glendevon Cl. BL3: Bolt 7A 38
M22: Wyth 2B 116
WN2: I Mak 3K 53
Glendevon Pl. M45: Whitef 4A 60
Glendon Ct. OL1: O'ham 8B 46
Glendon Cres. OL6: A Lyne 3M 81
Glendore M5: Sal 8J 77
Glendower Dr. M40: Man 5H 79
Glen Dr. WN6: App B 4J 33
Gleneagles BL3: Bolt 9A 38
Gleneagles Av. M11: Man 8A 80
OL10: H'ood 4J 43
Gleneagles Cl. SK7: Bram 8E 118
SK9: Wilm 6J 123
WA3: Low 2B 88
Gleneagles Dr. SK10: Macc 9G 129
Gleneagles Rd. M41: Urm 5M 91
SK8: H Grn 6H 117
Gleneagles Way BL0: Ram 9H 11
Glenfield WA14: Alt 3B 114
Glenfield Cl. OL4: O'ham 5A 64
Glenfield Dr. SK12: Poy 3H 125
Glenfield Rd. SK4: Stoc 4B 108
Glenfield Sq. BL4: Farn 1J 57
Glenfyne Rd. M6: Sal 5K 77
Glen Gdns. OL12: Roch 3D 28
Glengarth OL3: Upp 4L 65
Glengarth Dr. BL1: Bolt 6L 37
BL6: Los 6L 37
Glen Gro. M24: Mid 4A 62
OL2: O'ham 7H 45
Glenham Ct. M15: Man 5D 94
(off Moss La. W.)
Glenham Way OL9: Chad 7E 62
Glenhaven Av. M41: Urm 7C 92
Glenholme Rd. SK7: Bram 8B 118
Glenhurst Rd. M19: Man 3K 107
Glenilla Av. M28: Wors 5N 75
Glenlea Dr. M20: Man 8G 106
Glenluce Wlk. BL3: Bolt 7N 37
Glenmay Ct. M32: Stre 7J 93
Glen Maye M33: Sale 4J 105
Glenmaye Gro. WN2: Hin 6C 54
Glenmere Cl. M25: Pres 5M 59
Glenmere Rd. M20: Man 8H 107
Glenmoor Rd. SK1: Stoc 3N 9 (7E 108)
Glen Morag Gdns. OL11: Roch 7M 27
Glenmore Av. BL4: Farn 1H 57
M20: Man 4D 106
Glenmore Bungs. SK16: Duk 2N 97
(off Glenmore Gro.)
Glenmore Cl. BL3: Bolt 7N 37
OL11: Roch 8K 27
Glenmore Dr. M8: Man 3G 79
M35: Fail 2F 80
Glenmore Gro. SK16: Duk 1N 97
Glenmore Rd. BL0: Ram 3F 24
Glenmore St. BL9: Bury 9J 7 (3L 41)
Glenmuir Cl. M44: Irl 7H 91
Glenolden St. M11: Man 8B 80
Glenpark WN7: Lei 4K 73
Glenpark Wlk. M9: Man 3K 79
(off Craigend Dr.)
Glenridding Cl. OL1: O'ham 2L 63
Glenridge Cl. BL1: Bolt 2G 38
Glen Ri. WA15: Tim 2G 115
Glen Rd. OL4: O'ham 5N 63
Glen Royd OL12: Roch 4A 28
Glenroyd HD7: Mars 1G 48
Glensdale Dr. M40: Man 1C 80
Glenshee Dr. BL3: Bolt 7A 38
Glenside WN6: App B 2F 32
Glenside Av. M18: Man 6B 96
Glenside Dr. BL3: Bolt 1G 57
SK6: Wood 3M 109
SK9: Wilm 8H 123
Glenside Gdns. M35: Fail 3E 80
Glenside Gro. M28: Walk 8M 57
Glen St. BL0: Ram 7H 11
M50: Sal 2N 93
Glenthorn Av. M9: Man 5J 61
Glenthorne Dr. OL7: A Lyne 6L 81
Glenthorne St. BL1: Bolt 3F 38
(off Nebraska St.)
Glenthorn Gro. M33: Sale 5H 105
Glen Trad. Est. OL4: O'ham 5A 64
Glentress M. BL1: Bolt 4B 38
Glentrool M. BL1: Bolt 5B 38
Glent Vw. SK15: Stal 6D 82
Glent Wakefield Rd. SK15: Stal 7E 82
Glentwood WA14: Hale 6E 114
Glenvale Cl. M26: Rad 9H 41
Glen Vw. OL2: O'ham 7H 45
OL12: Whitw 4A 14
OL15: Lit 7N 15
Glenview Rd. M29: Tyld 9A 56
Glenville Cl. SK8: Chea H 8L 117
Glenville Rd. M8: Man 5E 78
Glenville Ter. M43: Droy 7C 80
(off Greenside La.)
Glenville Wlk. SK15: Stal 9D 82
(off Forester Dr.)
Glenville Way M34: Dent 7L 97
Glenwood Av. SK14: Hyde 4A 98
Glenwood Cl. M26: Rad 1H 59
Glenwood Dr. M9: Man 3K 79
M24: Mid 1A 62
Glenwood Gro. SK2: Stoc 4F 118
Glenwyn Av. M9: Man 7K 61
Globe Cl. M16: Old T 4C 94
Globe Ind. Est. M26: Rad 9H 41
Globe La. BL7: Eger 2E 22
SK16: Duk 2L 97
Globe La. Ind. Est. SK16: Duk 3M 97
Globe Pk. OL16: Roch 7F 28
Globe Sq. SK16: Duk 2L 97
Globe St. OL4: O'ham 4M 63
GLODWICK 6M 63
Glodwick OL4: O'ham 6M 63
GLODWICK BROOK 7L 63
Glodwick Rd. OL4: O'ham 6M 63
Glodwick Swimming Pool 5M 63
GLOSSOP 8E 100
Glossop & District Golf Course 9J 101
Glossop & District Sailing Club 8M 85
Glossop Brook Bus. Pk.
SK13: Glos 8D 100
Glossop Brook Rd. SK13: Glos 8D 100
Glossop Climbing Wall 8F 100
(off High St. East)
Glossop Leisure Cen. 9F 100
Glossop Rd. SK6: Mar B 8E 110
SK13: Char, Gam 1N 111
Glossop Station (Rail) 8E 100
Glossop Swimming Pool 7E 100
Glossop Ter. M40: Man 8B 62
Glossop Way WN2: Hin 7A 54
Gloster St. BL2: Bolt 3N 7 (5H 39)
Gloucester Av. BL6: Hor 2F 36
M19: Man 9N 95
M45: Whitef 3N 59
OL10: H'ood 4H 43
OL12: Roch 1H 29
SK6: Mar 1C 120
WA3: Gol 9L 71
Gloucester Cl. OL6: A Lyne 2A 82
SK10: Macc 9J 129
Gloucester Ct. BL6: Hor 2F 36
Gloucester Cres. WN2: Hin 5A 54
Gloucester Dr. M33: Sale 4D 104
OL3: Dig 8M 47
Gloucester Ho. M7: Sal 4B 78
(off Bk. Duncan St.)
Gloucester Pl. M6: Sal 7N 77
M46: Ath 7M 55
Gloucester Ri. SK16: Duk 2D 98
Gloucester Rd. M6: Sal 6J 77
M24: Mid 5M 61
M34: Dent 7E 96
M41: Urm 7D 92
M43: Droy 7E 80
SK8: H Grn 8H 117
SK12: Poy 2H 125
SK14: Hyde 9B 98
WA16: Knut 8F 132
WN5: Wig 5N 51
Gloucester St. M1: Man 8G 4 (2E 94)
M5: Sal 1B 94
M6: Sal 6N 77
M46: Ath 8K 55
SK3: Stoc 9B 108
Gloucester St. Nth. OL9: O'ham 6G 62
Gloucester St. Sth. OL9: O'ham 6G 62
Gloucester Way SK13: Glos 9H 101
Glover Av. M8: Man 4G 79
Glover Cen. OL5: Mos 2G 82
Glover Ct. M7: Sal 2E 78
WN7: Lei 2E 72
Glover Dr. SK14: Hyde 7B 98
Glover Fld. M7: Sal 4C 78
Glover Ho. Cl. WN7: Lei 8G 73
Glover Rd. PR7: Cop 6A 18
Glover St. BL6: Hor 9D 20
WA12: N Wil 6F 86
WN7: Lei 2E 72
Glyn Av. WA15: Hale 5G 114
Glynis Cl. SK3: Stoc 1D 118
Glynne St. BL4: Farn 3K 57
Glynn Gdns. M20: Man 4C 106
Glynrene Dr. M27: Ward 1C 76
Glynwood Pk. BL4: Farn 2K 57
Gnat Bank Fold OL11: Roch 8L 27
Goadsby St.
M4: Man 2J 5 (8F 78)
Goals Soccer Cen.
Manchester 5B 60
Goathland Way SK11: Macc 7H 131
GOATS 4N 45
Goats Ga. Ter. M45: Whitef 1K 59
Godbert Av. M21: Cho H 3B 106
Goddard La. SK13: Had 3C 100
SK22: Row 9N 111
Goddard Rd. SK13: Had 5C 100
Goddard St. OL8: O'ham 7K 63
Godfrey Av. M43: Droy 7B 80
Godfrey Mill SK14: Hyde 6B 98
Godfrey Range M18: Man 5D 96
Godfrey Rd. M6: Sal 5J 77
Godlee Dr. M27: Swin 3E 76
GODLEY 6C 98
Godley Cl. M11: Man 1A 96
Godley Ct. SK14: Hyde 7C 98
(off Mottram Rd.)
GODLEY GREEN 8D 98
GODLEY HILL 7E 98
Godley Hill SK14: Hyde 7E 98
Godley Hill Rd. SK14: Hyde 6E 98
Godley Station (Rail) 6D 98
Godley St. SK14: Hyde 5C 98
Godmond Hall Dr. M28: Wors 5G 75
Godolphin Cl. M30: Ecc 6F 76
Godson St. OL1: O'ham 2J 63
Godward Rd. SK22: N Mil 7L 121
Godwin St. M18: Man 3C 96
Goit Pl. OL16: Roch 7D 8 (6D 28)
GOLBORNE 1M 87
Golborne Av. M20: Man 1E 106
Golborne Dale Rd. WA12: N Wil 4K 87
Golborne Dr. OL2: Shaw 4M 45
Golborne Ent. Pk. WA3: Gol 9K 71
Golborne Gallery WN1: Wig 7J 9
(off The Galleries)
Golborne Ho. OL2: Shaw 4M 45
(off Cowie St.)
WA3: Gol 1L 87
Golborne Pl. WN1: Wig 7N 9 (3H 53)
Golborne Rd. WA2: Win 9K 87
WA3: Low 1N 87
WN4: A Mak 6G 70
Golborne St. WA12: N Wil 5H 87
GOLBURN CLOUGH 5L 65
Goldbrook Cl. OL10: H'ood 3K 43
Goldcraft Cl. OL10: H'ood 3K 43
Goldcrest Cl. M22: Shar 2E 116
M28: Wors 3J 75
Goldenhill Av. M11: Man 7A 80
Golden Sq. M30: Ecc 9D 76
(off Golden St.)
Golden St. M30: Ecc 9D 76
OL2: Shaw 4B 46
Golden Way M41: Urm 7D 92
Goldenways WN1: Wig 1F 52
Goldfinch Dr. BL9: Bury 9B 26
Goldfinch Way M43: Droy 7G 81
Goldie Av. M22: Wyth 6E 116
Goldrill Av. BL2: Bolt 4N 39
Goldrill Gdns. BL2: Bolt 4N 39
Goldsmith Av. M5: Sal 8K 77
OL1: O'ham 8B 46
Goldsmith Pl. WN3: Wig 7D 52
Goldsmith Rd. SK5: Stoc 8B 96
Goldsmith St. BL3: Bolt 8E 38
Goldsmith Way M34: Dent 1L 109
(off Wordsworth Rd.)
Goldstein Rd. BL6: Los 8K 37
Gold St. M1: Man 5J 5 (9F 78)
Goldsworth Rd. OL1: O'ham 9A 46
Goldsworthy Rd. M41: Urm 6M 91
Goldswick Wlk. M23: Wyth 7L 105
Golf Rd. M33: Sale 4M 105
WA15: Hale 4F 114
Golfview Dr. M30: Ecc 6D 76
Golinrod BL9: Bury 1K 25
Gomer Wlk. M8: Man 4H 79
(off Smedley Rd.)
Gonville Av. SK11: Sut E 9K 131
Gooch Dr. WA12: N Wil 7G 86
Gooch St. BL6: Hor 2E 36
Goodacre SK14: Hyde 3E 98
Goodall St. BL9: Bury 7M 7
SK11: Macc 5J 131
Gooden St. OL10: H'ood 3K 43
Goodhope Mill OL6: A Lyne 8B 6
Goodier Ho. Fold SK14: Hyde 5C 98
(off Victoria St.)
Goodiers Dr. M5: Sal 1N 93
Goodier St. M33: Sale 4G 105
M40: Man 6L 79
Goodier Vw. SK14: Hyde 4C 98
Good Intent OL16: Roch 8L 29
Goodison Cl. BL9: Bury 9A 42
Goodlad St. BL8: Bury 9H 25
Goodman St. M9: Man 2K 79
Goodrich OL11: Roch 7C 28
Goodridge Av. M22: Wyth 6B 116
Goodrington Rd. SK9: Hand 3K 123
Goodshaw Rd. M28: Wors 2K 75
Good Shepherd Cl.
OL16: Roch 6G 8 (5F 28)
Goodwill Cl. M27: Swin 3F 76
Goodwin Ct. OL9: Chad 7G 62
Goodwin St. BL1: Bolt 1M 7 (4H 39)
Goodwood Av. M23: Wyth 8K 105
M33: Sale 4C 104
Goodwood Cl. BL3: Lit L 9N 39
SK11: Macc 6J 131
Goodwood Ct. M7: Sal 4C 78
Goodwood Cres. WA15: Tim 1J 115
Goodwood Dr. M27: Pen 3H 77
OL1: O'ham 2M 63
SK3: Stoc 3C 118
Goodwood Rd. SK6: Mar 2B 120
Goodworth Wlk. M40: Man 3N 79
(off Egbert St.)
Goole St. M11: Man 1M 95
Goose Cote Hill BL7: Eger 3F 22
GOOSE GREEN 8B 52
Goose Grn. WA14: Alt 4D 6 (3D 114)
Goose Grn. Av. PR7: Cop 4C 18
Goosehouse Grn. SK6: Rom 5A 110
Goose La. OL12: Roch 5C 8 (5D 28)
Goosetrey Cl. SK9: Wilm 5K 123
Goostrey Av. M20: Man 9F 94
Goostrey Way WA16: Mob 4N 133
Gordon Av. BL3: Bolt 7D 38
M19: Man 8N 95
M33: Sale 2H 105
OL4: O'ham 5M 63
OL9: Chad 8E 62
SK7: H Gro 4H 119
WA11: Hay 2C 86
WN4: Gars 6B 70
Gordon Cl. WN5: Wig 3B 52
Gordon Pl. M20: Man 3G 106
Gordon Rd. M27: Swin 4C 76
M30: Ecc 7D 76
Gordonstoun Cres. WN5: Orr 4K 51
Gordon St. BL9: Bury 5K 7 (9L 25)
M7: Sal 6C 78
M16: Old T 4C 94
M18: Man 3C 96
OL2: Shaw 5N 45
(not continuous)
OL4: Lees 6B 64
OL4: Spri 5D 64
OL6: A Lyne 6A 82
OL9: Chad 7D 62
OL11: Roch 8E 28
OL16: Miln 9M 29
SK4: Stoc 6C 108
SK14: Hyde 7B 98
SK15: Stal 9E 82
WN1: I Mak, Wig 9N 9 (4H 53)
WN7: Lei 4H 73
Gordon Ter. M9: Man 2K 79
(off Kingscliffe St.)
SK15: Stal 8D 82
Gordon Way OL10: H'ood 3E 42
Gore Av. M5: Sal 8K 77
M35: Fail 3F 80
Gorebrook Ct. M12: Man 5M 95
Gore Cl. BL9: Bury 3B 42
Gore Cres. M5: Sal 7K 77
Goredale Av. M18: Man 6C 96
Gore Dr. M5: Sal 7K 77
Gore La. SK9: A Edg 2A 126
Gore's La. WA11: Cra 4D 68
Gore St. M1: Man 5K 5 (9G 78)
M3: Sal 4D 4 (9D 78)
M6: Sal 7N 77
(off Up. Gloucester St.)
WN5: Wig 5M 51
Goring Av. M18: Man 3B 96
Gorman St. WN6: Wig 2D 52
Gorman Wlk. WN3: Wig 6C 52
Gorrells Cl. OL11: Roch 1B 44
Gorrels Way OL11: Roch 1B 44
Gorrels Way Ind. Est.
OL11: Roch 1B 44
Gorse, The WA14: Bow 7B 114
Gorse Av. M32: Stre 6M 93
M43: Droy 8G 80
OL5: Mos 1H 83
OL8: O'ham 8N 63
SK6: Mar 1B 120
Gorse Bank BL9: Bury 1B 42
Gorse Bank Rd.
WA15: Haleb 8J 115
Gorse Cres. M32: Stre 6M 93
Gorse Dr. M32: Stre 6M 93
M38: Lit H 5G 56
Gorsefield Cl. M26: Rad 8G 41
Gorsefield Dr. M27: Swin 3F 76
Gorsefield Hey SK9: Wilm 6K 123
Gorse Hall Cl. SK16: Duk 2C 98
Gorse Hall Dr. SK15: Stal 9D 82
Gorse Hall Rd. SK16: Duk 2B 98
GORSE HILL 5L 93
Gorselands SK8: Chea H 1N 123
Gorse La. M32: Stre 6M 93
Gorse Pit BL9: Bury 1B 42
Gorse Rd. M27: Swin 4E 76
M28: Walk 9M 57
OL16: Miln 7L 29
Gorses BL9: Bury 9F 26
Gorses Dr. WN2: Asp 6M 35
Gorses Mt. BL2: Bolt 7K 39
Gorse Sq. M31: Part 5E 102
Gorses Rd. BL2: Bolt 7L 39
Gorse St. M32: Stre 6L 93
OL9: Chad 7D 62
Gorse Wlk. WN7: Lei 5D 72
Gorse Way SK13: Glos 9G 101
Gorseway SK5: Stoc 4F 108
Gorsey Av. M22: Wyth 2B 116
Gorsey Bank OL15: Lit 7N 15
Gorsey Bank Rd.
SK3: Stoc 8M 107
Gorsey Brow
M41: Urm 7F 92
SK1: Stoc 3N 9 (7E 108)
SK6: Rom 6L 109
SK14: B'tom 8K 99
WN5: Bil 5H 69
WN6: Stan 2M 33
(off Almond Brook Rd.)
Gorsey Brow Cl. WN5: Bil 5H 69
Gorsey Clough Wlk.
BL8: Tot 8F 24
Gorsey Dr. M22: Wyth 3B 116
Gorseyfields M43: Droy 1E 96
Gorsey Gro. BL5: W'ton 4F 54
Gorsey Hey BL5: W'ton 4G 55
Gorsey Hill St. OL10: H'ood 3J 43
Gorsey Intakes SK14: B'tom 9K 99
Gorsey La. OL6: A Lyne 4C 82
WA13: Warb 1H 113
WA14: Alt 3A 6 (2B 114)

Gorsey Mt. St.
SK1: Stoc 3N **9** (7E **108**)
(St Andrews Ct.)
SK1: Stoc 3M **9** (7D **108**)
(Up. Brook St.)
Gorsey Rd. M22: Wyth 3B **116**
SK9: Wilm 7E **122**
Gorsey Way OL6: A Lyne 4B **82**
Gorston Wlk. M22: Wyth 7B **116**
Gort Cl. BL9: Bury 2N **59**
GORTON 5B **96**
Gorton Cres. M34: Dent 7G **97**
Gorton Fold BL6: Hor 1E **36**
Gorton Gro. M28: Walk 6K **57**
Gorton Ind. Est. M18: Man 3A **96**
Gorton La. M12: Man 3M **95**
M18: Man 3M **95**
Gorton Parks M18: Man 3A **96**
Gorton Rd. M11: Man 2L **95**
M12: Man 2L **95**
SK5: Stoc 6D **96**
Gorton Station (Rail) 3B **96**
Gorton St. BL2: Bolt 4M **7** (6H **39**)
BL4: Farn 4J **57**
M3: Sal 2F **4** (8E **78**)
M30: Ecc 9A **76**
OL7: A Lyne 9K **81**
OL9: Chad 5F **62**
OL10: H'ood 2K **43**
Gortonvilla Wlk. *M12: Man* *3L 95*
(off Clowes St.)
Gosforth Cl. BL8: Bury 8J **25**
OL1: O'ham 2L **63**
Gosforth Wlk. M23: Wyth 7M **105**
Goshen La. BL9: Bury 6M **41**
Goshen Sports Cen. 6N **41**
Gosport Sq. M7: Sal 5C **78**
Gosport Wlk. *M8: Man* *4H 79*
(off Smeaton St.)
Goss Hall St. OL4: O'ham 5N **63**
Gotha Wlk. M13: Man 9N **5**
Gotherage Cl. SK6: Rom 6B **110**
Gotherage La. SK6: Rom 7B **110**
Gothic Cl. SK6: Rom 6C **110**
Goudhurst Ct. BL6: Hor 9G **21**
Gough's La. WA16: Knut 9H **133**
Gough St. *OL10: H'ood* *2K 43*
(off Adelaide St. E.)
SK3: Stoc 3H **9** (7B **108**)
Goulden Rd. M20: Man 2F **106**
Goulden St. M4: Man 2K **5** (8G **78**)
M6: Sal 8L **77**
Goulder Rd. M18: Man 6C **96**
Gould St. M4: Man 1J **5** (7G **79**)
M34: Dent 6J **97**
OL1: O'ham 3M **63**
Gourham Dr. SK8: Chea H 5L **117**
Govan St. M22: Nor 7D **106**
Govind Ruia Ct. M16: Whall R 7D **94**
Gowan Dr. M24: Mid 2J **61**
Gowanlock's St. BL1: Bolt 2F **38**
Gowan Rd. M16: Whall R 8D **94**
Gower Av. SK7: H Gro 4G **119**
Gower Ct. SK14: Hyde 9B **98**
Gowerdale Rd. SK5: Stoc 3G **109**
Gower Hey Gdns. SK14: Hyde 8B **98**
Gower Rd. SK4: Stoc 4B **108**
SK14: Hyde 8A **98**
Gowers St. OL16: Roch 5F **28**
Gower St. BL1: Bolt 4E **38**
BL4: Farn 2K **57**
M27: Pen 1G **77**
OL1: O'ham 1F **8** (4L **63**)
OL6: A Lyne 7F **6** (7N **81**)
WN5: Wig 5D **52**
WN7: Lei 6G **73**
Gowran Pk. OL4: O'ham 5A **64**
Gowy Cl. SK9: Wilm 5K **123**
Goya Ri. OL1: O'ham 8A **46**
Goyt Av. SK6: Mar 3C **120**
Goyt Cres. SK1: Stoc 5F **108**
SK6: Bred 5K **109**
Goyt Hey Av. WN5: Bil 5J **69**
Goyt Mill SK6: Mar 3C **120**
Goyt Rd. SK1: Stoc 5F **108**
SK6: Mar 3C **120**
SK22: N Mil 9M **121**
Goyt Valley SK6: Bred, Rom 6J **109**
Goyt Valley Rd. SK6: Bred 5K **109**
Goyt Valley Wlk. SK6: Bred 5K **109**
Goyt Vw. SK6: Rom 6K **109**
SK22: N Mil 9L **121**
Goyt Wlk. M45: Whitef 1A **60**
Grace St. BL6: Hor 1D **36**
OL12: Roch 3E **28**
WN7: Lei 5E **72**
Grace Wlk. M4: Man 9J **79**
Gracie Av. OL1: O'ham 2M **63**
Gradwell St.
SK3: Stoc 4H **9** (8B **108**)
Grafton Av. M30: Ecc 6G **76**
Grafton Ct. *M15: Man* *4C 94*
(off Chorlton Rd.)
OL16: Roch *7F 28*
(off Basil St.)
Graftons, The WA14: Alt 4C **6**
Grafton St. BL1: Bolt 4E **38**
BL9: Bury 4M **41**
M13: Man 4G **95**
M35: Fail 2E **80**
M46: Ath 1J **73**
OL1: O'ham 8B **46**
OL6: A Lyne 8G **6** (8A **82**)
(not continuous)
OL16: Roch 7F **28**
PR7: Adl 7J **19**
SK4: Stoc 5C **108**
SK14: Hyde 6A **98**
SK15: Mill 7G **82**
WA12: N Wil 6E **86**
WA14: Alt 4D **6** (3D **114**)
Graham Av. WN6: App B 2G **32**
Graham Cres. M44: Cad 4D **102**
Graham Dr. SK12: Dis 8F **120**
Graham Rd. M6: Sal 6J **77**
SK1: Stoc 8F **108**
Graham St. BL1: Bolt 4G **38**
M11: Man 1M **95**
OL7: A Lyne 9K **81**
WN2: Abr 1K **71**
Grainger Av. M12: Man 6M **95**
GRAINS BAR 6D **46**
Grains Rd.
OL1: O'ham, Shaw 5N **45**
OL2: O'ham, Shaw 5N **45**
OL3: Del 7D **46**
Grain Vw. M5: Sal 1N **93**
Gralam Cl. M33: Sale 7L **105**
Grammar, The 5D **114**
Grammar School Rd.
OL8: O'ham 9F **62**
WA13: Lym 5A **112**
Grampian Cl. OL9: Chad 6E **62**
Grampian Way OL2: Shaw 4L **45**
WA3: Low 9N **71**
WN2: P Bri 9L **53**
Granada M. M16: Whall R 8D **94**
Granada Rd. M34: Dent 6D **96**
Granada Studios 6D **4** (1D **94**)
Granada TV Cen. 5D **4** (9D **78**)
Granary La. M28: Wors 6N **75**
Granary M. SK12: Poy 3J **125**
Granary Way M33: Sale 6F **104**
Granby Ho. M1: Man 7J **5**
Granby Rd. M27: Swin 3C **76**
M32: Stre 8K **93**
SK2: Stoc 2F **118**
SK8: Chea H 7N **117**
WA15: Tim 7H **105**
Granby Row M1: Man 7J **5** (1F **94**)
(not continuous)
Granby St. BL8: Bury 9F **24**
OL9: Chad 8E **62**
Granby Village M1: Man 7J **5**
Grandale St. M14: Man 6H **95**
Grand Arc. WN1: Wig 8K **9** (3F **52**)
Grand Central Pools 3K **9** (8C **108**)
Grand Central Sq.
SK1: Stoc 3K **9** (7C **108**)
Grandidge St. OL11: Roch 8C **28**
Grand Stand OL2: Shaw 4B **46**
Grand Union Way M30: Ecc 1D **92**
Granford Cl. WA14: Alt 9D **104**
GRANGE 5J **47**
Grange, The BL5: W'ton 3E **54**
M14: Man 6H **95**
OL1: O'ham 3M **63**
SK3: Stoc *9A 108*
(off Edgeley Rd.)
SK11: Macc 6E **130**
SK14: Hyde 8C **98**
WN2: Hin 7N **53**
Grange Arts Cen. 1A **8** (4J **63**)
Grange Av. BL3: Lit L 9C **40**
M19: Man 9L **95**
M27: Swin 9D **58**
M30: Ecc 6D **76**
M32: Stre 7K **93**
M34: Dent 7M **97**
M41: Urm 7M **91**
OL8: O'ham 7G **63**
OL16: Miln 9K **29**
SK4: Stoc 3B **108**
SK8: Chea H 4L **117**
WA15: Hale 5G **115**
WA15: Tim 9H **105**
WN3: Wig 6E **52**
WN5: Orr 4M **51**
Grange Cl. SK14: Hyde 8C **98**
WA3: Low 3M **87**
Grange Ct. BL8: Bury 2H **41**
OL8: O'ham 7H **63**
WA14: Bow 6C **114**
Grange Cres. M41: Urm 8C **92**
Grange Dr. M9: Man 8L **61**
M30: Ecc 6D **76**
PR7: Cop 5A **18**
Grangeforth Rd. M8: Man 2E **78**
Grange Gdns. M30: Ecc 7E **76**
Grange Gro. M45: Whitef 3M **59**
Grangelands SK10: Macc 2D **130**
Grange La. M20: Man 6G **106**
OL3: Del 6J **47**
Grange Mnr. BL7: Bro X 5K **23**
Grange Mill Wlk. M40: Man 4N **79**
Grange Pk. Av. OL6: A Lyne 4C **82**
SK8: Chea 2J **117**
SK9: Wilm 6F **122**
Grange Pk. Rd. BL7: Bro X 7K **23**
M9: Man 8L **61**
SK8: Chea 2J **117**
Grange Pl. M44: Cad 3E **102**
Grange Rd. BL3: Bolt 7C **38**
BL4: Farn 2H **57**
BL7: Bro X 6K **23**
BL8: Bury 2H **41**
M21: Cho H 7N **93**
M24: Mid 6B **44**
M28: Wors 3F **74**
M30: Ecc 6N **75**
M33: Sale 4F **104**
M41: Urm 8C **92**
OL12: Whitw 3B **14**
SK7: Bram 4D **118**
SK11: Macc 6G **131**
WA11: Hay, N Wil 4A **86**
WA14: Bow 6C **114**
WA15: Tim 9H **105**
WN2: B'haw 1A **72**
WN4: A Mak 4C **70**
Grange Rd. Nth. SK14: Hyde 7C **98**
Grange Rd. Sth. SK14: Hyde 8C **98**
Grange St. M6: Sal 8L **77**
M35: Fail 4B **80**
OL9: O'ham 1B **8** (4J **63**)
WN2: Hin 7N **53**
WN7: Lei 7G **73**
Grangethorpe Dr. M19: Man 1K **107**
Grangethorpe Rd. M14: Man 7H **95**
M41: Urm 8C **92**
Grange Valley WA11: Hay 3A **86**
Grange Wlk. M24: Mid 1K **61**
Grangeway SK9: Hand 2H **123**
WN2: Hin 6C **54**
Grangewood BL7: Bro X 6K **23**
Grangewood Dr. M9: Man 3J **79**
Granite Ct. *M25: Pres* *6N 59*
(off Longfield Cen.)
Granite St. OL1: O'ham 3M **63**
Gransden Dr. M8: Man 4H **79**
Granshaw St. M40: Man 7K **79**
Gransmoor Av. M11: Man 2D **96**
Gransmoor Rd. M11: Man 2D **96**
M43: Droy 1D **96**
Grantchester Pl. BL4: Farn 2G **57**
Grantchester Way BL2: Bolt 3M **39**
Grant Cl. M9: Man 9J **61**
Grantham Cl. BL1: Bolt 3F **38**
Grantham Ct. *M34: Dent* *8K 97*
(off Stockport Rd.)
Grantham Dr. BL8: Bury 8K **25**
Grantham Gro. WN2: Wig 1J **53**
Grantham Rd. SK4: Stoc 6A **108**
Grantham St. M14: Man 6F **94**
OL4: O'ham 5G **8** (6L **63**)
Grantley St. WN4: A Mak 5D **70**
Grant M. BL0: Ram 7H **11**
Grant Rd. WN3: Wig 7D **52**
Grants Entry *BL0: Ram* *8H 11*
(off Young St.)
Grants La. BL0: Ram 8J **11**
Grant St. BL4: Farn 1J **57**
OL11: Roch 2B **44**
Grantwood WN4: A Mak 5D **70**
Granville Av. M7: Sal 2D **78**
M16: Whall R 7B **94**
Granville Cl. OL9: Chad 4G **62**
Granville Ct. M16: Whall R 6B **94**
OL16: Miln 1M **45**
Granville Gdns. M20: Man 6F **106**
Granville Rd. BL3: Bolt 9D **38**
M14: Man 9H **95**
M34: Aud 9F **80**
M41: Urm 6E **92**
SK8: Chea H 2N **117**
SK9: Wilm 9E **122**
WA15: Tim 1J **115**
Granville St. BL4: Farn 1L **57**
M27: Swin 2F **76**
M28: Walk 8K **57**
(not continuous)
M30: Ecc 7D **76**
OL1: O'ham 2J **63**
OL6: A Lyne 8A **82**
OL9: Chad 3G **62**
PR6: Adl 6K **19**
WN2: Hin 6A **54**
WN7: Lei 3H **73**
Granville Wlk. OL9: Chad 3G **62**
Grapes St. SK11: Macc 5H **131**
Graphite Way SK13: Had 4A **100**
Grasdene Av. M9: Man 8K **61**
Grasmere SK11: Macc 6D **130**
Grasmere Av. BL3: Lit L 8A **40**
BL4: Farn 4G **56**
M27: Ward 9C **58**
M41: Urm 8M **91**
M45: Whitef 4J **59**
OL10: H'ood 4J **43**
SK4: Stoc 2C **108**
WN2: Hin 7A **54**
WN2: I Mak 4K **53**
WN5: Orr 3K **51**
WN8: Uph 4F **50**
Grasmere Cl. SK15: Stal 6D **82**
Grasmere Ct. BL9: Bury 5N **41**
Grasmere Cres. M30: Ecc 7B **76**
SK6: H Lan 6B **120**
SK7: Bram 7C **118**
Grasmere Dr. BL9: Bury 5N **41**
WN4: A Mak 5E **70**
Grasmere Gro.
OL7: A Lyne 5A **6** (6K **81**)
Grasmere Rd. M27: Swin 4F **76**
M31: Part 5F **102**
M32: Stre 6K **93**
M33: Sale 6J **105**
OL2: O'ham 6G **45**
OL4: O'ham 5N **63**
SK8: Gat 4G **117**
SK9: A Edg 4F **126**
WA13: Lym 3A **112**
WA15: Tim 1J **115**
WN5: Wig 4N **51**
Grasmere St. BL1: Bolt 2G **38**
M12: Man 6N **95**
OL12: Roch 4D **28**
WN7: Lei 5G **73**
Grasmere Ter. WN2: Abr 2L **71**
Grasmere Wlk. M24: Mid 1L **61**
Grason Av. SK9: Wilm 5H **123**
GRASSCROFT 5F **64**
Grasscroft SK5: Stoc 2G **109**
Grasscroft Cl. M14: Man 7E **94**
GRASSCROFT CLOUGH 5H **65**
Grasscroft Rd. SK15: Stal 9D **82**
WN2: Hin 7C **54**
Grassfield Av. M7: Sal 4B **78**
Grassfield Way WA16: Knut 8G **133**
Grassholme Dr. SK2: Stoc 1L **119**
Grassingham Gdns. M6: Sal 7M **77**
Grassington Av. M40: Man 1M **79**
Grassington Ct. BL8: Bury 9F **24**
Grassington Dr. BL9: Bury 3C **42**
Grassington Pl. BL2: Bolt 3H **39**
Grassland Ri. M38: Lit H 7F **56**
Grass Mead M34: Dent 9L **97**
Grassmoor Cres. SK13: Gam 7N **99**
Grathome Wlk. *BL3: Bolt* *8F 38*
(off Belford Dr.)
Gratrix Av. M5: Sal 2A **94**
Gratrix La. M33: Sale 5M **105**
Gratrix St. M18: Man 5C **96**
Gratten Ct. M28: Walk 7K **57**
Gravel Bank Rd. SK6: Wood 2M **109**
GRAVEL HOLE 4G **45**
Gravel La. M3: Sal 3E **4** (8E **78**)
SK9: Wilm 1D **126**
Gravel Walks OL4: O'ham 4M **63**
Gravenmoor Dr. M7: Sal 4D **78**
Grave Oak La. WN7: Lei 9J **73**
Graver La. M40: Man 5B **80**
(not continuous)
Graves St. M26: Rad 6F **40**
Gray Av. WA11: Hay 3A **86**
Gray Cl. SK14: Mot 6J **99**
WN2: Wig 1K **53**
Graymar Rd. M38: Lit H 7H **57**
Graymarsh Dr. SK12: Poy 4J **125**
Grayrigg Wlk. *M9: Man* *3J 79*
(off Ruskington Dr.)
Graysands Rd. WA15: Hale 4F **114**
Grayson Av. M45: Whitef 3N **59**
Grayson Rd. M38: Lit H 7J **57**
Grayson's Cl. WN1: Wig 5K **9** (2F **52**)
Grayson Way OL3: G'fld 5L **65**
Grayston Ct. SK6: Mar 9D **110**
Gray St. BL1: Bolt 1J **7** (4F **38**)
Gray St. Nth. BL1: Bolt 4F **38**
Graythorpe Wlk. M5: Sal 9N **77**
Graythorp Wlk. *M14: Man* *6G 95*
(off Whickham Cl.)
Graythwaite Rd. BL1: Bolt 2A **38**
Grazing Dr. M44: Irl 6J **91**
Greame St. M14: Man 6E **94**
M16: Whall R 6E **94**
Great Acre WN1: Wig 5M **9** (2G **53**)
Gt. Ancoats St. M4: Man . . . 3K **5** (8G **78**)
Gt. Arbor Way M24: Mid 2L **61**
Gt. Bank Rd. BL5: W'ton 9F **36**
Gt. Bent Cl. OL12: Roch 1H **29**
Gt. Boys Cl. M29: Tyld 1F **74**
Gt. Bridgewater St.
M1: Man 7E **4** (1E **94**)
Gt. Cheetham St. E. M7: Sal 4D **78**
Gt. Cheetham St. W. M7: Sal 5B **78**
Gt. Clowes St. M3: Sal 1C **4** (7C **78**)
M7: Sal 4C **78**
Great Delph WA11: Hay 2A **86**
Gt. Ducie St. M3: Man 1F **4** (7E **78**)
Gt. Eaves Rd. BL0: Ram 7J **11**
Gt. Egerton St.
SK1: Stoc 2J **9** (7C **108**)
SK4: Stoc 2J **9** (7C **108**)
Greater Manchester Fire Service Mus.
. . . . 9D **8** (7D **28**)
Greater Manchester Police Mus.
. . . . 4K **5** (9G **78**)
Greatfield Rd. M22: Wyth 4A **116**
Great Flatt OL12: Roch 4N **27**
Great Fold WN7: Lei 6N **73**
Gt. Gable Cl. OL1: O'ham 3L **63**
Gt. Gates Cl. OL11: Roch 9D **28**
Gt. Gates Rd. OL11: Roch 1E **44**
Gt. George St. M3: Sal 3B **4** (8C **78**)
OL16: Roch 9C **8** (7D **28**)
(not continuous)
WN3: Wig 8G **9** (3E **52**)
Gt. Hall Cl. M26: Rad 8G **41**
Gt. Heaton Cl. M24: Mid 4H **61**
Great Holme BL3: Bolt 8G **39**
GREAT HORROCKS 6F **78**
Great Ho. Av. BB4: Has 1D **10**
Great House Barn 5B **20**
GREAT HOWARTH 1F **28**
Great Howarth OL12: Roch 1F **28**
Gt. Howarth Rd. OL12: Roch 1F **28**
Gt. Jackson St.
M15: Man 8D **4** (2D **94**)
Gt. John St. M3: Man 6D **4** (1D **94**)
Gt. Jones St. M12: Man 3M **95**
Gt. King St. SK11: Macc 4G **130**
Great Lee OL12: Roch 2B **28**
Gt. Lee Wlk. OL12: Roch 2B **28**
GREAT LEVER 9G **38**
Great Lever & Farnworth Golf Course
. . . . 2E **56**
Gt. Marlborough St.
M1: Man 8H **5** (2F **94**)
Gt. Marld Cl. BL1: Bolt 2A **38**
Great Meadow OL2: Shaw 4K **45**
Gt. Moor St. BL1: Bolt 4K **7** (6G **38**)
BL3: Bolt 4K **7** (6G **38**)
SK2: Stoc 2F **118**
Gt. Moss Rd. M29: Ast 8C **74**
Gt. Newton St. M40: Man 5A **80**
Gt. Norbury St. SK14: Hyde 6N **97**
Great Northern 6F **4** (1D **94**)
Gt. Northern Sq. Amphitheatre
M3: Man 6F **4**
Great Oak Dr. WA15: Alt . . . 3E **6** (3E **114**)
Great Oak Sq. WA16: Mob 4N **133**
Gt. Portwood St.
SK1: Stoc 1M **9** (6D **108**)
Gt. Queen St. SK11: Macc 4G **130**
Gt. Southern St. M14: Man 6G **94**
Greatstone Apartments
M32: Stre *6L 93*
(off Portland Rd.)
Gt. Stone Cl. M26: Rad 9D **40**
Gt. Stone Rd. M16: Old T 6N **93**
M32: Stre 5M **93**
Gt. Stones Cl. BL7: Eger 3F **22**
Great Underbank
SK1: Stoc 2K **9** (7D **108**)
Gt. Western St. M14: Man 5E **94**
M16: Whall R 5D **94**
Great Wood Local Nature Reserve
. . . . 9H **99**
GREAVE 5N **27**
Greave SK6: Rom 4A **110**
Greave Av. OL11: Roch 5N **27**
GREAVEFOLD 4A **110**
Greave Fold SK6: Rom 4N **109**
Greave Pk. OL3: Upp 4L **65**
Greave Rd. SK1: Stoc 8G **108**
Greaves Av. M35: Fail 4B **80**
Greaves Cl. WN6: App B 4K **33**
Greaves Rd. SK9: Wilm 7C **122**
Greaves St. OL1: O'ham 2D **8** (4K **63**)
(not continuous)
OL2: Shaw 5N **45**
OL4: Lees 5C **64**
OL5: Mos 9F **64**
Grebe Cl. SK12: Poy 2F **124**
WA16: Knut 5H **133**
WN3: Wig 7M **51**
Grebe Wlk. SK2: Stoc 3L **119**
Grecian Cres. BL3: Bolt 8G **38**
Grecian St. M7: Sal 5B **78**
Grecian St. Nth. M7: Sal 5B **78**
Grecian Ter. *M7: Sal* *5B 78*
(off Albert Pk. Rd.)
Gredle Cl. M41: Urm 7F **92**
Greeba Rd. M23: Wyth 1L **115**
Greek St. M1: Man 9K **5**
SK3: Stoc 5K **9** (8C **108**)
Green, The BL8: G'mount 4F **24**
HD7: Mars 1H **49**
M27: Clif 9H **59**
M28: Wors 5N **75**
M31: Part 4G **102**
OL8: O'ham 8L **63**
OL11: Roch 1A **44**
PR6: H Char 3J **19**
SK4: Stoc 5A **108**
SK6: Mar 4D **120**
SK8: Chea H 7L **117**
SK9: Hand 3K **123**
SK14: Hyde 3D **98**
SK15: Mill 6H **83**
WA15: Tim *9H 105*
(off Whitley Gdns.)
WN5: Wig 5M **51**
(not continuous)
WN8: Par 2A **32**
Green Acre BL5: W'ton 4H **55**
Greenacre SK8: H Grn 8H **117**
WN1: Wig 2G **53**
Greenacre Cl. BL0: Ram 7L **11**
WA16: Knut 8H **133**
Greenacre La. M28: Wors 6N **75**
Green Acre Pk. BL1: Bolt 3G **39**
GREENACRES 4N **63**
Greenacres WN6: Stan 3B **34**
Greenacres, The WA13: Lym 3B **112**
Greenacres Cl. WN7: Lei 1D **88**
Greenacres Ct. OL12: Roch 1H **29**
Greenacres Dr. M19: Man 4K **107**
GREENACRES HILL 3N **63**
GREENACRES MOOR 3N **63**
Greenacres Rd. OL4: O'ham 4M **63**
Greenall St. WN4: A Mak 5E **70**
Green & Slater Homes
SK4: Stoc 5M **107**
Green Av. BL3: Bolt 9J **39**
M27: Swin 3F **76**
M29: Ast 6A **74**
M38: Lit H 6F **56**
Green Bank BL2: Bolt 1M **39**
BL4: Farn 2K **57**
SK4: Stoc 1B **108**
SK13: Glos 9B **100**
Greenbank BL6: Hor 3F **36**
OL12: Whitw *9A 14*
(off Tonacliffe Rd.)
SK13: Had 4B **100**
WN2: Abr 3L **71**
WN2: Hin 8C **54**
Greenbank Av. M27: Swin 4D **76**
OL3: Upp 2M **65**
SK4: Stoc 6K **107**
SK8: Gat 2F **116**
WN5: Bil 8H **51**
Greenbank Bus. Pk. WN2: Hin 7D **54**
Greenbank Cres. SK6: Mar 2C **120**
Greenbank Dr. OL15: Lit 2K **29**
SK10: Boll 5L **129**
Greenbank Ho. *WA14: Bow* *4D 114*
(off Albert Sq.)
WN2: Hin 7D **54**
Greenbank Ind. Est. WN2: Hin 8C **54**
Greenbank Rd. BL3: Bolt 7C **38**
(not continuous)
M6: Sal 7L **77**
M26: Rad 7F **40**
M33: Sale 3E **104**
OL12: Roch 4D **28**
(not continuous)
SK6: Mar B 7E **110**
SK8: Gat 1F **116**
Greenbank Ter. M24: Mid 2A **62**
SK4: Stoc 1K **9**
Greenbarn Way BL6: Bla 2N **35**
Greenbeech Cl. SK6: Mar 9B **110**
Greenbooth Cl. SK16: Duk 2C **98**
Greenbooth Rd. OL12: Roch 2J **27**
Green Bri. Cl. OL11: Roch 9D **28**
Greenbridge La. OL3: G'fld 6K **65**
Greenbrook Bus. Pk.
BL9: Bury 9N **25**
Greenbrook Cl. BL9: Bury 9N **25**
Greenbrook St. BL9: Bury 9N **25**
Greenbrow Rd. M23: Wyth 2N **115**
(not continuous)
Green Bldg., The M1: Man 8G **5**
Greenburn Av. WA11: St H 9G **68**
Greenburn Dr. BL2: Bolt 2M **39**
Green Cl. M46: Ath 1N **73**
SK8: Gat 1F **116**
Green Clough OL15: Lit 6A **16**
Green Comn. La.
BL5: W'ton 4K **55**
Green Ct. WN7: Lei 9D **72**
Greencourt Dr. M38: Lit H 7G **56**
Green Courts WA14: Bow 4B **114**
Greencourts Bus. Pk.
M22: Wyth 7F **116**
Green Cft. SK6: Rom 5A **110**
Greencroft Mdw.
OL2: O'ham 7K **45**
Greencroft Rd. M30: Ecc 6B **76**
Greencroft Way M7: Sal 3C **78**
OL16: Roch 2H **29**
Greendale M46: Ath 7N **55**
Greendale Cres. WN7: Lei 6L **73**
Greendale Dr. M9: Man 8K **61**
M26: Rad 2H **59**
Greendale Gro. M34: Dent 9M **97**
Greendale La. SK10: P'bury 5B **128**

Green Dr. BL6: Los 5L 37
M19: Man 8L 95
SK9: Wilm 4J 123
WA15: Tim 9G 104
GREEN END 3L 107
Green End M34: Dent 9M 97
Green End Rd. M19: Man 3K 107
Greene Way M7: Sal 2N 77
GREENFIELD 6L 65
Greenfield Av. M30: Ecc 1A 92
M41: Urm 7D 92
WN2: I Mak 4H 53
WN8: Par 1A 32
Greenfield Cl. BL5: W'ton 2J 55
BL8: Bury 3G 41
SK3: Stoc 1C 118
SK22: N Mil 7K 121
WA15: Tim 1J 115
Greenfield Ct. OL10: H'ood 3J 43
Greenfield La. OL2: Shaw 6M 45
OL11: Roch 9E 28
OL16: Roch 2H 29
Greenfield Rd. M38: Lit H 7H 57
M46: Ath 6N 55
PR6: Adl 5K 19
SK10: Boll 6L 129
Greenfields WN6: Wig 8D 34
Greenfields Cl. WA12: N Wil 5F 86
WN2: Hin 5B 54
Greenfields Cres. WN4: A Mak 6F 70
Greenfield Station (Rail) 5K 65
Greenfield St. M34: Aud 2H 97
OL11: Roch 9E 28
SK13: Had 3C 100
SK14: Hyde 7A 98
Greenfield Ter. M41: Urm 7M 91
Greenfield Vw. OL16: Roch 2H 29
WN5: Bil 6H 69
Greenfinch Gdns.
WA14: W Tim 7C 104
Green Fold M18: Man 3D 96
Greenfold Av. BL4: Farn 4J 57
Green Fold La. BL5: W'ton 4G 55
Green Fold Way WN7: Lei 7J 73
Greenford Cl. SK8: Chea H 3N 117
WN5: Orr 5H 51
Greenford Rd. M8: Man 3F 78
Green Gables Cl. SK8: H Grn 6G 117
Greengage M13: Man 3H 95
GREEN GATE 1G 45
GREENGATE 2H 29
Green Ga. WA15: Haleb 8K 115
Greengate M3: Sal 1F 4 (7E 78)
M24: Man 8A 62
SK14: Hyde 9A 98
Greengate Cl. BL9: Bury 2B 42
OL12: Roch 1H 29
Greengate E. M40: Man 8A 62
Greengate Ind. Est. M24: Mid 6A 62
Greengate La. BL2: Bolt 4N 39
M25: Pres 7N 59
Greengate Rd. M34: Dent 5L 97
Greengate Rdbt. M40: Man 8A 62
Greengates SK10: Macc 2C 130
(off Priory La.)
Greengate St. OL4: O'ham 5F 8 (5L 63)
(not continuous)
Greengate W. M3: Sal 1D 4 (7D 78)
Greengrove Bank OL16: Roch 2G 29
Greenhalgh La. PR6: And 5L 19
Greenhalgh Moss La. BL8: Bury 8H 25
Greenhalgh St. M35: Fail 4A 80
SK4: Stoc 1K 9 (6C 108)
Green Hall Cl. M46: Ath 6A 56
Green Hall M. SK9: Wilm 8G 122
Greenham Rd. M23: Wyth 6M 105
Greenhaven WN8: Uph 4F 50
(off Tower Hill Rd.)
Greenhaven Cl. M28: Walk 8N 57
Green Hayes Av. WN1: Wig 9F 34
Greenhead Fold SK6: Rom 7L 109
Greenhead Wlk. BL3: Bolt 9F 38
(off Settle St.)
Greenhey WN5: Orr 4M 51
GREENHEYS
M15 4F 94
M38 5F 56
Greenheys BL2: Bolt 1M 39
M43: Droy 8E 80
Greenheys Bus. Cen. M15: Man 4F 94
(off Pencroft Way)
Greenheys Cres. BL8: G'mount 4E 24
Greenheys La. M15: Man 4E 94
Greenheys La. W. M15: Man 4D 94
Greenheys Rd. M38: Lit H 5F 56
GREEN HILL
M24 4B 62
OL2 3J 45
Green Hill M25: Pres 7N 59
Greenhill Av. BL3: Bolt 7C 38
BL4: Farn 5K 57
M33: Sale 2G 105
OL2: Shaw 3J 45
OL12: Roch 5C 28
Greenhill Cotts. OL5: Mos 9G 64
Greenhill Cres. WN5: Bil 5K 69
Greenhill La. BL3: Bolt 8A 38
Greenhill Pas. OL1: O'ham 3F 8
Green Hill Pl. SK3: Stoc 9B 108
Green Hill Rd. SK14: Hyde 6C 98
Greenhill Rd. BL8: Bury 3G 40
M8: Man 3F 78
M24: Mid 4A 62
WA15: Tim 1J 115
WN5: Bil 5K 69
Greenhills Cl. SK11: Macc 5J 131
Green Hill St. SK3: Stoc 9B 108
Green Hill Ter. SK3: Stoc 9B 108
Greenhill Ter. M24: Mid 4A 62
Greenhill Terraces
OL4: O'ham 4G 8 (5L 63)
Greenhill Wlk. SK12: Dis 9C 121
Green Hollow Fold SK15: C'ook 5G 83
Greenholme Cl. M40: Man 1B 80
Greenhow St. M43: Droy 1D 96
Greenhurst Cres. OL8: O'ham 9L 63
Greenhurst La. OL6: A Lyne 4B 82
Greenhurst Rd. OL6: A Lyne 3A 82
Greenhythe Rd. SK8: H Grn 9H 117
Greening Rd. M19: Man 7N 95
Greenland Av. WN6: Stan 4B 34
Greenland Cl. M29: Ast 3C 74
Greenland La. PR6: And, Hor 8N 19
Greenland Rd. BL3: Bolt 1H 57
BL4: Farn 1H 57
M29: Ast 4C 74
Greenlands Cl. SK8: Chea H 7K 117
Greenland St. M6: Sal 8L 77
M8: Man 3E 78
Green La. BL1: Bolt 2L 7 (5G 39)
BL3: Bolt 9G 39
BL4: Kea 4A 58
BL6: Hor 8D 20
M18: Man 3B 96
M24: Mid 1A 62
(Birch Rd.)
M24: Mid 4B 62
(Lees St.)
M30: Ecc 8C 76
M33: Sale 2E 104
M35: Fail 6C 80
M44: Cad 3F 102
M45: Whitef 2M 59
OL3: Del 8H 47
(off Church St.)
OL4: O'ham 1C 64
OL5: Mos 7E 64
OL6: A Lyne 5M 81
OL8: O'ham 9H 63
OL10: H'ood 2K 43
OL12: Roch 5C 28
PR7: Cop 6C 18
SK4: Stoc 5N 107
SK6: Rom 7M 109
SK7: H Gro 4H 119
SK9: A Edg 5E 126
SK9: Wilm 7G 122
SK10: Boll 4M 129
SK12: Poy 2N 125
SK13: Glos 9B 100
SK13: Had 5B 100
SK14: Holl 3N 99
SK14: Hyde 7D 98
(Alvon Ct.)
SK14: Hyde 7D 98
(Crossbridge Rd.)
WA3: Low 8C 72
WA5: Burt 9B 86
WA15: Tim 4H 115
(not continuous)
WA16: Knut 5D 132
WN2: Hin 6D 54
WN5: Bil 8H 51
WN6: Stan 3A 34
WN7: Lei 3L 73
(not continuous)
Green La. Ind. Est. SK4: Stoc 6B 108
Green La. Nth. WA15: Tim 2H 115
Greenlaw Ct. M16: Old T 4B 94
Greenlea Av. M18: Man 6B 96
Greenleach La. M28: Wors 2M 75
Greenlea Cl. WN5: Orr 6H 51
Greenleaf Cl. M28: Wors 4G 74
Greenleas BL6: Los 6L 37
Greenlees St. OL12: Roch 5D 28
Greenleigh Cl. BL1: Bolt 8E 22
Greenmans OL3: G'fld 8K 65
Greenmans La. OL3: G'fld 8K 65
Green Mdw. OL12: Roch 1H 29
Green Mdws. BL5: W'ton 4F 54
SK6: Mar 9C 110
SK11: Macc 6D 130
WA3: Low 4A 88
Green Mdws. Dr. SK6: Mar 8C 110
Green Mdws. Wlk. M22: Wyth 6D 116
GREENMOUNT 4F 24
Greenmount Cl. BL1: Bolt 5B 38
BL8: G'mount 3F 24
Greenmount Ct. BL1: Bolt 4B 38
Greenmount Dr. BL8: G'mount 3F 24
OL10: H'ood 5L 43
Greenmount Golf Course 4E 24
Greenmount La. BL1: Bolt 3A 38
Greenmount Pk. BL4: Kea 4A 58
Greenoak M26: Rad 4C 58
Greenoak Cl. WN2: Abr 3L 71
Greenoak Dr. M28: Walk 6K 57
M33: Sale 7J 105
Greenock Cl. BL3: Bolt 7N 37
Greenock Dr. OL10: H'ood 3E 42
Greenough St. M46: Ath 9M 55
WN1: Wig 7L 9 (3G 52)
Green Pk. Cl. BL8: G'mount 4F 24
Greenpark Rd. M22: Nor 7C 106
Green Pk. Vw. OL1: O'ham 1A 64
Green Pastures SK4: Stoc 7J 107
Greenrigg Cl. WN6: Stan 5C 34
Green Rd. M31: Part 5F 102
Greenroom Theatre 7G 5 (2E 94)
Greenroyd Av. BL2: Bolt 2M 39
Greenroyde OL11: Roch 8C 28
Greens, The OL12: Whitw 5A 14
Greens Arms Rd. BL7: Tur 1K 23
Greensbridge Gdns. BL5: W'ton 2H 55
Greenshank Cl. OL11: Roch 6L 27
WA12: N Wil 5F 86
WN7: Lei 5K 73
GREENSIDE 7D 80
Greenside BL2: Ain 3C 40
BL4: Farn 2K 57
M28: Wors 5A 76
SK4: Stoc 7M 107
Greenside Av. BL4: Kea 5N 57
OL4: O'ham 1A 64
Greenside Cl. BL8: Haw 2B 24
SK16: Duk 1D 98
Greenside Ct. M30: Ecc 7D 76
Greenside Cres. M43: Droy 8D 80
Greenside Dr. BL8: G'mount 4F 24
M44: Irl 8G 91
WA14: Hale 6E 114
Greenside La. M43: Droy 7C 80
Greenside Pl. M34: Dent 9L 97
Greenside Shop. Cen.
M43: Droy 9E 80
Greenside St. BL2: Ain 3C 40
M11: Man 9N 79
Greenside Trad. Cen.
M43: Droy 8E 80
Greenside Vw. SK14: Hyde 4D 98
Greenside Way M24: Mid 6A 62
Greens La. WN5: Bil 9J 51
Greenslate Av. WN6: App B 4J 33
Greenslate Ct. WN5: Bil 8H 51
(not continuous)
Greenslate Rd. WN5: Bil 8J 51
Greensmith Way BL5: W'ton 1G 54
Greenson Dr. M24: Mid 4K 61
Greenstead Av. M8: Man 2F 78
Greenstone Av. BL6: Hor 1C 36
Greenstone Dr. M6: Sal 5M 77
Green St. BL0: Eden 3L 11
BL4: Farn 2K 57
BL8: Bury 9H 25
(Elterwater Cl.)
BL8: Bury 9F 24
(Neston Rd.)
M14: Man 1J 107
M24: Mid 2N 61
M26: Rad 9G 41
M29: Tyld 1B 74
M30: Ecc 1B 92
M32: Stre 9J 93
M46: Ath 1N 73
OL8: O'ham 4A 8 (5H 63)
PR6: And 5L 19
PR7: Chor 1D 18
SK3: Stoc 1D 118
SK9: A Edg 4F 126
SK10: Macc 5J 131
SK14: Hyde 8B 98
WA16: Knut 6G 132
WN2: P Bri 9L 53
WN3: Wig 5F 52
Greensward Cl. WN6: Stan 3M 33
Greensway Shop. Cen.
OL2: Shaw 5M 45
(off Milnrow Rd.)
Greenthorne Av. SK4: Stoc 1B 108
Greenthorn Wlk. M15: Man 4E 94
(off Botham Cl.)
Green Top HD7: Mars 2G 48
Green Tree Gdns. SK6: Rom 6M 109
Greenvale OL11: Roch 5J 27
WN6: She 8K 33
Greenvale Bus. Pk. OL15: Lit 7N 15
Greenvale Ct. SK8: Chea 1H 117
Greenvale Dr. SK8: Chea 1H 117
Green Vw. M7: Sal 3C 78
WA13: Lym 2C 112
Green Vw. Chase OL4: Grot 6E 64
Greenview Dr. M20: Man 8H 107
OL11: Roch 5M 27
Green Villa Pk. SK9: Wilm 1D 126
Green Wlk. BL6: Bla 3N 35
M16: Whall R 7B 94
M31: Part 5F 102
M32: Stre 7H 93
SK8: Gat 1F 116
SK14: Mot 7J 99
WA14: Bow 4A 114
WA15: Tim 9F 104
Green Walks M25: Pres 8B 60
Greenwatch Cl. M30: Ecc 9C 76
Greenwater Mdw. SK14: Holl 4N 99
Green Way BL1: Bolt 9H 23
SK14: Mot 7J 99
Greenway BL6: Hor 1H 37
M22: Nor 8D 106
M24: Mid 6L 61
OL2: Shaw 3K 45
OL11: Roch 3N 43
SK6: Rom 7B 110
SK7: Bram 9B 118
SK9: Wilm 8G 122
SK14: Hyde 8A 98
WA14: Alt 2A 114
WN4: A Mak 6D 70
Greenway Av. M19: Man 9N 95
WN8: Skel 4A 50
Green Way Cl. BL1: Bolt 9H 23
Greenway Cl. BL8: Bury 1H 41
M33: Sale 5E 104
Greenway Dr. OL5: Mos 9F 64
Greenway M. BL0: Ram 1J 25
Greenway Rd. SK8: H Grn 8H 117
WA15: Tim 8F 104
Greenways M40: Man 1B 80
OL7: A Lyne 4K 81
WN5: Bil 8J 51
WN6: Stan 6D 34
WN7: Lei 4J 73
Greenwich Cl. M40: Man 6B 80
OL11: Roch 7L 27
Greenwood Av. BL6: Hor 3F 36
M27: Clif 1H 77
M28: Walk 8K 57
OL6: A Lyne 4N 81
(not continuous)
SK2: Stoc 1G 118
WN5: Wig 4B 52
Greenwood Bus. Cen. M5: Sal 1N 93
Greenwood Cl. M28: Wors 3F 74
WA15: Tim 2K 115
Greenwood Ct. WA3: Ris 7H 89
(Cedar Ct.)
WA3: Ris 9G 89
(Warrington Rd.)
Greenwood Dr. SK9: Wilm 6J 123
WA12: N Wil 7G 86
Greenwood Gdns. SK6: Bred 5K 109
Greenwood Pl. M30: Ecc 6E 76
OL15: Lit 9M 15
(off Hare Hill Rd.)
Greenwood Rd. M22: Wyth 4A 116
WA13: Lym 5A 112
WN6: Stan 2B 34
Greenwoods La. BL2: Bolt 9N 23
Greenwood St. BL4: Farn 3L 57
M6: Sal 6M 77
OL4: O'ham 3N 63
(not continuous)
OL4: Spri 6C 64
OL8: O'ham 1K 81
OL15: Lit 9M 15
OL16: Roch 8D 8 (6D 28)
WA14: Alt 3C 6 (3D 114)
Greenwood Ter. M5: Sal 2A 94
WA16: Mob 4N 133
Greenwood Va. BL1: Bolt 1G 38
(off Beryl St.)
Greer St. M11: Man 1A 96
Greetland Dr. M9: Man 7L 61
Greg Av. SK10: Boll 6J 129
Gregge St. OL10: H'ood 3K 43
(not continuous)
Gregg M. SK9: Wilm 4G 123
Gregory Av. BL2: Bolt 4M 39
M46: Ath 6L 55
SK6: Rom 7N 109
Gregory Row WA3: Low 9C 72
(off Sandy La.)
Gregory St. BL5: W'ton 4C 54
M12: Man 3L 95
OL8: O'ham 8G 62
SK14: Hyde 4B 98
WN2: Hin 5M 53
WN7: Lei 6G 73
Gregorys Yd. BL6: Bla 1M 35
(off Chorley Rd.)
Gregory Wlk. SK14: Hyde 4B 98
(off Gregory St.)
Gregory Way SK5: Stoc 2D 108
Gregson Fld. BL3: Bolt 8F 38
(not continuous)
Gregson Rd. SK5: Stoc 2C 108
Gregson St. OL1: O'ham 3E 8 (5K 63)
Greg St. SK5: Stoc 3C 108
Greg St. Ind. Est. SK4: Stoc 3C 108
Grelley Wlk. M14: Man 6G 95
(off Ellanby Cl.)
Grenaby Av. WN2: Hin 6D 54
Grendale Av. SK1: Stoc 7F 108
SK7: H Gro 6J 119
Grendale Dr. M16: Old T 4B 94
Grendon Av. OL8: O'ham 7J 63
Grendon St. BL3: Bolt 9D 38
Grendon Wlk. M12: Man 3M 95
(off Birch St.)
Grenfell Cl. WN3: Wig 6D 52
Grenfell Rd. M20: Man 5F 106
Grenham Av. M15: Man 3C 94
Grenville Rd. SK7: H Gro 4G 119
Grenville St. SK3: Stoc 4G 9 (8B 108)
SK15: Mill 6G 83
SK16: Duk 1N 97
Grenville Ter. OL6: A Lyne 8A 82
Grenville Wlk. OL15: Lit 5N 15
Gresford Cl. M21: Cho H 9N 93
Gresham Cl. M45: Whitef 4K 59
Gresham Dr. OL9: O'ham 4G 63
Gresham St. BL1: Bolt 1G 38
M34: Dent 5K 97
Gresham Wlk. SK4: Stoc 5C 108
(off Hesketh St.)
Gresham Way M33: Sale 7G 104
Gresley Av. BL6: Hor 1D 36
Gresley Cl. WN1: Wig 8N 9 (3H 53)
Gresty Av. M22: Wyth 6E 116
Greswell St. M34: Dent 5K 97
Greta Av. SK8: H Grn 9H 117
Greta Wlk. WN2: P Bri 9K 53
Gretna Rd. M46: Ath 1J 73
Greton Cl. M13: Man 5K 95
Gretton Cl. OL2: O'ham 8K 45
Greville St. M13: Man 5K 95
Grey Cl. SK6: Bred 4L 109
Greyfriars WN4: A Mak 6C 70
Greyfriars Ct. M3: Sal 1D 4 (7D 78)
Greyfriars Rd. M22: Wyth 5A 116
Greyhound Dr. M6: Sal 5B 78
Greyhound Rd. SK10: O Ald 8N 127
Grey Knotts M28: Wors 5H 75
Greylag Cres. M28: Wors 2L 75
Greylands Cl. M33: Sale 4F 104
Greylands Rd. M20: Man 8H 107
Grey Mare La. M11: Man 9L 79
Greymont Rd. BL9: Bury 7M 25
Grey Rd. WA14: Alt 2A 6 (2B 114)
WN4: A Mak 6D 70
Greysham Ct. M16: Whall R 7D 94
Greystoke Av. M19: Man 8A 96
M33: Sale 5B 105
WA15: Tim 1K 115
Greystoke Cres. M45: Whitef 1L 59
Greystoke Dr. BL1: Bolt 7E 22
M24: Mid 1J 61
SK9: A Edg 3F 126
Greystoke La. M35: Fail 4B 80
Greystoke Rd. SK10: Macc 2K 131
Greystoke St. SK1: Stoc 7E 108
Greystone Av. M21: Cho H 9E 94
WN2: Asp 7M 35
Greystone Cl. BL5: W'ton 1J 55
Greystone Wlk. SK4: Stoc 1B 108
Grey St. M12: Man 3K 95
M24: Mid 2L 61
M25: Pres 7B 60
M26: Rad 9H 41
M34: Dent 6H 97
OL6: A Lyne 8E 6 (8N 81)
SK15: Stal 9F 82
Greyswood Av. M8: Man 3E 78
Greytown Cl. M6: Sal 5M 77
Greywood Av. BL9: Bury 2A 42
Grierson St. BL1: Bolt 1F 38
M16: Whall R 5D 94
Griffe La. BL9: Bury 9B 42
Griffin Cl. BL9: Bury 9N 25
SK22: N Mil 9M 121
Griffin Farm Dr. SK8: H Grn 8J 117
Griffin Gro. M19: Man 9M 95
Griffin Ho. BL9: Bury 9N 25
Griffin La. SK8: H Grn 8J 117
Griffin Rd. M35: Fail 3B 80
Griffin St. M7: Sal 4B 78
Griffiths Cl. M7: Sal 6C 78
Griffiths St. M40: Man 5A 80
Grimeford La. BL6: Bla 8L 19
PR6: And 8L 19
GRIMEFORD VILLAGE 7N 19
Grimes Cotts. OL12: Roch 4L 27
Grimes St. OL12: Roch 4L 27
Grime St. BL0: Ram 1G 25
Grimscott Cl. M9: Man 1L 79
Grimshaw Av. M35: Fail 2E 80
SK10: Boll 6L 129
Grimshaw Cl. SK6: Bred 4L 109
Grimshaw Ct. WA3: Gol 9K 71
Grimshaw La. M24: Mid 3N 61
M40: Man 5L 79
SK10: Boll 6K 129
Grimshaw Rd. WN8: Skel 3A 50
Grimshaw St. M35: Fail 2C 80
SK1: Stoc 7E 108
WA3: Gol 9K 71
Grimstead Cl. M23: Wyth 1L 115
Grindall Av. M40: Man 9N 61
Grindleford Gdns. SK13: Gam 7A 100
(off Buxton M.)
Grindleford Gro. SK13: Gam 7A 100
(off Edale Cres.)
Grindleford Lea SK13: Gam 7A 100
(off Edale Cres.)
Grindleford Wlk. M21: Cho H 3C 106
SK13: Gam 7A 100
(off Buxton M.)
Grindle Grn. M30: Ecc 1C 92
Grindleton Av. M22: Wyth 4C 116
Grindley Av. M21: Cho H 3C 106
Grindlow St. M13: Man 4K 95
Grindlow Wlk. WN3: Wins 9N 51
Grindon Av. M7: Sal 3N 77
Grindrod La. OL12: W'le 9F 14
Grindrod St. M26: Rad 8G 40
Grindsbrook Rd. M26: Rad 5F 40
Grinton Av. M13: Man 7K 95
Grisdale Dr. M24: Mid 1K 61
Grisdale Rd. BL3: Bolt 7D 38
Grisebeck Way
OL1: O'ham 1C 8 (4J 63)
Grisedale Av. OL2: O'ham 4G 45
Grisedale Cl. M18: Man 5A 96
M24: Mid 9J 43
Grisedale Rd. OL11: Roch 9N 27
Grisedale Way SK11: Macc 7E 130
Gristlehurst La. BL9: Bury 8E 26
OL10: H'ood 8E 26
Gritley Wlk. M22: Wyth 6B 116
Gritstone Dr. SK10: Macc 3E 130
Grizebeck Cl. M18: Man 3A 96
Grizedale Cl. BL1: Bolt 2A 38
SK15: C'ook 3J 83
Grizedale Dr. WN2: I Mak 4K 53
Grizedale Rd. SK6: Wood 4M 109
Groby Ct. WA14: Alt 4B 6 (3C 114)
Groby Pl. WA14: Alt 2B 6 (2C 114)
Groby Rd. M21: Cho H 9A 94
M34: Aud 2J 97
WA14: Alt 4A 6 (4B 114)
Groby Rd. Nth. M34: Aud 1H 97
Groby St. OL8: O'ham 8L 63
SK15: Stal 9F 82
Groom St. M1: Man 8K 5
Grosvenor Av. M45: Whitef 3L 59
WA3: Low 1N 87
Grosvenor Casino
Bolton 4J 7 (6F 38)
Manchester, George St. 6H 5
Manchester, Ramsgate St.
6D 78
Manchester, Whitworth St. 7H 5
(off Whitworth St.)
Salford 7B 4 (1C 94)
Grosvenor Cen. SK11: Macc 4H 131
Grosvenor Cl. M28: Walk 6K 57
SK9: Wilm 1F 126
Grosvenor Ct. M7: Sal 2C 78
M16: Whall R 6D 94
M33: Sale 3F 104
OL7: A Lyne 9L 81
SK8: Chea 1J 117
WN5: Orr 5M 51
Grosvenor Cres. SK14: Hyde 8N 97
Grosvenor Dr. M28: Walk 6K 57
SK12: Poy 3G 125
Grosvenor Gdns. M7: Sal 6C 78
M22: Shar 1D 116
SK15: Stal 9D 82
WA12: N Wil 7F 86
Grosvenor Ho. M16: Whall R 8D 94
(off Arnold Rd.)
M33: Sale 4F 104
(off Grosvenor Sq.)
OL7: A Lyne 9A 6
Grosvenor Ho. M. M8: Man 9E 60
Grosvenor Ho. St. SK15: Stal 9D 82
Grosvenor Ind. Est. OL7: A Lyne 9L 81
Grosvenor Lodge SK7: H Gro 6F 118
(off Dorchester Rd.)
Grosvenor Pl. M13: Man 9J 5 (2F 94)
OL7: A Lyne 9L 81
Grosvenor Rd. M16: Whall R 7C 94
M27: Swin 3H 77
M28: Walk 6K 57
M30: Ecc 7A 76
M33: Sale 3F 104
M41: Urm 7C 92
M45: Whitef 2L 59
SK4: Stoc 5M 107
(not continuous)
SK6: Mar 9C 110
SK8: Chea H 3A 118
SK14: Hyde 8A 98
WA14: Alt 2E 6 (2E 114)
WN7: Lei 4F 72
Grosvenor Sq. M15: Man 9J 5 (2F 94)
M33: Sale 4G 104
OL3: Upp 3L 65
(off Watergate)

Grosvenor Sq. SK15: Stal 9D 82
(off Grosvenor St.)
Grosvenor St. BL2: Bolt . . . 5M 7 (6H 39)
BL3: Lit L 8A 40
BL4: Kea 3M 57
BL9: Bury 4M 41
M1: Man 9J 5 (2F 94)
M13: Man 9K 5 (2G 94)
M25: Pres 7B 60
M26: Rad 8F 40
M27: Pen 9F 58
M32: Stre 7K 93
M34: Dent 5H 97
OL7: A Lyne 9K 81
(not continuous)
OL10: H'ood 3H 43
OL11: Roch 3A 44
SK3: Stoc 8D 108
SK7: H Gro 4H 119
SK10: Macc 4G 130
SK15: Stal 9D 82
WN2: Hin 6N 53
WN5: Wig 5C 52
Grosvenor Way BL6: Hor 1E 36
OL2: O'ham 1H 63
GROTTON 6E 64
Grotton Hollow OL4: Grot 5D 64
Grotton Mdws. OL4: Grot 6E 64
Grouse St. OL12: Roch 4D 28
Grove, The BL2: Bolt 7J 39
BL3: Lit L 9B 40
BL5: W'ton 3F 54
M20: Man 7G 107
M30: Ecc 9F 76
M33: Sale 5H 105
M41: Urm 8N 91
OL2: Shaw 6L 45
OL3: Dob 2J 65
SK2: Stoc 9C 108
SK8: Chea H 9M 117
SK13: Had 5B 100
WA3: Low 9N 71
WA14: Alt 1C 6 (2D 114)
WA16: Knut 4J 133
WN2: I Mak 4H 53
WN6: App B 2G 32
Grove Arc. SK9: Wilm 7G 122
Grove Av. M35: Fail 5C 80
PR6: Adl 6K 19
SK9: Wilm 7F 122
Grove Bank OL4: Gras 6H 65
Grove Cl. M14: Man 6H 95
WN8: Uph 3G 50
Grove Cotts. BL5: W'ton 3G 54
OL3: Dig 6N 47
OL15: Lit 6N 15
Grove Ct. M33: Sale 4K 105
SK7: H Gro 4J 119
Grove Cres. PR6: Adl 6K 19
Grove Hill M28: Wors 4G 74
Grove Ho. M15: Man 4G 95
SK4: Stoc 7K 107
Grovehurst M27: Swin 4B 76
Grove La. M20: Man 5G 106
SK8: Chea H 9M 117
WA15: Hale 4G 114
WA15: Tim 9F 104
WN6: Stan 4C 34
Grove M. M28: Walk 8L 57
(off Malvern Gro.)
Grove Pk. 1M 123
Grove Pk. M33: Sale 4F 104
WA16: Knut 7G 133
Grove Pl. WN6: Stan 4C 34
Grove Rd. M24: Mid 1N 61
OL3: Upp 4L 65
SK15: Mill 6G 82
WA15: Hale 4E 114
WN8: Uph 3G 50
Groves Av. M5: Sal 2A 94
Grove St. BL1: Bolt 2E 38
BL4: Kea 3M 57
M7: Sal 5D 78
M43: Droy 1D 96
OL3: G'fld 6L 65
OL7: A Lyne 5J 81
OL10: H'ood 2K 43
OL11: Roch 8C 28
SK7: H Gro 4J 119
SK9: Wilm 7G 122
SK16: Duk 9A 82
SK22: N Mil 8L 121
WN4: A Mak 6D 70
WN7: Lei 6K 73
Grove Ter. OL4: O'ham 3B 64
Grove Way SK9: Wilm 7G 122
Grovewood Cl. OL7: A Lyne 5J 81
Grovewood Dr. WN6: App B 4J 33
Grovewood M. SK11: Macc 6G 131
Grundey St. SK7: H Gro 5J 119
Grundy Av. M25: Pres 9L 59
Grundy Cl. BL9: Bury 3N 41
Grundy La. BL9: Bury 3N 41
Grundy Rd. BL4: Kea 4M 57
Grundy's Cl. M29: Ast 5D 74
Grundy's La. PR7: Chor 4F 18
Grundy St. BL3: Bolt 8E 38
(off High St.)
BL5: W'ton 2G 55
M28: Walk 9N 57
OL10: H'ood 4K 43
SK4: Stoc 6K 107
WA3: Gol 2K 87
Guardian Cl. OL12: Roch 9H 15
Guardian Ct. M33: Sale 3G 104
Guardian Lodge SK8: Gat 2F 116
Guardian M. M23: Wyth 7J 105
Guernsey Cl. M19: Man 2M 107
Guest Rd. M25: Pres 5N 59
Guest St. M4: Man 4N 5 (9J 79)
WN7: Lei 5J 73
GUIDE BRIDGE 1K 97
Guide Bridge Station (Rail) 1K 97
Guide Bridge Theatre 1J 97
Guide Bri. Trad. Est.
OL7: A Lyne 1J 97
Guide Ct. BL0: Eden 2K 11
Guide La. M34: Aud 1K 97
Guide Post Rd. M13: Man 3J 95
Guide St. M50: Sal 9J 77
Guido St. BL1: Bolt 2E 38
M35: Fail 3C 80
Guild Av. M28: Walk 9L 57
Guildford Av. SK8: Chea H 9M 117
Guildford Cl. SK1: Stoc 9F 108
Guildford Cres. WN6: Wig 9L 33
Guildford Dr. OL6: A Lyne 3N 81
Guildford Gro. M24: Mid 9A 44
Guildford Rd. BL1: Bolt 2C 38
M6: Sal 6H 77
M19: Man 7N 95
M41: Urm 5E 92
SK16: Duk 2D 98
Guildford St. OL5: Mos 1G 83
Guildhall Cl. M15: Man 4F 94
Guild St. BL7: Bro X 6J 23
Guilford Rd. M30: Ecc 9B 76
Guinness Circ. M17: T Pk 1G 93
Guinness Ho. OL16: Roch 7F 28
Guinness Rd. M17: T Pk 1F 92
Guinness Rd. Trad. Est.
M17: T Pk 1F 92
Guiseley Cl. BL9: Bury 5L 25
Gullane Cl. M40: Man 3A 80
SK10: Macc 9F 128
Gull Cl. SK12: Poy 3F 124
Gulvain Pl. OL9: Chad 3D 62
Gunco La. SK10: P'bury 5G 128
SK11: Macc 6J 131
Gun Rd. SK6: Mel 9M 111
SK13: Chis 5L 111
Gunson Ct. M40: Man 1N 5 (7H 79)
Gunson St. M40: Man 1N 5 (7H 79)
Gun St. M4: Man 3L 5 (8G 79)
Gunters Av. BL5: W'ton 5H 55
Gurner Av. M5: Sal 2A 94
GURNETT 8K 131
Gurney St. M4: Man 9J 79
Gutter End BL9: Bury 7L 7 (2M 41)
Gutter La. BL0: Ram 7H 11
Guy Fawkes St. M5: Sal 2A 94
Guywood Cotts. SK6: Rom 5N 109
Guywood La. SK6: Rom 5N 109
Gwelo St. M11: Man 2L 97
Gwenbury Av. SK1: Stoc 7F 108
Gwendor Av. M8: Man 8E 60
Gwladys St. SK15: C'ook 4H 83
Gwynant Pl. M20: Man 1H 107
Gwyneth Morley Ct. SK9: Hand . . 3J 123
Gylden Cl. SK14: Hyde 3E 98
Gypsy La. SK2: Stoc 1G 119
(not continuous)
Gypsy Wlk. SK2: Stoc 1G 119
Gyte's La. M19: Man 7A 96

H

Habergham Cl. M28: Wors 3K 75
Hacienda, The M1: Man 7F 4
Hackberry Cl. WA14: B'ath 8B 104
Hacken Bri. Rd. BL3: Bolt 8K 39
Hacken La. BL3: Bolt 8K 39
Hackford Cl. BL1: Bolt 4D 38
BL8: Bury 8K 25
Hacking St. BL9: Bury 8N 7 (2N 41)
M7: Sal 4D 78
M25: Pres 7N 59
Hackle St. M11: Man 8A 80
Hackleton Cl. M4: Man 9J 79
Hackness Rd. M21: Cho H 9M 93
Hackney Av. M40: Man 6A 80
Hackney Cl. M26: Rad 7G 40
Hackwood Wlk. M8: Man 3E 78
(off Levenhurst Rd.)
Hackworth Cl. WN1: Wig 8N 9
Hadbutt La. M29: Ast 5A 74
Haddington Dr. M9: Man 8K 61
Haddon Av. M40: Man 1D 80
Haddon Cl. BL9: Bury 7N 41
SK6: H Lan 9B 120
SK9: A Edg 3E 126
SK11: Macc 7F 130
Haddon Grn. SK13: Gam 7N 99
(off Grassmoor Cres.)
Haddon Gro. M33: Sale 5G 105
SK5: Stoc 1C 108
WA15: Tim 9F 104
Haddon Hall Rd. M43: Droy 8C 80
Haddon Ho. M5: Sal 7K 77
Haddon Lea SK13: Gam 7N 99
(off Grassmoor Cres.)
Haddon M. SK13: Gam 7N 99
Haddon Rd. M21: Cho H 3C 106
M28: Wors 4C 76
M30: Ecc 1B 92
SK7: H Gro 6J 119
SK8: H Grn 8H 117
WA3: Low 8N 71
WN3: Wig 8B 52
Haddon St. M6: Sal 5A 78
M32: Stre 5K 93
OL11: Roch 8C 28
WN4: A Mak 5C 70
Haddon Way M34: Dent 8L 97
OL2: Shaw 4N 45
HADFIELD 4C 100
Hadfield Av. OL9: Chad 7F 62
Hadfield Cl. M14: Man 6J 95
Hadfield Cres. OL6: A Lyne 5B 82
Hadfield Ind. Est. SK13: Had 3B 100
Hadfield Pl. SK13: Glos 9E 100
Hadfield Rd. SK13: Had 5A 100
Hadfields Av. SK14: Holl 4N 99
Hadfield Sq. SK13: Glos 9E 100
(off Kershaw St.)
Hadfield Station (Rail) 5C 100
Hadfield St. M7: Sal 4C 78
M16: Old T 3B 94
OL8: O'ham 8J 63
SK13: Glos 9E 100
SK16: Duk 2L 97
Hadfield Ter. OL6: A Lyne 5B 82
Hadleigh Cl. BL1: Bolt 7H 23
Hadleigh Grn. BL6: Los 8K 37
Hadley Av. M13: Man 7K 95
Hadley Cl. SK8: Chea H 6L 117
Hadley St. M6: Sal 5A 78
Hadlow Grn. SK5: Stoc 2F 108
Hadlow Wlk. M40: Man 7K 79
(off Sabden Cl.)
Hadrian Ho. OL1: O'ham . . . 1D 8 (4K 63)
Hadwin St. BL1: Bolt 3G 38
Hafton Rd. M7: Sal 4A 78
Hag End Brow BL2: Bolt 7K 39
HAG FOLD 6L 55
Hag Fold Station (Rail) 6L 55
HAGGATE 9G 45
Haggate OL2: O'ham 9G 44
Haggate Cres. OL2: O'ham 9G 45
Hagg Bank La. SK12: Dis 8G 120
Hagley Rd. M5: Sal 3N 93
Hags, The BL9: Bury 7N 41
HAGUE, THE 7M 99
HAGUE BAR 7J 121
Hague Bar Ho. SK22: N Mil 7J 121
Hague Bar Rd. SK22: N Mil 7J 121
Hague Bush Cl. WA3: Low 9A 72
Hague Ct. M20: Man 3F 106
Hague Fold Rd.
SK22: N Mil 7J 121
Hague Ho. OL8: O'ham 6K 63
(off Eldon St.)
Hague Pl. SK15: Stal 8D 82
Hague Rd. M20: Man 3F 106
SK14: B'tom 9L 99
Hague St. OL4: O'ham 3B 64
OL6: A Lyne 5F 6 (6N 81)
SK13: Glos 9F 100
Haig Av. M44: Cad 4D 102
Haig Ct. BL8: Bury 3H 41
WA16: Knut 4J 133
HAIGH 6L 35
Haigh Av. SK4: Stoc 3C 108
Haigh Country Pk. 7J 35
Haigh Country Pk. Info. Cen. 6J 35
Haigh Hall 6J 35
Haigh Hall Cl. BL0: Ram 1H 25
Haigh Hall Golf Course 7J 35
Haigh La. OL1: Chad 2C 62
Haigh Lawn WA14: Alt 5A 6 (4B 114)
Haigh Pk. SK4: Stoc 3C 108
Haigh Rd. WN2: Asp, Hai 5L 35
Haigh St. OL11: Roch 7E 28
Haigh Vw. WN1: Wig 1G 52
WN3: I Mak 5H 53
Haig Rd. BL8: Bury 2H 41
M32: Stre 6K 93
WA16: Knut 5J 133
Haig St. WN3: Wig 4E 52
Haile Dr. M28: Wors 4G 74
Hailsham Cl. BL8: Bury 6J 25
Hail St. BL0: Ram 1G 25
Hailwood St. OL11: Roch 9C 28
Halbury Gdns. OL9: Chad 5E 62
Halbury Wlk. BL1: Bolt 2G 39
(off Fairhaven Rd.)
Halcyon Cl. OL12: Roch 3N 27
Haldane Rd. M50: Sal 9N 77
Haldene Wlk. M8: Man 4E 78
(off Felthorpe Dr.)
Haldon Rd. M20: Man 3J 107
HALE 5E 114
Hale Av. SK12: Poy 4H 125
Hale Bank BL5: W'ton 2H 55
Halebank Av. M20: Man 1E 106
HALEBARNS 7J 115
Hale Cl. WN7: Lei 8K 73
Hale Ct. WA14: Alt 5D 114
Hale Golf Course 8G 114
Hale Grn. Ct. WA15: Hale 4G 115
Hale Gro. WN4: A Mak 5C 70
Hale La. M35: Fail 2C 80
Hale Low Rd. WA15: Hale 4F 114
HALE MOSS 4F 114
Hale Rd. SK4: Stoc 5A 108
WA14: Alt 4D 114
WA15: Hale, Haleb 4D 114
Hales Cl. M43: Droy 7D 80
Halesden Rd. SK4: Stoc 3B 108
Halesfield WN2: Hin 9D 54
Hale Station (Rail) 5D 114
Halesworth Wlk. M40: Man 6H 79
(off Talgarth Rd.)
Hale Top M22: Wyth 5C 116
Hale Vw. WA14: Alt 5D 114
(off Ashley Rd.)
Hale Wlk. SK8: Chea 3M 117
Halewood Av. WA3: Gol 9J 71
Haley Cl. SK5: Stoc 9D 96
Haley St. M8: Man 3G 78
HALF ACRE 5A 60
Half Acre M26: Rad 6E 40
Half Acre Dr. OL11: Roch 7A 28
Half Acre La. BL6: Bla 3M 35
OL11: Roch 7N 27
Half Acre M. OL11: Roch 7N 27
Half Acre Rd. OL11: Roch 7N 27
Halfacre Rd. M22: Wyth 3B 116
Half Edge La. M30: Ecc 7E 76
Half Lea Grange M30: Ecc 7E 76
(off Half Edge La.)
Half Moon La. SK2: Stoc 1H 119
Half Moon St. M2: Man 4G 4
Halford Dr. M40: Man 2A 80
Halfpenny Bri. Ind. Est.
OL11: Roch 9E 8 (7E 28)
Half St. M3: Sal 1E 4 (7D 78)
SK11: Macc 6H 131
Halifax Rd. OL12: Roch 4F 28
OL15: Lit 8N 15
OL16: Roch 4F 28
Halifax St. OL6: A Lyne 6M 81
Hallacres La. SK8: Chea H 7K 117
Hallam Mill SK2: Stoc 1E 118
(off Hallam St.)
Hallam Rd. M40: Man 5N 79
Hallams Pas. SK2: Stoc 1E 118
Hallam St. M26: Rad 8K 41
SK2: Stoc 1E 118
Hallas Gro. M23: Wyth 7A 106
Hall Av. M14: Man 6J 95
M33: Sale 2E 104
SK15: H'rod 5F 82
WA15: Tim 9F 104
Hall Bank M30: Ecc 8C 76
Hall Bank Ho. OL3: G'fld 6J 65
Hallbottom St. SK14: Hyde 4C 98
Hallbridge Gdns. BL1: Bolt 1H 39
WN8: Uph 3F 50
Hall Cl. SK10: Macc 9H 129
SK14: Mot 4K 99
WN6: She 6M 33
Hall Coppice, The BL7: Eger 3E 22
Hallcroft M31: Part 4G 102
WN8: Skel 1A 50
Hallcroft Gdns. OL16: Miln 7J 29
Hall Dr. M24: Mid 4L 61
SK14: Mot 4K 99
Hallefield Cres. SK11: Macc 5J 131
Hallefield Dr. SK11: Macc 5J 131
Hallefield Rd. SK11: Macc 5J 131
Halle Sq. M4: Man 3H 5
Hall Farm Av. M41: Urm 6B 92
Hall Farm Cl. SK7: H Gro 4L 119
HALLFOLD 6A 14
Hall Fold OL12: Whitw 6N 13
Hall Gdns. OL12: Roch 3N 27
Hallgate BL5: W'ton 6G 55
WN1: Wig 7J 9 (3F 52)
Hallgate Dr. SK8: H Grn 5F 116
Hallgate Rd. SK1: Stoc 8F 108
HALL GREEN 4E 50
Hall Grn. WN8: Uph 4F 50
Hall Grn. Cl. SK16: Duk 9N 81
WN8: Uph 4F 50
Hall Grn. Rd. SK16: Duk 9N 81
Hall Gro. M14: Man 6J 95
SK8: Chea 1H 117
SK10: Macc 9H 129
Hall Hill SK10: Boll 6J 129
Hall Ho. La. WN7: Lei 6M 73
Halliday Ct. OL15: Lit 1J 29
Halliday Rd. M40: Man 6N 79
Halliford Rd. M40: Man 4M 79
Hallington Cl. BL3: Bolt 7G 38
HALL I' TH' WOOD 9H 23
Hall i' th' Wood BL1: Bolt 9H 23
Hall i' th' Wood La. BL2: Bolt 1J 39
Hall i' th' Wood Mus. 9H 23
Hall i' th' Wood Station (Rail) 1J 39
HALLIWELL 2E 38
Halliwell Av. OL8: O'ham 8J 63
Halliwell Ind. Est. BL1: Bolt 1E 38
Halliwell La. M8: Man 3E 78
Halliwell Rd. BL1: Bolt 1D 38
M25: Pres 1M 77
Halliwell St. BL1: Bolt 2E 38
(off Hobart St.)
OL12: Roch 6A 8 (5C 28)
(not continuous)
OL16: Miln, Roch 6J 29
Halliwell St. W. M8: Man 3E 78
Halliwell Wlk. M25: Pres 1M 77
Hallkirk Wlk. M40: Man 9B 62
Hall La. BL4: Farn 1L 57
(not continuous)
BL6: Los 5G 37
BL6: R'ton 3C 20
M23: Wyth 1A 116
M31: Part 4G 102
SK6: Wood 2M 109
SK11: Sut E 8K 131
WA5: Burt 9D 86
WN1: Wig 8G 34
WN2: Asp, Hin 4N 53
WN3: Wig 7K 51
WN5: Bil 7J 51
WN5: Wig 7K 51
WN6: App B 2F 32
Hall La. Gro. WN2: Hin 3N 53
Hall Lee Dr. BL5: W'ton 2J 55
Hall Mdw. SK8: Chea H 6K 117
Hall Mdw. Rd. SK13: Glos 7F 100
Hall Moss La. SK7: Bram 1N 123
Hall Moss Rd. M9: Man 8M 61
Hallows Av. M21: Cho H 3B 106
Hall Pool Dr. SK2: Stoc 9J 109
Hall Rd. M14: Man 6J 95
OL6: A Lyne 5N 81
SK7: Bram 6B 118
SK9: Hand 3K 123
SK9: Wilm 7F 122
WA11: Hay 2B 86
WA14: Bow 6C 114
Hallroyd Brow OL1: O'ham 3J 63
(off Sunfield Rd.)
Halls Barn OL3: G'fld 5L 65
(off Halls Way)
Halls Cotts. OL3: G'fld 5L 65
Hall's Ct. SK13: Glos 8E 100
Hallside Pk. WA16: Knut 8J 133
Hall's Pl. OL4: Spri 5C 64
Hallstead Av. M38: Lit H 7F 56
Hallstead Gro. M38: Lit H 7F 56
Hall St. BL3: Bolt 1L 57
BL4: Bolt 1L 57
BL8: Bury 8E 24
(Parkgate)
BL8: Bury 9J 25
(Rowans St.)
BL9: Sum 3J 25
M1: Man 6G 5 (1E 94)
M24: Mid 3M 61
M26: Rad 6F 40
M27: Pen 9F 58
M35: Fail 4B 80
OL2: O'ham 8H 45
OL4: O'ham 4M 63
(off Gravel Wlks.)
OL6: A Lyne 8B 82
OL10: H'ood 3K 43
OL12: Whitw 6A 14
SK1: Stoc 7E 108
Hall St. SK8: Chea 1J 117
SK10: Macc 4G 130
SK14: Hyde 6M 97
SK22: N Mil 7L 121
WN1: Wig 9L 9 (4G 52)
WN2: Bam 3H 71
WN2: I Mak 4J 53
Hallsville Rd. M19: Man 8A 96
Halls Way OL3: G'fld 5L 65
Hallsworth Rd. M30: Ecc 9A 76
Hall Ter. SK11: Lang 8M 131
Hallview Way M28: Walk 8G 57
Hall Wood Av. WA11: Hay 1C 86
Hallwood Av. M6: Sal 6J 77
Hallwood Rd. M23: Wyth 1N 115
SK9: Hand 3J 123
Hallworth Av. M34: Aud 9F 80
Hallworth Rd. M8: Man 2G 78
Hallworthy Cl. WN7: Lei 9D 72
Halmore Rd. M40: Man 8J 79
Halsall Cl. BL9: Bury 7M 25
Halsall Dr. BL3: Bolt 1F 56
Halsbury Cl. M12: Man 3K 95
Halsey Cl. OL9: Chad 9C 62
Halsey Wlk. M8: Man 3E 78
(off Greyswood Av.)
Halshaw La. BL4: Kea 4N 57
Halsmere Dr. M9: Man 8K 61
Halstead Av. M6: Sal 6K 77
M21: Cho H 1N 105
Halstead Dr. M44: Irl 8J 91
Halstead Gro. SK8: Gat 3E 116
WN7: Lei 5K 73
Halstead St. BL2: Bolt 3N 7 (5H 39)
BL9: Bury 8N 25
Halstead Wlk. BL9: Bury 8N 25
Halstock Wlk. M40: Man 5J 79
(off Foreland Cl.)
Halstone Av. SK9: Wilm 1D 126
Halston St. M15: Man 3D 94
Halter Cl. M26: Rad 7G 41
Halton Bank M6: Sal 6M 77
Halton Dr. WA15: Tim 7H 105
Halton Flats OL10: H'ood 2H 43
(off Meadow Cl.)
Halton Ho. M5: Sal 9M 77
(off Amersham St.)
Halton Rd. M11: Man 8A 80
Halton St. BL2: Bolt 5J 39
SK14: Hyde 6C 98
WA11: Hay 3B 86
Halvard Av. BL9: Bury 7M 25
Halvard Ct. BL9: Bury 7M 25
Halvis Gro. M16: Old T 7A 94
Hamble Cft. M26: Rad 3B 58
(off Stoneclough Ri.)
Hambleden Cl. BL3: Bolt 7A 38
Hambledon Cl. M46: Ath 6N 55
Hambleton Cl. BL8: Bury 3F 40
Hambleton Dr. M33: Sale 3D 104
Hambleton Rd. SK8: H Grn 7H 117
Hamblett St. WN7: Lei 5D 72
Hamble Way SK10: Macc 3C 130
Hambridge Cl. M8: Man 3F 78
Hamel St. BL3: Bolt 9E 38
SK14: Hyde 4C 98
Hamer Ct. OL16: Roch 4F 28
Hamer Dr. M16: Old T 4C 94
Hamer Hall Cres. OL12: Roch 3F 28
Hamer Hill M9: Man 8H 61
Hamer La. OL16: Roch 4F 28
Hamer St. BL0: Ram 3H 25
BL2: Bolt 3J 39
M26: Rad 8J 41
Hamer Ter. BL9: Sum 2J 25
(off Waterside Rd.)
Hamerton Rd. M40: Man 6H 79
Hamer Va. OL12: Roch 3F 28
Hamilcar Av. M30: Ecc 8E 76
Hamilton Av. M30: Ecc 9E 76
M44: Cad 4E 102
OL2: O'ham 9F 44
Hamilton Cl. BL8: Bury 1H 41
M25: Pres 8N 59
SK4: Stoc 1B 108
SK10: Macc 4L 131
Hamilton Ct. BL3: Lit L 9B 40
(off Heywood St.)
M33: Sale 4H 105
WN5: Wig 3B 52
Hamilton Cres. SK4: Stoc 7N 107
Hamilton Gro. M16: Old T 4C 94
(off Hamilton St.)
Hamilton Ho. WA14: Alt . . . 1D 6 (2D 114)
Hamilton Lodge M14: Man 6H 95
Hamilton M. M25: Pres 8N 59
M30: Ecc 7B 76
Hamilton Rd. M13: Man 6L 95
M25: Pres 8N 59
M29: Ast 4E 74
M45: Whitef 3L 59
WN2: Hin 7B 54
WN4: Gars 6N 69
Hamilton Sq. SK4: Stoc 6C 108
WN5: Wig 3B 52
Hamilton St. BL1: Bolt 8F 22
BL9: Bury 9M 25
M7: Sal 3C 78
M16: Old T 4C 94
M27: Swin 1D 76
M30: Ecc 7B 76
M46: Ath 9K 55
OL1: O'ham 5L 63
OL4: O'ham 5L 63
OL7: A Lyne 9K 81
OL9: Chad 4E 62
SK15: Stal 8E 82
WN7: Lei 4F 72
Hamilton Way OL10: H'ood 3J 43
Hamlet, The BL6: Los 4K 37
PR7: H Char 4J 19
Hamlet Dr. M33: Sale 2E 104
Hammerstone Rd. M18: Man 3A 96
Hammer St. OL10: H'ood 2G 43
Hammett Rd. M21: Cho H 9N 93
Hammond Av. SK4: Stoc 3C 108

Hammond Ct. SK4: Stoc . . . 3C 108
Hammond Flats OL10: H'ood . . . 2H 43
(off Meadow Cl.)
Hamnet Cl. BL1: Bolt . . . 8H 23
Hamnett St. M11: Man . . . 9B 80
M43: Droy . . . 9B 80
SK14: Hyde . . . 6A 98
Hamon Rd. WA15: Alt . . . 4E 6 (3E 114)
Hampden Ct. M30: Ecc . . . 8D 76
Hampden Cres. M18: Man . . . 4A 96
(not continuous)
Hampden Gro. M30: Ecc . . . 8D 76
Hampden Pl. WN5: Wig . . . 2A 52
(not continuous)
Hampden Rd. M25: Pres . . . 7A 60
M33: Sale . . . 5G 104
OL2: Shaw . . . 6A 46
Hampden St. OL10: H'ood . . . 3J 43
OL11: Roch . . . 9D 8
Hampden Wlk. WN5: Wig . . . 2A 52
Hampshire Cl. BL9: Bury . . . 4N 41
SK5: Stoc . . . 3G 109
SK13: Glos . . . 9H 101
Hampshire Ho. SK5: Stoc . . . 3G 109
Hampshire Rd. M31: Part . . . 6E 102
M43: Droy . . . 7E 80
OL9: Chad . . . 6F 62
SK5: Stoc . . . 3G 109
Hampshire Wlk. M8: Man . . . 4G 78
(off Appleford Dr.)
SK10: Macc . . . 2D 130
(off Kennedy Av.)
Hampson Av. WA3: Cul . . . 6H 89
Hampson Cl. M30: Ecc . . . 9B 76
WN4: A Mak . . . 8E 70
Hampson Cres. SK9: Hand . . . 2H 123
Hampson Fold M26: Rad . . . 8F 40
HAMPSON GREEN . . . 4H 35
Hampson Mill La. BL9: Bury . . . 7M 41
Hampson Pl. OL6: A Lyne . . . 4B 82
Hampson Rd. M32: Stre . . . 7J 93
OL6: A Lyne . . . 4B 82
Hampson Sq. M26: Rad . . . 8G 40
(off Water St.)
Hampson St. BL6: Hor . . . 9D 20
M5: Sal . . . 5B 4 (9C 78)
M26: Rad . . . 8G 41
M27: Pen . . . 1G 76
M30: Ecc . . . 9B 76
M33: Sale . . . 4K 105
M40: Man . . . 6J 79
M43: Droy . . . 8E 80
M46: Ath . . . 8L 55
SK1: Stoc . . . 8F 108
Hampstead Av. M41: Urm . . . 8M 91
Hampstead Dr. M45: Whitef . . . 2L 59
SK2: Stoc . . . 2G 118
Hampstead La. SK2: Stoc . . . 2G 118
Hampstead Rd. WN6: Stan . . . 3A 34
Hampton Ct. SK9: Hand . . . 1J 123
(off Wilmslow Rd.)
Hampton Gro. BL9: Bury . . . 7M 25
SK8: Chea H . . . 5K 117
WA14: Tim . . . 7F 104
WN7: Lei . . . 3N 73
Hampton Ho. M33: Sale . . . 4J 105
(off Northenden Rd.)
Hampton M. SK3: Stoc . . . 3D 118
Hampton Rd. BL3: Bolt . . . 9H 39
M21: Cho H . . . 8M 93
M35: Fail . . . 2E 80
M41: Urm . . . 8D 92
M44: Cad . . . 4E 102
Hampton St. OL8: O'ham . . . 7H 63
Hamsell Ct. M13: Man . . . 9M 5 (2H 95)
Hamsell Rd. M13: Man . . . 9M 5 (2H 95)
Hamson Dr. SK10: Boll . . . 5M 129
Hamsterley Av. M18: Man . . . 7B 96
Hanborough Ct. M29: Tyld . . . 2N 73
Hancock Cl. M14: Man . . . 6G 95
Hancock St. M32: Stre . . . 9K 93
Handel Av. M41: Urm . . . 7A 92
Handel M. M33: Sale . . . 4J 105
Handel St. BL1: Bolt . . . 1E 38
OL12: Whitw . . . 6N 13
Handford Ho. M41: Urm . . . 7E 92
(off Cavendish Rd.)
HANDFORTH . . . 2J 123
Handforth By-Pass
SK8: Chea H . . . 5K 123
SK9: Wilm, Hand . . . 5K 123
Handforth Dean SK9: Hand . . . 2K 123
Handforth Gro. M13: Man . . . 8K 95
Handforth Rd. SK5: Stoc . . . 3D 108
SK9: Wilm . . . 4K 123
Handforth Station (Rail) . . . 3J 123
Handley Av. M14: Man . . . 8G 94
Handley Cl. SK3: Stoc . . . 2A 118
Handley Gdns. BL1: Bolt . . . 5C 38
Handley Rd. SK7: Bram . . . 4C 118
Handley St. BL9: Bury . . . 4M 41
OL12: Roch . . . 5B 28
Hands La. OL11: Roch . . . 6M 27
Hand St. SK11: Macc . . . 4G 130
Handsworth St. M12: Man . . . 2J 95
Hanging Birch M24: Mid . . . 4G 60
Hanging Bri. M3: Man . . . 3G 4
(off Cateaton St.)
HANGING CHADDER . . . 5G 45
Hanging Chadder La.
OL2: O'ham . . . 5G 45
Hanging Lees Cl. OL16: Miln . . . 9N 29
Hani Ct. M8: Man . . . 1E 78
Hani Wells Bus. Pk. M19: Man . . . 1N 107
SK4: Man . . . 1N 107
Hankinson Cl. M31: Part . . . 6G 102
Hankinson Way M6: Sal . . . 7N 77
Hanley Cl. M24: Mid . . . 6M 61
SK12: Dis . . . 9G 121
Hanlith M. M19: Man . . . 9L 95
Hanlon St. M8: Man . . . 1E 78
Hanmer St. WN2: Hin . . . 6N 53
Hannah Baldwin Cl. M11: Man . . . 1L 95
Hannah Bus. Pk. WA15: Hale . . . 5E 6
Hannah Lodge M20: Man . . . 4F 106
(off Palatine Rd.)
Hannah St. M12: Man . . . 7M 95
Hannerton Rd. OL2: Shaw . . . 4A 46
Hannet Rd. M22: Wyth . . . 5C 116
Hanover Bus. Pk.
WA14: B'ath . . . 9B 104
Hanover Ct. BL3: Bolt . . . 7C 38
(off Greenbank Rd.)
M28: Wors . . . 4B 76
OL7: A Lyne . . . 9L 81
(off Aitken St.)
Hanover Cres. M14: Man . . . 5J 95
Hanover Gdns. M7: Sal . . . 2D 78
Hanover Ho. BL3: Bolt . . . 9D 38
M14: Man . . . 9J 95
(off Ladybarn La.)
OL8: O'ham . . . 4B 8
Hanover Rd. WA14: B'ath . . . 9B 104
WN2: Hin . . . 5M 53
Hanover St. BL1: Bolt . . . 3H 7 (5F 38)
M4: Man . . . 2H 5 (8F 78)
OL5: Mos . . . 1F 82
OL11: Roch . . . 2A 44
OL15: Lit . . . 9L 15
SK15: Stal . . . 8C 82
WN7: Lei . . . 4J 73
Hanover St. Nth. M34: Aud . . . 1J 97
Hanover St. Sth. M34: Aud . . . 1J 97
Hanover Towers SK5: Stoc . . . 5D 108
Hansby Cl. OL1: O'ham . . . 2J 63
WN8: Skel . . . 3C 50
Hansdon Cl. M8: Man . . . 4F 78
Hansen Wlk. M22: Wyth . . . 5B 116
Hanslope Wlk. M9: Man . . . 2K 79
(off Swainsthorpe Dr.)
Hansom Dr. M46: Ath . . . 1J 73
Hanson Cl. M24: Mid . . . 2M 61
Hanson Cl. Ind. Est. M24: Mid . . . 2M 61
Hanson M. SK1: Stoc . . . 6F 108
Hanson Rd. M40: Man . . . 3M 79
Hanson St. BL9: Bury . . . 9M 25
M24: Mid . . . 2M 61
OL4: O'ham . . . 4N 63
PR7: Adl . . . 8J 19
Hanstock Cl. WN5: Orr . . . 6J 51
Hanwell Cl. WN7: Lei . . . 9F 72
Hanworth Cl. M13: Man . . . 9L 5 (2G 95)
Hapsford Wlk. M40: Man . . . 5M 79
Hapton Av. M32: Stre . . . 8K 93
Hapton Pl. SK4: Stoc . . . 5C 108
Hapton St. M19: Man . . . 9M 95
Harbern Cl. M30: Ecc . . . 6D 76
Harbern Dr. WN7: Lei . . . 9F 54
Harborne Wlk. BL8: G'mount . . . 5F 24
Harboro Ct. M33: Sale . . . 5F 104
Harboro Gro. M33: Sale . . . 4F 104
Harboro Rd. M33: Sale . . . 3E 104
Harboro Way M33: Sale . . . 4F 104
Harbour City Stop (Metro) . . . 1M 93
Harbour Farm Rd. SK14: Hyde . . . 3B 98
Harbour La. OL16: Miln . . . 8K 29
Harbour La. Nth. OL16: Miln . . . 7K 29
Harbourne Av. M28: Wors . . . 2K 75
Harbourne Cl. M28: Wors . . . 2K 75
Harbrook Gro. WN2: Hin . . . 2E 72
Harburn Wlk. M22: Wyth . . . 7D 116
Harbury Cl. BL3: Bolt . . . 9B 38
WN6: Wig . . . 1C 52
Harbury Cres. M22: Wyth . . . 2B 116
Harbury Wlk. WN6: Wig . . . 1C 52
Harcles Dr. BL0: Ram . . . 3H 25
Harcombe Rd. M20: Man . . . 2H 107
Harcourt Av. M41: Urm . . . 8F 92
Harcourt Cl. M41: Urm . . . 8F 92
Harcourt Ind. Cen. M28: Walk . . . 6L 57
Harcourt M. BL6: Hor . . . 9D 20
(off Mottram St.)
Harcourt Rd. M33: Sale . . . 2G 104
WA14: Alt . . . 1D 114
Harcourt St. BL4: Farn . . . 1L 57
M28: Walk . . . 6L 57
M32: Stre . . . 6L 93
OL1: O'ham . . . 3M 63
SK5: Stoc . . . 9D 96
Harcourt St. Sth. M28: Walk . . . 6L 57
Hardacre St. WN3: I Mak . . . 5G 53
Hardberry Pl. SK2: Stoc . . . 1J 119
Hardcastle Av. M21: Cho H . . . 2B 106
Hardcastle Cl. BL2: Bolt . . . 7K 23
Hardcastle Gdns. BL2: Bolt . . . 7K 23
Hardcastle Rd. SK3: Stoc . . . 9B 108
Hardcastle St. BL1: Bolt . . . 2G 39
OL1: O'ham . . . 2F 8 (4L 63)
Harden Dr. BL2: Bolt . . . 2L 39
Harden Hills OL2: Shaw . . . 4A 46
HARDEN PARK . . . 2F 126
Harden Pk. SK9: A Edg . . . 2F 126
Hardfield Rd. M24: Mid . . . 6M 61
Hardfield St. OL10: H'ood . . . 2J 43
Hardicker St. M19: Man . . . 1N 107
Hardie Av. BL4: Farn . . . 4J 57
Harding St. M3: Sal . . . 2F 4
M4: Man . . . 9J 79
M6: Sal . . . 6N 77
PR6: Adl . . . 6K 19
SK1: Stoc . . . 7F 108
SK14: Hyde . . . 4A 98
Hard La. OL12: W'le . . . 6H 15
Hardman Av. M25: Pres . . . 9C 60
SK6: Bred . . . 5L 109
Hardman Blvd. M3: Man . . . 5E 4 (9D 78)
Hardman Cl. M26: Rad . . . 6F 40
Hardman Fold BL3: Bolt . . . 1J 57
Hardman La. M35: Fail . . . 2C 80
Hardman Rd. SK5: Stoc . . . 9D 96
Hardmans BL7: Bro X . . . 6G 23
Hardman's La. BL7: Bro X . . . 5G 22
Hardman's M. M45: Whitef . . . 5M 59
Hardman Sq. M3: Man . . . 5E 4 (9D 78)
Hardman's Rd. M45: Whitef . . . 5M 59
Hardman St. BL4: Farn . . . 4M 57
BL9: Bury . . . 9M 25
M3: Man . . . 5E 4 (9D 78)
M26: Rad . . . 6F 40
M35: Fail . . . 3B 80
OL9: Chad . . . 8F 62
OL10: H'ood . . . 2J 43
OL16: Miln . . . 8L 29
Hardman St. SK3: Stoc . . . 3H 9 (7B 108)
(not continuous)
WN3: Wig . . . 5E 52
Hardon Gro. M13: Man . . . 7L 95
Hardrow Cl. WN3: Wig . . . 9E 52
Hardrush Fold M35: Fail . . . 4E 80
Hardshaw Cl. M13: Man . . . 3G 95
Hardsough Fold BL0: Ram . . . 1J 11
(off Aitken St.)
Hardsough La. BL0: Eden . . . 1J 11
Hardwick Cl. M26: Rad . . . 7B 40
SK6: H Lan . . . 9C 120
Hardwick Dr. SK11: Macc . . . 7F 130
Hardwicke Rd. SK12: Poy . . . 2K 125
Hardwicke St. OL11: Roch . . . 9C 28
Hardwick Rd. M31: Part . . . 5H 103
WN4: A Mak . . . 5D 70
Hardwick St. OL7: A Lyne . . . 8K 81
Hardwood Cl. M8: Man . . . 3F 78
Hardy Av. M21: Cho H . . . 9N 93
Hardybutts WN1: Wig . . . 8L 9 (3G 52)
(not continuous)
Hardy Cl. BL5: W'ton . . . 9G 36
OL11: Roch . . . 1D 44
SK16: Duk . . . 1N 97
WA15: Tim . . . 9F 104
Hardy Dr. SK7: Bram . . . 8B 118
WA15: Tim . . . 9F 104
Hardy Farm M21: Cho H . . . 2A 106
Hardy Gro. M27: Swin . . . 5D 76
M28: Wors . . . 2N 75
Hardy La. M21: Cho H . . . 2A 106
Hardy Mill Rd. BL2: Bolt . . . 9N 23
Hardy St. M30: Ecc . . . 1B 92
OL4: O'ham . . . 5G 8 (6L 63)
OL6: A Lyne . . . 4B 82
WN6: Wig . . . 2D 52
Hardywood Rd. M34: Dent . . . 1L 109
Harebell Av. M38: Lit H . . . 8G 57
Harebell Cl. OL12: Roch . . . 2B 28
Harecastle Av. M30: Ecc . . . 1E 92
Haredale Dr. M8: Man . . . 4G 78
Hare Dr. BL9: Bury . . . 8A 42
Harefield Av. OL11: Roch . . . 8E 28
Harefield Dr. M20: Man . . . 6F 106
OL10: H'ood . . . 2L 43
SK9: Wilm . . . 9F 122
Harefield Rd. SK9: Hand . . . 2K 123
Harehill Cl. M13: Man . . . 8L 5 (2G 95)
Hare Hill Ct. OL15: Lit . . . 8M 15
Hare Hill Gdns. . . . 7M 127
Hare Hill Rd. OL15: Lit . . . 8L 15
SK14: Hat . . . 6F 98
(not continuous)
Harehill Wlk. SK14: Hat . . . 6F 98
Hareshill Bus. Pk. OL10: H'ood . . . 4G 43
Hareshill Rd. OL10: H'ood . . . 4G 42
Hare St. M4: Man . . . 3J 5
OL11: Roch . . . 8D 28
(not continuous)
Harewood SK14: B'tom . . . 9K 99
Harewood Av. M33: Sale . . . 4D 104
OL11: Roch . . . 3J 27
Harewood Cl. OL11: Roch . . . 3J 27
Harewood Ct. M9: Man . . . 6F 60
(off Deanswood Dr.)
M33: Sale . . . 5J 105
Harewood Dr. OL2: O'ham . . . 7G 44
OL11: Roch . . . 3H 27
Harewood Gro. SK5: Stoc . . . 9C 96
Harewood Rd. M44: Irl . . . 7J 91
OL2: Shaw . . . 4N 45
OL11: Roch . . . 3H 27
WN2: Hin . . . 5M 53
Harewood Wlk. M34: Dent . . . 8L 97
(off Tatton Rd.)
Harewood Way M27: Clif . . . 9F 58
OL11: Roch . . . 3H 27
SK11: Macc . . . 7F 130
Harford Cl. SK7: H Gro . . . 6E 118
Hargate Av. OL12: Roch . . . 3M 27
Hargate Cl. BL9: Sum . . . 3J 25
Hargate Dr. M44: Irl . . . 6H 91
WA15: Hale . . . 6G 114
Hargate Hill La. SK13: Char . . . 1N 111
Hargrave Cl. M9: Man . . . 8H 61
Hargreaves Ho. BL3: Bolt . . . 4J 7 (6F 38)
Hargreaves Rd. WA15: Tim . . . 1J 115
Hargreaves St. BL1: Bolt . . . 2F 38
M4: Man . . . 7F 78
OL1: O'ham . . . 1D 8 (4K 63)
OL9: O'ham . . . 5G 63
OL11: Roch . . . 9A 28
Harkerside Cl. M21: Cho H . . . 9B 94
Harkness St. M12: Man . . . 9N 5 (2H 95)
Harland Dr. M8: Man . . . 3G 78
WN4: A Mak . . . 7F 70
Harland Way OL12: Roch . . . 3M 27
Harlea Av. WN2: Hin . . . 8C 54
Harlech Av. M45: Whitef . . . 5A 60
WN2: Hin . . . 7C 54
Harlech Dr. SK7: H Gro . . . 6G 119
Harlech St. WN4: A Mak . . . 5C 70
Harleen Gro. SK2: Stoc . . . 9H 109
Harlesden Cres. BL3: Bolt . . . 7D 38
(off Langshaw Wlk.)
Harley Av. BL2: Ain . . . 3D 40
BL2: Bolt . . . 1M 39
M14: Man . . . 6K 95
Harley Ct. M24: Mid . . . 2L 61
Harley Rd. M24: Mid . . . 2L 61
M33: Sale . . . 3H 105
Harley St. M11: Man . . . 1B 96
OL6: A Lyne . . . 6D 6 (7M 81)
Harling Rd. M22: Shar . . . 9C 106
Harlington Cl. M23: Wyth . . . 9K 105
(off Petersfield Dr.)
Harlow Dr. M18: Man . . . 6B 96
Harlyn Av. SK7: Bram . . . 8D 118
Harmer Cl. M40: Man . . . 5M 79
Harmol Gro. OL7: A Lyne . . . 4K 81
Harmony Sq. M13: Man . . . 4J 95
Harmony St. OL4: O'ham . . . 4F 8 (5L 63)
OL16: Miln . . . 7K 29
Harmsworth Dr. SK4: Stoc . . . 3N 107
Harmsworth St. M6: Sal . . . 8L 77
Harmuir Cl. WN6: Stan . . . 8B 34
Harold Av. M18: Man . . . 5D 96
SK16: Duk . . . 1A 98
WN4: A Mak . . . 5D 70
Haroldene St. BL2: Bolt . . . 1J 39
Harold Lees Rd. OL10: H'ood . . . 1L 43
Harold Priestnall Cl. M40: Man . . . 4N 79
Harold Rd. WA11: Hay . . . 2C 86
Harold St. BL1: Bolt . . . 2E 38
M16: Old T . . . 3B 94
M24: Mid . . . 2K 61
M25: Pres . . . 7M 59
M35: Fail . . . 3C 80
OL9: O'ham . . . 4H 63
OL16: Roch . . . 3G 28
SK1: Stoc . . . 8F 108
WN2: Asp . . . 7N 35
Harper Cl. SK11: Macc . . . 6H 131
Harper Ct. SK3: Stoc . . . 9C 108
Harper Fold Cl. M26: Rad . . . 9E 40
Harper Fold Rd. M26: Rad . . . 9D 40
HARPER GREEN . . . 2J 57
Harper Green Community Leisure Cen.
. . . 2J 57
Harper Grn. Rd. BL4: Farn . . . 1J 57
Harper Ho. M19: Man . . . 8L 95
Harper Mill OL6: A Lyne . . . 7F 6 (7N 81)
Harper Pl. OL6: A Lyne . . . 7F 6 (7N 81)
Harper Rd. M22: Shar . . . 9D 106
Harper's La. BL1: Bolt . . . 2C 38
Harper Sq. OL2: Shaw . . . 5N 45
Harper St. BL4: Farn . . . 1J 57
OL8: O'ham . . . 7J 63
OL11: Roch . . . 8C 28
SK3: Stoc . . . 9C 108
WN1: Wig . . . 9N 9 (4H 53)
WN2: Hin . . . 7M 53
Harpford Cl. BL2: Bolt . . . 7A 40
Harpford Dr. BL2: Bolt . . . 7A 40
Harp Ind. Est. OL11: Roch . . . 2B 44
Harp Rd. M17: T Pk . . . 1G 92
Harp St. M11: Man . . . 2C 96
Harp Trad. Est. M17: T Pk . . . 1G 92
Harptree Gro. WN7: Lei . . . 3F 72
HARPURHEY . . . 3J 79
Harpurhey Rd. M8: Man . . . 2H 79
M9: Man . . . 2H 79
Harridge, The OL12: Roch . . . 2A 28
Harridge Av. OL12: Roch . . . 2A 28
SK15: Stal . . . 8G 83
Harridge Bank OL12: Roch . . . 2A 28
Harridge St. OL12: Roch . . . 2A 28
Harrier Cl. M22: Shar . . . 2D 116
M28: Wors . . . 2L 75
WN7: Lei . . . 5K 73
Harrier Dr. WN8: Skel . . . 3C 50
Harriet St. BL3: Bolt . . . 1C 56
M28: Walk . . . 7L 57
(not continuous)
M44: Cad . . . 3F 102
Harriett St. M4: Man . . . 2N 5 (8H 79)
OL16: Roch . . . 8E 8 (6E 28)
Harringay Rd. M40: Man . . . 5N 79
Harrington Cl. BL9: Bury . . . 5N 41
Harrington Rd. WA14: Alt . . . 2B 114
Harrington St. M18: Man . . . 4C 96
Harris Av. M34: Dent . . . 6F 96
M41: Urm . . . 4D 92
Harris Cl. M34: Dent . . . 6F 96
OL10: H'ood . . . 3D 42
Harris Dr. BL9: Bury . . . 1A 60
SK14: Hyde . . . 5D 98
Harrison Av. M19: Man . . . 7N 95
Harrison Cl. OL12: Roch . . . 4L 27
Harrison Cres. BL6: Bla . . . 1M 35
Harrison Rd. PR7: Adl . . . 7K 19
Harrisons Dr. SK6: Wood . . . 3N 109
Harrison St. BL0: Ram . . . 7J 11
BL6: Hor . . . 9D 20
M4: Man . . . 9J 79
M7: Sal . . . 6C 78
M30: Ecc . . . 1B 92
M38: Lit H . . . 7H 57
OL1: O'ham . . . 3D 8 (5K 63)
SK1: Stoc . . . 9D 108
SK14: Hyde . . . 5D 98
SK15: Stal . . . 8C 82
WN2: Hin . . . 8D 54
WN5: Wig . . . 4C 52
Harrison Way WA12: N Wil . . . 5F 86
Harris Rd. WN6: Stan . . . 1M 33
Harris St. BL3: Bolt . . . 6F 38
M8: Man . . . 6D 78
Harrogate Av. M25: Pres . . . 9C 60
Harrogate Cl. M11: Man . . . 2C 96
Harrogate Dr. SK5: Stoc . . . 9C 96
Harrogate Rd. SK5: Stoc . . . 9C 96
Harrogate Sq. BL8: Bury . . . 3F 40
Harrogate St. WN1: Wig . . . 9L 9 (4G 52)
Harroll Ga. M27: Swin . . . 3G 77
Harrop Ct. OL3: Dig . . . 7N 47
Harrop Ct. Rd. OL3: Dig . . . 7N 47
HARROP DALE . . . 7N 47
HARROP EDGE . . . 4H 99
Harrop Edge La. OL3: Dig . . . 8K 47
Harrop Edge Rd. SK14: Mot . . . 5H 99
Harrop Fold OL8: O'ham . . . 1L 81
HARROP GREEN . . . 7N 47
Harrop Grn. La. OL3: Dig . . . 7M 47
Harrop La. SK10: Adl . . . 1J 129
HARROP RIDGE . . . 6N 47
Harrop Rd. SK10: Boll . . . 5N 129
WA15: Hale . . . 5E 114
Harrops Pl. SK11: Macc . . . 6F 130
(off Park La.)
Harrop St. BL3: Bolt . . . 8B 38
M18: Man . . . 3D 96
M28: Walk . . . 8J 57
SK1: Stoc . . . 9E 108
SK15: Stal . . . 8D 82
Harrow Av. M19: Man . . . 2M 107
OL8: O'ham . . . 8H 63
OL11: Roch . . . 7M 27
Harrowby Cl. WN5: Wig . . . 5B 52
Harrowby Ct. BL4: Farn . . . 3J 57
Harrowby Dr. M40: Man . . . 5J 79
Harrowby Fold BL4: Farn . . . 3K 57
Harrowby La. BL4: Farn . . . 3K 57
Harrowby Rd. BL1: Bolt . . . 2A 38
BL3: Bolt . . . 9B 38
M27: Swin . . . 3E 76
Harrowby St. BL4: Farn . . . 3J 57
WN5: Wig . . . 5B 52
Harrow Cl. BL9: Bury . . . 7M 41
SK9: Wilm . . . 6J 123
WN5: Orr . . . 3K 51
Harrow Cres. WN7: Lei . . . 7H 73
Harrowdene Wlk. M9: Man . . . 2J 79
(off Alderside Rd.)
Harrow Dr. M33: Sale . . . 6G 105
SK8: Chea . . . 5H 117
Harrow M. OL2: Shaw . . . 5M 45
Harrow Pl. WN3: I Mak . . . 7J 53
Harrow Rd. BL1: Bolt . . . 4C 38
M33: Sale . . . 6G 105
WN5: Wig . . . 2A 52
Harrow St. M8: Man . . . 1G 78
OL11: Roch . . . 2F 44
Harrycroft Rd. SK6: Wood . . . 3M 109
Harryfields SK14: B'tom . . . 8J 99
Harry Hall Gdns. M7: Sal . . . 6B 78
Harry Lawson Ct. SK10: Macc . . . 3J 131
Harry Piggott Ct. M9: Man . . . 8H 61
Harry Rd. SK5: Stoc . . . 9D 96
Harry Rowley Cl. M22: Wyth . . . 5B 116
Harry's Ct. WN7: Lei . . . 5F 72
Harry St. OL2: O'ham . . . 1J 63
OL11: Roch . . . 1N 43
Harry Thorneycroft Wlk.
M11: Man . . . 1K 95
(off Rylance St.)
Harrytown SK6: Rom . . . 6L 109
Harry Whitehead Ct. BL9: Bury . . . 7M 25
Harsnips WN8: Skel . . . 1A 50
Harswell Cl. WN5: Orr . . . 6J 51
Hart Av. M33: Sale . . . 4M 105
M43: Droy . . . 9F 80
HART COMMON . . . 4D 54
Hart Comn. Caravan Pk.
BL5: W'ton . . . 4D 54
Hart Common Golf Course . . . 4D 54
Hart Ct. OL5: Mos . . . 9E 64
Hart Dr. BL9: Bury . . . 8A 42
Harter St. M1: Man . . . 6H 5 (1F 94)
Hartfield Cl. M13: Man . . . 3H 95
Hartfield Wlk. BL2: Bolt . . . 4K 39
Hartford Av. OL10: H'ood . . . 2G 42
SK4: Stoc . . . 2B 108
SK9: Wilm . . . 9E 122
Hartford Cl. OL10: H'ood . . . 1G 42
Hartford Dr. BL8: Bury . . . 7G 25
Hartford Gdns. WA15: Tim . . . 2K 115
Hartford Grn. BL5: W'ton . . . 5H 55
Hartford Ind. Est. OL9: O'ham . . . 5G 63
Hartford Rd. BL5: W'ton . . . 5H 55
M33: Sale . . . 6D 104
M41: Urm . . . 5E 92
Hartford St. M34: Dent . . . 4J 97
Hartford Wlk. M9: Man . . . 4H 79
(off Mannington Dr.)
Hart Hill Dr. M5: Sal . . . 7K 77
Harthill St. M8: Man . . . 5E 78
Hartington Cl. M41: Urm . . . 7E 92
Hartington Ct. OL2: O'ham . . . 8J 45
Hartington Dr. M11: Man . . . 7N 79
SK7: H Gro . . . 7J 119
WN6: Stan . . . 5C 34
Hartington Rd. BL1: Bolt . . . 5D 38
M21: Cho H . . . 9A 94
M30: Ecc . . . 7A 76
SK2: Stoc . . . 2H 119
SK6: H Lan . . . 8B 120
SK7: Bram . . . 9C 118
SK8: H Grn . . . 7J 117
SK12: Dis . . . 8B 120
WA14: B'ath . . . 9D 104
Hartington St. M14: Man . . . 6E 94
Hartis Av. M7: Sal . . . 4D 78
Hartland WN8: Skel . . . 1A 50
Hartland Av. M41: Urm . . . 7G 92
Hartland Cl. M29: Ast . . . 2C 74
SK2: Stoc . . . 8G 109
SK12: Poy . . . 1H 125
Hartland Ct. BL1: Bolt . . . 1F 38
(off Blackburn Rd.)
Hartland St. OL10: H'ood . . . 2J 43
Hartlebury OL11: Roch . . . 7C 28
Hartlepool Cl. M14: Man . . . 6G 95
Hartley Av. M25: Pres . . . 8B 60
WN1: Wig . . . 9N 9 (4H 53)
Hartley Cl. WA13: Lym . . . 4A 112
Hartley Grn. SK10: Boll . . . 5K 129
Hartley Grn. Gdns. WN5: Bil . . . 9H 51
Hartley Gro. M44: Irl . . . 5J 91
WN5: Orr . . . 4M 51
Hartley Hall Gdns. M16: Whall R . . . 8D 94
Hartley La. OL11: Roch . . . 9C 28
Hartley Pl. OL16: Roch . . . 6H 29
Hartley Rd. M21: Cho H . . . 8N 93
WA14: Alt . . . 1A 6 (2C 114)
Hartley St. BL6: Hor . . . 2D 36
M40: Man . . . 2L 79
OL10: H'ood . . . 2J 43
OL12: Roch . . . 4N 27
OL12: W'le . . . 8G 15
OL15: Lit . . . 9L 15
OL16: Roch . . . 6H 29
SK3: Stoc . . . 8B 108
SK15: Mill . . . 7G 83
WN5: Wig . . . 5M 51
Hartley Ter. OL11: Roch . . . 1C 44
OL15: Lit . . . 9L 15
(off Featherstall Rd.)
WN3: Wig . . . 9J 9 (4F 52)
Hartley Way WN5: Bil . . . 9H 51
Hart Mill Cl. OL5: Mos . . . 9E 64
Harton Av. M18: Man . . . 6A 96
Harton Cl. OL2: Shaw . . . 6L 45
Hart Rd. M14: Man . . . 7F 94
Harts Farm M. WN7: Lei . . . 3H 73
Hartshead WN8: Skel . . . 1A 50
Hartshead Av. OL6: A Lyne . . . 4N 81
SK15: Stal . . . 7D 82

Hartshead Cl. M11: Man .2E 96
Hartshead Cres. M35: Fail .4G 80
HARTSHEAD GREEN .2C 82
Hartshead Rd. OL6: A Lyne .4N 81
Hartshead St. OL4: Lees .6B 64
Hartshead Vw. SK14: Hyde .8C 98
Hart's Ho's. BL6: Hor .8F 20
Hart's La. WN8: Uph .3D 50
Hartsop Dr. M24: Mid .1H 61
Hartspring Av. M27: Swin .3G 77
Hart St. BL5: W'ton .4D 54
M1: Man .6H 5 (1F 94)
(Abingdon St.)
M1: Man .5J 5 (9F 78)
(Minshull St.)
M29: Tyld .2D 74
M43: Droy .8E 80
WA14: Alt .1E 6 (2E 114)
Hartswell Cl. WA3: Gol .8K 71
Hartswood Cl. M34: Dent .5L 97
Hartswood Rd. M20: Man .2J 107
Hartwell Cl. BL2: Bolt .2K 39
M11: Man .1L 95
Hartwell Gro. SK3: Stoc .3D 118
Harty Ho. M30: Ecc .8E 76
(off Monton La.)
Harvard Cl. SK6: Wood .3N 109
Harvard Gro. M6: Sal .7J 77
Harvard Rd. M18: Man .4N 95
Harvard St. OL11: Roch .9E 28
Harvest Cl. M6: Sal .5L 77
M33: Sale .5N 105
Harvest Pk. BL1: Bolt .4D 38
Harvest Rd. SK10: Macc .1G 131
Harvest Way WN2: Hin .8E 54
Harvey Av. WA12: N Wil .6C 86
Harvey Cl. WA3: Gol .9K 71
WN7: Lei .9D 72
Harvey La. WA3: Gol .9J 71
Harvey St. BL1: Bolt .1E 38
BL8: Bury .1J 41
OL12: Roch .3F 28
SK1: Stoc .2M 9 (7D 108)
WN3: I Mak .5H 53
Harvin Gro. M34: Dent .7L 97
Harwell Rd. WA14: W Tim .7C 104
Harwich Cl. M19: Man .8N 95
SK5: Stoc .2G 109
Harwin Cl. OL12: Roch .2B 28
HARWOOD .9N 23
Harwood Ct. M6: Sal .6A 78
SK4: Stoc .6K 107
Harwood Cres. BL8: Tot .6E 24
Harwood Dr. BL8: Bury .3G 41
Harwood Gdns. OL10: H'ood .3J 43
(off Mount St.)
Harwood Golf Course .1A 40
Harwood Gro. BL2: Bolt .3J 39
Harwood Ho. BL8: Tot .6E 24
HARWOOD LEE .8M 23
Harwood Mdw. BL2: Bolt .1N 39
Harwood Pk. OL10: H'ood .3J 43
Harwood Rd. BL8: Tot .9C 24
M19: Man .2K 107
SK4: Stoc .6K 107
Harwood St. OL15: Lit .9K 15
SK4: Stoc .5C 108
Harwood Va. BL2: Bolt .1M 39
Harwood Va. Ct. BL2: Bolt .1M 39
Harwood Wlk. BL8: Tot .6E 24
Haseldine St. WN4: A Mak .4C 70
Haseley Cl. M26: Rad .7B 40
M29: Tyld .2B 74
SK12: Poy .1J 125
Hasguard Cl. BL1: Bolt .4A 38
Haskoll St. BL6: Hor .3F 36
Haslam Brow BL9: Bury .4L 41
Haslam Ct. BL3: Bolt .7C 38
M7: Sal .1C 78
Haslam Hall M. BL1: Bolt .5N 37
Haslam Hey Cl. BL8: Bury .2F 40
Haslam Rd. SK3: Stoc .1C 118
Haslam St. BL3: Bolt .7E 38
BL9: Bury .9N 25
M24: Mid .4A 62
OL12: Roch .5B 28
Haslemere Av. WA15: Haleb .9J 115
Haslemere Dr. SK8: Chea H .6M 117
Haslemere Ind. Est.
WN4: A Mak .2D 70
Haslemere Rd. M20: Man .2J 107
M41: Urm .8B 92
Haslington Rd. M22: Wyth .5D 116
Hasper Av. M20: Man .1F 106
Hassall Av. M20: Man .1E 106
Hassall St. M26: Rad .7L 41
SK15: Stal .9E 82
Hassall Way SK9: Hand .1K 123
(off Spath La.)
Hassness Cl. WN3: Wig .9E 52
Hassop Av. M7: Sal .3N 77
Hassop Cl. M11: Man .9K 79
Hassop Rd. SK5: Stoc .8E 96
Hastings Av. M21: Cho H .9N 93
M45: Whitef .4A 60
Hastings Cl. M45: Whitef .4A 60
SK1: Stoc .9F 108
SK8: Chea H .6A 118
Hastings Dr. M41: Urm .6M 91
Hastings Rd. BL1: Bolt .4C 38
M25: Pres .6B 60
M30: Ecc .6A 76
Hastings St. OL11: Roch .8D 28
Haston Cl. SK5: Stoc .4D 108
Hasty La. WA15: Ring .8L 115
(not continuous)
Hatchett Rd. M22: Wyth .6C 116
Hatchings, The WA13: Lym .5A 112
Hatchley St. M13: Man .4J 95
Hatchmere Cl. SK8: Chea H .3L 117
WA15: Tim .1K 115
Hateley Rd. M16: Old T .7N 93
Hatfield Av. M19: Man .2L 107
Hatfield Cl. WN3: I Mak .7J 53
Hatfield Rd. BL1: Bolt .3D 38
Hatford Cl. M29: Tyld .1D 74
Hathaway Cl. SK8: H Grn .8G 117
Hathaway Dr. BL1: Bolt .8H 23
SK11: Macc .7G 131
Hathaway Gdns. SK6: Bred .5K 109
Hathaway Rd. BL9: Bury .9N 41
Hathaway Wlk. WN3: I Mak .7J 53
Hatherleigh Wlk. BL2: Bolt .7N 39
Hatherley Rd. M20: Man .2J 107
HATHERLOW .6M 109
Hatherlow SK6: Rom .6L 109
Hatherlow Ct. BL5: W'ton .1J 55
Hatherlow Hgts. SK6: Rom .7L 109
Hatherlow La. SK7: H Gro .5H 119
Hatherop Cl. M30: Ecc .9B 76
Hathersage Av. M6: Sal .7K 77
Hathersage Cres. SK13: Gam .7A 100
Hathersage Dr. SK13: Glos .9H 101
Hathersage Rd. M13: Man .5H 95
Hathersage St. OL9: O'ham .5G 62
Hathersage Way M34: Dent .9L 97
HATHERSHAW .7K 63
Hathershaw La. OL8: O'ham .8K 63
Hathershaw Sports Cen. .9K 63
Hatherton Ct. M28: Walk .5L 57
Hatherway Ct. WN7: Lei .4K 73
Hatro Ct. M41: Urm .8G 92
Hatters Ct. SK1: Stoc .5M 9 (8D 108)
HATTERSLEY .7H 99
Hattersley Cen., The SK14: Hat .7H 99
(off Hattersley Rd. E.)
Hattersley Ind. Est. SK14: Hat .8G 99
Hattersley Rd. E. SK14: Hat .8H 99
Hattersley Rd. W. SK14: Hat .7F 98
Hattersley Station (Rail) .8F 98
Hattersley Wlk. SK14: Hat .6F 98
(off Wardle Brook Av.)
Hatter St. M4: Man .2K 5
Hatton Av. M7: Sal .7C 78
M46: Ath .6M 55
Hatton Brow Ter. SK11: Sut E .8K 131
Hatton Fold M46: Ath .8K 55
Hattonfold M33: Sale .7J 105
Hatton Gro. BL1: Bolt .8H 23
Hattons Ct. M32: Stre .6J 93
Hattons Rd. M17: T Pk .3H 93
Hatton St. M12: Man .6M 95
PR7: Adl .7J 19
SK1: Stoc .1K 9 (6C 108)
SK4: Stoc .1K 9 (6C 108)
SK11: Macc .5G 131
Hatton Ter. SK16: Duk .9M 81
(off Queen St.)
Hat Works (The Mus. of Hatting)
.3K 9 (7C 108)
HAUGH .9N 29
Haugh Fold OL16: Miln .9N 29
Haugh Hill Rd. OL4: O'ham .9B 46
Haugh La. OL16: Miln .9N 29
Haugh Sq. OL16: Miln .9N 29
Haughton Cl. SK6: Wood .2L 109
SK10: Macc .3D 130
HAUGHTON DALE .1L 109
Haughton Dale Local Nature Reserve
.1M 109
Haughton Dr. M22: Nor .7C 106
HAUGHTON GREEN .9M 97
Haughton Grn. Rd. M34: Dent .9L 97
Haughton Hall Rd. M34: Dent .6L 97
Haughton St. M34: Aud .4K 97
SK14: Hyde .8B 98
Havana Cl. M11: Man .9L 79
Haveley Rd. M22: Wyth .2B 116
Havelock Dr. M7: Sal .6C 78
Havelock St. OL8: O'ham .6K 63
Haven, The BL3: Lit L .9A 40
(off Independent St.)
WA15: Hale .4F 114
Haven Bank BL1: Bolt .1G 39
Havenbrook Gro. BL0: Ram .2G 25
Haven Cl. M26: Rad .7D 40
OL4: Gras .5G 64
SK7: H Gro .6G 118
Haven Dr. M43: Droy .8C 80
Haven La. OL4: O'ham .9B 46
Havenscroft Av. M30: Ecc .1D 92
Havenside Cl. OL4: O'ham .9B 46
Haven St. M6: Sal .9L 77
Havenwood Rd. WN1: Wig .8E 34
Havercroft Cl. WN3: Wig .8B 52
Havercroft Pk. BL1: Bolt .4M 37
Haverfield Rd. M9: Man .8K 61
Haverford St. M12: Man .3L 95
Havergate Walks SK2: Stoc .3K 119
Haverhill Gro. BL2: Bolt .2J 39
(off Scawfell Av.)
Haversham Rd. M8: Man .9D 60
Havers Rd. M18: Man .4C 96
Haverty Pct. WA12: N Wil .8E 86
Havisham Cl. BL6: Los .8K 37
Hawarde Cl. WA12: N Wil .5D 86
Hawarden Av. M16: Whall R .7B 94
Hawarden Rd. WA14: Alt .1D 114
Hawarden St. BL1: Bolt .8F 22
Haw Clough La. OL3: G'fld .5M 65
Hawdraw Grn. SK2: Stoc .1J 119
Hawes Av. BL4: Farn .3F 56
M14: Man .1K 107
M27: Swin .3F 76
WA11: St H .9G 69
Hawes Cl. BL8: Bury .8H 25
SK2: Stoc .1E 118
Hawes Cres. WN4: A Mak .5E 70
Haweswater Av. M29: Ast .3C 74
WN2: I Mak .4L 53
Haweswater Cl. M34: Dent .7E 96
Haweswater Cres. BL9: Bury .7A 42
Haweswater Dr. M24: Mid .1K 61
Haweswater M. M24: Mid .1K 61
Hawfinch Gro. M28: Wors .2L 75
Hawick Gro. OL10: H'ood .3D 42
Hawk Cl. BL9: Bury .9A 26
Hawker Av. BL3: Bolt .9E 38
Hawker Dr. WN8: Skel .3C 50
Hawkeshead Rd. M8: Man .4G 79
(not continuous)
Hawke St. SK15: Stal .9F 82
HAWK GREEN .4C 120
Hawk Grn. Cl. SK6: Mar .4C 120
Hawk Grn. Rd. SK6: Mar .4C 120
Hawkhurst Ct. WN7: Lei .5K 73
Hawkhurst Pk. WN7: Lei .5K 73
Hawkhurst Rd. M13: Man .6L 95
Hawkhurst St. WN7: Lei .5K 73
Hawkinge Vw. OL10: H'ood .5L 43
Hawkins Cl. M9: Man .1H 79
Hawkins La. SK10: Rain .1N 131
Hawkins St. SK5: Stoc .4C 108
Hawkins Way OL15: Lit .5N 15
HAWKLEY .9E 52
Hawkley Av. WN3: Wig .9C 52
Hawkley Brook Ct. WN3: Wig .9C 52
Hawkridge Cl. BL5: W'ton .6H 55
Hawkridge Dr. M23: Wyth .6M 105
Hawkrigg Cl. WN6: Stan .5C 34
Hawk Rd. M44: Irl .6H 91
SK22: N Mil .7N 121
Hawksclough WN8: Skel .1B 50
HAWKSHAW .2B 24
Hawkshaw Cl. BL8: Haw .2B 24
WN2: Asp .9K 35
Hawkshaw Ct. M5: Sal .9N 77
Hawkshaw La. BL8: Haw .8B 10
Hawkshaw St. BL6: Hor .1D 36
Hawkshead Cl. SK15: Stal .6C 82
Hawkshead Dr. BL3: Bolt .9B 38
M24: Mid .2K 61
OL2: O'ham .6H 45
Hawkshead Fold SK13: Glos .6G 101
Hawkshead Rd. OL2: Shaw .4L 45
SK13: Glos .7G 101
Hawksheath Cl. BL7: Eger .4G 22
Hawksley Ct. OL8: O'ham .8G 62
(off Maple St.)
Hawksley Ind. Est. OL8: O'ham .8G 62
Hawksley St. BL6: Hor .2F 36
OL8: O'ham .8G 62
Hawksmoor Dr. OL2: Shaw .4M 45
Hawkstone Av. M43: Droy .7C 80
M45: Whitef .4K 59
Hawkstone Cl. BL2: Bolt .1M 39
Hawkswick Dr. M23: Wyth .6N 105
Hawkworth M29: Ast .5C 74
Hawk Yd. OL3: G'fld .6N 65
Hawk Yd. La. OL3: G'fld .6N 65
Hawley Brook Trad. Est.
WN3: Wig .9B 52
Hawley Dr. WA15: Haleb .7H 115
Hawley Grn. OL12: Roch .3B 28
Hawley La. WA15: Haleb .7H 115
Hawley St. M19: Man .9N 95
Haworth Av. BL0: Ram .3H 25
Haworth Cl. SK11: Macc .7F 130
Haworth Ct. M26: Rad .9H 41
(off Crook St.)
Haworth Dr. M32: Stre .6F 92
Haworth Rd. M18: Man .5A 96
Haworth St. BL8: Bury .9E 24
M26: Rad .9H 41
OL1: O'ham .2J 63
WN2: Hin .5N 53
Haworth Wlk. M26: Rad .9H 41
Hawsworth Cl. M15: Man .4G 94
Hawthorn Apartments M26: Rad .8H 41
(off Bury Rd.)
Hawthorn Av. BL0: Eden .4K 11
BL0: Ram .3G 25
BL8: Bury .9J 25
M26: Rad .2H 59
M28: Walk .1M 75
M30: Ecc .7D 76
M41: Urm .8F 92
SK6: Mar .1A 120
SK9: Wilm .7F 122
WA12: N Wil .6G 86
WA15: Tim .9F 104
WN1: Stan .6E 34
WN2: Hin .8C 54
WN4: Gars .5N 69
WN5: Orr .5K 51
WN5: Wig .5A 52
Hawthorn Bank BL2: Bolt .9M 23
SK13: Had .5B 100
SK22: N Mil .9L 121
Hawthorn Cl. M29: Tyld .1E 74
WA15: Tim .9F 104
WN5: Bil .5H 69
Hawthorn Ct. PR6: Adl .5J 19
SK6: Bred .5H 109
Hawthorn Cres. BL8: Tot .6F 24
OL2: Shaw .6M 45
OL8: O'ham .9K 63
Hawthornden M20: Man .4E 106
Hawthorn Dr. M6: Sal .6H 77
M19: Man .1L 107
M27: Pen .3J 77
M44: Cad .3E 102
SK15: Stal .1C 98
Hawthorne Av. BL4: Farn .3J 57
BL6: Hor .3G 37
WA3: Cul .4L 89
Hawthorne Dr. M28: Wors .3A 76
Hawthorne Gro. OL9: Chad .3F 62
SK6: Bred .4J 109
SK12: Poy .2N 125
Hawthorne Rd. BL3: Bolt .7C 38
Hawthorne St. BL3: Bolt .7C 38
Hawthorn Grn. SK9: Wilm .7F 122
(off Kennerley's La.)
Hawthorn Gro. OL7: A Lyne .9K 81
SK4: Stoc .5N 107
SK7: Bram .9A 118
SK9: Wilm .7G 122
SK14: Holl .3N 99
SK14: Hyde .8A 98
WN7: Lei .3G 73
Hawthorn La. M21: Cho H .9M 93
M32: Stre .9K 93
M33: Sale .2D 104
OL16: Miln .9L 29
SK9: Wilm .7F 122
Hawthorn Lodge SK3: Stoc .3D 118
Hawthorn Pk. SK9: Wilm .7F 122
Hawthorn Ri. SK10: P'bury .7C 128
Hawthorn Rd. BL4: Kea .6B 58
BL5: W'ton .4H 55
M32: Stre .9K 93
(off Hancock St.)
M34: Dent .5F 96
M40: Man .1C 80
M43: Droy .8G 80
(not continuous)
OL8: O'ham .9F 62
OL11: Roch .7K 27
SK4: Stoc .6L 107
SK8: Gat .2F 116
SK10: Boll .5K 129
WA15: Hale .5E 6 (4E 114)
Hawthorn Rd. Sth. M43: Droy .8G 80
Hawthorns, The M34: Aud .3H 97
M34: Dent .5F 96
(off Hawthorn Rd.)
M46: Ath .8M 55
(off Water St.)
OL4: O'ham .8D 46
Hawthorn St. M18: Man .4C 96
M34: Aud .3J 97
SK9: Wilm .8F 122
Hawthorn Ter. SK4: Stoc .5N 107
(off Hawthorn Gro.)
SK9: Wilm .8F 122
Hawthorn Vw. SK9: Wilm .7F 122
Hawthorn Wlk. M31: Part .5F 102
OL15: Lit .9K 15
SK9: Wilm .7F 122
Hawthorn Way SK10: Macc .2J 131
Hawthorpe Gro. OL3: Upp .3L 65
Haxby Rd. M18: Man .6B 96
Haxey Wlk. BL6: Hor .1B 36
Haybarn Rd. M23: Wyth .9A 106
Hayburn Rd. SK2: Stoc .8G 109
Haycock Cl. SK15: Stal .2H 99
Hay Cft. SK8: Chea H .7K 117
Hayden Ct. M40: Man .5J 79
(off Sedgeford Rd.)
SK13: Glos .9E 100
Haydn Av. M14: Man .5G 94
Haydn Fold SK13: Char .1N 111
HAYDOCK .2A 86
Haydock Av. M33: Sale .6B 104
Haydock Cl. M32: Stre .5M 93
SK10: Macc .1G 131
Haydock Cross WA11: Hay .9C 70
Haydock Dr. M28: Wors .4J 75
SK7: H Gro .5K 119
WA15: Tim .2H 115
Haydock Ind. Est. WA11: Hay .1B 86
Haydock La. BL7: Bro X .5J 23
(Broad Mdw.)
BL7: Bro X .5H 23
(Gledhill Way)
WA11: Hay .2A 86
(not continuous)
Haydock M. M7: Sal .4C 78
(off Rigby St.)
Haydock Pk. Gdns. WA12: N Wil .9E 70
Haydock Pk. Golf Course .4J 87
Haydock Pk. Racecourse .9G 70
Haydock St. BL1: Bolt .1K 7 (4G 38)
(not continuous)
WA12: N Wil .5D 86
WN4: A Mak .8E 70
Haydock Wlk. OL9: Chad .4G 62
(off Middleton Rd.)
Haye's Rd. M44: Cad .3F 102
(not continuous)
Hayes Row WA3: Low .9C 72
Hayes St. WN7: Lei .6C 72
(Horrocks St.)
WN7: Lei .3G 73
(Linden Gro.)
Hayeswater Circ. M41: Urm .6C 92
Hayeswater Rd. M41: Urm .6C 92
Hayfell Rd. WN3: Wig .1D 70
Hayfield Av. M29: Ast .4D 74
SK6: Bred .4L 109
Hayfield Cl. BL8: G'mount .4F 24
M12: Man .2K 95
M24: Mid .9A 44
OL4: O'ham .8C 46
SK10: Macc .1F 130
Hayfield Rd. M6: Sal .6H 77
SK6: Bred .4L 109
SK22: Bir V, N Mil .6N 121
Hayfields WA16: Knut .6J 133
Hayfield St. M33: Sale .3G 105
Hayfield Wlk. M34: Dent .9L 97
WA15: Tim .1J 115
Haygrove Wlk. M9: Man .2J 79
(off Alfred St.)
Hay Ho. OL4: O'ham .3B 64
(off Huddersfield Rd.)
Hayle Cl. SK10: Macc .3B 130
Hayle Rd. OL1: O'ham .8A 46
Hayley St. M13: Man .5K 95
Hayling Cl. BL8: Bury .7J 25
Hayling Rd. M33: Sale .3E 104
Haymaker Ri. OL12: W'le .8G 15
Hayman Av. WN7: Lei .8F 72
Haymans Wlk. M13: Man .9L 5 (2G 95)
Haymarket, The
BL9: Bury .8K 7 (2M 41)
Haymarket St.
BL9: Bury .8K 7 (2L 41)
M13: Man .4H 95
Haymill Av. M38: Lit H .5H 57
Haymond Cl. M6: Sal .4N 77
Haynes St. BL3: Bolt .9C 38
OL12: Roch .5D 28
Haysbrook Av. M28: Walk .7G 57
Haysbrook Cl. OL7: A Lyne .3L 81
Haythorp Av. M22: Wyth .4D 116
Hayton St. WA16: Knut .7F 132
Hayward Av. BL3: Lit L .9C 40
Hayward Gro. WN6: Stan .2A 34
Haywards Cl. SK13: Glos .6E 100
Hayward St. BL8: Bury .1J 41
Haywood Cl. WA3: Low .9A 72
Haywood Ho. M46: Ath .8M 55
Hazel Av. BL0: Ram .4H 25
BL5: W'ton .4H 55
BL8: Tot .8G 24
BL9: Bury .2A 42
M16: Whall R .7C 94
M26: Rad .3A 58
M27: Swin .3G 76
M33: Sale .5H 105
M38: Lit H .6F 56
OL6: A Lyne .4B 82
OL16: Miln .1L 45
SK6: Rom .6A 110
SK8: Chea .2K 117
SK11: Macc .7E 130
WN6: Wig .9D 34
Hazelbadge Cl. SK12: Poy .2G 125
Hazelbadge Rd. SK12: Poy .2G 125
Hazelbank Av. M20: Man .1G 107
Hazelbottom Rd. M8: Man .3G 79
Hazel Bus. Pk. WA11: R'ford .6A 68
Hazel Cl. M43: Droy .8G 80
SK6: Mar .3B 120
Hazel Ct. M16: Whall R .6C 94
(off Dudley Rd.)
Hazelcroft SK9: A Edg .5F 126
Hazelcroft Gdns. SK9: A Edg .5F 126
Hazeldean Ct. SK9: Wilm .5J 123
Hazeldene BL5: W'ton .6F 54
Hazel Dene Cl. BL9: Bury .5M 41
Hazeldene Rd. M40: Man .1C 80
Hazel Dr. M22: Wyth .7F 116
SK2: Stoc .1H 119
SK12: Poy .3K 125
WA13: Lym .5A 112
Hazelfields M28: Wors .3B 76
Hazel Gdns. SK8: Chea H .6N 117
(off Hazel Rd.)
HAZEL GROVE .4H 119
Hazel Gro. BL4: Farn .3J 57
M5: Sal .8J 77
M26: Rad .3F 58
M41: Urm .7E 92
OL9: Chad .3F 62
WA3: Gol .1L 87
WN7: Lei .3G 73
Hazel Grove (Park & Ride) .5H 119
Hazel Grove Golf Course .6M 119
Hazel Grove Pool and
Target Fitness Cen. .6E 118
Hazel Grove Recreation Cen. .7G 118
Hazel Grove Station (Rail) .5H 119
Hazelhall Cl. M28: Wors .3B 76
Hazel Hall Cotts. BL0: Ram .4H 25
Hazel Hall La. BL0: Ram .4H 25
HAZELHURST
BL0 .9H 11
M27 .3C 76
OL6 .4C 82
Hazelhurst Cl. BL0: Ram .1H 25
BL1: Bolt .2F 38
Hazelhurst Dr. M24: Mid .8L 43
SK10: Boll .5L 129
Hazelhurst Fold M28: Wors .3C 76
Hazelhurst Gro. WN4: A Mak .6F 70
Hazelhurst M. OL9: Chad .8D 62
Hazelhurst Rd. M28: Wors .3B 76
OL6: A Lyne .4C 82
SK15: Stal .6D 82
Hazelhurst Wlk. M23: Wyth .6M 105
Hazel La. OL8: O'ham .9H 63
Hazelmere Av. M30: Ecc .6B 76
Hazelmere Gdns. WN2: Hin .7A 54
Hazel Mt. BL7: Eger .3F 22
Hazel Pear Cl. BL6: Hor .1B 36
Hazel Rd. M24: Mid .1N 61
M45: Whitef .3A 60
M46: Ath .7L 55
SK8: Chea H .6N 117
SK15: Stal .7F 82
WA14: Alt .1D 6 (2D 114)
Hazels, The PR7: Cop .4B 18
Hazel St. BL0: Ram .1G 25
M34: Aud .3J 97
SK7: H Gro .4J 119
Hazel Ter. M9: Man .7J 61
Hazelton Cl. WN7: Lei .9G 72
Hazel Vw. SK6: Mar .4C 120
Hazel Wlk. M31: Part .5F 102
Hazelwell M33: Sale .5H 105
Hazelwood OL9: Chad .3C 62
Hazelwood Av. BL2: Bolt .1M 39
Hazelwood Cl. SK13: Had .3C 100
SK14: Hyde .7D 98
Hazelwood Ct. M41: Urm .6D 92
Hazelwood Dr. BL9: Bury .6M 25
M34: Aud .3K 97
Hazelwood Rd. BL1: Bolt .2C 38
M22: Wyth .7C 116
SK2: Stoc .3E 118
SK7: H Gro .5J 119
SK9: Wilm .6H 123
WA15: Hale .5E 114
WN1: Wig .8E 34
Hazlemere BL4: Kea .4A 58
Hazlemere Av. SK11: Macc .6E 130
Headen Av. WN5: Wig .6M 51
Head Farm Ct. WA12: N Wil .6D 86
Headingley Dr. M16: Old T .6N 93
Headingley Rd. M14: Man .1J 107
Headingley Way BL3: Bolt .9E 38
Headland Cl. WA3: Low .3A 88
Headlands Dr. M25: Pres .1N 77
Headlands Rd. SK7: Bram .6D 118
Headlands St. OL12: Roch .4C 28
HEADY HILL .2E 42
Heady Hill Cl. OL10: H'ood .3F 42
Heady Hill Ct. OL10: H'ood .2F 42
Heady Hill Rd. OL10: H'ood .2F 42
Heald Av. M14: Man .6G 95
Heald Cl. OL12: Roch .2A 28
OL15: Lit .2L 29
WA14: Bow .5C 114
Heald Dr. OL12: Roch .2A 28
WA14: Bow .5C 114
HEALD GREEN .7G 116
Heald Grn. Ho. M22: Wyth .7F 116

Heald Green Station (Rail) 7F 116
Heald Gro. M14: Man 5G 95
SK8: H Grn 6F 116
Heald La. OL15: Lit 2L 29
Heald Pl. M14: Man 5G 95
Heald Rd. WA14: Bow 5C 114
HEALDS GREEN 9D 44
Healds Grn. OL1: Chad 9D 44
Heald St. WA12: N Wil 6C 86
Healdwood Rd.
SK6: Rom, Wood 4N 109
HEALEY 1B 28
Healey Av. OL10: H'ood 1K 43
OL12: Roch 1A 28
Healey Bottoms
OL12: Roch 2N 27
Healey Cl. M7: Sal 2B 78
M23: Wyth 6M 105
Healey Dell OL12: Roch 1N 27
Healey Dell Nature Reserve 1N 27
Healey Gro. OL12: Whitw 9A 14
Healey Hall M. OL12: Roch 1A 28
Healey La. OL12: Roch 1C 28
Healey Stones OL12: Roch 1C 28
Healey St. OL16: Roch 9B 8 (7C 28)
Healing St. OL11: Roch 8E 28
Healthy Living Zone of the
Wigan Life Cen. 8K 9 (3F 52)
Heanor Av. M34: Dent 9L 97
HEAP BRIDGE 3B 42
Heap Brow BL9: Bury 3C 42
Heape St. OL11: Roch 3A 44
Heapfold OL12: Roch 3N 27
Heaplands BL8: G'mount 4F 24
Heapriding Bus. Pk.
SK3: Stoc 3G 9 (7B 108)
Heap Rd. OL12: Roch 3J 27
Heaps Farm Ct. SK15: Stal 1G 98
Heap St. BL3: Bolt 8F 38
BL9: Bury 3C 42
M26: Rad 9H 41
M45: Whitef 4M 59
OL4: O'ham 4N 63
Heapworth Av. BL0: Ram 8H 11
Heapy Cl. BL8: Bury 3F 40
Heapy St. SK11: Macc 6J 131
Heardman Av. WN6: Wig 2D 52
Heart, The M50: Sal 2L 93
Hearthstone Cl. SK8: Chea 9H 107
Heath, The M24: Mid 5N 61
OL7: A Lyne 4L 81
SK13: Glos 6E 100
Heath Av. BL0: Ram 4H 25
M7: Sal 6B 78
M41: Urm 6E 92
Heathbank Rd. M9: Man 7H 61
SK3: Stoc 9N 107
SK8: Chea H 8L 117
HEATH CHARNOCK 4J 19
Heath Cl. BL3: Bolt 1C 56
Heathcote Av. SK4: Stoc 5A 108
Heathcote Gdns. SK6: Rom 7B 110
Heathcote Rd. M18: Man 5A 96
Heath Cotts. BL1: Bolt 7E 22
Heath Cres. SK2: Stoc 2D 118
Heath Dr. WA16: Knut 6F 132
Heather Av. M43: Droy 8G 81
M44: Cad 2E 102
OL2: Shaw 4A 46
Heather Bank BL8: Tot 6E 24
OL15: Lit 8A 16
Heatherbell Cl. WA14: W Tim 7B 104
Heather Brae WA12: N Wil 5D 86
Heather Brow SK15: Stal 2H 99
Heather Cl. BL6: Hor 9D 20
OL4: O'ham 2B 64
OL10: H'ood 4J 43
SK11: Lym G 9G 131
Heather Ct. SK4: Stoc 3B 108
WA14: Bow 4B 114
Heatherdale Dr. M8: Man 4F 78
Heather Falls SK22: N Mil 7L 121
Heatherfield BL1: Bolt 8D 22
(not continuous)
Heatherfield Ct. SK9: Wilm 6K 123
Heather Gro. M43: Droy 1F 96
SK14: Holl 3N 99
WN4: A Mak 6H 71
WN5: Wig 4B 52
WN7: Lei 3G 73
Heatheridge Cl. SK10: Macc 9G 128
Heatherlands BB4: Has 1G 10
OL12: Whitw 2B 14
Heather Lea M34: Dent 7L 97
Heatherlea Cl. WN8: Uph 4G 50
Heathermount WA14: W Tim 8B 104
Heather Rd. WA14: Hale 6E 114
WA15: Hale 6E 114
Heathers, The SK2: Stoc 3F 118
Heatherside SK5: Stoc 8E 96
SK15: Stal 8G 82
Heatherside Av. OL5: Mos 1H 83
Heatherside Rd. BL0: Ram 7H 11
Heather St. M11: Man 8N 79
Heather Wlk. M31: Part 5F 102
(off Gorse Sq.)
Heather Way OL3: Dig 8M 47
SK6: Mar 1B 120
Heatherway M14: Man 5G 95
(off Parkfield St.)
M33: Sale 3D 104
Heath Farm La. M31: Part 5H 103
Heathfield BL2: Bolt 9N 23
BL4: Farn 2M 57
M28: Wors 5N 75
PR6: H Char 4J 19
SK9: Wilm 9F 122
Heathfield Av. M34: Dent 7H 97
SK4: Stoc 3A 108
SK8: Gat 2G 117
Heathfield Cl. M33: Sale 4M 105
Heathfield Ct. BL3: Bolt 9B 38
(off Linnyshaw Cl.)
Heathfield Dr. BL3: Bolt 1C 56
M27: Swin 3G 77
M29: Tyld 1E 74
Heathfield Rd. BL9: Bury 9M 41
M45: Whitef 9M 41
SK2: Stoc 1D 118
HEATHFIELDS 3M 65
Heathfield Sq. WA16: Knut 6F 132
Heathfields Rd. OL3: Upp 3M 65
Heathfields Sq. OL3: Upp 3M 65
Heathfield St. M40: Man 5A 80
Heath Gdns. WN2: Hin 8E 54
Heathgate WN8: Skel 1A 50
Heath Ho. Cl. WA3: Low 2M 87
Heathland WN8: Uph 4F 50
Heathland Rd. M7: Sal 2A 78
Heathlands Dr. M25: Pres 1N 77
Heathlands Ho. WA16: Knut 6F 132
Heathlands Village M25: Pres 1N 77
Heathland Ter. SK3: Stoc 9C 108
Heath La. WA3: Cro 7C 88
WA3: Low 2M 87
(not continuous)
WN7: Lei 5D 72
Heathlea WN2: Hin 9E 54
Heathlea Cl. BL1: Bolt 7F 22
Heathlea Gdns. WN2: Hin 9E 54
Heathmoor Av. WA3: Low 3N 87
Heath Rd. OL12: W'le 8G 14
SK2: Stoc 1D 118
SK10: Boll 7J 129
SK13: Glos 6E 100
WA14: Hale 5D 114
WA15: Tim 8F 104
WN4: A Mak 8E 70
Heathside Gro. M28: Walk 8M 57
Heathside Pk. Rd. SK3: Stoc 8L 107
Heathside Rd. M20: Man 3H 107
SK3: Stoc 9M 107
Heath St. M8: Man 3E 78
OL11: Roch 9A 8 (7B 28)
WA3: Gol 1K 87
WN4: A Mak 8F 70
Heath Vw. M7: Sal 2N 77
WA14: Alt 4D 114
(off Tipping St.)
Heathway Av. M11: Man 8B 80
Heathwood OL3: Upp 3M 65
Heathwood Rd. M19: Man 4K 107
HEATLEY 1D 112
Heatley Cl. M34: Dent 7F 96
WA13: Lym 3B 112
Heatley Rd. OL16: Roch 7H 29
Heatley Way SK9: Hand 2J 123
(off Delamere Rd.)
HEATON 4B 38
Heaton Av. BL1: Bolt 3A 38
BL2: Bolt 8M 23
BL3: Lit L 8A 40
BL4: Farn 3K 57
SK7: Bram 4B 118
HEATON CHAPEL 3A 108
Heaton Chapel Station (Rail) 3A 108
Heaton Cl. BL9: Bury 7N 41
SK4: Stoc 5M 107
WN8: Uph 4E 50
Heaton Ct. BL9: Bury 5M 41
M25: Pres 8B 60
M33: Sale 4J 105
SK4: Stoc 4N 107
Heaton Ct. Gdns. BL1: Bolt 5N 37
Heaton Dr. BL9: Bury 7N 41
Heaton Fold BL9: Bury 4L 41
Heaton Gdns. SK4: Stoc 4A 108
Heaton Grange BL1: Bolt 5B 38
Heaton Grange Dr. BL1: Bolt 5B 38
Heaton Gro. BL9: Bury 5M 41
Heaton Hall 6D 60
Heaton La. SK4: Stoc 2H 9 (7B 108)
HEATON MERSEY 6K 107
Heaton Mersey Ind. Est.
SK4: Stoc 7K 107
HEATON MOOR 4N 107
Heaton Moor Golf Course 3M 107
Heaton Moor Rd. SK4: Stoc 5N 107
Heaton Mt. BL1: Bolt 5B 38
HEATON NORRIS 1G 9 (6B 108)
HEATON PARK 7B 60
Heaton Park 6D 60
Heaton Park Bowling Pavilion 5B 60
Heaton Park Farm Animal Cen. . . .6C 60
Heaton Park Golf Course 6E 60
Heaton Park Horticultural Cen. . . .6C 60
Heaton Pk. Rd. M9: Man 6F 60
Heaton Pk. Rd. W. M9: Man 6F 60
Heaton Park Stop (Metro) 7B 60
Heaton Park Tramway Mus. 6E 60
Heaton Rd. BL2: Bolt 7B 40
BL6: Los 7L 37
M20: Man 1H 107
SK4: Stoc 5A 108
Heatons Gro. BL5: W'ton 1J 55
Heatons Sports Club 5N 107
Heaton St. M7: Sal 3D 78
M24: Mid 4G 60
M25: Pres 7A 60
M34: Dent 6H 97
OL16: Miln 8L 29
WN1: Wig 1F 52
WN2: Asp 7N 35
WN3: I Mak 5H 53
WN6: Stan 3B 34
Heaton Towers SK4: Stoc 6C 108
(off Wilkinson Rd.)
HEAVILEY 1E 118
Heaviley Gro. BL6: Hor 8C 20
SK2: Stoc 1E 118
Hebble Butt Cl. OL16: Miln 7J 29
Hebble Cl. BL2: Bolt 8J 23
Hebburn Dr. BL8: Bury 8J 25
Hebburn Wlk. M14: Man 5G 95
(off Gt. Western St.)
Hebden Av. M6: Sal 7J 77
SK6: Bred 4L 109
WA3: Cul 4K 89
Hebden Ct. BL1: Bolt 1H 7 (4F 38)
Hebden Dr. SK13: Glos 9H 101
Hebden Wlk. M15: Man 4E 94
(off Arnott Cres.)
Hebdon Cl. WN4: A Mak 5D 70
Hebers Ct. M24: Mid 9L 43
Heber St. M26: Rad 9G 41
WN2: I Mak 4J 53
Hebron St. OL2: O'ham 9L 45
Hector Av. OL16: Roch 5F 28
Hector Rd. M13: Man 6L 95
WN5: Wig 2A 52
Heddles Ct. WN7: Lei 6G 73
Heddon Cl. SK4: Stoc 5K 107
Heddon Wlk. M8: Man 4H 79
(off Smedley Rd.)
Hedgelands Wlk. M33: Sale 3C 104
(off Epping Dr.)
Hedgemead WN6: Wig 2D 52
Hedge Row SK10: Rain 4N 129
Hedgerow Gdns. WN6: Stan 3A 34
Hedge Rows, The SK14: Hyde 6D 98
Hedgerows, The OL12: Whitw 5A 14
WA11: Hay 2C 86
Hedges St. M35: Fail 2E 80
Hedingham Cl. SK10: Macc 4D 130
Hedley St. BL1: Bolt 2D 38
Hedley Wlk. M8: Man 3E 78
(off Halliwell La.)
Heeley St. WN1: Wig 1E 52
Heginbottom Cres. OL6: A Lyne . . .5N 81
HEIGHTS 6H 47
Heights, The BL6: Hor 3F 36
Heights Av. OL12: Roch 3C 28
Heights Cl. OL12: Roch 3C 28
Heights Ct. OL12: Roch 4C 28
Heightside WA15: Tim 2H 115
(off Edenhurst Dr.)
Heights La. OL1: Chad 1D 62
OL3: Del 5G 47
OL12: Roch 3C 28
Helena Cl. WA16: Knut 6J 133
Helena St. M6: Sal 5J 77
Helen St. BL4: Farn 3L 57
M7: Sal 5B 78
M30: Ecc 1B 92
WA3: Gol 8J 71
WN4: A Mak 6D 70
Helensville Av. M6: Sal 5M 77
Helga St. M40: Man 5M 79
Helias Cl. M28: Walk 8G 56
Hellidon Cl. M12: Man 3J 95
Hell Nook WA3: Gol 9H 71
Helmclough Way M28: Wors 2K 75
Helmet St. M1: Man 7N 5 (1H 95)
Helmsdale M28: Walk 9K 57
WN8: Skel 1A 50
Helmsdale Av. BL3: Bolt 6A 38
Helmsdale Cl. BL0: Ram 2G 24
Helmshore Av. OL4: O'ham 9B 46
Helmshore Ho. OL2: Shaw 4M 45
(off Helmshore Way)
Helmshore Rd. BB4: Has 1G 11
BL8: Holc 8G 11
Helmshore Wlk.
M13: Man 9L 5 (2G 95)
Helmshore Way OL2: Shaw 4M 45
Helmsman Way WN3: Wig 6E 52
Helsby Cl. OL4: Spri 5D 64
Helsby Gdns. BL1: Bolt 9G 23
Helsby Rd. M33: Sale 6L 105
Helsby Wlk. M12: Man 1J 95
Helsby Way SK9: Hand 2J 123
WN3: Wins 9N 51
Helston Cl. M44: Irl 7J 91
SK7: Bram 8D 118
SK14: Hat 8G 99
Helston Dr. OL2: O'ham 8K 45
Helston Gro. SK8: H Grn 7H 117
Helston Wlk. SK14: Hat 8G 99
Helston Way M29: Ast 2D 74
Helton Wlk. M24: Mid 2H 61
Helvellyn Dr. M24: Mid 1J 61
Helvellyn Rd. WN5: Wig 5M 51
Helvellyn Wlk. OL1: O'ham 2L 63
Hembury Av. M19: Man 2L 107
Hembury Cl. M24: Mid 1N 61
Hemfield Bus. Pk. WN2: I Mak 3L 53
Hemfield Cl. WN2: I Mak 3L 53
Hemfield Ct. WN2: I Mak 3M 53
Hemfield Rd. WN2: I Mak 3L 53
(not continuous)
Hemley Cl. BL5: W'ton 5F 54
Hemlock Av. OL8: O'ham 8J 63
Hemming Dr. M30: Ecc 9E 76
Hemmington Dr. M9: Man 3J 79
Hemmons Rd. M12: Man 7N 95
Hempcroft Rd. WA15: Tim 2J 115
Hempshaw Bus. Cen.
SK1: Stoc 9F 108
Hempshaw La. SK1: Stoc 9D 108
SK2: Stoc 8E 108
Hemsby Cl. BL3: Bolt 8B 38
Hemsley St. M9: Man 1K 79
Hemsley St. Sth. M9: Man 2K 79
Hemswell Cl. M6: Sal 6L 77
Hemsworth Rd. BL1: Bolt . . .1G 7 (4E 38)
M18: Man 6B 96
HENBURY 4A 130
Henbury Dr. SK6: Wood 2M 109
Henbury La. SK8: Chea H 9L 117
Henbury Ri. SK11: Hen 4A 130
Henbury Rd. SK9: Hand 2J 123
Henbury St. M14: Man 6F 94
SK2: Stoc 3G 119
Henderson Av. M27: Pen 1F 76
Henderson St. M19: Man 9N 95
OL12: Roch 3F 28
OL15: Lit 9L 15
SK11: Macc 5G 131
Henderville St. OL15: Lit 8L 15
Hendham Cl. SK7: H Gro 5E 118
Hendham Dr. WA14: Alt 2B 114
Hendham Va. M9: Man 3H 79
Hendham Va. Ind. Pk. M8: Man . . .3H 79
Hendon Cl. SK9: Wilm 6J 123
Hendon Dr. BL9: Bury 7M 41
SK3: Stoc 9M 107
Hendon Gro. OL10: H'ood 5K 43
WN7: Lei 2H 73
Hendon Rd. M9: Man 7H 61
WN5: Wig 3A 52
Hendon St. WN7: Lei 2H 73
Hendriff Pl. OL12: Roch 4D 28
Henfield Wlk. M22: Wyth 4B 116
(off Cornfield Dr.)
Hen Fold Rd. M29: Ast 3D 74
Hengist St. BL2: Bolt 5K 39
M18: Man 5B 96
Henley Av. M16: Old T 6A 94
M44: Irl 2F 102
SK8: Chea H 5K 117
Henley Cl. BL8: Bury 4H 41
SK10: Macc 9F 128
Henley Dr. OL7: A Lyne 6K 81
WA15: Tim 9F 104
Henley Grange
SK8: Chea 2H 117
Henley Gro. BL3: Bolt 9D 38
Henley Pl. M19: Man 2M 107
Henley St. OL1: O'ham 3H 63
OL9: Chad 8E 62
OL12: Roch 4C 28
WN2: Asp 6L 35
Henley Ter. OL11: Roch 8C 28
Henlow Wlk. M40: Man 9B 62
Hennicker St. M28: Walk 1L 75
Henniker Rd. BL3: Bolt 1B 56
Henniker St. M27: Swin 4E 76
Hennon St. BL1: Bolt 3E 38
Henrietta St. BL3: Bolt 8C 38
M16: Old T 5B 94
OL6: A Lyne 5D 6 (6M 81)
WN7: Lei 5H 73
Henry Herman St. BL3: Bolt 9B 38
Henry Lee St. BL3: Bolt 9D 38
Henry Pk. St. WN1: I Mak 4H 53
Henry Sq. OL6: A Lyne 9B 6
Henry St. BL0: Ram 7K 11
BL2: Bolt 6H 39
BL5: W'ton 2G 55
(off Winward St.)
M4: Man 3K 5 (8G 78)
(not continuous)
M16: Old T 4B 94
M24: Mid 3L 61
M25: Pres 6B 60
M29: Tyld 1B 74
M30: Ecc 9C 76
M34: Dent 9M 97
M35: Fail 3D 80
M43: Droy 9F 80
(off Church St.)
OL11: Roch 9C 8 (7D 28)
OL12: W'le 7G 14
OL15: Lit 2K 29
SK1: Stoc 8F 108
SK13: Glos 8E 100
SK14: Hyde 7A 98
WN3: I Mak 7H 53
WN7: Lei 7J 73
(not continuous)
Henshall La. WA14: D Mas 1J 113
Henshall Rd. SK10: Boll 6J 129
Henshaw Ct. M16: Old T 5A 94
Henshaw La. OL9: Chad 9D 62
Henshaw St. M32: Stre 7K 93
OL1: O'ham 2C 8 (4J 63)
Henshaw Wlk. BL1: Bolt 2F 38
(off Hargreaves St.)
M13: Man 9L 5
Henson Gro. WA15: Tim 3G 115
Henthorn St. OL1: O'ham 3L 63
OL2: Shaw 6M 45
Henton Wlk. M40: Man 6H 79
(off Rimworth Dr.)
Henty Cl. M30: Ecc 9B 76
Henwick Hall Av. BL0: Ram 1H 25
Henwood Rd. M20: Man 3H 107
Hepburn Ct. M6: Sal 6L 77
(off Monroe Cl.)
Hepley Rd. SK12: Poy 3L 125
Hepple Cl. SK4: Stoc 5L 107
Heppleton Rd. M40: Man 1B 80
Hepple Wlk. OL7: A Lyne 5J 81
Heptonstall Wlk. M18: Man 4A 96
(off Hampden Cres.)
Hepton St. OL1: O'ham 3J 63
Hepworth Cl. WA3: Gol 8J 71
Hepworth St. SK14: Hyde 1B 110
Heraldic Ct. M6: Sal 5N 77
Herbert St. BL3: Lit L 9B 40
BL5: W'ton 1G 55
BL6: Hor 9C 20
M8: Man 5E 78
M25: Pres 7M 59
M26: Rad 7F 40
M32: Stre 7K 93
M34: Dent 5L 97
M43: Droy 9D 80
OL4: O'ham 2A 64
OL9: Chad 4F 62
SK3: Stoc 9B 108
WN3: Wig 4E 52
Hereford Av. WA3: Gol 9L 71
Hereford Cl. OL2: Shaw 5K 45
OL6: A Lyne 3A 82
SK10: Macc 3D 130
WN4: A Mak 8G 70
Hereford Cres. BL3: Lit L 8B 40
Hereford Dr. BL9: Bury 4M 41
M25: Pres 8B 60
M27: Swin 4F 76
SK9: Hand 3K 123
Hereford Gro. M41: Urm 7C 92
WN8: Uph 5F 50
Hereford Rd. BL1: Bolt 4C 38
M30: Ecc 5G 76
SK5: Stoc 3G 108
SK8: Chea 3M 117
WN2: Hin 5B 54
Hereford St. BL1: Bolt 2G 39
M33: Sale 4H 105
(not continuous)
OL9: O'ham 6F 62
OL11: Roch 8E 28
Hereford Wlk. M34: Dent 8K 97
(off Norwich Av.)
SK6: Rom 7L 109
Hereford Way M24: Mid 2A 62
SK15: Stal 2G 99
Herevale Grange M28: Wors 3J 75
Herevale Hall Dr. BL0: Ram 1H 25
Heristone Av. M34: Dent 6K 97
Heritage Gdns. M20: Man 6G 107
SK4: Stoc 4A 108
(off Heaton Moor Rd.)
Heritage Pk. OL16: Roch 8F 8 (6E 28)
Heritage Way WN3: Wig 9H 9 (4E 52)
Heritage Wharf OL7: A Lyne 9B 6
Herle Dr. M22: Wyth 6B 116
Hermitage Av. SK6: Rom 6C 110
Hermitage Cl. WN6: App B 5J 33
Hermitage Ct. WA15: Hale 4G 114
(off Bancroft Rd.)
Hermitage Gdns. SK6: Rom 6C 110
HERMITAGE GREEN 9L 87
Hermitage Grn. La. WA2: Win 8J 87
Hermitage Rd. M8: Man 1F 78
WA15: Hale 4F 114
Hermon Av. OL8: O'ham 7J 63
Herne St. M11: Man 1M 95
Heron Av. BL4: Farn 3G 57
SK16: Duk 2B 98
Heron Cl. SK13: Glos 9G 101
WA16: Knut 5H 133
Heron Ct. M6: Sal 7H 77
SK3: Stoc 9C 108
(off Lomas St.)
Herondale Cl. M40: Man 5N 79
Heron Dr. M34: Aud 9G 81
M44: Irl 6H 91
SK12: Poy 3E 124
WN3: Wins 9B 52
Heron La. OL5: Mos 8G 65
Heron Mill OL8: O'ham 8H 63
Heron Pl. WN5: Wig 3N 51
Herons Reach BL0: Ram 2H 11
WA3: G'ury 3L 89
Heron St. M15: Man 4D 94
M27: Pen 1G 77
OL8: O'ham 7G 62
SK3: Stoc 8B 108
Heron's Way BL2: Bolt 6H 39
Herons Wharf WN6: App B 5H 33
Heron Vw. SK13: Glos 9B 100
Herries St. OL6: A Lyne 6A 82
Herriots Bus. Pk. SK16: Duk 2L 97
Herristone Rd. M8: Man 9F 60
Herrod Av. SK4: Stoc 3C 108
Herschel St. M40: Man 2M 79
Hersey St. M6: Sal 8L 77
Hersham Wlk. M9: Man 2K 79
(off Hemsley St. Sth.)
Hertford Dr. M29: Tyld 8B 56
Hertford Gro. M44: Cad 2D 102
Hertford Ind. Est. OL7: A Lyne 9L 81
Hertford Rd. M9: Man 1J 79
Hertfordshire Pk. Cl. OL2: Shaw . . .4M 45
Hertford St. OL7: A Lyne 9L 81
Hesford Av. M9: Man 3L 79
Hesketh Av. BL1: Bolt 8G 22
M20: Man 5F 106
OL2: Shaw 7L 45
Hesketh Ct. M46: Ath 8L 55
Hesketh Dr. WN6: Stan 2L 33
Hesketh Ho. BL4: Farn 3L 57
(off Hesketh Wlk.)
Hesketh Mnr. M46: Ath 8L 55
(off Hesketh Ct.)
Hesketh Mdw. La.
WA3: Low 1B 88
Hesketh Pl. SK7: H Gro 3H 119
(off Fenton Av.)
Hesketh Rd. M33: Sale 5F 104
OL16: Roch 6G 28
Hesketh St. M46: Ath 7M 55
SK4: Stoc 4C 108
(Bourne St.)
SK4: Stoc 5C 108
(Old Rd.)
WN5: Wig 4C 52
WN7: Lei 5F 72
Hesketh Wlk. BL4: Farn 3L 57
M24: Mid 1K 61
Hesnall Cl. WA3: G'ury 1L 89
Hessel St. M50: Sal 9K 77
Hester Wlk. M15: Man 3E 94
(off Brindle Pl.)
Heston Av. M13: Man 7K 95
Heston Dr. M41: Urm 6C 92
Heswall Av. M20: Man 1G 106
WA3: Cul 6G 89
Heswall Dr. BL8: Bury 8E 24
Heswall Rd. SK5: Stoc 8D 96
Heswall St. BL2: Bolt 5N 39
Hetherington Wlk.
M12: Man 5M 95
(off Norman Gro.)
Hethorn St. M40: Man 5A 80
Hetton Av. M13: Man 7K 95
Heversham WN8: Skel 1A 50
Heversham Av. OL2: Shaw 5A 46
Heversham Wlk. M18: Man 3A 96
(off Grizebeck Cl.)
Hewart Cl. M40: Man 6H 79
Hewart Dr. BL9: Bury 1B 42
Hewetson Cres.
SK11: Macc 5C 130
Hewitt Av. M34: Dent 6D 96
Hewitt Bus. Pk. WN5: Bil 7J 51
Hewitt St. M15: Man 8E 4 (2D 94)
Hewlett Av. PR7: Cop 4A 18
Hewlett Ct. BL0: Ram 3G 25
Hewlett Rd. M21: Cho H 8N 93
Hewlett St. BL2: Bolt 3M 7 (5H 39)
BL5: W'ton 4D 54
PR7: Cop 4B 18
WN1: Wig 8K 9 (3F 52)
Hexagon Cl. M9: Man 9H 61
Hexham Av. BL1: Bolt 3A 38
WN3: Wig 8C 52

Hexham Cl. M33: Sale 5D 104
M46: Ath 7N 55
OL9: Chad 4G 62
SK2: Stoc 2J 119
Hexham Rd. M18: Man 6A 96
Hexham Way SK10: Macc 9G 129
Hexon Cl. M6: Sal 7L 77
Hexworth Wlk. SK7: Bram 5E 118
Hey, The OL2: Shaw 4A 46
Hey Bottom La. OL12: W'le 9D 14
Heybridge La. SK10: P'bury 6F 128
Heybrook OL16: Roch 4F 28
Heybrook Cl. M45: Whitef 3B 60
Heybrook Rd. M23: Wyth 2A 116
Heybrook St. OL16: Roch 5F 28
Heybrook Wlk. M45: Whitef 3B 60
Heybury Cl. M11: Man 1L 95
Hey Cres. OL4: Lees 4C 64
Hey Cft. M45: Whitef 4J 59
Heycrofts Vw. BL0: Eden 3K 11
Heyden Bank *SK13: Gam 7N 99*
(off Grassmoor Cres.)
Heyden Cl. SK10: Macc 4C 130
Heyden Fold *SK13: Gam 7N 99*
(off Grassmoor Cres.)
Heyden Ter. SK13: Gam 7N 99
Heyes Av. WA11: Hay 4A 86
WA15: Tim 9H 105
Heyes Dr. WA15: Tim 9H 105
Heyes Farm Rd. SK11: Macc 5C 130
Heyes Ho. SK11: Macc 4C 130
Heyes Junc. WN8: Skel 4C 50
Heyes La. SK9: A Edg 3F 126
WA15: Tim 9H 105
Heyes Leigh WA15: Tim 9H 105
Heyes Rd. WN5: Orr 5J 51
Heyes St. WN6: App B 5G 32
Heyes Ter. *WA15: Tim 8H 105*
(off The Old Orchard)
Heyeswood WA11: Hay 3A 86
Hey Flake La. OL3: Del 5H 47
Heyford Av. M40: Man 9B 62
Heyford Rd. WN5: Wig 3A 52
Hey Head OL2: Shaw 4B 46
Hey Head Cotts. BL2: Bolt 8B 24
Hey Head La. OL15: Lit 5M 15
HEYHEADS 3H 83
Heyheads New Rd. SK15: C'ook 3H 83
Hey Hill Cl. OL2: O'ham 7L 45
Heyland Rd. M23: Wyth 1N 115
Hey La. OL3: Upp 2M 65
Heylee *OL7: A Lyne 1K 97*
(off South St.)
Hey Lock Cl. WA12: N Wil 9F 86
Heyridge Dr. M22: Nor 7C 106
HEYROD 5F 82
Heyrod Fold SK15: H'rod 5F 82
Heyrod Hall Est. SK15: H'rod 6F 82
Heyrod St. M1: Man 6M 5 (1H 95)
SK15: C'ook 5G 83
Heyrose Wlk. *M15: Man 3C 94*
(off Shawheath Cl.)
Heys, The M25: Pres 6A 60
OL6: A Lyne 6A 82
PR7: Cop 3C 18
SK5: Stoc 8E 96
WN8: Par 1A 32
Heys Av. M23: Wyth 7N 105
M27: Ward 9C 58
SK6: Rom 5B 110
Heysbank Rd. SK12: Dis 9G 121
Heys Cl. OL16: Miln 8M 29
Heys Cl. Nth. M27: Ward 9C 58
Heys Ct. SK3: Stoc 8N 107
Heyscroft Rd. M20: Man 2H 107
SK4: Stoc 6M 107
Heys Farm Cotts. SK6: Rom 5B 110
Heysham Av. M20: Man 1E 106
Heysham Rd. WN5: Orr 4M 51
Heyshaw Wlk. M23: Wyth 7M 105
Heyshoot La. WA3: Cul, G'ury 4L 89
(not continuous)
HEYSIDE 9L 45
Heyside OL2: O'ham 9L 45
Heyside Av. OL2: O'ham 9L 45
Heyside Cl. SK15: C'ook 4H 83
Heyside Way BL9: Bury 9M 7 (3M 41)
Heys La. OL10: H'ood 2F 42
SK6: Rom 5B 110
Heysome Cl. WA11: Cra 6C 68
Heys Rd. M25: Pres 6N 59
OL6: A Lyne 7A 82
Heys St. BL8: Bury 2K 41
WN2: Hin 5M 53
Hey St. OL16: Roch 6G 8 (5F 28)
WN3: I Mak 7J 53
WN6: Wig 3E 52
Heys Vw. M25: Pres 6A 60
Heythrop Cl. M45: Whitef 2L 59
Hey Top OL3: G'fld 7N 65
HEYWOOD 2J 43
Heywood Av. M27: Clif 9H 59
OL4: Aus 3D 64
WA3: Gol 9L 71
Heywood Cl. SK9: A Edg 3G 126
WA12: N Wil 9F 86
Heywood Ct. M24: Mid 4F 60
Heywood Distribution Pk.
OL10: H'ood 4E 42
Heywood Fold Rd. OL4: Spri 4C 64
Heywood Gdns. BL3: Bolt 8F 38
M25: Pres 7A 60
WA3: Gol 9L 71
Heywood Gro. M33: Sale 2G 105
Heywood Hall Rd. OL10: H'ood 1J 43
Heywood Ho. *M6: Sal 7J 77*
(off Edgehill Rd.)
OL8: O'ham 6K 63
Heywood Ind. Pk. OL10: H'ood 4F 42
Heywood La. OL4: Aus 4D 64
Heywood M. *BL3: Lit L 9B 40*
(off Heywood St.)
M25: Pres 7A 60
Heywood Old Rd. M24: Mid 1F 60
OL10: H'ood 1F 60
Heywood Pk. Vw. BL3: Bolt 8F 38
Heywood Rd. M25: Pres 6A 60
M33: Sale 5H 105
OL11: Roch 2N 43
SK9: A Edg 3G 126
Heywood's Hollow BL1: Bolt 1G 38
Heywood Sports Village 1H 43
Heywood Station
East Lancashire Railway 3K 43
Heywood St. BL1: Bolt 4G 38
BL3: Lit L 9B 40
BL9: Bury 9N 7 (3N 41)
M8: Man 3F 78
M27: Swin 2E 76
M35: Fail 3B 80
OL4: O'ham 3B 64
Heywood Way M6: Sal 7M 77
Heyworth Av. SK6: Rom 5A 110
Heyworth St. *M5: Sal 9L 77*
(off Bridson St.)
Hibbert Av. M34: Dent 4J 97
SK14: Hyde 8B 98
Hibbert Cres. M35: Fail 3E 80
Hibbert La. SK6: Mar 2C 120
Hibbert St. BL1: Bolt 2G 38
M14: Man 6H 95
OL4: Lees 4B 64
SK4: Stoc 3C 108
SK5: Stoc 3C 108
SK22: N Mil 9L 121
Hibel Rd. SK10: Macc 3H 131
Hibernia St. BL3: Bolt 7D 38
Hibernia Way M32: Stre 4G 92
Hibson Av. OL12: Roch 3J 27
Hibson Cl. OL12: W'le 8G 15
Hic-Bibi La. PR7: Cop 7B 18
Hic-Bibi Local Nature Reserve 7C 18
Hickenfield Rd. SK14: Hyde 4C 98
Hicken Pl. SK14: Hyde 4C 98
Hickory Cl. WA12: N Wil 7F 86
Hickton Dr. WA14: Alt 1B 114
Hidden Gem
Manchester St Mary's Catholic Church
5F 4
Hieland Rd. WN1: Wig 1H 53
Higginbotham Grn. SK11: Macc 6J 131
HIGGINSHAW 1L 63
Higginshaw La. OL1: O'ham 1L 63
OL2: O'ham 1L 63
Higginshaw Rd.
OL1: O'ham 1F 8 (2K 63)
Higginson Rd. SK5: Stoc 1C 108
Higginson St. WN7: Lei 5J 73
Higgs Cl. OL4: O'ham 4A 64
Higham Cl. OL2: O'ham 7L 45
Higham Cotts. SK14: Hyde 9E 98
Higham La. SK14: Hyde 9C 98
Higham St. SK8: Chea H 6M 117
Higham Vw. *M6: Sal 7N 77*
(off Broad St.)
High Ash Gro. M34: Aud 2H 97
High Av. BL2: Bolt 4M 39
High Bank BL7: Bro X 6G 23
BL8: Bury 4J 41
M18: Man 4C 96
M34: Dent 7F 96
M46: Ath 5B 56
WA14: Alt 2C 6 (2D 114)
WA15: Hale 5G 115
Highbank M27: Pen 3J 77
SK13: Tin 2B 100
High Bank Av. SK15: Stal 2G 98
High Bank Cl. M44: Cad 2E 102
High Bank Cres. M25: Pres 8B 60
Highbank Cres. OL4: Gras 6H 65
Highbank Dr. M20: Man 8G 107
High Bank Gro. M25: Pres 8B 60
High Bank La. BL6: Los 5K 37
High Bank Rd. BL9: Bury 9M 41
M27: Pen 2H 77
M43: Droy 1D 96
SK14: Hyde 6C 98
Highbank Rd. OL16: Miln 9N 29
SK13: Glos 9H 101
High Bank Side
SK1: Stoc 2L 9 (7D 108)
High Bank St. BL2: Bolt 5K 39
High Barn Cl. OL11: Roch 8C 28
Highbarn Ho. *OL2: O'ham 8J 45*
(off High Barn St.)
High Barn La. OL12: Whitw 2A 14
(Kiln Bank La.)
OL12: Whitw 5N 13
(New Rd.)
High Barn Rd. M24: Mid 4M 61
OL2: O'ham 8K 45
High Barn St. OL2: O'ham 8J 45
High Beeches BL2: Bolt 7B 40
High Beeches Cres.
WN4: A Mak 4D 70
High Bent Av. SK8: Chea H 9M 117
High Birch Ter. OL11: Roch 9N 27
Highbridge Cl. BL2: Bolt 6A 40
Highbrook Gro. *BL1: Bolt 3F 38*
(off Lindfield Dr.)
High Brow M38: Lit H 8F 56
Highbury SK4: Stoc 6L 107
Highbury Av. M41: Urm 7M 91
M44: Irl 8H 91
Highbury Cl. BL5: W'ton 5F 54
Highbury Ct. M25: Pres 6A 60
Highbury Rd. M16: Whall R 8D 94
SK4: Stoc 2A 108
Highbury Way OL2: O'ham 6H 45
Highclere Av. M7: Sal 4E 78
M8: Man 4E 78
Highclere Rd. M8: Man 9E 60
Highcliffe Ct. WN6: Stan 5C 34
Highcliffe Rd. M9: Man 8F 60
Highclove La. M28: Wors 5G 74
Highcrest Av. SK8: Gat 2E 116
Highcrest Gro. M29: Tyld 1E 74
Highcroft BL1: Bolt 1H 39
SK14: Hyde 1B 110
Highcroft Av. M20: Man 4D 106
High Cft. Cl. SK16: Duk 1D 98
Highcroft Rd. SK6: Rom 5N 109
Highcroft Way OL12: Roch 1D 28
HIGH CROMPTON 5K 45
Highdales Rd. M23: Wyth 2A 116
Highdown Wlk. *M9: Man 2K 79*
(off Augustine Webster Cl.)
High Elm Dr. WA15: Haleb 7J 115
High Elm Rd. WA15: Haleb 7J 115
High Elms SK8: Chea H 1N 123
Higher Ainsworth Rd. M26: Rad 5E 40
Higher Alt Hill OL6: A Lyne 1N 81
Higher Ardwick
M12: Man 9N 5 (2H 95)
Higher Arthurs OL3: G'fld 5L 65
Higher Austin's BL6: Los 3H 37
Higher Bank Rd. OL15: Lit 2L 29
HIGHER BANKS 4H 121
Higher Barlow Row
SK1: Stoc 4M 9 (8D 108)
Higher Barn BL6: Hor 1H 37
Higher Barn Rd. SK13: Had 5A 100
HIGHER BARROWSHAW 1A 64
Higher Bents La. SK6: Bred 5K 109
HIGHER BLACKLEY 7G 61
HIGHER BOARSHAW 1A 62
Higher Bri. St. BL1: Bolt 1K 7 (3G 38)
Higherbrook Cl. BL6: Hor 3F 36
HIGHER BROUGHTON 4C 78
Higher Bury St.
SK4: Stoc 1G 9 (6B 108)
Higher Calderbrook OL15: Lit 5N 15
Higher Calderbrook Rd.
OL15: Lit 5N 15
Higher Cambridge St. M15: Man 3F 94
Higher Carr La. OL3: G'fld 4L 65
Higher Chatham St.
M15: Man 9H 5 (3F 94)
HIGHER CHISWORTH 4L 111
Higher Cleggswood Av.
OL15: Lit 2L 29
Higher Clough Cl. BL3: Bolt 8B 38
Higher Counthill OL4: O'ham 1B 64
Higher Cft. M30: Ecc 1C 92
M45: Whitef 5J 59
Higher Crossbank OL4: Lees 3C 64
Higher Cross La. OL3: Upp 4M 65
HIGHER CRUMPSALL 1F 78
Higher Damshead BL5: W'ton 3H 55
Higher Darcy St. BL2: Bolt 7K 39
(not continuous)
Higher Dean St. M26: Rad 9E 40
HIGHER DINTING 7C 100
Higher Dinting SK13: Glos 7C 100
Higher Downs WA14: Alt 4C 114
WA16: Knut 7J 133
Higher Drake Mdw. BL5: W'ton 6G 54
Higher Dunscar BL7: Eger 4F 22
HIGHER END 8H 51
HIGHERFENCE 3K 131
Higher Fence Rd. SK10: Macc 3K 131
Higher Fold M24: Mid 9N 43
Higherfold Farm SK6: H Lan 6A 120
Higher Fold La. BL0: Ram 7L 11
HIGHER FOLDS 4N 73
Higher Fullwood OL1: O'ham 8A 46
HIGHER GAMESLEY 9N 99
HIGHER GREEN 5D 74
Higher Grn. OL6: A Lyne 6A 82
Higher Grn. La. M29: Ast 6D 74
Higher Greenshall La.
SK12: Dis 9J 121
HIGHER HARTSHEAD 9C 64
Higher Henry St. SK14: Hyde 8A 98
Higher Highfield Ct. WN2: Asp 6L 35
Higher Hillgate
SK1: Stoc 4M 9 (8D 108)
Higher Ho. Cl. OL9: Chad 7D 62
HIGHER HURDSFIELD 2L 131
HIGHER HURST 4B 82
HIGHER HYDEGREEN 5J 83
HIGHER INCE 4K 53
Higher Kinders OL3: G'fld 5L 65
Higher Knowles BL6: Hor 2G 36
Higher Landedmans *BL5: W'ton 3H 55*
(off George St.)
Higher La. M45: Whitef 3L 59
SK10: Kerr 7M 129
WA11: Cra, R'ford 5A 68
WA13: Lym 5A 112
WN2: Asp 8K 35
WN8: Dal 4A 32
WN8: Uph 4G 50
Higher Lime Rd. OL8: O'ham 2G 80
Higher Lodge OL11: Roch 3H 27
Higher Lomax La. OL10: H'ood 2F 42
Higher Lydgate Pk. OL4: Gras 5F 64
Higher Mkt. St. BL4: Farn 3M 57
Higher Mdws. M19: Man 9A 96
Higher Moulding BL9: Bury 8D 26
Higher Newtons OL5: Mos 9G 65
HIGHER OGDEN 8B 30
HIGHER OPENSHAW 2D 96
Higher Ormond St. M15: Man 9J 5
Higher Oswald St. M4: Man 2J 5
Higher Pk. OL2: Shaw 2N 45
Higher Pit La. M26: Rad 4D 40
HIGHER POYNTON 3N 125
Higher Ridings BL7: Bro X 5G 22
Higher Ri. OL2: Shaw 3L 45
Higher Rd. M41: Urm 7D 92
Higher Row BL9: Bury 1A 42
HIGHER RUSHCROFT 4K 45
Higher Shady La. BL7: Bro X 6J 23
Higher Shore Rd. OL15: Lit 7J 15
Higher Southfield BL5: W'ton 4G 55
Higher Sq. *SK13: Tin 2C 100*
(off Stocks Brow)
HIGHER STAKE HILL 8C 44
HIGHER SUMMERSEAT 4H 25
Higher Summerseat BL0: Ram 3H 25
Higher Swan La. BL3: Bolt 8E 38
Higher Tame St. SK15: Stal 8E 82
Higher Turf La. OL4: Scout 3E 64
Higher Turf Pk. OL2: O'ham 9J 45
Higher Vw. WN8: Uph 5G 50
Higher Wharf St.
OL7: A Lyne 9C 6 (8M 81)
Higher Wheat La. OL16: Roch 5G 28
HIGHER WOODHILL 8K 25
Higher Wood St. M24: Mid 2L 61
(not continuous)
Higher York St.
M13: Man 9K 5 (3G 94)
HIGHFIELD
BL4 3G 56
WN3 7N 51
High Fld. WA14: Lit B 5J 113
Highfield M20: Man 6G 106
M33: Sale 5J 105
SK8: Chea 4H 117
SK10: P'bury 8E 128
WN5: Wig 7A 52
Highfield Av. BL2: Bolt 1A 40
M26: Rad 2J 59
M28: Wors 2F 74
M33: Sale 5J 105
M46: Ath 6N 55
OL10: H'ood 2F 42
SK6: Rom 6K 109
WA3: Gol 1J 87
WN1: Wig 2H 53
WN6: She 6L 33
WN7: Lei 7L 73
Highfield Cl. M32: Stre 9J 93
PR6: Adl 6K 19
SK3: Stoc 3D 118
SK14: Hyde 3C 98
Highfield Country Pk. 9A 96
Highfield Ct. BL4: Farn 4J 57
M25: Pres 6A 60
SK14: Mot 5K 99
Highfield Cres. SK9: Wilm 5H 123
Highfield Dr. BL4: Farn 3H 57
M24: Mid 4L 61
M27: Pen 3J 77
M30: Ecc 6D 76
M41: Urm 6C 92
OL2: O'ham 1J 63
OL5: Mos 2F 82
SK10: Macc 2E 130
WA11: Cra 6C 68
WN6: Stan 5C 34
Highfield Est. SK9: Wilm 5H 123
Highfield Gdns. SK14: Holl 4N 99
SK14: Hyde 6C 98
Highfield Glen OL6: A Lyne 5C 82
Highfield Grange Av.
WN3: Wig, Wins 9A 52
Highfield Gro. WN2: Asp 7M 35
Highfield Ho. BL4: Farn 3G 56
SK3: Stoc 2D 118
Highfield La. BL9: Bury 9M 41
M45: Whitef 9M 41
WA2: Win 9M 87
WA3: Low 4M 87
Highfield Mdw. *OL5: Mos 2F 82*
(off Highfield Dr.)
Highfield Pk. SK4: Stoc 6L 107
Highfield Pk. Rd. SK6: Bred 4J 109
Highfield Parkway SK7: Bram 2B 124
Highfield Pl. *M18: Man 5D 96*
(off Debdale La.)
M25: Pres 6N 59
Highfield Range M18: Man 5D 96
Highfield Rd. BL0: Eden 4K 11
BL1: Bolt 2C 38
BL4: Farn 3F 56
BL6: Bla 3A 36
M6: Sal 7M 77
M19: Man 8A 96
M25: Pres 5N 59
M30: Ecc 6D 76
M32: Stre 9J 93
M38: Lit H 6G 56
OL11: Roch 4K 27
OL16: Miln 7L 29
PR6: Adl 5K 19
SK6: Mar 1C 120
SK6: Mel 1E 120
SK7: Bram 4D 118
SK7: H Gro 5L 119
SK8: Chea H 6K 117
SK10: Boll 5L 129
SK11: Macc 5G 130
SK12: Poy 2E 124
SK13: Glos 9F 100
WA15: Hale 5G 115
WA15: Tim 2H 115
WN2: Hin 4N 53
Highfield Rd. Ind. Est.
M38: Lit H 6G 56
Highfield Rd. Nth. PR6: Adl 5K 19
Highfield St. BL4: Kea 5A 58
M8: Man 3E 78
M24: Mid 3N 61
M34: Aud 3K 97
M34: Dent 4J 97
OL9: O'ham 2A 8 (4H 63)
(not continuous)
SK3: Stoc 8A 108
SK16: Duk 9M 81
Highfield St. W. SK16: Duk 9M 81
Highfield Ter. M9: Man 2J 79
OL4: O'ham 1A 64
OL7: A Lyne 3K 81
SK22: N Mil 7N 121
High Gables BL1: Bolt 4C 38
Highgate BL3: Bolt 1L 55
Highgate Av. M41: Urm 5A 92
Highgate Cen. SK6: Bred 5K 109
Highgate Cres. M18: Man 6B 96
WN6: App B 5J 33
High Gate Dr. OL2: O'ham 5G 44
Highgate Dr. M38: Lit H 6F 56
Highgate Ho. *OL8: O'ham 9H 63*
(off Marple Cl.)
Highgate La. M38: Lit H 6F 56
OL12: Whitw 8A 14
Highgate Rd. WA14: Alt 3B 114
WN8: Uph 4F 50
High Gates M33: Sale 3K 105
Highgrove M33: Sale 7G 104
Highgrove, The BL1: Bolt 3M 37
Highgrove Cl. BL1: Bolt 1G 38
Highgrove Ct. M9: Man 6F 60
Highgrove M. SK9: Wilm 8F 122
High Gro. Rd. OL3: G'fld 6H 65
OL4: Gras 6H 65
SK8: Chea 2H 117
High Hill Rd. SK22: Bir V, N Mil 6N 121
High Houses BL1: Bolt 7E 22
High Hurst Cl. M24: Mid 3H 61
High Knowles OL4: O'ham 7D 64
Highland Lodge WN6: Stan 4A 34
Highland M. SK6: Rom 4N 109
Highland Rd. BL6: Hor 3G 36
BL7: Bro X 5J 23
Highlands OL2: O'ham 9G 45
(not continuous)
OL15: Lit 2L 29
Highlands, The OL5: Mos 1E 82
Highlands Dr. SK2: Stoc 1K 119
Highlands Ho. *OL5: Mos 1E 82*
(off Old Brow)
Highlands Rd. OL2: O'ham 9G 45
OL2: Shaw 4K 45
OL11: Roch 8K 27
SK2: Stoc 1K 119
Highland Vw. *OL5: Mos 9F 64*
(off Quickedge Rd.)
Highland Wlk. M40: Man 4B 80
Highland Way WA16: Knut 9G 133
HIGH LANE 8B 120
High La. M21: Cho H 9N 93
SK6: Wood 3M 109
SK13: Glos 1N 111
High Lawn WA14: Bow 5C 114
High Lea PR6: Adl 6K 19
SK8: Chea 2H 117
SK9: A Edg 4H 127
High Lea Rd. SK22: N Mil 7K 121
HIGH LEE 7K 121
High Lee Ho. *M33: Sale 3K 105*
(off Broad Rd.)
High Lee La. OL4: O'ham 9E 46
HIGH LEGH 9D 112
High Legh Park Golf Course 9E 112
High Legh Rd. M11: Man 1B 96
WA13: Lym 7D 112
High Level Rd.
OL11: Roch 9D 8 (7D 28)
Highmarsh Cres. M20: Man 3E 106
WA12: N Wil 4E 86
High Mdw. M27: Swin 3H 77
SK8: Chea H 7K 117
Highmeadow M26: Rad 2F 58
WN8: Uph 4E 50
High Mdws. BL7: Bro X 5J 23
SK6: Rom 5N 109
SK13: Glos 9D 100
Highmead St. M18: Man 4B 96
Highmead Wlk. *M16: Old T 4C 94*
(off Hamer Dr.)
High Moor Cres. OL4: O'ham 2B 64
High Moor La. WN6: Wrig 1F 32
Highmoor Vw. OL4: O'ham 2B 64
Highmore Dr. M9: Man 8K 61
High Mt. BL2: Bolt 1M 39
Highnam Wlk. M22: Wyth 6N 115
High Pk. WN6: She 6N 33
High Peak OL15: Lit 9C 16
High Peak Rd. OL6: A Lyne 4D 82
OL12: Whitw 8A 14
High Peak St. M40: Man 4N 79
High Rid La. BL6: Los 4J 37
Highshore Dr. M8: Man 3E 78
High Stile La. OL3: Dob 1N 65
High Stile St. BL4: Kea 4M 57
Highstone Dr. M8: Man 4H 79
Highstones Gdns. SK13: Glos 7G 101
High St. BL3: Bolt 7E 38
BL3: Lit L 9B 40
BL6: Hor 9D 20
BL7: Bel 1L 21
BL7: Tur 1K 23
BL8: Bury 1F 40
M4: Man 4H 5 (9F 78)
M24: Mid 1M 61
(not continuous)
M28: Walk 8K 57
M29: Ast 5C 74
M29: Tyld 1A 74
M43: Droy 9E 80
M46: Ath 9L 55
OL1: O'ham 2D 8 (4K 63)
OL2: O'ham 8H 45
OL2: Shaw 6M 45
OL3: Del 8J 47
OL3: Upp 2L 65
OL4: Lees 5B 64
OL5: Mos 9G 64
OL10: H'ood 2G 43
OL12: Roch 6C 8 (5D 28)
OL15: Lit 9K 15
SK1: Stoc 2L 9 (7D 108)
SK7: H Gro 5K 119
SK8: Chea 1J 117
SK10: Boll 5M 129
SK11: Macc 6H 131
(not continuous)
SK14: Hyde 6C 98
SK15: Stal 8E 82
SK22: N Mil 7M 121
WA3: Gol 1K 87
WA12: N Wil 5G 87
WA14: Alt 3C 6 (3D 114)
WN1: Wig 1G 52
WN2: Asp 9L 35
WN3: I Mak 5H 53
WN6: Stan 3B 34
WN7: Lei 5J 73
High St. East SK13: Glos 8F 100
High St. West SK13: Glos 8C 100
Highthorne Grn. OL2: O'ham 4G 44
HIGHTOWN 3D 78
Hightree Dr. SK11: Hen 4A 130
Hightrees Dr. M20: Man 3E 106
High Vw. M25: Pres 8A 60
Highview SK13: Glos 9C 100

High Vw. St. BL1: Bolt 7F 22
BL3: Bolt 7D 38
Highview Wlk. M9: Man 8K 61
High Wardle La. OL12: W'le 6E 14
Highwood OL11: Roch 4K 27
Highwood Cl. BL2: Bolt 3N 39
SK13: Glos 9D 100
High Wood Fold SK6: Mar B 8F 110
Highwoods Cl. WN4: A Mak 5D 70
Highworth Cl. BL3: Bolt 7F 38
(off Parrot St.)
Highworth Dr. M40: Man 9B 62
Higson Av. M21: Cho H 1A 106
M30: Ecc 1C 92
SK6: Rom 6K 109
Hilary Av. M46: Ath 6L 55
OL8: O'ham 1K 81
SK8: H Grn 7J 117
WA3: Low 9N 71
Hilary Cl. SK4: Stoc 6B 108
Hilary Gro. BL4: Farn 4K 57
Hilary Rd. M22: Wyth 6B 116
Hilary St. OL11: Roch 3B 44
Hilberry Ho. OL5: Mos 8H 65
Hilbre Av. OL2: O'ham 1H 63
Hilbre Rd. M19: Man 9L 95
Hilbre Way SK9: Hand 2K 123
Hilbury Av. M9: Man 1J 79
Hilda Av. BL8: Tot 7F 24
SK8: Chea 2K 117
Hilda Gro. SK5: Stoc 4D 108
Hilda Rd. SK14: Hyde 1A 110
Hilda St. BL3: Bolt 8H 39
OL9: O'ham 1A 8 (4H 63)
(not continuous)
OL10: H'ood 2J 43
SK5: Stoc 4D 108
WN7: Lei 4E 72
Hilden Ct. M16: Whall R 5C 94
Hilden St. BL2: Bolt 4N 7 (6H 39)
WN7: Lei 5H 73
Hilditch Cl. M23: Wyth 1A 116
Hildyard St. WN5: Wig 5C 52
Hiley Rd. M30: Ecc 1N 91
Hilgay Cl. WN3: Wins 8A 52
Hill, The WA16: Knut 8H 133
Hillam Cl. M41: Urm 7C 92
Hillary Av. OL7: A Lyne 5M 81
WN5: Wig 6A 52
Hillary Rd. SK14: Hyde 4D 98
Hillbank WN6: Stan 5D 34
Hill Bank Cl. SK15: C'ook 5G 83
Hillbank Cl. BL1: Bolt 1D 38
Hillbank St. M24: Mid 6B 44
Hill Barn La. OL3: Dig 9N 47
Hillbeck Cres. WN4: Gars 6A 70
Hillbrae Av. WA11: St H 9E 68
Hillbrook Av. M40: Man 9N 61
Hillbrook Grange SK7: Bram 9B 118
Hillbrook Rd. SK1: Stoc 8G 108
SK7: Bram 9B 118
Hillbrow Wlk. M8: Man 3E 78
(off Highshore Dr.)
Hillbury Rd. SK7: Bram 6D 118
Hill Carr WA14: Alt 4A 6 (3B 114)
Hill Cl. OL4: O'ham 6N 63
WN6: App B 5J 33
Hillcote Wlk. M18: Man 3N 95
(off Marjorie Cl.)
Hill Cot Rd. BL1: Bolt 8G 22
Hill Ct. M. SK6: Rom 6M 109
Hillcourt Rd. SK6: H Lan 8B 120
SK6: Rom 4N 109
Hillcourt St. M1: Man 9J 5 (2F 94)
Hill Cres. M9: Man 8F 60
WN7: Lei 2E 72
Hill Crest M46: Ath 6A 56
Hillcrest M6: Sal 7G 77
M24: Mid 9L 43
SK14: Hyde 1C 110
WN2: P Bri 9L 53
WN8: Skel 4A 50
Hill Crest Av. WN7: Lei 2E 72
Hillcrest Av. OL10: H'ood 1F 42
SK4: Stoc 6M 107
Hillcrest Cres. OL10: H'ood 1F 42
Hillcrest Dr. M19: Man 1A 108
M34: Dent 8M 97
Hillcrest Rd. M25: Pres 9M 59
M29: Tyld 2E 74
OL11: Roch 2A 44
(not continuous)
SK2: Stoc 1G 118
SK7: Bram 6D 118
SK10: Boll 6K 129
SK11: Gaws 8E 130
Hill Cft. SK2: Stoc 1J 119
Hillcroft OL8: O'ham 1L 81
Hillcroft Cl. M8: Man 2F 78
Hillcroft Rd. WA14: Alt 2A 114
Hilldale Av. M9: Man 7J 61
Hilldean WN8: Uph 3G 50
Hill Dr. SK9: Hand 3K 123
Hillel Ho. M15: Man 4F 94
Hill End SK6: Rom 4A 110
Hillend SK14: Mot 8K 99
Hill End La. SK14: Mot 8J 99
Hillend Pl. M23: Wyth 6N 105
Hill End Rd. OL3: Del 7J 47
Hillend Rd. M23: Wyth 6N 105
Hill Farm Cl. OL8: O'ham 8L 63
Hillfield M5: Sal 8K 77
Hillfield Cl. M13: Man 4J 95
Hillfield Dr. BL2: Bolt 3J 39
M28: Wors 3H 75
Hillfield Wlk. BL2: Bolt 3J 39
Hillfoot Wlk. M15: Man 3C 94
(off Shawgreen Cl.)
Hillgate Av. M5: Sal 2A 94
Hillgate Bus. Cen. SK1: Stoc 8D 108
(off Swallow St.)
Hillgate St. OL6: A Lyne 5F 6 (6N 81)
Hillhead Wlk. M8: Man 4F 78
(off Barnsdale Dr.)
Hillhouse Ct. OL11: Roch 1N 43
Hillier St. M9: Man 2K 79
Hillier St. Nth. M9: Man 2K 79
Hillingdon Cl. OL8: O'ham 2F 80
Hillingdon Dr. M9: Man 9N 61
Hillingdon Ho. BL1: Bolt 3F 38
(off Enfield Cl.)
Hillingdon Rd. M32: Stre 8L 93
M45: Whitef 4J 59
Hillington Rd. M33: Sale 4E 104
SK3: Stoc 8A 108
Hillkirk Dr. OL12: Roch 2A 28
Hillkirk St. M11: Man 9K 79
Hill La. BL2: Bolt 1N 7 (4H 39)
BL6: Bla 1L 35
M9: Man 8J 61
Hillman Cl. M40: Man 5J 79
Hill Mt. SK16: Duk 1D 98
Hillock, The BL2: Bolt 8L 23
M29: Ast 5C 74
Hillock La. WN8: Dal 6A 32
Hillock Pl. M46: Ath 9M 55
(off Miller's La.)
Hillreed WN6: Wig 2C 52
Hillridge Rd. WN5: Wig 1N 51
Hill Ri. BL0: Ram 1G 24
SK6: Rom 6M 109
WA14: Alt 2A 114
Hillsborough Dr.
BL9: Bury 1A 60
Hill's Ct. BL8: Bury 9H 25
Hillsdale Gro. BL2: Bolt 1M 39
Hill Side BL1: Bolt 5A 38
Hillside WA13: Lym 6F 112
Hillside Av. BL4: Farn 4J 57
BL6: Bla 3A 36
BL6: Hor 9E 20
BL7: Bro X 4J 23
M7: Sal 2N 77
M28: Walk 7K 57
M45: Whitef 1L 59
M46: Ath 7N 55
OL2: O'ham 7J 45
OL2: Shaw 5A 46
OL3: Dig 8L 47
OL4: Grot 6D 64
OL4: O'ham 4N 63
SK14: Hyde 2C 110
SK15: C'ook 4J 83
WA12: N Wil 7C 86
WN4: A Mak 2C 70
Hillside Cl. BL2: Bolt 8M 23
BL3: Bolt 1M 55
M40: Man 1M 79
SK7: Bram 8E 118
SK12: Dis 9G 121
SK13: Had 6A 100
WN3: Wins 8A 52
WN5: Bil 5H 69
Hillside Ct. BL1: Bolt 5A 38
M25: Pres 8N 59
M46: Ath 7N 55
SK10: Macc 3L 131
(off Springhill)
Hillside Cres. BL6: Hor 9E 20
BL9: Bury 7M 25
OL6: A Lyne 5C 82
Hillside Dr. M24: Mid 2N 61
M27: Pen 4K 77
SK10: Macc 3L 131
Hillside Gdns. BL9: Sum 3J 25
Hillside Gro. SK6: Mar B 7E 110
Hillside Ho. BL1: Bolt 5A 38
Hillside Rd. BL0: Ram 9G 11
SK2: Stoc 9H 109
SK6: Wood 3N 109
SK14: Hyde 3N 109
WA15: Hale 4G 115
WA16: Knut 6G 132
Hillside St. BL3: Bolt 7E 38
Hillside Vw. M34: Dent 1L 109
OL16: Miln 7L 29
SK22: N Mil 7K 121
Hillside Wlk. OL12: Roch 1B 28
Hillside Way OL12: Whitw 5A 14
Hills La. BL9: Bury, Whitef 1B 60
Hillspring Rd. OL4: Spri 5D 64
Hillstone Av. OL12: Roch 1A 28
Hillstone Cl. BL8: G'mount 3F 24
Hill St. BL8: Bury 9F 24
BL9: Sum 2J 25
M7: Sal 4C 78
(not continuous)
M20: Man 1G 106
M24: Mid 9M 43
M26: Rad 2H 59
(Rupert St.)
M26: Rad 8F 40
(Wilson St.)
OL2: Shaw 6N 45
OL4: O'ham 4M 63
OL7: A Lyne 9B 6 (8L 81)
OL10: H'ood 1F 42
OL16: Roch 8E 8 (6E 28)
SK6: Rom 6M 109
SK11: Macc 6H 131
SK14: Hyde 9C 98
SK16: Duk 9M 81
WA14: B'ath 8C 104
WN2: Hin 5N 53
WN6: Wig 5G 9 (2E 52)
WN7: Lei 5G 73
HILL TOP
M28 . . . . .6L 57
SK9 . . . . .6G 123
Hill Top BL1: Bolt 1E 38
BL3: Lit L 8A 40
M46: Ath 6A 56
OL1: Chad 1D 62
OL12: Whitw 9A 14
SK6: Rom 5M 109
WA15: Hale 7G 115
Hill Top Av. M25: Pres 7A 60
SK8: Chea H 6N 117
SK9: Wilm 6G 123
Hilltop Av. M9: Man 8J 61
M45: Whitef 3A 60
Hill Top Ct. SK8: Chea H 6N 117
Hilltop Ct. M8: Man 9E 60
M14: Man 8J 95
M28: Walk 7L 57
(off Fereday St.)
Hill Top Dr. OL11: Roch 2C 44
WA15: Hale 6G 115
Hilltop Dr. BL8: Tot 7E 24
OL2: O'ham 1J 63
SK6: Mar 1N 119
Hill Top Fold WN2: Hin 5A 54
Hilltop Gro. M45: Whitef 3A 60
HILLTOP LANE 1K 121
Hill Top La. OL3: Del 7E 46
Hill Top Rd. M28: Walk 7L 57
OL10: H'ood 5G 43
WA11: R'ford 8A 68
Hilltop Rd. SK13: Glos 7D 100
Hill Vw. OL3: Del 8J 47
(off St Annes Sq.)
OL15: Lit 5A 16
SK10: Boll 6K 129
SK15: Stal 3G 99
WN7: Lei 2G 72
Hill Vw. Cl. OL1: O'ham 1N 63
Hill Vw. Ct. BL1: Bolt 9F 22
Hill Vw. Dr. PR7: Cop 5A 18
Hill Vw. Rd. BL1: Bolt 9F 22
M34: Dent 8E 96
Hillwood Av. M8: Man 8E 60
Hillwood Dr. SK13: Glos 9H 101
Hillyard St. BL8: Bury 1J 41
Hilly Cft. BL7: Bro X 5G 22
Hilmarton Cl. BL2: Bolt 8M 23
Hilrose Av. M41: Urm 7F 92
Hilson Ct. M43: Droy 9E 80
Hilton Arc. OL1: O'ham 2D 8
Hilton Av. BL6: Hor 1C 36
M41: Urm 7D 92
Hilton Bank M28: Walk 8J 57
Hilton Cl. SK11: Macc 5D 130
WN7: Lei 5J 73
Hilton Ct. SK3: Stoc 4J 9 (8C 108)
Hilton Cres. M25: Pres 9A 60
M28: Wors 4J 75
OL6: A Lyne 5N 81
Hilton Dr. M25: Pres 9A 60
M44: Cad 3D 102
Hilton Fold La. M24: Mid 2N 61
Hilton Gro. M28: Walk 8J 57
SK12: Poy 2H 125
HILTON HOUSE 6C 36
Hilton Ho. SK1: Stoc 3L 9 (7D 108)
Hilton La. M25: Pres 9N 59
M28: Walk 9J 57
Hilton Lodge M25: Pres 9A 60
HILTON PARK 9A 60
Hilton Pl. WN2: Asp 6M 35
Hilton Rd. BL9: Bury 8L 7 (2M 41)
M22: Shar 2D 116
SK7: Bram 6D 118
SK12: Dis 8E 120
SK12: Poy 1N 125
(not continuous)
Hiltons Cl. OL8: O'ham 6J 63
Hiltons Farm Cl. M34: Aud 3J 97
Hiltons Sq. M27: Pen 1G 77
Hilton St. BL2: Bolt 5K 39
BL9: Bury 9M 25
M1: Man 4K 5 (9G 78)
M4: Man 3J 5 (8F 78)
M7: Sal 4C 78
M24: Mid 1L 61
M38: Lit H 7H 57
OL1: O'ham 3N 63
SK3: Stoc 4H 9 (8B 108)
SK14: Hyde 4C 98
WN1: Wig 6L 9 (2G 52)
WN3: I Mak 5H 53
WN4: A Mak 7F 70
Hilton St. Nth. M7: Sal 4C 78
Hilton Wlk. M24: Mid 3H 61
Himley Rd. M11: Man 7A 80
Hincaster Wlk. M18: Man 4A 96
(off Hampden Cres.)
Hinchcombe Cl. M38: Lit H 5H 57
(off Haymill Av.)
Hinchley Rd. M9: Man 9N 61
Hinchley Way M27: Pen 9F 58
Hinckley St. M11: Man 1L 95
Hindburn Cl. M45: Whitef 2A 60
Hindburn Dr. M28: Wors 2H 75
Hindburn Wlk. M45: Whitef 2A 60
Hinde St. M40: Man 2M 79
Hindhead Wlk. M40: Man 6B 80
(off Thaxmead Dr.)
Hind Hill St. OL10: H'ood 3J 43
Hindle Dr. OL2: O'ham 9G 45
Hindles Cl. M46: Ath 9J 55
Hindle St. M26: Rad 9G 40
Hindle Ter. OL3: Del 8J 47
HINDLEY 6N 53
Hindley Av. M22: Wyth 5A 116
Hindley Bus. Cen. WN2: Hin 6N 53
Hindley Cl. OL7: A Lyne 9K 81
HINDLEY GREEN 8E 54
Hindley Grn. Bus. Pk. WN2: Hin 9D 54
Hindley Hall Golf Course 3N 53
Hindley Ho. WN3: Wig 6D 52
Hindley Ind. Est. WN2: Hin 7E 54
Hindley Mill La. WN2: Hin 4A 54
Hindley Pool 6B 54
Hindley Rd. BL5: W'ton 6H 55
WN2: W'ton 6E 54
Hindley Sports Cen. 6B 54
Hindley Station (Rail) 4A 54
Hindley St. OL7: A Lyne 9K 81
(not continuous)
SK1: Stoc 8D 108
Hindley Wlk. WN1: Wig 7J 9
Hind Rd. WN5: Wig 3A 52
HINDSFORD 9M 55
Hindsford Bri. M. M46: Ath 1A 74
Hindsford Cl. M23: Wyth 7K 105
Hindsford St. M46: Ath 1A 74
Hinds La. BL8: Bury 4J 41
M26: Bury, Rad 5J 41
Hind St. BL2: Bolt 5L 39
Hinkler Av. BL3: Bolt 9F 38
Hinstock Cres. M18: Man 4B 96
Hinton OL12: Roch 5B 8 (5D 28)
Hinton Cl. OL11: Roch 7K 27
Hinton Gro. SK14: Hyde 9D 98
Hinton M. SK1: Stoc 7F 108
Hinton St. M4: Man 1L 5 (7G 79)
OL8: O'ham 5D 8 (6K 63)
Hipley Cl. SK6: Bred 3L 109
Hirons La. OL4: Spri 6D 64
Hirst Av. M28: Walk 6K 57
Hitchen Cl. SK16: Duk 2C 98
Hitchen Dr. SK16: Duk 2C 98
Hitchen St. M13: Man 4H 95
Hitch Lowes SK11: Chel 9A 126
Hives, The M17: T Pk 2H 93
Hive St. OL8: O'ham 9F 62
HMP & YOI Forest Bank
M27: Pen 1L 77
HMP Buckley Hall
OL12: Roch 2E 28
HMP Manchester M3: Man 6E 78
HMP Risley WA3: Ris 9G 89
HMP Styal SK9: Sty 4F 122
HMYOI Hindley
WN2: B'haw 9N 53
Hoade St. WN2: Hin 4A 54
Hobart Cl. SK7: Bram 2D 124
Hobart St. BL1: Bolt 2E 38
M18: Man 4B 96
Hobberley Dr. WN8: Skel 3C 50
Hobby Gro. WN7: Lei 5K 73
Hobcroft La. WA16: Mob 1M 133
Hob Hey La. WA3: Cul 5F 88
Hob Hill SK15: Stal 9C 82
Hob Mill Ri. OL5: Mos 7H 65
Hobson Ct. M34: Aud 3J 97
Hobson Cres. M34: Aud 3J 97
Hobson Moor Rd. SK14: Mot 3J 99
Hobson St. M11: Man 2E 96
M35: Fail 4A 80
OL1: O'ham 3D 8 (5K 63)
SK5: Stoc 7D 96
SK11: Macc 5H 131
Hockenhull Cl. M22: Wyth 5D 116
Hocker La. SK10: N Ald, O Ald 8G 127
Hockerley Cl. M33: Sale 3D 104
Hockery Vw. WN2: Hin 7M 53
HOCKLEY 3K 125
Hockley Cl. SK12: Poy 3L 125
Hockley Paddock SK12: Poy 3K 125
Hockley Rd. M23: Wyth 2M 115
SK12: Poy 3L 125
Hodder Av. OL15: Lit 8K 15
PR7: Chor 1E 18
Hodder Bank SK2: Stoc 2J 119
Hodder Cl. WN5: Wig 4A 52
Hodder Way M45: Whitef 3B 60
(not continuous)
Hoddesdon St. M8: Man 3G 79
Hodge Brow BL6: R'ton 1B 20
Hodge Clough Rd. OL1: O'ham 8N 45
HODGEFOLD 1J 111
Hodge Fold SK14: B'tom 9J 99
Hodge La. M5: Sal 9M 77
SK14: B'tom 1J 111
Hodge Rd. M28: Walk 9L 57
OL1: O'ham 9A 46
Hodges St. WN6: Wig 9D 34
Hodge St. M9: Man 1L 79
Hodgson Ct. M19: Man 1F 107
Hodgson Dr. WA15: Tim 8G 104
Hodgson St. M8: Man 5E 78
OL6: A Lyne 9A 6 (8L 81)
Hodnet Dr. WN4: A Mak 7F 70
Hodnett Av. M41: Urm 8M 91
Hodnet Wlk. M34: Dent 8J 97
Hodson Fold OL8: O'ham 1L 81
Hodson Rd. M27: Swin 9E 58
Hodson St. M3: Sal 2D 4 (8D 78)
WN3: Wig 9H 9 (4E 52)
(not continuous)
Hogarth Ri. OL1: O'ham 8A 46
Hogarth Rd. OL11: Roch 1D 44
SK6: Mar B 8E 110
Hogarth Wlk. M8: Man 4H 79
(off Smeaton St.)
Hoggs Bri. Cl. M27: Pen 2K 77
Holbeach Cl. BL8: Bury 8K 25
WN2: Hin 7A 54
Holbeck M29: Ast 5C 74
Holbeck Av. OL12: Roch 1B 28
Holbeck Cl. BL6: Hor 4F 36
Holbeck Gro. M14: Man 5K 95
Holbeton Cl. M8: Man 5G 78
SK7: Bram 4D 118
Holborn Av. M26: Rad 8D 40
M35: Fail 3F 80
WN3: Wig 6E 52
WN7: Lei 2H 73
Holborn Dr. M8: Man 5G 78
Holborn Gdns. OL11: Roch 8B 28
Holborn Sq. OL11: Roch 8B 28
Holborn St. OL11: Roch 8B 28
Holbrook Av. M38: Lit H 5H 57
Holbrook St. M1: Man 7J 5
HOLCOMBE 8G 11
Holcombe Av. BL8: Bury 2K 41
WA3: Gol 1M 87
HOLCOMBE BROOK 3G 24
Holcombe Brook BL0: Ram 2F 24
(off Redisher Cft.)
Holcombe Brook Sports Club 2F 24
Holcombe Cl. BL4: Kea 5A 58
M6: Sal 8N 77
OL4: Spri 4D 64
WA14: Alt 1B 114
Holcombe Ct. BL0: Ram 3G 24
Holcombe Cres. BL4: Kea 5A 58
Holcombe Dr. SK10: Macc 1F 130
Holcombe Gdns. M19: Man 3K 107
Holcombe Lee BL0: Ram 1G 24
Holcombe M. BL0: Ram 2F 24
Holcombe Old Rd. BL8: Holc 2F 24
Holcombe Pct. BL0: Ram 2F 24
Holcombe Rd. BL3: Lit L 9N 39
BL8: Ram, Tot 6F 24
M14: Man 1K 107
Holcombe Vw. Cl. OL4: O'ham 1A 64
Holcombe Village BL8: Holc 8G 10
Holcombe Wlk. SK4: Stoc 1B 108
Holcroft Dr. WN2: Abr 3M 71
Holcroft La. WA3: Cul 6K 89
Holden Av. BL0: Ram 9G 11
BL1: Bolt 7F 22
BL9: Bury 9D 26
M16: Whall R 8D 94
Holden Brook Cl. WN7: Lei 5K 73
Holden Clough Dr. OL7: A Lyne 3L 81
HOLDEN FOLD 1G 63
Holden Fold La. OL2: O'ham 1G 63
(not continuous)
Holden Gallery 9J 5
Holden Lea BL5: W'ton 9G 36
Holden Rd. M7: Sal 1C 78
WN7: Lei 4H 73
Holden Rd. Trad. Est. WN7: Lei 4H 73
Holden St. OL6: A Lyne 5F 6 (6N 81)
(not continuous)
OL8: O'ham 8K 63
OL12: Roch 3E 28
PR7: Adl 6J 19
Holden Wlk. WN5: Wig 6B 52
Holder Av. BL3: Lit L 7B 40
Holderness Dr. OL2: O'ham 1G 62
Holdgate Cl. M15: Man 4D 94
Holding St. WN2: Hin 5N 53
Holdsworth St. M27: Swin 3D 76
Holebottom OL6: A Lyne 4N 81
HOLEHOUSE 3L 111
Hole Ho. Fold SK6: Rom 6M 109
Holehouse La. SK10: Adl, Boll 3F 128
SK11: Lang 8N 131
Holford Av. M14: Man 7G 94
Holford Ct. M34: Dent 6K 97
Holford Cres. WA16: Knut 7G 133
Holford Wlk. OL16: Roch 6H 29
Holford Way WA12: N Wil 6J 87
Holgate Dr. WN5: Orr 5J 51
Holgate St. OL4: O'ham 2B 64
Holhouse La. BL8: G'mount 3F 24
Holiday La. SK2: Stoc 1K 119
Holkar Mdws. BL7: Bro X 5J 23
Holker Cl. M13: Man 4J 95
SK12: Poy 2K 125
Holker Way M34: Dent 8L 97
(off Two Trees La.)
Holkham Cl. M4: Man 3N 5 (8H 79)
Holland Av. SK15: Stal 8D 82
Holland Cl. OL3: Del 8H 47
SK12: Poy 3J 125
Holland Ct. M8: Man 9E 60
M26: Rad 8J 41
SK1: Stoc 9E 108
WN8: Skel 9B 50
Holland Gro. OL6: A Lyne 4M 81
Holland Ho. WN8: Uph 5G 50
HOLLAND LEES 7G 33
HOLLAND MOOR 4C 50
Holland Pk. SK7: Bram 8B 118
Holland Ri. OL12: Roch 6B 8 (5C 28)
Holland Rd. M8: Man 9E 60
SK7: Bram 8C 118
SK14: Hyde 4C 98
Hollands Pl. SK11: Macc 5K 131
Holland St. BL1: Bolt 9G 22
M6: Sal 5N 77
M26: Rad 8J 41
M34: Dent 5H 97
M40: Man 8J 79
M46: Ath 9M 55
OL10: H'ood 4J 43
OL12: Roch 7A 8 (6C 28)
OL16: Roch 1H 29
SK11: Macc 5G 131
Holland St. E. M34: Dent 5H 97
Holland St. W. M34: Dent 5H 97
Holland Wlk. M6: Sal 5N 77
Hollie La. M5: Sal 2A 94
Hollies, The BL2: Bolt 4N 39
M6: Sal 7H 77
M20: Man 5E 106
M27: Swin 4D 76
(Moorfield Cl.)
M27: Swin 3H 77
(West Dr.)
M46: Ath 8M 55
OL8: O'ham 7H 63
SK4: Stoc 5N 107
SK8: Gat 2G 116
WN1: Wig 9G 34
WN2: Asp 7M 35
Hollies Ct. M33: Sale 4H 105
Hollies Dr. SK6: Mar 2D 120
Hollies La. SK9: Wilm 7L 123
Hollin Acre BL5: W'ton 4H 55
Hollin Bank SK4: Stoc 1B 108
Hollinbrook WN6: Wig 1C 52
Hollin Cres. OL3: G'fld 7H 65
Hollincross La. SK13: Glos 9E 100
Holliney Rd. M22: Wyth 6E 116
HOLLINFARE 5C 102
Hollingford Pl. WA16: Knut 8G 132
Hollington Way WN3: Wins 9N 51
Hollingwood Cl. WN4: A Mak 7D 70
HOLLINGWORTH
OL15 . . . . .2L 29
SK14 . . . . .4M 99
Hollingworth Av. M40: Man 9D 62
Hollingworth Cl. SK1: Stoc 4L 9
Hollingworth Ct. OL15: Lit 9L 15
(off Stubley Mill Rd.)
Hollingworth Dr. SK6: Mar 4C 120
Hollingworth Fold OL15: Lit 3N 29
Hollingworth Lake Caravan Pk.
OL15: Lit 4M 29
Hollingworth Lake Country Pk. . . .3M 29
Hollingworth Lake Nature Reserve
. . . . .3M 29
Hollingworth Lake Sailing Club . . .3L 29
Hollingworth Lake Vis. Cen. 2M 29

Hollingworth Lake Water Activity Cen. ... 2L 29
Hollingworth Rd. OL15: Lit ... 1M 29
SK6: Bred ... 4J 109
Hollingworth St. OL9: Chad ... 8F 62
Hollinhall St. OL4: O'ham ... 4N 63
Hollin Hey Cl. WN5: Bil ... 7H 69
Hollin Hey Rd. BL1: Bolt ... 1N 37
Hollinhey Ter. SK14: Holl ... 4M 99
Hollin Ho. M24: Mid ... 9M 43
Hollinhurst Dr. BL6: Los ... 5L 37
Hollinhurst Rd. M26: Rad ... 1J 59
Hollin La. M24: Mid ... 7K 43
OL11: Roch ... 7K 27
SK9: Sty ... 9E 116
SK11: Sut E ... 9K 131
Hollin Rd. SK10: Boll ... 6L 129
HOLLINS
BL9 ... 7N 41
M24 ... 9M 43
OL8 ... 8G 63
HOLLINS, THE ... 6C 54
Hollins BL4: Farn ... 3E 56
Hollins, The SK6: Mar ... 1C 120
Hollins Av. OL4: Lees ... 3C 64
SK13: Gam ... 7N 99
(off Hollins M.)
SK14: Hyde ... 1B 110
Hollins Bank *SK13: Gam ... 7N 99*
(off Brassington Cres.)
Hollins Brook Cl. BL9: Bury ... 7A 42
Hollins Brook Way BL9: Bury ... 6A 42
Hollins Brow BL9: Bury ... 8M 41
Hollins Cl. BL9: Bury ... 8A 42
M29: Ast ... 2B 74
SK13: Gam ... 7N 99
(off Brassington Cres.)
WN4: Gars ... 6A 70
Hollinsclough Cl. M22: Shar ... 2D 116
Hollinscroft Av. WA15: Tim ... 2K 115
Hollins Dr. M24: Mid ... 8K 43
Hollins Fold *SK13: Gam ... 7N 99*
(off Brassington Cres.)
Hollins Gdns. *SK13: Gam ... 7N 99*
(off Hollins M.)
HOLLINS GREEN
OL8 ... 9J 63
WA3 ... 6B 102
Hollins Grn. M24: Mid ... 9M 43
Hollins Grn. Gdns. *SK6: Mar ... 1C 120*
(off Station Rd.)
Hollins Grn. Rd. SK6: Mar ... 1C 120
Hollins Gro. M12: Man ... 6M 95
M33: Sale ... 4G 104
SK13: Gam ... 7N 99
(off Brassington Cres.)
Hollinshead *M7: Sal ... 4D 78*
(off Wilmur Av.)
Hollins Ind. Pk. SK13: Had ... 4D 100
Hollins La. BL0: Ram ... 5L 11
BL9: Bury ... 7N 41
OL3: G'fld ... 6N 65
OL5: Mos ... 1G 83
SK6: Mar ... 1C 120
SK6: Mar B ... 9E 110
SK13: Gam ... 7N 99
Hollins M. BL9: Bury ... 8B 42
SK13: Gam ... 7N 99
Hollinsmoor Rd. SK22: Row ... 9M 111
Hollins Mt. SK6: Mar B ... 8E 110
Hollins Rd. OL4: Lees ... 3C 64
OL8: O'ham ... 9F 62
SK11: Macc ... 6K 131
WN2: Hin ... 6C 54
Hollins Sq. BL9: Bury ... 9A 42
Hollins St. BL2: Bolt ... 6J 39
OL4: Spri ... 5C 64
SK15: Stal ... 1C 98
Hollins Ter. SK6: Mar ... 1C 120
SK11: Macc ... 6K 131
HOLLINS VALE ... 7A 42
Hollins Vw. SK11: Macc ... 6H 131
Hollins Wlk. M22: Wyth ... 5C 116
Hollins Way *SK13: Gam ... 7N 99*
(off Hollins M.)
Hollinswood Rd. BL2: Bolt ... 6J 39
M28: Wors ... 4J 75
Hollin Well Cl. M24: Mid ... 8L 43
HOLLINWOOD ... 9G 62
Hollinwood Av. M40: Man ... 8B 62
OL9: Chad ... 8B 62
Hollinwood Bus. Cen.
OL8: O'ham ... 1F 80
Hollinwood La. SK6: Mar ... 5E 120
(not continuous)
Hollinwood Rd. SK12: Dis ... 9G 120
Hollinwood Stop (Metro) ... 9E 62
Holloway Dr. M28: Ward ... 1C 76
Hollowbrook Way OL12: Roch ... 3B 28
Hollowell La. BL6: Hor ... 3F 36
Hollow End SK5: Stoc ... 1F 108
Hollow End Towers
SK5: Stoc ... 1F 108
Hollow Fld. OL11: Roch ... 4J 27
Hollowgate M27: Swin ... 4C 76
Hollow La. WA16: Knut ... 7H 133
Hollow Mdws. M26: Rad ... 5C 58
Hollows, The SK8: H Grn ... 6H 117
Hollows Ct. *SK14: Hyde ... 7B 98*
(off Ridling La.)
Hollows Farm Av. OL12: Roch ... 3B 28
Hollowspell OL12: Roch ... 2G 29
Hollow Va. Dr. SK5: Stoc ... 8D 96
Holly Av. M28: Walk ... 9M 57
M41: Urm ... 7B 92
SK8: Chea ... 2J 117
WA12: N Wil ... 6G 87
Holly Bank M40: Man ... 3A 80
OL2: O'ham ... 8H 45
(off Church St.)
OL2: O'ham ... 6H 45
(Fir La.)
OL6: A Lyne ... 9G 6 (8A 82)
SK13: Glos ... 9G 100
SK14: Holl ... 4N 99
WN7: Lei ... 3J 73
Hollybank M33: Sale ... 5J 105
M43: Droy ... 7G 80
SK15: Mill ... 6G 83
Holly Bank Caravan Pk.
WA3: Rix ... 7B 102
Holly Bank Cl. M15: Man ... 3B 94
Holly Bank Cotts. *M31: Part ... 4G 103*
(off Manchester Rd.)
SK6: Wood ... 3M 109
(off High La.)
Holly Bank Ct. SK8: Chea H ... 6M 117
Hollybank Dr. BL6: Los ... 5K 37
Holly Bank Ind. Est. M26: Rad ... 9F 40
Holly Bank Ri. SK16: Duk ... 1C 98
Holly Bank Rd. SK9: Wilm ... 5G 122
Holly Bank St. M26: Rad ... 9F 40
Hollybrook OL1: Chad ... 9F 44
Hollybrook Dene SK6: Rom ... 6B 110
Holly Bush Sq. WA3: Low ... 9A 72
Hollybush St. M18: Man ... 3C 96
Holly Cl. WA15: Tim ... 1G 115
Holly Ct. BL9: Bury ... 2N 41
M20: Man ... 2G 106
M44: Irl ... 6J 91
SK3: Stoc ... 2C 118
SK14: Hyde ... 7D 98
Holly Cres. PR7: Cop ... 3B 18
Hollycroft Av. BL2: Bolt ... 7M 39
M22: Wyth ... 1C 116
Hollydene WN2: Asp ... 7L 35
Holly Dene Dr. BL6: Los ... 5K 37
Holly Dr. M33: Sale ... 4G 105
Hollyedge Dr. M25: Pres ... 9N 59
Hollyfern Rd. WA14: W Tim ... 7B 104
Holly Fold M45: Whitef ... 2M 59
Hollygate, The SK3: Stoc ... 3G 9
Holly Grange SK7: Bram ... 4D 118
WA14: Bow ... 5D 114
Holly Gro. BL1: Bolt ... 3D 38
BL4: Farn ... 3H 57
M33: Sale ... 4K 105
M34: Dent ... 6L 97
OL3: Dig ... 9M 47
OL3: Dob ... 1M 65
OL4: Lees ... 3B 64
OL9: Chad ... 3F 62
SK15: Stal ... 1B 98
WA16: Tab ... 5A 132
WN7: Lei ... 3G 73
Holly Heath Dr. WN1: Wig ... 8E 34
Hollyhedge Av. M22: Wyth ... 2C 116
Hollyhedge Ct. M22: Shar ... 2D 116
Hollyhedge Ct. Rd. M22: Shar ... 2D 116
Hollyhedge Rd.
M22: Shar, Wyth ... 2B 116
M23: Wyth ... 2M 115
SK8: Gat ... 3D 116
Hollyhey Dr. M23: Wyth ... 7B 106
Holly Ho. Dr. M41: Urm ... 7N 91
Hollyhouse Dr. SK6: Wood ... 3L 109
Hollyhurst M28: Wors ... 4B 76
Holly La. OL8: O'ham ... 9G 63
SK9: Sty ... 2D 122
Holly Mill Cres. BL1: Bolt ... 9G 22
Hollymount M16: Old T ... 5A 94
Hollymount Av. SK2: Stoc ... 2G 119
Hollymount Dr. OL4: O'ham ... 9B 46
SK2: Stoc ... 2G 119
Hollymount Gdns. SK2: Stoc ... 2H 119
Holly Mt. La. BL8: G'mount ... 4D 24
Hollymount Rd. SK2: Stoc ... 2G 119
HOLLY NOOK ... 6M 35
Holly Oak Gdns. OL10: H'ood ... 3H 43
Holly Rd. M27: Swin ... 4D 76
SK4: Stoc ... 3A 108
SK6: H Lan ... 8C 120
SK7: Bram ... 1C 124
SK11: Macc ... 5F 130
SK12: Poy ... 3J 125
WA3: Gol ... 1M 87
WA13: Lym ... 2C 112
WN2: Asp ... 7L 35
WN5: Wig ... 4B 52
Holly Rd. Nth. SK9: Wilm ... 8F 122
Holly Rd. Sth. SK9: Wilm ... 9F 122
Holly Royde Cl. M20: Man ... 2G 106
Holly St. BL1: Bolt ... 9G 22
BL8: Tot ... 7F 24
BL9: Bury ... 2N 41
BL9: Sum ... 2J 25
M11: Man ... 1K 95
M43: Droy ... 8B 80
OL12: W'le ... 8G 15
OL16: Roch ... 2F 44
SK1: Stoc ... 7E 108
Hollythorn Av. SK8: Chea H ... 8N 117
Holly Va. Cotts. SK6: Mar B ... 8H 111
Holly Vw. M22: Shar ... 3D 116
Holly Wlk. M31: Part ... 5E 102
Hollyway M22: Nor ... 8D 106
Hollywood BL1: Bolt ... 2C 38
WA14: Bow ... 5D 114
Hollywood Bowl
Ashton-under-Lyne ... 7K 81
Bolton ... 4F 36
Hollywood Rd. BL1: Bolt ... 2C 38
SK6: Mel ... 8H 111
Hollywood Towers
SK3: Stoc ... 3H 9 (8B 108)
Hollywood Way SK4: Stoc ... 7B 108
Holmbrook M29: Tyld ... 1D 74
Holmbrook Wlk. *M8: Man ... 4F 78*
(off Heywood St.)
Holm Ct. *M6: Sal ... 8N 77*
(off Mulberry Rd.)
Holmcroft Rd. M18: Man ... 6B 96
Holmdale Av. M19: Man ... 3K 107
Holmdale Ct. M33: Sale ... 4J 105
Holme Av. BL8: Bury ... 7J 25
WN1: Wig ... 1F 52
Holmebrook Dr. BL6: Hor ... 3F 36
Holme Ct. WN1: Wig ... 1F 52
Holme Cres. OL2: O'ham ... 1G 62
Holmecroft Chase BL5: W'ton ... 9J 37
Holmefield M33: Sale ... 4H 105
Holmefield Dr. SK8: Chea H ... 7N 117
Holme Ho. OL15: Lit ... 5A 16
Holme Ho. St. OL15: Lit ... 4A 16
Holme Pk. Cl. WN3: I Mak ... 6J 53
Holmepark Gdns. M28: Wors ... 5H 75
Holme Pk. Way M35: Fail ... 3F 80
Holme Rd. M20: Man ... 5E 106
Holmes Cotts. BL1: Bolt ... 1D 38
Holmes Ct. SK1: Stoc ... 3M 9
Holmes Ho. Av. WN3: Wins ... 8N 51
Holmes Rd. OL12: Roch ... 6B 28
Holmes St. BL3: Bolt ... 8H 39
OL12: Roch ... 2G 29
(Hollowspell)
OL12: Roch ... 5B 28
(Primrose St.)
SK2: Stoc ... 9C 108
SK8: Chea ... 1K 117
Holme St. SK14: Hyde ... 7A 98
Holmes Way M34: Dent ... 1K 109
Holmeswood Cl. SK9: Wilm ... 6H 123
Holmeswood Rd. BL3: Bolt ... 1E 56
Holme Ter. OL15: Lit ... 5A 16
WN1: Wig ... 9E 34
Holmfield Av. M9: Man ... 3L 79
M25: Pres ... 8B 60
Holmfield Av. W. M9: Man ... 3L 79
Holmfield Cl. SK4: Stoc ... 5B 108
Holmfield Grn. BL3: Bolt ... 9A 38
Holmfirth Rd. OL3: G'fld ... 6M 65
Holmfirth St. M13: Man ... 5L 95
Holmfoot Wlk. *M9: Man ... 3J 79*
(off Foleshill Av.)
Holmlea Rd. M43: Droy ... 8C 80
Holmlee Way SK10: P'bury ... 7B 128
Holmleigh Av. M9: Man ... 1K 79
Holmpark Rd. M11: Man ... 2D 96
Holmrook WA14: Alt ... 2B 114
Holmsfield Cl. WN2: Asp ... 1K 53
Holmside Gdns. M19: Man ... 4K 107
Holmwood WA14: Bow ... 4A 114
Holmwood Cl. WN4: A Mak ... 5D 70
Holmwood Ct. M20: Man ... 4G 106
Holmwood Rd. M20: Man ... 3G 106
Holroyd St. M11: Man ... 1M 95
OL16: Roch ... 8E 8 (6E 28)
Holset Dr. WA14: Alt ... 2B 114
Holset Wlk. SK7: H Gro ... 5E 118
Holst Av. M8: Man ... 4F 78
Holstein Av. OL12: Roch ... 1B 28
Holstein St. M13: Man ... 4J 95
Holt Av. PR7: Cop ... 3C 18
WN5: Bil ... 6H 69
Holtby St. M9: Man ... 1K 79
Holt Cres. WN5: Bil ... 6H 69
Holthouse Rd. BL8: Tot ... 8E 24
Holt La. M35: Fail ... 3F 80
HOLT LANE END ... 3F 80
Holt La. M. M35: Fail ... 3F 80
Holton Way WN3: Wins ... 1B 70
HOLTS ... 7B 64
Holts La. OL4: O'ham ... 7A 64
SK9: Sty ... 3E 122
Holts Pas. OL15: Lit ... 9L 15
Holts Ter. OL12: Roch ... 3C 28
Holt St. BL0: Ram ... 8K 11
BL3: Bolt ... 7E 38
M27: Clif ... 9F 58
M29: Tyld ... 1B 74
M30: Ecc ... 1C 92
M34: Aud ... 1J 97
M40: Man ... 5L 79
OL4: O'ham ... 3N 63
OL12: Whitw ... 5A 14
OL15: Lit ... 4A 16
OL16: Miln ... 8L 29
SK1: Stoc ... 5M 9 (8D 108)
WA14: B'ath ... 8C 104
WN1: I Mak ... 3J 53
WN2: Hin ... 6M 53
WN3: Wig ... 7D 52
WN5: Orr ... 6H 51
WN6: Wig ... 1C 52
WN7: Lei ... 3G 72
Holt St. W. BL0: Ram ... 9H 11
Holtswell Cl. WA3: Low ... 9A 72
HOLT TOWN ... 8K 79
Holt Town M40: Man ... 8J 79
Holt Town Ind. Est. M11: Man ... 8K 79
Holt Town Stop (Metro) ... 8K 79
Holtwood Wlk. SK5: Stoc ... 1G 109
Holway Wlk. *M9: Man ... 3H 79*
(off Hendham Va.)
Holwick Rd. M23: Wyth ... 6M 105
Holwood Dr. M16: Whall R ... 9D 94
Holybourne Wlk. M23: Wyth ... 8K 105
Holy Harbour St. BL1: Bolt ... 2D 38
Holyhurst Wlk. *BL1: Bolt ... 2F 38*
(off Rix St.)
Holyoake Rd. M28: Walk ... 9L 57
Holyoake St. M43: Droy ... 8G 80
Holyoak St. M40: Man ... 4A 80
Holyrood Cl. M25: Pres ... 5B 60
WN7: Lei ... 3N 73
Holyrood Ct. M25: Pres ... 5A 60
Holyrood Dr. M25: Pres ... 5B 60
M27: Swin ... 3D 76
Holyrood Gro. M25: Pres ... 5B 60
Holyrood Rd. M25: Pres ... 6B 60
Holyrood St. M40: Man ... 6C 80
OL1: O'ham ... 2L 63
Holy St. M14: Man ... 6G 94
Homebeck Ho. SK8: Gat ... 2F 116
Homebury Dr. M11: Man ... 8N 79
Home Dr. M24: Mid ... 4L 61
Home Farm WA16: Mere ... 1B 132
Home Farm Av. SK10: Macc ... 3D 130
SK14: Mot ... 8J 99
Homelands Cl. M33: Sale ... 6F 104
Homelands Rd. M33: Sale ... 6F 104
Homelands Wlk. *M9: Man ... 3J 79*
(off Shiredale Dr.)
Homelaurel Ho. M33: Sale ... 6H 105
Homelyme Ho. SK12: Poy ... 3K 125
Homer Dr. SK6: Mar B ... 8E 110
Homer St. M26: Rad ... 8E 40
Homerton Rd. M40: Man ... 6N 79
Homestead, The M33: Sale ... 3F 104
Homestead Av. WA11: Hay ... 2B 86
Homestead Cl. M31: Part ... 4H 103
Homestead Cres. M19: Man ... 5J 107
Homestead Gdns. OL12: Roch ... 9H 15
Homestead Rd. SK12: Dis ... 9F 120
Homewood Av. M22: Nor ... 7C 106
Homewood Rd. M22: Nor ... 7B 106
Honduras St. OL4: O'ham ... 4M 63
Hondwith Cl. BL2: Bolt ... 8J 23
Honeybourne Cl. M29: Tyld ... 1D 74
Honeycombe Cotts. *SK8: Chea ... 2K 117*
(off Oak Rd.)
Honey Hill OL4: Lees ... 6C 64
Honey St. M8: Man ... 6G 78
Honeysuckle Av. WN6: Wig ... 9C 34
Honeysuckle Cl. M23: Wyth ... 7K 105
SK6: Wood ... 3L 109
Honeysuckle Dr. SK15: Stal ... 8E 82
Honeysuckle Wlk. M33: Sale ... 2D 104
Honeysuckle Way OL12: Roch ... 2B 28
Honeywell La. OL8: O'ham ... 8K 63
Honeywood Cl. BL0: Ram ... 2G 24
Honford Ct. SK9: Hand ... 3J 123
Honford Rd. M22: Wyth ... 3B 116
Hong Kong Av. M90: Man A ... 7N 115
Honister Av. WA11: St H ... 9G 68
Honister Dr. M24: Mid ... 1L 61
Honister Rd. M9: Man ... 3L 79
WN5: Wig ... 5M 51
Honister Way OL11: Roch ... 9N 27
Honiton Av. SK14: Hat ... 7F 98
Honiton Cl. OL9: Chad ... 2C 62
OL10: H'ood ... 4H 43
WN7: Lei ... 9F 54
Honiton Dr. BL2: Bolt ... 6A 40
Honiton Gro. M26: Rad ... 7D 40
Honiton Ho. *M6: Sal ... 7G 77*
(off Devon Cl.)
Honiton Wlk. *SK14: Hat ... 7G 98*
(off Honiton Av.)
Honiton Way WA14: Alt ... 1A 114
Honor St. M13: Man ... 6L 95
Honsham Wlk. M23: Wyth ... 7L 105
Hood Cl. M29: Tyld ... 1E 74
Hood Gro. WN7: Lei ... 7K 73
Hood Sq. OL4: Grot ... 6D 64
Hood St. M4: Man ... 3L 5 (8G 79)
Hood Wlk. M34: Dent ... 1L 109
Hook St. WN2: I Mak ... 4J 53
Hoole Cl. SK8: Chea ... 2M 117
HOOLEY BRIDGE ... 9H 27
Hooley Bri. Ind. Est.
OL10: H'ood ... 9H 27
HOOLEY BROW ... 1J 43
Hooley Clough OL10: H'ood ... 9J 27
HOOLEY HILL ... 2K 97
Hooley Range SK4: Stoc ... 5N 107
Hooper St. M12: Man ... 1J 95
OL4: O'ham ... 5L 63
SK4: Stoc ... 3K 9 (7C 108)
HOOTEN GARDENS ... 7L 73
Hooten La. WN7: Lei ... 7L 73
Hooton St. BL3: Bolt ... 9D 38
M40: Man ... 7L 79
Hooton Way *SK9: Hand ... 1J 123*
(off Beeston Rd.)
Hopcroft Cl. M9: Man ... 5G 61
Hope Av. BL2: Bolt ... 8M 23
(Heaton Av.)
BL2: Bolt ... 6J 39
(Willowbank Av.)
M32: Stre ... 6H 93
M38: Lit H ... 7K 57
SK9: Hand ... 3H 123
Hope Carr La. WN7: Lei ... 8J 73
Hope Carr Nature Reserve ... 8H 73
Hope Carr Rd. WN7: Lei ... 7J 73
(not continuous)
Hope Carr Ter. WN7: Lei ... 8J 73
Hope Carr Way WN7: Lei ... 7J 73
Hope Chapel *OL6: A Lyne ... 6A 82*
(off Curzon Rd.)
Hope Ct. *OL12: Roch ... 5D 28*
(off Hope St.)
Hopecourt Cl. M6: Sal ... 6J 77
Hope Cres. M6: Sal ... 7J 77
WN6: She ... 6M 33
Hopedale Cl. M11: Man ... 9L 79
Hopedale Rd. SK5: Stoc ... 2D 108
Hope Dr. SK10: Macc ... 4F 130
Hope Ent. Cen. WN5: Wig ... 2B 52
Hopefield Rd. WA13: Lym ... 3C 112
Hopefield St. BL3: Bolt ... 8E 38
Hope Fold Av. M46: Ath ... 9K 55
Hopefold Dr. M28: Walk ... 9M 57
HOPE GREEN ... 5H 125
Hope Grn. Way SK10: Adl ... 4H 125
Hope Hey La. M38: Lit H ... 6G 57
Hope La. SK10: Adl ... 5H 125
WA3: G'ury ... 8M 73
WN7: Lei ... 8N 73
Hopelea St. M20: Man ... 1G 106
Hope Pk. Cl. M25: Pres ... 8A 60
Hope Pk. Rd. M25: Pres ... 8A 60
Hope Rd. M14: Man ... 5J 95
M25: Pres ... 9N 59
M33: Sale ... 5H 105
Hopes Carr SK1: Stoc ... 3M 9 (7D 108)
Hope St. BL0: Ram ... 9H 11
BL4: Farn ... 3M 57
BL6: Bla ... 4A 36
BL6: Hor ... 9D 20
M1: Man ... 5J 5 (9F 78)
M5: Sal ... 4A 4 (9B 78)
M7: Sal ... 3C 78
M27: Pen ... 2G 77
M27: Swin ... 3D 76
M29: Ast ... 2C 74
M30: Ecc ... 8F 76
M34: Aud ... 4J 97
M38: Lit H ... 7H 57
OL1: O'ham ... 4M 63
OL2: Shaw ... 5M 45
OL6: A Lyne ... 6A 82
OL10: H'ood ... 4L 43
Hope St. OL11: Roch ... 3A 44
OL12: Roch ... 5D 28
PR6: Adl ... 5L 19
SK4: Stoc ... 2H 9 (7B 108)
SK7: H Gro ... 4H 119
SK10: Macc ... 4J 131
SK13: Glos ... 7G 101
SK16: Duk ... 1M 97
(not continuous)
WA12: N Wil ... 6E 86
WN1: Wig ... 7J 9
WN2: Asp ... 9B 36
WN2: Hin ... 5B 54
WN3: I Mak ... 7H 53
WN4: A Mak ... 5G 71
WN7: Lei ... 5H 73
Hope St. Nth. BL6: Hor ... 8D 20
Hope St. W. SK10: Macc ... 4H 130
Hope Ter. SK3: Stoc ... 5K 9 (8C 108)
SK16: Duk ... 1M 97
(off Hope St.)
Hopgarth Wlk. *M40: Man ... 5B 80*
(off Terence St.)
Hopkin Av. OL1: O'ham ... 3M 63
Hopkins Bldgs. OL5: Mos ... 8H 65
Hopkins Fld. WA14: Bow ... 6B 114
Hopkinson Av. M34: Dent ... 4H 97
Hopkinson Cl. OL3: Upp ... 3L 65
Hopkinson Rd. M9: Man ... 6J 61
Hopkins St. M12: Man ... 6M 95
SK14: Hyde ... 5B 98
Hopkin St. OL1: O'ham ... 2E 8 (4K 63)
Hoppet La. M43: Droy ... 8G 80
Hopton Av. M22: Wyth ... 4D 116
Hopton Ct. *M15: Man ... 3F 94*
(off Booth St. W.)
HOPWOOD ... 3K 43
Hopwood Av. BL6: Hor ... 9E 20
M30: Ecc ... 7D 76
OL10: H'ood ... 4J 43
Hopwood Cl. BL9: Bury ... 9M 41
WA3: Low ... 1B 88
Hopwood Ct. M24: Mid ... 8M 43
OL2: Shaw ... 5K 45
Hopwood Ct. M. OL10: H'ood ... 4K 43
Hopwood Rd. M24: Mid ... 8M 43
Hopwood St. M27: Pen ... 2G 77
M40: Man ... 4N 79
Horace Barnes Cl. M14: Man ... 6F 94
Horace Gro. SK4: Stoc ... 4C 108
Horace St. BL1: Bolt ... 2E 38
(not continuous)
Horatio St. M18: Man ... 3D 96
Horbury Av. M18: Man ... 6B 96
Horbury Dr. BL8: Bury ... 2J 41
Horden Wlk. *OL2: O'ham ... 8J 45*
(off Shaw St.)
Hordern Cl. SK13: Had ... 5C 100
Horeb St. BL3: Bolt ... 7E 38
Horest La. OL3: Dens ... 4E 46
Horizons, The BL6: Bla ... 2B 36
Horley Cl. BL8: Bury ... 6J 25
Horlock Ct. M5: Sal ... 7A 78
Hornbeam Cl. M33: Sale ... 3C 104
WA15: Tim ... 2L 115
Hornbeam Ct. M6: Sal ... 7N 77
Hornbeam Cres. WN4: A Mak ... 7E 70
Hornbeam Rd. M19: Man ... 7N 95
Hornbeam Way M4: Man ... 7F 78
Hornby Av. M9: Man ... 6K 61
Hornby Dr. BL3: Bolt ... 1M 55
Hornby Gro. WN7: Lei ... 3M 73
Hornby Lodge *M25: Pres ... 8A 60*
(off Prestwich Pk. Rd. Sth.)
Hornby Rd. M32: Stre ... 5M 93
Hornby St. BL9: Bury ... 5L 7 (8M 25)
M8: Man ... 6E 78
M24: Mid ... 3M 61
OL8: O'ham ... 5A 8 (6H 63)
OL10: H'ood ... 3J 43
WN1: Wig ... 1F 52
Horncastle Cl. BL8: Bury ... 8K 25
WA3: Low ... 1B 88
Horncastle Rd. M40: Man ... 9N 61
Hornchurch Ct. *M15: Man ... 3E 94*
(off Bonsall St.)
OL10: H'ood ... 5K 43
Hornchurch Ho. SK2: Stoc ... 1E 118
Hornchurch St. M15: Man ... 3D 94
Horne Gro. WN3: Wig ... 6C 52
Horne St. BL9: Bury ... 4L 41
Hornet Cl. OL11: Roch ... 1E 44
Horniman Ho. M13: Man ... 4G 95
Hornsea Cl. BL8: Bury ... 2F 40
OL9: Chad ... 2D 62
Hornsea Rd. SK2: Stoc ... 2L 119
Hornsea Wlk. *M11: Man ... 9M 79*
(off Grey Mare La.)
Hornsey Gro. WN3: Wins ... 8A 52
Horridge Av. WA12: N Wil ... 4F 86
Horridge Fold BL7: Eger ... 2F 22
Horridge Fold Av. BL5: O Hul ... 1A 56
Horridge St. BL8: Bury ... 9H 25
Horrobin BL7: Tur ... 3K 23
Horrobin Fold BL7: Tur ... 3K 23
Horrobin La. BL6: R'ton ... 4N 19
BL7: Tur ... 3K 23
PR6: And ... 4N 19
HORROCKS FOLD ... 6D 22
Horrocks Fold Av. BL1: Bolt ... 7E 22
Horrocks St. BL3: Bolt ... 7B 38
M26: Rad ... 8J 41
M29: Tyld ... 1A 74
M46: Ath ... 1N 73
WN7: Lei ... 6C 72
Horrocks Woods ... 7C 22
Horsa St. BL2: Bolt ... 3J 39
Horsedge St. OL1: O'ham ... 1D 8 (3K 63)
Horsefield Av. OL12: Whitw ... 8A 14
Horsefield Cl. M21: Cho H ... 1D 106
Horseshoe Dr. SK11: Macc ... 5F 130
Horseshoe La. BL7: Bro X ... 5H 23
M24: Mid ... 5D 62
SK9: A Edg ... 3F 126
Horsfield St. BL3: Bolt ... 8B 38
Horsfield Way SK6: Bred ... 2J 109

Horsforth La. OL3: G'fld 7K 65
Horsham Av. SK7: H Gro 6G 118
Horsham Cl. BL5: W'ton 5H 55
BL8: Bury 6J 25
Horsham Gro. WN2: Wig 1J 53
Horsham St. M6: Sal 8L 77
Horstead Wlk. *M19: Man 7M 95*
(off Deepcar St.)
Horticultural Centre, The
in Wythenshawe Pk. 8M 105
Horton Av. BL1: Bolt 7F 22
Horton Rd. M14: Man 7F 94
Horton Sq. OL2: Shaw 6M 45
Horton St. SK1: Stoc 9E 108
WN6: Wig 9B 34
Hortree Rd. M32: Stre 7L 93
HORWICH 9D 20
Horwich Bus. Pk. BL6: Hor 2D 36
Horwich Golf Course 2F 36
Horwich Heritage Cen. *9E 20*
(off Longworth Rd.)
Horwich Leisure Cen. 1E 36
Horwich Parkway (Park & Ride) 5E 36
Horwich Parkway Station (Rail) 5E 36
Horwood Cres. M20: Man 3J 107
Hoscar Dr. M19: Man 1L 107
Hoskers, The BL5: W'ton 4E 54
HOSKERS NOOK 6E 54
Hoskers Nook BL5: W'ton 4F 54
Hoskins Cl. M12: Man 4M 95
Hospital Av. M30: Ecc 8E 76
Hospital Rd. BL7: Bro X 5G 23
M23: Wyth 2L 115
M27: Pen 3H 77
Hotel Rd. M90: Man A 8B 116
Hotel St. BL1: Bolt 3K 7 (5G 38)
WA12: N Wil 6E 86
Hothersall Rd. SK5: Stoc 1D 108
Hothersall St. *M7: Sal 7D 78*
(off Jonas St.)
Hotspur Cl. M14: Man 9F 94
HOUGH 4J 127
Hough Cl. OL8: O'ham 9L 63
Hough End Av. M21: Cho H 2B 106
Hough End Cen., The
M21: Cho H 1D 106
Houghend Cres. M21: Cho H 1D 106
Hough Fold Way BL2: Bolt 8L 23
Hough Grn. WA15: Ash 9E 114
Hough Hall Rd. M40: Man 2L 79
Hough Hill Rd. SK15: Stal 9D 82
(not continuous)
Hough La. BL7: Bro X 6G 23
M24: Mid 8D 44
M29: Tyld 2D 74
SK9: A Edg, Wilm 4J 127
SK14: Hyde 4C 98
Houghley Cl. SK10: Macc 2G 131
Hough Rd. M20: Man 1F 106
Hough St. BL3: Bolt 7B 38
M29: Tyld 2E 74
Houghton Av. OL8: O'ham 9H 63
WN5: Wig 1B 52
Houghton Cl. OL16: Roch 7G 28
WA12: N Wil 6E 86
Houghton La. M27: Swin 5D 76
WN6: She 6K 33
Houghton Rd. M8: Man 1F 78
Houghton's La. WN8: Skel 2A 50
(not continuous)
Houghtons Rd. WN8: Skel 9A 32
Houghton St. BL3: Bolt 7F 38
BL9: Bury 9J 7 (3L 41)
M27: Pen 4K 77
OL2: O'ham 1J 63
WA12: N Wil 6E 86
WN7: Lei 4H 73
Hough Wlk. M7: Sal 1A 4 (7B 78)
(not continuous)
Houghwood Golf Course 3F 68
Houghwood Grange WN4: A Mak 7C 70
Houldsworth Av. WA14: Tim 9E 104
Houldsworth Golf Course 9B 96
Houldsworth Mill SK5: Stoc 1C 108
Houldsworth Sq. SK5: Stoc 1C 108
Houldsworth St. M1: Man 3K 5 (8G 78)
M26: Rad 7F 40
SK5: Stoc 1C 108
Hounslow Ho. *BL1: Bolt 3F 38*
(off Kenton Cl.)
Hourigan Ho. WN7: Lei 2G 73
Houseley Av. OL9: Chad 8E 62
Houseman Cres. M20: Man 3E 106
Houseman Gro. WN6: Wig 1D 52
Housesteads SK14: Hat 8G 99
Housley Cl. WN3: Wig 7D 52
Houson St. OL8: O'ham 5D 8 (6K 63)
Houston Pk. M50: Sal 9M 77
Hove Cl. BL8: G'mount 4F 24
Hoveden St. M8: Man 6E 78
Hove Dr. M14: Man 1K 107
Hove St. BL3: Bolt 7D 38
Hove St. Nth. BL3: Bolt 6D 38
Hovey Cl. M8: Man 3E 78
Hoviley SK14: Hyde 6B 98
Hovingham St.
OL16: Roch 6G 8 (5F 28)
Hovington Gdns.
M19: Man 2K 107
Hovis Mill SK11: Macc 5J 131
Hovis St. M11: Man 1A 96
Howard Av. BL3: Bolt 8B 38
BL4: Kea 4N 57
M30: Ecc 7D 76
SK4: Stoc 2A 108
SK8: Chea H 6M 117
WA13: Lym 3C 112
Howard Cl. SK6: Rom 6L 109
SK13: Glos 7D 100
Howard Ct. OL6: A Lyne 7E 6 (7N 81)
WA15: Tim 9J 105
(off Bedford Dr.)
Howard Dr. WA15: Hale 6G 114
Howard Hill BL9: Bury 8N 41
Howardian Cl. OL8: O'ham 9J 63
Howard La. M34: Dent 5K 97
Howard Pl. OL16: Roch 6C 8 (5D 28)
SK13: Glos 8C 100
SK14: Hyde 7A 98
(off Rutherford Way)
Howard Rd. M22: Nor 7C 106
WA3: Cul 7J 89
Howard's WN5: Orr 4K 51
Howard's La. OL5: Mos 1H 83
WN5: Orr 4K 51
(not continuous)
Howards Mdw. SK13: Glos 9D 100
Howard Spring Wlk. *M8: Man 2E 78*
(off Absalom Dr.)
Howard St. BL1: Bolt 3G 38
M5: Sal 1N 93
M8: Man 6E 78
M26: Rad 9H 41
M32: Stre 7K 93
M34: Aud 3K 97
M34: Dent 4J 97
OL2: Shaw 5L 45
OL4: O'ham 3B 64
OL7: A Lyne 5B 6 (6L 81)
OL12: Roch 5D 28
SK1: Stoc 1L 9 (6D 108)
SK13: Glos 8E 100
SK15: Mill 6G 82
WN5: Wig 6N 51
Howard Way OL15: Lit 5N 15
Howarth Av. M28: Wors 3C 76
Howarth Cl. BL9: Bury 6M 41
M11: Man 9M 79
Howarth Ct. BL6: Hor 9G 21
SK2: Stoc 2F 118
HOWARTH CROSS 3F 28
Howarth Cross St. OL16: Roch 3F 28
Howarth Dr. M44: Irl 8G 91
Howarth Farm Rd. M43: Droy 5H 81
Howarth Farm Way OL12: Roch 2G 29
Howarth Grn. OL12: Roch 2H 29
Howarth Knowl OL12: Roch 9G 14
Howarth Sq. OL16: Roch 6F 8 (5E 28)
Howarth St. BL4: Farn 4L 57
BL5: W'ton 3H 55
M16: Old T 5B 94
OL15: Lit 8M 15
WN7: Lei 6K 73
Howbridge Cl. M28: Wors 2K 75
Howbro Dr. OL7: A Lyne 5J 81
Howbrook Wlk. *M15: Man 3E 94*
(off Brindle Pl.)
Howclough Cl. M28: Walk 9N 57
How Clough Dr. M28: Walk 9N 57
Howcroft Cl. BL1: Bolt 1J 7 (4F 38)
Howcroft St. BL3: Bolt 7E 38
Howden Cl. SK5: Stoc 7C 96
Howden Dr. WN3: Wig 7D 52
Howden Rd. M9: Man 6H 61
SK22: N Mil 6M 121
HOWE BRIDGE 1J 73
Howe Bri. Cl. M46: Ath 1J 73
Howe Bridge Crematorium
M46: Ath 9H 55
Howe Bridge Sports Cen. 1K 73
Howe Dr. BL0: Ram 3H 25
Howell Cft. Nth.
BL1: Bolt 2K 7 (5G 38)
Howell Cft. Sth. BL1: Bolt 3K 7 (5G 38)
Howells Av. M33: Sale 3H 105
Howell's Yd. BL1: Bolt 3K 7
Howe St. M7: Sal 3B 78
OL7: A Lyne 1K 97
SK10: Macc 3K 131
Howgill Cres. OL8: O'ham 8J 63
Howgill St. M11: Man 9B 80
How La. BL9: Bury 7L 25
How Lea Dr. BL9: Bury 7M 25
Howley Cl. M44: Irl 8J 91
Howsin Av. BL2: Bolt 9J 23
Howton Cl. M12: Man 5M 95
Howty Cl. SK9: Wilm 5J 123
Hoxton Cl. SK6: Bred 4L 109
Hoy Dr. M41: Urm 4D 92
Hoylake Cl. M40: Man 2B 80
WN7: Lei 8F 72
Hoylake Rd. M33: Sale 6M 105
SK3: Stoc 8M 107
Hoyland Cl. M12: Man 3L 95
Hoyle Av. OL8: O'ham 6J 63
Hoyles Ct. M26: Rad 8J 41
Hoyle's Ter. OL16: Miln 7J 29
Hoyle St. BL1: Bolt 9F 22
M12: Man 7N 5 (1H 95)
M24: Mid 5A 62
M26: Rad 2H 59
OL12: Whitw 3B 14
Hoyle St. Ind. Est. M12: Man 8N 5
Hoyle Wlk. *M13: Man 3H 95*
(off Glenbarry Cl.)
Hubert Worthington Ho.
SK9: A Edg 4F 126
(off George St.)
Hucclecote Av. M22: Wyth 5B 116
Hucklow Av. M23: Wyth 5N 115
Hucklow Bank *SK13: Gam 7N 99*
(off Grassmoor Cres.)
Hucklow Cl. *SK13: Gam 7N 99*
(off Grassmoor Cres.)
Hucklow Fold *SK13: Gam 7N 99*
(off Grassmoor Cres.)
Hucklow Lanes *SK13: Gam 7N 99*
(off Grassmoor Cres.)
Hudcar La. BL9: Bury 9N 25
Huddart Cl. M5: Sal 1A 94
Huddersfield Narrow Canal
Sculpture Trail 7H 65
Huddersfield Rd. OL1: O'ham 4M 63
OL3: Del 8J 47
OL3: Dens 2G 46
OL3: Dig 9L 47
OL4: Aus, Lees, O'ham, Scout
4M 63
OL5: Mos 1H 83
OL16: Miln 9M 29
SK15: C'ook 5H 83
SK15: Mill, Stal 8E 82
Hudson Cl. BL3: Bolt 9C 38
Hudson Ct. M9: Man 8H 61
Hudson Gro. WA3: Low 1A 88
Hudson Rd. BL3: Bolt 9C 38
SK14: Hyde 1B 110
Hudsons Pas. OL15: Lit 7N 15
Hudson St. OL9: Chad 1E 80
Hudsons Wlk. OL11: Roch 6N 27
Hudswell Cl. M45: Whitef 3L 59
Hughenden Ct. BL8: Tot 6F 24
Hughes Av. BL6: Hor 9C 20
Hughes Cl. BL9: Bury 1N 41
M35: Fail 2C 80
Hughes St. BL1: Bolt 2D 38
(Arnold St.)
BL1: Bolt 2E 38
(Thorpe St.)
M11: Man 1K 95
Hughes Way M30: Ecc 9A 76
Hugh Fold *OL4: Lees 6B 64*
(off Hartshead St.)
Hughley Cl. OL2: O'ham 8K 45
Hugh Lupus St. BL1: Bolt 8H 23
Hugh Oldham Dr. M7: Sal 4B 78
Hugh St. OL16: Roch 6E 8 (5E 28)
SK13: Glos 8D 100
Hughtrede St. OL16: Roch 1F 44
Hugo St. BL4: Farn 1J 57
M40: Man 3M 79
OL11: Roch 2B 44
Hulbert St. BL8: Bury 3J 41
M24: Mid 2N 61
Hullet Cl. WN6: App B 4J 33
Hulley Pl. *SK10: Macc 3K 131*
(off Hurdsfield Rd.)
Hulley Rd. SK10: Macc 1J 131
Hull Mill La. OL3: Del 7J 47
Hull Sq. M3: Sal 2B 4 (8C 78)
Hully St. SK15: Stal 8C 82
HULME 3E 94
Hulme Ct. M15: Man 9D 4
Hulme Dr. WA15: Tim 9J 105
Hulme Gro. WN7: Lei 4E 72
Hulme Hall M14: Man 5H 95
Hulme Hall Av. SK8: Chea H 7M 117
Hulme Hall Cl. SK8: Chea H 6M 117
Hulme Hall Cres. SK8: Chea H 7M 117
Hulme Hall La. M40: Man 6K 79
Hulme Hall Rd.
M15: Man 9B 4 (2C 94)
SK8: Chea H 5M 117
Hulme High St. M15: Man 4E 94
Hulme Mkt. Hall M15: Man 4E 94
Hulme Pl. M5: Sal 4A 4
Hulme Rd. BL2: Bolt 7M 23
M26: Rad 4C 58
M33: Sale 5K 105
M34: Dent 6F 96
SK4: Stoc 2B 108
WN7: Lei 4E 72
Hulme's La. M34: Dent 9J 97
Hulme Sq. SK11: Macc 7H 131
Hulmes Rd. M35: Fail 6D 80
M40: Man 6C 80
(not continuous)
Hulmes Ter. BL2: Ain 4C 40
Hulme St. BL1: Bolt 1L 7 (4G 39)
BL8: Bury 5G 7 (1K 41)
M1: Man 9G 4 (2E 94)
M5: Sal 4A 4 (9B 78)
M15: Man 9E 4 (2D 94)
(Jackson Cres.)
M15: Man 9G 4 (2E 94)
(Newcastle St.)
OL6: A Lyne 6A 82
OL8: O'ham 7J 63
SK1: Stoc 9F 108
Hulmeswood Ter. *M34: Dent 1L 109*
(off Tennyson Av.)
Hulme Wlk. *M15: Man 3D 94*
(off Stretford Rd.)
Hulton Av. M28: Walk 8H 57
Hulton Cl. BL3: Bolt 8B 38
Hulton District Cen. M28: Walk 7H 57
Hulton Dr. BL3: Bolt 9B 38
Hulton La. BL3: Bolt 1B 56
HULTON LANE ENDS 3B 56
Hulton Pk. 4N 55
Hulton St. M5: Sal 2N 93
M16: Whall R 5D 94
M34: Dent 5J 97
M35: Fail 3B 80
Hulton Vale BL3: Bolt 1A 56
Humber Dr. BL9: Bury 6M 25
Humber Pl. WN5: Wig 4N 51
Humber Rd. M29: Ast 3D 74
OL16: Miln 7L 29
Humberstone Av.
M15: Man 9E 4 (3E 94)
Humber St. M8: Man 3G 78
M50: Sal 9K 77
Hume St. M19: Man 9N 95
OL16: Roch 7E 28
Humphrey Booth Gdns. M6: Sal 7L 77
Humphrey Cres. M41: Urm 7G 92
Humphrey La. M41: Urm 7G 92
Humphrey Pk. M41: Urm 7G 92
Humphrey Park Station (Rail) 6G 93
Humphrey Rd. M16: Old T 4A 94
SK7: Bram 4C 118
Humphrey St. M8: Man 2E 78
WN2: I Mak 4K 53
Humphries Ct. M40: Man 6H 79
Huncoat Av. SK4: Stoc 3B 108
Huncote Dr. *M9: Man 1K 79*
(off Hemsley St. Sth.)
Hungerford Wlk. *M23: Wyth 9K 105*
(off Butcher La.)
HUNGER HILL
BL3 1M 55
WN6 1K 33
Hunger Hill OL12: W'le 8H 15
Hunger Hill Av. BL3: Bolt 1N 55
Hunger Hill La. OL12: Roch 2L 27
Hunmanby Av. M15: Man 9F 4 (2E 94)
Hunstanton Dr. BL8: Bury 8K 25
Hunston Rd. M33: Sale 5F 104
Hunt Av. OL7: A Lyne 5M 81
Hunter Dr. M26: Rad 8G 41
Hunter Rd. WN5: Wig 2B 52
Hunters Chase WN5: Bil 1J 69
Hunters Cl. SK6: Bred 5K 109
SK9: Wilm 5L 123
Hunters Ct. SK15: Stal 2G 99
SK16: Duk 2C 98
Hunters Grn. BL0: Ram 2F 24
HUNTERS HILL 6M 47
Hunters Hill BL9: Bury 8A 42
Hunters Hill La. OL3: Dig 6L 47
Hunters La. OL1: O'ham 2E 8 (4K 63)
OL16: Roch 6C 8 (5D 28)
SK13: Glos 9B 100
Hunters Lodge *SK9: Wilm 5L 123*
(off Hunters Cl.)
Hunters M. M33: Sale 3G 104
SK9: Wilm 7H 123
Hunters Pool La. SK10: P'bury 5A 128
Hunterston Av. M30: Ecc 8G 76
Hunters Vw. SK9: Hand 3H 123
Hunt Fold BL8: G'mount 4F 24
Hunt Fold Dr. BL8: G'mount 4F 24
Huntingdon Av. OL9: Chad 6F 62
Huntingdon Cres. SK5: Stoc 3H 109
Huntingdon Wlk. *BL1: Bolt 2F 38*
(off Draycott St.)
Huntingdon Way M34: Dent 8K 97
Huntington Av. M20: Man 1F 106
Hunt La. OL9: Chad 3D 62
Huntley Ho. BL9: Bury 9A 26
Huntley Mt. Rd. BL9: Bury 9A 26
Huntley Rd. M8: Man 9D 60
SK3: Stoc 9N 107
Huntley St. BL9: Bury 1A 42
Huntley Way OL10: H'ood 3D 42
Huntly Chase SK9: Wilm 7H 123
Hunt Rd. SK14: Hyde 4D 98
WA11: Hay 3B 86
Huntroyde Av. BL2: Bolt 3K 39
Hunt's Bank BL5: W'ton 5H 55
M3: Man 2G 5 (8E 78)
Huntsham Cl. WA14: Alt 1B 114
Huntsman Dr. M44: Irl 1G 102
Huntsman Rd. M9: Man 2L 79
Huntspill Rd. WA14: W Tim 8D 104
Hunts Rd. M6: Sal 5K 77
Hunt St. M9: Man 1J 79
M46: Ath 8M 55
WN1: Wig 9N 9 (4H 53)
Hurdlow Av. M7: Sal 3N 77
Hurdlow Grn. *SK13: Gam 8N 99*
(off Brassington Cres.)
Hurdlow Lea *SK13: Gam 8N 99*
(off Brassington Cres.)
Hurdlow M. SK13: Gam 8N 99
Hurdlow Wlk. M9: Man 3J 79
Hurdlow Way *SK13: Gam 8N 99*
(off Brassington Cres.)
HURDSFIELD 3J 131
Hurdsfield Grn. *SK10: Macc 2J 131*
(off Brocklehurst Av.)
Hurdsfield Ind. Est.
SK10: Macc 1J 131
(Charter Way)
SK10: Macc 2H 131
(Melville Rd.)
Hurdsfield Rd. SK2: Stoc 3G 119
SK10: Macc 3J 131
Hurford Av. M18: Man 3B 96
Hurlbote Cl. SK9: Hand 1J 123
Hurley Dr. SK8: Chea H 5K 117
Hurlston Av. WN8: Skel 3A 50
Hurlston Rd. BL3: Bolt 1E 56
HURST 5A 82
Hurst Av. M33: Sale 5C 104
SK8: Chea H 9A 118
Hurstbank Av. M19: Man 4J 107
Hurst Bank Rd. OL6: A Lyne 6B 82
Hurstbourne Av. M11: Man 7N 79
HURST BROOK 6N 81
Hurstbrook PR7: Cop 4C 18
Hurst Brook Cl. OL6: A Lyne 6N 81
Hurstbrook Cl. SK13: Glos 8H 101
Hurstbrook Dr. M32: Stre 7F 92
Hurst Cl. BL5: O Hul 4A 56
SK13: Glos 8H 101
Hurst Ct. M23: Wyth 3M 115
OL6: A Lyne 5A 82
Hurst Cres. SK13: Glos 9G 101
Hurst Cross OL6: A Lyne 5A 82
HURSTEAD 1H 29
Hurstead Cl. M8: Man 4F 78
Hurstead Cotts. OL12: Roch 1H 29
Hurstead Grn. OL12: Roch 1H 29
Hurstead M. *OL12: Roch 1H 29*
(off Braddocks Cl.)
Hursted Rd. OL16: Miln 7K 29
Hurstfield Ind. Est. SK5: Stoc 2C 108
Hurstfield Rd. M28: Wors 2J 75
Hurst Fold M44: Irl 6J 91
Hurstfold Av. M19: Man 5J 107
Hurst Grn. Cl. BL8: Bury 4F 40
Hurst Gro. OL6: A Lyne 5B 82
Hurst Hall Dr. OL6: A Lyne 5B 82
Hursthead Rd.
SK8: Chea H 8N 117
Hurstheads La. SK6: Rom 7M 109
Hursthead Wlk. M13: Man 9L 5
Hurst Hill Cres. OL6: A Lyne 6A 82
HURST KNOLL 5N 81
Hurst La. SK10: Boll 5L 129
WA3: G'ury 3K 89
Hurst Lea Ct. SK9: A Edg 3F 126
Hurst Lea Rd. SK22: N Mil 8L 121
Hurst Mdw. OL6: A Lyne 5A 82
OL16: Roch 2F 44
Hurstmead Ter. *M20: Man 6G 106*
(off South Rd.)
Hurst Mill La. WA3: G'ury 1L 89
Hurst Mills Ind. Est.
SK13: Glos 9H 101
HURST NOOK 4B 82
Hurst Rd. SK13: Glos 8H 101
Hurst St. BL3: Bolt 9D 38
BL9: Bury 8N 7 (2N 41)
(not continuous)
M28: Walk 5K 57
OL9: O'ham 2A 8 (4H 63)
OL11: Roch 8E 28
(not continuous)
SK5: Stoc 1C 108
WN2: Hin 5M 53
WN7: Lei 8K 73
Hurstvale Av. SK8: H Grn 6G 116
Hurstville Rd. M21: Cho H 2A 106
Hurst Wlk. M22: Wyth 5N 115
Hurstway Dr. M9: Man 8K 61
Hurstwood BL1: Bolt 8E 22
OL6: A Lyne 4C 82
Hurstwood Cl. OL8: O'ham 7N 63
Hurstwood Ct. BL3: Bolt 8J 39
Hurstwood Gro. SK2: Stoc 1K 119
Huskisson Way WA12: N Wil 5E 86
Hus St. M43: Droy 1D 96
Husteads OL3: Dob 2H 65
Husteads La. OL3: Dob 2H 65
Hutchins La. OL4: O'ham 2A 64
Hutchinson Rd. OL11: Roch 4J 27
Hutchinson St. M26: Rad 8J 41
OL11: Roch 7A 28
Hutchinson Way M26: Rad 1F 58
Hut La. PR6: H Char 1L 19
Hutton Av. M28: Wors 4G 74
OL6: A Lyne 8B 82
Hutton Cl. WA3: Cul 4G 88
Hutton Ho. OL11: Roch 9C 8
Hutton Lodge *M20: Man 1H 107*
(off Wilmslow Rd.)
Hutton St. WN1: Stan 1D 34
Hutton Wlk. *M13: Man 3H 95*
(off Glenbarry Cl.)
Huxley Av. M8: Man 4F 78
Huxley Cl. SK7: Bram 8C 118
SK10: Macc 2F 130
Huxley Dr. SK7: Bram 8C 118
Huxley Pl. WN3: Wig 6D 52
Huxley St. BL1: Bolt 2D 38
OL4: O'ham 6N 63
WA14: B'ath 9D 104
Huxton Grn. SK7: H Gro 5E 118
Huyton Rd. PR7: Adl 7K 19
(not continuous)
Huyton Ter. PR6: Adl 6L 19
Hyacinth Cl. SK3: Stoc 2B 118
WA11: Hay 3C 86
Hyacinth Wlk. *M31: Part 6F 102*
(off Redbrook Rd.)
Hyatt Cres. WN6: Stan 1N 33
HYDE 7A 98
Hydebank SK6: Rom 7A 110
Hyde Bank Ct. SK22: N Mil 8M 121
Hyde Bank Mill SK22: N Mil 7M 121
Hyde Bank Rd. SK22: N Mil 7M 121
Hyde Central Station (Rail) 7N 97
Hyde Cl. WN3: Wig 6D 52
Hyde Dr. M28: Walk 9K 57
Hyde Festival Theatre 7A 98
Hyde Fold Cl. M19: Man 2L 107
Hyde Gro. M13: Man 4H 95
M28: Walk 9K 57
M33: Sale 4H 105
Hyde Ho. SK4: Stoc 3A 108
Hyde Leisure Pool 7C 98
Hyde North Station (Rail) 4N 97
Hyde Pk. Pl. *OL16: Roch 6G 28*
(off Belfield La.)
Hyde Pl. M13: Man 4H 95
Hyde Point SK14: Hyde 5N 97
Hyde Rd. M12: Man 9N 5 (2H 95)
M18: Man 2H 95
M24: Mid 5C 62
M28: Walk 9K 57
M34: Dent 5K 97
SK6: Wood 3L 109
SK14: Mot 6J 99
Hyde's Cross M4: Man 2G 5
Hyde Sq. M24: Mid 2K 61
Hydes Ter. SK15: Stal 8E 82
Hyde St. BL3: Bolt 9D 38
M43: Droy 6G 81
SK16: Duk 1A 98
Hyde United FC 7C 98
Hyde Way SK14: Mot 6J 99
Hydon Brook Wlk. OL11: Roch 9A 28
Hydra Cl. M7: Sal 1A 4 (7B 78)
Hydrangea Cl. BL5: W'ton 5H 55
M33: Sale 3C 104
Hyldavale Av. SK8: Gat 1G 116
Hylton Dr. OL7: A Lyne 5K 81
SK8: Chea H 6A 118
Hyman Goldstone Wlk.
M8: Man 3E 78
(off Carstairs Cl.)
Hyndelle Lodge WN2: Hin 5N 53
Hyndman Ct. *M5: Sal 8K 77*
(off Sheader Dr.)
Hypatia St. BL2: Bolt 4J 39
Hythe Cl. M14: Man 6H 95
Hythe Rd. SK3: Stoc 8N 107
Hythe St. BL3: Bolt 8B 38
Hythe Wlk. OL9: Chad 5F 62

I

Ian Frazer Ct. OL11: Roch 9D 28
Ibberton Wlk. *M9: Man 1L 79*
(off Carnaby St.)
Ibsley OL12: Roch 6B 8 (5C 28)
Ice Ho. Cl. M28: Walk 8G 57
Iceland St. M6: Sal 8M 77
Idonia St. BL1: Bolt 1E 38
Ifco Cen. M14: Man 6H 95
Ilex Gro. M7: Sal 4C 78
Ilford St. M11: Man 8N 79
Ilford Way WA16: Mob 4N 133
Ilfracombe Rd. SK2: Stoc 8H 109
Ilfracombe St. M40: Man 4B 80
Ilkeston Dr. WN2: Asp 9B 36

Ilkeston Wlk. M34: Dent 9L 97
M40: Man 4M 79
(off Halliford Rd.)
Ilkley Cl. BL2: Bolt 5K 39
OL9: Chad 5F 62
Ilkley Cres. SK5: Stoc 9C 96
Ilkley Dr. M41: Urm 5A 92
Ilkley St. M40: Man 1M 79
Ilk St. M11: Man 8N 79
Illingworth Av. SK15: Stal 9F 82
Illona Dr. M7: Sal 2N 77
Ilminster OL11: Roch 9B 8 (7C 28)
Ilminster Wlk. *M9: Man 6K 61*
(off Crossmead Dr.)
Ilthorpe Wlk. M40: Man 4M 79
IMAX Cinema
Manchester 2H 5
(within The Printworks)
Imex Bus. Pk. M13: Man 6L 95
Imogen Ct. M5: Sal 7A 4 (1B 94)
Imperial Dr. WN7: Lei 4M 73
Imperial Point M50: Sal 2M 93
Imperial Ter. *M33: Sale 2G 105*
(off Woodfield Gro.)
Imperial War Mus. North 2L 93
Imperial Way M9: Man 9H 61
Ina Av. BL1: Bolt 3A 38
Ince Cl. M20: Man 1G 106
SK4: Stoc 5C 108
Ince Grn. La. WN2: I Mak 5H 53
WN3: I Mak 5H 53
Ince Hall Av. WN2: I Mak 3J 53
INCE-IN-MAKERFIELD 5H 53
Ince Station (Rail) 5H 53
Ince St. SK4: Stoc 5C 108
Ince Wlk. WN1: Wig 7J 9
Inchcape Dr. M9: Man 7G 60
Inchfield Cl. OL11: Roch 5K 27
Inchfield Rd. M40: Man 1M 79
Inchley Rd. M13: Man 9K 5 (2G 94)
Inchwood M. OL4: O'ham 8B 46
Incline Rd. OL8: O'ham 9F 62
Independent Ho. SK8: Chea 4H 117
Independent St. BL3: Lit L 9A 40
India Ho. M1: Man 7H 5 (1F 94)
India St. BL9: Sum 2J 25
Indigo St. M6: Sal 5M 77
Indigo Wlk. M6: Sal 5M 77
Indus Pl. M7: Sal 6B 78
Industrial Est., The *BL1: Bolt 2E 38*
(off Raphael St.)
Industrial St. BL0: Ram 5J 11
BL5: W'ton 4H 55
Industry Rd. OL12: Roch 4D 28
Industry St. OL11: Roch 4K 27
OL12: Whitw 4B 14
OL15: Lit 9M 15
Infant St. M25: Pres 7B 60
Infirmary St. BL1: Bolt 3L 7 (5G 39)
Ingersley Ct. SK10: Boll 5M 129
Ingersley Rd. SK10: Boll 5M 129
INGERSLEY VALE 6N 129
Ingersley Va. SK10: Boll 5M 129
Ingham Av. WA12: N Wil 8F 86
Ingham Rd. WA14: W Tim 8D 104
Inghams La. OL15: Lit 9M 15
Ingham's Rd. WA3: Cro 8C 88
Ingham St. BL9: Bury 9N 7 (3N 41)
M40: Man 6C 80
OL1: O'ham 2F 8 (4L 63)
WN7: Lei 2G 72
Inghamwood Cl. M7: Sal 3E 78
Ingleby Av. M9: Man 7L 61
Ingleby Cl. BL5: W'ton 1H 55
OL2: Shaw 4L 45
WN6: Stan 2A 34
Ingleby Ct. M32: Stre 8L 93
Ingleby Way OL2: Shaw 4L 45
Ingledene Av. M7: Sal 1D 78
Ingledene Ct. M7: Sal 1D 78
Ingledene Gro. BL1: Bolt 2B 38
Ingle Dr. SK2: Stoc 9G 109
Inglefield OL11: Roch 4L 27
Inglehead Cl. M34: Dent 7L 97
Inglemoss Dr. WA11: R'ford 9A 68
Ingle Nook Cl. M31: C'ton 2N 103
Inglenook Ct. WN7: Lei 2J 73
Ingle Rd. SK8: Chea 1M 117
Ingles Fold M28: Wors 2J 75
Inglesham Cl. M23: Wyth 1A 116
WN7: Lei 9G 72
Inglestone Cl. WA12: N Wil 5E 86
Ingleton Av. M8: Man 9G 60
Ingleton Cl. BL2: Bolt 9L 23
OL2: O'ham 7H 45
SK8: Chea 1H 117
Ingleton Dr. WA11: St H 9F 68
Ingleton M. BL8: Bury 9H 25
Ingleton Rd. SK3: Stoc 9A 108
Inglewhite Av. WN1: Wig 1F 52
Inglewhite Cl. BL9: Bury 5K 41
Inglewhite Cres. WN1: Wig 1F 52
Inglewhite Pl. WN1: Wig 1F 52
Inglewood WA14: Alt 5A 6 (4B 114)
Inglewood Av. WN1: Wig 9N 9 (4H 53)
Inglewood Cl. BL9: Bury 9B 26
M31: Part 4F 102
OL7: A Lyne 5K 81
Inglewood Ct. WN5: Wig 6A 52
Inglewood Hollow SK15: Stal 1F 98
Inglewood Rd. OL9: Chad 2C 62
WA11: R'ford 9A 68
Inglewood Wlk. *M13: Man 3H 95*
(off Brunswick St.)
Inglis St. OL15: Lit 8M 15
Ingoe Cl. OL10: H'ood 1L 43
Ingoldsby Av. M13: Man 5J 95
Ingram Dr. SK4: Stoc 5K 107
Ingram St. WN2: P Bri 8K 53
WN6: Wig 2C 52
Ings Av. OL12: Roch 3N 27
Ings La. OL12: Roch 3N 27
Inkerman St. M40: Man 4J 79
OL12: Roch 4D 28
(off Industry Rd.)
SK14: Hyde 5A 98
Inman St. BL9: Bury 4L 41
M34: Dent 6K 97
Innes St. M12: Man 6N 95
Innis Av. M40: Man 5A 80
Institute of Gymnastics 4A 96
Institute St. BL1: Bolt 3L 7 (5H 39)
Instow Cl. OL9: Chad 2D 62
Intake Head HD7: Mars 1F 48
Intake La. OL3: G'fld 8J 65
International App. M90: Man A 8B 116
Invar Rd. M27: Swin 1D 76
Inverbeg Dr. BL2: Bolt 5A 40
Invergarry Wlk. *M11: Man 9A 80*
(off Bob Massey Cl.)
Inverlael Av. BL1: Bolt 4C 38
Inverness Av. M9: Man 7M 61
Inverness Cl. WN2: Asp 7N 35
Inverness Rd. SK16: Duk 2N 97
Inver Wlk. M40: Man 9B 62
Inward Dr. WN6: She 7L 33
Inwood Wlk. *M8: Man 4H 79*
(off Smedley Rd.)
Inworth Cl. BL5: W'ton 5H 55
Inworth Wlk. *M8: Man 3E 78*
(off Highshore Dr.)
Iona Pl. BL2: Bolt 2K 39
Iona Way M41: Urm 4D 92
Ionian Gdns. M7: Sal 5B 78
Ipswich St. OL11: Roch 8D 28
Ipswich Wlk. *M12: Man 4K 95*
(off Chipstead Av.)
M34: Dent 8L 97
(off Lancaster Rd.)
Iqbal Cl. M12: Man 4M 95
Irby Wlk. SK8: Chea 3M 117
Ireby Cl. M24: Mid 1H 61
Iredale Cres. WN6: Stan 5C 34
Iredine St. M11: Man 5K 81
Irene Av. SK14: Hyde 5B 98
Iris Av. BL4: Farn 2H 57
BL4: Kea 6N 57
(not continuous)
M11: Man 1B 96
Iris St. BL0: Ram 8H 11
OL8: O'ham 9K 63
Iris Wlk. *M31: Part 6G 102*
(off Cross La. W.)
Irkdale St. M8: Man 4H 79
Irk St. M4: Man 1J 5 (7F 78)
Irk Va. Dr. OL1: Chad 2C 62
Irk Way M45: Whitef 1A 60
IRLAM 7J 91
Irlam Av. M30: Ecc 9D 76
Irlam Ind. Est. M44: Irl 1F 102
Irlam Locks Circ. M44: Irl 8J 91
Irlam Rd. M33: Sale 3J 105
M41: Urm 8J 91
IRLAMS O'TH' HEIGHT 4J 77
Irlam Sq. M6: Sal 5K 77
Irlam Station (Rail) 1F 102
Irlam St. BL1: Bolt 1F 38
M40: Man 5K 79
Irlam Wharf Rd. M44: Irl 1H 103
Irmass Ind. Est. M17: T Pk 3K 93
Irma St. BL1: Bolt 1G 38
Ironmonger La. WN3: Wig 9J 9 (4F 52)
Iron St. BL6: Hor 2E 36
M40: Man 7K 79
Irvin Dr. M22: Wyth 7F 116
Irvine Av. M28: Wors 4H 75
Irvine St. WN7: Lei 4H 73
Irving Cl. SK2: Stoc 4E 118
Irving Ho. *BL1: Bolt 2F 38*
(off Irving St.)
Irving St. BL1: Bolt 2F 38
OL8: O'ham 9F 62
Irvin St. M40: Man 4A 80
Irwell Av. M30: Ecc 9F 76
M38: Lit H 7J 57
Irwell Cl. M26: Rad 1H 59
Irwell Gro. M30: Ecc 9F 76
Irwell Ho. M15: Man 8C 4
M44: Irl 8J 91
Irwell Pk. Way M30: Ecc 9F 76
Irwell Pl. M5: Sal 8B 78
M26: Rad 3B 58
M30: Ecc 9F 76
WN5: Wig 5N 51
Irwell Ri. SK10: Boll 5K 129
Irwell Rd. WN5: Orr 4K 51
Irwell St. BL0: Ram 7J 11
BL9: Bury 8J 7 (2L 41)
M3: Sal 4D 4 (9D 78)
M6: Sal 4N 77
M8: Man 6D 78
M26: Rad 3A 58
(Ford St.)
M26: Rad 1H 59
(St John's St.)
IRWELL VALE 1J 11
Irwell Va. Rd. BB4: Has 1J 11
Irwell Vale Station
East Lancashire Railway 1J 11
Irwell Wlk. OL8: O'ham 8G 62
Irwin Dr. SK9: Hand 1H 123
Irwin Pl. SK8: Chea H 4L 117
Irwin Rd. WA14: B'ath 8D 104
Irwin St. M34: Dent 6J 97
Isaac Cl. M5: Sal 1N 93
Isaac St. BL1: Bolt 4D 38
Isaac Way M4: Man 9J 79
Isabella Cl. M16: Old T 5B 94
Isabella Sq. WN1: Wig 7N 9 (3H 53)
Isabella St. OL12: Roch 3D 28
Isabel Wlk. BL3: Bolt 7E 38
Isaiah St. OL8: O'ham 7K 63
Isa St. BL0: Ram 1G 25
Isca St. M11: Man 9L 79
Isel Wlk. M24: Mid 1J 61
Isherwood Cl. OL10: H'ood 3J 43
Isherwood Dr. SK6: Mar 1A 120
Isherwood Rd. M31: C'ton 2N 103
Isherwood St. OL10: H'ood 3K 43
OL11: Roch 7E 28
WN7: Lei 2G 72
Isis Cl. M7: Sal 2M 77
Island Row WN2: I Mak 4L 53
Islington Rd. SK2: Stoc 3G 118
Islington St. M3: Sal 3C 4 (9C 78)
Islington Way M3: Sal 4B 4 (9C 78)
Isobel Baillie Lodge *M16: Old T 4C 94*
(off Whitchurch Dr.)
Isobel Cl. *M16: Whall R 5E 94*
(off Crosshill St.)
M30: Ecc 9B 76
Ivanhoe Av. WA3: Low 9N 71
Ivanhoe Ct. BL3: Bolt 1K 57
Ivanhoe St. BL3: Bolt 1K 57
OL1: O'ham 2N 63
Iveagh Ct. OL16: Roch 7F 28
Iver Ho. *M5: Sal 9M 77*
(off Amersham St.)
Ivor St. OL11: Roch 1N 43
Ivy Av. WA12: N Wil 7F 86
Ivy Bank OL5: Mos 1H 83
OL12: Whitw 3B 14
Ivy Bank Cl. BL1: Bolt 8F 22
Ivy Bank Rd. BL1: Bolt 8F 22
Ivybridge Cl. M13: Man 4J 95
Ivybridge Ho. BL3: Bolt 7D 38
Ivy Cl. M43: Droy 7D 80
OL2: Shaw 5M 45
Ivy Cotts. M34: Dent 1L 109
OL12: Roch 4B 28
Ivy Ct. M21: Cho H 1A 106
Ivycroft SK13: Had 5A 100
Ivydale Dr. WN7: Lei 5L 73
Ivy Dr. M24: Mid 4L 61
Ivy Farm Gdns. WA3: Cul 5F 88
Ivy Gdns. M7: Sal 2E 78
Ivy Graham Cl. M40: Man 4N 79
Ivygreen Dr. OL4: Spri 5C 64
Ivygreen Rd. M21: Cho H 9M 93
Ivy Gro. BL4: Farn 3J 57
BL4: Kea 4N 57
M38: Lit H 7G 56
Ivy Ho. SK9: A Edg 6G 126
SK11: Macc 5E 130
Ivy Ho. Rd. WA3: Low 9N 71
Ivy La. SK11: Macc 6E 130
Ivy Leaf Sq. M7: Sal 4D 78
Ivylea Rd. M19: Man 4K 107
Ivy Lodge Cl. SK15: Mill 6H 83
Ivymeade Cl. SK11: Macc 5D 130
Ivy Meade Rd. SK11: Macc 6D 130
Ivynook Cl. WA14: W Tim 7B 104
Ivy Rd. BL1: Bolt 3D 38
BL5: W'ton 4H 55
BL8: Bury 2H 41
SK11: Macc 6D 130
SK12: Poy 3J 125
WA3: Gol 1L 87
Ivy St. BL0: Ram 2F 24
BL3: Bolt 8D 38
M30: Ecc 9D 76
M40: Man 2M 79
WN1: Wig 8H 9 (3E 52)
WN4: A Mak 7E 70
Ivy Ter. OL15: Lit 4A 16
WN6: Stan 1N 33
Ivy Wlk. M31: Part 5E 102

J

J2 Business Pk. BL9: Bury 2B 42
Jack Brady Cl. M23: Wyth 3L 115
Jackdaw Rd. BL8: G'mount 3F 24
Jackie Brown Wlk. *M40: Man 5J 79*
(off Thornton St. Nth.)
Jackies La. WA13: Lym 3A 112
Jack La. M41: Urm 9K 91
(Dunster Dr.)
M41: Urm 7E 92
(Falcon Av.)
M43: Droy 8F 80
(not continuous)
Jack Lane Nature Reserve 9K 91
Jack McCann Ct. *OL16: Roch 5E 28*
(off Trafalgar St.)
Jackman Av. OL10: H'ood 5J 43
Jacks La. BL5: W'ton 4C 54
Jackson Av. SK16: Duk 1A 98
WA3: Cul 6G 88
Jackson Cl. BL8: Bury 1H 41
OL8: O'ham 6J 63
WA15: Tim 9J 105
Jackson Ct. M21: Cho H 8M 93
M41: Urm 6A 92
Jackson Cres. M15: Man 9D 4 (3D 94)
Jackson Gdns. M34: Dent 7H 97
Jackson La. SK10: Boll 6M 129
Jackson M. OL4: O'ham 2A 64
Jackson Pit OL1: O'ham 3C 8 (5J 63)
Jacksons' Brickworks
Local Nature Reserve 9A 120
Jacksons Bldgs. *SK13: Glos 8F 100*
(off Victoria St.)
Jacksons Cl. SK10: Boll 6M 129
Jacksons Edge Rd. SK6: Dis 8D 120
SK12: Dis 8D 120
Jacksons La. SK7: H Gro 6E 118
Jacksons Pl. OL16: Roch 6G 8 (5F 28)
Jackson's Row M2: Man 5F 4 (9E 78)
Jackson St. BL3: Bolt 7E 38
BL4: Farn 3L 57
BL4: Kea 4N 57
M24: Mid 2N 61
M26: Rad 1H 59
M28: Walk 7K 57
M32: Stre 7J 93
M33: Sale 4K 105
M35: Fail 4B 80
M45: Whitef 4M 59
OL4: O'ham 4M 63
OL4: Spri 5C 64
OL6: A Lyne 5D 6
OL12: W'le 8G 15
OL16: Roch 7F 28
SK8: Chea 1K 117
SK11: Macc 6H 131
SK13: Had 4E 100
Jackson St. SK14: Hyde 7A 98
SK14: Mot 6K 99
WN2: I Mak 4K 53
Jack St. BL2: Bolt 3K 39
Jack Taylor Ct. OL12: Roch 4F 28
Jacob Bright M. OL12: Roch 3D 28
Jacob Cl. WN5: Bil 9H 51
Jacobite Cl. M7: Sal 1B 78
Jacobsen Av. SK14: Hyde 5C 98
Jacob's Ladder *OL5: Mos 1F 82*
(off Hanover St.)
Jacob St. WN2: Hin 5N 53
Jaffrey St. WN7: Lei 5G 73
James Andrew St. M24: Mid 2N 61
James Bentley Wlk. *M40: Man 5A 80*
(off Lastingham St.)
James Brindley Basin
M1: Man 5M 5 (9H 79)
James Butterworth Ct.
OL16: Roch 7F 28
(off James Butterworth St.)
James Butterworth St.
OL16: Roch 7F 28
James Cl. SK16: Duk 1B 98
WN3: Wig 4F 52
James Corbett Rd. M50: Sal 9J 77
James Ct. *M18: Man 4B 96*
(off Wellington St.)
James Dr. SK14: Hyde 7B 98
James Henry Av. M5: Sal 1A 94
James Hill St. OL15: Lit 9M 15
James Leech St.
SK3: Stoc 4K 9 (8C 108)
James Leigh St. M1: Man 7H 5
James Nasmyth Way M30: Ecc 8C 76
Jameson Cl. M8: Man 5D 78
Jameson St. OL11: Roch 2N 43
James Pl. PR7: Cop 5A 18
SK11: Macc 4G 131
WN6: Stan 2A 34
James Rd. OL2: Shaw 4M 45
WA11: Hay 2C 86
James Sq. WN6: Stan 2A 34
James St. BL3: Lit L 9B 40
BL4: Kea 3N 57
BL5: W'ton 1G 54
BL6: Hor 1B 36
BL7: Eger 2E 22
BL9: Bury 9N 7 (3N 41)
M3: Sal 4B 4 (9C 78)
M25: Pres 6N 59
(not continuous)
M26: Rad 2G 59
M29: Tyld 2A 74
M33: Sale 4K 105
M34: Aud 1J 97
M34: Dent 5L 97
M35: Fail 2E 80
M40: Man 7J 79
M43: Droy 8F 80
M46: Ath 1N 73
OL2: O'ham 7L 45
OL4: O'ham 2A 64
OL10: H'ood 1J 43
OL12: Roch 5E 28
(Flannel St.)
OL12: Roch 1G 28
(Wardle Rd.)
OL12: Whitw 4B 14
OL15: Lit 1J 29
SK3: Stoc 9C 108
SK6: Bred 3L 109
SK11: Macc 5H 131
(not continuous)
SK13: Glos 9E 100
SK15: Stal 1B 98
WN2: Bam 3H 71
WN3: I Mak 5G 53
James St. Nth. M26: Rad 1H 59
James St. Sth. OL9: Chad 4E 62
Jameston Ri. *BL6: Hor 9D 20*
(off Wright St.)
Jammy La. OL9: Chad 5G 62
Jane Barter Ho. *BL4: Farn 3L 57*
(off Hesketh Wlk.)
Jane St. OL9: Chad 5F 62
OL12: Roch 5C 28
Japan St. M7: Sal 2E 78
Jardine Way OL9: Chad 7D 62
Jarman Rd. SK11: Sut E 8K 131
Jarvis St. OL4: O'ham 5L 63
OL12: Roch 4D 28
Jasmine Av. M43: Droy 8G 80
SK10: Macc 4C 130
Jasmine Cl. M23: Wyth 7L 105
Jasmine Ct. BL3: Bolt 9F 38
Jasmine Rd. WN5: Wig 4A 52
Jasmine Wlk. *M31: Part 6G 102*
(off Erskine Wlk.)
Jauncey St. BL3: Bolt 7D 38
Jaxons Ct. WN1: Wig 7J 9
Jayton Av. M20: Man 8G 107
Jean Av. WN7: Lei 8G 72
Jean Cl. M19: Man 7M 95
Jedburgh Av. BL1: Bolt 4C 38
Jefferson Pl. M4: Man 8J 79
Jefferson Way OL12: Roch 2D 28
Jeffreys Dr. SK16: Duk 1A 98
Jeffrey St. WN2: I Mak 3K 53
Jeffrey Wlk. *OL10: H'ood 2F 42*
(off Gaskill St.)
Jehlum Cl. M8: Man 3G 79
Jellicoe Av. M44: Cad 2F 102
Jenkin Hall OL1: Chad 1D 62
Jenkinson St. M15: Man 9J 5 (3F 94)
WN2: Hin 5N 53
Jenkyn Wlk. *M11: Man 9L 79*
(off Newcombe Cl.)
Jennaby Wlk. BL1: Bolt 2F 38
Jennet Hey WN4: A Mak 4C 70
Jennet's La. WA3: G'ury 9L 73
Jennings Av. M5: Sal 1N 93
Jennings Cl. SK14: Hyde 4E 98
Jennings Pk. Av. WN2: Abr 3M 71
Jennings St. SK3: Stoc 9B 108
Jennison Cl. M18: Man 3N 95
Jenny Beck Gro. *BL3: Bolt 8F 38*
(off Aldsworth Dr.)
JENNY GREEN 7H 91
Jenny La. SK7: W'ford 3C 124
Jenny Lind Cl. BL3: Bolt 1K 57
Jenny St. OL8: O'ham 9G 62
Jepheys Pl. OL12: Roch 4D 28
Jepheys St. OL12: Roch 4D 28
Jepson St. SK2: Stoc 1E 118
JERICHO 9D 26
Jericho Rd. BL9: Bury 9D 26
Jermyn St. OL12: Roch 5E 28
Jerrold St. OL15: Lit 9M 15
Jersey Cl. M19: Man 1L 107
Jersey Rd. SK5: Stoc 4D 108
Jersey St. M4: Man 3L 5 (8G 79)
OL6: A Lyne 5D 6 (7M 81)
Jerusalem Pl. M2: Man 6F 4
Jesmond Av. M25: Pres 9A 60
Jesmond Dr. BL8: Bury 8J 25
Jesmond Gro. SK8: Chea H 7N 117
Jesmond Rd. BL1: Bolt 9C 22
Jesmond Wlk. *M9: Man 6J 61*
(off Claygate Dr.)
Jessamine Av. M7: Sal 6C 78
Jessel Cl. M13: Man 3H 95
Jessica Way WN7: Lei 6D 72
Jessie St. BL3: Bolt 7D 38
M40: Man 4M 79
Jessop Dr. SK6: Mar 8C 110
Jessop Forge BL3: Lit L 9A 40
Jessop St. M18: Man 4B 96
Jethro St. BL2: Bolt 9K 23
(Galindo St.)
BL2: Bolt 4J 39
(Kelstern Cl.)
Jetson St. M18: Man 3D 96
Jevington Wlk. M13: Man 3H 95
Jewel Cl. M41: Urm 7B 92
Jibcroft Brook La. WA3: Cul 4G 88
Jimmy McMullen Wlk.
M14: Man 6F 94
(off Fred Tilson Cl.)
Jinnah Cl. M11: Man 1A 96
OL4: O'ham 6N 63
JJ Thomson M. M14: Man 9J 95
Joan Lestor Ho. M38: Lit H 8K 57
Joan St. M40: Man 3M 79
Jobling St. M11: Man 1L 95
Jocelyn St. M40: Man 4K 79
Joddrell St. M3: Man 5E 4 (9D 78)
Jodrell Cl. SK11: Macc 5J 131
Jodrell St. SK11: Macc 5J 131
SK22: N Mil 8L 121
Joel La. SK14: Hyde 1B 110
Johannesburg Dr. M23: Wyth 3M 115
Johannesburg Gdns.
M23: Wyth 3M 115
John Ashworth St. OL12: Roch 4F 28
John Atkinson Ct. M5: Sal 8K 77
John Av. SK8: Chea 2K 117
John Beeley Av. M11: Man 1B 96
John Booth St. OL4: Spri 6C 64
John Boste Ct. BL3: Bolt 9K 39
John Boyd Dunlop Dr.
OL16: Roch 9H 29
John Brown St. BL1: Bolt 1H 7 (4F 38)
John Clynes Av. M40: Man 7H 79
John Collier Av. OL16: Roch 1J 45
John Cross St. BL3: Bolt 8F 38
John Dalton St. M2: Man 5F 4 (9E 78)
SK13: Had 4A 100
John Derby Ho. M16: Old T 5N 93
John Foran Cl. M40: Man 4N 79
John Gilbert Way M17: T Pk 4K 93
John Grundy Ho. *SK14: Hyde 7B 98*
(off Reynold St.)
John Henry St. OL12: Whitw 2B 14
John Heywood St. M11: Man 8N 79
John Howarth Countryside Cen. 4J 81
John Kemble Ct. OL11: Roch 9B 28
John Kennedy Gdns. SK14: Mot 6K 99
John Kennedy Rd. SK14: Mot 6K 99
John Knott St. OL4: Lees 5C 64
JOHN LEE FOLD 2N 61
John Lee Fold M24: Mid 2M 61
John Lester Ct. *M6: Sal 7N 77*
(off Belvedere Rd.)
John Lloyd Ct. *M44: Irl 9G 91*
(off Alexandra Gro.)
John May Ct. SK10: Macc 2F 130
John Milne Av. OL16: Roch 1H 45
Johnny King Cl. M40: Man 5J 79
John Paine Ct. *M27: Pen 9F 58*
(off Pott St.)
John Roberts Cl. OL11: Roch 8C 28
John Robinson Wlk. *M40: Man 3M 79*
(off Shelderton Cl.)
Johns Av. WA11: Hay 2B 86
Johns Cl. M21: Cho H 9A 94
John Shepley St. SK14: Hyde 7B 98
John Smeaton Ct.
M1: Man 5M 5 (9H 79)
Johnson Av. OL1: O'ham 7B 46
WA12: N Wil 4E 86
WN2: B'haw 1A 72
Johnsonbrook Rd.
SK14: Duk, Hyde 4N 97
Johnson Cl. WN7: Lei 6D 72
JOHNSON FOLD 2A 38
Johnson Fold Av. BL1: Bolt 2N 37
Johnson Gro. M24: Mid 3K 61
Johnson's Sq. M40: Man 6J 79
Johnson St. BL1: Bolt 4L 7 (6G 39)
M3: Sal 3E 4 (8D 78)
M15: Man 3C 94
M26: Rad 1H 59
M27: Pen 4K 77
M29: Tyld 1B 74
M46: Ath 1J 73
OL11: Roch 9A 28
(off Burnaby St.)
WN5: Wig 5M 51
Johnson St. Sth. M29: Tyld 2B 74
Johnson Ter. *SK16: Duk 9M 81*
(off Hill St.)

John's Pl. SK6: Rom 6N 109
Johnston OL12: Roch 5B 8 (5C 28)
Johnston Av. OL15: Lit 2K 29
John Stone Ct. M32: Stre 6G 93
John St. BL3: Lit L 9B 40
BL4: Farn 3M 57
BL7: Bro X 6H 23
BL9: Bury 6M 7 (1M 41)
M3: Sal 2E 4 (8D 78)
M4: Man 3J 5 (8F 78)
M7: Sal 6C 78
(not continuous)
M25: Pres 3D 60
M27: Swin 2G 76
M28: Walk 7L 57
M29: Tyld 1B 74
M30: Ecc 9B 76
M33: Sale 3H 105
M34: Dent 5K 97
M35: Fail 1D 80
M43: Droy 1D 96
M44: Cad 3F 102
OL2: O'ham 8H 45
OL2: Shaw 7L 45
OL4: Spri 5D 64
OL7: A Lyne 1K 97
OL8: O'ham 3B 8 (5J 63)
OL10: H'ood 2J 43
(not continuous)
OL12: Whitw 4B 14
OL15: Lit 9L 15
OL16: Roch 2G 29
(Mitchell St.)
OL16: Roch 6D 8 (5D 28)
(Pagan St.)
PR7: Cop 4B 18
SK1: Stoc 4L 9 (8D 108)
(not continuous)
SK6: Bred 3L 109
SK6: Comp 5E 110
SK6: Mar 2D 120
SK6: Rom 6N 109
SK7: H Gro 4H 119
SK10: Boll 5M 129
SK11: Macc 6H 131
SK13: Glos 9E 100
SK14: Holl 5N 99
SK14: Hyde 6A 98
(Clarendon St.)
SK14: Hyde 6A 98
(Tinker St.)
SK15: H'rod 5E 82
WA3: Gol 1K 87
WA14: Alt 4C 6 (3D 114)
WN1: Wig 8M 9 (3G 53)
WN2: Hin 8D 54
WN4: A Mak 5G 70
WN5: Wig 6A 52
WN7: Lei 5H 73
John St. W. OL7: A Lyne 1K 97
John William St. M11: Man 9A 80
M30: Ecc 8F 76
Joiner St. M4: Man 4J 5 (9F 78)
M5: Sal 4A 4 (9B 78)
Join Rd. M33: Sale 4K 105
Jolly Brows BL2: Bolt 1L 39
Jolly Tar La. PR7: Cop 6C 18
Jonas St. M7: Sal 7D 78
M9: Man 2K 79
Jonathan Fold WN7: Lei 5M 73
Jones Sq. SK1: Stoc 9E 108
Jones St. BL1: Bolt 4G 38
BL6: Hor 9D 20
M6: Sal 7M 77
M26: Rad 8H 41
OL1: O'ham 1G 8 (3L 63)
OL2: O'ham 1J 63
OL16: Roch 7E 28
SK13: Had 4C 100
Jones Way OL16: Roch 8G 29
Jonquil Dr. M28: Walk 9G 56
Jopson St. M24: Mid 2N 61
Jordan Av. OL2: Shaw 3N 45
Jordangate SK10: Macc 4H 131
Jordan St. M15: Man 8E 4 (2D 94)
SK13: Glos 8G 100
Joseph Adamson Ind. Est.
SK14: Hyde 7N 97
Joseph Dean Ct. M40: Man 3M 79
Josephine Dr. M27: Swin 3G 76
Joseph Jennings Ct.
OL7: A Lyne 4L 81
Joseph Johnson M. M22: Nor 7D 106
Joseph Lister Dr. OL12: Roch 9H 15
Joseph Mamlock Ho. M8: Man 1D 78
Joseph St. BL4: Farn 2L 57
M24: Mid 2L 61
M26: Rad 1H 59
M30: Ecc 9B 76
M35: Fail 2D 80
OL12: Roch 3B 28
OL15: Lit 8M 15
SK6: Mar 1D 120
Joshua La. M24: Mid 4B 62
Josslyn Rd. M5: Sal 7K 77
Jo St. M5: Sal 9N 77
Joule Cl. M5: Sal 1N 93
Joules Ct. SK1: Stoc 3M 9 (7D 108)
Joule St. M9: Man 1K 79
Jowett St. OL1: O'ham 2N 63
SK5: Stoc 4D 108
Jowett's Wlk.
OL7: A Lyne 9A 6 (8K 81)
Jowkin La. OL11: Roch 6J 27
Joyce St. M40: Man 3N 79
Joynson Av. M7: Sal 6C 78
Joynson St. M33: Sale 3H 105
Joy Pl. OL12: Roch 3D 28
Joy St. BL0: Ram 8H 11
OL12: Roch 3D 28
JUBILEE 2N 45
Jubilee OL2: Shaw 2N 45
Jubilee Av. M26: Rad 2J 59
SK16: Duk 9B 82
WN5: Orr 7H 51
Jubilee Cl. M30: Ecc 7D 76
Jubilee Cotts. M28: Walk 8K 57
SK7: H Gro 5J 119
(off Brook St.)
Jubilee Ct. M16: Old T 5A 94
SK5: Stoc 7D 96
SK9: Hand 1K 123
(off Chelford Rd.)
WA3: Gol 9K 71
(off Grimshaw St.)
Jubilee Cres. WA11: Hay 2C 86
Jubilee Gdns. SK22: N Mil 8M 121
Jubilee Ho.
BL1: Bolt 3J 7 (6F 38)
Jubilee Ho's. M29: Tyld 2N 73
Jubilee Pk. M24: Mid 2N 61
Jubilee Pool 3E 38
Jubilee Rd. M24: Mid 2N 61
Jubilee Sq. *M34: Dent 6J 97*
(off Market St.)
Jubilee St. BL3: Bolt 9D 38
M6: Sal 8M 77
OL2: Shaw 6N 45
OL7: A Lyne 9K 81
SK22: N Mil 8M 121
Jubilee Ter. M24: Mid 2N 61
Jubilee Wlk. OL12: Whitw 3B 14
Jubilee Way BL9: Bury 7H 7 (2K 41)
Judith St. OL12: Roch 2A 28
Judson Av. M21: Cho H 2B 106
Judy La. SK11: Sut E 9K 131
Julia M. *BL6: Hor 9D 20*
(off Wright St.)
Julian Ho. OL1: O'ham 1D 8 (4J 63)
Julia St. BL6: Hor 9D 20
M3: Man 1F 4 (7E 78)
OL12: Roch 6B 8 (5C 28)
Julius St. M19: Man 9N 95
July St. M13: Man 4J 95
Jumbles Beck BL7: Tur 1L 23
Jumbles Country Pk. 3L 23
Jumbles Country Pk. Vis. Cen. 4L 23
Jumbles Sailing Club 3K 23
Jumbles Wlk. BL7: Tur 1L 23
Junction 19 Ind. Pk.
OL10: H'ood 3L 43
Junction 22 Bus. Pk. OL9: Chad 1D 80
Junction All. OL16: Roch 8D 8 (6D 28)
Junction Ho. M1: Man 5L 5
Junction La. WA12: N Wil 7D 86
Junction Rd. BL3: Bolt 7A 38
SK1: Stoc 9D 108
Junction Rd. W. BL6: Los 7L 37
Junction St. SK14: Hyde 4N 97
Junction Ter. WN3: I Mak 5H 53
Junction Works M1: Man 5L 5
June Av. SK4: Stoc 6N 107
WN7: Lei 4E 72
June St.
OL7: A Lyne 9A 6 (8L 81)
Juniper Bank SK5: Stoc 9E 96
Juniper Cl. BL1: Bolt 3F 38
M33: Sale 2G 104
OL4: O'ham 8C 46
Juniper Cres. M43: Droy 1D 96
Juniper Dr. OL16: Roch 6H 29
WN2: Hin 8B 54
Juniper Ri. SK10: Macc 3C 130
Jupiter Gro. WN3: Wig 9B 52
Jupiter Wlk. M40: Man 5M 79
Jura Cl. SK16: Duk 1A 98
Jura Dr. M41: Urm 4E 92
Jura Gro. OL10: H'ood 3G 43
Jurby Av. M9: Man 7J 61
Jury St. M8: Man 6E 78
WN7: Lei 3G 72
Justene Cl. WA3: Gol 8K 71
Justice St. SK10: Macc 3H 131
Justin Cl. M13: Man 9K 5 (2G 94)
Jutland Av. OL11: Roch 5A 28
Jutland Gro. BL5: W'ton 2H 55
Jutland Ho. M1: Man 5L 5
Jutland St. M1: Man 5L 5 (9G 79)

K

Kale St. M13: Man 9L 5 (2G 95)
Kalmia Gro. M7: Sal 4C 78
Kandel Pl. OL12: Whitw 5B 14
Kane Ct. WA3: Low 1C 88
Kansas Av. M50: Sal 1L 93
Kara St. M6: Sal 8L 77
Karen Rd. WN1: I Mak 3H 53
Karmo Ind. Est.
OL11: Roch 9A 8 (7B 28)
Karting 2000
Manchester 3A 96
Kate St. BL0: Ram 8H 11
Kathan Cl. OL16: Roch 6F 28
Katherine Ct. *M16: Old T 4B 94*
(off Humphrey Rd.)
Katherine Ho.
OL6: A Lyne 7B 6 (7L 81)
Katherine Rd. SK2: Stoc 2G 119
Katherine St.
OL6: A Lyne 7C 6 (7M 81)
OL7: A Lyne 8A 6 (8K 81)
Kathkin Av. M8: Man 9G 60
Kathleen Gro. *M14: Man 7J 95*
(off Stanley Av.)
Kathleen St. OL12: Roch 6B 28
Kay Av. SK6: Bred 5H 109
Kay Brow BL0: Ram 8J 11
OL10: H'ood 2H 43
Kay Cl. WN1: Wig 8M 9 (3G 53)
Kaye Av. WA3: Cul 6H 89
Kayes Av. SK1: Stoc 7F 108
Kayfields BL2: Bolt 9M 23
Kay Gdn. Shop. Cen.
BL9: Bury 8K 7 (2L 41)
Kay La. WA13: Lym 7B 112
Kayley Ind. Est.
OL7: A Lyne 7A 6 (7K 81)
Kay Lodge *M14: Man 9H 95*
(off Lombard Gro.)
Kays Gdns. M3: Sal 2C 4 (8C 78)
Kay St. BL0: Eden 4K 11
BL1: Bolt 1L 7 (4G 39)
(Folds Rd.)
BL1: Bolt 1L 7 (3G 38)
(Turton St.)
BL3: Lit L 9A 40
BL7: Tur 1K 23
BL9: Bury 1N 41
(not continuous)
BL9: Sum 2J 25
M6: Sal 4M 77
M11: Man 2L 95
M46: Ath 9M 55
OL10: H'ood 2H 43
OL11: Roch 8C 28
OL15: Lit 3K 29
SK15: Stal 9D 82
Kayswood Rd. SK6: Mar 1A 120
Keadby Cl. M30: Ecc 1D 92
Keal Dr. M44: Irl 5H 91
Keane Ct. M8: Man 3F 78
Keane St. OL7: A Lyne 6B 6 (7L 81)
Kean Pl. M30: Ecc 9D 76
Kearnes Cl. WN2: Abr 3M 71
KEARSLEY 5A 58
Kearsley Community Leisure Cen. 5M 57
Kearsley Dr. BL3: Bolt 9J 39
Kearsley Grn. M26: Rad 5C 58
Kearsley Hall Rd. M26: Rad 4C 58
Kearsley Mt. Shop. Pct.
BL4: Kea 5B 58
Kearsley Rd. M8: Man 9F 60
M26: Rad 3C 58
Kearsley Station (Rail) 4A 58
Kearsley St. M30: Ecc 8B 76
WN6: Wig 6G 9 (2E 52)
WN7: Lei 5F 72
Kearsley Va. M26: Rad 3B 58
Kearton Dr. M30: Ecc 9G 76
Keary Cl. M18: Man 3B 96
Keasdon Av. M22: Wyth 3C 116
Keaton Cl. M6: Sal 6L 77
Keats Av. M34: Dent 9L 97
M43: Droy 8E 80
OL12: Roch 3M 27
WN3: Wig 6D 52
WN5: Bil 1H 69
WN6: Stan 9B 34
Keats Cl. M46: Ath 6N 55
Keats Cres. M26: Rad 8E 40
Keats Dr. SK10: Macc 3C 130
Keats Fold SK16: Duk 2E 98
Keats Ho. SK5: Stoc 9C 96
Keats M. M23: Wyth 8J 105
Keats Rd. BL8: G'mount 3F 24
M30: Ecc 9D 76
OL1: O'ham 2M 63
Keats St. WN7: Lei 3F 72
Keats Wlk. *BL1: Bolt 2F 38*
(off Irving St.)
Keats Way WN2: Abr 1L 71
Keb La. OL8: O'ham 2L 81
Keble Av. OL8: O'ham 8J 63
Keble Gro. WN7: Lei 2E 72
Keble St. WN2: I Mak 4J 53
Kedington Cl. *M40: Man 5H 79*
(off Ribblesdale Dr.)
Kedleston Av. M14: Man 5K 95
Kedleston Grn. SK2: Stoc 9H 109
Kedleston Wlk. M34: Dent 8K 97
Keel Dr. SK14: Hyde 3B 98
Keele Cl. M40: Man 7H 79
SK2: Stoc 1F 118
Keele Cres. SK11: Macc 6F 130
Keeley Cl. M40: Man 6A 80
Keep, The BL1: Bolt 5N 37
Keepers Cl. WA16: Knut 5K 133
Keepers Dr. OL12: Roch 3K 27
Keighley Av. M43: Droy 7E 80
Keighley Cl. BL8: Bury 2F 40
Keighley St. BL1: Bolt 2D 38
Keilder M. BL1: Bolt 5B 38
Keith Dr. SK3: Stoc 9N 107
Keith Wlk. M40: Man 7J 79
Kelboro Av. M34: Aud 2H 97
Kelbrook Ct. SK2: Stoc 2J 119
Kelbrook Rd. M11: Man 1N 95
Kelby Av. M23: Wyth 9A 106
Kelday Wlk. *M8: Man 4H 79*
(off Smedley Rd.)
Keld Cl. BL8: Bury 8H 25
Keld Wlk. *M18: Man 4A 96*
(off Hampden Cres.)
Kelfield Av. M23: Wyth 6N 105
Kelham Wlk. M40: Man 1A 80
Kellaton Cl. WN3: I Mak 5H 53
Kellbank Rd. WN3: Wig 8B 52
Kellbrook Cres. M7: Sal 1A 78
(not continuous)
Kellet's Row M28: Walk 6K 57
Kellett Cl. WN5: Wig 2A 52
Kellett St. BL1: Bolt 7G 22
OL16: Roch 6G 8 (5F 28)
Kellett Wlk. *M11: Man 8N 79*
(off Trimdon Cl.)
Kelley Pit La. WN1: I Mak 4G 53
Kelling Wlk. M15: Man 9C 4
Kells, The SK13: Chis 3K 111
Kells Gro. WN6: Wig 1D 52
Kellmarsh Cl. M11: Man 2B 96
Kelmscott Lodge *M41: Urm 6B 92*
(off Cornhill Rd.)
Kelsall Cl. SK3: Stoc 1B 118
Kelsall Dr. M43: Droy 7D 80
WA15: Tim 1J 115
Kelsall Rd. SK8: Chea 2M 117
Kelsall St. M12: Man 3L 95
M33: Sale 4H 105
OL9: O'ham 5H 63
OL16: Roch 6D 8 (5D 28)
Kelsall Way *SK9: Hand 1J 123*
(off Spath La.)
Kelsey Flats *OL10: H'ood 2H 43*
(off Meadow Cl.)
Kelsey Wlk. M9: Man 6G 61
Kelso Cl. OL8: O'ham 1K 81
Kelso Gro. WN2: Hin 7N 53
Kelson Av. OL7: A Lyne 5L 81
Kelso Pl. M15: Man 8B 4 (2C 94)
Kelso Way SK10: Macc 9G 129
Kelstern Av. M13: Man 6K 95
Kelstern Cl. BL2: Bolt 4K 39
Kelstern Sq. M13: Man 6K 95
Kelton Cl. SK5: Stoc 3D 108
Kelverlow St. OL4: O'ham 4N 63
Kelvin Av. M24: Mid 5G 60
M33: Sale 4H 105
Kelvin Cl. WN4: Gars 6A 70
Kelvindale Dr.
WA15: Tim 9J 105
Kelvin Gro. M8: Man 4F 78
SK15: Mill 6H 83
WN3: Wig 9B 52
(not continuous)
Kelvington Dr. M9: Man 4J 79
Kelvin St. M4: Man 3J 5
OL7: A Lyne 1J 97
Kelway Ter. WN1: Wig 2G 53
Kelwood Av. BL9: Bury 8C 26
Kemball M30: Ecc 8F 76
Kemble Av. M23: Wyth 7B 106
Kemble Cl. BL6: Hor 8D 20
Kemmel Av. M22: Shar 2D 116
Kemnay Wlk. *M11: Man 9A 80*
(off Edith Cavell Cl.)
Kemp Av. OL11: Roch 8B 28
Kempley Cl. M12: Man 3L 95
Kempnough Hall Rd.
M28: Wors 3M 75
Kemp Rd. SK6: Mar B 9F 110
Kempsey Ct. OL9: Chad 4F 62
Kempsey Wlk. *M40: Man 1B 80*
(off Enstone Dr.)
Kempsford Cl. M23: Wyth 1A 116
Kempston Gdns. *BL1: Bolt 2F 38*
(off Wolfenden St.)
Kemp St. M24: Mid 3L 61
SK14: Hyde 5B 98
Kempton Av. BL3: Lit L 1A 58
M33: Sale 5D 104
Kempton Cl. M43: Droy 8G 80
SK7: H Gro 6L 119
WA12: N Wil 4G 86
Kempton Ct. M33: Sale 5C 104
Kempton Ho. *M7: Sal 4B 78*
(off Griffin St.)
Kempton Rd. M19: Man 9M 95
Kempton Way OL9: Chad 4G 62
SK10: Macc 9G 129
Kemsing Wlk. M5: Sal 9N 77
Kenchester Av. M11: Man 1B 96
Kendal Av. M33: Sale 5J 105
M34: Dent 8L 97
M41: Urm 5M 91
OL7: A Lyne 6K 81
OL12: Roch 3K 27
SK14: Hyde 4N 97
Kendal Cl. OL10: H'ood 4K 43
SK11: Macc 6C 130
WA15: Tim 2K 115
Kendal Ct. *M22: Shar 1D 116*
(off Downes Way)
M30: Ecc 9B 76
(off New La.)
SK15: Stal 7D 82
Kendal Dr. BL9: Bury 5K 41
OL2: Shaw 5A 46
SK7: Bram 1A 124
SK8: Gat 3H 117
Kendal Gdns. SK6: Wood 4M 109
Kendal Gro. M28: Walk 9N 57
M45: Whitef 3M 59
WN4: A Mak 7D 70
WN7: Lei 5F 72
Kendal Ho. SK15: Stal 7D 82
WN2: I Mak 3K 53
Kendall Rd. M8: Man 8E 60
Kendal Rd. BL0: Ram 3G 24
BL1: Bolt 4D 38
M6: Sal 5J 77
M28: Wors 3F 74
M32: Stre 6K 93
SK11: Macc 6D 130
WN2: Hin 6A 54
WN2: I Mak 3K 53
Kendal Rd. W. BL0: Ram 3F 24
Kendal St. WN6: Wig 2E 52
Kendal Ter. *SK16: Duk 9N 81*
(off Astley St.)
Kendal Wlk. M24: Mid 2K 61
Kendon Gro. M34: Dent 6J 97
Kendrew Rd. BL3: Bolt 8B 38
Kendrew Wlk. *M9: Man 1K 79*
(off Shepherd St.)
Kendrick Pl. WN1: Wig 7N 9 (3H 53)
Kenford Dr. WN3: Wins 9B 52
Kenford Wlk. *M8: Man 4E 78*
(off Ermington Dr.)
Kenhall Rd. WN7: Lei 6L 73
Kenilworth OL11: Roch 9B 8 (7C 28)
Kenilworth Av. M20: Man 3E 106
M27: Clif 8H 59
M45: Whitef 5N 59
OL9: Chad 2C 62
SK8: Chea H 4M 117
SK9: Hand 3J 123
WA16: Knut 6J 133
Kenilworth Cl. M26: Rad 6F 40
OL4: O'ham 6D 64
SK6: Mar 8C 110
SK11: Macc 6D 130
Kenilworth Dr. SK7: H Gro 7H 119
WN2: Hin 7B 54
WN7: Lei 3N 73
Kenilworth Gdns. WA12: N Wil 7F 86
Kenilworth Grn. SK11: Macc 6D 130
Kenilworth Gro. M34: Aud 1J 97
Kenilworth Rd. M33: Sale 4E 104
M41: Urm 8K 91
OL16: Roch 4G 44
SK3: Stoc 9L 107
Kenilworth Rd. SK11: Macc 7D 130
WA3: Low 2A 88
Kenilworth Sq. BL1: Bolt 3C 38
Kenion Rd. OL11: Roch 7N 27
Kenion St. OL16: Roch 8D 8 (6D 28)
Kenley Dr. OL10: H'ood 5L 43
Kenley Lodge SK7: Bram 8B 118
Kenley Wlk. *M8: Man 4H 79*
(off Gransden Dr.)
Kenmay Av. BL3: Bolt 7A 38
Kenmere Gro. M40: Man 1N 79
Kenmor Av. BL8: Bury 4G 41
Kenmore Cl. M45: Whitef 3A 60
Kenmore Dr. WA15: Tim 4G 115
Kenmore Gro. M44: Cad 2E 102
WN4: Gars 6A 70
Kenmore Rd. M22: Nor 9C 106
M33: Sale 7C 104
M45: Whitef 3A 60
Kenmore Way M45: Whitef 3A 60
Kennard Cl. M9: Man 1L 79
Kennard Pl. WA14: Alt 1E 114
Kennedy Av. SK10: Macc 3C 130
Kennedy Cl. WN6: Stan 4C 34
Kennedy Dr. BL3: Lit L 9C 40
BL9: Bury 1A 60
Kennedy Rd. M5: Sal 8J 77
M29: Ast 3E 74
Kennedy Sq. SK14: Mot 6J 99
Kennedy St. BL2: Bolt 5K 39
M2: Man 5G 5 (9E 78)
OL8: O'ham 6J 63
Kennedy Way M34: Dent 7H 97
SK4: Stoc 6A 108
Kennerley Ct. SK2: Stoc 2E 118
Kennerley Lodge SK3: Stoc 2D 118
Kennerley Rd. SK2: Stoc 2E 118
Kennerley's La. SK9: Wilm 7F 122
Kennet Cl. BL5: W'ton 2G 55
SK9: Wilm 4J 123
Kennet Flats *OL10: H'ood 2H 43*
(off Meadow Cl.)
Kenneth Av. WN7: Lei 4F 72
Kenneth Collis Ct. M22: Wyth 4B 116
Kenneth Gro. WN7: Lei 4F 72
Kenneth Sq. M7: Sal 4D 78
Kennett Dr. SK6: Bred 4K 109
Kennett Rd. M23: Wyth 4N 115
Kennet Way SK11: Macc 4D 130
WN7: Lei 3H 73
Kenninghall Rd. M22: Wyth 4C 116
Kennington Av. M40: Man 6N 79
Kennington Fold BL3: Bolt 9E 38
Kenny Cl. OL4: Lees 6A 64
Kenside St. M16: Whall R 6E 94
Kensington, The M20: Man 3G 106
Kensington Av. M14: Man 5J 95
M26: Rad 8D 40
OL2: O'ham 6G 44
OL6: A Lyne 6B 82
OL9: Chad 3C 62
SK14: Hyde 8B 98
Kensington Cl. BL8: G'mount 4G 24
OL16: Miln 7L 29
Kensington Ct. BL1: Bolt 2H 7 (5F 38)
M7: Sal 2B 78
M34: Dent 5F 96
SK9: Wilm 8F 122
SK14: Hyde 8B 98
Kensington Dr. BL6: Hor 1F 36
BL8: Bury 4G 41
M5: Sal 7K 77
WN7: Lei 3N 73
Kensington Gdns. SK14: Hyde 8C 98
WA15: Hale 6F 114
Kensington Gro. M34: Dent 5F 96
SK15: Stal 9D 82
WA14: Tim 8E 104
Kensington Pl. BL1: Bolt 2H 7 (5F 38)
Kensington Rd. M21: Cho H 7N 93
M35: Fail 2F 80
OL8: O'ham 7H 63
SK3: Stoc 9N 107
WN5: Wig 6A 52
Kensington Sq. SK10: Macc 4D 130
Kensington St. M14: Man 6F 94
OL11: Roch 9C 28
SK14: Hyde 8B 98
Kenslow Av. M8: Man 9E 60
Kensworth Cl. BL1: Bolt 3E 38
M23: Wyth 1K 115
Kensworth Dr. BL1: Bolt 3E 38
Kent Av. M43: Droy 9C 80
OL9: Chad 5E 62
SK8: Chea H 2A 118
SK10: Boll 7J 129
WN2: P Bri 9K 53
Kent Cl. M28: Walk 9J 57
OL3: Dig 8M 47
Kent Ct. BL1: Bolt 1J 7 (4F 38)
M14: Man 6H 95
Kent Dr. BL4: Kea 5B 58
BL9: Bury 4M 41
Kentfield Dr. BL1: Bolt 1H 39
Kentford Dr. M40: Man 6H 79
Kentford Gro. *BL4: Farn 3K 57*
(off Westminster St.)
Kentford Rd. BL1: Bolt 3F 38
Kent Gro. M35: Fail 4C 80
Kentmere Av. OL12: Roch 2F 28
WA11: St H 9G 68
Kentmere Cl. SK8: Gat 4G 117
Kentmere Ct. M9: Man 7N 61
Kentmere Dr. M24: Mid 9K 43
M29: Ast 3C 74
Kentmere Gro. BL4: Farn 4G 56
Kentmere Rd. BL2: Bolt 3N 39
WA15: Tim 1K 115
(not continuous)
Kent M. *OL7: A Lyne 9L 81*
(off Victoria St.)
Kentmore Cl. M12: Man 2N 95
SK4: Stoc 6K 107
Kenton Av. M18: Man 6A 96
Kenton Cl. BL1: Bolt 3E 38
M34: Aud 2H 97

Kenton Rd. OL2: Shaw 5L 45
Kenton St. OL8: O'ham 6M 63
Kent Rd. M29: Tyld 9B 56
M31: Part 6F 102
M34: Dent 7E 96
M44: Cad 3D 102
M46: Ath 7L 55
SK3: Stoc 8N 107
SK13: Glos 8F 100
Kent Rd. E. M14: Man 6J 95
Kent Rd. W. M14: Man 6H 95
Kentsford Dr. M26: Rad 7B 40
Kentstone Av. SK4: Stoc 5J 107
Kent St. BL1: Bolt 1J 7 (4F 38)
M2: Man 4G 5
M7: Sal 6C 78
M27: Pen 9F 58
OL11: Roch 7D 28
WN1: Wig 9M 9 (4G 53)
WN7: Lei 6N 73
Kentucky St. OL4: O'ham 5N 63
Kent Wlk. OL10: H'ood 3F 42
SK10: Macc 3D 130
(off Kennedy Av.)
Kentway WA12: N Wil 8F 86
Kentwell Cl. SK16: Duk 2M 97
Kentwell Dr. SK10: Macc 2G 131
Ken Ward Sports Centre, The 8G 99
Kenwick Dr. M40: Man 9C 62
Kenwood Av. M19: Man 2L 107
SK7: Bram 1B 124
SK8: Gat 1F 116
WA15: Hale 5F 114
WN7: Lei 6L 73
Kenwood Cl. M32: Stre 7L 93
WN7: Lei 5L 73
Kenwood Ct. M32: Stre 8L 93
Kenwood La. M28: Wors 5N 75
Kenwood Rd. BL1: Bolt 1C 38
M32: Stre 8L 93
OL1: O'ham 2G 63
SK5: Stoc 6C 96
KENWORTHY 6A 106
Kenworthy Av. OL6: A Lyne 5A 82
Kenworthy Gdns. OL3: Upp 3L 65
Kenworthy La. M22: Nor 6C 106
Kenworthy St. OL16: Roch 6G 28
SK15: Stal 9D 82
(not continuous)
Kenworthy Ter. OL16: Roch 6G 28
Kenwright St. M4: Man 2J 5 (8F 78)
Kenwyn St. M40: Man 7K 79
KENYON 5B 88
Kenyon Av. M33: Sale 6L 105
OL8: O'ham 8K 63
SK16: Duk 2B 98
Kenyon Bus. Pk. BL3: Bolt 7F 38
Kenyon Cl. SK14: Hyde 4C 98
Kenyon Clough BB4: Has 1G 11
Kenyon Ct. M40: Man 2M 79
Kenyon Cres. BL9: Bury 7M 25
KENYON FOLD 8K 27
Kenyon Fold OL11: Roch 8K 27
Kenyon Gro. M38: Lit H 7F 56
Kenyon Ho. *SK16: Duk 9M 81*
(off Astley St.)
Kenyon La. M24: Mid 3A 62
M25: Pres 7B 60
M40: Man 2M 79
SK16: Duk 2B 98
(off Kenyon Av.)
WA3: Cro 7B 88
WA3: Cul, Low 3A 88
Kenyon Rd. BL2: Bolt 7B 40
WN1: Wig 1F 52
WN6: Stan 2A 34
Kenyons La. Nth. WA11: Hay 1C 86
Kenyons La. Sth. WA11: Hay 2C 86
Kenyon St. BL0: Ram 7J 11
BL9: Bury 1N 41
M18: Man 3C 96
M26: Rad 9H 41
OL6: A Lyne 7A 6 (7L 81)
OL10: H'ood 2H 43
SK16: Duk 1M 97
WN7: Lei 2F 72
Kenyon Ter. M38: Lit H 8F 56
Kenyon Way BL8: Tot 8F 24
M38: Lit H 7F 56
Keppel Rd. M21: Cho H 8A 94
Keppel St. OL6: A Lyne 7F 6 (7N 81)
Kepplecove Mdw. M28: Wors 5G 75
Kepwick Dr. M22: Wyth 6D 116
Kerans Dr. BL5: W'ton 2G 54
Kerenhappuch St. BL0: Ram 9H 11
Kerfield Wlk. M13: Man 9L 5
Kerfoot Cl. M22: Nor 8D 106
Kerfoot St. WN7: Lei 6L 73
Kermishaw Nook M29: Ast 4B 74
Kermoor Av. BL1: Bolt 7F 22
Kerne Gro. M23: Wyth 7N 105
Kerrera Dr. M5: Sal 9K 77
KERRIDGE 7M 129
Kerridge Dr. SK6: Bred 4K 109
KERRIDGE-END 1N 131
Kerridge Rd. SK10: Rain 1M 131
Kerrier Cl. *M30: Ecc 8G 76*
(off Kearton Dr.)
Kerris Cl. M22: Wyth 6D 116
Kerr St. M9: Man 8J 61
Kerry Gro. BL2: Bolt 4J 39
Kerry Wlk. M23: Wyth 4M 115
KERSAL 2N 77
Kersal Av. M27: Pen 2J 77
M38: Lit H 7J 57
Kersal Bank M7: Sal 2B 78
Kersal Bar M7: Sal 1B 78
Kersal Cell *M7: Sal 2M 77*
(off White Water Dr.)
Kersal Cl. M7: Sal 1B 78
M25: Pres 1N 77
Kersal Crag M7: Sal 1B 78
KERSAL DALE 2B 78
Kersal Dr. WA15: Tim 9J 105
Kersal Gdns. M7: Sal 1B 78
Kersal Hall Av. M7: Sal 2N 77
Kersal Rd. M7: Sal 1N 77
M25: Pres 1N 77
Kersal Va. M25: Pres 2M 77
Kersal Va. Ct. M7: Sal 2N 77
Kersal Va. Rd. M25: Pres 1M 77
Kersal Way M7: Sal 3A 78
Kerscott Cl. WN3: I Mak 6J 53
Kerscott Rd. M23: Wyth 7L 105
Kersh Av. M19: Man 9N 95
Kershaw Av. BL3: Lit L 8A 40
M25: Pres 9M 59
M33: Sale 6K 105
Kershaw Bus. Cen. *BL3: Bolt 7E 38*
(off Baldwin St.)
Kershaw Dr. OL9: Chad 8B 62
Kershaw Gro. M34: Aud 1F 96
SK11: Macc 4F 130
Kershaw Hey OL5: Mos 3G 82
Kershaw La. M34: Aud 1F 96
Kershaw Rd. M35: Fail 3D 80
Kershaw St. BL2: Bolt 8K 23
BL3: Bolt 7E 38
BL9: Bury 8N 7 (2N 41)
M29: Tyld 1B 74
M43: Droy 9D 80
OL2: O'ham 7H 45
OL2: Shaw 5M 45
(not continuous)
OL7: A Lyne 1K 97
OL10: H'ood 2G 43
OL12: Roch 5D 28
SK13: Glos 9E 100
WN5: Orr 5M 51
Kershaw St. E. OL2: Shaw 5M 45
Kershaw Wlk. *M12: Man 3J 95*
(off Aked Cl.)
Kershaw Way WA12: N Wil 4F 86
Kershope Gro. M5: Sal 1N 93
Kersley St. OL4: O'ham 5L 63
Kerswell Wlk. *M40: Man 5M 79*
(off Troydale Dr.)
Kerwin Wlk. *M11: Man 1M 95*
(off Mill St.)
Kerwood Dr. OL2: O'ham 9J 45
Kesteven Rd. M9: Man 3J 79
Keston Av. M9: Man 8M 61
M43: Droy 9K 80
Keston Cres. SK5: Stoc 2F 108
Keston Rd. OL1: O'ham 2N 63
Kestor St. BL2: Bolt 1N 7 (4H 39)
(not continuous)
Kestrel Av. BL4: Farn 4G 57
M27: Clif 9H 59
M34: Aud 9G 81
M38: Lit H 6H 57
OL4: O'ham 6N 63
WA16: Knut 5H 133
Kestrel Cl. M45: Whitef 5N 59
SK6: Mar 4D 120
SK14: Hyde 5B 98
Kestrel Ct. M50: Sal 1K 93
Kestrel Dr. BL9: Bury 9A 26
M44: Irl 6H 91
WN4: A Mak 4F 70
Kestrel M. OL11: Roch 6L 27
WN8: Skel 8A 32
Kestrel Pk. WN8: Skel 8A 32
Kestrel Rd. M17: T Pk 1F 92
Kestrel St. BL1: Bolt 1M 7 (4H 39)
Kestrel Vw. SK13: Glos 9B 100
Kestrel Wlk. *M12: Man 3M 95*
(off Flamingo Cl.)
Keswick Av. M34: Dent 5H 97
M41: Urm 8M 91
OL7: A Lyne 5K 81
OL8: O'ham 7L 63
OL9: Chad 4E 62
SK8: Gat 4G 116
SK11: Macc 7D 130
SK14: Hyde 5N 97
Keswick Cl. M13: Man 4J 95
M24: Mid 1J 61
M44: Cad 4E 102
SK11: Macc 6D 130
SK15: Stal 6D 82
Keswick Ct. *M22: Shar 1D 116*
(off Downes Way)
M24: Mid 1J 61
Keswick Dr. BL9: Bury 5K 41
SK7: Bram 1A 124
Keswick Gro. M6: Sal 7M 77
Keswick Pl. WN2: I Mak 4K 53
Keswick Rd. M28: Walk 9N 57
M32: Stre 6J 93
SK4: Stoc 1B 108
SK6: H Lan 7B 120
WA15: Tim 1K 115
Keswick St. BL1: Bolt 2G 38
OL11: Roch 2N 43
Kesworthy Cl. SK14: Hat 7H 99
Ketley Wlk. M22: Wyth 4E 116
Kettering Rd. M19: Man 7N 95
Kettleshulme Wlk. *SK9: Wilm 5K 123*
(off Picton Dr.)
Kettleshulme Way SK12: Poy 4K 125
Kettlewell Wlk. *M18: Man 4A 96*
(off Hampden Cres.)
Ketton Cl. M11: Man 2C 96
Kevin Av. OL2: O'ham 1J 63
Kevin Cl. SK2: Stoc 3F 118
Kevin St. M19: Man 9M 95
Kew Av. SK14: Hyde 8B 98
Kew Dr. M41: Urm 5A 92
SK8: Chea H 5K 117
Kew Gdns. M40: Man 1M 79
Kew Rd. M35: Fail 2E 80
OL4: O'ham 5M 63
(not continuous)
OL11: Roch 1E 44
Key Ct. M34: Dent 9L 97
Keyhaven Wlk. *M40: Man 5J 79*
(off Glendower Dr.)
Keymer St. M11: Man 8K 79
Keynsham Rd. M11: Man 7N 79
Keystone Cl. M6: Sal 6L 77
Key West Cl. M11: Man 9L 79
Keyworth Wlk. *M40: Man 6K 79*
(off Kirkhaven Sq.)
Khartoum St. M11: Man 8B 80
M16: Old T 5C 94
Khubsuret Ho.
OL11: Roch 9B 8 (7C 28)
Kibbles Brow BL7: Bro X 5J 23
Kibboth Crew BL0: Ram 7H 11
Kibworth Cl. M45: Whitef 3K 59
Kibworth Wlk. *M9: Man 6K 61*
(off Crossmead Dr.)
Kidacre Wlk. *M40: Man 3M 79*
(off Ravelston Dr.)
Kidderminster Way OL9: Chad 2D 62
Kid Glove Rd. WA3: Gol 9L 71
Kidnall Wlk. M9: Man 1L 79
Kid St. M24: Mid 2L 61
Kiel Cl. M30: Ecc 1E 92
Kielder Cl. WN4: A Mak 3C 70
Kielder Hill M24: Mid 8L 43
Kielder Sq. M5: Sal 9M 77
Kiers Ct. BL6: Hor 9G 21
Kilbride Av. BL2: Bolt 6N 39
Kilbuck La. WA11: Hay 1C 86
Kilburn Av. M9: Man 6J 61
WN4: A Mak 6G 70
Kilburn Cl. SK8: H Grn 8G 117
WN7: Lei 1F 72
Kilburn Ct. *M14: Man 5J 95*
(off Hope Rd.)
Kilburn Dr. WN6: She 5L 33
Kilburn Gro. WN3: Wins 8A 52
Kilburn Rd. M26: Rad 8D 40
SK3: Stoc 9A 108
WN5: Orr 6G 51
Kilburn St. OL1: O'ham 2N 63
Kilcoby Av. M27: Pen 2K 77
Kildale Cl. BL3: Bolt 8N 37
Kildare Cres. OL11: Roch 2D 44
Kildare Grange WN2: Hin 6M 53
Kildare Rd. M21: Cho H 9C 94
M27: Swin 3E 76
Kildare St. BL4: Farn 4K 57
WN2: Hin 6M 53
WN5: Wig 5C 52
Kildonan Dr. BL3: Bolt 6A 38
Killer St. BL0: Ram 8J 11
Killington Cl. WN3: Wig 9E 52
Killingworth M. BL6: Hor 3F 36
Killon St. BL9: Bury 3N 41
Kilmaine Av. M9: Man 8N 61
Kilmaine Dr. BL3: Bolt 7N 37
Kilmarsh Wlk. *M8: Man 3E 78*
(off Halliwell La.)
Kilmington Dr. M8: Man 4E 78
Kilmory Dr. BL2: Bolt 6N 39
Kilmory Fold SK13: Glos 6G 100
Kiln Bank OL12: Whitw 4A 14
Kiln Bank La. OL12: Whitw 4A 14
Kilnbrook Cl. OL4: Grot 7E 64
Kiln Brow BL7: Bro X 5K 23
Kiln Cft. SK6: Rom 7K 109
Kiln Cft. La. SK9: Hand 2K 123
Kilner Cl. BL9: Bury 8A 42
Kilnerdeyne Ter.
OL16: Roch 9B 8 (7C 28)
Kilner Wlk. *M40: Man 6H 79*
(off Talgarth Rd.)
Kiln Fld. BL7: Bro X 5G 22
KILN GREEN 8N 47
Kiln Hill Cl. OL1: Chad 1D 62
Kiln Hill La. OL1: Chad 1D 62
Kilnhurst Wlk. BL1: Bolt 1G 7
Kiln La. OL16: Miln 7K 29
SK13: Had 4C 100
Kiln Mt. OL16: Miln 7K 29
Kilnsey Wlk. *M18: Man 4A 96*
(off Hampden Cres.)
Kilnside Dr. M9: Man 3J 79
Kiln St. BL0: Ram 9H 11
BL3: Lit L 9A 40
Kiln Wlk. OL12: Roch 3C 28
Kilnwick Cl. M18: Man 6N 95
Kilphin, The BL6: Los 4K 37
Kilrush Av. M30: Ecc 1D 92
Kilsby Cl. BL4: Farn 1J 57
BL6: Los 6M 37
Kilsby Wlk. M40: Man 6J 79
Kilshaw St. WN5: Wig 6N 51
Kilton Wlk. *M40: Man 6H 79*
(off Rimworth Dr.)
Kilvert Dr. M33: Sale 3F 104
Kilworth Av. M33: Sale 5F 104
Kilworth Dr. BL6: Los 7M 37
Kilworth St. OL11: Roch 9B 28
Kimberley Av. SK6: Rom 6M 109
Kimberley Pl. WN4: A Mak 7F 70
Kimberley Rd. BL1: Bolt 8F 22
Kimberley St. M7: Sal 3D 78
OL8: O'ham 8G 63
PR7: Cop 4B 18
SK3: Stoc 9C 108
WN6: Wig 2D 52
Kimberley Wlk. M15: Man 9C 4
Kimble Cl. BL8: G'mount 3F 24
Kimbolton Cl. M12: Man 2M 95
Kinburn Rd. M19: Man 6J 107
Kinbury Wlk. *M40: Man 6H 79*
(off Kingsfold Av.)
Kincardine Ct. M13: Man 9L 5 (3G 95)
Kincardine Rd. M13: Man 9K 5 (2G 94)
Kincraig Cl. BL3: Bolt 8N 37
M11: Man 9A 80
Kinder Av. OL4: O'ham 6A 64
OL6: A Lyne 4D 82
Kinder Cl. SK13: Glos 9C 100
Kinder Ct. *SK3: Stoc 9C 108*
(off James St.)
Kinder Dr. SK6: Mar 1D 120
Kinder Fold SK15: Stal 3G 99
Kinder Gro. SK6: Rom 6B 110
WN4: A Mak 4C 70
Kinder Ho. *M5: Sal 7K 77*
(off Medway Cl.)
Kinderlee Way SK13: Chis 3K 111
Kinders OL3: G'fld 6L 65
Kinders Cl. M31: C'ton 2L 103
Kinders Cres. OL3: G'fld 6L 65
Kinders Fold OL15: Lit 7K 15
Kinders La. OL3: G'fld 6L 65
Kinders M. OL3: G'fld 6L 65
Kinder St. SK3: Stoc 9C 108
SK15: Stal 8D 82
Kinderton Av. M20: Man 1G 106
Kinder Vw. SK22: N Mil 8M 121
Kinder Way M24: Mid 1L 61
Kineton Wlk. *M13: Man 3H 95*
(off Lauderdale Cres.)
King Albert St. OL2: Shaw 5M 45
(not continuous)
Kingcombe Wlk. *M9: Man 2K 79*
(off Thornsett Cl.)
King Cup Cl. SK13: Glos 9G 101
King Edward Av. SK13: Glos 8F 100
King Edward Rd. SK10: Macc 4G 131
SK14: Hyde 1B 110
WA16: Knut 6G 132
King Edwards Bldgs. *M7: Sal 2E 78*
(off Bury Old Rd.)
King Edwards Ct. SK14: Hyde 9C 98
King Edward St. M5: Sal 1A 94
M19: Man 8N 95
M30: Ecc 8C 76
SK10: Macc 4G 131
King Edward Vs. *WN2: Hin 6A 54*
(off Arthur St.)
Kingfisher Av. M34: Aud 9G 81
Kingfisher Cl. M12: Man 4K 95
Kingfisher Ct. M50: Sal 1K 93
OL12: Roch 1G 28
WN4: A Mak 4E 70
WN6: Wig 2D 52
Kingfisher Ct. Ind. Est.
WN4: A Mak 4E 70
Kingfisher Dr. BL4: Farn 4G 57
BL9: Bury 9A 26
Kingfisher M. SK6: Mar 1D 120
Kingfisher Pk. WN8: Skel 8A 32
Kingfisher Rd. SK2: Stoc 3K 119
Kingfisher Way SK13: Glos 9B 100
King George Cl. WN4: A Mak 7E 70
King George Rd. SK14: Hyde 8B 98
WA11: Hay 2D 86
Kingham Dr. M4: Man 2N 5 (8H 79)
Kingholm Gdns. *BL1: Bolt 3E 38*
(off Kirkhope Dr.)
King La. OL1: O'ham 8B 46
(Sholver Hill Cl.)
OL1: O'ham 7B 46
(Wells Rd.)
Kingmoor Av. M26: Rad 8H 41
King of Prussia Yd. WN1: Wig 8J 9
Kings Acre WA14: Bow 6A 114
Kings Av. M8: Man 2F 78
M45: Whitef 1L 59
SK8: Gat 3F 116
WA3: Low 2B 88
Kingsbridge Av. BL2: Ain 4D 40
SK14: Hat 7F 98
Kingsbridge Cl. SK6: Mar 9B 110
Kingsbridge Ct. M9: Man 3H 79
Kingsbridge Dr. SK16: Duk 2M 97
Kingsbridge Ho. BL3: Bolt 7D 38
Kingsbridge Rd. M9: Man 3H 79
OL8: O'ham 6M 63
Kingsbridge Wlk. SK14: Hat 7F 98
Kingsbrook Ct. *M16: Whall R 9D 94*
(off St Austell Rd.)
Kingsbrook Rd. M16: Whall R 9D 94
Kingsbury Av. BL1: Bolt 3B 38
Kingsbury Cl. BL8: Bury 7G 25
Kingsbury Ct. BL1: Bolt 3B 38
WN8: Skel 8A 32
Kingsbury Ct. Lodge *BL1: Bolt 3B 38*
(off Kingsbury Av.)
Kingsbury Dr. SK9: Wilm 6J 123
Kingsbury Rd. M11: Man 8A 80
Kingscliffe St. M9: Man 2K 79
Kings Cl. M18: Man 3D 96
M25: Pres 6B 60
SK7: Bram 5D 118
SK9: Wilm 8F 122
Kings Ct. *M6: Sal 6N 77*
(off St Georges Way)
M29: Tyld 1A 74
(off Market St.)
SK5: Stoc 5D 108
SK13: Glos 9E 100
WA14: Alt 4C 6
Kingscourt Av. BL1: Bolt 2D 38
King's Cres. M16: Old T 6A 94
M29: Tyld 2N 73
Kingscroft Ct. WN1: Wig 9M 9 (4G 53)
Kingsdale Cl. BL9: Bury 5N 41
Kingsdale Rd. M18: Man 5E 96
Kingsdown Cres. WN1: Wig 8F 34
Kingsdown Dr. BL1: Bolt 3G 38
Kingsdown Gdns. *BL1: Bolt 3G 38*
(off Kingsdown Dr.)
Kingsdown Rd. M22: Wyth 6B 116
WN2: Abr 3L 71
Kingsdown Wlk. SK5: Stoc 3F 108
Kings Dr. M24: Mid 3K 61
SK4: Stoc 5M 107
SK6: Mar 9B 110
SK8: Chea H 4M 117
Kingsfield Dr. M20: Man 6H 107
Kingsfield Way M29: Ast 2C 74
Kings Fold M46: Ath 8N 55
Kingsfold Av. M40: Man 6H 79
Kingsfold Cl. BL2: Bolt 6M 39
Kingsford St. M5: Sal 8K 77
King's Gdns. WN7: Lei 5L 73
Kingsgate BL1: Bolt 2J 7 (5F 38)
Kingsgate Rd. M22: Wyth 6B 116
Kings Gro. M32: Stre 6M 93
OL12: Roch 1G 28
Kingsheath Av. M11: Man 7N 79
Kingshill Ct. WN6: Stan 5C 34
Kingshill Rd. M21: Cho H 9N 93
Kingsholme Rd. M22: Wyth 5B 116
Kingsland OL11: Roch 1A 44
Kingsland Cl. M40: Man 7J 79
Kingsland Rd. BL4: Farn 2H 57
OL11: Roch 9N 27
SK3: Stoc 9M 107
Kings La. M32: Stre 6M 93
Kings Lea PR7: Adl 5J 19
Kingslea Rd. M20: Man 3H 107
Kingsleigh Rd. SK4: Stoc 5K 107
Kingsley Av. M7: Sal 3N 77
M9: Man 3L 79
M32: Stre 6M 93
M41: Urm 7B 92
M45: Whitef 4N 59
SK4: Stoc 4C 108
SK9: Wilm 4H 123
WN3: Wig 8C 52
Kingsley Cl. M34: Dent 8H 97
OL6: A Lyne 5C 82
Kingsley Ct. M5: Sal 9N 77
Kingsley Dr. OL4: Lees 4B 64
SK8: Chea H 4M 117
Kingsley Gro. M34: Aud 1G 96
Kingsley Rd. M22: Nor 8C 106
M24: Mid 1N 61
M27: Swin 1D 76
M28: Walk 7K 57
OL4: O'ham 5N 63
WA15: Tim 9H 105
WN2: Hin 6B 54
Kingsley St. BL1: Bolt 2E 38
BL8: Bury 2H 41
WN7: Lei 3E 72
Kings Lynn Cl. M20: Man 5G 106
Kingsmead PR7: Chor 1F 18
Kingsmead Ct. WA3: Cro 9C 88
Kingsmead M. M9: Man 6H 61
Kingsmede WN1: Wig 9G 34
Kingsmere Av. M19: Man 8L 95
Kingsmill Av. M19: Man 9N 95
Kingsmoor Flds. SK13: Glos 6F 100
Kingsmoor Rd. SK13: Glos 7F 100
KINGS MOSS 3D 68
Kings Moss La. WA11: K Mos 3C 68
Kingsnorth Cl. *BL1: Bolt 3G 38*
(off Adisham Dr.)
Kingsnorth Rd. M41: Urm 5M 91
Kings Oak Cl. WN1: Wig 7L 9 (3G 52)
Kings Pk. M17: T Pk 4H 93
WN7: Lei 2J 73
King Sq. OL8: O'ham 3C 8 (5J 63)
Kings Reach Bus. Pk.
SK4: Stoc 7A 108
Kings Reach Rd. SK4: Stoc 7A 108
Kings Rd. M16: Old T 6N 93
M21: Cho H 9B 94
M25: Pres 9B 60
M32: Stre 8L 93
M33: Sale 4F 104
M34: Aud 4E 96
M44: Irl 2F 102
OL2: Shaw 6L 45
OL6: A Lyne 6N 81
OL8: O'ham 6K 63
OL9: Chad 8C 62
OL16: Roch 8F 28
SK6: Rom 5L 109
SK7: H Gro 4J 119
SK8: Chea H 4L 117
SK9: Wilm 6D 122
WA3: Gol 2K 87
WN4: A Mak 5D 70
Kings Ter. M32: Stre 6M 93
SK16: Duk 9M 81
(off Queen St.)
KINGSTON 6M 97
Kingston Arc. SK14: Hat 7H 99
Kingston Av. BL2: Bolt 3K 39
M20: Man 7G 107
OL1: O'ham 2M 63
OL9: Chad 7E 62
SK11: Macc 5K 131
Kingston Cl. BL8: Bury 4H 41
M7: Sal 2C 78
M33: Sale 5D 104
OL2: Shaw 4M 45
SK14: Hat 7H 99
WN3: Wig 8E 52
Kingston Ct. *M20: Man 7G 107*
(off Kingston Rd.)
Kingston Dr. M33: Sale 3K 105
M41: Urm 9B 92
OL2: O'ham 6G 44
Kingston Gdns. SK14: Hyde 6M 97
Kingston Gro. M9: Man 7L 61
Kingston Hill SK8: Chea 3J 117
Kingston M. M35: Fail 3F 80
Kingston Mill SK3: Stoc 3H 9 (7B 108)
Kingston Pl. SK8: Chea H 5K 117
Kingston Rd. M20: Man 7G 107
M26: Rad 6J 41
M35: Fail 3F 80
SK9: Hand 2H 123
Kingston St. SK3: Stoc 3H 9 (7B 108)
King St. BL0: Ram 8J 11
BL1: Bolt 2J 7 (5F 38)
BL2: Bolt 8L 23
BL4: Farn 3L 57
BL5: W'ton 3H 55
BL6: Hor 9C 20
BL7: Bro X 5G 22
M2: Man 4F 4 (9E 78)
(not continuous)
M3: Sal 2E 4 (8D 78)
M6: Sal 5K 77
M7: Sal 3D 78
M24: Mid 2M 61
M26: Rad 1H 59
M30: Ecc 9F 76
M32: Stre 8K 93
M34: Aud 3K 97
M34: Dent 6K 97
M35: Fail 4B 80
M43: Droy 1E 96
(not continuous)
OL3: Del 8J 47
OL5: Mos 1G 83

King St. OL8: O'ham 4C 8 (5J 63)
OL9: O'ham 3C 8 (5J 63)
OL10: H'ood 3J 43
OL12: Whitw 3B 14
OL16: Roch 7C 8 (6D 28)
SK7: W'ford 5N 123
SK10: Macc 4J 131
SK13: Glos 9E 100
SK14: B'tom 9K 99
SK14: Holl 4N 99
SK14: Hyde 6A 98
SK15: Stal 8D 82
SK16: Duk 9D 6 (9M 81)
WA12: N Wil 6E 86
WA16: Knut 6G 132
WN1: Wig 8J 9 (3F 52)
WN2: Hin 5N 53
WN2: I Mak 4K 53
WN7: Lei 6H 73
King St. E. OL11: Roch 8D 28
SK1: Stoc 1L 9 (6D 108)
King St. Rdbt. OL1: O'ham 5J 63
OL4: O'ham 5J 63
OL8: O'ham 4C 8 (5J 63)
King St. Sth. OL11: Roch 8C 28
(not continuous)
King St. W. M3: Man 4F 4 (9E 78)
SK3: Stoc 2J 9 (7C 108)
WN1: Wig 8J 9 (3F 52)
Kings Vw. SK4: Stoc 7A 108
Kings Wlk. M43: Droy 1E 96
(off King St.)
OL6: A Lyne 5A 82
(off King's Rd.)
Kingsway BL4: Kea 5N 57
M19: Man 3K 107
M20: Man 1H 117
M24: Mid 5L 61
M27: Pen 4J 77
M28: Walk 2L 75
M32: Stre 8J 93
OL16: Roch 8F 28
SK6: Bred 5J 109
SK7: Bram 5D 118
SK8: Chea, Gat 1H 117
SK8: Chea, H Grn 5J 117
SK10: Boll 6J 129
SK16: Duk 2B 98
WA11: St H 9E 68
WA12: N Wil 7F 86
WA14: Alt 2D 6 (2D 114)
WN1: Wig 1G 52
WN2: I Mak 4J 53
Kingsway Av. M19: Man 8L 95
Kingsway Bldgs. M19: Man 3K 107
Kingsway Bus. Pk. OL16: Roch 9H 29
(not continuous)
Kingsway Cl. OL8: O'ham 6J 63
Kingsway Cres. M19: Man 3K 107
Kingsway Pk. M41: Urm 4C 92
Kingsway Pk. Sports Cen. 8G 28
Kingsway Retail Pk. OL16: Roch . . .6H 29
Kingsway Sth. SK8: Chea H 8K 117
Kingsway W. Ind. Pk.
OL16: Roch 8F 28
Kingswear Dr. BL1: Bolt 3D 38
Kingswood Ct. SK9: Wilm 7G 122
(off Grove Av.)
Kingswood Gro. SK5: Stoc 8D 96
Kingswood Rd. M14: Man 9J 95
M24: Mid 9L 43
M25: Pres 6M 59
M30: Ecc 6B 76
Kingthorpe Gdns. BL3: Bolt 8G 38
(off Lever St.)
King William Ent. Pk. M50: Sal 1N 93
King William St. M29: Tyld 2A 74
M30: Ecc 7A 76
M50: Sal 1N 93
Kingwood Av. BL1: Bolt 4A 38
Kingwood Cres. WN5: Wig 5A 52
Kinlet Rd. WN3: Wig 7N 51
Kinlett Wlk. M40: Man 9B 62
Kinley Cl. M12: Man 3L 95
(off Clowes St.)
Kinley Rd. BL4: Farn 2G 56
Kinloch Dr. BL1: Bolt 5C 38
Kinloch Gdns. OL8: O'ham 7K 63
Kinloch St. OL8: O'ham 7L 63
Kinmel Av. SK5: Stoc 4G 108
Kinmel Wlk. M23: Wyth 1M 115
Kinmount Wlk. M9: Man 4J 79
(off Lathbury Rd.)
Kinnaird Cres. SK1: Stoc 8F 108
Kinnaird Rd. M20: Man 3H 107
Kinnerley Gro. M28: Wors 1H 75
Kinniside Rd. WN3: Wig 9D 52
Kinross M30: Ecc 8F 76
(off Peel St.)
Kinross Av. SK2: Stoc 4E 118
WN4: Gars 6N 69
Kinross Cl. BL0: Ram 3G 25
Kinross Dr. BL3: Bolt 7A 38
Kinross Rd. M14: Man 6K 95
Kinsale Wlk. M23: Wyth 4M 115
Kinsey Av. M23: Wyth 9M 105
Kinsley Cl. WN3: I Mak 6H 53
Kinsley Dr. M28: Walk 9K 57
Kintbury St. WN2: Bam 3J 71
Kintore Av. SK7: H Gro 4K 119
Kintore Wlk. M40: Man 5H 79
(off Ribblesdale Dr.)
Kintyre Av. M5: Sal 9K 77
Kintyre Cl. M11: Man 9A 80
(off Coatbridge St.)
Kintyre Dr. BL3: Bolt 7N 37
Kinver Cl. BL3: Bolt 9D 38
(off Woodbine Rd.)
Kinver Rd. M40: Man 9A 62
Kipling Av. M34: Dent 1L 109
M43: Droy 7E 80
WN3: Wig 7D 52
Kipling Cl. SK2: Stoc 9K 109
Kipling Gro. WN7: Lei 3F 72
Kipling Rd. OL1: O'ham 1M 63
Kipling St. M7: Sal 4C 78
Kippax St. M14: Man 6G 94
Kirby Av. M27: Swin 5D 76
M46: Ath 6L 55
OL9: Chad 8B 62
Kirby Rd. WN7: Lei 5G 72
Kirby Wlk. OL2: Shaw 4M 45
Kiribati Way WN7: Lei 4G 72
Kirkacre Av. WA12: N Wil 9F 86
Kirkbank St. OL9: O'ham . . .1A 8 (4H 63)
Kirkbeck WN7: Lei 7L 73
Kirkburn Vw. BL8: Bury 8J 25
Kirkby Av. M33: Sale 6J 105
M40: Man 3N 79
Kirkby Cl. BL9: Bury 5L 41
Kirkby Dr. M33: Sale 6K 105
Kirkby Rd. BL1: Bolt 4C 38
WA3: Cul 6H 89
Kirkdale Av. M40: Man 9B 62
Kirkdale Dr. OL2: O'ham 7G 44
Kirkdale Gdns. WN8: Uph 4E 50
Kirkebrok Rd. BL3: Bolt 8B 38
Kirkfell Dr. M29: Ast 3C 74
SK6: H Lan 7B 120
Kirkfell Wlk. OL1: O'ham 2K 63
(not continuous)
Kirkgate Cl. M40: Man 1N 5
Kirkhall La. BL1: Bolt 4D 38
WN7: Lei 3G 72
Kirkhall Workshops BL1: Bolt 4D 38
(off Bilbao St.)
Kirkham Av. M18: Man 3B 96
WA3: Low 3A 88
Kirkham Cl. M34: Dent 6K 97
Kirkham Rd. SK8: H Grn 6H 117
WN7: Lei 8F 72
KIRKHAMS 4A 60
Kirkham St. BL2: Bolt 3J 39
M5: Sal 9L 77
M38: Lit H 6H 57
OL9: O'ham 1B 8 (4J 63)
WN2: Abr 2L 71
Kirkhaven Sq. M40: Man 6K 79
Kirkhill Grange BL5: W'ton 1J 55
Kirkhill Wlk. M40: Man 9B 62
(off Blandford Dr.)
KIRKHOLT .2D 44
Kirkholt Wlk. M9: Man 8K 61
(off Woodmere Dr.)
Kirkhope Dr. BL1: Bolt 3E 38
Kirkhope Wlk. BL1: Bolt 3E 38
Kirklands BL2: Bolt 2L 39
M33: Sale 6G 105
Kirklee Av. OL9: Chad 2E 62
Kirklee Rd. OL11: Roch 2B 44
Kirklees BL8: Tot 6G 25
Kirklees Cl. BL8: Tot 6G 24
Kirklees St. BL8: Tot 6F 24
Kirklees Wlk. M45: Whitef 3A 60
Kirkless Ind. Est. WN2: Asp 2L 53
Kirkless La. WN2: I Mak 2L 53
Kirkless St. WN1: Wig 3H 53
WN2: Asp 9K 35
Kirkless Vs. WN2: Asp 1K 53
Kirkley St. SK14: Hyde 8A 98
Kirklinton Dr. M9: Man 4J 79
Kirkman Av. M30: Ecc 1C 92
Kirkman Cl. M18: Man 5B 96
Kirkmanshulme La. M12: Man 5L 95
M18: Man 5M 95
Kirkman St. BL9: Bury 9M 41
Kirkpatrick St. WN2: Hin 8D 54
Kirk Rd. M19: Man 1N 107
Kirkstall OL12: Roch 5B 8 (5C 28)
Kirkstall Av. OL10: H'ood 1H 43
OL15: Lit 8L 15
Kirkstall Cl. SK10: Macc 2F 130
SK12: Poy 2G 125
Kirkstall Gdns. M26: Rad 7E 40
Kirkstall Rd. M24: Mid 9L 43
M41: Urm 6E 92
PR7: Chor 1G 18
Kirkstall Sq. M13: Man 3H 95
Kirkstead Rd. SK8: Chea H 8A 118
Kirkstead Way WA3: Gol 1K 87
Kirkstile Cres. WN3: Wins 9A 52
Kirkstile Pl. M27: Clif 7E 58
Kirkstone WN5: Wig 4N 51
Kirkstone Av. M28: Walk 1N 75
WA11: St H 9G 68
Kirkstone Cl. OL1: O'ham 2K 63
Kirkstone Dr. M24: Mid 1K 61
OL2: O'ham 6H 45
Kirkstone Rd. M40: Man 9A 62
SK14: Hyde 4N 97
Kirk St. M18: Man 4B 96
Kirktown Wlk. M11: Man 1A 96
(off Greenside St.)
Kirkwall Dr. BL2: Bolt 7J 39
Kirkway M9: Man 7M 61
M24: Mid 4N 61
OL11: Roch 2D 44
Kirkwood Cl. WN2: Wig 1J 53
Kirkwood Dr. M40: Man 6H 79
Kirtley Av. M30: Ecc 7D 76
Kirtlington Cl. OL2: O'ham 7J 45
Kirton Lodge M25: Pres 7B 60
Kirton Wlk. M9: Man 6H 61
Kitchener Av. M44: Cad 4D 102
Kitchener St. BL3: Bolt 9J 39
BL8: Bury 3H 41
Kitchener Way BL4: Farn 2G 56
Kitchen St. OL16: Roch 6E 8 (5E 28)
Kite Gro. WN7: Lei 5K 73
Kitepool St. M30: Ecc 6A 76
Kitter St. OL12: Roch 2F 28
KITT GREEN 2M 51
Kitt Grn. Rd. WN5: Wig 2M 51
Kittiwake Cl. M29: Ast 3B 74
Kittiwake Ct. SK2: Stoc 2K 119
KITT'S MOSS 9B 118
Kitt's Moss La. SK7: Bram 9B 118
Kittybert Av. M18: Man 3C 96
Kitty Wheeldon Gdns.
M33: Sale 3G 104
(off Ashton La.)
Kiveton Cl. M28: Walk 9K 57
Kiveton Dr. WN4: A Mak 8F 70
Kiwi St. M6: Sal 8N 77
KK5 Play Cen. 9M 81
Knacks La. OL12: Roch 9M 13
Knaresborough Cl. SK5: Stoc 8C 96
Knaresborough Rd. WN2: Hin 7A 54
Knarr Barn La. OL3: Dob 9G 47
Knarr La. OL3: Del 1H 65
Kneller Wlk. OL1: O'ham 8A 46
Knight Cres. M24: Mid 8J 43
Knightley Wlk. M40: Man 5J 79
(off Thornton St. Nth.)
Knightsbridge SK1: Stoc . . .1L 9 (6D 108)
Knightsbridge Cl. M7: Sal 2C 78
SK9: Wilm 5J 123
Knightsbridge M. M20: Man 4G 107
Knightsbridge Sq. SK10: Macc 4D 130
Knightscliffe Cres. WN6: She 6H 33
Knights Cl. M25: Pres 6A 60
SK11: Macc 5J 131
Knights Ct. M5: Sal 8G 77
Knights Gro. M27: Swin 4D 76
Knightshill Cres. WN6: Wig 2C 52
Knight St. BL1: Bolt 4G 38
BL8: Bury 2J 41
M20: Man 6G 107
OL7: A Lyne 8K 81
SK11: Macc 5J 131
SK14: Hyde 8C 98
Knightswood BL3: Bolt 9A 38
Knightswood Rd. M8: Man 3F 78
Knightwake Rd. SK22: N Mil 7K 121
Kniveton Cl. M12: Man 3L 95
(off Kniveton Rd.)
Kniveton Rd. M12: Man 3L 95
Knivton St. SK14: Hyde 6C 98
Knob Hall Gdns. M23: Wyth 4M 115
Knole Av. SK12: Poy 2K 125
Knoll, The OL2: Shaw 6N 45
OL5: Mos 1E 82
WA14: Alt 2A 6 (2B 114)
Knoll Cl. OL3: G'fld 5K 65
Knoll St. M7: Sal 3C 78
OL11: Roch 1N 43
SK22: N Mil 7L 121
Knoll St. Ind. Pk. M7: Sal 3C 78
(off Knoll St.)
Knott Fold SK14: Hyde 9A 98
Knott Hill OL12: Whitw 1B 14
Knott Hill La. OL3: Del 9H 47
Knott Hill Local Nature Reserve . . .3C 82
Knott Hill St. OL12: Whitw 1C 14
Knott La. BL1: Bolt 2A 38
SK14: Hyde 9A 98
KNOTT LANES 3J 81
Knott Lanes OL8: O'ham 2K 81
KNOTT MILL 8E 4 (2D 94)
Knotts Brow BL7: Edg 2N 23
Knott's Ho's. WN7: Lei 9E 72
Knowe Av. M22: Wyth 6C 116
Knowl Cl. BL0: Ram 1J 25
M34: Dent 7F 96
Knowldale Way M12: Man 4K 95
(off Dillon Dr.)
Knowle Av. OL7: A Lyne 6K 81
Knowle Dr. M25: Pres 9N 59
Knowle Grn. SK9: Hand 3H 123
Knowle Pk. SK9: Hand 3H 123
Knowle Rd. SK6: Mel 1F 120
Knowles Av. WN3: Wig 7C 52
Knowles Ct. M6: Sal 7H 77
Knowles Edge St. BL1: Bolt 2D 38
Knowles Farm Cl. WN8: Roby M . . .1F 50
Knowles Pl. M15: Man 9A 5
WN1: Wig 7N 9 (3H 53)
Knowles St. BL1: Bolt 3H 39
M26: Rad 8G 40
WN3: I Mak 5G 53
Knowle's Vs. WN3: Wig 7C 52
Knowle Way SK14: Mot 7J 99
(off Chain Bar La.)
Knowl Hill Dr. OL12: Roch 3K 27
Knowl Hill Vw. OL10: H'ood 2F 42
Knowl La. OL12: Roch 9G 12
Knowl Rd. OL16: Roch 7H 29
Knowls, The OL8: O'ham 1F 80
KNOWLS LANE 6C 64
Knowls La. OL4: O'ham 6C 64
Knowl St. OL8: O'ham 9G 62
SK15: Stal 8E 82
Knowl Syke St. OL12: W'le 7G 14
Knowl Top La. OL3: Upp 4N 65
Knowl Vw. BL8: Tot 7G 24
OL15: Lit 3K 29
Knowsley OL4: Spri 4D 64
Knowsley Av. M5: Sal 1A 94
M41: Urm 5C 92
M46: Ath 7L 55
OL4: Spri 4D 64
WA3: Gol 1L 87
Knowsley Cres. OL12: Whitw 1C 14
SK1: Stoc 8F 108
Knowsley Dr. M27: Swin 5D 76
OL4: Spri 4D 64
WN7: Lei 8F 72
Knowsley Grange BL1: Bolt 5M 37
Knowsley Grn. OL4: Spri 4D 64
Knowsley Gro. BL6: Hor 3F 36
Knowsley La. BL6: R'ton 2N 19
PR6: H Char 2N 19
Knowsley Rd. BL1: Bolt 2C 38
BL2: Ain 3C 40
M45: Whitef 2M 59
SK1: Stoc 8F 108
SK7: H Gro 7K 119
SK11: Macc 7G 130
WN6: Wig 9D 34
Knowsley St. BL1: Bolt 1K 7 (4G 38)
BL9: Bury 9J 7 (3L 41)
M8: Man 6E 78
OL12: Roch 5C 28
WN7: Lei 5F 72
Knowsley Ter. OL4: Spri 4D 64
SK1: Stoc 8F 108
(off Knowsley Rd.)
KNUTSFORD 6G 132
Knutsford Av. M16: Old T 5C 94
M33: Sale 4L 105
SK4: Stoc 1B 108
Knutsford Bus. Pk. WA16: Knut . . .4K 133
Knutsford Dr. WA16: Knut, Mere . . .1F 132
Knutsford Golf Course 5G 132
Knutsford Heath Nature Reserve
. . . . .6F 132
Knutsford Heritage Cen. 6G 132
(off King St.)
Knutsford Leisure Cen. 7F 132
Knutsford Moor Nature Reserve
. . . . .5G 133
Knutsford Rd. M18: Man 4A 96
SK9: A Edg, Wilm 2D 126
WA16: Mob 3A 126
(Foden La.)
WA16: Mob 5K 133
(Longridge)
KNUTSFORD SERVICE AREA 7C 132
Knutsford Sports Club 5F 132
Knutsford Station (Rail) 7G 133
Knutsford St. M6: Sal 8L 77
Knutsford Vw. WA15: Haleb 7J 115
Knutsford Wlk. SK11: Macc 5J 131
(off Bank St.)
KNUTSHAW BRIDGE 9N 37
Knutshaw Cres. BL3: Bolt 1M 55
Knypersley Av. SK2: Stoc 9G 108
Krokus Sq. OL9: Chad 4E 62
Kyle Ct. SK7: H Gro 6K 119
Kylemore Av. BL3: Bolt 7C 38
Kylemore Pl. BL4: Farn 4K 57
Kylemore Way M11: Man 1L 95
Kyle Rd. SK7: H Gro 6K 119
Kynder St. M34: Dent 6K 97

L

Labrador Quay M50: Sal 2N 93
Labtec St. M27: Pen 1H 77
Laburnam St. WN4: A Mak 8E 70
Laburnum Av. BL8: Tot 6F 24
M27: Swin 4E 76
M30: Ecc 1A 92
(off Wilfred Rd.)
M34: Aud 9G 80
M35: Fail 4D 80
M45: Whitef 5M 59
M46: Ath 8N 55
OL2: Shaw 6M 45
OL6: A Lyne 4N 81
OL9: Chad 2F 62
SK14: Hyde 9A 98
SK15: Stal 1C 98
SK16: Duk 1C 98
WN3: I Mak 5J 53
WN7: Lei 2G 73
Laburnum Cl. WA15: Tim 2H 115
Laburnum Ct. BL8: Tot 6F 24
WA13: Lym 3C 112
Laburnum Dr. BL9: Bury 2N 59
Laburnum Gro. BL6: Hor 3G 37
M25: Pres 6N 59
M29: Tyld 1E 74
WN6: Wig 8D 34
Laburnum Ho. OL2: Shaw 6M 45
Laburnum La. OL16: Miln 1L 45
WA15: Hale 7E 114
Laburnum Lodge BL2: Bolt 4N 39
Laburnum Pk. BL2: Bolt 8J 23
Laburnum Rd. BL4: Farn 3J 57
M18: Dent 6D 96
M18: Man 5B 96
M24: Mid 3A 62
M28: Walk 9M 57
M34: Dent 6D 96
M41: Urm 5B 92
M44: Cad 3E 102
OL8: O'ham 2G 81
SK11: Macc 7J 131
WA3: Low 2B 88
Laburnum St. BL1: Bolt 4E 38
M6: Sal 8M 77
M46: Ath 8N 55
Laburnum Ter. OL11: Roch 9C 28
Laburnum Vs. OL8: O'ham 1L 81
(off Simkin Way)
Laburnum Wlk. M33: Sale 3C 104
(off Epping Dr.)
Laburnum Way OL15: Lit 8K 15
SK3: Stoc 8N 107
Laceby Av. OL8: O'ham 7J 63
Lacerta M. M7: Sal 7B 78
Lacey Av. SK9: Wilm 5G 123
Lacey Cl. SK9: Wilm 5G 123
Lacey Ct. SK9: Wilm 5G 123
LACEY GREEN 5G 122
Lacey Grn. SK9: Wilm 6G 123
Lacey Gro. SK9: Wilm 5H 123
Lackford Dr. M40: Man 6H 79
Lacrosse Av. OL8: O'ham 7G 63
Lacy Gro. M32: Stre 8K 93
Lacy St. M32: Stre 8K 93
SK1: Stoc 4L 9 (8D 108)
Lacy Wlk. M12: Man 1K 95
(off Alderman Sq.)
Ladbrooke Cl. OL6: A Lyne 6N 81
Ladbrooke Rd. OL6: A Lyne 5N 81
Ladcastle Rd. OL3: Dob, Upp 2J 65
Ladhill La. OL3: G'fld 6L 65
Ladies La. WN2: Hin 5N 53
Ladies Mile WA16: Knut 6F 132
Ladies' Wlk. M46: Ath 1L 73
LADYBARN 1J 107
Ladybarn Av. WA3: Gol 2J 87
Ladybarn Cres. M14: Man 1J 107
SK7: Bram 9D 118
Ladybarn Ho. M14: Man 8J 95
Ladybarn La. M14: Man 9J 95
Ladybarn Mnr. SK7: Bram 7C 118
Ladybarn Rd. M14: Man 9J 95
Ladybower SK8: Chea H 3A 118
Ladybower Ct. SK13: Glos 8E 100
Ladybridge Av. M28: Wors 2K 75
Lady Bri. Brow BL1: Bolt 5A 38
Ladybridge Community Leisure Cen.
. . . . .8A 38
Lady Bri. La. BL1: Bolt 5A 38
BL3: Bolt 6A 38
Ladybridge Ri. SK8: Chea H 4A 118
Ladybridge Rd. SK8: Chea H 5N 117
Ladybrook Av. WA15: Tim 9H 105
Ladybrook Ct. SK8: Chea H 4N 117
(off Ladybridge Rd.)
Ladybrook Gro. SK9: Wilm 4J 123
Ladybrook Rd. SK7: Bram 6A 118
Ladyfield St. SK9: Wilm 7G 123
Ladyfield Ter. SK9: Wilm 7G 123
Lady Harriet Wlk. M28: Walk 8K 57
(off Ellesmere Shop. Cen.)
Ladyhill Vw. M28: Wors 2K 75
LADY HOUSE 9J 29
Ladyhouse Cl. OL16: Miln 8L 29
Ladyhouse La. OL16: Miln 8K 29
(not continuous)
Lady Kelvin Rd. WA14: Alt 1C 114
Ladylands Av. M11: Man 8A 80
Lady La. M34: Aud 2G 96
WA3: Cro 8E 88
WN3: Wig 7B 52
Ladymeadow Cl. BL1: Bolt 1J 39
Ladymere Dr. M28: Wors 2J 75
Lady Rd. OL4: Lees 5B 64
Ladys Cl. SK12: Poy 2J 125
Ladyshore Cl. M5: Sal 9M 77
Ladyshore Rd. BL3: Lit L 1C 58
Lady's Incline SK12: Poy 2J 125
Ladysmith, The OL6: A Lyne 5C 82
Ladysmith Av. BL9: Bury 8N 25
WN4: A Mak 7F 70
Ladysmith Cen.
OL6: A Lyne 7D 6 (7M 81)
Ladysmith Dr. OL6: A Lyne 5C 82
Ladysmith Rd. M20: Man 5H 107
OL6: A Lyne 5C 82
SK15: Stal 6D 82
Ladysmith St. OL8: O'ham 8G 63
SK3: Stoc 9C 108
Ladythorn Av. SK6: Mar 2D 120
Ladythorn Ct. M25: Pres 9N 59
(off Ladythorne Dr.)
Ladythorn Cres. SK7: Bram 9D 118
Ladythorne Av. M25: Pres 9N 59
Ladythorne Dr. M25: Pres 9N 59
Ladythorn Gro. SK7: Bram 9D 118
Ladythorn Rd. SK7: Bram 8C 118
Ladywell (Park & Ride) 9G 77
Ladywell Av. M38: Lit H 7H 57
Ladywell Cl. SK7: H Gro 5E 118
Ladywell Gro. M38: Lit H 6H 57
Ladywell Point M50: Ecc 9G 77
Ladywell Rdbt. M30: Ecc 8G 76
Ladywell Stop (Metro) 8G 77
Ladywell Trad. Est. M50: Sal 8H 77
Lafford La. WN8: Roby M, Uph 9G 32
LA Fitness
Manchester 4G 5
Sale, Washway Rd. 3G 105
Sale, Whitehall Rd. 6H 105
Lagan Wlk. M22: Wyth 5D 116
Lagos Cl. M14: Man 5F 94
Laindon Rd. M14: Man 5K 95
Lainton Ct. SK3: Stoc 8A 108
LAITHWAITE 3B 52
Laithwaite Rd. WN5: Wig 4A 52
Lake Bank OL15: Lit 2L 29
Lake Dr. M24: Mid 4L 61
Lake Ho. M15: Man 9B 4 (2C 94)
Lakeland Av. WN4: A Mak 6F 70
Lakeland Ct. M24: Mid 1J 61
Lakeland Cres. BL9: Bury 6L 41
Lakeland Dr. OL2: O'ham 4G 44
Lakelands Cl. SK10: Macc 4K 131
Lakelands Dr. BL3: Bolt 7A 38
Lakenheath Dr. BL1: Bolt 7G 23
Lake Rd. M17: T Pk 2J 93
M34: Dent 5K 97
SK15: Stal 6C 82
Lakes Dr. WN5: Orr 5J 51
Lake Side OL15: Lit 3L 29
SK13: Had 3C 100
WN7: Lei 4F 72
Lakeside BL9: Bury 7M 41
SK8: Chea 5H 117
Lakeside Av. BL3: Bolt 1H 57
M28: Walk 6L 57
OL7: A Lyne 6K 81
WN5: Bil 8J 51
Lakeside Bldg. SK8: Chea 4H 117
Lakeside Cl. M18: Man 3D 96
Lakeside Cotts. WN1: Stan 3F 34
Lakeside Ct. M7: Sal 1C 78
Lakeside Dr. SK12: Poy 1J 125
Lakeside Grn. SK2: Stoc 1G 118
Lakeside Ri. M9: Man 8F 60
Lakeside Way
BL9: Bury 9L 7 (3M 41)
Lakes Rd.
SK6: Mar, Mar B, Mel 1D 120
SK16: Duk 1N 97
Lakes Ter. WN2: I Mak 4K 53
Lake St. BL3: Bolt 7G 38
OL11: Roch 7D 28
SK2: Stoc 2F 118
WN7: Lei 4J 73
Lakes Vw. SK15: Stal 6C 82
Lakeswood SK16: Duk 1M 97
Lake Vw. M9: Man 9M 61
OL15: Lit 7K 15
Lake Wlk. WN5: Wig 4M 51
Lakin St. M40: Man 3M 79
Laleham Grn. SK7: Bram 4B 118
Lamb Cl. M12: Man 4L 95
Lamb Ct. M3: Sal 3D 4 (8D 78)
LAMBERHEAD GREEN 5M 51
Lamberhead Ho. WN5: Orr 5M 51
Lamberhead Ind. Est.
WN5: Wig 6M 51
Lamberhead Rd. WN5: Wig 5M 51
Lambert Dr. M33: Sale 2D 104

Lambert Hall *M1: Man* 7K 5
(off Granby Row)
Lamberton Dr. M23: Wyth 1L 115
Lambert St. OL7: A Lyne 9K 81
Lambeth Av. M35: Fail 2F 80
Lambeth Cl. BL6: Hor 1F 36
Lambeth Gro. SK6: Wood 3L 109
Lambeth Rd. M40: Man 6A 80
SK5: Stoc 1D 108
Lambeth St. M46: Ath 8K 55
Lambeth Ter. OL11: Roch 8B 28
Lambgates SK13: Had 4C 100
Lambgates La. SK13: Had 4C 100
Lamb La. M3: Sal 3D 4 (8D 78)
Lambley Cl. WN7: Lei 2F 72
Lambourn Cl. *BL3: Bolt* 7F 38
(off Parrot St.)
SK12: Poy 2H 125
Lambourne Cl. M22: Wyth 7C 116
Lambourne Gro. OL16: Miln 8K 29
Lambourn Rd. M41: Urm 5L 91
Lambrook Wlk. *M40: Man* 6B 80
(off Eastmoor Dr.)
Lambs Fold SK4: Stoc 3B 108
Lamb St. WN1: Wig 2H 53
Lambton Rd. M21: Cho H 9C 94
M28: Wors 3C 76
Lambton St. BL3: Bolt 1D 56
M30: Ecc 6B 76
WN5: Wig 6N 51
Lamburn Av. M40: Man 9B 62
Lamb Wlk. *M34: Dent* 1L 109
(off Wordsworth Rd.)
Lamerton Way SK9: Wilm 4K 123
Lamorna Cl. M7: Sal 2A 78
Lamphey Cl. BL1: Bolt 4M 37
Lamplight Way M27: Pen 3L 77
Lamport Cl. M1: Man 8K 5 (2G 94)
Lamport Ct. M1: Man 8K 5
Lamprey Dr. WA14: W Tim 7B 104
Lampson St. M8: Man 6D 78
Lampton Cl. WA14: Alt 9D 104
Lampwick La. M4: Man 4N 5 (9H 79)
Lamsholme Cl. M19: Man 7M 95
Lanark Av. M22: Nor 8C 106
Lanark Cl. OL10: H'ood 3E 42
SK7: H Gro 5L 119
Lanark Wlk. SK10: Macc 2D 130
Lanbury Dr. M8: Man 3E 78
Lancashire County Cricket Club 5M 93
Lancashire County Cricket Club Mus. 5N 93
Lancashire Ct. OL9: O'ham 6G 62
LANCASHIRE HILL 5C 108
Lancashire Hill SK4: Stoc 5C 108
SK5: Stoc 5C 108
Lancashire Rd. M31: Part 6F 102
Lancaster Av. BL0: Ram 1G 25
BL4: Farn 2G 57
BL6: Hor 2F 36
M24: Mid 4A 62
M29: Tyld 8B 56
M35: Fail 3C 80
M41: Urm 6E 92
M45: Whitef 4N 59
M46: Ath 8N 55
SK15: Stal 7D 82
WA3: Gol 1M 87
Lancaster Cl. BL1: Bolt 3M 7 (5H 39)
PR6: Adl 6L 19
SK6: Rom 7L 109
SK7: H Gro 7H 119
WA12: N Wil 5C 86
Lancaster Ct. M19: Man 9L 95
M40: Man 6N 79
WN7: Lei 6K 73
Lancaster Dr. BL3: Lit L 8B 40
BL9: Bury 5M 25
M25: Pres 9B 60
Lancaster Ho. M1: Man 7J 5
OL2: O'ham 7H 45
SK3: Stoc 8C 108
(off York St.)
Lancaster La. WN8: Par 1A 32
Lancaster Lodge M27: Swin 4H 77
Lancaster Pl. PR6: Adl 5K 19
Lancaster Rd. M6: Sal 4H 77
M20: Man 5F 106
M34: Dent 8K 97
M43: Droy 7D 80
M44: Cad 3D 102
SK9: Wilm 5K 123
WN2: Hin 5A 54
WN5: Wig 2N 51
Lancaster Sq. OL2: O'ham 7H 45
Lancaster St. M26: Rad 9E 40
OL5: Mos 1E 82
OL9: Chad 7E 62
PR7: Cop 4C 18
SK1: Stoc 1N 9 (6E 108)
WN3: I Mak 5H 53
Lancaster Ter. *BL1: Bolt* 2F 38
(off Boardman St.)
OL11: Roch 3J 27
Lancaster Wlk. *BL1: Bolt* 2F 38
(off Halliwell Rd.)
WN5: Wig 2A 52
Lancaster Way BL5: W'ton 1F 54
Lancelot Rd. M22: Wyth 5E 116
Lancelyn Dr. SK9: Wilm 6J 123
Lancewood Pl. WN5: Wig 5A 52
Lanchester Dr. BL3: Bolt 7E 38
Lancing Av. M20: Man 5J 107
Lancing Wlk. OL9: Chad 5E 62
Landau Dr. M28: Walk 8G 57
Landcross Rd. M14: Man 8H 95
Landedmans BL5: W'ton 4H 55
Landells Wlk. *M40: Man* 5M 79
(off Peckford Dr.)
Lander Gro. M9: Man 8L 61
LAND GATE 2D 70
Land Ga. OL12: Whitw 1C 14
Landgate Ind. Est. WN4: A Mak 2D 70
Landgate La. WN4: A Mak 3C 70
Landkey Cl. M23: Wyth 6M 105
Land La. SK9: Wilm 8H 123
Landmark, The *M26: Rad* 1H 59
(off New Rd.)
Landmark Ct. BL1: Bolt 3A 38
Landmark Ho. SK8: Chea H 5N 117
L & M Bus. Pk. WA14: Alt 1C 114
Landor Cl. WA3: Low 1A 88
Landor Ct. M34: Dent 6D 96
Landore Cl. M26: Rad 8H 41
Landos Ct. M40: Man 1N 5 (7H 79)
Landos Rd. M40: Man 1N 5 (7H 79)
Landrace Dr. M28: Wors 4J 75
Landsberg Rd. M35: Fail 2F 80
Landsberg Ter. M35: Fail 2F 80
Landseer Dr. SK6: Mar B 9E 110
SK10: Macc 4C 130
Landseer St. OL4: O'ham 5F 8 (6L 63)
(not continuous)
Lands End Rd. M24: Mid 4G 60
LAND SIDE 9H 73
Landside WN7: Lei 8H 73
LANDSLOW GREEN 2L 99
Landstead Dr. M40: Man 8K 79
Land St. WN6: Wig 3E 52
Lane, The BL1: Bolt 5M 37
LANE BOTTOM 8B 30
Lane Brow OL4: Grot 6E 64
Lane Dr. OL4: Grot 6E 64
LANE END 5L 43
Lane End M30: Ecc 9F 76
OL10: H'ood 4L 43
Lane End Cl. M35: Fail 4E 80
Lane End Rd. M19: Man 4J 107
LANE ENDS
SK6, Marple Bridge 7F 110
SK6, Romiley 5A 110
Lane Ends SK6: Rom 5A 110
Lanegate SK14: Hyde 9A 98
LANE HEAD
OL3 8J 65
WA3 3A 88
Lane Head HD7: Mars 2J 49
Lane Head Av. WA3: Low 9A 72
Lane Head Rd. OL4: O'ham 7C 64
Lane Mdw. OL2: Shaw 6L 45
Lanesfield Wlk. *M8: Man* 2H 79
(off Stakeford Dr.)
LANE SIDE 5A 46
Laneside Av. OL2: Shaw 5A 46
Laneside Cl. OL15: Lit 8L 15
Laneside Dr. SK7: Bram 6E 118
Laneside Rd. M20: Man 8H 107
SK22: N Mil 8N 121
SK22: Row 1N 121
Laneside Wlk. OL16: Miln 6K 29
Lanfield Dr. M8: Man 3E 78
Langbourne Cl. M26: Rad 3B 58
Langcliffe Cl. WA3: Cul 6G 88
Langcliffe Pl. M26: Rad 3C 58
Langcliffe Wlk. *M18: Man* 4A 96
(off Hampden Cres.)
Langcroft Dr. M40: Man 5A 80
Langdale Av. M19: Man 9N 95
OL8: O'ham 7H 63
OL16: Roch 4G 44
WA3: Gol 9M 71
WA13: Lym 3A 112
WN1: Wig 9E 34
WN2: I Mak 3L 53
Langdale Cl. M34: Dent 8J 97
SK6: H Lan 7B 120
SK8: Gat 4H 117
SK11: Macc 7D 130
WA15: Tim 1F 6 (2E 114)
Langdale Ct. M8: Man 4G 78
Langdale Cres. WN2: Abr 2L 71
WN5: Orr 3M 51
Langdale Dr. BL9: Bury 9N 41
M24: Mid 9L 43
M28: Walk 1N 75
Langdale Gro. WN2: P Bri 9L 53
Langdale Hall *M14: Man* 6H 95
(off Upper Pk. Rd.)
Langdale M. BL9: Bury 8M 25
Langdale Rd. M14: Man 5J 95
M31: Part 5F 102
M32: Stre 6J 93
M33: Sale 7E 104
SK4: Stoc 2A 108
SK6: Wood 3M 109
SK7: Bram 1A 124
WN2: Hin 6A 54
WN5: Orr 4M 51
Langdale St. BL3: Bolt 9F 38
BL4: Farn 4K 57
WN7: Lei 5G 73
Langdale Ter. *SK15: Stal* 6D 82
(off Springs La.)
Langden Cl. OL2: Shaw 4L 45
WA3: Cul 5F 88
Langdon Cl. BL1: Bolt 4E 38
Langfield WA3: Low 2A 88
Langfield Av. M16: Whall R 6C 94
Langfield Cres. M43: Droy 8G 81
Langfield Wlk. M6: Sal 8N 77
Langford Dr. M44: Irl 8H 91
WN7: Lei 8G 73
Langford Gdns. *BL3: Bolt* 8F 38
(off Aldsworth Dr.)
Langford Rd. M20: Man 2F 106
SK4: Stoc 4A 108
Langford St. M34: Dent 6K 97
SK11: Macc 4G 130
Langham Cl. BL1: Bolt 7H 23
Langham Ct. M20: Man 4E 106
M32: Stre 5G 93
Langham Gro. WA15: Tim 8H 105
Langham Rd. M6: Sal 8M 77
OL8: O'ham 7J 63
SK4: Stoc 7N 107
WA14: Bow 5B 114
WN6: Stan 3A 34
Langham St. OL7: A Lyne 5L 81
Langham St. Ind. Est.
OL7: A Lyne 5L 81
Langholm Cl. WN3: Wins 8B 52
Langholm Dr. BL2: Bolt 6N 39
Langholme Cl.
M15: Man 9C 4 (2C 94)
Langholme Pl. M30: Ecc 8B 76
Langholme Way OL10: H'ood 3E 42
Langholm Rd. WN4: Gars 6N 69
Langland Cl. *M9: Man* 7K 61
(off Leconfield Dr.)
M19: Man 8B 96
Langland Dr. M30: Ecc 2C 92
LANGLEY
M24 2K 61
SK11 8N 131
Langley Av. M24: Mid 8K 43
M25: Pres 6A 60
OL4: Grot 6E 64
SK7: H Gro 6F 118
WA12: N Wil 8F 86
Langley Cl. M41: Urm 7E 92
WA3: Gol 9M 71
WN6: Stan 2B 34
Langley Ct. M7: Sal 1D 78
SK13: Had 4C 100
Langley Cres. M25: Pres 5A 60
Langley Dr. BL3: Bolt 7D 38
M28: Wors 4G 74
SK9: Hand 3K 123
SK11: Macc 8F 130
SK13: Glos 9H 101
Langley Gdns. M25: Pres 5A 60
Langley Grange M25: Pres 5A 60
Langley Gro. M25: Pres 5A 60
Langley Hall SK11: Lang 8M 131
Langley Hall Cl. SK11: Lang 8M 131
Langley Hall Cotts.
SK11: Lang 8M 131
Langley Hall Rd. M25: Pres 5A 60
Langley Ho. M24: Mid 9M 43
Langley La. M24: Mid 8H 43
OL10: H'ood 8H 43
Langley Platt La. M46: Ath 2L 73
Langley Rd. M6: Sal 2M 77
M14: Man 8H 95
M25: Pres 6N 59
M27: Pen 2M 77
M33: Sale 5E 104
SK11: Lang 9L 131
Langley Rd. Sth. M6: Sal 4M 77
Langley St. WN5: Wig 5A 52
Langness St. M11: Man 9A 80
Lango St. *M16: Old T* 4B 94
(off Howarth St.)
Langport Av. M12: Man 3K 95
Langroyd Wlk. *M8: Man* 3E 78
(off Highshore Dr.)
Langset Av. WN2: Hin 5N 53
Langsett Av. M6: Sal 7J 77
SK13: Gam 8N 99
(off Wardlow M.)
Langsett Grn. *SK13: Gam* 8N 99
(off Wardlow M.)
Langsett Gro. *SK13: Gam* 8N 99
(off Wardlow M.)
Langsett La. SK13: Gam 8N 99
Langsett Lea *SK13: Gam* 8N 99
(off Youlgreave Cres.)
Langsett Ter. *SK13: Gam* 8N 99
(off Youlgreave Cres.)
Langshaw Rd. BL3: Bolt 7D 38
Langshaw St. M6: Sal 9M 77
M16: Old T 5B 94
Langshaw Wlk. BL3: Bolt 7D 38
Langside Av. M9: Man 7K 61
Langside Dr. BL3: Bolt 8N 37
Langstone Cl. BL6: Hor 1D 36
Langston Grn. SK7: H Gro 6E 118
Langston St. M3: Man 7E 78
Langthorne St. M19: Man 9N 95
Langthorne Wlk. *BL3: Bolt* 6E 38
(off Deane Rd.)
Langton Av. WN6: Stan 3B 34
Langton Cl. M35: Fail 2F 80
WA12: N Wil 5D 86
Langton Ct. *WN2: P Bri* 8K 53
(off Moss La.)
Langton Pl. WN6: Stan 3B 34
Langton St. M6: Sal 8L 77
M24: Mid 3M 61
OL10: H'ood 1J 43
Langton Ter. OL11: Roch 9C 28
LANGTREE 1A 34
Langtree Cl. M28: Wors 2J 75
Langtree La. WN6: Stan 1A 34
Langwood La.
WA11: R'ford 1A 68
Langworthy Av. M38: Lit H 7J 57
Langworthy Rd. M6: Sal 6M 77
M40: Man 3M 79
Langworthy Stop (Metro) 9L 77
Lanhill Dr. M8: Man 4H 79
Lankro Way M30: Ecc 9F 76
Lanley Cl. BL3: Lit L 9B 40
Lanreath Cl. SK10: Macc 3B 130
Lanreath Wlk. *M8: Man* 4G 79
(off Moordown Cl.)
Lansbury Ho. *M16: Whall R* 6C 94
(off Whalley Rd.)
Lansbury St. WN5: Orr 5L 51
Lansdale Gdns. M19: Man 3K 107
Lansdale St. BL4: Farn 3M 57
M28: Walk 6L 57
M30: Ecc 1A 92
Lansdown Cl. SK8: Chea H 8A 118
Lansdowne WA3: Cul 7G 89
Lansdowne Av. M34: Aud 9G 80
SK6: Rom 6A 110
Lansdowne Cl. BL0: Ram 9H 11
BL2: Bolt 3J 39
Lansdowne Ct. OL9: Chad 5F 62
Lansdowne Dr. M28: Wors 2K 75
Lansdowne Ho. *M20: Man* 6G 106
(off Wilmslow Rd.)
Lansdowne Rd. BL2: Bolt 2J 39
M8: Man 1F 78
M30: Ecc 7D 76
M33: Sale 2G 104
M41: Urm 9M 91
Lansdowne Rd. M46: Ath 6A 56
OL9: Chad 5G 62
WA14: Alt 1C 6 (1D 114)
Lansdowne Rd. Nth. M41: Urm 8M 91
Lansdowne St. OL11: Roch 6A 28
SK10: Macc 3J 131
Lansdowne Ter. *WN1: Wig* 2F 52
(off Earl St.)
Lantern Cl. SK5: Stoc 3G 109
Lantern Vw. SK22: N Mil 6L 121
Lapwing Cl. OL11: Roch 6K 27
SK15: Stal 6D 82
WA3: Low 1N 87
WA12: N Wil 5F 86
Lapwing Ct. M20: Man 3F 106
Lapwing La. M20: Man 3F 106
M34: A Lyne 9H 81
SK5: Stoc 1F 108
Larch Av. M26: Rad 2H 59
M27: Swin 4C 76
M32: Stre 8K 93
SK8: Chea H 6M 117
SK11: Macc 7E 130
WA12: N Wil 7F 86
WN5: Wig 5A 52
Larch Cl. M23: Wyth 8J 105
M35: Fail 4D 80
SK6: Mar 2B 120
SK12: Poy 3K 125
WA3: Low 3B 88
WN5: Bil 5H 69
Larches, The OL5: Mos 1G 83
Larch Gdns. M8: Man 5F 78
Larch Gro. M27: Ward 9B 58
M46: Ath 7L 55
OL4: Lees 3B 64
OL9: Chad 3F 62
Larch Ho. *M14: Man* 5H 95
(off Rusholme Pl.)
Larchlea WA15: Alt 3F 114
Larch Ri. SK10: P'bury 7B 128
Larch Rd. M30: Ecc 6A 76
M31: Part 5F 102
M34: Dent 6L 97
WA11: Hay 2B 86
WN7: Lei 2G 73
Larch St. BL9: Bury 2A 42
OL8: O'ham 5A 8 (5H 63)
Larchview Rd. M24: Mid 3A 62
Larch Way SK13: Glos 9H 101
Larchway OL16: Roch 6H 29
SK6: H Lan 8C 120
SK7: Bram 8A 118
Larchwood OL9: Chad 3C 62
SK8: Chea 1J 117
Larchwood Av. M9: Man 3L 79
Larchwood Cl. M33: Sale 4C 104
Larchwood Dr. SK9: Wilm 6K 123
WN1: Wig 8E 34
Larchwood St. BL1: Bolt 2G 39
Larden Wlk. *M8: Man* 4E 78
(off Greyswood Av.)
Largs Wlk. M23: Wyth 1M 115
Larke Ri. M20: Man 5E 106
Larkfield Av. M38: Lit H 6G 57
WN1: Wig 8E 34
Larkfield Cl. BL8: G'mount 3F 24
OL7: A Lyne 3M 81
Larkfield Gro. BL2: Bolt 4J 39
M38: Lit H 6G 57
Larkfield M. M38: Lit H 6G 57
Lark Hall Cl. SK10: Macc 5L 131
Lark Hall Cres. SK10: Macc 5L 131
Larkhall Ri. M22: Shar 2D 116
Lark Hall Rd. SK10: Macc 5L 131
Lark Hall Yd. SK10: Macc 5L 131
LARK HILL
M24 3M 61
M29 5C 74
LARKHILL 5D 90
Lark Hill BL4: Farn 4L 57
SK3: Stoc 8A 108
Larkhill SK15: Stal 5D 82
Larkhill Av. WN6: Stan 4C 34
Larkhill Cl. WA15: Tim 1H 115
Lark Hill Cotts. SK22: N Mil 7K 121
Lark Hill Ct. M24: Mid 3M 61
Lark Hill La. OL3: Del, Dig 8K 47
Lark Hill Pl. OL12: Roch 4C 28
Lark Hill Rd. OL3: Dob 1J 65
SK3: Stoc 8A 108
Larkhill Rd. SK8: Chea H 2A 118
Larkhill Wlk. *M8: Man* 4G 78
(off Appleford Dr.)
Lark M. OL3: G'fld 7M 65
Larkside Av. M28: Walk 8M 57
Larkspur Cl. BL1: Bolt 1J 39
WN7: Lei 7H 73
Larks Ri. M43: Droy 7H 81
Lark St. BL1: Bolt 1L 7 (4G 39)
BL4: Farn 4L 57
OL1: O'ham 9A 46
Larkswood Dr. SK2: Stoc 2K 119
Larkwood Cl. SK15: C'ook 3H 83
Larkwood Way SK10: Boll 8J 129
Larmuth Av. M21: Cho H 2B 106
Larne Av. M32: Stre 7J 93
SK3: Stoc 9N 107
Larne St. M11: Man 1M 95
Larwood Av. SK4: Stoc 7N 107
Lascar Av. M5: Sal 1N 93
Laser Quest
Rochdale 9C 28
Laser Quest & The Rock
The Trafford Centre 3D 92
Lashbrook Cl. M40: Man 6J 79
Lassell Fold SK14: Hyde 3E 98
Lassell St. M11: Man 2D 96
(not continuous)
Lastingham St. M40: Man 4A 80
Latchford St. OL7: A Lyne 6L 81
Latchmere Rd. M14: Man 9H 95
LATELY COMMON 9L 73
Latham Av. WA12: N Wil 5F 86
Latham Cl. SK6: Bred 3K 109
Latham La. WN5: Orr 2L 51
Latham Rd. BL6: Bla 1M 35
Latham Row BL6: Hor 1H 37
Latham St. BL1: Bolt 2G 38
M11: Man 2D 96
Lathbury Rd. M9: Man 4J 79
M40: Man 4J 79
Lathom Av. WN8: Par 1A 32
Lathom Gro. M33: Sale 5L 105
Lathom Hall Av. OL4: Spri 4D 64
Lathom Rd. M20: Man 1J 107
M44: Irl 9G 91
Lathom St. BL9: Bury 9N 25
Lathom Way SK10: Macc 2K 131
Latimer Cl. WN5: Orr 4K 51
Latimer St. OL4: O'ham 5L 63
Latin St.
OL16: Roch 9B 8 (7C 28)
Latrigg Cres. M24: Mid 1H 61
Latrobe St. M43: Droy 1E 96
Lauderdale Cres. M13: Man 3H 95
Launceston Cl. OL8: O'ham 7N 63
SK7: Bram 8D 118
Launceston Rd. M26: Rad 7D 40
WN2: Hin 8E 54
Laundry St. M6: Sal 6M 77
Laura St. BL9: Sum 3J 25
Laureate's Pl. OL4: Spri 4E 64
Laureate Way M34: Dent 1L 109
Laurel Av. BL3: Bolt 7M 39
M14: Man 7F 94
OL9: Chad 3B 62
SK8: Chea 2J 117
WA12: N Wil 7G 86
Laurel Bank SK14: Hyde 9N 97
SK15: Stal 1E 98
Laurel Bank Gdns. M9: Man 8J 61
Laurel Ct. *BL1: Bolt* 4G 38
(off Haydock St.)
M20: Man 2G 106
OL16: Roch 7F 28
(off Vavasour St.)
SK4: Stoc 4N 107
Laurel Cres. WN2: Hin 8C 54
Laurel Dr. M38: Lit H 7H 57
WA15: Tim 3H 115
Laurel End La. SK4: Stoc 5M 107
Laurel Grn. M34: Dent 7L 97
Laurel Gro. M5: Sal 8J 77
WA3: Low 1N 87
WN4: A Mak 6E 70
WN7: Lei 2G 73
Laurel Ho. M6: Sal 6H 77
SK4: Stoc 4N 107
Laurel Rd. SK4: Stoc 4N 107
Laurels, The OL5: Mos 1G 83
PR7: Cop 2C 18
SK6: H Lan 7C 120
Laurels Dr. OL15: Lit 2K 29
Laurel St. BL1: Bolt 5D 38
BL8: Tot 7F 24
BL9: Bury 2A 42
M24: Mid 3B 62
OL4: O'ham 5M 63
SK4: Stoc 1J 9 (6C 108)
WN5: Wig 4C 52
Laurel Trad. Est. OL2: O'ham 1L 63
Laurel Wlk. M31: Part 6F 102
Laurel Way SK7: Bram 7A 118
Laurence Cl. M12: Man 3N 95
Laurence Lowry Ct. *M27: Pen* 1F 76
(off Lowry Dr.)
Lauren Cl. OL4: Spri 5C 64
Lauria Ter. BL2: Ain 3D 40
Laurie Pl. *OL12: Roch* 4D 28
(off Whitehall St.)
Laurieston Ct. SK8: Chea 2H 117
Lauriston Cl. M22: Shar 1D 116
Lauriston Gallery, The 3H 105
(within Waterside Arts Cen.)
Lausanne Rd. M20: Man 1G 107
SK7: Bram 4C 118
Lavender Cl. M23: Wyth 7L 105
M33: Sale 3C 104
Lavender Rd. BL4: Farn 2H 57
OL4: O'ham 7B 64
WN6: Wig 9C 34
Lavenders Brow
SK1: Stoc 2M 9 (7D 108)
Lavender St. M26: Rad 9D 40
Lavender Wlk. M31: Part 6F 102
WN4: Gars 5A 70
Lavenham Av. M11: Man 9B 80
Lavenham Bus. Cen.
OL9: O'ham 5G 63
(off Parsons St.)
Lavenham Cl. BL9: Bury 9M 41
SK7: H Gro 6J 119
SK10: Macc 2G 131
Laverton Cl. BL9: Bury 3D 42
Lavington Av. SK8: Chea 1M 117
Lavington Gro. M18: Man 5B 96
Lavinia St. M30: Ecc 8B 76
Lavister Av. M19: Man 5J 107
Lawefield Cres. M27: Clif 6D 58
Lawers Av. OL9: Chad 3E 62
Lawfield Ct. SK7: Bram 5B 118
Lawflat OL12: W'le 8G 14
Lawler Av. M5: Sal 3A 94
Lawnbank Cl. M24: Mid 2K 61
Lawn Closes OL8: O'ham 8N 63
Lawndale Cl. M26: Rad 1H 59
Lawndale Dr. M28: Wors 2J 75
Lawn Dr. M27: Swin 3E 76
WA15: Tim 1E 114
Lawnfold SK13: Had 5A 100
Lawngreen Av. M21: Cho H 1N 105
Lawnhurst Av. M23: Wyth 8M 105
Lawnhurst Cl. SK8: Chea H 8L 117
Lawnhurst Trad. Est. SK3: Stoc 2N 117
Lawns, The SK9: Wilm 1D 126
WA14: Bow 4C 114
WN2: Hin 6M 53
Lawns Av. WN5: Orr 6G 51
Lawnside M. M20: Man 3F 106
Lawn St. BL1: Bolt 3E 38
Lawnswood OL11: Roch 1A 44

Lawnswood Dr. M27: Swin 4H 77
M29: Tyld 1E 74
Lawnswood Pk. Rd.
M27: Swin 4G 77
Lawrence Cl. OL12: Roch 4M 27
Lawrence Ct. WN2: Abr 1L 71
Lawrence Pl. SK12: Poy 4H 125
Lawrence Rd. M41: Urm 6M 91
SK7: H Gro 4J 119
WA14: Alt 1C 114
Lawrence St. BL9: Bury 8M 41
SK1: Stoc 3K 9 (7C 108)
Lawrie Av. BL0: Ram 9H 11
Lawson Av. BL6: Hor 9E 20
SK8: Gat 2G 116
WN7: Lei 1G 72
Lawson Cl. M24: Mid 8M 43
M28: Wors 3C 76
Lawson Dr. WA15: Tim 1G 114
Lawson Gro. M33: Sale 2G 105
Lawson Rd. BL1: Bolt 2D 38
Lawson St. BL1: Bolt 9F 22
M9: Man 9H 61
OL1: O'ham 3L 63
(off Mortimer St.)
Lawson Wlk. M34: Dent 9K 97
Laws Ter. OL15: Lit 9K 15
Law St. OL11: Roch 9A 28
Lawton Av. SK7: Bram 7C 118
Lawton Cl. SK6: Rom 7K 109
WA3: Cul 6G 89
Lawton Fold OL4: Grot 4E 64
Lawton Moor Rd. M23: Wyth 7N 105
Lawton Rd. SK4: Stoc 4A 108
Lawton Sq. OL3: Del 8J 47
Lawton St. M11: Man 2B 96
M43: Droy 8F 80
OL3: Del 8H 47
(off King St.)
OL12: Roch 4E 28
SK14: Hyde 6B 98
(off Hopkins St.)
SK15: Stal 9E 82
Laxey Av. M46: Ath 9N 55
Laxey Cl. OL9: Chad 6F 62
Laxey Cres. WN7: Lei 3E 72
Laxey St. M40: Man 3N 79
Laxfield Dr. M41: Urm 6L 91
Laxford Gro. BL3: Bolt 6N 37
Layard St. OL6: A Lyne 7A 6 (7L 81)
Laycock Av. BL2: Bolt 1J 39
SK15: Mill 6H 83
Laycock Cres. M35: Fail 3D 80
Laycock Dr. SK16: Duk 2D 98
Laycock Gro. M35: Fail 3D 80
Laycock St. OL16: Roch 2H 29
Laycock Way M34: Dent 1K 109
Layfield Cl. BL8: Tot 5D 24
Layland Av. WA3: Cul 5G 88
Laystall St. M1: Man 4L 5 (9G 79)
Laythe Barn Cl. OL16: Miln 7J 29
Layton Av. SK14: Hyde 6N 97
Layton Cl. SK1: Stoc 4N 9 (8E 108)
WN5: Wig 6A 52
Layton Dr. BL4: Kea 5N 57
SK6: Rom 5N 109
Layton St. M40: Man 8J 79
Lazenby Cres. WN4: A Mak 7C 70
Lazonby Av. WN2: Asp 9B 36
Lazonby Wlk. M13: Man 5L 95
(off Bates St.)
Lea Bank Cl. SK11: Macc 4E 130
Leabank St. M19: Man 8M 95
Leabrook Dr. M40: Man 2C 80
Leaburn Dr. M19: Man 4K 107
Leach Cl. OL16: Roch 3G 29
Leaches Rd. BL0: Eden, Ram 6K 11
(not continuous)
Leach M. M25: Pres 7M 59
Leach St. BL3: Bolt 7F 38
BL4: Farn 2M 57
M18: Man 3N 95
M25: Pres 7M 59
OL2: O'ham 7L 45
OL2: Shaw 6N 45
OL16: Miln 8K 29
OL16: Roch 9G 8 (7F 28)
Leach Wlk. OL4: O'ham 3B 64
Leaconfield Dr. M28: Wors 3N 75
Lea Ct. M35: Fail 3C 80
SK4: Stoc 4N 107
Leacroft WN4: A Mak 4C 70
Leacroft Av. BL2: Bolt 7L 39
Leacroft Rd. M21: Cho H 3C 106
Leadale Cl. WN6: Stan 3A 34
Leadale Ri. OL4: Spri 5D 64
Leadbeaters Cl. SK11: Macc 5K 131
Leadbeaters Rd. SK11: Macc 5K 131
Leader St. WN1: Wig 8N 9 (3H 53)
WN5: Wig 5N 51
Leader Williams Rd. M44: Irl 8G 91
Lea Dr. M9: Man 8L 61
Leafield M29: Tyld 1D 74
Leafield Av. M20: Man 4J 107
Lea Fld. Cl. M26: Rad 9E 40
Leafield Dr. M28: Wors 4H 75
SK8: Chea H 9L 117
Leafield Rd. SK12: Dis 9F 120
Leaford Av. M34: Dent 5H 97
Leaford Cl. M34: Dent 5H 97
Leaf St. BL2: Bolt 7K 39
M15: Man 9F 4 (3E 94)
SK5: Stoc 1C 108
Leaf Ter. OL12: Roch 1B 28
Lea Ga. BL2: Bolt 8L 23
Leagate M41: Urm 8E 92
Lea Ga. Cl. BL2: Bolt 8L 23
Leagate Cl. WN3: Wig 8B 52
League St. OL16: Roch 8E 28
Leaholme Cl. M40: Man 5B 80
Leah St. OL15: Lit 9M 15
Leaks Ter. WA16: Knut 6G 132
(off Red Cow Yd.)
Leak St. M16: Old T 3B 94
(off Hadfield St.)
Lealholme Av. WN2: Asp 9K 35
Leamington Av. BL9: Bury 5L 25
M20: Man 4E 106
WA12: N Wil 8F 86
Leamington Ct. SK5: Stoc 1C 108
Leamington Ho. M15: Man 4G 95
(off Denmark Rd.)
Leamington Rd. M30: Ecc 7B 76
M41: Urm 6B 92
SK5: Stoc 1C 108
(not continuous)
SK10: Macc 3D 130
Leamington St. M11: Man 2B 96
OL4: O'ham 3N 63
OL12: Roch 5C 28
Leamore Wlk. M9: Man 8K 61
(off Leconfield Dr.)
Lea Mt. Dr. BL9: Bury 9C 26
Leam St. OL6: A Lyne 6A 82
Leander Cl. M9: Man 9K 61
M26: Rad 6E 40
Leander Dr. OL11: Roch 3B 44
Lea Rd. SK4: Stoc 4N 107
SK8: H Grn 6G 117
Leas, The WA15: Hale 4H 115
Leaside Av. OL1: Chad 1F 62
Leaside Cl. OL12: Roch 3B 28
Leaside Dr. M20: Man 3J 107
Leaside Gro. M28: Walk 8M 57
Leaside Way SK9: Wilm 8H 123
Lea St. SK22: N Mil 7L 121
WN3: Wig 4D 52
Leatham Royd HD7: Mars 1H 49
(off Manchester Rd.)
Leaton Av. M23: Wyth 1N 115
Leavale Cl. M38: Lit H 7G 56
Leavengreave Ct. OL12: Whitw 2B 14
Lea Vw. OL2: O'ham 9G 44
Leaview WN1: Wig 2J 53
Leaway OL12: W'le 8G 15
WN2: I Mak 4J 53
Le Bas Ho. M20: Man 2E 106
Lecester Rd. M8: Man 4G 79
Leckenby Cl. M28: Wors 4H 75
(off Border Brook La.)
Leconfield Dr. M9: Man 7K 61
Leconfield Rd. M30: Ecc 6N 75
LECTURERS CLOSE 7G 38
Lecturers Cl. BL3: Bolt 7G 38
Ledbroke Cl. M5: Sal 2A 94
Ledburn WN8: Skel 9A 32
Ledburn Cl. M15: Man 9C 4 (3C 94)
Ledburn Ct. M15: Man 9C 4
Ledbury Av. M41: Urm 6C 92
Ledbury Cl. M24: Mid 5M 61
Ledbury Rd. M35: Fail 6C 80
Ledbury St. WN7: Lei 3H 73
(Orchard La.)
WN7: Lei 4H 73
(Sandgate Cl.)
Ledbury Wlk. M9: Man 8H 61
Ledgard Av. WN7: Lei 6F 72
Ledge Ley SK8: Chea H 7K 117
Ledley St. SK10: Boll 6K 129
Ledmore Gro. WN4: Gars 7A 70
Ledsham Av. M9: Man 6F 60
Ledson Rd. M23: Wyth 2M 115
Ledward La. WA14: Bow 5B 114
Lee Av. BL3: Bolt 9E 38
WA14: B'ath 9B 104
Leebangs Rd. SK14: B'tom 9K 99
Lee Bank BL5: W'ton 3J 55
Leech Av. OL6: A Lyne 5B 82
Leech Brook Av. M34: Aud 3J 97
Leech Brook Cl. M34: Aud 3J 97
Leech St. SK14: Hyde 6C 98
SK15: Stal 9D 82
Lee Cl. M44: Irl 8G 91
WA16: Knut 7F 132
Lee Ct. M22: Nor 8D 106
Lee Cres. M32: Stre 6L 93
Lee Cross OL3: Dig 8N 47
Lee Dale Cl. M34: Dent 7L 97
Leedale St. M12: Man 7M 95
Leeds Cl. BL9: Bury 9A 42
Leeds St. WN3: Wig 9G 9 (4E 52)
Leeds St. Ind. Est.
WN3: Wig 9G 9 (4E 52)
Lee Flds. OL3: Upp 3L 65
Leefields Cl. OL3: Upp 3L 65
Lee Fold M29: Ast 3D 74
Leegate Cl. SK4: Stoc 4L 107
Leegate Dr. M9: Man 7L 61
Leegate Gdns. SK4: Stoc 4L 107
Leegate Ho. SK4: Stoc 4M 107
Leegate Rd. SK4: Stoc 4L 107
(not continuous)
Leegrange Rd. M9: Man 1K 79
Lee Gro. BL4: Farn 3G 57
LEE HEAD 2M 111
Lee Head SK13: Char 3M 111
Leek Old Rd. SK11: Sut E 9J 131
Leek St. M26: Rad 9E 40
Lee La. BL6: Hor 9C 20
WN2: Abr 2L 71
Leemans Hill St. BL8: Tot 8G 25
Lee Rd. M9: Man 2K 79
LEES 5B 64
Lees Av. M34: Dent 7J 97
LEESBROOK 5A 64
Lees Brook Pk. OL4: O'ham 5A 64
Lees Cotts. BL7: Tur 3K 23
Lee's Ct. SK1: Stoc 3L 9 (7D 108)
LEESFIELD 6A 64
Leesfield OL6: A Lyne 5D 6 (6M 81)
Lees Gro. OL4: O'ham 6A 64
Lees Hall Ct. M14: Man 9J 95
Lees Hall Cres. M14: Man 9J 95
Lees Ho. OL4: Lees 4B 64
Lee Side OL3: Dig 9N 47
Leeside SK4: Stoc 7M 107
Lees La. SK9: Wilm 7N 123
SK10: P'bury 7N 123
WN8: Dal, Roby M 4A 32
Lees New Rd. OL4: O'ham 9A 64
Leeson Av. PR7: Char R 1A 18
(not continuous)
Lees Pk. Av. M43: Droy 8G 80
Lees Pk. Way M43: Droy 8G 80
Lees Rd. OL4: O'ham 4M 63
OL5: Mos 8E 64
OL6: A Lyne 4A 82
PR6: And 5L 19
SK7: Bram 1B 124
Lees Row SK13: Had 4E 100
Lees Sq. OL6: A Lyne 7F 6 (7N 81)
Lees St. M11: Man 2B 96
M18: Man 2B 96
M24: Mid 4B 62
M27: Pen 1F 76
M43: Droy 8F 80
OL2: Shaw 5M 45
(not continuous)
OL5: Mos 9F 64
OL6: A Lyne 6M 81
OL8: O'ham 2L 81
SK15: Stal 8D 82
Lees St. E. OL2: Shaw 5N 45
(off Lees St.)
Lees St. Ent. Trad. Est.
M18: Man 3C 96
Leestone Rd. M22: Shar 1D 116
Lee St. BL9: Bury 5N 25
M24: Mid 9L 43
M46: Ath 9M 55
OL3: Upp 3L 65
OL8: O'ham 5B 8 (5H 63)
OL15: Lit 8M 15
SK1: Stoc 3L 9 (7D 108)
Leesway OL4: Lees 6B 64
Leesway Dr. M34: Dent 7L 97
Leeswood Av.
M21: Cho H 2B 106
Lee Va. Dr. SK13: Char 1N 111
Leewood M27: Clif 7D 58
Leewood Ct. SK4: Stoc 5N 107
Left Bank M3: Man 5D 4 (9D 78)
Leftbank M3: Man 4D 4 (9D 78)
Le Gendre St. BL2: Bolt 3J 39
Le Gendre St. Sth. BL2: Bolt 3K 39
Legh Cl. SK12: Poy 2J 125
Legh Ct. M33: Sale 5K 105
WA3: Gol 1K 87
WA16: Knut 5K 133
(off Montmorency Rd.)
Legh Dr. M34: Aud 9F 80
SK6: Wood 2M 109
Legh Gdns. WA16: Knut 7H 133
Legh Ho. WA16: Knut 7H 133
Leghorn Wlk. M11: Man 9L 79
(off Yeoman Wlk.)
Legh Rd. M7: Sal 2C 78
M33: Sale 5L 105
SK10: Adl 9G 125
SK10: P'bury 5E 128
SK12: Dis 9D 120
WA16: Knut 7H 133
Legh St. M7: Sal 3C 78
M13: Man 4H 95
M30: Ecc 9C 76
WA3: Gol 1K 87
WA12: N Wil 6C 86
(not continuous)
WN4: A Mak 8E 70
Legion Gro. M7: Sal 4D 78
Legwood Ct. M41: Urm 7C 92
Leicester Av. BL6: Hor 1C 36
M7: Sal 2E 78
M34: Dent 8K 97
M43: Droy 7D 80
WA15: Tim 8G 104
WN2: Hin 5B 54
Leicester Ct. M7: Sal 1D 78
Leicester Dr. SK13: Glos 9H 101
Leicester Rd. M7: Sal 4D 78
M29: Tyld 9B 56
M33: Sale 3H 105
M35: Fail 5E 80
M45: Whitef 2K 59
WA15: Hale 5E 114
Leicester St. OL4: O'ham 5M 63
OL7: A Lyne 5C 6 (6M 81)
OL11: Roch 8E 28
SK5: Stoc 7D 96
Leicester Wlk. M7: Sal 4D 78
(off Brighton Av.)
LEIGH 5H 73
Leigh & Lowton Sailing Club 8C 72
Leigh Arc. WN1: Wig 7J 9
Leigh Av. M27: Swin 5D 76
SK6: Mar 2B 120
WA16: Knut 5J 133
Leighbrook Rd. M14: Man 9G 95
Leigh Bus. Pk. WN7: Lei 7K 73
Leigh Centurions RLFC 7F 72
Leigh Cl. BL8: Tot 6E 24
Leigh Commerce Pk. WN7: Lei 8K 73
Leigh Comn. BL5: W'ton 2G 54
Leigh Cotts. WA15: Tim 3J 115
LEIGH END 1L 89
Leigh Fold SK14: Hyde 4B 98
Leigh Golf Course 5E 88
Leigh Indoor Sports Cen. 7F 72
Leigh La. BL8: Bury 1G 40
Leigh Rd. BL5: W'ton 3H 55
(not continuous)
M28: Wors 4H 75
(not continuous)
M46: Ath 3H 73
SK9: Wilm 9C 122
WA15: Hale 5E 114
WN2: Hin 1D 72
WN7: Lei 3H 73
Leigh Sports Village 6F 72
Leigh St. BL4: Farn 3L 57
BL5: W'ton 2G 54
BL8: Bury 9F 24
OL10: H'ood 2G 43
OL16: Roch 6H 29
SK11: Macc 5J 131
SK14: Hyde 7B 98
WN1: Wig 9M 9 (4G 53)
WN2: Asp 9B 36
Leigh St. WN2: Hin 1D 72
WN7: Lei 5E 72
Leighton Av. BL1: Bolt 4C 38
M24: Mid 6N 61
M46: Ath 8K 55
OL15: Lit 3K 29
Leighton Dr. SK6: Mar B 8F 110
WN7: Lei 9D 72
Leighton Rd. M16: Old T 5B 94
Leighton St. M40: Man 2M 79
M46: Ath 8K 55
Leinster Rd. M27: Swin 3E 76
Leinster St. BL4: Farn 3K 57
Leith Av. M33: Sale 4L 105
Leith Pl. OL8: O'ham 9J 63
Leith Rd. M33: Sale 4L 105
Le Mans Cres.
BL1: Bolt 3K 7 (5G 38)
Lemnos St. OL1: O'ham 1F 8 (4L 63)
Lemonpark Ind. Est.
OL10: H'ood 3K 43
Lemon St. M29: Tyld 2A 74
Lena St. BL1: Bolt 2G 38
M1: Man 5K 5 (9G 78)
Len Cox Wlk. M4: Man 3K 5
Lenfield La. OL1: O'ham 2J 63
Leng Rd. M40: Man 5B 80
Lenham Av. M30: Ecc 8B 76
(off Dover St.)
Lenham Cl. SK5: Stoc 2F 108
Lenham Gdns. BL2: Bolt 6M 39
Lenham Towers SK5: Stoc 2F 108
Lenham Wlk. M22: Wyth 7C 116
Lennox Gdns. BL3: Bolt 7A 38
Lennox Ho. OL6: A Lyne 5E 6 (6M 81)
Lennox St. M34: Aud 3J 97
OL6: A Lyne 6E 6 (7N 81)
Lennox Wlk. OL10: H'ood 3E 42
Lenora St. BL3: Bolt 8C 38
Lenten Gro. OL10: H'ood 5J 43
Lenthall Wlk. M8: Man 3E 78
(off Crookhill Dr.)
Lentmead Dr. M40: Man 1M 79
Lenton Gdns. M22: Shar 2D 116
Lentworth Dr. M28: Walk 6K 57
Leominster Dr. M22: Wyth 4D 116
Leominster Rd. M24: Mid 5N 61
Leonard Ct. WN7: Lei 5D 72
Leonardin Cl. OL2: Shaw 4K 45
Leonard Pl. WN7: Lei 6D 72
Leonard St. BL3: Bolt 9F 38
OL11: Roch 3A 44
Leonard Way OL2: O'ham 9K 45
Leopold Av. M20: Man 3F 106
Leopold Ct. OL11: Roch 6B 28
Leopold St. OL11: Roch 6B 28
WN5: Wig 6M 51
(not continuous)
Lepp Cres. BL8: Bury 7J 25
Leroy Dr. M9: Man 9J 61
Lerryn Dr. SK7: Bram 6B 118
Lesley Rd. M32: Stre 8G 93
Leslie Av. BL9: Bury 9M 41
OL9: Chad 8F 62
Leslie Gro. WA15: Tim 1G 114
Leslie Hough Way M6: Sal 6A 78
Leslie St. BL2: Bolt 3J 39
M14: Man 6G 94
Lessingham Av. WN1: Wig 9E 34
Lester Rd. M38: Lit H 6F 56
Lester St. M32: Stre 7K 93
Letchworth Av. OL11: Roch 8E 28
Letchworth St. M14: Man 6G 94
Letcombe Cl. WN7: Lei 3H 73
Letham St. OL8: O'ham 9K 63
Letitia St. BL6: Hor 1C 36
Levedale Rd. M9: Man 7K 61
Leven Cl. BL4: Kea 5B 58
Levengreave Cl. WN2: Hin 8E 54
Levenhurst Rd. M8: Man 3E 78
Levens Cl. SK8: Gat 3G 116
Levens Dr. BL2: Bolt 3M 39
LEVENSHULME 8M 95
Levenshulme Rd. M18: Man 5B 96
Levenshulme Station (Rail) 8M 95
Levenshulme Swimming Pools 8N 95
Levenshulme Ter. M19: Man 8M 95
(off Stockport Rd.)
Levenshulme Trad. Est.
M19: Man 7A 96
Levens Pl. WN2: I Mak 3K 53
WN5: Wig 4N 51
Levens Rd. SK7: H Gro 5G 118
Levens St. M6: Sal 5A 78
M40: Man 3M 79
Levens Wlk. OL9: Chad 6E 62
WN5: Wig 4N 51
Leven Wlk. M23: Wyth 1N 115
M45: Whitef 3B 60
Lever Av. M27: Clif 9H 59
Lever Bri. Pl. BL3: Bolt 7L 39
Lever Chambers BL1: Bolt 4K 7
Lever Cl. M29: Tyld 1A 74
Lever Ct. M7: Sal 2N 77
Lever Dr. BL3: Bolt 8F 38
LEVER EDGE 9F 38
Lever Edge La. BL3: Bolt 1D 56
Leverett Cl. WA14: Alt 2A 114
Lever Gdns. BL3: Lit L 9A 40
Lever Gro. BL2: Bolt 7H 39
Lever Hall Rd. BL2: Bolt 5L 39
Leverhulme Av. BL3: Bolt 9H 39
Lever Pk. 5C 20
Lever Pk. Av.
BL6: Hor, R'ton 9C 20
Lever Shop. Pde. BL3: Bolt 8F 38
Lever St. BL0: Ram 8H 11
BL2: Bolt 7H 39
BL3: Bolt 8F 38
(not continuous)
BL3: Lit L 8A 40
BL5: W'ton 9G 37
M1: Man 4J 5 (9G 78)
M24: Mid 2M 61
M26: Rad 7F 40
M29: Tyld 1A 74
Lever St. OL10: H'ood 1J 43
SK7: H Gro 5H 119
WN1: Wig 7J 9 (3F 52)
Lever Wlk. M24: Mid 4L 61
Levington Dr. OL8: O'ham 2L 81
Levi St. BL1: Bolt 3A 38
Lewes Av. M34: Dent 8K 97
Lewes Wlk. OL9: Chad 5F 62
Lewis Av. M9: Man 1K 79
M41: Urm 4D 92
Lewis Cl. PR7: Adl 7H 19
WN3: Wig 6D 52
Lewis Dr. OL10: H'ood 3E 42
Lewisham Av. M40: Man 6N 79
Lewisham Cl. OL2: O'ham 6G 44
Lewisham Ho. BL1: Bolt 3F 38
(off Kenton Cl.)
Lewis Rd. M43: Droy 8C 80
SK5: Stoc 8D 96
Lewis St. M30: Ecc 9D 76
M40: Man 7J 79
OL2: Shaw 7M 45
OL10: H'ood 1K 43
SK14: Hyde 6B 98
Lewtas St. M30: Ecc 9E 76
Lexton Av. M8: Man 9G 60
Leybourne Av. M19: Man 7N 95
Leybourne M. M7: Sal 4D 78
(off Gt. Cheetham St. E.)
Leybourne St. BL1: Bolt 2F 38
Leybrook Rd. M22: Wyth 4B 116
Leyburn Av. M32: Stre 6J 93
M41: Urm 8A 92
OL2: O'ham 8H 45
Leyburn Cl. M45: Whitef 3L 59
WN1: Wig 2J 53
Leyburne Rd. SK2: Stoc 1H 119
Leyburn Gro. BL4: Farn 2L 57
(off Spring St.)
SK6: Rom 6N 109
Leyburn Ho. M13: Man 5J 95
Leyburn Rd. M40: Man 9A 62
Leycester Cl. WA16: Knut 8J 133
Leycester Dr. WA16: Mob 1M 133
Leycester Rd. WA16: Knut 9H 133
Leycett Dr. M23: Wyth 7N 105
Ley Cres. M29: Ast 4C 74
Leycroft St. M1: Man 6L 5 (1G 95)
Leyden Wlk. M23: Wyth 3N 115
Ley Dr. OL10: H'ood 5K 43
Leyfield Av. SK6: Rom 6N 109
Leyfield Ct. SK6: Rom 6N 109
Leyfield Rd. OL16: Miln 7H 29
Leygate Vw. SK22: N Mil 7L 121
Ley Hey Av. SK6: Mar 9C 110
Ley Hey Ct. SK6: Mar 9C 110
LEY HEY PARK 9B 110
Ley Hey Rd. SK6: Mar 9C 110
Leyland Av. M20: Man 5J 107
M44: Irl 5J 91
SK8: Gat 1G 116
WN2: Hin 8N 53
LEYLAND GREEN 5M 69
Leyland Grn. Rd. WN4: Gars 5N 69
LEYLAND MILL BROW 8G 34
Leyland Mill La. WN1: Wig 9F 34
Leylands La. SK14: B'tom 2H 111
Leyland St. BL9: Bury 8M 41
SK4: Stoc 2J 9 (7C 108)
WN2: Abr 1K 71
WN2: Hin 7M 53
Ley La. SK6: Mar B 7F 110
Ley Rd. M29: Ast 3A 74
(not continuous)
Leys Rd. WA14: Tim 8E 104
Leyton Av. M40: Man 3N 79
Leyton Cl. BL4: Farn 2G 57
Leyton Dr. BL9: Bury 7M 41
Leyton St. OL12: Roch 3D 28
Leywell Dr. OL1: O'ham 9A 46
Leywell Rd. M9: Man 2L 79
Liberty OL6: A Lyne 8B 6
Library La. OL9: O'ham 1A 8 (3H 63)
Library St. BL5: W'ton 3H 55
WN1: Wig 8K 9 (3F 52)
Library Theatre
Manchester 6G 4
(off St Peter's Sq.)
Library Wlk. M2: Man 5G 4
Libra St. BL1: Bolt 2E 38
(off Darwin St.)
Lichen Cl. PR7: Char R 1A 18
Lichens Cres. OL8: O'ham 8L 63
Lichfield Av. BL2: Bolt 2J 39
M29: Ast 3D 74
OL6: A Lyne 3A 82
SK5: Stoc 1C 108
WA3: Low 1N 87
WA15: Hale 4J 115
Lichfield Cl. BL4: Farn 2H 57
M26: Rad 7D 40
OL3: Dens 2F 46
WA16: Knut 6K 133
Lichfield Dr. BL8: Bury 9K 25
M8: Man 3G 79
M25: Pres 9B 60
M27: Swin 4F 76
OL9: Chad 2E 62
Lichfield Gro. WN4: A Mak 8F 70
Lichfield Rd. M26: Rad 7D 40
M30: Ecc 6F 76
M41: Urm 5D 92
Lichfield St. M6: Sal 5N 77
WN5: Wig 6N 51
Lichfield Ter. OL16: Roch 9G 28
Lichfield Wlk. SK6: Rom 7L 109
Lidbrook Wlk. M12: Man 3K 95
Liddington Hall Dr. BL0: Ram 1H 25
Lidgate Cl. WN3: Wins 8A 52
Lidgate Gro. BL4: Farn 3K 57
(off Westminster St.)
M20: Man 5F 106
Lidgett Cl. M38: Lit H 6K 57
Lidgetts La. SK10: Rain 9N 129
Lidiard St. M8: Man 1F 78
Lido Ho. OL4: Grot 5D 64

Lieutenant Wlk. *M5: Sal 1A 94*
(off Tatton St.)
Lifestyle Fitness Cen. 6F 130
Liffey Av. M22: Wyth 4D 116
Lifton Av. M40: Man 6K 79
Light Alders La. SK12: Dis 8D 120
Lightbirches La. OL5: Mos 9E 64
Lightborne Rd. M33: Sale 4D 104
Lightbounds Rd. BL1: Bolt 1A 38
Lightbourne Av. M27: Swin 3F 76
LIGHTBOURNE GREEN 3F 76
Lightbowne Rd. M40: Man 4M 79
Lightburn Av. OL15: Lit 1J 29
Lightburne Av. BL1: Bolt 5C 38
WN7: Lei 7G 72
Lightfoot Wlk. *M11: Man 9L 79*
(off Newcombe Cl.)
Lighthorne Av. SK3: Stoc 9L 107
Lighthorne Gro. SK3: Stoc 9L 107
Lighthorne Rd. SK3: Stoc 9L 107
Lighthouse OL15: Lit 5N 15
Lighthurst La. PR7: Chor 1G 18
Light Oaks Rd. M6: Sal 6H 77
WA3: G'ury 3L 89
Lightowlers La. OL15: Lit 7A 16
Lightshaw La. WA3: Gol, Low 6L 71
Lightwood M28: Wors 2J 75
Lightwood Cl. BL4: Farn 2M 57
Lignum Av. OL9: Chad 3F 62
Lilac Av. BL9: Bury 5K 41
M27: Swin 2G 76
OL16: Miln 1L 45
SK14: Hyde 9A 98
WA16: Knut 7E 132
WN4: Gars 5A 70
WN6: Wig 9D 34
WN7: Lei 3G 73
Lilac Ct. M6: Sal 8N 77
Lilac Gdns. BL3: Bolt 9J 39
WN3: I Mak 7J 53
Lilac Gro. M25: Pres 5N 59
M40: Man 1M 79
OL9: Chad 3F 62
WN5: Bil 6H 69
Lilac La. OL8: O'ham 9H 63
Lilac Rd. OL11: Roch 2D 44
WA3: Gol 9K 71
WA15: Hale 4G 114
Lilac St. SK2: Stoc 1D 118
Lilac Vw. Cl. OL2: Shaw 6N 45
Lilac Wlk. M31: Part 5F 102
Lila St. M9: Man 3L 79
Lilburn Cl. BL0: Ram 1J 25
Liley St. OL16: Roch 8F 8 (6E 28)
LILFORD 4J 73
Lilford Cl. M12: Man 3M 95
Lilford Sq. SK11: Macc 7H 131
Lilford St. M46: Ath 9K 55
WN7: Lei 6G 72
Lilian Dr. WN6: Wig 9D 34
Lilian St. M16: Old T 5B 94
Lillian Gro. SK5: Stoc 9D 96
Lilly St. BL1: Bolt 4E 38
SK14: Hyde 9C 98
Lilmore Av. M40: Man 4A 80
Lilstock Wlk. *M9: Man 8K 61*
(off Woodmere Dr.)
Lily Av. BL4: Farn 2J 57
Lilybrook Dr. WA16: Knut 7H 133
Lily Cl. SK3: Stoc 2B 118
LILY HILL 1M 59
Lily Hill St. M45: Whitef 1L 59
Lily La. M9: Man 3L 79
WN2: Bam, P Bri 3J 71
LILY LANES 2A 82
Lily Lanes OL5: Mos 2B 82
OL6: A Lyne 2B 82
Lily Pl. WN4: A Mak 8F 70
Lily Rose Cl. BL1: Bolt 2N 37
Lily St. M24: Mid 3A 62
M30: Ecc 9B 76
OL1: O'ham 2J 63
OL2: O'ham 8K 45
OL16: Miln 7K 29
WN4: A Mak 5H 71
Lily Thomas Ct. M11: Man 2B 96
Lima St. BL9: Bury 1A 42
Lime Av. M27: Swin 4C 76
M41: Urm 7B 92
M45: Whitef 4M 59
SK22: N Mil 6N 121
WN7: Lei 2G 73
Lime Bank St. M12: Man 1J 95
Limebrook Cl. M11: Man 2C 96
Lime Cl. M6: Sal 7N 77
SK16: Duk 3A 98
WA3: Rix 6B 102
WN2: Abr 3M 71
Lime Ct. M6: Sal 7N 77
Lime Cres. M16: Old T 5A 94
Limeditch Rd. M35: Fail 1E 80
LIME FIELD 3K 61
LIMEFIELD 7M 25
Lime Fld. SK10: Boll 4M 129
Limefield M24: Mid 3K 61
OL5: Mos 9E 64
OL15: Lit 7B 16
OL16: Roch 6J 29
WN1: Wig 7L 9 (3G 52)
Limefield Av. BL4: Farn 2L 57
WA13: Lym 5A 112
Limefield Brow BL9: Bury 6M 25
Limefield Cl. BL1: Bolt 9C 22
SK6: Mar 9C 110
Limefield Ct. M7: Sal 1C 78
Limefield Dr. WN8: Skel 4C 50
Limefield Rd. BL1: Bolt 9B 22
BL9: Bury 6M 25
M7: Sal 1C 78
M26: Rad 9D 40
Limefield Ter. M19: Man 8M 95
Lime Gdns. M24: Mid 3K 61
SK16: Duk 1M 97
LIME GATE 1G 80
Lime Ga. OL8: O'ham 9G 63
Lime Grn. OL8: O'ham 1H 81
Lime Grn. Pde. *OL8: O'ham 1H 81*
(off Lime Grn.)
Lime Grn. Rd. OL8: O'ham 2G 81
Lime Gro. BL0: Ram 7K 11
BL9: Bury 6M 25
M15: Man 4G 94
M16: Old T 5A 94
M20: Man 5F 106
M25: Pres 5N 59
M28: Walk 1L 75
M34: Dent 5K 97
OL2: O'ham 6H 45
OL6: A Lyne 5N 81
OL10: H'ood 1H 43
OL15: Lit 8K 15
SK8: Chea 1J 117
SK10: Macc 4J 131
SK15: Stal 1B 98
WA3: Low 3N 87
WA15: Tim 9H 105
WN2: Hin 8B 54
LIMEHURST 4L 81
Limehurst WA14: Alt 4A 6 (3C 114)
Limehurst Av. M20: Man 9E 94
OL7: A Lyne 4L 81
Limehurst Ct. OL8: O'ham 1H 81
Limehurst Rd. OL7: A Lyne 4L 81
Lime Kiln La. SK6: Mar 2D 120
Limekiln La. M12: Man 1J 95
Lime Kilns, The M28: Wors 5A 76
Lime La. M35: Fail 3G 80
OL8: O'ham 1G 80
Lime Pl. *SK16: Duk 1M 97*
(off Railway St.)
Lime Rd. M32: Stre 8K 93
Limers Ga. OL12: Whitw 1E 14
OL12: W'le 9D 14
Limerston Dr. M40: Man 5L 79
Limes, The OL5: Mos 1E 82
(The Knoll)
OL5: Mos 1H 83
(The Willows)
OL11: Roch 1A 44
SK3: Stoc 9B 108
WA3: Cul 5F 88
WA3: Low 3A 88
WN6: Stan 6D 34
WN7: Lei 3J 73
Limes Av. WN6: Stan 6E 34
Limesdale Cl. BL2: Bolt 7B 40
LIME SIDE 1H 81
Limeside Rd. OL8: O'ham 9G 62
Limestead Av. M8: Man 2F 78
Lime St. BL4: Farn 3M 57
BL9: Bury 7M 25
M29: Tyld 1A 74
M30: Ecc 9D 76
M46: Ath 8H 55
OL1: Chad 2G 63
OL11: Roch 9A 28
SK6: Bred 4J 109
SK16: Duk 1M 97
(not continuous)
WN1: Wig 7L 9 (3G 52)
Lime Tree Cl. M41: Urm 8E 92
Limetree Dr. BL2: Bolt 2N 39
Lime Tree Gro. M35: Fail 3F 80
Lime Tree La. WA16: H Leg 9E 112
Limetree La. WA13: Lym 8E 112
Limetrees Rd. M24: Mid 3L 61
Limetree Wlk. *M11: Man 9L 79*
(off Albert St.)
Lime Va. WN3: I Mak 7J 53
Lime Va. Rd. WN5: Bil 7G 68
Lime Wlk. M31: Part 5E 102
SK9: Wilm 5J 123
(off Malpas Cl.)
Limewood Mdw. M29: Ast 4D 74
Limley Gro. M21: Cho H 1B 106
Linacre Av. BL3: Bolt 1F 56
Linacre Way SK13: Glos 9H 101
Linbeck Gro. WA3: Low 9A 72
Linby St. M15: Man 9D 4 (2D 94)
Lincoln Av. BL3: Lit L 9A 40
M19: Man 8N 95
M32: Stre 6F 92
M34: Dent 8K 97
M43: Droy 7E 80
M44: Cad 4D 102
SK8: H Grn 8G 116
WA3: Low 9N 71
Lincoln Cl. M29: Tyld 9B 56
OL6: A Lyne 2A 82
OL11: Roch 7E 28
SK10: Macc 2D 130
WN7: Lei 1E 88
Lincoln Cl. Ind. Est.
OL11: Roch 7E 28
Lincoln Ct. M7: Sal 1D 78
M40: Man 6N 79
Lincoln Dr. BL9: Bury 4M 41
M25: Pres 9B 60
OL15: Lit 2L 29
WA15: Tim 2H 115
WN2: Asp 7M 35
WN4: A Mak 8F 70
Lincoln Grn. SK5: Stoc 2F 108
Lincoln Gro. BL2: Bolt 9N 23
M13: Man 4H 95
M33: Sale 4L 105
M46: Ath 8K 55
Lincoln Leach Ct.
OL11: Roch 8D 28
Lincoln Minshull Cl.
M23: Wyth 6M 105
Lincoln Pl. M1: Man 8H 5
SK10: Macc 2D 130
WN5: Wig 2N 51
Lincoln Ri. SK6: Rom 7L 109
Lincoln Rd. BL1: Bolt 4C 38
M24: Mid 6A 62
M27: Swin 3E 76
M35: Fail 4E 80
SK9: Wilm 5K 123
WN2: Hin 6A 54
Lincoln Sq. M2: Man 5F 4 (9E 78)
Lincoln St. M13: Man 5L 95
M30: Ecc 9C 76
OL9: O'ham 6F 62
OL11: Roch 7E 28
Lincoln Towers
SK1: Stoc 4M 9 (8D 108)
Lincoln Wlk. OL10: H'ood 2F 42
SK10: Macc 2D 130
Lincoln Way SK13: Glos 9H 101
Lincombe Hey SK10: P'bury 5G 128
Lincombe Rd. M22: Wyth 7B 116
Lincroft Rd. WN2: Hin 8C 54
Linda Dr. SK7: H Gro 5H 119
Lindale SK14: Hyde 4N 97
Lindale Av. BL1: Bolt 4A 38
BL9: Bury 9N 41
M40: Man 9B 62
M41: Urm 6N 91
OL2: O'ham 4G 45
OL9: Chad 5E 62
Lindale Cl. M28: Wors 3F 74
Lindale Dr. M24: Mid 9K 43
Lindale Ri. OL2: Shaw 5A 46
Lindale Rd. M28: Wors 3F 74
Lindbury Av. SK2: Stoc 9G 108
Linden Av. BL0: Ram 8K 11
BL3: Lit L 7A 40
M6: Sal 4L 77
M27: Swin 3D 76
M33: Sale 4F 104
M34: Aud 2H 97
M46: Ath 9K 55
OL4: O'ham 3A 64
WA15: Alt 1F 6 (2E 114)
WN4: A Mak 5C 70
WN5: Orr 5J 51
Linden Cl. BL0: Ram 4K 11
M34: Dent 6L 97
WA13: Lym 3B 112
Linden Ct. *SK10: Macc 2F 130*
(off Collingwood Cl.)
WN5: Orr 5J 51
Linden Cres. BL8: Tot 8F 24
Linden Dr. M5: Sal 1N 93
Linden Gro. M14: Man 9J 95
M44: Cad 3E 102
SK2: Stoc 3F 118
SK7: Bram 2B 124
WN5: Bil 7G 69
WN5: Orr 5J 51
(not continuous)
WN7: Lei 3G 73
Linden Lea M33: Sale 6H 105
Linden M. M28: Wors 4G 75
Linden Pk. M19: Man 9L 95
Linden Rd. M20: Man 4F 106
M28: Wors 4G 75
M34: Dent 6L 97
SK8: Chea H 4M 117
SK15: Stal 2G 98
WN2: Hin 4A 54
Lindens WN8: Skel 8A 32
Linden St. WN5: Wig 6N 51
Linden Wlk. BL2: Bolt 8J 23
WN5: Orr 5J 51
Linden Way M43: Droy 1C 96
SK6: H Lan 8D 120
Lindenwood OL9: Chad 3C 62
Lindeth Av. M18: Man 5B 96
Lindfield Dr. BL1: Bolt 3F 38
Lindfield Est. Nth. SK9: Wilm 8F 122
Lindfield Est. Sth. SK9: Wilm 8E 122
Lindfield Rd. SK5: Stoc 8D 96
Lindholme WN8: Skel 9A 32
Lindinis Av. M6: Sal 8N 77
Lindisfarne OL12: Roch 5B 8
Lindisfarne Av. WA3: Low 1E 88
Lindisfarne Cl. M33: Sale 7H 105
Lindisfarne Dr. SK12: Poy 2H 125
Lindisfarne Pl. BL2: Bolt 2K 39
Lindisfarne Rd. OL7: A Lyne 5J 81
Lindley Av. WN5: Orr 6G 51
Lindley Dr. WN8: Par 1A 32
Lindley Gro. SK3: Stoc 2B 118
Lindley St. BL3: Lit L 9B 40
BL4: Kea 5B 58
Lindleywood Rd. M14: Man 9K 95
Lindon Av. M34: Dent 7H 97
Lindop Cl. WA16: Knut 6J 133
Lindop Rd. WA15: Hale 6F 114
Lindow Cl. BL8: Bury 7H 25
Lindow Common Local Nature Reserve 7D 122
Lindow Ct. *M33: Sale 5M 105*
(off Northenden Rd.)
SK6: Bred 5H 109
SK9: Wilm 6D 122
Lindow Ct. Farm Caravan Pk.
WA16: Mob 9A 122
LINDOW END 3A 126
Lindow Fold Dr. SK9: Wilm 1C 126
Lindow La. SK9: Wilm 7D 122
LINDOW MOSS 8B 122
Lindow Pde. SK9: Wilm 8E 122
Lindow Rd. M16: Old T 7A 94
Lindow St. M33: Sale 5M 105
WN7: Lei 4F 72
Lindrick Av. M45: Whitef 5K 59
Lindrick Cl. M40: Man 3A 80
SK10: Macc 9G 128
Lindrick Ter. BL3: Bolt 7E 38
Lindrum Av. SK11: Lym G 9H 131
Lindsay Av. M19: Man 8L 95
M27: Swin 3E 76
SK8: Chea H 6N 117
Lindsay Cl. OL4: O'ham 1A 64
Lindsay Rd. M19: Man 9L 95
Lindsay St. BL6: Hor 3F 36
SK15: Stal 8E 82
Lindsay Ter. WN2: Asp 7L 35
Lindsell Rd. WA14: W Tim 8C 104
Lindsgate Dr. WA15: Tim 9H 105
Lindside Wlk. *M9: Man 8K 61*
(off Woodmere Dr.)
Lind St. M40: Man 8K 79
Lindum Av. M16: Old T 5B 94
Lindum Ct. OL10: H'ood 2K 43
Lindum St. M14: Man 6G 95
Lindwall Cl. M23: Wyth 6A 106
Lindy Av. M27: Clif 8F 58
Linear Vw. WA12: N Wil 8F 86
Linear Walkway M30: Ecc 7D 76
Linebank Grn. *WA14: Alt 1E 114*
(off Grosvenor Rd.)
Linehan Cl. SK4: Stoc 6J 107
Lineholme OL2: O'ham 1G 62
Linen Ct. M3: Sal 1B 4 (7C 78)
Lines Rd. M43: Droy 9F 80
M44: Irl 9G 90
Linfield Cl. BL2: Bolt 9L 23
Linfield St. M11: Man 9N 79
Linford Av. M40: Man 9A 62
Lingard Cl. M34: Aud 1G 96
Lingard La. SK6: Bred 3H 109
Lingard Rd. M22: Nor 7C 106
Lingards Dr. M29: Ast 6B 74
Lingards La. M29: Ast 6B 74
(not continuous)
Lingard St. SK5: Stoc 9D 96
WN7: Lei 6K 73
Lingard Ter. M34: Aud 1G 96
Lingcrest Cl. M19: Man 1A 108
Lingdale Rd.
SK8: Chea H 5L 117
Lingdale Wlk. M40: Man 3M 79
SK11: Macc 7H 131
(off London Rd.)
Ling Dr. M46: Ath 9M 55
Lingfield *M16: Whall R 6C 94*
(off Whalley Rd.)
Lingfield Av. M33: Sale 6B 104
SK7: H Gro 5K 119
Lingfield Cl. BL4: Farn 4K 57
BL8: Bury 6J 25
SK10: Macc 9G 128
Lingfield Cres. WN6: Wig 9B 34
Lingfield Rd. M11: Man 8A 80
Lingfield Wlk. *OL9: Chad 4G 62*
(off Kempton Way)
Lingheath M. WA14: W Tim 7B 104
Lingholme Dr. M24: Mid 1H 61
Lingmell Av. WA11: St H 9F 68
Lingmell Cl. BL1: Bolt 4A 38
M24: Mid 1J 61
M41: Urm 5N 91
Lingmoor Cl. M24: Mid 1H 61
WN3: Wig 1D 70
Lingmoor Dr. M29: Ast 3C 74
Lingmoor Rd. BL1: Bolt 3A 38
Lingmoor Wlk. *M15: Man 4E 94*
(off Arnott Cres.)
Lings Wlk. M22: Wyth 6D 116
Linguard Bus. Pk.
OL16: Roch 9E 8 (7E 28)
Linhope Cl. SK4: Stoc 5K 107
Link, The OL2: Shaw 4K 45
SK5: Stoc 2G 108
SK9: Hand 3J 123
Link Av. M41: Urm 8G 92
Linkfield Dr. M28: Wors 4G 74
Link La. OL8: O'ham 9J 63
Link Rd. M33: Sale 7D 104
OL4: Spri 4C 64
Links, The M40: Man 3A 80
SK14: Hyde 3D 98
Links Av. M35: Fail 5D 80
Links Cres. M25: Pres 9D 60
Links Dr. BL6: Los 5K 37
Linksfield M34: Dent 4K 97
Linkside Av. OL2: O'ham 7H 45
Links Pl. OL6: A Lyne 4B 82
Links Ri. M41: Urm 5A 92
Links Rd. BL2: Bolt 9A 24
BL6: Los 5K 37
OL10: H'ood 4J 43
SK6: Mar 3C 120
SK6: Rom 5A 110
SK9: Wilm 2D 126
Links Vw. M25: Pres 1N 77
OL11: Roch 7N 27
Links Vw. Ct. M45: Whitef 4K 59
Links Way OL9: Chad 3G 62
Linksway M25: Pres 9C 60
M27: Swin 4G 76
SK8: Gat 3F 116
Linksway Cl. SK4: Stoc 3M 107
Linksway Dr. BL9: Bury 9N 41
Link Wlk. M31: Part 6F 102
Linkway, The BL6: Hor 4E 36
Linkway Av. WN4: A Mak 5H 71
Linkway Ind. Est. M24: Mid 3N 61
Linley Cl. WN6: Stan 8N 33
Linley Dr. OL4: O'ham 7A 64
Linley Gro. BL0: Ram 3G 25
Linley Rd. M33: Sale 3H 105
SK8: Chea H 7N 117
WN5: Wig 6B 52
Linley St. M26: Rad 7L 41
Linnell Dr. OL11: Roch 5K 27
Linnet Cl. M34: Aud 9G 81
SK2: Stoc 2K 119
WA12: N Wil 6F 86
Linnet Dr. BL9: Bury 9A 26
M44: Irl 6H 91
WN7: Lei 5K 73
Linnet Gro. SK10: Macc 3E 130
Linnet Hill OL11: Roch 7A 28
Linnets Wood M. M28: Walk 8M 57
Linnett Cl. M12: Man 5L 95
Linney La. OL2: Shaw 5N 45
Linney Rd. SK7: Bram 5B 118
Linney Sq. WN1: Wig 7N 9
Linn St. M8: Man 1F 78
LINNYSHAW 8M 57
Linnyshaw Cl. BL3: Bolt 9B 38
Linnyshaw Ind. Est. M28: Walk 8N 57
Linnyshaw La. M28: Walk 7M 57
Linsford Ct. BL3: Bolt 1B 56
Linslade Gdns. *BL3: Bolt 7F 38*
(off Derby St.)
Linslade Ho. *M5: Sal 9M 77*
(off Buckingham St.)
Linslade Wlk. *M9: Man 3J 79*
(off Carisbrook St.)
Linstead Dr. M8: Man 4E 78
Linstock Way M46: Ath 8J 55
Linthorpe Wlk. BL3: Bolt 8C 38
Linton Av. BL9: Bury 8M 25
M34: Dent 6E 96
WA3: Gol 8J 71
Linton Cl. M4: Man 1J 95
Linton Rd. M33: Sale 2J 105
Linton Va. M26: Rad 3B 58
Linton Wlk. M7: Sal 2M 77
(not continuous)
Linwood Cl. WN2: Hin 7N 53
Linwood Gro. M12: Man 7M 95
Linwood St. M35: Fail 4A 80
Lion Brow M9: Man 9J 61
Lion Fold La. M9: Man 8J 61
Lion La. BL6: Bla 2M 35
Lions Dr. M27: Swin 3G 76
Lion St. M9: Man 9J 61
Liptrot St. WN5: Wig 4C 52
Liptrott Rd. PR7: Chor 1D 18
Lisbon St. OL12: Roch 4A 28
Lisburn Av. M21: Cho H 8B 94
M33: Sale 5G 104
Lisburne Av. SK2: Stoc 1H 119
Lisburne Cl. SK2: Stoc 1H 119
Lisburne Ct. SK2: Stoc 1H 119
Lisburne La. SK2: Stoc 2G 119
Lisburn Rd. M40: Man 2M 79
Liscard Av. M14: Man 8G 94
Liscard St. M46: Ath 8K 55
Lisetta Av. OL4: O'ham 6M 63
Liskeard Av. OL2: O'ham 9K 45
Liskeard Cl. OL16: Roch 4G 28
Liskeard Dr. SK7: Bram 8D 118
Lisle St. OL12: Roch 4E 28
Lismore Av. BL3: Bolt 7A 38
SK3: Stoc 9N 107
Lismore Rd. SK16: Duk 2A 98
Lismore Wlk. M22: Wyth 7D 116
Lismore Way M41: Urm 4D 92
Lissadel Science Pk. M6: Sal 7A 78
Lissadel St. M6: Sal 6N 77
Lisson Gro. WA15: Hale 5E 114
Lister Rd. M24: Mid 5G 60
Lister St. BL3: Bolt 9C 38
Liston St. SK16: Duk 1B 98
Litcham Cl. M1: Man 8K 5 (2G 94)
Litchfield Ct. M24: Mid 4G 61
Litchfield Gro. M28: Wors 3A 76
Litherland Av. M22: Wyth 5D 116
Litherland Rd. BL3: Bolt 1F 56
M33: Sale 5L 105
Little 66 BL9: Bury 5A 42
Lit. Ancoats St. M1: Man 3K 5 (8G 78)
Lit. Aston Cl. SK10: Macc 9G 128
Littlebank St. OL4: O'ham 5M 63
LITTLE BOLLINGTON 5J 113
LITTLE BOLTON 9H 77
Lit. Bolton Ter. M5: Sal 8J 77
LITTLEBOROUGH 9M 15
Littleborough Coach House & Heritage Cen. 9M 15
Littleborough Ind. Est. OL15: Lit 9L 15
Littleborough Sports Cen. 7M 15
Littleborough Station (Rail) 9M 15
Littlebourne Wlk. BL1: Bolt 7H 23
Littlebrook Cl. SK8: Chea H 3A 118
SK13: Had 5C 100
Littlebrooke Cl. BL2: Bolt 4J 39
Lit. Brook Rd. M33: Sale 7C 104
Little Brow BL7: Bro X 6H 23
Lit. Carr La. PR7: Chor 1G 19
Lit. Church St. WN5: Wig 5M 51
LITTLE CLEGG 3K 29
Lit. Clegg Rd. OL15: Lit 3K 29
Littledale St. OL12: Roch 6A 8 (5C 28)
(not continuous)
Lit. David St. M1: Man 6J 5 (1F 94)
Little Delph WA11: Hay 2A 86
Lit. Ees La. M33: Sale 2F 104
Lit. Egerton St.
SK1: Stoc 1K 9 (6D 108)
Lit. Factory St. M29: Tyld 1A 74
Littlefields SK14: Mot 5K 99
Little Flatt OL12: Roch 4N 27
Littlegate BL5: W'ton 6G 54
LITTLE GREEN 2A 62
Littlegreen Gdns. M6: Sal 7M 77
Little Grn. Vw. M24: Mid 2N 61
Littleham Wlk. *M18: Man 4A 96*
(off Hampden Cres.)
Lit. Harwood Lee BL2: Bolt 1L 39
Littlehaven Cl. M12: Man 4K 95
Lit. Heath La. WA14: D Mas 2L 113
Lit. Hey St. OL2: O'ham 8L 45
Littlehills Cl. M24: Mid 2K 61
Lit. Holme St. M4: Man 8J 79
Lit. Holme Wlk. BL3: Bolt 8G 39
Lit. Howarth Way OL12: Roch 1G 29
LITTLE HULTON 6H 57
Lit. John St. M3: Man 6D 4 (9D 78)
Little La. M9: Man 7G 61
WN3: Wig 6B 52
WN5: Wig 6B 52
LITTLE LEVER 9B 40
Little Lever Leisure Cen. 9N 39
Lit. Lever St. M1: Man 4K 5 (9G 78)
(not continuous)
Little London WN1: Wig 6K 9 (2F 52)
Lit. Meadow Cl. SK10: P'bury 6F 128
Lit. Meadow Rd. WA14: Bow 6B 114
Little Mdws. BL7: Bro X 6G 22
Lit. Moor Clough BL7: Eger 3F 22
Lit. Moor Cotts. *SK1: Stoc 8F 108*
(off Hampson St.)
Littlemoor Ct. SK13: Glos 9E 100
Littlemoor Ho. OL4: O'ham 3N 63
Littlemoor La. OL3: Dig 8L 47
OL4: O'ham 3N 63
Littlemoor Rd. SK14: Mot 7K 99
LITTLEMOSS 7G 81
Littlemoss Bus. Pk. M43: Droy 7G 80
Lit. Moss La. M27: Clif 9F 58

Littlemoss Rd. M43: Droy 7G 80
Lit. Nelson St. M4: Man 1J 5 (7F 78)
Lit. Oak Cl. OL4: Lees 5B 64
Little Overwood WA14: W Tim 7B 104
LITTLE PARK 3M 61
Little Pasture WN7: Lei 1G 73
Lit. Peter St. M15: Man 8E 4 (2D 94)
Lit. Pitt St. M1: Man 4L 5
Lit. Quay St. M3: Man 5F 4 (9E 78)
Littler Av. M21: Cho H 3B 106
Littlers Point M17: T Pk 4K 93
LITTLE SCOTLAND 2L 35
Little Scotland BL6: Bla 3L 35
Lit. Stones Rd. BL7: Eger 3F 22
Little St. SK2: Stoc 8F 108
SK10: Macc 4G 131
Little Theatre 2A 74
Littleton Gro. WN6: Stan 2B 34
Littleton Rd. M6: Sal 2M 77
M7: Sal 2M 77
LITTLE TOWN 8E 88
Little Town OL8: O'ham 7G 62
Little Underbank
SK1: Stoc 2L 9 (7D 108)
LITTLEWOOD 8M 25
Littlewood *OL2: O'ham* 8L 45
(off Oldham Rd.)
Littlewood Av. BL9: Bury 8M 25
Littlewood Rd. M22: Wyth 3B 116
Littlewood St. M6: Sal 8L 77
Litton Bank *SK13: Gam* 8A 100
(off Riber Bank)
Littondale Cl. OL2: O'ham 7J 45
Litton Fold *SK13: Gam* 8A 100
(off Litton M.)
Litton Gdns. SK13: Gam 8A 100
Litton M. SK13: Gam 8A 100
Liverpool Castle 7B 20
Liverpool Cl. SK5: Stoc 1C 108
Liverpool Rd. M3: Man 6C 4 (1C 94)
M30: Ecc 4L 91
M44: Cad, Irl 5D 102
WA11: Hay 9M 69
(not continuous)
WN2: Hin, P Bri 9L 53
WN4: A Mak, Gars 9M 69
Liverpool Row WA12: N Wil 9G 86
Liverpool St. M5: Sal 9A 78
(Brunel Av.)
M5: Sal 8K 77
(Weaste La.)
M6: Sal 5A 4 (8L 77)
SK5: Stoc 1C 108
Liverstudd Av. SK5: Stoc 9D 96
Liverton Ct. *M9: Man* 6G 61
(off Liverton Dr.)
Liverton Dr. M9: Man 6G 61
Livesey St. M4: Man 1M 5 (7H 79)
M19: Man 9N 95
OL1: O'ham 3N 63
Livingston Av. M22: Wyth 5A 116
Livingstone Av. OL5: Mos 1E 82
Livingstone Cl. SK10: Macc 4D 130
Livingstone Ho. WN1: Wig 2H 53
Livingstone Pl. *M16: Old T* 4A 94
(off Carver St.)
Livingstone St. OL4: Lees 6B 64
OL4: Spri 5D 64
WN4: A Mak 5D 70
LivingWell Health Club
Manchester 7E 4
(off Deansgate)
Livsey Ct. BL1: Bolt 4G 38
Livsey La. OL10: H'ood 2F 42
Livsey St. M45: Whitef 3M 59
OL16: Roch 8E 8 (6E 28)
Lizard St. M1: Man 4K 5
Liza St. WN7: Lei 2G 73
Lizmar Ter. M9: Man 2L 79
Llanberis Rd. SK8: Chea H 6K 117
Llanfair Rd. SK3: Stoc 8A 108
Lloyd Av. SK8: Gat 1F 116
Lloyd Ct. *M12: Man* 3L 95
(off Kelsall St.)
WN7: Lei 3G 72
Lloyd Cres. WA12: N Wil 6C 86
Lloyd Gdns. WA14: Alt 5D 6 (4D 114)
Lloyd Rd. M19: Man 1N 107
Lloyds Ct. WA14: Alt 4C 6 (3D 114)
Lloyd Sq. WA14: Alt 4C 6 (3D 114)
Lloyd St. M2: Man 5F 4 (9E 78)
(not continuous)
M43: Droy 9D 80
OL10: H'ood 3J 43
OL11: Roch 9B 28
OL12: Whitw 5A 14
SK4: Stoc 5B 108
WA14: Alt 4C 6 (3D 114)
WA15: Alt 4D 6 (3D 114)
Lloyd St. Nth. M14: Man 5F 94
M15: Man 5F 94
Lloyd St. Sth. M14: Man 8F 94
Lloyd Wright Av. M11: Man 1K 95
LOBDEN 7C 14
Lobden Cres. OL12: Whitw 7A 14
Lobden Golf Course 7C 14
Lobelia Av. BL4: Farn 2H 57
Lobelia Wlk. *M31: Part* 6F 102
(off Redbrook Rd.)
Lobley Cl. OL12: Roch 3F 28
Local Board St. WN2: I Mak 4J 53
Lochawe Cl. OL10: H'ood 3F 42
Lochinver Gro. OL10: H'ood 3F 42
Lochmaddy Cl. SK7: H Gro 6K 119
Loch St. WN5: Orr 5M 51
Lock 50 Bus. Cen. *OL16: Roch* 8E 28
(off League St.)
Lock Bldg., The M1: Man 7G 5 (1E 94)
Lock Cl. OL10: H'ood 4K 43
Locke Ind. Est. *BL6: Hor* 1D 36
(off Winter Hey La.)
Lockerbie Pl. WN3: Wins 9B 52
Locker La. WN4: A Mak 5J 71
Lockes Yd. M1: Man 8G 5
Lockett Gdns. M3: Sal 2C 4 (8C 78)
Lockett Rd. WN4: A Mak 4E 70
Lockett St. M6: Sal 5N 77
M8: Man 6D 78
Lockhart Cl. M12: Man 4M 95
Lockhart St. OL16: Roch 8F 28
Lockingate St. OL6: A Lyne 4M 81
Locking Ga. Ri. OL4: O'ham 2B 64
Lock Keepers Ct. M43: Droy 1E 96
Lock Keepers M. M27: Pen 2K 77
Locklands La. M44: Irl 7H 91
Lock La. BL3: Bolt 8L 37
BL6: Los 8L 37
M31: Part 5E 102
Lock Mill Pl. OL16: Roch 8E 28
Lock Rd. WA14: Alt 1C 114
Locks, The M44: Irl 8J 91
Lock Side *SK15: Stal* 8E 82
(off Mottram Rd.)
Lockside OL15: Lit 8N 15
SK6: Mar 1D 120
Lockside M. WN1: Wig 9M 9 (4G 53)
Lockside Vw. OL5: Mos 8H 65
SK15: Stal 8E 82
Locksley Cl. SK4: Stoc 6A 108
Locks Vw. WN1: I Mak 3J 53
Lockton Cl. M1: Man 8L 5 (2G 95)
SK5: Stoc 2C 108
Lockton Ct. M1: Man 8K 5
Lock Vw. M26: Rad 3B 58
Lockwood St. M12: Man 6N 95
Locomotion Ind. Est. BL6: Hor 2E 36
Loddon Wlk. *M9: Man* 2K 79
(off Hillier St.)
Lodge, The SK13: Had 3C 100
Lodge Av. M41: Urm 7E 92
Lodge Bank BL6: Hor 1B 36
SK13: Had 3C 100
Lodge Bank Est. BL6: Hor 1B 36
Lodge Bank Rd. OL15: Lit 2K 29
Lodge Brow M26: Rad 1H 59
SK10: Boll 4L 129
Lodge Cl. SK16: Duk 2B 98
WA13: Lym 3C 112
Lodge Ct. SK4: Stoc 6L 107
SK14: Mot 5K 99
Lodge Dr. M29: Ast 4C 74
WA3: Cul 6H 89
Lodge Farm Cl. SK7: Bram 5C 118
Lodge Fold M43: Droy 8F 80
Lodge Grn. SK16: Duk 2B 98
Lodge Gro. M46: Ath 1N 73
Lodge La. M46: Ath 1M 73
OL3: Del 7H 47
SK14: Hyde 3A 98
SK16: Duk 1A 98
WA12: N Wil 9E 70
(not continuous)
WN7: Lei 5N 73
Lodge M. BL0: Ram 8J 11
Lodge Mill La. BL0: Ram 6N 11
Lodgepole Cl. M30: Ecc 1N 91
Lodge Rd. M26: Rad 1H 59
M46: Ath 1N 73
WA16: Knut 5J 133
WN5: Orr 7J 51
Lodges, The M28: Wors 2A 76
Lodgeside Cl. M43: Droy 8F 80
Lodge St. BL0: Ram 6L 11
(Edith St.)
BL0: Ram 8J 11
(Kay Brow)
M24: Mid 2M 61
M40: Man 5K 79
OL7: A Lyne 9A 6 (9K 81)
OL12: W'le 8G 15
OL15: Lit 8M 15
SK14: Hyde 4B 98
Lodge Vw. BL0: Ram 6N 11
BL2: Bolt 1N 7 (4H 39)
M43: Droy 8F 80
Loeminster Pl. WN2: I Mak 4J 53
Loen Cres. BL1: Bolt 1D 38
Loganberry Av. M6: Sal 7N 77
Logan St. BL1: Bolt 8F 22
Logwood Av. BL8: Bury 1K 41
WN5: Wig 4A 52
Logwood Ho. WN5: Wig 3B 52
Logwood Pl. WN5: Wig 3B 52
Loire Dr. WN5: Wig 3C 52
Loisine Cl. OL11: Roch 1N 43
Lok Fu Gdns. M8: Man 5D 78
Lomas Cl. M19: Man 5K 107
Lomas Ct. OL6: A Lyne 7B 6 (7L 81)
Lomas Sq. SK11: Macc 7H 131
Lomas St. M24: Mid 2N 61
M35: Fail 1E 80
SK3: Stoc 9B 108
Lomax's Bldgs. BL2: Bolt 4L 7 (6G 39)
Lomax St. BL1: Bolt 2F 38
BL4: Farn 2K 57
BL8: G'mount 2F 24
BL9: Bury 6N 7 (1N 41)
M1: Man 4M 5 (9H 79)
M26: Rad 1G 59
M45: Whitef 1L 59
OL12: Roch 2F 28
OL15: Lit 7L 15
WN2: P Bri 9L 53
Lombard Cl. SK6: Bred 4K 109
Lombard Gro. M14: Man 9H 95
Lombard St. M46: Ath 3L 73
OL1: O'ham 1C 8 (4J 63)
OL12: Roch 5B 28
Lombardy Ct. M6: Sal 7N 77
Lomond Av. M32: Stre 6K 93
WA15: Hale 4G 114
Lomond Cl. SK2: Stoc 4E 118
Lomond Dr. BL8: Bury 9H 25
Lomond Lodge M8: Man 9E 60
Lomond Pl. BL3: Bolt 6N 37
Lomond Rd. M22: Wyth 5E 116
SK8: H Grn 5E 116
Lomond Ter. OL16: Roch 9G 28
London Cl. WN5: Wig 3A 52
London Flds. WN5: Bil 5J 69
London Pl. SK1: Stoc 3L 9 (7D 108)
SK22: N Mil 5M 121
London Rd. M1: Man 5K 5 (1G 94)
OL1: O'ham 2M 63
SK7: H Gro 4H 119
SK9: A Edg 4F 126
SK10: Adl, P'bury 4F 128
SK11: Lym G, Macc 9N 131
London Rd. Nth. SK12: Poy 2J 125
(not continuous)
London Rd. Sth. SK12: Poy 4H 125
London Rd. Ter. SK11: Macc 7H 131
London Row WA12: N Wil 9G 86
London Sq. SK1: Stoc 3L 9 (7D 108)
London St. BL3: Bolt 8F 38
M6: Sal 6A 78
M45: Whitef 4M 59
Loney St. SK11: Macc 5G 130
Longacre WN2: Hin 2D 72
Longacres Dr. OL12: Whitw 5B 14
Longacres La. OL12: Whitw 4B 14
Longacres Rd. WA15: Haleb 8J 115
Longacre St. M1: Man 6M 5 (9H 79)
SK10: Macc 4G 130
Longbow Ct. M7: Sal 5C 78
Longbridge Rd. M17: T Pk 3G 92
Longbrook WN6: She 5M 33
Longbutt La. WA13: Lym 4A 112
(not continuous)
Long Causeway M46: Ath 3J 73
Longcauseway BL4: Farn 4L 57
Longcliffe Wlk. *BL1: Bolt* 2G 38
(off Hibbert St.)
Long Clough OL2: O'ham 1G 63
Longclough Dr. SK13: Glos 9C 100
Longcrag Wlk. *M15: Man* 4F 94
(off Botham Cl.)
Longcroft M29: Ast 6N 73
Longcroft Dr. WA14: Alt 3B 114
Longcroft Gro. M23: Wyth 9N 105
M34: Aud 1F 96
Long Cft. La. SK8: Chea H 7K 117
Longcroft Pl. WA13: Lym 2D 112
Longdale Cl. OL2: O'ham 8G 45
Longdale Dr. SK14: Mot 6K 99
Longdale Gdns. SK14: Mot 6K 99
Longdell Wlk. *M9: Man* 2K 79
(off Dalbeattie St.)
Longden Av. OL4: O'ham 9B 46
Longden Ct. SK7: Bram 1C 124
Longden La. SK11: Macc 6L 131
Longden Rd. M12: Man 7M 95
WN4: A Mak 7D 70
Longden St. BL1: Bolt 4D 38
SK10: Macc 5J 131
Longendale Rd. WN6: Stan 4A 34
Longfellow Av. BL3: Bolt 9C 38
Longfellow Cl. WN3: Wig 6D 52
Longfellow Cres. OL1: O'ham 8A 46
Longfellow Wlk. *M34: Dent* 1L 109
(off Wordsworth Rd.)
Longfield BL9: Bury 8N 25
M25: Pres 6N 59
Longfield Av. M41: Urm 8C 92
PR7: Cop 3B 18
SK8: H Grn 8H 117
WA15: Tim 1J 115
Longfield Cen. M25: Pres 6N 59
Longfield Ct. SK14: Hyde 3B 98
Longfield Cotts. *M41: Urm* 7B 92
(off Stamford Rd.)
Longfield Cres. OL4: O'ham 2N 63
Longfield Dr. M41: Urm 7B 92
Longfield Gdns. M44: Cad 4E 102
Longfield La. OL4: O'ham 2A 64
Longfield Pk. OL2: Shaw 6L 45
Longfield Rd. BL3: Bolt 1B 56
M23: Wyth 8M 105
OL2: Shaw 6L 45
OL11: Roch 5A 28
Longfield St. WN2: Asp 1K 53
Longford Av. BL1: Bolt 2D 38
M32: Stre 7L 93
Longford Cl. M32: Stre 6L 93
OL9: O'ham 5G 63
Longford Cotts. M32: Stre 7M 93
Longford Ho. M21: Cho H 8M 93
Longford Pk. 7M 93
Longford Pl. M14: Man 5K 95
Longford Rd. M21: Cho H 8M 93
M32: Stre 6L 93
SK5: Stoc 8D 96
Longford Rd. W. M19: Man 8B 96
SK5: Stoc 8B 96
Longford St. M18: Man 3B 96
OL10: H'ood 2J 43
Longford Trad. Est. M32: Stre 6K 93
Longford Wharf M32: Stre 7L 93
Long Grain Pl. SK2: Stoc 2H 119
Longham Cl. M11: Man 9K 79
SK7: Bram 6B 118
Long Hey WA15: Hale 4G 115
WN8: Skel 8A 32
Longhey Rd. M22: Wyth 2C 116
Long Heys La. WN8: Dal 8C 32
Long Hill OL11: Roch 9B 28
Longhill Wlk. *M40: Man* 4M 79
(off Halliford Rd.)
Longhirst Cl. BL1: Bolt 1C 38
Longhope Rd. M22: Wyth 4A 116
Longhurst La. SK6: Mar B, Mel 9E 110
Longhurst Rd. M9: Man 7G 60
WN2: Hin 7B 54
Longlands Cl. OL3: Del 8J 47
Longlands Dr. SK14: Hyde 6E 98
SK22: N Mil 7L 121
Longlands Rd. SK22: N Mil 7L 121
Long La. BL2: Bolt 7L 39
BL5: W'ton 1F 54
BL9: Bury 6L 25
OL3: Dob 1K 65
OL3: G'fld 5N 65
OL9: Chad 8D 62
PR6: H Char 1K 19
SK10: Boll, P Shr 2M 129
SK13: Char 9L 99
WN2: Hin 7C 54
WN8: Uph 8C 50
Longlevens Rd. M22: Wyth 5B 116
Longley Dr. M28: Wors 4B 76
Longley La. M22: Nor, Shar 8C 106
Longley Rd. M28: Walk 9L 57
Longley St. OL1: O'ham 4D 8
OL2: Shaw 7M 45
Long Marl Dr. SK9: Hand 2L 123
Longmead Av. SK7: H Gro 5H 119
WN4: A Mak 6F 70
Longmeade Gdns. SK9: Wilm 8H 123
Long Meadow BL7: Bro X 6K 23
SK14: Hyde 3C 98
Longmeadow SK8: Chea H 8A 118
Longmeadow Gro. M34: Dent 7J 97
Long Mdw. Pas. SK14: Hyde 6A 98
Longmead Rd. M6: Sal 5K 77
Longmead Way M24: Mid 2N 61
Longmere Av. M22: Wyth 4C 116
Long Millgate M3: Man 2G 5 (8E 78)
Longmoor Rd. SK13: Glos 9C 100
LONGMOSS 3B 130
Longnor Grn. *SK13: Gam* 7N 99
(off Brassington Cres.)
Longnor M. SK13: Gam 7N 99
Longnor Rd. SK7: H Gro 7J 119
SK8: H Grn 8J 117
Longnor Way *SK13: Gam* 7N 99
(off Brassington Cres.)
Longport Av. M20: Man 1F 106
Longridge BL7: Bro X 5K 23
WA16: Knut 5K 133
Longridge Av. SK15: Stal 6D 82
WN6: Stan 4C 34
Longridge Cres. BL1: Bolt 2A 38
Longridge Dr. BL8: Bury 4G 40
OL10: H'ood 2E 42
Longridge Trad. Est.
WA16: Knut 5L 133
Longridge Way WN6: Stan 4C 34
Long Row SK10: Boll 5J 129
SK15: C'ook 3J 83
Long Rushes OL2: Shaw 4K 45
LONGSHAW 9H 51
Longshaw Av. M27: Pen 1G 76
WN5: Bil 1J 69
LONGSHAW BOTTOM 1J 69
Longshaw Cl. M8: Man 1H 79
WN5: Bil 1J 69
LONGSHAW COMMON 2J 69
Longshaw Comn. WN5: Bil 1J 69
(not continuous)
Longshaw Dr. M28: Walk 7H 57
Longshaw Ford Rd. BL1: Bolt 8N 21
Longshaw Old Rd. WN5: Bil 1J 69
LONGSHOOT 6M 9 (2G 53)
Longshoot Cl. WN1: Wig 6N 9 (2G 53)
Longshut La. SK1: Stoc 9D 108
Longshut La. W. SK2: Stoc 9D 108
Longsides Rd. WA15: Haleb 8J 115
LONG SIGHT 2J 63
LONGSIGHT 5M 95
Longsight BL2: Bolt 8M 23
Longsight Ind. Est. M12: Man 5L 95
Longsight La. BL2: Bolt 1L 39
(not continuous)
SK8: Chea H 1L 123
Longsight Lodge BL2: Bolt 9M 23
Longsight Rd. BL0: Ram 2G 24
BL8: G'mount 2G 24
M18: Man 6N 95
Longsight Shop. Cen. M12: Man 5L 95
Longsons, The SK5: Stoc 5D 108
Longson St. BL1: Bolt 3H 39
Longstone Rd. M22: Wyth 7F 116
Long St. M18: Man 3C 96
M24: Mid 2M 61
M27: Swin 3F 76
Longthwaite Cl. M24: Mid 1J 61
Longton Av. M20: Man 3F 106
WA3: Low 1M 87
Longton Rd. M6: Sal 5J 77
M9: Man 6H 61
Longton St. BL9: Bury 8M 41
WN2: Hin 7M 53
Longtown Gdns. *BL1: Bolt* 2F 38
(off Gladstone St.)
Longview Dr. M27: Ward 1C 76
Long Wlk. M31: Part 5E 102
Longwall Av. M28: Wors 2J 75
Longwood Av. SK2: Stoc 1F 118
Longwood Cl. SK6: Rom 5B 110
WA11: R'ford 9A 68
Long Wood Rd. M17: T Pk 3H 93
Longwood Rd. M22: Wyth 4D 116
Long Wood Rd. Est. M17: T Pk 3H 93
Longworth Av. BL6: Bla 1M 35
PR7: Cop 3C 18
(not continuous)
Longworth Cl. M41: Urm 8M 91
Longworth Clough BL7: Eger 3E 22
Longworth Clough Nature Reserve
2B 22
Longworth La. BL7: Eger 3D 22
Longworth Rd. BL6: Hor 9E 20
BL7: Bel, Eger 1A 22
Longworth Rd. Nth. BL7: Bel 1N 21
Longworth St. BL2: Bolt 5K 39
M3: Man 6E 4 (1D 94)
Lonsdale Av. M27: Swin 5D 76
M41: Urm 5B 92
OL16: Roch 8F 28
SK5: Stoc 6D 96
WN7: Lei 8F 72
Lonsdale Ct. M24: Mid 4A 62
Lonsdale Gro. *BL4: Farn* 3K 57
(off Westminster St.)
Lonsdale Rd. BL1: Bolt 4C 38
M19: Man 7N 95
OL8: O'ham 9G 62
Lonsdale St. BL8: Bury 2J 41
M40: Man 4A 80
Lonsdale Wlk. WN5: Orr 3M 51
Loom St. M4: Man 3L 5 (8G 79)
Loonies Ct. SK1: Stoc 3L 9 (8D 108)
Lord Av. M46: Ath 1A 74
Lord Byron Sq. M50: Sal 9M 77
Lord Derby Rd. SK14: Hyde 3A 110
Lord Gro. M46: Ath 1A 74
Lord Kitchener Ct. M33: Sale 2H 105
Lord La. M34: Aud 2G 96
M35: Fail 6C 80
Lord La. M. M35: Fail 4D 80
Lord Napier Dr. M5: Sal 2A 94
Lord Nth. St. M40: Man 6K 79
Lord's Av. M5: Sal 8K 77
Lordsfield Av. OL7: A Lyne 6M 81
Lord's Fold *BL1: Bolt* 2A 38
(off New Church Rd.)
Lord Sheldon Way
OL6: A Lyne 6A 6 (7K 81)
OL7: A Lyne 9H 81
Lordship Cl. M9: Man 1L 79
Lordsmead St. M15: Man 9C 4 (3C 94)
Lord Sq. OL16: Roch 7C 8 (6D 28)
Lord's Stile La. BL7: Bro X 5H 23
Lords St. M44: Cad 3D 102
Lord St. BL3: Lit L 9B 40
BL4: Kea 3M 57
BL5: W'ton 2G 55
BL6: Hor 9D 20
BL9: Bury 3B 42
(Roach St.)
BL9: Bury 8M 7 (2M 41)
(Spring St.)
M3: Man 6E 78
M4: Man 6E 78
M7: Sal 6C 78
M24: Mid 1M 61
M26: Rad 9G 40
M29: Ast 4A 74
M34: Dent 5E 96
M46: Ath 1N 73
OL1: O'ham 1D 8 (3K 63)
(not continuous)
OL6: A Lyne 5D 6 (6M 81)
OL15: Lit 9N 15
SK1: Stoc 3K 9 (7D 108)
SK10: Boll 5M 129
SK11: Macc 5H 131
(not continuous)
SK13: Glos 8E 100
SK14: Holl 5N 99
SK15: Duk, Stal 1B 98
SK16: Duk 1B 98
WA3: Cro 9C 88
WA12: N Wil 6D 86
WN1: Wig 2F 52
WN2: Hin 6N 53
WN2: I Mak 4K 53
WN4: A Mak 6G 71
WN7: Lei 5H 73
Lord St. Sth. WN7: Lei 5J 73
Lordy Cl. WN6: Stan 5E 34
Loretto Rd. M41: Urm 8F 92
Lorgill Cl. SK3: Stoc 3D 118
Loring St. M40: Man 5A 80
Lorland Rd. SK3: Stoc 9N 107
Lorna Gro. SK8: Gat 1E 116
Lorna Rd. SK8: Chea H 5N 117
Lorna Way M44: Irl 9J 91
Lorne Av. OL2: O'ham 9F 44
Lorne Gro. M41: Urm 7E 92
SK3: Stoc 1C 118
Lorne Rd. M14: Man 9H 95
Lorne St. BL1: Bolt 2K 7 (5G 38)
BL4: Farn 1K 57
M30: Ecc 1B 92
OL5: Mos 1F 82
OL8: O'ham 7J 63
OL10: H'ood 2J 43
OL12: Roch 2F 28
WN1: Wig 8N 9 (3H 53)
Lorne Way OL10: H'ood 3E 42
Lorraine Cl. OL10: H'ood 4K 43
Lorraine Rd. WA15: Tim 2G 115
Lorton Av. WA11: St H 9E 68
Lorton Cl. M24: Mid 1H 61
M28: Wors 4G 75
Lorton Gro. BL2: Bolt 4N 39
LOSTOCK 6L 37
Lostock (Park & Ride) 6L 37
Lostock Av. M19: Man 8N 95
M33: Sale 4L 105
M41: Urm 6B 92
SK7: H Gro 6F 118
SK12: Poy 2F 124
Lostock Circ. M41: Urm 5F 92
Lostock Cl. OL10: H'ood 1G 42
WN5: Bil 5J 69
Lostock Ct. M32: Stre 5F 92
SK9: Hand 2J 123
Lostock Dr. BL9: Bury 7M 25
Lostock Gro. M32: Stre 6H 93
LOSTOCK HALL FOLD 5H 37
Lostock Hall Rd. SK12: Poy 3F 124
Lostock Ind. Est. BL6: Los 5F 36
(Cranfield Rd.)
BL6: Los 6H 37
(Lynstock Way)
LOSTOCK JUNCTION 7M 37
Lostock Junc. La. BL6: Los 6L 37
Lostock La. BL5: W'ton 7F 36
BL6: Los 7F 36
Lostock Pk. Dr. BL6: Los 5J 37
Lostock Rd. BL5: W'ton 8E 36
M5: Sal 8L 77
M41: Urm 5C 92
SK9: Hand 2J 123
SK12: Poy 4H 125
Lostock Station (Rail) 6L 37
Lostock St. M40: Man 7J 79
Lostock Wlk. M45: Whitef 2B 60
WN7: Lei 4F 72
Lothian Av. M30: Ecc 7N 75
Lottery Row BL1: Bolt 3L 7 (5G 39)
Lottery St. SK3: Stoc 3H 9 (7B 108)
Lottie St. M27: Pen 2G 77
Loughborough Cl. M33: Sale 5D 104
Loughfield M41: Urm 7A 92
Loughrigg Av. OL2: O'ham 4G 44
WA11: St H 9F 68
Loughrigg Cl. M29: Ast 3C 74

Louisa M. M34: Dent 7F 96
Louisa St. BL1: Bolt 2F 38
M11: Man 1A 96
M28: Walk 7L 57
Louis Av. BL9: Bury 9M 25
Louise Cl. OL12: Roch 2G 28
Louise Gdns. BL5: W'ton 5H 55
OL12: Roch 2G 28
Louise St. OL12: Roch 2F 28
(not continuous)
Louis St. BL0: Eden 1K 11
Louvaine Av. BL1: Bolt 9A 22
Louvaine Cl. M18: Man 3C 96
Louvain St. M35: Fail 3C 80
Lovalle St. BL1: Bolt 3D 38
Lovat Dr. WA16: Knut 9H 133
Lovat Rd. BL2: Bolt 5N 39
Lovatt Ct. WA13: Lym 3C 112
Love La. BL0: Eden, Ram 5L 11
SK4: Stoc 6C 108
Loveless Ho. M46: Ath 7M 55
(off Brooklands Av.)
Lovell Ct. M8: Man 9E 60
Lovell Dr. SK14: Hyde 5C 98
Lovers La. M46: Ath 9H 55
OL4: Gras 5F 64
Lovett Wlk. M22: Nor 8D 106
Low Bank OL12: Roch 2G 28
Low Bank Rd. WN4: A Mak 6B 70
Lowbrook Av. M9: Man 8N 61
Lowbrook La. OL4: Wat 2C 64
Lowcock St. M7: Sal 6D 78
Lowcroft WN8: Skel 9A 32
Lowcroft Cres. OL9: Chad 3D 62
LOW CROMPTON 6J 45
Low Crompton Rd. OL2: O'ham 7H 45
Lowcross Rd. M40: Man 4M 79
Lowe Av. M46: Ath 6L 55
Lowe Dr. WA16: Knut 6H 133
Lowe Grn. OL2: O'ham 7J 45
Lowe Mill La. WN2: Hin 6N 53
Lwr. Albion St. M1: Man 7K 5 (1G 94)
Lwr. Alma St. SK16: Duk 9C 6 (9M 81)
Lwr. Alt Hill OL6: A Lyne 2N 81
LOWER ARTHURS 5L 65
Lower Austins BL6: Los 3H 37
Lwr. Bamford Cl. M24: Mid 1M 61
Lower Bank SK13: Glos 9F 100
Lowerbank M34: Dent 4K 97
Lwr. Bank Cl. SK13: Had 6B 100
Lwr. Bank St. BL9: Bury 7J 7 (2L 41)
SK11: Macc 5H 131
(not continuous)
Lwr. Barn Rd. SK13: Had 5A 100
Lower Beechwood OL11: Roch 8B 28
Lower Beestow OL5: Mos 4F 82
Lwr. Bennett St. SK14: Hyde 5N 97
Lwr. Bents La. SK6: Bred 4K 109
Lower Birches OL4: O'ham 7C 64
LOWER BREDBURY 6J 109
Lwr. Bridgeman St.
BL2: Bolt 5M 7 (6H 39)
Lower Broadacre SK15: Stal 3H 99
Lowerbrook Cl. BL6: Hor 3F 36
Lwr. Brook Farm BL5: O Hul 4A 56
Lwr. Brooklands Pde. M8: Man 9D 60
(off Counthill Dr.)
Lwr. Brook La. M28: Wors 5A 76
LOWER BROUGHTON 6D 78
Lwr. Broughton Rd. M7: Sal 5B 78
Lwr. Burgh Way PR7: Chor 1D 18
Lwr. Bury St. SK4: Stoc 1G 9 (6B 108)
Lwr. Byrom St. M3: Man 6D 4 (1D 94)
Lower Calderbrook OL15: Lit 5N 15
(off Calderbrook Rd.)
Lwr. Carr La. OL3: G'fld 5L 65
Lower Carrs OL6: A Lyne 5A 82
SK1: Stoc 3M 9 (7D 108)
Lwr. Chatham St.
M1: Man 8H 5 (2F 94)
M15: Man 9H 5 (2F 94)
Lower Chesham BL9: Bury 1A 42
(off Chesham Cres.)
Lower Crimble OL11: Roch 9K 27
Lower Cft. M45: Whitef 5J 59
Lowercroft Ind. Pk. BL8: Bury 1F 40
Lowercroft Rd. BL8: Bury 2E 40
Lower Crossbank OL4: Lees 3C 64
LOWER CRUMPSALL 2H 79
Lwr. Darcy St. BL2: Bolt 7K 39
Lower Dingle OL1: O'ham 8N 45
LOWER DINTING 8D 100
Lwr. Drake Fold BL5: W'ton 6G 54
Lwr. Edge Av. OL1: O'ham 3J 63
Lwr. Exchange St. SK11: Macc 5H 131
(off Boden St.)
Lowerfield Dr. SK2: Stoc 2K 119
Lowerfield Gdns. WA3: Gol 9M 71
Lowerfield Rd. SK10: Macc 3J 131
Lowerfields OL3: Dob 2K 65
OL8: O'ham 7M 63
Lwr. Fields Ri. OL2: Shaw 4M 45
LOWER FOLD 2A 28
Lower Fold BL2: Bolt 9N 23
BL8: Haw 2A 24
M34: Dent 6L 97
SK6: Mar B 8E 110
Lower Fold Av. OL2: O'ham 8L 45
Lowerfold Cl. OL12: Roch 1A 28
Lwr. Fold Cotts. SK6: H Lan 8A 120
Lowerfold Cres. OL12: Roch 1A 28
Lowerfold Dr. OL12: Roch 1A 28
Lowerfold Way OL12: Roch 1A 28
Lwr. Frenches Dr. OL3: G'fld 6K 65
Lower Gate OL16: Roch 7C 8
Lwr. Goodwin Cl. BL2: Bolt 1M 39
Lwr. Goodwin Fold BL2: Bolt 1M 39
(off Lwr. Goodwin Cl.)
LOWER GREEN 7D 74
Lower Grn. M24: Mid 6L 61
OL6: A Lyne 6N 81
OL12: Roch 4A 28
Lower Grn. La. M29: Ast 8D 74
Lwr. Greenshall La. SK12: Dis 8H 121
Lower Hague SK22: N Mil 7H 121
LOWER HEALEY 2C 28
Lwr. Healey La. OL12: Roch 2C 28
Lwr. Hey La. OL5: Mos 8H 65
Lower Higham Vis. Cen. 9D 98
Lwr. Hill Dr. PR6: H Char 4K 19
Lower Hillgate
SK1: Stoc 2L 9 (7D 108)
LOWER HINDS 4J 41
LOWERHOUSE 5J 129
Lowerhouse SK10: Boll 5J 129
Lower Ho. Dr. BL6: Los 5L 37
Lower Ho. La. OL12: W'le 7F 14
Lower Ho. St. OL1: O'ham 3M 63
Lower Ho. Wlk. BL7: Bro X 5H 23
Lwr. Hyde Grn. SK15: Mill 6H 83
LOWER INCE 6H 53
LOWER IRLAM 9G 90
Lwr. Jowkin La. OL11: Roch 6J 27
LOWER KERSAL 4A 78
Lwr. Knoll Rd. OL3: Dig 7M 47
Lower Knotts BL2: Bolt 7N 23
Lwr. Knowl La. OL12: Roch 9H 13
Lower Landedmans BL5: W'ton 4H 55
Lower La. OL16: Miln, Roch 1G 44
Lower Lea SK12: Dis 9F 120
Lwr. Leigh Rd. BL5: W'ton 5H 55
Lwr. Lime Rd. OL8: O'ham 2G 80
Lower Longshoot
WN1: Wig 7M 9 (3G 53)
Lwr. Lyndon Av. WN6: She 6L 33
Lwr. Makinson Fold BL6: Hor 3F 36
Lwr. Market St. SK14: B'tom 9K 99
Lower Marlands BL7: Bro X 5G 22
Lower Mead BL7: Eger 4G 22
Lwr. Meadow Rd. SK9: Hand 2K 123
Lwr. Moat Cl. SK4: Stoc 5C 108
Lwr. Monton Rd. M30: Ecc 8E 76
LOWER MOOR 3L 63
Lwr. Mosley St. M2: Man 7F 4 (1E 94)
Lwr. Moss La. M15: Man 9C 4 (2C 94)
M45: Whitef 3M 59
Lwr. New Row M28: Wors 1H 75
Lwr. Nuttall Rd. BL0: Ram 1K 25
LOWER OGDEN 9B 30
Lwr. Ormond St. M1: Man 8H 5 (2F 94)
M15: Man 9H 5 (2F 94)
Lwr. Park Cres. SK12: Poy 9G 118
Lwr. Park Rd. M14: Man 5H 95
SK12: Poy 1F 124
LOWER PLACE 9E 28
LOWER POOLS 2B 38
Lower Pools BL1: Bolt 2A 38
Lwr. Rawson St. BL4: Farn 2M 57
Lower Rd. BL0: Ram 6K 11
Lwr. Rock St. SK22: N Mil 8M 121
LOWER ROE CROSS 4J 99
LOWER RUSHCROFT 3L 45
Lower Rushcroft OL2: Shaw 4M 45
Lwr. St Stephen St. WN6: Wig 3D 52
Lwr. Seedley Rd. M6: Sal 7L 77
Lwr. Sheriff St.
OL12: Roch 6A 8 (5C 28)
Lower Southfield BL5: W'ton 4G 54
Lower Sq. SK13: Tin 2C 100
Lower Standrings OL11: Roch 5M 27
(off Bagslate Moor Rd.)
Lower Stones OL3: Del 9H 47
Lower St. BL4: Farn 4K 57
OL16: Roch 9E 28
Lwr. Strines Rd. SK6: Mar 2D 120
LOWER SUMMERSEAT 4J 25
Lwr. Sutherland St. M27: Swin 2E 76
Lower Tenterfield OL11: Roch 3J 27
(off Hutchinson Rd.)
Lower Tong BL7: Bro X 6G 23
Lwr. Turf La. OL4: Scout 4D 64
Lwr. Tweedale St.
OL11: Roch 9D 8 (7D 28)
Lwr. Vickers St. M40: Man 7J 79
Lwr. Victoria St. OL9: Chad 4F 62
Lwr. Wharf St.
OL6: A Lyne 8D 6 (8M 81)
Lwr. Wheat End OL16: Roch 5F 28
Lwr. Woodhill Rd.
BL8: Bury 5G 7 (1K 41)
(not continuous)
Lowerwood La. BL2: Bolt 3J 39
Lwr. Wrigley Grn. OL3: Dig 9M 47
Lowes, The WA14: Bow 6B 114
Lowes La. M34: Dent 8L 97
(off Nottingham Way)
SK11: Gaws 9C 130
Lowes Pk. Golf Course 7N 25
Lowes Rd. BL9: Bury 7M 25
Lowestead Rd. M11: Man 8A 80
Lowestoft St. M14: Man 7G 95
Lowe St. M26: Rad 8F 40
M34: Dent 6M 97
SK1: Stoc 3L 9 (7D 108)
SK11: Macc 5H 131
WA3: Gol 1K 87
Loweswater Av. M29: Ast 3B 74
Loweswater Cl. OL7: A Lyne 6K 81
Loweswater Rd. BL4: Farn 4F 56
SK8: Gat 4G 117
Loweswater Ter. SK15: Stal 6D 82
(off Ullswater Ter.)
Lowfell Wlk. M18: Man 6B 96
Lowfield Av. M43: Droy 7D 80
OL6: A Lyne 5C 82
Lowfield Gdns. WA3: G'ury 2L 89
Lowfield Gro. SK2: Stoc 9D 108
Lowfield Rd. SK2: Stoc 1C 118
SK3: Stoc 1C 118
Lowfield Wlk. M9: Man 8K 61
(off Normanton Dr.)
Low Gate La. OL3: Del 3J 47
Lowgill Wlk. M18: Man 4A 96
(off Beyer Cl.)
Low Green M46: Ath 6A 56
Low Gro. La. OL3: G'fld 6H 65
Low Hall Gdns. WN2: P Bri 8L 53
Low Hill OL12: Roch 2G 28
Lowhouse Cl. OL16: Miln 6L 29
Lowick Av. BL3: Bolt 9H 39
Lowick Cl. SK7: H Gro 5H 119
Lowick Grn. SK6: Wood 3K 109
Lowland Gro. OL7: A Lyne 4L 81
Lowland Rd. SK2: Stoc 3F 118
Lowlands Cl. M24: Mid 6A 62
Lowland Way WA16: Knut 9G 133
Low Lea Rd. SK6: Mar B 9E 110
LOW LEIGHTON 7N 121
Low Leighton Rd.
SK22: N Mil 8N 121
Low Mdws. OL2: O'ham 6H 45
Lowndes Cl. SK2: Stoc 1F 118
Lowndes La. SK2: Stoc 9F 108
Lowndes St. BL1: Bolt 4C 38
Lowndes Wlk. M13: Man 3H 95
(off Copeman Cl.)
Lownorth Rd. M22: Wyth 7D 116
Lowood Av. M41: Urm 5N 91
Lowood Cl. OL16: Miln 7K 29
Lowood St. WN7: Lei 5F 72
Lowrey Wlk. M9: Man 3K 79
(off Craigend Dr.)
Lowry, The 2L 93
Lowry, The M14: Man 9H 95
Lowry Ct. M45: Whitef 1K 59
SK14: Mot 5K 99
Lowry Dr. M27: Pen 1F 76
SK6: Mar B 8E 110
Lowry Gro. SK14: Mot 6K 99
Lowry Ho. M30: Ecc 8E 76
(off Monton La.)
Lowry Lodge M16: Old T 4C 94
(off Hamer Dr.)
Lowry Outlet Mall M50: Sal 2M 93
Lowry Wlk. BL1: Bolt 3E 38
Lows, The OL4: O'ham 6M 63
LOW SIDE 7N 63
Lowside Av. BL1: Bolt 6L 37
SK6: Wood 3N 109
Lowside Dr. OL4: O'ham 6M 63
Low's Pl. OL12: Roch 3E 28
Lowstern Cl. BL7: Eger 4E 22
Lowther Av. M18: Man 6N 95
OL2: O'ham 4G 44
WA3: Cul 5N 89
WA15: Tim 1G 115
Lowther Cl. M25: Pres 8M 59
Lowther Ct. M25: Pres 8M 59
Lowther Cres. M24: Mid 2K 61
Lowther Dr. WN7: Lei 3N 73
Lowther Gdns. M41: Urm 6L 91
Lowther Rd. M8: Man 1F 78
M25: Pres 8M 59
OL11: Roch 9C 28
Lowther St. BL3: Bolt 1H 57
SK10: Boll 5M 129
Lowther Ter. WN6: App B 4G 33
Lowthorpe St. M14: Man 7F 94
LOWTON 2B 88
Lowton Av. M9: Man 3L 79
Lowton Bus. Pk. WA3: Low 1C 88
LOWTON COMMON 9C 72
Lowton Gdns. WA3: Low 4L 87
LOWTON HEATH 3L 87
Lowton Rd. M33: Sale 6D 104
WA3: Gol 8L 71
LOWTON ST MARY'S 2C 88
Lowton St Mary's By-Pass
WN7: Lei 2E 88
Lowton St. M26: Rad 8G 40
Low Wood Cl. SK7: Bram 6A 118
Low Wood Rd. M34: Dent 5E 96
Loxford Ct. M15: Man 9G 4
Loxford St. M15: Man 9G 4 (3E 94)
Loxham St. BL3: Bolt 1L 57
Loxley Chase BL1: Bolt 2F 38
Loxley Cl. SK11: Macc 5F 130
Loxley Wlk. M40: Man 6K 79
(off Filby Wlk.)
Loxton Cres. WN3: Wig 8E 52
Loynd St. BL0: Ram 8J 11
Lubeck St. M9: Man 2K 79
Lucas Rd. BL4: Farn 3H 57
Lucas St. BL9: Bury 1N 41
OL4: O'ham 4M 63
Lucerne Cl. OL9: Chad 5G 62
Lucerne Rd. SK7: Bram 4C 118
Lucien Cl. M12: Man 4K 95
Luciol Cl. M29: Tyld 1D 74
Lucknow St. OL11: Roch 8D 28
Lucy St. BL1: Bolt 3B 38
M7: Sal 5C 78
M15: Man 3C 94
SK3: Stoc 8C 108
Ludford Gro. M33: Sale 6F 104
Ludgate Hill M4: Man 1K 5 (7G 78)
Ludgate Rd. M40: Man 6A 80
OL11: Roch 2E 44
Ludgate St. M4: Man 1J 5 (7F 78)
Ludlow WN8: Skel 8A 32
Ludlow Av. M27: Clif 9G 59
M45: Whitef 5A 60
WN2: Hin 7C 54
Ludlow Cl. SK10: Macc 2J 131
Ludlow Dr. WN7: Lei 3N 73
Ludlow Pk. OL4: O'ham 5A 64
(off Lees Brook Pk.)
Ludlow Rd. SK2: Stoc 8G 108
Ludlow St. WN6: Stan 1N 33
Ludlow Towers SK5: Stoc 1G 109
Ludovic Ter. WN1: Wig 8F 34
Ludwell Wlk. M8: Man 4F 78
(off Barnsdale Dr.)
Lugano Rd. SK7: Bram 4C 118
Luke Fold SK15: Stal 1H 99
Luke Kirby Ct. M27: Pen 1F 76
Luke Rd. M43: Droy 9F 80
Luke St. WN4: A Mak 5G 71
Luke Wlk. M8: Man 4G 78
(off Appleford Dr.)
Lullington Cl. M22: Wyth 6B 116
Lullington Rd. M6: Sal 6K 77
Lulworth WN8: Skel 8A 32
Lulworth Av. M41: Urm 7N 91
Lulworth Cl. BL8: Bury 7J 25
Lulworth Cres. M35: Fail 2F 80
Lulworth Dr. WN2: Hin 7C 54
Lulworth Gdns. M23: Wyth 8M 105
Lulworth Rd. BL3: Bolt 9B 38
M24: Mid 1M 61
M30: Ecc 7C 76
LUMB 2H 11
Lumb Carr Av. BL0: Ram 1G 24
Lumb Carr Rd. BL8: Holc 2G 24
Lumb Cl. SK7: Bram 9C 118
Lumb Cotts. BL0: Ram 2H 11
Lumber La. M28: Wors 2M 75
WA5: Burt 9B 86
Lumb Ho. SK7: Bram 9C 118
Lumb La. M34: Aud 9G 80
(not continuous)
M43: Droy 7G 80
(not continuous)
OL7: Droy 7G 80
SK7: Bram 9C 118
Lumley Cl. M14: Man 5G 95
Lumley Rd. SK11: Macc 5D 130
Lumn Hollow SK14: Hyde 7B 98
(not continuous)
Lumn Rd. SK14: Hyde 7B 98
Lumn's La. M27: Clif, Pen 9J 59
Lumn St. BL9: Bury 5M 25
Lumsdale Rd. M32: Stre 4G 93
Lumsden St. BL3: Bolt 7F 38
Lum St. BL1: Bolt 1M 7 (4H 39)
Lumwood BL1: Bolt 1C 38
Luna St. M4: Man 3K 5 (8G 78)
Lundale Wlk. M40: Man 4M 79
(off Craiglands Av.)
Lund Av. M26: Rad 3H 59
Lund St. M16: Old T 3B 94
Lundy Av. M21: Cho H 3B 106
Lune Cl. M45: Whitef 3N 59
Lunedale WN2: P Bri 9L 53
Lunedale Grn. SK2: Stoc 1J 119
Lune Dr. M45: Whitef 2N 59
Lune Gro. OL10: H'ood 1F 42
WN7: Lei 5E 72
Lunehurst WA3: Low 1A 88
Lune Rd. WN2: P Bri 9J 53
Lune St. M29: Tyld 2A 74
OL8: O'ham 7J 63
Lune Wlk. M43: Droy 1F 96
(off Ellen St.)
M45: Whitef 3N 59
Lune Way SK5: Stoc 3D 108
Lunn Av. M18: Man 3D 96
Luntswood Gro. WA12: N Wil 5D 86
Lupin Av. BL4: Farn 2H 57
Lupin Cl. OL1: O'ham 9B 46
Lupin Dr. WA11: Hay 3C 86
Lupton St. M34: Dent 5K 97
Lurden Wlk. OL9: Chad 7F 62
Lurdin La. WN1: Stan 5E 34
WN6: Stan 5D 34
Lurgan Av. M33: Sale 5J 105
Lutener Av. WA14: W Tim 8C 104
Luton Dr. M23: Wyth 3N 115
Luton Gro. M46: Ath 8K 55
Luton Rd. SK5: Stoc 9D 96
Luton St. BL3: Bolt 8H 39
BL8: Bury 9G 25
Lutyens Cl. SK10: Macc 4D 130
Luxhall Wlk. M40: Man 6N 79
Luxor Gro. M34: Dent 6D 96
LUZLEY 3E 82
LUZLEY BROOK 7L 45
Luzley Brook Rd. OL2: O'ham 7L 45
Luzley Rd. OL5: Mos 2E 82
OL6: A Lyne, Mos 5E 82
SK15: Stal 7E 82
Lyceum Pas. OL16: Roch 7C 8 (6D 28)
Lyceum Pl. M15: Man 9H 5 (2F 94)
Lychgate WN5: Wig 6B 52
Lychgate Ct. BL2: Bolt 4M 39
OL4: O'ham 7B 64
Lychgate M. M21: Cho H 9N 93
SK4: Stoc 6K 107
Lychwood SK6: Mar 1C 120
Lydbrook Cl. BL1: Bolt 4H 7 (6F 38)
Lydden Av. M11: Man 7B 80
Lydford OL11: Roch 9B 8 (7C 28)
Lydford Gdns. BL2: Bolt 7N 39
Lydford Grn. WN6: Stan 4C 34
Lydford St. M6: Sal 6A 78
Lydford Wlk. M13: Man 3H 95
(off Beckhampton Cl.)
LYDGATE
OL4 5F 64
OL15 9B 16
Lydgate PR7: Chor 1D 18
Lydgate Av. BL2: Bolt 4M 39
Lydgate Cl. M34: Dent 8M 97
M45: Whitef 2N 59
SK15: C'ook 4H 83
Lydgate Dr. OL4: O'ham 6N 63
Lydgate Fold OL4: Lyd 6F 64
Lydgate Rd. M33: Sale 6J 105
M43: Droy 7C 80
Lydgate Wlk. M45: Whitef 2N 59
Lydiate Cl. BL3: Bolt 9G 38
Lydiat La. SK9: A Edg 5F 126
Lydney Av. SK8: H Grn 8H 117
Lydney Rd. M41: Urm 6L 91
Lyefield Av. WN1: Wig 2J 53
Lyefield Wlk. OL16: Roch 7F 28
Lymbridge Dr. BL6: Bla 2N 35
Lyme Av. SK9: Wilm 5G 122
SK11: Macc 7H 131
Lyme Clough Way M24: Mid 8L 43
Lyme Ct. SK7: H Gro 4H 119
SK14: Hyde 6B 98
Lymefield Ct. SK2: Stoc 9H 109
Lymefield Dr. M28: Wors 3M 75
Lymefield Gro. SK2: Stoc 1F 118
Lymefield Ter. SK14: B'tom 9L 99
Lymefield Vis. Cen. 9L 99
LYME GREEN 9H 131
Lyme Grn. Bus. Pk.
SK11: Lym G 9G 130
Lyme Gro. M33: Sale 5J 105
M43: Droy 9D 80
SK2: Stoc 9D 108
SK6: Mar 2C 120
Lyme Gro. SK6: Rom 6A 110
WA14: Alt 4B 6 (3C 114)
Lyme Ho. SK4: Stoc 7K 107
Lyme Lea Cl. SK8: Chea H 7N 117
Lyme Pl. SK16: Duk 1M 97
Lyme Rd. SK7: H Gro 6J 119
SK12: Dis 8D 120
SK12: Poy 3N 125
Lymes, The WA14: Bow 6B 114
Lyme St. SK4: Stoc 6K 107
SK7: H Gro 4H 119
WA11: Hay 3B 86
WA12: N Wil 5B 86
Lyme Ter. SK16: Duk 9M 81
Lyme Vw. Ct. SK6: Rom 6A 110
Lymewood Ct. WA11: Hay 2B 86
Lymewood Dr. SK9: Wilm 6K 123
SK12: Dis 9E 120
Lymington Cl. M24: Mid 6N 61
Lymington Dr. M23: Wyth 7K 105
LYMM 4A 112
Lymm Cl. M28: Walk 8H 57
SK3: Stoc 1B 118
Lymm Hall WA13: Lym 4A 112
Lymm Leisure Cen. 5C 112
Lymm Quay WA13: Lym 4A 112
Lymm Rd. WA13: Lym 6F 112
WA14: Lit B 6F 112
Lymm Wlk. SK8: Chea 3M 117
Lynn St. WN2: P Bri 8L 53
Lynbridge Cl. WN5: Orr 6J 51
Lyncombe Cl. SK8: Chea H 9N 117
Lyndale WN8: Skel 8A 32
Lyndale Av. M27: Swin 4D 76
SK5: Stoc 6D 96
Lyndale Dr. OL15: Lit 8L 15
Lyndene Av. M28: Wors 2A 76
Lyndene Ct. OL10: H'ood 1H 43
Lyndene Gdns. SK8: Gat 1G 117
Lyndene Rd. M22: Wyth 2C 116
Lyndhurst Av. M25: Pres 8D 60
M33: Sale 5F 104
M34: Dent 6J 97
M41: Urm 5C 92
M44: Irl 6J 91
OL6: A Lyne 5M 81
OL9: Chad 6D 62
OL11: Roch 4B 44
SK6: Bred 4K 109
SK7: H Gro 6G 118
Lyndhurst Cl. SK9: Wilm 9C 122
Lyndhurst Dr. WA15: Hale 5G 115
Lyndhurst Gdns. M24: Mid 3K 61
Lyndhurst Rd. M20: Man 4F 106
M32: Stre 7H 93
OL8: O'ham 8H 63
SK5: Stoc 7C 96
Lyndhurst St. M6: Sal 8L 77
Lyndhurst Vw. SK16: Duk 9N 81
Lyndon Av. WN6: She 6L 33
Lyndon Cl. BL8: Tot 7F 24
OL4: Scout 3E 64
Lyndon Cft. OL8: O'ham 7G 63
Lyndon Rd. M44: Irl 8G 91
Lyne Av. SK13: Glos 9C 100
Lyne Edge Cres. SK16: Duk 2C 98
Lyne Edge Rd. SK16: Duk 2D 98
Lyneham Wlk. M7: Sal 4E 78
(off Highclere Av.)
Lyne Vw. SK14: Hyde 3C 98
Lyngard Cl. SK9: Wilm 5K 123
Lyngarth Ho. WA14: Alt 1E 114
(off Grosvenor Rd.)
Lyngate Cl. SK1: Stoc 4N 9 (8E 108)
Lyn Gro. OL10: H'ood 1F 42
Lynham Dr. OL10: H'ood 4J 43
Lynmouth Av. M20: Man 2F 106
M41: Urm 9B 92
OL2: O'ham 9G 44
OL8: O'ham 8K 63
SK5: Stoc 1C 108
Lynmouth Cl. M26: Rad 8J 41
OL9: Chad 2C 62
WN6: Wig 9D 34
Lynmouth Ct. M25: Pres 8M 59
Lynmouth Gro.
M25: Pres 8M 59
Lynn Av. M33: Sale 2J 105
Lynn Dr. M43: Droy 8C 80
Lynne Cl. SK13: Glos 9H 101
Lynnfield Ho. WA14: Alt 1D 6
Lynn Gro. SK11: Macc 6G 130
Lynn St. OL9: O'ham 7G 62
Lynnwood Dr.
OL11: Roch 5M 27
Lynnwood Rd. M19: Man 6J 107
Lynroyle Way OL11: Roch 1B 44
Lynside Wlk. M22: Wyth 8C 116
Lynsted Av. BL3: Bolt 9H 39
Lynstock Way BL6: Los 6G 37
Lynthorpe Av. M44: Cad 2E 102
Lynthorpe Rd. M40: Man 9B 62
Lynton Av. M27: Pen 1F 76
M41: Urm 7K 91
M44: Cad 2F 102
OL2: O'ham 9G 44
OL8: O'ham 9G 62
OL11: Roch 1N 43
SK14: Hat 7F 98
WN6: Wig 9D 34
Lynton Cl. OL9: Chad 2D 62
WA16: Knut 7J 133
Lynton Ct. SK9: A Edg 3F 126
Lynton Cres. M28: Walk 2L 75
Lynton Dr. M19: Man 1L 107
M25: Pres 5B 60
SK6: H Lan 7B 120
Lynton Gro. WA15: Tim 2F 114
Lynton La. SK9: A Edg 3F 126
Lynton Lea M26: Rad 8J 41
Lynton M. SK9: A Edg 3F 126
Lynton Pk. Rd. SK8: Chea H 7L 117
Lynton Rd. BL3: Bolt 1D 56
M21: Cho H 8N 93
M27: Pen 1F 76
M29: Tyld 2E 74

Lynton Rd. SK4: Stoc 3A 108
SK8: Gat 2H 117
WN2: Hin 5B 54
Lynton St. M14: Man 7G 95
WN7: Lei 5F 72
Lynton Ter. M26: Rad 4B 58
Lyntonvale Av. SK8: Gat 1G 116
Lynton Wlk. SK14: Hat 7F 98
Lyn Town Trad. Est. M30: Ecc 8D 76
Lynway Dr. M20: Man 3G 107
Lynway Gro. M24: Mid 1N 61
Lynwell Rd. M30: Ecc 8D 76
Lynwood SK9: Wilm 8F 122
WA15: Hale 7G 114
Lynwood Av. BL3: Bolt 1J 57
M16: Whall R 7B 94
M30: Ecc 8D 76
WA3: Low 3A 88
Lynwood Cl. OL7: A Lyne 3L 81
WN8: Skel 4B 50
Lynwood Ct. M8: Man 9E 60
Lynwood Dr. OL4: O'ham 3A 64
Lynwood Gro. BL2: Bolt 9L 23
M33: Sale 3J 105
M34: Aud 9G 80
M46: Ath 8K 55
SK4: Stoc 2A 108
Lynwood Ter. *WN2: Hin* *5N 53*
(off Jenkinson St.)
Lyon Gro. M28: Wors 2A 76
Lyon Ind. Est. WA14: B'ath 9B 104
Lyon Rd. BL4: Kea 5M 57
WA14: B'ath 9C 104
WN6: Wig 1C 52
Lyon Rd. Ind. Est. BL4: Kea 5M 57
Lyons Dr. BL8: Bury 3G 41
Lyon's Fold M33: Sale 2H 105
Lyons Rd. M17: T Pk 2G 93
Lyon St. M27: Swin 3E 76
OL2: Shaw 5M 45
SK11: Macc 5G 131
WN3: Wig 9H 9 (4E 52)
(not continuous)
WN4: A Mak 3C 70
Lyon Way SK5: Stoc 2C 108
Lyra Pl. M7: Sal 7B 78
Lyric Theatre
Salford Quays *2L 93*
(in The Lowry)
Lysander Cl. M14: Man 9G 94
Lytham Av. M21: Cho H 1B 106
Lytham Cl. OL6: A Lyne 4B 82
Lytham Ct. OL6: A Lyne 4B 82
Lytham Dr. OL10: H'ood 3H 43
SK7: Bram 8E 118
Lytham Rd. M14: Man 8K 95
M19: Man 8K 95
M41: Urm 7K 91
SK8: H Grn 6G 117
WN4: A Mak 5C 70
Lytham St. OL12: Roch 2C 28
SK3: Stoc 1D 118
Lytherton Av. M44: Cad 4E 102
Lytle St. M14: Man 1J 107
Lytton Av. M8: Man 4F 78
Lytton Rd. M43: Droy 8E 80
Lytton St. BL1: Bolt 2E 38

M

Mabel Av. BL3: Bolt 9H 39
M28: Wors 3A 76
Mabel Rd. M35: Fail 1E 80
Mabel's Brow BL4: Kea 4M 57
Mabel St. BL1: Bolt 4D 38
BL5: W'ton 5H 55
M40: Man 5B 80
OL12: Roch 3B 28
WN5: Wig 5B 52
Maberry Cl. WN6: She 5H 33
Mabfield Rd. M14: Man 8H 95
Mabledon Cl. SK8: H Grn 7J 117
Mabs Ct. OL6: A Lyne 8G 6 (8A 82)
Mab's Cross 5L 9
Mabs Cross Ct. WN1: Wig 5K 9
Mab's Cross Ho. WN1: Wig 5K 9
Macaulay St. OL2: O'ham 8J 45
Macauley Cl. SK16: Duk 2D 98
Macauley Pl. WN3: Wig 7C 52
Macauley Rd. M16: Old T 7A 94
SK5: Stoc 8B 96
Macauley St. OL11: Roch 2B 44
Macauley Way M34: Dent 9L 97
Mc Bride Riverside Pk.
M24: Mid 3L 61
McCall Wlk. *M11: Man* *8N 79*
(off Trimdon Cl.)
MACCLESFIELD 5H 131
Macclesfield Cl. WN2: Hin 6M 53
Macclesfield Crematorium
SK10: Macc 3F 130
Macclesfield Golf Course 6K 131
Macclesfield Leisure Cen. 3C 130
Macclesfield Rd. SK7: H Gro 8K 119
SK9: A Edg 4F 126
SK9: Wilm 7H 123
SK10: O Ald 4F 126
SK10: P'bury 1D 130
Macclesfield Silk Mus. & Heritage Cen.
....5H 131
Macclesfield Station (Rail) 4H 131
Macclesfield Town FC 8H 131
Macclesfield West Pk. Mus. 3G 130
Maccoll Av. M7: Sal 6C 78
McConnell Rd. M40: Man 3M 79
McCormack Dr.
WN1: Wig 8M 9 (3G 53)
Mac Ct. SK1: Stoc 5L 9
McCready Dr. M5: Sal 1A 94
Macdonald Av. BL4: Farn 4H 57
WN3: Wig 8D 52
Macdonald Rd. M44: Irl 1F 102
Macdonald St. OL8: O'ham 7K 63
WN5: Orr 5M 51
McDonna St. BL1: Bolt 1D 38
McDonough Cl. OL8: O'ham 8L 63
McDowall Wlk. M8: Man 9G 61
Macefin Av. M21: Cho H 4C 106
McEllen Rd. WN2: Abr 3M 71
McEvoy St. BL1: Bolt 2G 38
Macfarren St. M12: Man 6M 95
McGinty Pl. M1: Man 7H 5
Macintosh Mills
M15: Man 8G 4 (2E 94)
McKean St. BL3: Bolt 8H 39
Mackenzie Av. WN3: Wig 8D 52
Mackenzie Gro. BL1: Bolt 9E 22
Mackenzie Ind. Pk. SK3: Stoc 1N 117
Mackenzie Rd. M7: Sal 4A 78
Mackenzie St. BL1: Bolt 8E 22
M12: Man 6M 95
Mackenzie Wlk. OL1: O'ham 7B 46
Mackeson Dr. OL6: A Lyne 6B 82
Mackeson Rd. OL6: A Lyne 6B 82
McKie Cl. OL8: O'ham 8L 63
Mackintosh Way
OL1: O'ham 1D 8 (4K 63)
Mackworth St. M15: Man 4D 94
McLaren Ct. M21: Cho H 8N 93
Maclaren Dr. M8: Man 1D 78
McLean Dr. M44: Irl 5H 91
Maclure Rd. OL11: Roch 9D 8 (7D 28)
Macnair Ct. SK6: Mar 2D 120
Macnair M. SK6: Mar 2D 120
McNaught St. OL16: Roch 7F 28
Mconnel Apartments M4: Man 3L 5
Madams Wood Rd. M28: Walk 8G 56
Maddison Rd. M43: Droy 1D 96
Madeira Pl. M30: Ecc 8B 76
Madeley Cl. WA14: Hale 7E 114
WN3: Wig 8B 52
Madeley Dr. OL9: Chad 5F 62
Madeley Gdns. *BL1: Bolt* *2F 38*
(off Hargreaves St.)
OL12: Roch 4B 28
Maden's Sq. OL15: Lit 9M 15
Maden St. M29: Ast 4A 74
Maden Vw. OL11: Roch 4A 44
Maden Wlk. OL9: Chad 3F 62
Madison Apartments M16: Old T 4A 94
Madison Av. M34: Aud 1G 96
SK8: Chea H 5M 117
Madison Gdns. BL5: W'ton 1J 55
M35: Fail 3C 80
Madison Pk. BL5: W'ton 1J 55
Madison St. M18: Man 3C 96
Madras Rd. SK3: Stoc 9A 108
Madron Av. SK10: Macc 3B 130
Maesbrook Dr. M29: Tyld 2B 74
Mafeking Av. BL9: Bury 8N 25
Mafeking Pl. WN4: A Mak 7F 70
Mafeking Rd. BL2: Bolt 5M 39
Mafeking St. OL8: O'ham 8G 63
Magdala St. OL1: O'ham 3J 63
OL10: H'ood 4K 43
Magdalen Dr. WN4: A Mak 6C 70
Magda Rd. SK2: Stoc 2G 119
Magenta Av. M44: Irl 2F 102
Magistrates' Court
Bolton 3J 7 (5F 38)
Bury 8H 7 (2K 41)
Macclesfield 3H 131
Manchester City 5E 4 (9D 78)
Oldham 2C 8 (4J 63)
Stockport 3L 9 (8D 108)
Tameside 8B 6 (8L 81)
Trafford 3G 105
Wigan & Leigh 9L 9 (4G 52)
Mag La. WA13: Lym 9A 112
WA16: H Leg 9A 112
Magna Carta Ct. M6: Sal 4H 77
Magnetic Ho. M50: Sal 2M 93
Magnolia Cl. *M31: Part* *6F 102*
(off Redbrook Rd.)
M33: Sale 3C 104
Magnolia Ct. M6: Sal 8N 77
M33: Sale *2C 104*
(off Magnolia Cl.)
Magnolia Dr. M8: Man 4F 78
Magnolia Ri. SK10: P'bury 7C 128
Magnum Cen.
OL16: Roch 9F 8 (7E 28)
Magpie Cl. M43: Droy 7G 81
Magpie La. OL4: O'ham 7B 64
Magpie Wlk. *M11: Man* *9L 79*
(off Newcombe Cl.)
Maguire Av. SK13: Had 3C 100
Maher Gdns. M15: Man 5D 94
Mahogany Wlk. *M33: Sale* *3C 104*
(off Epping Dr.)
Mahood St. SK3: Stoc 9B 108
Maida St. M12: Man 7N 95
Maiden Cl. OL7: A Lyne 4L 81
Maiden M. M27: Swin 3F 76
Maidford Cl. M4: Man 9J 79
M32: Stre 7L 93
Maidstone Av. M21: Cho H 8N 93
Maidstone Cl. SK10: Macc 2F 130
WN7: Lei 9E 54
Maidstone M. M21: Cho H 8N 93
Maidstone Rd. SK4: Stoc 5J 107
Maidstone Wlk. *M34: Dent* *8L 97*
(off Worcester Av.)
Main Av. M17: T Pk 4J 93
M19: Man 1L 107
Main Dr. WA14: Bow, D Mas 4L 113
Maine Rd. M14: Man 7F 94
(not continuous)
Mainhill Wlk. *M40: Man* *5A 80*
(off Marlinford Dr.)
Main La. WA3: Cro 6A 88
Mainprice Cl. M6: Sal 7M 77
Main Rd. M27: Clif 8J 59
OL9: O'ham 4G 63
SK11: Lang 8N 131
Mains Av. WN2: Bam 3J 71
Main St. M35: Fail 2D 80
SK14: Hyde 5A 98
WN5: Bil 6H 69
Mainwaring Dr. SK9: Wilm 6J 123
Mainwaring Ter. M23: Wyth 6N 105
Mainway M24: Mid 5L 61
Mainway E. M24: Mid 5A 62
Mainwood Rd. WA15: Tim 2J 115
Mainwood Sq. M13: Man 9L 5
Maismore Rd. M22: Wyth 6N 115
Maitland Av. M21: Cho H 3B 106
Maitland Cl. OL12: Roch 2G 28
Maitland St. SK1: Stoc 9F 108
Maitland Wlk. OL9: Chad 3F 62
Maizefield Cl. M33: Sale 4M 105
Majestic M. WN5: Orr 6H 51
Major St. BL0: Ram 8H 11
M1: Man 6H 5 (1F 94)
OL16: Miln 7K 29
WN5: Wig 5N 51
Major Wlk. *M5: Sal* *1A 94*
(off Robert Hall St.)
Makants Cl. M29: Tyld 2F 74
M46: Ath 6A 56
Makant St. BL1: Bolt 1D 38
Makepeace Wlk. M8: Man 9D 60
Makerfield Dr. WA12: N Wil 4D 86
Makerfield Way WN2: I Mak 3M 53
Makin Ct. OL10: H'ood 3J 43
Makinson Arc. WN1: Wig 7J 9
Makinson Av. BL6: Hor 2G 36
WN2: Hin 4N 53
Makinson La. BL6: Hor 9H 21
Makinson Yd. BL1: Bolt 2J 7
Makin St. M1: Man 7H 5 (1F 94)
Makkah Cl. M40: Man 5M 79
Malaga Av. M90: Man A 8A 116
Malakoff St. SK15: Stal 1B 98
Malbern Ind. Est. M34: Dent 5H 97
Malbrook Wlk. *M13: Man* *3H 95*
(off Jessel Cl.)
Malby St. OL1: O'ham 3K 63
Malcolm Av. M27: Clif 8G 58
Malcolm Dr. M27: Clif 9G 58
Malcolm St. OL11: Roch 1B 44
Malden Gro. M23: Wyth 9N 105
Maldon Cl. BL3: Lit L 9A 40
SK2: Stoc 1L 119
WN2: Wig 1J 53
Maldon Cres. M27: Swin 4F 76
Maldon Dr. M30: Ecc 6E 76
Maldon Rd. WN6: Stan 4C 34
Maldon St. OL11: Roch 8D 28
Maldwyn Av. BL3: Bolt 1C 56
M8: Man 9F 60
Malgam Dr. M20: Man 8G 106
Malham Av. WN3: Wig 9D 52
Malham Cl. OL2: O'ham 8H 45
WN7: Lei 5E 72
Malham Ct. SK2: Stoc 1H 119
Malham Dr. M45: Whitef 3N 59
Malham Gdns. *BL3: Bolt* *9D 38*
(off Maltby Dr.)
Malika Pl. WN4: A Mak 4B 70
Malimson Bourne *M7: Sal* *4C 78*
(off Hilton St. Nth.)
Mall, The BL9: Bury 8L 7 (2M 41)
M30: Ecc 8F 76
M33: Sale 4H 105
SK14: Hyde 7A 98
SK15: Stal 3H 99
Mallaig Wlk. *M11: Man* *1A 96*
(off Brigham St.)
Mallard Cl. OL8: O'ham 9H 63
SK2: Stoc 2L 119
SK16: Duk 2B 98
WA16: Knut 6H 133
Mallard Ct. M50: Sal 1K 93
SK8: H Grn 7H 117
Mallard Cres. SK12: Poy 2E 124
Mallard Dr. BL6: Hor 1C 36
Mallard Grn. WA14: B'ath 8B 104
Mallards, The SK11: Macc 4F 130
Mallards Reach SK6: Rom 6M 109
Mallard St. M1: Man 8H 5 (1F 94)
Mallett Cres. BL1: Bolt 2A 38
Malley Gdns. OL5: Mos 2G 83
Malley Wlk. *M9: Man* *8K 61*
(off Greendale Dr.)
Malling Rd. M23: Wyth 3N 115
Mallison St. BL1: Bolt 1G 38
Mallory Av. OL7: A Lyne 5M 81
Mallory Cl. WA16: Mob 4M 133
Mallory Ct. WA14: Bow 4C 114
Mallory Dr. WN7: Lei 5L 73
Mallory Rd. SK14: Hyde 4D 98
Mallory Wlk. M23: Wyth 8K 105
Mallow Cft. OL16: Roch 9G 28
Mallowdale M28: Wors 2J 75
Mallowdale Av. M14: Man 9G 94
Mallowdale Cl. BL1: Bolt 5M 37
Mallowdale Rd. SK2: Stoc 2J 119
Mallow St. M15: Man 3D 94
Mallow Wlk. *M31: Part* *6G 102*
(off Broom Rd.)
Malmesbury Cl. SK12: Poy 2H 125
Malmesbury Rd.
SK8: Chea H 9N 117
Malpas Av. WN1: Wig 5N 9 (2G 53)
Malpas Cl. SK8: Chea 3M 117
SK9: Wilm 5J 123
Malpas Dr. WA14: Tim 8E 104
Malpas St. M12: Man 3M 95
OL1: O'ham 1E 8 (4K 63)
Malpas Wlk. *M16: Old T* *4C 94*
(off Clifton Cl.)
Malsham Rd. M23: Wyth 6M 105
Malta Cl. M24: Mid 4B 62
Malta St. M4: Man 9J 79
OL4: O'ham 5A 64
Maltby Ct. OL4: Lees 6C 64
Maltby Dr. BL3: Bolt 9D 38
Maltby Rd. M23: Wyth 1M 115
Maltings La. OL11: Roch 2A 44
Malton Av. BL3: Bolt 8B 38
M21: Cho H 9A 94
M45: Whitef 1M 59
WA3: Low 2A 88
Malton Cl. M45: Whitef 1M 59
OL9: Chad 2D 62
WN7: Lei 4E 72
Malton Dr. SK7: H Gro 8H 119
WA14: Alt 1A 114
Malton Rd. M28: Wors 3F 74
SK4: Stoc 4M 107
Malton St. OL8: O'ham 5A 8 (6H 63)
Malt St. M15: Man 9B 4 (2C 94)
WA16: Knut 6G 133
Malus Ct. M6: Sal 7N 77
Malvern Av. BL1: Bolt 3B 38
BL9: Bury 8M 25
M41: Urm 6B 92
M43: Droy 8G 81
M46: Ath 6A 56
OL6: A Lyne 3N 81
SK8: Gat 2E 116
WN2: Hin 7C 54
Malvern Cl. BL4: Farn 3G 57
BL6: Hor 8E 20
M25: Pres 6B 60
M27: Pen 4K 77
OL2: O'ham 9G 45
OL2: Shaw 4K 45
OL16: Miln 6L 29
SK4: Stoc 5B 108
WN3: Wins 8N 51
WN4: A Mak 6E 70
Malvern Cres. WN3: I Mak 7J 53
Malvern Dr. M27: Pen 4K 77
SK10: Macc 9J 129
WA14: Alt 2B 114
Malvern Gro. M6: Sal 7J 77
M20: Man 2F 106
M28: Walk 8L 57
Malvern Ri. SK13: Had 4C 100
Malvern Rd. M24: Mid 6L 61
WA16: Knut 8F 132
Malvern Row *M15: Man* *3C 94*
(off Cornbrook Pk. Rd.)
Malvern St. M15: Man 3C 94
OL8: O'ham 6H 63
WN6: Stan 1N 33
Malvern St. E. OL11: Roch 6A 28
Malvern St. W. OL11: Roch 6A 28
Malvern Ter. WN7: Lei 7H 73
Manby Rd. M18: Man 5N 95
Manby Sq. M18: Man 5N 95
Mancentral Trad. Est.
M5: Sal 4C 4 (9C 78)
MANCHESTER 4H 5 (9E 78)
Manchester Airport Eastern Link Rd.
SK7: Bram 2A 124
SK8: Chea H 9K 117
SK9: Hand 9K 117
Manchester Airport Station (Rail)
....8A 116
Manchester Aquatics Cen.
....9J 5 (2G 94)
Manchester Art Gallery 5H 5 (9F 78)
Manchester Bus. Pk.
M22: Wyth 7C 116
Manchester Cathedral 2G 5 (8E 78)
Manchester Cathedral Vis. Cen. 3G 4
Manchester Central 7F 4 (1E 94)
Manchester Chambers
OL1: O'ham 2C 8 (4J 63)
Manchester City FC 8L 79
Manchester Climbing Cen. 2L 95
Manchester Craft & Design Cen. *3J 5*
(off Oak St.)
Manchester Crematorium
M21: Cho H 2B 106
Manchester Evening News Arena
....1G 5 (7E 78)
Manchester Fort Shop. Pk.
M8: Man 5G 78
Manchester Golf Course 6A 44
Manchester Gorton Mkt.
M18: Man 4B 96
Manchester Ind. Cen.
M3: Man 6C 4 (1C 94)
(not continuous)
Manchester Ind. Pk. M40: Man 5L 79
MANCHESTER INTERNATIONAL AIRPORT
....9A 116
Manchester Intl. Bus. Cen.
M22: Wyth 8F 116
Manchester Jewish Mus. 6F 78
Manchester Leisure Sports
Development Centre, The 5F 94
Manchester Maccabi Community &
Sports Club 8C 60
Manchester Metropolitan University
All Saints Building 9H 5 (2F 94)
Aytoun Building 6J 5 (1G 94)
Bellhouse Building *9H 5*
(off Lwr. Ormond St.)
Chatham Building 9J 5 (3F 94)
Didsbury Campus 6G 107
Elizabeth Gaskell Campus 5H 95
Geoffrey Manton Building *9J 5*
(off Rosamond Rd. W.)
Grosvenor Building 9J 5
Hollings Campus 7J 95
John Dalton Building
....8H 5 (2F 94)
Loxford Tower 9H 5
Ormond Building 9H 5
St Augustine's *9H 5*
(off Lwr. Chatham St.)
Manchester Mus. 3G 94
Manchester New Rd. M24: Mid 6K 61
M31: Part 5G 102
Manchester Old Rd. BL9: Bury 3L 41
M24: Mid 4G 60
M31: C'ton 2L 103
Manchester Rd. BL0: Ram 8L 11
BL2: Bolt 4M 7 (6H 39)
BL3: Bolt 6H 39
BL4: Kea, Swin 5A 58
BL5: Bolt, W'ton 9G 37
BL6: Bla 2N 35
BL9: Bury 9J 7 (2L 41)
(Moss St., not continuous)
BL9: Bury 8L 11
(Whitelow Rd.)
HD7: Mars ....4C 48 & 1G 48
Manchester Rd. M16: Whall R 8A 94
M21: Cho H 8A 94
(Barlow Moor Rd.)
M21: Cho H 9N 93
(High La.)
M27: Clif 5A 58
M27: Pen, Swin 3G 76
M27: Ward 9B 58
M28: Walk 9L 57
M29: Ast 4D 74
M29: Tyld 1B 74
M31: C'ton, Part 4G 102
M34: Aud 2E 96
M34: Dent 5E 96
M43: Droy 9C 80
OL2: Shaw 7L 45
OL3: G'fld 7J 65
OL5: Mos 4F 82
OL7: A Lyne 9A 6 (8K 81)
OL8: O'ham 9F 62
OL9: O'ham 9F 62
OL10: H'ood 7H 43
OL11: Roch 9A 8 (1A 44)
OL16: Roch 9A 8 (8B 28)
SK4: Stoc 3A 108
SK8: Chea 8J 107
SK9: Wilm 7G 123
SK10: Boll, Macc 7G 129
SK13: Tin 3A 100
SK14: Holl 3A 100
SK14: Hyde 6M 97
WA3: Rix 8A 102
WA14: Alt, B'ath, Tim
....1C 6 (1D 114)
WA16: Knut, Mere 2D 132
WN1: I Mak 3H 53
WN2: I Mak 3H 53
WN7: Lei 6L 73
Manchester Rd. E. M38: Lit H 7H 57
Manchester Rd. Nth. M34: Dent 5G 97
Manchester Rd. Sth. M34: Dent 6G 97
Manchester Rd. W. M38: Lit H 5E 56
Manchester Row WA12: N Wil 9G 86
Manchester Rugby Club 1M 123
Manchester Science Pk.
M15: Man 4F 94
Manchester St. M16: Old T 4B 94
OL1: O'ham 3C 8 (5J 63)
OL8: O'ham 4A 8 (6H 63)
OL9: O'ham 3B 8 (5J 63)
OL10: H'ood, Mid 2J 43
Manchester St. Rdbt. OL9: O'ham 3B 8
Manchester Tennis Cen. 8L 79
Manchester United FC 4M 93
Manchester United Mus. & Tour
....4M 93
Manchester Velodrome
National Cycling Cen. 8M 79
Manchet St. OL11: Roch 3N 43
Mancroft Av. BL3: Bolt 8E 38
Mancroft Ter. BL3: Bolt 8E 38
Mancroft Wlk. M1: Man 8K 5
Mancunian Rd. M34: Dent 8L 97
Mancunian Way M1: Man 8J 5 (2F 94)
M12: Man 9D 4 (2D 94)
M15: Man 9D 4 (2D 94)
Mandalay Gdns. SK6: Mar 9A 110
Mandale Pk. 9A 8 (8B 28)
Mandarin Grn. WA14: B'ath 8B 104
Mandarin Wlk. *M6: Sal* *7A 78*
(off Milton Pl.)
Manderville Cl. WN3: Wins 9A 52
Mandeville St. M19: Man 9N 95
Mandeville Ter. BL8: Haw 3B 24
Mandley Av. M40: Man 9B 62
Mandley Cl. BL3: Lit L 7A 40
Mandley Pk. Av. M7: Sal 3D 78
Mandon Cl. M26: Rad 7E 40
Manesty Cl. M24: Mid 1H 61
Manet Cl. M7: Sal 2A 78
Mangle St. M1: Man 4K 5 (9G 78)
Mango Pl. M6: Sal 8N 77
Manifold Dr. SK6: H Lan 9C 120
Manifold St. M6: Sal 5A 78
Manilla Wlk. *M11: Man* *9L 79*
(off Abernant Cl.)
Manley Av. M27: Clif 7E 58
WA3: Gol 8J 71
Manley Cl. BL9: Sum 3J 25
WN7: Lei 2F 72
Manley Cres. BL5: W'ton 2K 55
Manley Gro. SK7: Bram 9C 118
SK14: Mot 6J 99
MANLEY PARK 7B 94
Manley Pk. WN7: Lei 6J 73
Manley Rd. M16: Whall R 8A 94
M21: Cho H 8A 94
M33: Sale 7E 104
OL8: O'ham 7J 63
OL11: Roch 1A 44
(not continuous)
SK11: Gaws 7E 130
Manley Row BL5: W'ton 3K 55
Manley St. M7: Sal 4C 78
WN3: I Mak 5H 53
Manley Ter. BL1: Bolt 9F 22
Manley Way SK14: Mot 6K 99
Manning Av. WN6: Wig 1D 52
Manningford Ct. WN3: I Mak 6H 53
Manningham Rd. BL3: Bolt 7C 38
Mannington Dr. M9: Man 3H 79
Mannion Ho. WN1: Wig 8L 9 (3G 52)
Mannock St. OL8: O'ham 4A 8 (5H 63)
Manns, The OL3: G'fld 6J 65
Manor, The WA11: R'ford 6A 68
Manor Av. BL3: Lit L 9C 40
M16: Whall R 7C 94
M33: Sale 3D 104
M41: Urm 8D 92
WA3: Gol 1M 87
WA12: N Wil 5C 86
Manor Cl. M34: Dent 7M 97
OL4: Gras 5H 65
OL9: Chad 3G 62
SK8: Chea H 7A 118
SK9: Wilm 6D 122

Manor Cl. WA13: Lym 5A 112
WN4: Gars 7N 69
Manor Cotts. OL5: Mos 9F 64
Manor Ct. BL2: Bolt 9L 23
M32: Stre 8H 93
M33: Sale 4D 104
SK1: Stoc 7E 108
(off Hall St.)
WA3: Gol 1M 87
Manor Cres. SK10: Macc 1H 131
WA16: Knut 6H 133
Manordale Wlk. M40: Man 4H 79
(off Westmount Cl.)
Manor Dr. M21: Cho H 4C 106
OL2: O'ham 9J 45
Mnr. Farm Cl. OL7: A Lyne 4K 81
Mnr. Farm Ri. OL4: O'ham 4A 64
Manorfield Cl. BL1: Bolt 3B 38
Manor Fold M46: Ath 8L 55
Manor Gdns. SK9: Wilm 7J 123
Manor Ga. Rd. BL2: Bolt 4A 40
Manor Golf Course 7B 58
Manor Gro. WN2: Asp 7L 35
WN5: Orr 3M 51
WN7: Lei 7L 73
Mnr. Hill Rd. SK6: Mar 9C 110
Manor Ho. Cl. WA11: St H 9E 68
Manor Ho. Dr. WN8: Skel 8C 50
Manorial Dr. M38: Lit H 6F 56
Manor Ind. Est. M32: Stre 9J 93
Manor La. OL3: Del 4A 48
WA16: Olle 9L 133
Manor Lodge M27: Pen 2K 77
SK8: Chea H 6A 118
Manor Mill OL9: Chad 3G 62
Mnr. Mill Cl. OL16: Roch 2H 29
Manor Pk. M41: Urm 8D 92
Manor Pk. Nth. WA16: Knut 6J 133
Manor Pk. Rd. SK13: Glos 8G 100
Manor Pk. Sth. WA16: Knut 7H 133
Manor Pk. Vw. SK13: Glos 7G 100
Manor Pl. WN3: I Mak 5J 53
Manor Rd. BL6: Hor 9F 20
M6: Sal 6K 77
M19: Man 7N 95
M24: Mid 5L 61
M27: Swin 4F 76
M29: Ast 4D 74
M32: Stre 8H 93
M33: Sale 3H 105
M34: Aud 2F 96
M34: Dent 7M 97
M43: Droy 9C 80
OL2: Shaw 5L 45
OL4: O'ham 7N 63
SK5: Stoc 3F 108
SK6: Mar 9C 110
SK6: Wood 3M 109
SK7: Bram 6A 118
SK8: Chea H 6A 118
SK9: Wilm 6D 122
SK14: Hyde 4C 98
WA11: Hay 2C 86
WA13: Lym 5A 112
(not continuous)
WA15: Alt 4E 6 (3E 114)
WN2: Hin 6B 54
WN6: She 6K 33
Manor St. BL0: Ram 7H 11
BL1: Bolt 2L 7 (5G 39)
BL4: Farn 4K 57
BL4: Kea 6B 58
BL9: Bury 7N 7 (2N 41)
M12: Man 8M 5 (1H 95)
M24: Mid 1M 61
M34: Aud 2K 97
OL2: O'ham 1L 63
OL5: Mos 9F 64
SK13: Glos 8F 100
WA3: Gol 9L 71
WN1: Wig 8J 9 (3F 52)
WN5: Wig 5C 52
Manor Ter. SK11: Lang 9M 131
Manor Vw. SK6: Wood 3M 109
Manor Wlk. M34: Aud 2K 97
(off Mt. Pleasant St.)
Manor Way PR7: Cop 5A 18
Manor Yd. OL3: Upp 3L 65
(off Wade Row)
Mansart Cl. WN4: A Mak 7G 70
Manse, The OL5: Mos 2F 82
Manse Gdns. WA12: N Wil 5G 86
Mansell Way BL6: Hor 3F 36
Mansfield Av. BL0: Ram 3H 25
M9: Man 7J 61
M34: Dent 5H 97
Mansfield Cl. M34: Dent 4H 97
OL7: A Lyne 9K 81
Mansfield Cres. M34: Dent 5H 97
Mansfield Dr. M9: Man 7K 61
Mansfield Grange OL11: Roch 7A 28
Mansfield Gro. BL1: Bolt 2C 38
Mansfield Rd. M9: Man 7J 61
M41: Urm 8B 92
OL5: Mos 1H 83
OL8: O'ham 6M 63
OL11: Roch 6K 27
SK14: Hyde 8B 98
Mansfield St. OL7: A Lyne 1J 97
WA3: Gol 9J 71
Mansfield Vw. OL5: Mos 1H 83
Mansford Dr. M40: Man 5L 79
Manshaw Cres. M34: Aud 2E 96
Manshaw Rd. M11: Man 2E 96
Mansion Av. M45: Whitef 9L 41
Mansion Dr. WA16: Knut 6H 133
Mansion Ho., The WA14: Alt 9D 104
Manson Av. M15: Man 9B 4 (2C 94)
Manstead Wlk. M40: Man 8K 79
Manston Dr. SK8: Chea H 5M 117
Manston Lodge SK2: Stoc 2F 118
Manswood Dr. M8: Man 3F 78
Mantell Wlk. M40: Man 5M 79
(off Bower St.)
Manthorpe Av. M28: Wors 3A 76
Mantley La. OL3: Dens 5D 46
Manton Av. M9: Man 9N 61
M34: Dent 6E 96
Manton Cl. M7: Sal 4E 78
Manton Ho. SK5: Stoc 4F 108
Manvers St. SK5: Stoc 5C 108
Manwaring St. M35: Fail 2C 80
Manway Bus. Pk. WA14: Tim 8E 104
Maple Av. BL1: Bolt 3C 38
BL6: Hor 3G 37
BL9: Bury 2A 42
M21: Cho H 9A 94
M30: Ecc 6A 76
M32: Stre 8K 93
M34: Aud 9F 80
M34: Dent 6J 97
M45: Whitef 4M 59
M46: Ath 7K 55
SK6: Mar 3C 120
SK8: Chea H 5L 117
SK11: Macc 7H 131
SK12: Dis 9K 121
SK12: Poy 3K 125
SK15: Stal 1C 98
WA3: Low 2B 88
WA12: N Wil 7G 86
WN2: Hin 8B 54
WN2: I Mak 5J 53
Maple Bank WA14: Bow 4B 114
Maple Cl. BL4: Kea 6N 57
M6: Sal 7M 77
M24: Mid 3B 62
M33: Sale 4C 104
OL2: Shaw 4K 45
OL9: Chad 2F 62
SK2: Stoc 1F 118
WN5: Bil 5H 69
Maple Ct. M16: Old T 5A 94
SK4: Stoc 4A 108
Maple Cres. WN7: Lei 3G 73
Maplecroft SK1: Stoc 8F 108
Mapledon Rd. M9: Man 2L 79
Maple Dr. WA15: Tim 2L 115
WN2: Abr 3L 71
Maplefield Dr. M28: Wors 3J 75
Maple Gro. BL0: Ram 9K 11
BL8: Tot 8G 24
M25: Pres 5N 59
M28: Walk 2L 75
M35: Fail 5C 80
M40: Man 9C 62
WN6: Wig 9D 34
Maple Ho. M14: Man 5H 95
SK14: Hyde 9C 98
Maple Rd. BL4: Farn 3H 57
M23: Wyth 8J 105
M27: Swin 4E 76
M31: Part 5F 102
OL9: Chad 2F 62
SK7: Bram 1C 124
SK9: A Edg 2G 126
Maple Rd. W. M23: Wyth 8J 105
Maple St. BL2: Bolt 8K 23
BL3: Bolt 7E 38
OL8: O'ham 8G 62
OL11: Roch 9A 8 (7B 28)
WN4: A Mak 4D 70
Maple Wlk. BL3: Bolt 7M 39
M23: Wyth 8J 105
Maplewood SK11: Macc 7H 131
(off Briarwood Av.)
Maplewood Cl. M9: Man 9H 61
OL2: O'ham 1G 63
Maplewood Ct. M7: Sal 3C 78
Maplewood Gdns. BL1: Bolt 2F 38
Maplewood Gro. SK15: Stal 7F 82
Maplewood Ho. BL1: Bolt 3F 38
(off Prospect St.)
Maplewood Rd. SK9: Wilm 6K 123
Mapley Av. M22: Nor 8C 106
Maplin Cl. M13: Man 9M 5 (2H 95)
Maplin Dr. SK2: Stoc 2L 119
Maranatha Ct. M30: Ecc 1D 92
Marble St. M2: Man 4H 5 (9F 78)
OL1: O'ham 3M 63
Marbury Av. M14: Man 8G 94
Marbury Cl. M41: Urm 6L 91
SK3: Stoc 9M 107
Marbury Dr. WA14: Tim 7E 104
Marbury Gro. WN6: Stan 4B 34
Marbury Rd. SK4: Stoc 2B 108
SK9: Wilm 5G 122
Marcer Rd. M40: Man 8J 79
March Av. SK4: Stoc 6N 107
Marchbank WN2: Asp 1K 53
Marchbank Dr. SK8: Chea 1H 117
March Dr. BL8: Bury 8K 25
Marchers M. M30: Ecc 9B 76
Marches Cl. OL2: O'ham 8M 45
Marchioness St. M18: Man 3D 96
Marchmont Cl. M13: Man 3J 95
March St. OL16: Roch 7F 8 (6E 28)
Marchwood Av. M21: Cho H 8C 94
Marchwood Cl. BL6: Bla 5B 36
Marcliffe Dr. M19: Man 8A 96
OL11: Roch 7N 27
Marcliffe Ind. Est. SK7: H Gro 6J 119
Marcliff Gro. SK4: Stoc 6N 107
WA16: Knut 7G 132
Marcroft Pl. OL11: Roch 9E 28
Marcus Garvey Ct. M16: Whall R 7D 94
Marcus Gro. M14: Man 6H 95
Marcus St. BL1: Bolt 3C 38
Mardale Av. M20: Man 3H 107
M27: Ward 9C 58
M41: Urm 6N 91
OL2: O'ham 4G 45
WA11: St H 9F 68
Mardale Cl. BL2: Bolt 3N 39
M25: Pres 4B 60
M46: Ath 6L 55
OL4: O'ham 3A 64
SK15: Stal 7D 82
Mardale Cres. WA13: Lym 4A 112
Mardale Dr. BL2: Bolt 3N 39
M24: Mid 2K 61
SK8: Gat 1G 117
Mardale Rd. M27: Swin 4D 76
Marden Rd. M23: Wyth 2N 115
Mardon Cl. WA16: Knut 5K 133
Mardyke OL12: Roch 6B 8 (5C 28)
Marfield Av. OL9: Chad 6E 62
Marfield Ct. M41: Urm 8L 91
Marford Cl. M22: Wyth 1C 116
Marford Cres. M33: Sale 6F 104
Margaret Ashton Cl. M9: Man 3L 79
Margaret Av. OL16: Roch 6G 28
WN6: Stan 8N 33
Margaret Ho. OL6: A Lyne 8A 6 (8L 81)
Margaret Rd. M34: Dent 5L 97
M43: Droy 8C 80
Margaret Sands St. M15: Man 3C 94
Margaret St. BL9: Bury 9M 7 (3M 41)
OL2: Shaw 6M 45
OL6: A Lyne 7A 6 (7L 81)
OL7: A Lyne 9B 6 (8L 81)
OL8: O'ham 9F 62
OL10: H'ood 2G 43
SK5: Stoc 1C 108
WN2: Hin 5N 53
WN6: Wig 2D 52
Margaret Ter. OL6: A Lyne 8A 6
Margaret Ward Ct. OL11: Roch 8E 28
(off Wellfield St.)
Margate Av. M40: Man 5N 79
Margate Rd. SK5: Stoc 1D 108
Margrove Chase BL6: Los 7L 37
Margrove Cl. M35: Fail 2G 80
Margrove Rd. M6: Sal 6J 77
Margroy Cl. OL12: Roch 3E 28
Marguerita Rd. M40: Man 6B 80
(not continuous)
Marham Cl. M21: Cho H 2D 106
Marian Av. WA12: N Wil 6C 86
Marian Pl. WN2: Bam 2J 71
Marian Rd. WA11: Hay 2B 86
Maria Sq. BL7: Bel 1M 21
Maria St. BL1: Bolt 2F 38
Marie Cl. M34: Dent 7K 97
Marie St. M7: Sal 3D 78
Marigold Cl. SK11: Macc 4D 130
Marigold St. OL11: Roch 8D 28
WN5: Wig 4A 52
Marigold Ter. M24: Mid 4B 62
(off Sundew Pl.)
Mariman Dr. M8: Man 9F 60
Marina Av. M34: Dent 8L 97
Marina Cl. SK9: Hand 2J 123
Marina Cres. M11: Man 7N 79
Marina Dr. SK6: Mar 9N 109
WN5: Wig 6A 52
Marina Rd. M43: Droy 8F 80
SK6: Bred 4L 109
Marine Av. M31: Part 5E 102
Mariners Way M44: Irl 9G 90
Marion Dr. WA16: Mob 4N 133
Marion St. BL3: Bolt 1K 57
OL8: O'ham 8K 63
Maritime Cl. WA12: N Wil 4F 86
Maritime Ct. M33: Sale 4F 104
Marjorie Cl. M18: Man 3N 95
Mark Av. M6: Sal 6A 78
Markenfield Dr. OL2: Shaw 5K 45
Market App. WN4: A Mak 7E 70
Market Arc. SK13: Glos 8E 100
WN7: Lei 5H 73
Market Av. OL6: A Lyne 7D 6 (7M 81)
Market Chambers BL0: Ram 7J 11
(off Ramsbottom La.)
Marketgate Shop. Cen.
WN1: Wig 7J 9 (3F 52)
Market Hall BL1: Bolt 2K 7 (5G 38)
Market Pde. BL9: Bury 8L 7 (2M 41)
Market Pl. BL0: Eden 3K 11
BL0: Ram 7H 11
BL1: Bolt 1K 7 (4G 38)
BL4: Farn 3L 57
BL9: Bury 7K 7 (2L 41)
HD7: Mars 1H 49
M22: Wyth 4C 116
M24: Mid 2M 61
M26: Rad 1H 59
M27: Pen 1G 76
M34: Dent 6J 97
M43: Droy 9E 80
M46: Ath 8M 55
OL1: O'ham 2C 8 (4J 63)
OL2: O'ham 8H 45
OL2: Shaw 6M 45
OL5: Mos 1F 82
(off Market St.)
OL6: A Lyne 7D 6 (7M 81)
OL10: H'ood 2J 43
OL16: Roch 7C 8 (6D 28)
PR7: Adl 6K 19
SK1: Stoc 1L 9 (6D 108)
(not continuous)
SK6: Comp 6D 110
SK10: Boll 5M 129
SK10: Macc 4H 131
SK13: Glos 9E 100
SK14: Hyde 7A 98
(not continuous)
SK14: Mot 6K 99
WA12: N Wil 6D 86
WN1: Wig 8J 9 (3F 52)
WN6: Stan 3B 34
WN7: Lei 5H 73
Market Pl., The OL6: A Lyne 7D 6
Market Pct. BL4: Farn 3L 57
Market Sq. OL2: O'ham 8H 45
WA14: Alt 3C 6
(not continuous)
Market St. BL0: Eden 2K 11
BL1: Bolt 2K 7 (5G 38)
BL3: Lit L 9A 40
BL4: Farn 2L 57
BL5: W'ton 3G 55
BL8: Tot 6F 24
BL9: Bury 7K 7 (2L 41)
(Market Pl.)
BL9: Bury 9L 7 (3M 41)
(Trinity St.)
Market St. M1: Man 4H 5 (9F 78)
M2: Man 3G 4 (9E 78)
M24: Mid 2L 61
(not continuous)
M26: Rad 3B 58
M27: Pen 1G 76
M29: Tyld 1A 74
(Charles St.)
M29: Tyld 1A 74
(Shuttle St.)
M34: Dent 6J 97
(not continuous)
M43: Droy 1E 96
M46: Ath 8L 55
OL2: O'ham 8H 45
OL2: Shaw 6M 45
OL5: Mos 1F 82
OL6: A Lyne 7D 6 (7M 81)
OL10: H'ood 2H 43
OL12: Bac, Whitw 9A 14
PR7: Adl 7K 19
SK6: Mar 2C 120
SK12: Dis 9G 120
SK13: Glos 9E 100
SK14: B'tom 9K 99
SK14: Holl 4N 99
SK14: Hyde 6A 98
SK14: Mot 5K 99
SK15: Stal 8D 82
SK22: N Mil 8L 121
WA12: N Wil 5D 86
WA14: Alt 3C 6 (3D 114)
WN1: Wig 7J 9 (3F 52)
WN2: Hin 6N 53
WN6: Stan 3B 34
WN7: Lei 5H 73
Market Street Stop (Metro)
4H 5 (9F 78)
Market Wlk. HD7: Mars 1H 49
(off Market Pl.)
M33: Sale 4H 105
Market Way M6: Sal 7M 77
OL16: Roch 6C 8 (5D 28)
Markfield Av. M13: Man 4J 95
Markham Cl. M12: Man 1K 95
SK14: Hyde 3A 98
Markham St. SK14: Hyde 3A 98
Markington St. M14: Man 6F 94
Mark Jones Wlk. M40: Man 5N 79
(off Mitchell St.)
Markland Ct. WN6: Wig 2D 52
MARKLAND HILL 4N 37
Markland Hill BL1: Bolt 4N 37
Markland Hill Cl. BL1: Bolt 3A 38
Markland Hill La. BL1: Bolt 3N 37
Marklands Rd. BL6: Hor 8G 20
M29: Ast 6B 74
Markland St. BL0: Ram 8H 11
BL3: Bolt 4K 7 (6G 38)
SK14: Hyde 8B 98
(not continuous)
WN1: Wig 4H 53
Markland Tops BL1: Bolt 3A 38
Mark La. M4: Man 3H 5
OL2: Shaw 6N 45
Marks St. M26: Rad 9G 41
Mark St. M28: Wors 3G 75
OL9: O'ham 1A 8 (4H 63)
OL12: Roch 4F 28
Mark Wood OL3: Del 8J 47
MARLAND 9N 27
Marland Av. OL8: O'ham 1L 81
OL11: Roch 9N 27
SK8: Chea H 5L 117
Marland Cl. OL11: Roch 8N 27
Marland Cres. SK5: Stoc 9D 96
Marland Fold OL11: Roch 9N 27
Marland Fold La. OL8: O'ham 1K 81
Marland Golf Course 8M 27
Marland Grn. OL11: Roch 9N 27
Marland Hill Rd. OL11: Roch 8A 28
Marland Old Rd. OL11: Roch 9N 27
Marland Ri. OL11: Roch 8N 27
Marland St. OL9: Chad 8E 62
Marland Tops OL11: Roch 9N 27
Marland Way M32: Stre 6K 93
Marlborough Av. M16: Whall R 7B 94
SK8: Chea H 5N 117
SK9: A Edg 3G 127
WN3: I Mak 7J 53
Marlborough Cl. BL0: Ram 2J 25
M34: Dent 6K 97
OL7: A Lyne 1J 97
OL12: Whitw 7A 14
SK6: Mar 9A 110
SK10: Macc 9H 129
WA16: Knut 4J 133
Marlborough Ct. BL1: Bolt 2N 37
M9: Man 6F 60
SK11: Macc 5H 131
(off Pickford St.)
Marlborough Dr. M35: Fail 4C 80
SK4: Stoc 4B 108
SK10: Macc 9H 129
Marlborough Gdns. BL4: Farn 3H 57
Marlborough Gro. M43: Droy 8G 80
Marlborough Rd. M7: Man, Sal 4E 78
M7: Sal 4E 78
M30: Ecc 6G 76
M32: Stre 6J 93
M33: Sale 4H 105
M41: Urm 6N 91
M44: Irl 6J 91
M46: Ath 7N 55
OL2: O'ham 1J 63
SK14: Hyde 9B 98
WA14: Bow 5D 114
Marlborough St. BL1: Bolt 4D 38
OL4: O'ham 4F 8 (5L 63)
OL7: A Lyne 1J 97
(not continuous)
OL10: H'ood 4K 43
OL12: Roch 4A 28
Marlborough Way WA11: Hay 1B 86
Marlbrook Dr. BL5: W'ton 6G 55
Marlbrook M. BL5: W'ton 6H 55
Marlbrook Wlk. BL3: Bolt 8G 39
Marlcroft Av. SK4: Stoc 6N 107
Marld Cres. BL1: Bolt 2A 38
Marle Av. OL5: Mos 1H 83
Marle Cft. M45: Whitef 5J 59
Marlecroft Cl. M23: Wyth 9N 105
Marl Edge SK10: P'bury 8E 128
Marle Earth Cotts. OL5: Mos 1H 83
(off Micklehurst Rd.)
Marle Ri. OL5: Mos 1H 83
Marler Rd. SK14: Hyde 5B 98
Marley Cl. WA15: Tim 9F 104
Marley Dr. M33: Sale 2G 104
Marleyer Cl. M40: Man 3A 80
Marleyer Ri. SK6: Rom 8L 109
Marley Rd. M19: Man 9N 95
SK12: Poy 4J 125
Marlfield Av. WA13: Lym 5B 112
Marlfield Rd. OL2: Shaw 4J 45
WA15: Haleb 8K 115
Marlfield St. M9: Man 1K 79
Marl Gro. WN5: Orr 7H 51
Marlhill Cl. SK2: Stoc 2J 119
Marlhill Ct. SK2: Stoc 2J 119
Marlinford Dr. M40: Man 5A 80
Marloes WA14: Bow 5B 114
Marlor Ct. OL10: H'ood 2G 42
Marlor St. M34: Dent 5J 97
Marlow Brow SK13: Had 5C 100
Marlow Cl. BL2: Bolt 3N 39
M41: Urm 5B 92
SK8: Chea H 5L 117
Marlow Ct. PR7: Adl 7J 19
Marlow Dr. M27: Swin 4E 76
M44: Irl 6H 91
SK9: Hand 1H 123
WA14: Bow 5N 113
Marlowe Cl. WN3: Wig 6D 52
Marlowe Ct. SK11: Macc 7G 131
Marlowe Dr. M20: Man 4G 106
Marlowe Wlk. M34: Dent 1K 109
Marlowe Walks SK6: Bred 6J 109
Marlow Ho. M5: Sal 9M 77
(off Hodge La.)
Marlow Rd. M9: Man 1L 79
Marlow St. SK13: Had 5C 100
Marlton Wlk. M9: Man 7K 61
(off Leconfield Dr.)
Marlwood Rd. BL1: Bolt 2A 38
Marlwood Way OL2: O'ham 1G 63
Marmion Cl. WA3: Low 9A 72
Marmion Dr. M21: Cho H 9N 93
Marne Av. M22: Shar 2D 116
OL6: A Lyne 5C 82
Marne Cres. OL11: Roch 5A 28
Marnland Gro. BL3: Bolt 8N 37
Marnock Cl. WN2: B'haw 2B 72
Maroon Rd. M22: Wyth 8E 116
MARPLE 1C 120
Marple Av. BL1: Bolt 9H 23
MARPLE BRIDGE 9E 110
Marple Cl. OL8: O'ham 9H 63
WN6: Stan 2M 33
Marple Ct. SK1: Stoc 9E 108
MARPLE DALE 8A 110
Marple Golf Course 4B 120
Marple Gro. M32: Stre 6J 93
Marple Hall Dr. SK6: Mar 9A 110
Marple Old Rd. SK2: Stoc 1L 119
Marple Packhorse Bridge 4E 120
Marple Rd. SK2: Stoc 9H 109
SK13: Char, Chis 3J 111
Marple Station (Rail) 9D 110
Marple St. M15: Man 4C 94
Marquess Way M24: Mid 4G 60
Marquis Av. BL9: Bury 9L 25
Marquis Dr. SK8: H Grn 8J 117
Marquis St. M19: Man 8B 96
Marrick Av. SK8: Chea 2H 117
Marrick Cl. WN3: Wig 9D 52
Marriott St. M20: Man 2G 107
SK1: Stoc 5M 9 (8D 108)
Marryat Ct. M12: Man 3L 95
(off Gregory St.)
Mars Av. BL3: Bolt 9D 38
MARSDEN 1H 49
Marsden Cl. OL5: Mos 7E 64
OL7: A Lyne 5J 81
OL16: Roch 4G 44
Marsden Dr. WA15: Tim 1J 115
Marsden Golf Course 3G 49
Marsden Ho. BL1: Bolt 2J 7
Marsden Rd. BL1: Bolt 2J 7 (5F 38)
SK6: Rom 5N 109
Marsden's Sq. OL15: Lit 8M 15
(off Sutcliffe St.)
Marsden St. BL5: W'ton 3G 55
BL9: Bury 5L 7 (1M 41)
M2: Man 4G 5 (9E 78)
M24: Mid 4A 62
(off Lancaster Av.)
M28: Walk 9B 58
M28: Wors 3G 75
M30: Ecc 7C 76
SK13: Had 5C 100
(off Queen St.)
WN1: Wig 7J 9 (3F 52)
WN3: I Mak 7J 53
WN5: Wig 4C 52
Marsden Ter. SK11: Macc 6H 131
Marsden Wlk. M26: Rad 8F 40
Marsett Cl. OL12: Roch 4M 27
Marsett Wlk. M23: Wyth 6M 105
Marshall Ct. OL1: O'ham 3J 63
(off Bradford St.)
OL6: A Lyne 8A 82
Marshall Rd. M19: Man 8M 95
Marshall Stevens Way
M17: T Pk 4H 93
Marshall St. M4: Man 2K 5 (8G 78)
M12: Man 9N 5 (3H 95)
OL16: Roch 6G 28
WN7: Lei 5H 73
Marsham Cl. M13: Man 4K 95
OL4: Grot 6E 64
Marsham Dr. SK6: Mar 2D 120

Marsham Rd. BL5: W'ton 5H 55
SK7: H Gro 6G 118
Marshbank BL5: W'ton 2G 55
Marsh Brook Cl. WA3: Rix 6B 102
Marshbrook Cl. WN2: Hin 5C 54
Marshbrook Dr. M9: Man 9H 61
Marsh Brook Fold BL5: W'ton 4C 54
Marshbrook Rd. M41: Urm 6C 92
Marsh Cl. SK3: Stoc 1B 118
Marshdale WN7: Lei 4F 72
(off Norbury St.)
Marshdale Rd. BL1: Bolt 4A 38
Marshes Fold M28: Walk 9K 57
Marshfield Rd. WA15: Tim 2J 115
Marshfield St. M13: Man 3H 95
Marshfield Wlk. M13: Man 3H 95
(off Lauderdale Cres.)
Marsh Fold BL5: W'ton 2G 55
(off Marsh St.)
Marsh Fold La. BL1: Bolt 4D 38
MARSH GREEN 2A 52
Marsh Grn. WN5: Wig 2A 52
Marsh Head OL3: Dig 7A 48
Marsh Hey Cl. M38: Lit H 5G 57
Marsh La. BL3: Lit L 8B 40
BL4: Farn 3J 57
SK22: N Mil 8N 121
WN1: Wig 7K 9 (3F 52)
Marsh La. Trad. Est.
SK22: N Mil 8N 121
Marsh Lea OL3: Dig 7N 47
Marsh Rd. BL3: Lit L 8A 40
M38: Lit H 7J 57
Marsh Row WN2: Hin 7C 54
Marsh St. BL1: Bolt 2F 38
BL5: W'ton 2G 55
BL6: Hor 9C 20
M28: Walk 9N 57
Marshway Dr. WA12: N Wil 5E 86
Marsland Av. WA15: Tim 8H 105
Marsland Cl. M34: Dent 6F 96
MARSLAND GREEN 6N 73
Marsland Grn. La. M29: Ast 6N 73
Marsland Rd. M33: Sale 5G 104
SK6: Mar 9A 110
WA15: Tim 1H 115
MARSLANDS 1L 65
Marslands OL3: Dig 9L 47
Marsland St. SK1: Stoc 5D 108
(not continuous)
SK7: H Gro 5H 119
Marsland St. Ind. Est.
SK7: H Gro 5J 119
Marsland St. Nth. M7: Sal 3E 78
Marsland St. Sth. M7: Sal 3E 78
Marsland Ter. SK1: Stoc 8F 108
Mars St. OL9: O'ham 4G 63
Marston Bentley Ind. Est.
WN2: Asp 1L 53
Marston Cl. BL6: Los 4J 37
M35: Fail 4G 80
M45: Whitef 3B 60
Marston Dr. M44: Irl 7J 91
Marston Ho. M5: Sal 9M 77
(off Cypress Cl.)
Marston Rd. M7: Sal 2D 78
M32: Stre 7M 93
Marston St. M40: Man 5J 79
Martens Rd. M44: Irl 3F 102
Marthall Dr. M33: Sale 6L 105
Marthall La. WA16: Mart, Olle 9M 133
Marthall Way SK9: Hand 1K 123
Martham Dr. SK2: Stoc 1L 119
Martha's Ter. OL16: Roch 2G 28
Martha St. BL3: Bolt 8E 38
OL1: O'ham 3H 63
Martial Art Studio, The 9F 68
Martin Av. BL3: Lit L 9C 40
BL4: Farn 4G 57
OL4: O'ham 5N 63
WA12: N Wil 4E 86
Martin Cl. M34: Dent 4K 97
SK2: Stoc 2K 119
Martindale Cl. OL2: O'ham 7J 45
Martindale Cres. M12: Man 3K 95
M24: Mid 9J 43
WN5: Wig 5B 52
Martindale Gdns. BL1: Bolt 2F 38
(off Jennaby Wlk.)
Martindale Rd. WA11: St H 8F 68
Martin Dr. M44: Irl 5H 91
Martingale Cl. M26: Rad 7G 41
Martingale Ct. M8: Man 3F 78
Martingale Way M43: Droy 7H 81
Martin Gro. BL4: Kea 4N 57
Martin Ho. M14: Man 6J 95
Martin La. OL12: Roch 4N 27
Martin Rd. M27: Clif 9H 59
Martins Av. PR7: H Char 3H 19
Martinsclough BL6: Los 6L 37
Martins Ct. WN2: Hin 5C 54
Martinscroft Rd. M23: Wyth 2N 115
Martins Fld. OL12: Roch 4L 27
Martins La. WN8: Skel 4B 50
Martin St. BL7: Tur 1L 23
BL9: Bury 1C 42
M5: Sal 8L 77
M34: Aud 2K 97
M46: Ath 8M 55
SK14: Hyde 7B 98
Martins Way M43: Droy 9D 80
Martland Av. WA3: Low 2N 87
WN6: She 7K 33
Martland Bus. Pk. WN5: Wig 2A 52
Martland Ct. WN5: Orr 1M 51
Martland Cres. WN6: Wig 9B 34
MARTLAND MILL 9A 34
Martland Mill Ind. Est.
WN5: Wig 1N 51
Martland Mill La. WN5: Wig 1A 52
(not continuous)
Martland Point WN5: Orr 1M 51
Martlesham Wlk. M4: Man 3J 5
Martlet Av. SK12: Dis 9F 120
Martlet Cl. M14: Man 8G 94
Martlett Av. OL11: Roch 6K 27
Martlew Dr. M46: Ath 7A 56
Martock Av. M22: Wyth 4D 116
Marton Av. BL2: Bolt 4K 39
M20: Man 6H 107
Marton Cl. SK10: Macc 3D 130
WA3: Cul 5G 89
Marton Dr. M46: Ath 7N 55
Marton Grange M25: Pres 8C 60
Marton Grn. SK3: Stoc 2B 118
Marton Gro. SK4: Stoc 2C 108
Marton Pl. M33: Sale 4G 105
Marton St. WN1: Wig 6K 9 (2F 52)
Marton Way SK9: Hand 1K 123
(off Spath La.)
Marus Av. WN3: Wig 8C 52
Marus Bri. Retail Pk. WN3: Wig 9C 52
Marus Bri. Rdbt. WN3: Wig 8C 52
Marvic Ct. M13: Man 6K 95
Marwick Cl. WN6: Stan 2A 34
Marwood Cl. M26: Rad 3A 58
WA14: Alt 1B 114
Marwood Dr. M23: Wyth 4M 115
Maryfield Cl. WA3: Gol 2K 87
Maryfield Ct. M16: Whall R 9D 94
Mary France St. M15: Man 3D 94
Mary Hulton Ct. BL5: W'ton 3J 55
Maryland Av. BL2: Bolt 5L 39
MARYLEBONE 9G 34
Marylebone Ct. WN1: Wig 9G 34
Marylebone Pl. WN1: Wig 9F 34
Marylon Dr. M22: Nor 8D 106
Maryport Dr. WA15: Tim 9K 105
Mary St. BL0: Ram 9H 11
BL4: Farn 4L 57
M3: Man 1F 4 (7E 78)
M29: Tyld 2B 74
M34: Dent 5L 97
M43: Droy 9F 80
OL10: H'ood 2H 43
OL16: Roch 1H 29
SK1: Stoc 1N 9 (6E 108)
SK8: Chea 1J 117
SK14: Hyde 6N 97
SK16: Duk 9M 81
Mary St. E. BL6: Hor 9D 20
Mary St. W. BL6: Hor 9C 20
Masboro St. M8: Man 3E 78
Masbury Cl. BL1: Bolt 6F 22
Masefield Av. M25: Pres 8M 59
M26: Rad 8E 40
WN5: Orr 5L 51
WN7: Lei 3F 72
Masefield Cl. SK16: Duk 2E 98
Masefield Cres. M43: Droy 9E 80
Masefield Dr. BL4: Farn 4J 57
SK4: Stoc 6M 107
WN3: Wig 7C 52
Masefield Gro. SK5: Stoc 8C 96
Masefield Rd. BL3: Lit L 8B 40
M43: Droy 9E 80
OL1: O'ham 1M 63
Mason Cl. WN4: A Mak 6G 70
Mason Clough BL1: Bolt 8G 23
Mason Gdns. BL3: Bolt 4H 7 (6F 38)
Mason La. M46: Ath 9N 55
Mason Row BL7: Eger 3E 22
Masons Gro. SK13: Had 3C 100
Masons La. SK10: Macc 3K 131
Mason St. BL6: Hor 1C 36
BL7: Eger 4F 22
BL9: Bury 8N 7 (2N 41)
M4: Man 2K 5 (8G 78)
OL7: A Lyne 9K 81
OL10: H'ood 2G 42
OL16: Roch 8D 8 (6D 28)
WN2: Abr 2L 71
WN3: Wig 9G 9 (4E 52)
Mason St. Ind. Est. WN3: Wig 9G 9
Massey Av. M35: Fail 2F 80
OL6: A Lyne 4N 81
Massey Cft. OL12: Whitw 6A 14
Massey Rd. M33: Sale 4L 105
WA15: Alt 4E 6 (3E 114)
Massey St. BL9: Bury 1A 42
M5: Sal 4A 4
SK1: Stoc 3L 9 (7D 108)
SK9: A Edg 4F 126
Massey Wlk. M22: Wyth 6E 116
Massie St. SK8: Chea 1J 117
Masson Pl. M4: Man 1H 5
Masters Ct. WA16: Knut 7F 132
Matchmoor La. BL6: Hor 9H 21
Matham Wlk. M15: Man 9H 5
Mather Av. M25: Pres 1B 78
M30: Ecc 8E 76
M45: Whitef 1N 59
WA3: Low 3A 88
Matherbank BL5: W'ton 6H 55
(off Lwr. Leigh Rd.)
Mather Cl. M45: Whitef 2M 59
Mather Fold Cotts. BL7: Eger 4F 22
Mather Fold Rd. M28: Wors 1J 75
Mather La. WN7: Lei 6J 73
Mather Rd. BL9: Bury 6M 25
M30: Ecc 8E 76
Mather St. BL3: Bolt 6F 38
BL4: Kea 3M 57
M26: Rad 9G 41
M35: Fail 3B 80
M46: Ath 8M 55
Mather Way M6: Sal 7N 77
(off Salford Shop. City)
Matheson Dr. WN5: Wig 3A 52
Matisse Way M7: Sal 2A 78
MATLEY 3G 98
Matley Cl. SK14: Hyde 4E 98
Matley Ct. SK15: Mot 3H 99
Matley Grn. SK5: Stoc 2G 109
Matley La. SK14: Hyde 4E 98
SK15: Mat 4E 98
Matley Pk. La. SK15: Stal 3G 99
Matlock Av. M7: Sal 3N 77
M20: Man 2E 106
M34: Dent 9L 97
M41: Urm 9B 92
OL6: A Lyne 4C 82
Matlock Bank SK13: Gam 8A 100
(off Castleton Cres.)
Matlock Cl. BL4: Farn 2M 57
M33: Sale 4J 105
M46: Ath 9M 55
Matlock Ct. BL6: Hor 9G 21
Matlock Dr. SK7: H Gro 7J 119
Matlock Gdns. SK13: Gam 8A 100
(off Castleton Cres.)
Matlock La. SK13: Gam 8A 100
(off Castleton Cres.)
Matlock M. WA14: Alt 1E 6
Matlock Pl. SK13: Gam 8A 100
(off Castleton Cres.)
Matlock Rd. M32: Stre 6G 93
SK5: Stoc 8E 96
SK8: H Grn 8H 117
Matlock St. M30: Ecc 1C 92
Matson Wlk. M22: Wyth 5N 115
Matt Busby Cl. M27: Pen 3H 77
Matterdale Ter. SK15: Stal 6D 82
(off Ullswater Ter.)
Matthew Cl. OL8: O'ham 7N 63
SK13: Tin 2B 100
Matthew Moss La. OL11: Roch 9N 27
Matthews Av. BL4: Kea 4N 57
Matthews La. M12: Man 7M 95
M18: Man 7M 95
M19: Man 7M 95
Matthew's St. M12: Man 2L 95
Matthias Ct. M3: Sal 1B 4 (7C 78)
Mattison St. M11: Man 2C 96
Maudsley Cl. M7: Sal 4E 78
Maudsley St. BL9: Bury 9J 7 (3L 41)
Maud St. BL2: Bolt 8K 23
OL12: Roch 3E 28
Mauldeth Cl. SK4: Stoc 5M 107
Mauldeth Ct. SK4: Stoc 5M 107
Mauldeth Rd. M14: Man 1H 107
M19: Man 2K 107
M19: Man, Stoc 4L 107
M20: Man 1H 107
SK4: Stoc 6L 107
Mauldeth Road Station (Rail) 2K 107
Mauldeth Rd. W. M20: Man 9E 94
M21: Cho H 2B 106
Maunby Gdns. M38: Lit H 8K 57
Maureen Av. M8: Man 2F 78
Maureen St. OL12: Roch 3E 28
Maurice Cl. SK16: Duk 1B 98
Maurice Dr. M6: Sal 6M 77
Maurice Pariser Wlk. M8: Man 3E 78
(off Squire Rd.)
Maurice St. M6: Sal 6M 77
Maveen Ct. SK2: Stoc 3E 118
Maveen Gro. SK2: Stoc 3E 118
Mavis Dr. PR7: Cop 4B 18
Mavis Gro. OL16: Miln 7L 29
Mavis St. OL11: Roch 3A 44
Mawdsley Dr. M8: Man 2E 79
Mawdsley St. BL1: Bolt 3K 7 (5G 38)
Maxfield Cl. SK11: Macc 4D 130
Maxton Ho. BL4: Farn 3M 57
(off Bridgewater St.)
Maxwell Av. SK2: Stoc 2G 119
Maxwell St. BL1: Bolt 9F 22
BL9: Bury 1A 42
Mayall St. OL5: Mos 1F 82
Mayall St. E. OL4: O'ham 4N 63
Mayan Av. M3: Sal 2B 4 (8C 78)
May Av. SK4: Stoc 6A 108
SK8: Chea H 9N 117
WN2: Abr 3L 71
WN7: Lei 4F 72
Maybank St. BL3: Bolt 7E 38
Mayberth Av. M8: Man 9F 60
Maybreck Cl. BL3: Bolt 7D 38
Maybrook Wlk. M9: Man 2J 79
(off Alfred St.)
Mayburn Cl. M24: Mid 6A 62
Maybury Cl. BL0: Ram 9H 11
Maybury St. M18: Man 3C 96
May Ct. M16: Whall R 6C 94
Maycroft SK5: Stoc 2F 108
Maycroft Av. M20: Man 3H 107
Maydews Pas. SK11: Macc 5H 131
(off Brook St.)
May Dr. M19: Man 2L 107
Mayer St. SK2: Stoc 9G 109
Mayes Ct. M14: Man 1J 107
(off Sheringham Rd.)
Mayes Gdns. M4: Man 9J 79
Mayes St. M4: Man 2H 5 (8F 78)
(not continuous)
Mayfair BL6: Hor 1F 36
M7: Sal 1B 78
Mayfair, The M20: Man 3G 106
Mayfair Av. M6: Sal 7H 77
M26: Rad 8D 40
M41: Urm 7B 92
M45: Whitef 4M 59
Mayfair Cl. SK12: Poy 2J 125
SK16: Duk 1C 98
Mayfair Ct. M14: Man 9H 95
WA15: Tim 9H 105
Mayfair Cres. M35: Fail 2F 80
Mayfair Dr. M33: Sale 6E 104
M44: Irl 7H 91
M46: Ath 7A 56
OL2: O'ham 1H 63
WN2: Asp 1N 53
WN3: Wig 9C 52
Mayfair Gdns. M45: Whitef 4M 59
(off Bury New Rd.)
OL11: Roch 8B 28
Mayfair Gro. M45: Whitef 4N 59
Mayfair Pk. M20: Man 4E 106
Mayfair Rd. M22: Wyth 4D 116
MAYFIELD 4F 28
Mayfield BL2: Bolt 8L 23
M26: Rad 1E 58
Mayfield Av. BL3: Bolt 9J 39
BL4: Farn 4K 57
M27: Swin 4C 76
M28: Walk 8L 57
M32: Stre 8H 93
Mayfield Av. M33: Sale 4L 105
M34: Dent 1L 109
OL4: Spri 4D 64
PR6: Adl 6K 19
SK5: Stoc 3D 108
SK11: Macc 7G 130
Mayfield Cl. BL0: Ram 3G 25
WA15: Tim 1H 115
Mayfield Ct. WA15: Tim 1H 115
WN5: Orr 2M 51
Mayfield Dr. WN7: Lei 1E 88
Mayfield Gro. M18: Man 6D 96
SK5: Stoc 3D 108
SK9: Wilm 9D 122
Mayfield Ind. Pk. M44: Irl 6K 91
Mayfield Mans. M16: Whall R 6D 94
Mayfield Rd. BL0: Ram 3G 24
M7: Sal 1B 78
M16: Whall R 6D 94
OL1: O'ham 2M 63
SK6: Mar B 7E 110
SK7: Bram 2C 124
WA15: Tim 1H 115
WA16: Mob 4M 133
WN5: Orr 3M 51
WN8: Uph 4E 50
(not continuous)
Mayfield St. M34: Aud 4J 97
M46: Ath 8L 55
OL16: Roch 4F 28
(not continuous)
WN4: A Mak 7D 70
Mayfield Ter. OL16: Roch 4F 28
SK11: Macc 7G 130
Mayfield Vw. WA13: Lym 5A 112
Mayflower Av. M5: Sal 1N 93
Mayflower Cl. SK13: Glos 9G 101
Mayflower Cotts. WN1: Stan 4F 34
Mayflower Gdns. PR7: Chor 2E 18
Mayford Rd. M19: Man 7M 95
Maygate OL9: O'ham 3H 63
May Gro. M19: Man 9N 95
Mayhill Dr. M6: Sal 6G 77
M28: Wors 2A 76
Mayhurst Av. M21: Cho H 5C 106
Maynard Rd. WA14: W Tim 8C 104
Mayorlowe Av. SK5: Stoc 4G 108
Mayor's Rd. WA15: Alt 4E 6 (3E 114)
Mayor St. BL1: Bolt 6E 38
BL3: Bolt 5G 7 (6E 38)
BL8: Bury 1J 41
OL9: O'ham 4G 62
Mayo St. M12: Man 1J 95
May Pl. OL11: Roch 9E 28
(off Burlington St.)
OL15: Lit 1J 29
Maypole, The M6: Sal 6N 77
(off Broughton Rd.)
Maypole Cl. M31: C'ton 2L 103
Maypole Cres. WN2: Abr 3M 71
Maypool Dr. SK5: Stoc 2D 108
May Rd. M16: Whall R 6C 94
M27: Pen 4H 77
SK8: Chea H 9N 117
Maysmith M. M7: Sal 4C 78
May St. BL2: Bolt 3N 7 (5H 39)
M26: Rad 9G 41
M30: Ecc 6C 76
M40: Man 5A 80
(not continuous)
OL8: O'ham 7G 62
OL10: H'ood 4K 43
(not continuous)
WA3: Gol 8L 71
WN7: Lei 5E 72
Maythorn Av. WA3: Cro 9C 88
Mayton St. M11: Man 1M 95
Maytree Ct. PR6: Adl 5J 19
May Tree Dr. WN1: Wig 8E 34
Mayville Dr. M20: Man 3G 106
May Wlk. M31: Part 5F 102
Maywood SK9: Wilm 1D 126
Maywood Av. M20: Man 8G 107
Maze St. BL3: Bolt 7K 39
(not continuous)
Meachin Av. M21: Cho H 3B 106
Mead, The M5: Sal 8K 77
Mead Cl. WA16: Knut 7F 132
Meade, The BL3: Bolt 1F 56
M21: Cho H 1A 106
SK9: Wilm 6H 123
Meade Cl. M41: Urm 7C 92
Meade Gro. M13: Man 6L 95
Meade Hill Rd. M8: Man 8D 60
M25: Pres 8D 60
Meade Mnr. M21: Cho H 1A 106
Meadfoot Av. M25: Pres 8D 60
Meadfoot Rd. M18: Man 3B 96
Meadland Gro. BL1: Bolt 9G 23
Meadon Av. M27: Clif 1H 77
Meadow, The BL1: Bolt 5L 37
OL3: Del 7J 47
Meadow Av. WA15: Hale 4H 115
Meadow Bank M21: Cho H 1N 105
SK4: Stoc 6N 107
SK6: Bred 5K 109
SK13: Glos 9B 100
WA15: Tim 9G 104
Meadowbank OL7: A Lyne 4L 81
SK14: Holl 3N 99
Meadowbank Av. M46: Ath 7N 55
Meadowbank Cl. M35: Fail 4E 80
OL4: O'ham 7B 64
Meadow Bank Ct. M32: Stre 8H 93
Meadowbank Gdns. WA3: G'ury 2L 89
Meadowbank Rd. BL3: Bolt 1C 56
Meadowbrook Cl. BL6: Los 9L 37
BL9: Bury 9B 26
Meadowbrook Way
SK8: Chea H 3N 117
Meadow Brow SK9: A Edg 3F 126
Meadowburn Nook M30: Ecc 6B 76
Meadow Cl. BL3: Lit L 1B 58
M32: Stre 8L 93
M34: Dent 1L 109
OL5: Mos 8H 65
Meadow Cl. OL10: H'ood 2H 43
OL12: Roch 4M 27
PR7: Cop 6C 18
SK6: H Lan 7C 120
SK6: Wood 3L 109
SK9: Wilm 1D 126
WA12: N Wil 6C 86
WA15: Hale 4H 115
WN7: Lei 8G 72
WN8: Skel 4B 50
Meadow Cotts. OL12: Whitw 3B 14
Meadow Ct. M6: Sal 7H 77
M21: Cho H 9M 93
WA15: Hale 4J 115
WN6: Wig 2D 52
Meadow Cft. M45: Whitef 5J 59
SK7: H Gro 3J 119
Meadowcroft BL5: W'ton 4H 55
M26: Rad 7F 40
SK14: Mot 5K 99
WN4: A Mak 4C 70
Meadowcroft Ho. OL11: Roch 7L 27
Meadowcroft La. OL1: O'ham 2M 63
OL11: Roch 7L 27
Meadowcroft Way WN7: Lei 8K 73
Meadow Dr. SK10: P'bury 6F 128
WA16: Knut 7F 132
Meadow Fld. WN2: Hin 2D 72
Meadowfield BL6: Los 5K 37
OL16: Roch 1F 44
WN8: Uph 4E 50
Meadowfield Ct. SK13: Had 6B 100
Meadowfield Cl. SK14: Hyde 5A 98
Meadowfield Dr. M28: Wors 4J 75
Meadow Fold OL3: Upp 3M 65
Meadowgate M28: Wors 2N 75
M41: Urm 8D 92
WN6: Wig 1B 52
Meadowgate Rd. M6: Sal 7H 77
Meadow Head Av. OL12: Whitw 8B 14
Meadow Head La. OL11: Roch 3F 26
Meadow Hgts. BL0: Ram 8K 11
(off Fir St.)
Meadow Ind. Est. M35: Fail 6C 80
(Banbury Rd.)
M35: Fail 4A 80
(Hobson St.)
SK1: Stoc 5D 108
Meadowlands PR7: Char R 1A 18
Meadow La. BL2: Bolt 5A 40
M28: Wors 5N 75
M34: Dent 9L 97
OL8: O'ham 9J 63
SK12: Dis 9G 121
SK16: Duk 1A 98
WA14: D Mas 3H 113
Meadow Mill SK1: Stoc 5D 108
Meadow Pk. BL0: Ram 2J 11
Meadow Pit La. WN2: Hai 4H 35
Meadow Ri. OL2: Shaw 3L 45
SK13: Glos 9B 100
Meadow Rd. M7: Sal 1A 4 (7B 78)
M24: Mid 5K 61
M41: Urm 8D 92
Meadows, The BL5: W'ton 8D 36
M24: Mid 5N 61
M25: Pres 7A 60
M26: Rad 7E 40
M44: Cad 2F 102
M45: Whitef 4J 59
(off Old Hall La.)
OL3: Upp 4L 65
OL4: Grot 5D 64
OL12: Roch 1F 26
OL12: Whitw 5A 14
SK6: Bred 4M 109
SK13: Had 5B 100
Meadows Cl. SK7: H Gro 4J 119
WN2: Hin 6N 53
Meadowside OL16: Miln 9N 29
SK7: Bram 5A 118
SK10: Adl 6M 125
SK12: Dis 9K 121
Meadowside Av. BL2: Bolt 4K 39
M22: Wyth 3C 116
M28: Walk 7M 57
M44: Irl 7H 91
WN4: A Mak 2D 70
Meadowside Cl. M26: Rad 7G 40
Meadowside Gro. M28: Walk 8M 57
Meadowside Rd. WN2: Hin 7B 54
Meadows La. BL2: Bolt 1N 39
Meadows Rd. M33: Sale 2J 105
SK4: Stoc 1A 108
(not continuous)
SK8: Chea H 7L 117
SK8: H Grn 6G 116
Meadow St. PR7: Adl 7K 19
SK2: Stoc 2G 118
SK14: Hyde 8B 98
SK22: N Mil 7L 121
WN6: Wig 2D 52
Meadowsweet La. M28: Walk 7G 57
Meadowsweet Rd.
WA16: Mob 5M 133
Meadowvale Dr. WN5: Wig 5N 51
Meadow Vw. OL12: Roch 4M 27
PR6: H Char 5J 19
WN5: Orr 3J 51
Meadow Wlk. BL4: Farn 3H 57
M29: Ast 6C 74
(not continuous)
M31: Part 5F 102
OL15: Lit 9K 15
SK6: Bred 5K 109
Meadow Way BL6: Bla 3A 36
BL8: Tot 7E 24
BL9: Sum 3J 25
M40: Man 1M 79
PR7: Cop 5A 18
SK9: Wilm 1D 126
SK10: Macc 2J 131
WA15: Hale 4H 115
Meads, The OL9: Chad 5E 62
Meads Ct. M27: Swin 2F 76
Meadscroft Dr. SK9: A Edg 4E 126

Meads Gro. BL4: Farn 3E 56
M29: Ast 4D 74
Mead Way M34: Dent 9K 97
Meadway BL0: Ram 5J 11
BL4: Kea 2N 57
BL9: Bury 6M 41
M29: Tyld 1E 74
M33: Sale 6E 104
OL9: Chad 9C 62
OL11: Roch 9A 28
SK6: H Lan 7C 120
SK7: Bram 1C 124
SK10: P'bury 8E 128
SK12: Poy 1F 124
SK15: Stal 3H 99
SK16: Duk 2B 98
WA3: Low 1N 87
WN2: I Mak 4J 53
Meadway Cl. M33: Sale 6E 104
Meadway Ct. SK7: Bram 1C 124
Meadway Rd. SK8: Chea H 4N 117
Mealhouse Brow SK1: Stoc 2L 9
Mealhouse Ct. M46: Ath 8L 55
Mealhouse La. BL1: Bolt 2K 7 (5G 38)
M46: Ath 8L 55
Meal St. SK4: Stoc 5C 108
SK22: N Mil 7M 121
Meanley Rd. M29: Ast 3N 73
Meanley St. M29: Tyld 1B 74
Meanwood Brow *OL12: Roch* *5B 28*
(off Rooley Moor Rd.)
Meanwood Fold OL12: Roch 5B 28
Mecca Bingo
Bolton 4J 7 (6F 38)
Breightmet 5N 39
Oldham 3C 8 (5J 63)
Rochdale 7E 8 (6E 28)
Sale 4G 105
West Gorton 3M 95
Meddings Cl. SK9: A Edg 5F 126
MediaCityUk Stop (Metro) 2L 93
Medina Cl. SK8: Chea H 3N 117
Medlar Way WN4: A Mak 5C 70
Medley St. OL12: Roch 4D 28
Medlock Cl. BL4: Farn 3J 57
Medlock Ct. M11: Man 2N 95
OL4: Lees 4B 64
Medlock Dr. OL8: O'ham 1L 81
Medlock Gates M35: Fail 6D 80
Medlock Ho. M15: Man 8C 4
Medlock Leisure Cen. 8F 80
Medlock Pl. M43: Droy 9F 80
Medlock Rd. M35: Fail 6D 80
Medlock St. M15: Man 8F 4 (2E 94)
M43: Droy 8E 80
OL1: O'ham 4L 63
MEDLOCK VALE 6D 80
Medlock Way M45: Whitef 3B 60
OL4: Lees 5B 64
WN2: P Bri 9K 53
Medtia Sq. OL1: O'ham 4D 8
Medway, The OL10: H'ood 1G 42
Medway Cl. BL6: Hor 1F 36
M5: Sal 7K 77
OL8: O'ham 8G 62
SK9: Wilm 4J 123
WN4: A Mak 4C 70
WN7: Lei 1E 88
Medway Cres.
WA14: Alt 1A 6 (1C 114)
Medway Dr. BL4: Kea 6B 58
BL6: Hor 1F 36
Medway Pl. WN5: Wig 4A 52
Medway Rd. M28: Wors 2J 75
OL2: Shaw 4L 45
OL8: O'ham 8G 63
WA3: Cul 7J 89
Medway Wlk. *M40: Man* *7J 79*
(off Naylor St.)
WN5: Wig 4A 52
Meech St. M11: Man 1A 96
Meek St. OL2: O'ham 1L 63
Meerbrook Rd. SK3: Stoc 8M 107
Mee's Sq. M30: Ecc 1D 92
Mee St. SK11: Macc 7J 131
Megabowl
Bury 6A 42
Megan Ho. OL6: A Lyne 8C 6
Megfield BL5: W'ton 5G 54
Meg La. SK10: Macc 4C 130
Megna Cl. OL9: O'ham 4H 63
Melandra Castle 6N 99
Melandra Castle Rd. SK13: Gam 7N 99
Melandra Cres. SK14: Hat 7H 99
Melandra Rd. SK13: Had 6N 99
Melanie Cl. SK13: Glos 9C 100
Melanie Dr. SK5: Stoc 9D 96
Melba St. M11: Man 1C 96
Melbecks Wlk. M23: Wyth 6M 105
Melbourne Av. M32: Stre 7K 93
M90: Man A 7N 115
OL9: Chad 4E 62
Melbourne Cl. BL6: Hor 1E 36
OL11: Roch 2E 44
Melbourne Gro. BL6: Hor 1E 36
Melbourne M. *M7: Sal* *5D 78*
(off Arrow St.)
OL9: Chad 4F 62
Melbourne Rd. BL3: Bolt 7C 38
OL11: Roch 2E 44
SK7: Bram 9C 118
Melbourne St. M7: Sal 5D 78
M9: Man 2K 79
M15: Man 9E 4 (2D 94)
M27: Pen 2H 77
M34: Dent 7J 97
OL9: Chad 4F 62
SK5: Stoc 9D 96
SK15: Stal 8D 82
Melbourne St. Nth. OL6: A Lyne 6N 81
Melbourne St. Sth.
OL6: A Lyne 6E 6 (6N 81)
Melbury Av. M20: Man 4J 107
Melbury Dr. BL6: Los 4H 37
Melbury Rd. SK8: Chea H 9N 117
Meldon Rd. M13: Man 7K 95
Meldreth Dr. M12: Man 5L 95
Meldrum St. OL8: O'ham 7K 63
Melford Av. M40: Man 1C 80
Melford Dr. SK10: Macc 2G 131
WN4: A Mak 6D 70
WN5: Bil 8H 51
Melford Gro. OL4: O'ham 5A 64
Melford Rd. SK7: H Gro 6K 119
Melfort Av. M32: Stre 8L 93
Melia Ho. *M4: Man* *7F 78*
(off Lord St.)
Meliden Cres. BL1: Bolt 3C 38
M22: Wyth 4D 116
Melksham Cl. *M5: Sal* *8A 78*
(off Culverwell Dr.)
SK11: Macc 5E 130
Mellalieu St. M24: Mid 2K 61
OL2: O'ham 1J 63
Melland Av. M21: Cho H 3B 106
Melland Rd. M18: Man 6A 96
Mellands Ct. *M18: Man* *6B 96*
(off Levenshulme Rd.)
Melland Sports Cen. 6A 96
Meller Rd. M13: Man 7L 95
Melling Av. OL9: Chad 2C 62
SK4: Stoc 2C 108
Melling Cl. PR6: Adl 6L 19
WN7: Lei 9H 73
Melling Rd. OL4: O'ham 5N 63
Mellings Av. WN5: Bil 1J 69
Melling St. M12: Man 5M 95
WN5: Wig 6B 52
Mellington Av. M20: Man 8G 107
Melling Way WN3: Wins 1A 70
Mellodew Dr. OL1: O'ham 8A 46
MELLOR 1H 121
Mellor & Townscliffe Golf Course
2G 121
Mellor Brook Dr. WN2: P Bri 9K 53
Mellor Brow OL10: H'ood 2H 43
Mellor Cl. OL6: A Lyne 8B 82
WN6: Stan 2B 34
Mellor Ct. SK2: Stoc 9J 109
Mellor Cres. WA16: Knut 7E 132
Mellor Dr. BL9: Bury 5K 41
M28: Wors 1K 75
Mellor Gro. BL1: Bolt 3C 38
Mellor Ho. *OL2: O'ham* *8J 45*
(off Royton Hall Pk.)
Mellor Rd. OL6: A Lyne 6C 82
SK8: Chea H 6N 117
SK22: N Mil 2L 121
Mellor Sports Club 1G 120
Mellors Rd. M17: T Pk 2H 93
Mellor St. M25: Pres 7M 59
M26: Rad 1H 59
(not continuous)
M30: Ecc 9D 76
M32: Stre 5L 93
M35: Fail 4B 80
M40: Man 1N 5 (7J 79)
M43: Droy 9D 80
OL2: O'ham 7H 45
OL4: Lees 5B 64
OL8: O'ham *9G 62*
(off Limeside Rd.)
OL11: Roch 5B 28
OL12: Roch 8A 8 (5B 28)
Mellor Vw. SK12: Dis 9C 121
Mellor Way OL9: Chad 7F 62
Mellow Cl. BL1: Bolt 6E 38
Mellowstone Dr. M21: Cho H 9E 94
Melloy Pl. M8: Man 6F 78
Melmerby Cl. WN4: A Mak 7C 70
Melmerby Ct. M5: Sal 9M 77
Melon Pl. M6: Sal 8A 78
Melrose OL12: Roch 6B 8 (5C 28)
Melrose Apartments M13: Man 5H 95
Melrose Av. BL1: Bolt 3B 38
BL8: Bury 1J 41
M20: Man 5H 107
M30: Ecc 6A 76
M33: Sale 4H 105
OL10: H'ood 1H 43
OL15: Lit 7L 15
SK3: Stoc 9L 107
WN7: Lei 1F 72
Melrose Cl. M45: Whitef 1M 59
Melrose Ct. OL9: Chad 7E 62
Melrose Cres. SK3: Stoc 3B 118
SK12: Poy 9A 120 & 1N 125
WA15: Hale 6H 115
WN4: Gars 7N 69
Melrose Dr. WN3: Wins 8N 51
Melrose Gdns. M26: Rad 7E 40
Melrose Rd. BL3: Lit L 9N 39
M26: Rad 7E 40
Melrose St. BL9: Sum 3H 25
M40: Man 5A 80
OL1: O'ham 2M 63
OL11: Roch 6B 28
Melrose Way PR7: Chor 1G 19
Melsomby Rd. M23: Wyth 6N 105
Meltham Av. M20: Man 2F 106
Meltham Cl. SK4: Stoc 7K 107
Meltham Pl. *BL3: Bolt* *8E 38*
(off Bk. Willows La.)
Meltham Rd. SK4: Stoc 7K 107
Melton Av. M34: Dent 6E 96
M41: Urm 6K 91
Melton Cl. M28: Walk 9K 57
M29: Ast 2C 74
OL10: H'ood 3G 43
Melton Dr. BL9: Bury 7N 41
Melton Rd. M8: Man 1D 78
Melton Row *M26: Rad* *8F 40*
(off Melton St.)
Melton St. *M9: Man* *1L 79*
(off Gilmour Ter.)
M26: Rad 8F 40
OL10: H'ood 3G 43
SK5: Stoc 4D 108
Melton Wlk. *M26: Rad* *8F 40*
(off Melton St.)
Melton Way *M26: Rad* *8F 40*
(off Melton St.)
Melverley Dr. WN7: Lei 5L 73
Melverley Rd. M9: Man 6F 60
Melverley St. WN3: Wig 4D 52
Melville Cl. M11: Man 2C 96
Melville Rd. BL4: Kea 5N 57
M32: Stre 6H 93
M44: Cad 3D 102
SK6: Wood 2J 131
Melville St. BL3: Bolt 8H 39
M3: Sal 3C 4 (8C 78)
OL4: Lees 6B 64
OL6: A Lyne 5D 6 (7M 81)
OL11: Roch 3B 44
Melvin Av. M22: Wyth 3D 116
Melyncourt Dr. SK14: Hat 6H 99
Memorial Pk. Dr. *SK6: Mar* *1C 120*
(off Stockport Rd.)
Memorial Rd. M28: Walk 9L 57
Menai Gro. SK8: Chea 1M 117
Menai Rd. SK3: Stoc 1C 118
Menai St. BL3: Bolt 8C 38
Mendip Av. M22: Wyth 3E 116
WN3: Wins 8N 51
Mendip Cl. BL2: Bolt 5A 40
BL6: Hor 8E 20
OL2: O'ham 9G 44
OL9: Chad 6E 62
SK4: Stoc 5C 108
SK8: H Grn 8G 116
Mendip Ct. SK4: Stoc 5C 108
Mendip Cres. BL8: Bury 1H 41
Mendip Dr. BL2: Bolt 6A 40
OL16: Miln 6L 29
Mendip Rd. OL8: O'ham 8H 63
Mendips Cl. OL2: Shaw 4K 45
Menston Av. M40: Man 1C 80
Mentmore Rd. OL16: Roch 5H 29
Mentone Cres. M22: Wyth 3D 116
Mentone Rd. SK4: Stoc 5N 107
Mentor St. M13: Man 6L 95
Menzies Ct. *M21: Cho H* *8A 94*
(off Ransfield Rd.)
Mercer Ct. PR7: H Char 4J 19
Mercer La. OL11: Roch 5K 27
Mercer Rd. M18: Man 4B 96
WA11: Hay 3A 86
Mercer's Rd. OL10: H'ood 5J 43
Mercer St. M19: Man 8N 95
M43: Droy 8F 80
WA12: N Wil 5G 86
Merchants Cres. WA3: Low 9A 72
Merchants Quay M50: Sal 3M 93
Merchants Quay Ct. M30: Ecc 7C 76
Mercian Mall
OL6: A Lyne 7D 6 (7M 81)
Mercian Way SK3: Stoc 9B 108
Mercia St. BL3: Bolt 7D 38
Mercury Bldgs. M1: Man 5K 5
Mercury Bus. Pk. M41: Urm 3F 92
Mercury Way M41: Urm 4F 92
SK6: Wood 3C 50
Mere, The OL6: A Lyne 4B 82
SK8: Chea H 3M 117
Mere Av. M6: Sal 8L 77
M24: Mid 5M 61
M43: Droy 1C 96
WN7: Lei 5F 72
Mere Bank Cl. M28: Walk 8K 57
Merebank Cl. OL11: Roch 5K 27
Merebrook Cl. M26: Rad 1H 59
SK11: Macc 4D 130
Merebrook Rd. SK11: Macc 4D 130
Mere Cl. BL9: Bury 7A 42
M33: Sale 5M 105
M34: Dent 7F 96
Mereclough Av. M28: Walk 1N 75
Mere Ct. WA16: Knut 6G 133
Meredew Av. M27: Swin 4E 76
Meredith Ct. *M15: Man* *3F 94*
(off Epsley Cl.)
Meredith St. BL3: Bolt 9G 38
M14: Man 1J 107
Mere Dr. M20: Man 4G 107
M27: Clif 9G 58
Merefield Av. OL11: Roch 8C 28
Merefield Cl. WN2: Hin 7A 54
Merefield Rd. WA15: Tim 2J 115
Merefield St. OL11: Roch 8C 28
Merefield Ter. OL11: Roch 8C 28
Mere Fold M28: Walk 8J 57
PR7: Char R 2A 18
Merefold BL6: Hor 1B 36
Mere Gdns. BL1: Bolt 4F 38
Mere Golf Course 1C 132
Mere Gro. WA11: St H 9F 68
Mere Hall WA16: Mere 1A 132
Merehall Cl. BL1: Bolt 4F 38
Merehall Dr. BL1: Bolt 4F 38
Merehall St. BL1: Bolt 3E 38
Mereheath Dr. WA16: Mere 1E 132
Mereheath La.
WA16: Knut, Mere 1D 132
Mereheath Pk. WA16: Knut 5F 132
Mere Ho. M15: Man 9A 4 (2C 94)
SK4: Stoc 7K 107
Mereland Av. M20: Man 4H 107
Mereland Cl. WN5: Orr 5J 51
Mere La. OL11: Roch 8D 28
Meremanor M28: Walk 1N 75
Mere Oaks WN1: Stan 7E 34
Merepool Cl. SK6: Mar 9N 109
Mere Rd. WA12: N Wil 5J 87
WN4: A Mak 6F 70
Mere Side SK15: Stal 6C 82
(not continuous)
Mereside Cl. SK8: Chea H 3L 117
SK10: Macc 3E 130
Mereside Gro. M28: Walk 8M 57
Mereside Rd. WA16: Mere 1D 132
Mereside Wlk. *M15: Man* *3C 94*
(off Mosshall Cl.)
Mere St. OL11: Roch 9C 8 (7D 28)
WN5: Wig 5C 52
WN7: Lei 5F 72
Mere Wlk. BL1: Bolt 4F 38
Merewood Av. M22: Wyth 1C 116
Meriden Cl. M26: Rad 6F 40
Meriden Gro. BL6: Los 6M 37
Meridian Cen. OL8: O'ham 5C 8
Meridian Pl. M20: Man 4F 106
Merinall Cl. OL16: Roch 6G 29
Meriton Rd. SK9: Hand 2H 123
Meriton Wlk. M18: Man 5N 95
Merlewood BL0: Eden 3L 11
Merlewood Av. M19: Man 1A 108
M34: Aud 9F 80
OL3: Upp 3L 65
Merlewood Dr. M27: Swin 4C 76
M29: Ast 2C 74
Merlin Av. WA16: Knut 5H 133
Merlin Cl. OL8: O'ham 2L 81
(not continuous)
OL15: Lit 3L 29
SK2: Stoc 1L 119
Merlin Dr. M27: Clif 9H 59
Merlin Gro. BL1: Bolt 3C 38
Merlin Ho. M19: Man 4J 107
Merlin Rd. M44: Irl 6H 91
OL16: Miln 7K 29
Merlyn Av. M20: Man 4H 107
M33: Sale 2J 105
M34: Dent 7J 97
Merlyn Ct. *M20: Man* *4H 107*
(off Milden Cl.)
Merrick Av. M22: Wyth 3D 116
Merrick St. OL10: H'ood 3K 43
Merridale, The WA15: Hale 7G 114
Merridale Rd. M40: Man 1A 80
Merriden Rd. SK10: Macc 2F 130
Merridge Wlk. *M8: Man* *4E 78*
(off Brentfield Av.)
Merrill St. M4: Man 9J 79
Merriman Av. WA16: Knut 5J 133
Merriman St. M16: Whall R 5D 94
Merrion St. BL4: Farn 1K 57
Merrow Wlk. M1: Man 8K 5
Merrybent Cl. SK2: Stoc 2H 119
Merrybower Rd. M7: Sal 2D 78
Merrydale Av. M30: Ecc 6E 76
Merrydale Cl. SK10: Macc 3D 130
Merryfield Grange BL1: Bolt 5B 38
Merryman Hall OL16: Roch 3F 28
Merryman's La. SK9: A Edg 6A 126
Mersey Bank Av. M21: Cho H 4C 106
Mersey Bank Lodge SK13: Had 4B 100
Mersey Bank Rd. SK13: Had 5B 100
Mersey Cl. M45: Whitef 2A 60
WN2: Hin 8E 54
Mersey Ct. M33: Sale 3L 105
Mersey Cres. M20: Man 5C 106
Mersey Dr. M31: Part 4H 103
M45: Whitef 2A 60
Mersey Ferries Terminal 2M 93
Mersey Mdws. M20: Man 5E 106
Mersey Rd. M20: Man 5E 106
M33: Sale 2H 105
SK4: Stoc 6L 107
WN2: P Bri 9J 53
WN5: Orr 4K 51
Mersey Rd. Ind. Est. M35: Fail 1F 80
Mersey Rd. Nth. M35: Fail 1E 80
Mersey Sq. M45: Whitef 2A 60
SK1: Stoc 2K 9 (7C 108)
(not continuous)
Mersey St. M11: Man 1C 96
(not continuous)
SK1: Stoc 1N 9 (6E 108)
WN7: Lei 5E 72
Mersey Valley Vis. Cen. 2M 105
Mersey Vw. M41: Urm 9M 91
Merseyway SK1: Stoc 2K 9 (7C 108)
Merston Dr. M20: Man 8H 107
Merton Av. OL8: O'ham 8H 63
SK6: Bred 4L 109
SK7: H Gro 7K 119
Merton Cl. BL3: Bolt 7D 38
Merton Dr. M43: Droy 9C 80
Merton Gro. M29: Ast 4D 74
OL9: Chad 8B 62
WA15: Tim 1H 115
Merton Rd. M25: Pres 6B 60
M33: Sale 2G 105
SK3: Stoc 8N 107
SK12: Poy 2F 124
WN3: Wig 2A 70
Merton St. BL8: Bury 1K 41
Merton Wlk. *M9: Man* *3K 79*
(off Nethervale Dr.)
Merville Av. M40: Man 1L 79
Mervyn Pl. WN3: Wig 7D 52
Mervyn Rd. M7: Sal 4N 77
Merwell Rd. M41: Urm 8M 91
Merwood Av. SK8: H Grn 7J 117
Merwood Gro. M14: Man 5K 95
Meshaw Cl. M23: Wyth 6L 105
Mesnefield Rd. M7: Sal 2N 77
Mesne Lea Gro. M28: Wors 2M 75
Mesne Lea Rd. M28: Walk 2M 75
Mesnes Av. WN3: Wig 6D 52
Mesnes Pk. 5H 9 (2E 52)
Mesnes Pk. Ter.
WN1: Wig 6J 9 (2F 52)
Mesnes Rd. WN1: Wig 1F 52
Mesnes St. WN1: Wig 6J 9 (2F 52)
Mesnes Ter. WN1: Wig 6K 9 (2F 52)
Met, The 7K 7
Metal Box Way BL5: W'ton 1J 55
Metcalfe Ct. M38: Lit H 7G 57
SK6: Rom *6M 109*
(off Metcalfe Dr.)
Metcalfe Dr. SK6: Rom 6M 109
Metcalfe St. OL16: Roch 6H 29
Metcalf M. OL3: Upp 3L 65
Metcalf's Yd. BL6: Bla 2N 35
Metcalf Ter. BL2: Ain 3D 40
Metfield Pl. BL1: Bolt 4D 38
Metfield Wlk. M40: Man 9B 62
Methodist Intl. Ho. *M14: Man* *5K 95*
(off Daisy Bank Rd.)
Methuen St. M12: Man 6N 95
Methwold St. BL3: Bolt 8D 38
Metroplex Bus. Pk. M50: Sal 1L 93
Mevagissey Wlk. OL4: O'ham 3N 63
Mews, The BL1: Bolt 4C 38
M4: Man 5N 5 (9J 79)
M25: Pres 8A 60
M28: Wors 4M 75
M33: Sale 5J 105
M40: Man 7L 79
M45: Whitef 3K 59
SK8: Gat 2G 117
WN2: Hin 6N 53
Mexborough St. OL4: O'ham 3A 64
Meyer St. SK3: Stoc 1D 118
Meynell Dr. WN7: Lei 8H 73
Meyrick Cl. WN3: Wins 9N 51
Meyrick Ct. WA12: N Wil 6D 86
Meyrick Rd. M6: Sal 7N 77
Meyrick St. WN5: Wig 5C 52
Miall St. OL11: Roch 7D 28
Micawber Rd. SK12: Poy 4J 125
Michael Ct. M19: Man 6J 107
Michaels Hey Pde. M23: Wyth 8J 105
Michael St. M24: Mid 3L 61
Michael Wife La.
BL0: Eden, Ram 2L 11
(not continuous)
Michigan Av. M50: Sal 1M 93
Michigan Pk. M50: Sal 1M 93
Mickleby Wlk. M40: Man 1N 5
MICKLEHURST 1H 83
Micklehurst Av. M20: Man 4D 106
Micklehurst Grn. SK2: Stoc 2J 119
Micklehurst Rd. OL5: Mos 2G 82
Mickleton M46: Ath 7N 55
Midbrook Wlk. M22: Wyth 5A 116
Middlebourne St. M6: Sal 8L 77
MIDDLEBROOK 4E 36
Middlebrook Dr. BL6: Los 6L 37
Middlebrook Retail & Leisure Pk.
BL6: Hor 4E 36
Middle Calderbrook OL15: Lit 5N 15
Middlecot Cl. WN5: Orr 6J 51
Middledale Cl. M8: Man 2H 79
Middle Fld. OL11: Roch 4J 27
Middlefield OL8: O'ham 2L 81
Middlefields SK8: Chea H 3N 117
Middlegate M40: Man 8B 62
OL8: O'ham 9J 63
Middle Grn. OL6: A Lyne 6N 81
Middleham St. M14: Man 7F 94
MIDDLE HEALEY 1B 28
Middle Hill OL12: Roch 1D 28
Middle Hillgate
SK1: Stoc 3M 9 (7D 108)
Middlehills SK11: Macc 6L 131
MIDDLE HULTON 2D 56
Middle La. M31: Part 6E 102
Middle Newgate OL15: Lit 6L 15
Middlesex Dr. BL9: Bury 4M 41
Middlesex Rd. M9: Man 9J 61
SK5: Stoc 2F 108
Middlesex Wlk.
OL9: O'ham 3A 8 (5H 63)
Middlestone Dr. M9: Man 3J 79
Middle St. OL12: Whitw 5A 14
MIDDLETON 3L 61
Middleton Arena 3M 61
Middleton Av. M35: Fail 3D 80
Middleton Cen. Ind. Est.
M24: Mid 3L 61
Middleton Cl. M26: Rad 5F 40
Middleton Dr. BL9: Bury 9M 41
Middleton Gdns. M24: Mid 3L 61
MIDDLETON JUNCTION 5C 62
Middleton Old Rd. M9: Man 9J 61
Middleton Rd. M8: Man 1E 78
M24: Mid 5F 60
(not continuous)
OL1: Chad 2C 62
OL2: O'ham 7L 45
OL9: Chad, O'ham 2A 8 (2C 62)
(not continuous)
OL10: H'ood, Mid 4K 43
SK5: Stoc 7D 96
Middleton Shop. Cen. M24: Mid 3L 61
Middleton Vw. M24: Mid 3N 61
Middleton Way M24: Mid 3L 61
Middle Wlk. WA16: Knut 6H 133
Middleway OL4: Grot 6E 64
Middlewich Wlk. *M18: Man* *4A 96*
(off Peacock Cl.)
MIDDLEWOOD 1N 125
Middlewood WA3: Low 1A 88
Middlewood Cl. OL9: Chad 3E 62
Middlewood Dr. SK4: Stoc 7M 107
Middlewood Grn. OL9: Chad 3E 62
Middle Wood La. OL15: Lit 8J 15
Middlewood Rd. SK6: H Lan 8A 120
SK12: Poy 8M 119
Middlewood Station (Rail) 9A 120
Middlewood St. M5: Sal 5A 4 (9B 78)
Middlewood Vw. SK6: H Lan 7A 120
Middlewood Wlk. *M9: Man* *3J 79*
(off Fernclough Rd.)
SK6: Mar 2A 120
Midfield Ct. M7: Sal 3D 78
Midford Av. M30: Ecc 8B 76
Midford Dr. BL1: Bolt 6F 22
Midford Wlk. *M8: Man* *4F 78*
(off Barnsdale Dr.)
Midge Hall Dr. OL11: Roch 7M 27
Midge Hill OL5: Mos 7G 64
Midgley Av. M18: Man 3C 96
Midgley Cres. OL6: A Lyne 6B 82
Midgley Dr. OL16: Roch 2G 44
Midgley St. M27: Swin 4D 76
Midgreave Av. OL3: Del 8J 47
Midgrove OL3: Del 8J 47
Midgrove La. OL3: Del 9J 47
Midhurst Av. M40: Man 6N 79
Midhurst Cl. *BL1: Bolt* *3F 38*
(off Bk. Ashford Wlk.)
SK8: Chea H 7L 117
Midhurst St. OL11: Roch 8D 28
Midhurst Way *OL9: Chad* *5F 62*
(off Petworth Rd.)
Midland Cl. WN7: Lei 4E 72

Midland Cotts. SK7: H Gro ... 6N 119
Midland Rd. SK5: Stoc ... 7D 96
SK7: Bram ... 3C 118
Midland St. M12: Man ... 2J 95
Midland Ter. SK22: N Mil ... 8M 121
WA14: Alt ... 5D 114
(off Ashley Rd.)
Midland Wlk. SK7: Bram ... 4C 118
(not continuous)
Midlothian St. M11: Man ... 8N 79
Midmoor Wlk. M9: Man ... 8K 61
(off Stockfield Dr.)
MID REDDISH ... 9D 96
Midville Rd. M11: Man ... 7A 80
MIDWAY ... 4H 125
Midway SK8: Chea H ... 1N 123
Midway Dr. SK12: Poy ... 4H 125
Midway St. M12: Man ... 7M 95
Midwood Hall M6: Sal ... 7M 77
(off Eccles Old Rd.)
Milan St. M7: Sal ... 4D 78
Milbourne Rd. BL9: Bury ... 7M 25
Milburn Av. M23: Wyth ... 6A 106
Milburn Dr. BL2: Bolt ... 4N 39
Milbury Dr. OL15: Lit ... 3L 29
Milden Cl. M20: Man ... 4H 107
Mildred Av. M25: Pres ... 1B 78
OL2: O'ham ... 1J 63
OL4: Grot ... 6E 64
Mildred St. M7: Sal ... 5B 78
Mild St. M9: Man ... 8J 61
MILE END ... 1F 118
Mile End La. SK2: Stoc ... 2F 118
Mile La. BL8: Bury ... 3F 40
Miles La. WN6: App B, She ... 4H 33
(not continuous)
MILES PLATTING ... 7K 79
Miles Platting Swimming Pool & Fitness Cen. ... 7J 79
Miles St. BL1: Bolt ... 2E 38
BL4: Farn ... 3K 57
M12: Man ... 2M 95
OL1: O'ham ... 3M 63
SK14: Hyde ... 7C 98
Milford Av. OL8: O'ham ... 9G 63
Milford Brow OL4: Lees ... 4B 64
Milford Cres. OL15: Lit ... 8M 15
Milford Dr. M19: Man ... 1N 107
Milford Gro. SK2: Stoc ... 9G 109
Milford Rd. BL2: Bolt ... 9N 23
BL3: Bolt ... 9F 38
WN2: Wig ... 1J 53
Milford St. M6: Sal ... 9L 77
M9: Man ... 7G 61
OL12: Roch ... 4D 28
WN3: I Mak ... 5H 53
Milking Grn. Ind. Est. OL4: Lees ... 6C 64
Milking La. BL3: Farn ... 1E 56
Milkstone Pl. OL11: Roch ... 7D 28
Milkstone Rd.
OL11: Roch ... 9C 8 (7D 28)
Milk St. BL0: Ram ... 9H 11
M2: Man ... 4H 5 (9F 78)
M29: Tyld ... 1B 74
OL4: O'ham ... 4N 63
OL11: Roch ... 9C 8 (7D 28)
SK14: Hyde ... 7A 98
WN3: Wig ... 9J 9 (4F 52)
Milkwood Gro. M18: Man ... 5B 96
Mill, The SK15: Stal ... 9D 82
Millais St. M40: Man ... 2M 79
Millard St. OL9: Chad ... 4E 62
Millard Wlk. M18: Man ... 5B 96
Mill Bank M26: Rad ... 1H 59
Millbank WN6: App B ... 5H 33
Millbank Ct. OL10: H'ood ... 2G 42
Millbank Dr. SK10: Macc ... 2D 130
Millbank Gdns. BL1: Bolt ... 3C 38
(off Ivy Rd.)
Millbank St. M1: Man ... 5M 5 (9H 79)
OL10: H'ood ... 2G 42
Millbeck Ct. M24: Mid ... 1J 61
Millbeck Cres. WN5: Wig ... 6A 52
Millbeck Gdns. M24: Mid ... 1J 61
Millbeck Gro. BL3: Bolt ... 8F 38
(off Roxalina St.)
WA11: St H ... 8F 68
Millbeck Rd. M24: Mid ... 1J 61
Millbeck St. M15: Man ... 3F 94
(off Fenwick St.)
Millbrae Gdns. OL2: Shaw ... 5K 45
Mill Bri. Gdns. WA12: N Wil ... 6H 87
Millbridge Gdns. OL16: Roch ... 8E 28
MILLBROOK ... 6G 83
Millbrook SK14: Holl ... 3N 99
Millbrook Av. M34: Dent ... 8H 97
M46: Ath ... 6N 55
Millbrook Bank OL11: Roch ... 4J 27
Millbrook Bus. Cen. M23: Wyth ... 1L 115
Mill Brook Bus. Pk.
WA11: R'ford ... 7A 68
Millbrook Cl. OL2: Shaw ... 6A 46
WA3: G'ury ... 4L 89
Millbrook Fold SK7: H Gro ... 7K 119
Millbrook Gro. SK9: Wilm ... 5J 123
(off Bankside Cl.)
Millbrook Ho. BL4: Farn ... 3M 57
(off Lime St.)
Mill Brook Ind. Est. M23: Wyth ... 1L 115
Millbrook Rd. M23: Wyth ... 4N 115
Millbrook Row PR6: H Char ... 4L 19
Millbrook St. SK1: Stoc ... 4L 9 (8D 108)
Millbrook Towers
SK1: Stoc ... 4L 9 (8D 108)
MILL BROW
M28 ... 4H 75
SK6 ... 8G 111
Mill Brow M9: Man ... 9H 61
M28: Wors ... 4N 75
OL1: Chad ... 1E 62
OL6: A Lyne ... 1N 81
SK6: Mar B ... 8G 111
SK14: B'tom ... 9K 99
Mill Brow Rd. SK6: Mar B ... 8H 111
Millbrow Ter. OL1: Chad ... 1E 62
Mill Bldg., The BL7: Eger ... 4E 22
Mill Cl. WA16: Knut ... 4K 133
Mill Cotts. BB4: Water ... 1E 12
Mill Ct. M41: Urm ... 7E 92
SK13: Glos ... 8D 100
Mill Ct. Dr. M26: Rad ... 3B 58
Millcrest Cl. M28: Wors ... 5G 75
Mill Cft. BL1: Bolt ... 4E 38
OL2: Shaw ... 6N 45
Millcroft Av. WN5: Orr ... 6H 51
Mill Cft. Cl. OL12: Roch ... 3H 27
Millcroft La. OL3: Del ... 6J 47
Milldale Cl. BL6: Los ... 5K 37
M46: Ath ... 8L 55
Milldale Rd. WN7: Lei ... 9D 72
Millennium Ct. BL3: Bolt ... 9C 38
Millennium Ho. M16: Old T ... 3B 94
(off Chester Rd.)
M34: Dent ... 9K 97
Millennium Tower M50: Sal ... 1M 93
Miller Hey OL5: Mos ... 3G 83
Miller Ho. OL2: Shaw ... 7M 45
Miller Mdw. Cl. OL2: Shaw ... 4N 45
Miller Rd. OL8: O'ham ... 8J 63
Millers Brook Cl. OL10: H'ood ... 1J 43
Millers Brow Wlk. M9: Man ... 9H 61
Millers Cl. M33: Sale ... 5N 105
Millers Ct. M5: Sal ... 8G 77
SK10: Macc ... 4G 130
SK15: Stal ... 1C 98
Millersdale Ct. SK13: Glos ... 8H 101
Millers La. M46: Ath ... 9M 55
WA13: Lym ... 2C 112
WN2: P Bri ... 9K 53
Millers Nook WN8: Uph ... 4F 50
Millers Row SK4: Stoc ... 4C 108
Millers St. M30: Ecc ... 9C 76
Miller St. BL1: Bolt ... 9F 22
BL6: Bla ... 5A 36
BL9: Sum ... 3J 25
M4: Man ... 1H 5 (8F 78)
M26: Rad ... 8F 40
OL6: A Lyne ... 6M 81
OL10: H'ood ... 2J 43
(not continuous)
Millers Wharf SK15: Stal ... 8E 82
Millervale Ho. WN2: P Bri ... 1J 71
Millett St. BL0: Ram ... 7K 11
BL9: Bury ... 7H 7 (2K 41)
Millett Ter. BL9: Bury ... 6D 26
Millfield OL10: H'ood ... 2J 43
(off Hornby St.)
WN8: Par ... 3A 32
Millfield Bus. Pk. WA11: Hay ... 1B 86
Millfield Ct. WA15: Hale ... 5E 114
Millfield Dr. M28: Wors ... 4J 75
Millfield Gro. OL16: Roch ... 7F 28
Millfield La. WA11: Hay ... 8B 70
WN4: A Mak ... 8B 70
Millfield Rd. BL2: Bolt ... 5A 40
Millfield Wlk. M40: Man ... 9A 62
(off Pleasington Dr.)
Millfold OL12: Whitw ... 4B 14
Mill Fold Gdns. OL15: Lit ... 1L 29
Mill Fold Rd. M24: Mid ... 3L 61
Millford Av. M41: Urm ... 7M 91
(not continuous)
Millford Gdns. M41: Urm ... 7M 91
MILLGATE ... 1C 14
Mill Ga. OL8: O'ham ... 8H 63
Millgate BL7: Eger ... 3E 22
OL3: Del ... 8J 47
OL16: Roch ... 3G 28
SK1: Stoc ... 1L 9 (6D 108)
WN1: Wig ... 8K 9 (3F 52)
Mill Ga. Cen. BL9: Bury ... 7L 7 (2M 41)
Millgate Cen. OL3: Del ... 8J 47
Millgate La. M20: Man ... 7G 107
(Kingston Rd.)
M20: Man ... 8F 106
(Parrs Wood Rd.)
Millgate Ter. OL12: Whitw ... 1C 14
Mill Grn. SK11: Macc ... 6J 131
(off Cross St.)
Millgreen Cl. WN8: Uph ... 4E 50
Mill Grn. St. M12: Man ... 7N 5 (1J 95)
Millhalf Cl. M15: Man ... 4D 94
Millhead Av. M40: Man ... 8K 79
MILL HILL ... 3N 7 (4H 39)
Mill Hill M38: Lit H ... 5F 56
Mill Hill Av. SK12: Poy ... 8H 119
Mill Hill Caravan Pk.
BL2: Bolt ... 1N 7 (4H 39)
Mill Hill Gro. SK14: Mot ... 7J 99
Mill Hill Hollow SK12: Poy ... 8H 119
Mill Hill St. BL2: Bolt ... 1N 7 (4H 39)
Mill Hill Way SK14: Mot ... 7J 99
(off Chain Bar La.)
Mill Ho. BL9: Bury ... 5M 25
Millhouse Av. M23: Wyth ... 3N 115
Mill Ho. Cl. OL12: Roch ... 1H 29
Millhouse St. BL0: Ram ... 6L 11
Mill Ho. Vw. WN8: Uph ... 4G 51
Milliner Ct. SK2: Stoc ... 9H 109
Milliners Wharf M4: Man ... 9J 79
Millingford Av. WA3: Gol ... 8J 71
Millingford Gro. WN4: A Mak ... 7E 70
Millingford Ind. Est. WA3: Gol ... 2K 87
Milling St. M1: Man ... 7G 5 (1E 94)
Millington Gdns. WA13: Lym ... 2D 112
Millington Hall La.
WA14: M'ton ... 9J 113
Millington La. WA14: M'ton ... 8H 113
Millington Rd. M17: T Pk ... 2J 93
Millington Wlk. M15: Man ... 3C 94
(off Mosshall Cl.)
Mill La. BL5: W'ton ... 6G 54
BL6: Hor ... 9F 20
BL6: Los ... 5H 37
BL8: Bury ... 9H 25
M22: Nor ... 7D 106
M34: Dent ... 8M 97
M35: Fail ... 3A 80
OL2: O'ham ... 8G 44
OL3: Dob ... 2G 65
OL5: Mos ... 9F 64
Mill La. OL6: A Lyne ... 8C 6 (8M 81)
OL9: Chad ... 7G 62
PR7: Cop ... 4B 18
SK5: Stoc ... 8D 96
SK6: Rom ... 9L 109
SK6: Wood ... 2L 109
(Botany Rd.)
SK6: Wood ... 2L 109
(Wood Cotts.)
SK7: H Gro ... 7K 119
SK8: Chea ... 1J 117
SK8: Chea H ... 4N 117
SK9: A Edg ... 6A 126
SK10: Adl ... 8C 124
SK10: Boll ... 5N 129
SK10: Mot S A, P'bury ... 2N 127
SK11: Macc ... 5H 131
SK14: Hyde ... 8M 97
WA11: R'ford ... 7A 68
WA12: N Wil ... 6H 87
WA13: Lym ... 1D 112
WN2: Asp ... 9B 36
WN6: App B ... 5G 33
WN7: Lei ... 6K 73
WN8: Dal, Uph ... 1D 50
WN8: Par ... 3A 32
Mill Leat Cl. WN8: Par ... 2A 32
Mill Leat M. WN8: Par ... 2A 32
Mill Mdw. WA12: N Wil ... 6H 87
Mill Nook OL12: Roch ... 2D 28
Millom Av. M23: Wyth ... 7A 106
Millom Cl. OL16: Roch ... 4G 28
Millom Ct. WA15: Tim ... 1K 115
Millom Dr. BL9: Bury ... 1N 59
Millom Pl. SK8: Gat ... 4G 117
Millow St. M4: Man ... 1H 5 (7F 78)
Mill Pond Av. BL3: Bolt ... 9H 39
(off Cotton Lodge Cl.)
SK22: N Mil ... 6N 121
Mill Pond Cl. OL2: Shaw ... 6M 45
Millpond Cl. SK6: Stri ... 5F 120
Mill Pool Cl. SK6: Wood ... 3M 109
Millpool Wlk. M9: Man ... 2J 79
(off Alderside Rd.)
Millrace Cl. SK8: Chea ... 9H 107
Millrise OL1: O'ham ... 1C 8
Mill Rd. BL9: Bury ... 5M 25
SK9: Wilm ... 7G 123
SK11: Macc ... 6H 131
WN5: Orr ... 6H 51
Mills Farm Cl. OL8: O'ham ... 1L 81
MILLS HILL ... 3C 62
Mills Hill Rd. M24: Mid ... 2B 62
Mills Hill Station (Rail) ... 2B 62
Millside OL6: A Lyne ... 7F 6
WN3: Wig ... 9H 9
Mills St. OL10: H'ood ... 2G 42
OL12: Whitw ... 5B 14
Millstone Cl. PR7: Cop ... 4C 18
SK12: Poy ... 1K 125
Millstone Ct. SK6: Bred ... 5L 109
WA3: Gol ... 9J 71
Millstone Pas. SK11: Macc ... 6J 131
Millstone Rd. BL1: Bolt ... 3A 38
Millstream La. M40: Man ... 7C 80
Mill St. BL0: Ram ... 1G 25
BL1: Bolt ... 2M 7 (4H 39)
BL2: Bolt ... 4H 39
BL4: Farn ... 3K 57
BL5: W'ton ... 3H 55
BL7: Bro X ... 5G 22
BL8: Tot ... 6F 24
M6: Sal ... 6N 77
M11: Man ... 1M 95
(not continuous)
M26: Rad ... 1H 59
(not continuous)
M28: Wors ... 3H 75
M35: Fail ... 3A 80
M46: Ath ... 1N 73
OL2: O'ham ... 8H 45
OL3: Upp ... 3L 65
OL5: Mos ... 2F 82
OL15: Lit ... 2K 29
PR6: Adl ... 5K 19
PR7: Cop ... 4B 18
SK6: Wood ... 3L 109
SK7: H Gro ... 4H 119
SK9: Wilm ... 7G 123
SK11: Macc ... 4H 131
SK13: Glos ... 8F 100
SK14: Hyde ... 4B 98
SK15: Stal ... 9F 82
WA3: Gol ... 1K 87
WA14: Alt ... 1E 6 (2E 114)
WN2: Hin ... 5N 53
WN3: Wig ... 9H 9 (4E 52)
WN4: A Mak ... 8F 70
Mill St. Ind. Est.
BL2: Bolt ... 2M 7 (4H 39)
Mill St. Mall SK11: Macc ... 4H 131
(off Grosvenor Cen.)
Mill Town SK13: Glos ... 8F 100
Milltown SK13: Glos ... 8F 100
Milltown Cl. M26: Rad ... 1H 59
Milltown St. M26: Rad ... 1H 59
Mill Vw. Ct. OL8: O'ham ... 8H 63
Mill Vw. La. BL6: Hor ... 9G 21
Millwain Ho. SK4: Stoc ... 4M 107
Millwall Cl. M18: Man ... 4B 96
Millway WA15: Haleb ... 8J 115
Millway Wlk. M40: Man ... 5A 80
(off Orford Rd.)
Millwell La. BL1: Bolt ... 2K 7
Millwood Cl. SK8: Chea H ... 7K 117
WN4: A Mak ... 5D 70
Millwood Ct. BL9: Bury ... 6M 41
OL2: O'ham ... 8H 45
Millwood Ter. SK14: Hyde ... 7A 98
Millwood Vw. SK15: Stal ... 8E 82
Millwright Cl. HD7: Mars ... 1G 49
Millwright St. M40: Man ... 5N 79
Mill Yd. BL6: Hor ... 9F 20
BL9: Bury ... 6N 7 (1N 41)
Milne Cl. M12: Man ... 3M 95
SK16: Duk ... 1N 97
Milne Gro. OL16: Miln ... 8M 29
Milner Av. BL9: Bury ... 8M 25
WA14: B'ath ... 9B 104
Milner St. M16: Old T ... 5C 94
M26: Rad ... 9E 40
M27: Swin ... 2F 76
OL12: Whitw ... 6A 14
Milnes Av. WN7: Lei ... 8H 73
Milne St. BL0: Ram ... 1J 11
M12: Man ... 3M 95
(off Milne Cl.)
OL1: O'ham ... 1L 63
OL2: Shaw ... 6M 45
OL9: Chad ... 4F 62
(Bentley St.)
OL9: Chad ... 2G 62
(Victoria Wlk.)
OL9: O'ham ... 6G 62
OL11: Roch ... 2A 44
Milnes Yd. OL16: Miln ... 8K 29
(off Dale St.)
Milngate Cl. OL16: Roch ... 1G 44
Milnholme BL1: Bolt ... 1C 38
MILNROW ... 7J 29
Milnrow Cl. M13: Man ... 8L 5 (2G 95)
Milnrow Rd. OL2: Shaw ... 5M 45
OL15: Lit ... 3K 29
OL16: Roch ... 8D 8 (6E 28)
OL16: Shaw ... 4N 45
Milnrow Stop (Metro) ... 8K 29
Milnthorpe Rd. BL2: Bolt ... 4M 39
Milnthorpe St. M6: Sal ... 5A 78
Milnthorpe Way M12: Man ... 3K 95
Milsom Av. BL3: Bolt ... 9D 38
Milstead Wlk. M40: Man ... 5M 79
(off Peckford Dr.)
Milston Wlk. M8: Man ... 4F 78
(off Barnsdale Dr.)
Milton Av. BL3: Bolt ... 9C 38
BL3: Lit L ... 8B 40
M5: Sal ... 8K 77
M43: Droy ... 9E 80
M44: Irl ... 2F 102
SK15: Mill ... 6H 83
WA12: N Wil ... 6E 86
Milton Cl. M32: Stre ... 6L 93
M46: Ath ... 6M 55
SK6: Mar ... 3C 120
SK16: Duk ... 2E 98
(not continuous)
Milton Ct. M7: Sal ... 1D 78
M19: Man ... 4K 107
M30: Ecc ... 8D 76
PR7: Cop ... 4B 18
SK7: Bram ... 9C 118
Milton Cres. BL4: Farn ... 5J 57
SK8: Chea ... 2H 117
Milton Dr. M33: Sale ... 2G 105
OL9: Chad ... 5E 62
SK12: Poy ... 2H 125
WA15: Tim ... 7G 104
Milton Gro. M16: Whall R ... 7B 94
M33: Sale ... 2G 105
WN1: Wig ... 9F 34
WN5: Bil ... 1H 69
WN5: Orr ... 5L 51
Milton Lodge M16: Whall R ... 7B 94
Milton Mt. M18: Man ... 5B 96
(off Old Hall Dr.)
Milton Pl. M6: Sal ... 7A 78
Milton Rd. M25: Pres ... 6B 60
M26: Rad ... 8D 40
M27: Swin ... 1D 76
M32: Stre ... 6L 93
M34: Aud ... 9H 81
PR7: Cop ... 5B 18
SK7: Bram ... 8C 118
WA3: Low ... 2N 87
Milton St. BL0: Ram ... 8H 11
M7: Sal ... 6D 78
M24: Mid ... 2L 61
M30: Ecc ... 8D 76
OL2: O'ham ... 7J 45
OL5: Mos ... 9F 64
OL16: Roch ... 6D 8 (5D 28)
SK14: Hyde ... 5A 98
WN7: Lei ... 5G 72
Milton Vw. OL5: Mos ... 9F 64
Milverton Av. SK14: Hat ... 8F 98
Milverton Cl. BL6: Los ... 7M 37
Milverton Dr. SK7: Bram ... 1N 123
Milverton Rd. M14: Man ... 5J 95
Milverton Wlk. SK14: Hat ... 7F 98
Milwain Dr. SK4: Stoc ... 2A 108
Milwain Rd. M19: Man ... 9L 95
M32: Stre ... 8J 93
Mimosa Dr. M27: Pen ... 9F 58
Mincing St. M4: Man ... 1J 5 (7F 78)
Minden Cl. BL8: Bury ... 2H 41
M20: Man ... 4H 107
Minden Pde.
BL9: Bury ... 8L 7 (2M 41)
Minden St. M6: Sal ... 4L 77
Minehead Av. M20: Man ... 1E 106
M41: Urm ... 9B 92
WN7: Lei ... 9F 54
Miners M., The M28: Wors ... 3J 75
Minerva Rd. BL4: Farn ... 2G 57
OL6: A Lyne ... 9E 6 (8N 81)
Minerva Ter. OL15: Lit ... 9L 15
(off William St.)
Mine St. OL10: H'ood ... 9H 27
Mine Way WA11: Hay ... 2C 86
Minford Cl. M40: Man ... 5N 79
Minnie St. BL3: Bolt ... 9C 38
OL12: Whitw ... 4B 14
Minoan Gdns. M7: Sal ... 5B 78
Minor Av. SK11: Lym G ... 9H 131
Minorca Av. M11: Man ... 8B 80
Minorca Cl. OL11: Roch ... 5K 27
Minorca St. BL3: Bolt ... 8F 38
Minor St. M35: Fail ... 2E 80
(not continuous)
OL11: Roch ... 3A 44
Minshull St. M1: Man ... 5J 5 (9F 78)
WA16: Knut ... 6G 132
Minshull St. Sth.
M1: Man ... 6K 5 (1G 94)
Minsmere Cl. M8: Man ... 4F 78
Minsmere Walks SK2: Stoc ... 2K 119
Minstead Cl. SK14: Hyde ... 8D 98
Minstead Wlk. M22: Wyth ... 5A 116
Minster Cl. BL2: Bolt ... 2K 39
SK16: Duk ... 3A 98
Minster Dr. M41: Urm ... 6A 92
SK8: Chea ... 2M 117
WA14: Bow ... 7A 114
Minster Gro. M29: Ast ... 3C 74
Minster Rd. BL2: Bolt ... 2K 39
M9: Man ... 2L 79
Minster Way OL9: Chad ... 2E 62
Minstrel Cl. M27: Swin ... 3E 76
WN2: Abr ... 3L 71
Minton Ct. BL3: Bolt ... 8B 38
(off Hough St.)
Minton St. M40: Man ... 2A 80
OL4: O'ham ... 5F 8 (6L 63)
Minto St. OL7: A Lyne ... 5B 6 (6L 81)
(not continuous)
Mintridge Cl. M11: Man ... 2C 96
Mint St. BL0: Ram ... 4J 11
Mirabel St. M3: Man ... 1F 4 (7E 78)
Miranda Ct. M5: Sal ... 7A 4 (1B 94)
Mirfield Av. M9: Man ... 7J 61
OL8: O'ham ... 7J 63
SK4: Stoc ... 6N 107
Mirfield Cl. WA3: Low ... 2N 87
Mirfield Dr. M24: Mid ... 2L 61
M30: Ecc ... 6D 76
M41: Urm ... 5C 92
Mirfield Rd. M9: Man ... 7J 61
Miriam Gro. WN7: Lei ... 6J 73
Miriam St. BL3: Bolt ... 8C 38
M35: Fail ... 4B 80
Mirrlees Dr. SK7: H Gro ... 5F 118
Miry La. BL5: W'ton ... 6F 54
(Dunham Cl.)
BL5: W'ton ... 4G 54
(Lower Southfield)
WN3: Wig ... 9G 9 (4D 52)
WN6: Wig ... 3D 52
WN8: Par ... 2B 32
Missenden Ho. M5: Sal ... 9M 77
(off Cyprus Cl.)
Mission St. OL10: H'ood ... 2H 43
Missouri Av. M50: Sal ... 9L 77
Misterton Wlk. M23: Wyth ... 9L 105
(off Sandy La.)
Mistletoe Gro. M3: Sal ... 1C 4
Mistral Ct. M30: Ecc ... 7E 76
Mitcham Av. M9: Man ... 8M 61
Mitchell Cl. SK8: Gat ... 1E 116
Mitchell Gdns. M22: Shar ... 2D 116
MITCHELL HEY ... 8A 8 (6C 28)
Mitchell Hey OL12: Roch ... 7A 8 (6C 28)
Mitchell Ho. SK8: Gat ... 1E 116
(off Mitchell Cl.)
Mitchell Rd. WN5: Bil ... 5J 69
Mitchells Quay M35: Fail ... 3C 80
Mitchell St. BL8: Bury ... 9J 25
M30: Ecc ... 7C 76
M40: Man ... 5N 79
OL1: O'ham ... 3J 63
OL12: Roch ... 6A 8 (5B 28)
OL16: Roch ... 2G 29
WA3: Gol ... 2K 87
WN2: I Mak ... 4K 53
WN4: A Mak ... 8F 70
WN5: Wig ... 5B 52
WN7: Lei ... 5D 72
Mitcheson Gdns. M6: Sal ... 7M 77
Mitford Ct. M14: Man ... 1H 107
Mitford Rd. M14: Man ... 1H 107
Mitford St. M32: Stre ... 8J 93
Mitre Rd. M13: Man ... 5L 95
Mitre St. BL1: Bolt ... 9J 23
M35: Fail ... 2D 80
Mitton Cl. BL8: Bury ... 2E 40
OL10: H'ood ... 2E 42
WA3: Cul ... 4G 88
Mizpah Gro. BL8: Bury ... 2H 41
Mizzy Rd. OL12: Roch ... 4C 28
Moadlock SK6: Rom ... 4N 109
Moat Av. M22: Wyth ... 2B 116
Moat Gdns. M22: Wyth ... 3B 116
Moat Hall Av. M30: Ecc ... 1A 92
Moat Ho. St. WN2: I Mak ... 4K 53
Moat Rd. M22: Wyth ... 3B 116
Moat Wlk. SK5: Stoc ... 1G 109
MOBBERLEY ... 4N 133
Mobberley Cl. M19: Man ... 4K 107
Mobberley Golf Course ... 8A 122
Mobberley Rd. BL2: Bolt ... 4L 39
SK9: Wilm ... 6A 122
WA16: Knut ... 6H 133
Mobberley Station (Rail) ... 1M 133
Moberly Hall M15: Man ... 4G 94
(off Burlington St. E.)
Mocha Pde. M7: Sal ... 7C 78
Modbury Cl. SK7: H Gro ... 6E 118
Modbury Ct. M26: Rad ... 4A 58
Modbury Wlk. M8: Man ... 4F 78
(off Brinsworth Dr.)
Mode Hill La. M45: Whitef ... 3B 60
Mode Hill Wlk. M45: Whitef ... 3B 60
Model Lodging Ho. M3: Sal ... 3D 4
Model Ter. WN2: P Bri ... 8K 53
Mode Wheel Circ. M17: T Pk ... 2J 93
Mode Wheel Ind. Est. M50: Sal ... 1K 93
Mode Wheel Rd. M5: Sal ... 9K 77
Mode Wheel Rd. Sth. M50: Sal ... 1K 93
Modwen Rd. M5: Sal ... 3A 94
Moelfre Dr. SK8: Chea H ... 8A 118
Moffat Cl. BL2: Bolt ... 6N 39
Moggie La. SK10: Adl ... 5K 125
Moisant St. BL3: Bolt ... 9E 38
Moison Ho. SK2: Stoc ... 1E 118
(off Canada St.)
Mold St. BL1: Bolt ... 1F 38
OL1: O'ham ... 3J 63
Molesworth St.
OL16: Roch ... 7E 8 (6E 28)

Mollets Wood M34: Dent 4L 97
Mollington Rd. M22: Wyth 7D 116
Mollis Gro. OL1: O'ham 9B 46
Molly Potts Cl. WA16: Knut 8H 133
Molyneux Rd. BL5: W'ton 2J 55
M19: Man 8A 96
Molyneux St. OL12: Roch 5A 8 (5B 28)
WN1: Wig 7M 9 (3G 53)
Mona Av. M32: Stre 6J 93
SK8: H Grn 6J 117
Monaco Dr. M22: Nor 6C 106
Monarch Cl. M44: Irl 2F 102
OL2: O'ham 1H 63
Mona Rd. OL9: Chad 6F 62
Monart Rd. M9: Man 1K 79
Mona St. *M6: Sal* *6N 77*
(off Gloucester St.)
SK14: Hyde 7B 98
WN1: Wig 7H 9 (3E 52)
Mona Way M44: Irl 9J 91
Moncrieffe St. BL3: Bolt 6G 39
(not continuous)
Monde Trad. Est. M17: T Pk 3G 93
Mond Rd. M44: Irl 5J 91
Money Ash Rd. WA15: Alt 4D 114
Monfa Av. SK2: Stoc 3E 118
Monica Av. M8: Man 8E 60
Monica Ct. M30: Ecc 7F 76
Monica Gro. M19: Man 9L 95
Monica Ter. WN4: A Mak 8E 70
Monks Cl. M8: Man 9G 60
OL16: Miln 7J 29
Monks Ct. M5: Sal 8H 77
Monksdale Av. M41: Urm 7B 92
Monks Hall Gro. M30: Ecc 8F 76
Monks La. BL2: Bolt 2L 39
Monkswood OL1: O'ham 1B 8 (4J 63)
Monkton Av. M18: Man 6A 96
Monkwood Dr. *M9: Man* *2K 79*
(off Dalbeattie St.)
Monmouth Av. BL9: Bury 8M 25
M33: Sale 3F 104
Monmouth Cres. WN4: A Mak 8F 70
Monmouth Rd. SK8: Chea H 6N 117
Monmouth St. M18: Man 3C 96
M24: Mid 3A 62
OL9: O'ham 6G 62
OL11: Roch 7D 28
Monroe Cl. M6: Sal 6L 77
WN3: Wig 8D 52
Monsal Av. M7: Sal 3N 77
SK2: Stoc 9H 109
Monsall Cl. BL9: Bury 1N 59
SK11: Macc 5K 131
Monsall Dr. SK11: Macc 5K 131
Monsall Rd. M40: Man 4K 79
Monsall Stop (Metro) 4K 79
Monsall St. M40: Man 5J 79
OL8: O'ham 8J 63
Mons Av. OL11: Roch 5A 28
Montague Bus. Pk. M16: Old T 5N 93
Montague Ct. *M33: Sale* *4J 105*
(off Montague Rd.)
Montague Ho.
SK3: Stoc 4H 9 (7B 108)
Montague Rd. M16: Old T 4N 93
M33: Sale 4H 105
OL6: A Lyne 8A 82
Montague St. BL3: Bolt 9C 38
Montague Way SK15: Stal 8D 82
Montagu Rd. SK2: Stoc 9H 109
Montagu St. SK6: Comp 6E 110
Montana Sq. M11: Man 2C 96
MONTCLIFFE 8G 21
Montcliffe Cres. M16: Whall R 8E 94
Monteagle St. M9: Man 7G 61
Montford Ent. Cen. *M50: Sal* *9M 77*
(off Wynford Sq.)
Montford Ri. WN2: Asp 1K 53
Montford St. M50: Sal 9M 77
Montfort Cl. BL5: W'ton 5F 54
Montgomery OL11: Roch 9B 8 (7C 28)
Montgomery Cl. WA16: Knut 4J 133
Montgomery Dr. BL9: Bury 1A 60
Montgomery Ho. M16: Whall R 7E 94
OL8: O'ham 1F 80
Montgomery Rd. M13: Man 7L 95
Montgomery St. OL8: O'ham 9F 62
OL11: Roch *9A 28*
(off Manchester Rd.)
Montgomery Way M26: Rad 7C 40
Montmano Dr. M20: Man 2E 106
Montmorency Rd. WA16: Knut 5K 133
MONTON 6D 76
Monton Av. M30: Ecc 7E 76
Monton Bri. Ct. M30: Ecc 6C 76
Montondale M30: Ecc 7C 76
Montonfields Rd. M30: Ecc 7C 76
Monton Grn. M30: Ecc 6D 76
Monton La. M30: Ecc 8E 76
Montonmill Gdns. M30: Ecc 7C 76
Monton Rd. M30: Ecc 7D 76
(not continuous)
SK5: Stoc 4G 108
Monton St. BL3: Bolt 9F 38
M14: Man 5F 94
M26: Rad 9F 40
Montpellier M. M7: Sal 1D 78
Montpellior Rd. M22: Wyth 5C 116
Montreal St. M19: Man 8N 95
OL8: O'ham 7K 63
WN7: Lei 6A 72
Montrey Cres. WN4: Gars 7N 69
Montrose *M30: Ecc* *8E 76*
(off Monton La.)
Montrose Av. BL0: Ram 3G 24
BL2: Bolt 3K 39
M20: Man 3F 106
M32: Stre 7H 93
SK2: Stoc 4E 118
SK16: Duk 2N 97
WN5: Wig 3M 51
Montrose Cl. SK10: Macc 3E 130
Montrose Cres. M19: Man 8L 95
Montrose Dr. BL7: Bro X 6J 23
Montrose Gdns. OL2: O'ham 8K 45
Montrose St. OL11: Roch 4A 44
MONTSERRAT 2N 37
Montserrat Brow BL1: Bolt 2M 37
Montserrat Rd. BL1: Bolt 2N 37
Monument Mans. *WN1: Wig* *1F 52*
(off Wigan La.)
Monument Rd. WN1: Wig 1G 52
Monyash Ct. *SK13: Gam* *8N 99*
(off Youlgreave Cres.)
Monyash Gro. *SK13: Gam* *8N 99*
(off Youlgreave Cres.)
Monyash Lea *SK13: Gam* *8N 99*
(off Ashford M.)
Monyash M. SK13: Gam 8N 99
Monyash Pl. *SK13: Gam* *8N 99*
(off Monyash M.)
Monyash Vw. WN2: Hin 8B 54
Monyash Way *SK13: Gam* *8A 100*
(off Ashford M.)
Moody St. WN6: Stan 3B 34
Moon Gro. M14: Man 6J 95
Moon St. OL9: O'ham 4G 63
Moor Av. WN6: App B 4J 33
Moor Bank La. OL16: Roch 9H 29
Moorbottom Rd. BL8: Holc 8E 10
Moorby Av. M19: Man 4K 107
Moorby St. OL1: O'ham 3L 63
Moorby Wlk. *BL3: Bolt* *7G 38*
(off Fletcher St.)
MOORCLOSE 4A 62
Moor Cl. M26: Rad 7E 40
Moorclose St. M24: Mid 3A 62
Moorclose Wlk. *M9: Man* *3J 79*
(off Conran St.)
Moorcock Av. M27: Pen 2H 77
Moorcot Ct. M23: Wyth 8M 105
Moor Cres. OL3: Dig 9L 47
Moorcroft BL0: Ram 4K 11
OL11: Roch 1D 44
Moorcroft Dr. M19: Man 4L 107
Moorcroft Rd. M23: Wyth 7M 105
Moorcroft Sq. SK14: Hyde 3B 98
Moorcroft St. M43: Droy 1E 96
OL8: O'ham 9G 63
Moorcroft Wlk. M19: Man 4K 107
Moordale Av. OL4: O'ham 2B 64
Moordale Rd. WA16: Knut 6H 133
Moordale St. M20: Man 3F 106
Moordown Cl. M8: Man 4G 79
Moor Dr. WN8: Skel 4B 50
Moor Edge Rd. OL5: Mos 1J 83
Mooredge Ter. OL2: O'ham 1J 63
Moore Dr. WA11: Hay 2C 86
Moore Gro. WA13: Lym 2C 112
Moore Ho. M30: Ecc 1D 92
MOOREND 1K 121
Moor End M22: Nor 8C 106
Moor End Av. M7: Sal 2B 78
Moor End Ct. M7: Sal 2B 78
Moorend Golf Course 3D 124
Moor End Rd. SK6: Mel 1J 121
Moore's Ct. BL1: Bolt 4D 38
Moores La. WN6: Stan 2A 34
Moore St. OL16: Roch 8D 8 (6D 28)
WN1: Wig 1J 53
Moore St. E. WN1: Wig 5N 9 (2H 53)
Moore Wlk. *M34: Dent* *1L 109*
(off Wordsworth Rd.)
Moorfield *M7: Sal* *1B 78*
(off Moor La.)
M26: Rad 8E 40
M28: Wors 3G 75
(Brindley St.)
M28: Wors 2N 75
(Old Clough La.)
Moorfield Av. M20: Man 1H 107
M34: Dent 8L 97
OL15: Lit 7L 15
SK15: Stal 2G 98
Moorfield Chase BL4: Farn 4L 57
Moorfield Cl. M27: Swin 4D 76
M30: Ecc 8D 76
M44: Irl 6J 91
Moorfield Ct. *SK14: Holl* *4N 99*
(off Moorfield Ter.)
Moorfield Cres. WA3: Low 2C 88
Moorfield Dr. SK9: Wilm 9D 122
SK14: Hyde 4C 98
Moorfield Gro. BL2: Bolt 3J 39
M33: Sale 5K 105
SK4: Stoc 4N 107
Moorfield Hamlet OL2: Shaw 5K 45
Moorfield Hgts. SK15: C'ook 3H 83
Moorfield M. OL2: Shaw 5M 45
Moorfield Pde. M44: Irl 6J 91
Moorfield Pl. *OL12: Roch* *4D 28*
(off Turner St.)
Moorfield Rd. M6: Sal 6K 77
M20: Man 4E 106
M27: Swin 4C 76
M44: Irl 6J 91
OL8: O'ham 9F 62
Moorfield St. M20: Man 1G 107
SK14: Holl 4N 99
WN2: P Bri 8L 53
Moorfield Ter. SK14: Holl 4N 99
SK15: C'ook 3H 83
Moorfield Vw. OL15: Lit 8L 15
MOORGATE 3J 83
Moor Ga. BL2: Bolt 8L 23
Moorgate BL9: Bury 6M 7 (1M 41)
Moorgate Av. M20: Man 1E 106
OL11: Roch 6M 27
Moorgate Cotts. SK15: C'ook 3J 83
Moorgate Ct. *BL2: Bolt* *3J 39*
(off Starkie Rd.)
Moorgate Dr. M29: Ast 5D 74
SK15: C'ook 4H 83
Moor Ga. La. OL15: Lit 6J 15
Moorgate M. SK15: C'ook 3H 83
Moorgate Retail Pk.
BL9: Bury 6N 7 (1N 41)
Moorgate Rd. M26: Rad 4E 40
SK15: C'ook 3H 83
Moorgate St. OL3: Upp 3L 65
Moorhead St. M4: Man 1L 5 (7G 79)
MOORHEY 5N 63
Moorhey Ind. Est. OL4: O'ham 5M 63
Moorhey Rd. M38: Lit H 5G 56
Moorhey St. OL4: O'ham 5M 63
Moor Hill OL11: Roch 5L 27
Moorhill Ct. M7: Sal 1B 78
Moorhill Rd. SK11: Macc 8G 131
Moorhouse Farm OL16: Miln 7J 29
Moorhouse Fold OL16: Miln 7J 29
Moorings, The M28: Wors 5A 76
OL5: Mos 8H 65
SK12: Dis 9H 121
Moorings Cl. WN1: I Mak 3J 53
Moorings Rd. M17: T Pk 1H 93
Moorland Av. M8: Man 9E 60
M33: Sale 5J 105
M43: Droy 9C 80
OL3: Del 9J 47
OL11: Roch 5L 27
OL12: Whitw 7A 14
OL16: Miln 7L 29
Moorland Cres. OL12: Whitw 7A 14
Moorland Dr. BL6: Hor 1H 37
M38: Lit H 5H 57
SK8: Chea H 7L 117
Moorland Fold SK15: Stal 2H 99
Moorland Gro. BL1: Bolt 2B 38
Moorland Ho. *M27: Swin* *3F 76*
(off Worsley Rd.)
Moorland Rd. M20: Man 5G 106
SK2: Stoc 3E 118
SK15: C'ook 5H 83
WN2: Hin 6M 53
WN4: A Mak 6H 71
Moorlands Av. M41: Urm 6B 92
WN7: Lei 7H 73
Moorlands Caravan Pk.
OL3: Dens 1G 46
Moorlands Cl. SK10: Macc 1G 130
Moorlands Cres. OL5: Mos 8H 65
Moorlands Dr. OL5: Mos 8H 65
Moorland St. OL2: Shaw 5N 45
OL12: Roch 4C 28
OL15: Lit 7N 15
Moorlands Vw. BL0: Eden 1K 11
BL3: Bolt 1B 56
Moorland Ter. OL12: Roch 4M 27
Moor La. BL1: Bolt 4J 7 (6F 38)
BL3: Bolt 4J 7 (6F 38)
M7: Sal 2N 77
M23: Wyth 6N 105
M41: Urm 6A 92
OL3: Del 3K 47
OL3: Dob 1M 65
OL12: Roch 2L 27
SK7: W'ford 3B 124
SK9: Wilm 3A 126
WN7: Lei 2G 72
Moorlea M35: Fail 2D 80
Moor Lodge SK4: Stoc 4N 107
Moor Nook M33: Sale 5K 105
Moor Pk. SK2: Stoc 1D 118
Moor Pk. Av. OL11: Roch 2N 43
Moor Pk. Rd. M20: Man 8H 107
Moor Platt *M33: Sale* *5K 105*
(off Derbyshire Rd. Sth.)
Moor Platt Cl. BL6: Hor 1H 37
Moor Rd. BB4: Has 1F 10
BL8: Holc 3F 10
M23: Wyth 7L 105
OL15: Lit 5N 15
PR6: H Char 1A 20
PR7: Chor 1D 18
WN5: Orr 6H 51
Moorsbrook Gro. *SK9: Wilm* *5K 123*
(off Lyngard Cl.)
Moorsholme Av. M40: Man 3M 79
MOORSIDE
M28 2C 76
OL4 9B 46
Moorside OL11: Roch 1D 44
OL15: Lit 8A 16
WA16: Knut 6G 133
WN2: Asp 7M 35
Moorside Av. BL1: Bolt 2B 38
BL2: Ain 3D 40
BL4: Farn 4J 57
BL6: Hor 9E 20
M43: Droy 9E 81
Moorside Cl. SK13: Glos 9D 100
Moorside Ct. *M33: Sale* *4H 105*
(off Sibson Rd.)
M34: Dent 5K 97
Moorside Cres. M43: Droy 8E 80
Moorside Ho. *WA15: Tim* *9J 105*
(off Oakleigh Ct.)
Moor Side La. BL0: Ram 7N 11
Moorside La. M34: Dent 5L 97
(not continuous)
Moorside Lodge M27: Swin 2D 76
Moorside Rd. BL8: Tot 7E 24
M7: Sal 2B 78
M8: Man 1F 78
M27: Swin 3C 76
M41: Urm 6M 91
OL5: Mos 1H 83
SK4: Stoc 6M 107
Moorside Station (Rail) 1D 76
Moorside St. M43: Droy 8F 80
Moorside Vw. BL8: Tot 7F 24
OL2: Shaw *4N 45*
(off Small Brook Rd.)
SK13: Glos *8F 100*
(off Station St.)
Moorside Wlk. WN5: Orr 3M 51
Moorsley Dr. M9: Man 7L 61
Moor St. BL9: Bury 5M 7 (1M 41)
M27: Swin 3F 76
M30: Ecc 9B 76
OL1: O'ham 4M 63
OL2: Shaw 6L 45
OL10: H'ood 2G 42
WN2: Asp 7N 35
Moors Vw. BL0: Ram 8H 11
Moorton Av. M19: Man 1L 107
Moorton Pk. M19: Man 1L 107
Moortop Cl. M9: Man 6H 61
Moor Top Pl. SK4: Stoc 5N 107
Moor Vw. BB4: Water 1E 12
Moor Vw. Cl. OL12: Roch 3L 27
Moorville Rd. M6: Sal 5J 77
Moor Way BL8: Haw 2B 24
Moorway SK9: Wilm 9D 122
Moorway Dr. M9: Man 7M 61
Moorwood Dr. M33: Sale 5E 104
OL8: O'ham 7N 63
Mopmakers Grn. SK9: Wilm 7G 123
Mora Av. OL9: Chad 2F 62
Moran Cl. SK9: Wilm 4K 123
Moran Cres. SK11: Macc 5F 130
Morano Dr. WN2: P Bri 8K 53
Moran Rd. SK11: Macc 5F 130
Moran Wlk. *M15: Man* *3E 94*
(off Crediton Cl.)
Morar Dr. BL2: Bolt 5A 40
Morar Rd. SK16: Duk 2A 98
Mora St. M9: Man 2L 79
Moravian Cl. SK16: Duk 9N 81
Moravian Fld. M43: Droy 1E 96
Moray Cl. BL0: Ram 1G 24
Moray Rd. OL9: Chad 7E 62
Morbourne Cl. M12: Man 3K 95
Morden Av. M11: Man 8A 80
WN4: A Mak 6D 70
Morecambe Cl. M40: Man 4N 79
Morelands, The BL1: Bolt 5B 38
Moresby Cl. WN7: Lei 5F 72
Moresby Dr. M20: Man 8G 106
Morestead Wlk. *M40: Man* *7H 79*
(off New Allen St.)
Moreton Av. M32: Stre 7K 93
M33: Sale 5E 104
M45: Whitef 2M 59
SK7: Bram 1C 124
Moreton Cl. SK16: Duk 3A 98
WA3: Gol 9J 71
WN3: Wins 9N 51
Moreton Dr. BL8: Bury 1H 41
SK9: Hand 3K 123
SK12: Poy 2K 125
WN7: Lei 9G 72
Moreton Ho. WA14: Alt 4A 6
Moreton La. SK2: Stoc 9G 109
Moreton St. OL9: Chad 3D 62
Moreton Wlk. SK2: Stoc 9G 109
Morgan Pl. SK5: Stoc 4D 108
Morgan St. OL15: Lit 9M 15
Morgans Way WA3: Low 1C 88
Morillon Rd. M44: Irl 5H 91
Morland Rd. M16: Old T 5B 94
MORLEY 4B 122
Morley Av. M14: Man 8F 94
M27: Swin 4E 76
MORLEY GREEN 5B 122
Morley Grn. Rd. SK9: Wilm 4B 122
Morley Rd. M26: Rad 8D 40
Morley's La. M29: Ast 7A 74
(not continuous)
Morley St. BL3: Bolt 6E 38
BL9: Bury 4M 41
M45: Whitef 3M 59
M46: Ath 8L 55
OL4: O'ham 2B 64
OL16: Roch 4F 28
SK13: Glos 9F 100
Morley Way OL3: G'fld 6L 65
Morna Wlk. M12: Man 1J 95
Morningside WA14: Alt 2B 114
Morningside Cl. M43: Droy 2E 96
OL16: Roch 9G 8 (7F 28)
Morningside Dr. M20: Man 8H 107
Mornington Av. SK8: Chea 3J 117
Mornington Ct. *OL1: O'ham* *3J 63*
(off Bradford St.)
Mornington Cres. M14: Man 9F 94
Mornington Rd. BL1: Bolt 4C 38
M33: Sale 3K 105
M46: Ath 5A 56
OL11: Roch 2D 44
PR6: Adl 5L 19
SK8: Chea 3J 117
WN2: Hin 6B 54
Morpeth Cl. M12: Man 4K 95
OL7: A Lyne 6J 81
Morpeth St. M27: Swin 4E 76
Morrell Rd. M22: Nor 8C 106
Morris Fold Dr. BL6: Los 7K 37
MORRIS GREEN 1D 56
Morris Grn. BL3: Bolt 1D 56
Morris Grn. Bus. Pk. *BL3: Bolt* *8D 38*
(off Fearnhead St.)
Morris Grn. La. BL3: Bolt 9D 38
Morris Grn. St. BL3: Bolt 1D 56
Morris Gro. M41: Urm 9M 91
Morris Hall *M14: Man* *5J 95*
(off Daisy Bank Hall)
Morris Ho. WN1: Wig 7L 9
Morrison St. BL3: Bolt 9F 38
Morrison Wlk. *M40: Man* *5M 79*
(off Eldridge Dr.)
Morris Rd. WN8: Uph 4E 50
Morris St. BL1: Bolt 2M 7 (5H 39)
BL2: Bolt 5H 39
M20: Man 1G 107
M26: Rad 7L 41
M29: Tyld 1A 74
OL4: O'ham 6L 63
WN1: Wig 7L 9 (3G 53)
WN2: Hin 6N 53
WN3: I Mak 7H 53
Morrowfield Av. M8: Man 3E 78
Morse Rd. M40: Man 5N 79
Morston Cl. M28: Wors 2J 75
Mortar St. OL4: O'ham 3N 63
(not continuous)
Mort Ct. *BL1: Bolt* *1D 38*
(off Halliwell Rd.)
Mortfield Gdns. BL1: Bolt 4E 38
Mortfield La. BL1: Bolt 4E 38
(not continuous)
Mort Fold M38: Lit H 6H 57
Mortimer Av. M9: Man 7K 61
Mortimer Ho. *BL6: Hor* *1D 36*
(off Chorley New Rd.)
Mortimer St. OL1: O'ham 2L 63
Mortlake Cl. M28: Walk 8G 56
Mortlake Dr. M40: Man 5N 79
Mort La. M29: Tyld 1F 74
Morton Av. WN3: Wig 6E 52
Morton Dr. SK11: Sut E 9K 131
Morton Moss Ct. *BL3: Bolt* *8B 38*
(off Higher Clough Cl.)
Mortons, The BL5: W'ton 1G 55
Morton St. M24: Mid 1M 61
M26: Rad 1H 59
M35: Fail 4A 80
SK4: Stoc 4C 108
Morton Ter. *M34: Dent* *8L 97*
(off Tatton Rd.)
SK6: Wood 3M 109
Mort St. BL4: Farn 3J 57
BL6: Hor 9D 20
WN2: Hin 6C 54
WN6: Wig 2D 52
WN7: Lei 5D 72
Morven Av. SK7: H Gro 4K 119
Morven Dr. M23: Wyth 2N 115
Morven Gro. BL2: Bolt 5N 39
Morville Dr. WN3: Wig 7E 52
Morville Rd. M21: Cho H 8C 94
Moschatel Wlk. M31: Part 5G 103
Moscow Rd. SK3: Stoc 9B 108
Moscow Rd. E. SK3: Stoc 9B 108
Mosedale Av. WA11: St H 9F 68
Mosedale Cl. M23: Wyth 1L 115
M29: Ast 4D 74
Mosedale Rd. M24: Mid 1J 61
Moseldene Rd. SK2: Stoc 2H 119
Moseley Ct. M19: Man 8L 95
SK8: Chea H 4L 117
Moseley Grange SK8: Chea H 4L 117
Moseley Rd. M14: Man 9J 95
M19: Man 9L 95
SK8: Chea H 4L 117
Moseley St. SK3: Stoc 5J 9 (8C 108)
MOSES GATE 1K 57
Moses Gate Country Pk. 8L 39
Moses Gate Station (Rail) 1K 57
Moses Ga. Workshops *BL3: Bolt* *1L 57*
(off Gladys St.)
Mosley Arc. *M1: Man* *5H 5*
(off Parker St.)
Mosley Av. BL0: Ram 3H 25
BL9: Bury 8M 25
Mosley Cl. WA15: Tim 9F 104
MOSLEY COMMON 3G 75
Mosley Comn. Rd. M28: Wors 2F 74
M29: Tyld 2F 74
Mosley Rd. M17: T Pk 5J 93
WA15: Tim 1H 115
Mosley St. M2: Man 6G 5 (9F 78)
M26: Rad 8F 40
Moss, The M24: Mid 5N 61
Mossack Av. M22: Wyth 6C 116
Moss Av. OL16: Roch 7G 29
WN5: Bil 8H 51
WN7: Lei 5K 73
MOSS BANK 9E 68
Moss Bank M8: Man 2F 78
OL2: Shaw *6M 45*
(off Queen St.)
PR7: Cop 4B 18
SK7: Bram 1A 124
Moss Bank Av. M43: Droy 8G 80
Moss Bank Cl. BL1: Bolt 9E 22
Mossbank Cl. SK13: Had 5A 100
Moss Bank Ct. M43: Droy 8G 80
WN7: Lei 5E 72
Moss Bank Gro. M27: Ward 9D 58
Mossbank Gro. OL10: H'ood 1H 43
Moss Bank Rd. M27: Ward 9D 58
WA11: St H 9E 68
Moss Bank Trad. Est.
M28: Walk 7M 57
Moss Bank Way BL1: Bolt 3N 37
Moss Bower Rd. SK11: Macc 8G 131
Mossbray Av. M19: Man 4J 107
Moss Bri. Rd. OL16: Roch 7F 28
Moss Brook Ct. M40: Man 6H 79
Mossbrook Dr. M38: Lit H 5F 56
Moss Brook Rd. M9: Man 3K 79
MOSSBROW 9E 102
Moss Brow SK10: Boll 6J 129
Moss Chase SK11: Macc 8G 130
Moss Cl. M26: Rad 7D 40
Mossclough Ct. M9: Man 3K 79
Moss Colliery Rd. M27: Clif 8E 58
Moss Cft. Cl. M41: Urm 6M 91
Mossdale Av. BL1: Bolt 5M 37
Mossdale Rd. M23: Wyth 7M 105
M33: Sale 7F 104
WN4: A Mak 2D 70
Mossdown Rd. OL2: O'ham 9L 45
Moss Dr. BL6: Hor 1H 37
Mosses Ho. BL9: Bury 9L 7 (3M 41)
Moss Farm Cl. M24: Mid 5N 61
Mossfield Cl. BL9: Bury 1A 42
M29: Tyld 2C 74
SK4: Stoc 6N 107
Mossfield Ct. BL1: Bolt 4F 38
Mossfield Grn. M30: Ecc 5F 76
Mossfield Rd. BL4: Farn 3J 57
BL4: Kea 5N 57
M27: Pen, Swin 3G 58
WA15: Tim 1K 115
Moss Fold M29: Ast 3D 74
OL6: A Lyne 6F 6
Mossgate Rd. OL2: Shaw 4K 45
Moss Grange Av. M16: Whall R 5C 94
Moss Grn. M31: C'ton 2N 103
MOSS GROVE 9H 63
Moss Gro. OL2: Shaw 3J 45
WA13: Lym 3C 112
WN6: Stan 4B 34
Moss Gro. Ct. *M15: Man* *5D 94*
(off Moss La. W.)
Mossgrove Rd. WA15: Tim 1F 114
Mossgrove St. OL8: O'ham 9H 63

Mosshall Cl. M15: Man 3C 94
Moss Hall Farm Cotts.
BL5: O Hul 3E 56
Moss Hall Rd. BL9: Bury 3C 42
OL10: H'ood, Mid 5E 42
MOSS HEY 6N 45
Moss Hey Dr. M23: Wyth 7A 106
Mosshey St. OL2: Shaw 6N 45
Moss Ho. La. M28: Wors 5G 75
(off Vicars Hall La.)
Moss Ho. Ter. M9: Man 1H 79
Moss Ind. Est. OL16: Roch 8F 28
WN7: Lei 9D 72
Mossland Cl. OL10: H'ood 4J 43
Mossland Gro. BL3: Bolt 1M 55
MOSS LANE 8H 131
Moss La. BL1: Bolt 2B 38
BL4: Kea 6B 58
BL6: Bla 2B 36
M9: Mid 6M 61
M17: Urm 4E 92
M24: Mid 6L 61
(not continuous)
M27: Ward 1D 76
M28: Walk 7M 57
(not continuous)
M29: Ast 9A 74
M31: Part, Warb 5G 103
M33: Sale 5D 104
(Edinburgh Cl.)
M33: Sale 5B 104
(Moss Rd.)
M44: Cad 3E 102
M45: Whitef 3M 59
OL2: O'ham 9L 45
OL7: A Lyne 6H 81
OL12: Whitw 7N 13
OL16: Roch 9E 8 (7E 28)
PR7: Cop 4B 18
SK7: Bram 1A 124
SK9: A Edg 4G 126
SK9: Sty 1C 122
SK10: Boll 5J 129
SK10: Mot S A 3M 127
SK11: Macc 7F 130
SK14: B'tom 9J 99
WA3: G'ury 4M 89
(not continuous)
WA3: Low 4L 87
WA3: Rix 3A 102
WA11: Cra 5C 68
WA13: Warb 7F 102
WA14: Alt 3D 6 (3D 114)
WA15: Alt, Hale 3D 6 (3D 114)
WA15: Tim 9F 104
WA16: H Leg 9F 112
WA16: Mere, O Tab 2C 132
WN2: P Bri 8K 53
WN6: Wrig 1H 33
Moss La. E. M14: Man 5E 94
M15: Man, Whall R 5E 94
M16: Man, Whall R 5D 94
Moss Lane Ground 4F 114
Moss La. Ind. Est. M45: Whitef . . . 2M 59
OL2: O'ham 9L 45
Moss La. Trad. Est. M45: Whitef . . . 2N 59
Moss La. W. M15: Man 5D 94
Moss Lea BL1: Bolt 9E 22
(not continuous)
Mosslee Av. M8: Man 8E 60
MOSSLEY 1F 82
MOSSLEY BROW 1G 83
MOSSLEY CROSS 1E 82
Mossley Industrial Heritage Cen.
. . . . 1F 82
Mossley Rd. OL4: Gras 7G 65
OL6: A Lyne 7F 6 (7N 81)
Mossley Station (Rail) 1F 82
Moss Lodge La. OL7: A Lyne 8H 81
Moss Mnr. M33: Sale 5E 104
Moss Mdw. BL5: W'ton 2G 55
Moss Mdw. Rd. M6: Sal 6J 77
Mossmere Rd. SK8: Chea H 3M 117
Moss Mill St. OL16: Roch 8F 28
MOSS NOOK 8E 116
Moss Nook Ind. Area
M22: Wyth 7E 116
Moss Pk. Rd. M32: Stre 7G 93
Moss Pit Row WN2: Asp 8L 35
Moss Pl. BL9: Bury 4L 41
Moss Rd. BL4: Farn 4M 57
M32: Stre 5J 93
M33: Sale 4B 104
M44: Cad 7C 90
SK9: A Edg 3G 127
WN5: Bil 8H 51
Moss Rose SK9: A Edg 3G 127
Moss Rose Stadium 8H 131
Moss Row BL9: Bury 9M 7 (3M 41)
OL11: Roch 4J 27
Moss Shaw Way M26: Rad 7E 40
(not continuous)
MOSS SIDE 5F 94
Moss Side BL8: Bury 8G 25
Moss Side La. OL16: Roch 8G 29
WA3: Rix 5A 102
Moss Side Leisure Cen. 4E 94
Moss Side Rd. M44: Cad 2E 102
Moss Side St. OL12: Whitw 1C 14
Moss Sq. SK11: Macc 8H 131
Moss St. BL4: Farn 2M 57
BL9: Bury 8K 7 (2L 41)
BL9: Sum 3K 25
M7: Sal 5C 78
M34: Aud 9F 80
M43: Droy 8F 80
OL4: O'ham 3B 64
OL10: H'ood 2H 43
OL16: Roch 9G 8 (7F 28)
SK14: Holl 4N 99
WN2: P Bri 8K 53
WN3: I Mak 8J 53
WN5: Wig 5M 51
WN6: Wig 2D 52
Moss St. E. OL6: A Lyne . . . 7C 6 (7M 81)
Moss St. W. OL7: A Lyne . . . 8A 6 (8K 81)
Moss Ter. OL6: A Lyne 8A 6 (8L 81)
OL16: Roch 9G 8 (7F 28)
SK9: Wilm 6L 123
SK11: Gaws 7E 130
WN5: Wig 6M 51
Moss Va. Cres. M32: Stre 5F 92
Moss Va. Rd. M41: Urm 7E 92
Moss Vw. M29: Tyld 2B 74
M40: Man 9A 62
Moss Vw. Rd. BL2: Bolt 4M 39
M31: Part 5H 103
SK11: Gaws 8E 130
Moss Way M33: Sale 4E 104
OL7: A Lyne, Aud 9J 81
Mossway M24: Mid 6L 61
Mossways Caravan Pk.
SK9: Wilm 7B 122
MOSSWAYS PARK 6B 122
Mosswood Pk. M20: Man 8G 106
Mosswood Rd. SK9: Wilm 5K 123
Mossylea Cl. M24: Mid 6N 61
Mossy Lea Fold WN6: Wrig 1L 33
Mossy Lea Rd. WN6: Wrig 1K 33
MOSTON 2M 79
Moston Bank Av. M9: Man 3K 79
Moston Fairway Nature Reserve
. . . . 2A 80
Moston La. M9: Man 2K 79
M40: Man 2M 79
Moston La. E. M40: Man 9B 62
Moston Rd. M24: Mid 6B 62
Moston Station (Rail) 9B 62
Moston St. M7: Sal 3E 78
SK5: Stoc 1D 108
Mostyn Av. BL9: Bury 8M 25
M14: Man 9K 95
SK8: Chea H 6K 117
Mostyn Rd. SK7: H Gro 6F 118
Mostyn St. SK15: Duk, Stal 1C 98
SK16: Duk 1C 98
Motcombe Farm Rd.
SK8: H Grn 6G 116
Motcombe Gro. SK8: H Grn 4F 116
Motcombe Rd. SK8: H Grn 5F 116
Motherwell Av. M19: Man 8M 95
Mottershead Av. BL3: Lit L 8A 40
Mottershead Rd. M22: Wyth 3B 116
Mottram Av. M21: Cho H 3B 106
Mottram Cl. SK8: Chea 2M 117
Mottram Dr. WA15: Tim 2G 114
WN3: Wig 6E 52
Mottram Fold SK1: Stoc . . . 4L 9 (8D 108)
SK14: Mot 6K 99
Mottram Hall Golf Course 1B 128
MOTTRAM IN LONGDENDALE 5K 99
Mottram M. BL6: Hor 9D 20
(off Wright St.)
Mottram Moor SK14: Holl, Mot 5K 99
Mottram Old Rd. SK14: Hyde 9C 98
SK15: Stal 9F 82
MOTTRAM RISE 2H 99
Mottram Rd. M33: Sale 5L 105
SK9: A Edg 4G 126
SK14: B'tom 9J 99
SK14: Hat, Hyde 6B 98
SK15: Mat, Stal 9E 82
MOTTRAM ST ANDREW 3M 127
Mottram St. BL6: Hor 9D 20
SK1: Stoc 4M 9 (8D 108)
(Bamford St.)
SK1: Stoc 4L 9 (8D 108)
(Mottram Fold)
Mottram Towers
SK1: Stoc 4L 9 (8D 108)
Mottram Vw. SK15: Stal 3H 99
Mottram Way SK1: Stoc 4L 9
SK10: Macc 2J 131
Mough La. OL9: Chad 8B 62
Moulding Moss BL9: Bury 7E 26
Mouldsworth Av. M20: Man 1F 106
SK4: Stoc 2B 108
Moulton Cl. WA16: Knut 7J 133
Moulton St. M8: Man 6D 78
Moulton St. Pct. M8: Man 6D 78
Mount, The M7: Sal 2C 78
OL6: A Lyne 7G 6 (7A 82)
SK5: Stoc 4F 108
WA14: Alt 1C 6 (2D 114)
WA15: Haleb 7J 115
WN8: Skel 3A 50
Mountain Ash OL12: Roch 2N 27
Mountain Ash Cl. M33: Sale 3C 104
OL12: Roch 2N 27
Mountain Gro. M28: Walk 7K 57
Mountain Rd. PR7: Cop 5B 18
Mountain St. M28: Walk 7K 57
M40: Man 6B 80
OL5: Mos 1F 82
SK1: Stoc 6E 108
Mount Av. OL12: Roch 1J 29
OL15: Lit 7L 15
Mountbatten Av. SK16: Duk 2C 98
Mountbatten Cl. BL9: Bury 1A 60
Mountbatten St. M18: Man 4A 96
Mt. Carmel Ct. M5: Sal 2B 94
(off Mt. Carmel Cres.)
Mt. Carmel Cres. M5: Sal 2B 94
Mount Cres. WN5: Orr 5K 51
Mount Dr. M41: Urm 7F 92
SK6: Mar 2C 120
Mountfield M25: Pres 7A 60
Mountfield Ct. WN5: Orr 4K 51
Mountfield Rd. SK3: Stoc 9A 108
SK7: Bram 1C 124
Mountfield Wlk. BL1: Bolt 3F 38
(off Kentford Rd.)
M11: Man 9L 79
(off Hopedale Cl.)
Mountfold M24: Mid 4N 61
Mountford Av. M8: Man 9E 60
Mount Gro. SK8: Gat 1E 116
Mountheath Ind. Pk.
M25: Pres 1A 78
Mount La. OL3: Dob 3H 65
Mountmorres Cl. BL5: O Hul 4A 56
Mount Pl. OL12: Roch 6A 8
Mt. Pleasant BL3: Bolt 7K 39
(off Lever Bri. Pl.)
BL7: Edg 1L 23
BL9: Bury 2M 25
M24: Mid 3H 61
M25: Pres 3D 60
PR6: Adl 5K 19
SK2: Stoc 1K 119
SK6: Wood 3M 109
SK7: H Gro 4H 119
SK9: Wilm 5G 122
(Egerton Rd.)
SK9: Wilm 2D 126
(Knutsford Rd.)
SK10: Boll 4M 129
SK10: Macc 3F 130
SK13: Tin 2C 100
SK14: Hyde 6D 98
Mt. Pleasant Bus. Cen.
OL4: O'ham 4M 63
Mt. Pleasant Ho.
M27: Swin 2G 77
Mt. Pleasant Rd. BL4: Farn 3G 56
M34: Dent 7K 97
Mt. Pleasant St. BL6: Hor 3F 36
M34: Aud 2K 97
(not continuous)
OL4: O'ham 4M 63
OL6: A Lyne 5E 6 (6N 81)
(not continuous)
Mt. Pleasant Trad. Est.
OL6: A Lyne 5F 6
Mt. Pleasant Wlk. M26: Rad 8G 40
Mount Rd. HD7: Mars 3D 48
M18: Man 4A 96
M19: Man 4A 96
M24: Mid 4L 61
M25: Pres 4B 60
SK4: Stoc 6A 108
SK14: Hyde 2D 110
Mountroyal Cl. SK14: Hyde 4C 98
Mt. St Joseph's Rd. BL3: Bolt 7C 38
Mountside BL7: Eger 5F 22
Mountside Cl. OL12: Roch 3C 28
Mountside Cres. M25: Pres 7M 59
Mt. Sion Rd. M26: Rad 1D 58
Mt. Skip La. M38: Lit H 7H 57
Mountsorrel Rd. WA14: W Tim . . . 7C 104
Mount St. BL0: Ram 7H 11
BL1: Bolt 3F 38
BL6: Hor 3F 36
M2: Man 6G 4 (1E 94)
M3: Sal 2C 4 (8C 78)
M27: Swin 3F 76
M30: Ecc 1C 92
M34: Dent 8M 97
OL2: O'ham 9J 45
OL10: H'ood 3J 43
OL11: Roch 3A 44
OL12: Roch 6A 8 (5C 28)
SK13: Glos 9E 100
SK14: Hyde 7B 98
WN7: Lei 6E 72
Mount Ter. M43: Droy 7C 80
SK11: Macc 5K 131
WA14: Alt 3C 6
Mount Vw. OL3: Upp 3K 65
WN3: I Mak 6G 53
Mount Vw. Rd. OL2: Shaw 6A 46
Mt. Zion Rd. BL9: Bury 7M 41
Mousell St. M8: Man 6F 78
Mouselow Cl. SK13: Had 6B 100
Mousley Bottom SK22: N Mil 8K 121
Mowbray Av. M25: Pres 9B 60
M33: Sale 5J 105
Mowbray St. BL1: Bolt 3C 38
OL1: O'ham 3E 8 (5K 63)
OL7: A Lyne 8A 6 (8L 81)
OL11: Roch 1N 43
SK1: Stoc 4M 9 (8D 108)
Mowbray Wlk. M24: Mid 1K 61
Mow Halls La. OL3: Dob 2K 65
Mowpen Brow WA16: H Leg 9C 112
Moxley Rd. M8: Man 1D 78
Moxon Way WN4: A Mak 6G 70
Moy Hill OL16: Miln 8M 29
Moyse Av. BL8: Bury 8F 24
Mozart Cl. M4: Man 2N 5 (8H 79)
MUDD 7K 99
Muirfield Av. SK6: Bred 4L 109
Muirfield Cl. BL3: Bolt 9A 38
M25: Pres 6A 60
M40: Man 2A 80
OL10: H'ood 3J 43
SK9: Wilm 6J 123
Muirfield Dr. M29: Ast 2D 74
SK10: Macc 9H 129
Muirhead Ct. M6: Sal 5N 77
Mulberry OL10: H'ood 5E 42
Mulberry Av. OL10: H'ood 5E 42
WA3: Low 2B 88
Mulberry Cl. M26: Rad 1G 58
OL10: H'ood 5E 42
OL11: Roch 8C 28
SK8: H Grn 8H 117
WN5: Wig 5A 52
Mulberry Ct. BL6: Hor 3F 36
(off Dale St. E.)
M6: Sal 7N 77
(off Mulberry Rd.)
M41: Urm 7C 92
SK11: Macc 8H 131
WA14: Alt 1D 6
Mulberry Dr. SK10: Macc 3J 131
Mulberry Ho. OL3: Del 8J 47
Mulberry M. SK4: Stoc . . . 1J 9 (6B 108)
Mulberry Mt. St.
SK3: Stoc 5K 9 (8C 108)
Mulberry Rd. M6: Sal 8N 77
Mulberry St. M2: Man 5F 4 (9E 78)
OL6: A Lyne 7E 6 (7N 81)
Mulberry Wlk. M33: Sale 2D 104
M43: Droy 1C 96
Mulberry Way OL10: H'ood 5E 42
Mule St. BL2: Bolt 1N 7 (4H 39)
Mulgrave Rd. M28: Wors 2A 76
Mulgrave St. BL3: Bolt 1D 56
M27: Swin 1D 76
Mulgrove Wlk. M9: Man 8K 61
(off Haverfield Rd.)
Mullacre Rd. M22: Wyth 1C 116
Mull Av. M12: Man 4L 95
Mullein Cl. WA3: Low 1N 87
Mulliner St. BL1: Bolt 3G 38
(off Prospect St.)
Mullineux St. M28: Walk 9L 57
Mullins Av. WA12: N Wil 4F 86
Mullion Cl. M19: Man 7B 96
Mullion Dr. WA15: Tim 1E 114
Mullion Wlk. M8: Man 4G 78
Mulmount Cl. OL8: O'ham 8G 63
MUMPS 2F 8 (4L 63)
Mumps OL1: O'ham 2G 8 (4L 63)
Mumps M. OL1: O'ham 4L 63
(off Garden St.)
Mumps Rdbt.
OL1: O'ham 2G 8 (4L 63)
OL4: O'ham 4L 63
Munday St. M4: Man 9J 79
Municipal Cl. OL10: H'ood 2J 43
(off Hartland St.)
Munn Rd. M9: Man 6G 61
Munro Av. M22: Wyth 5E 116
WN5: Orr 5J 51
Munslow Wlk. M9: Man 8L 61
Munster St. M4: Man 1H 5 (7F 78)
Muriel St. M7: Sal 5C 78
OL10: H'ood 2K 43
OL16: Roch 8F 28
Murieston Rd. WA15: Hale 5E 114
Murphy Cl. WN3: Wig 6D 52
Murray Cl. SK10: Macc 3E 130
Murrayfield OL11: Roch 7K 27
SK10: P'bury 8E 128
Murray Rd. BL9: Bury 8L 7 (2M 41)
Murray St. M4: Man 3L 5 (8G 79)
M7: Sal 4C 78
M46: Ath 9K 55
Murrow Wlk. M9: Man 2J 79
(off Alderside Rd.)
Murton Ter. BL1: Bolt 9F 22
Musabbir Sq. OL12: Roch 5E 28
(off Jermyn St.)
Musbury Av. SK8: Chea H 5N 117
Muscle & Fitness Gymnasium 9F 58
(off Station Rd.)
Musden Wlk. SK4: Stoc 1B 108
Mus. of Science & Industry
. . . . 6D 4 (1D 94)
Mus. of the Manchester Regiment, The
. . . . 7D 6 (7M 81)
Mus. of Transport 4G 78
Mus. of Wigan Life 9K 9 (4F 52)
Museum St. M2: Man 6F 4 (1E 94)
Musgrave Gdns. BL1: Bolt 4D 38
Musgrave Rd. BL1: Bolt 4C 38
M22: Wyth 4C 116
Muslin St. M5: Sal 5A 4 (9B 78)
Mustard La. WA3: Cro 9C 88
Muter Av. M22: Wyth 5E 116
Mutual St. OL10: H'ood 1K 43
Mycroft Cl. WN7: Lei 2G 72
Myerscroft Cl. M40: Man 1C 80
Myles Standish Way PR7: Chor 1F 18
Myrrh St. BL1: Bolt 1F 38
Myrrh Wlk. BL1: Bolt 1F 38
(off Myrrh St.)
Myrtle Av. WN4: A Mak 4C 70
WN7: Lei 2G 73
Myrtle Bank M25: Pres 1N 77
Myrtle Cl. OL8: O'ham 6J 63
Myrtle Gdns. BL9: Bury 2A 42
Myrtle Gro. M25: Pres 9A 60
M34: Dent 6D 96
M43: Droy 8G 80
M45: Whitef 1K 59
WN5: Bil 6H 69
Myrtleleaf Gro. M5: Sal 8K 77
Myrtle Pl. M7: Sal 6B 78
Myrtle Rd. M24: Mid 1A 62
M31: Part 5E 102
Myrtle St. BL1: Bolt 4E 38
M11: Man 1K 95
M16: Old T 5B 94
(off Langshaw St.)
SK3: Stoc 8N 107
WN1: Wig 7H 9
Myrtle St. Nth. BL9: Bury 2A 42
Myrtle St. Sth. BL9: Bury 2A 42
My St. M5: Sal 9L 77
Mytham Gdns. BL3: Lit L 1B 58
Mytham Rd. BL3: Lit L 9B 40
Mytholme Av. M44: Cad 5D 102
Mythorn Wlk. M40: Man 5M 79
(off Harmer Cl.)
Mytton Rd. BL1: Bolt 9C 22
Mytton St. M15: Man 4E 94

N

Nabbs Fold BL8: G'mount 2F 24
Nabbs Way BL8: G'mount 4G 24
Nab Cl. SK10: Boll 4N 129
Nab La. SK6: Mar 8B 110
SK10: Boll 4N 129
Naburn Cl. SK5: Stoc 2G 109
Naburn Dr. WN5: Orr 6J 51
Naburn St. M13: Man 5J 95
Nada Lodge M8: Man 1E 78
(off St Mary's Hall Rd.)
Nada Rd. M8: Man 1E 78
Naden Vw. OL11: Roch 4J 27
Naden Wlk. M45: Whitef 3N 59
Nadine St. M6: Sal 7L 77
Nadin St. OL8: O'ham 8J 63
Nailers Grn. BL8: G'mount 4F 24
(off Brandlesholme Rd.)
Nairn Cl. M40: Man 7K 79
(off Eastfield Av.)
WN6: Stan 3A 34
Nall Ga. OL16: Roch 2G 44
Nall St. M19: Man 1N 107
OL16: Miln 6J 29
Nameplate Cl. M30: Ecc 8B 76
Nancy St. M15: Man 9B 4 (3C 94)
Nancy Vw. SK10: Boll 5M 129
Nandywell BL3: Lit L 9B 40
Nangreave Rd. SK2: Stoc 1E 118
NANGREAVES 2M 25
Nangreaves St. WN7: Lei 5E 72
Nan Nook Rd. M23: Wyth 7M 105
Nansen Av. M30: Ecc 7C 76
Nansen Cl. M32: Stre 5L 93
Nansen Rd. SK8: Gat 3F 116
Nansen St. M6: Sal 8L 77
M32: Stre 6K 93
Nansmoss La. SK9: Wilm 5C 122
Nantes Ct. BL1: Bolt 2E 38
Nantwich Av. OL12: Roch 2D 28
Nantwich Cl. SK8: Chea 2M 117
Nantwich Rd. M14: Man 8F 94
Nantwich Wlk. BL3: Bolt 8F 38
Nantwich Way SK9: Hand 1K 123
(off Spath La.)
Napier Ct. M15: Man 3B 94
(off City Rd.)
SK4: Stoc 5N 107
SK14: Hyde 8B 98
(off Napier St.)
Napier Grn. M5: Sal 2A 94
Napier Rd. M21: Cho H 9A 94
M30: Ecc 7C 76
SK4: Stoc 5N 107
Napier St. M27: Swin 3D 76
OL2: Shaw 4M 45
SK7: H Gro 4H 119
SK14: Hyde 8B 98
Napier St. E. OL8: O'ham . . . 5A 8 (6H 63)
Napier St. W. OL8: O'ham 6H 63
Naples Rd. SK3: Stoc 1N 117
Naples St. M4: Man 1J 5 (7F 78)
NAR 9C 14
Narbonne Av. M30: Ecc 6G 76
Narborough Cl. WN2: Hin 7A 54
Narborough Wlk. M40: Man 5H 79
(off Westmount Cl.)
Narbuth Dr. M8: Man 3E 78
Narcissus Wlk. M28: Walk 8G 56
NARROW GATE BROW 5H 45
Narrow La. SK10: Adl 5L 125
Narrows, The WA14: Alt . . . 5B 6 (4C 114)
Narrow Wlk. WA14: Bow 5C 114
Naseby Av. M9: Man 7L 61
Naseby Ct. M25: Pres 6B 60
Naseby Pl. M25: Pres 6B 60
Naseby Rd. SK5: Stoc 9C 96
Naseby Wlk. M45: Whitef 3B 60
(not continuous)
Nash Rd. M17: T Pk 1E 92
Nash St. M15: Man 3D 94
Nasmyth Av. M34: Dent 5L 97
Nasmyth Bus. Cen. M30: Ecc 7C 76
Nasmyth Rd. M30: Ecc 1C 92
Nasmyth St. BL6: Hor 1E 36
M8: Man 5F 79
Nathan Dr. M3: Sal 2D 4 (8D 78)
WA11: Hay 3B 86
Nathaniel Ct. WN2: P Bri 8L 53
(off Ridyard St.)
Nathans Rd. M22: Wyth 3B 116
National Cycling Cen.
Manchester Velodrome 8M 79
National Dr. M5: Sal 1N 93
National Football Mus. . . . 2G 5 (8E 78)
National Indoor BMX Arena 8M 79
National Ind. Est. OL7: A Lyne 8K 81
National Squash Cen. 8L 79
National Trad. Est. SK7: H Gro . . 4G 119
Naunton Av. WN7: Lei 5E 72
Naunton Rd. M24: Mid 4N 61
Naunton Wlk. M9: Man 2K 79
(off Jonas St.)
Naval St. M4: Man 2M 5 (8H 79)
Nave Ct. M6: Sal 6M 77
Navenby Av. M16: Old T 5B 94
Navenby Rd. WN3: Wig 9D 52
Navigation Bank WN6: Stan 9A 34
Navigation Cl. WN7: Lei 6G 73
Navigation Ho. M1: Man 5L 5
WN7: Lei 6J 73
(off Siddow Comn.)
Navigation Rd. WA14: Alt 9D 104
Navigation Road Station (Rail & Metro)
. . . . 1E 114
Navigation Trad. Est. M40: Man . . . 5L 79
Navigation Vw. OL16: Roch 8F 28
Navigators Wharf M43: Droy 1E 96
Naylor Av. WA3: Gol 1L 87
Naylor Ct. M40: Man 1N 5 (7H 79)
Naylor Farm Av. WN6: She 7K 33
Naylors Ter. BL7: Bel 1L 21
Naylor St. M40: Man 1N 5 (7J 79)
M46: Ath 8L 55
OL1: O'ham 1C 8 (4J 63)
Nazeby Wlk. OL9: O'ham 6G 63
Naze Ct. OL1: O'ham 3J 63
(off Bradford St.)
Naze Wlk. SK5: Stoc 2G 108
Neal Av. OL6: A Lyne 6G 6 (7A 82)
SK8: H Grn 7F 116
Neale Av. OL3: G'fld 6M 65
Neale Rd. M21: Cho H 1N 105
NEAR BARROWSHAW 2A 64
Near Birches Pde. OL4: O'ham 7B 64
Nearbrook Rd. M22: Wyth 3B 116
Nearcroft Rd. M23: Wyth 9N 105
Neargates PR7: Char R 2A 18
Near Hey Cl. M26: Rad 9E 40
Nearmaker Av. M22: Wyth 3B 116
Nearmaker Rd. M22: Wyth 3B 116
Neary Way M41: Urm 4C 92
Neasden Gro. BL3: Bolt 7D 38
(off Langshaw Wlk.)
Neath Av. M22: Nor 9C 106
Neath Cl. M45: Whitef 4B 60
SK12: Poy 1H 125
Neath Fold BL3: Bolt 9E 38

Neath St. OL9: O'ham 2A 8 (4H 63)
Nebo St. BL3: Bolt 8E 38
Nebraska St. BL1: Bolt 3F 38
Neden Cl. M11: Man 1N 95
Needham Av. M21: Cho H 9A 94
Needham Ct. M45: Whitef 4M 59
Needhams Wharf Cl.
SK10: Macc 3L 131
Needwood Cl. M40: Man 5J 79
Needwood Rd. SK6: Wood 3N 109
Neem Ho. M14: Man 5H 95
(off Rusholme Pl.)
Neenton Sq. M12: Man 3M 95
Neild Gdns. WN7: Lei 6G 73
Neild St. M1: Man 7L 5 (1H 95)
OL8: O'ham 7J 63
Neill St. M7: Sal 6D 78
Neilson Cl. M24: Mid 4A 62
Neilson Ct. M23: Wyth 1N 115
Neilston Av. M40: Man 3N 79
Neilston Ri. BL1: Bolt 5L 37
Nell Carrs BL0: Ram 6L 11
Nellie St. OL10: H'ood 2G 42
Nell La. M20: Man 3D 106
M21: Cho H 1B 106
Nell St. BL1: Bolt 9G 22
Nel Pan La. WN7: Lei 2E 72
Nelson Av. M30: Ecc 7D 76
SK12: Poy 3L 125
Nelson Bus. Cen. M34: Dent 5K 97
Nelson Cl. M15: Man 5D 94
SK12: Poy 3L 125
Nelson Ct. M40: Man 6J 79
(off Droitwich Rd.)
Nelson Dr. M43: Droy 8B 80
M44: Cad 2F 102
WN2: I Mak 3K 53
Nelson Fold M27: Pen 1G 76
Nelson Mandela Ct.
M16: Whall R 6D 94
(off Range Rd.)
Nelson Pit Vis. Cen. 3N 125
Nelson Rd. M9: Man 6J 61
Nelson Sq. BL1: Bolt 3L 7 (5G 39)
Nelson St. BL3: Bolt 7H 39
BL3: Lit L 9B 40
BL4: Farn 3M 57
BL6: Hor 1F 36
BL9: Bury 4M 41
(not continuous)
M5: Sal 9L 77
M7: Sal 5C 78
M13: Man 4G 95
M24: Mid 4A 62
M29: Tyld 2C 74
M30: Ecc 8D 76
M32: Stre 8K 93
M34: Aud 3K 97
M34: Dent 5K 97
(not continuous)
M40: Man 7K 79
M46: Ath 7K 55
(not continuous)
OL4: Lees 6B 64
OL10: H'ood 3J 43
OL15: Lit 9M 15
OL16: Roch 8C 8 (6D 28)
SK7: H Gro 3K 119
SK11: Macc 5H 131
SK14: Hyde 7B 98
WA12: N Wil 6D 86
(not continuous)
WN2: Hin 5N 53
Nelson Way OL9: Chad 7F 62
Nelstrop Cres. SK4: Stoc 2B 108
Nelstrop Rd. SK4: Stoc 2A 108
Nelstrop Rd. Nth. SK4: Stoc 1A 108
Nelstrop Wlk. SK4: Stoc 2A 108
Nene Gro. WN2: Hin 7A 54
Nepaul Rd. M9: Man 1K 79
Neptune Gdns. M7: Sal 5B 78
Nero St. BL0: Ram 7L 11
Nesbit St. BL2: Bolt 1K 39
Nesfield Rd. M23: Wyth 6M 105
Neston Av. BL1: Bolt 8G 23
M20: Man 2F 106
M33: Sale 6L 105
Neston Cl. OL2: Shaw 5A 46
Neston Gro. SK3: Stoc 2B 118
Neston Rd. BL8: Bury 9F 24
OL16: Roch 9G 28
Neston St. M11: Man 2D 96
Neston Way SK9: Hand 3J 123
Neswick Wlk. M23: Wyth 6M 105
NETHER ALDERLEY 7F 126
Nether Alderley Mill 8F 126
Netherbury Cl. M18: Man 6A 96
Netherby Rd. WN6: Wig 9D 34
Nethercote Av. M23: Wyth 1A 116
Nethercott Ct. M29: Tyld 1N 73
Nethercroft OL11: Roch 4K 27
Nethercroft Ct.
WA14: Alt 2A 6 (2C 114)
Nethercroft Rd. WA15: Tim 2J 115
Netherfield Cl. OL8: O'ham 7G 63
Netherfield Rd. BL3: Bolt 1E 56
Netherfields SK9: A Edg 5F 126
WN7: Lei 3F 72
Nether Fold SK10: P'bury 5E 128
Netherhey La. OL2: O'ham 1G 63
Nether Hey St. OL8: O'ham 6M 63
(not continuous)
Netherhouse Rd. OL2: Shaw 5L 45
Netherland St. M50: Sal 1N 93
NETHER LEES 6A 64
Netherlees OL4: Lees 6A 64
NETHERLEY 2G 49
Netherley Dr. HD7: Mars 2G 49
Netherley Rd. PR7: Cop 5B 18
Netherlow Ct. SK14: Hyde 7B 98
(off Union St.)
Nether St. M12: Man 7M 5 (1H 95)
SK14: Hyde 9C 98
Netherton Gro. BL4: Farn 1J 57
Netherton Rd. M14: Man 8F 94
Nethervale Dr. M9: Man 3K 79
Netherwood M35: Fail 2F 80
Netherwood Ct. WN6: She 6L 33
Netherwood Gro. WN3: Wins 1B 70
Netherwood Rd. M22: Nor 9B 106
Netherwood Way BL5: W'ton 1J 55
Netley Av. OL12: Roch 2D 28
Netley Gdns. M26: Rad 8E 40
Netley Rd. M23: Wyth 3N 115
Nettlebarn Rd. M22: Wyth 2B 116
Nettleford Rd. M16: Whall R 9D 94
Nettleton Gro. M9: Man 1L 79
Nevada St. BL1: Bolt 3F 38
(off St Ann St.)
M13: Man 4J 95
Nevendon Dr. M23: Wyth 3M 115
Nevern Cl. BL1: Bolt 4A 38
Nevile Ct. M7: Sal 2A 78
Nevile Rd. M7: Sal 2A 78
Neville Cardus Wlk. M14: Man 7H 95
(off Taylor St.)
Neville Cl. BL1: Bolt 1J 7 (4F 38)
Neville Dr. M44: Irl 5H 91
Neville St. OL9: Chad 4G 63
SK7: H Gro 4H 119
WA12: N Wil 5D 86
WN2: P Bri 8K 53
Nevill Rd. SK7: Bram 5C 118
Nevin Av. SK8: Chea H 6K 117
Nevin Cl. SK7: Bram 8E 118
Nevin Rd. M40: Man 1B 80
Nevis Gro. BL1: Bolt 8E 22
Nevis St. OL11: Roch 2E 44
Nevy Fold Av. BL6: Hor 1H 37
New Acre Ct. SK6: Rom 6M 109
(off Metcalfe Dr.)
New Allen St. M40: Man . . .1M 5 (7H 79)
NEWALL GREEN 3N 115
Newall Gro. WN7: Lei 3H 73
Newall Rd. M23: Wyth 4M 115
Newall St. OL9: Chad 9F 62
OL15: Lit 8M 15
Newark Av. M14: Man 6G 94
M26: Rad 7C 40
Newark Pk. Way OL2: O'ham 5G 44
Newark Rd. M27: Clif 9H 59
OL12: Roch 2D 28
SK5: Stoc 3D 108
WN2: Hin 7M 53
Newark Sq. OL12: Roch 2D 28
Newark St. WN6: Wig 2C 52
Newarth Dr. WA13: Lym 5B 112
New Bailey St. M3: Sal 3D 4 (9D 78)
Newbank Chase OL9: Chad 3E 62
New Bank Cl. OL3: Dob 2J 65
Newbank Cl. M24: Mid 4A 62
New Bank St. M12: Man 3K 95
M29: Tyld 2B 74
SK13: Had 4B 100
Newbank Twr. M3: Sal 1D 4 (7D 78)
New Barn OL3: Del 5F 46
New Barn Av. WN4: A Mak 7F 70
New Barn Cl. OL2: Shaw 5L 45
New Barn La. OL11: Roch 8B 28
WN7: Lei 8G 72
New Barn Rd. OL8: O'ham 9L 63
New Barns Av. M21: Cho H 2B 106
New Barn St. BL1: Bolt 3C 38
OL2: Shaw 5L 45
OL16: Roch 8E 28
New Barton St. M6: Sal 5J 77
Newbeck Cl. BL6: Hor 3F 36
Newbeck St. M4: Man 2J 5
New Beech Rd. SK4: Stoc 6K 107
New Belvedere Cl. M32: Stre 7K 93
Newberry Gro. SK3: Stoc 2B 118
Newbiggin Wlk. SK10: Macc 4G 130
(off Longacre St.)
NEWBOLD .6G 28
NEWBOLD BROW 5F 28
Newbold Cl. SK16: Duk 1N 97
Newbold Hall Dr. OL16: Roch 6G 28
Newbold Hall Gdns. OL16: Roch . . .6G 28
Newbold Moss OL16: Roch 6F 28
Newbold Stop (Metro) 7G 28
Newbold St. BL8: Bury 2J 41
OL16: Roch 6G 29
Newbold Wlk. M15: Man 9G 4
NEW BOSTON 3B 86
Newboult Rd. SK8: Chea 1K 117
Newbourne Cl. SK7: H Gro 4H 119
Newbreak Cl. OL4: O'ham 3A 64
Newbreak St. OL4: O'ham 3A 64
Newbridge Cl. M26: Rad 8H 41
WN4: Gars 7A 70
New Bridge Gdns.
BL9: Bury 7L 41
Newbridge Gdns. BL2: Bolt 9M 23
New Bridge La.
SK1: Stoc 2M 9 (7D 108)
New Bridge St. M3: Sal 1F 4 (7E 78)
Newbridge Vw. OL5: Mos 2G 83
New Briggs Fold BL7: Eger 3F 22
New Brighton Cotts.
OL12: Whitw 5B 14
(off Ruth St.)
SK11: Lang 9M 131
New Broad La. OL16: Roch 1G 44
Newbrook Av. M21: Cho H 5C 106
Newbrook Rd. BL5: O Hul 6A 56
M46: Ath 6A 56
New Brunswick St.
BL6: Hor 1D 36
New Bldgs. Pl. OL16: Roch 6C 8
Newburn Av. M9: Man 7L 61
Newburn Cl. WN3: Wig 7B 52
NEW BURY 4J 57
Newbury Av. M33: Sale 4C 104
Newbury Cl. SK8: Chea H 9M 117
Newbury Ct. WA15: Tim 9F 104
(off Tulip Dr.)
Newbury Dr. M30: Ecc 7B 76
M41: Urm 4C 92
Newbury Gro. OL10: H'ood 4H 43
Newbury Pl. M7: Sal 3C 78
Newbury Rd. BL3: Lit L 9N 39
SK8: H Grn 8G 117
Newbury Wlk. BL1: Bolt 3F 38
M9: Man 4J 79
(off Ravelston Dr.)
OL9: Chad 4G 62
(off Kempton Way)
Newby Cl. BL9: Bury 5N 41
Newby Dr. M24: Mid 9L 43
M33: Sale 5L 105
SK8: Gat 1F 116
WA14: Alt 1D 114
Newby Rd. BL2: Bolt 3M 39
SK4: Stoc 6A 108
SK7: H Gro 5G 119
Newby Rd. Ind. Est.
SK7: H Gro 5G 119
Newby Sq. WN5: Wig 6M 51
Newcastle St. M15: Man . . .9G 4 (2E 94)
(not continuous)
Newcastle Wlk. M34: Dent 8L 97
(off Trowbridge Rd.)
New Cateaton St.
BL9: Bury 1M 41
New Cathedral St.
M1: Man 3G 4 (8E 78)
New Century Ho.
M34: Dent 6G 97
New Chapel La. BL6: Hor 2G 37
Newchurch OL8: O'ham 2L 81
New Church Ct. M26: Rad 9G 41
M45: Whitef 4M 59
(off Elizabeth St.)
Newchurch La. WA3: Cul 7H 89
New Church Rd. BL1: Bolt 2A 38
New Church St. M26: Rad 9H 41
Newchurch St. M11: Man 1L 95
(off Blackrock St.)
OL11: Roch 3A 44
Newchurch Wlk. M26: Rad 9H 41
New City Rd. M28: Wors 2H 75
Newcliffe Rd. M9: Man 7L 61
New Coin St. OL2: O'ham 9H 45
New College St.
M3: Man 5D 4 (9D 78)
New Colliers Row BL1: Bolt 7N 21
Newcombe Cl. M11: Man 9L 79
Newcombe Ct. M33: Sale 4F 104
(off Beech Gro.)
Newcombe Dr. M38: Lit H 5G 57
Newcombe Rd. BL0: Ram 4G 25
Newcombe St. M3: Man 7E 78
New Copper Moss
WA15: Alt 4G 6 (3F 114)
New Ct. Dr. BL7: Eger 2F 22
New Ct. St. M3: Man 5E 4 (9D 78)
Newcroft M35: Fail 4F 80
Newcroft Cres. M41: Urm 8F 92
Newcroft Dr. M9: Man 1H 79
M41: Urm 8G 92
SK3: Stoc 1B 118
Newcroft Rd. M41: Urm 8F 92
New Cross M4: Man 3K 5 (8G 78)
New Cross St. M5: Sal 8J 77
M27: Swin 3G 76
Newdale Rd. M12: Man 7N 95
NEW DELPH 9J 47
New Devonshire Sq. M7: Sal 4D 78
New Drake Grn. BL5: W'ton 6G 54
NEW EARTH 6N 63
Newearth Rd. M28: Walk, Wors 2J 75
New Earth St. OL4: O'ham 6N 63
OL5: Mos 9G 64
New Ellesmere App. M28: Walk 7K 57
New Elm Rd. M3: Man 6C 4 (1C 94)
Newenden Rd. WN1: Wig 8E 34
New Field Cl. M26: Rad 9E 40
OL16: Roch 6F 28
Newfield Ct. BL5: W'ton 2G 55
WA13: Lym 2B 112
Newfield Head La. OL16: Miln 8M 29
Newfield Vw. OL16: Miln 7L 29
(not continuous)
New Fold WN5: Orr 7G 51
New Forest Rd. M23: Wyth 8J 105
New Gartside St.
M3: Man 5D 4 (9D 78)
NEWGATE .4E 50
Newgate OL16: Roch 7B 8 (6C 28)
SK9: Wilm 7C 122
Newgate Av. WN6: App B 4J 33
Newgate Cotts. BL5: O Hul 2B 56
Newgate Dr. M38: Lit H 5G 57
Newgate Rd. M33: Sale 7B 104
WN8: Uph 4D 50
New George St. BL8: Bury 1J 41
M4: Man 2J 5 (8F 78)
New Grn. BL2: Bolt 7M 23
New Hall Av. M7: Sal 2C 78
SK8: H Grn 8G 116
Newhall Av. BL2: Bolt 6B 40
M30: Ecc 2A 92
Newhall Dr. M23: Wyth 6N 105
New Hall La. BL1: Bolt 3B 38
WA3: Cul, Ris 8G 89
(not continuous)
New Hall M. BL1: Bolt 3M 37
Newhall Pl. BL1: Bolt 4B 38
New Hall Rd. BL9: Bury 9D 26
M7: Sal 2C 78
M33: Sale 4M 105
Newhall Rd. SK5: Stoc 7E 96
New Hall St. SK10: Macc 3G 131
Newham Av. M11: Man 8N 79
Newham Cl. SK11: Sut E 9K 131
Newham Dr. BL8: Bury 4H 41
Newhart Gro. M28: Walk 9K 57
Newhaven Av. M11: Man 2D 96
WN7: Lei 2H 73
Newhaven Bus. Pk. M30: Ecc 9E 76
Newhaven Cl. BL8: Bury 6J 25
SK8: Chea H 5A 118
Newhaven Wlk. BL2: Bolt 3H 39
New Herbert St. M6: Sal 5J 77
NEWHEY 9M 29
New Hey HD7: Mars 1G 48
Newhey Av. M22: Wyth 2C 116
New Hey Rd. SK8: Chea 1K 117
Newhey Rd. M22: Wyth 3C 116
OL16: Miln 8L 29
(not continuous)
Newhey Stop (Metro) 9M 29
New Heys Way BL2: Bolt 7L 23
New Holder St. BL1: Bolt 3H 7 (5F 38)
Newholme Ct. M32: Stre 7L 93
Newholme Gdns. M28: Walk 8K 57
Newholme Rd. M20: Man 3E 106
Newhouse Cl. OL12: W'le 8G 15
Newhouse Cres. OL11: Roch 5K 27
Newhouse Dr. WN3: Wins 1A 70
Newhouse Rd. OL10: H'ood 4J 43
NEW HOUSES 9N 51
New Houses OL4: Scout 3F 64
Newhouse St. OL12: W'le 8G 15
Newick Wlk. M9: Man 8K 61
(off Leconfield Dr.)
Newington Av. M8: Man 8E 60
Newington Ct. WA14: Bow 4C 114
Newington Dr. BL1: Bolt 3G 38
BL8: Bury 4G 40
Newington Wlk. BL1: Bolt 3G 38
(off Kentford Rd.)
New Islington M4: Man 3N 5 (8H 79)
New Islington Stop (Metro)
. . . . .4N 5 (9J 79)
New Kings Head Yd.
M3: Sal 2F 4 (8E 78)
Newland Av. WN5: Wig 6A 52
Newland Dr. BL5: O Hul 4A 56
Newland M. WA3: Cul 4G 88
Newlands M35: Fail 6C 80
Newlands Av. BL2: Bolt 3N 39
M29: Ast 4B 74
M30: Ecc 1N 91
M44: Irl 7H 91
M45: Whitef 2L 59
OL12: Roch 2D 28
SK7: Bram 7D 118
SK8: Chea H 8M 117
Newlands Cl. OL12: Roch 2D 28
SK8: Chea H 8M 117
Newlands Dr. BL6: Bla 5A 36
M20: Man 8H 107
M25: Pres 6N 59
M27: Pen 4J 77
SK9: Wilm 9D 122
SK13: Had 5B 100
WA3: Low 1N 87
Newlands Rd. M23: Wyth 8M 105
SK8: Chea 1J 117
SK10: Macc 5C 130
WN7: Lei 7H 73
(not continuous)
Newland St. M8: Man 1G 78
Newlands Wlk. M24: Mid 8K 43
New La. BL2: Bolt 3L 39
M24: Mid 2M 61
M30: Ecc 8B 76
OL2: O'ham 8H 45
New La. Ct. BL2: Bolt 2M 39
NEW LANE END 7C 88
New La. End WA3: Cro 7C 88
New Lawns SK5: Stoc 8E 96
Newlea Cl. BL1: Bolt 2D 38
New Lees St. OL6: A Lyne 5A 82
(not continuous)
New Lester Cl. M29: Tyld 1C 74
New Lester Way M38: Lit H 7F 56
New Lodge WN1: Wig 1G 52
New Lodge, The M46: Ath 8L 55
Newlyn Av. SK10: Macc 3B 130
SK15: Stal 7G 83
Newlyn Cl. SK7: H Gro 6H 119
Newlyn Dr. M33: Sale 7J 105
SK6: Bred 5L 109
WN4: A Mak 8E 70
WN8: Skel 4B 50
Newlyn St. M14: Man 7G 94
Newman Av. WN6: Wig 1D 52
NEW MANCHESTER 1H 75
Newman Cl. WN2: Hin 5N 53
New Mansion Ho. SK1: Stoc 9D 108
(off Wellington Rd. Sth.)
Newman St. OL6: A Lyne . . .7B 6 (7L 81)
OL16: Roch 2G 28
SK14: Hyde 6B 98
WN1: Wig 1H 53
New Market M2: Man 4G 5 (9E 78)
Newmarket Cl. M33: Sale 6B 104
SK10: Macc 9G 129
Newmarket Gro. OL7: A Lyne 5J 81
New Mkt. Hall WN1: Wig 6J 9 (2F 52)
New Mkt. La. M2: Man 4H 5 (9F 78)
Newmarket M. M7: Sal 4C 78
Newmarket Rd. BL3: Lit L 1A 58
OL7: A Lyne 5J 81
New Mkt. St. WN1: Wig 7J 9 (3F 52)
New Mdw. BL6: Los 5L 37
New Medlock Ho.
M15: Man 9G 5 (2E 94)
New Miles La. WN6: She 6K 33
New Mill OL16: Roch 3H 29
NEW MILLS 7M 121
New Mills Art Theatre 8L 121
New Mills Central (Rail) 8L 121
New Mills Golf Course 6L 121
New Mills Heritage & Information Cen.
. . . . .8L 121
New Mills Leisure Cen. 7M 121
New Mills Newtown Station (Rail)
. . . . .9L 121
New Mills Rd. SK13: Chis 5L 111
New Mill St. OL15: Lit 9L 15
Newmill Wlk. M8: Man 4F 78
(off Brentfield Av.)
New Moor La. SK7: H Gro 4H 119
New Moss Rd. M44: Cad 2E 102
NEW MOSTON 1C 80
New Mount St. M4: Man 1J 5
Newnham St. BL1: Bolt 1G 38
New North Manchester Golf Course
. . . . .3J 61
New Oak Cl. M35: Fail 2G 80
New Pk. Ct. SK22: N Mil 8N 121
New Pk. Rd. M5: Sal 2A 94
Newpark Wlk. M8: Man 4F 78
(off Tamerton Dr.)
New Parsons St. OL9: O'ham 5G 63
Newport Av. SK5: Stoc 1C 108
Newport M. BL4: Farn 4L 57
(off Newport St.)
Newport Rd. BL3: Bolt 9H 39
M21: Cho H 8N 93
M34: Dent 9M 97
Newport St. BL1: Bolt 3K 7 (5G 38)
BL3: Bolt 4K 7 (5G 38)
BL4: Farn 4L 57
BL8: Tot 8G 24
M6: Sal 8L 77
M14: Man 6G 95
M24: Mid 2A 62
OL8: O'ham 6H 63
Newquay Av. BL2: Ain 3D 40
SK5: Stoc 1C 108
Newquay Dr. SK7: Bram 8D 118
SK10: Macc 4B 130
New Quay St. M3: Man 5D 4 (9D 78)
New Radcliffe St.
OL1: O'ham 2B 8 (4J 63)
New Ridd Ri. SK14: Hyde 9A 98
New Riven Ct. BL3: Lit L 9A 40
New Rd. M26: Rad 1H 59
OL8: O'ham 7J 63
OL12: Whitw 5N 13
OL15: Lit 1J 29
PR6: And, H Char 3M 19
PR7: Cop 3C 18
SK10: P'bury 6E 128
SK13: Tin 2B 100
WA13: Lym 4A 112
WN2: Hai 6K 35
New Rock BL5: W'ton 6H 55
New Royd Av. OL4: Lees 3C 64
Newry Rd. M30: Ecc 1E 92
Newry St. BL1: Bolt 1E 38
Newry Wlk. M9: Man 8G 60
(off Riverdale Rd.)
Newsham Cl. BL3: Bolt 7E 38
Newsham Rd. SK3: Stoc 1C 118
Newsham Wlk. M12: Man 6N 95
WN6: Wig 2C 52
Newshaw La. SK13: Had 6B 100
Newsholme Cl. WA3: Cul 6H 89
Newsholme St. M8: Man 3E 78
New Smithfield Mkt. M11: Man 2A 96
NEW SPRINGS 1K 53
New Springs BL1: Bolt 1C 38
Newstead OL12: Roch 6B 8 (5C 28)
Newstead Av. M20: Man 3J 107
OL6: A Lyne 3N 81
Newstead Cl. SK12: Poy 1H 125
Newstead Dr. BL3: Bolt 1B 56
Newstead Gro. SK6: Bred 5K 109
Newstead Rd. M41: Urm 6E 92
WN3: Wig 8B 52
Newstead Ter. WA15: Tim 9F 104
New St. BL1: Bolt 4J 7 (6F 38)
BL6: Bla 2N 35
BL8: Tot 7F 24
M26: Rad 1H 59
M27: Pen 1G 77
M30: Ecc 9C 76
M40: Man 6K 79
M43: Droy 1E 96
OL3: Upp 3L 65
OL4: Lees 5B 64
OL12: Roch 3C 28
OL15: Lit 1K 29
OL16: Miln 8L 29
SK9: Wilm 9D 122
SK14: B'tom 9K 99
SK15: Stal 1D 98
SK22: N Mil 8M 121
WA14: Alt 5B 6 (3C 114)
WN2: P Bri 9K 53
WN4: A Mak 6F 70
WN5: Wig 6M 51
New Tame OL3: Del 5F 46
New Tempest Rd. BL6: Los 8L 37
New Ter. SK9: Wilm 6G 122
SK14: Hyde 8B 98
(Ashley M.)
SK14: Hyde 4C 98
(Hamel St.)
New Thomas St. M6: Sal 6N 77
NEWTON 5C 98
Newton Av. M12: Man 5L 95
M20: Man 2F 106
Newton Bus. Pk. SK14: Hyde 4D 98
Newton Cl. WN1: Wig 1G 52
NEWTON COMMON 6B 86
Newton Ct. SK14: Hyde 4A 98
(off Markham St.)
Newton Cres. M24: Mid 1J 61
Newtondale Av. OL2: O'ham 8G 45
Newton Dr. BL8: G'mount 4G 24
Newton for Hyde Station (Rail) . . .5C 98
Newton Gdns. WA3: Low 1C 88
New Tong Fld. BL7: Bro X 6G 23
Newton Grn. SK14: Hyde 4C 98
Newton Hall 5N 97
Newton Hall Ct. SK14: Hyde 4N 97
Newton Hall Rd. SK14: Hyde 4N 97
NEWTON HEATH 4N 79
Newton Heath & Moston Stop (Metro)
. . . . .4N 79
Newton La. WA12: N Wil 3H 87
NEWTON-LE-WILLOWS 5G 87
Newton-le-Willows Station (Rail)
. . . . .6H 87
Newton Moor Ind. Est.
SK14: Hyde 4B 98
Newtonmore Wlk. M11: Man 9N 79
(off Kincraig Cl.)
Newton Pk. Dr. WA12: N Wil 6J 87
Newton Rd. M24: Mid 4G 60
M35: Fail 6C 80
M41: Urm 7C 92
SK9: Wilm 5F 122
WA2: Win 8J 87

Newton Rd. WA3: Low 5K 87
WA14: Alt 9E 104
WN5: Bil 4J 69
Newton St. BL1: Bolt 2F 38
BL9: Bury 7M 25
M1: Man 4K 5 (9G 78)
M32: Stre 8K 93
M35: Fail 4A 80
M40: Man 4A 80
M43: Droy 7F 80
OL6: A Lyne 6E 6 (7N 81)
OL16: Roch 8F 28
SK3: Stoc 8C 108
SK11: Macc 5G 131
SK14: Hyde 6A 98
SK15: Stal 8C 82
WN7: Lei 5H 73
Newton Ter. BL1: Bolt 2F 38
(off Newton Wlk.)
SK16: Duk 9M 81
(off Queen St.)
Newton Wlk. BL1: Bolt 2F 38
NEWTON WOOD 3N 97
Newton Wood Rd. SK16: Duk 3M 97
NEW TOWN 6M 45
NEWTOWN
M4 . . . . . 7G 78
M27 . . . . . 9E 58
SK12 . . . . . 3L 125
SK22 . . . . . 9L 121
WN5 . . . . . 5C 52
Newtown Av. M34: Dent 7L 97
Newtown Cl. M11: Man 1N 95
M27: Pen 9F 58
Newtown Ct. M25: Pres 7B 60
Newtown M. M25: Pres 7B 60
Newtown St. M25: Pres 7B 60
OL2: Shaw 6M 45
New Union St. M4: Man . . . 3M 5 (8H 79)
New Vernon St. BL9: Bury 9M 25
New Viaduct St. M11: Man 8K 79
Newville Dr. M20: Man 3J 107
New Vine St. M15: Man 9F 4 (3E 94)
New Wakefield St.
M1: Man 8H 5 (2F 94)
New Way OL12: Whitw 5A 14
New Welcome St. M15: Man 3E 94
New William Cl. M31: Part 4G 103
(off Moss La.)
NEW WINDSOR 4A 4 (8A 78)
New York BL3: Bolt 8A 38
New York St. M1: Man 5H 5 (9F 78)
OL10: H'ood 2G 43
New Zealand Rd. SK1: Stoc 7E 108
Neyland Cl. BL1: Bolt 5A 38
Ney St. OL7: A Lyne 4K 81
Niagara St. SK2: Stoc 1E 118
Nicholas Cft. M4: Man 3J 5 (8F 78)
Nicholas Owen Cl. M11: Man 1A 96
Nicholas Rd. OL8: O'ham 7J 63
Nicholas St. BL2: Bolt 1N 7 (4H 39)
M1: Man 5H 5 (9F 78)
Nicholson Av. SK10: Macc 3J 131
Nicholson Cl. SK10: Macc 3J 131
Nicholson Rd. SK14: Hyde 4N 97
Nicholson Sq. SK16: Duk 1M 97
Nicholson St. OL4: Lees 5B 64
OL11: Roch 8D 28
SK4: Stoc 6C 108
Nichols St. M6: Sal 7A 78
(off Gerrard St.)
Nicker Brow OL3: Dob 2K 65
Nick Hilton's La. PR6: H Char 2N 19
Nickleby Rd. SK12: Poy 3H 125
Nickleton Brow PR6: H Char 3M 19
(not continuous)
Nick Rd. La. OL12: W'le 7D 14
Nico Ditch M18: Man 7A 96
Nicolas Rd. M21: Cho H 8M 93
Nicola St. BL7: Eger 5F 22
Nicol Mere Dr. WN4: A Mak 4D 70
Nicol Rd. WN4: A Mak 5D 70
Nield Rd. M34: Dent 6K 97
Nield's Brow WA14: Bow 5C 114
Nield St. OL5: Mos 9E 64
Nields Way SK6: Mel 3G 120
Nigel Rd. M9: Man 3L 79
Nigher Moss Av. OL16: Roch 6G 29
Nightingale Cl. SK2: Stoc 3K 119
SK9: Wilm 5G 122
Nightingale Ct. WN6: Wig 2D 52
Nightingale Dr. M34: Aud 8G 81
Nightingale Gdns. M23: Wyth 7N 105
Nightingale Rd. BL6: Bla 1M 35
Nightingale St. M3: Man 1F 4 (7E 78)
PR6: Adl 5K 19
Nightingales Wlk. BL3: Bolt 9G 39
Nile, The M15: Man 8F 4
Nile St. BL3: Bolt 7G 38
OL1: O'ham 1C 8 (3J 63)
OL7: A Lyne 1K 97
OL16: Roch 6F 8 (5E 28)
Nile Ter. M7: Sal 5C 78
NIMBLE NOOK 6E 62
Nimble Nook OL9: Chad 6E 62
Nina Dr. M40: Man 8A 62
Nine Acre Ct. M5: Sal 2A 94
(off Taylorson St.)
Nine Acre Dr. M5: Sal 2A 94
Ninehouse La. BL3: Bolt 8G 38
Ninfield Rd. M23: Wyth 3A 116
Ninian Ct. M24: Mid 2L 61
Ninian Gdns. M28: Walk 8L 57
Ninth Av. OL8: O'ham 1H 81
Nipper La. M45: Whitef 2L 59
Nisbet Av. M22: Wyth 4D 116
Nithe Wlk. BL8: Bury 7G 25
Niven St. M12: Man 8M 5 (2H 95)
Nixon Rd. BL3: Bolt 9D 38
Nixon Rd. Sth. BL3: Bolt 9D 38
Nixons La. WN8: Skel 4B 50
Nixon St. M35: Fail 3C 80
OL11: Roch 1N 43
SK3: Stoc 5K 9 (8C 108)
SK11: Macc 4F 130
Noahs Ark La. WA16: Mob 4A 126
NOB END 1A 58
Noble Mdw. OL12: Roch 9H 15
Noble St. BL3: Bolt 7F 38
OL8: O'ham 7K 63
WN7: Lei 5J 73
(not continuous)
Noel Dr. M33: Sale 4K 105
Noel St. BL1: Bolt 2J 7 (5F 38)
Nolan St. M9: Man 2K 79
Nona St. M6: Sal 8L 77
NOOK 5N 45
Nook, The BL9: Bury 3C 42
M28: Wors 2N 75
M30: Ecc 7A 76
M41: Urm 8D 92
OL3: G'fld 7M 65
SK7: Bram 1B 124
WN6: App B 5J 33
Nook Cotts. OL4: Aus 3D 64
Nook Farm Av. OL12: Roch 2D 28
Nook Flds. BL2: Bolt 1M 39
Nook La. M29: Ast 8D 74
OL6: A Lyne 5A 82
WA3: Gol 1L 87
Nook Side OL12: Roch 2D 28
Nook Ter. OL12: Roch 2D 28
Noon Ct. WA12: N Wil 8E 86
Noon Sun Cl. OL3: G'fld 7K 65
Noon Sun St. OL12: Roch 4D 28
Norbet Wlk. M9: Man 3K 79
(off Broadwell Dr.)
Norbreck Av. M21: Cho H 1A 106
SK8: Chea 1M 117
Norbreck Cres. WN6: Wig 1D 52
Norbreck Gdns. BL2: Bolt 4K 39
Norbreck St. BL2: Bolt 4K 39
Norburn Rd. M13: Man 7L 95
Norbury Av. M6: Sal 5K 77
M33: Sale 4F 104
OL4: Gras 5F 64
SK6: Mar 1B 120
SK14: Hyde 7A 98
WN5: Bil 4H 69
Norbury Cl. M40: Man 6K 79
(off Giltbrook Av.)
WA16: Knut 5J 133
Norbury Ct. M11: Man 2A 96
Norbury Cres. SK7: H Gro 5H 119
Norbury Dr. SK6: Mar 1B 120
Norbury Gro. BL1: Bolt 9H 23
M27: Pen 1F 76
SK7: H Gro 5H 119
Norbury Hollow Caravan Site
SK12: Poy 9N 119
Norbury Hollow Rd.
SK7: H Gro 7M 119
Norbury Ho. OL4: O'ham 6M 63
Norbury La. OL8: O'ham 8A 64
Norbury M. SK6: Mar 1B 120
NORBURY MOOR 7H 119
Norbury St. M7: Sal 4D 78
OL16: Roch 9F 28
SK1: Stoc 3L 9 (7D 108)
SK11: Macc 5G 130
WN7: Lei 5F 72
Norburys Yd. WA16: Knut 6G 133
(off King St.)
Norbury Way SK9: Hand 1J 123
(off Chelford Rd.)
Norcliffe Hall M. SK9: Sty 2C 122
Norcliffe Wlk. M18: Man 5N 95
Norcot Wlk. M15: Man 3C 94
(off Royce Rd.)
Norcross Cl. SK2: Stoc 2H 119
Nordale Pk. OL12: Roch 3J 27
Nordek Cl. OL2: O'ham 7H 45
Nordek Dr. OL2: O'ham 7H 45
NORDEN 4K 27
Norden Av. M20: Man 2F 106
Norden Cl. OL11: Roch 3H 27
Norden Ct. BL3: Bolt 8F 38
Norden Lodge OL11: Roch 5K 27
Norden Rd. OL11: Roch 8J 27
Nordens Dr. OL9: Chad 2D 62
Nordens Rd. OL9: Chad 3D 62
Nordens St. OL9: Chad 3E 62
Norden Way OL11: Roch 3H 27
Noreen Av. M25: Pres 6B 60
Norfield Cl. SK16: Duk 1N 97
Norfolk Av. M18: Man 5A 96
M34: Dent 6D 96
M43: Droy 7D 80
M45: Whitef 3N 59
OL10: H'ood 2F 42
SK4: Stoc 2A 108
Norfolk Cl. BL3: Lit L 8B 40
M44: Cad 3D 102
OL2: Shaw 5K 45
OL15: Lit 6N 15
WN2: Hin 5C 54
Norfolk Cres. M35: Fail 4C 80
Norfolk Dr. BL4: Farn 2L 57
Norfolk Gdns. M41: Urm 6L 91
OL10: H'ood 1F 42
Norfolk Ho. M7: Sal 1D 78
M33: Sale 4K 105
Norfolk Rd. M18: Man 5A 96
M46: Ath 6K 55
WN5: Bil 1J 69
Norfolk Sq. SK13: Glos 8E 100
Norfolk St. M2: Man 4G 5 (9E 78)
M6: Sal 5N 77
M28: Walk 5L 57
OL9: O'ham 7F 62
(not continuous)
OL11: Roch 9B 8 (7C 28)
SK13: Glos 8F 100
SK14: Hyde 7A 98
WN5: Wig 5C 52
WN6: Wig 1D 52
Norfolk Wlk. SK10: Macc 2D 130
(off Wiltshire Cl.)
Norfolk Way OL2: O'ham 1H 63
Norford Way OL11: Roch 5K 27
Norgate St. M20: Man 5G 106
Norlan Av. M34: Aud 2J 97
Norland Wlk. M40: Man 5M 79
(off Bower St.)
Norleigh Rd. M22: Nor 8C 106
NORLEY 5N 51
Norley Av. M32: Stre 6M 93
Norley Cl. OL1: Chad 1F 62
Norley Dr. M19: Man 7A 96
M33: Sale 4L 105
Norley Hall Av. WN5: Wig 4N 51
Norley Rd. WN5: Wig 4M 51
WN7: Lei 6D 72
Norman Av. SK7: H Gro 4G 119
WA11: Hay 2D 86
WA12: N Wil 6H 87
Normanby Chase WA14: Alt 3B 114
Normanby Gro. M27: Swin 1E 76
Normanby Rd. M28: Wors 1K 75
Normanby St. BL3: Bolt 1C 56
M14: Man 5F 94
M27: Swin 1E 76
WN5: Wig 5M 51
Norman Cl. M24: Mid 2A 62
Normandale Av. BL1: Bolt 3B 38
Normandy Cres. M26: Rad 9F 40
Norman Gro. M12: Man 5L 95
SK5: Stoc 1C 108
Norman Rd. M7: Sal 3D 78
M14: Man 7H 95
M33: Sale 5H 105
OL6: A Lyne 4N 81
OL11: Roch 9A 8 (7B 28)
SK4: Stoc 5N 107
SK15: Stal 8C 82
WA14: Alt 1C 114
Norman Rd. W. M9: Man 3L 79
Norman's Pl. WA14: Alt . . . 4C 6 (3D 114)
Norman St. BL3: Bolt 8G 38
(off Rishton La.)
BL9: Bury 9A 26
M12: Man 4N 95
M24: Mid 2N 61
M26: Rad 8K 41
(off Sandford St.)
M35: Fail 1E 80
OL1: O'ham 3H 63
SK14: Hyde 7B 98
Normanton Av. M6: Sal 7J 77
Normanton Cl. WN6: Stan 8B 34
Normanton Dr. M9: Man 7K 61
Normanton Rd. SK3: Stoc 9M 107
Norman Weall Ct. M24: Mid 1M 61
Normington St. OL4: O'ham 4M 63
Norreys Av. M41: Urm 6M 91
Norreys St. OL16: Roch 6E 8 (5E 28)
Norris Av. SK4: Stoc 7A 108
NORRIS BANK 6A 108
Norris Bank Ter. SK4: Stoc 7A 108
NORRIS HILL 6N 107
Norris Hill Dr. SK4: Stoc 6A 108
Norris Rd. M33: Sale 6H 105
Norris St. BL3: Bolt 7F 38
BL3: Lit L 9A 40
BL4: Farn 4L 57
M29: Tyld 2B 74
Norris Towers SK4: Stoc 1K 9
Nortex Bus. Cen. BL1: Bolt 4E 38
Northallerton Rd. M7: Sal 4N 77
Northam Cl. WN6: Stan 3A 34
Northampton Rd. M40: Man 4L 79
Northampton Way M34: Dent 8L 97
(off Leicester Av.)
NORTH ASHTON 4A 70
North Av. BL4: Farn 3H 57
BL8: G'mount 4F 24
BL9: Bury 8A 42
M19: Man 1L 107
OL3: G'fld 6L 65
SK15: Stal 7D 82
WN7: Lei 7L 73
(East Av.)
WN7: Lei 6B 72
(South Av.)
Northavon Cl. M30: Ecc 9G 76
(off Andoc Av.)
North Bk. Rock BL9: Bury 7K 7
(not continuous)
Northbank Gdns. M19: Man 2K 107
Northbank Ho. M28: Wors 5A 76
Northbank Ind. Est. M44: Irl 3G 102
Northbank Ind. Pk. M44: Irl 2G 103
(not continuous)
Northbank Wlk. M20: Man 5C 106
Nth. Blackfield La. M7: Sal 2B 78
Northbourne St. M6: Sal 8L 77
Northbrook Av. M8: Man 7E 60
Nth. Brook Rd. SK13: Had 5A 100
Nth. Broughton St. M3: Sal 3D 4
Nth. Butts St. WN7: Lei 6K 73
North Circ. M45: Whitef 5N 59
North City Family & Fitness Cen.
. . . . . 2K 79
Nth. City Shop. Cen. M9: Man 2K 79
Nth. Clifden La. M7: Sal 4D 78
Northcliffe Rd. SK2: Stoc 8G 109
North Cl. SK13: Tin 2B 100
Northcombe Rd. SK3: Stoc 2C 118
Northcote Av. M22: Wyth 3C 116
Northcote Rd. SK7: Bram 8D 118
North Cres. M11: Man 7B 80
North Cft. M46: Ath 6K 55
OL8: O'ham 8L 63
Northcroft WN1: Wig 2J 53
Northdale Rd. M9: Man 6G 60
Nth. Dean St. M27: Pen 1G 76
Northdene WN8: Par 2A 32
(off Burnside)
Northdene Dr. OL11: Roch 7L 27
Nth. Dene Pk. OL9: Chad 4E 62
Northdown Av. M15: Man 3C 94
SK6: Wood 3N 109
North Downs WA16: Knut 7J 133
Nth. Downs Rd. OL2: Shaw 4K 45
SK8: Chea H 4L 117
North Dr. M27: Swin 3H 77
M34: Aud 9G 80
WN6: App B 2G 32
North Edge WN7: Lei 4K 73
NORTHENDEN 7C 106
Northenden Golf Course 6D 106
Northenden Pde. M22: Nor 7C 106
Northenden Rd. M33: Sale 3H 105
PR7: Cop 4B 18
SK8: Gat 1F 116
Northenden Vw. M20: Man 6G 106
(off South Rd.)
North End Rd. SK15: Stal 8E 82
Northen Gro. M20: Man 4E 106
Northerly Cres. M40: Man 8B 62
Northern, The
(Tennis & Squash Club) 4F 106
Northern Av. M27: Clif 8J 59
Northern Gro. BL1: Bolt 3D 38
NORTHERN MOOR 7M 105
Northfield WN8: Skel 8A 32
Northfield Av. M40: Man 9D 62
Northfield Ct. WA3: Gol 9M 71
Northfield Dr. SK9: Wilm 6J 123
Northfield Rd. BL9: Bury 7M 25
M40: Man 9D 62
Northfields WA16: Knut 5J 133
Northfield St. BL3: Bolt 7D 38
Northfleet Rd. M30: Ecc 1N 91
NORTH FLORIDA 1A 86
Nth. Florida Rd. WA11: Hay 1A 86
North Gate OL8: O'ham 9J 63
Northgate OL12: Whitw 7A 14
Northgate Av. SK10: Macc 3G 131
Northgate Cl. BL6: Hor 3E 36
Northgate La. OL1: O'ham 9B 46
Northgate Rd. SK3: Stoc 8A 108
Nth. George St. M3: Sal . . . 1B 4 (8C 78)
North Gro. M13: Man 4J 95
M28: Walk 8K 57
M41: Urm 7C 92
Nth. Harvey St.
SK1: Stoc 2M 9 (7D 108)
North Hill St. M3: Sal 1C 4 (7C 78)
Northland Rd. BL1: Bolt 7G 22
M9: Man 8M 61
Northlands M26: Rad 7E 40
North La. M29: Ast 4B 74
OL12: Roch 5D 8 (5D 28)
Northleach Cl. BL8: Bury 1H 41
Northleigh Dr. M25: Pres 8C 60
Northleigh Ho. M16: Old T 7A 94
Northleigh Rd. M16: Old T 6A 94
Nth. Lonsdale St. M32: Stre 6L 93
Nth. Manchester Bus. Pk.
M40: Man 4K 79
Northmead SK10: P'bury 8E 128
North Meade M21: Cho H 1A 106
NORTH MOOR 1A 8 (4H 63)
Northmoor Rd. M12: Man 5M 95
North Nook OL4: Aus 3C 64
Northolme Gdns. M19: Man 3K 107
Northolt Av. WN7: Lei 2H 73
Northolt Ct. M11: Man 8B 80
Northolt Dr. BL3: Bolt 8G 39
Northolt Fold OL10: H'ood 5K 43
Northolt Rd. M23: Wyth 7M 105
North Pde. M3: Man 4F 4
M33: Sale 6K 105
OL16: Miln 9N 29
North Pk. Rd. SK7: Bram 5C 118
Nth. Phoebe St. M5: Sal 9A 78
North Pl. SK1: Stoc 2L 9 (7D 108)
Northpoint Ind. Est. SK16: Duk 3M 97
Nth. Quarry Bus. Pk.
WN6: App B 3H 33
Nth. Quarry Bus. Village
WN6: App B 3H 33
NORTH REDDISH 8C 96
Northridge Rd. M9: Man 5J 61
North Ri. OL3: G'fld 6L 65
(not continuous)
North Rd. M11: Man 8N 79
M25: Pres 6M 59
M31: C'ton 4L 103
M34: Aud 9H 81
M43: Droy 8N 79
M46: Ath 7K 55
SK13: Glos 5E 100
SK15: Stal 8E 82
WA15: Hale 7G 114
Northside Av. M41: Urm 7N 91
North Stage M50: Sal 1M 93
Nth. Star Dr. M3: Sal 4B 4 (9C 78)
Northstead Av. M34: Dent 7M 97
North St. BL0: Ram 5J 11
M8: Man 5F 78
M24: Mid 1M 61
M26: Rad 8J 41
OL2: O'ham 8H 45
(not continuous)
OL6: A Lyne 7B 6 (7M 81)
(Katherine St.)
OL6: A Lyne 8A 6 (8L 81)
(Welbeck St. Nth.)
OL10: H'ood 2G 42
OL12: Whitw 5A 14
OL15: Lit 9N 15
(off East St.)
OL16: Roch 5E 8 (5E 28)
WA11: Hay 3B 86
WA12: N Wil 5C 86
WN4: A Mak 6G 71
WN7: Lei 6K 73
Northumberland Av.
OL7: A Lyne 6M 81
Northumberland Cl. M16: Old T 4B 94
Northumberland Cres.
M16: Old T 4B 94
(off Henry St.)
Northumberland Ho.
OL9: O'ham 6G 62
(off Milne St.)
Northumberland Rd. M16: Old T . . . 5B 94
M31: Part 6F 102
SK5: Stoc 1F 108
Northumberland St. M7: Sal 3C 78
WN1: Wig 6N 9 (2H 53)
(not continuous)
Northumberland Way
M22: Shar 1D 116
Northumbria St. BL3: Bolt 7D 38
Northurst Dr. M8: Man 8E 60
North Vale PR6: H Char 4J 19
Nth. Vale Rd.
WA15: Tim 1G 6 (1F 114)
North Vw. BL0: Ram 4J 11
BL9: Sum 3H 25
M45: Whitef 1L 59
OL5: Mos 1H 83
OL12: Whitw 4B 14
North Vw. Cl. OL4: Lyd 6F 64
Northward Rd. SK9: Wilm 8E 122
North Way BL1: Bolt 9J 23
SK14: Hyde 7B 98
Northway M30: Ecc 8F 76
M43: Droy 1E 96
SK5: Stoc 2G 108
WA14: Alt 1E 114
WN1: Wig 6K 9 (2F 52)
WN8: Skel 2A 50
Northways WN6: Stan 2A 34
Northwell St. WN7: Lei 2G 72
Nth. Western St.
M1: Man 7M 5 (1H 95)
M12: Man 2J 95
M19: Man 9M 95
Northwich Rd. WA16: Knut, Tab . . . 7A 132
Northwold Cl. WN3: Wins 8A 52
Northwold Dr. BL1: Bolt 4N 37
M9: Man 8N 61
Northwood BL2: Bolt 9L 23
Northwood Av. WA12: N Wil 5J 87
Northwood Cl. SK6: Mar 2B 120
Northwood Cres. BL3: Bolt 7D 38
Northwood Gro. M33: Sale 4H 105
North Woodley M26: Rad 2J 59
Norton Av. M12: Man 6N 95
M33: Sale 2D 104
M34: Dent 6E 96
M41: Urm 5D 92
Norton Grange M25: Pres 8C 60
Norton Gro. SK4: Stoc 7N 107
Norton Rd. M28: Wors 3F 74
OL12: Roch 2D 28
Norton St. BL1: Bolt 1G 38
M1: Man 5N 5 (9H 79)
M3: Sal 2F 4 (8E 78)
M7: Sal 3D 78
M16: Old T 5B 94
M40: Man 6K 79
SK10: Macc 4J 131
Norview Dr. M20: Man 9G 107
Norville Av. M40: Man 8B 62
Norway Gro. SK5: Stoc 4D 108
Norway St. BL1: Bolt 2E 38
M6: Sal 8L 77
M32: Stre 6L 93
Norweb Way WN7: Lei 7K 73
Norwell Rd. M22: Shar 2D 116
Norwich Av. M34: Dent 8K 97
OL9: Chad 2E 62
OL11: Roch 6M 27
WA3: Low 1N 87
WN4: A Mak 8G 71
Norwich Cl. OL6: A Lyne 2A 82
SK16: Duk 2D 98
Norwich Dr. BL8: Bury 1K 41
Norwich Rd. M32: Stre 6F 92
Norwich St. OL11: Roch 8E 28
Norwick Cl. BL3: Bolt 8N 37
Norwood M25: Pres 9A 60
Norwood Av. M7: Sal 2A 78
M20: Man 4J 107
M29: Ast 4B 74
SK6: H Lan 8A 120
SK7: Bram 1B 124
SK8: Chea H 4M 117
WA3: Low 2B 88
WN4: A Mak 4C 70
WN6: Wig 9D 34
Norwood Cl. M28: Walk 2M 75
OL2: Shaw 4L 45
PR6: Adl 5K 19
Norwood Ct. M32: Stre 8L 93
(off Norwood Rd.)
Norwood Cres. OL2: O'ham 1J 63
Norwood Dr. M27: Swin 3C 76
WA15: Tim 2K 115
Norwood Gro. BL1: Bolt 4E 38
OL2: O'ham 1J 63
Norwood Lodge M7: Sal 2B 78
Norwood Pk. WA14: Alt . . . 2A 6 (2C 114)
Norwood Rd. M32: Stre 8L 93
SK2: Stoc 3F 118
SK8: Gat 1G 116
Nostell Rd. WN4: A Mak 5D 70
Nottingham Av. SK5: Stoc 2G 108
Nottingham Cl. SK5: Stoc 3G 108
Nottingham Dr. BL1: Bolt 3F 38
M35: Fail 5E 80
OL6: A Lyne 3M 81
Nottingham Pl. WN1: Wig 2H 53
Nottingham Ter. SK5: Stoc 2G 108
Nottingham Way M34: Dent 8L 97
Nowell Ct. M24: Mid 9M 43
Nowell Ho. M24: Mid 9M 43
Nowell Rd. M24: Mid 9M 43
Nudger Cl. OL3: Dob 1J 65
Nudger Grn. OL3: Dob 1J 65
Nuffield Cl. BL1: Bolt 3C 38
Nuffield Ho. BL1: Bolt 3C 38
Nuffield Rd. M22: Wyth 3D 116
Nugent Rd. BL3: Bolt 9F 38
Nugget St. OL4: O'ham 5M 63
No. 2 Passage
SK3: Stoc 3H 9 (7B 108)
Number One M50: Sal 2L 93
Nuneaton Dr. M40: Man 7J 79
Nuneham Av. M20: Man 1H 107
Nunfield Cl. M40: Man 9N 61
Nunnery Rd. BL3: Bolt 8C 38
Nunthorpe Dr. M8: Man 2H 79
Nursery Av. WA15: Hale 7E 114
Nursery Brow M45: Whitef 2H 59

Nursery Cl. M33: Sale 4K 105
PR7: Char R 1B 18
SK2: Stoc 9H 109
SK13: Glos 9E 100
Nursery Dr. SK12: Poy 2H 125
Nursery Gdns. OL16: Roch 5G 29
Nursery Gro. M31: Part 4G 103
Nursery La. SK3: Stoc 9M 107
SK9: Wilm 8E 122
SK10: N Ald 8B 126
Nursery Rd. M25: Pres 5N 59
M35: Fail 3E 80
M41: Urm 5A 92
SK4: Stoc 6A 108
SK8: Chea H 6L 117
SK10: Boll 6J 129
SK14: Hyde 6N 97
Nursery St. M6: Sal 7M 77
M16: Whall R 6E 94
Nutbank La. M9: Mid 5K 61
Nuthatch Av. M28: Wors 2L 75
Nuthurst Rd. M40: Man 9A 62
NUTSFORD VALE 5N 95
Nutsford Va. M12: Man 5N 95
Nut St. BL1: Bolt 2E 38
NUTTALL 1J 25
Nuttall Av. BL3: Lit L 9C 40
BL6: Hor 1C 36
M45: Whitef 3M 59
Nuttall Cl. BL0: Ram 9J 11
Nuttall Hall Cotts. BL0: Ram 9K 11
Nuttall Hall Rd. BL0: Ram 1K 25
NUTTALL LANE 9J 11
Nuttall La. BL0: Ram 9H 11
Nuttall M. M45: Whitef 3M 59
Nuttall Sq. BL9: Bury 7M 41
Nuttall St. BL9: Bury 9N 7 (3N 41)
M11: Man 2M 95
M16: Old T 4B 94
M44: Cad 2F 102
M46: Ath 8N 55
OL8: O'ham 7M 63
OL16: Roch 8E 8 (6E 28)
Nutt La. M25: Pres 3D 60
Nutt St. WN1: Wig 1H 53
Nutwood Ct. SK5: Stoc 1C 108
NW Regional Basketball Cen. 9E 96

O

O2 Apollo Manchester 9N 5 (2H 95)
Oadby Cl. M12: Man 5M 95
Oadby Pl. SK5: Stoc 7D 96
Oak Av. BL0: Ram 3G 25
BL3: Lit L 9B 40
BL6: Hor 3G 37
M21: Cho H 9A 94
M24: Mid 4M 61
M44: Cad 3E 102
M45: Whitef 4M 59
OL2: O'ham 6H 45
SK4: Stoc 6N 107
SK6: Rom 6N 109
SK8: Chea H 5M 117
SK9: Wilm 9E 122
SK11: Macc 7E 130
SK12: Dis 9K 121
WA3: Gol 1L 87
WA11: Hay 2B 86
WA12: N Wil 6F 86
WN2: Abr 3M 71
WN2: Hin 8C 54
WN6: Stan 4C 34
OAK BANK 3N 59
Oak Bank M9: Man 2J 79
M25: Pres 1M 77
(Cumbria Ct.)
M25: Pres 6N 59
(Stanhope Av.)
SK9: A Edg 2F 126
SK12: Dis 9K 121
SK15: C'ook 3J 83
Oakbank WN2: P Bri 8L 53
Oak Bank Av. M9: Man 1L 79
Oakbank Av. OL9: Chad 3C 62
Oak Bank Cl. M45: Whitef 3A 60
Oak Bank Ct. SK10: Boll 4M 129
Oakbank Dr. BL1: Bolt 7E 22
Oakbarton BL6: Los 8L 37
Oakcliffe Rd. M23: Wyth 9N 105
OL12: Roch 1G 29
Oak Cl. OL12: Whitw 2B 14
SK9: Wilm 8E 122
SK14: Mot 5K 99
Oak Coppice BL1: Bolt 5B 38
Oak Cotts. SK9: Sty 2D 122
Oak Ct. SK6: Bred 4L 109
Oakcroft SK15: Stal 2H 99
Oakcroft Way M22: Shar 1D 116
Oakdale BL2: Bolt 9L 23
Oakdale Cl. M45: Whitef 3K 59
Oakdale Ct. OL3: Del 9H 47
WA14: Alt 2A 6 (2C 114)
Oakdale Dr. M20: Man 7H 107
M29: Ast 4D 74
SK8: H Grn 5G 116
Oakdean Ct. SK9: Wilm 5G 122
Oakden Dr. M34: Dent 7G 97
Oakdene M27: Swin 4B 76
WN7: Lei 5J 73
Oakdene Av. SK4: Stoc 3B 108
SK8: H Grn 8G 117
Oak Dene Cl. OL3: G'fld 7K 65
Oakdene Cres. SK6: Mar 9C 110
Oakdene Gdns. SK6: Mar 9C 110
Oakdene Rd. M24: Mid 3A 62
SK6: Mar 1C 120
WA15: Tim 8H 105
Oakdene St. M9: Man 2L 79
Oak Dr. M14: Man 8J 95
M34: Dent 5E 96
SK6: Mar 1A 120
SK7: Bram 8A 118
Oakenbank La.
SK10: Boll, Rain 5N 129
Oaken Bank Rd. OL10: H'ood 7L 43
OAKEN BOTTOM 5L 39
Oakenbottom Rd. BL2: Bolt 6L 39
Oaken Clough OL7: A Lyne 4K 81
Oakenclough OL1: O'ham 1C 8
Oakenclough Cl. SK9: Wilm 4J 123
Oaken Clough Dr. OL7: A Lyne 4K 81
Oakenclough Dr. BL1: Bolt 2A 38
Oaken Clough Ter. OL7: A Lyne 4K 81
Oakenden Cl. WN4: A Mak 4D 70
Oakengates WN6: Stan 3C 34
Oakenrod Hill OL11: Roch 6A 28
Oakenrod Vs. OL11: Roch 6B 28
Oakenshaw Av. OL12: Whitw 8A 14
Oakenshaw Ct. OL12: Whitw 8A 14
Oakenshaw Vw. OL12: Whitw 8A 14
Oaken St. OL7: A Lyne 4L 81
Oaker Av. M20: Man 4D 106
Oakes St. BL4: Kea 4N 57
Oakfield M25: Pres 8C 60
M33: Sale 3G 104
SK16: Duk 3B 98
Oakfield Av. M16: Old T 6N 93
M16: Whall R 6C 94
M43: Droy 9D 80
M46: Ath 7L 55
SK8: Chea 1K 117
SK15: C'ook 4H 83
WA3: Gol 9J 71
WA16: Knut 5J 133
Oakfield Cl. BL6: Hor 2H 37
SK7: Bram 2C 124
SK9: A Edg 2G 127
Oakfield Ct. WA15: Tim 1F 114
Oakfield Cres. WN2: Asp 7M 35
Oakfield Dr. M38: Lit H 6F 56
Oakfield Gro. BL4: Farn 5K 57
M18: Man 5B 96
Oakfield Ho. WA15: Alt 3E 6
Oakfield M. M33: Sale 4G 104
SK3: Stoc 2D 118
Oakfield Rd. M20: Man 5F 106
SK3: Stoc 2D 118
SK8: Chea 5H 117
SK9: A Edg 3G 127
SK12: Poy 2K 125
SK13: Had 6A 100
SK14: Hyde 4B 98
WA15: Alt 2E 6 (2E 114)
Oakfield St. M8: Man 4F 78
WA15: Alt 2E 6 (2E 114)
Oakfield Ter. OL11: Roch 5A 28
Oakfield Trad. Est.
WA15: Alt 2E 6 (2E 114)
Oak Fold SK10: Kerr 7L 129
Oakfold Av. OL6: A Lyne 4A 82
Oakford Av. M40: Man 1N 5 (7H 79)
Oakford Ct. SK13: Had 5B 100
Oakford Wlk. BL3: Bolt 8D 38
Oak Gates BL7: Eger 4F 22
Oak Grn. SK8: Chea H 1K 123
Oak Gro. M30: Ecc 9B 76
M41: Urm 7E 92
OL6: A Lyne 4A 82
SK8: Chea 2K 117
SK12: Poy 2H 125
Oakham Av. M20: Man 9F 94
Oakham Cl. BL8: Bury 8L 25
Oakham M. M7: Sal 1B 78
Oakham Rd. M34: Dent 8L 97
Oakhead WN7: Lei 7L 73
Oak Hill OL15: Lit 9K 15
Oak Hill Cl. WN1: Wig 9E 34
Oakhill Cl. BL2: Bolt 5A 40
SK10: Macc 9F 128
Oakhill Ct. M7: Sal 3D 78
Oakhill Trad. Est. M28: Walk 5K 57
Oakhill Way *M8: Man 3E 78*
(off Greenland St.)
Oak Ho. M14: Man 8J 95
Oakhouse Dr. M21: Cho H 1A 106
Oakhurst Av. OL12: Roch 9H 15
Oakhurst Chase SK9: A Edg 3F 126
Oakhurst Dr. SK3: Stoc 2N 117
Oakhurst Gdns. M25: Pres 7N 59
Oakhurst Gro. BL5: W'ton 4F 54
Oakington Av. *M14: Man 6G 95*
(off Heald Pl.)
Oakland Av. M6: Sal 6G 77
M16: Old T 5N 93
M19: Man 4K 107
SK2: Stoc 1G 119
Oakland Ct. SK12: Poy 2H 125
WN2: Hin 8C 54
(off Basswood Grn.)
Oakland Gro. BL1: Bolt 2B 38
Oakland Ho. M16: Old T 4N 93
Oaklands BL1: Bolt 5A 38
Oaklands, The OL11: Roch 3A 44
Oaklands Av. SK6: Mar B 8F 110
SK8: Chea H 5M 117
Oaklands Cl. SK9: Wilm 5K 123
Oaklands Ct. OL4: G'fld 6J 65
Oaklands Dene SK14: Hyde 7D 98
Oaklands Dr. M25: Pres 7A 60
M33: Sale 3G 105
SK7: H Gro 6J 119
Oaklands Ho. M14: Man 8H 95
Oaklands Pk. OL4: G'fld 6H 65
Oaklands Rd. BL0: Ram 4K 11
M7: Sal 3N 77
M27: Swin 4D 76
OL2: O'ham 1J 63
OL3: G'fld 6J 65
OL4: G'fld 6J 65
SK14: Hyde 7D 98
WA3: Low 2B 88
WA16: Olle 9M 133
Oakland Ter. OL11: Roch 3A 44
Oak La. M45: Whitef 3A 60
SK9: Wilm 8E 122
SK10: Kerr 8L 129
Oak Lea *M16: Old T 6B 94*
(off Up. Chorlton Rd.)
Oaklea WN6: Stan 2L 33
Oak Lea Av. SK9: Wilm 9F 122
Oaklea Rd. M33: Sale 3E 104
Oakleigh SK3: Stoc 3D 118
SK4: Stoc 5N 107
(off Heaton Moor Rd.)
WA16: Knut 9J 133
WN8: Skel 9B 50
Oakleigh Av. BL3: Bolt 1H 57
M19: Man 1L 107
WA15: Tim 9G 105
Oakleigh Cl. OL10: H'ood 5K 43
Oakleigh Ct. WA15: Tim 9J 105
Oakleigh Ho. M33: Sale 5E 104
SK10: Boll 5M 129
(off Hamson Dr.)
Oakleigh M. M33: Sale 5E 104
Oakleigh Rd. SK8: Chea H 7K 117
Oakley Av. WN5: Bil 4J 69
Oakley Cl. M26: Rad 3G 58
M40: Man 5A 80
Oakley Dr. OL1: O'ham 8A 46
WN5: Wig 5B 52
Oakley Pk. BL1: Bolt 5A 38
Oakley St. OL15: Lit 1J 29
Oakley Vs. SK4: Stoc 5N 107
Oaklings, The WN2: Hin 8C 54
Oak Lodge SK7: Bram 8D 118
Oakmere Av. M30: Ecc 6C 76
Oakmere Cl. M22: Wyth 3C 116
Oakmere Rd. SK8: Chea H 3L 117
SK9: Hand 1J 123
Oak M. SK9: Wilm 5H 123
Oakmoor Dr. M7: Sal 2N 77
Oakmoor Rd. M23: Wyth 1N 115
Oakridge Wlk. *M9: Man 3J 79*
(off Carisbrook St.)
Oak Rd. M7: Sal 4B 78
M20: Man 3G 106
M31: Part 6E 102
M33: Sale 4K 105
M35: Fail 4D 80
OL8: O'ham 9G 63
SK8: Chea 1K 117
SK10: Mot S A, P'bury 4N 127
WA15: Hale 4E 114
WA16: Mob 9A 122
Oaks, The PR7: Chor 1E 18
SK8: H Grn 5F 116
SK13: Glos 9C 100
SK14: Hyde 6D 98
Oaks Av. BL2: Bolt 8K 23
Oaks Bus. Pk. WN8: Uph 7D 50
Oaks Bus. Pk., The M23: Wyth 8L 105
Oakshaw Cl. M9: Man 9J 61
Oakshaw Dr. OL12: Roch 4M 27
Oakside Cl. SK8: Chea 1K 117
Oaks La. BL2: Bolt 8J 23
Oak St. BL0: Ram 9J 11
M4: Man 3J 5 (8F 78)
(not continuous)
M24: Mid 4B 62
M26: Rad 2J 59
M27: Pen 1G 77
M29: Tyld 1B 74
M30: Ecc 9D 76
M34: Aud 3K 97
M46: Ath 1J 73
OL2: Shaw 5N 45
OL10: H'ood 1G 43
OL12: Whitw 2B 14
OL15: Lit 2K 29
(Wesley Ct.)
OL15: Lit 9N 15
(West Vw.)
OL16: Miln 1L 45
OL16: Roch 8C 8 (6D 28)
SK3: Stoc 8N 107
SK7: H Gro 4H 119
SK13: Glos 8E 100
SK14: Hyde 5B 98
WA3: Cro 9C 88
WN1: Wig 8N 9 (3H 53)
WN7: Lei 7H 73
Oak Ter. OL15: Lit 4A 16
Oakthorn Gro. WA11: Hay 3A 86
Oak Tree Cl. M46: Ath 1J 73
SK2: Stoc 8H 109
SK14: Hyde 7D 98
Oaktree Cotts. SK8: Chea H 4L 117
Oak Tree Ct. SK8: Chea 2K 117
WN8: Skel 9B 32
Oak Tree Cres. SK15: Stal 1D 98
Oak Tree Dr. SK16: Duk 2C 98
Oak Vw. OL12: Whitw 1B 14
WA16: Knut 7J 133
Oak Vw. Rd. OL3: G'fld 6L 65
Oak Vs. SK15: C'ook 3K 83
Oakville Dr. M6: Sal 6G 77
Oakville Ter. M40: Man 1L 79
Oak Wlk. M34: Aud 3J 97
Oakwater Av. SK8: H Grn 5H 117
Oakway M20: Man 8H 107
M24: Mid 8L 43
Oakwell Dr. BL9: Bury 9A 42
M7: Sal 1D 78
Oakwell Mans. M7: Sal 1D 78
Oakwood M27: Clif 7E 58
M33: Sale 4C 104
OL9: Chad 4C 62
SK13: Glos 9B 100
WN8: Skel 9B 32
Oakwood Av. M27: Clif 7E 58
M28: Walk 9N 57
M34: Aud 2J 97
M40: Man 1B 80
SK8: Gat 2G 116
SK9: Wilm 8D 122
WN4: A Mak 8D 70
WN6: She 7K 33
Oakwood Cl. BL8: Bury 1H 41
Oakwood Ct. OL7: A Lyne 5C 6 (6M 81)
WA14: Bow 7B 114
Oakwood Dr. BL1: Bolt 4A 38
M6: Sal 5H 77
M28: Walk 9N 57
SK10: P'bury 7G 128
WN7: Lei 9G 73
Oakwood Est. M5: Sal 9K 77
Oakwood Gro. M26: Rad 7J 41
Oakwood Ho. M21: Cho H 9B 94
Oakwood La. WA14: Bow 6A 114
Oakwood Rd. PR7: Cop 3C 18
SK6: Rom 6N 109
SK12: Dis 9G 121
Oakwood Sq. SK8: H Grn 5H 117
Oakwood Vw. PR7: Chor 1E 18
Oakworth Cft. OL4: O'ham 8C 46
Oakworth Dr. BL1: Bolt 8E 22
Oakworth St. M9: Man 9H 61
Oatlands SK9: A Edg 5G 127
Oatlands Rd. M22: Wyth 6B 116
Oat St. SK1: Stoc 9E 108
Oban Av. M40: Man 6N 79
OL1: O'ham 2M 63
Oban Cres. SK3: Stoc 3B 118
Oban Dr. M33: Sale 5L 105
WN4: Gars 6N 69
Oban Gro. BL1: Bolt 8F 22
Oban St. BL1: Bolt 1E 38
Oban Way WN2: Asp 7N 35
Oberlin St. OL4: O'ham 4A 64
OL11: Roch 8B 28
Oberon Cl. *M30: Ecc 8D 76*
(off Shakespeare Cres.)
Observer Bldg. WN1: Wig 8K 9
Occleston Cl. M33: Sale 7L 105
Occupation Rd. WA14: Alt 1D 114
Occupiers La. SK7: H Gro 6L 119
Ocean Ho. *M15: Man 4F 94*
(off Boundary La.)
Ocean St. WA14: B'ath 1B 114
Ocean St. Trad. Est.
WA14: B'ath 1B 114
Ocean Wlk. *M15: Man 4E 94*
(off Crediton Cl.)
Ockendon Dr. M9: Man 3K 79
Octagon Ct. BL1: Bolt 3K 7 (5G 38)
Octagon Theatre 3K 7 (5G 38)
Octavia Dr. M40: Man 6A 80
Oddfellow Hall OL6: A Lyne 8C 6
Oddies Yd. *OL12: Roch 3E 28*
(off Isabella St.)
Odell St. M11: Man 2N 95
Odeon Cinema
Manchester 2H 5 (8F 78)
Rochdale 9C 28
The Trafford Cen. 3E 92
Odessa Av. M6: Sal 6H 77
Odette St. M18: Man 5A 96
OFFERTON 2J 119
Offerton Dr. SK2: Stoc 1H 119
Offerton Fold SK2: Stoc 9G 109
OFFERTON GREEN 1L 119
Offerton Grn. SK2: Stoc 1K 119
Offerton Ind. Est. SK2: Stoc 9G 108
Offerton La. SK2: Stoc 8F 108
Offerton Rd. SK2: H Gro, Stoc 4L 119
SK7: H Gro 4L 119
Offerton St. BL6: Hor 1C 36
SK1: Stoc 6F 108
Off Green St. M24: Mid 2N 61
Off Grove Rd. SK15: Mill 6G 82
Off Kershaw St. *OL2: Shaw 5M 45*
(off Kershaw St. E.)
Off Ridge Hill La. *SK15: Stal 8C 82*
(off Ridge Hill La.)
Off Stamford St. *SK15: Mill 6G 83*
(off Stamford St.)
Off Vaudrey La. M34: Dent 7L 97
Ogbourne Wlk. *M13: Man 3H 95*
(off Lauderdale Cres.)
OGDEN 8C 30
Ogden Cl. M45: Whitef 2N 59
OL10: H'ood 2F 42
Ogden Ct. *SK14: Hyde 7B 98*
(off Frank St.)
Ogden Gdns. SK16: Duk 1B 98
Ogden Gro. SK8: Gat 3E 116
Ogden La. M11: Man 2B 96
OL16: Miln 8A 30
Ogden Rd. M35: Fail 4D 80
SK7: Bram 1A 124
Ogden Sq. SK16: Duk 1M 97
Ogden St. M20: Man 5G 107
M24: Mid 3M 61
M25: Pres 7B 60
M27: Swin 3F 76
OL4: O'ham 5A 64
OL9: Chad 3F 62
OL11: Roch 2A 44
SK14: B'tom 9L 99
Ogden Wlk. M45: Whitef 3N 59
Ogmore Wlk. M40: Man 9A 62
Ogwen Dr. M25: Pres 6A 60
Ohio Av. M50: Sal 1M 93
O'Kane Ho. *M30: Ecc 9D 76*
(off Cawdor St.)
Okehampton Cl. M26: Rad 7C 40
Okehampton Cres.
M33: Sale 3D 104
Okell Gro. WN7: Lei 4F 72
Okeover Rd. M7: Sal 2C 78
Olaf St. BL2: Bolt 3J 39
Olanyian Dr. M8: Sal 5D 78
Old Bakery, The BL5: W'ton 3H 55
Old Bank Cl. SK6: Bred 5L 109
Old Bank St. M2: Man 4G 4 (9E 78)
Old Bank Vw. OL1: O'ham 8N 45
Old Barn Pl. BL7: Bro X 5H 23
Old Barton Rd. M41: Urm 2D 92
Old Beechfield Gdns.
WN6: Stan 4A 34
Old Bent La. OL12: W'le 7E 14
Old Birley St. M15: Man 4E 94
OLD BIRTLE 6D 26
Old Boat Yd., The M28: Wors 5A 76
OLD BOSTON 2C 86
Old Boston WA11: Hay 1D 86
Old Boston Trad. Est. WA11: Hay 1E 86
Oldbridge Dr. WN2: Hin 5N 53
Old Broadway M20: Man 3G 107
Old Brook Cl. OL2: Shaw 4A 46
Oldbrook Fold WA15: Tim 3H 115
Old Brow OL5: Mos 1F 82
(Mayall St.)
OL5: Mos 2F 82
(Round Hey)
Old Brow Ct. OL5: Mos 2F 82
Old Brow La. *OL16: Roch 2G 29*
(off Wheelwright Dr.)
Oldbury Cl. M40: Man 1N 5 (7J 79)
OL10: H'ood 5J 43
Oldcastle Av. M20: Man 9F 94
Old Chapel Ct. PR6: Adl 6K 19
Old Chapel St. SK3: Stoc 9A 108
Old Church M. SK16: Duk 1B 98
Old Church St. M40: Man 4N 79
OL1: O'ham 2E 8 (4K 63)
Old Clay Dr. OL12: Roch 1G 29
Old Clough La. M28: Walk, Wors 1N 75
(not continuous)
Old Colliers Row BL1: Bolt 8N 21
Old Colliery Yd. WN4: Gars 7N 69
Oldcott Cl. M28: Wors 5G 75
Old Court House, The M3: Sal 3B 4
Old Court St. SK14: Hyde 7A 98
Old Courtyard, The M22: Shar 2D 116
Old Croft OL4: Spri 5D 64
Oldcroft M. SK1: Stoc 9F 108
Old Crofts Bank M41: Urm 5C 92
Old Cross *SK13: Glos 7G 100*
(off Shepley St.)
Old Cross St. OL6: A Lyne 7E 6 (7N 81)
Old Dairy M. SK14: Hyde 4N 97
Old Delph Rd. OL11: Roch 4K 27
Old Doctors St. BL8: Tot 6F 24
Old Eagley M. BL1: Bolt 7G 22
Old Edge La. OL2: O'ham 1J 63
Old Elm St. M12: Man 3H 95
Old Engine La. BL0: Ram 8K 11
Oldershaw Dr. M9: Man 4J 79
Olde Stoneheath Ct.
PR6: H Char 1L 19
Old Farm Cl. SK10: Macc 2E 130
Old Farm Cres. M43: Droy 1D 96
Old Farm Dr. SK2: Stoc 1K 119
Old Farm M. SK8: Chea H 8A 118
OLDFIELD BROW 1A 114
Oldfield Cl. BL5: W'ton 3H 55
Oldfield Dr. WA15: Tim 1F 114
WA16: Mob 4N 133
Oldfield Gro. M33: Sale 3J 105
Oldfield La. WA14: D Mas 3M 113
Oldfield M. WA14: Alt 2A 6 (2C 114)
Oldfield Rd. M5: Sal 7A 4 (2B 94)
M25: Pres 4B 60
M33: Sale 3J 105
WA14: Alt 1A 6 (2A 114)
Oldfield St. M11: Man 9N 79
Old Fold M30: Ecc 6C 76
SK7: H Gro 3H 119
WN5: Wig 5M 51
Old Fold Rd. BL5: W'ton 4D 54
WN2: Asp 7N 35
Old Garden, The WA15: Tim 9H 105
Old Gardens St.
SK1: Stoc 4M 9 (8D 108)
Oldgate Wlk. *M15: Man 3C 94*
(off Shawheath Cl.)
OLD GLOSSOP 7G 101
Old Green BL2: Bolt 7M 23
BL8: G'mount 4F 24
Old Greenwood La. BL6: Hor 3F 36
Old Ground St. BL0: Ram 8J 11
Old Hall 1H 133
Old Hall Cl. BL8: Bury 6H 25
SK13: Glos 7C 100
SK14: Mot 4K 99
Old Hall Clough BL6: Los 5L 37
(not continuous)
Old Hall Ct. M33: Sale 4L 105
M45: Whitef 4J 59
Old Hall Cres. SK9: Hand 3K 123
Old Hall Dr. M18: Man 5B 96
SK2: Stoc 1J 119
WN4: A Mak 8D 70
Old Hall Fold SK13: Had 4B 100
Old Hall La. BL5: W'ton 6G 55
BL6: Bolt 3L 37
M13: Man 7K 95
M14: Man 8J 95
M19: Man 7K 95
M24: Man 5F 60
M25: Pres 3E 60
M28: Wors 3M 75
M45: Whitef 4J 59
SK6: Mel 2E 120
SK7: W'ford 5B 124
SK14: Mot 4K 99
WA16: O Tab 4K 133
Old Hall M. BL1: Bolt 3M 37
Old Hall Mill La. M46: Ath 2J 73
Old Hall Rd. M7: Sal 1C 78
M32: Stre 5G 92
M33: Sale 4L 105
M40: Man 3N 79
M45: Whitef 4J 59
SK8: Gat 1F 116
Old Hall Sq. SK13: Had 4C 100
Old Hall St. BL4: Farn 4M 57
M11: Man 2C 96
M24: Mid 2M 61
SK10: Macc 3H 131
SK16: Duk 2L 97
WN3: I Mak 5H 53
Old Hall St. Nth.
BL1: Bolt 2K 7 (5G 38)
OLDHAM 2D 8 (4K 63)
Oldham Athletic FC 1H 63
Oldham Av. SK1: Stoc 7F 108
Oldham B'way. Bus. Pk.
OL9: Chad 7C 62
Oldham Bus. Cen. OL1: O'ham 4D 8
Oldham Central Trad. Pk.
OL1: O'ham 3L 63
Oldham Climbing Wall 2D 8
Oldham Coliseum Theatre
2E 8 (4K 63)
Oldham Ct. M40: Man 1N 5 (7H 79)

Oldham Crematorium
OL8: O'ham 1G 81
Oldham Dr. SK6: Bred 4L 109
OLDHAM EDGE 3K 63
Oldham Golf Course 7C 64
Oldham Ho. OL2: Shaw 7M 45
Oldham Mumps Stop (Metro) 3G 8 (5L 63)
Oldham Rd. M4: Man 2L 5 (8G 79)
M24: Mid 3M 61
M35: Fail 4N 79
M40: Man 2L 5 (8G 79) (Addington St.)
M40: Man 4N 79 (Erwin St.)
OL1: Dens 6D 46
OL2: O'ham 8J 45
OL2: O'ham, Shaw 8M 45
OL3: Del, Dob 2G 64
OL3: Dens 6D 46
OL3: Upp 5K 65
OL4: Gras, G'fld, Grot, Lyd, Spri 5C 64
OL6: A Lyne 6C 6 (7M 81)
OL7: A Lyne 5B 6 (3L 81)
OL11: Roch 9E 28 (not continuous)
OL16: Roch 8D 8 (7E 28)
Oldham Roughyeds RLFC 1J 81
Oldhams La. BL1: Bolt 8E 22 (not continuous)
Oldham Sports Cen. 2D 8 (4K 63)
Oldham Sq. SK22: N Mil 8M 121
Oldhams Ri. SK10: Macc 9H 129
Oldhams Ter. BL1: Bolt 8E 22
Oldham St. M1: Man 4J 5 (9F 78)
M4: Man 8G 78
M34: Dent 7G 97
M43: Droy 8F 80
SK5: Stoc 1C 108
SK10: Boll 5M 129
SK14: Hyde 7A 98
Oldham Way OL1: O'ham 4D 8 (3H 63)
OL4: O'ham 4D 8 (3H 63)
OL8: O'ham 1A 8 (3H 63)
OL9: O'ham 1A 8 (3H 63)
Oldham Werneth Stop (Metro) 4A 8 (5H 63)
Old Heyes Rd. WA15: Tim 8H 105
Old Hey Wlk. WA12: N Wil 8F 86
Old House Ter. OL6: A Lyne 5B 82
Old Kays BL8: Tot 5E 24
Old Kiln La. BL1: Bolt 2L 37
OL4: Grot 7E 64
Oldknow Rd. SK6: Mar 1D 120
Old La. BL5: W'ton 4F 54
BL6: Hor 2H 37
BL9: Bury 5M 25
M11: Man 1B 96
M38: Lit H 5G 57
OL3: Dob 1L 65
OL3: Upp 2N 65
OL4: Aus 3D 64
OL4: Gras 5H 65
OL9: Chad 7F 62
OL12: Bac, Whitw 1B 14
WN1: Wig 8E 34
WN6: She 6M 33
Old Lansdowne Rd. M20: Man 4E 106
Old Lees St. OL6: A Lyne 5A 82
Old Links Cl. BL1: Bolt 2N 37
Old Lord's Cres. BL6: Hor 8D 20
Old Manor, The OL12: Roch 4C 28
Old Manor Pk. M46: Ath 9J 55
Old Market Pl.
WA14: Alt 2D 6 (2D 114)
WA16: Knut 6G 132
Old Market St. M9: Man 9H 61
Old Meadow SK11: Macc 4G 131
Old Meadow Dr. M34: Dent 4K 97
Old Meadow La. WA15: Hale 4H 115
Old Medlock St. M3: Man 6C 4 (1C 94)
Old Mill Cl. M27: Pen 2H 77
WA13: Lym 1D 112
Old Mill Ho. OL4: Grot 6D 64
Old Mill La. OL4: Grot 6D 64
SK7: H Gro 7L 119
SK11: Macc 6J 131
Old Mills Hill M24: Mid 2B 62
Old Mill St. M4: Man 4M 5 (9H 79)
Oldmill St. OL12: Roch 5C 8 (5D 28)
Old Mill Wharf M43: Droy 1E 96
Old Moat La. M20: Man 1F 106
Oldmoor Rd. SK6: Bred 3J 109
Old Moss La. WA3: G'ury 3M 89
Old Mount Rd. HD7: Mars 3F 48
Old Mount St. M4: Man 1J 5 (7G 78)
Old Nans La. BL2: Bolt 2N 39
Old Nursery Fold BL2: Bolt 9M 23
Old Oak Cl. BL2: Bolt 7B 40
Old Oak Cotts. BL8: Haw 3E 24
Old Oak Dr. M34: Dent 6L 97
Old Oake Cl. M28: Walk 9M 57
Old Oak St. M20: Man 5G 107
Old Orchard SK9: Wilm 7F 122
Old Orchard, The WA15: Tim 8H 105
Old Pack Horse Rd. OL3: Del 6L 47
Old Packhorse Rd. HX6: Ripp 8D 16
OL15: Lit 8C 16
Old Park La. M17: Urm 3C 92
Old Parrin La. M30: Ecc 7B 76
Old Pasture Cl. SK2: Stoc 9J 109
Old Penny La. WA11: Hay 1E 86
Old Pepper La. WN6: Stan 2M 33
Old Quarry La. BL7: Eger 4G 22
Old Rake BL6: Hor 8F 20
Old Rectory Gdns. SK8: Chea 1J 117
Old Ribbon Mill, The
SK11: Macc 6H 131 (off Pitt St.)
Old River Cl. M44: Irl 7H 91
Old Rd. BL1: Bolt 9F 22
M9: Man 9J 61
M35: Fail 3C 80
OL6: A Lyne 5C 82
OL16: Roch 1J 29
Old Rd. SK4: Stoc 5C 108
SK8: Chea 1L 117
SK9: Hand 3J 123
SK9: Wilm 6G 123
SK13: Tin 2C 100
SK14: Hyde 4A 98
SK14: Mot 3J 99
SK15: Stal 1F 98
SK16: Duk 9N 81 (not continuous)
WN4: A Mak 6D 70
Old School Ct. M9: Man 9H 61 (off Old School Dr.)
M30: Ecc 6D 76
Old School Dr. M9: Man 9H 61
Old School Ho., The OL15: Lit 8K 15
Old School La. PR7: Adl 8H 19
SK8: Chea H 7M 117
Old School M. SK16: Duk 1B 98 (off Vicarage Dr.)
Old School Pl. OL12: W'le 8G 15
WN4: A Mak 8D 70
Old School Rooms, The BL1: Bolt 4L 7
Old Shaw St. M5: Sal 1N 93
OLD SIRS 7G 55
Old Sirs BL5: W'ton 6H 55
Old Smithy Rd. SK22: N Mil 8M 121
Old Square OL6: A Lyne 7E 6 (7N 81)
Old Stables, The M34: Aud 3K 97
Old Station St. M30: Ecc 9C 76
Oldstead Gro. BL3: Bolt 8A 38
Oldstead Wlk. M9: Man 4J 79 (off Kelvington Dr.)
Old St. OL4: O'ham 6A 64
OL6: A Lyne 8B 6 (8L 81)
SK14: B'tom 9K 99
SK15: Stal 8D 82
Old Swan Cl. BL7: Eger 3F 22
OLD TAME 4E 46
Old Tannery, The SK14: Hyde 9C 98
Old Thorn La. OL3: G'fld 5N 65
Old Towns Cl. BL8: Tot 6F 24
OLD TRAFFORD 4A 94
Old Trafford 4M 93
Old Trafford Cricket Ground 6M 93
Old Trafford Sports Barn 5A 94
Old Trafford Stop (Metro) 5N 93
Old Vicarage BL5: W'ton 6G 55
Old Vicarage Gdns. M28: Walk 8L 57
Old Vicarage M. BL5: W'ton 6G 55
Old Vicarage Rd. BL6: Hor 1H 37
Old Wargrave Rd. WA12: N Wil 6E 86
Oldway Wlk. M40: Man 5N 79
Old Wellington Rd. M30: Ecc 8D 76
Old Wells Cl. M38: Lit H 5H 57
Old Well Wlk. M33: Sale 6C 104
Old Will's La. BL6: R'ton 7D 20
Old Wood La. BL2: Ain, Bolt 4A 40
Oldwood Rd. M23: Wyth 4N 115
Old Wool La. SK8: Chea H 2L 117 (not continuous)
Old York St. M15: Man 3D 94
Oleo Ter. M44: Irl 6K 91
Olga St. BL1: Bolt 2E 38
Olivant St. BL9: Bury 4L 41
Olive Bank BL8: Bury 9H 25
Olive Gro. WN6: Wig 9C 34
Oliver Cl. OL15: Lit 9K 15
SK10: Boll 6K 129
Oliver Fold Cl. M28: Wors 4F 74
Oliver La. HD7: Mars 1H 49
Olive Rd. WA15: Tim 8G 104
Olivers Ct. OL9: O'ham 5G 63
Oliver St. M46: Ath 8K 55
SK1: Stoc 5K 9 (8D 108)
Olive Shapley Av. M20: Man 5G 107
Olive Stanring Ho. OL15: Lit 8N 15
Olive St. BL3: Bolt 8E 38
BL8: Bury 2K 41
M26: Rad 9J 41
M35: Fail 2C 80
OL10: H'ood 2K 43
OL11: Roch 3A 44
Olive Ter. SK14: B'tom 9K 99
Olive Wlk. M33: Sale 2C 104 (off Epping Dr.)
Olivia Ct. M5: Sal 7A 4 (1B 94)
Olivia Gro. M14: Man 6J 95
Olivier Ho. WA14: Alt 4D 6
Ollerbarrow Rd. WA15: Hale 5E 114
Ollerbrook Ct. BL1: Bolt 2G 38
Ollerenshaw Hall M14: Man 5J 95 (off Daisy Bank Hall)
Ollersett Av. SK22: N Mil 7M 121
Ollersett Dr. SK22: N Mil 7N 121
Ollersett Ho. SK22: N Mil 7N 121 (off Ollersett Dr.)
Ollersett La. SK22: N Mil 6N 121
OLLERTON 9M 133
Ollerton BL2: Bolt 5B 8
Ollerton Av. M16: Old T 6B 94
M33: Sale 2D 104
Ollerton Cl. M22: Nor 7D 106
WN2: Asp 1K 53
Ollerton Ct. M16: Old T 7A 94 (off Manchester Rd.)
Ollerton Dr. M35: Fail 4D 80
Ollerton Rd. SK9: Hand 1J 123
Ollerton St. BL1: Bolt 7G 22
PR6: Adl 4K 19
Ollerton Ter. BL1: Bolt 7G 23
Ollier Av. M12: Man 7M 95
Olney OL11: Roch 9B 8 (7C 28)
Olney Av. M22: Wyth 1C 116
Olney St. M13: Man 5J 95
Olsberg Cl. M26: Rad 8J 41
Olwen Av. M12: Man 4M 95
Olwen Cres. SK5: Stoc 9D 96
Olympia Ct. M44: Irl 7H 91
Olympia Trad. Est.
M15: Man 8E 4 (2D 94)
Olympic Ct. M50: Sal 1M 93
Olympic Ho. M90: Man A 8A 116
Olympic St. M11: Man 1K 95
Omega Circ. M44: Irl 2G 103
Omega Dr. M44: Irl 2G 103
Omer Av. M13: Man 7L 95
Omer Dr. M19: Man 1K 107
Onchan Av. OL4: O'ham 5M 63
One Ash Cl. OL12: Roch 3D 28
One Oak Ct. SK7: Bram 5A 118
One Oak La. SK9: Wilm 7L 123
Ongar Wlk. M9: Man 8G 61
Onslow Av. M40: Man 1C 80
Onslow Cl. OL1: O'ham 3J 63
Onslow Rd. SK3: Stoc 8A 108
Onslow St. OL11: Roch 9A 28
Ontario Ho. M50: Sal 2N 93
Onward St. SK14: Hyde 7A 98
OOZEWOOD 6G 45
Oozewood Rd. OL2: O'ham 7E 44
Opal Ct. M14: Man 9J 95
Opal Gdns. M14: Man 5J 95
Opal Gro. WN7: Lei 6G 73
Opal Hall M15: Man 9H 5 (3F 94)
Opal St. M19: Man 9N 95
OPENSHAW 1N 95
Openshaw Ct. M27: Clif 9G 58
Openshaw Fold BL9: Bury 5K 41
Openshaw Fold Rd.
BL9: Bury 4K 41
Openshaw La. M44: Cad 2F 102 (off Prospect Av.)
Openshaw Pl. BL4: Farn 3J 57
Openshaw St. BL9: Bury 9N 7 (3N 41)
Openshaw Wlk. M11: Man 9A 80 (off Greenside St.)
Opera House 5E 4 (9D 78)
Oracle Ct. M28: Walk 9L 57 (off Sparta Av.)
Orama Av. M6: Sal 6G 77
Oram St. BL9: Bury 9N 25 (not continuous)
Orange Hill Rd. M25: Pres 6B 60
Orbital 24 M34: Dent 6H 97
Orbital Way M34: Dent 6H 97
Orbit Ho. M30: Ecc 8F 76 (off Albert St.)
Orchard, The BL5: W'ton 2G 54
OL8: O'ham 8N 63
SK9: A Edg 5G 126
Orchard Av. BL1: Bolt 2C 38
M18: Man 5C 96 (off Woodland Rd.)
M28: Wors 3J 75
M31: Part 4G 103
WA13: Lym 4A 112
Orchard Brow OL2: Shaw 5K 45 (off Surrey Av.)
WA3: Rix 6B 102
Orchard Cl. SK8: Chea H 8A 118
SK9: Wilm 9E 122
SK11: Macc 6F 130
SK12: Poy 3J 125
WN6: She 5L 33
WN7: Lei 3H 73
Orchard Ct. BL9: Bury 5L 41
SK2: Stoc 1H 119
WA3: Cro 9C 88
WA15: Tim 9H 105
WN5: Bil 8H 51
Orchard Cres. SK10: N Ald 6E 126
Orchard Dr. SK9: Hand 4K 123
SK13: Gam 8A 100
WA15: Hale 4G 114
Orchard Gdns. BL2: Bolt 1N 39
SK8: Gat 1E 116
Orchard Grn. SK9: A Edg 4G 126
Orchard Gro. M20: Man 3E 106
OL2: Shaw 5L 45
Orchard Ind. Est. M6: Sal 6N 77
Orchard La. WN7: Lei 3H 73
Orchard Pl. M33: Sale 3H 105
SK12: Poy 2H 125
WA15: Tim 9H 105
Orchard Ri. SK14: Hyde 1C 110
Orchard Rd. M35: Fail 3D 80
SK6: Comp 6E 110
WA13: Lym 2C 112
WA15: Alt 1F 6 (2E 114)
Orchard Rd. E. M22: Nor 6C 106
Orchard Rd. W. M22: Nor 6C 106
Orchards, The OL2: Shaw 5L 45
OL10: H'ood 2K 43 (off Orchard St.)
SK3: Stoc 3D 118
WN5: Orr 6J 51
Orchard St. BL4: Farn 4M 57
M6: Sal 5N 77 (not continuous)
M20: Man 3E 106
OL10: H'ood 1K 43
SK1: Stoc 3M 9 (7D 108)
SK14: Hyde 7B 98
WN1: Wig 7L 9 (3G 52)
WN4: A Mak 7F 70
Orchard Trad. Est. M6: Sal 5M 77
Orchard Va. SK3: Stoc 1A 118
Orchard Wlk. BL8: G'mount 4F 24 (off Lomax St.)
Orchid Av. BL4: Farn 2J 57
Orchid Cl. M44: Irl 9F 90
OL1: O'ham 2H 63
WN8: Uph 5F 50
Orchid Dr. BL9: Bury 4N 41
Orchid St. M9: Man 3J 79
Orchid Way OL12: Roch 2B 28
Ordell Wlk. M9: Man 8K 61
Ordinal St. M17: T Pk 3K 93
Ordnance St. M30: Ecc 8D 76
ORDSALL 2A 94
Ordsall Av. M38: Lit H 7J 57
Ordsall District Cen. M5: Sal 1A 94
Ordsall Hall Mus. 3A 94
Ordsall La. M5: Sal 8A 4 (3A 94)
Oregon Av. OL1: O'ham 2J 63
Oregon Cl. M13: Man 3H 95
Orford Av. SK12: Dis 9G 121
Orford Cl. SK6: H Lan 8B 120
WA3: Gol 2K 87
Orford Ct. WN7: Lei 8K 73
Orford Pk. WN7: Lei 8K 73
Orford Rd. M25: Pres 6A 60
M40: Man 5A 80
Organ St. WN2: Hin 8D 54
WN7: Lei 5G 73
Organ Way SK14: Holl 4N 99
Oriel Av. OL8: O'ham 8J 63
Oriel Cl. OL9: Chad 6E 62
SK2: Stoc 1F 118
Oriel Ct. M33: Sale 3H 105
Oriel Rd. M20: Man 4F 106
WN4: A Mak 6C 70
Oriel St. BL3: Bolt 7D 38
OL11: Roch 8D 28
Orient, The M17: Urm 3D 92 (in The Trafford Cen.)
Orient Dr. OL7: A Lyne 7K 81
Orient Ho. M1: Man 7J 5
Orient Rd. M6: Sal 6G 77
Orient St. M7: Sal 3E 78
Oriole Dr. M28: Wors 2J 75
Oriole Ho. M19: Man 5J 107
Orion Bus. Pk. SK3: Stoc 2A 118
Orion Pl. M7: Sal 6B 78
Orion Trad. Est. M17: T Pk 1G 93
Orkney Cl. M23: Wyth 3N 115
M26: Rad 8H 41
Orkney Dr. M41: Urm 4D 92
Orlanda Av. M6: Sal 6G 77
Orlanda Dr. M7: Sal 4E 78
Orlando St. BL2: Bolt 7H 39 (not continuous)
BL3: Bolt 7H 39
Orleans Way OL1: O'ham 1C 8 (4J 63)
Orley Wlk. OL1: O'ham 8A 46
Orme Av. M6: Sal 5H 77
M24: Mid 4M 61
Orme Cl. M11: Man 9K 79
M41: Urm 7F 92
SK10: Macc 1H 131
SK10: P'bury 5E 128
Orme Cres. SK10: Macc 1H 131
Ormerod Av. OL2: O'ham 9J 45
Ormerod Cl. SK6: Rom 7K 109
Ormerod St. OL10: H'ood 3K 43
Ormeston Lodge M41: Urm 8D 92
Orme St. M11: Man 9K 79
OL4: O'ham 5F 8 (6L 63)
SK9: A Edg 4F 126
Ormonde Av. M6: Sal 6H 77
Ormonde Ct. OL6: A Lyne 6N 81
Ormonde St. OL6: A Lyne 6N 81
Ormond St. BL3: Bolt 7L 39
BL9: Bury 6N 7 (1N 41)
Ormrods, The BL9: Bury 8E 26
Ormrod St. BL2: Bolt 9K 23
BL3: Bolt 4J 7 (6F 38)
BL4: Farn 3K 57
BL9: Bury 8N 7 (2N 41)
Ormsby Av. M18: Man 5N 95
Ormsby Cl. SK3: Stoc 3C 118
WN6: Stan 2B 34
Orms Gill Pl. SK2: Stoc 1J 119
Ormsgill St. M15: Man 4E 94
Ormside Cl. WN2: Hin 7D 54
Ormskirk Av. M20: Man 2E 106
Ormskirk Cl. BL8: Bury 4F 40
Ormskirk Rd. SK5: Stoc 2D 108
WN5: Wig 5M 51
WN8: Skel 3A 50
WN8: Uph 4D 50
Ormston Av. BL6: Hor 8D 20
Ormston Gro. WN7: Lei 3H 73
Ormstons La. BL6: Hor 7F 20
Ornatus St. BL1: Bolt 8G 23
Ornsay Wlk. M11: Man 9A 80 (off Bob Massey Cl.)
Oronsay Gro. M5: Sal 9K 77
Orphanage St. SK4: Stoc 5C 108
Orpington Dr. BL8: Bury 3H 41
Orpington Rd. M9: Man 3K 79 (off Vernon St.)
Orpington St. WN5: Wig 5N 51
ORRELL 6H 51
Orrell Gdns. WN5: Orr 5K 51
Orrell Hall Cl. WN5: Orr 3M 51
ORRELL POST 4J 51
Orrell Rd. WN5: Orr 4H 51
Orrell Station (Rail) 7J 51
Orrell St. BL8: Bury 1K 41
M11: Man 1B 96
WN1: Wig 4G 52
Orrell Water Pk. 8J 51
Orrel St. M6: Sal 8L 77
Orrishmere Rd. SK8: Chea H 4L 117
Orron St. OL15: Lit 9L 15
Orsett Cl. M40: Man 1N 5 (7H 79)
Orthes Gro. SK4: Stoc 3B 108
Orton Av. M23: Wyth 7N 105
Orton Rd. M23: Wyth 7N 105
Orton Way WN4: A Mak 7C 70
Orvietto Av. M6: Sal 6G 77
Orville Dr. M19: Man 1L 107
Orwell Av. M22: Wyth 1C 116
M34: Dent 6E 96
Orwell Cl. BL8: Bury 9K 25
SK9: Wilm 4J 123
WN6: Stan 9B 34
Orwell Rd. BL1: Bolt 2C 38
Osborne Cl. BL8: Bury 4H 41
SK9: Wilm 8J 123
Osborne Ct. M46: Ath 8L 55
Osborne Dr. M27: Pen 3J 77
Osborne Gro. BL1: Bolt 3D 38
SK8: H Grn 4F 116
WN7: Lei 4M 73
Osborne Ho. M26: Rad 9E 40 (off Bolton Rd.)
M30: Ecc 8C 76 (off Queen Victoria St.)
Osborne Pl. SK13: Had 4C 100
Osborne Rd. M6: Sal 8G 77
M9: Man 3K 79
M19: Man 8L 95
M34: Dent 5K 97
OL8: O'ham 6H 63
SK2: Stoc 9D 108
Osborne Rd. SK14: Hyde 8B 98
WA3: Low 2A 88
WA15: Alt 2E 6 (2E 114)
WN4: A Mak 6D 70
Osborne St. M6: Sal 7M 77
M20: Man 5F 106
M40: Man 6H 79
OL2: Shaw 6M 45
OL9: O'ham 3G 63
OL10: H'ood 3J 43
OL11: Roch 8C 28
SK6: Bred 5H 109
Osborne Ter. M33: Sale 4H 105
OL6: A Lyne 6E 6
Osborne Trad. Est. OL9: O'ham 3G 63
Osborne Wlk. M26: Rad 8E 40
Osbourne Cl. BL4: Farn 2L 57
Osbourne Pl. WA14: Alt 4C 6
Oscar St. BL1: Bolt 2D 38
M40: Man 3M 79
Oscott Av. M38: Lit H 5H 57
Oscroft Cl. M8: Man 4E 78
Oscroft Wlk. M14: Man 1J 107 (off Lyth St.)
Osman Ho. BL1: Bolt 4G 38 (off Prince St.)
Osmond St. OL4: O'ham 4N 63
Osmund Av. BL2: Bolt 5L 39
Osprey Av. BL5: W'ton 5E 54
Osprey Cl. M15: Man 4D 94
SK16: Duk 2B 98
Osprey Ct. M15: Man 4D 94 (off Osprey Cl.)
Osprey Dr. M43: Droy 7G 80
M44: Irl 6H 91
SK9: Wilm 6H 123
Osprey Ho. M50: Sal 1J 93
Osprey's, The WN3: Wig 7N 51
Ossington Wlk. M23: Wyth 6N 105
Ossory St. M14: Man 6G 95
Osterley Rd. M9: Man 8L 61
Ostlers Ga. M43: Droy 8H 81
Ostrich La. M25: Pres 8B 60
Oswald Cl. M6: Sal 5N 77
Oswald La. M21: Cho H 8A 94
Oswald Rd. M21: Cho H 8N 93
Oswald St. BL3: Bolt 8D 38 (not continuous)
M4: Man 1H 5 (7F 78) (Munster St.)
M4: Man 9J 79 (Tame St.)
OL2: Shaw 4N 45
OL16: Roch 5G 8 (5E 28)
SK5: Stoc 6D 96
Oswestry Cl. BL8: G'mount 5E 24
Otago St. OL4: O'ham 2N 63
Othello Dr. M30: Ecc 8D 76
Otley Av. M6: Sal 7J 77
Otley Cl. OL9: Chad 5F 62
Otley Gro. SK3: Stoc 3B 118
Otmoor Way OL2: O'ham 8L 45
Otranto Av. M6: Sal 6H 77
Ottawa Cl. M23: Wyth 3M 115
Otterburn Ho. M30: Ecc 7E 76
Otterburn Pl. SK2: Stoc 1J 119
Otterbury Cl. BL8: Bury 2F 40
Otter Dr. BL9: Bury 8A 42
M8: Man 5D 78
Otterham Wlk. M40: Man 5B 80
Otterspool Rd. SK6: Rom 7M 109
Otterswood Sq. Ind. Est.
WN5: Wig 1N 51
Ottery Wlk. M40: Man 9B 62
Ottiwells Ter. HD7: Mars 1H 49
OUGHTRINGTON 3C 112
Oughtrington Cres. WA13: Lym 3C 112
Oughtrington La. WA13: Lym 5B 112
Oughtrington Vw. WA13: Lym 3C 112
Oulder Hill OL11: Roch 6N 27
Oulder Hill Community Complex 5M 27
Oulder Hill Dr. OL11: Roch 6M 27
Ouldfield Cl. OL16: Roch 7F 28
Oulton Av. M33: Sale 3L 105
Oulton Cl. WN7: Lei 6J 73
Oulton St. BL1: Bolt 8H 23
Oulton Wlk. M40: Man 7J 79 (off Dinsdale Cl.)
Oundle Cl. M14: Man 6H 95
Ouse St. M50: Sal 9J 77
Outram Cl. SK6: Mar 3C 120
Outram Ho. M1: Man 5M 5
Outram M. OL3: Upp 2L 65
Outram Rd. SK16: Duk 3M 97
Outram Sq. M43: Droy 1E 96
Outrington Dr. M11: Man 1M 95
Outterside St. PR7: Adl 7K 19
OUTWOOD 3F 58
Outwood Av. M27: Clif 7D 58
Outwood Dr. SK8: H Grn 7F 116
Outwood Gro. BL1: Bolt 8F 22
Outwood La. M90: Man A 7B 116
Outwood La. W. M90: Man A 7A 116
Outwood Rd. M26: Rad 1G 59
SK8: H Grn 7G 116
Oval, The SK8: H Grn 7G 116
WN6: She 7K 33
Oval Dr. SK16: Duk 2M 97
Oval Vw. SK6: Wood 3M 109
Ovenhouse La. SK10: Boll 7J 129
Over Ashberry WA14: W Tim 7B 104
Overbeck Cl. WN6: Wig 8D 34
Overbridge Rd. M3: Sal 6D 78
M7: Sal 6D 78
M8: Man 6D 78
Overbrook Av. M40: Man 5J 79
Overbrook Dr. M25: Pres 8A 60
Overcombe Wlk. M40: Man 5H 79 (off Glendower Dr.)
Overdale M27: Swin 4G 76
SK6: Mar 1C 120
WA14: Alt 2B 114
Overdale Cl. OL1: O'ham 2J 63
Overdale Crematorium BL1: Bolt 6B 38
Overdale Cres. M41: Urm 7N 91

Overdale Dr. BL1: Bolt 5B **38**
SK13: Glos 9D **100**
Overdale Ho. M6: Sal 6H **77**
Overdale Rd. M22: Wyth 2C **116**
SK6: Rom 7K **109**
SK12: Dis 9J **121**
Overdell Dr. OL12: Roch 1A **28**
Overdene Cl. BL6: Los 6K **37**
Overens St. OL4: O'ham 4M **63**
Overfields WA16: Knut 5K **133**
Overfield Way OL12: Roch 3D **28**
Overgreen BL2: Bolt 1M **39**
Overhill Dr. SK9: Wilm 7K **123**
Overhill La. SK9: Wilm 7K **123**
Overhill Rd. OL9: Chad 3D **62**
SK9: Wilm 7J **123**
Overhill Way WN3: Wins 8A **52**
OVER HULTON 4A **56**
OVER KNUTSFORD 7J **133**
Overlea Dr. M19: Man 3K **107**
Overlinks Dr. M6: Sal 5H **77**
Overman Way M27: Pen 3L **77**
Over Pl. WA16: Knut 8J **133**
Overstone Dr. M8: Man 3E **78**
OVER TABLEY 4A **132**
Overton Av. M22: Wyth 2C **116**
Overton Cl. M26: Rad 2H **59**
Overton Cres. M33: Sale 6D **104**
SK7: H Gro 3J **119**
Overton La. BL1: Bolt 5M **37**
Overton Rd. M22: Wyth 2C **116**
Overton St. WN7: Lei 6G **72**
Overton Way SK9: Hand 1J **123**
Over Town La. OL12: Roch 2F **26**
Overt St. OL11: Roch 8D **28**
Overwood Rd. M22: Nor 8C **106**
Ovington Wlk. *M40: Man* *5H* ***79***
(off Ribblesdale Dr.)
Owen Fold OL4: Lees 5C **64**
(not continuous)
Owen Ho. OL6: A Lyne 9B **6**
Owenington Gro. M38: Lit H 6H **57**
Owens Cl. OL9: Chad 3C **62**
Owens Farm Dr. SK2: Stoc 9J **109**
Owens Pk. M14: Man 8J **95**
Owens Row *BL6: Hor* *1E* ***36***
(off Bk. George St.)
Owen St. M6: Sal 5N **77**
M30: Ecc 9B **76**
OL1: O'ham 9B **46**
SK3: Stoc 3H **9** (7B **108**)
WN7: Lei 5F **72**
OWLER BARROW 1G **41**
Owlerbarrow Rd. BL8: Bury 1G **40**
Owler La. OL9: Chad 8B **62**
Owlsfield WA12: N Wil 6H **87**
Owls Ga. OL4: Lees 5B **64**
Owlwood Cl. M38: Lit H 8F **56**
Owlwood Dr. M38: Lit H 8F **56**
Owsten Ct. BL6: Hor 1A **36**
Oxbow Way M45: Whitef 3N **59**
Oxbridge Cl. M33: Sale 5D **104**
Oxburgh Rd. WN3: I Mak 7J **53**
Oxendale Dr. M24: Mid 2J **61**
Oxendon Av. M11: Man 7N **79**
Oxenholme Wlk. *M18: Man* *4B* ***96***
(off Borwell St.)
Oxenhurst Grn. SK2: Stoc 2J **119**
Oxford Av. M33: Sale 4D **104**
M43: Droy 7D **80**
M45: Whitef 3N **59**
OL11: Roch 7M **27**
Oxford Cl. BL4: Farn 3G **56**
Oxford Ct. M2: Man 6G **5** (1E **94**)
M15: Man 3E **94**
M16: Old T *4C* ***94***
(off Globe Cl.)
WN1: Wig 6M **9** (2G **53**)
Oxford Dr. M24: Mid 1A **62**
SK6: Wood 4N **109**
Oxford Gro. BL1: Bolt 3D **38**
(not continuous)
M44: Cad 2D **102**
Oxford Pk. Community Sports Cen.
. . . . .1K **97**
Oxford Pl. M14: Man 5H **95**
OL16: Roch 8E **28**
Oxford Rd. BL3: Lit L 9N **39**
BL6: Los 4H **37**
M1: Man 8H **5** (2F **94**)
M6: Sal 6G **77**
M13: Man 9J **5** (2F **94**)
M15: Man 2F **94**
M46: Ath 6K **55**
SK11: Macc 6F **130**
SK14: Hyde 9B **98**
SK16: Duk 1A **98**
WA14: Alt 5C **6** (4D **114**)
WN5: Orr 3K **51**
Oxford Road Station (Rail)
. . . . .8H **5** (2F **94**)
Oxford St. BL1: Bolt 2K **7** (5G **38**)
BL9: Bury 9N **7** (3N **41**)
M1: Man 6G **5** (1E **94**)
M16: Old T 4C **94**
M30: Ecc 9E **76**
OL2: Shaw 5M **45**
OL7: A Lyne 1K **97**
OL9: O'ham 6F **62**
PR7: Adl 7K **19**
SK15: Mill 6G **83**
SK15: Stal 9F **82**
WA12: N Wil 6D **86**
WN2: Hin 4B **54**
WN7: Lei 3H **73**
Oxford St. E. OL7: A Lyne 1K **97**
Oxford St. W. OL7: A Lyne 1K **97**
Oxford Wlk. *M34: Dent* *8L* ***97***
(off Worcester Av.)
Oxford Way OL12: Roch 3C **28**
SK4: Stoc 5B **108**
Ox Ga. BL2: Bolt 8L **23**
Ox Hey Cl. BL0: Ram 7J **11**
BL6: Los 4G **37**
Ox Hey La. BL6: Los 4G **37**
OL3: Del, Dens 3G **47**
Oxhill Wlk. *M40: Man* *9B* ***62***
(off Blandford Dr.)
Oxhouse Rd. WN5: Orr 7H **51**
Oxlea Gro. BL5: W'ton 4G **54**
Oxney Cl. SK11: Macc 4D **130**
Oxney Rd. M14: Man 5H **95**
Ox St. BL0: Ram 9H **11**
Oxted Wlk. *M8: Man* *4F* ***78***
(off Dinnington Dr.)
Oxton Av. M22: Wyth 3B **116**
Oxton St. M11: Man 2D **96**
Oxygrains Packhorse Bridge 1M **31**
Ozanam Ct. M7: Sal 3C **78**

P

PACIFIC QUAYS 1K **93**
Pacific Rd. WA14: B'ath 1A **114**
Pacific Way M50: Sal 1J **93**
Packer St. BL1: Bolt 2D **38**
OL16: Roch 7C **8** (6D **28**)
Packhorse Ct. HD7: Mars 1H **49**
Pack Horse Yd. OL16: Roch 7C **8**
Packsaddle Pk. SK10: P'bury 8C **128**
Packwood Chase OL9: Chad 3D **62**
Padbury Cl. M41: Urm 6L **91**
Padbury Ho. *M5: Sal* *9M* ***77***
(off Cypress Cl.)
Padbury Wlk. *M40: Man* *5L* ***79***
(off Mansford Dr.)
Padbury Way BL2: Bolt 2L **39**
Padden Brook SK6: Rom 6M **109**
Padden Brook M. SK6: Rom 6M **109**
Paddington Av. M40: Man 5N **79**
Paddington Cl. M6: Sal 8N **77**
Paddison St. M27: Swin 3E **76**
Paddock, The BL0: Ram 7H **11**
M28: Wors 3M **75**
M45: Whitef 4J **59**
OL3: G'fld 7J **65**
SK7: Bram 6B **118**
SK8: Chea 2K **117**
SK9: Hand 2J **123**
SK13: Had 4B **100**
SK14: Holl 4A **100**
WA13: Lym 4D **112**
WA15: Tim 3H **115**
WN4: A Mak 4C **70**
Paddock Brow SK10: P'bury 8E **128**
Paddock Chase SK12: Poy 9K **119**
Paddock Cl. M46: Ath 6N **55**
Paddock Ct. M35: Fail 5D **80**
Paddock Fld. M5: Sal 1A **94**
Paddock Head OL15: Lit 1J **29**
PADDOCKHILL 2A **126**
Paddock Hill WA16: Mob 2A **126**
Paddock La. M35: Fail 5D **80**
WA13: Warb 8C **102**
WA14: D Mas 2H **113**
Paddock Ri. WN6: Wig 9B **34**
Paddock Rd. SK14: Hyde 9A **98**
WN8: Skel 6A **50**
Paddocks, The SK3: Stoc 3E **118**
SK10: P'bury 8E **128**
WA15: Haleb 7H **115**
Paddock St. M12: Man 8M **5** (2H **95**)
Paderborn Ct. BL1: Bolt 4H **7** (6F **38**)
PADFIELD 4E **100**
Padfield Ga. SK13: Glos 9F **100**
Padfield Main Rd.
SK13: Had 3C **100**
Padiham Cl. BL9: Bury 5K **41**
WN7: Lei 5J **73**
Padstow Cl. SK10: Macc 4C **130**
SK14: Hat 6G **99**
Padstow Dr. SK7: Bram 8D **118**
Padstow St. M40: Man 7K **79**
Padstow Wlk. SK14: Hat 6G **99**
Padworth Wlk. M23: Wyth 8K **105**
Pagan St. OL16: Roch 6D **8** (5D **28**)
Pagefield Cl. WN6: Wig 2D **52**
Pagefield Ind. Est.
WN6: Wig 2C **52**
Pagefield St. WN6: Wig 2D **52**
Paget St. M40: Man 5J **79**
OL6: A Lyne 6N **81**
Pagnall Ct. OL9: Chad 6F **62**
Paignton Av. M19: Man 9L **95**
SK14: Hat 7F **98**
Paignton Cl. WN5: Bil 2J **69**
Paignton Dr. M33: Sale 3D **104**
Paignton Gro. SK5: Stoc 1C **108**
Paignton Wlk. SK14: Hat 7F **98**
Pailin Dr. M43: Droy 8G **81**
Pailton Cl. BL6: Los 6M **37**
Painswick Rd. M22: Wyth 6A **116**
Paisley Pk. BL4: Farn 2L **57**
Paiton St. BL1: Bolt 5D **38**
Palace Arc. *WN4: A Mak* *7E* ***70***
(off Foy St.)
Palace Ct. BL1: Bolt 1K **7** (4G **38**)
Palace Gdns. OL2: O'ham 1H **63**
Palace Gro. WN7: Lei 4M **73**
Palace Rd. M33: Sale 3G **105**
OL6: A Lyne 5B **82**
Palace St. BL1: Bolt 1K **7** (4G **38**)
BL9: Bury 2N **41**
(not continuous)
OL9: O'ham 4G **63**
Palace Theatre
Manchester 7H **5** (1F **94**)
Palatine Av. M20: Man 2G **106**
OL11: Roch 5M **27**
Palatine Cl. M44: Irl 8G **91**
WN3: Wig 7B **52**
Palatine Ct. M34: Dent 4J **97**
Palatine Cres. M20: Man 3G **106**
Palatine Dr. BL9: Bury 5M **25**
Palatine Ho. SK3: Stoc 8C **108**
Palatine M. M20: Man 2G **107**
M34: Dent 5J **97**
Palatine Rd. M20: Man 4F **106**
M22: Nor 7C **106**
OL11: Roch 5M **27**
Palatine Sq. WN7: Lei 5F **72**
Palatine St. BL0: Ram 8J **11**
BL1: Bolt 2K **7** (5G **38**)
M34: Dent 4J **97**
(not continuous)
OL16: Roch 6G **29**
Palatine Ter. OL11: Roch 5M **27**
Palewood Cl. WN1: Wig 2H **53**
Paley St. BL1: Bolt 2L **7** (5G **39**)
Palfrey Pl. M12: Man 9N **5** (2H **95**)
Palgrave Av. M40: Man 5J **79**
Palin St. WN2: Hin 8D **54**
Palin Wood Rd. OL3: Del 7J **47**
Palladium Dr. M9: Man 2J **79**
Palladium Ho. *M9: Man* *2J* ***79***
(off Rochdale Rd.)
Pall Mall BL6: R'ton 6C **20**
M2: Man 5G **5**
(not continuous)
Pall Mall Ct. M2: Man 4G **5**
Pallotine Wlk. OL11: Roch 8B **28**
Palma Av. M90: Man A 7N **115**
Palm Av. WN4: Gars 5A **70**
Palm Bus. Cen. OL9: Chad 5F **62**
Palm Cl. M33: Sale 3C **104**
Palmer Av. SK8: Chea 1L **117**
Palmer Cl. M8: Man 9G **60**
OL8: O'ham 7K **63**
Palmer Gro. WN7: Lei 1G **72**
Palmerston Av. M16: Whall R 7C **94**
Palmerston Cl. BL0: Ram 1H **25**
M34: Dent 6F **96**
WN2: Hin 7M **53**
Palmerstones Ct. BL1: Bolt 5B **38**
Palmerston Rd. M34: Dent 6F **96**
SK2: Stoc 4E **118**
SK11: Macc 5E **130**
Palmerston St. M12: Man 1J **95**
SK10: Boll 5L **129**
Palmer St. M7: Sal 5B **78**
M33: Sale 4G **105**
SK16: Duk 9M **81**
Palm Gro. OL9: Chad 3F **62**
WN5: Wig 5A **52**
Palm St. BL1: Bolt 1G **38**
M13: Man 6L **95**
M43: Droy 8B **80**
OL4: O'ham 3N **63**
Pamir Dr. OL7: A Lyne 8K **81**
Pandora St. M20: Man 3F **106**
Panfield Rd. M22: Wyth 3B **116**
Pangbourne Av. M41: Urm 6E **92**
Pangbourne Cl. SK3: Stoc 1A **118**
Pankhurst Centre, The 4G **95**
Pankhurst Wlk. *M14: Man* *6G* ***95***
(off Ellanby Cl.)
Panmure St. OL8: O'ham 7K **63**
Pansy Rd. BL4: Farn 3H **57**
Panton St. BL6: Hor 3F **36**
Paperhouse Cl. OL11: Roch 4J **27**
Paper Mill Rd. BL7: Bro X 6H **23**
Paprika Cl. M11: Man 2B **96**
Parade, The M27: Swin 2F **76**
SK6: Rom 7L **109**
SK9: A Edg 4F **126**
Parade Rd. M90: Man A 8B **116**
Paradise St. BL0: Ram 8J **11**
M34: Aud 2J **97**
SK11: Macc 5G **131**
SK13: Had 4B **100**
Paradise Wlk. M1: Man 5L **5**
Paradise Wharf M1: Man . . .5L **5** (9G **79**)
Paragon Bus. Pk. BL6: Hor 3G **36**
Paramel Av. BL3: Lit L 7B **40**
PARBOLD 2A **32**
Parbold Av. M20: Man 2F **106**
Parbold Hill WN8: Par 2B **32**
Parbold Station (Rail) 2A **32**
Parchments, The WA12: N Wil 5G **87**
Pardoner's Ct. M5: Sal 8H **77**
Pares Land Wlk. *OL16: Roch* *7F* ***28***
(off McNaught St.)
Pargate Chase OL11: Roch 5M **27**
Parham Wlk. *M9: Man* *8K* ***61***
(off Stockfield Dr.)
Paris Av. M5: Sal 2A **94**
WN3: Wins 8N **51**
Parish Vw. M5: Sal 1A **94**
Parish Wlk. BL2: Ain 3D **40**
Paris St. BL3: Bolt 8C **38**
Park, The BL0: Ram 4J **11**
M32: Stre 5L **93**
OL3: G'fld 6M **65**
OL4: Gras 6G **65**
Park 66 BL9: Bury 6A **42**
Park & Ride
Broadbottom 9K **99**
Brooklands 5G **105**
Cheadle Hulme 5N **117**
Davenport 2D **118**
Hazel Grove 5H **119**
Horwich Parkway 5E **36**
Ladywell 9G **77**
Lostock 6L **37**
Radcliffe 9H **41**
Romiley 6N **109**
Smithy Bridge 2K **29**
Westhoughton 1H **55**
Park Av. BL0: Ram 8K **11**
BL1: Bolt 9F **22**
M7: Sal 2E **78**
M11: Man 1L **95**
M16: Old T 4B **94**
M19: Man 8M **95**
M25: Pres 7A **60**
M26: Rad 8K **41**
M27: Swin 3D **76**
M33: Sale 2G **105**
M35: Fail 2B **80**
M41: Urm 7C **92**
M45: Whitef 5K **59**
OL9: Chad 2F **62**
SK3: Stoc 9L **107**
SK6: Rom 6N **109**
SK7: Bram 1B **124**
SK8: Chea H 6L **117**
SK9: Wilm 6H **123**
Park Av. SK12: Poy 2J **125**
SK14: Hyde 5A **98**
WA3: Gol 8J **71**
WA14: Tim 8E **104**
WA15: Hale 6F **114**
WN5: Bil 1J **69**
WN6: She 5M **33**
Park Av. Nth. WA12: N Wil 7F **86**
Park Av. Sth. WA12: N Wil 7F **86**
Park Bank M5: Sal 8K **77**
M46: Ath 5A **56**
PARK BRIDGE 9N **63**
Park Bridge Heritage Cen. 1N **81**
Park Bri. Rd. OL6: A Lyne 3L **81**
OL7: A Lyne 3L **81**
Parkbridge Wlk. M13: Man 9L **5**
Park Brook La. WN6: She 5M **33**
Park Brook Rd. SK11: Macc 5E **130**
Parkbrook Rd. M23: Wyth 9A **106**
Park Brow Cl. M21: Cho H 9B **94**
Park Bungs. SK6: Mar 2C **120**
Park Cl. M45: Whitef 5M **59**
OL9: Chad 2F **62**
SK13: Glos 7F **100**
SK15: Stal 7C **82**
WA14: Tim 8F **104**
WN8: Par 1B **32**
Park Cotts. BL1: Bolt 1D **38**
OL2: Shaw 4K **45**
OL3: G'fld 6H **65**
Park Ct. M28: Walk 1M **75**
M33: Sale 3G **104**
OL11: Roch 9C **8** (7D **28**)
Park Ct. M. SK8: Chea 3K **117**
Park Cres. M14: Man 6H **95**
OL6: A Lyne 8B **82**
OL9: Chad 2D **62**
SK9: Wilm 5G **123**
SK13: Glos 6D **100**
WN1: Wig 6H **9** (2E **52**)
Park Cres. W. WN1: Wig 5G **9** (2E **52**)
Parkdale M29: Ast 5C **74**
OL9: Chad 2F **62**
Parkdale Av. M18: Man 4A **96**
M34: Aud 2H **97**
Parkdale Rd. BL2: Bolt 3K **39**
Parkdene Cl. BL2: Bolt 9L **23**
Park Dene Dr. SK13: Glos 7E **100**
Park Dr. M16: Whall R 7B **94**
M30: Ecc 6D **76**
SK4: Stoc 6N **107**
SK9: Wilm 5G **123**
SK14: Hyde 5A **98**
WA15: Hale 5F **114**
WA15: Tim 9G **105**
Park Edge BL5: W'ton 4J **55**
Parkedge Cl. WN7: Lei 7G **72**
Parkend Dr. WN7: Lei 8G **72**
Parkend Rd. M23: Wyth 3N **115**
Parker Arc. *M1: Man* *5H* ***5***
(off Parker St.)
Parker St. BL9: Bury 8N **7** (2N **41**)
M1: Man 5J **5** (9F **78**)
SK11: Macc 5J **131**
(not continuous)
Parkett Heyes Rd. SK11: Macc . . .5C **130**
Parkfield M5: Sal 8K **77**
M24: Mid 3L **61**
M30: Ecc 5K **91**
M43: Droy 8E **80**
OL9: Chad 2E **62**
WN6: She 5M **33**
Parkfield Av. BL4: Farn 4J **57**
M14: Man 6G **95**
M25: Pres 8C **60**
M29: Ast 4C **74**
M41: Urm 8B **92**
OL8: O'ham 9F **62**
SK6: Mar 1C **120**
Parkfield Cl. M29: Ast 4C **74**
OL16: Roch 2F **44**
WN7: Lei 3J **73**
Parkfield Ct. WA14: Alt 4B **6** (3C **114**)
Parkfield Dr. M24: Mid 3K **61**
M29: Tyld 1E **74**
Parkfield Est. M27: Swin 4G **76**
Parkfield Ind. Est. M24: Mid 3K **61**
Parkfield Rd. BL3: Bolt 9G **39**
OL4: Gras 5H **65**
SK8: Chea H 6L **117**
WA14: Alt 4A **6** (3C **114**)
WA16: Knut 8H **133**
Parkfield Rd. Nth. M40: Man 9C **62**
Parkfield Rd. Sth. M20: Man 4F **106**
Parkfields SK15: Stal 7G **82**
WN2: Abr 3L **71**
Parkfield St. M14: Man 5G **95**
(Gateshead Cl.)
M14: Man 6G **95**
(Heald Av.)
OL16: Roch 2F **44**
Parkgate BL8: Bury 8E **24**
OL9: Chad 2F **62**
WA16: Knut 5J **133**
Park Ga. Av. M20: Man 2G **106**
Park Ga. Cl. SK6: Bred 3J **109**
Parkgate Dr. BL1: Bolt 8G **23**
M27: Swin 3G **77**
SK2: Stoc 3F **118**
Parkgate La. WA16: Knut 5J **133**
Parkgate Rd. SK11: Macc 8G **131**
WA14: W Tim 8C **104**
Park Gates Av. SK8: Chea H 6A **118**
Park Gates Dr. SK8: Chea H 6A **118**
Parkgate Trad. Est. WA16: Knut . . .4J **133**
Parkgate Way OL2: Shaw 5A **46**
SK9: Hand *2J* ***123***
(off Davenham Rd.)
Park Grange WN2: Hin 8A **54**
Park Grn. SK11: Macc 5H **131**
(not continuous)
Park Gro. M19: Man 7M **95**
M26: Rad 8F **40**
M28: Walk 2L **75**
SK4: Stoc 4N **107**
SK11: Macc 6G **131**
Park Hall *M14: Man* *6H* ***95***
(off Thurloe St.)
Parkham Cl. BL5: W'ton 5H **55**
Park Hey Dr. WN6: App B 5J **33**
Park Hill M25: Pres 9C **60**
OL12: Roch 4D **28**
Parkhill Av. M8: Man 9G **60**
Park Hill Cl. SK22: N Mil 6M **121**
Parkhill Ct. WA16: Knut 7H **133**
Park Hill Dr. M45: Whitef 3L **59**
Parkhill Rd. WA15: Hale 6G **114**
Parkhills Cl. BL9: Bury 4M **41**
Parkhills Rd. BL9: Bury 9M **7** (4L **41**)
Park Hill St. BL1: Bolt 4E **38**
Park Ho. *M23: Wyth* *9J* ***105***
(off Bridge Rd.)
M29: Tyld 1A **74**
M43: Droy 1E **96**
Park Ho. Bri. Est. M6: Sal 3L **77**
Park Ho. Bri. Rd. M6: Sal 4L **77**
Park Ho. Dr. SK10: P'bury 5E **128**
Park Ho. La. SK10: P'bury 5E **128**
Parkhouse St. M11: Man 1N **95**
Parkhouse St. Ind. Est.
M11: Man 1N **95**
Parkhurst Av. M40: Man 1C **80**
Parkin Cl. SK16: Duk 1N **97**
Park Ind. Est. WN4: A Mak 8B **70**
Parkinson St. BL3: Bolt 7D **38**
BL9: Bury 8M **25**
Parkin St. M12: Man 6M **95**
Parklake Av. M7: Sal 2D **78**
Parkland Av. SK22: N Mil 6M **121**
Parklands BL6: Los 5F **36**
M33: Sale *3J* ***105***
(off Charlton Dr.)
M45: Whitef 3L **59**
(Pinfold Ct.)
M45: Whitef 1M **59**
(Well La.)
OL2: O'ham 5G **44**
OL2: Shaw 4A **46**
OL4: Gras 5H **65**
OL10: H'ood 4F **42**
SK6: Rom 5B **110**
SK7: Bram 6C **118**
SK9: Wilm 7H **123**
WA14: Alt 3B **114**
WN8: Skel 1B **50**
Parklands, The M26: Rad 4B **58**
SK4: Stoc 4C **108**
Parklands Cres. OL10: H'ood 4F **42**
Parklands Dr. M33: Sale 6D **104**
WN2: Asp 6M **35**
Parklands Ho. OL2: O'ham 5G **44**
Parklands Rd. M23: Wyth 9M **105**
Parklands Sports Cen. 4B **116**
Parklands Way OL10: H'ood 4F **42**
SK12: Poy 2J **125**
PARK LANE 4K **59**
Park Lane 5L **59**
Park La. BL6: Hor 1F **36**
M6: Sal 5J **77**
M7: Sal 2C **78**
M27: Pen 3K **77**
M28: Wors 3E **74**
M45: Whitef 4K **59**
OL2: O'ham 7H **45**
(not continuous)
OL3: G'fld 6M **65**
OL8: O'ham 9K **63**
OL16: Roch 6C **8** (5D **28**)
SK1: Stoc 8F **108**
SK11: Macc 6F **130**
SK12: Poy 2J **125**
SK16: Duk 1N **97**
WA13: Warb 7D **102**
WA14: Lit B 5J **113**
WA15: Hale 6G **114**
WN2: Abr 3L **71**
WN7: Lei 6L **73**
Park La. Ct. M7: Sal 2C **78**
M45: Whitef 4K **59**
Park La. W. M27: Pen 3K **77**
Park Lea Ct. M7: Sal 1D **78**
Parkleigh Dr. M40: Man 9C **62**
Park Lodge M7: Sal 2C **78**
M16: Whall R 7D **94**
M19: Man 8M **95**
Park Lodge Cl. SK8: Chea 3K **117**
Park Mdw. BL5: W'ton 3J **55**
Park M. M16: Whall R 7B **94**
M26: Rad 8J **41**
Park Mill Ind. Est. OL5: Mos 8G **65**
Park Mt. SK8: Gat 2F **116**
SK11: Macc 6E **130**
Park Mt. Cl. SK11: Macc 6E **130**
Park Mt. Dr. SK11: Macc 6E **130**
Parkmount Rd. M9: Man 1K **79**
Park Pde. OL2: Shaw 3N **45**
OL6: A Lyne 9B **6** (8L **81**)
Park Pde. Ind. Est.
OL6: A Lyne 9B **6** (8L **81**)
Park Pl. M4: Man 7F **78**
M6: Sal 7G **77**
M25: Pres 6B **60**
SK4: Stoc 6L **107**
Park Range M14: Man 6J **95**
Park Ri. SK6: Rom 5N **109**
SK15: Stal 7C **82**
Park Rd. BL0: Ram 2F **24**
BL1: Bolt 5D **38**
BL3: Lit L 8N **39**
BL5: W'ton 3H **55**
BL9: Bury 9L **25**
M6: Sal 6G **77**
M8: Man 8C **60**
M24: Mid 3L **61**
M25: Pres 8C **60**
M28: Walk 1K **75**
M30: Ecc 6G **77**
(Dante Cl.)
M30: Ecc 6D **76**
(Monton Grn.)
M31: Part 5H **103**
M32: Stre 5H **93**

Park Rd. M33: Sale .2G **104**
M34: Aud .1H **97**
M34: Dent .6J **97**
OL4: O'ham .4D **8** (5J **63**)
OL8: O'ham .4D **8** (5J **63**)
OL12: Roch .4E **28**
OL15: Lit .8M **15**
PR7: Adl .7J **19**
PR7: Cop .4B **18**
SK4: Stoc .3N **107**
SK6: Rom .5N **109**
SK8: Chea .1K **117**
SK8: Chea H .6A **118**
SK8: Gat .1E **116**
SK9: Wilm .7E **122**
SK12: Dis .8C **120**
SK13: Had .5C **100**
SK14: Hyde .5A **98**
SK16: Duk .9N **81**
SK22: N Mil .8M **121**
WA3: Gol .2J **87**
WA13: Lym .7E **112**
WA13: Warb .8C **102**
(not continuous)
WA14: Bow .4A **114**
WA14: Tim .8E **104**
WA15: Hale .6E **114**
WA15: Tim .8E **104**
WN1: Wig .5G **9** (2D **52**)
WN2: Hin .7N **53**
WN5: Bil .1J **69**
(not continuous)
WN5: Orr .5L **51**
WN6: Stan .4B **34**
WN6: Wig .5G **9** (2D **52**)
Park Rd. Nth. M41: Urm .6C **92**
WA12: N Wil .6H **87**
Park Rd. Sth. M41: Urm .7C **92**
WA12: N Wil .7F **86**
Park Row BL1: Bolt .7G **22**
SK4: Stoc .7K **107**
Parks, The WA12: N Wil .9E **70**
Park Seventeen M45: Whitef .2M **59**
Parkside M14: Man .8H **95**
M24: Mid .5K **61**
OL12: Whitw .4B **14**
WN2: Hin .5A **54**
Park Side Av. OL2: Shaw .4N **45**
Parkside Av. M7: Sal .2D **78**
M28: Walk .1L **75**
M30: Ecc .9C **76**
M35: Fail .5C **80**
WN4: A Mak .2C **70**
Parkside Cl. M26: Rad .8K **41**
SK6: H Lan .7A **120**
Parkside Cres. WN5: Orr .5K **51**
Parkside Ind. Est. OL2: O'ham .8J **45**
Parkside Ind. Pk. WA3: Gol .1K **87**
Parkside La. SK6: Mel .1F **120**
Parkside M. M45: Whitef .2M **59**
Parkside Pl. WN8: Uph .7D **50**
Parkside Rd. M14: Man .7E **94**
M33: Sale .5K **105**
WA2: Win .5K **87**
WA3: Win .5K **87**
Parkside St. BL2: Bolt .3K **39**
Parkside Wlk.
BL9: Bury .9M **7** (3M **41**)
SK7: Bram .4C **118**
(not continuous)
Parks Nook BL4: Farn .4K **57**
Park Sq. M16: Old T .7N **93**
OL6: A Lyne .6B **82**
Parkstead Dr. M9: Man .4J **79**
Parkstone Av. M18: Man .3D **96**
M45: Whitef .5K **59**
Parkstone Cl. BL8: Bury .2F **40**
Parkstone Ct. BL3: Lit L .9C **40**
Parkstone Dr. M27: Swin .4H **77**
Parkstone La. M28: Wors .6N **75**
Parkstone Rd. M44: Irl .6H **91**
Park St. BL1: Bolt .4E **38**
BL4: Farn .2L **57**
M3: Man .1G **5** (7E **78**)
M3: Sal .4B **4**
M7: Sal .2C **78**
M25: Pres .7B **60**
M26: Rad .8J **41**
M27: Swin .3G **76**
M29: Tyld .1B **74**
M34: Dent .6H **97**
M43: Droy .8G **80**
M46: Ath .7N **55**
OL2: O'ham .8J **45**
OL2: Shaw .4J **45**
OL5: Mos .2F **82**
OL6: A Lyne .9C **6** (8L **81**)
OL7: A Lyne .9A **6** (8L **81**)
OL8: O'ham .5B **8** (6J **63**)
(not continuous)
OL10: H'ood .4K **43**
OL16: Roch .9C **8** (7D **28**)
SK1: Stoc .1L **9** (6D **108**)
SK6: Bred .5K **109**
SK10: Boll .5M **129**
SK11: Macc .5H **131**
SK15: Stal .9E **82**
WN3: Wig .5E **52**
Parksway M9: Man .6G **60**
M25: Pres .9B **60**
M27: Pen .4J **77**
Parks Yd. BL9: Bury .7K **7** (2L **41**)
Park Ter. BL1: Bolt .6G **22**
BL5: W'ton .2H **55**
M45: Whitef .4K **59**
OL5: Mos .2F **82**
OL10: H'ood .1J **43**
SK13: Glos .9E **100**
WN6: Stan .1A **34**
Park Va. Rd. SK11: Macc .6G **131**
Park Vw. BL1: Bolt .7G **22**
(not continuous)
BL4: Farn .2L **57**
BL4: Kea .4N **57**
HD7: Mars .1J **49**
M9: Man .4H **79**
Park Vw. M14: Man .5G **94**
(Fairbank Av.)
M14: Man .1K **107**
(Green St.)
M34: Aud .1H **97**
OL2: Shaw .4J **45**
OL6: A Lyne .6C **82**
OL9: Chad .2E **62**
OL15: Lit .8M **15**
SK1: Stoc .9F **108**
SK3: Stoc .9L **107**
SK6: Bred .5G **109**
SK7: H Gro .7M **119**
SK8: Gat .1F **116**
WA14: Lit B .4J **113**
WN2: Abr .1L **71**
WN2: I Mak .4L **53**
WN4: A Mak .8E **70**
Park Vw. Ct. M21: Cho H .8M **93**
M25: Pres .8A **60**
SK6: Rom .6N **109**
Parkview Ct. M32: Stre .8M **93**
Park Vw. Ho. M46: Ath .8L **55**
Parkview Pk. WA13: Lym .6E **112**
Park Vw. Ri. SK22: N Mil .6M **121**
Park Vw. Rd. BL3: Bolt .8D **38**
M25: Pres .8A **60**
Parkville Rd. M20: Man .3H **107**
M25: Pres .4B **60**
Park Way M17: T Pk .5F **92**
M32: Stre .5F **92**
M41: Urm .5F **92**
Parkway BL5: W'ton .5F **54**
M34: Dent .6G **97**
M38: Lit H .7F **56**
OL9: Chad .1E **62**
OL11: Roch .5N **27**
SK3: Stoc .9L **107**
SK7: Bram .5C **118**
SK9: Wilm .8G **122**
SK22: N Mil .6M **121**
WN6: Stan .2L **33**
Parkway Bus. Cen. M14: Man .7E **94**
Parkway Circ. M17: T Pk .3G **93**
Parkway Four Ind. Est.
M17: T Pk .3G **93**
Parkway Gro. M38: Lit H .7F **56**
Parkway Ind. Est. M17: T Pk .3G **92**
Parkway Trad. Est. M32: Stre .4G **92**
Parkwood BL7: Eger .3E **22**
Parkwood Cl. WN3: I Mak .5H **53**
Parkwood Cotts. M25: Pres .3E **60**
Parkwood Dr. BL5: O Hul .4A **56**
Parkwood Rd. M23: Wyth .9K **105**
Parlane St. M4: Man .1K **5** (7G **78**)
Parliament Pl. BL9: Bury .3L **41**
Parliament St. BL9: Bury .3L **41**
WN3: I Mak .5G **53**
WN8: Uph .3G **50**
Parndon Dr. SK2: Stoc .9G **109**
Parnell Av. M22: Nor .8C **106**
Parnell Cl. M29: Ast .5C **74**
Parnham Cl. M26: Rad .7B **40**
Parrbrook Cl. M45: Whitef .2N **59**
Parrbrook Wlk. M45: Whitef .2A **60**
PARR BROW .3F **74**
Parr Cl. BL4: Farn .3J **57**
Parrenthorn Rd. M25: Pres .4B **60**
Parrfield Rd. M28: Wors .3A **76**
PARR FOLD .1K **75**
Parr Fold BL9: Bury .1A **60**
Parr Fold Av. M28: Wors .1K **75**
(not continuous)
Parr Ho. *OL8: O'ham .6K 63*
(off Eldon St.)
Parrin La. M30: Ecc .7B **76**
Parr La. BL9: Bury .2N **59**
Parrot St. BL3: Bolt .7F **38**
M11: Man .9A **80**
Parrs Ct. M44: Irl .7G **91**
Parrs Mt. M. SK4: Stoc .6L **107**
Parr St. M11: Man .2C **96**
M29: Tyld .2A **74**
M30: Ecc .9D **76**
SK11: Macc .5G **130**
Parrs Wood Av. M20: Man .6H **107**
Parrs Wood Ct. M20: Man .7H **107**
Parrs Wood Entertainment Cen.
.7J **107**
Parrs Wood La. M20: Man .7H **107**
Parrs Wood Rd. M20: Man .8G **106**
Parrs Wood Sports Cen. .7J **107**
Parry Mead SK6: Bred .4L **109**
Parry Rd. M12: Man .5M **95**
Parry Wlk. OL6: A Lyne .6A **82**
Parslow Av. M8: Man .2F **78**
Parsonage M3: Man .3F **4** (9E **78**)
Parsonage, The *WN2: Hin .4A 54*
(off Hoade St.)
Parsonage Brow WN8: Uph .3D **50**
Parsonage Cl. BL9: Bury .1N **41**
M5: Sal .7A **4**
WN8: Uph .4E **50**
Parsonage Ct. M20: Man .2G **107**
SK4: Stoc .4N **107**
Parsonage Dr. M28: Walk .9K **57**
Parsonage Gdns. M3: Man .4F **4**
SK6: Mar .3D **120**
Parsonage Grn. *SK9: Wilm .7G 122*
(off Green La.)
Parsonage La. M3: Man .3F **4**
Parsonage Retail Pk. WN7: Lei .4G **72**
Parsonage Rd. M20: Man .2G **107**
M26: Rad .4C **58**
M28: Walk .9K **57**
M41: Urm .8M **91**
(not continuous)
SK4: Stoc .4N **107**
WN8: Uph .4E **50**
Parsonage St. BL9: Bury .1N **41**
M8: Man .1E **78**
M15: Man .4D **94**
M26: Rad .8G **41**
SK4: Stoc .1J **9** (6C **108**)
SK11: Macc .5H **131**
SK14: Hyde .7A **98**
Parsonage Ter. *OL16: Miln .7K 29*
(off Parsonage Wlk.)
Parsonage Wlk. OL16: Miln .6K **29**
WA3: Cul .7H **89**
Parsonage Way SK8: Chea .2N **117**
WN7: Lei .4G **72**
Parson's Bullough Rd.
BL6: R'ton .1A **20**
Parson's Dr. M24: Mid .1L **61**
Parsons Fld. M6: Sal .5N **77**
Parsons La. BL9: Bury .7L **7** (2M **41**)
Parsons St. OL9: O'ham .5G **63**
Parson's Wlk. WN1: Wig .5H **9** (2E **52**)
Parsons Way M9: Man .3K **79**
Parth St. BL9: Bury .3C **42**
PARTINGTON .5G **103**
Partington Ct. BL4: Farn .2L **57**
SK13: Glos .8H **101**
Partington La. M27: Swin .3E **76**
Partington Leisure Cen. .6G **102**
Partington Pk. OL11: Roch .4A **44**
SK13: Glos .6E **100**
Partington Pl. *M33: Sale .3H 105*
(off School Rd.)
Partington Players Theatre .8E **100**
Partington Shop. Cen.
M31: Part .5G **103**
Partington St. BL3: Bolt .1D **56**
M28: Wors .3C **76**
M30: Ecc .7D 76
(off Monton Rd.)
M35: Fail .3D **80**
M40: Man .3A **80**
OL1: O'ham .2F **8** (4L **63**)
OL10: H'ood .2F **42**
OL11: Roch .2N **43**
WN5: Wig .3B **52**
Partridge Av. M23: Wyth .1A **116**
Partridge Cl. M44: Irl .5H **91**
OL11: Roch .6L **27**
Partridge Ct. SK2: Stoc .2F **118**
Partridge Ri. M43: Droy .7H **81**
Partridge Rd. M35: Fail .4G **80**
Partridge St. M32: Stre .4M **93**
Partridge Way OL9: Chad .3B **62**
Part St. BL5: W'ton .1G **55**
Parvet Av. M43: Droy .7D **80**
Parvey La. SK11: Sut E .9J **131**
Pascal St. M19: Man .9M **95**
Pass, The OL16: Roch .6F **8** (5E **28**)
PASSMONDS .4N **27**
Passmonds Cres. OL11: Roch .5N **27**
Passmonds Way OL11: Roch .5N **27**
Pass St. OL9: O'ham .5H **63**
Pass Way *WA11: St H .9G 68*
(off Honister Av.)
Paston Rd. M22: Shar .9C **106**
Pasture Cl. OL10: H'ood .3G **43**
SK10: Macc .1G **131**
WN4: A Mak .4B **70**
Pasture Dr. WA3: Cro .9D **88**
Pasturefield Cl. M33: Sale .5M **105**
Pasture Fld. Rd. M22: Wyth .6E **116**
Pasturegreen Way M44: Irl .6J **91**
Pastures La. OL4: Scout .3E **64**
Patch Cft. Rd. M22: Wyth .6E **116**
Patchett St. M12: Man .3L **95**
M29: Tyld .1B **74**
Patch La. SK7: Bram .1B **124**
(not continuous)
Pateley Sq. WN6: Wig .1E **52**
Patey St. M12: Man .6M **95**
Pathfield Wlk. *M9: Man .2J 79*
(off Smallfield Dr.)
Patience St. OL12: Roch .4A **28**
Patmos St. BL0: Ram .8K **11**
Paton Av. BL3: Bolt .9H **39**
Paton M. BL3: Bolt .9H **39**
Paton St. M1: Man .5K **5** (9G **78**)
OL12: Roch .2B **28**
Patricia Dr. M28: Walk .9M **57**
Patrick Roddy Ct. M18: Man .4A **96**
PATRICROFT .9D **76**
Patricroft Bri. M30: Ecc .9C **76**
Patricroft Rd. M30: Ecc .8C **76**
WN2: I Mak .5J **53**
Patricroft Station (Rail) .8C **76**
Patten St. M20: Man .2G **107**
Patterdale SK8: Chea .2H **117**
Patterdale Av. M41: Urm .5B **92**
OL7: A Lyne .5K **81**
Patterdale Cl. OL1: O'ham .2L **63**
OL11: Roch .1N **43**
SK15: Stal .7D **82**
Patterdale Dr. BL9: Bury .5L **41**
M24: Mid .1K **61**
Patterdale Pl. WN2: I Mak .4K **53**
Patterdale Rd. BL2: Bolt .9N **23**
M22: Nor .8D **106**
M31: Part .5F **102**
OL7: A Lyne .5K **81**
SK1: Stoc .9F **108**
SK6: Wood .4M **109**
WN4: A Mak .2D **70**
WN7: Lei .6L **73**
Patterdale Wlk. *WA15: Tim .2K 115*
(off Bowness Rd.)
Pattern Av. OL11: Roch .5B **28**
Pattern Ho. SK15: Stal .8D **82**
Patterson Av. M21: Cho H .8N **93**
Patterson St. BL3: Bolt .8B **38**
BL5: W'ton .4D **54**
M34: Dent .5K **97**
WA12: N Wil .6E **86**
Patting Cl. M44: Irl .6K **91**
Pattishall Cl. M4: Man .9J **79**
Pattison Cl. OL12: Roch .2A **28**
Patton Cl. BL9: Bury .1A **60**
Patton Ct. M7: Sal .6B **78**
Paul Ct. *SK1: Stoc .7E 108*
(off Hall St.)
Paulden Av. M23: Wyth .1A **116**
OL4: O'ham .2B **64**
Paulden Dr. M35: Fail .3E **80**
Paulette St. BL1: Bolt .2F **38**
Paulhan Rd. M20: Man .4J **107**
Paulhan St. BL3: Bolt .9E **38**
Pauline St. WN2: Hin .1D **72**
Paul Row OL15: Lit .5N **15**
Pavement La. WA16: Mob .4L **133**
Pavilion Cl. OL12: Roch .3D **28**
Pavilion Ct. WA12: N Wil .6D **86**
Pavilion Dr. OL6: A Lyne .5A **82**
Pavilion Gdns. BL5: W'ton .3G **55**
Pavilion Lodge *M16: Old T .6N 93*
(off Edgbaston Dr.)
Pavilions, The M21: Cho H .8B **94**
SK8: Chea .3J **117**
Pavilion Sq. BL5: W'ton .3G **55**
Pavilion Wlk. M26: Rad .8F **40**
Pavilion Way SK10: Macc .3D **130**
Paxford Pl. SK9: Wilm .9F **122**
Paxton Pl. M11: Man .1K **95**
WN8: Skel .7A **50**
Paythorne Cl. WA3: Cul .6H **89**
Paythorne Grn. SK2: Stoc .2J **119**
Peabody St. BL3: Bolt .8F **38**
Peacefield SK6: Mar .2B **120**
Peacehaven Av. M11: Man .8A **80**
Peace St. BL3: Bolt .7E **38**
M29: Ast .4A **74**
M35: Fail .1E **80**
M46: Ath .8N **55**
Peaceville Rd. M19: Man .8L **95**
Peach Bank M24: Mid .3M **61**
Peach Bank Ho. M24: Mid .3M **61**
Peach Gro. WA11: Hay .2B **86**
Peach Rd. OL4: O'ham .2A **64**
Peach St. M25: Pres .6B **60**
Peach Tree Cl. *M7: Sal .4E 78*
(off Brakenhurst Dr.)
Peach Tree Ct. M6: Sal .8N **77**
Peacock Av. M6: Sal .5K **77**
Peacock Cl. M18: Man .3A **96**
SK13: Had .5A **100**
Peacock Dr. SK8: H Grn .9G **117**
Peacock Fold WN7: Lei .4F **72**
Peacock Gro. M18: Man .5B **96**
Peacock La. OL14: Wals .1M **15**
WA16: H Leg .9D **112**
Peacock Way *SK9: Hand .1J 123*
(off Pickmere Rd.)
Peak Av. M46: Ath .6L **55**
Peak Bank SK6: Rom .6L **109**
Peak Cl. OL4: O'ham .2K **65**
Peakdale Av. M8: Man .2G **79**
SK8: H Grn .6G **116**
Peakdale Rd. M43: Droy .7C **80**
SK6: Mar .3D **120**
SK13: Had .6A **100**
Peak District National Pk.
.5F **48** & 5F **84**
Peaknaze Cl. M27: Pen .2H **77**
SK13: Glos .9D **100**
Peak Rd. SK22: N Mil .7M **121**
Peak St. BL1: Bolt .2E **38**
M1: Man .5L **5** (9G **79**)
OL9: O'ham .5G **62**
SK1: Stoc .2N **9** (7E **108**)
Peak Vw. SK13: Had .5B **100**
Peanock La. OL15: Lit .3L **29**
Pear Av. BL9: Bury .1B **42**
Pear Cl. M24: Mid .5N **61**
Peardale Cl. M30: Ecc .1C **92**
Pearl Av. M7: Sal .1D **78**
Pearl Brook Ind. Est. BL6: Hor .1D **36**
Pearle St. SK10: Macc .3H **131**
Pearl Mill Cl. OL8: O'ham .7M **63**
Pearl St. M34: Dent .6J **97**
OL11: Roch .5A **28**
SK7: H Gro .3J **119**
SK10: P'bury .6E **128**
WN6: Wig .9E **34**
Pearl Way SK14: Mot .6K **99**
Pearly Bank OL1: O'ham .7A **46**
Pear Mill Ind. Est. SK6: Bred .6G **109**
Pearn Av. M19: Man .3L **107**
Pearn Rd. M19: Man .3L **107**
Pearson Cl. M31: Part .5H **103**
OL16: Miln .6K **29**
Pearson Gro. OL4: Lees .5B **64**
Pearson Ho. M30: Ecc .1D **92**
Pearson's Flash .7F **52**
Pearson St. BL9: Bury .1A **42**
OL16: Roch .5G **29**
SK5: Stoc .5D **108**
SK11: Macc .5J **131**
SK16: Duk .3N **97**
Peart Av. SK6: Wood .2N **109**
Pear Tree Av. PR7: Cop .2B **18**
Pear Tree Cl. M6: Sal .8N **77**
SK6: Mar B .8E **110**
SK13: Had .5A **100**
Pear Tree Ct. M6: Sal .8N **77**
WN2: Asp .6M **35**
Peartree Cres. WA12: N Wil .7F **86**
Pear Tree Dr. BL4: Farn .4H **57**
SK15: Stal .8E **82**
Pear Tree Gro. M29: Tyld .1E **74**
Pear Tree Pl. BL4: Farn .4H **57**
Pear Tree Wlk. *M33: Sale .3C 104*
(off Mountain Ash Cl.)
Peartree Wlk. M22: Wyth .3A **116**
Peart St. M34: Dent .6J **97**
Peary St. M4: Man .1L **5** (7G **79**)
Peaslake Cl. SK6: Rom .6A **110**
Peatfield Av. M27: Ward .9D **58**
Peatfield Wlk. *M15: Man .4E 94*
(off Botham Cl.)
Pebble Cl. SK15: Stal .6D **82**
Pebworth Cl. M24: Mid .6L **61**
Peckford Dr. M40: Man .5M **79**
Peckforton Cl. SK8: Gat .2F **116**
Peckforton Wlk. *SK9: Wilm .5K 123*
(off Colshaw Dr.)
Peckmill Cl. SK9: Wilm .4K **123**
Pedder St. BL1: Bolt .3D **38**
Pedler Brow La. OL12: Lit .8J **15**
OL15: Lit .8J **15**
Pedley Hill SK10: Adl .7K **125**
Pedley Wlk. M13: Man .8L **5**
Peebles Cl. WN4: Gars .6N **69**
Peebles Dr. M40: Man .6B **80**
PEEL .7F **56**
Peel Av. BL0: Ram .9G **11**
M17: Urm .3D 92
(in The Trafford Cen.)
WA14: Hale .5D **114**
Peel Bri. BL0: Ram .8J **11**
PEEL BROW .8K **11**
Peel Brow BL0: Ram .8K **11**
Peel Centre, The
SK1: Stoc .1N **9** (6E **108**)
Peel Circ. M41: Urm .3E **92**
Peel Cl. M46: Ath .8N **55**
Peel Cotts. BL8: Aff .5A **24**
Peel Ct. *SK2: Stoc .1E 118*
(off Peel St.)
Peel Cross Rd. M5: Sal .9N **77**
Peel Dr. M33: Sale .4L **105**
M38: Lit H .7G **57**
Peelgate Dr. SK8: H Grn .5F **116**
PEEL GREEN .1B **92**
Peel Grn. Cemetery & Crematorium
M30: Ecc .1N **91**
Peel Grn. Rd. M30: Ecc .1B **92**
Peel Grn. Trad. Est. M30: Ecc .1B **92**
Peel Gro. M12: Man .5M **95**
M28: Wors .2M **75**
PEEL HALL .5E **116**
Peel Hall Av. M29: Tyld .1C **74**
Peel Hall Rd. BL9: Sum .3H **25**
M22: Wyth .4D **116**
Peel Ho. M30: Ecc .8F **76**
Peel Ho. Cl. M38: Lit H .8G **56**
Peel Ind. Est. BL9: Bury .5K **7** (9L **25**)
Peel La. M8: Man .6F **78**
M28: Walk .8G **56**
M29: Ast .6C **74**
M38: Lit H .8G **56**
OL10: H'ood .1G **43**
Peel Mills BL9: Bury .1L **41**
Peel Moat Ct. SK4: Stoc .3A **108**
Peel Moat Rd. SK4: Stoc .3N **107**
Peel Moat Sports and
Target Fitness Cen. .3N **107**
Peel Monument .9F **10**
Peel Mt. BL0: Ram .1G **24**
M6: Sal .7A **78**
Peel Pk. Cres. M38: Lit H .7G **56**
Peel Rd. WA15: Hale .4E **114**
WN8: Skel .6B **50**
Peels Av. OL4: Spri .4D **64**
Peel Sq. M18: Man .5B **96**
Peel St. BL4: Farn .3M **57**
BL5: W'ton .2G **55**
HD7: Mars .1H **49**
M26: Rad .1H **59**
M30: Ecc .8F **76**
M34: Aud .3J **97**
M34: Dent .5J **97**
M35: Fail .4B **80**
M43: Droy .1D **96**
OL2: Shaw .5L **45**
OL6: A Lyne .7C **6** (7M **81**)
OL9: Chad .5F **62**
OL10: H'ood .2G **43**
OL12: Roch .5A **8** (5C **28**)
OL15: Lit .9M **15**
PR6: Adl .6L **19**
SK2: Stoc .1D **118**
SK11: Macc .6H **131**
SK13: Had .4E **100**
SK14: Hyde .8B **98**
SK15: Stal .9C **82**
SK16: Duk .9N **81**
WA12: N Wil .6D **86**
WN2: P Bri .9K **53**
WN7: Lei .5G **73**
Peel Ter. BL5: W'ton .1G **54**
SK16: Duk .9M 81
(off Queen St.)
Peel Theatre .9K **7** (3L **41**)
Peel Vw. BL8: Tot .7G **24**
Peel Way BL9: Bury .7J **7** (2L **41**)
Peelwood Av. M38: Lit H .6H **57**
Peelwood Gro. M46: Ath .9N **55**
Peerglow Pk. Est. WA14: Tim .8E **104**
Peers Cl. M41: Urm .5L **91**
Peers St. BL8: Bury .2J **41**
Pegamoid St. BL2: Bolt .3J **39**
Pegasus Ct. *M33: Sale .3K 105*
(off Broad Rd.)
OL11: Roch .6A **28**
Pegasus Sq. M7: Sal .7B **78**
Peggie's La. SK10: White G .2H **129**
Pegwell Dr. M7: Sal .5D **78**
Pekin St. OL6: A Lyne .6N **81**
Pelham Gro. WN2: Hin .7N **53**
Pelham Pl. M8: Man .9G **60**
Pelham St. BL3: Bolt .9D **38**
OL7: A Lyne .1J **97**
OL8: O'ham .9K **63**
Pellowe Rd. OL8: O'ham .8J **63**
Pelton Av. M27: Ward .9D **58**
Pelton Wlk. *M40: Man .5J 79*
(off Pitsford Rd.)
Pemberlei Rd. WN2: Asp .1N **53**
PEMBERTON .6N **51**
Pemberton Bus. Cen.
WN5: Wig .5N **51**
Pemberton Ho. *OL2: Shaw .4M 45*
(off Napier St.)
Pemberton Rd. WN3: Wins .2L **69**
WN5: Wins .2L **69**
Pemberton Station (Rail) .7A **52**
Pemberton St. BL1: Bolt .9F **22**
M16: Old T .5B **94**
M38: Lit H .7J **57**
OL11: Roch .2A **44**
Pemberton Way OL2: Shaw .4M **45**
Pembridge Fold M24: Mid .3A **62**
Pembridge Rd. M9: Man .7L **61**
Pembroke Av. M30: Ecc .8D **76**
M33: Sale .3F **104**
Pembroke Cl. BL6: Hor .9C **20**
M13: Man .3J **95**
SK8: Chea H .5K **117**

Pembroke Ct. M27: Pen . . . 2H 77
OL12: Roch . . . 4D 28
(off Alma St.)
SK6: Rom . . . 6K 109
SK7: H Gro . . . 5J 119
Pembroke Dr. BL9: Bury . . . 5L 41
OL4: O'ham . . . 8B 46
Pembroke Gro. M44: Cad . . . 2D 102
Pembroke Ho. SK3: Stoc . . . 8C 108
(off York St.)
Pembroke Rd. SK11: Macc . . . 5D 130
WN2: Hin . . . 8E 54
WN5: Wig . . . 2A 52
Pembroke St. BL1: Bolt . . . 1G 7 (4E 38)
M6: Sal . . . 9L 77
M7: Sal . . . 4D 78
OL8: O'ham . . . 4A 8 (5H 63)
OL15: Lit . . . 8M 15
Pembroke Way M34: Dent . . . 8L 97
(off Worcester Av.)
Pembry Cl. SK5: Stoc . . . 3F 108
Pembury Cl. M22: Wyth . . . 4B 116
Penarth Rd. BL3: Bolt . . . 8C 38
M22: Nor . . . 8C 106
Penbury Rd. WN1: Wig . . . 7E 34
Pencarrow Cl. M20: Man . . . 5E 106
Pencombe Cl. M12: Man . . . 4M 95
Pencroft Way M15: Man . . . 4F 94
Pendeen Cl. M22: Wyth . . . 6D 116
M29: Ast . . . 3B 74
Pendennis OL11: Roch . . . 9B 8 (7C 28)
Pendennis Av. BL6: Los . . . 7M 37
Pendennis Cl. M26: Rad . . . 7C 40
Pendennis Cres. WN2: Hin . . . 8C 54
Pendennis Rd. SK4: Stoc . . . 5A 108
Pendle Av. BL1: Bolt . . . 7F 22
PENDLEBURY . . . 2H 77
Pendlebury Cl. M25: Pres . . . 9M 59
Pendlebury Ct. M27: Pen . . . 1G 76
Pendlebury Fold BL3: Bolt . . . 1M 55
Pendlebury La. WN1: Hai . . . 7F 34
WN2: Hai . . . 7F 34
Pendlebury Rd. M27: Swin, Pen . . . 2F 76
SK8: Gat . . . 1F 116
Pendlebury St. BL1: Bolt . . . 1G 39
Pendlebury Towers SK5: Stoc . . . 5D 108
Pendle Cl. BL8: Bury . . . 1H 41
OL4: O'ham . . . 6A 64
WN5: Wig . . . 6A 52
Pendle Ct. BL1: Bolt . . . 1E 38
WN7: Lei . . . 6K 73
WN8: Skel . . . 8B 50
Pendlecroft Av. M27: Pen . . . 3J 77
Pendle Dr. BL6: Hor . . . 8E 20
Pendle Gdns. WA3: Cul . . . 7G 88
Pendle Gro. OL2: O'ham . . . 9G 45
Pendle Ho. M34: Dent . . . 7K 97
Pendle Pl. WN8: Skel . . . 7B 50
Pendle Rd. M34: Dent . . . 7K 97
WA3: Gol . . . 9M 71
PENDLETON . . . 7N 77
Pendleton Grn. M6: Sal . . . 7M 77
(off Nursery St.)
Pendleton Ho. M6: Sal . . . 7N 77
(off Broughton Rd.)
Pendleton Way M6: Sal . . . 7M 77
Pendle Wlk. M40: Man . . . 7J 79
SK5: Stoc . . . 3E 108
Pendleway M27: Pen . . . 1G 77
Pendragon Pl. M35: Fail . . . 3E 80
Pendrell Wlk. M9: Man . . . 8K 61
(off Sanderstead Dr.)
Penelope Rd. M6: Sal . . . 5K 77
Penerley Dr. M9: Man . . . 4J 79
Penfair Cl. M11: Man . . . 9M 79
Penfield Cl. M1: Man . . . 8K 5 (2G 94)
Penfield Rd. WN7: Lei . . . 9E 72
Penfold Wlk. M12: Man . . . 3L 95
(off Witterage Cl.)
Pengarth Rd. BL6: Hor . . . 9E 20
Pengham Wlk. M23: Wyth . . . 7N 105
Pengwern Av. BL3: Bolt . . . 8C 38
Penhale M. SK7: Bram . . . 8D 118
Penhall Wlk. M40: Man . . . 5M 79
(off Mansford Dr.)
Peninsula M7: Sal . . . 3A 78
Penistone Av. M6: Sal . . . 7J 77
M9: Man . . . 8M 61
OL16: Roch . . . 7G 29
Penketh Av. M18: Man . . . 5N 95
M29: Ast . . . 4C 74
Penketh Pl. WN8: Skel . . . 6A 50
Penketh St. WN6: Wig . . . 1D 52
Penkford La. WA5: Coll G . . . 8A 86
Penkford St. WA12: N Wil . . . 6B 86
Penleach Av. WN7: Lei . . . 5K 73
Penmere Gro. M33: Sale . . . 7E 104
Penmoor Chase SK7: H Gro . . . 6F 118
Penmore Cl. OL2: Shaw . . . 5N 45
Pennant Dr. M25: Pres . . . 6N 59
Pennant Ind. Est.
OL1: O'ham . . . 3M 63
Pennant St. OL1: O'ham . . . 3M 63
Pennell Dr. WN3: Wig . . . 6C 52
Pennell St. M11: Man . . . 9B 80
Penn Grn. SK8: Chea H . . . 6N 117
Penn Ho. Cl. SK7: Bram . . . 7C 118
Pennine Av. OL9: Chad . . . 6E 62
WN3: Wins . . . 8N 51
Pennine Bus. Pk.
OL10: H'ood . . . 4G 43
Pennine Cl. BL6: Hor . . . 8E 20
BL8: Bury . . . 1H 41
M9: Man . . . 7L 61
Pennine Ct. M27: Pen . . . 1G 76
SK10: Macc . . . 2J 131
SK15: Stal . . . 7G 82
Pennine Dr. OL6: A Lyne . . . 6B 82
OL12: W'le . . . 8G 14
OL16: Miln . . . 6L 29
WA14: Alt . . . 2B 114
Pennine Gro. OL6: A Lyne . . . 4B 82
WN7: Lei . . . 2E 72
Pennine La. WA3: Gol . . . 9M 71
Pennine Pl. WN8: Skel . . . 5A 50
Pennine Pct. OL16: Miln . . . 8K 29
Pennine Rd. BL6: Hor . . . 8E 20
SK6: Wood . . . 2N 109
SK7: H Gro . . . 6F 118
SK13: Glos . . . 9C 100
Pennine Ter. SK16: Duk . . . 9N 81
(off Peel St.)
Pennine Va. OL2: Shaw . . . 4N 45
Pennine Vw. M34: Aud . . . 4J 97
OL2: O'ham . . . 8J 45
OL5: Mos . . . 1G 83
OL15: Lit . . . 4A 16
OL16: Roch . . . 5E 8
SK15: H'rod . . . 6F 82
Pennine Wlk. WN2: P Bri . . . 9L 53
PENNINGTON . . . 6G 73
Pennington Av. WN7: Lei . . . 7G 73
Pennington Cl. M38: Lit H . . . 7F 57
WN2: Asp . . . 2A 54
Pennington Ct. WN7: Lei . . . 9D 72
Pennington Dr. WA12: N Wil . . . 6H 87
Pennington Flash Country Pk. . . . 8D 72
Pennington Flash Country Pk. Vis. Cen.
. . . 7E 72
Pennington Gdns. WN7: Lei . . . 7G 73
Pennington Golf Course . . . 7E 72
PENNINGTON GREEN . . . 1N 53
Pennington Grn. La. WN2: Asp . . . 1A 54
Pennington Ho. WN7: Lei . . . 6G 73
Pennington La.
WA9: Coll G, St H . . . 7A 86
WN2: Hai . . . 4H 35
WN2: I Mak . . . 3K 53
Pennington M. WN7: Lei . . . 8G 73
Pennington Rd. BL3: Bolt . . . 9G 38
WN7: Lei . . . 7H 73
Penningtons La. SK11: Gaws . . . 7C 130
Pennington Sq. WN7: Lei . . . 6J 73
Pennington St. BL8: Bury . . . 9E 24
M12: Man . . . 7M 95
M28: Walk . . . 9M 57
OL9: Chad . . . 6H 63
WN2: Hin . . . 5N 53
Pennistone Cl. M44: Irl . . . 6J 91
Pennon Cl. M7: Sal . . . 4C 78
Penn St. BL4: Farn . . . 3K 57
BL6: Hor . . . 1E 36
M40: Man . . . 2L 79
OL8: O'ham . . . 6H 63
OL10: H'ood . . . 3J 43
OL16: Roch . . . 6D 8 (5D 28)
Penny Black Chambers
M28: Wors . . . 5N 75
(off Barton Rd.)
Penny Bri. La. M41: Urm . . . 7A 92
(not continuous)
Penny Brook Fold SK7: H Gro . . . 4K 119
Pennybutts Cl. WA3: Gol . . . 8J 71
Pennygate Cl. WN2: Hin . . . 5N 53
Pennyhurst St. WN3: Wig . . . 4D 52
Penny La. SK5: Stoc . . . 6D 108
WA5: Coll G . . . 9A 86
WA11: Hay . . . 2C 86
Penny Mdw. OL6: A Lyne . . . 7E 6 (7N 81)
Pennymoor Dr. WA14: Alt . . . 1B 114
Penrhos Av. SK8: Gat . . . 2E 116
Penrhyn Av. M24: Mid . . . 4M 61
SK8: Chea H . . . 6K 117
Penrhyn Cres. SK7: H Gro . . . 7G 119
Penrhyn Dr. M25: Pres . . . 7A 60
Penrhyn Gro. M46: Ath . . . 6L 55
Penrhyn Rd. SK3: Stoc . . . 8N 107
Penrice Cl. M26: Rad . . . 7D 40
Penrice Fold M28: Wors . . . 3J 75
Penrith Av. BL1: Bolt . . . 3B 38
M11: Man . . . 7B 80
M28: Walk . . . 9N 57
M33: Sale . . . 6J 105
M45: Whitef . . . 4A 60
OL7: A Lyne . . . 5K 81
OL8: O'ham . . . 7G 63
SK5: Stoc . . . 8D 96
SK11: Macc . . . 7D 130
Penrith Cl. M31: Part . . . 4F 102
Penrith Cres. WN4: A Mak . . . 6E 70
Penrith St. OL11: Roch . . . 8D 28
Penrod Pl. M6: Sal . . . 6A 78
Penrose Cl. M8: Man . . . 4F 78
Penrose Gdns. M24: Mid . . . 2N 61
Penrose Pl. WN8: Skel . . . 7C 50
Penrose St. BL2: Bolt . . . 5K 39
Penrose Wlk. M24: Mid . . . 8M 43
Penroy Av. M20: Man . . . 5C 106
Penroyson Cl. M12: Man . . . 3L 95
Penruddock Wlk. M13: Man . . . 5L 95
(off Bates St.)
Penry Av. M44: Cad . . . 2F 102
Penryn Av. M33: Sale . . . 7J 105
OL2: O'ham . . . 8K 45
Penryn Ct. M7: Sal . . . 1C 78
Pensarn Av. M14: Man . . . 9K 95
Pensarn Gro. SK5: Stoc . . . 4D 108
Pensby Cl. M27: Pen . . . 3J 77
Pensby Wlk. M40: Man . . . 5J 79
(off Tollard Av.)
Pensford Ct. BL2: Bolt . . . 7M 23
Pensford Rd. M23: Wyth . . . 4M 115
Penshaw Av. WN3: Wig . . . 8E 52
Penshurst Rd. SK5: Stoc . . . 2F 108
Penshurst Wlk. M34: Dent . . . 8L 97
(off Two Trees La.)
Penson St. WN1: Wig . . . 1G 52
Penswick Rd. WN2: Hin . . . 8E 54
Penthorpe Dr. OL2: O'ham . . . 9K 45
Pentland Av. M40: Man . . . 9A 62
Pentland Cl. SK7: H Gro . . . 6F 118
Pentlands, The OL2: Shaw . . . 4K 45
Pentlands Av. M7: Sal . . . 5C 78
Pentland Ter. BL1: Bolt . . . 3F 38
Pentland Way SK14: Hyde . . . 3E 98
Pentwyn Gro. M23: Wyth . . . 9A 106
Penwell Fold OL1: O'ham . . . 2J 63
WN8: Skel . . . 3C 50
Penydarren Vw. BL3: Bolt . . . 1K 57
Penzance Cl. SK10: Macc . . . 4C 130
Penzance St. M40: Man . . . 7K 79
People's History Mus. . . . 4E 4 (9D 78)
Peover Av. M33: Sale . . . 4L 105
Peover Rd. SK9: Hand . . . 1K 123
Peover Wlk. SK8: Chea . . . 2M 117
Pepler Av. M23: Wyth . . . 6A 106
Peploe Wlk. M23: Wyth . . . 7K 105
Pepper Cl. M22: Wyth . . . 1C 116
Pepper Ct. SK9: Wilm . . . 8F 122
Pepperhill Rd. M16: Whall R . . . 5E 94
Pepper La. WN6: She, Stan . . . 1M 33
Pepper Mill La.
WN1: Wig . . . 9L 9 (4G 52)
Peppermint Cl. OL16: Miln . . . 9N 29
Pepper Rd. SK7: H Gro . . . 5F 118
Peppers, The WA13: Lym . . . 4A 112
Pepper St. SK11: Hen . . . 4A 130
WA13: Lym . . . 4A 112
Pepperwood Dr. WN3: Wins . . . 9B 52
Pepys Pl. WN3: Wig . . . 7D 52
Perceval Way WN2: Hin . . . 7N 53
Perch St. WN1: Wig . . . 6N 9 (2H 53)
Percival Cl. M8: Man . . . 4E 78
Percival Rd. M43: Droy . . . 9F 80
Percival Wlk. OL2: O'ham . . . 9J 45
Percy Dr. M5: Sal . . . 2A 94
Percy Rd. M34: Dent . . . 7J 97
Percy St. BL0: Ram . . . 9H 11
BL1: Bolt . . . 2G 39
BL4: Farn . . . 4M 57
BL9: Bury . . . 1N 41
M15: Man . . . 3C 94
OL4: O'ham . . . 4N 63
OL12: Whitw . . . 1C 14
OL16: Roch . . . 8F 28
SK1: Stoc . . . 1L 9 (6D 108)
SK15: Stal . . . 9E 82
Percyvale St. SK10: Macc . . . 4J 131
Peregrine Cres. M43: Droy . . . 7G 80
Peregrine Dr. M44: Irl . . . 6H 91
WN7: Lei . . . 5K 73
Peregrine Rd. SK2: Stoc . . . 3L 119
Peregrine St. M15: Man . . . 4E 94
Peregrine Vw. M43: Droy . . . 7G 81
(off Bittern Dr.)
Perendale Ri. BL1: Bolt . . . 9F 22
Periton Wlk. M9: Man . . . 8K 61
(off Leconfield Dr.)
Perivale Dr. OL8: O'ham . . . 7M 63
Perkins Av. M7: Sal . . . 5D 78
Pernham St. OL4: O'ham . . . 4N 63
Perranwell Cl. M22: Wyth . . . 6A 116
Perrin St. SK14: Hyde . . . 7A 98
Perry Av. SK14: Hyde . . . 5D 98
Perrybrook Wlk. WN4: A Mak . . . 6G 70
(off North St.)
Perry Cl. OL11: Roch . . . 8B 28
Perrygate Av. M20: Man . . . 2F 106
Perrymead M25: Pres . . . 5B 60
Perryn Pl. WN6: Stan . . . 3C 34
Perry Rd. WA15: Tim . . . 1H 115
Pershore OL12: Roch . . . 6B 8 (5C 28)
Pershore Rd. M24: Mid . . . 9M 43
Perth M30: Ecc . . . 8E 76
(off Monton La.)
Perth Av. OL9: Chad . . . 7E 62
WN2: I Mak . . . 3K 53
Perth Cl. SK7: Bram . . . 1C 124
Perth Rd. OL11: Roch . . . 2F 44
Perth St. BL3: Bolt . . . 9D 38
M27: Swin . . . 3D 76
OL2: O'ham . . . 8L 45
Peru St. M3: Sal . . . 2B 4 (8C 78)
Peterborough Cl. OL6: A Lyne . . . 4M 81
SK10: Macc . . . 2E 130
Peterborough Dr. BL1: Bolt . . . 3G 38
Peterborough St. M18: Man . . . 3D 96
Peterborough Wlk. BL1: Bolt . . . 3F 38
(off Charnock Dr.)
BL1: Bolt . . . 3G 38
(off Peterborough Dr.)
Peterchurch Wlk. M11: Man . . . 1A 96
(off Eccles Cl.)
Peterhead Cl. BL1: Bolt . . . 3E 38
Peterhead Wlk. M5: Sal . . . 9N 77
Peterhouse Gdns.
SK6: Wood . . . 4N 109
Peterhouse Rd. SK11: Sut E . . . 9K 131
Peterhouse Wlk. WN4: A Mak . . . 6C 70
Peter Kane Sq. WA3: Gol . . . 1K 87
(off Heath St.)
Peterloo Ct. M6: Sal . . . 8L 77
(off St Luke's Rd.)
Peterloo Ter. M24: Mid . . . 1M 61
Peter Martin St. BL6: Hor . . . 9D 20
Peter Moss Way M19: Man . . . 8A 96
Petersburg Rd. SK3: Stoc . . . 1A 118
Peters Cl. SK10: P'bury . . . 6E 128
Peters Ct. WA15: Tim . . . 2K 115
Petersfield Dr. M23: Wyth . . . 9K 105
Petersfield Gdns. WA3: Cul . . . 5G 88
Petersfield Wlk. BL1: Bolt . . . 4F 38
(off Bk. Ashford Wlk.)
Peter St. BL5: W'ton . . . 4C 54
BL9: Bury . . . 5M 7 (1M 41)
M2: Man . . . 6F 4 (1E 94)
M3: Man . . . 6F 4 (1E 94)
M29: Tyld . . . 1A 74
M30: Ecc . . . 9D 76
M34: Dent . . . 6L 97
OL1: O'ham . . . 3D 8 (5K 63)
SK1: Stoc . . . 6E 108
SK7: H Gro . . . 4H 119
(not continuous)
SK11: Macc . . . 6G 130
SK13: Had . . . 3C 100
WA3: Gol . . . 1K 87
WA14: Alt . . . 5C 6 (4D 114)
WN2: Hin . . . 6N 53
WN4: A Mak . . . 7F 70
WN5: Wig . . . 3M 51
WN7: Lei . . . 6K 73
Peter St. W. SK11: Macc . . . 5G 130
Peterswood Cl. M22: Wyth . . . 4A 116
Peter Wood Gdns.
M32: Stre . . . 8G 93
PETRE BANK . . . 2L 125
Petrel Av. SK12: Poy . . . 2F 124
Petrel Cl. M29: Ast . . . 2B 74
M43: Droy . . . 7G 80
OL11: Roch . . . 6L 27
SK3: Stoc . . . 1B 118
Petrel Ho. M19: Man . . . 4J 107
Petrie Ct. M6: Sal . . . 6A 78
Petrie St. OL12: Roch . . . 4D 28
Petrock Wlk. M40: Man . . . 5A 80
(off Gaskell St.)
Petticoat La. WN2: I Mak . . . 4L 53
Petts Cres. OL15: Lit . . . 8L 15
Petunia Gro. SK11: Macc . . . 7F 130
Petunia Wlk. M38: Lit H . . . 8G 57
(off Madams Wood Rd.)
Petworth Av. WN3: Wins . . . 9A 52
Petworth Cl. M22: Shar . . . 2D 116
Petworth Rd. OL9: Chad . . . 5F 62
Pevensey Ct. M9: Man . . . 9M 61
Pevensey Dr. WA16: Knut . . . 8G 132
Pevensey Rd. M6: Sal . . . 5L 77
Pevensey Wlk. OL9: Chad . . . 5F 62
Peveril Av. SK22: N Mil . . . 6M 121
Peveril Cl. M45: Whitef . . . 4B 60
Peveril Cl. SK13: Glos . . . 9H 101
Peveril Cres. M21: Cho H . . . 7N 93
Peveril Dr. SK7: H Gro . . . 7K 119
Peveril Gdns. SK12: Dis . . . 9K 121
Peveril M. SK12: Dis . . . 9K 121
Peveril Rd. M5: Sal . . . 8K 77
OL1: O'ham . . . 2N 63
WA14: B'ath . . . 9C 104
Peveril St. BL3: Bolt . . . 9C 38
Peveril Ter. SK14: Hyde . . . 9C 98
Peveril Wlk. SK11: Macc . . . 5D 130
PEWFALL . . . 9N 69
Pewfist, The BL5: W'ton . . . 4G 54
Pewfist Grn. BL5: W'ton . . . 5G 55
Pewfist Spinney, The BL5: W'ton . . . 4F 54
Pewsey Rd. M22: Wyth . . . 4E 116
Pexhill Ct. SK4: Stoc . . . 6M 107
Pexhill Dr. SK10: Macc . . . 5C 130
Pexhill Rd. SK10: Macc . . . 7A 130
SK11: Gaws, Hen . . . 7A 130
Pexwood OL1: Chad . . . 2C 62
Phaeton Cl. M46: Ath . . . 1J 73
Pheasant Cl. M28: Wors . . . 4H 75
Pheasant Dr. M21: Cho H . . . 1C 106
Pheasant Ri. WA14: Bow . . . 6D 114
Phelan Cl. M40: Man . . . 5H 79
Phethean St. BL2: Bolt . . . 2N 7 (5H 39)
BL4: Farn . . . 2K 57
Philip Av. M34: Dent . . . 4J 97
Philip Cl. WN5: Wig . . . 6A 52
Philip Dr. M33: Sale . . . 6H 105
Philip Godlee Lodge M20: Man . . . 6G 106
Philip Howard Ct. BL4: Farn . . . 3K 57
(off Glynne St.)
Philip Howard Rd. SK13: Glos . . . 9E 100
Philips Av. BL4: Farn . . . 4L 57
Philips Ct. M14: Man . . . 5J 95
(off Hope Rd.)
Philips Dr. M45: Whitef . . . 5K 59
PHILIPS PARK . . . 7M 79
Philips Pk.
Manchester . . . 7M 79
Prestwich . . . 6K 59
Philips Pk. Rd. M11: Man . . . 8K 79
Philips Pk. Rd. E. M45: Whitef . . . 5L 59
Philips Pk. Rd. W. M45: Whitef . . . 6J 59
Philip St. BL3: Bolt . . . 7E 38
M30: Ecc . . . 9D 76
OL4: O'ham . . . 3N 63
OL11: Roch . . . 8D 28
Phillimore St. OL4: Lees . . . 6B 64
Phillip & Pauline Gordon Ho.
M25: Pres . . . 1A 78
Phillips Pl. M45: Whitef . . . 4M 59
Phillips St. WN7: Lei . . . 2G 72
Phillip Way SK14: Hat . . . 8H 99
Phipps' La. WA5: Burt . . . 9B 86
Phipps St. M28: Walk . . . 7K 57
Phoebe St. BL3: Bolt . . . 8D 38
(off Church Av.)
M5: Sal . . . 1N 93
Phoenix, The M7: Sal . . . 5C 78
Phoenix Cl. OL10: H'ood . . . 3L 43
Phoenix Ct. SK4: Stoc . . . 3C 108
Phoenix Ind. Est. M35: Fail . . . 2E 80
Phoenix Pk. Ind. Est.
OL10: H'ood . . . 3L 43
Phoenix Pl. OL4: Spri . . . 5C 64
Phoenix St. BL1: Bolt . . . 1M 7 (4H 39)
BL4: Farn . . . 4L 57
BL9: Bury . . . 7J 7 (2L 41)
M2: Man . . . 4H 5 (9F 78)
OL1: O'ham . . . 3D 8 (5K 63)
OL4: Spri . . . 5C 64
OL12: Roch . . . 4A 28
OL15: Lit . . . 8M 15
Phoenix Way M15: Man . . . 4E 94
M26: Rad . . . 1G 58
M41: Urm . . . 3E 92
WN3: I Mak . . . 6H 53
Phyllis St. M24: Mid . . . 4A 62
OL12: Roch . . . 4N 27
Picadilly WN5: Bil . . . 5J 69
Piccadilly M1: Man . . . 4J 5 (9F 78)
SK1: Stoc . . . 2L 9 (7D 108)
Piccadilly Gdns. . . . 4J 5 (9F 78)
Piccadilly Gardens Stop (Metro)
. . . 5J 5 (9F 78)
Piccadilly Lofts M1: Man . . . 5K 5
Piccadilly Pl. M1: Man . . . 6K 5 (1G 94)
Piccadilly Plaza M1: Man . . . 5H 5 (9F 78)
Piccadilly Sth. M1: Man . . . 5K 5 (9G 78)
Piccadilly Station (Rail & Metro)
. . . 6L 5 (1G 95)
Piccadilly Trad. Est.
M1: Man . . . 6N 5 (1H 95)
PICCADILLY VILLAGE . . . 5M 5 (9H 79)
Piccard Cl. M40: Man . . . 5J 79
Pickenham Cl. SK11: Macc . . . 6D 130
Pickering Cl. BL8: Bury . . . 8H 25
M26: Rad . . . 3A 58
M41: Urm . . . 7B 92
WA15: Tim . . . 9G 104
Pickering St. M15: Man . . . 4D 94
Pickford Av. BL3: Lit L . . . 9C 40
Pickford Ct. M15: Man . . . 4D 94
SK16: Duk . . . 1N 97
Pickford La. SK16: Duk . . . 1N 97
Pickford M. SK16: Duk . . . 1N 97
(off Pickford La.)
Pickford's Brow SK1: Stoc . . . 2L 9
Pickford St. M4: Man . . . 3L 5 (8G 79)
SK11: Macc . . . 5H 131
Pickford Wlk. OL2: O'ham . . . 9J 45
Pickhill OL3: Upp . . . 3L 65
Pickhill M. OL3: Upp . . . 3L 65
Pickley Ct. WN7: Lei . . . 1G 73
PICKLEY GREEN . . . 1G 72
Pickley Grn. WN7: Lei . . . 1G 72
Pickmere Av. M20: Man . . . 9G 94
Pickmere Cl. M33: Sale . . . 6M 105
M43: Droy . . . 9F 80
SK3: Stoc . . . 1A 118
Pickmere Gdns. SK8: Chea H . . . 2L 117
Pickmere La. WA16: Tab . . . 5A 132
Pickmere M. OL3: Upp . . . 3L 65
Pickmere Rd. SK9: Hand . . . 1J 123
Pickmere Ter. SK16: Duk . . . 9M 81
Picksley St. WN7: Lei . . . 6K 73
Pickthorn Cl. WN2: P Bri . . . 8L 53
Pickup St. OL16: Roch . . . 8E 8 (6E 28)
WN2: I Mak . . . 4J 53
Pickwick Rd. SK12: Poy . . . 3H 125
Pickworth St. OL8: O'ham . . . 7K 63
Picton Cl. M3: Sal . . . 2D 4 (8D 78)
Picton Dr. SK9: Wilm . . . 5K 123
Picton Sq. OL4: O'ham . . . 4F 8 (5L 63)
Picton St. M7: Sal . . . 7C 78
OL7: A Lyne . . . 4L 81
Picton Wlk. M16: Whall R . . . 6E 94
(off Bedwell St.)
Piele Rd. WA11: Hay . . . 2A 86
Pier, The WN3: Wig . . . 4E 52
(off Pottery Rd.)
Pierce St. OL1: O'ham . . . 2N 63
SK11: Macc . . . 4G 130
Piercy St. M4: Man . . . 4N 5 (9J 79)
M35: Fail . . . 3C 80
Piethorne Cl. OL16: Miln . . . 9N 29
Pigeon St. M1: Man . . . 4L 5 (9G 79)
Piggott St. BL4: Farn . . . 4K 57
Pigot St. WN5: Orr . . . 5M 51
Pike Av. M35: Fail . . . 4G 80
M46: Ath . . . 9J 55
Pike Fold Golf Course . . . 1C 60
Pike Fold La. M9: Man . . . 8H 61
Pikelaw Pl. WN8: Skel . . . 6A 50
Pike Mill Est. BL3: Bolt . . . 8F 38
Pike Nook Workshops BL3: Bolt . . . 7F 38
Pike Rd. BL3: Bolt . . . 8E 38
Pike's La. SK13: Glos . . . 9D 100
Pike St. OL11: Roch . . . 8D 28
Pike Vw. BL6: Hor . . . 9F 20
Pike Vw. Cl. OL4: O'ham . . . 6M 63
Pilgrim Dr. M11: Man . . . 9L 79
Pilgrims Way M50: Ecc, Sal . . . 8G 77
WN6: Stan . . . 5D 34
Pilgrim Way OL1: O'ham . . . 9A 46
Pilkington Dr. M45: Whitef . . . 1A 60
Pilkington Rd. BL4: Kea . . . 5N 57
M9: Man . . . 9M 61
M26: Rad . . . 7F 40
Pilkington St. BL0: Ram . . . 9H 11
BL3: Bolt . . . 7F 38
M24: Mid . . . 2N 61
WN2: Hin . . . 5N 53
Pilkington Way M26: Rad . . . 9G 41
Pilling Fld. BL7: Eger . . . 4F 22
Pilling Pl. WN8: Skel . . . 6A 50
Pilling St. BL8: Bury . . . 1J 41
M34: Dent . . . 6K 97
OL12: Roch . . . 5B 28
WN7: Lei . . . 5F 72
Pilling Wlk. OL9: Chad . . . 5E 62
Pilning St. BL3: Bolt . . . 8H 39
Pilot Ind. Est. BL3: Bolt . . . 8J 39
Pilot St. BL9: Bury . . . 3N 41
Pilsley Cl. WN5: Orr . . . 2L 51
Pilsworth Cotts. BL9: Bury . . . 7B 42
Pilsworth Ind. Est.
BL9: Bury . . . 5A 42
Pilsworth Rd. BL9: Bury . . . 6N 41
(not continuous)
OL10: H'ood . . . 5E 42
Pilsworth Rd. Ind. Est.
BL9: Bury . . . 6N 41
Pilsworth Way BL9: Bury . . . 6N 41
Pimblett Rd. WA11: Hay . . . 2B 86
Pimblett St. M3: Man . . . 1G 5 (7E 78)
WA3: Gol . . . 2K 87
Pimbo Ind. Est. WN8: Skel . . . 6A 50
(not continuous)
Pimbo Junc. WN8: Skel . . . 6C 50
Pimbo La. WN8: Uph . . . 2D 68
Pimbo Rd. WA11: K Mos . . . 3C 68
WN8: Skel . . . 6A 50
PIMHOLE . . . 3N 41
Pimhole Fold BL9: Bury . . . 3N 41
Pimhole Rd. BL9: Bury . . . 2N 41
Pimlico Cl. M7: Sal . . . 4C 78
(off Hilton St. Nth.)
Pimlott Gro. M25: Pres . . . 9L 59
SK14: Hyde . . . 4A 98
Pimlott Rd. BL1: Bolt . . . 1J 39
Pimmcroft Way M33: Sale . . . 5M 105
Pincher Wlk. M11: Man . . . 9A 80
(off Edith Cavell Cl.)
Pincroft La. PR7: Adl . . . 7K 19
Pinder Wlk. M15: Man . . . 3E 94
(off Brindle Pl.)
Pineacre Cl. WA14: W Tim . . . 8B 104
Pineapple St. SK7: H Gro . . . 5J 119
Pine Av. M45: Whitef . . . 4M 59
WA12: N Wil . . . 7F 86
Pine Cl. M34: Aud . . . 3J 97
SK6: Mar . . . 3B 120
SK10: Macc . . . 3K 131
Pine Ct. M20: Man . . . 4F 106
SK7: Bram . . . 5B 118

Pine Gro. BL4: Farn 3J 57
BL5: W'ton 4G 55
M14: Man 5K 95
M25: Pres 5N 59
M27: Swin 3D 76
M28: Wors 2M 75
M30: Ecc 6E 76
M33: Sale 2D 104
M34: Dent 6L 97
OL2: O'ham 6H 45
SK16: Duk 1C 98
WA3: Gol 1M 87
Pinehurst SK10: P'bury 7C 128
Pinehurst Rd. M40: Man 5K 79
Pinelea WA15: Alt 3F 114
Pine Lodge SK7: Bram 8D 118
Pine Mdws. M26: Rad 5B 58
Pine Rd. M20: Man 4F 106
SK7: Bram 7D 118
SK10: Macc 3K 131
SK12: Poy 3K 125
SK15: Stal 1B 98
WN5: Wig 5B 52
Pines, The M23: Wyth 7A 106
M33: Sale 6H 105
OL10: H'ood 2J 43
(off Pine St.)
WN7: Lei 7H 73
Pine St. BL1: Bolt 2G 39
BL9: Bury 2A 42
M1: Man 5H 5 (9F 78)
M24: Mid 4A 62
M26: Rad 8H 41
M29: Tyld 1B 74
OL6: A Lyne 6M 81
OL9: Chad 3E 62
OL10: H'ood 2J 43
OL15: Lit 8M 15
OL16: Miln 1M 45
OL16: Roch 6F 28
SK6: Wood 3M 109
SK14: Hyde 4A 98
Pine St. Nth. BL9: Bury 1A 42
(not continuous)
Pine St. Sth. BL9: Bury 2A 42
Pinetop Cl. M21: Cho H 2C 106
Pine Tree Rd. OL8: O'ham 1H 81
Pinetree St. M18: Man 4A 96
Pinevale WN6: Stan 5D 34
Pine Vw. WN3: Wins 1M 69
Pine Wlk. M31: Part 5F 102
(off Wood La.)
Pine Way OL4: Lees 5C 64
Pinewood M33: Sale 4D 104
OL9: Chad 4C 62
WA14: Bow 5A 114
WN4: A Mak 8D 70
WN8: Skel 9B 32
Pinewood Cl. BL1: Bolt 2F 38
SK4: Stoc 5M 107
SK16: Duk 9N 81
WN2: Abr 3M 71
Pinewood Ct. M33: Sale 3K 105
SK9: Wilm 5K 123
(off Brackenwood M.)
WA14: Hale 6E 114
Pinewood Cres. BL0: Ram 3H 25
WN2: I Mak 5J 53
WN5: Orr 5J 51
Pinewood Rd. M21: Cho H 1N 105
SK9: Wilm 5K 123
Pinewoods, The SK6: Wood 3M 109
Pinfold BL0: Eden 1K 11
SK13: Had 5A 100
Pinfold Av. M9: Man 9M 61
Pinfold Cl. BL5: W'ton 5F 54
WA15: Haleb 8K 115
Pinfold Ct. M32: Stre 8J 93
(off Barton Rd.)
M45: Whitef 3L 59
Pinfold Dr. M25: Pres 6M 59
SK8: Chea H 6M 117
Pinfold La. M45: Whitef 3L 59
M90: Man A 9M 115
SK6: Rom 4A 110
Pinfold Pl. WN8: Skel 7B 50
Pinfold Rd. M28: Walk 1K 75
Pinfold St. SK11: Macc 4G 131
WN2: I Mak 4K 53
Pingate Dr. SK8: Chea H 9M 117
Pingate La. SK8: Chea H 9M 117
Pingate La. Sth. SK8: Chea H 9M 117
Pingle La. OL3: Del 7G 47
Pingot OL2: Shaw 3A 46
Pingot, The M44: Irl 6J 91
WN7: Lei 5F 72
Pingot Av. M23: Wyth 7A 106
Pingot Ct. WN7: Lei 5F 72
(off Cooperative St.)
Pingot La. SK14: B'tom 8L 99
Pingot Rd. SK22: N Mil 7N 121
WN5: Bil 5J 69
Pingott La. SK13: Had 4C 100
Pinhigh Pl. M6: Sal 4H 77
Pink Bank La. M12: Man 5M 95
(not continuous)
Pin Mill Brow M12: Man 1J 95
Pinnacle Dr. BL7: Eger 3F 22
Pinner Fold SK15: Stal 7G 82
Pinner Pl. M19: Man 2M 107
Pinners Cl. BL0: Ram 7H 11
Pinnington La. M32: Stre 7K 93
Pinnington Rd. M18: Man 3B 96
Pintail Av. SK3: Stoc 1B 118
Pintail Cl. OL12: Roch 3N 27
Pioneer Cl. BL6: Hor 9D 20
Pioneer Ct. OL7: A Lyne 9A 6
Pioneer Ind. Est. WN5: Wig 5B 52
Pioneer Rd. M27: Clif 9K 59
Pioneer St. BL6: Hor 9E 20
M11: Man 7N 79
M24: Mid 7B 44
OL11: Roch 7E 28
OL15: Lit 9M 15
Pioneers Villa OL16: Miln 9B 30
Pioneers Yd. OL16: Miln 8K 29
Piperhill Av. M22: Nor 6C 106
Pipers, The WA3: Low 1B 88
Pipers Cl. OL11: Roch 5J 27
Pipers Ct. M44: Irl 6K 91
Pipewell Av. M18: Man 4A 96
Pipit Av. WA12: N Wil 6F 86
Pipit Cl. M34: Aud 8G 81
Pirie Wlk. M40: Man 4A 80
(off Queensferry St.)
Pitcairn Ho. M30: Ecc 9D 76
(off Adelaide St.)
Pitchcombe Rd. M22: Wyth 5A 116
Pitcombe Cl. BL1: Bolt 6E 22
Pitfield Cotts. SK14: Hyde 6N 97
Pitfield Gdns. M23: Wyth 9M 105
Pitfield La. BL2: Bolt 1N 39
Pitfield St. BL2: Bolt 5J 39
Pit Hey Pl. WN8: Skel 6A 50
Pit La. OL2: O'ham, Shaw 4G 45
Pitman Cl. M11: Man 1M 95
Pitmore Wlk. M40: Man 9B 62
PITSES 7A 64
Pits Farm Av. OL11: Roch 6A 28
Pitsford Rd. M40: Man 5K 79
Pitshouse OL12: Roch 3K 27
Pitshouse La. OL12: Roch 3K 27
Pit St. OL9: Chad 7F 62
Pittbrook St. M12: Man 2J 95
Pitt St. M26: Rad 9E 40
M34: Dent 6K 97
OL4: O'ham 5L 63
OL10: H'ood 2H 43
OL12: Roch 5E 8 (5D 28)
SK3: Stoc 5H 9 (8B 108)
SK11: Macc 6H 131
SK14: Hyde 6A 98
WN3: I Mak 5G 53
WN3: Wig 9H 9 (4E 52)
Pitt St. E. OL4: O'ham 6M 63
Pixmore Av. BL1: Bolt 9J 23
Place, The M1: Man 5L 5 (9G 79)
Place Rd. WA14: Alt 1C 114
Plain Pitt St. SK14: Hyde 4N 97
(not continuous)
Plainsfield St. M16: Whall R 5D 94
Plane Av. WN5: Wig 4B 52
Plane Ct. M6: Sal 8N 77
Plane Rd. M35: Fail 5D 80
Plane St. OL4: O'ham 4N 63
Plane Tree Cl. SK6: Mar 2A 120
Plane Tree Gro. WA11: Hay 2D 86
Planetree Rd. M31: Part 5E 102
WA15: Hale 5G 114
Planetree Wlk. M23: Wyth 8J 105
Planet Way M34: Aud 4J 97
Planewood Gdns. WA3: Low 2B 88
PLANK LANE 6D 72
Plank La. WN7: Lei 6C 72
Plantagenet Wlk. M40: Man 6B 80
(off Marguerita Rd.)
Plantagent St. OL5: Mos 8G 64
Plantation Av. M28: Walk 7K 57
Plantation Gates WN1: Wig 1H 53
Plantation Gro. BL9: Bury 8B 42
Plantation Ind. Est.
OL6: A Lyne 9F 6 (8A 82)
Plantation Rd. BL7: Edg 7A 10
Plantation St. M18: Man 4C 96
OL6: A Lyne 8A 82
Plantation Vw. BL9: Sum 2J 25
Plant Cl. M33: Sale 3G 104
Plant Hill Rd. M9: Man 6H 61
Plasman Ind. Cen. M19: Man 8A 96
Plate St. OL1: O'ham 2E 8 (4K 63)
Platinum Rd. M41: Urm 4F 92
Plato St. OL9: O'ham 1A 8 (4H 63)
Platt Av. OL6: A Lyne 4N 81
PLATT BRIDGE 9K 53
Plattbrook Cl. M14: Man 8G 95
Platt Cl. OL16: Miln 8L 29
Platt Ct. M14: Man 7H 95
Platt Cft. WN7: Lei 6L 73
Platt Fields Pk. 7H 95
Platt Fold Rd. WN7: Lei 4J 73
Platt Fold St. WN7: Lei 5J 73
Platt Hall (The Gallery of Costume)
7H 95
Platt Hill Av. BL3: Bolt 8B 38
Platt Ho. M5: Sal 3N 93
(off Elmira Way)
Platting Gro. OL7: A Lyne 5K 81
Platting La. OL11: Roch 9E 28
Platting Rd. OL4: Lyd, Scout 3F 64
Platt La. BL5: W'ton 3K 55
M14: Man 8F 94
OL3: Del, Dob 9J 47
WN1: Stan 1E 34
WN1: Wig 6N 9 (2H 53)
WN2: Hin 6N 53
Platt Lane Complex 7G 95
Platts Dr. M44: Irl 7H 91
Platt St. OL4: Spri 5C 64
SK8: Chea 1K 117
SK13: Had 4C 100
SK16: Duk 2L 97
WN2: P Bri 9K 53
WN7: Lei 4H 73
Platt Wlk. M34: Dent 8J 97
Plattwood Wlk. M15: Man 3C 94
(off Shawgreen Cl.)
Playfair Cl. OL10: H'ood 5K 43
Playfair St. BL1: Bolt 7G 22
M14: Man 5G 94
Playgolf Manchester 3C 92
Pleachway SK4: Stoc 6L 107
Pleasance Way WA12: N Wil 5F 86
Pleasant Ct. OL11: Roch 2A 44
Pleasant Gdns. BL1: Bolt 1H 7 (4F 38)
Pleasant Rd. M30: Ecc 9E 76
Pleasant St. BL8: Bury 9F 24
M9: Man 3J 79
OL10: H'ood 9H 27
OL11: Roch 2N 43
SK10: Macc 3K 131
Pleasant Ter. SK16: Duk 9N 81
(off Peel St.)
PLEASANT VIEW 2F 44
Pleasant Vw. M9: Man 7G 61
M26: Rad 3H 59
OL2: Shaw 6A 46
OL4: Lees 4C 64
PR7: Cop 3C 18
SK6: Comp 5E 110
SK10: Macc 4A 130
Pleasant Way SK8: Chea H 9A 118
Pleasington Dr. BL8: Bury 2E 40
M40: Man 9A 62
Plevna St. BL2: Bolt 2N 7 (5H 39)
Plodder La. BL4: Farn 2B 56
BL5: O Hul 2B 56
Ploughbank Dr. M21: Cho H 1C 106
Plough Cl. M41: Urm 7K 91
Ploughfields BL5: W'ton 9G 36
M28: Wors 5H 75
Ploughmans Way SK10: Macc 1F 130
Plough St. SK16: Duk 1A 98
Plover Cl. OL11: Roch 6K 27
SK10: Macc 8F 128
SK13: Glos 9H 101
WA12: N Wil 6F 86
Plover Dr. BL9: Bury 9A 26
M44: Irl 5H 91
WA14: B'ath 8B 104
Plover Ter. M21: Cho H 1C 106
Plover Way WA3: Low 1A 88
Plowden Cl. BL3: Bolt 9D 38
Plowden Rd. M22: Wyth 5A 116
Plowley Cl. M20: Man 6G 106
Plucksbridge Rd. SK6: Mar 4E 120
Plumbley Dr. M16: Old T 6B 94
Plumbley St. M11: Man 2C 96
Plumley Cl. M33: Sale 5M 105
SK3: Stoc 2D 118
SK11: Macc 5J 131
Plumley Rd. SK9: Hand 1J 123
Plummer Av. M21: Cho H 2A 106
Plumpton Cl. OL2: O'ham 2J 63
Plumpton Dr. BL9: Bury 7L 25
Plumpton Rd. OL11: Roch 4F 44
Plumpton Wlk. M13: Man 5L 95
Plum St. OL8: O'ham 5A 8 (6H 63)
Plumtree Cl. M30: Ecc 8E 76
PLUNGEBROOK 2M 131
Plunge Rd. BL0: Eden 3L 11
Pluto Cl. M6: Sal 6B 78
Plymouth Av. M13: Man 4K 95
Plymouth Cl. OL6: A Lyne 3M 81
Plymouth Dr. BL4: Farn 3G 57
SK7: Bram 8C 118
Plymouth Gro. M13: Man 3H 95
M26: Rad 7D 40
SK3: Stoc 9N 107
WN6: Stan 5D 34
Plymouth Gro. W. M13: Man 4K 95
Plymouth Rd. M33: Sale 3D 104
Plymouth St. OL8: O'ham 7K 63
Plymouth Vw. M13: Man 3H 95
Plymouth Village M13: Man 4J 95
(off Plymouth Gro.)
Plymtree Cl. M8: Man 9D 60
POBGREEN 2N 65
Pobgreen La. OL3: Upp 2N 65
Pochard Dr. SK12: Poy 2E 124
WA14: B'ath 9B 104
Pochin St. M40: Man 7K 79
POCKET 6D 38
Pocket Nook BL6: Los 9L 37
Pocket Nook La. WA3: Low 1C 88
Pocket Nook Rd. BL6: Los 9K 37
Pocket Workshops, The
BL3: Bolt 6D 38
Pocklington Dr. M23: Wyth 9M 105
Podnor La. SK6: Mel 1K 121
Podsmead Rd. M22: Wyth 5A 116
Poets Nook WN7: Lei 6G 73
Point, The OL6: A Lyne 8E 6 (8N 81)
Point Retail Pk., The
OL16: Roch 7E 8 (6E 28)
Poise Brook Dr. SK2: Stoc 2K 119
Poise Brook Rd. SK2: Stoc 2K 119
Poise Cl. SK7: H Gro 4L 119
Poke St. WN5: Wig 5M 51
Poland St. M4: Man 2M 5 (8H 79)
M34: Aud 1J 97
Poland St. Ind. Est.
M4: Man 2M 5 (8H 79)
Polden Cl. OL8: O'ham 9J 63
Polden Wlk. M9: Man 1L 79
(off Glen Av.)
Polding St. WN3: I Mak 7H 53
Poleacre La. SK6: Wood 2N 109
Polebrook Av. M12: Man 3J 95
Polefield App. M25: Pres 5A 60
Polefield Circ. M25: Pres 5A 60
Polefield Gdns. M25: Pres 5A 60
Polefield Grange M25: Pres 5A 60
Polefield Gro. M25: Pres 5A 60
Polefield Hall Rd. M25: Pres 5A 60
Polefield Rd. M9: Man 9J 61
M25: Pres 5B 60
Polegate Dr. WN7: Lei 9E 54
Pole La. BL9: Bury 9B 42
M35: Fail 2D 80
SK6: Mel 4L 121
SK22: N Mil 4L 121
Pole La. Ct. BL9: Bury 9B 42
Pole St. BL2: Bolt 3J 39
OL7: A Lyne 5C 6 (6M 81)
WN6: Stan 3B 34
Polesworth Cl. M12: Man 3M 95
Police St. M2: Man 4F 4 (9E 78)
M6: Sal 7N 77
M30: Ecc 8C 76
WA14: Alt 2D 6 (2D 114)
Pollard Ct. OL1: O'ham 3J 63
(off Bradford St.)
Pollard Gro. OL15: Lit 6N 15
Pollard Ho. BL3: Bolt 1C 56
Pollards La. BL9: Sum 3J 25
Pollard Sq. M31: Part 5H 103
Pollard St. M4: Man 5N 5 (9H 79)
Pollard St. E. M40: Man 8J 79
Pollen Cl. M33: Sale 6K 105
Pollen Rd. WA14: Alt 1C 114
Polletts Av. SK5: Stoc 2G 109
Pollit Cft. SK6: Rom 7K 109
Pollitt Av. OL6: A Lyne 5N 81
Pollitt Cl. M12: Man 3L 95
Pollitts Cl. M30: Ecc 8B 76
Pollitt St. M26: Rad 9J 41
Polly Grn OL12: Roch 2D 28
Polonia Ct. OL8: O'ham 8G 62
Polo Rd. M17: T Pk 1G 93
Polperro Cl. OL2: O'ham 8L 45
SK10: Macc 3B 130
Polperro Wlk. SK14: Hat 6G 99
Polruan Rd. M21: Cho H 7N 93
Polruan Wlk. SK14: Hat 6H 99
Polworth Rd. M9: Man 1K 79
Polygon, The M7: Sal 4B 78
M30: Ecc 8G 76
Polygon Av. M13: Man 3H 95
Polygon Rd. M8: Man 1E 78
Polygon St. M13: Man 9N 5 (2H 95)
Pomfret St. M6: Sal 5J 77
M12: Man 3M 95
Pomona Cres. M5: Sal 2A 94
Pomona Docks
M16: Old T 9A 4 (3B 94)
Pomona Stop (Metro) 3A 94
Pomona Strand
M16: Old T 9A 4 (4N 93)
(not continuous)
Pomona St. OL11: Roch 8D 28
Ponds Cl. M21: Cho H 8A 94
Pond St. WA3: Low 1C 88
Pondwater Cl. M28: Walk 8G 57
Ponsford Av. M9: Man 8M 61
Ponsonby Rd. M32: Stre 6K 93
Pontefract Cl. M27: Swin 3H 77
Poolbank Cl. WN2: Hin 8E 54
Pool Bank St. M24: Mid 4G 61
(not continuous)
Poolcroft M33: Sale 5M 105
Poole Cl. SK7: Bram 6B 118
Pool End Cl. SK10: Macc 9H 129
Pool End Rd. SK10: Macc 9H 129
Pooley Cl. M24: Mid 2G 61
Pool Fld. Cl. M26: Rad 9D 40
Pool Fold M35: Fail 4E 80
Pool Fold Cl. BL1: Bolt 2B 38
Pool Grn. BL6: Bla 2N 35
Pool Ho. Rd. SK12: Poy 1N 125
Pool Pl. BL1: Bolt 2B 38
Pool Rd. WA3: Rix 5B 102
POOLSTOCK 5E 52
Poolstock WN3: Wig 6E 52
Poolstock La. WN3: Wig 8C 52
Pool St. BL1: Bolt 1J 7
(Back La.)
BL1: Bolt 2J 7 (5F 38)
(St George's Rd.)
OL8: O'ham 7K 63
SK11: Macc 6J 131
WN2: Hin 7N 53
WN3: Wig 5E 52
Pool Ter. BL1: Bolt 2B 38
Poolton Rd. M9: Man 7G 61
Poorfield St. OL8: O'ham 5C 8
Poot Hall OL12: Roch 2D 28
Pope Way M34: Dent 1L 109
(off Kipling Av.)
Poplar Av. BL1: Bolt 9G 22
BL2: Bolt 7K 23
BL6: Hor 3G 37
BL9: Bury 1A 42
M19: Man 1N 107
OL4: Lyd 7F 64
OL8: O'ham 9H 63
OL12: Roch 4A 28
SK9: Wilm 9E 122
SK22: N Mil 6N 121
WA3: Cul 6H 89
WA12: N Wil 6G 86
WA14: Alt 1E 6 (1E 114)
WN4: Gars 5A 70
WN5: Wig 5A 52
Poplar Cl. M29: Tyld 1B 74
SK8: Gat 2G 116
Poplar Ct. M34: Aud 3K 97
SK3: Stoc 2D 118
(off Garners La.)
Poplar Dr. M25: Pres 9N 59
PR7: Cop 4C 18
Poplar Gro. BL0: Ram 7K 11
BL5: W'ton 3G 55
M18: Man 5B 96
M29: Tyld 2B 74
M33: Sale 5H 105
M41: Urm 7E 92
M44: Cad 2E 102
OL6: A Lyne 5N 81
SK2: Stoc 3G 119
SK10: Boll 5L 129
WA11: Hay 3A 86
WN2: Hin 8D 54
Poplar Rd. M19: Man 5J 107
M27: Swin 3D 76
M28: Walk 1M 75
M30: Ecc 6E 76
M32: Stre 9J 93
SK11: Macc 6H 131
SK16: Duk 2C 98
WA11: Hay 3A 86
Poplars, The BL8: Bury 7J 25
OL5: Mos 1H 83
PR7: Adl 7J 19
WA3: Gol 9L 71
WA14: Alt 3C 6 (3C 114)
WN7: Lei 1E 88
Poplars Rd. SK15: Stal 7G 83
Poplar St. M24: Mid 4B 62
M29: Tyld 1A 74
M34: Aud 2K 97
M35: Fail 4B 80
SK4: Stoc 6K 107
WA3: Gol 9L 71
WN7: Lei 6H 73
Poplar Wlk. M31: Part 5E 102
(off Long Wlk.)
M34: Aud 3K 97
(off Poplar St.)
OL9: Chad 3F 62
Poplar Way SK6: H Lan 8D 120
Poplin Dr. M3: Sal 1E 4 (7D 78)
Poppy Cl. M23: Wyth 7L 105
OL9: Chad 4B 62
Poppyfield Vw. OL11: Roch 4K 27
Poppythorn Ct. M25: Pres 6N 59
Poppythorn La. M25: Pres 6N 59
(not continuous)
Poppywood Av. WA14: W Tim 7B 104
Porchester Dr. M26: Rad 7C 40
Porchfield Sq. M3: Man 6E 4 (1D 94)
Porlock Av. M34: Aud 1G 96
SK14: Hat 7F 98
Porlock Cl. SK1: Stoc 8G 108
WN2: P Bri 1K 71
Porlock Rd. M23: Wyth 1A 116
M41: Urm 9A 92
Porlock Wlk. SK14: Hat 7F 98
Porritt Cl. OL11: Roch 7K 27
Porritt St. BL9: Bury 9N 25
(not continuous)
Porritt Way BL0: Ram 7J 11
Portal Ct. M24: Mid 3A 62
Portal Gro. M34: Dent 8M 97
Portal Wlk. M9: Man 2J 79
(off Alderside Rd.)
Porter Av. WA12: N Wil 4F 86
Porter Dr. M40: Man 4J 79
Porterfield Dr. M29: Tyld 2B 74
Porter St. BL9: Bury 9M 25
OL9: O'ham 6G 63
Porters Wood Cl. WN5: Orr 4M 51
Portfield Cl. BL1: Bolt 4A 38
Portfield Wlk. M40: Man 5N 79
(off Harmer Cl.)
Portford Cl. SK10: Macc 3D 130
Portgate Wlk. M13: Man 4J 95
(off St Stephens Cl.)
Porthleven Cres. M29: Ast 2D 74
Porthleven Dr. M23: Wyth 1L 115
Porthtowan Wlk. SK14: Hat 6H 99
(off Underwood Rd.)
Portico Library, The & Gallery
5H 5 (9F 78)
Portinscale Cl. BL8: Bury 1H 41
Portland, The M14: Man 9J 95
Portland Arc. M1: Man 5J 5
(off Parker St.)
Portland Basin Mus. 9B 6 (9L 81)
Portland Chambers SK15: Stal 8E 82
(off Portland Pl.)
Portland Cl. SK7: H Gro 6F 118
WN2: P Bri 1K 71
Portland Ct. M20: Man 5G 106
Portland Cres. M13: Man 4J 95
Portland Gro. SK4: Stoc 4N 107
Portland Ho. M6: Sal 7G 77
OL6: A Lyne 8B 6 (8L 81)
SK6: Mar 2B 120
Portland Ind. Est. BL9: Bury 9N 25
(off Portland St.)
Portland Mill OL6: A Lyne 8B 6
Portland Pl. BL6: Hor 1E 36
OL7: A Lyne 9B 6 (8L 81)
SK15: Stal 8E 82
Portland Rd. M13: Man 6L 95
M27: Swin 3G 77
M28: Walk 6K 57
M30: Ecc 7F 76
M32: Stre 5L 93
SK22: N Mil 6N 121
WA14: Bow 4C 114
Portland St. BL1: Bolt 2F 38
BL9: Bury 9N 25
M1: Man 6H 5 (1F 94)
WA12: N Wil 5C 86
WN5: Wig 5B 52
WN7: Lei 5H 73
Portland St. Nth.
OL6: A Lyne 7A 6 (7L 81)
Portland St. Sth.
OL6: A Lyne 8B 6 (8L 81)
OL7: A Lyne 9B 6 (8L 81)
Portland Ter. OL6: A Lyne 8B 6
Portland Wlk. SK11: Macc 5D 130
Portloe Rd. SK8: H Grn 8G 117
Portman Rd. M16: Whall R 6D 94
Portman St. OL5: Mos 1F 82
Portmarnock Cl. SK10: Macc 1F 130
Porton Wlk. M22: Wyth 6A 116
Portrea Cl. SK3: Stoc 2C 118
Portree Cl. M30: Ecc 8B 76
Portree Ct. OL10: H'ood 4F 42
Portrush Cl. SK10: Macc 9G 128
Portrush Rd. M22: Wyth 5D 116
Portside Cl. M28: Wors 5J 75
Portslade Wlk. M23: Wyth 2M 115
Portsmouth Cl. M7: Sal 5C 78
Portsmouth St. M13: Man 4G 95
(not continuous)
Port Soderick Av. M5: Sal 9N 77
Portstone St. M16: Whall R 5D 94
Port St. M1: Man 4K 5 (9G 78)
SK1: Stoc 1J 9 (7C 108)
SK14: Hyde 7A 98
(off Market St.)
Portugal Rd. M25: Pres 9A 60
Portugal St. BL2: Bolt 3N 7 (5J 39)
M4: Man 1N 5 (7H 79)
(Butler St.)
M4: Man 2M 5 (8H 79)
(Radium St.)
OL7: A Lyne 9K 81
Portugal St. E. M1: Man 6M 5 (1H 95)
Portville Rd. M19: Man 7M 95
Portway M22: Wyth 5A 116
PORTWOOD 5F 108
Portwood Ind. Est. SK1: Stoc 6F 108
Portwood Pl. SK1: Stoc 6D 108
Portwood Wlk. M9: Man 3J 79
(off Shiredale Dr.)

Posnett St. SK3: Stoc 8A 108
Postal St. M1: Man 4K 5
Post Office St.
WA14: Alt 2D 6 (2D 114)
Post St. SK13: Had 4D 100
Potato Wharf
M3: Man 7C 4 (1C 94)
POT GREEN 2G 24
Pot Hill OL6: A Lyne 6N 81
Pothill OL10: H'ood 3H 43
Pot Hill Sq. OL6: A Lyne 6N 81
Pot Ho. La. OL12: W'le 9D 14
Potter Ho. *OL8: O'ham 6K 63*
(off Eldon St.)
Potter Pl. WN8: Skel 6B 50
Potter Rd. SK13: Had 6A 100
Potter's La. M9: Man 3K 79
Potter St. BL9: Bury 1N 41
M26: Rad 8K 41
Pottery La. M11: Man 4L 95
M12: Man 4L 95
Pottery Rd. WN3: Wig 9G 9 (4D 52)
Pottery Ter. WN3: Wig 4E 52
Pottinger St. OL7: A Lyne 9K 81
Pott La. SK11: Macc 6K 131
POTT SHRIGLEY 2N 129
Pott St. M27: Pen 9F 58
M40: Man 5B 80
WA14: Alt 3C 6 (3D 114)
Poulton Av. BL2: Bolt 5M 39
Poulton Dr. WN4: A Mak 5C 70
Poulton St. M11: Man 2C 96
Poundswick La. M22: Wyth 4B 116
Powder Mill Cl. M44: Irl 8J 91
Powell Av. SK14: Hyde 6B 98
Powell Dr. WN5: Bil 7H 69
Powell Ho. *BL9: Bury 1M 41*
(off Walmersley Rd.)
Powell St. BL8: Bury 3H 41
M11: Man 8B 80
M16: Old T 5B 94
WN1: Wig 6K 9 (2F 52)
WN2: Abr 1L 71
Powerhouse Health & Fitness Cen.
. . . .*6A 98*
(off Borough Arc.)
Powerleague Soccer Cen.
Ardwick 8N 5 (2J 95)
Bolton 6L 39
Manchester 9E 94
Stockport 7N 107
Trafford 3B 92
Wigan 2B 52
Powicke Dr. SK6: Rom 7K 109
Powis Rd. M41: Urm 8K 91
Pownall Av. M20: Man 9F 94
SK7: Bram 8D 118
Pownall Ct. SK9: Wilm 6D 122
POWNALL GREEN 8C 118
POWNALL PARK 6E 122
Pownall Pl. *SK7: Bram 8C 118*
(off Bramhall La. Sth.)
Pownall Rd. SK8: Chea H 6M 117
SK9: Wilm 6E 122
WA14: Alt 5D 6 (4D 114)
Pownall Sq. SK11: Macc 4G 130
Pownall St. SK7: H Gro 4H 119
SK10: Macc 3H 131
WN7: Lei 5J 73
Powys St. M46: Ath 1N 73
Poynings Dr. M22: Wyth 6B 116
Poynt Chase M28: Wors 5J 75
Poynter St. M40: Man 1A 80
Poynter Wlk. OL1: O'ham 8A 46
POYNTON 2H 125
Poynton Cl. BL9: Bury 3N 41
Poynton Ind. Est. SK12: Poy 5J 125
Poynton Leisure Cen. 4K 125
Poynton Sports Club 2J 125
Poynton Station (Rail) 2G 124
Poynton St. M15: Man 3E 94
SK10: Macc 4G 130
Praed Rd. M17: T Pk 4J 93
Pratt Wlk. *M11: Man 9L 79*
(off Raglan Cl.)
Precinct, The SK2: Stoc 1H 119
SK3: Stoc 9B 108
SK8: Chea H 5N 117
SK14: Holl 4N 99
Precinct Cen. M13: Man 3J 94
Preece Cl. SK14: Hyde 5D 98
Preesall Av. SK8: H Grn 7G 117
Preesall Cl. BL8: Bury 3F 40
Prefect Pl. WN5: Wig 3N 51
Premier Rd. M8: Man 6E 78
Premier St. M16: Old T 5C 94
Prentice Wlk. M11: Man 9M 79
Prenton St. M11: Man 1C 96
Prenton Way BL8: Tot 8F 24
Presall St. BL2: Bolt 4K 39
Presbyterian Fold WN2: Hin 5N 53
Prescot Av. M29: Tyld 1E 74
M46: Ath 6N 55
Prescot Cl. BL9: Bury 3N 41
Prescot Rd. M9: Man 3J 79
WA15: Hale 5F 114
Prescott Av. WA3: Gol 8J 71
Prescott Ct. *M28: Walk 8J 57*
(off Prescott St.)
Prescott La. WN5: Orr 2M 51
Prescott Rd. SK9: Wilm 5G 122
WN8: Skel 6D 50
Prescott St. BL3: Bolt 8D 38
M28: Walk 8J 57
OL16: Roch 3G 28
WA3: Gol 9K 71
WN2: Hin 6N 53
WN6: Wig 7G 9 (3D 52)
WN7: Lei 4H 73
Prescott Wlk. M34: Dent 8M 97
Press St. M11: Man 2B 96
Presswood Ct. *M6: Sal 4J 77*
(off Swinton Pk. Rd.)
Prestage St. M12: Man 7N 95
M16: Old T 4C 94
PRESTBURY 7E 128
Prestbury Av. M14: Man 8E 94
WA15: Alt 1E 6 (1E 114)
WN3: Wig 8B 52
Prestbury Cl. BL9: Bury 3N 41
SK2: Stoc 3H 119
Prestbury Dr. OL1: O'ham 2H 63
SK6: Bred 5J 109
Prestbury Golf Course 9D 128
Prestbury La. SK10: P'bury 6E 128
Prestbury Link Rd. SK9: Wilm 9H 123
Prestbury Pk. SK10: P'bury 7C 128
Prestbury Rd. BL1: Bolt 8H 23
SK9: Wilm 9J 123
SK10: Macc 1D 130
SK10: O Ald 7L 127
(not continuous)
Prestbury Station (Rail) 6E 128
Prestfield Rd. M45: Whitef 4N 59
Presto Gdns. BL3: Bolt 8C 38
PRESTOLEE 3A 58
Prestolee Rd. BL3: Lit L 2A 58
M26: Rad 2A 58
Preston Av. M30: Ecc 7G 76
M44: Irl 1G 102
Preston Cl. M30: Ecc 7G 76
Preston Rd. M19: Man 9M 95
PR7: Char R 4A 18
PR7: Cop 4A 18
WN6: Stan 4A 18
Preston St. BL3: Bolt 8J 39
M18: Man 3A 96
M24: Mid 3M 61
OL4: O'ham 4F 8 (5L 63)
OL12: Roch 4A 28
Preston St. W. SK11: Macc 6F 130
Presto St. BL3: Bolt 8C 38
BL4: Farn 2M 57
Prestt Gro. WN3: Wig 6D 52
PRESTWICH 6N 59
Prestwich Av. WA3: Cul 6G 88
WN7: Lei 5K 73
Prestwich Cl. SK2: Stoc 9F 108
Prestwich Forest Pk. 7J 59
Prestwich Golf Course 9N 59
Prestwich Hills M25: Pres 8N 59
Prestwich Ind. Est. M46: Ath 7K 55
PRESTWICH PARK 8N 59
Prestwich Pk. Rd. Sth.
M25: Pres 8N 59
Prestwich Stop (Metro) 6N 59
Prestwich St. M46: Ath 7K 55
Prestwick Cl. SK10: Macc 8G 128
Prestwick Wlk. *M40: Man 9A 62*
(off Pleasington Dr.)
Prestwood Cl. BL1: Bolt 3E 38
Prestwood Dr. BL1: Bolt 3E 38
Prestwood Pl. WN8: Skel 7D 50
Prestwood Rd. BL4: Farn 2H 57
M6: Sal 6J 77
Pretoria Rd. BL2: Bolt 4M 39
OL8: O'ham 8G 63
WN4: A Mak 6E 70
Pretoria St. OL12: Roch 4A 28
PRETTYWOOD 2D 42
Price St. BL4: Farn 2L 57
BL9: Bury 3N 41
M4: Man 9J 79
SK16: Duk 1N 97
PRICKSHAW 8N 13
Prickshaw La. OL12: Roch 8N 13
Pride Cl. WA12: N Wil 7H 87
Pridmouth Rd. M20: Man 2H 107
Priest Av. SK8: Gat 3F 116
Priestfields WN7: Lei 5K 73
Priest Hill OL1: O'ham 2C 8
Priest Hill St. OL1: O'ham . . .2C 8 (4J 63)
Priest La. SK10: Mot S A 4M 127
Priestley Rd. M28: Ward 2C 76
Priestley Way OL2: Shaw 2M 45
Priestnall Ct. *SK4: Stoc 5L 107*
(off Priestnall Rd.)
Priestnall Rd. SK4: Stoc 5L 107
Priestners Way WN7: Lei 4G 72
Priest St. OL9: Chad 7F 62
Priestwood Av. OL4: O'ham 8C 46
Primary Cl. M44: Cad 3E 102
Primley Wlk. *M9: Man 2K 79*
(off Edward St.)
Primrose Av. BL4: Farn 2H 57
M28: Walk 9J 57
M41: Urm 7D 92
OL3: Upp 2M 65
SK6: Mar 1B 120
SK11: Macc 7F 130
SK14: Hyde 1A 110
PRIMROSE BANK 5B 8 (6J 63)
Primrose Bank BL8: Tot 6E 24
M28: Walk 9J 57
OL3: G'fld 6L 65
OL8: O'ham 6J 63
WA14: Bow 6C 114
Primrose Cl. BL2: Bolt 9A 24
M5: Sal 8M 77
Primrose Cotts. *WA14: Bow 6C 114*
(off Brickkiln Row)
Primrose Cres. SK13: Glos 9C 100
SK14: Hyde 9A 98
Primrose Dr. BL9: Bury 9C 26
M43: Droy 7G 81
Primrose Gro. WA11: Hay 2B 86
WN5: Wig 4B 52
Primrose Hill SK13: Glos 9D 100
Primrose Hill Cotts.
OL5: Mos 1H 83
(off Micklehurst Rd.)
OL10: H'ood 9M 27
Primrose Hill Ct. OL2: Shaw 4K 45
Primrose La. SK6: Mel 5C 110
SK13: Glos 8C 100
WN6: Stan 2A 34
Primrose Pl. *WN4: A Mak 8E 70*
(off Haydock St.)
Primrose St. BL1: Bolt 9G 22
BL4: Kea 4M 57
M4: Man 2L 5 (8G 79)
M29: Tyld 1B 74
Primrose St. OL12: Roch 5B 28
WN7: Lei 5F 72
Primrose St. Nth. M29: Tyld 1B 74
Primrose St. Sth. M29: Tyld 2B 74
Primrose Ter. SK13: Glos 9D 100
SK15: Stal 8E 82
Primrose Vw. WN4: A Mak 8E 70
Primrose Wlk. OL8: O'ham 6J 63
SK6: Mar 1B 120
Primula Dr. WA3: Low 1N 87
Primula St. BL1: Bolt 9G 22
Prince Albert Av. *M19: Man 7M 95*
(off Belvoir Av.)
Prince Charlie St. OL1: O'ham 3M 63
Princedom St. M9: Man 2K 79
Prince Edward Av. M34: Dent 7K 97
OL4: O'ham 4N 63
Prince George St. OL1: O'ham 2N 63
Prince Lee Gdns. SK4: Stoc 3M 107
Princemead Pl. M17: T Pk 4H 93
Prince of Wales Ind. Units
OL1: O'ham 2N 63
Prince Rd. SK12: Poy 1N 125
Princes Av. BL3: Lit L 8B 40
M20: Man 4H 107
M29: Ast 4B 74
M44: Irl 6K 91
SK6: Bred 5L 109
Prince's Bri. M3: Man 6C 4 (1C 94)
Princes Ct. *BL0: Ram 8J 11*
(off Silver St.)
M30: Ecc 7D 76
Princes Dr. M33: Sale 5K 105
SK6: Mar 9B 110
Princes Gdns. WN7: Lei 5L 73
Prince's Incline SK12: Poy 2J 125
Prince's Pk. WN6: She 8K 33
Princes Rd. M33: Sale 5J 105
SK4: Stoc 4M 107
SK6: Bred 5L 109
WA14: Alt 1D 114
Princess Av. BL4: Kea 5N 57
M25: Pres 9B 60
M34: Dent 6J 97
M46: Ath 6L 55
OL12: Roch 1G 28
SK8: Chea H 4M 117
WA11: Hay 2D 86
WN4: A Mak 7F 70
Princess Cl. OL5: Mos 2H 83
OL10: H'ood 3J 43
SK16: Duk 1A 98
Princess Ct. *M15: Man 3C 94*
(off Cornbrook Pk. Rd.)
M25: Pres 8A 60
Princess Dr. M24: Mid 3K 61
SK10: Boll 7J 129
Princess Gold M34: Aud 2F 96
Princess Gro. BL4: Farn 3L 57
Princess Pde. BL9: Bury . . .8L 7 (2M 41)
M14: Man 8E 94
Princess Parkway M22: Nor 8B 106
M23: Wyth 8B 106
Princess Rd. BL6: Los 5K 37
M14: Man 3E 94
M15: Man 9F 4 (3E 94)
M16: Whall R 3E 94
M20: Man 5C 106
M21: Cho H 5C 106
M25: Pres 7B 60
M41: Urm 6B 92
OL2: Shaw 6L 45
OL9: Chad 8C 62
OL16: Roch 6H 29
PR6: And 5L 19
SK9: Wilm 9E 122
WN4: A Mak 7E 70
WN6: Stan 8N 33
Princess St. BL1: Bolt 3L 7 (5G 39)
M1: Man 6H 5 (9E 78)
M2: Man 5G 4 (9E 78)
M6: Sal 6N 77
(off Cheltenham St.)
M15: Man 9A 4 (3B 94)
M26: Rad 9E 40
M27: Swin 3G 76
M30: Ecc 8C 76
M35: Fail 3C 80
OL4: Lees 5B 64
OL6: A Lyne 6A 82
OL12: Roch 5D 28
OL12: Whitw 6A 14
(off Albert St.)
SK10: Boll 6K 129
SK13: Glos 9D 100
SK14: Hyde 7B 98
WA14: B'ath 8C 104
WA16: Knut 6G 132
WN2: Hin 6M 53
WN3: Wig 9J 9 (4F 52)
WN7: Lei 5J 73
(not continuous)
Princes St. SK1: Stoc 2K 9 (7C 108)
WA12: N Wil 6E 86
Prince St. BL0: Ram 8J 11
BL1: Bolt 4F 38
OL1: O'ham 2F 8 (4L 63)
OL10: H'ood 2J 43
OL16: Roch 8E 28
WN4: A Mak 5D 70
Princes Wlk. SK7: Bram 8E 118
Princes Way SK11: Macc 4C 130
Princes Wood Rd. SK12: Poy 1N 125
Princethorpe Cl. BL6: Los 6M 37
Princeton Cl. M6: Sal 7J 77
Prince Way OL2: O'ham 6G 45
Pringle St. OL16: Roch 8F 8 (6E 28)
Prinknash Rd. M22: Wyth 5C 116
Printers Brow SK14: Holl 4A 100
Printers Cl. M19: Man 6J 107
SK4: Stoc 6J 107
Printer's Ct. BL7: Tur 1L 23
Printers Dr. SK6: Stri 5F 120
SK15: C'ook 4K 83
Printers Fold SK14: Holl 4N 99
Printers La. BL2: Bolt 7K 23
Printers Pk. SK14: Holl 4A 100
Printer St. M11: Man 1B 96
OL1: O'ham 3D 8 (5K 63)
Printon Av. M9: Man 7G 60
Printshop La. M29: Tyld 1N 73
M46: Ath 1N 73
Printworks, The M4: Man . . .2H 5 (8F 78)
Printworks La. M19: Man 8A 96
Printworks Rd. SK15: H'rod 7E 82
Prior St. OL8: O'ham 6M 63
Priorswood Pl. WN8: Skel 7D 50
Priory, The M7: Sal 4B 78
Priory Av. M7: Sal 4B 78
M21: Cho H 9A 94
WN7: Lei 1F 72
Priory Cl. M33: Sale 2K 105
OL8: O'ham 8H 63
SK16: Duk 3A 98
WN5: Wig 6M 51
Priory Ct. *M30: Ecc 8E 76*
(off Abbey Gro.)
SK5: Stoc 9C 96
SK10: Macc 3D 130
WA14: Bow 6C 114
(off Priory St.)
Priory Dr. SK10: Macc 2C 130
Priory Gdns. M20: Man 4G 107
Priory Gro. M7: Sal 4B 78
OL9: Chad 7E 62
Priory La. SK5: Stoc 9C 96
SK10: Macc 2C 130
Priory Nook WN8: Uph 4G 51
Priory Pl. BL2: Bolt 2K 39
M7: Sal 4B 78
Priory Rd. M27: Swin 1E 76
M33: Sale 3J 105
SK8: Chea 2M 117
SK9: Wilm 6D 122
WA14: Bow 7B 114
WN4: A Mak 5C 70
WN8: Uph 4G 51
Priory St. WA14: Bow 7C 114
Pritchard St. M1: Man 7J 5 (1F 94)
M32: Stre 7K 93
Privet St. OL4: O'ham 2A 64
Proctor Cl. WN5: Wig 2B 52
Proctor St. BL8: Bury 3J 41
Proctor Way M30: Ecc 2N 91
(not continuous)
Prodesse Ct. WN2: Hin 5N 53
Proe's Ct. WN1: Wig 7H 9 (3E 52)
Progress Av. M34: Aud 3K 97
Progress Ho. WN3: Wig 5F 52
Progressive Bus. Pk. M34: Aud 1J 97
Progress St. BL1: Bolt 3G 38
OL6: A Lyne 7A 6 (7L 81)
OL11: Roch 3A 44
WN2: Hin 6N 53
Progress Way M34: Dent 7G 96
Promenade St. OL10: H'ood 2K 43
Propps Hall Dr. M35: Fail 4B 80
Prospect Av. BL2: Bolt 1N 39
BL4: Farn 4K 57
M44: Cad 2F 102
Prospect Cotts. WN2: Hai 6K 35
Prospect Ct. BL8: Tot 6F 24
Prospect Dr. M35: Fail 5D 80
WA15: Haleb 8K 115
Prospect Ho. *M9: Man 3K 79*
(off Church La.)
WN6: Stan 4B 34
Prospect Ind. Cen. WN2: Hin 6N 53
Prospect La. SK9: A Edg 3A 126
Prospect Pl. BL4: Farn 2K 57
BL9: Bury 8N 41
M27: Swin 3G 76
(off Manchester Rd.)
OL6: A Lyne 5A 82
OL10: H'ood 1J 43
WN8: Skel 6D 50
Prospect Rd. M44: Cad 2F 102
OL6: A Lyne 5B 82
OL9: O'ham 4G 63
SK16: Duk 9A 82
WN6: Stan 5B 34
Prospect St. BL1: Bolt 3G 38
M29: Tyld 1A 74
OL10: H'ood 3K 43
OL11: Roch 9C 28
OL15: Lit 8M 15
WN2: Hin 6N 53
Prospect Ter. BL8: Bury 9K 25
OL12: Roch 3H 27
Prospect Va. SK8: H Grn 6G 116
Prospect Vw. *M27: Swin 3G 76*
(off Manchester Rd.)
Prospect Vs. M9: Man 1L 79
Prosperity M29: Ast 2E 74
Prosser Av. M46: Ath 9J 55
Protector Way M44: Irl 9G 90
Prout St. M12: Man 6M 95
Provender Cl. WA14: B'ath 8D 104
Providence Ho. *OL4: O'ham 3B 64*
(off Huddersfield Rd.)
Providence St. BL3: Bolt 7G 39
M4: Man 9J 79
M34: Aud 2K 97
OL6: A Lyne 6A 82
Provident Av. M19: Man 8A 96
Provident St. OL2: Shaw 5M 45
Provident Way WA15: Tim 9G 105
Provis Rd. M21: Cho H 1A 106
Prubella Av. M34: Dent 4J 97
Pryce Av. WN2: I Mak 4J 53
Pryce St. BL1: Bolt 3E 38
Pryme St. M15: Man 8D 4 (2D 94)
Pudding Fold SK14: Hat 6F 98
Pudding La. SK14: Hat 6F 98
(not continuous)
Puffin Av. SK12: Poy 2F 124
Puffingate Cl. SK15: C'ook 3J 83
Pugin Wlk. *M9: Man 4J 79*
(off Oldershaw Dr.)
Pulborough Cl. BL8: Bury 6H 25
Pulford Av. M21: Cho H 4C 106
Pulford Rd. M33: Sale 6J 105
Pullman Cl. M19: Man 9N 95
Pullman Ct. BL2: Bolt 7H 39
Pullman Dr. M32: Stre 7F 92
Pullman St. OL11: Roch 8D 28
Pump St. OL9: O'ham 9F 62
WN2: Hin 6N 53
Pumptree M. SK11: Macc 5C 130
Pump Yd. M4: Man 2H 5
Punch La. BL3: Bolt 1M 55
BL3: O Hul 2M 55
Punch St. BL3: Bolt 6E 38
PUNGLE, THE 6F 54
Pungle, The BL5: W'ton 6F 54
Purbeck Cl. M22: Wyth 6B 116
Purbeck Dr. BL6: Los 3H 37
BL8: Bury 7J 25
Purbeck Way M29: Ast 3C 74
Purcell Cl. BL1: Bolt 3E 38
Purcell St. M12: Man 6M 95
Purdon St. BL9: Bury 7M 25
Purdy Ho. OL8: O'ham 5C 8 (6J 63)
Puritan Wlk. *M40: Man 5H 79*
(off Ribblesdale Dr.)
Purley Av. M23: Wyth 7A 106
Purley Dr. M44: Cad 3D 102
Purple St. BL1: Bolt 2L 7
Purslow Cl. M12: Man 9K 79
Purton Wlk. *M9: Man 3K 79*
(off Broadwell Dr.)
Putney Cl. OL1: O'ham 2J 63
Puzzletree Ct. SK2: Stoc 9G 108
Pye Cl. WA11: Hay 1E 86
Pyegrove SK13: Glos 8H 101
Pyegrove Rd. SK13: Glos 8G 101
Pyke St. WN1: Wig 2G 53
Pymgate Dr. SK8: H Grn 5F 116
Pymgate La. SK8: H Grn 5F 116
Pym St. M30: Ecc 8D 76
M40: Man 2L 79
OL10: H'ood 3J 43
Pyramid Ct. M7: Sal 4C 78
Pyrus Cl. M30: Ecc 1N 91
Pytha Fold Rd. M20: Man 3H 107

Q

Quadrangle, The M21: Cho H 8A 94
Quadrant, The M9: Man 8M 61
M43: Droy 9D 80
OL10: H'ood 2K 43
SK1: Stoc 7F 108
SK6: Rom 6L 109
Quail Dr. M44: Irl 6H 91
Quail St. OL4: O'ham 6N 63
Quainton Ho. *M5: Sal 9M 77*
(off Amersham St.)
Quakerfields BL5: W'ton 4F 54
Quakersfield BL8: Tot 5E 24
Quakers Pl. WN6: Stan 3B 34
Quakers Ter. WN6: Stan 1A 34
Quantock Cl. SK4: Stoc 6C 108
WN3: Wins 9N 51
Quantock Dr. OL8: O'ham 8K 63
Quantock St. M16: Whall R 5D 94
Quarlton Dr. BL8: Haw 2B 24
Quarmby Rd. M18: Man 5D 96
Quarry Bank Mill 3D 122
Quarry Bank Rd. SK9: Sty 3D 122
Quarry Cl. SK13: Glos 8F 100
Quarry Clough SK15: Stal 1G 98
Quarry Hgts. SK15: Stal 1C 98
Quarry Hill OL12: Roch 2C 28
Quarry Junc. WN8: Skel 3A 50
Quarry La. OL3: Dob 2G 64
OL4: Scout 2G 64
Quarrymans Vw. WA15: Tim 1H 115
Quarry Pl. WN1: Wig 3H 53
Quarry Pond Rd. M28: Walk 8G 57
Quarry Ri. SK6: Rom 5M 109
SK15: Stal 1C 98
Quarry Rd. BL4: Kea 4A 58
SK6: Rom 6M 109
SK22: N Mil 8N 121
Quarry St. BL0: Ram 8K 11
(not continuous)
M26: Rad 9H 41
OL12: Roch 4C 28
OL12: Whitw 1C 14
SK6: Wood 3M 109
SK15: Stal 9C 82
Quarry Vw. OL12: Roch 2C 28
Quarry Wlk. *M11: Man 9L 79*
(off Redfield Cl.)
Quay 5 M5: Sal 2A 94
Quay Ct. *M44: Irl 8J 91*
(off Bankquay Ct.)
Quays, The M50: Sal 2M 93
Quayside WN7: Lei 6G 73
Quayside Cl. M28: Wors 5J 75
Quayside M. WA13: Lym 4A 112
Quayside Way
SK11: Macc 5J 131
Quays Reach M50: Sal 9L 77
Quays Theatre *2L 93*
(In The Lowry)
Quay St. M3: Man 5D 4 (9D 78)
M3: Sal 3E 4 (8D 78)
OL10: H'ood 3K 43
Quayview M5: Sal 1N 93
Quay West M17: T Pk 3L 93
Quebec Bldg. M3: Sal 2E 4
Quebec Pl. BL3: Bolt 7D 38
Quebec St. BL3: Bolt 7E 38
M34: Dent 5J 97
OL9: O'ham 3G 63
WN7: Lei 5A 72
Queen Alexandra Cl.
M5: Sal 1B 94
Queen Anne Cl. BL9: Bury 8B 42
Queen Anne Ct. SK9: Wilm 8H 123
Queen Anne Dr. M28: Wors 3J 75
Queen Annes Ct.
SK11: Macc 6F 130
Queenhill Dr. SK14: Hyde 4C 98
Queenhill Rd. M22: Nor 7D 106

Queens Av. BL3: Lit L 8A 40
BL7: Bro X 6H 23
M18: Man 4N 95
M46: Ath 6L 55
OL12: Roch 1G 28
SK6: Bred 5L 109
SK10: Macc 2J 131
WA3: G'ury 2L 89
WN4: A Mak 7E 70
Queensbrook BL1: Bolt 3H 7 (5F 38)
Queensbury Cl. BL1: Bolt 8E 22
SK9: Wilm 6J 123
Queensbury Ct. M40: Man 7K 79
(off Wardle St.)
Queensbury Pde. M40: Man 7K 79
(off Eastfield Av.)
Queens Cl. M28: Walk 8L 57
M28: Wors 3G 74
SK4: Stoc 6M 107
SK10: Boll 7J 129
SK10: Macc 2J 131
SK14: Hyde 1B 110
Queens Ct. M20: Man 4F 106
M40: Man 5J 79
M41: Urm 7L 91
SK4: Stoc 6M 107
SK6: Mar 1D 120
SK9: Wilm 8F 122
(off Queens Rd.)
WN5: Wig 5M 51
(off Wardley St.)
Queenscroft M30: Ecc 7E 76
Queens Dr. M25: Pres 9B 60
OL11: Roch 1C 44
SK4: Stoc 6M 107
SK8: Chea H 4M 117
SK13: Glos 8H 101
SK14: Hyde 1C 110
WA3: Gol 1M 87
WA12: N Wil 4E 86
Queensferry St. M40: Man 4A 80
Queens Gdns. SK8: Chea 1K 117
WN7: Lei 5L 73
Queensgate BL1: Bolt 4C 38
SK7: Bram 1C 124
Queensgate Dr. OL2: O'ham 6G 45
Queen's Gro. M12: Man 5M 95
Queens Hall Pas. WN1: Wig 7J 9
Queensland Rd. M18: Man 4N 95
Queensmead Pl. M17: T Pk 4H 93
Queensmere Dr. M27: Clif 9G 58
QUEENS PK. 4H 79
Queens Pk. Mus. & Art Gallery 4H 79
Queen's Pk. Rd. OL10: H'ood 9J 27
Queens Pk. St. BL1: Bolt 4E 38
Queens Pl. BL9: Sum 3J 25
SK15: Stal 8D 82
(off Queen St.)
Queen Sq. OL6: A Lyne 7A 82
Queens Rd. BL3: Bolt 8C 38
M8: Man 5F 78
M9: Man 4H 79
M33: Sale 3F 104
M40: Man 4J 79
M41: Urm 8D 92
OL6: A Lyne 5A 82
OL8: O'ham 6K 63
OL9: Chad 4E 62
OL15: Lit 9M 15
SK6: Bred 5L 109
SK7: H Gro 4J 119
SK8: Chea H 3L 117
(not continuous)
SK9: Wilm 8F 122
WA11: Hay 2D 86
WA15: Hale 5G 6 (4E 114)
WN4: A Mak 6E 70
WN5: Orr 6G 51
Queen's Rd. Ter. OL15: Lit 9M 15
(off Queen's Rd.)
Queens Ter. SK9: Hand 2J 123
SK16: Duk 9M 81
Queenston Rd. M20: Man 4F 106
Queen St. BL0: Ram 8H 11
BL1: Bolt 3J 7 (5F 38)
BL4: Farn 3L 57
BL5: W'ton 3G 55
BL6: Hor 1D 36
BL8: Tot 8G 24
BL9: Bury 7N 7 (2N 41)
M2: Man 5F 4 (9E 78)
M3: Sal 2E 4 (8D 78)
M6: Sal 5K 77
M24: Mid 3A 62
M26: Rad 1J 59
M34: Aud 3K 97
M34: Dent 5J 97
M35: Fail 3C 80
M38: Lit H 8J 57
OL1: O'ham 2E 8 (4K 63)
OL2: O'ham 8H 45
OL2: Shaw 6M 45
OL4: Spri 5C 64
OL5: Mos 1F 82
OL6: A Lyne 7F 6 (7N 81)
OL10: H'ood 1J 43
OL12: Roch 5D 28
OL15: Lit 9M 15
SK6: Mar 1D 120
SK8: Chea 1L 117
SK10: Boll 5M 129
SK10: Macc 4J 131
SK13: Glos 9D 100
SK13: Had 5C 100
SK14: Hyde 8B 98
SK15: Stal 8D 82
SK16: Duk 9M 81
WA3: Gol 1L 87
WA12: N Wil 6E 86
WA16: Knut 6F 132
WN2: Hin 5N 53
WN2: P Bri 9K 53
WN3: Wig 9J 9 (4F 52)
WN5: Orr 5L 51
WN5: Wig 6A 52
WN7: Lei 5J 73
Queen St. Mills OL5: Mos 1G 82
Queen St. W. M20: Man 1G 107
Queens Vw. OL15: Lit 2L 29
Queen's Wlk. M43: Droy 9E 80
Queensway BL4: Kea 6N 57
M19: Man 6J 107
M27: Clif 9G 58
M28: Wors 2J 75
M31: Part 4G 103
M41: Urm 5E 92
M44: Irl 7G 91
OL3: G'fld 5L 65
OL5: Mos 2G 83
OL11: Roch 2B 44
SK8: H Grn 7G 117
SK12: Poy 3H 125
SK16: Duk 2C 98
WA16: Knut 5E 132
WN1: Wig 1E 52
WN2: I Mak 3J 53
WN6: She 8K 33
WN7: Lei 5L 73
Queensway Neighbourhood Cen.
OL11: Roch 8E 28
Queen Victoria St. M30: Ecc 3E 76
OL11: Roch 9E 28
SK11: Macc 4H 131
Quenby St. M15: Man 9C 4 (2C 94)
Quendon Av. M7: Sal 6D 78
Quest Pk. OL10: H'ood 5E 42
QUICK 7G 64
QUICK EDGE 8F 64
Quickedge La. OL4: Grot 7E 64
Quickedge Rd. OL4: Lyd 9F 64
OL5: Mos 9F 64
Quick Rd. OL5: Mos 7G 64
Quick Vw. OL5: Mos 8H 65
QUICKWOOD 9F 64
Quickwood OL5: Mos 9G 64
(off Roughtown Rd.)
Quill Ct. M44: Irl 2F 102
(off Magenta Av.)
Quilter Gro. M9: Man 9H 61
Quince Ho. M6: Sal 7A 78
(off Milton Pl.)
Quinney Cres. M16: Whall R 5D 94
Quinn St. M11: Man 9M 79
Quinton OL12: Roch 6B 8 (5C 28)
Quinton Wlk. M13: Man 3H 95
(off Rudcroft Cl.)
Quintrell Brow BL7: Bro X 5H 23

R

Rabbit La. SK14: Mot 3K 99
Raby St. M14: Man 5E 94
M16: Whall R 5D 94
Race, The SK9: Hand 4J 123
Racecourse Pk. SK9: Wilm 8E 122
Racecourse Rd. SK9: Wilm 7D 122
Racecourse Wlk. M26: Rad 8F 40
Racefield Cl. WA13: Lym 4A 112
Racefield Hamlet OL1: Chad 8E 44
Racefield Rd. WA14: Alt 3A 6 (3C 114)
WA16: Knut 7F 132
Rachel Rosing Wlk. M8: Man 2E 78
(off Grangeforth Rd.)
Rachel St. M12: Man 7N 5 (1H 95)
Rackhouse Rd. M23: Wyth 7A 106
Radbourne Cl. M12: Man 3M 95
Radbourne Gro. BL3: Bolt 8A 38
Radbourne Ho. BL2: Bolt 6J 39
RADCLIFFE 9G 41
Radcliffe (Park & Ride) 9H 41
Radcliffe Av. WA3: Cul 6G 88
Radcliffe Borough FC 8E 40
Radcliffe Bri. M26: Rad 1G 59
Radcliffe Gro. WN7: Lei 3H 73
Radcliffe Moor Rd. BL2: Bolt 6D 40
M26: Bolt, Rad 6B 40
Radcliffe New Rd. M26: Rad 1J 59
M45: Whitef 1J 59
Radcliffe Pk. Cres. M6: Sal 5J 77
Radcliffe Pk. Rd. M6: Sal 5H 77
Radcliffe Pool & Fitness Cen. 9G 41
Radcliffe Rd. BL2: Bolt 5J 39
BL3: Bolt 7L 39
BL9: Bury 5K 41
OL4: O'ham 1A 64
Radcliffe Stop (Metro) 9H 41
Radcliffe St. OL1: O'ham 1D 8 (3K 63)
(not continuous)
OL2: O'ham 8H 45
OL4: Spri 5D 64
Radcliffe Vw. M5: Sal 2A 94
(off Ordsall Dr.)
Radclyffe Athletics Cen. 4D 62
Radclyffe M. M5: Sal 2A 94
Radclyffe St. M24: Mid 1M 61
OL9: Chad 3F 62
Radclyffe Ter. M24: Mid 1M 61
Radelan Gro. M26: Rad 8D 40
Radford Cl. SK2: Stoc 9H 109
Radford Dr. M9: Man 2K 79
(off Hemsley St. Sth.)
M44: Irl 6H 91
Radford Ho. SK2: Stoc 9J 109
Radford St. M7: Sal 2B 78
Radium St. M4: Man 2M 5 (8H 79)
Radlet Dr. WA15: Tim 8G 104
Radlett Wlk. M13: Man 4H 95
(off Plymouth Gro.)
Radley Cl. BL1: Bolt 3B 38
M33: Sale 5D 104
Radley St. M16: Whall R 6E 94
M43: Droy 1C 96
Radnor Av. M34: Dent 6F 96
Radnor Cl. WN2: Hin 8C 54
Radnor Dr. WN7: Lei 5E 72
Radnor Ho. SK3: Stoc 5J 9
Radnormere Dr. SK8: Chea H 3L 117
Radnor St. M15: Man 4E 94
M18: Man 5A 96
M32: Stre 7K 93
OL9: O'ham 6G 62
Radstock Cl. BL1: Bolt 6F 22
M14: Man 8G 94
Radstock Rd. M32: Stre 7J 93
Radway M29: Tyld 1D 74
Raeburn Dr. SK6: Mar B 8E 110
Rae St. SK3: Stoc 8A 108
Raglan Av. M27: Clif 9H 59
M45: Whitef 4A 60
Raglan Cl. M11: Man 9L 79
Raglan Dr. WA14: Tim 8E 104
Raglan Rd. M32: Stre 6H 93
M33: Sale 5F 104
SK10: Macc 2K 131
Raglan St. BL1: Bolt 2E 38
OL11: Roch 3A 44
SK14: Hyde 7N 97
Raglan Wlk. M15: Man 3E 94
(off Eden Cl.)
Ragley Cl. SK12: Poy 2K 125
Raikes Clough Ind. Est.
BL3: Bolt 8K 39
Raikes La. BL3: Bolt 8J 39
Raikes La. Ind. Est. BL3: Bolt 8J 39
Raikes Rd. BL3: Bolt 7L 39
Raikes Way BL3: Bolt 7L 39
Railside Ter. M30: Ecc 8G 76
(off St Mary's Rd.)
Railton Av. M16: Whall R 6C 94
Railton Ter. M9: Man 3L 79
Railway App. OL11: Roch 2A 44
Railway Bank SK14: Hyde 7N 97
(off Bowling Grn. St.)
Railway Brow OL11: Roch 3A 44
Railway Cotts. SK6: Bred 4K 109
(off Kennett Dr.)
Railway Rd. M32: Stre 4L 93
M41: Urm 7D 92
OL9: Chad 9E 62
OL9: O'ham 5H 63
PR6: Adl 6K 19
PR7: Adl 6K 19
SK1: Stoc 4K 9 (8C 108)
SK6: Mar 1A 120
WA3: Gol 9L 71
WN7: Lei 5G 73
Railway St. BL0: Ram 8J 11
BL4: Farn 2M 57
BL9: Sum 3J 25
M18: Man 3A 96
M26: Rad 1G 59
M46: Ath 7K 55
(not continuous)
OL10: H'ood 3K 43
OL15: Lit 9M 15
OL16: Miln 9M 29
OL16: Roch 9E 8 (7E 28)
SK4: Stoc 1J 9 (6C 108)
SK13: Glos 8E 100
SK13: Had 4C 100
SK14: Hyde 7A 98
SK16: Duk 9M 81
WA12: N Wil 6E 86
WA14: Alt 4C 6 (3D 114)
WN2: Hin 4N 53
WN6: Wig 2D 52
Railway St. Ind. Est. M18: Man 3B 96
Railway St. W. BL9: Sum 3H 25
Railway Ter. BL8: Bury 3J 41
BL9: Sum 3J 25
M21: Cho H 7A 94
(off Manchester Rd.)
OL10: H'ood 3J 43
PR7: Cop 4C 18
SK12: Dis 9G 121
Railway Vw. OL2: Shaw 4N 45
OL4: Spri 5C 64
PR7: Adl 6K 19
SK5: Stoc 7C 96
Raimond St. BL1: Bolt 1D 38
Rainbow Cl. M21: Cho H 1A 106
Rainbow Dr. M46: Ath 6M 55
Raincliff Av. M13: Man 7L 95
Raines Crest OL16: Miln 7L 29
Rainford Av. M20: Man 9F 94
WA15: Tim 1G 115
Rainford By-Pass
WA11: R'ford, Wind 8A 68
Rainford Hall Cotts. WA11: Cra 8D 68
Rainford Ho. BL1: Bolt 1K 7
Rainford Ind. Est. WA11: R'ford 6A 68
(not continuous)
Rainford Rd. WN5: Bil 5F 68
Rainford St. BL2: Bolt 7K 23
Rainforth St. M13: Man 6L 95
Rainham Dr. BL1: Bolt 3F 38
M8: Man 3F 78
Rainham Gro. BL1: Bolt 3F 38
(off Rainham Dr.)
Rainham Way OL9: Chad 5F 62
SK5: Stoc 2F 108
Rainhill Wlk. M40: Man 6B 80
(off Eastmoor Dr.)
Rainow Av. M43: Droy 9C 80
Rainow Dr. SK12: Poy 4L 125
Rainow Rd. SK3: Stoc 1A 118
SK10: Macc, Rain 2L 131
Rainow Vw. SK10: Boll 4N 129
Rainow Way SK9: Wilm 5K 123
(off Malpas Cl.)
Rainsdale Flats OL10: H'ood 2H 43
(off Meadow Cl.)
Rainshaw La. M18: Man 6B 96
Rainshaw St. BL1: Bolt 9G 22
OL2: O'ham 8H 45
OL4: O'ham 3A 64
RAIN SHORE 1H 27
RAINSOUGH 1M 77
Rainsough Av. M25: Pres 1N 77
Rainsough Brow M25: Pres 1M 77
Rainsough Cl. M25: Pres 1N 77
Rainsough Hill M25: Pres 1M 77
Rainton Wlk. M40: Man 9B 62
(off Enstone Dr.)
Rainwood OL9: Chad 3C 62
Raithby Dr. WN3: Wig 8D 52
Raja Cl. M8: Man 3G 79
Rajar Wlk. WA16: Mob 4N 133
Rake OL11: Roch 6J 27
Rake, The BL0: Ram 8H 11
Rake Fold BL8: Holc 8G 11
Rakehead Wlk. M15: Man 4F 94
(off Botham Cl.)
Rake La. M27: Clif 8G 58
Rake St. BL9: Bury 9M 25
Rake Ter. OL15: Lit 8N 15
Rake Top OL12: Roch 4N 27
RAKEWOOD 4A 30
Rakewood Dr. OL4: O'ham 8B 46
Rakewood Rd. OL15: Lit 2M 29
Raleigh Cl. M20: Man 3F 106
OL1: O'ham 3K 63
WA12: N Wil 8G 86
Raleigh Gdns. OL15: Lit 5N 15
Raleigh St. M32: Stre 7K 93
SK5: Stoc 4C 108
Ralli Courts M3: Sal 4D 4 (9D 78)
Ralli Quays M3: Sal 4D 4 (9D 78)
Ralph Av. SK14: Hyde 1B 110
Ralph Grn. St. OL9: O'ham 8F 62
Ralph Sherwin Ct. OL12: Roch 1H 29
Ralphs La. OL3: Dens 2G 47
SK16: Duk 2N 97
Ralph St. BL1: Bolt 2E 38
M11: Man 9B 80
OL12: Roch 4E 28
Ralston Cl. M7: Sal 2E 78
Ralstone Av. OL8: O'ham 7K 63
Ramage Wlk. M12: Man 9K 79
Ramillies Av. SK8: Chea H 6N 117
Rampit Cl. WA11: Hay 2C 86
Ramp Rd. E. M90: Man A 8B 116
Ramp Rd. Sth. M90: Man A 8B 116
(off Outwood La.)
Ramp Rd. W. M90: Man A 8A 116
Ramsay Av. BL4: Farn 4H 57
Ramsay Pl. OL16: Roch 6E 8 (5E 28)
Ramsay St. BL1: Bolt 9F 22
OL16: Roch 6E 8 (5E 28)
Ramsay Ter. OL16: Roch 6E 8 (5E 28)
RAMSBOTTOM 8J 11
Ramsbottom Heritage Cen. 7H 11
(off Carr St.)
Ramsbottom La. BL0: Ram 7J 11
Ramsbottom Pool & Fitness Cen.
....7J 11
Ramsbottom Rd. BL6: Hor 1E 36
BL7: Edg 3N 23
BL8: Haw 3N 23
Ramsbottom Row M25: Pres 7N 59
Ramsbottom Station
East Lancashire Railway 8J 11
Ramsbury Dr. M40: Man 9B 62
Ramsdale Rd. SK7: Bram 7C 118
Ramsdale St. OL9: Chad 4E 62
Ramsden Cl. OL1: O'ham 1B 8 (4J 63)
SK13: Glos 7E 100
WN3: Wig 8B 52
Ramsden Cres.
OL1: O'ham 1B 8 (4J 63)
Ramsden Fold M27: Clif 9F 58
Ramsden Rd. OL12: W'le 5G 14
Ramsden St. BL3: Bolt 7L 39
OL1: O'ham 1B 8 (4J 63)
OL6: A Lyne 6M 81
Ramsey Av. M19: Man 8B 96
Ramsey Cl. M46: Ath 9N 55
WN4: A Mak 8E 70
Ramsey Gro. BL8: Bury 2H 41
Ramsey St. M40: Man 3N 79
OL1: O'ham 3M 63
OL9: Chad 6F 62
WN7: Lei 5J 73
Ramsgate Rd. M40: Man 6A 80
SK5: Stoc 1D 108
Ramsgate St. M7: Sal 5D 78
M8: Man 5D 78
Ramsgill Cl. M23: Wyth 7M 105
Ramsgreave Cl. BL9: Bury 5K 41
Ram St. M38: Lit H 7G 56
Ramswell Cl. BL3: Bolt 9J 39
Ramwell Gdns. BL3: Bolt 7E 38
Ramwells Brow BL7: Bro X 5G 23
Ramwells Ct. BL7: Bro X 5H 23
Ramwells M. BL7: Bro X 5J 23
(off Windy Harbour La.)
Ranby Av. M9: Man 7L 61
Randale Dr. BL9: Bury 9N 41
Randall Av. WN6: She 7L 33
Randall Cl. WA12: N Wil 5E 86
Randall Wlk. M11: Man 9L 79
(off Raglan Cl.)
Randal St. BL3: Bolt 8D 38
SK14: Hyde 6B 98
Randerson St. M12: Man 8M 5
Randlesham St. M25: Pres 7B 60
Randle St. WN2: Hin 5N 53
Randolph Pl. SK3: Stoc 9C 108
Randolph Rd. BL4: Kea 4N 57
Randolph St. BL3: Bolt 6E 38
M19: Man 7N 95
OL8: O'ham 9G 63
Rands Clough Dr. M28: Wors 4J 75
Rand St. OL1: O'ham 2A 64
Ranelagh Rd. M27: Pen 3J 77
Ranelagh St. M11: Man 8N 79
Raneley Gro. OL11: Roch 2E 44
Ranford Rd. M19: Man 9M 95
Range Ct. SK10: Macc 3J 131
Range Dr. SK6: Wood 2N 109
Range Hall Ct. SK1: Stoc 7E 108
(off Hall St.)
Range La. OL3: Dens 3G 46
Rangemore Av. M22: Nor 8D 106
Range Rd. M16: Whall R 6D 94
SK3: Stoc 1C 118
SK15: Duk, Stal 1E 98
Range Stadium 9E 94
Range St. BL3: Bolt 8E 38
M11: Man 1A 96
Ranicar St. WN2: Hin 8E 54
Rankin Cl. M15: Man 4D 94
Rankine Ter. BL3: Bolt 7E 38
Ranmore Av. M11: Man 1B 96
WN4: Gars 6A 70
Rannoch Rd. BL2: Bolt 5N 39
Ransfield Rd. M21: Cho H 8A 94
Ranulph Ct. M6: Sal 5K 77
(off King St.)
Ranworth Av. SK4: Stoc 6L 107
Ranworth Cl. BL1: Bolt 7H 23
Ranworth Dr. WA3: Low 2A 88
Raper St. OL4: O'ham 3N 63
Rapes Highway OL3: Dens 8H 31
Raphael St. BL1: Bolt 2E 38
Rappax Rd. WA15: Hale 7G 114
Rasbottom St. BL3: Bolt 7E 38
Raspberry La. M30: Irl 4J 91
M44: Irl 5G 91
Rassbottom Brow SK15: Stal 8C 82
Rassbottom Ind. Est. SK15: Stal 8C 82
Rassbottom St. SK15: Stal 8C 82
Rassey Cl. WN6: Stan 5D 34
Rastell Wlk. M9: Man 8K 61
(off Ravenswood Dr.)
Ratcliffe Av. M44: Irl 7H 91
Ratcliffe Rd. WN2: Asp 6M 35
Ratcliffe St. M19: Man 8N 95
M29: Tyld 1C 74
SK1: Stoc 5L 9 (8D 108)
WN6: Wig 2D 52
WN7: Lei 4H 73
Ratcliffe Ter. OL5: Mos 2F 82
Ratcliffe Towers
SK1: Stoc 4L 9 (8D 108)
Rathan Rd. M41: Urm 5C 92
Rathbone St. OL16: Roch 6G 28
Rathbourne Av. M9: Man 7J 61
Rathen Av. WN2: I Mak 2K 53
Rathen Rd. M20: Man 3G 107
Rathmell Cl. WA3: Cul 6G 89
Rathmell Rd. M23: Wyth 6M 105
Rathmore Av. M40: Man 5K 79
Rathvale Dr. M22: Wyth 7B 116
Rath Wlk. M40: Man 5A 80
(off Orford Rd.)
Rathybank Cl. BL1: Bolt 3D 38
Rattenbury Ct. M6: Sal 5J 77
Raveden Cl. BL1: Bolt 1D 38
Raveley Av. M14: Man 9J 95
Ravelston Dr. M9: Man 6J 61
Raven Av. OL9: Chad 6E 62
Raven Cl. M43: Droy 7G 81
PR7: Chor 1C 18
Raven Ct. M15: Man 4D 94
(off Dudley Cl.)
Ravendale Cl. OL12: Roch 4M 27
Raven Dr. M44: Irl 6H 91
Ravenfield Gro. BL1: Bolt 1G 7
Ravenglass Dr. M24: Mid 9J 43
Ravenhead Cl. M14: Man 9J 95
Ravenhead Dr. WN8: Uph 4E 50
Ravenhead Sq. SK15: C'ook 5H 83
Ravenhead Way WN8: Uph 5D 50
Ravenhurst M7: Sal 1D 78
Ravenhurst Dr. BL1: Bolt 6M 37
Ravenna Av. M23: Wyth 9K 105
Ravenoak Av. M19: Man 9A 96
Ravenoak Dr. M35: Fail 2E 80
Ravenoak Pk. Rd. SK8: Chea H 7N 117
Ravenoak Rd. SK2: Stoc 3E 118
SK8: Chea H 7N 117
Raven Rd. BL3: Bolt 8B 38
WA15: Tim 7H 105
Ravensbury St. M11: Man 8N 79
Ravenscar Cres. M22: Wyth 7C 116
Ravenscar Wlk. BL4: Farn 4L 57
(off Norris St.)
Ravens Cl. M25: Pres 9D 60
SK13: Glos 9B 100
Ravenscourt WA13: Lym 4A 112
(off Pepper St.)
Ravenscraig Rd. M38: Lit H 5J 57
Ravensdale Gdns. M30: Ecc 7E 76
Ravensdale Rd. BL1: Bolt 5M 37
Ravensdale St. M14: Man 6H 95
Ravensfield Ind. Est. SK16: Duk 9L 81
Ravensfield Way SK16: Duk 1M 97
Ravens Holme BL1: Bolt 5N 37
Ravenside Pk. OL9: Chad 6E 62
Ravens Pl. M25: Pres 9D 60
Ravenstonedale Dr. OL2: O'ham 7J 45
Ravenstone Dr. M33: Sale 3L 105
Ravenstones Dr. OL3: Dig 9M 47
Raven St. BL9: Bury 9M 25
M12: Man 7N 5 (1H 95)
OL11: Roch 4K 27
Ravensway M25: Pres 9C 60
Ravens Wood BL1: Bolt 5N 37
Ravenswood M20: Man 4E 106
Ravenswood Av. SK4: Stoc 7M 107
WN3: Wins 8A 52
Ravens Wood Brow WN5: Bil 5J 69
Ravenswood Ct. SK3: Stoc 3D 118
Ravenswood Dr. BL1: Bolt 5N 37
M9: Man 8K 61
SK8: Chea H 7N 117
WN2: Hin 4A 54
Ravenswood Rd. M32: Stre 4M 93
SK9: Wilm 1D 126
Raven Ter. SK16: Duk 9N 81
(off Peel St.)
Raven Way M6: Sal 7M 77
(off Salford Shop. City)
Ravenwood OL9: Chad 4B 62
Ravenwood Dr. M34: Aud 3J 97
WA15: Haleb 8J 115
Ravine Av. M9: Man 3K 79
(not continuous)
Rawcliffe Av. BL2: Bolt 5N 39
Rawcliffe St. M14: Man 6G 94
Rawdon Cl. M19: Man 8N 95
Rawlinson La. PR6: H Char 4J 19
PR7: H Char 3H 19
Rawlinson St. BL6: Hor 9D 20
(off Winter Hey La.)
Rawlyn Rd. BL1: Bolt 2A 38
Rawpool Gdns. M23: Wyth 9N 105
Rawson Av. BL4: Farn 2M 57

Rawson Rd. BL1: Bolt .3D 38
Rawsons Rake BL0: Ram .8G 11
Rawson St. BL4: Farn .2L 57
Rawsthorne Av. BL0: Eden .4K 11
M18: Man .7B 96
Rawsthorne St. BL1: Bolt .2F 38
M29: Tyld .2E 74
Rawstron St. OL12: Whitw .5A 14
Rayburn Way M8: Man .5F 78
(not continuous)
Raycroft Av. M9: Man .9M 61
Raydale Cl. WA3: Low .9A 72
Rayden Cres. BL5: W'ton .5G 55
Raydon Av. *M40: Man* .*5J 79*
(off Sedgeford Rd.)
Raylees BL0: Ram .1J 25
Rayleigh Av. M11: Man .2D 96
Rayleigh Cl. SK10: Macc .3C 130
Raymond Av. BL9: Bury .8M 25
OL9: Chad .7F 62
Raymond Rd. M23: Wyth .6A 106
Raymond St. M27: Pen .1F 76
Rayner La. OL7: A Lyne .9H 81
Rayners Cl. SK15: Stal .9C 82
Rayner St. SK1: Stoc .8F 108
Raynham Av. M20: Man .5G 107
Raynham St. OL6: A Lyne . .6F 6 (7N 81)
Raysonhill Dr. M9: Man .9H 61
Reabrook Av. M12: Man .3L 95
Reach, The M28: Walk .9M 57
Read Cl. BL9: Bury .5K 41
OL2: Shaw .6M 45
Reade Av. M41: Urm .8M 91
Reade Ho. *M41: Urm* .*8N 91*
(off Flixton Rd.)
Reading Cl. M11: Man .1A 96
Reading Dr. M33: Sale .4D 104
Reading St. M6: Sal .5A 78
Reading Wlk. M34: Dent .8K 97
Readitt Wlk. *M11: Man* .*8N 79*
(off Coghlan Cl.)
Read St. SK14: Hyde .6N 97
Read St. W. SK14: Hyde .6N 97
Reaney Wlk. *M12: Man* .*3M 95*
(off Stonehurst Cl.)
Reather Wlk. M40: Man .1N 5
Rebecca Ct. *OL16: Miln* .*8K 29*
(off Harbour La.)
Rebecca St. M8: Man .2F 78
Recreation Av. WN4: A Mak .6G 71
Recreation Dr. WN5: Bil .5J 69
Recreation Rd. M35: Fail .1E 80
Recreation St. BL2: Bolt .8M 23
BL3: Bolt .8F 38
M25: Pres .7B 60
Rectory Av. M8: Man .1F 78
M25: Pres .7A 60
WA3: Low .1M 87
Rectory Cl. M26: Rad .8K 41
M34: Dent .7L 97
Rectory Ct. SK6: Mar .2C 120
Rectory Flds. SK1: Stoc . .2N 9 (7E 108)
Rectory Gdns. BL5: W'ton .6G 55
M25: Pres .7A 60
Rectory Grn. M25: Pres .6N 59
SK1: Stoc .2N 9 (7E 108)
Rectory Gro. M25: Pres .8A 60
Rectory Hill BL9: Bury .9C 26
Rectory La. BL9: Bury .9C 26
M25: Pres .6N 59
M26: Rad .9H 41
WN1: Stan .3B 34
WN6: Stan .3B 34
Rectory Rd. M8: Man .1E 78
WN4: Gars .5A 70
Rectory St. M24: Mid .2L 61
Redacre SK12: Poy .9K 119
Redacre Rd. M18: Man .3C 96
RED BANK .8H 87
Red Bank BL9: Bury .7D 26
M4: Man .1H 5 (7F 78)
M8: Man .7F 78
PR7: Chor .1G 19
WA12: N Wil .8H 87
Red Bank Av. WA12: N Wil .8J 87
Red Bank Rd. M26: Rad .7F 40
Redbarn Cl. SK6: Bred .4K 109
Red Barn Rd. WN5: Bil .4F 68
Redbourne Dr. M41: Urm .5N 91
Redbrick Ct. OL7: A Lyne .9L 81
Red Bri. BL2: Bolt .3A 40
Redbridge Gro. *M21: Cho H* .*9N 93*
(off Crossland Rd.)
Redbrook Av. M40: Man .5K 79
Redbrook Cl. BL4: Farn .2M 57
Redbrook Gro. *SK9: Wilm* .*5J 123*
(off Colshaw Dr.)
Redbrook Rd. M31: Part .6F 102
WA15: Tim .1K 115
WN3: I Mak .5G 53
Red Brook St. OL11: Roch .6B 28
Redbrook Way SK10: Adl .9G 125
Redbrow Hollow SK6: Comp .6D 110
Redburn Cl. WN3: Wig .5E 52
Redburn Rd. M23: Wyth .9A 106
Redby St. M11: Man .2N 95
Redcar Av. M20: Man .2G 106
M41: Urm .5A 92
Redcar Cl. OL1: O'ham .2M 63
SK7: H Gro .6L 119
Redcar Lodge *M27: Pen* .*3J 77*
(off Redcar Rd.)
Redcar Rd. BL1: Bolt .9C 22
BL3: Lit L .9A 40
M27: Pen .3J 77
Redcar St. OL12: Roch .5C 28
Red Cat La. WA11: Cra .6C 68
Redcedar Pk. BL2: Bolt .7L 39
Redcliffe Ct. M25: Pres .9A 60
Redclyffe Av. M14: Man .6H 95
Redclyffe Circ. M41: Urm .3C 92
Redclyffe Rd. M20: Man .3F 106
M41: Urm .2D 92
Redcot BL1: Bolt .5C 38
Redcot Ct. M45: Whitef .4J 59
Redcote St. M40: Man .2M 79
Redcourt SK13: Glos .9E 100
Redcourt Av. M20: Man .4G 106
Red Cow Yd. WA16: Knut .6G 132
Redcroft Gdns. M19: Man .4K 107
Redcroft Rd. M33: Sale .2E 104
Redcross St.
OL12: Roch .5C 8 (4D 28)
Redcross St. Nth. OL12: Roch .4C 28
Reddaway Cl. M6: Sal .5N 77
REDDISH
SK5 .1D 108
WA13 .2B 112
Reddish Cl. BL2: Bolt .7M 23
Reddish Cres. WA13: Lym .3A 112
REDDISH GREEN .1B 108
Reddish La. M18: Man .5C 96
M34: Man .6C 96
WA13: Lym .3A 112
(not continuous)
Reddish North Station (Rail) .7D 96
Reddish Rd. SK5: Stoc .1D 108
(not continuous)
Reddish South Station (Rail) .1D 108
REDDISH VALE .1E 108
Reddish Vale Country Pk. .1F 108
Reddish Vale Farm .1E 108
Reddish Vale Golf Course .2E 108
Reddish Vale Nature Reserve .9F 96
Reddish Va. Rd. SK5: Stoc .1D 108
Reddish Vale Sports Cen.
(NW Regional Basketball Cen.)
.9E 96
Reddish Vale Vis. Cen. .1F 108
Reddy La. WA14: Lit B, M'ton .8H 113
(not continuous)
Reddyshore Brow OL15: Lit .6N 15
Reddyshore Scout Ga.
OL14: Wals .1M 15
Redesmere Cl. M43: Droy .9F 80
SK10: Macc .3E 130
WA15: Tim .1K 115
Redesmere Dr.
SK8: Chea H .3L 117
SK9: A Edg .4E 126
Redesmere Pk. M41: Urm .9B 92
Redesmere Rd. SK9: Hand .1J 123
Redfearn Wood OL12: Roch .3N 27
Redfern Av. M33: Sale .5L 105
Redfern Cl. SK13: Had .3C 100
Redfern Cotts. OL11: Roch .4J 27
Redfern Ho. SK6: Rom .6L 109
Redfern St. M4: Man .2H 5 (8F 78)
Redfern Way OL11: Roch .4J 27
Redfield Cl. M11: Man .9L 79
Redfield Cft. WN7: Lei .5J 73
Redford Cl. WN7: Lei .5J 73
Redford Dr. SK7: Bram .5E 118
Redford Rd. M8: Man .7E 60
Redford St. BL8: Bury .1J 41
Red Gables OL7: A Lyne .6L 81
Redgate SK13: Had .5E 100
SK14: Hyde .9A 98
Redgate La. M12: Man .3L 95
(not continuous)
Redgate Rd. WN4: A Mak .4E 70
Redgates Wlk. *M21: Cho H* .*8A 94*
(off Ransfield Rd.)
Redgate Way BL4: Farn .2G 56
Redgrave Ho. WA14: Alt .4D 6
Redgrave Pas. OL4: O'ham .3A 64
Redgrave Ri. WN3: Wins .8A 52
Redgrave St. OL4: O'ham .3N 63
Redgrave Wlk. M19: Man .8A 96
Red Hall St. OL4: O'ham .5N 63
Redhill Dr. SK6: Bred .5H 109
Redhill Gro. *BL1: Bolt* .*3F 38*
(off Vernon St.)
Redhill St. M4: Man .4L 5 (9G 79)
Red Hill Way WN2: Hin .5N 53
Red Ho. SK10: Macc .3J 131
Red Ho. Bri. PR7: Adl .7J 19
Redhouse Farm Maize Maze .9L 103
Red Ho. La. WA14: D Mas .8K 103
Redhouse La. SK6: Bred .4K 109
SK12: Dis .9H 121
Redington Cl. M28: Wors .4H 75
Redisher Cl. BL0: Ram .2F 24
Redisher Cft. BL0: Ram .2F 24
Redisher La. BL8: Haw .1E 24
Redland Av. SK5: Stoc .3D 108
Redland Cl. OL15: Lit .8M 15
Redland Ct. WN2: Bam .3J 71
Redland Cres. M21: Cho H .2A 106
Red La. BL2: Bolt .3L 39
(not continuous)
OL3: Dig .6M 47
OL12: Roch .3F 28
SK12: Dis .9F 120
Red Lion St. M4: Man .3J 5 (8F 78)
RED LUMB .1F 26
Red Lumb St. OL12: Roch .1F 26
Redlynch Wlk. M8: Man .3F 78
Redmain Gro. WA3: Low .1A 88
Redman Gate BL8: Aff .7B 24
Redmans Cl. M30: Ecc .9B 76
Redmayne Cl. WA12: N Wil .5E 86
Redmere Dr. BL9: Bury .4N 41
Redmere Gro. M14: Man .9H 95
Redmire M. SK16: Duk .2C 98
Redmires Ct. M5: Sal .9N 77
Redmond Cl. M34: Aud .2J 97
Redmoor La. SK22: Dis .9L 121
SK22: N Mil .9L 121
Redmoor Mill SK22: N Mil .9L 121
Redmoor Sq. M13: Man .8L 5
Redmoss Row M27: Pen .2K 77
Rednal Wlk. WN3: Wig .5E 52
Red Pike Wlk. OL1: O'ham .3L 63
Redpol Av. WN7: Lei .4K 73
Redpoll Cl. M28: Wors .3L 75
RED ROCK .4F 34
Red Rock Brow WN1: Hai .4F 34
Red Rock La. M26: Rad .5D 58
WN1: Hai, Stan .4E 34
WN2: Hai .4E 34
Red Rose Cres. M19: Man .1A 108
Red Rose Gdns. M33: Sale .2H 105
M38: Walk .*7H 57*
(off County Rd.)
Red Rose Retail Cen. M5: Sal .9A 78
Red Row SK7: H Gro .7M 119
Redruth Av. SK10: Macc .3C 130
Redruth St. M14: Man .7G 95
Redscar Wlk. M24: Mid .2K 61
Redshank Cl. WA12: N Wil .5F 86
Redshank Dr. SK10: Macc .9F 128
Redshank Gro. WN7: Lei .4J 73
Redshaw Av. BL2: Bolt .7J 23
Redshaw Cl. M14: Man .8J 95
Redstart Cl. WA3: Low .1A 88
Redstart Gro. M28: Wors .2L 75
Redstock Cl. BL5: W'ton .2J 55
Redstone Rd. M19: Man .5J 107
Redthorn Av. M19: Man .1L 107
Redthorpe Cl. BL2: Bolt .3J 39
Redvale Dr. M7: Sal .4D 78
REDVALES .5L 41
Redvales Rd. BL9: Bury .5L 41
Redvers St. OL1: O'ham . . .1A 8 (3H 63)
Redwater Cl. M28: Wors .4H 75
Red Waters WN7: Lei .4J 73
Redway SK10: Kerr .6M 129
Redwing Cen. M17: T Pk .3J 93
Redwing Rd. BL8: G'mount .3F 24
REDWOOD .5L 51
Redwood BL5: W'ton .5F 54
M33: Sale .4C 104
OL9: Chad .4B 62
WN6: She .6M 33
Redwood Av. WN5: Orr .5L 51
WN6: Wig .9C 34
Redwood Cl. BL3: Bolt .7M 39
OL12: Roch .2N 27
SK3: Stoc .8N 107
Redwood Ct. SK10: Boll .8J 129
Redwood Dr. M8: Man .5G 78
M34: Aud .3J 97
SK6: Bred .5K 109
Redwood Ho. M22: Nor .7D 106
Redwood La. OL4: Lees .4B 64
Redwood Pk. Gro. OL16: Roch .6H 29
Redwood Rd. OL3: Upp .4M 65
Redwood St. M6: Sal .6M 77
Reebok Stadium .5F 36
Reece Ct. SK16: Duk .1A 98
Reeceton Gdns. BL1: Bolt .5C 38
Reedbank M26: Rad .3G 58
Reed Cl. BL4: Farn .3K 57
Reed Ct. *OL1: O'ham* .*3J 63*
(off Bradford St.)
Reed Cres. WN3: Wig .7D 52
Reedham Cl. BL1: Bolt .4D 38
Reedham Wlk. *M40: Man* .*6K 79*
(off Giltbrook Av.)
OL9: O'ham .7F 62
Reed Hill OL16: Roch .6C 8 (5D 28)
Reedley Dr. M28: Wors .2K 75
Reedmace Cl. M28: Walk .1M 75
Reedmaker Pl. M27: Swin .2D 76
Reeds Brow WA11: R'ford .2A 68
Reedshaw Bank SK2: Stoc .2H 119
Reedshaw Rd. M9: Man .4H 79
Reedsmere Cl. WN5: Wig .5C 52
Reed St. M18: Man .3B 96
OL1: O'ham .2F 8
Reedymoor BL5: W'ton .7G 54
Reeman Cl. SK6: Bred .4L 109
Reeman Ct. SK9: Wilm .4G 122
Reepham Cl. WN3: Wins .8A 52
Reeve Cl. SK2: Stoc .2K 119
Reeve's Ct. M5: Sal .8G 77
Reeves Rd. M21: Cho H .1A 106
Reeves St. WN7: Lei .4H 73
Reeve St. WA3: Low .1D 88
Reevey Av. SK7: H Gro .5G 119
Reform Club, The *SK4: Stoc* .*4N 107*
(off Heaton Moor Rd.)
Reform St. OL12: Roch .4D 28
Reform Wlk. M11: Man .1N 95
Refuge St. OL2: Shaw .6M 45
Regaby Gro. WN2: Hin .6C 54
Regal Cl. M45: Whitef .3A 60
Regal Fold OL12: Roch .1F 28
Regal Ind. Est. M12: Man .2M 95
Regal Wlk. *M40: Man* .*4A 80*
(off Lastingham St.)
Regan Av. M21: Cho H .1C 106
Regan St. BL1: Bolt .1E 38
M26: Rad .1H 59
Regatta Cl. OL9: Chad .8E 62
Regatta St. M6: Sal .4M 77
Regency Chambers
BL9: Bury .8J 7
Regency Cl. M40: Man .5J 79
OL8: O'ham .7H 63
SK13: Glos .8F 100
Regency Ct. M33: Sale .4F 104
OL11: Roch .6L 27
SK2: Stoc .1E 118
SK8: Chea H .5M 117
SK15: Stal .*8D 82*
(off Waterloo Rd.)
WA15: Hale .4J 115
WN1: Wig .7L 9 (3G 52)
Regency Gdns.
SK8: Chea H .7K 117
SK14: Hyde .5C 98
Regency Lodge M25: Pres .7N 59
Regency Pk. SK9: Wilm .9E 122
Regency Wharf WN7: Lei .6L 73
Regent Av. M14: Man .7F 94
M38: Lit H .7K 57
SK11: Macc .6F 130
WN4: A Mak .5C 70
Regent Bank SK9: Wilm .9E 122
Regent Caravan Pk. M6: Sal .6M 77
Regent Cinema
Marple .1C 120
Regent Cl. OL10: H'ood .3G 43
SK7: Bram .2B 124
SK8: Chea H .3A 118
SK9: Wilm .9E 122
Regent Ct. M7: Sal .1C 78
SK4: Stoc .3A 108
WA14: Alt .3C 6 (3D 114)
WA15: Haleb .*7J 115*
(off Dial Rd.)
Regent Cres. *M17: Urm* .*3D 92*
(in The Trafford Cen.)
M35: Fail .4C 80
OL2: O'ham .1H 63
Regent Dr. BL6: Los .5K 37
M34: Dent .8H 97
OL5: Mos .3G 83
WN7: Lei .3M 73
Regent Fold OL5: Mos .3G 83
Regent Ho. M14: Man .6J 95
SK4: Stoc .2J 9
Regent Pk. Golf Course .5K 37
Regent Pl. M14: Man .5H 95
Regent Retail Pk.
M5: Sal .6A 4 (1B 94)
Regent Rd. BL6: Los .5K 37
M5: Sal .6A 4 (9A 78)
SK2: Stoc .1E 118
WA14: Alt .3B 6 (3C 114)
Regents, The SK9: Wilm .6H 123
Regents Hill BL6: Los .6L 37
Regents Pl. M5: Sal .9A 78
Regent Sq. M5: Sal .1A 94
(not continuous)
Regent St. BL0: Ram .9G 11
BL9: Bury .9M 25
M24: Mid .1L 61
M30: Ecc .8F 76
M40: Man .5B 80
M46: Ath .9N 55
OL1: O'ham .2F 8 (4L 63)
OL2: Shaw .*5M 45*
(off Kershaw St. E.)
OL10: H'ood .3G 42
OL12: Roch .4D 28
OL15: Lit .9M 15
PR7: Cop .4B 18
SK13: Glos .8F 100
SK13: Had .4D 100
WA12: N Wil .6D 86
WA16: Knut .6G 132
WN2: Hin .6M 53
(not continuous)
Regent Trad. Est. M5: Sal . .4B 4 (9C 78)
Regent Wlk. BL4: Farn .3L 57
Regina Av. SK15: Stal .8D 82
Regina Ct. M6: Sal .7G 77
Regina Cres. WN7: Lei .4N 73
Reginald Latham Ct. *M40: Man* .*7J 79*
(off Berkshire Rd.)
Reginald St. BL3: Bolt .1B 56
M11: Man .2D 96
M27: Swin .1D 76
M30: Ecc .1C 92
Reid Cl. M34: Dent .9L 97
Reigate Cl. BL8: Bury .3H 41
Reigate Rd. M41: Urm .9M 91
Reilly St. M15: Man .3E 94
Reins Lee Av. OL8: O'ham .9L 63
Reins Lee Rd. OL7: A Lyne .4L 81
Reliance St. M40: Man .3A 80
Reliance St. Ent. Pk. M40: Man .4A 80
Reliance Trad. Est. M40: Man . .4A 80
Rembrandt Wlk. OL1: O'ham .8A 46
Rena Cl. SK4: Stoc .5B 108
Rena Ct. SK4: Stoc .5B 108
Rendel Cl. M32: Stre .7K 93
WA12: N Wil .7G 86
Renfrew Cl. SK10: Macc .2D 130
WN3: Wig .8D 52
Renfrew Dr. BL3: Bolt .9A 38
Renfrew Rd. WN2: Asp .7N 35
Rennie Cl. M32: Stre .7K 93
Renolds Ho. M5: Sal .8A 4
Renshaw Av. M30: Ecc .9D 76
Renshaw Dr. BL9: Bury .1B 42
Renshaw St. M30: Ecc .9D 76
WA14: Alt .1E 6 (2E 114)
Renshaw Pl. WA16: H Leg .9D 112
Renton Rd. BL3: Bolt .9C 38
M22: Wyth .3C 116
M32: Stre .7L 93
Renwick Gro. *BL3: Bolt* .*9D 38*
(off Maltby Dr.)
Renwick Sq. WN4: A Mak .7C 70
Repton Av. M34: Dent .6E 96
M40: Man .1C 80
M41: Urm .7L 91
M43: Droy .7B 80
OL8: O'ham .8H 63
SK14: Hyde .6B 98
WN3: I Mak .7J 53
Repton Cl. M33: Sale .5D 104
Reservoir Gdns. *M28: Walk* .*7L 57*
(off Worsley Rd. Nth.)
Reservoir Rd. SK3: Stoc .9B 108
Reservoir St. M3: Sal .1E 4 (7D 78)
M6: Sal .8M 77
OL16: Roch .5G 28
WN2: Asp .9B 36
WN2: I Mak .3K 53
Residences, The M25: Pres .8B 60
Restormel Av. WN2: Asp .7N 35
Retford Av. OL16: Roch .9F 28
Retford Cl. BL8: Bury .8L 25
Retford St. OL4: O'ham .6M 63
Retiro St.
OL1: O'ham .2E 8 (4K 63)
Retley Pas. OL1: O'ham .2C 8
Retreat, The M28: Wors .2N 75
SK6: Rom .7N 109
Reuben St. SK4: Stoc .4C 108
Revers St. BL8: Bury .5G 7 (1K 41)
Reveton Grn. SK7: Bram .5E 118
Rex Bldgs. SK9: Wilm .8G 122
Rexcine Way SK14: Hyde .4D 98
Rex Ct. OL4: Grot .5E 64
Reynard Ct. M13: Man .5K 95
Reynard Rd. M21: Cho H .1A 106
Reynard St. SK14: Hyde .6A 98
Reynell Rd. M13: Man .7L 95
Reyner St. M1: Man .6H 5
OL6: A Lyne .8B 82
Reynolds Cl. BL5: O Hul .5A 56
Reynolds Dr. BL5: O Hul .4A 56
M18: Man .3B 96
SK6: Mar B .8E 110
Reynolds M. SK9: Wilm .6K 123
Reynolds Rd. M16: Old T .5B 94
Reynold St. SK14: Hyde .7A 98
Rhine, The M15: Man .8F 4
Rhine Cl. BL8: Tot .6F 24
Rhine Dr. M8: Man .5D 78
Rhiwlas Dr. BL9: Bury .4M 41
Rhode Ho's. SK6: Mar .4C 120
RHODES .4H 61
Rhodes Av. OL3: Upp .2M 65
OL4: Lees .6C 64
RHODES BANK .3E 8 (5L 63)
Rhodes Bank OL1: O'ham . . .3E 8 (5K 63)
Rhodes Bus. Pk. M24: Mid .4H 61
Rhodes Cres. OL11: Roch .1D 44
Rhodes Dr. BL9: Bury .1N 59
RHODES GREEN .3G 60
Rhodes Hill OL4: Lees .6C 64
Rhodes St. OL1: O'ham .2F 8 (4L 63)
OL2: O'ham .9L 45
OL12: Roch .2F 28
SK13: Had .4D 100
SK14: Hyde .6N 97
Rhodes St. Nth. SK14: Hyde .6N 97
Rhodes Top SK13: Had .4D 100
Rhode St. BL8: Tot .7F 24
Rhodeswood Dr. SK13: Had .3C 100
Rhos Av. M14: Man .9K 95
M24: Mid .4M 61
SK8: Chea H .6L 117
Rhos Dr. SK7: H Gro .6H 119
Rhosleigh Av. BL1: Bolt .9F 22
Rhyddings, The BL9: Bury .6D 26
Rial Pl. *M15: Man* .*3F 94*
(off Eden Cl.)
Rialto Gdns. M7: Sal .4D 78
Ribbesford Rd. WN3: Wig .7N 51
Ribble Av. BL2: Bolt .5M 39
OL9: Chad .2C 62
OL15: Lit .8K 15
Ribble Cl. WA3: Cul .7H 89
Ribble Cres. WN5: Bil .7G 69
Ribble Dr. BL4: Kea .6A 58
BL9: Bury .5M 25
M28: Wors .4G 74
M45: Whitef .2N 59
WN5: Wig .4N 51
Ribble Gro. OL10: H'ood .1F 42
WN7: Lei .5E 72
Ribblehead Ct. M26: Rad .3C 58
Ribble Rd. OL8: O'ham .8G 62
WN2: P Bri .9J 53
WN6: Stan .2M 33
Ribblesdale Cl. OL10: H'ood .5K 43
Ribblesdale Dr. M40: Man .5H 79
Ribblesdale Rd. BL3: Bolt .8E 38
Ribble St. OL11: Roch .9C 28
Ribbleton Cl. BL8: Bury .3F 40
Ribble Wlk. *M43: Droy* .*1E 96*
(off Ellen St.)
Ribchester Dr. BL9: Bury .5K 41
Ribchester Gdns. WA3: Cul .6J 89
Ribchester Gro. BL2: Bolt .3M 39
Riber Bank SK13: Gam .8A 100
Riber Cl. *SK13: Gam* .*8A 100*
(off Baslow M.)
Riber Fold *SK13: Gam* .*8A 100*
(off Baslow M.)
Riber Grn. *SK13: Gam* .*8A 100*
(off Baslow M.)
Ribston St. M15: Man .3D 94
Rice St. M3: Man .6D 4 (1D 94)
Richard Burch St. BL9: Bury .1M 41
Richard Gwyn Cl. BL5: W'ton .5F 54
Richard Reynolds Ct.
M44: Cad .*2F 102*
(off Dean Rd.)
Richards Cl. M34: Aud .2J 97
Richardson Cl. M45: Whitef .2M 59
Richardson Rd. M30: Ecc .8E 76
Richardson St. M11: Man .2C 96
SK1: Stoc .9E 108
Richards Rd. WN6: Stan .1M 33
Richard St. BL0: Ram .7L 11
M26: Rad .9F 40
OL11: Roch .9D 8 (7D 28)
SK1: Stoc .5D 108
WN3: I Mak .5G 53
Richbell Cl. M44: Irl .1F 102
Richborough Cl. M7: Sal .5D 78
Richelieu St. BL3: Bolt .8H 39
Richmal Ter. BL0: Ram .7H 11
Richmond Av. M25: Pres .1B 78
M41: Urm .7E 92
OL2: O'ham .8H 45
OL9: Chad .7E 62
SK9: Hand .1J 123
Richmond Cl. BL8: Tot .7F 24
M33: Sale .5M 105
M45: Whitef .4K 59
OL2: Shaw .7M 45
OL5: Mos .2H 83
OL16: Roch .1G 44
SK13: Had .4C 100
SK15: Stal .9D 82
SK16: Duk .3A 98
WA3: Cul .5F 88
WA13: Lym .3C 112
WN1: Stan .5E 34
Richmond Ct. M3: Sal .2B 4
M9: Man .*6F 60*
(off Deanswood Dr.)
M13: Man .5J 95
M34: Aud .3J 97
SK2: Stoc .2H 119
WA14: Bow .5B 114
Richmond Cres. OL5: Mos .2H 83
Richmond Dr. M28: Wors .2C 76
WA13: Lym .3C 112
WN7: Lei .3N 73

Richmond Gdns. BL3: Bolt 9J 39
WA12: N Wil 7F 86
Richmond Grn. SK7: Bram 9D 118
WA14: Bow 5B 114
Richmond Gro. BL4: Farn 2H 57
M13: Man 5J 95
M30: Ecc 7E 76
SK8: Chea H 5L 117
WN7: Lei 4M 73
Richmond Gro. E. M12: Man 4K 95
Richmond Hill M3: Sal 1D 4
SK11: Macc 6J 131
SK14: Hyde 8C 98
WA14: Bow 5B 114
WA16: Knut 7H 133
WN5: Wig 5N 51
Richmond Hill Rd. SK8: Chea 2H 117
Richmond Ho. M27: Pen 9F 58
(off Berry St.)
SK15: Stal 9D 82
(off Grosvenor St.)
Richmond Pk. M14: Man 8J 95
Richmond Pl. SK11: Macc 6J 131
Richmond Rd. M14: Man 9J 95
M17: T Pk 2G 92
M28: Wors 3F 74
M34: Dent 6E 96
M35: Fail 2E 80
SK4: Stoc 6L 107
SK6: Rom 5N 109
SK16: Duk 3A 98
WA14: Alt 1C 6 (2D 114)
WA14: Bow 5B 114
WN2: Hin 8C 54
WN4: A Mak 5C 70
Richmond St. BL6: Hor 1D 36
BL9: Bury 4L 41
M1: Man 6J 5 (1F 94)
M3: Sal 1D 4 (7D 78)
M34: Aud 3J 97
M43: Droy 8G 80
M46: Ath 8L 55
OL6: A Lyne 8A 6 (7K 81)
OL7: A Lyne 7A 6 (6K 81)
SK14: Hyde 7B 98
SK15: Stal 8E 82
WN1: Wig 7H 9 (3E 52)
WN3: Wig 6D 52
Richmond Ter. SK6: Mar 6E 120
Richmond Vw. OL5: Mos 1H 83
(off Bk. Micklehurst Rd.)
Richmond Wlk. M26: Rad 6E 40
OL9: O'ham 3A 8 (5H 63)
Ricroft Rd. SK6: Comp 5E 110
Ridd Cotts. OL11: Roch 5H 27
Riddell Ct. M5: Sal 8J 77
Ridding Av. M22: Wyth 4D 116
Ridding Cl. SK2: Stoc 1H 119
Riddings Ct. WA15: Tim 8F 104
Riddings Rd. WA15: Hale 6F 114
WA15: Tim 8F 104
Riddiough Ct. OL12: Whitw 6A 14
Riders Ga. BL9: Bury 9E 26
Rides, The WA11: Hay 3A 86
Ridge, The SK6: Mar 4D 120
Ridge Av. SK6: Mar 3D 120
WA15: Haleb 9J 115
WN1: Stan 5E 34
Ridge Cl. SK6: Rom 6B 110
SK13: Had 5A 100
Ridge Cres. M45: Whitef 3A 60
SK6: Mar 4D 120
Ridgecroft OL7: A Lyne 4M 81
Ridgedale Cen. SK6: Mar 1C 120
Ridgedales, The OL1: O'ham 8B 46
Ridge-End SK6: Mar 5E 120
Ridge End Fold SK6: Mar 6D 120
Ridgefield M2: Man 5F 4 (9E 78)
Ridgefield St. M35: Fail 3B 80
(not continuous)
Ridgegreen M28: Wors 5H 75
Ridge Gro. M45: Whitef 3A 60
RIDGE HILL 7D 82
Ridge Hill SK11: Sut E 9L 131
Ridge Hill La. SK15: Stal 8C 82
Ridge La. OL3: Dig 7N 47
Ridgemont Av. SK4: Stoc 6N 107
Ridgemont Wlk. M23: Wyth 6M 105
Ridge Pk. SK7: Bram 9B 118
Ridge Rd. SK6: Mar 3D 120
Ridge Vw. SK11: Macc 7G 130
Ridge Wlk. M9: Man 8J 61
Ridgeway M27: Clif 1H 77
SK9: Wilm 7L 123
WA3: Low 2B 88
Ridgeway, The SK12: Dis 8F 120
Ridgeway Gates
BL1: Bolt 2K 7 (5G 38)
Ridgeway Rd. WA15: Tim 2J 115
Ridgewell Av. WA3: Low 1M 87
Ridgewood Av. M40: Man 5J 79
OL9: Chad 3C 62
Ridgewood Ct. WN2: Hin 8E 54
Ridgmont Cl. BL6: Hor 1H 37
Ridgmont Dr. BL6: Hor 1H 37
M28: Wors 4G 75
Ridgmont Rd. SK7: Bram 1C 124
Ridgway BL6: Bla 2M 35
Ridgway, The SK6: Rom 7L 109
Ridgway St. M40: Man 8J 79
Ridgway St. E. M4: Man 8J 79
Riding Cl. M29: Ast 3E 74
M33: Sale 4M 105
Riding Fold M43: Droy 7H 81
Ridingfold La. M28: Wors 5A 76
Riding Ga. BL2: Bolt 7M 23
Riding Ga. M. BL2: Bolt 7M 23
Riding Head La. BL0: Ram 6M 11
Riding La. WN4: A Mak 4H 71
Ridings, The SK9: Wilm 1C 126
Ridings Ct. OL3: Dob 1K 65
Ridings Rd. SK13: Had 4B 100
Ridings St. M11: Man 1N 95
M40: Man 5L 79
Riding St. PR6: Adl 6K 19
Ridings Way OL9: Chad 5F 62
Ridley Dr. WA14: Tim 7E 104
Ridley Gro. M33: Sale 5M 105
Ridley Rd. SK10: Boll 5J 129
Ridley St. OL4: O'ham 5L 63
Ridley Wlk. M15: Man 4F 94
(off Wellhead Cl.)
Ridling La. SK14: Hyde 7B 98
Ridsdale Av. M20: Man 2F 106
Ridsdale Wlk. M6: Sal 5N 77
(off Langley Rd. Sth.)
Ridyard St. M38: Lit H 6J 57
WN2: P Bri 8L 53
WN5: Wig 4A 52
Riefield BL1: Bolt 1C 38
Rifle Rd. M33: Sale 3M 105
Rifle St. OL1: O'ham 1D 8 (3K 63)
Riga Rd. M14: Man 8H 95
Riga St. M4: Man 2J 5 (8F 78)
Rigby Av. BL6: Bla 2M 35
M26: Rad 7J 41
Rigby Ct. BL3: Bolt 8G 38
OL12: Roch 3K 27
Rigby Gro. M38: Lit H 7F 56
Rigby La. BL2: Bolt 7K 23
Rigby's Ho's. PR7: Adl 7H 19
Rigbys La. WN4: A Mak 7G 70
Rigby St. BL3: Bolt 8G 38
M7: Sal 3C 78
WA3: Gol 1K 87
WA14: Alt 5D 6 (4D 114)
WN2: Hin 5A 54
WN4: A Mak 7D 70
Rigby's Yd. WN5: Wig 5M 51
Rigby Wlk. M7: Sal 4D 78
Rigel Pl. M7: Sal 7B 78
(off Indus Pl.)
Rigel St. M4: Man 1N 5 (7H 79)
Rigi Mt. OL2: O'ham 6H 45
RIGSHAW BRIDGE 6J 19
Rigshaw Bri. Cotts. PR7: Adl 6J 19
Rigton Cl. M12: Man 4M 95
Riley Cl. M33: Sale 7B 104
Riley Ct. BL1: Bolt 5E 38
BL8: Bury 2J 41
Riley La. WN2: Hai 4L 35
Riley Sq. WN1: Wig 7M 9 (3G 53)
Rileys Snooker Club
Manchester, Deansgate
. . . . .4F 4 (9E 78)
Manchester, Kirkmanshulme La.
. . . . .4N 95
Stockport 9D 108
(off Wellington Rd. Sth.)
Trafford 9D 104
Whitefield 3N 59
Riley St. M46: Ath 1J 73
Rileywood Cl. SK6: Rom 7K 109
Rilldene Wlk. OL11: Roch 5J 27
Rilston Av. WA3: Cul 6F 88
Rimington Av. WA3: Gol 9M 71
Rimington Cl. WA3: Cul 6G 89
Rimington Fold M24: Mid 9J 43
Rimmer Cl. M11: Man 1K 95
Rimmington Cl. M9: Man 9M 61
Rimmon Cl. OL3: G'fld 6L 65
Rimsdale Cl. SK8: Gat 4F 116
Rimsdale Dr. M40: Man 2A 80
Rimsdale Wlk. BL3: Bolt 7N 37
Rimworth Dr. M40: Man 6H 79
Rindle Rd. M29: Ast 8D 74
Ringcroft Gdns. M40: Man 1N 79
Ringford Wlk. M40: Man 5K 79
RINGLEY .4C 58
Ringley Av. WA3: Gol 9J 71
RINGLEY BROW 3D 58
Ringley Chase M45: Whitef 3K 59
Ringley Cl. M45: Whitef 3K 59
Ringley Dr. M45: Whitef 3K 59
Ringley Gro. BL1: Bolt 8F 22
Ringley Hey M45: Whitef 3K 59
Ringley Mdws. M26: Rad 4C 58
Ringley M. M26: Rad 3H 59
Ringley Old Brow M26: Rad 4C 58
Ringley Pk. M45: Whitef 3K 59
Ringley Pk. Vw. M45: Whitef 3K 59
Ringley Rd. M26: Rad 4C 58
(Fold Rd.)
M26: Rad 3B 58
(Market St.)
M45: Whitef 3J 59
Ringley Rd. W. M26: Rad 3E 58
Ringley St. M9: Man 2J 79
Ringlow Av. M27: Swin 3C 76
Ringlow Pk. Rd. M27: Swin 4C 76
Ring Lows La. OL12: Roch 1D 28
Ringmer Dr. M22: Wyth 6B 116
Ringmere Ct. OL1: O'ham 3J 63
(off Godson St.)
Ringmore Rd.
SK7: Bram, H Gro 5E 118
Ring O'Bells La. SK12: Dis 9G 120
Rings Cl. M35: Fail 4D 80
Ringstead Cl. SK9: Wilm 5J 123
Ringstead Dr. M40: Man 6H 79
SK9: Wilm 5J 123
Ringstone Cl. M25: Pres 8N 59
RINGWAY 9M 115
Ringway Av. WN7: Lei 2H 73
Ringway Cl. SK10: Macc 9F 128
Ringway Golf Course 6J 115
Ringway Gro. M33: Sale 6L 105
Ringway M. M22: Shar 2D 116
Ringway Rd. M22: Wyth 8D 116
M90: Man A 8B 116
Ringway Rd. W. M22: Man A 7B 116
M90: Man A 7B 116
Ringway Trad. Est.
M22: Wyth 7D 116
Ringwood Av. BL0: Ram 1G 24
M12: Man 7N 95
M26: Rad 2H 59
M34: Aud 9G 80
SK7: H Gro 6F 118
SK14: Hyde 8D 98
Ringwood Way OL9: Chad 3G 62
Rink St. M14: Man 1J 107
Ripley Av. SK2: Stoc 3F 118
SK8: Chea H 1N 123
Ripley Cl. M4: Man 1J 95
SK7: H Gro 7J 119
Ripley Cres. M41: Urm 4N 91
Ripley Dr. WN3: Wig 7N 51
WN7: Lei 4H 73
Ripley St. BL2: Bolt 9J 23
Ripley Way M34: Dent 9K 97
Ripon Av. BL1: Bolt 3A 38
BL9: Bury 1M 59
M45: Whitef 1M 59
WA3: Low 1N 87
WN6: Wig 9E 34
Ripon Cl. BL3: Lit L 9N 39
M26: Rad 7K 41
M45: Whitef 1M 59
OL9: Chad 5F 62
SK1: Stoc 5L 9 (8D 108)
SK10: Macc 1G 131
WA12: N Wil 5F 86
WA15: Hale 6J 115
Ripon Cres. M32: Stre 6F 92
Ripon Dr. BL1: Bolt 3A 38
WN4: A Mak 8G 70
Ripon Gro. M33: Sale 2F 104
Ripon Hall Av. BL0: Ram 1H 25
Ripon Rd. M32: Stre 6F 92
Ripon St. M15: Man 4F 94
OL1: O'ham 3H 63
OL6: A Lyne 6F 6 (7N 81)
Ripon Wlk. SK6: Rom 7L 109
Rippenden Av. M21: Cho H 7N 93
Rippingham Rd. M20: Man 1G 107
Rippleton Rd. M22: Wyth 3D 116
Ripponden Rd. OL1: O'ham 3N 63
OL3: Dens 2F 46
OL4: O'ham 3N 63
Ripponden St. OL1: O'ham 2N 63
Ripton Wlk. M9: Man 7G 60
(off Selston Rd.)
Risbury Wlk. M40: Man 4A 80
(off Bridlington Cl.)
Rise, The OL4: Spri 4C 64
WN6: Stan 9N 33
Riseley's Pas. SK10: Macc 4H 131
(off King Edward St.)
Riseley St. SK10: Macc 4G 130
Rises, The SK13: Had 4B 100
Rishton Av. BL3: Bolt 1G 57
Rishton La. BL3: Bolt 8G 38
(Rupert St.)
BL3: Bolt 9G 38
(Walker Av.)
Rishworth Cl. SK2: Stoc 2H 119
Rishworth Dr. M40: Man 2C 80
Rishworth Ri. OL2: Shaw 3K 45
Rising La. OL8: O'ham 9J 63
Rising La. Cl. OL8: O'ham 9J 63
Risings, The SK22: N Mil 7L 121
Rising Sun Cl. SK11: Gaws 7E 130
Rising Sun Rd. SK11: Gaws 8E 130
Risley Av. M9: Man 2J 79
Risley St. OL1: O'ham 3K 63
Rissington Av. M23: Wyth 1A 116
Rita Av. M14: Man 6G 94
Ritson Cl. M18: Man 3N 95
Riva Rd. M19: Man 6J 107
River Bank, The M26: Rad 3A 58
Riverbank OL3: Dob 2J 65
Riverbank Cl. SK10: Boll 5K 129
Riverbank Ct. OL4: O'ham 2A 64
Riverbank Dr. BL8: Bury 5H 7 (1K 41)
Riverbank Garden BL8: Bury 1K 41
(off Tottington Rd.)
Riverbank Lawns M3: Sal 1D 4
Riverbanks BL2: Bolt 7K 39
Riverbank Twr. M3: Sal 1D 4
Riverbank Wlk. M20: Man 5C 106
River Bank Way SK13: Glos 9H 101
Riverbend Technology Cen.
M44: Irl 2H 103
Riverbrook Rd. WA14: W Tim 7B 104
Riverdale Cl. WN6: Stan 8A 34
Riverdale Rd. M9: Man 8F 60
River Ho. M43: Droy 8E 80
(off Medlock St.)
River La. M31: Part 4G 103
M34: Dent 6M 97
Rivermead OL16: Miln 1M 45
Rivermead Av. WA15: Haleb 8J 115
Rivermead Cl. M34: Dent 1L 109
Rivermead Rd. M34: Dent 9L 97
Rivermead Way M45: Whitef 3N 59
Riverpark Rd. M40: Man 7M 79
River Pl. M15: Man 8E 4 (2D 94)
OL16: Miln 7K 29
Riversdale Ct. M25: Pres 7N 59
Riversdale Dr. OL8: O'ham 1L 81
Riversdale Rd. SK8: Chea 1H 117
Riversdale Vw. SK6: Wood 3L 109
Riversedge OL12: Whitw 5A 14
Rivershill M33: Sale 2G 105
Rivershill Dr. OL10: H'ood 3G 43
Rivershill Gdns. WA15: Haleb 9J 115
Riverside BL1: Bolt 2H 39
M7: Sal 1A 4 (7B 78)
OL1: Chad 2C 62
SK16: Duk 9E 6 (9N 81)
Riverside, The BL1: Bolt 3H 39
Riverside Av. M21: Cho H 5C 106
M44: Irl 8J 91
WN1: Wig 5M 9 (2G 53)
Riverside Bus. Pk. SK9: Wilm 7H 123
Riverside Cl. M26: Rad 8K 41
SK13: Glos 8F 100
Riverside Ct. M20: Man 5E 106
M50: Sal 1N 93
OL12: Whitw 2B 14
SK6: Mar B 8D 110
SK11: Lang 8N 131
Riverside Dr. BL9: Sum 3H 25
M26: Rad 3B 58
M41: Urm 9B 92
OL16: Roch 3G 28
SK10: P'bury 8E 128
Riverside Ho. OL3: Upp 3L 65
Riverside Ind. Est. OL7: A Lyne 9L 81
Riverside M. M15: Man 8E 4
Riverside Pk. Caravan Site
M22: Nor 7D 106
Riverside Rd. M26: Rad 8K 41
Rivers La. M41: Urm 4C 92
Riversleigh Cl. BL1: Bolt 1A 38
Riversmeade BL7: Bro X 6K 23
WN7: Lei 4J 73
Rivers St. WN5: Orr 5J 51
Riverstone Bri. OL15: Lit 9L 15
Riverstone Dr. M23: Wyth 9K 105
River St. BL0: Ram 9J 11
BL2: Bolt 3M 7 (5H 39)
M1: Man 8G 5
M12: Man 7N 5 (1H 95)
M15: Man 9F 4 (2E 94)
M26: Rad 9H 41
OL10: H'ood 1J 43
OL16: Roch 7D 8 (6D 28)
SK1: Stoc 5F 108
SK9: Wilm 6G 123
SK11: Macc 6J 131
Riverton Rd. M20: Man 8G 106
River Vw. M24: Mid 5A 62
SK5: Stoc 1E 108
Riverview SK4: Stoc 8L 107
River Vw. Cl. M25: Pres 9M 59
Riverview Cotts. SK13: Glos 9E 100
(off Turnlee Dr.)
River Vw. Ct. BL2: Bolt 4J 39
Riverview Ct. M7: Sal 2B 78
Riverview Wlk. BL1: Bolt 6E 38
(off Bridgewater St.)
Riverway WN1: Wig 9K 9 (4F 52)
Riviera Ct. OL12: Roch 3H 27
RIVINGTON 4B 20
Rivington M6: Sal 6J 77
Rivington Av. M27: Pen 2J 77
PR6: Adl 6L 19
WA3: Gol 9M 71
WN1: Wig 1E 52
WN2: P Bri 8L 53
Rivington Country Pk. 4B 20
Rivington Ct. M45: Whitef 4J 59
Rivington Cres. M27: Pen 2J 77
Rivington Dr. BL8: Bury 3G 40
OL2: Shaw 5A 46
WN2: B'haw 1B 72
WN8: Uph 4G 50
Rivington Gro. M34: Aud 1G 96
M44: Cad 2E 102
Rivington Hall Cl. BL0: Ram 1J 25
Rivington Ho. BL6: Hor 9D 20
Rivington La. BL6: R'ton 4B 20
PR6: And 7N 19
Rivington Pike Tower 5E 20
Rivington Pl. PR7: Cop 7A 18
Rivington Rd. BL6: R'ton 1G 21
BL7: Bel, R'ton 1G 21
M6: Sal 6J 77
OL4: Spri 4D 64
WA15: Hale 5F 114
Rivington St. BL6: Bla 2N 35
M46: Ath 9J 55
OL1: O'ham 2K 63
OL12: Roch 4D 28
Rivington Terraced Gdns. 4D 20
Rivington Wlk. M12: Man 4L 95
Rivington Way WN6: Stan 4C 34
Rixson St. OL4: O'ham 4N 63
Rix St. BL1: Bolt 2F 38
RIXTON 6A 102
Rixton Claypits Local Nature Reserve
. . . . .6A 102
Rixton Ct. M16: Old T 6A 94
(off Basford Rd.)
Rixton Dr. M29: Tyld 2C 74
Rixtonleys Dr. M44: Irl 9J 91
Rixton Pk. Homes WA3: Rix 6A 102
Roach Bank Ind. Est.
BL9: Bury 5A 42
Roach Bank Rd. BL9: Bury 5A 42
Roach Ct. M40: Man 6H 79
(off Hamerton Rd.)
ROACHES 8H 65
Roaches Ind. Est. OL5: Mos 8H 65
Roaches M. OL5: Mos 8G 65
Roaches Way OL5: Mos 8H 65
SK11: Macc 7F 130
Roach Grn. WN1: Wig 6N 9 (2H 53)
Roachill Cl. WA14: Alt 2B 114
Roach Pl. OL16: Roch 6E 8 (5E 28)
Roach St. BL9: Bury 8M 41
(Hollins Brow)
BL9: Bury 2B 42
(Lord St.)
Roach Va. OL16: Roch 3G 29
Roachwood Cl. OL9: Chad 4C 62
ROAD END 6M 65
Roading Brook Rd. BL2: Bolt 1A 40
Road Knowl OL2: Shaw 6N 45
Road La. OL12: Roch 1B 28
Roads Ford Av. OL16: Miln 6K 29
Roadside Ct. WA3: Low 1M 87
Roan Ct. SK11: Macc 5K 131
Roan Ho. Way SK11: Macc 5K 131
Roan M. SK11: Macc 5J 131
Roan Way SK9: A Edg 5G 126
Roaring Ga. La.
WA15: Hale, Ring 4L 115
(not continuous)
Robert Bolt Theatre, The 3H 105
(within Waterside Arts Cen.)
Robert Hall St. M5: Sal 1A 94
Robert Harrison Av. M20: Man 2E 106
Robert Lawrence Ct. M41: Urm 8A 92
Robert Malcolm Cl. M40: Man 5J 79
Robert Owen Gdns. M22: Nor 8C 106
Robert Owen St. M43: Droy 8G 80
Robert Powell Theatre 7A 78
Robert Salt Ct.
WA14: Alt 1E 6 (1E 114)
Roberts Av. M14: Man 5G 95
Robert Saville Ct. OL11: Roch 7A 28
(off Half Acre M.)
Robertscroft Cl. M22: Wyth 3B 116
Robertshaw Av. M21: Cho H 2A 106
Robertshaw St. WN7: Lei 3G 72
Robertson St. M26: Rad 8G 40
Roberts Pas. OL15: Lit 4A 16
Roberts Pl. OL15: Lit 2K 29
(off Wordsworth Cres.)
Roberts St. M30: Ecc 9D 76
Robert St. BL0: Ram 5J 11
BL2: Bolt 8M 23
BL8: Bury 1J 41
M3: Man 7E 78
M25: Pres 7B 60
M26: Rad 8G 40
M33: Sale 4L 105
M35: Fail 1E 80
M46: Ath 1N 73
OL8: O'ham 8F 62
OL10: H'ood 4K 43
OL16: Roch 6D 8 (5E 28)
SK14: Hyde 6N 97
SK16: Duk 1M 97
WN2: P Bri 8K 53
Robeson Way M22: Shar 1D 116
Robe Wlk. M18: Man 3B 96
(off Briercliffe Cl.)
Robin Cl. BL4: Farn 4G 57
PR7: Char R 2A 18
Robin Cres. SK11: Lym G 9H 131
Robin Cft. SK6: Bred 5H 109
Robin Dr. M44: Irl 6H 91
Robin Hill Dr. WN6: Stan 2M 33
Robin Hill La. WN6: Stan 1N 33
ROBIN HOOD 1F 32
Robin Hood Av. SK11: Macc 7G 131
Robin Hood La. WN6: Wrig 1F 32
Robin Hood St. M8: Man 2E 78
Robinia Cl. M30: Ecc 1N 91
Robin La. M45: Whitef 4M 59
SK11: Lym G 9H 131
ROBIN PARK 3C 52
Robin Pk. Arena 3C 52
Robin Pk. Retail Pk. WN5: Wig 3C 52
Robin Pk. Rd. WN5: Wig 3B 52
Robin Pk. Sports & Tennis Cen. 3C 52
Robin Rd. BL9: Sum 2H 25
WA14: W Tim 7C 104
Robinsbay Rd. M22: Wyth 7D 116
Robins Cl. M43: Droy 7G 81
SK7: Bram 8C 118
Robins La. SK7: Bram 8B 118
WA3: Cul 7F 88
WA11: K Mos 2E 68
Robinson Pk. SK15: Stal 9B 82
(off Robinson St.)
Robinsons Fold OL4: Spri 4E 64
Robinson's Pl. OL4: Spri 4E 64
Robinson St. BL6: Hor 9D 20
M29: Tyld 1B 74
OL6: A Lyne 6M 81
OL9: Chad 5F 62
OL16: Roch 7D 8 (6E 28)
SK3: Stoc 9B 108
SK14: Hyde 6C 98
SK15: Stal 1B 98
WN7: Lei 6J 73
Robin St. OL1: O'ham 3J 63
Robins Way SK10: Boll 6L 129
Robinsway WA14: Bow 6C 114
Robinswood Rd. M22: Wyth 5C 116
Robinwood Lodge SK13: Gam 8A 100
(off Bleaklow La.)
Rob La. WA12: N Wil 5H 87
Robson Av. M41: Urm 2E 92
Robson Pl. WN2: Abr 2L 71
Robson St. OL1: O'ham 3E 8 (5K 63)
Robson Way WA3: Low 1B 88
ROBY MILL 9F 32
Roby Mill WN8: Roby M 8F 32
Roby Rd. M30: Ecc 1C 92
Roby St. M1: Man 5K 5
Roby Well Way WN5: Bil 5H 69
Roch Av. OL10: H'ood 2F 42
Roch Bank M9: Man 8E 60
Rochbury Cl. OL11: Roch 7L 27
Roch Cl. M45: Whitef 2A 60
Roch Cres. M45: Whitef 1A 60
ROCHDALE 6C 8 (5D 28)
Rochdale Cen. Retail Cen.
OL11: Roch 9E 8 (7E 28)
Rochdale Crematorium
OL11: Roch 6N 27
Rochdale Ent. Generation Cen.
OL12: Roch 8A 8 (6C 28)
Rochdale Exchange Shop. Cen.
OL16: Roch 7B 8 (5C 28)
Rochdale FC 5A 28
Rochdale Golf Course 5M 27
Rochdale Hornets RLFC 5A 28
Rochdale Ho. M15: Man 7D 4
Rochdale Ind. Cen. OL11: Roch . . .7B 28
Rochdale La. OL2: O'ham 7H 45
OL10: H'ood 2J 43
Rochdale Old Rd. BL9: Bury 1A 42
Rochdale Pioneers Mus. . . .6C 8 (5D 28)
Rochdale Rd. BL0: Eden, Ram 3L 11
BL9: Bury 7M 7 (2M 41)
HX6: Ripp 5G 17
M4: Man 2K 5 (7G 78)
M9: Man 3J 79
M24: Mid 1M 61
M40: Man 8F 78
OL1: O'ham 1B 8 (2J 63)
OL2: O'ham 5G 44
OL2: Shaw 5M 45
OL3: Dens 1E 46
OL9: O'ham 1B 8 (2J 63)
OL10: H'ood 2J 43
OL14: Wals 1N 15
OL16: Miln, Roch 6J 29
OL16: Shaw 3J 45
Rochdale Rd. E. OL10: H'ood 2K 43
Rochdale Station (Rail) . . .9D 8 (7D 28)
Rochdale Stop (Metro) . . .9D 8 (7D 28)
Roche Gdns. SK8: Chea H 9N 117
Roche Rd. OL3: Del 7H 47

Rochester Av. BL2: Bolt 3M 39
M21: Cho H 2C 106
M25: Pres 9B 60
M28: Wors 1K 75
Rochester Cl. OL6: A Lyne 3N 81
SK16: Duk 2D 98
WA3: Gol 1K 87
Rochester Dr. WA14: Tim 7E 104
Rochester Gro. SK7: H Gro 4J 119
Rochester Rd. M41: Urm 5D 92
Rochester Way OL9: Chad 5F 62
Rochford Av. M45: Whitef 4K 59
Rochford Cl. M45: Whitef 4K 59
Rochford Ho. *M34: Aud* 3J 97
(off Denton Rd.)
Rochford Pl. OL10: H'ood 5L 43
Rochford Rd. M30: Ecc 1N 91
Roch Mills Cres. OL11: Roch 8A 28
Roch Mills Gdns. OL11: Roch 8A 28
Roch St. OL16: Roch 4F 28
Roch Vale Caravan Pk.
OL16: Roch 8F 8 (6E 28)
Roch Valley Way OL11: Roch 7A 28
Roch Vw. BL9: Bury 2B 42
Roch Wlk. M45: Whitef 2A 60
Roch Way M45: Whitef 2A 60
Rock, The BL9: Bury 7K 7 (2L 41)
Rockall Wlk. *M11: Man* 9L 79
(off Fairisle Cl.)
Rock Av. BL1: Bolt 2D 38
Rock Bank M7: Sal 4B 78
OL5: Mos 1F 82
Rock Bank Ri. SK10: Boll 4M 129
Rockbourne Cl. WN2: Hin 7N 53
Rockdove Av. M15: Man 9F 4 (2E 94)
Rocket St. M3: Sal 4C 4 (9C 78)
Rockfield Dr. *M9: Man* 2K 79
(off Dalbeattie St.)
Rock Fold BL7: Eger 4G 23
Rockford Lodge WA16: Knut 7J 133
Rock Gdns. SK14: Hyde 1B 110
Rock Hall Vis. Cen. 1M 57
Rockhampton St. M18: Man 4B 96
Rockhaven Av. BL6: Hor 9E 20
Rockhouse Cl. M30: Ecc 1C 92
Rockingham Cl. M12: Man 3J 95
OL2: Shaw 4J 45
Rockingham Dr. WN2: Hin 7M 53
Rockland Wlk. M40: Man 9A 62
Rockley Gdns. M6: Sal 6A 78
Rocklyn Av. M40: Man 9A 62
Rocklynes SK6: Rom 6M 109
Rockmead Dr. M9: Man 8K 61
Rock Mill La. SK22: N Mil 8L 121
Rock Nook OL15: Lit 5A 16
Rock Pl. BL9: Bury 7M 7 (2M 41)
Rock Rd. M28: Wors 7H 75
M41: Urm 7F 92
Rock St. BL0: Ram 7L 11
BL6: Hor 1D 36
M7: Sal 4C 78
M11: Man 1C 96
OL1: O'ham 2D 8 (4K 63)
(not continuous)
OL7: A Lyne 5L 81
(not continuous)
OL10: H'ood 3K 43
SK14: Hyde 1B 110
SK22: N Mil 8M 121
WA3: Gol 8K 71
Rock Ter. BL7: Eger 4G 22
OL5: Mos 4F 82
(Manchester Rd.)
OL5: Mos 8G 64
(Stockport Rd.)
SK16: Duk 9N 81
Rock Vw. HD7: Mars 1H 49
Rocky Bank Ter. *WN3: I Mak* 6H 53
(off Warrington Rd.)
Rocky La. M27: Swin 5D 76
M30: Ecc 5D 76
Roda St. M9: Man 3L 79
Rodborough Gdns. M23: Wyth . . .4M 115
Rodborough Rd. M23: Wyth 4M 115
Rodeheath Cl. SK9: Wilm 7J 123
Rodenhurst Dr. M40: Man 3M 79
Rodepool Cl. SK9: Wilm 4J 123
Rodgers Cl. BL5: W'ton 5G 55
Rodgers Way BL5: W'ton 5G 55
Rodmell Av. M40: Man 5J 79
Rodmell Cl. BL7: Bro X 6G 22
Rodmill Ct. M14: Man 8H 95
Rodmill Dr. SK8: Gat 3F 116
Rodney Ct. M4: Man 1M 5
Rodney Dr. SK6: Bred 3L 109
Rodney St. M3: Sal 4C 4 (9C 78)
M4: Man 2N 5 (8H 79)
M46: Ath 9L 55
OL6: A Lyne 6A 82
OL11: Roch 2N 43
SK11: Macc 5H 131
WN1: Wig 9K 9 (4F 52)
Roeacre Bus. Pk. OL10: H'ood 2K 43
Roeacre Ct. OL10: H'ood 2J 43
Roeacre St. OL10: H'ood 2K 43
Roebuck Gdns. M33: Sale 4G 105
Roebuck La. M33: Sale 4G 105
OL4: O'ham 9D 46
Roebuck Low OL4: O'ham 9D 46
Roebuck M. M33: Sale 5H 105
Roebuck St. WN2: Hin 8E 54
Roeburn Wlk. M45: Whitef 3B 60
Roecliffe Cl. WN3: Wig 5E 52
ROE CROSS 3J 99
Roe Cross Grn. SK14: Mot 4J 99
Roe Cross Ind. Pk.
SK14: Mot 4K 99
Roe Cross Rd. SK14: Mot 3J 99
Roedean Gdns. M41: Urm 7K 91
Roefield OL12: Roch 5A 28
Roefield Ter. OL12: Roch 5A 28
ROE GREEN 2A 76
Roe Grn. M28: Wors 2N 75
Roe Grn. Av. M28: Wors 2A 76
Roe Hey Dr. PR7: Cop 3C 18
Roe La. OL4: O'ham 2A 64
Roe St. M4: Man 1M 5 (7H 79)
OL12: Roch 4A 28
SK11: Macc 5G 131
Roewood La. SK10: Macc 3L 131
(Clarendon Dr.)
SK10: Macc 4M 131
(Ecton Av.)
Rogate Dr. M23: Wyth 2N 115
Roger Byrne Cl. M40: Man 5N 79
Roger Cl. SK6: Rom 7K 109
Roger Hay SK8: Chea H 4N 117
Rogerson Cl. WA15: Tim 9J 105
Rogerstead BL3: Bolt 6D 38
Roger St. M4: Man 7F 78
Rogerton Cl. WN7: Lei 6K 73
Rokeby Av. M32: Stre 8K 93
WA3: Low 9N 71
Rokeden WA12: N Wil 5G 87
Roker Av. M13: Man 7L 95
Roker Ind. Est. OL1: O'ham 3M 63
Roker Pk. Av. M34: Aud 2H 97
Roland Rd. BL3: Bolt 8D 38
SK5: Stoc 1D 108
Rolla St. M3: Sal 2E 4 (8D 78)
Rollesby Cl. BL8: Bury 8K 25
Rolleston Av. M40: Man 8J 79
Rollins La. SK6: Mar B 7D 110
Rolls Cres. M15: Man 3D 94
Rollswood Dr. M40: Man 4M 79
Romana Sq. WA14: Tim 8E 104
Roman Cl. WA12: N Wil 7F 86
WN3: Wig 7C 52
Roman Ct. M7: Sal 5C 78
Roman Lakes Leisure Pk. 3E 120
Roman Rd. M25: Pres 1N 77
M35: Fail 2E 80
OL2: O'ham 9H 45
OL8: O'ham 2E 80
SK4: Stoc 1K 9 (6C 108)
WN4: A Mak 5D 70
Roman St. M4: Man 3J 5
M26: Rad 9E 40
OL5: Mos 8G 64
Romer Av. M40: Man 1C 80
Rome Rd. M40: Man 1M 5 (7H 79)
Romer St. BL2: Bolt 5K 39
Romford Av. M34: Dent 5L 97
WN7: Lei 4H 73
Romford Cl. OL8: O'ham 6J 63
Romford Pl. WN2: Hin 6A 54
Romford Rd. M33: Sale 2E 104
Romford St. WN2: Hin 6N 53
Romford Wlk. M9: Man 8F 60
ROMILEY 6N 109
Romiley (Park & Ride) 6N 109
Romiley Cres. BL2: Bolt 4L 39
Romiley Dr. BL2: Bolt 4L 39
Romiley Golf Course 5A 110
Romiley Pools & Target Fitness Cen.
. . . . .6M 109
Romiley Pct. SK6: Rom 6N 109
Romiley Sq. WN6: Stan 4B 34
Romiley Station (Rail) 6N 109
Romiley St. M6: Sal 5K 77
SK1: Stoc 6F 108
Romley Rd. M41: Urm 5D 92
Romney Av. OL11: Roch 2D 44
Romney Chase BL1: Bolt 9F 22
Romney Rd. BL1: Bolt 2N 37
Romney St. M6: Sal 5A 78
M40: Man 2M 79
OL6: A Lyne 6E 6 (7N 81)
Romney Towers SK5: Stoc 2F 108
Romney Wlk. OL9: Chad 5F 62
Romney Way SK5: Stoc 2F 108
WN1: Wig 9E 34
Romsdal Vs. SK6: Rom 6M 109
Romsey OL12: Roch 6B 8 (5C 28)
Romsey Av. M24: Mid 9L 43
Romsey Dr. SK8: Chea H 9A 118
Romsey Gdns. M23: Wyth 1N 115
Romsey Gro. WN3: Wins 9A 52
Romsley Cl. M12: Man 3M 95
Romsley Dr. BL3: Bolt 9D 38
Ronaldsay Gdns. M5: Sal 9L 77
Ronald St. M11: Man 9B 80
OL4: O'ham 4N 63
OL11: Roch 3A 44
Rona Wlk. M12: Man 4L 95
Rondin Rd. M11: Man 1K 95
M12: Man 1K 95
Ronnie Taylor Cl. OL16: Miln 7K 29
Ronnis Mt. OL7: A Lyne 3K 81
Ronton Wlk. *M8: Man* 2H 79
(off Mawdsley Dr.)
Roocroft Ct. BL1: Bolt 3E 38
Roocroft Sq. BL6: Bla 2M 35
Rooden Ct. M25: Pres 7B 60
Roods La. OL11: Roch 4H 27
Rookery, The WA12: N Wil 5G 86
Rookery Av. M18: Man 3D 96
WN4: A Mak 8E 70
WN6: App B 4J 33
Rookery Cl. SK15: Stal 2H 99
Rookerypool Cl. SK9: Wilm 4J 123
Rooke St. M30: Ecc 1A 92
Rookfield M33: Sale 3J 105
Rookfield Av. M33: Sale 3J 105
Rookley Wlk. *M14: Man* 6H 95
(off Whitecliffe Cl.)
Rook St. BL0: Ram 8J 11
M15: Man 4D 94
OL4: O'ham 6N 63
Rookswood Dr. OL11: Roch 1N 43
Rookswood Way WA16: Knut 4K 133
Rookway M24: Mid 4M 61
Rookwood OL1: Chad 2C 62
Rookwood Av. M23: Wyth 9M 105
Rookwood Hill SK7: Bram 6C 118
Rooley Moor Rd. OL12: Roch 4J 13
(not continuous)
OL13: Bac, Roch 1F 12
Rooley St. OL12: Roch 4A 28
Rooley Ter. OL12: Roch 4A 28
Roosevelt Rd. BL4: Kea 4N 57
Rooth St. SK4: Stoc 1G 9 (6B 108)
Ropefield Way OL12: Roch 2C 28
Rope Race 3C 120
Rope St. OL12: Roch 5C 8 (5D 28)
Ropewalk M3: Sal 1E 4 (7D 78)
Ropley Wlk. *M9: Man* 1L 79
(off Oak Bank Av.)
Rosa Gro. M7: Sal 4C 78
Rosalind Ct. M5: Sal 7A 4 (1B 94)
Rosamond Dr. M3: Sal 3C 4 (8C 78)
Rosamond St. BL3: Bolt 8D 38
M15: Man 3F 94
Rosamond St. W.
M15: Man 3F 94
Rosary Cl. OL8: O'ham 1K 81
Rosary Rd. OL8: O'ham 1L 81
Roscoe Av. WA12: N Wil 6H 87
Roscoe Ct. BL5: W'ton 4H 55
Roscoe Lowe Brow PR6: And 6N 19
Roscoe Rd. M44: Irl 8F 90
Roscoe St.
OL1: O'ham 3E 8 (5L 63)
SK3: Stoc 4H 9 (8B 108)
WN1: Wig 9N 9 (4H 53)
Roscow Av. BL2: Bolt 4M 39
ROSCOW FOLD 4L 39
Roscow Rd. BL4: Kea 4A 58
Rose Acre M28: Wors 3J 75
Roseacre Cl. BL2: Bolt 4J 39
Roseacre Dr. SK8: H Grn 6H 117
Rose Av. BL4: Farn 2K 57
M44: Irl 8G 90
OL11: Roch 3J 27
OL15: Lit 2K 29
WA11: Hay 3B 86
WN2: Abr 3L 71
WN6: Wig 9C 34
Rose Bank SK10: Boll 6K 129
WA13: Lym 4A 112
Rosebank BL0: Ram 5K 11
BL6: Los 5L 37
Rose Bank Cl. SK14: Holl 4N 99
WN1: Wig 8E 34
Rosebank Cl. BL2: Ain 3C 40
Rose Bank Rd. M40: Man 6N 79
Rosebank Rd. M44: Cad 4D 102
Rosebay Cl. OL2: O'ham 8K 45
Rosebeck Wlk. *WA14: W Tim* 7B 104
(off Over Ashberry)
Roseberry Av. OL1: O'ham 2M 63
Roseberry Cl. BL0: Ram 2J 25
Roseberry Rd. WN4: A Mak 5D 70
Roseberry St. BL3: Bolt 8D 38
OL8: O'ham 4A 8 (5H 63)
Rosebery St. BL5: W'ton 3H 55
M14: Man 6E 94
SK2: Stoc 3H 119
ROSE BRIDGE 3J 53
Rosebridge Ct. WN1: I Mak 4J 53
Rose Bridge Sports & Community Cen.
. . . . .3H 53
Rosebridge Way WN1: I Mak 4J 53
Rosebury Av. WN7: Lei 5J 73
Rose Cott. Rd. M14: Man 9G 95
Rose Cotts. *M14: Man* 9J 95
(off Ladybarn La.)
OL3: G'fld 5M 65
Rose Ct. WN1: I Mak 4J 53
Rose Cres. M44: Irl 8G 91
Rosecroft Cl. SK3: Stoc 3C 118
Rosedale Av. BL1: Bolt 8F 22
M46: Ath 8L 55
WA3: Low 2M 87
Rosedale Cl. OL1: O'ham 2M 63
Rosedale Ct. M34: Dent 6J 97
Rosedale Dr. WN7: Lei 5L 73
Rosedale Rd. M14: Man 7F 94
SK4: Stoc 3B 108
Rosedale Way SK16: Duk 3N 97
Rosefield Cl. SK3: Stoc 2C 118
Rosefield Cres. OL16: Roch 6G 28
Rosefinch Rd. WA14: W Tim 7C 104
Rosegarth Av. M20: Man 4C 106
Rose Grn. SK13: Glos 8G 100
Rose Gro. BL4: Kea 4N 57
BL8: Bury 2G 41
SK13: Char 1J 111
Rosehay Av. M34: Dent 7K 97
Rose Hey La. M35: Fail 6C 80
ROSE HILL
BL2 . . . . .7H 39
WN4 .3C 70
WN5 .5N 51
ROSEHILL 5C 114
Rose Hill BL0: Ram 8J 11
BL2: Bolt 7H 39
M34: Dent 6H 97
OL3: Del 9J 47
SK15: Stal 1C 98
Rose Hill Av. M40: Man 6N 79
WN5: Wig 5N 51
Rose Hill Cl. BL7: Bro X 6H 23
OL6: A Lyne 5B 82
Rosehill Cl. M6: Sal 8M 77
Rosehill Ct. M6: Sal 8M 77
OL4: O'ham 3B 64
Rose Hill Cres. OL6: A Lyne 5C 82
Rose Hill Dr. BL7: Bro X 6H 23
Rose Hill Marple Station (Rail)
. . . . .1B 120
Rosehill M. *M27: Clif* 9F 58
(off Lit. Moss La.)
Rose Hill Rd. OL6: A Lyne 5C 82
Rosehill Rd. M27: Pen 9F 58
(not continuous)
Rose Hill St. OL10: H'ood 2G 42
Rose Hill Ter. M46: Ath 8M 55
Rosehill Vw. WN4: A Mak 3C 70
Roseland Av. M20: Man 4G 107
Roseland Dr. M25: Pres 5B 60
Roselands Av. M33: Sale 6F 104
Rose La. SK6: Mar 1B 120
Rose Lea BL2: Bolt 9M 23
Rose Leigh *M41: Urm* 6D 92
(off Crofts Bank Rd.)
Roseleigh Av. M19: Man 1L 107
Rosemary Cres. WN1: Wig 1G 53
Rosemary Dr. OL15: Lit 8K 15
SK14: Hyde 1A 110
WA12: N Wil 6H 87
Rosemary Gro. M7: Sal 5B 78
Rosemary La. BL5: O Hul 6B 56
SK1: Stoc 3N 9 (7E 108)
Rosemary Rd. OL9: Chad 3C 62
Rosemary Wlk. *M31: Part* 6G 102
(off Broom Rd.)
Rosemead Ct. SK5: Stoc 2D 108
Rose Mt. WA2: Win 9L 87
Rosemount M24: Mid 1L 61
SK14: Hyde 4A 98
Rosemount Cres. SK14: Hyde 4N 97
Roseneath SK7: Bram 6B 118
Roseneath Av. M19: Man 8A 96
Roseneath Gro. BL3: Bolt 1E 56
Roseneath Rd. BL3: Bolt 9E 38
M41: Urm 6C 92
Rosen Sq. OL9: Chad 4F 62
Rose St. BL2: Bolt 7H 39
M24: Mid 3A 62
OL9: Chad 8E 62
SK5: Stoc 5D 108
WN1: I Mak 4J 53
WN2: Hin 6N 53
Rose Ter. SK15: Stal 9D 82
Rosethorns Cl. M24: Mid 8L 43
Rosette Wlk. M27: Swin 3F 76
Rose Va. SK8: H Grn 6G 116
Rosevale Av. M19: Man 3K 107
Rosevale Cl. WN2: Hin 7N 53
Roseville M. M33: Sale 4H 105
Rose Wlk. M31: Part 5F 102
SK6: Mar 1B 120
Roseway SK7: Bram 5D 118
SK11: Macc 7H 131
Rosewell Cl. M40: Man 6J 79
Rose Wharf SK11: Macc 5J 131
Rosewood BL5: W'ton 5F 54
M34: Dent 6H 97
OL11: Roch 4K 27
SK14: Holl 4N 99
Rosewood Av. BL8: Tot 7G 24
M43: Droy 8F 80
SK4: Stoc 7M 107
Rosewood Cl. SK16: Duk 3A 98
WN2: Abr 3L 71
Rosewood Cres. OL9: Chad 2F 62
Rosewood Gdns. *M33: Sale* 5M 105
(off Hart Av.)
SK8: Gat 1E 116
Rosewood Rd. M9: Man 6J 61
Rosewood Wlk. M23: Wyth 8J 105
Rosford Av. M14: Man 7G 94
Rosgill Cl. SK4: Stoc 6K 107
Rosgill Dr. M24: Mid 2J 61
Rosgill Wlk. *M18: Man* 4A 96
(off Hampden Cres.)
Rosina Cl. WN4: A Mak 4C 70
Rosina St. M11: Man 2D 96
Rosley Rd. WN3: Wig 8E 52
Roslin Gdns. BL1: Bolt 8B 22
Roslin St. M11: Man 8B 80
Roslyn Av. M41: Urm 8M 91
Roslyn Rd. SK3: Stoc 2C 118
Rossall Av. M26: Rad 3J 59
M32: Stre 6J 93
Rossall Cl. BL2: Bolt 4K 39
Rossall Ct. SK7: Bram 9C 118
Rossall Cres. WN7: Lei 7J 73
Rossall Dr. SK7: Bram 9C 118
Rossall Rd. BL2: Bolt 4K 39
(not continuous)
OL12: Roch 3E 28
Rossall St. BL2: Bolt 4K 39
Rossall Way M6: Sal 7N 77
Ross Av. M19: Man 8L 95
M45: Whitef 5M 59
OL9: Chad 8D 62
SK3: Stoc 2C 118
Ross Cl. WN2: Wig 1J 53
WN5: Bil 4J 69
Rossdale Gro. WN6: Stan 5D 34
Ross Dr. M27: Clif 7E 58
Rossenclough Cl. SK9: Wilm 5H 123
Rossendale Av. M9: Man 1L 79
Rossendale Cl. OL2: Shaw 5A 46
Rossendale Rd. SK8: H Grn 7H 117
Rossendale Way OL2: Shaw 4M 45
Rosset Cl. WN3: Wins 9A 52
Rossett Av. M22: Wyth 7C 116
WA15: Tim 8G 105
Rossett Dr. M41: Urm 5N 91
Rossetti Wlk. *M34: Dent* 1L 109
(off Wordsworth Rd.)
Ross Gro. M41: Urm 7C 92
Rosshill Wlk. *M15: Man* 3C 94
(off Shawgreen Cl.)
Rossington Pk. SK13: Had 3B 100
Rossington Pl. SK13: Had 4B 100
Rossington St. M40: Man 5B 80
Rossini St. BL1: Bolt 1E 38
Rosslare Rd. M22: Wyth 5D 116
Ross Lave La. M34: Dent 9F 96
SK5: Dent 9F 96
Rosslave Wlk. SK5: Stoc 1G 109
Rosslyn Bldg., The OL11: Roch . . .2N 43
Rosslyn Gro. WA15: Tim 1G 115
Rosslyn Rd. M16: Old T 7N 93
M40: Man 1M 79
SK8: H Grn 6J 117
Rossmere Av. OL11: Roch 7A 28
Rossmill La. WA15: Haleb 8H 115
Ross St. OL8: O'ham 5A 8 (6H 63)
Rostherne Av. M14: Man 8F 94
M16: Old T 6B 94
SK6: H Lan 7B 120
WA3: Low 1N 87
Rostherne Ct. WA14: Alt 4D 114
Rostherne Dr. WA16: Mere 1F 132
Rostherne Gdns. BL3: Bolt 8C 38
Rostherne Mere 9M 113
Rostherne Rd. M33: Sale 5M 105
SK3: Stoc 2C 118
SK9: Wilm 9D 122
Rostherne St. *M6: Sal* 8L 77
(off White St.)
WA14: Alt 4D 114
Rosthernmere Rd. SK8: Chea H . . .3L 117
Rosthwaite Cl. M24: Mid 2H 61
WN3: Wig 9D 52
Rosthwaite Gro. WA11: St H 9F 68
Roston Ct. M7: Sal 2D 78
Roston Rd. M7: Sal 2D 78
Rostrevor Rd. SK3: Stoc 2C 118
(not continuous)
Rostron Av. M12: Man 3K 95
Rostron Brow SK1: Stoc 2L 9
Rostron Rd. BL0: Ram 8H 11
Rostron St. M19: Man 8N 95
Rothay Cl. BL2: Bolt 3N 39
M45: Whitef 3B 60
Rothay Dr. M24: Mid 9K 43
SK5: Stoc 9D 96
Rothay St. WN7: Lei 6K 73
Rothbury Av. OL7: A Lyne 6J 81
Rothbury Cl. BL8: Bury 2F 40
Rothbury Ct. BL3: Bolt 9C 38
Rotherby Rd. M22: Shar 2D 116
Rotherdale Av. WA15: Tim 2K 115
Rotherhead Cl. BL6: Hor 2B 36
Rotherhead Dr. SK11: Macc 7F 130
Rothermere Wlk. *M23: Wyth* 9L 105
(off Sandy La.)
Rotherwood Av. M32: Stre 6L 93
Rotherwood Rd. SK9: Wilm 8B 122
Rothesay Av. SK16: Duk 2N 97
Rothesay Cres. M33: Sale 6C 104
Rothesay Rd. BL3: Bolt 9C 38
M8: Man 9D 60
M27: Pen 3J 77
OL1: O'ham 2N 63
Rothesay Ter. OL16: Roch 9G 28
Rothiemay Rd. M41: Urm 7M 91
Rothley Av. M22: Wyth 2C 116
Rothman Cl. M40: Man 4A 80
Rothwell Cres. M38: Lit H 6F 56
Rothwell La. M38: Lit H 6F 56
Rothwell Rd. PR6: And 6L 19
WA3: Gol 9M 71
Rothwell St. BL0: Ram 8H 11
BL3: Bolt 7F 38
(not continuous)
M28: Walk 8N 57
M35: Fail 4D 80
M40: Man 4A 80
OL2: O'ham 9G 45
OL12: Roch 4F 28
Rottingdene Dr. M22: Wyth 6B 116
ROUGH BANK 8A 30
Rough Bank OL12: Whitw 9A 14
Roughey Gdns. M22: Wyth 3C 116
Rough Hey La. OL3: Dens 1G 46
Rough Hey Wlk. OL16: Roch 7F 28
Roughhill La. BL9: Bury 9C 26
Roughlea Av. WA3: Cul 5F 88
Roughlee Av. M27: Swin 2D 76
ROUGHTOWN 9G 65
Roughtown Ct. OL5: Mos 9G 65
Roughtown Rd. OL5: Mos 9G 64
Roundcroft SK6: Rom 5B 110
Round Gdns. SK10: Boll 4L 129
Roundham Wlk. *M9: Man* 2K 79
(off Hillier St.)
Round Hey OL5: Mos 2F 82
Roundhey SK8: H Grn 7G 117
Round Hill Cl. SK13: Had 6B 100
Round Hill Way BL1: Bolt 4G 39
Roundhill Way OL4: O'ham 2B 64
Roundhouse Av. WN1: Wig 2H 53
Roundmoor Rd. WN6: Stan 5D 34
ROUNDTHORN
M23 .3L 115
OL4 . . . . .7A 64
Round Thorn WA3: Cro 9C 88
Roundthorn Ind. Est.
M23: Wyth 1L 115
(not continuous)
Roundthorn La. BL5: W'ton 4G 54
Roundthorn Rd. M23: Wyth 1M 115
M24: Mid 4N 61
OL4: O'ham 5M 63
Roundway SK7: Bram 9B 118
SK22: N Mil 7N 121
Roundwood Rd. M22: Nor 9C 106
Roundy La. SK10: Adl 9K 125
Rountree Ho. *OL9: O'ham* 5H 63
(off Manchester St.)
Rousdon Cl. M40: Man 5J 79
Rouse Cl. M11: Man 9L 79
Rouse St. OL11: Roch 9A 28
Routledge Wlk. M9: Man 2K 79
Roving Bri. Ri. M27: Pen 2K 77
Rowan Av. BL6: Hor 3G 37
M16: Whall R 6C 94
M33: Sale 6J 105
M41: Urm 6D 92
WA3: Low 2B 88
WN6: Wig 9C 34
Rowan Cl. M35: Fail 4D 80
OL12: Roch 2M 27
Rowan Ct. M14: Man 1J 107
SK14: Hyde 8B 98
(off Stockport Rd.)
Rowan Cres. SK16: Duk 2C 98
Rowandale St. M1: Man 7F 4
Rowan Dr. BL9: Bury 1A 42
SK8: Chea H 7A 118
Rowanhill WN1: Wig 2G 53
Rowan Ho. OL6: A Lyne 8D 6
Rowanlea M25: Pres 7B 60
Rowan Lodge SK7: Bram 8D 118
Rowan Pl. M25: Pres 8A 60
Rowans, The BL1: Bolt 5N 37
M28: Wors 3F 74
OL5: Mos 1G 83
PR6: Adl 5K 19
Rowans Cl. SK15: Stal 7E 82
Rowanside SK10: P'bury 7C 128
Rowanside Dr. SK9: Wilm 6K 123
Rowans St. BL8: Bury 9J 25

Rowan St. SK14: Hyde 8C 98
Rowanswood Dr. SK14: Hyde 6D 98
Rowan Tree Dr. M33: Sale 7H 105
Rowan Tree Rd. OL8: O'ham 1H 81
WA16: Mob 9A 122
Rowan Wlk. M31: Part 6F 102
SK13: Had 5A 100
Rowan Way M7: Sal 3C 78
SK10: Macc 3J 131
Rowanwood OL9: Chad 4C 62
Rowany Cl. M25: Pres 9N 59
ROWARTH 9N 111
Rowarth Av. M34: Dent 9L 97
SK13: Gam 7N 99
(off Grassmoor Cres.)
Rowarth Bank *SK13: Gam 7N 99*
(off Grassmoor Cres.)
Rowarth Cl. *SK13: Gam 7N 99*
(off Grassmoor Cres.)
Rowarth Fold *SK13: Gam 7N 99*
(off Grassmoor Cres.)
Rowarth Rd. M23: Wyth 5M 115
Rowarth Way *SK13: Gam 7N 99*
(off Grassmoor Cres.)
Rowbotham St. SK14: Hyde 9B 98
Rowbottom Sq. WN1: Wig 8J 9 (3F 52)
Rowcon Cl. M34: Aud 4J 97
(not continuous)
Rowdell Wlk. M23: Wyth 6A 106
Rowden Rd. OL4: O'ham 7B 64
Rowe Grn. M34: Dent 6K 97
Rowena St. BL3: Bolt 1K 57
Rowe St. M29: Tyld 1C 74
Rowfield Dr. M23: Wyth 4M 115
Rowland Av. M41: Urm 6E 92
Rowland Ct. OL16: Roch 7F 28
Rowland Ho. OL2: O'ham 8K 45
ROWLANDS 3K 25
Rowlands Rd. BL9: Bury, Sum 3J 25
Rowland St. M5: Sal 1N 93
OL16: Roch 7F 28
Rowland St. Nth. M46: Ath 8M 55
Rowland St. Sth. M46: Ath 9M 55
Rowlandsway M22: Wyth 5C 116
Rowland Way OL4: Lees 4B 64
Rowley Dr. SK7: H Gro 7J 119
Rowley St. OL6: A Lyne 4A 82
Rowley Way WA16: Knut 9H 133
ROW-OF-TREES 2C 126
Rowood Av. M8: Man 4G 79
SK5: Stoc 7D 96
Rowrah Cres. M24: Mid 2G 61
Rowsley Av. BL1: Bolt 3B 38
M20: Man 4D 106
Rowsley Cl. SK13: Gam 7A 100
Rowsley Grn. *SK13: Gam 7A 100*
(off Edale Cres.)
Rowsley Gro. SK5: Stoc 1C 108
SK13: Gam 7A 100
(off Rowsley Cl.)
Rowsley M. SK13: Gam 7A 100
Rowsley Rd. M30: Ecc 1C 92
M32: Stre 6G 93
Rowsley St. M6: Sal 5A 78
M11: Man 8L 79
Rowsley Wlk. *SK13: Gam 7A 100*
(off Rowsley Cl.)
Rowson Ct. *M33: Sale 4K 105*
(off Oak Rd.)
Rowson Dr. M44: Cad 2E 102
Rowton Ri. WN1: Stan 4E 34
Rowton St. BL2: Bolt 1J 39
Roxalina St. BL3: Bolt 8F 38
Roxburgh Cl. SK10: Macc 3E 130
Roxburgh St. M18: Man 4B 96
ROXBURY 6N 63
Roxbury Av. OL4: O'ham 6A 64
Roxby Cl. M28: Walk 8J 57
Roxby Wlk. *M40: Man 9B 62*
(off Blandford Dr.)
Roxby Way WA16: Knut 9G 133
Roxholme Wlk. M22: Wyth 7B 116
Roxton Cl. BL6: Hor 8D 20
Roxton Rd. SK4: Stoc 2A 108
Roxwell Wlk. *M9: Man 2J 79*
(off Alderside Rd.)
Royal, The M3: Sal 3B 4
Royal Arc. WN1: Wig 7K 9
Royal Av. BL9: Bury 8M 25
M21: Cho H 1N 105
M41: Urm 7D 92
M43: Droy 8F 80
OL10: H'ood 3J 43
Royal Ct. SK11: Macc 5J 131
Royal Ct. Dr. BL1: Bolt 1G 7 (4E 38)
Royal Cres. SK8: Chea 5H 117
Royal Dr. WN7: Lei 4H 73
Royal Exchange M2: Man 4G 4 (9E 78)
Royal Exchange Arc. *M2: Man 4G 4*
(within Royal Exchange)
Royal Exchange Theatre 4G 4 (9E 78)
Royal Gdns. BL0: Ram 2G 24
WA14: Bow 5N 113
ROYAL GEORGE 7H 65
Royal George Cotts. OL3: G'fld 6H 65
Royal George St.
SK3: Stoc 5K 9 (8C 108)
Royal Ho. *BL1: Bolt 2E 38*
(off Tennyson St.)
Royal Mdws. SK10: Macc 3E 130
Royal Oak Ind. Est. *SK1: Stoc 9D 108*
(off Cooper St.)
Royal Oak Rd. M23: Wyth 9M 105
(not continuous)
Royal Oak Yd. SK1: Stoc 2L 9
Royal St. OL16: Roch 3G 28
Royalthorn Av. M22: Wyth 1C 116
Royalthorn Dr. M22: Wyth 1B 116
Royalthorn Rd. M22: Wyth 1B 116
Royce Av. WA15: Alt 1F 6 (2E 114)
Royce Ct. *M15: Man 3C 94*
(off Erskine St.)
WA16: Knut 6G 132
Royce Rd. M15: Man 3D 94
Royce Trad. Est. M17: T Pk 2E 92
Roydale St. M40: Man 7K 79
Royden Av. M9: Man 6J 61
M44: Irl 9G 90
WN3: Wig 9D 52
Royden Cres. WN5: Bil 5J 69
Royden Rd. WN5: Bil 5J 69
Roydes St. M24: Mid 1N 61
Royds Cl. BL8: Tot 8G 25
M13: Man 4K 95
Royds Pl. OL16: Roch 8E 28
Royds St. BL8: Tot 6F 24
HD7: Mars 1H 49
OL16: Miln 8L 29
OL16: Roch 8F 28
Royds St. W. OL16: Roch 8E 28
Royd St. BL9: Bury 9C 26
OL8: O'ham 7G 63
Roy Grainger Ct. M16: Whall R 6D 94
Roy Ho. OL2: O'ham 6H 45
Royland Av. BL3: Bolt 9H 39
Royland Ct. BL3: Bolt 9G 39
Royle Av. SK13: Glos 8F 100
Royle Barn Rd. OL11: Roch 2A 44
Royle Cl. OL8: O'ham 8K 63
SK2: Stoc 2E 118
Royle Grn. Rd. M22: Nor 8D 106
Royle Higginson Ct. M41: Urm 7C 92
Roylelands Bungs. OL11: Roch 1A 44
Royle Pennine Trad. Est.
OL11: Roch 1B 44
Royle Rd. OL11: Roch 1A 44
Royles Cotts. M33: Sale 5H 105
Royles Sq. *SK9: A Edg 4F 126*
(off South St.)
Royle St. M6: Sal 9M 77
M14: Man 1J 107
M28: Walk 9L 57
M34: Dent 4K 97
SK1: Stoc 9D 108
ROYLEY 9G 44
Royley OL2: O'ham 9G 44
Royley Carr Flats *SK6: Bred 5K 109*
(off Field St.)
Royley Clough OL2: O'ham 8G 44
Royley Cres. OL2: O'ham 9G 44
Royley Ho. *OL2: O'ham 9G 44*
(off Lea Vw.)
Royley Rd. OL8: O'ham 7J 63
Royley Way OL2: O'ham 9G 44
Roynton Rd. BL6: R'ton 6D 20
Royon Dr. SK3: Stoc 9N 107
Royston Av. BL2: Bolt 4J 39
M16: Whall R 6C 94
M34: Dent 6E 96
Royston Cl. BL8: G'mount 4F 24
WA3: Low 1A 88
Royston Ct. M16: Whall R 6C 94
Royston Rd. M16: Old T 6A 94
M41: Urm 6E 92
Roy St. BL3: Bolt 8C 38
OL2: O'ham 8H 45
ROYTON 8H 45
Royton Av. M33: Sale 6L 105
Royton Hall Pk. OL2: O'ham 8J 45
Royton Hall Wlk. OL2: O'ham 8J 45
Royton Ho. OL2: Shaw 7M 45
Royton Sports Cen. 8J 45
Rozel Sq. M3: Man 6E 4 (1D 94)
Ruabon Cres. WN2: Hin 7B 54
Ruabon Fold WN2: Hin 7C 54
Ruabon Rd. M20: Man 6H 107
Rubens Cl. SK6: Mar B 8F 110
Ruby Gro. WN7: Lei 6G 73
Ruby St. BL1: Bolt 1G 38
BL9: Sum 2J 25
M15: Man 3F 94
M34: Dent 7J 97
Ruby St. Pas. OL11: Roch 9A 8
Rudcroft Cl. M13: Man 9L 5 (3G 95)
Rudding St. OL2: O'ham 1L 63
Ruddpark Rd. M22: Wyth 6C 116
Rudd St. M40: Man 3M 79
Rudford Gdns. BL3: Bolt 8G 38
Rudgwick Dr. BL8: Bury 6J 25
Rudheath Av. M20: Man 1F 106
Rudman Dr. M5: Sal 1B 94
Rudman St. OL7: A Lyne 9L 81
OL12: Roch 3C 28
Rudolph St. BL3: Bolt 9G 39
Rudston Av. M40: Man 9N 61
Rudyard Av. M24: Mid 9A 44
WN6: Stan 2B 34
Rudyard Cl. SK11: Macc 6F 130
Rudyard Gro. M33: Sale 6E 104
OL11: Roch 2D 44
SK4: Stoc 2B 108
Rudyard Rd. M6: Sal 5J 77
Rudyard St. M7: Sal 4C 78
Ruecroft Cl. WN6: App B 4H 33
Rufford Av. OL11: Roch 9B 28
SK14: Hyde 7C 98
Rufford Cl. M45: Whitef 1N 59
OL2: Shaw 5K 45
OL6: A Lyne 3N 81
PR7: Chor 2E 18
Rufford Dr. BL3: Bolt 1E 56
M45: Whitef 1M 59
Rufford Gro. BL3: Bolt 1E 56
Rufford Pde. M45: Whitef 1M 59
Rufford Pl. M18: Man 5D 96
M29: Ast 6A 74
Rufford Rd. M16: Whall R 6C 94
Rufford St. WN4: A Mak 5C 70
Rufus St. M14: Man 1K 107
Rugby Cl. SK10: Macc 9J 129
WN5: Orr 6J 51
Rugby Dr. M33: Sale 6G 105
SK10: Macc 1J 131
WN5: Orr 3K 51
Rugby Ho. SK10: Macc 1H 131
Rugby Pk. SK4: Stoc 7K 107
Rugby Rd. M6: Sal 7G 77
OL12: Roch 4E 28
WN7: Lei 7H 73
Rugby Rd. Ind. Est. OL12: Roch 4E 28
Rugby St. M8: Man 6D 78
Rugeley St. M6: Sal 5A 78
RUINS 9M 23
Ruins La. BL2: Bolt 9M 23
Ruislip Av. M40: Man 5K 79
Ruislip Cl. OL8: O'ham 7M 63
Rumbles La. OL3: Del 8J 47
Rumble Tumble Activity Cen.
8H 9 (3E 52)
Rumbold St. M18: Man 3C 96
Rumworth Rd. BL6: Los 6L 37
Rumworth St. BL3: Bolt 8E 38
Runcorn St. M15: Man 9A 4 (2B 94)
Runfield Cl. WN7: Lei 5H 73
Runger La. M90: Man A 8M 115
Runhall Cl. M12: Man 3M 95
Running Hill Ga. OL3: Upp 2N 65
RUNNING HILL HEAD 1A 66
Running Hill La. OL3: Dob 1N 65
Runnymead Ct. OL2: O'ham 8J 45
Runnymeade M6: Sal 5H 77
M27: Swin 4G 77
Runnymede Cl. SK3: Stoc 9A 108
Runnymede Ct. BL3: Bolt 7E 38
SK3: Stoc 1A 118
Runshaw Av. WN6: App B 4J 33
Runway Visitor Park, The 9N 115
Rupert St. BL3: Bolt 8G 38
M26: Rad 2H 59
M40: Man 6C 80
OL12: Roch 4A 28
SK5: Stoc 1C 108
WN1: Wig 9N 9 (4H 53)
Rupert Ter. SK5: Stoc 1C 108
Ruscombe Fold M24: Mid 9J 43
Rush Acre Cl. M26: Rad 9E 40
Rushall Wlk. M23: Wyth 5M 115
Rush Bank OL2: Shaw 4K 45
Rushberry Av. M40: Man 9A 62
Rushbrooke Av. M11: Man 8A 80
Rushbury Dr. OL2: O'ham 8L 45
Rushcroft Ct. M9: Man 9M 61
Rushcroft Rd. OL2: Shaw 4K 45
Rushdene WN3: Wig 7D 52
Rushden Rd. M19: Man 7N 95
Rushen St. M11: Man 9A 80
Rushes, The SK13: Had 5B 100
Rushes Mdw. WA13: Lym 2C 112
Rushey Av. WA15: Haleb 1B 116
Rushey Cl. WA15: Haleb 8K 115
Rushey Fld. BL7: Bro X 5G 22
Rushey Fold Ct. BL1: Bolt 2E 38
Rushey Fold La. BL1: Bolt 2E 38
Rusheylea Cl. BL1: Bolt 2D 38
Rushey Rd. M22: Wyth 2B 116
Rushfield Dr. M13: Man 6L 95
Rushfield Rd. SK8: Chea H 9M 117
Rushford Av. M19: Man 7M 95
Rushford Ct. *M19: Man 7M 95*
(off Rushford Av.)
Rushford Gro. BL1: Bolt 9G 22
RUSHFORD PARK 7M 95
Rushford St. M12: Man 5M 95
Rush Gdns. WA13: Lym 3B 112
RUSHGREEN 3B 112
Rushgreen Rd. WA13: Lym 3A 112
Rush Gro. OL3: Upp 4L 65
Rush Hill Rd. OL3: Upp 4L 65
Rush Hill Ter. OL3: Upp 4L 65
Rushlake Dr. BL1: Bolt 3F 38
Rushlake Gdns. OL11: Roch 5K 27
Rush La. SK6: Mel 1L 121
Rushley Av. M7: Sal 4A 78
Rushmere OL6: A Lyne 4B 82
SK13: Glos 9G 101
Rushmere Av. M19: Man 8N 95
Rushmere Cl. SK10: White G 2K 129
Rushmere Dr. BL8: Bury 8J 25
Rushmere Wlk. M16: Old T 4C 94
Rushmoor Av. WN4: A Mak 6H 71
Rushmoor Cl. M44: Irl 7H 91
Rush Mt. OL2: Shaw 4K 45
RUSHOLME 6J 95
Rusholme Gdns. *M14: Man 7H 95*
(off Wilmslow Rd.)
Rusholme Gro. M14: Man 6H 95
Rusholme Gro. W. M14: Man 6H 95
Rusholme Pl. M14: Man 5H 95
Rushside Rd. SK8: Chea H 9L 117
Rush St. SK16: Duk 1C 98
Rushton Av. WA12: N Wil 5E 86
WN7: Lei 2F 72
Rushton Cl. SK6: Mar 2D 120
Rushton Dr. SK6: Mar 3C 120
SK6: Rom 5N 109
SK7: Bram 5B 118
Rushton Fold SK10: Mot S A 3M 127
Rushton Gdns. SK7: Bram 4B 118
Rushton Gro. M11: Man 2C 96
OL4: O'ham 9B 46
Rushton Rd. BL1: Bolt 3C 38
SK3: Stoc 9N 107
SK8: Chea H 9M 117
Rushton St. M20: Man 6G 107
M28: Walk 9L 57
Rushway Av. M9: Man 9N 61
Rushwick Av. M40: Man 5K 79
Rushwood Pk. WN6: Stan 2A 34
Rushworth Ct. SK4: Stoc 3A 108
Rushycroft SK14: Mot 5K 99
Rushyfield Cres. SK6: Rom 5A 110
Rushy Hill Vw. OL12: Roch 3A 28
Rushy Vw. WA12: N Wil 5D 86
Ruskin Av. BL4: Kea 4A 58
M14: Man 5G 94
M34: Aud 2G 96
M34: Dent 8H 97
OL9: Chad 8D 62
WA12: N Wil 5F 86
WN3: Wig 8C 52
Ruskin Ct. *BL4: Farn 4M 57*
(off Corn Mill Dr.)
WA16: Knut 6G 132
Ruskin Cres. M25: Pres 8M 59
WN2: Abr 1L 71
Ruskin Dr. M33: Sale 4C 104
Ruskin Gdns. SK6: Bred 5L 109
Ruskin Gro. SK6: Bred 5L 109
Ruskington Dr. M9: Man 3J 79
Ruskin Rd. BL3: Lit L 8B 40
M16: Old T 6B 94
M25: Pres 8M 59
M43: Droy 8E 80
OL11: Roch 2C 44
SK5: Stoc 8C 96
Ruskin St. M26: Rad 3C 58
OL1: O'ham 3H 63
Ruskin Way WA16: Knut 5G 132
Rusland Ct. M9: Man 8M 61
M33: Sale 3G 104
SK2: Stoc 9F 108
(off Sylvester Av.)
Rusland Dr. BL2: Bolt 2M 39
Rusland Wlk. M22: Wyth 5B 116
Russeldene Rd. WN3: Wig 8B 52
Russell Av. M16: Whall R 7C 94
M33: Sale 3K 105
SK6: H Lan 8B 120
Russell Cl. *BL1: Bolt 4D 38*
(off Russell St.)
Russell Ct. *BL4: Farn 3M 57*
(off Russell St.)
M16: Whall R 6B 94
M38: Lit H 8K 57
Russell Dr. M44: Irl 7H 91
Russell Fox Ct. *SK5: Stoc 1C 108*
(off Broadstone Rd.)
Russell Gdns. SK4: Stoc 7N 107
Russell Pl. M33: Sale 3H 105
Russell Rd. M6: Sal 5H 77
M16: Whall R 6C 94
M31: Part 5H 103
Russell St. BL1: Bolt 4D 38
BL4: Farn 3M 57
BL9: Bury 9M 25
M8: Man 6D 78
M16: Whall R 6E 94
M25: Pres 7A 60
M30: Ecc 8F 76
M38: Lit H 8K 57
M46: Ath 8L 55
OL6: A Lyne 6A 82
OL9: Chad 4F 62
OL10: H'ood 2K 43
OL11: Roch 8C 28
(off Grove St.)
SK2: Stoc 1E 118
SK6: Comp 5E 110
SK14: Hyde 6A 98
SK16: Duk 1N 97
WN2: Hin 9E 54
WN2: I Mak 3K 53
Russet Rd. M9: Man 1J 79
Russet Wlk. BL1: Bolt 9F 22
Russet Way SK9: A Edg 2D 126
Rustons Wlk. *M40: Man 1C 80*
(off Glensdale Dr.)
Ruth Av. M40: Man 1C 80
Ruthen La. M16: Old T 5A 94
Rutherford Av. M14: Man 6G 94
Rutherford Cl. SK14: Hyde 7N 97
Rutherford Dr. BL5: O Hul 4A 56
WA16: Knut 9J 133
Rutherford Way
SK14: Hyde 7A 98
Rutherglade Cl. M40: Man 4H 79
Rutherglen Dr. BL3: Bolt 6A 38
Rutherglen Wlk. M40: Man 5K 79
Ruthin Av. M9: Man 6H 61
M24: Mid 5M 61
SK8: Chea H 5K 117
Ruthin Cl. M6: Sal 8N 77
OL8: O'ham 9F 62
Ruthin Ct. M6: Sal 8N 77
Ruth St. BL0: Eden 4K 11
BL1: Bolt 1H 7 (4F 38)
BL9: Bury 9M 25
M18: Man 6B 96
OL1: O'ham 1E 8 (3K 63)
Rutland OL11: Roch 7C 28
Rutland Av. M16: Old T 6N 93
M20: Man 2F 106
M27: Pen 9F 58
M34: Dent 7L 97
M41: Urm 6C 92
M46: Ath 6A 56
WA3: Low 2N 87
Rutland Cl. BL3: Lit L 8B 40
OL6: A Lyne 8A 82
SK8: Gat 1G 116
Rutland Ct. M20: Man 3G 107
SK2: Stoc 2E 118
Rutland Cres. SK5: Stoc 3H 109
Rutland Dr. BL9: Bury 4N 41
M7: Sal 2B 78
WN4: A Mak 6F 70
Rutland Gro. BL1: Bolt 3D 38
BL4: Farn 4K 57
Rutland La. M33: Sale 4M 105
(not continuous)
Rutland Rd. M28: Walk 1K 75
M29: Tyld 9A 56
M30: Ecc 6F 76
M31: Part 6F 102
M43: Droy 8D 80
M44: Cad 3E 102
SK7: H Gro 7J 119
SK11: Macc 8G 131
WA14: Alt 1C 6 (1D 114)
WN2: Hin 5B 54
Rutland St. BL3: Bolt 8E 38
M18: Man 3C 96
M27: Swin 1E 76
M35: Fail 2D 80
OL6: A Lyne 8A 82
OL9: O'ham 6G 62
OL10: H'ood 1J 43
SK14: Hyde 4A 98
WN7: Lei 6N 73
Rutland Way OL2: Shaw 4N 45
Rutter's La. SK7: H Gro 5G 118
Ryall Av. M5: Sal 1A 94
Ryall Av. Sth. M5: Sal 1A 94
Ryan St. M11: Man 2C 96
Ryburn Flats *OL10: H'ood 2H 43*
(off Meadow Cl.)
Ryburn Rd. SK11: Macc 7E 130
Ryburn Sq. OL11: Roch 7K 27
Rydal Av. M24: Mid 5L 61
M30: Ecc 6B 76
M33: Sale 3F 104
M41: Urm 9A 92
M43: Droy 9C 80
OL2: O'ham 4G 44
OL9: Chad 2C 62
SK6: H Lan 7B 120
SK7: H Gro 4G 119
SK14: Hyde 4N 97
WN2: Hin 6A 54
WN5: Orr 4K 51
Rydal Cl. BL6: Bla 1M 35
BL9: Bury 5L 41
M29: Ast 3B 74
M34: Dent 7F 96
SK8: Gat 3G 117
WN4: A Mak 6F 70
Rydal Ct. BL1: Bolt 3A 38
Rydal Cres. M27: Swin 4F 76
M28: Walk 1M 75
Rydal Dr. WA15: Haleb 7K 115
Rydal Gdns. M24: Mid 1J 61
Rydal Gro. BL4: Farn 4G 56
M45: Whitef 3N 59
OL7: A Lyne 6L 81
OL10: H'ood 4J 43
Rydal Ho. *M28: Walk 9L 57*
(off Sandwich St.)
Rydal Mt. SK5: Stoc 7D 96
SK9: A Edg 2D 126
Rydal Pl. SK11: Macc 6E 130
WN2: Abr 2L 71
WN2: I Mak 3L 53
Rydal Rd. BL1: Bolt 3B 38
BL3: Lit L 9A 40
M32: Stre 6K 93
OL4: O'ham 4N 63
Rydal St. WA12: N Wil 6F 86
WN7: Lei 5G 73
Rydal Wlk. OL4: O'ham 4A 64
SK15: Stal 7D 82
WN5: Wig 4M 51
Ryde Av. M34: Dent 9M 97
SK4: Stoc 6N 107
Ryder Av. WA14: Alt 9E 104
RYDER BROW 6B 96
Ryder Brow M18: Man 5B 96
Ryder Brow Rd. M18: Man 5B 96
Ryder Brow Station (Rail) 5B 96
Ryder Gro. WN7: Lei 8L 73
Ryder St. BL1: Bolt 2D 38
M40: Man 6H 79
OL10: H'ood 2J 43
Ryde St. BL3: Bolt 8B 38
WN5: Wig 5B 52
Rydings La. OL12: W'le 8E 14
Rydings Rd. OL12: Roch 9E 14
Rydley St. BL2: Bolt 4N 7 (6J 39)
Ryebank Gro. OL6: A Lyne 5A 82
Ryebank M. M21: Cho H 8M 93
Rye Bank Rd. M16: Old T 7N 93
Ryebank Rd. M21: Cho H 8M 93
Ryebank Way SK10: Macc 1G 131
Ryeburn Av. M22: Wyth 4C 116
Ryeburn Dr. BL2: Bolt 8J 23
Ryeburne St. OL4: O'ham 4N 63
Ryeburn Wlk. M41: Urm 5N 91
Ryecroft M45: Whitef 4J 59
Ryecroft Av. BL8: Tot 7F 24
M6: Sal 7J 77
OL10: H'ood 2K 43
WA3: Low 9A 72
Ryecroft Bus. Cen. *OL7: A Lyne 9K 81*
(off Ryecroft St.)
Ryecroft Cl. OL9: Chad 8D 62
Ryecroft Dr. BL5: W'ton 9F 36
Ryecroft Gro. M23: Wyth 9N 105
Ryecroft Ho. OL7: A Lyne 9A 6
Ryecroft La. BL7: Bel 1L 21
M28: Wors 6N 75
M34: Aud 2J 97
WA16: Mob 4L 133
Ryecroft Pk. Sports Club 6L 117
Ryecroft Rd. M32: Stre 8J 93
Ryecroft St. OL7: A Lyne 9A 6 (9K 81)
Ryecroft Vw. M34: Aud 1G 96
Ryedale Av. M40: Man 5K 79
Ryedale Cl. SK4: Stoc 5N 107
Ryefield OL7: A Lyne 9K 81
Ryefield Cl. WA15: Tim 1J 115
Ryefield Rd. M33: Sale 6C 104
Ryefields OL12: Roch 1H 29
Ryefields Dr. OL3: Upp 2L 65
Ryefield St. BL1: Bolt 3H 39
Ryeford Cl. WN3: I Mak 5J 53
Rye Hill BL5: W'ton 3H 55
Ryelands BL5: W'ton 3H 55
Ryelands Cl. OL16: Roch 9F 28
Ryelands Ct. *BL5: W'ton 3H 55*
(off Ryelands)
Rye St. OL10: H'ood 1K 43
Rye Top La. OL3: Upp 4N 65
Rye Wlk. *M13: Man 4H 95*
(off Carmoor Rd.)
OL9: Chad 5E 62
Rygate Wlk. *M8: Man 4E 78*
(off Felthorpe Dr.)
Rylance Rd. WN3: Wins 1A 70
Rylance St. M11: Man 9K 79
Ryland Cl. SK5: Stoc 8D 96
Rylands Ct. *M15: Man 3C 94*
(off Stretford Rd.)
Rylands St. WN6: Wig 1D 52
Rylane Wlk. M40: Man 5K 79
Rylatt Ct. *M33: Sale 3F 104*
(off Ashton La.)
Ryles Cl. SK11: Macc 7G 130
Ryles Cres. SK11: Macc 7G 131
Ryles Ho. SK11: Macc 7G 131
Ryle's Pk. Rd. SK11: Macc 7G 130
Ryle St. SK11: Macc 6H 131

Ryley Av. BL3: Bolt 7C 38
Ryleys La. SK9: A Edg 4E 126
Ryley St. BL3: Bolt 6D 38
Rylstone Av. M21: Cho H 5C 106
Ryther Gro. M9: Man 6G 61
Ryton Av. M18: Man 6A 96
Ryton Cl. WN3: Wig 5E 52

S

Sabden Brook Dr. WN2: P Bri 9J 53
Sabden Cl. BL9: Bury 6M 25
M40: Man 7K 79
OL10: H'ood 2F 42
Sabden Rd. BL1: Bolt 2N 37
Sable Way M11: Man 8M 79
Sabrina St. M8: Man 5D 78
Sack St. SK14: Hyde 4A 98
Sackville Cl. OL2: Shaw 3L 45
Sackville Pl. M1: Man 7J 5
Sackville St. BL2: Bolt 5K 39
BL9: Bury 6N 7 (1N 41)
M1: Man 6J 5 (1F 94)
M3: Sal 3D 4
OL11: Roch 2A 44
Saddleback Cl. M28: Wors 4J 75
Saddleback Cres. WN5: Wig 5M 51
Saddleback Dr. SK10: P'bury 6D 128
Saddleback Rd. WN5: Wig 4M 51
Saddlecote M28: Wors 6A 76
Saddlecote Cl. M8: Man 2G 79
Saddle Ct. WN5: Wig 5C 52
Saddle Gro. M43: Droy 7H 81
Saddle Junc. WN5: Wig 4C 52
Saddle St. BL2: Bolt 2J 39
Saddle Tree Fold WA3: Low 8B 72
Saddlewood Av. M19: Man 6J 107
SADDLEWORTH 3K 65
Saddleworth Bus. Cen. OL3: Del . . . 8J 47
Saddleworth Bus. Pk. OL3: Dig . . . 8M 47
Saddleworth Fold OL3: Upp 2M 65
Saddleworth Golf Course 3K 65
Saddleworth Llama Trekking Centre & Animal Farm 3H 47
Saddleworth Mus. & Art Gallery . . . 3L 65
Saddleworth Swimming Pool 4L 65
Saddleworth Youth Cen. 4L 65
Sadie Av. M32: Stre 5G 93
Sadler Ct. M15: Man 4D 94
Sadler St. BL3: Bolt 8H 39
M24: Mid 2L 61
Safflower Av. M27: Swin 2D 76
Saffron Cl. WA3: Low 1A 88
Saffron Dr. OL4: O'ham 1A 64
Saffron Wlk. M22: Wyth 7C 116
M31: Part 6G 102
(off Cross La. W.)
Sagars Rd. SK9: Hand, Sty 2G 123
Sagar St. M8: Man 6E 78
Sahal Ct. M7: Sal 6C 78
St Agnes Ct. M24: Mid 9L 43
St Agnes Rd. M13: Man 7L 95
St Agnes St. SK5: Stoc 6D 96
St Aidans Cl. M26: Rad 2F 58
OL11: Roch 8B 28
WN5: Bil 4J 69
St Aidan's Gro. M7: Sal 4A 78
St Albans Av. M40: Man 5N 79
OL6: A Lyne 4M 81
SK4: Stoc 3A 108
St Albans Cl. OL8: O'ham 7K 63
WA11: Hay 2C 86
St Albans Ct. OL11: Roch . . . 9A 8 (7C 28)
St Alban's Cres. WA14: W Tim . . . 8C 104
St Albans Ho. OL16: Roch 9B 8
St Albans St. OL16: Roch . . . 9B 8 (7C 28)
SK22: N Mil 7M 121
St Alban's Ter. M8: Man 5D 78
OL11: Roch 9A 8 (7C 28)
St Aldates SK6: Rom 6K 109
St Aldwyn's Rd. M20: Man 3G 106
St Ambrose Ct. OL1: O'ham 2N 63
St Ambrose Gdns. *M6: Sal 8M 77*
(off Blodwell St.)
St Ambrose Rd. M29: Ast 5B 74
OL1: O'ham 2N 63
St Andelm Hall M14: Man 6J 95
St Andrews Av. M30: Ecc 9E 76
M43: Droy 9C 80
WA15: Tim 9E 104
St Andrews Cl. BL0: Ram 9J 11
M33: Sale 7C 104
OL15: Lit 9J 15
SK4: Stoc 4N 107
SK6: Rom 7M 109
SK13: Had 5A 100
St Andrews Ct. *BL1: Bolt 3L 7*
(off Exchange St.)
SK1: Stoc 3N 9 (7E 108)
SK11: Macc 5F 130
(off Brough St. W.)
SK13: Had 5A 100
(Springfield Cl.)
SK13: Had 5C 100
(off Church St.)
WA15: Hale 4F 114
St Andrew's Cres. WN2: Hin 6N 53
St Andrews Dr. OL10: H'ood 3J 43
WN6: Wig 1C 52
WN7: Lei 5L 73
St Andrews Ho. M38: Walk 8J 57
St Andrews Rd. BL6: Los 5J 37
M26: Rad 6F 40
M32: Stre 7H 93
SK4: Stoc 4N 107
SK8: H Grn 6H 117
SK11: Macc 5F 130
St Andrew's Sq. M1: Man . . . 6N 5 (1H 95)
St Andrew's St. M1: Man . . . 6M 5 (1H 95)
M26: Rad 6F 40
St Andrews Vw. M26: Rad 6F 40
St Andrews Wlk. SK22: N Mil . . . 7M 121
St Annes Av. M6: Sal 7L 77
M46: Ath 1N 73
OL2: O'ham 9H 45
St Annes Ct. *M6: Sal 6M 77*
(off Brindle St.)
M33: Sale 4J 105
M34: Aud 3J 97
WN6: She 7K 33
St Anne's Cres. OL4: Gras 6F 64
St Anne's Dr. M34: Dent 5L 97
WN6: She 7L 33
St Annes Gdns. OL10: H'ood 2L 43
St Annes Mdw. BL8: Tot 6F 24
St Annes M. OL10: H'ood 2K 43
St Annes Rd. BL6: Hor 9E 20
M21: Cho H 1A 106
M34: Aud 3K 97
M34: Dent 4K 97
St Annes Sq. OL3: Del 8J 47
St Annes St. BL9: Bury 9M 25
(not continuous)
SK14: B'tom 9K 99
(off Lwr. Market St.)
St Ann's All. M2: Man 4F 4
St Ann's Arc. M2: Man 4G 4
St Ann's Chyd. M2: Man 4G 4
St Anns Cl. M25: Pres 8N 59
St Anns Pde. SK9: Wilm 7G 123
St Ann's Pas. M2: Man 4G 4
St Ann's Pl. M2: Man 4F 4
St Anns Rd. M25: Pres 8M 59
OL16: Roch 5H 29
SK7: H Gro 5G 118
St Ann's Rd. Nth. SK8: H Grn . . . 6H 117
St Ann's Rd. Sth. SK8: H Grn . . . 6H 117
St Ann's Sq. M2: Man . . . 4G 4 (9E 78)
SK8: H Grn 7H 117
St Ann's St. M27: Swin 2E 76
M33: Sale 5M 105
St Ann St. BL1: Bolt 3F 38
M2: Man . . . 4F 4 (9E 78)
St Anthony's Dr. OL5: Mos 9G 64
St Asaph's Dr. M7: Sal 2E 78
OL6: A Lyne 4M 81
St Aubin's Rd. BL2: Bolt 6J 39
St Aubyn's Rd. WN1: Wig 8F 34
St Augustine's Ct. *BL2: Bolt 3J 39*
(off Thicketford Rd.)
St Augustine's Rd. SK3: Stoc . . . 8N 107
St Augustine St. BL1: Bolt 2E 38
M40: Man 5J 79
St Austell Av. M29: Ast 2D 74
SK10: Macc 3B 130
St Austell Dr. BL8: G'mount 3F 24
SK8: H Grn 7G 117
St Austell Rd. M16: Whall R 8D 94
St Austells Dr. M25: Pres 6A 60
M27: Pen 3J 77
St Barnabas Ct. SK11: Macc 6H 131
St Barnabas Dr. OL15: Lit 8L 15
St Barnabas Sq. M11: Man 1N 95
St Bartholomew's Dr.
M5: Sal 7A 4 (1B 94)
St Bartholomew St. BL3: Bolt 8H 39
St Bede's Av. BL3: Bolt 1C 56
St Bees Cl. M14: Man 5F 94
SK8: Gat 4G 116
St Bees Rd. BL2: Bolt 2K 39
St Bees Wlk. M24: Mid 1K 61
St Benedicts Av. M12: Man 3L 95
St Bernards Av. M6: Sal 5B 78
St Bernards Cl. M6: Sal 5B 78
St Boniface Rd. M7: Sal 6B 78
St Brannocks Rd. M21: Cho H . . . 8B 94
SK8: Chea H 8N 117
St Brelades Dr. M7: Sal 2E 78
St Brendan's Rd. M20: Man 1G 106
St Brendan's Rd. Nth.
M20: Man 1G 106
St Brides Cl. BL6: Hor 9C 20
St Bride St. M16: Old T 4C 94
St Brides Way M16: Old T 4C 94
St Catherines Ct. *BL6: Hor 1D 36*
(off Richmond St.)
St Catherines Dr. BL4: Farn 3G 56
St Catherine's Rd. M20: Man . . . 1G 106
St Chads Av. SK6: Rom 6N 109
St Chad's Cl. OL16: Roch . . . 8D 8 (6D 28)
St Chad's Ct. OL16: Roch 8D 8
St Chads Cres. OL3: Upp 3M 65
OL8: O'ham 1H 81
St Chads Gro. SK6: Rom 6N 109
St Chads Rd. M20: Man 1J 107
St Chad's St. M8: Man 6F 78
St Charles Cl. SK13: Had 4B 100
St Christopher Cl. WN6: Stan . . . 8N 33
St Christopher's Av. OL6: A Lyne . . . 4B 82
St Christophers Cl. M20: Man . . . 2E 106
St Christopher's Dr. SK6: Rom . . . 6L 109
St Christophers Ho. *SK1: Stoc . . . 9D 108*
(off Wellington Rd. Sth.)
St Christopher's Rd.
OL6: A Lyne 4A 82
St Clair Rd. BL8: G'mount 2F 24
St Clare Ter. *BL6: Los 4H 37*
(off Chorley New Rd.)
St Clement Cl. *M41: Urm 8D 92*
(off Manor Av.)
St Clements Ct. M25: Pres 7B 60
M44: Irl 6J 91
OL8: O'ham 6K 63
(off Falcon St.)
OL11: Roch 5A 28
SK11: Macc 6H 131
(off Hobson St.)
WN3: Wig 6D 52
St Clements Dr. M5: Sal 2A 94
St Clements Fold M41: Urm 7E 92
St Clement's Rd. M21: Cho H 9N 93
WN1: Wig 8F 34
St Clement's St. WN3: I Mak 7J 53
St Cuthbert's Fold OL8: O'ham . . . 1L 81
St Davids Av. SK6: Rom 6M 109
St Davids Cl. M33: Sale 5G 105
OL6: A Lyne 3A 82
St Davids Ct. M8: Man 5F 78
St David's Cres. WN2: Asp 7L 35
St Davids Rd. SK7: H Gro 6G 118
SK8: Chea 2M 117
St David's Wlk. M32: Stre 7G 93
St Domingo Pl. OL1: O'ham 2C 8
St Domingo St.
OL9: O'ham 2B 8 (4J 63)
St Dominic's M. BL3: Bolt 9D 38
St Dominics Way M24: Mid 4M 61
St Dunstan Wlk. *M40: Man 4M 79*
(off Craiglands Av.)
St Edmund Hall Cl. BL0: Ram 1J 25
St Edmund's Rd. M40: Man 4K 79
St Edmund St.
BL1: Bolt 2J 7 (5F 38)
St Edmund's Wlk. M38: Lit H 7J 57
St Edwards Cl. SK11: Macc 6H 131
St Edwards Rd. M14: Man 7F 94
St Elisabeth's Way SK5: Stoc 1C 108
St Elizabeth Pk. M34: Dent 6H 97
St Elizabeth's Rd. WN2: Asp 6L 35
St Elmo Av. SK2: Stoc 9H 109
St Elmo Pk. SK12: Poy 2N 125
St Ethelbert's Av. BL3: Bolt 7C 38
St Gabriel Cl. WN8: Roby M 9F 32
St Gabriels Ct. OL11: Roch 3B 44
St Gabriel's Ct. OL11: Roch 2A 44
St Gabriel's Hall M14: Man 5H 95
St Gabriels Rd. M24: Mid 4A 62
ST GEORGES 9B 4 (3C 94)
St George's Av. BL5: W'ton 5G 54
M15: Man 9B 4 (3C 94)
WA15: Tim 9G 105
St George's Cl. WA16: Knut 8J 133
St Georges Ct. BL1: Bolt 1K 7
(All Saints St.)
BL1: Bolt 1H 7
(Back La.)
BL9: Bury 9B 42
M15: Man 9C 4
M29: Tyld 2A 74
(off Lemon St.)
M30: Ecc 9F 76
(off Bentcliffe Way)
M32: Stre 8J 93
SK14: Hyde 7B 98
WA14: B'ath 9B 104
St George's Cres. M6: Sal 7G 77
M28: Walk 9L 57
WA15: Tim 8G 105
St Georges Dr. M40: Man 3N 79
SK14: Hyde 8A 98
St George's Gdns. M34: Dent 8L 97
St George's Ho. *SK15: Stal 8D 82*
(off Cambridge St.)
St Georges Pl. *M6: Sal 5N 77*
(off Gerald Rd.)
M46: Ath 7K 55
SK11: Macc 6H 131
St Georges Rd. BL1: Bolt . . . 1G 7 (4F 38)
BL9: Bury 8B 42
M14: Man 1K 107
M31: C'ton 2L 103
M32: Stre 7J 93
M43: Droy 7D 80
OL11: Roch 5L 27
SK22: N Mil 7M 121
St Georges Sq. BL1: Bolt . . . 1L 7 (4G 39)
OL9: Chad 8C 62
St George's St. BL1: Bolt . . . 1K 7 (4G 38)
M29: Tyld 2A 74
SK11: Macc 6H 131
SK15: Stal 7C 82
St Georges Ter. BB4: Water 1F 12
St Georges Way M6: Sal 6N 77
St Germain St. BL4: Farn 3K 57
St Giles Dr. SK14: Hyde 7C 98
St Gregorys Cl. BL4: Farn 4K 57
St Gregory's Pl. PR7: Chor 1F 18
St Gregory's Rd.
M12: Man 8N 5 (2H 95)
St Helena Rd. BL1: Bolt . . . 2H 7 (5F 38)
St Helens Cl. WA3: Rix 5C 102
St Helens Rd. BL3: Bolt 3B 56
BL5: O Hul 3B 56
WA11: R'ford 8A 68
WN7: Lei 1D 88
St Helier's Dr. M7: Sal 2E 78
St Helier Sq. M19: Man 3L 107
St Helier St. BL3: Bolt 8E 38
St Herberts Ct. OL9: Chad 4F 62
St Hilarys Pk. SK9: A Edg 4F 126
St Hilda's Cl. M22: Nor 7D 106
PR7: Chor 1F 18
St Hilda's Dr. OL1: O'ham 3H 63
St Hilda's Rd. M16: Old T 4B 94
M22: Nor 7C 106
M34: Aud 3J 97
St Hilda's Vw. M34: Aud 4J 97
St Hilda's Way PR7: Chor 1F 18
St Hugh's Cl. WA14: Tim 8E 104
St Ignatius Wlk. *M5: Sal 1A 94*
(off King Edward St.)
St Ives Av. SK8: Chea 1M 117
St Ives Cl. SK10: Macc 3C 130
St Ives Cres. M33: Sale 7G 105
St Ives Rd. M14: Man 7G 95
St Ives Way OL2: O'ham 8L 45
St James Av. BL2: Bolt 4M 39
BL8: Bury 9H 25
St James Cl. M6: Sal 7H 77
OL16: Roch 4G 44
SK13: Glos 9E 100
St James Ct. *BL8: Bury 9H 25*
(off St James Av.)
M2: Man 4H 5
M6: Sal 7H 77
M20: Man 5G 107
(off Moorland Rd.)
M20: Man 7G 107
(Millgate La.)
OL4: O'ham 3N 63
SK8: Chea H 9L 117
SK14: Hat 7G 98
WA15: Alt . . . 3F 6 (3E 114)
WN6: Stan 2A 34
St James Cres. WN2: B'haw 2B 72
St James Dr. M33: Sale 5G 104
SK9: Wilm 8F 122
St James Gro. *OL10: H'ood 2H 43*
(off W. Church St.)
WA14: Tim 7F 104
WN3: Wig 5E 52
St James Hill SK10: P'bury 7B 128
St James Ho. *M6: Sal 7M 77*
(off Pendleton Way)
SK4: Stoc 5B 108
St James Lodge *SK3: Stoc 3E 118*
(off The Crescent)
St James Rd. M7: Sal 4D 78
SK4: Stoc 3N 107
WN5: Orr 7H 51
St James Sq. *SK22: N Mil 7M 121*
(off Spring Bank)
St James's Sq. M2: Man 5G 4
St James St. BL4: Farn 4H 57
BL5: W'ton 6H 55
M1: Man . . . 6G 5 (1F 94)
M30: Ecc 8E 76
OL1: O'ham 4M 63
OL2: Shaw 5M 45
OL6: A Lyne 8A 82
OL10: H'ood 2H 43
OL16: Miln 7K 29
St James Ter. OL10: H'ood 2H 43
St James Way OL12: W'le 7G 14
SK8: Chea H 9L 117
St Johns Av. BL5: W'ton 9F 36
M43: Droy 8F 80
WA16: Knut 7F 132
St Johns Cl. SK6: Rom 6M 109
SK16: Duk 1B 98
St Johns Ct. *BL0: Ram 8J 11*
(off Cross St.)
BL5: W'ton 9G 37
M6: Sal 8M 77
(off Milford St.)
M7: Sal 4C 78
(off Wellington St. W.)
M26: Rad 1J 59
OL4: Lees 4C 64
OL16: Roch 7F 28
(off St John's Dr.)
SK14: Hyde 6C 98
WA14: Bow 4D 114
WA16: Knut 6J 133
(off Churchfields)
WN2: Abr 1L 71
St Johns Dr. OL16: Roch 7F 28
SK14: Hyde 6C 98
St John's Gdns.
BL9: Bury . . . 6M 7 (1M 41)
OL5: Mos 9G 64
St John's Ind. Est. OL4: Lees 5B 64
St Johns M. *BL8: Tot 6F 24*
(off Kirklees St.)
St John's Pas. M3: Man . . . 6E 4 (1D 94)
St John's Pl. SK4: Stoc 6K 107
St Johns Rd. BL6: Los 9K 37
M13: Man 5L 95
M16: Old T 5B 94
M28: Wors 3G 74
M34: Dent 4K 97
SK4: Stoc 6K 107
SK7: H Gro 6F 118
SK9: Wilm 2D 126
SK11: Macc 5G 131
WA14: Alt . . . 5B 6 (4C 114)
WA16: Knut 7F 132
WN2: Asp 7L 35
St Johns Sq. BL9: Bury . . . 7M 7 (2M 41)
M3: Sal 3C 4
St John's St. BL4: Kea 3M 57
M7: Sal 4C 78
M26: Rad 1H 59
OL9: O'ham 6G 63
WN2: Abr 2L 71
St John St. BL6: Hor 1D 36
M3: Man . . . 6E 4 (1D 94)
M27: Pen 4K 77
M28: Walk 7K 57
M30: Ecc 9D 76
M44: Irl 7H 91
M46: Ath 8M 55
OL4: Lees 5B 64
SK16: Duk 1B 98
(not continuous)
WA12: N Wil 6D 86
WN5: Wig 5M 51
St Johns Wlk. *SK3: Stoc 8N 107*
(off Oak St.)
St John's Wood BL6: Los 8K 37
St Joseph's Av. M45: Whitef 4A 60
St Josephs Cl. OL2: Shaw 4N 45
St Joseph's Dr. M5: Sal 1A 94
OL16: Roch 9F 28
St Joseph St. *BL1: Bolt 2E 38*
(off Hobart St.)
St Katherine's Dr. BL6: Bla 1M 35
St Kilda Av. BL4: Kea 5N 57
St Kilda's Av. M43: Droy 7D 80
St Kilda's Dr. M7: Sal 2E 78
St Lawrence Cl. M34: Dent 7K 97
St Lawrence Quay M50: Sal 2M 93
St Lawrence Rd. M34: Dent 6K 97
St Lawrence St. M15: Man 3C 94
St Leonard's Av. BL6: Los 3H 37
St Leonard's Ct. M33: Sale 1E 104
St Leonards Dr.
WA15: Tim . . . 1F 6 (1F 114)
St Leonards Rd. SK4: Stoc 3B 108
St Leonards Sq. *M24: Mid 2M 61*
(off Clarke Brow)
St Leonards St. M24: Mid 2M 61
St Lesmo Ct. SK3: Stoc 9A 108
St Lesmo Rd. SK3: Stoc 8N 107
St Lukes Av. WA3: Low 1N 87
St Lukes Ct. BL1: Bolt 4D 38
OL9: Chad 4E 62
OL11: Roch 8D 28
St Lukes Cres. SK16: Duk 1N 97
St Luke's Dr. WN5: Orr 7H 51
St Lukes Ho. SK10: Macc 4D 130
WN4: A Mak 6F 70
St Luke's Rd. M6: Sal 8K 77
St Luke St. OL11: Roch 8D 28
St Lukes Wlk. *M40: Man 4M 79*
(off Rollswood Dr.)
St Malo Rd. WN1: Wig 8F 34
St Margaret's Av. M19: Man 2L 107
St Margarets Cl. BL1: Bolt 4C 38
M25: Pres 5B 60
WA14: Alt . . . 3A 6 (3C 114)
St Margaret's Gdns.
OL8: O'ham 8G 62
St Margaret's Rd. BL1: Bolt 4C 38
M25: Pres 5B 60
M40: Man 8B 62
SK8: Chea 1M 117
WA14: Alt . . . 5A 6 (3C 114)
St Marks Av. OL2: O'ham 8L 45
WA14: Alt 2A 114
WN5: Wig 4C 52
(not continuous)
St Marks Cl. OL2: O'ham 8L 45
St Marks Ct. *M22: Wyth 5B 116*
(off Stoneacre Rd.)
OL9: Chad 3F 62
SK16: Duk 9M 81
St Marks Cres. M28: Walk 1L 75
St Mark's La. M7: Sal 3E 78
M8: Man 3E 78
St Marks Sq. BL9: Bury 9M 25
St Marks St. BL3: Bolt 7G 38
M19: Man 8A 96
SK6: Bred 4L 109
SK16: Duk 9M 81
St Mark's Wlk. BL3: Bolt 8F 38
St Martin's Av. SK4: Stoc 6A 108
St Martin's Cl. M43: Droy 7D 80
SK14: Hyde 7D 98
St Martin's Dr. M7: Sal 2E 78
St Martins Rd. M33: Sale 2D 104
OL8: O'ham 9L 63
SK6: Mar 1D 120
St Martins St. OL11: Roch 3B 44
St Mary's Apartments *M25: Pres . . . 7N 59*
(off The Coppice)
St Mary's Av. BL3: Bolt 7C 38
M34: Dent 9L 97
WN5: Bil 6G 68
St Mary's Cl. M25: Pres 7N 59
M46: Ath 9N 55
OL16: Roch 9F 28
St Marys' Cl. SK1: Stoc . . . 2N 9 (7E 108)
St Mary's Cl. WN2: Asp 7L 35
St Marys Ct. *M8: Man 1E 78*
(off St Mary's Hall Rd.)
M19: Man 8M 95
(off Elbow St.)
M25: Pres 7N 59
M40: Man 2N 79
OL1: O'ham 1C 8
WA3: Low 9D 72
St Mary's Crest OL3: G'fld 6M 65
St Mary's Dr. OL3: G'fld 6M 65
SK5: Stoc 2D 108
SK8: Chea 1L 117
St Mary's Est. OL1: O'ham 1D 8
St Marys Ga. M1: Man . . . 3G 4 (8E 78)
OL2: Shaw 5M 45
OL3: Upp 3L 65
OL12: Roch . . . 8B 8 (6C 28)
OL16: Roch . . . 8B 8 (6C 28)
SK1: Stoc . . . 2M 9 (6D 108)
St Mary's Hall Rd. M8: Man 1E 78
St Marys Ind. Pk. SK14: Hyde 3D 98
St Mary's Parsonage
M3: Man . . . 4E 4 (9D 78)
St Mary's Pl. BL9: Bury . . . 8J 7 (2L 41)
St Marys Rd. M25: Pres 7N 59
M28: Walk 7K 57
M30: Ecc 8F 76
M33: Sale 3F 104
M40: Man 3N 79
SK12: Dis 9G 120
SK13: Glos 8E 100
SK14: Hyde 4B 98
SK22: N Mil 7L 121
WA14: Bow 5B 114
(not continuous)
WN2: Asp 6L 35
St Mary's St. M3: Man . . . 4F 4 (9E 78)
M15: Man 4D 94
OL1: O'ham . . . 1D 8 (3K 63)
St Mary St. M3: Sal 3C 4
St Mary's Vw. *SK14: Hyde 4C 98*
(off Bradley Grn. Rd.)
St Marys Way OL1: O'ham . . . 1B 8 (4J 63)
SK1: Stoc . . . 5N 9 (6E 108)
WN7: Lei 5H 73
St Matthew's Cl. WN3: Wig 7N 51
St Matthews Ct. M32: Stre 8J 93
St Matthews Dr. OL1: Chad 1E 62
St Matthews Grange *BL1: Bolt . . . 3F 38*
(off Mount St.)
St Matthew's Rd. SK3: Stoc 8B 108
St Matthews Ter. *BL1: Bolt 3F 38*
(off Barnwood Dr.)
SK3: Stoc 8B 108
St Matthews Wlk. *BL1: Bolt 3F 38*
(off Rushlake Dr.)
St Mawes Ct. M26: Rad 7C 40
SK10: Macc 3C 130
St Michaels & All Angels Church . . . 8E 6
St Michael's Av. BL3: Bolt 1J 57
M46: Ath 1J 73
SK7: Bram 8C 118
St Michael's Cl. BL8: Bury 4F 40
St Michael's Ct. M27: Ward 9D 58
M30: Ecc 1A 92
M33: Sale 2E 104
WN1: Wig 1F 52
St Michaels Gdns. M45: Whitef 2A 60
St Michael's Pl. M4: Man 1J 5
St Michaels Rd. SK14: Hyde 7D 98
St Michael's Sq. M4: Man . . . 1J 5 (7F 78)
OL6: A Lyne . . . 7E 6 (7N 81)
St Michaels Ter. *SK10: Macc 4H 131*
(off Churchside)
St Modwen Rd. M32: Stre 4F 92

St Nicholas Rd.
M15: Man 9D 4 (2D 94)
WA3: Low 9C 72
St Osmund's Dr. BL2: Bolt 5M 39
St Osmund's Gro. BL2: Bolt 5M 39
St Oswalds Ct. PR7: Cop 5B 18
St Oswalds Rd. M19: Man 7N 95
WN4: A Mak 8D 70
St Patrick St. WN1: Wig 8M 9 (3G 53)
St Patricks Way
WN1: Wig 8M 9 (3G 53)
St Paul's Av. WN3: Wig 7C 52
St Pauls Cl. M26: Rad 2G 58
PR6: Adl 5K 19
SK15: Stal 8F 82
St Pauls Ct. BL9: Bury 1N 41
M7: Sal 1B 78
M28: Walk 8L 57
OL8: O'ham 7K 63
SK11: Macc 5J 131
(off St Paul's Rd.)
St Paul's Gdns. M7: Sal 1B 78
(off St Paul's Rd.)
SK14: Hyde 6B 98
(off St Paul's St.)
St Paul's Hill Rd. SK14: Hyde 7C 98
St Paul's M. SK1: Stoc 5F 108
(off St Paul's St.)
St Paul's Pl. BL1: Bolt 1D 38
St Paul's Ri. M7: Sal 1B 78
(off St Paul's Rd.)
St Paul's Rd. M7: Sal 1B 78
M20: Man 2H 107
M28: Walk 9M 57
SK4: Stoc 4N 107
SK11: Macc 5J 131
St Pauls St. BL0: Ram 8J 11
BL9: Bury 6N 7 (1N 41)
SK1: Stoc 5E 108
SK14: Hyde 6B 98
SK15: Stal 8F 82
St Pauls Trad. Est. SK15: Stal 8F 82
St Paul's Vs. BL9: Bury 1N 41
St Peter's Av. BL1: Bolt 2B 38
WA16: Knut 7F 132
St Petersburgh Way M22: Wyth 4B 116
St Peters Cl. OL7: A Lyne 8K 81
WA13: Lym 3B 112
St Peter's Ct. BL2: Bolt 4N 7
M32: Stre 6L 93
(off Burleigh Rd.)
St Peter's Dr. SK14: Hyde 7C 98
St Petersgate SK1: Stoc 3K 9 (7C 108)
St Peters Ho. BL2: Bolt 6J 39
St Peter's Rd. BL9: Bury 5M 41
M27: Swin 3E 76
St Peter's Sq. M2: Man 6G 5 (1E 94)
SK1: Stoc 2K 9 (7C 108)
St Peter's Square Stop (Metro)
6G 5 (1E 94)
St Peters St. OL6: A Lyne 9A 6 (8L 81)
OL16: Roch 7F 28
St Peter's Ter. BL4: Farn 4L 57
St Peter's Way BL1: Bolt 1L 7 (4G 39)
BL2: Bolt 1L 7 (4G 39)
BL3: Bolt 4G 39
St Philip's Av. BL3: Bolt 8E 38
St Philip's Pl. M3: Sal 3B 4 (8C 78)
St Philip's Rd. M18: Man 5B 96
St Philips Sq. M3: Sal 3B 4
St Phillip's Dr. OL2: O'ham 2J 63
St Richard's Cl. M46: Ath 7L 55
St Saviour's Rd. SK2: Stoc 2G 118
Saintsbridge Rd. M22: Wyth 5B 116
St Simons Cl. SK2: Stoc 8G 108
St Simon St. M3: Sal 1C 4 (7C 78)
St Stephen's Av. M34: Aud 1J 97
WN1: Wig 1H 53
St Stephens Cl. BL2: Bolt 7K 39
M13: Man 4J 95
M29: Ast 5B 74
St Stephens Ct. M9: Man 3J 79
(off Shieldborn Dr.)
St Stephens Gdns. BL4: Kea 5A 58
M24: Mid 1M 61
St Stephens Rd. WN6: Stan 3N 33
St Stephens St. BL4: Kea 5A 58
OL1: O'ham 3L 63
St Stephen St. M3: Sal 1D 4 (8C 78)
St Stephens Vw. M43: Droy 8E 80
St Teresa's Rd. M16: Old T 6N 93
St Thomas Circ. OL8: O'ham 6H 63
St Thomas Cl. M26: Rad 9G 41
St Thomas Ct. BL9: Bury 2N 41
OL3: Del 8H 47
(off Church St.)
St Thomas More Sports Hall 7J 97
(off Town La.)
St Thomas Pde. OL4: Lees 5B 64
(off High St.)
St Thomas' Pl. M8: Man 6F 78
St Thomas's Ct. WN8: Uph 4G 51
St Thomas's Pl. SK1: Stoc 8D 108
St Thomas St. BL1: Bolt 2E 38
WN3: Wig 9J 9 (4F 52)
St Thomas St. Nth.
OL8: O'ham 5A 8 (6H 63)
St Thomas St. Sth. OL8: O'ham 6H 63
St Vincent St. M4: Man 3N 5 (8H 79)
St Werburgh's Rd. M21: Cho H 8B 94
St Werburgh's Road Stop (Metro)
9B 94
St Wilfred's Dr. OL12: Roch 2B 28
St Wilfrid's Pl. WN6: Stan 3C 34
St Wilfrid's Rd. WN6: Stan 3C 34
St Wilfrid's St. M15: Man 9D 4 (3D 94)
St Wilfrids Way WN6: Stan 3C 34
St Williams Av. BL3: Bolt 9F 38
St Winifred's Pl. SK15: Stal 8C 82
(off West St.)
Salcombe Av. BL2: Ain 3D 40
Salcombe Cl. M33: Sale 3E 104
WN1: Wig 1H 53
Salcombe Gro. BL2: Bolt 6N 39
Salcombe Rd. M11: Man 1B 96
SK2: Stoc 8G 108
Salco Sq. WA14: Alt 1D 114
Salcot Wlk. M40: Man 7H 79
(off Eastburn Av.)
SALE 3H 105
Sale Circ. M23: Wyth 6A 106
Sale Golf Course 3M 105
Sale Heys Rd. M33: Sale 5F 104
Sale La. M29: Tyld 2E 74
Sale Leisure Cen. 3J 105
SALEM 5A 64
Salem Cotts. SK22: N Mil 7M 121
Salem Gro. OL4: O'ham 5A 64
Sale Rd. M23: Wyth 6M 105
Salesbury Way WN3: Wig 8D 52
Sale Sharks RUFC 9C 108
Sales's La. BL9: Bury 4N 25
Sale Stop (Metro) 4H 105
Sale St. OL15: Lit 8M 15
Sale Water Pk. 1K 105
Sale Way WN7: Lei 6F 72
SALFORD 3C 4 (1A 94)
Salford App. M3: Sal 2F 4 (8E 78)
Salford Central Station (Rail)
4D 4 (9D 78)
Salford City Red RLFC 2A 92
Salford Crescent Station (Rail) 8A 78
Salford Ent. Cen. M50: Sal 9J 77
Salford Foyer M6: Sal 7M 77
Salford Mus. & Art Gallery 8B 78
SALFORD QUAYS 2M 93
Salford Quays Stop (Metro) 2N 93
Salford Rd. BL5: O Hul 3B 56
Salford Roman Catholic Cathedral
3C 4 (8C 78)
Salford Shop. City M6: Sal 7M 77
Salford Sports Village 3N 77
Salford St. BL9: Bury 9N 25
OL4: O'ham 6N 63
Salford University
MediaCityUK 2L 93
Salford University Bus. Pk.
M6: Sal 7A 78
Salford University Climbing Wall
7A 78
(within Tom Husband Leisure Complex)
Salford Watersports Cen. 2M 93
Salik Gdns. OL11: Roch 8D 28
Salisbury Av. OL10: H'ood 4H 43
WN2: Hin 5B 54
Salisbury Cotts. SK13: Had 4C 100
(off Salisbury St.)
Salisbury Cres. OL6: A Lyne 3A 82
Salisbury Dr. M25: Pres 9B 60
SK16: Duk 1D 98
Salisbury Ho. M1: Man 7J 5
M3: Sal 2D 4
Salisbury Pl. SK10: Macc 9J 129
Salisbury Rd. BL6: Hor 3H 37
M21: Cho H 8A 94
M26: Rad 7E 40
M27: Swin 3E 76
M30: Ecc 6F 76
M41: Urm 5D 92
OL4: O'ham 5M 63
WA11: Hay 1B 86
WA14: B'ath 9D 104
WN4: A Mak 5D 70
Salisbury St. BL3: Bolt 5G 7 (6E 38)
M14: Man 5F 94
M24: Mid 2N 61
M45: Whitef 3M 59
OL2: Shaw 4K 45
SK5: Stoc 9D 96
SK13: Had 4C 100
WA3: Gol 1K 87
Salisbury Ter. BL3: Lit L 9C 40
Salisbury Way M29: Ast 2C 74
Salix Ct. M6: Sal 7N 77
Salkeld Av. WN4: A Mak 7C 70
Salkeld St. OL11: Roch 8D 28
Salley St. OL15: Lit 4N 15
Sallowfields WN5: Orr 6H 51
Sally's Yd. M1: Man 8H 5
Salmesbury Hall Cl. BL0: Ram 9H 11
Salmon Flds. OL2: O'ham 9J 45
Salmon Flds. Bus. Village
OL2: O'ham 9K 45
Salmon St. M4: Man 3J 5 (8F 78)
WN1: Wig 5N 9 (2H 53)
Salop St. BL2: Bolt 4M 7 (6H 39)
M6: Sal 6N 77
Salop Wlk. SK10: Macc 2D 130
Saltash Cl. M22: Wyth 6C 116
Saltburn Wlk. M9: Man 2K 79
(off Princedom St.)
Saltdene Rd. M22: Wyth 6B 116
Saltergate Cl. BL3: Bolt 8N 37
Saltergate M. M5: Sal 9N 77
(off Cavell Way)
Saltersbrook Gro. SK9: Wilm 5J 123
(off Fairywell Cl.)
Salters Ct. M46: Ath 8M 55
Saltersley La. SK9: Wilm 7A 122
Salterton Dr. BL3: Bolt 8L 37
Salterton Wlk. M40: Man 3M 79
(off Hugo St.)
Salteye Rd. M30: Ecc 9A 76
Saltford Av. M4: Man 3N 5 (8H 79)
Saltford Ct. M4: Man 3N 5 (8J 79)
Salthill Av. OL10: H'ood 5K 43
Salthill Dr. M22: Wyth 5D 116
Salthouse Cl. BL8: Bury 7J 25
Saltire Gdns. M7: Sal 2D 78
Saltney Av. M20: Man 1E 106
Saltram Cl. M26: Rad 7C 40
Saltram Rd. WN3: Wig 7N 51
Saltrush Rd. M22: Wyth 5C 116
Salts Dr. OL15: Lit 8L 15
Salts St. OL2: Shaw 5L 45
Saltwood Gro. BL1: Bolt 3G 38
(off Kentford Rd.)
Salutation St. M15: Man 3E 94
Salvin Cl. WN4: A Mak 7G 71
Salvin Wlk. M9: Man 8K 61
(off Rockmead Dr.)
Salwick Cl. WN3: Wig 7B 52
Salwick Way M18: Man 7B 96
Sam Cowan Cl. M14: Man 6F 94
Samian Gdns. M7: Sal 5B 78
Samlesbury Cl. M20: Man 5E 106
OL2: Shaw 5K 45
Sammy Cookson Cl. M14: Man 6F 94
Samouth Cl. M40: Man 7J 79
Sampson Sq. M14: Man 5F 94
Sam Rd. OL3: Dig 7M 47
Samson St. OL16: Roch 5G 29
Sam Swire St. M15: Man 4E 94
Samuel La. OL2: Shaw 4J 45
Samuel Ogden St.
M1: Man 7J 5 (1F 94)
Samuel St. BL9: Bury 5N 7 (1N 41)
M19: Man 9N 95
M24: Mid 1M 61
M35: Fail 2D 80
M46: Ath 1A 74
OL11: Roch 2A 44
SK4: Stoc 5B 108
SK11: Macc 5H 131
SK14: Holl 4M 99
Samwoods Ho. WN4: A Mak 5D 70
(off Whitledge Grn.)
Sanby Av. M18: Man 5A 96
Sanby Rd. M18: Man 5A 96
Sanctuary, The M15: Man 3D 94
Sanctuary Cl. M15: Man 4G 94
Sandacre Rd. M23: Wyth 9A 106
Sandal St. M40: Man 7K 79
Sandalwood BL5: W'ton 5F 54
Sandalwood Dr. WN6: Wig 9C 34
Sandbach Av. M14: Man 9E 94
Sandbach Rd. M33: Sale 5M 105
SK5: Stoc 7C 96
Sandbach Wlk. SK8: Chea 3M 117
Sandbank Gdns. OL12: Whitw 4A 14
Sand Banks BL1: Bolt 7G 22
SANDBED 9E 64
Sandbed La. OL3: Del 7K 47
OL5: Mos 9F 64
Sand Beds La.
BL0: Eden, Roch 2M 11
Sandbrook Gdns. WN5: Orr 6H 51
Sandbrook Pk. OL11: Roch 9C 28
Sandbrook Rd. WN5: Orr 6G 51
Sandbrook Way M34: Dent 4K 97
OL11: Roch 9C 28
(not continuous)
Sandby Dr. SK6: Mar B 8E 110
Sanderling Cl. BL5: W'ton 5F 54
Sanderling Dr. M8: Man 5D 78
WN7: Lei 4J 73
Sanderling Rd. SK2: Stoc 2L 119
WA12: N Wil 5F 86
Sanderson Cl. M28: Wors 2B 76
Sanderson Ct. M40: Man 5K 79
(off Redbrook Av.)
Sanderson's Cft. WN7: Lei 6L 73
Sanderson St. BL9: Bury 1N 41
M40: Man 5K 79
WN7: Lei 5F 72
Sanders Sq. SK11: Macc 7H 131
Sanderstead Dr. M9: Man 8K 61
Sandfield Cl. WA3: Low 1A 88
Sandfield Cres. WA3: G'ury 2L 89
Sandfield Dr. BL6: Los 6L 37
Sandfield Rd. OL16: Roch 8F 28
Sandfold SK5: Stoc 7C 96
Sandfold La. M19: Man 7A 96
SK5: Stoc 7C 96
Sandford Av. M18: Man 3B 96
Sandford Cl. BL2: Bolt 9M 23
Sandford Rd. M33: Sale 5M 105
WN5: Orr 6G 51
Sandford St. M3: Sal 1D 4
M26: Rad 8K 41
Sandgate Av. M11: Man 8B 80
M26: Rad 4B 58
Sandgate Cl. WN7: Lei 4H 73
Sandgate Dr. M41: Urm 5C 92
Sandgate Rd. M45: Pres, Whitef 4A 60
OL9: Chad 5F 62
SK10: Macc 2K 131
Sandham St. BL3: Bolt 8G 38
Sandham Wlk. BL3: Bolt 8G 38
(off Teal St.)
Sandheys M34: Dent 4K 97
Sandheys Gro. M18: Man 5C 96
Sandhill Cl. BL3: Bolt 8G 38
Sandhill La. SK6: Mar B 6G 111
SK13: Chis 6G 111
Sandhill St. SK14: Hyde 5C 98
Sandhill Wlk. M22: Wyth 5A 116
Sand Hole La. OL11: Roch 3D 44
Sandhole La. OL11: Roch 8K 27
Sandhole Rd. BL4: Kea 5A 58
Sandhurst Av. M20: Man 2F 106
Sandhurst Cl. BL8: Bury 1H 41
Sandhurst Ct. BL2: Bolt 6M 39
Sandhurst Dr. BL2: Bolt 6M 39
SK9: Wilm 5H 123
Sandhurst Rd. M20: Man 6G 107
SK2: Stoc 2F 118
Sandhurst St. OL8: O'ham 7N 63
Sandhutton St. M9: Man 1J 79
Sandiacre WN6: Stan 4B 34
Sandilands Rd. M23: Wyth 8K 105
Sandilea Ct. M7: Sal 1N 77
Sandileigh Av. M20: Man 3G 106
SK5: Stoc 4F 108
SK8: Chea 1M 117
WA15: Hale 4F 114
WA16: Knut 6F 132
Sandileigh Dr. BL1: Bolt 1J 39
WA15: Hale 4F 114
Sandimoss Ct. M33: Sale 4F 104
Sandiway M44: Irl 7H 91
OL10: H'ood 2K 43
SK6: Bred 5K 109
SK7: Bram 5C 118
SK13: Glos 9H 101
WA16: Knut 6H 133
Sandiway Cl. SK6: Mar 8C 110
Sandiway Dr. M20: Man 5F 106
Sandiway Pl. WA14: Alt 1C 6 (2D 114)
Sandiway Rd. M33: Sale 4F 104
SK9: Hand 1J 123
WA14: Alt 1C 6 (1D 114)
Sand La. SK10: N Ald 7E 126
Sandling Dr. WA3: Gol 8J 71
Sandmere Wlk. M9: Man 8K 61
(off Rockmead Dr.)
Sandmoor Pl. WA13: Lym 5B 112
Sandon St. BL3: Bolt 8E 38
Sandown Av. M6: Sal 8L 77
Sandown Cl. OL1: O'ham 2L 63
SK9: Wilm 6J 123
WA3: Cul 5H 89
Sandown Cres. BL3: Lit L 1A 58
M18: Man 6B 96
Sandown Dr. M33: Sale 5E 104
M34: Dent 9M 97
WA15: Haleb 9K 115
Sandown Gdns. M41: Urm 7A 92
Sandown Pl. SK11: Macc 5C 130
Sandown Rd. BL2: Bolt 1M 39
BL9: Bury 9N 41
SK3: Stoc 8N 107
SK7: H Gro 5K 119
WN6: Wig 9B 34
Sandown St. M18: Man 3C 96
Sandpiper Cl. BL4: Farn 4G 57
OL11: Roch 6L 27
SK10: Macc 9F 128
SK16: Duk 2B 98
WA12: N Wil 5F 86
Sandpiper Dr. SK3: Stoc 1B 118
Sandpiper Rd. WN3: Wig 7M 51
Sandpits OL10: H'ood 4L 43
Sandpits Bus. Pk. SK14: Hat 6H 99
Sandra Dr. WA12: N Wil 6G 87
Sandray Cl. BL3: Bolt 7A 38
Sandray Gro. M5: Sal 9L 77
Sandridge Cl. BL4: Kea 3M 57
Sandridge Wlk. M12: Man 3K 95
(off Martindale Cres.)
Sandringham Av. M34: Aud 3H 97
M34: Dent 6E 96
SK15: Stal 7D 82
Sandringham Cl. PR7: Adl 7H 19
WA14: Bow 6N 113
WN5: Wig 6B 52
Sandringham Ct. M9: Man 6F 60
(off Deanswood Dr.)
M23: Wyth 8J 105
SK9: Wilm 8F 122
(off Cavendish M.)
WA3: Low 2A 88
(off Thurlow)
Sandringham Dr. BL8: G'mount 4G 24
OL16: Miln 7L 29
SK4: Stoc 7M 107
SK12: Poy 3H 125
SK16: Duk 2C 98
WN7: Lei 3N 73
Sandringham Grange
M25: Pres 8D 60
Sandringham Ho. SK6: Mar 1A 120
Sandringham Rd. BL6: Hor 2F 36
M28: Wors 4H 75
SK6: Bred 5G 109
SK7: H Gro 5K 119
SK8: Chea H 4M 117
SK10: Macc 3K 131
SK14: Hyde 1B 110
WN2: Hin 7A 54
Sandringham St. M18: Man 5A 96
Sandringham Way OL2: O'ham 6G 44
SK9: Wilm 8F 122
Sands Av. OL9: Chad 2B 62
Sands Cl. SK14: Hat 8G 98
Sandsend Cl. M8: Man 6D 78
Sandsend Rd. M41: Urm 6C 92
Sandstone Rd. OL16: Miln 6K 29
WN3: Wins 9B 52
Sandstone Way M21: Cho H 1C 106
Sand St. M40: Man 6H 79
SK15: Stal 1C 98
Sands Wlk. SK14: Hat 8G 99
Sandusky Dr. BL1: Bolt 1H 39
Sandwash Cl. WA11: R'ford 6A 68
Sandway WN6: Wig 1C 52
Sandwell Dr. M33: Sale 2H 105
Sandwich Dr. SK10: Macc 9G 128
Sandwich Rd. M30: Ecc 7F 76
Sandwich St. M28: Walk 9L 57
Sandwick Cres. BL3: Bolt 7E 38
Sandwith Cl. WN3: Wig 9E 52
Sandwood Av. BL3: Bolt 7N 37
Sandy Acre OL5: Mos 2F 82
Sandyacre Cl. BL5: O Hul 5B 56
Sandy Bank OL2: Shaw 4K 45
Sandy Bank Av. SK14: Hat 8G 98
Sandybank Cl. SK13: Had 5A 100
Sandy Bank Rd. BL7: Edg 1L 23
M8: Man 2E 78
Sandybrook Cl. BL8: Tot 7F 24
Sandybrook Dr. M9: Man 9H 61
Sandy Brow M9: Man 9J 61
Sandy Brow La. WA3: Cro 7N 87
Sandy Cl. BL9: Bury 8M 41
SK10: Boll 6K 129
Sandy Ct. WN7: Lei 9C 72
Sandycroft Av. M22: Wyth 4C 116
WN1: Wig 1F 52
Sandygate Cl. M27: Swin 3E 76
Sandy Gro. M6: Sal 7L 77
M27: Swin 2F 76
WA3: Cul 1A 98
Sandy Haven Cl. SK14: Hat 8G 99
Sandy Haven Wlk. SK14: Hat 8G 99
Sandyhill Ct. M9: Man 8F 60
Sandyhill Rd. M9: Man 8F 60
Sandyhills BL3: Bolt 8F 38
Sandylands Dr. M25: Pres 1N 77
Sandy La. M6: Sal 7L 77
M21: Cho H 9A 94
M23: Wyth 9L 105
M24: Mid 3A 62
M25: Pres 8M 59
Sandy La. M29: Ast 6B 74
(Abbotts Grn.)
M29: Ast 9C 74
(Gt. Moss Rd.)
M32: Stre 8H 93
M43: Droy 7G 81
M44: Irl 6H 91
OL2: O'ham 8H 45
OL3: Dob 1K 65
OL11: Roch 6A 28
PR7: Adl 6G 19
SK5: Stoc 5C 108
SK6: Rom 6N 109
SK9: Wilm 6C 122
SK10: Macc 2A 130
SK13: Chis 3K 111
SK16: Duk 1A 98
WA3: Cro 9C 88
WA3: Gol 1J 87
WA3: Low 8C 72
WA11: St H 9C 68
WA13: Lym 2C 112
WN2: Hin 5B 54
WN5: Orr 7H 51
Sandy Meade M25: Pres 8N 59
Sandy Nook SK15: Stal 1D 98
Sandy Pk. WN2: Hin 5C 54
Sandys Av. OL8: O'ham 8H 63
Sandyshot Wlk. M22: Wyth 4E 116
Sandy Va. SK16: Duk 9B 82
Sandy Wlk. OL2: O'ham 8H 45
Sandywarps M44: Irl 9H 91
Sandy Way WN2: Hin 5B 54
Sandyway M25: Pres 8N 59
Sandyway Cl. BL5: W'ton 3F 54
Sandywell Cl. M11: Man 2B 96
Sandywell St. M11: Man 1B 96
Sandywood M6: Sal 7L 77
Sangster Ct. M5: Sal 1N 93
Sankey Gro. M9: Man 8G 61
Sankey St. BL9: Bury 7H 7 (2K 41)
WA3: Gol 1K 87
WA12: N Wil 6D 86
Sankey Valley Country Pk. 6A 86
Sankey Valley Ind. Est.
WA12: N Wil 7D 86
Santiago St. M14: Man 6G 94
Santley St. M12: Man 6M 95
Santon Av. M14: Man 9K 95
Santon Dr. WA3: Low 1A 88
Sapling Gro. M33: Sale 6D 104
Sapling Rd. BL3: Bolt 1C 56
M27: Swin 5D 76
Sarah Butterworth Ct.
OL16: Roch 7F 28
(off Sarah Butterworth St.)
Sarah Butterworth St.
OL16: Roch 7F 28
SARAH MOOR 2K 63
Sarah St. BL0: Eden 3L 11
M11: Man 9L 79
M24: Mid 3L 61
M30: Ecc 9B 76
OL2: Shaw 7L 45
OL8: O'ham 9H 63
OL11: Roch 7E 28
WN2: Hin 9D 54
Sargent Dr. M16: Whall R 5D 94
Sargent Rd. SK6: Bred 6H 109
Sark Rd. M21: Cho H 7N 93
Sarn Av. M22: Wyth 3C 116
Sarnesfield Cl. M12: Man 5M 95
Sarnia Ct. M7: Sal 3C 78
(off Bk. Hope St.)
Sarsfield Av. WA3: Low 1N 87
Satinwood Cl. WN4: A Mak 7C 70
Satinwood Wlk. M3: Sal 1D 4
Saturn Gro. M6: Sal 6B 78
Saunders M. PR7: Chor 2F 18
Saunton Av. BL2: Bolt 1N 39
Saunton Rd. M11: Man 1B 96
Sautridge Cl. M24: Mid 5B 44
Savernake Rd. SK6: Wood 3N 109
Savick Av. BL2: Bolt 5N 39
Saville Rd. M26: Rad 5F 40
SK8: Gat 1G 116
Saville St. BL2: Bolt 3M 7 (6H 39)
M24: Mid 4B 62
SK11: Macc 6J 131
Saviours Ter. BL3: Bolt 7D 38
(off Bankfield St.)
Savio Way M24: Mid 4M 61
Savoy Cinema
Stockport 5N 107
Savoy Ct. M45: Whitef 1L 59
Savoy Dr. OL2: O'ham 1L 63
Savoy St. OL4: O'ham 6M 63
OL11: Roch 5A 28
Sawley Av. M45: Whitef 1M 59
OL4: O'ham 7A 64
OL15: Lit 7L 15
WA3: Low 9N 71
WN6: Wig 1C 52
Sawley Cl. WA3: Cul 7H 89
Sawley Dr. SK8: Chea H 9N 117
Sawley Rd. M40: Man 6J 79
Sawmill, The BL9: Bury 9M 7 (3M 41)
Saw Mill Way OL15: Lit 1L 29
Sawpit St. WA13: Warb 9H 103
WA14: D Mas 9H 103
Sawston Wlk. M40: Man 8A 62
Saw St. BL1: Bolt 2F 38
Sawyer Brow SK14: Hyde 5C 98
Sawyer Dr. WN4: A Mak 7G 70
Sawyer St. BL8: Bury 9H 25
OL12: Roch 4D 28
Saxbrook Wlk. M22: Wyth 4E 116
Saxby Av. BL7: Bro X 5G 23
Saxby St. M6: Sal 5J 77
Saxelby Dr. M8: Man 4G 79
Saxfield Dr. M23: Wyth 1B 116
Saxholme Wlk.
M22: Wyth 5B 116
Saxon Av. M8: Man 1F 78
SK16: Duk 1N 97
Saxon Cl. BL8: Bury 2H 41

Saxon Ct. M33: Sale 5H 105
Saxon Dr. M34: Aud 2J 97
M43: Droy 8F 80
OL9: Chad 3C 62
Saxonholme Rd. OL11: Roch 5A 44
Saxon Ho. M16: Whall R 6C 94
OL15: Lit 9N 15
Saxonside M24: Mid 9K 43
Saxon St. M24: Mid 3N 61
M26: Rad 9F 40
M34: Dent 6K 97
M40: Man 7K 79
M43: Droy 8F 80
OL4: O'ham 4N 63
OL5: Mos 8G 64
Saxthorpe Cl. M33: Sale 3D 104
WN3: Wins 8A 52
Saxthorpe Wlk. M12: Man 4K 95
(off Britnall Av.)
Saxwood Av. M9: Man 1J 79
Saxwood Cl. OL12: Roch 4L 27
Scafell Av. OL7: A Lyne 6K 81
Scafell Cl. OL1: O'ham 2K 63
(not continuous)
SK6: H Lan 7B 120
Scafell Dr. WN5: Wig 5M 51
Scafell Gro. WN2: P Bri 9L 53
Scalby Wlk. M22: Wyth 6C 116
Scale St. M5: Sal 9N 77
(off Christopher St.)
Scaliot Cl. SK22: N Mil 7L 121
Scant Row BL6: Hor 1L 37
Scarborough St. M40: Man 2M 79
Scarcroft Rd. M12: Man 4M 95
Scarfield Dr. OL11: Roch 4K 27
Scargill Cl. M14: Man 9H 95
Scargill Rd. BL3: Bolt 8B 38
Scarisbrick Av. M20: Man 5J 107
WN8: Par 2A 32
Scarisbrick Rd. M19: Man 9L 95
Scarisbrick St. WN1: Wig 2F 52
Scarr Av. M26: Rad 1J 59
Scarr Dr. OL12: Roch 2D 28
Scarr La. OL2: Shaw 5N 45
Scarr Ter. OL12: Whitw 4B 14
Scarr Wheel M7: Sal 3B 78
Scarsdale Av. BL1: Bolt 3B 38
Scarsdale Rd. M14: Man 5K 95
Scarsdale St. M6: Sal 7A 78
Scarth Pk. WN8: Skel 4A 50
Scarthwood Cl. BL2: Bolt 8M 23
Scawfell Av. BL2: Bolt 2J 39
Scawton Wlk. M9: Man 6G 61
Sceptre Cl. WA12: N Wil 6D 86
Schofield Cl. M24: Mid 9M 43
OL16: Miln 7K 29
Schofield Gdns. WN7: Lei 7G 72
Schofield Hall Rd. OL15: Lit 4A 30
Schofield La. M46: Ath 8H 55
Schofield Pl. OL15: Lit 4A 16
Schofield Rd. M30: Ecc 9A 76
M43: Droy 9F 80
Schofield St. M11: Man 9A 80
M26: Rad 8H 41
M35: Fail 2D 80
OL2: O'ham 7H 45
OL8: O'ham 8J 63
OL10: H'ood 2J 43
OL11: Roch 9E 28
OL15: Lit 8N 15
(Blackstone Edge Ct.)
OL15: Lit 4A 16
(Schofield Pl.)
OL16: Miln 8L 29
WN7: Lei 7G 72
Scholar Grn. Rd. M32: Stre 4G 93
Scholars Cl. SK10: Macc 4B 130
Scholars Ct. M27: Clif 8E 58
Scholars Dr. M20: Man 1F 106
SK3: Stoc 8N 107
Scholars Grn. La. WA13: Lym 4A 112
Scholars Ri. BL7: Bolt 6G 23
Scholars Way BL9: Bury 9N 25
(off Taylor St.)
M24: Mid 2L 61
Scholefield La. WN1: Wig 7M 9 (3G 53)
SCHOLES 8M 9 (3G 53)
Scholes WN1: Wig 8L 9 (3G 52)
(not continuous)
Scholes Bank BL6: Hor 9C 20
Scholes Cl. M7: Sal 2E 78
Scholes Dr. M40: Man 9C 62
Scholes La. M25: Pres 8A 60
Scholes Pct. WN1: Wig 8M 9 (3G 53)
Scholes St. BL8: Bury 1J 41
M27: Swin 2G 76
M35: Fail 1E 80
OL1: O'ham 2F 8 (4L 63)
OL9: Chad 7E 62
OL11: Roch 3A 44
Scholes Wlk. M25: Pres 8A 60
Scholey St. BL2: Bolt 7H 39
Scholfield Av. M41: Urm 8F 92
School Av. M32: Stre 6M 93
OL6: A Lyne 4A 82
WN1: Wig 5N 9 (2H 53)
School Brow BL9: Bury 6K 7 (1L 41)
(not continuous)
M28: Wors 4N 75
SK6: Rom 6L 109
WN5: Bil 5J 69
School Cl. SK12: Poy 3K 125
SK13: Had 4A 100
WA16: Knut 7E 132
School Ct. BL0: Ram 5K 11
BL7: Eger 3F 22
M4: Man 3M 5 (8H 79)
SK3: Stoc 1D 118
School Cres. SK15: Stal 7C 82
School Dr. SK16: Duk 3B 98
WA13: Lym 2D 112
WN5: Bil 5J 69
Schoolfold La. SK10: Adl 7L 125
School Gro. M20: Man 2H 107
M25: Pres 8M 59
School Hill BL1: Bolt 1J 7 (4F 38)
School Ho. BL7: Bolt 6G 23
(off School St.)
School Ho. Flats OL8: O'ham 9F 62
School Ho. Rd. OL4: O'ham 6N 63
School La. BL9: Bury 5L 25
M9: Man 9H 61
M19: Man 5G 107
M20: Man 5G 107
M31: C'ton 2M 103
M44: Cad 3E 102
M44: Irl 7G 91
OL11: Roch 5H 27
OL16: Roch 8D 8 (6D 28)
SK4: Stoc 3A 108
SK6: Comp 4E 110
SK8: Chea H 7L 117
(not continuous)
SK10: O Ald 7L 127
SK12: Poy 2K 125
SK14: Hyde 1B 110
SK15: C'ook 3H 83
WA3: Rix 6B 102
WA14: D Mas 9L 103
WN1: Wig 8L 9 (3G 52)
WN2: Hai 5H 35
WN4: Gars 7N 69
WN6: Stan 4A 34
WN8: Roby M 9F 32
WN8: Uph 4G 51
School M. SK7: Bram 8C 118
School Rd. M30: Ecc 1C 92
M32: Stre 7J 93
M33: Sale 3H 105
(not continuous)
M35: Fail 3D 80
OL8: O'ham 9F 62
SK9: Hand 2J 123
WA15: Hale 5G 6 (4F 114)
Schools Hill SK8: Chea 4J 117
Schoolside Cl. M8: Man 4G 78
Schoolside La. M24: Mid 4G 61
Schools Rd. M18: Man 4C 96
School St. BL0: Ram 9H 11
BL3: Lit L 9B 40
BL5: W'ton 3G 54
BL6: Hor 1E 36
BL7: Bro X 6G 23
BL9: Bury 3A 42
M4: Man 1K 5 (7F 78)
M7: Sal 6D 78
M26: Rad 9F 40
M29: Ast 3A 74
M29: Tyld 2A 74
M30: Ecc 7B 76
M46: Ath 9K 55
OL3: Upp 3L 65
OL4: Spri 5D 64
OL8: O'ham 6H 63
OL10: H'ood 2H 43
OL12: Roch 6C 8 (5D 28)
OL15: Lit 9J 15
SK7: H Gro 5J 119
WA3: Gol 1K 87
WA12: N Wil 6E 86
WN1: Wig 7L 9 (3G 52)
WN2: Abr 1L 71
WN2: I Mak 4J 53
WN4: A Mak 5G 71
WN7: Lei 2G 72
School St. Ind. Est.
SK7: H Gro 5J 119
School Ter. OL12: Whitw 5A 14
(off Lloyd St.)
WA3: Gol 1K 87
School Vw. SK11: Sut E 9K 131
(off Hollin La.)
School Wlk. M16: Old T 4C 94
School Way WN5: Wig 5N 51
School Yd. SK4: Stoc 6K 107
Schuster Rd. M14: Man 6J 95
Schwabe St. M24: Mid 3H 61
Scobell St. BL8: Tot 8F 24
Scoltock Way OL1: O'ham 1D 8 (4K 63)
Scope o' th' La. BL2: Bolt 9K 23
Score St. M11: Man 9M 79
Scorton Av. BL2: Bolt 5N 39
Scorton St. BL1: Bolt 4D 38
(off Wyresdale Rd.)
Scorton Wlk. M40: Man 9B 62
(off Blandford Dr.)
Scotforth Cl. M15: Man 9D 4 (2D 94)
Scotia Wlk. WA3: Low 1B 88
Scotland Hall Rd. M40: Man 5N 79
Scotland La. BL9: Bury 5B 26
Scotland Pl. BL0: Ram 8J 11
Scotland Rd. M4: Man 1H 5 (7F 78)
Scotland St. M40: Man 5A 80
OL6: A Lyne 8E 6 (7N 81)
Scot La. BL6: Bla 6N 35
WN2: Asp 6N 35
WN5: Wig 2B 52
(not continuous)
WN6: Wig 2B 52
SCOT LANE END 5A 36
Scotman's Flash 7E 52
Scotson Fold M26: Rad 1F 58
Scotta Rd. M30: Ecc 1B 92
Scott Av. BL9: Bury 6M 41
M21: Cho H 7A 94
M30: Ecc 7C 76
WN1: Wig 7E 34
WN2: Hin 5A 54
Scott Cl. SK5: Stoc 4D 108
SK10: Macc 5L 131
Scott Dr. SK6: Mar B 8F 110
WA15: Alt 4G 6 (3F 114)
Scottfield OL8: O'ham 6J 63
Scottfield Rd. OL8: O'ham 6K 63
Scott Ga. M34: Aud 2J 97
Scotthope Cl. SK11: Macc 6D 130
Scott Pl. M3: Man 5F 4 (9D 78)
Scott Rd. M25: Pres 8M 59
M34: Dent 8J 97
M43: Droy 9E 80
SK10: P'bury 6E 128
WA3: Low 9N 71
Scotts Ind. Pk.
OL16: Roch 9F 8 (7E 28)
Scott St. BL5: W'ton 1G 55
M26: Rad 4D 58
M29: Ast 6D 74
OL8: O'ham 6K 63
WN6: Wig 2E 52
WN7: Lei 5F 72
Scott Wlk. WA12: N Wil 8F 86
Scotty Brook Cres. SK13: Glos 9G 101
SCOUT
HD7 1K 49
OL5 3F 82
Scout Dr. M23: Wyth 3M 115
Scout Grn. M24: Mid 9M 43
SCOUTHEAD 3E 64
Scout Rd. BL0: Ram 4M 11
BL1: Bolt 7B 22
Scout Vw. BL8: Tot 7G 24
Scovell St. M7: Sal 4C 78
Scowcroft La. OL2: Shaw 7L 45
Scowcroft St. BL2: Bolt 3J 39
Scribe Pl. M44: Irl 2F 102
Scroggins La. M31: Part 4G 102
Scropton St. M40: Man 4J 79
Seabright Wlk. M11: Man 9L 79
(off Pilgrim Dr.)
Seabrook Cres. M41: Urm 5C 92
Seabrook Rd. M40: Man 6A 80
Seacombe Av. M14: Man 8F 94
Seacombe Gro. SK3: Stoc 8N 107
Seaford Rd. BL2: Bolt 7M 23
M6: Sal 5A 78
Seaford Wlk. M9: Man 8H 61
OL9: Chad 5F 62
Seaforth Av. M46: Ath 7L 55
Seaforth Rd. BL1: Bolt 8F 22
Seaham Dr. BL8: Bury 8J 25
Seaham Wlk. M14: Man 6G 95
(off Head Pl.)
Sealand Cl. M33: Sale 6L 105
Sealand Dr. M30: Ecc 1A 92
Sealand Ho. M25: Pres 6B 60
Sealand Rd. M23: Wyth 6M 105
Sealand Way SK9: Hand 2J 123
(off Henbury Rd.)
Seale Av. M34: Aud 2H 97
Sealey Wlk. M40: Man 6K 79
(off Filby Wlk.)
Seal Rd. SK7: Bram 7D 118
Seaman Way WN2: I Mak 5K 53
Seamons Dr. WA14: Alt 1B 114
Seamons Rd. WA14: Alt, D Mas 1A 114
Seamons Wlk. WA14: Alt 2B 114
(off Seamons Rd.)
Searby Rd. M18: Man 5N 95
Searness Rd. M24: Mid 1H 61
Seascale Av. M11: Man 7N 79
Seascale Cres. WN1: Wig 9F 34
Seascale Wlk. M24: Mid 1K 61
Seathwaite Cl. M24: Mid 1J 61
M29: Ast 3B 74
Seathwaite Rd. BL4: Farn 4G 56
Seathwaite Wlk. M18: Man 4A 96
(off Hampden Cres.)
Seatoller Ct. OL2: O'ham 8J 45
Seatoller Dr. M24: Mid 2H 61
Seatoller Pl. WN5: Wig 4M 51
Seaton Cl. SK7: H Gro 6H 119
Seaton M. OL7: A Lyne 6J 81
Seaton Rd. BL1: Bolt 2D 38
Seaton Way M14: Man 5F 94
Sebastian Cl. SK6: Mar B 9E 110
Second Av. BL1: Bolt 5C 38
BL3: Lit L 8N 39
BL9: Bury 2C 42
M11: Man 7B 80
M17: T Pk 4K 93
M27: Swin 5D 76
M29: Ast 6C 74
M46: Ath 7M 55
OL8: O'ham 9G 63
SK12: Poy 5H 125
SK15: C'ook 5H 83
WN6: Wig 1D 52
Second St. BL1: Bolt 9A 22
Section St. BL3: Bolt 4K 7 (6G 38)
Sedan Cl. M5: Sal 9N 77
Sedburgh Cl. M33: Sale 6D 104
Sedbury Cl. M23: Wyth 7M 105
Seddon Av. M18: Man 3C 96
M26: Rad 7K 41
Seddon Cl. M26: Rad 8G 41
M46: Ath 8L 55
Seddon Gdns. M26: Rad 3A 58
Seddon Ho. Dr. WN6: Wig 9B 34
Seddon La. M26: Rad 3A 58
Seddon Rd. WA14: Hale 5D 114
Seddons Av. BL8: Bury 4G 40
Seddon St. BL3: Lit L 9B 40
BL5: W'ton 9G 37
M12: Man 7N 95
M26: Rad 9G 41
M38: Lit H 6G 57
Sedgeborough Rd. M16: Whall R 5D 94
Sedge Cl. SK5: Stoc 9E 96
Sedgefield Cl. M5: Sal 8M 77
SK10: Macc 9G 129
Sedgefield Dr. BL1: Bolt 1C 38
WN6: Wig 9B 34
Sedgefield Pk. OL4: O'ham 5A 64
Sedgefield Rd. M26: Rad 3F 58
Sedgefield Wlk. M23: Wyth 6M 105
Sedgeford Cl. SK9: Wilm 5H 123
Sedgeford Rd. M40: Man 5J 79
Sedgely WN6: Stan 5D 34
Sedgemoor Cl. SK8: Chea H 5N 117
Sedgemoor Va. BL2: Bolt 2N 39
Sedgemoor Way
OL1: O'ham 1C 8 (4J 63)
Sedgley Av. M25: Pres 9B 60
OL16: Roch 9F 28
Sedgley Cl. M24: Mid 4A 62
Sedgley Dr. BL5: W'ton 6G 55
SEDGLEY PARK 9B 60
Sedgley Pk. Rd. M25: Pres 9B 60
Sedgley Park RUFC 5L 59
Sedgley Pk. Trad. Est. M25: Pres 1A 78
Sedgley Rd. M8: Man 2F 78
Sedgley St. M24: Mid 4A 62
Sedgwick Cl. BL5: W'ton 5H 55
M46: Ath 8N 55
Sedley Av. M25: Pres 6M 59
Sedwyn St. WN1: Wig 5N 9 (2H 53)
SEEDFIELD 8M 25
Seedfield Rd. BL9: Bury 8M 25
SEEDLEY 8L 77
Seedley Av. M38: Lit H 7J 57
Seedley Pk. Rd. M6: Sal 8L 77
Seedley Rd. M6: Sal 7L 77
Seedley St. M14: Man 6G 94
Seedley Ter. M6: Sal 7L 77
Seedley Vw. Rd. M6: Sal 7L 77
Seed St. BL1: Bolt 5D 38
Seel St. OL5: Mos 1E 82
Sefton Av. M46: Ath 6L 55
WN5: Orr 6H 51
Sefton Cl. M13: Man 3G 95
M24: Mid 3K 61
OL1: O'ham 8A 46
WN5: Orr 6H 51
Sefton Ct. BL1: Bolt 1J 7
BL9: Bury 7M 25
(off Sefton St.)
Sefton Cres. M33: Sale 2H 105
Sefton Dr. BL9: Bury 7N 25
M27: Swin 4D 76
M28: Wors 5A 76
SK9: Wilm 4H 123
Sefton Fold Dr. WN5: Bil 5H 69
Sefton Fold Gdns. WN5: Bil 5H 69
Sefton La. BL6: Hor 4F 36
Sefton Rd. BL1: Bolt 2C 38
M21: Cho H 9A 94
M24: Mid 3K 61
M27: Pen 1F 76
M33: Sale 3H 105
WN3: Wig 7C 52
WN4: A Mak 4C 70
WN5: Orr 6H 51
Sefton St. BL9: Bury 7M 25
M8: Man 2F 78
M26: Rad 2J 59
M45: Whitef 4M 59
OL9: O'ham 9F 62
OL10: H'ood 3K 43
OL11: Roch 8D 28
SK13: Glos 9E 100
WA12: N Wil 6C 86
WN7: Lei 5H 73
Sefton Vw. WN5: Orr 6H 51
Segal Cl. M7: Sal 3C 78
Selborne Rd. M21: Cho H 8A 94
Selbourne Cl. BL5: W'ton 2J 55
SK5: Stoc 7C 96
Selbourne St. OL8: O'ham 1L 81
WN7: Lei 3H 73
Selby Av. M45: Whitef 1M 59
OL9: Chad 2D 62
Selby Cl. M26: Rad 7K 41
M32: Stre 6G 92
OL16: Miln 7J 29
SK12: Poy 1H 125
Selby Ct. WN7: Lei 5G 73
(off Boughey St.)
Selby Dr. M6: Sal 7H 77
M41: Urm 4N 91
WN3: Wig 7N 51
Selby Gdns. SK8: Chea H 9A 118
Selby Rd. M24: Mid 9L 43
M32: Stre 6G 92
Selby St. M11: Man 1N 95
OL16: Roch 5F 28
SK4: Stoc 4B 108
Selby Wlk. BL8: Bury 3F 40
Selden St. OL8: O'ham 6H 63
Selham Wlk. M13: Man 9M 5
Selhurst Av. M11: Man 8A 80
Selkirk Av. OL8: O'ham 7H 63
WN4: Gars 6A 70
Selkirk Cl. SK10: Macc 2D 130
Selkirk Dr. M9: Man 8L 61
Selkirk Gro. WN5: Wig 3M 51
Selkirk Pl. OL10: H'ood 3F 42
Selkirk Rd. BL1: Bolt 8E 22
OL9: Chad 7D 62
Sellars Sq. M43: Droy 1E 96
Sellars St. M11: Man 1C 96
Selsby Av. M30: Ecc 8B 76
Selsey Av. M33: Sale 5F 104
SK3: Stoc 9L 107
Selsey Dr. M20: Man 8H 107
Selside WN3: Wig 9E 52
Selside Ct. M26: Rad 3B 58
Selside Wlk. M14: Man 9H 95
(off Boland Dr.)
Selstead Rd. M22: Wyth 6B 116
Selston Rd. M9: Man 7G 60
Selwood Wlk. M9: Man 3J 79
(off Carisbrook St.)
Selworth Av. M33: Sale 4L 105
Selworth Cl. WA15: Tim 1E 114
Selworthy Rd. M16: Whall R 5D 94
Selwyn Av. M9: Man 2J 79
Selwyn Cl. WA12: N Wil 4E 86
Selwyn Dr. SK8: Chea H 8A 118
SK11: Sut E 9K 131
Selwyn Jones Sports Cen. 3F 86
Selwyn St. BL2: Bolt 4N 7 (6H 39)
OL8: O'ham 6J 63
WN7: Lei 4H 73
Semple Way OL9: Chad 8D 62
Senecar Cl. WN2: Asp 1L 53
Senior Av. M14: Man 1K 107
Senior Rd. M30: Ecc 1N 91
Senior St. M3: Sal 1E 4 (7D 78)
Sennicar La. WN1: Hai, Wig 7F 34
WN2: Hai 7F 34
Sepal Cl. SK5: Stoc 8E 96
Sephton Av. WA3: Cul 6G 88
Sephton St. WN3: I Mak 5J 53
Sepia Gro. M24: Mid 2L 61
Sequoia St. M9: Man 2K 79
Sergeants La. M45: Whitef 4J 59
Serin Cl. SK2: Stoc 2K 119
WA12: N Wil 6F 86
Serpentine Wlk. WA12: N Wil 1G 87
Service St. SK3: Stoc 8N 107
Sesame Gdns. M44: Irl 6K 91
Setantii Mus. 7D 6 (7M 81)
Set St. SK15: Stal 9C 82
Sett Cl. SK22: N Mil 7L 121
Settle Cl. BL8: Bury 2F 40
Settle St. BL3: Bolt 9E 38
BL3: Lit L 9C 40
Settstones La. OL3: Upp 2N 65
Seven Acres OL3: Del 7J 47
Seven Acres Country Pk. 3L 39
Seven Acres La. OL12: Roch 3K 27
Sevenoaks PR7: Chor 5F 18
WN7: Lei 4J 73
Sevenoaks Av. M41: Urm 5D 92
SK4: Stoc 3M 107
Sevenoaks Cl. SK10: Macc 2F 130
Sevenoaks Dr. BL3: Bolt 9F 38
M27: Swin 4G 77
Sevenoaks Rd. SK8: Gat 1G 116
Sevenoaks Wlk. M13: Man 4H 95
(off Beckhampton Cl.)
Seven Stars Rd. WN3: Wig 4D 52
Seven Stiles Dr. SK6: Mar 9B 110
Seventh Av. OL8: O'ham 1G 81
Severn Cl. BL9: Bury 6M 25
SK10: Macc 2D 130
WA14: Alt 1B 6 (1C 114)
WN5: Bil 7H 69
Severn Dr. OL16: Miln 7L 29
SK7: Bram 9A 118
WN2: Hin 8E 54
WN5: Wig 5N 51
Severn Rd. OL8: O'ham 1F 80
(not continuous)
OL9: Chad 3D 62
OL10: H'ood 1F 42
WA3: Cul 7H 89
WN4: A Mak 5H 71
Severnside Trad. Est. M17: T Pk 4H 93
Severn St. WN7: Lei 6K 73
Severn Way BL4: Kea 5B 58
SK5: Stoc 3E 108
Seville's Bldgs. OL5: Mos 8F 64
Sevilles Pl. OL4: Lees 6B 64
(off Church St.)
Seville St. OL2: O'ham 1J 63
OL2: Shaw 7L 45
Sewell Way M38: Lit H 8G 56
Sewerby St. M16: Whall R 5E 94
Sexa St. M11: Man 1B 96
Sexton St. OL10: H'ood 2H 43
SK13: Tin 2C 100
Seymour Av. M11: Man 8B 80
Seymour Chase WA16: Knut 8G 133
Seymour Cl. M16: Old T 4B 94
Seymour Ct. M7: Sal 2E 78
M26: Rad 9H 41
SK4: Stoc 6K 107
Seymour Dr. BL2: Bolt 7K 23
Seymour Gro. BL4: Farn 2H 57
M16: Old T 4A 94
M33: Sale 4H 105
OL16: Roch 1F 44
SK6: Mar 1B 120
WA15: Tim 2G 115
Seymour Pl. M16: Old T 4A 94
Seymour Rd. BL1: Bolt 1G 38
M8: Man 1E 78
SK2: Stoc 2F 118
SK8: Chea H 7M 117
Seymour Rd. Sth. M11: Man 8B 80
Seymour St. BL2: Bolt 7K 23
M18: Man 3B 96
M26: Rad 9H 41
(Darbyshire St.)
M26: Rad 9H 41
(Quarry St.)
M34: Dent 6H 97
OL10: H'ood 3G 43
(not continuous)
Seymour Wlk. M26: Rad 9H 41
(off Haworth Wlk.)
Shackleton Ct. M40: Man 6A 80
Shackleton Gro. BL1: Bolt 2N 37
Shackleton St. M30: Ecc 7C 76
Shackliffe Rd. M40: Man 9N 61
Shaddock Av. OL12: Roch 4L 27
Shade Av. OL4: Spri 6C 64
Shade La. PR7: Chor 3G 19
Shade Ter. SK6: H Lan 8C 120
Shadewood Rd. SK11: Macc 6E 130
Shadowbrook Av. M23: Wyth 3N 115
Shadowbrook Cl. OL1: O'ham 2J 63
Shadowmoss Rd. M22: Wyth 8D 116
Shadows La. OL5: Mos 7H 65
Shadows M. OL5: Mos 7H 65
Shadwell Gro. WN7: Lei 2E 72
Shadwell St. E. OL10: H'ood 1J 43
Shadwell St. W. OL10: H'ood 1J 43
Shadworth Cl. OL5: Mos 7H 65
Shadworth La. OL5: Mos 7J 65
Shady La. BL7: Bro X 7J 23
M23: Wyth 9K 105
Shady Oak Rd. SK2: Stoc 1K 119
Shaftesbury Av. BL6: Los 4H 37
M30: Ecc 1C 92
OL15: Lit 2K 29
SK8: Chea H 6A 118
WA15: Tim 2G 115
Shaftesbury Cl. BL1: Bolt 3F 38
(off Ashford Wlk.)
BL6: Los 4H 37
Shaftesbury Dr. OL10: H'ood 4H 43
OL12: W'le 8H 15
Shaftesbury Gdns. M41: Urm 7K 91
Shaftesbury Rd. M8: Man 3F 78
M27: Swin 3F 76
SK3: Stoc 1M 117
Shafton Wlk. M40: Man 9B 62
(off Blandford Dr.)

Shaftsbury Rd. WN5: Orr 3L 51
Shaftsbury St. WN6: Wig 9C 34
Shaftway Cl. WA11: Hay 2C 86
SHAKERLEY 9B 56
Shakerley La. M46: Ath 7A 56
Shakerley Rd. M29: Tyld 1A 74
Shakespeare Av. BL9: Bury 6M 41
M26: Rad 8E 40
M34: Dent 9K 97
SK15: Mill 6H 83
Shakespeare Cl. OL15: Lit 5N 15
Shakespeare Ct. SK11: Macc . . . 7G 131
Shakespeare Cres. M30: Ecc 8D 76
M43: Droy 8E 80
Shakespeare Dr. SK8: Chea 1L 117
Shakespeare Gro. WN3: Wig 7D 52
Shakespeare Rd. M25: Pres 8M 59
M27: Swin 2D 76
M43: Droy 8E 80
OL1: O'ham 1M 63
SK6: Bred 5J 109
Shakespeare Wlk. M13: Man 3H 95
Shakleton Av. M9: Man 8M 61
Shalbourne Rd. M28: Walk 8K 57
Shaldon Dr. M40: Man 6C 80
Shalebrook Cl. M46: Ath 9J 55
Shalefield Gdns. M46: Ath 9J 55
Shalemere Ct. M46: Ath 9J 55
Shalewood Ct. M46: Ath 9J 55
Shalfleet Cl. BL2: Bolt 8M 23
Shambles, The WA16: Knut 7H 133
Shamrock Ct. M28: Walk 8J 57
Shandon Av. M22: Nor 7C 106
Shanklin Cl. M21: Cho H 8N 93
M34: Dent 9M 97
Shanklin Ho. M21: Cho H 8N 93
Shanklin Wlk. BL3: Bolt 7K 39
Shanklyn Av. M41: Urm 7C 92
Shanley Ct. OL9: Chad 3F 62
Shannon Cl. OL10: H'ood 1F 42
Shannon Rd. M22: Wyth 4D 116
Shap Av. WA15: Tim 2K 115
Shap Cres. M28: Walk 1N 75
Shap Dr. M28: Walk 9N 57
Shap Ga. WN5: Wig 4M 51
Shapwick Cl. M9: Man 2J 79
(off Coningsby Dr.)
Sharcott Cl. M16: Whall R 5E 94
Shardlow Cl. M40: Man 6J 79
(off Thornden Rd.)
Shared St. WN1: Wig 9M 9 (4G 53)
Shargate Cl. SK9: Wilm 5H 123
Sharman St. BL3: Bolt 7J 39
Sharnbrook Wlk. BL2: Bolt 3J 39
M8: Man 9D 60
Sharnford Cl. BL2: Bolt 6J 39
Sharnford Sq. M12: Man 3M 95
(off Bridgend Cl.)
SHARON 6G 65
Sharon Av. OL4: Gras 6G 65
Sharon Cl. OL7: A Lyne 9J 81
Sharon Sq. WN2: Bam 2J 71
SHARPLES 9E 22
Sharples Av. BL1: Bolt 7F 22
Sharples Community Leisure Cen. 8G 23
Sharples Dr. BL8: Bury 9F 24
Sharples Hall BL1: Bolt 7G 23
Sharples Hall Dr. BL1: Bolt 7G 22
Sharples Hall Fold BL1: Bolt 8G 22
Sharples Hall M. BL1: Bolt 7G 23
Sharples Hall St. OL4: O'ham 3A 64
Sharples Pk. BL1: Bolt 9E 22
Sharples St. SK4: Stoc 5C 108
Sharples Va. BL1: Bolt 1F 38
Sharples St. SK10: Macc 4G 130
Sharp St. BL8: Bury 9H 25
M4: Man 1K 5 (7G 78)
M24: Mid 3M 61
M25: Pres 7N 59
M28: Walk 8M 57
WN3: I Mak 5H 53
Sharratt's Path PR7: Char R 1C 18
Sharrington Dr. M23: Wyth 1L 115
Sharrow Wlk. M9: Man 3J 79
(off Broadwell Dr.)
SHARSTON 1D 116
Sharston Cres. WA16: Knut 7H 133
Sharston Grn. Bus. Pk.
M22: Shar 1E 116
Sharston Ind. Area M22: Shar . . . 9C 106
(not continuous)
Sharston Rd. M22: Shar 1C 116
Shaving La. M28: Walk 1L 75
SHAW 6M 45
Shaw, The SK13: Had 6B 100
Shaw Av. SK14: Hyde 9C 98
Shawbrook Av. M28: Wors 2J 75
Shawbrook Rd. M19: Man 2L 107
Shawbury Cl. BL6: Bla 3N 35
Shawbury Gro. M33: Sale 6F 104
Shawbury Rd. M23: Wyth 3A 116
Shawbury St. M24: Mid 4A 62
SHAWCLOUGH 2C 28
Shawclough Cl. OL12: Roch 2B 28
Shawclough Dr. OL12: Roch 2A 28
Shawclough Ri. OL12: Roch 3B 28
(off Shawclough Rd.)
Shawclough Rd. OL12: Roch 1A 28
Shawclough Trad. Est.
OL12: Roch 2B 28
Shawclough Way OL12: Roch 2A 28
Shawcroft Cl. OL2: Shaw 7L 45
Shawcroft Vw. BL1: Bolt 1J 39
Shaw & Crompton Stop (Metro) . . 6N 45
Shawcross Fold SK1: Stoc 1L 9
Shawcross La. M22: Nor 8E 106
Shawcross St. M6: Sal 9M 77
SK1: Stoc 5N 9 (8E 108)
SK14: Hyde 9C 98
Shawdene Rd. M22: Nor 8B 106
Shaw Dr. WA16: Knut 5J 133
SHAW EDGE 8L 45
Shawe Hall Av. M41: Urm 9A 92
Shawe Hall Cres. M41: Urm 9A 92
Shawe Rd. M41: Urm 7A 92
Shawes Dr. PR6: And 6M 19
Shawe Vw. M41: Urm 7A 92
SHAWFIELD 3L 27
Shawfield Cl. M14: Man 9F 94
Shawfield Ct. SK2: Stoc 2H 119
Shawfield Gro. OL12: Roch 3L 27
Shawfield La. OL12: Roch 4K 27
Shawfield Rd. SK13: Had 6B 100
Shawfields SK15: Stal 7G 82
Shawfold OL2: Shaw 5M 45
Shawford Cres. M40: Man 9A 62
Shawford Rd. M40: Man 9A 62
SHAWFORTH 1C 14
Shaw Ga. OL3: Upp 4N 65
Shawgreen Cl. M15: Man 3C 94
SHAW HALL 5J 65
SHAWHALL 4D 98
Shaw Hall M14: Man 5J 95
(off Daisy Bank Hall)
Shaw Hall Av. SK14: Hyde 4E 98
SHAW HALL BANK 6J 65
Shaw Hall Bank Rd. OL3: G'fld 6J 65
Shaw Hall Cl. OL3: G'fld 6J 65
Shaw Head Dr. M35: Fail 4D 80
SHAW HEATH
SK3 . . . . 9C 108
WA16 . . . . 5K 133
Shaw Heath SK2: Stoc 9D 108
SK3: Stoc 5J 9 (8C 108)
Shawheath Cl. M15: Man 3C 94
Shaw Heath Vw. WA16: Knut 5J 133
Shawhill Wlk. M40: Man 8K 79
(off Millhead Av.)
Shaw Ho. BL4: Farn 4L 57
(off Moorfield Chase)
M46: Ath 7M 55
(off Brooklands Av.)
OL2: Shaw 7M 45
Shaw La. OL16: Miln 4L 29
SK13: Had 7A 100
(not continuous)
Shawlea Av. M19: Man 2K 107
Shaw Lee OL3: Dig 8N 47
Shaw Lodge OL12: W'le 8G 15
(off Lodge St.)
Shaw Moor Av. SK15: Stal 9F 82
Shaw Rd. BL6: Hor 8D 20
OL1: O'ham 2L 63
OL2: O'ham 9J 45
OL16: Miln 1M 45
OL16: Roch 3F 44
SK4: Stoc 3N 107
Shaw Rd. Sth. SK3: Stoc 1C 118
Shaws OL3: Upp 4M 65
Shaws Fold OL4: Spri 4E 64
SK9: Sty 3E 122
SHAW SIDE 7M 45
Shaws La. OL3: Upp 3M 65
SK10: P'bury 6N 127
Shaw's Rd. WA14: Alt 3C 6 (3D 114)
Shaw St. BL3: Bolt 7F 38
BL4: Farn 1K 57
BL9: Bury 1A 42
M3: Man 1G 5 (7E 78)
OL1: O'ham 1E 8 (3K 63)
OL2: O'ham 8J 45
OL3: G'fld 5L 65
OL4: Spri 5D 64
OL6: A Lyne 7G 6
OL12: Roch 3F 28
SK11: Macc 4G 131
SK13: Glos 9E 100
SK14: Mot 5K 99
WA3: Cul 6G 89
WA11: Hay 3B 86
WN1: Wig 2F 52
WN4: A Mak 5E 70
Shaw Ter. SK16: Duk 9N 81
Shay Av. WA15: Haleb 6L 115
Shayfield Av. M22: Wyth 2C 116
OL9: Chad 4C 62
Shayfield Dr. M22: Wyth 1C 116
Shayfield Rd. M22: Wyth 2C 116
Shay La. WA15: Haleb 6J 115
Sheader Dr. M5: Sal 3J 77
Sheaf Fld. Wlk. M26: Rad 8G 41
Sheard Av. OL6: A Lyne 4A 82
Sheard Ct. OL2: Shaw 6M 45
Sheardhall Av. SK12: Dis 9H 121
Shearer Way M27: Pen 2K 77
Shearing Av. OL12: Roch 4L 27
Shearsby Cl. M15: Man 4D 94
Shearwater Av. M29: Ast 2B 74
Shearwater Dr. BL5: W'ton 5F 54
M28: Walk 8K 57
Shearwater Gdns. M30: Ecc 1A 92
Shearwater Ho. M19: Man 4J 107
Shearwater Rd. SK2: Stoc 2K 119
Sheaves Cl. WN2: Abr 3M 71
Sheddings, The BL3: Bolt 8H 39
Shed St. OL12: Whitw 5B 14
Sheen Gdns. M22: Wyth 7F 116
Sheepfoot La. M25: Pres 8C 60
OL1: O'ham 2H 63
Sheep Gap OL12: Roch 4N 27
Sheep Ga. Dr. BL8: Tot 8E 24
Sheep Hey BL0: Ram 5K 11
Sheep Ho. La. BL6: R'ton 3B 20
Sheep La. M28: Wors 2G 74
Sheerness St. M18: Man 4B 96
Sheffield Rd. SK13: Glos 8G 100
SK14: Hyde 5C 98
(not continuous)
Sheffield Row WA12: N Wil 9G 86
Sheffield St. M1: Man 6L 5 (1G 95)
SK4: Stoc 5C 108
Shefford Cres. WN3: Wins 9N 51
Sheiling Ct. WA14: Alt 4B 6 (3C 114)
Sheilings, The WA3: Low 1B 88
Shelbourne Av. BL1: Bolt 2C 38
Shelbourne M. SK10: Macc 4D 130
Shelburne Dr. WN2: Hin 7M 53
Shelden Cl. SK13: Gam 8N 99
(off Brassington Cres.)
Shelden Fold SK13: Gam 8N 99
(off Brassington Cres.)
Shelden M. SK13: Gam 8N 99
Shelden Pl. SK13: Gam 8N 99
(off Brassington Cres.)
SHELDERSLOW 4D 64
Shelderton Cl. M40: Man 3M 79
Sheldon Av. M41: Urm 7B 92
WN6: Stan 2B 34
Sheldon Cl. BL4: Farn 1J 57
M31: Part 5G 102
Sheldon Ct. OL7: A Lyne 5M 81
Sheldon Dr. SK11: Macc 8F 130
Sheldon Pl. SK10: Boll 5M 129
Sheldon Rd. SK7: H Gro 8J 119
SK12: Poy 4N 125
Sheldon St. M11: Man 8N 79
Sheldrake Cl. SK16: Duk 2B 98
Sheldrake Rd. WA14: B'ath 8B 104
Sheldwich Cl. WN7: Lei 7H 73
Shelfield OL11: Roch 4L 27
Shelfield Cl. OL11: Roch 4L 27
Shelfield La. OL11: Roch 4K 27
Shelford Av. M18: Man 5N 95
Shellbrook Gro. SK9: Wilm 5J 123
(off Rossenclough Rd.)
Shelley Av. M24: Mid 1N 61
Shelley Cl. PR7: Cop 5C 18
Shelley Ct. SK8: Chea H 6M 117
Shelley Dr. WN2: Abr 1L 71
WN5: Orr 5L 51
Shelley Gro. M43: Droy 8E 80
SK14: Hyde 4A 98
SK15: Mill 6H 83
Shelley Ri. SK16: Duk 2E 98
Shelley Rd. M25: Pres 8M 59
M27: Swin 2D 76
M38: Lit H 6H 57
OL1: O'ham 2N 63
OL9: Chad 8D 62
SK5: Stoc 8B 96
Shelley St. M40: Man 2A 80
WN7: Lei 3E 72
Shelley Wlk. BL1: Bolt 3E 38
(off Darley St.)
M46: Ath 6M 55
Shelley Way M34: Dent 9K 97
Shellingford Cl. WN6: She 5H 33
Shelmerdine Cl. SK14: Mot 7J 99
(off Chain Bar La.)
Shelmerdine Gdns. M6: Sal 6J 77
Shelton Av. M33: Sale 4D 104
Shenfield Wlk. M40: Man 7J 79
(off Farnborough Rd.)
Shenhurst Cl. SK9: Wilm 1D 126
Shentonfield Rd. M22: Shar 1D 116
Shenton Pk. Av. M33: Sale 6C 104
Shenton St. SK14: Hyde 5N 97
Shepherd Ct. OL16: Roch . . . 9G 8 (7F 28)
Shepherd Cross St. BL1: Bolt 3D 38
Shepherd Cross St. Ind. Est.
BL1: Bolt 2E 38
(off Shepherd Cross St.)
Shepherds Brow WA14: Bow 4A 114
Shepherds Cl. BL6: Bla 1M 35
BL8: G'mount 4F 24
Shepherd's Dr. BL6: Hor 1J 37
Shepherds Grn. OL3: G'fld 6N 65
Shepherd St. BL8: G'mount 5F 24
BL9: Bury 9M 7 (3M 41)
M9: Man 1K 79
OL2: O'ham 9J 45
(Crompton St.)
OL2: O'ham 8J 45
(Oldham Rd.)
OL10: H'ood 2H 43
OL11: Roch 4J 27
OL12: Roch 5D 28
Shepherds Way OL16: Miln 8K 29
Shepherd Wlk. M34: Dent 9K 97
Shepley Av. BL3: Bolt 7D 38
Shepley Cl. SK7: H Gro 7H 119
SK16: Duk 1A 98
(off Jeffreys Dr.)
Shepley Dr. SK7: H Gro 6H 119
Shepley Ho. SK7: H Gro 6J 119
Shepley Ind. Est. Nth. M34: Aud . . . 2L 97
Shepley Ind. Est. Sth. M34: Aud . . . 3L 97
Shepley La. SK6: Mar 4C 120
Shepley La. Ind. Est. SK6: Mar . . . 4C 120
Shepley Rd. M34: Aud 3K 97
Shepley St. M34: Aud 2K 97
M35: Fail 1E 80
OL4: Lees 5B 64
SK13: Glos 7G 101
SK13: Had 6A 100
SK14: Hyde 7B 98
SK15: Stal 8D 82
Shepton Av. WN2: P Bri 1K 71
Shepton Cl. BL1: Bolt 6E 22
Shepton Dr. M23: Wyth 5N 115
Shepway Ct. M30: Ecc 8B 76
Sheraton Cl. WN5: Orr 2M 51
Sheraton Rd. OL8: O'ham 7J 63
Sherborne Av. WN2: Hin 6C 54
Sherborne Cl. M26: Rad 7D 40
Sherborne Ho. M24: Mid 9M 43
Sherborne Rd. SK3: Stoc 9M 107
WN5: Orr 3L 51
Sherborne St. M3: Man 6E 78
M8: Man 6E 78
Sherborne St. Trad. Est.
M8: Man 5F 78
Sherborne St. W. M3: Sal 7D 78
Sherbourne Cl. OL8: O'ham 7N 63
SK8: Chea H 9N 117
Sherbourne Ct. M25: Pres 7N 59
Sherbourne Dr. OL10: H'ood 1F 42
Sherbourne Pl. WN3: I Mak 6H 53
Sherbourne Rd. BL1: Bolt 3B 38
M24: Mid 9M 43
M41: Urm 6E 92
SK11: Macc 5D 130
Sherbourne St. M25: Pres 7N 59
Sherbrooke Av. OL3: Upp 2M 65
Sherbrooke Cl. M33: Sale 5F 104
Sherbrooke Rd. SK12: Dis 9G 121
Sherbrook Ri. SK9: Wilm 8H 123
Sherdley Ct. M8: Man 1F 78
Sherdley Rd. M8: Man 1F 78
Sherford Cl. SK7: H Gro 5E 118
Sheridan Av. WA3: Low 2N 87
Sheridan Ct. M40: Man 5K 79
(off Ridgewood Av.)
Sheridan Way M34: Dent 9K 97
OL9: Chad 3C 62
Sheri Dr. WA12: N Wil 7G 87
Sheriffs Dr. M29: Tyld 1E 74
Sheriff St. BL2: Bolt 3J 39
OL12: Roch 6A 8 (4C 28)
(not continuous)
OL16: Miln 8L 29
Sheringham Dr. BL8: Bury 8K 25
M27: Swin 4F 76
SK14: Hyde 6D 98
Sheringham Pl. BL3: Bolt 7E 38
Sheringham Rd. M14: Man 1J 107
Sherlock Av. WA11: Hay 2B 86
Sherlock St. M14: Man 1J 107
Sherratt St. M4: Man 2L 5 (8G 79)
Sherrington St. M12: Man 6M 95
Sherway Dr. WA15: Tim 9J 105
Sherwell Rd. M9: Man 8G 61
Sherwin Way OL11: Roch 3B 44
Sherwood Av. M7: Sal 3A 78
M14: Man 9H 95
M26: Rad 4F 40
M29: Ast 4B 74
M33: Sale 3J 105
M43: Droy 8G 80
SK4: Stoc 7M 107
SK8: Chea H 5L 117
WN4: A Mak 6F 70
Sherwood Bus. Pk. OL11: Roch . . . 2B 44
Sherwood Cl. BL8: Tot 6F 24
M5: Sal 7K 77
OL6: A Lyne 3N 81
SK6: Mar 3C 120
Sherwood Cres. WN2: P Bri 9K 53
WN5: Wig 4A 52
Sherwood Dr. M27: Pen 3H 77
WN5: Wig 5A 52
WN8: Skel 9B 32
Sherwood Fold SK13: Char 1N 111
Sherwood Gro. WN5: Wig 4A 52
WN7: Lei 8K 73
Sherwood Ho. WN2: P Bri 9K 53
Sherwood M. OL6: A Lyne 6A 82
(off Board St.)
Sherwood Rd. M34: Dent 6F 96
SK6: Wood 3M 109
SK11: Macc 8H 131
Sherwood St. BL1: Bolt 1G 38
M14: Man 9H 95
OL1: O'ham 2H 63
OL11: Roch 2B 44
(off Queensway)
Sherwood Way OL2: Shaw 4J 45
Shetland Circ. M41: Urm 4C 92
Shetland Rd. M40: Man 7J 79
Shetland Way M26: Rad 7G 40
M41: Urm 4C 92
SHEVINGTON 6L 33
Shevington Gdns. M23: Wyth 7A 106
Shevington La. WN6: She, Stan 6L 33
SHEVINGTON MOOR 2L 33
Shevington Moor WN6: Stan 2L 33
SHEVINGTON VALE 5H 33
Shieldborn Dr. M9: Man 2J 79
Shield Cl. OL8: O'ham 4B 8 (5J 63)
Shield Dr. M28: Ward 2C 76
Shield St. SK3: Stoc 4J 9 (8C 108)
Shiel St. M28: Walk 8L 57
Shiers Dr. SK8: Chea 3K 117
Shiffnall St. BL2: Bolt 4L 7 (6H 39)
Shildon Cl. WN2: Wig 1J 53
Shilford Dr. M4: Man 1M 5 (7H 79)
Shillingford Rd. BL4: Farn 3J 57
M18: Man 7B 96
OL9: Chad 7E 62
Shillingstone Cl. BL2: Bolt 1N 39
Shillington Cl. M28: Walk 8G 56
Shiloh La. OL4: O'ham 1D 64
Shiloh Rd. SK6: Mel 2L 121
Shilton Gdns. BL3: Bolt 7F 38
(off Derby St.)
Shilton St. BL0: Ram 9H 11
Shilton Wlk. M40: Man 9B 62
(off Blandford Dr.)
Ship Canal Ho.
M15: Man 7D 4 (1D 94)
Shipgate BL1: Bolt 2L 7
Shipham Cl. WN7: Lei 2F 72
Shipla Cl. OL9: O'ham 1B 8 (4J 63)
Ship La. OL3: Del 7D 46
OL4: Del 6D 46
Shipley Av. M6: Sal 7J 77
Shipley Vw. M41: Urm 4N 91
Shipperbottom La. BL0: Ram 9K 11
Shippey St. M14: Man 1J 107
Shipston Cl. BL8: Bury 1H 41
Shipton St. BL1: Bolt 1C 38
Shirburn OL11: Roch 7C 28
Shirebrook Dr. M26: Rad 8H 41
SK13: Glos 8F 100
SHIREBROOK PARK 9H 101
Shireburn Av. BL2: Bolt 4K 39
Shiredale Cl. SK8: Chea H 3N 117
Shiredale Dr. M9: Man 3J 79
Shire Gdns. M26: Rad 8F 40
Shiregreen Av. M40: Man 5H 79
Shirehills M25: Pres 8N 59
Shireoak Rd. M20: Man 1J 107
Shires, The M26: Rad 7G 41
M43: Droy 7H 81
Shires Cl. WN2: Hin 7A 54
Shires Vw. OL5: Mos 1F 82
Shire Way SK13: Glos 6G 100
Shirewell Rd. WN5: Orr 6J 51
Shirley Av. M7: Sal 3N 77
M27: Pen 3J 77
M30: Ecc 1C 92
M32: Stre 6M 93
M34: Aud 1G 97
Shirley Av. M34: Dent 6D 96
OL9: Chad 9C 62
SK6: Mar 1B 120
SK8: H Grn 8H 117
SK14: Hyde 4A 98
Shirley Cl. SK7: H Gro 5G 118
Shirley Ct. M33: Sale 4J 105
Shirley Gro. SK3: Stoc 2C 118
Shirley Rd. M8: Man 3F 78
Shirleys Cl. SK10: P'bury 7E 128
Shirleys Dr. SK10: P'bury 7E 128
Shirley St. OL11: Roch 2A 44
Shoecroft Av. M34: Dent 6J 97
Shoemaker Gdns. WN2: Asp 7M 35
SHOLVER 8A 46
Sholver Hey La. OL1: O'ham 8A 46
Sholver Hill Cl. OL1: O'ham 8B 46
Sholver La. OL1: O'ham 8A 46
Shone Av. M22: Wyth 5E 116
SHORE 8K 15
Shore Av. OL2: Shaw 3N 45
Shorecliffe Ri. M26: Rad 1J 59
Shoreditch Cl. SK4: Stoc 3N 107
SHORE EDGE 4B 46
Shorefield Cl. OL16: Miln 6K 29
(off Silver Hill)
Shorefield Mt. BL7: Eger 5F 22
Shore Fold OL15: Lit 8K 15
Shoreham Cl. M16: Whall R 5D 94
Shoreham Wlk. OL9: Chad 5E 62
Shore Hill OL15: Lit 8N 15
Shore La. OL15: Lit 9N 15
Shore Lea OL15: Lit 8K 15
Shore Mt. OL15: Lit 8K 15
Shore Rd. OL15: Lit 8K 15
Shore St. OL1: O'ham 4L 63
OL16: Miln 7K 29
Shoreswood BL1: Bolt 8E 22
Shorland St. M27: Swin 3C 76
Shorrocks St. BL8: Bury 1F 40
Short Av. M43: Droy 1D 96
Short Cl. WA12: N Wil 6B 86
Shortcroft St. M15: Man . . . 8F 4 (2E 94)
Shortland Cres. M19: Man 5J 107
Shortland Pl. WN2: B'haw 2C 72
Shortlands Av. BL9: Bury 3M 41
Short St. M4: Man 4J 5 (9F 78)
M7: Sal 7D 78
M46: Ath 1A 74
OL10: H'ood 3G 43
SK4: Stoc 5B 108
SK7: H Gro 4H 119
SK11: Macc 4H 131
WA3: Gol 9L 71
WA11: Hay 3B 86
WA12: N Wil 6B 86
WN5: Wig 5M 51
Short St. E. SK4: Stoc 5C 108
Short Wlk. M31: Part 6F 102
Shortwood Cl. M40: Man 5M 79
(off Harmer Cl.)
Shottery Walks SK6: Bred 5K 109
Shotton Wlk. M14: Man 6G 95
(off Ellanby Cl.)
Shottwood Fold OL15: Lit 6N 15
Showcase Cinema
Belle Vue 4N 95
Shrewsbury Cl. WN2: Hin 5B 54
Shrewsbury Ct. M16: Old T 4C 94
Shrewsbury Gdns. SK8: Chea H . . 9A 118
Shrewsbury Rd. BL1: Bolt 4C 38
M25: Pres 8N 59
M33: Sale 6G 104
M43: Droy 8E 80
Shrewsbury St. M16: Old T 4B 94
OL4: O'ham 3N 63
SK13: Glos 8E 100
Shrewsbury Way M34: Dent 8L 97
(off Trowbridge Rd.)
Shrigley Cl. SK9: Wilm 5J 123
Shrigley Ct. SK10: Boll 5M 129
(off Church St.)
Shrigley Hall Golf Course 1N 129
Shrigley Ri. SK10: Boll 4N 129
Shrigley Rd. SK10: Boll, P Shr . . . 4M 129
SK10: P Shr 9M 125
SK12: Poy 3N 125
Shrigley Rd. Nth. SK12: Poy 3N 125
Shrigley Rd. Sth. SK10: Macc 4J 131
Shrivenham Wlk. M23: Wyth 9M 105
(off Pitfield Gdns.)
Shropshire Av. SK5: Stoc 2G 108
Shropshire Dr. SK13: Glos 9H 101
Shropshire Rd. M35: Fail 4E 80
Shropshire Sq. M12: Man 3L 95
(off St Benedict's Av.)
Shrowbridge Wlk. M12: Man 3M 95
(off Clowes St.)
Shrubbery, The BL6: Los 5L 37
(off Old Hall Clough)
Shrub St. BL3: Bolt 1D 56
Shudehill M4: Man 3H 5 (8F 78)
Shudehill Rd. M28: Wors 1H 75
Shudehill Stop (Metro) 2H 5 (8F 78)
Shurdington Rd. BL5: O Hul 6A 56
M46: Ath 6A 56
Shurmer St. BL3: Bolt 8D 38
Shutlingsloe Way SK10: Macc . . . 4E 130
Shutt La. OL3: Dob 1J 65
Shuttle Cl. OL5: Mos 9G 64
Shuttle Dr. OL10: H'ood 3G 42
Shuttle Hillock Rd. WN2: B'haw . . . 3B 72
Shuttle St. M26: Rad 2J 59
M29: Tyld 1A 74
M30: Ecc 8F 76
WN2: Hin 5A 54
SHUTTLEWORTH 6L 11
Shuttleworth Cl.
M16: Whall R 9D 94
Shutts La. SK15: Stal 1G 98
Siam St. M11: Man 1L 95
Sibley Av. WN4: A Mak 6G 70
Sibley Rd. SK4: Stoc 5N 107
Sibley St. M18: Man 4B 96
Siblies Wlk. M22: Wyth 4A 116
Sibson Cl. M21: Cho H 8N 93

Sibson Rd. M21: Cho H . . . 8N 93
M33: Sale . . . 4G 105
Sicklefield WN1: Wig . . . 7F 34
Sickle St. M2: Man . . . 4H 5 (9F 78)
OL4: O'ham . . . 4F 8 (6L 63)
Sidbrook St. WN2: Hin . . . 6M 53
Sidbury Rd. M21: Cho H . . . 9B 94
Sidcup Rd. M23: Wyth . . . 2M 115
Siddall St. M12: Man . . . 7M 95
M26: Rad . . . 8G 40
M34: Dent . . . 6K 97
OL1: O'ham . . . 3K 63
OL2: Shaw . . . 5M 45
OL10: H'ood . . . 4K 43
SIDDAL MOOR . . . 5J 43
Siddeley Dr. WA12: N Wil . . . 6C 86
Siddeley St. WN7: Lei . . . 5F 72
Siddington Av. M20: Man . . . 1F 106
SK3: Stoc . . . 1A 118
Siddington Rd. SK9: Hand . . . 1J 123
SK12: Poy . . . 4K 125
SIDDOW COMMON . . . 7J 73
Siddow Comn. WN7: Lei . . . 7J 73
(not continuous)
Side Av. WA14: Bow . . . 6C 114
Sidebotham St. SK6: Bred . . . 4K 109
Sidebottom St. M43: Droy . . . 9D 80
OL4: O'ham . . . 3B 64
SK15: Stal . . . 8D 82
SIDE OF THE MOOR . . . 8M 23
Side St. M11: Man . . . 8N 79
OL8: O'ham . . . 9G 62
Sidford Cl. BL3: Bolt . . . 7L 39
Sidings, The BL7: Tur . . . 1K 23
BL9: Bury . . . 9K 7
M28: Wors . . . 5A 76
Sidlaw Cl. OL8: O'ham . . . 9K 63
Sidley Av. M9: Man . . . 7L 61
Sidley Pl. *SK14: Hyde* . . . *6C 98*
(off St John's Dr.)
Sidley St. SK14: Hyde . . . 6C 98
Sidmouth Av. M41: Urm . . . 6M 91
Sidmouth Dr. M9: Man . . . 9J 61
Sidmouth Gro.
SK8: Chea H . . . 8L 117
WN3: Wig . . . 8B 52
Sidmouth Rd. M33: Sale . . . 3D 104
Sidmouth St. M34: Aud . . . 2H 97
(not continuous)
OL9: O'ham . . . 6G 62
Sidney Rd. M9: Man . . . 1J 79
Sidney St. BL3: Bolt . . . 7G 39
M1: Man . . . 9J 5 (2F 94)
M3: Man . . . 5F 4 (9E 78)
M3: Sal . . . 3C 4 (8C 78)
OL1: O'ham . . . 2L 63
WN7: Lei . . . 5J 73
Sidwell Wlk. *M4: Man* . . . *9J 79*
(off Merrill St.)
Siebers Bank OL12: Roch . . . 3B 28
Siemens Rd. M20: Man . . . 3D 106
M44: Cad, Irl . . . 3F 102
Siemens St. BL6: Hor . . . 2E 36
Sienna Cl. M44: Irl . . . 2F 102
Sienna Ct. OL9: Chad . . . 3E 62
Sighthill Wlk. *M9: Man* . . . *2J 79*
(off Coningsby Dr.)
Signal Cl. M30: Ecc . . . 8B 76
Signal Dr. M40: Man . . . 4J 79
Signet Wlk. M8: Man . . . 5G 78
Silas St. OL6: A Lyne . . . 5A 82
Silburn Way M24: Mid . . . 4H 61
Silbury Wlk. *M8: Man* . . . *5E 78*
(off Barrow Hill Rd.)
Silchester Dr. M40: Man . . . 4J 79
Silchester Wlk. OL1: O'ham . . . 1D 8
Silchester Way BL2: Bolt . . . 3M 39
Silcock St. WA3: Gol . . . 1K 87
Silfield Cl. M11: Man . . . 9K 79
Silkhey Gro. M28: Walk . . . 1L 75
Silkin Cl. M13: Man . . . 9K 5
Silkin Ct. M13: Man . . . 9K 5
Silk Mill *SK11: Macc* . . . *6H 131*
(off Mill Rd.)
SK12: Poy . . . 2F 124
Silk Mill St. WA16: Knut . . . 6G 132
Silk Mill Way M24: Mid . . . 3L 61
Silk Rd., The SK10: Boll, Macc . . . 6G 129
SK11: Macc . . . 4H 131
Silk Rd. Bus. Pk. SK10: Macc . . . 1J 131
Silk Rd. Retail Pk. SK10: Macc . . . 1J 131
Silk St. BL5: W'ton . . . 2G 55
M3: Sal . . . 1B 4 (7C 78)
M4: Man . . . 2L 5 (8H 79)
M24: Mid . . . 3L 61
M30: Ecc . . . 9F 76
M40: Man . . . 4A 80
OL11: Roch . . . 9A 28
SK13: Glos . . . 8G 100
WN7: Lei . . . 5H 73
Sillitoe Dr. WN6: Wig . . . 2D 52
Silsbury Gro. WN6: Stan . . . 4D 34
Silsden Av. M9: Man . . . 6G 61
WA3: Low . . . 1D 88
Silsden Wlk. M7: Sal . . . 2M 77
Silton St. M9: Man . . . 3L 79
Silvamere Cl. M6: Sal . . . 7L 77
Silvan Ct. SK10: Macc . . . 3F 130
Silver Birch Cl. BL6: Los . . . 3J 37
Silverbirch Cl. M33: Sale . . . 6D 104
Silver Birches M34: Dent . . . 8M 97
Silver Birch Gro. M27: Pen . . . 4H 77
WN4: A Mak . . . 5D 70
Silver Birch M. SK16: Duk . . . 2B 98
Silverbirch Way M35: Fail . . . 3D 80
Silver Blades Ice Rink
Altrincham . . . 3E 6 (3E 114)
Silver Cl. SK16: Duk . . . 2M 97
Silver Ct. M45: Whitef . . . 2L 59
Silvercroft St. M15: Man . . . 8D 4 (2D 94)
Silverdale M27: Clif . . . 9G 59
WA14: Alt . . . 3A 6 (3C 114)
WN1: Wig . . . 1F 52
Silverdale Av. M25: Pres . . . 9D 60
M34: Dent . . . 7L 97
M38: Lit H . . . 6H 57
Silverdale Av. M44: Irl . . . 5J 91
OL9: Chad . . . 5E 62
WN2: I Mak . . . 3K 53
Silverdale Cl. BL9: Bury . . . 4N 41
SK6: H Lan . . . 7B 120
Silverdale Ct. WN1: Wig . . . 8L 9
Silverdale Dr. OL4: Lees . . . 5C 64
SK9: Wilm . . . 1F 126
Silverdale Gro. WA11: St H . . . 9E 68
Silverdale Rd. BL1: Bolt . . . 5D 38
BL4: Farn . . . 2H 57
M21: Cho H . . . 8B 94
SK4: Stoc . . . 4A 108
SK8: Gat . . . 3G 117
WA12: N Wil . . . 5E 86
WN2: Hin . . . 6B 54
WN5: Orr . . . 4M 51
Silverdale St. M11: Man . . . 2D 96
Silver Hill OL16: Miln . . . 6K 29
Silver Hill Rd. SK14: Hyde . . . 8B 98
Silver Jubilee Wlk. M4: Man . . . 3K 5
Silverlace Av. M11: Man . . . 2C 96
Silverlea Dr. M9: Man . . . 9H 61
Silvermere OL6: A Lyne . . . 4B 82
Silvermere Cl. BL0: Ram . . . 9H 11
Silver Springs SK14: Hyde . . . 9C 98
Silverstone Dr. M40: Man . . . 6B 80
Silver St. BL0: Ram . . . 8J 11
BL9: Bury . . . 8K 7 (2L 41)
M1: Man . . . 6H 5
(Abingdon St.)
M1: Man . . . 5J 5 (9F 78)
(Minshull St.)
M44: Irl . . . 5J 91
M45: Whitef . . . 2L 59
OL1: O'ham . . . 3C 8 (5J 63)
SK10: Boll . . . 5M 129
WN2: P Bri . . . 9K 53
Silver Ter. WN1: Wig . . . 9L 9 (3G 52)
Silverthorne Cl. SK15: Stal . . . 9D 82
Silverton Cl. SK14: Hat . . . 7H 99
(not continuous)
Silverton Gro. BL1: Bolt . . . 9G 22
M24: Mid . . . 8J 43
Silverton Ho. *M6: Sal* . . . *7G 77*
(off Devon Cl.)
Silverwell La. BL1: Bolt . . . 3L 7 (5G 39)
Silverwell St. BL1: Bolt . . . 3L 7 (5G 39)
BL6: Hor . . . 9D 20
M40: Man . . . 5B 80
Silverwell Yd. BL1: Bolt . . . 3L 7
Silverwood OL9: Chad . . . 4C 62
Silverwood Av. M21: Cho H . . . 9A 94
Silvester St. BL6: Bla . . . 2N 35
Silvine Wlk. M40: Man . . . 6J 79
Silvington Way WN2: Asp . . . 1K 53
Simeon St. M4: Man . . . 1K 5 (7G 78)
OL16: Miln . . . 7K 29
Simfield Cl. WN6: Stan . . . 3A 34
SIMISTER . . . 3D 60
Simister Dr. BL9: Bury . . . 1N 59
Simister Grn. M25: Pres . . . 3D 60
Simister La. M24: Mid . . . 2F 60
M25: Pres . . . 3C 60
Simister Rd. M35: Fail . . . 3D 80
Simister St. M9: Man . . . 2K 79
Simkin Way OL8: O'ham . . . 1K 81
SIMMONDLEY . . . 9C 100
Simmondley Gro. SK13: Glos . . . 9C 100
Simmondley La. SK13: Glos . . . 9C 100
Simmondley New Rd.
SK13: Glos . . . 9C 100
SIMMONDLEY VILLAGE . . . 9C 100
Simmons Ct. M16: Whall R . . . 6D 94
Simms Cl. BL0: Ram . . . 9G 11
M3: Sal . . . 3B 4 (8C 78)
SIMM'S LANE END . . . 5M 69
Simm's St. WN2: Asp . . . 8N 35
Simms Yd. WN2: Asp . . . 8A 36
Simonbury Cl. BL8: Bury . . . 2F 40
Simon Freeman Cl. M19: Man . . . 1A 108
Simon Ho. SK4: Stoc . . . 2A 108
Simon La. M24: Mid . . . 1F 60
Simons Cl. M33: Sale . . . 5G 105
SK13: Glos . . . 9C 100
Simons Wlk. SK13: Glos . . . 9C 100
Simonsway M22: Wyth . . . 4A 116
M23: Wyth . . . 4A 116
Simpkin St. WN2: Abr . . . 1L 71
Simpson Av. M27: Clif . . . 9J 59
SIMPSON CLOUGH . . . 8H 27
Simpson Gro. M28: Wors . . . 4H 75
Simpson Hill Cl. OL10: H'ood . . . 1L 43
Simpson La. SK10: P Shr . . . 7N 125
Simpson Rd. M28: Wors . . . 4H 75
Simpsons Ct. *SK11: Macc* . . . *4G 130*
(off Gt. King St.)
Simpsons Pl. *OL12: Roch* . . . *4D 28*
(off Victoria St.)
Simpson Sq. OL9: Chad . . . 8G 62
Simpson St. M4: Man . . . 1J 5 (7F 78)
M11: Man . . . 9M 79
OL9: Chad . . . 7F 62
SK9: Wilm . . . 8E 122
SK14: Hyde . . . 7A 98
Sinclair Av. M8: Man . . . 1E 78
Sinclair Pl. WN5: Wig . . . 3B 52
Sinclair St. OL11: Roch . . . 1B 44
SINDERLAND GREEN . . . 7K 103
Sinderland La. WA14: D Mas . . . 8J 103
Sinderland Rd. M31: Part . . . 4K 103
WA14: B'ath, D Mas . . . 7N 103
Sindsley Ct. *M27: Ward* . . . *1D 76*
(off Moss La.)
Sindsley Gro. BL3: Bolt . . . 9F 38
Sindsley Rd. M27: Ward . . . 9D 58
Singapore Av. M90: Man A . . . 7N 115
Singleton Av. BL2: Bolt . . . 5M 39
BL6: Hor . . . 8E 20
Singleton Cl. M7: Sal . . . 1B 78
Singleton Gro. BL5: W'ton . . . 3K 55
Singleton Lodge *M7: Sal* . . . *1C 78*
(off Cavendish Rd.)
Singleton Rd. M7: Sal . . . 1B 78
SK4: Stoc . . . 4N 107
Singleton St. M26: Rad . . . 8D 40
Sion St. M26: Rad . . . 1E 58
Sir Charles Groves Hall
M15: Man . . . *3F 94*
(off Booth St. W.)
Sirdar St. M11: Man . . . 1D 96
Sir Isaac Newton Way
OL16: Miln, Roch . . . 8G 28
Sirius Pl. M7: Sal . . . 7C 78
Sir Matt Busby Way M16: Old T . . . 4M 93
Sir Richard Fairey Rd.
SK4: Stoc . . . 2M 107
Sir Robert Thomas Ct. M9: Man . . . 2J 79
Sir Williams Ct. M23: Wyth . . . 1A 116
Siskin Cl. WA12: N Wil . . . 6F 86
WN7: Lei . . . 5K 73
Siskin Rd. SK2: Stoc . . . 2K 119
Sisley Cl. M7: Sal . . . 2A 78
Sisson St. M35: Fail . . . 3D 80
Sisters St. M43: Droy . . . 1E 96
Sittingbourne Rd. WN1: Wig . . . 8F 34
Sixpools Gro. M28: Wors . . . 2K 75
Sixth Av. BL1: Bolt . . . 5C 38
BL3: Lit L . . . 8N 39
BL9: Bury . . . 9C 26
OL8: O'ham . . . 1G 81
Sixth St. M17: T Pk . . . 4K 93
Size Ho. Pl. WN7: Lei . . . 6J 73
Size St. OL12: Whitw . . . 5B 14
SK14 Ind. Pk. SK14: Hyde . . . 4N 97
SKAGEN . . . 3F 38
Skaife Rd. M33: Sale . . . 4L 105
Skarratt Cl. M12: Man . . . 3L 95
Skegness Cl. BL8: Bury . . . 8K 25
SKELLORN GREEN . . . 6J 125
Skellorn Grn. La. SK10: Adl . . . 6J 125
SKELMERSDALE . . . 2A 50
Skelmersdale Sports Cen. . . . 4A 50
Skelton Gro. BL2: Bolt . . . 4N 39
M13: Man . . . 7L 95
Skelton Rd. M32: Stre . . . 6K 93
WA14: Tim . . . 9E 104
Skelton St. WN4: A Mak . . . 4C 70
Skelwith Av. BL3: Bolt . . . 1G 57
Skelwith Cl. M41: Urm . . . 5A 92
Skerry Cl. M13: Man . . . 9L 5 (2G 95)
Skerton Rd. M16: Old T . . . 4A 94
Skiddaw Cl. M24: Mid . . . 9J 43
Skiddaw Pl. WN5: Wig . . . 5N 51
Skilgate Wlk. *M40: Man* . . . *4A 80*
(off Queensferry St.)
Skip Pl. M3: Man . . . 1H 5 (7F 78)
Skipton Av. M40: Man . . . 1B 80
OL9: Chad . . . 2D 62
WN2: Hin . . . 7C 54
Skipton Cl. BL8: Bury . . . 2F 40
SK5: Stoc . . . 9C 96
SK7: H Gro . . . 7H 119
Skipton Dr. M41: Urm . . . 4N 91
Skipton St. BL2: Bolt . . . 4K 39
OL8: O'ham . . . 7M 63
Skipton Wlk. *BL2: Bolt* . . . *4K 39*
(off Skipton St.)
Skitters Gro. WN4: A Mak . . . 6B 70
Skull Ho. La. WN6: App B . . . 3G 33
Skull Ho. M. WN6: App B . . . 4G 33
Skye Cl. OL10: H'ood . . . 3E 42
Skye Rd. M41: Urm . . . 4D 92
Skyes Cres. WN3: Wins . . . 1N 69
Skye Wlk. M23: Wyth . . . 3N 115
SLACKCOTE . . . 5F 46
Slackcote La. OL3: Del . . . 5F 46
Slackey Brow BL4: Kea . . . 5C 58
Slackey Fold WN2: Hin . . . 1D 72
Slack Fold La. BL3: Bolt . . . 1D 56
BL4: Farn . . . 1D 56
Slack Ga. OL12: Whitw . . . 6C 14
OL12: W'le . . . 6C 14
Slackgate La. OL3: Dens . . . 3G 47
Slack Hall OL4: Aus . . . 3C 64
Slack La. BL2: Bolt . . . 6L 23
BL5: W'ton . . . 1H 55
BL8: Aff . . . 6A 24
M27: Pen . . . 1G 77
OL3: Del . . . 5F 46
Slack Rd. M9: Man . . . 1H 79
Slack's La. PR6: H Char . . . 3L 19
Slack St. OL16: Roch . . . 7D 8 (6E 28)
SK11: Macc . . . 7J 131
SK14: Hyde . . . 5C 98
Slade Gro. M13: Man . . . 6L 95
Slade Hall Rd. M12: Man . . . 7M 95
Slade La. M13: Man . . . 8L 95
M19: Man . . . 9L 95
SK10: O Ald . . . 9K 127
WA16: Mob . . . 1M 133
Slade Mt. M19: Man . . . 9L 95
Sladen St. OL12: Roch . . . 4D 28
Slades La. OL3: Upp . . . 2A 66
Slade St. BL3: Lit L . . . 9A 40
Slades Vw. Cl. OL3: Dig . . . 7M 47
Slag La. WA3: Low . . . 1N 87
Slaidburn Av. BL2: Bolt . . . 6N 39
Slaidburn Cl. OL16: Miln . . . 8K 29
WN3: Wig . . . 8D 52
Slaidburn Cres. WA3: Gol . . . 8J 71
Slaidburn Dr. BL8: Bury . . . 1E 40
Slaithwaite Dr. M11: Man . . . 8A 80
Slant Cl. SK13: Glos . . . 9F 100
Slateacre Rd. SK14: Hyde . . . 1C 110
Slatelands Av. SK13: Glos . . . 9D 100
Slatelands Rd. SK13: Glos . . . 9D 100
Slate La. M34: A Lyne . . . 1J 97
M34: Aud . . . 1G 96
Slater Av. BL6: Hor . . . 9E 20
Slaterfield BL3: Bolt . . . 7F 38
Slater Ho. M5: Sal . . . 8A 4 (2B 94)
Slater La. BL1: Bolt . . . 3H 39
Slater's Nook BL5: W'ton . . . 2G 55
Slater St. BL1: Bolt . . . 4G 38
BL4: Farn . . . 3L 57
M30: Ecc . . . 8B 76
M35: Fail . . . 1D 80
OL8: O'ham . . . 4B 8
OL9: O'ham . . . 3B 8
SK11: Macc . . . 6G 130
Slater St. Nth. WN7: Lei . . . 5F 72
Slater Way SK14: Mot . . . 7J 99
Slate Wharf M15: Man . . . 7C 4 (1C 94)
SLATTOCKS . . . 6B 44
Slattocks Link Rd. M24: Mid . . . 7B 44
Slaunt Bank OL12: Roch . . . 3J 27
Slawson Way OL10: H'ood . . . 1L 43
Sleaford Cl. BL8: Bury . . . 8K 25
M40: Man . . . 7J 79
Sledbrook St. WN5: Wig . . . 6N 51
Sleddale Cl. SK2: Stoc . . . 2H 119
Sledmere Cl. BL1: Bolt . . . 2G 38
M11: Man . . . 9M 79
Sledmoor Rd. M23: Wyth . . . 7M 105
Slimbridge Cl. BL2: Bolt . . . 3A 40
Sloane Av. OL4: Lees . . . 3B 64
Sloane St. BL3: Bolt . . . 9C 38
OL6: A Lyne . . . 7F 6 (7N 81)
Slough Ind. Est.
M5: Sal . . . 7A 4 (1B 94)
SMALLBRIDGE . . . 2G 29
Smallbridge Cl. M28: Wors . . . 2K 75
Smallbridge Ind. Pk.
OL16: Roch . . . 3G 28
Smallbrook La. WN7: Lei . . . 8G 54
Smallbrook Rd. OL2: Shaw . . . 2N 45
Smalldale Av. M16: Whall R . . . 6E 94
Smalley St. OL11: Roch . . . 2A 44
WN6: Stan . . . 3B 34
Smallfield Dr. M9: Man . . . 2J 79
Small La. WA16: Mob . . . 1N 133
Smallridge Cl. M40: Man . . . 7J 79
SMALLSHAW . . . 5N 81
Smallshaw Cl. WN4: A Mak . . . 8D 70
Smallshaw Fold OL6: A Lyne . . . 5M 81
Smallshaw La. OL6: A Lyne . . . 5N 81
Smallshaw Rd. OL12: Roch . . . 1M 27
Smallshaw Sq. OL6: A Lyne . . . 5M 81
Smallwood St. M40: Man . . . 4A 80
Smart St. M12: Man . . . 6M 95
Smeaton Cl. M32: Stre . . . 7L 93
Smeaton St. BL6: Hor . . . 2E 36
M8: Man . . . 4H 79
SMEDLEY . . . 4G 79
Smedley Av. BL3: Bolt . . . 9H 39
M8: Man . . . 4G 79
Smedley La. M8: Man . . . 4G 78
Smedley Pl. SK13: Glos . . . 7G 101
Smedley Rd. M8: Man . . . 4G 79
Smedley St. M8: Man . . . 4F 78
Smethurst Ct. *BL3: Bolt* . . . *1C 56*
(off Smethurst La.)
Smethurst Hall Pk. WN5: Bil . . . 9G 51
Smethurst Hall Rd. BL9: Bury . . . 9D 26
Smethurst La. BL3: Bolt, Farn . . . 1C 56
BL4: Farn . . . 1C 56
WN5: Wig . . . 6N 51
Smethurst Rd. WN5: Bil . . . 9F 50
Smethurst St. BL8: Bury . . . 9H 25
M9: Man . . . 1J 79
M24: Mid . . . 4B 62
OL10: H'ood . . . 2G 43
Smith Av. WN5: Orr . . . 3M 51
Smith Brow BL6: Bla . . . 1M 35
Smith Farm Cl. OL4: Aus . . . 3C 64
Smithfield Bldgs. M4: Man . . . 4J 5
Smithfield Ent. Est. *M11: Man* . . . *2B 96*
(off Press St.)
Smithfold La. M28: Walk . . . 8H 57
Smith Hill OL16: Miln . . . 7K 29
Smithies Av. M24: Mid . . . 1M 61
Smithies St. OL10: H'ood . . . 2K 43
Smithills Cft. Rd. BL1: Bolt . . . 1B 38
SMITHILLS DEAN . . . 7N 21
Smithills Dean Rd. BL1: Bolt . . . 7B 22
Smithills Dr. BL1: Bolt . . . 2A 38
Smithill's Hall . . . 9C 22
Smithills Hall Cl. BL0: Ram . . . 9H 11
Smithills Hall Country Pk. . . . 8C 22
Smithills Open Farm . . . 8D 22
Smith La. BL7: Eger . . . 4G 22
WA16: Mob . . . 1M 133
Smith's La. WN2: Hin . . . 2C 72
Smiths Lawn SK9: Wilm . . . 9F 122
Smith's Pl. M46: Ath . . . 8M 55
Smith's Rd. BL3: Bolt . . . 9L 39
Smiths Ter. SK11: Macc . . . 6J 131
Smith St. BL0: Ram . . . 9H 11
BL9: Bury . . . 9N 25
M16: Old T . . . 3B 94
M28: Walk . . . 8L 57
M34: Dent . . . 7K 97
M46: Ath . . . 8L 55
OL4: Lees . . . 3B 64
OL5: Mos . . . 9E 64
OL7: A Lyne . . . 9K 81
OL10: H'ood . . . 2J 43
OL15: Lit . . . *9M 15*
(off Barehill St.)
OL16: Roch . . . 7D 8 (6D 28)
PR7: Adl . . . 7J 19
SK8: Chea . . . 1L 117
SK11: Macc . . . 6H 131
SK14: Hyde . . . 4A 98
SK16: Duk . . . 1L 97
WN2: Asp . . . 7M 35
WN7: Lei . . . 5J 73
Smithwood Av. WN2: Hin . . . 5B 54
SMITHY BRIDGE . . . 2K 29
Smithy Bridge (Park & Ride) . . . 2K 29
Smithy Bri. Rd. OL15: Lit . . . 1J 29
OL16: Lit . . . 1J 29
Smithy Bridge Station (Rail) . . . 2K 29
Smithy Brook Rd. WN3: Wig . . . 7B 52
SMITHY BROW . . . 9B 88
Smithy Brow SK10: Boll . . . 5N 129
WA3: Cro . . . 9B 88
Smithy Cl. SK13: Glos . . . 8F 100
Smithy Ct. SK6: Mar . . . 1C 120
WN3: Wig . . . 7B 52
Smithy Cft. BL7: Bro X . . . 5G 23
Smithy Fld. OL15: Lit . . . 8L 15
Smithy Fold OL12: Roch . . . 4N 27
SK13: Glos . . . 8F 100
Smithy Fold Rd. SK14: Hyde . . . 8B 98
Smithy Glen Dr. WN5: Bil . . . 7J 51
SMITHY GREEN . . . 8M 117
Smithy Grn. OL16: Miln . . . 9B 30
SK6: Wood . . . 3M 109
SK8: Chea H . . . 7M 117
WN2: I Mak . . . 4J 53
Smithy Gro. OL6: A Lyne . . . 6N 81
Smithy Hill BL3: Bolt . . . 8B 38
Smithy La. M3: Man . . . 4F 4 (9E 78)
M31: Part . . . 5G 103
OL3: Upp . . . 3L 65
SK6: Mar B . . . 7J 111
SK10: Mot S A . . . 3A 128
SK14: Hyde . . . 8B 98
WA3: Cro . . . 9C 88
WA14: D Mas . . . 4L 113
Smithy Nook OL15: Lit . . . 5N 15
Smithy St. BL0: Ram . . . 8J 11
BL5: W'ton . . . 9G 37
SK7: H Gro . . . 4H 119
WN7: Lei . . . 6H 73
Smithy Yd. *OL3: Upp* . . . *3L 65*
(off Smithy La.)
Smock La. WN4: Gars . . . 6N 69
Smyrna St. M5: Sal . . . 9L 77
M26: Rad . . . 8F 40
OL4: O'ham . . . 5N 63
OL10: H'ood . . . 3H 43
Smyrna Wlk. *M26: Rad* . . . *8F 40*
(off Smyrna St.)
Snake Pass SK13: Glos . . . 8K 101
Snake Rd. SK13: Glos . . . 9K 101
Snapebrook Gro. *SK9: Wilm* . . . *5K 123*
(off Colshaw Dr.)
Snape Rd. SK10: Macc . . . 2J 131
Snape St. M26: Rad . . . 6F 40
(not continuous)
Snell St. M4: Man . . . 9J 79
Snipe Av. OL11: Roch . . . 6L 27
Snipe Cl. SK12: Poy . . . 2E 124
Snipe Retail Pk. OL7: A Lyne . . . 1H 97
Snipe Rd. OL8: O'ham . . . 9M 63
Snipe St. BL3: Bolt . . . 7G 39
Snipeway OL7: A Lyne . . . 1H 97
Snowberry Wlk. *M31: Part* . . . *5F 102*
(off Wood La.)
Snowden Av. M41: Urm . . . 9B 92
WN3: Wig . . . 7C 52
Snowden St. BL1: Bolt . . . 1H 7 (4F 38)
OL8: O'ham . . . 7K 63
OL10: H'ood . . . 4K 43
Snowden Wlk. *M40: Man* . . . *9A 62*
(off Pleasington Dr.)
Snowdon Dr. BL6: Hor . . . 8E 20
SK8: Chea H . . . 5K 117
Snowdon Rd. M30: Ecc . . . 7G 76
Snowdon St. OL11: Roch . . . 2E 44
Snowdrop Wlk. *M7: Sal* . . . *4C 78*
(off Bury New Rd.)
Snow Hill SK11: Macc . . . 6J 131
Snow Hill Rd. BL3: Bolt . . . 7L 39
Snowshill Dr. WN3: Wig . . . 7N 51
Snydale Cl. BL5: W'ton . . . 1J 55
Snydale Way BL3: Bolt, W'ton . . . 2L 55
Soane Cl. WN4: A Mak . . . 7G 71
Soapstone Way M44: Irl . . . 9H 91
Soap St. M4: Man . . . 3J 5
Soccer Village . . . 5K 29
Society St. OL2: Shaw . . . 5M 45
Sofa St. BL1: Bolt . . . 3C 38
Soham Cl. WN2: Hin . . . 7A 54
Soho St. BL3: Bolt . . . 4K 7 (6G 38)
OL4: O'ham . . . 4M 63
WN5: Wig . . . 4C 52
Solent Av. M8: Man . . . 9F 60
Solent Dr. BL3: Bolt . . . 7K 39
Sole St. WN1: Wig . . . 5N 9 (2H 53)
Solness St. BL9: Bury . . . 7M 25
Soloman Rd. WA14: W Tim . . . 7C 104
Solway Cl. BL3: Bolt . . . 9E 38
M27: Clif . . . 7E 58
WN4: A Mak . . . 6D 70
Solway Rd. M22: Wyth . . . 3D 116
Somerby Dr. M22: Wyth . . . 6B 116
Somerdale Av. BL1: Bolt . . . 5B 38
Somerfield Rd. M9: Man . . . 1J 79
Somerford Av. M20: Man . . . 9F 94
Somerford Rd. SK5: Stoc . . . 7D 96
Somerford Way *SK9: Hand* . . . *1J 123*
(off Spath La.)
Somersby Ct. SK7: Bram . . . 6C 118
Somersby Dr. BL7: Bro X . . . 5G 23
Somersby St. OL8: O'ham . . . 7J 63
Somersby Wlk. *BL3: Bolt* . . . *7G 38*
(off Hallington Cl.)
Somerset Av. M29: Tyld . . . 8A 56
OL2: Shaw . . . 5K 45
Somerset Cl. M44: Cad . . . 2E 102
SK5: Stoc . . . 4G 109
Somerset Dr. BL9: Bury . . . 4M 41
Somerset Gro. OL11: Roch . . . 5M 27
Somerset Ho. OL7: A Lyne . . . 5K 81
Somerset Pl. M33: Sale . . . 2H 105
Somerset Rd. BL1: Bolt . . . 4C 38
M30: Ecc . . . 6G 76
M35: Fail . . . 4C 80
M43: Droy . . . 7D 80
M46: Ath . . . 6K 55
WA14: Alt . . . 1D 114
WN5: Wig . . . 5N 51
Somerset St. OL4: O'ham . . . 5N 63
Somers Rd. SK5: Stoc . . . 8D 96
Somers Wlk. M9: Man . . . 8G 60
Somerton Av. M22: Wyth . . . 4B 116
M33: Sale . . . 5J 105
Somerton Cl. SK11: Macc . . . 5D 130
WN6: Stan . . . 3A 34
Somerton Ct. M9: Man . . . 8M 61
Somerton Rd. BL2: Bolt . . . 6N 39
SK11: Macc . . . 6D 130
Somerville Gdns. WA15: Tim . . . 9F 104
Somerville Rd. WN1: Wig . . . 8F 34
Somerville Sq. BL1: Bolt . . . 1D 38
Somerville St. BL1: Bolt . . . 1D 38
Somerwood Wlk. *M12: Man* . . . *3L 95*
(off Kelsall St.)
Sommerville Ct. *M7: Sal* . . . *2C 78*
(off Park La.)

Sonning Dr. BL3: Bolt 1B **56**
Sonning Wlk. M8: Man 4G **78**
Sopwith Dr. M14: Man 8F **94**
Sorby Rd. M44: Irl 1G **103**
Sorrel Bank M6: Sal 6M **77**
SK5: Stoc 8E **96**
Sorrel Dr. OL15: Lit 8K **15**
Sorrel St. M15: Man 9D **4** (3D **94**)
Sorrel Way OL4: O'ham 1B **64**
Sorton St. M1: Man 8J **5** (2F **94**)
SOSS MOSS 7C **126**
Soss Moss La. SK10: N Ald 7C **126**
Souchay Ct. *M20: Man 4G **106***
(off Clothorn Rd.)
Soudan Rd. SK2: Stoc 1E **118**
Soudan St. M24: Mid 2A **62**
Sougher's La. WN4: A Mak 4B **70**
Sound, The OL3: Del 8J **47**
SOURACRE 6D **82**
Souracre Fold SK15: H'rod 7E **82**
Sth. Acre Dr. SK11: Macc 5L **131**
Southacre Dr. SK9: Hand 3J **123**
Southall St. M3: Man 7E **78**
Southampton Cl. M7: Sal 5C **78**
Southam St. M7: Sal 3E **78**
South Av. BL4: Kea 5N **57**
M19: Man 1L **107**
M27: Swin 5D **76**
M45: Whitef 2L **59**
OL3: G'fld 5L **65**
OL10: H'ood 2G **42**
WN7: Lei 6B **72**
(North Av.)
WN7: Lei 7L **73**
(West Av.)
South Bk. Rock BL9: Bury 7K **7**
(not continuous)
Sth. Bank Cl. SK9: A Edg 3G **126**
Southbank Gdns. BL1: Bolt 2A **38**
Sth. Bank Rd. BL9: Bury 9J **7** (3L **41**)
Southbank Rd. M19: Man 3J **107**
Southbourne Av. M41: Urm 7F **92**
Southbourne St. M6: Sal 8L **77**
Southbrook Av. M8: Man 8E **60**
Southbrook Cl. SK13: Had 5A **100**
Southbrook Gro. BL3: Bolt 9G **39**
South Chadderton Stop (Metro) 8E **62**
Southchurch Pde. *M40: Man 6H **79***
(off Whitley Rd.)
Southcliffe Rd. SK5: Stoc 2D **108**
Sth. Cliffe St. M11: Man 2D **96**
South Cl. BL9: Bury 9N **41**
SK9: Wilm 8E **122**
SK13: Tin 2B **100**
Southcombe Wlk. M15: Man 4E **94**
South Ct. OL16: Roch 6E **8** (5E **28**)
WN7: Lei 4K **73**
South Cres. M11: Man 8B **80**
South Cft. OL8: O'ham 8M **63**
Southcross Rd. M18: Man 6B **96**
Sth. Cross St. BL9: Bury 8M **7** (2M **41**)
(not continuous)
Sth. Croston St. M16: Old T 5C **94**
Southdene WN8: Par 2A **32**
Southdene Av. M20: Man 4D **106**
Southdown Cl. OL11: Roch 9A **28**
SK4: Stoc 6B **108**
SK10: Macc 9H **129**
Southdown Cres. M9: Man 9M **61**
SK8: Chea H 7L **117**
Southdown Dr. M28: Wors 4G **74**
South Downs WA16: Knut 7J **133**
Sth. Downs Cl. OL2: Shaw 4K **45**
Sth. Downs Dr. WA14: Hale 7D **114**
Sth. Downs Rd.
WA14: Bow, Hale 6C **114**
South Dr. BL2: Bolt 1M **39**
M21: Cho H 2A **106**
M41: Urm 4N **91**
SK8: Gat 3F **116**
SK9: Wilm 8G **122**
WA15: Tim 9G **104**
WN6: App B 2G **32**
Southend Av. M15: Man 3C **94**
Southend St. BL3: Bolt 9D **38**
Southerly Cres. M40: Man 8B **62**
Southern App. M27: Clif 9J **59**
Southernby Cl. *M13: Man 9L **95***
(off Holmfirth St.)
Southern Cl. M34: Dent 9K **97**
SK7: Bram 6D **118**
Southern Cres. SK7: Bram 5D **118**
Southern Ho. *BL1: Bolt 3E **38***
(off Kirkhope Dr.)
Southern Ind. Est. M28: Walk 6L **57**
Southern Rd. M33: Sale 2G **105**
Southern's Fold WN2: Asp 9K **35**
Southern St. M3: Man 7E **4** (1D **94**)
M6: Sal 8L **77**
M28: Walk 6L **57**
WN5: Wig 6A **52**
Southery Av. WN3: Wins 8A **52**
Southey Cl. OL15: Lit 3K **29**
Southey Ct. M34: Dent 9L **97**
Southey Wlk. *M34: Dent 1L **109***
(off Burns Rd.)
Southfield SK10: P'bury 9E **128**
WN2: P Bri 9L **53**
Southfield Av. BL9: Bury 6M **25**
Southfield Cl. *SK9: Hand 3H **123***
(off Knowle Pk.)
SK16: Duk 3A **98**
Southfield Dr. BL5: W'ton 4G **54**
South Fld. Ind. Est. M17: T Pk 3J **93**
Southfield Rd. BL0: Ram 3G **24**
Southfields WA14: Bow 5C **114**
WA16: Knut 5J **133**
Southfields Av. M11: Man 8A **80**
Southfields Dr. WA15: Tim 9H **105**
Southfield St. BL3: Bolt 8J **39**
South Gdns. M29: Ast 5B **74**
Southgarth Rd. M6: Sal 7L **77**
South Gate PR7: Adl 6J **19**
Southgate BL2: Bolt 9M **23**
M3: Man 4F **4** (9E **78**)
M21: Cho H 1A **106**
Southgate M41: Urm 9B **92**
OL3: Dob 1K **65**
OL12: Whitw 7A **14**
SK4: Stoc 3A **108**
Southgate Av. M40: Man 6M **79**
Southgate Ct. M33: Sale 3J **105**
Southgate Ind. Est. OL10: H'ood 3K **43**
Southgate M. SK4: Stoc 3A **108**
Southgate Rd. BL9: Bury 9M **41**
OL9: Chad 8C **62**
Southgates PR7: Char R 2A **18**
Southgate St. OL1: O'ham 3E **8** (5K **63**)
Southgate Way *OL7: A Lyne 9L **81***
(off John St.)
South Gro. M13: Man 4J **95**
M28: Walk 9K **57**
M33: Sale 5H **105**
SK9: A Edg 4F **126**
Southgrove Av. BL1: Bolt 7F **22**
South Hall St. M5: Sal 7A **4** (1B **94**)
South Hey WN7: Lei 5E **72**
South Hill OL4: Spri 6C **64**
South Hill St. OL4: O'ham 4G **8** (5L **63**)
Sth. King St. M2: Man 4F **4** (9E **78**)
M30: Ecc 8B **76**
Sth. Lancashire Ind. Est.
WN4: A Mak 4E **70**
Southlands BL2: Bolt 4M **39**
*SK3: Stoc 3D **118***
(off Bramhall La.)
Southlands Av. M30: Ecc 1N **91**
WN6: Stan 4B **34**
Southlands Ct. SK3: Stoc 1D **118**
South La. M29: Ast 4A **74**
Sth. Langworthy Rd. M50: Sal 1L **93**
Southlea Rd. M19: Man 3J **107**
M20: Man 3J **107**
Southleigh Dr. BL2: Bolt 6A **40**
Southlink OL4: O'ham 5L **63**
Southlink Bus. Pk. OL4: O'ham 5L **63**
Southlink Bus. Pk. Workshops
OL4: O'ham 3G **8** (5L **63**)
Southlink Ind. Pk. OL4: O'ham 4M **63**
Sth. Lonsdale St. M32: Stre 6L **93**
South Manchester Gymnastics Cen.
2D **116**
Sth. Marlow St. SK13: Had 5C **100**
South Mead SK12: Poy 1F **124**
South Meade M21: Cho H 1A **106**
M25: Pres 9C **60**
M27: Swin 4E **76**
WA15: Tim 9G **104**
South Meadway SK6: H Lan 8C **120**
Southmere Cl. M40: Man 8A **62**
Sth. Mesnefield Rd. M7: Sal 3N **77**
Southmill St. M2: Man 6F **4** (1E **94**)
Southmoor M23: Wyth 9M **105**
Southmoor Bus. Pk. M23: Wyth 9L **105**
Southmoor Ind. Est.
M23: Wyth 1M **115**
Southmoor Rd. M23: Wyth 9M **105**
Southmoor Wlk. *BL3: Bolt 7F **38***
(off Parrot St.)
South Oak La. SK9: Wilm 8E **122**
Southolme Gdns. M19: Man 4K **107**
Southover BL5: W'ton 5G **55**
South Pde. OL16: Roch 7C **8** (6D **28**)
SK7: Bram 5D **118**
South Pk. Bus. Cen.
SK11: Macc 6H **131**
South Pk. Dr. SK12: Poy 2J **125**
South Pk. Rd. SK8: Gat 1G **117**
SK11: Macc 5G **131**
South Pl. OL16: Roch 5F **8** (5E **28**)
Southpoint SK4: Stoc 6M **107**
Southpool Cl. SK7: Bram 5E **118**
Sth. Pump St. M1: Man 6K **5** (1G **94**)
Sth. Radford St. M7: Sal 3N **77**
SOUTH REDDISH 2D **108**
South Ridge M34: Dent 4K **97**
South Rd. M20: Man 6G **106**
M27: Clif 9K **59**
PR7: Cop 4B **18**
WA14: Bow 5C **114**
(not continuous)
WA14: Hale 7D **114**
South Row M25: Pres 1M **77**
Sth. Royd St. BL8: Tot 6F **24**
Southsea St. M11: Man 2B **96**
South Side SK14: Hyde 5C **98**
Southside SK6: Bred 2J **109**
Southside Ind. Pk. M46: Ath 6J **55**
South Stage M50: Sal 1M **93**
South St. BL0: Ram 8K **11**
(Earl St.)
BL0: Ram 8K **11**
(Old Engine La.)
BL3: Bolt 9F **38**
BL9: Bury 7M **7** (2M **41**)
M11: Man 1N **95**
(not continuous)
M12: Man 4K **95**
OL7: A Lyne 1J **97**
OL8: O'ham 9F **62**
OL10: H'ood 2G **42**
OL16: Roch 6E **8** (5E **28**)
SK9: A Edg 4F **126**
South Ter. BL0: Ram 4J **11**
BL9: Bury 5K **41**
OL12: Roch 4L **27**
SK9: A Edg 5F **126**
South Ter. Ct. OL16: Roch 8E **28**
South Va. Cres.
WA15: Tim 1G **6** (2F **114**)
South Vw. *M14: Man 7H **95***
(off Taylor St.)
M46: Ath 8L **55**
OL11: Roch 7K **27**
SK5: Stoc 6D **96**
SK6: Wood 2N **109**
SK15: C'ook 4J **83**
SK16: Duk 9N **81**
SK22: N Mil 7L **121**
South Vw. Gdns. SK8: Chea 4H **117**
South Vw. Rd. OL16: Roch 2J **29**
SK13: Glos 9H **101**
South Vw. St. BL2: Bolt 5K **39**
South Vw. Ter. OL16: Roch 1J **29**
Southview Wlk. OL4: O'ham 2B **64**
Sth. Villa Ct. WN6: Stan 4B **34**
South Wlk. SK15: Stal 9D **82**
Southward Rd. WA11: Hay 2D **86**
Southwark Dr. SK16: Duk 3A **98**
Southway M30: Ecc 8F **76**
M40: Man 9D **62**
M43: Droy 1E **96**
OL7: A Lyne 4M **81**
OL8: O'ham 9J **63**
WA14: Alt 1E **114**
WN8: Skel 2A **50**
Southwell Cl.
BL1: Bolt 1G **7** (4E **38**)
SK6: Rom 7L **109**
WA3: Low 1M **87**
Southwell Ct. M32: Stre 8J **93**
Southwell Gdns. OL6: A Lyne 3M **81**
Southwell St. M9: Man 3K **79**
South West Av. SK10: Boll 6K **129**
South Whiteacre WN6: Stan 2L **33**
Southwick Rd. M23: Wyth 6N **105**
Sth. William St. M3: Sal 4B **4**
Southwold Cl. M19: Man 8A **96**
Southwood Cl. BL3: Bolt 9G **39**
SK6: Mar 2A **120**
Southwood Dr. M9: Man 6F **60**
Sth. Woodley Gdns. M26: Rad 3J **59**
Southwood Rd. SK2: Stoc 3F **118**
Southworth Ct. M3: Sal 3B **4**
Southworth La. WA3: Cro 9A **88**
Southworth Rd. WA12: N Wil 6H **87**
Southyard St. M19: Man 9N **95**
Sovereign Bus. Pk. WN1: Wig 9M **9**
Sovereign Cl. WA3: Low 2A **88**
Sovereign Ent. Pk. M50: Sal 1N **93**
Sovereign Fold Rd. WN7: Lei 1G **72**
Sovereign Hall Caravan Pk.
*OL5: Mos 1E **82***
(off Stamford St.)
Sovereign Ho. SK8: Chea 1L **117**
Sovereign Point M50: Sal 2M **93**
Sovereign Rd. WN1: Wig 9L **9** (4G **52**)
Sovereign St. M6: Sal 6N **77**
SOWCAR 5N **129**
Sowcar Way SK10: Boll 5N **129**
Sowerby Cl. BL8: Bury 2F **40**
Sowerby Wlk. *M9: Man 7G **60***
(off Chapel La.)
Spa Cl. SK5: Stoc 9C **96**
Spa Cres. M38: Lit H 5G **57**
Spa Gro. M38: Lit H 5H **57**
Spa La. M38: Lit H 5H **57**
OL4: Lees 6A **64**
Spalding Dr. M23: Wyth 5N **115**
Sparkford Av. M23: Wyth 7K **105**
Sparkle St. M1: Man 5L **5** (9G **79**)
Spark Rd. M23: Wyth 9M **105**
Spa Rd. BL1: Bolt 3G **7** (6E **38**)
M46: Ath 6L **55**
Spa Rd. Ind. Est.
BL1: Bolt 3H **7** (5F **38**)
Sparrow Cl. SK5: Stoc 7C **96**
Sparrowfield Cl. SK15: C'ook 3H **83**
Sparrow Hill OL16: Roch 8B **8** (6C **28**)
WN8: Par 2D **32**
Sparrow La. WA16: Knut 7H **133**
Sparrow St. M13: Man 4J **95**
OL2: O'ham 1J **63**
Sparta Av. M28: Walk 9K **57**
Sparta Wlk. *M11: Man 1M **95***
(off Mill St.)
Sparth Bottoms Rd.
OL11: Roch 9A **8** (7B **28**)
Sparth Cl. SK4: Stoc 5B **108**
Sparthfield Av. OL11: Roch 8C **28**
Sparthfield Rd. SK4: Stoc 5B **108**
Sparth Hall SK4: Stoc 5B **108**
Sparth La. SK4: Stoc 5B **108**
Sparth Rd. M40: Man 5B **80**
Spa St. M15: Man 4G **94**
Spathfield Ct. SK4: Stoc 5B **108**
Spath Holme M20: Man 5F **106**
Spath La. SK8: Chea H 2K **123**
SK9: Hand 1J **123**
Spath La. E. SK8: Chea H 1N **123**
Spath Rd. M20: Man 4E **106**
Spath Wlk. SK8: Chea H 1N **123**
Spawell Cl. WA3: Low 9A **72**
Spaw St. M3: Sal 3D **4** (8D **78**)
Speakman Av. WA12: N Wil 4F **86**
WN7: Lei 5K **73**
Speakmans Dr. WN6: App B 6G **33**
Spean Wlk. *M11: Man 9A **80***
(off Bill Williams Cl.)
Spear St. M1: Man 4J **5** (9F **78**)
Spectator St. M4: Man 9J **79**
Specton Wlk. M12: Man 6N **95**
Spectrum Bus. Pk. SK3: Stoc 1N **117**
Spectrum Way SK3: Stoc 1A **118**
Speedwell SK13: Tin 2B **100**
Speedwell Cl. SK13: Tin 2B **100**
WA3: Low 1A **88**
Speke Wlk. M34: Dent 8J **97**
Spelding Dr. WN6: Stan 8A **34**
Spencer Av. BL3: Lit L 9C **40**
M16: Whall R 7B **94**
M45: Whitef 1L **59**
SK14: Hyde 4A **98**
Spencer Brook SK10: P'bury 7D **128**
Spencer La. OL11: Roch 8K **27**
Spencer M. SK10: P'bury 7D **128**
Spencer Rd. WN1: Wig 9E **34**
Spencer Rd. W. WN6: Wig 9D **34**
Spencers La. WN5: Orr 4H **51**
WN8: Skel 4A **50**
Spencer St. BL0: Ram 9H **11**
BL8: Bury 1J **41**
M26: Rad 8J **41**
M30: Ecc 9C **76**
OL1: O'ham 1F **8** (4L **63**)
OL5: Mos 1E **82**
OL9: Chad 7F **62**
OL15: Lit 8N **15**
Spencer St. SK5: Stoc 9D **96**
SK16: Duk 1N **97**
Spencers Wood *BL7: Bro X 6G **23***
(off Hough La.)
Spender Av. M8: Man 4F **78**
Spendmore PR7: Cop 3C **18**
Spendmore La. PR7: Cop 5A **18**
Spen Fold BL8: Bury 4G **40**
OL15: Lit 1L **29**
Spenleach La. BL8: Haw 1C **24**
Spenlow WN7: Lei 7L **73**
Spenlow Cl. SK12: Poy 5J **125**
Spennithorne Rd. M41: Urm 7B **92**
Spenser Av. M26: Rad 8E **40**
M34: Dent 9L **97**
Spenwood Rd. OL15: Lit 9K **15**
Spey Cl. WA14: Alt 1C **114**
WN6: Stan 3A **34**
Spey Ho. SK5: Stoc 7D **96**
Speyside Cl. M45: Whitef 3N **59**
Spilsby Sq. WN3: Wig 9D **52**
Spindle Av. SK15: Stal 7F **82**
Spindle Ct. *OL2: O'ham 8J **45***
(off High Barn St.)
Spindle Cft. BL4: Farn 3L **57**
Spindle Hillock WN4: Gars 5A **70**
Spindlepoint Dr. M28: Wors 2K **75**
Spindles, The OL5: Mos 2G **83**
Spindles Shop. Cen.
OL1: O'ham 3C **8** (5J **63**)
Spindletree Av. M9: Man 7M **61**
Spindle Wlk. BL5: W'ton 1H **55**
Spindlewood Cl. SK15: Stal 8G **82**
Spindlewood Rd. WN3: I Mak 5H **53**
Spinks St. OL4: O'ham 6M **63**
Spinnerette Cl. WN7: Lei 5J **73**
Spinners Gdns. OL12: Roch 1G **28**
Spinners Grn. OL12: Roch 3D **28**
Spinners Hall BL1: Bolt 1K **7**
Spinners La. SK12: Poy 2G **124**
Spinners M. BL1: Bolt 4F **38**
Spinners Way OL4: O'ham 8B **46**
SK10: Boll 6K **129**
Spinney, The BL1: Bolt 5C **38**
BL7: Tur 3K **23**
M28: Wors 5B **76**
M41: Urm 7A **92**
M45: Whitef 4J **59**
OL4: Scout 3D **64**
OL12: Roch 2B **28**
SK8: Chea 4K **117**
SK12: Poy 2G **125**
WN5: Wig 6B **52**
Spinney Apartments WN8: Uph 2G **50**
Spinney Cl. SK9: Hand 3H **123**
SK13: Glos 7E **100**
Spinney Dr. BL9: Bury 7L **25**
M33: Sale 6D **104**
Spinney Gro. M34: Dent 4K **97**
Spinney La. WA16: Knut 6E **132**
Spinney Mead SK10: Macc 3J **131**
Spinney Nook BL2: Bolt 2L **39**
Spinney Rd. M23: Wyth 9A **106**
Spinningdale M38: Lit H 5E **56**
Spinningfields *BL1: Bolt 4E **38***
(off Vermont St.)
Spinningfield Way OL10: H'ood 5J **43**
Spinning Ga. Shop. Cen.
WN7: Lei 6H **73**
Spinning Jenny Way WN7: Lei 6H **73**
Spinning Mdw. BL1: Bolt 4E **38**
Spinnings, The BL9: Sum 2J **25**
Spion Kop WN4: A Mak 7D **70**
Spiredale Brow WN6: Stan 2C **34**
Spire Hollin SK13: Glos 7D **100**
Spires Cft. WN7: Lei 5K **73**
Spire Wlk. *M12: Man 1K **95***
(off Aden Cl.)
Spirewood Gdns. SK6: Rom 7L **109**
Spodden Cotts. OL12: Whitw 4B **14**
Spodden Fold OL12: Whitw 6A **14**
Spodden St. OL12: Roch 5B **28**
Spodden Wlk. M45: Whitef 2B **60**
Spode Grn. La. WA14: Lit B 6K **113**
Spod Rd. OL12: Roch 4A **28**
Spokeshave Way OL16: Roch 3G **28**
Spooner Rd. M30: Ecc 9C **76**
Sportaid Health & Fitness Club
*4H **131***
(off Sunderland St.)
SPORTCITY 8L **79**
Sporting Edge Community Sports Cen.
1C **96**
Sportside Av. M28: Walk 8M **57**
Sportside Cl. M28: Walk 7L **57**
Sportside Gro. M28: Walk 7L **57**
Sportsmans Dr. OL8: O'ham 8L **63**
Sportsman St. WN7: Lei 5F **72**
SPOTLAND BRIDGE 5B **28**
SPOTLAND FOLD 4A **28**
Spotland Rd. OL12: Roch 5A **8** (5B **28**)
Spotland Stadium 5A **28**
Spotland Tops OL12: Roch 4N **27**
Spout Brook Rd. SK15: H'rod 5E **82**
Spout Grn. *SK14: Mot 4K **99***
(off Old Rd.)
Spreadbury St. M40: Man 3M **79**
Spring Av. M45: Whitef 1L **59**
SK14: Hyde 9C **98**
SPRING BANK 5A **52**
Spring Bank M6: Sal 7L **77**
M29: Ast 4C **74**
OL3: Upp 3L **65**
OL12: Whitw 5B **14**
*SK13: Glos 9D **100***
(off Turnlee Rd.)
SK15: Stal 9E **82**
SK22: N Mil 7M **121**
WA14: Bow 4D **114**
WN6: App B 4G **33**
Springbank OL9: Chad 4E **62**
SK10: Boll 6J **129**
SK13: Had 4B **100**
Spring Bank Av. M34: Aud 2H **97**
OL6: A Lyne 5M **81**
Springbank Cl. SK6: Wood 2N **109**
Springbank Ct. M8: Man 9E **60**
SK6: Wood 3M **109**
Springbank Gdns. SK22: N Mil 7L **121**
WA13: Lym 2C **112**
Springbank Ind. Est. WN2: P Bri 8L **53**
Spring Bank La. OL11: Roch 5K **27**
(not continuous)
SK15: H'rod 5F **82**
Springbank La. SK10: Adl 8K **125**
Springbank Pl.
SK1: Stoc 4K **9** (8C **108**)
Springbank Rd. SK6: Wood 2N **109**
Spring Bank St. OL8: O'ham 7G **63**
Spring Bank Ter. M34: Aud 2G **97**
Springbourne WN6: Wig 1C **52**
Springbridge Ct. M16: Whall R 8E **94**
Spring Bri. Rd. M16: Whall R 7E **94**
Springburn Cl. BL6: Hor 3F **36**
M28: Wors 4H **75**
Springburn Way OL3: Upp 3L **65**
Spring Cl. BL0: Ram 8H **11**
BL8: Tot 7E **24**
OL4: Lees 6A **64**
Spring Clough M28: Wors 5B **76**
OL7: A Lyne 4L **81**
Spring Clough Av. M28: Walk 9N **57**
Spring Clough Dr. M28: Walk 9N **57**
Springclough Dr. OL8: O'ham 7M **63**
Spring Cotts. *OL5: Mos 9F **64***
(off Bk. Mill La.)
Spring Ct. OL12: Roch 4D **28**
Spring Ct. M. SK14: Holl 4M **99**
Springdale Gdns. M20: Man 5F **106**
SPRINGFIELD
BL2 6H **39**
WN6 1C **52**
Springfield BL2: Bolt 4N **7** (6H **39**)
M26: Rad 5C **58**
M41: Urm 7C **92**
*OL4: O'ham 4N **63***
(off Moorgate St.)
SK13: Char 2M **111**
Springfield Av. M8: Man 2G **79**
OL15: Lit 7L **15**
SK5: Stoc 1C **108**
SK6: Mar 1C **120**
SK7: H Gro 4H **119**
WA3: Gol 1J **87**
WA13: Lym 2C **112**
Springfield Cl. M35: Fail 2C **80**
OL10: H'ood 3K **43**
SK13: Had 5A **100**
Springfield Ct. BL3: Bolt 8J **39**
Springfield Dr. SK9: Wilm 9C **122**
Springfield Gdns. BL4: Kea 5A **58**
Springfield Ind. Est. M35: Fail 2C **80**
Springfield La. M3: Sal 1E **4** (7D **78**)
M44: Irl 7G **90**
OL2: O'ham 5G **44**
OL16: Roch 2H **29**
Springfield M. PR6: And 4M **19**
Springfield Pk. 8M **27**
Springfield Rd. BL0: Ram 3G **24**
BL1: Bolt 6F **22**
BL4: Farn 2H **57**
BL4: Kea 5M **57**
BL6: Hor 3F **36**
M24: Mid 2L **61**
M33: Sale 4H **105**
M43: Droy 8D **80**
M46: Ath 7N **55**
PR6: Adl 5L **19**
SK8: Gat 3G **116**
SK11: Macc 4D **130**
WA14: Alt 2D **6** (2D **114**)
WA16: Mob 4M **133**
WN2: Hin 5N **53**
WN6: Wig 9C **34**
Springfield Rd. Nth. PR7: Cop 4B **18**
Springfields SK10: P'bury 6E **128**
WA16: Knut 5J **133**
Springfield St. BL3: Bolt 8H **39**
M34: Aud 3K **97**
OL6: A Lyne 5B **82**
OL10: H'ood 2F **42**
WN1: Wig 1F **52**
Springfield Ter. PR6: H Char 4L **19**
Spring Gdns. BL2: Bolt 9N **23**
BL6: Hor 9D **20**
M2: Man 4H **5** (9F **78**)
M6: Sal 7M **77**
M24: Mid 1M **61**
*M46: Ath 8M **55***
(off Mather St.)
*OL3: Upp 3L **65***
(off Moorgate St.)
OL15: Lit 9M **15**
SK1: Stoc 3N **9** (7E **108**)
SK7: H Gro 4H **119**
SK10: Macc 3H **131**
SK13: Had 4B **100**
SK14: Hyde 5A **98**
WA15: Tim 2J **115**
WN1: Wig 7H **9** (3E **52**)
Spring Gdn. St. OL2: O'ham 8H **45**
Spring Gro. M45: Whitef 1L **59**
*OL3: G'fld 6L **65***
(off Chew Valley Rd.)
WN1: Wig 9M **9** (4G **53**)
Spring Hall Ri. OL4: O'ham 8C **46**
SPRINGHEAD 5C **64**
Springhead Av. M20: Man 1F **106**
OL4: Spri 6D **64**
SPRING HILL 2A **64**
Springhill OL2: O'ham 8H **45**
OL16: Roch 1F **44**
SK10: Macc 3L **131**
Spring Hill Ct. OL4: O'ham 3A **64**
Spring La. M26: Rad 9G **41**
OL4: Lees 6B **64**
WA13: Lym 4F **112**
Springlawns BL1: Bolt 4A **38**
Springlees Ct. OL4: Spri 5C **64**
Springmeadow SK13: Char 1N **111**
Springmeadow La.
OL3: Upp 3M **65**

Spring Mill Cl. BL3: Bolt 8F 38
(off Aldsworth Dr.)
Spring Mill Dr. OL5: Mos 8H 65
Spring Mill Wlk. OL16: Roch 3G 28
Spring Mt. SK22: N Mil 6M 121
Springmount WA3: Low 1A 88
Spring Pl. OL12: Whitw 3B 14
Springpool WN3: Wins 9M 51
Spring Ri. OL2: Shaw 3L 45
SK13: Glos 9B 100
Spring Rd. SK3: Stoc 8A 108
SK12: Poy 4K 125
WA14: Hale 5D 114
WN5: Orr 3K 51
Springs, The OL11: Roch 6K 27
WA14: Bow 5B 114
(not continuous)
Springs Brow PR7: Cop 8A 18
Spring Side OL12: Whitw 2B 14
Springside SK4: Stoc 1B 108
Springside Av. M28: Walk 8M 57
Springside Cl. M28: Walk 8M 57
Springside Cotts. BL7: Bel 3B 22
Springside Gro. M28: Walk 8M 57
Spring Side La. OL12: W'le 7E 14
Springside Rd. BL9: Bury 5K 25
Springside Vw. BL8: Bury 6H 25
Springside Vw. Cotts. BL8: Bury . . 6J 25
Springside Wlk. M15: Man 3C 94
(off Shawgreen Cl.)
Springs La. SK15: Stal 7C 82
Springs Ri. SK15: Stal 7C 82
(not continuous)
Springs Rd. M24: Mid 5C 62
Spring St. BL0: Ram 7K 11
(Millett St.)
BL0: Ram 8H 11
(Spring Cl.)
BL3: Bolt 7G 38
BL4: Farn 2L 57
BL6: Hor 9D 20
BL8: Bury 9F 24
BL8: Tot 6E 24
BL9: Bury 8M 7 (2M 41)
(not continuous)
HD7: Mars 1H 49
M12: Man 7M 95
OL3: Upp 3L 65
OL4: O'ham 3N 63
OL4: Spri 5D 64
OL5: Mos 9F 64
SK9: Wilm 7F 122
SK13: Glos 8D 100
SK14: B'tom 8K 99
SK14: Holl 4M 99
SK15: Stal 8D 82
WN1: Wig 9M 9 (4G 53)
WN3: I Mak 7H 53
Spring Ter. BL8: Tot 6F 24
(off Spring St.)
OL9: Chad 4E 62
OL11: Roch 5M 27
OL16: Miln 1M 45
Spring Thyme Fold OL15: Lit 9L 15
Spring Vale M24: Mid 3M 61
M25: Pres 9N 59
SK7: H Gro 5J 119
Springvale Cl. OL7: A Lyne 5K 81
Springvale Ct. M24: Mid 2N 61
Spring Vale Dr. BL8: Tot 6E 24
Spring Vale St. BL8: Tot 7E 24
Spring Vale Ter. OL15: Lit 9M 15
(off Church St.)
Spring Vale Way OL2: O'ham 7L 45
SPRING VIEW 7J 53
Spring Vw. BL3: Lit L 9B 40
BL4: Kea 5A 58
Springville Av. M9: Man 3L 79
Springwater Av. BL0: Ram 2G 24
Springwater Cl. BL2: Bolt 1M 39
Spring Water Dr. SK13: Had 6A 100
Springwater La. M45: Whitef 1L 59
Springwell Cl. M6: Sal 8L 77
Springwell Gdns. SK14: Hat 8H 99
Springwell Way SK14: Hat 8H 99
Springwood OL3: Del 7H 47
SK13: Glos 9B 100
Springwood Av. M27: Pen 4H 77
OL9: Chad 2C 62
WA16: Knut 5J 133
Springwood Cl. SK10: Boll 8H 129
Springwood Ct. SK10: Boll 8H 129
Springwood Cres. SK6: Rom 6B 110
Springwood Dr. PR7: Chor 1H 19
Springwood Est. OL3: Del 7H 47
Springwood Hall OL7: A Lyne 3L 81
Springwood Hall Rd.
OL8: O'ham 9L 63
Springwood La. SK6: Rom 6C 110
Springwood St. BL0: Ram 7H 11
Springwood Way OL7: A Lyne 4L 81
SK10: Boll 8H 129
Sprodley Dr. WN6: App B 2F 32
Spruce Av. BL9: Bury 2A 42
Spruce Cl. WA3: Low 2B 88
Spruce Ct. M6: Sal 8A 78
Spruce Cres. BL9: Bury 6M 25
Spruce Lodge SK8: Chea 1J 117
Spruce Rd. WN6: Wig 9C 34
Spruce St. BL0: Ram 1G 25
M15: Man 3D 94
OL16: Roch 9G 8 (7F 28)
Spruce Wlk. M33: Sale 2C 104
Sprucewood OL9: Chad 3B 62
Spuley La. SK10: Boll, P Shr 2N 129
Spur, The OL8: O'ham 1B 63
Spurn La. OL3: Dig 9L 47
Spurstow M. SK8: Chea H 7N 117
Spur Wlk. M8: Man 3E 78
(off Broomfield Dr.)
Square, The BL3: Bolt 9A 38
BL9: Bury 8L 7 (2M 41)
M27: Swin 5E 76
M29: Tyld 1B 74
M45: Whitef 3L 59
OL3: Dob 1K 65
Square, The OL3: Upp 3L 65
SK4: Stoc 5A 108
SK14: Hyde 7A 98
SK16: Duk 2C 98
WA13: Lym 4A 112
WA15: Haleb 7J 115
Square Fold M43: Droy 8F 80
Square St. BL0: Ram 8J 11
SK11: Macc 6J 131
Squire Rd. M8: Man 3E 78
Squire's Ct. M5: Sal 8G 77
Squires La. M29: Tyld 2N 73
Squires M. M31: Part 5F 102
Squirrel Dr. WA14: B'ath 8C 104
Squirrel La. BL6: Hor 9C 20
Squirrels Chase SK10: P'bury 8D 128
Squirrel's Jump SK9: A Edg 4G 127
Stable Fold M26: Rad 8G 41
Stablefold M28: Wors 5A 76
OL5: Mos 2F 82
Stableford Av. M30: Ecc 6C 76
Stables, The M25: Pres 8B 60
M43: Droy 7H 81
OL12: Whitw 5A 14
Stables Fitness & Leisure Club . . . 9G 25
Stable St. OL1: O'ham 3M 63
OL9: Chad 9E 62
Stable Yd., The M20: Man 1H 107
Stableyard Cotts. WA11: Cra 8C 68
Stablings, The SK9: Wilm 9F 122
Stadium Dr. M11: Man 1K 95
Stadium Way BL6: Hor 4E 36
WN5: Wig 2B 52
Stafford Cl. SK10: Macc 2D 130
SK13: Glos 9H 101
(off Shirebrook Dr.)
Stafford Ct. OL16: Lit 1J 29
Stafford Rd. M27: Swin 2F 76
M28: Wors 1K 75
M30: Ecc 7E 76
M35: Fail 5E 80
Staffordshire Cl. M31: Part 6F 102
Stafford St. BL8: Bury 9K 25
OL9: O'ham 7G 62
SK22: N Mil 6M 121
WN2: Hin 6M 53
WN7: Lei 6M 73
Stafford Wlk. M34: Dent 8L 97
(off Lancaster Rd.)
SK10: Macc 2D 130
(off Wiltshire Wlk.)
Stage La. WA13: Lym 3C 112
Stag Ind. Est. WA14: B'ath 1B 114
Stag Pasture Rd. OL8: O'ham 1H 81
Stainburn Cl. WN6: She 6J 33
Stainburne Rd. SK2: Stoc 1G 119
Stainburn Rd. M11: Man 1N 95
Staindale OL4: O'ham 5A 64
Stainer Cl. WA12: N Wil 4E 86
Stainer St. M12: Man 6M 95
Stainforth Cl. BL8: Bury 1F 40
WA3: Cul 5F 88
Stainforth St. M11: Man 1L 95
Stainmoor Ct. SK2: Stoc 1H 119
Stainmore Av. OL6: A Lyne 3A 82
Stainsbury St. BL3: Bolt 8D 38
Stainton Av. M18: Man 5C 96
Stainton Cl. M26: Rad 7F 40
Stainton Dr. M24: Mid 9J 43
Stainton Pk. 8E 40
Stainton Rd. M26: Rad 7E 40
Staithes Rd. M22: Wyth 7C 116
Stakeford Dr. M8: Man 2H 79
STAKEHILL 7B 44
Stake Hill Ind. Est. M24: Mid 8C 44
Stakehill Ind. Est. M24: Mid 7B 44
Stakehill La. M24: Mid 6B 44
Staley Cl. SK15: Stal 8F 82
Staley Farm Cl. SK15: Stal 6G 82
Staley Hall Cres. SK15: Stal 7F 82
Staley Hall Rd. SK15: Stal 7F 82
Staley Rd. OL5: Mos 2G 82
(not continuous)
Staley St. OL4: O'ham 5M 63
OL4: Spri 5C 64
Stalham Cl. M40: Man 7J 79
Stalmine Av. SK8: H Grn 7G 117
STALYBRIDGE 8D 82
Stalybridge Celtic FC 1F 98
Stalybridge Country Pk. 3K 83
Stalybridge Rd. SK14: Mot 5K 99
Stalybridge Station (Rail) 8C 82
Stalyhill Dr. SK15: Stal 2H 99
Staly Ind. Est. SK15: Stal 8E 82
Stambourne Dr. BL1: Bolt 9G 22
Stamford Arc. OL6: A Lyne 7E 6
Stamford Av. SK15: Stal 8B 82
WA14: Alt 2A 114
Stamford Brook Rd.
WA14: W Tim 8D 104
Stamford Cl. SK11: Macc 8G 130
SK15: Stal 8B 82
Stamford Ct. OL6: A Lyne 8A 82
SK11: Macc 8G 130
(off Stamford Rd.)
Stamford Dr. M35: Fail 4F 80
SK15: Stal 8B 82
Stamford Golf Course 3H 83
Stamford Grange
WA14: Alt 3C 6 (3C 114)
Stamford Gro. SK15: Stal 7C 82
Stamford New Rd.
WA14: Alt 4D 6 (3D 114)
Stamford Pk. 8B 82
Stamford Pk. Rd.
WA15: Alt, Hale 5E 6 (4E 114)
Stamford Pl. M33: Sale 4J 105
SK9: Wilm 7G 123
(off Manchester Rd.)
Stamford Rd. M7: Sal 4A 78
M13: Man 6K 95
M31: C'ton 2L 103
M34: Aud 2H 97
M41: Urm 7B 92
OL4: Lees 3C 64
OL5: Mos 9F 64
Stamford Rd. SK9: A Edg 4G 126
SK9: Wilm 5F 122
SK11: Macc 8G 130
WA14: Bow 5B 114
WA14: Lit B 5J 113
Stamford Sq. OL6: A Lyne 8A 82
WA14: Alt 3D 6
Stamford St. M16: Old T 4B 94
(not continuous)
M27: Pen 1G 76
M33: Sale 2G 105
M46: Ath 7N 55
OL4: Lees 5B 64
OL5: Mos 1E 82
OL6: A Lyne 8C 6 (8M 81)
OL10: H'ood 3K 43
OL16: Roch 7F 28
SK15: Mill 6G 83
SK15: Stal 8B 82
(not continuous)
WA14: Alt 2D 6 (2D 114)
Stamford St. Central
OL6: A Lyne 7E 6 (7N 81)
Stamford St. E.
OL6: A Lyne 7F 6 (7N 81)
(not continuous)
Stamford St. W.
OL6: A Lyne 9B 6 (8L 81)
Stamford Way
WA14: Alt 2D 6 (2D 114)
Stampstone St. OL1: O'ham 3M 63
Stanage Av. M9: Man 7L 61
Stanbank St. SK4: Stoc 4C 108
Stanbridge Ct. SK4: Stoc . . 1J 9 (6C 108)
Stanbrook St. M19: Man 9A 96
Stanbury Cl. BL9: Bury 3C 42
Stanbury Dr. SK16: Duk 1A 98
Stanbury Rd. BL1: Bolt 3F 38
Stanbury Wlk. M40: Man 7J 79
(off Berkshire Rd.)
Stancliffe Gro. WN2: Asp 6M 35
Stancliffe Rd. M22: Shar 2D 116
Stancross Rd. M23: Wyth 7J 105
STAND 3K 59
Standall Wlk. M9: Man 1K 79
(off Dalbeattie St.)
Stand Av. M45: Whitef 2L 59
Stand Cl. M45: Whitef 3J 59
STANDEDGE 3A 48
Standedge Foot Rd. OL3: Del 5M 47
Standedge Rd. OL3: Dig, Dob 9L 47
Standedge Wlk. SK15: C'ook 4H 83
(off Crowswood Dr.)
Standfield Cen. M28: Wors 4H 75
Standfield Dr. M28: Wors 3H 75
Stand Golf Course 2K 59
STANDISH 3B 34
Standish Av. WN5: Bil 5J 69
Standish Court Golf Court 3C 34
Standish Gallery WN1: Wig 7K 9
(off The Galleries)
Standishgate WN1: Wig . . . 7K 9 (3F 52)
STANDISH LOWER GROUND 8A 34
Standish Rd. M14: Man 9J 95
Standish St. M29: Ast 2B 74
Standish Wlk. M34: Dent 8J 97
Standish Wood La.
WN6: Stan, Wig 4B 34
Stand La. M26: Rad 1H 59
M45: Whitef 1H 59
Stand Lodge M26: Rad 2J 59
(off Stand La.)
Standmoor Ct. M45: Whitef 4K 59
Standmoor Rd. M45: Whitef 4K 59
Standon Wlk. M40: Man 9B 62
(off Blandford Dr.)
Standrick Hill Ri. SK15: C'ook 5H 83
Standring Av. BL8: Bury 4G 40
Stand Ri. M26: Rad 3H 59
Stanedge Gro. WN3: Wig 9E 52
Stanford Cl. M26: Rad 4C 58
Stanford Hall Cres. BL0: Ram 1H 25
Stanhope Av. M25: Pres 6N 59
M34: Aud 3J 97
Stanhope Cl. M34: Dent 4J 97
SK9: Wilm 6J 123
Stanhope Ct. M25: Pres 5N 59
Stanhope Rd. M6: Sal 5L 77
WA14: Bow 5A 114
Stanhope St. M19: Man 8N 95
M34: Aud 4J 97
OL5: Mos 2F 82
OL6: A Lyne 6A 82
OL11: Roch 8D 28
SK5: Stoc 1C 108
WN7: Lei 4F 72
Stanhope Way M35: Fail 2C 80
Stanhorne Av. M8: Man 9F 60
Stanhurst M30: Ecc 7E 76
Stanier Av. M30: Ecc 7D 76
Stanier Cl. SK11: Lym G 9H 131
Stanier Pl. BL6: Hor 2E 36
Stanier St. M9: Man 2K 79
Stanion Gro. SK16: Duk 1A 98
Stan Jolly Wlk. M11: Man 1A 96
Stanlaw Ho. M30: Ecc 9E 76
Stanley & Brocklehurst Ct.
SK10: Macc 4G 131
(off King Edward Rd.)
Stanley Av. M14: Man 6H 95
SK6: Mar 9A 110
SK7: H Gro 4H 119
SK14: Hyde 5B 98
Stanley Av. Nth. M25: Pres 5N 59
Stanley Av. Sth. M25: Pres 5N 59
Stanley Casino 1K 7
Stanley Cl. BL5: W'ton 4J 55
M16: Old T 4B 94
M45: Whitef 2M 59
Stanley Ct. BL9: Bury 6M 7 (1M 41)
Stanley Dr. M45: Whitef 5M 59
WA15: Tim 2G 115
WN7: Lei 2F 72
STANLEY GREEN 9K 117
Stanley Grn. Bus. Pk.
SK8: Chea H 1K 123
Stanley Grn. Ind. Est.
SK8: Chea H 9K 117
(not continuous)
Stanley Grn. Ind. Pk.
SK8: Chea H 1K 123
Stanley Grn. Retail Pk.
SK8: Chea H 9L 117
Stanley Gro. BL6: Hor 3F 36
M12: Man 5L 95
M18: Man 5L 95
M21: Cho H 9N 93
(off Crossland Rd.)
M41: Urm 7D 92
SK4: Stoc 4N 107
Stanley Hall La. SK12: Dis 8F 120
Stanley La. WN2: Asp, Hai 4L 35
Stanley M. BL2: Bolt 5L 39
Stanley Mt. M33: Sale 5G 104
Stanley Pk. Grange SK9: Hand . . . 1J 123
Stanley Pk. Wlk. BL2: Bolt 4K 39
Stanley Pl. OL12: Roch 5C 28
SK11: Macc 5H 131
(off Wood St.)
WN1: Wig 7N 9 (3H 53)
Stanley Rd. BL1: Bolt 3C 38
BL4: Farn 3F 56
M7: Sal 2D 78
M16: Old T 4A 94
M16: Whall R 7D 94
M26: Rad 6E 40
M27: Swin 2G 76
M28: Walk 9L 57
M30: Ecc 9C 76
M34: Dent 6F 96
M45: Whitef 2M 59
OL9: Chad 7F 62
SK4: Stoc 4N 107
SK8: Chea H 9J 117
SK9: Hand 9J 117
WA16: Knut 6F 132
WN2: Asp 6M 35
WN2: P Bri 8K 53
WN8: Uph 4F 50
Stanley Rd. Ind. Est.
M45: Whitef 2M 59
WA16: Knut 7G 132
Stanley Sq. SK15: Stal 9C 82
Stanley St. BL0: Ram 9H 11
M3: Sal 5D 4 (9D 78)
(not continuous)
M8: Man 6F 78
M11: Man 2B 96
M25: Pres 7B 60
M29: Tyld 1B 74
M40: Man 5L 79
M45: Whitef 2M 59
M46: Ath 9L 55
OL4: Lees 6B 64
OL4: Spri 5D 64
OL9: Chad 4F 62
OL10: H'ood 3J 43
OL12: Roch 4C 28
SK1: Stoc 1N 9 (6E 108)
SK11: Macc 4H 131
SK15: Stal 9C 82
WA12: N Wil 6D 86
WN5: Wig 5C 52
Stanley St. Sth. BL3: Bolt . . . 4H 7 (6F 38)
Stanley Way OL16: Roch 8G 28
Stanlo Ho. M1: Man 7J 5
Stanmere Ct. BL8: Haw 2B 24
Stanmoor Dr. WN2: Asp 6N 35
Stanmore Av. M32: Stre 7H 93
Stanmore Dr. BL3: Bolt 7D 38
Stanmore Ho. M34: Aud 1G 97
Stannanought Rd. WN8: Skel 8B 32
(not continuous)
Stannard Rd. M30: Ecc 9N 75
Stanneybrook Cl. OL16: Roch 5F 28
Stanney Cl. OL16: Miln 8J 29
Stanneylands Cl. SK9: Wilm 4H 123
Stanneylands Dr. SK9: Wilm 4G 123
Stanneylands Rd.
SK9: Sty, Wilm 2G 122
Stanney Rd. OL16: Roch 5F 28
Stannybrook Rd. M35: Fail 3H 81
Stanrose Cl. BL7: Eger 4E 22
Stanrose Vs. BL7: Eger 3F 22
Stansbury Pl. SK2: Stoc 1J 119
Stansby Gdns. M12: Man 3K 95
Stansfield Cl. BL2: Bolt 4J 39
WN7: Lei 8L 73
Stansfield Dr. OL11: Roch 4L 27
Stansfield Hall OL15: Lit 5N 15
Stansfield Rd. M35: Fail 2E 80
SK14: Hyde 5B 98
Stansfield St. M11: Man 1B 96
M40: Man 6B 80
OL1: O'ham 3J 63
OL9: Chad 6F 62
Stanstead Cl. WN2: Wig 1J 53
Stansted Wlk. M23: Wyth 7K 105
Stanthorne Av. M20: Man 1F 106
Stanton Av. M7: Sal 4A 78
M20: Man 4D 106
Stanton Cl. WA11: Hay 3A 86
WN3: Wig 8E 52
Stanton Ct. M32: Stre 5K 93
Stanton Gdns. M20: Man 4E 106
SK4: Stoc 7N 107
Stanton St. M11: Man 8A 80
M32: Stre 5K 93
OL9: Chad 8F 62
Stanway Av. BL3: Bolt 6E 38
Stanway Cl. BL3: Bolt 6E 38
M24: Mid 5N 61
Stanway Dr. WA15: Hale 4F 114
Stanway Rd. M45: Whitef 3A 60
Stanway St. M9: Man 2K 79
M32: Stre 5K 93
Stanwell Rd. M27: Swin 3F 76
M40: Man 1A 80
Stanwick Av. M9: Man 7F 60
Stanworth Av. BL2: Bolt 5M 39
Stanworth Cl. M16: Whall R 6D 94
Stanyard Ct. M5: Sal 1N 93
STANYCLIFFE 9A 44
Stanycliffe La. M24: Mid 9N 43
Stanyforth St. SK13: Had 5C 100
Stapleford Cl. BL5: O Hul 5B 56
BL8: Bury 2G 41
M23: Wyth 3M 115
M33: Sale 3L 105
Stapleford Wlk. M34: Dent 8J 97
Staplehurst Cl. WN7: Lei 9E 54
Staplehurst Rd. M40: Man 6M 79
Staplers Wlk. M14: Man 6H 95
(off Stenbury Cl.)
Stapleton Av. BL1: Bolt 3N 37
Stapleton Rd. SK10: Macc 2F 130
Stapleton St. M6: Sal 5J 77
WN2: P Bri 9K 53
Starbeck Cl. BL8: Bury 2F 40
Starcliffe St. BL3: Bolt 1L 57
Star Ct. OL16: Roch 8D 8
Starcross Wlk. M40: Man 4N 79
(off Morecambe Cl.)
Starfield Av. OL15: Lit 3K 29
Star Gro. M7: Sal 4D 78
Star Ind. Est. OL8: O'ham . . . 5D 8 (6K 63)
Starkey St. OL10: H'ood 1J 43
Starkie Rd. BL2: Bolt 5J 39
(Bury Rd.)
BL2: Bolt 3J 39
(Lowerwood La.)
Starkies BL9: Bury 5L 41
Starkie St. M28: Wors 3A 76
Star La. BL6: Hor 1B 36
SK11: Macc 8H 131
STARLING 2E 40
Starling Cl. M22: Shar 1D 116
M43: Droy 7H 81
Starling Dr. BL4: Farn 4G 57
Starling Rd. BL8: Bury 4E 40
M26: Rad 4E 40
Starmoor Dr. M8: Man 4F 78
Starmount Cl. BL2: Bolt 6A 40
Starring Gro. OL15: Lit 9K 15
(off Starring Rd.)
Starring La. OL15: Lit 9J 15
Starring Rd. OL15: Lit 8J 15
Starring Way OL15: Lit 9K 15
Starry Wlk. M7: Sal 6B 78
Stars Brow WN6: Stan 8A 18
Startham Av. WN5: Bil 7H 69
Starting Chair OL4: Scout 3F 64
Stash Gro. M23: Wyth 9A 106
Stately Dr. M24: Mid 4G 60
Statham Cl. M34: Dent 6L 97
Statham Fold SK14: Hyde 5D 98
Statham St. M6: Sal 7A 78
SK11: Macc 5G 131
Statham Wlk. M13: Man 8L 5
Station App. M1: Man 5K 5 (9G 78)
(Ducie St.)
M1: Man 7H 5 (1F 94)
(Whitworth St.)
M46: Ath 7N 55
OL3: Del 9J 47
SK8: H Grn 7F 116
WA15: Alt 2E 6 (2E 114)
Station App. Bus. Est.
OL11: Roch 7D 28
(off Station Rd.)
Station Av. WN2: B'haw 1N 71
WN5: Orr 6H 51
Station Bri. M41: Urm 7D 92
Station Cl. M26: Rad 7F 40
SK14: Hyde 7N 97
Station Cotts. M31: Part 4H 103
SK8: Chea H 5N 117
WA14: W Tim 8D 104
Stationers Entry
OL16: Roch 7C 8 (6D 28)
Station Ho. WA14: Alt 2D 6
Station Ho's. OL3: Dig 7N 47
Station La. OL3: G'fld 6K 65
OL4: Grot 6D 64
Station Lofts OL6: A Lyne 8D 6
Station M. M35: Fail 2C 80
WN4: Gars 7A 70
Station Rd. BL4: Kea 4N 57
BL6: Bla 3A 36
BL7: Tur 1K 23
BL8: G'mount 4F 24
M8: Man 1F 78
M27: Swin, Pen 2F 76
M30: Ecc 9D 76
M32: Stre 6K 93
M41: Urm 7D 92
M44: Irl 1F 102
OL3: Dig 7N 47
OL3: Upp 3L 65
OL4: Grot 6D 64
OL5: Mos 1G 82
OL11: Roch 9D 8 (7D 28)
OL12: Whitw 9N 13
(Market St.)
OL12: Whitw 3B 14
(Meadow Cotts.)
OL15: Lit 9M 15
OL16: Miln 8K 29
PR7: Adl 7J 19
PR7: Cop 4C 18
SK1: Stoc 3K 9 (8C 108)
SK3: Stoc 4J 9 (8C 108)
SK4: Stoc 7K 107
SK5: Stoc 7C 96
SK6: Mar 1C 120
SK6: Stri 6F 120
SK6: Wood 3M 109
SK8: Chea H 5M 117
SK9: Hand 3J 123
SK9: Sty 3F 122
SK9: Wilm 7G 123
SK13: Had 4C 100
SK14: Hyde 7E 98
SK22: N Mil 8L 121
(Mousley Bottom)
SK22: N Mil 6F 120
(Whitecroft Rd.)
WA11: Hay 3A 86

Station Rd. WA14: D Mas 1J 113
WA16: Mob 1M 133
WN1: Wig 9K 9 (3F 52)
WN4: Gars 7N 69
WN8: Par 2A 32
Station Rd. Ind. Est. SK5: Stoc 7C 96
Station Sq. OL5: Mos 1F 82
Station St. BL3: Bolt 5L 7 (6G 39)
OL4: Spri 5C 64
SK7: H Gro 5H 119
SK10: Macc 3H 131
SK13: Glos 8F 100
SK16: Duk 9M 81
Station Ter. WN1: Hai 4F 34
Station Vw. M19: Man 8M 95
M43: Droy 2E 96
SK7: H'Gro 5F 118
SK15: Stal 8C 82
(off Rassbottom St.)
Station Yd. SK22: N Mil 9L 121
Staton Av. BL2: Bolt 4K 39
Staton St. M11: Man 1A 96
Statter St. BL9: Bury 8N 41
Staveleigh Mall
OL6: A Lyne 7D 6 (7M 81)
Staveley Av. BL1: Bolt 7F 22
SK15: Stal 7D 82
Staveley Cl. M24: Mid 1K 61
OL2: Shaw 6A 46
Stavely Wlk. *OL2: O'ham 8J 45*
(off Royton Hall Wlk.)
Staverton Cl. M13: Man 9M 5 (2H 95)
Stavesacre WN7: Lei 7H 73
Staveton Cl. SK7: Bram 4D 118
Stavordale OL12: Roch 6B 8
Staycott St. M16: Whall R 5E 94
Stayley Cotts. *SK15: C'ook 3H 83*
(off School La.)
Stayley Dr. SK15: Stal 8F 82
Steadings Ri. WA16: Mere 2D 132
Stead St. BL0: Ram 8J 11
Steadway OL3: G'fld 6M 65
Stedman Cl. M11: Man 9K 79
Steele Ho. M5: Sal 8A 4 (2B 94)
Steeles Av. SK14: Hyde 6B 98
Steeple Cl. M8: Man 5E 78
Steeple Dr. M5: Sal 9N 77
Steeple St. SK10: Macc 3J 131
Steeple Vw. OL2: O'ham 8H 45
Stein Av. WA3: Low 1A 88
Stelfox Av. M14: Man 8F 94
WA15: Tim 9J 105
Stelfox La. M34: Aud 2J 97
Stelfox St. M30: Ecc 1B 92
Stella St. M9: Man 7G 61
Stelling St. M18: Man 4B 96
Stenbury Cl. M14: Man 6H 95
Stenner La. M20: Man 6F 106
Stenson Sq. *M11: Man 2B 96*
(off Ettrick Cl.)
Stephen Cl. BL8: Bury 2J 41
Stephen Lowry Wlk. *M40: Man 3M 79*
(off McConnell Rd.)
Stephen Oake Cl. M8: Man 5E 78
Stephenson Av. M43: Droy 9E 80
Stephenson Ct. SK5: Stoc 7D 96
Stephenson Rd. M32: Stre 7K 93
WA12: N Wil 7F 86
Stephenson St. BL6: Hor 2D 36
M35: Fail 1E 80
OL4: O'ham 3A 64
WN2: Abr 2L 71
Stephens Rd. M20: Man 3H 107
SK15: Stal 6C 82
Stephens St. BL2: Bolt 5L 39
Stephens Ter. *M20: Man 5G 107*
(off Kings Lynn Cl.)
Stephen St. BL8: Bury 2J 41
M3: Man 6E 78
M41: Urm 7E 92
SK1: Stoc 8F 108
WN2: P Bri 9K 53
Stephen St. Sth. BL8: Bury 3J 41
Stephen's Way WN3: Wig 6B 52
Stephen Wlk. *SK1: Stoc 8F 108*
(off Stephen St.)
Step Hill SK11: Macc 4H 131
STEPPING HILL 3H 119
Steps Mdw. OL12: Roch 1H 29
Stern Av. M5: Sal 1N 93
Sterndale Av. WN6: Stan 2B 34
Sterndale Rd. M28: Wors 4G 74
SK3: Stoc 2C 118
SK6: Rom 7M 109
Sterratt St. BL1: Bolt 5E 38
Stetchworth Dr. M28: Wors 4J 75
Steuber Dr. M44: Irl 3G 103
Stevenage Cl. SK11: Macc 5G 130
Stevenage Dr. SK11: Macc 5F 130
Steven Ct. M21: Cho H 9B 94
Stevenson Cl. BL4: Farn 4H 57
WN3: Wig 6D 52
Stevenson Ct. *BL4: Kea 4M 57*
(off Bent St.)
Stevenson Dr. OL1: O'ham 8B 46
Stevenson Pl. M1: Man 4K 5
Stevenson Rd. M27: Swin 2E 76
Stevenson Sq. M1: Man 4K 5 (9G 78)
OL12: Roch 2G 28
Stevenson St. M3: Sal 4B 4 (9C 78)
M28: Walk 8J 57
Stevens St. SK9: A Edg 4F 126
Stewart Av. BL4: Farn 4J 57
Stewart Rd. WN3: Wig 8D 52
Stewart St. BL1: Bolt 3F 38
BL8: Bury 1H 41
(not continuous)
OL7: A Lyne 8K 81
OL16: Miln 1M 45
Stewerton Cl. WA3: Gol 8J 71
Steynton Cl. BL1: Bolt 4A 38
Stickens Lock La. M44: Irl 9H 91
Stile Cl. M41: Urm 7K 91
Stiles Av. SK6: Mar 9C 110
Stiles Cl. SK13: Had 4A 100
Stillwater Dr. M11: Man 8M 79
Stirling *M30: Ecc 8E 76*
(off Monton La.)
Stirling Av. M20: Man 9E 94
SK6: Mar 2C 120
SK7: H Gro 6H 119
WN2: I Mak 3K 53
Stirling Cl. SK3: Stoc 1A 118
SK10: Macc 2D 130
WN7: Lei 4M 73
Stirling Ct. SK4: Stoc 3A 108
Stirling Dr. SK15: Stal 7D 82
WN4: Gars 6A 70
Stirling Gro. M45: Whitef 3N 59
Stirling Pl. OL10: H'ood 3E 42
Stirling Rd. BL1: Bolt 8F 22
OL9: Chad 7D 62
WN2: Hin 7B 54
Stirling St. OL9: O'ham 4G 63
WN1: Wig 1F 52
Stirrup Brook Gro.
M28: Wors 5G 74
Stirrup Fld. WA3: Gol 1K 87
Stirrup Ga. M28: Wors 5A 76
Stitch La. SK4: Stoc 5B 108
Stitch Mi La. BL2: Bolt 2M 39
Stiups La. OL16: Roch 9F 28
Stobart Av. M25: Pres 9B 60
STOCK BROOK 4F 62
Stockburn Dr. M35: Fail 3F 80
Stockbury Gro. *BL1: Bolt 3G 38*
(off Halliwell Rd.)
Stock Cl. OL12: Roch 3C 28
Stockdale Av. SK3: Stoc 2D 118
Stockdale Gro. BL2: Bolt 3N 39
Stockdale Rd. M9: Man 7K 61
Stockdove M. *WA14: W Tim 8B 104*
(off Daisygate Dr.)
Stockfield Mt. OL9: Chad 5F 62
Stockfield Rd. OL9: Chad 4F 62
Stock Gro. OL16: Miln 6K 29
Stockholm Rd. SK3: Stoc 1B 118
Stockholm St. M11: Man 8N 79
Stockland Cl. M13: Man 9K 5 (2G 94)
Stock La. OL9: Chad 6F 62
Stockley Av. BL2: Bolt 2M 39
Stockley Dr. WN6: App B 4J 33
Stockley Wlk. *M15: Man 3C 94*
(off Shawgreen Cl.)
Stockmar Grange BL1: Bolt 4N 37
STOCKPORT 3K 9 (7C 108)
Stockport Air Raid Shelters 2L 9
Stockport Art Gallery 4L 9 (8D 108)
Stockport County FC 9C 108
Stockport Crematorium
SK1: Stoc 9E 108
Stockport Garrick Theatre
. . . . .3K 9 (7C 108)
Stockport Golf Course 2M 119
STOCKPORT GREAT MOOR 3G 118
STOCKPORT LITTLE MOOR 8F 108
Stockport Plaza 2K 9
Stockport Rd. M12: Man 9N 5 (3H 95)
M13: Man 3H 95
M19: Man 6M 95
M34: Dent 6K 97
OL4: Lyd 6F 64
OL5: Mos 9F 64
OL7: A Lyne 9A 6 (1K 97)
SK3: Stoc 9L 107
SK6: Mar 1M 119
SK6: Rom 6M 109
SK8: Chea 1J 117
SK14: Hat, Mot 8H 99
SK14: Hyde 8B 98
WA15: Alt, Tim 2E 6 (2E 114)
Stockport Rd. E. SK6: Bred 4K 109
Stockport Rd. W. SK6: Bred 5G 108
Stockport Station (Rail) . . .4J 9 (8C 108)
Stockport Story Mus. & Staircase House
. . . . .1L 9
Stockport Trad. Est.
SK4: Stoc 7N 107
Stockport Viaduct 2H 9 (6B 108)
Stockport Village SK1: Stoc 2K 9
Stock Rd. OL12: Roch 3E 28
Stocks, The SK13: Tin 2C 100
Stocks Brow SK13: Tin 2C 100
Stocks Cotts. BL6: Hor 9F 20
Stocks Ct., The WA3: Low 1N 87
Stocksfield Dr. M9: Man 8H 61
M38: Lit H 6G 56
Stocks Gdns. SK15: Stal 9F 82
Stocksgate OL12: Roch 3N 27
Stocks Ind. Est. M30: Ecc 8C 76
Stocks La. SK15: Stal 9E 82
Stocks Pk. Dr. BL6: Hor 1E 36
Stocks St. M8: Man 7F 78
OL11: Roch 2N 43
Stocks St. E. M8: Man 7F 78
Stock St. BL8: Bury 8L 25
Stockton Av. SK3: Stoc 8N 107
Stockton Dr. BL8: Bury 8L 25
Stockton Pk. OL4: O'ham 5A 64
Stockton Rd. BL4: Farn 1K 57
M21: Cho H 9N 93
SK9: Wilm 1E 126
Stockton St. M16: Whall R 5D 94
M27: Swin 3E 76
OL15: Lit 9L 15
Stockwell Cl. WN3: Wins 8A 52
Stockwood Wlk. M9: Man 3J 79
Stoke Abbot Cl. SK7: Bram 8C 118
Stokesay Cl. BL9: Bury 7M 41
OL2: O'ham 8L 45
Stokesay Dr. SK7: H Gro 6G 119
Stokesay Rd. M33: Sale 3E 104
Stokesby Gdns. BL6: Los 4K 37
Stokesley Wlk. *BL3: Bolt 9F 38*
(off Belford Dr.)
Stokes Mill *SK15: Stal 8E 82*
(off Higher Tame St.)
Stokes St. M11: Man 8B 80
Stokoe Av. WA14: Alt 2A 114
Stonall Av. M15: Man 9C 4 (3C 94)
Stoneacre BL6: Los 4H 37
Stoneacre Ct. M27: Swin 3F 76
Stoneacre Dr. PR6: Adl 4K 19
Stoneacre Rd. M22: Wyth 6B 116
Stonebeck Cl. BL5: O Hul 3A 56
Stonebeck Rd. M23: Wyth 2M 115
Stonebottom Brow *OL3: Dob 1L 65*
(off Wool Rd.)
STONE BREAKS 4E 64
Stonebreaks Rd. OL4: Spri 5D 64
Stonebridge Cl. BL6: Los 6L 37
Stonebridge M. M29: Ast 5B 74
Stonechat Cl. M28: Wors 2J 75
M43: Droy 7G 81
WA3: Low 1A 88
Stonechurch BL3: Bolt 7E 38
Stonecliffe Av. SK15: Stal 8D 82
Stonecliffe Ter. SK15: Stal 7E 82
Stone Cl. BL0: Ram 1G 24
STONECLOUGH 4C 58
Stoneclough M. OL1: O'ham 2J 63
Stoneclough Ri. M26: Rad 3B 58
Stoneclough Rd. BL4: Kea 4N 57
M26: Rad 4N 57
Stonecroft OL1: O'ham 1C 8
Stonecrop WN6: App B 3H 33
Stone Cross La. Nth.
WA3: Low 2M 87
Stone Cross La. Sth.
WA3: Low 4M 87
STONE CROSS PARK 2L 87
Stonedelph Cl. BL2: Ain 3D 40
Stonefield M29: Tyld 1D 74
Stonefield Dr. M8: Man 5D 78
Stonefield St. OL16: Miln 8K 29
Stoneflat Ct. OL12: Roch 5B 28
Stonegate Fold PR6: H Char 4L 19
Stone Hall La. WN8: Dal 8D 32
Stonehaven BL3: Bolt 9A 38
WN3: Wins 9A 52
Stonehead St. M9: Man 3L 79
Stonehewer St. M26: Rad 1H 59
Stonehill Cres. OL12: Roch 2M 27
Stonehill Dr. OL12: Roch 2M 27
Stone Hill Ind. Est. BL4: Farn 5L 57
Stone Hill La. OL12: Roch 3M 27
Stone Hill Rd. BL4: Farn 5L 57
Stonehill Rd. OL12: Roch 2M 27
Stonehouse BL7: Bro X 6J 23
Stone Ho. Rd. WN5: Wig 2A 52
Stonehouse Wlk. *M23: Wyth 9L 105*
(off Sandy La.)
Stonehurst SK6: Mar 3B 120
Stonehurst Cl. M12: Man 3M 95
Stonelands Way OL4: Grot 7D 64
Stone Lea Way *M46: Ath 9J 55*
(off Gadbury Fold)
Stoneleigh Av. M33: Sale 3D 104
Stoneleigh Cl. SK10: Macc 2G 130
Stoneleigh Dr. M26: Rad 4B 58
Stoneleigh Rd. OL4: Spri 4D 64
Stoneleigh St. OL1: O'ham 2M 63
Stonelow Cl. M15: Man 3E 94
Stonemead SK6: Rom 5B 110
Stonemead Av. WA15: Haleb 8J 115
Stonemead Cl. BL3: Bolt 8G 38
Stonemead Dr. M9: Man 7J 61
Stonemere Dr. M26: Rad 2J 59
Stone Mill Cotts. BL7: Tur 2L 23
Stonemill Ri. WN6: App B 5H 33
Stonemill Ter. SK5: Stoc 5D 108
Stonepail Cl. SK8: Gat 2E 116
Stonepail Rd. SK8: Gat 2F 116
Stone Pale M45: Whitef 4M 59
Stone Pit Cl. WA3: Low 9B 72
Stone Pit La. WA3: Cro 7B 88
Stone Pits BL0: Eden 3L 11
Stone Pl. M14: Man 6H 95
Stoneridge SK13: Had 4B 100
Stone Row SK6: Mar 1D 120
WN2: Asp 9K 35
Stones Bank Rd. BL7: Bel 1A 22
Stonesby Cl. M16: Whall R 5C 94
Stonesdale Cl. OL2: O'ham 7J 45
Stonesteads Dr. BL7: Bro X 5H 23
Stonesteads Way BL7: Bro X 5H 23
Stone St. BL2: Bolt 8L 23
M3: Man 7E 4 (1D 94)
OL16: Miln 8K 29
Stoneswood Dr. OL5: Mos 9G 64
Stoneswood Rd. OL3: Del 9H 47
Stonethwaite Cl. WN3: Wig 9D 52
Stoney Bank M26: Rad 4C 58
Stoney Brow WN8: Roby M 9F 32
Stoneycroft Av. BL6: Hor 9F 20
Stoneycroft Cl. BL6: Hor 8F 20
STONEYFIELD 8D 28
Stoneyfield SK15: Stal 6D 82
Stoneyfield Cl. M16: Whall R 7E 94
Stoneyfold La. SK11: Macc 6L 131
Stoneygate La. WN6: App B 2F 32
Stoneygate Wlk. *M11: Man 2B 96*
(off Botha Cl.)
Stoneyholme Av. M8: Man 3G 79
Stoney Knoll M7: Sal 4C 78
Stoneyland Dr. SK22: N Mil 7L 121
Stoney La. OL3: Del 5H 47
PR7: Adl 9H 19
SK9: Wilm 9E 122
WN6: Wrig 1A 32
WN8: Par, Wrig 1A 32
Stoneyroyd OL12: Whitw 5B 14
Stoneyside Av. M28: Walk 7M 57
Stoneyside Gro. M28: Walk 7M 57
Stoneyvale Ct. OL11: Roch 9D 28
Stonie Heyes Av. OL12: Roch 3F 28
Stonor Rd. PR7: Adl 6J 19
Stony Bri. La. WA15: Tim 9G 105
Stonyford Rd. M33: Sale 4K 105
Stony Head *OL15: Lit 4N 15*
(off Higher Calderbrook Rd.)
Stonyhurst PR7: Chor 1F 18
Stonyhurst Av. BL1: Bolt 8F 22
WN3: I Mak 5G 53
Stonyhurst Cres. WA3: Cul 4F 88
Stopes Rd. BL3: Lit L 9C 40
M26: Rad 8C 40
Stopford Av. OL15: Lit 1J 29
Stopford St. M11: Man 2C 96
SK3: Stoc 8B 108
WN2: I Mak 4J 53
Stopford Wlk. M34: Dent 6K 97
Stopforth St. WN6: Wig 2D 52
Stopley Wlk. *M11: Man 1M 95*
(off Mill St.)
Store Pas. *OL15: Lit 9L 15*
(off John St.)
Stores Cotts. OL4: Gras 6H 65
Stores Rd. M90: Man A 9N 115
Stores St. M25: Pres 7B 60
Store St. BL6: Hor 9E 20
M1: Man 6L 5 (1G 95)
M11: Man 2N 95
M26: Rad 8K 41
OL2: Shaw 4N 45
OL7: A Lyne 4L 81
OL11: Roch 4K 27
SK2: Stoc 3G 118
SK10: Boll 5M 129
Storeton Cl. M22: Wyth 5D 116
Stormer Hill Fold BL8: Tot 5F 24
Stortford Dr. M23: Wyth 6A 106
Storth Bank SK13: Glos 9B 100
Storth Mdw. Rd. SK13: Glos 9B 100
Storwood Cl. WN5: Orr 6J 51
Stothard Rd. M32: Stre 8H 93
Stott Dr. M41: Urm 8L 91
Stottfield OL2: O'ham 9J 45
Stott Ho. OL8: O'ham 5C 8 (6K 63)
Stott La. BL2: Bolt 3J 39
M6: Sal 7H 77
M24: Mid 7L 43
Stott Milne St. OL9: Chad 6F 62
Stott Rd. M27: Swin 4D 76
OL9: Chad 8C 62
Stott's La. M40: Man 4B 80
Stott St. M35: Fail 4B 80
OL12: Roch 4D 28
OL16: Miln 9K 29
OL16: Roch 2H 29
Stott Wharf WN7: Lei 6K 73
Stourbridge Av. M38: Lit H 5H 57
Stour Cl. WA14: Alt 1A 6 (1C 114)
Stourport Cl. SK6: Rom 7L 109
Stour Rd. M29: Ast 2C 74
Stout St. WN7: Lei 5E 72
Stovell Av. M12: Man 7M 95
Stovell Rd. M40: Man 2M 79
Stowe Cl. BL8: Bury 8K 25
Stowe Gdns. WN7: Lei 5J 73
Stowell Ct. BL1: Bolt 3F 38
Stowell St. BL1: Bolt 3F 38
M5: Sal 9L 77
(off Dolbey St.)
Stowfield Cl. M9: Man 7G 61
Stow Gdns. M20: Man 2F 106
Stracey St. M40: Man 7K 79
(not continuous)
Stradbroke Cl. M18: Man 4A 96
WA3: Low 2C 88
Strain Av. M9: Man 7J 61
Straits, The M29: Ast 4D 74
Strand, The BL6: Hor 1F 36
OL11: Roch 2D 44
WN4: A Mak 6E 70
Strand Av. WN4: A Mak 6E 70
Strand Ct. M32: Stre 9J 93
Strandedge Cl. BL0: Ram 1J 25
Strand Way OL2: O'ham 1H 63
Strange Rd. WN4: Gars 7A 70
Strange St. WN7: Lei 6D 72
STRANGEWAYS 6E 78
Strangford St. M26: Rad 8D 40
Strang St. BL0: Ram 8J 11
Stranraer Rd. WN5: Wig 2N 51
Stranton Dr. M28: Wors 2C 76
Stratfield Av. M23: Wyth 7K 105
Stratford Av. BL1: Bolt 3B 38
BL9: Bury 5L 25
M20: Man 3E 106
M30: Ecc 1C 92
OL8: O'ham 8K 63
OL11: Roch 8C 28
Stratford Cl. BL4: Farn 2G 57
Stratford Gdns. SK6: Bred 5K 109
Stratford Rd. M24: Mid 6N 61
Stratford Sq. SK8: H Grn 8H 117
Stratford St. WN6: Wig 2D 52
Stratford Way SK11: Macc 7G 131
Strathaven Pl. OL10: H'ood 3E 42
Strathblane Cl. M20: Man 1G 107
Strathblane Ho. *SK8: Chea 1J 117*
(off Ashfield Rd.)
Strathfield Dr. M11: Man 8A 80
Strathmere Av. M32: Stre 6K 93
Strathmore Av. M16: Whall R 7A 94
M34: Dent 7M 97
WN4: A Mak 5D 70
Strathmore Cl. BL0: Ram 1J 25
Strathmore Rd. BL2: Bolt 3M 39
Stratton Dr. WN2: P Bri 1J 71
Stratton Gro. BL6: Hor 8D 20
Stratton Rd. M16: Whall R 7A 94
M27: Pen 1F 76
SK2: Stoc 8G 109
Strawberry Bank *M6: Sal 7A 78*
(off Strawberry Rd.)
Strawberry Cl. WA14: B'ath 9B 104
Strawberry Flds. M43: Droy 8G 80
Strawberry Hill M6: Sal 7A 78
Strawberry Hill Rd. BL2: Bolt 7J 39
Strawberry La. OL5: Mos 7F 64
SK9: Wilm 8D 122
Strawberry Rd. M6: Sal 7N 77
Stray, The BL1: Bolt 9J 23
Stray St. M11: Man 1C 96
Streamside Cl. WA15: Tim 3H 115
Stream Ter. SK1: Stoc 7F 108
Street, The OL2: Shaw 5B 46
STREET BRIDGE 9E 44
Street Bri. Rd. OL1: Chad 1E 62
STREET END 2E 80
Streetgate M38: Lit H 6G 57
Streethouse La. OL3: Dob 2J 65
Street La. M26: Rad 4E 40
SK10: Adl 6G 125
Street Lodge OL11: Roch 3N 43
Street With No Name, The *8M 95*
(off Levenshulme Station)
STRETFORD 8J 93
Stretford Ho. *M32: Stre 8J 93*
(off Chapel La.)
Stretford Leisure Cen. 5M 93
Stretford Mall M32: Stre 8J 93
Stretford Motorway Est.
M32: Stre 4G 92
Stretford Pl. OL12: Roch 2C 28
Stretford Rd. M15: Man 3D 94
M16: Old T 4B 94
M41: Urm 8D 92
Stretford Stop (Metro) 8K 93
Stretton Av. M20: Man 5H 107
M32: Stre 6G 93
M33: Sale 4E 104
WA3: Low 2A 88
WN5: Bil 5J 69
Stretton Cl. M40: Man 5J 79
WN6: Stan 4A 34
Stretton Rd. BL0: Ram 3G 24
BL3: Bolt 8C 38
BL8: G'mount 3G 24
Stretton Way *SK9: Hand 1J 123*
(off Sandiway Rd.)
Striding Edge Wlk. OL1: O'ham 2L 63
Strike Ten Bowl 9C 28
STRINE DALE 8C 46
STRINES .5F 120
Strines Cl. WN2: Hin 5N 53
Strines Ct. SK14: Hyde 5B 98
STRINESDALE 9E 46
Strinesdale Cen. 2C 64
Strines Rd. SK6: Mar, Dis 1D 120
Strines Station (Rail) 6G 121
Stringer Av. SK14: Mot 7J 99
Stringer Cl. SK14: Mot 7J 99
Stringer St. SK1: Stoc 6E 108
WN7: Lei 5M 73
Stringer Way SK14: Mot 7J 99
Stroma Gdns. M41: Urm 4C 92
Stromness Gro. OL10: H'ood 3E 42
Strong St. M7: Sal 6D 78
STRONGSTRY 4J 11
Strongstry Rd. BL0: Ram 4J 11
Strontian Wlk. *M11: Man 9A 80*
(off Edith Cavell Cl.)
Stroud Av. M30: Ecc 7B 76
Stroud Cl. M24: Mid 6M 61
WN2: Wig 1J 53
Struan Ct. WA14: Alt 2A 6 (2C 114)
Stuart Av. M44: Irl 7G 91
SK6: Mar 9N 109
WN2: Hin 8D 54
Stuart Cl. WN2: P Bri 9J 53
Stuart Ct. *SK10: Macc 2F 130*
(off Collingwood Cl.)
Stuart Cres. WN5: Bil 5H 69
Stuart Ho. M43: Droy 1E 96
Stuart Pl. M43: Droy 7B 80
Stuart Rd. M32: Stre 6K 93
SK6: Bred 2H 109
WA14: B'ath 9B 104
Stuart St. M11: Man 8M 79
M24: Mid 3A 62
OL8: O'ham 6J 63
OL16: Roch 9F 8 (7E 28)
(not continuous)
Stuart St. E. M11: Man 8M 79
Stuart Wlk. M24: Mid 4L 61
STUBBINS .5J 11
Stubbins Cl. M23: Wyth 7L 105
Stubbins La. BL0: Eden, Ram 7J 11
Stubbins St. BL0: Ram 5J 11
Stubbins Va. Rd. BL0: Ram 4J 11
Stubbins Va. Ter. BL0: Ram 5H 11
Stubbs Cl. M7: Sal 2A 78
Stubbs Ter. SK11: Macc 5J 131
STUBLEY .9K 15
Stubley Gdns. OL15: Lit 9L 15
Stubley La. OL15: Lit 9K 15
Stubley Mill Rd. OL15: Lit 1J 29
(not continuous)
STUBSHAW CROSS 5G 71
Studd Brow OL12: Whitw 3B 14
Student Village M1: Man 8G 5
M6: Sal 6B 78
Studforth Wlk. *M15: Man 4F 94*
(off Botham Cl.)
Studio Cinema, The *7G 133*
(off Toft Rd.)
Studland Rd. M22: Wyth 4E 116
Studley Cl. OL2: O'ham 8L 45
Studley Ct. M29: Tyld 1A 74
Sturgess St. WA12: N Wil 6C 86
Sturton Av. WN3: Wig 8B 52
STYAL 3E 122
Styal Av. M32: Stre 6G 93
SK5: Stoc 2D 108
Styal Country Pk. 4E 122
Styalgate SK8: Gat 2E 116
Styal Golf Course 1F 122
Styal Gro. SK8: Gat 4F 116
Styal Rd. M22: Wyth 9E 116
SK8: Gat, H Grn 2F 116
SK9: Sty, Wilm 3F 122
Styal Station (Rail) 2F 122
Styal St. BL1: Bolt 4C 38
Styal Vw. SK9: Wilm 4G 123
Stylehead Dr. M24: Mid 9J 43
Style St. M4: Man 1J 5 (7F 78)
STYPERSON 2L 129
Styperson Way SK12: Poy 3J 125
Sudbrook Cl. WA3: Low 1A 88
Sudbury Cl. *M16: Old T 4B 94*
(off Stanley Rd.)
WN3: Wig 9E 52
Sudbury Dr. BL6: Los 6L 37
SK8: H Grn 7J 117
Sudbury Rd. SK7: H Gro 7J 119
SUDDEN 9A 28
Sudden St. OL11: Roch 9A 28

Sudell St. M4: Man 1L 5 (7G 79)
(not continuous)
M40: Man 1M 5 (7H 79)
Sudell St. Ind. Est. M4: Man 1L 5
Sudley Rd. OL11: Roch 8A 28
Sudlow St. OL16: Roch 3F 28
Sudren St. BL8: Bury 1F 40
Sue Patterson Wlk. *M40: Man* 5J 79
(off Aldbourne Cl.)
Suez St. WA12: N Wil 6D 86
Suffield Wlk. M22: Wyth 6C 116
Suffolk Av. M43: Droy 7E 80
Suffolk Cl. BL3: Lit L 7B 40
SK10: Macc 3D 130
WN1: Stan 4E 34
Suffolk Dr. SK5: Stoc 2G 109
SK9: Wilm 5G 123
Suffolk Gro. WN7: Lei 5E 72
Suffolk Rd. WA14: Alt 3B 114
Suffolk St. M6: Sal 5N 77
OL9: O'ham 6F 62
OL11: Roch 9C 8 (7D 28)
Sugar La. OL3: Dob 1K 65
SK10: Adl, Boll 9K 125
Sugar Mill Sq. M5: Sal 8K 77
Sugar Pit La. WA16: Knut 5E 132
Sugden Sports Cen. 9J 5 (2F 94)
Sugden St. OL6: A Lyne 7A 82
Sulby Av. M32: Stre 7L 93
Sulby St. M26: Rad 4B 58
M40: Man 2M 79
Sulgrave Av. SK12: Poy 2K 125
Sullivan St. M12: Man 6M 95
Sullivan Way WN1: Wig 6M 9 (2G 53)
Sultan St. BL9: Bury 4M 41
Sulway Cl. M27: Swin 3G 76
Sumac St. M11: Man 8B 80
Sumbland Ho. M27: Clif 9H 59
Summer Av. M41: Urm 7E 92
Summerbottom SK14: B'tom 9K 99
Summer Castle
OL16: Roch 8E 8 (6E 28)
Summer Ct. M33: Sale 6C 104
Summercroft OL9: Chad 8F 62
Summercroft Cl. WA3: Gol 2K 87
Summerdale Dr. BL0: Ram 3H 25
Summerfield Av. M43: Droy 7C 80
Summerfield Ct. M21: Cho H 8M 93
Summerfield Dr. M24: Mid 1A 62
M25: Pres 1N 77
M29: Ast 2C 74
Summerfield Pl. SK9: Wilm 8F 122
Summerfield Rd. BL3: Bolt 8J 39
M22: Wyth 5B 116
M28: Wors 3A 76
WA16: Mob 4M 133
Summerfields PR7: Cop 6C 18
WA16: Knut 5J 133
Summerfields Village Cen.
SK9: Wilm 5J 123
Summerfield Vw. OL8: O'ham 8N 63
Summer Hill *OL5: Mos* 9G 64
(off Roughtown Rd.)
Summer Hill Cl. BL1: Bolt 7E 22
Summerhill Rd. SK10: P'bury 9D 128
Summerhill Vw. OL3: Dens 3G 46
Summerlea SK8: Chea H 7N 117
Summerlea Cl. SK10: Macc 3H 131
Summer Pl. M14: Man 7H 95
Summers Av. SK15: Stal 8F 82
Summers Cl. WA16: Knut 9G 133
SUMMERSEAT 3J 25
Summerseat Cl. M5: Sal 1N 93
OL4: Spri 4D 64
Summerseat La. BL0: Ram 2G 24
Summerseat Station
East Lancashire Railway 3J 25
Summersgill Cl. OL10: H'ood 3K 43
Summershades La. OL4: Gras 5G 65
Summershades Ri. OL4: Gras 5G 65
Summers St. OL9: Chad 4G 62
Summer St. BL6: Hor 9D 20
OL16: Roch 8E 8 (6E 28)
Summers Way WA16: Knut 9G 133
Summerton Ho. *M5: Sal* 9N 77
(off Buckingham St.)
Summervale Ho. OL9: O'ham 3A 8
Summerville Av. M9: Man 3L 79
Summerville Rd. M6: Sal 4L 77
SUMMIT
OL2 4G 44
OL10 2F 42
OL15 4A 16
Summit Cl. BL9: Bury 9E 26
Summit St. OL10: H'ood 2E 42
Sumner Av. BL2: Ain 3D 40
Sumner Rd. M6: Sal 5K 77
Sumners Pl. SK13: Glos 8D 100
Sumner St. BL3: Bolt 1C 56
M46: Ath 8L 55
OL2: Shaw 7M 45
SK13: Glos 9E 100
WN2: Asp 7N 35
Sumner Way M41: Urm 7D 92
Sunadale Cl. BL3: Bolt 7C 38
Sunbank Cl. OL12: Roch 3B 28
Sunbank La. WA15: Ring 9K 115
Sunbeam St. WA12: N Wil 6F 86
Sunbeam Wlk. *M11: Man* 9L 79
(off Hopedale Cl.)
Sunbury Cl. SK9: Wilm 4K 123
SK16: Duk 1C 98
Sunbury Dr. M40: Man 6B 80
Sundance Ct. M50: Sal 1L 93
Sunderland Arc. *SK11: Macc* 5H 131
(off Sunderland St.)
Sunderland Av. OL6: A Lyne 6N 81
Sunderland Pl. WN5: Wig 2A 52
(not continuous)
Sunderland St. SK11: Macc 5H 131
Sundew Cl. OL10: H'ood 2J 43
Sundew Pl. M24: Mid 4B 62
Sundial Cl. SK14: Hat 6G 98
Sundial Ho. WA3: Cul 6H 89
Sundial Rd. SK2: Stoc 9H 109
Sundial Wlk. SK14: Hat 6G 98
Sundown Cl. SK22: N Mil 7K 121
Sundridge Cl. BL3: Bolt 9B 38
Sun Dr. OL15: Lit 9N 15
Sunfield SK6: Rom 5M 109
Sunfield Av. OL4: O'ham 9B 46
Sunfield Cres. OL2: O'ham 9J 45
Sunfield Dr. OL2: O'ham 9K 45
Sunfield Est. OL3: Dig 8M 47
Sunfield La. OL3: Dig 8M 47
Sunfield Rd. OL1: O'ham 3J 63
Sunfield Way OL4: Lees 4B 64
Sunflower Gro. OL9: Chad 3D 62
Sunflower Mdw. M44: Irl 7J 91
Sun Ga. OL15: Lit 4K 29
SUN GREEN 6H 83
Sun Grn. SK15: Mill 6H 83
SUN HILL 4C 64
Sun Hill OL4: Lees 4C 64
Sunhill Cl. OL16: Roch 2F 44
Sunk La. M24: Mid 3M 61
Sunlaws Ct. SK13: Glos 9D 100
Sunlaws St. SK13: Glos 9D 100
Sunleigh Rd. WN2: Hin 5A 54
Sunlight Rd. BL1: Bolt 5D 38
Sunningdale Av. M11: Man 8N 79
M26: Rad 7D 40
M33: Sale 5L 105
M45: Whitef 4J 59
Sunningdale Cl. BL8: Bury 4G 41
SK14: Hyde 4C 98
Sunningdale Ct. BL3: Lit L 9B 40
M34: Dent 6F 96
Sunningdale Dr. M6: Sal 5G 77
M25: Pres 6N 59
M44: Irl 6G 91
OL10: H'ood 4J 43
SK7: Bram 8E 118
SK13: Glos 8G 101
(not continuous)
Sunningdale Gro. WN7: Lei 3M 73
Sunningdale Ho. M33: Sale 5L 105
Sunningdale Rd. M34: Dent 8L 97
M41: Urm 8B 92
SK8: Chea H 8M 117
SK11: Macc 6E 130
Sunningdale Wlk. *BL3: Bolt* 7E 38
(off Dinsdale Dr.)
Sunninghey Ct. SK9: A Edg 3E 126
Sunning Hill St. BL3: Bolt 8E 38
Sunny Av. BL9: Bury 8M 25
SUNNY BANK 9N 41
Sunny Bank M26: Rad 3A 58
OL4: Lees 6B 64
Sunnybank SK9: Wilm 8F 122
Sunnybank Av. M30: Ecc 7F 76
M43: Droy 9D 80
SK4: Stoc 4L 107
Sunnybank Cl. SK11: Macc 7H 131
WA12: N Wil 5F 86
Sunny Bank Cotts. BB4: Has 1F 10
Sunnybank Dr. SK9: Wilm 1C 126
Sunny Bank Rd. BB4: Has 1F 10
(not continuous)
BL9: Bury 9M 41
M13: Man 6K 95
Sunnybank Rd. BL1: Bolt 2D 38
M29: Ast 3C 74
M43: Droy 9D 80
WA14: Bow 6C 114
Sunny Banks SK13: Glos 9D 100
Sunny Bower St. BL8: Tot 7F 24
Sunny Brow PR7: Cop 3D 18
Sunny Brow Rd. M18: Man 4A 96
M24: Mid 3K 61
Sunny Dr. M25: Pres 7M 59
WN5: Orr 5K 51
Sunnyfield Rd. M25: Pres 4B 60
SK4: Stoc 5L 107
Sunnyfields WN3: Wins 9N 51
Sunny Gth. BL5: W'ton 3G 54
Sunnylea Av. M19: Man 3K 107
Sunny Lea M. *SK9: Wilm* 8F 122
(off Victoria Rd.)
Sunnymead Av. BL1: Bolt 9G 23
Sunnymede Va. BL0: Ram 2G 25
Sunnyside M43: Droy 7D 80
OL7: A Lyne 5K 81
Sunnyside Av. M43: Droy 6D 80
Sunny Side Cotts. M32: Stre 7M 93
OL12: Roch 3G 27
Sunnyside Ct. M20: Man 5H 107
M43: Droy 7D 80
Sunnyside Cres. OL6: A Lyne 8A 82
Sunnyside Gro. OL6: A Lyne 8A 82
Sunnyside Rd. BL1: Bolt 2D 38
M43: Droy 7D 80
WN4: A Mak 4C 70
Sunny Top BL8: Haw 3C 24
Sunnywood Cl. BL8: Tot 7F 24
Sunnywood Dr. BL8: Tot 7G 24
Sunnywood La. BL8: Tot 7G 24
Sunrise Vw. OL15: Lit 5A 16
Sunset Av. M22: Nor 6C 106
Sunset Bus. Pk. BL4: Kea 6C 58
Sunshine Pl. M14: Man 7F 94
Sun St. BL0: Ram 7H 11
OL5: Mos 1F 82
Sun Vw. OL2: O'ham 9L 45
Sunwell Ter. SK6: Mar 3C 120
Surbiton Rd. M40: Man 6N 79
Surma Cl. OL9: O'ham 4H 63
OL16: Roch 8F 28
Surrey Av. M43: Droy 7D 80
OL2: Shaw 5K 45
WN7: Lei 6N 73
Surrey Cl. BL3: Lit L 8B 40
Surrey Dr. BL9: Bury 4M 41
Surrey Pk. Cl. OL2: Shaw 4M 45
Surrey Rd. M9: Man 9J 61
SK11: Gaws 8E 130
Surrey St. M9: Man 9H 61
OL6: A Lyne 5A 82
OL9: O'ham 6G 62
SK13: Glos 8E 100
Surrey Way SK5: Stoc 4G 108
Surtees Rd. M23: Wyth 6N 105
Sussex Av. BL9: Bury 3D 42
M20: Man 4G 107
SK11: Gaws 7E 130
Sussex Cl. M27: Clif 9G 58
OL9: Chad 5F 62
WN1: Stan 3E 34
WN2: Hin 6C 54
Sussex Dr. BL9: Bury 4M 41
M43: Droy 7E 80
Sussex Pl. M29: Tyld 8B 56
SK14: Hyde 4C 98
Sussex Rd. M31: Part 6F 102
M44: Cad 2D 102
SK3: Stoc 8N 107
Sussex St. M2: Man 4G 5 (9E 78)
M7: Sal 6C 78
OL11: Roch 9C 8 (7D 28)
WN7: Lei 6N 73
Sutch La. WA13: Lym 4B 112
Sutcliffe Av. M12: Man 7N 95
Sutcliffe St. BL1: Bolt 2F 38
M24: Mid 3A 62
OL2: O'ham 9L 45
OL7: A Lyne 9K 81
OL8: O'ham 6J 63
OL15: Lit 8M 15
Sutherland Cl. OL8: O'ham 1K 81
Sutherland Dr. SK10: Macc 3E 130
Sutherland Flats *OL10: H'ood* 2H 43
(off Meadow Cl.)
Sutherland Gro. BL4: Farn 3K 57
Sutherland Rd. BL1: Bolt 3B 38
M16: Old T 6N 93
OL10: H'ood 3D 42
WN3: Wig 8D 52
Sutherland St. BL4: Farn 3K 57
M27: Swin 1E 76
M30: Ecc 7B 76
OL6: A Lyne 7B 82
WN2: Hin 6M 53
WN5: Wig 5C 52
Suthers St. M26: Rad 2J 59
OL9: O'ham 5G 62
Sutton Av. WA3: Cul 5G 89
Sutton Cl. BL8: Bury 4H 41
SK11: Macc 7H 131
Sutton Dr. M43: Droy 7C 80
Sutton Fold PR6: Adl 4K 19
Sutton Ho. M6: Sal 7M 77
Sutton La. PR6: Adl 5L 19
(Fielding Pl.)
PR6: Adl 4K 19
(Stoneacre Dr.)
SUTTON LANE ENDS 9K 131
Sutton Mnr. M21: Cho H 8N 93
Sutton Rd. BL3: Bolt 8A 38
M18: Man 6A 96
SK4: Stoc 5A 108
SK9: A Edg 4E 126
SK12: Poy 4L 125
Suttons La. SK6: Mar 2D 120
Sutton Wlk. SK14: Hat 7F 98
Sutton Way *M6: Sal* 7N 77
(off Salford Shop. City)
SK9: Hand 1K 123
(off Sandiway Rd.)
SK13: Had 4C 100
Swailes St. OL4: O'ham 5M 63
Swaindrod La. OL15: Lit 7B 16
Swaine St. SK3: Stoc 3J 9 (7C 108)
Swainsthorpe Dr. M9: Man 2K 79
Swain St. OL12: Roch 4C 28
Swains Wlk. WA16: O Tab, Tab 4A 132
Swalecliff Av. M23: Wyth 7K 105
Swale Cl. SK9: Wilm 4K 123
Swaledale Cl. OL2: O'ham 7J 45
Swale Dr. WA14: Alt 1A 6 (1C 114)
Swallow Bank Dr. OL11: Roch 1N 43
Swallow Cl. SK10: Macc 5L 131
SK15: C'ook 3J 83
Swallow Ct. SK9: Wilm 5G 123
Swallow Dr. BL9: Bury 9A 26
M44: Irl 6H 91
OL11: Roch 6L 27
Swallowfield M44: Irl 7H 91
WN7: Lei 5J 73
Swallow Fold SK13: Glos 9B 100
Swallow La. SK15: C'ook 3J 83
Swallow St. M11: Man 9L 79
M12: Man 7M 95
OL8: O'ham 9H 63
SK1: Stoc 9D 108
Swallows Wood Nature Reserve
1N 99
Swanage Av. M23: Wyth 7K 105
SK2: Stoc 1H 119
Swanage Cl. BL8: Bury 7J 25
Swanage Rd. M30: Ecc 7B 76
Swanbourne Gdns. SK3: Stoc 1A 118
Swan Cl. SK12: Poy 2F 124
Swan Ct. OL2: Shaw 6M 45
Swanfield Wlk. *WA3: Gol* 8J 71
(off Walters Grn. Cres.)
Swan Gro. M46: Ath 9K 55
Swanhill Cl. M18: Man 3D 96
Swan La. BL3: Bolt 8E 38
WN2: Hin 7D 54
Swanley Av. M40: Man 5K 79
Swan Mdw. Ind. Est. WN3: Wig 4E 52
Swan Mdw. Rd.
WN3: Wig 9G 9 (4E 52)
Swann Ct. SK8: Chea H 6N 117
Swann Gro. SK8: Chea H 6N 117
Swann La. SK8: Chea H 6M 117
Swann St. WN3: Wig 4E 52
Swan Rd. BL8: G'mount 3F 24
WA12: N Wil 5A 86
WA15: Tim 7G 105
SWANSCOE 1M 131
Swanscoe Av. SK10: Boll 6L 129
Swanscoe La. SK10: Rain 1M 131
Swansea St. OL8: O'ham 7M 63
Swan St. M4: Man 2J 5 (8F 78)
OL6: A Lyne 7E 6 (7N 81)
SK9: Wilm 7G 123
Swan Ter. M30: Ecc 1C 92
Swanton Wlk. *M8: Man* 4E 78
(off Kilmington Dr.)
Swan Wlk. M22: Wyth 5C 116
Swarbrick Dr. M25: Pres 9M 59
Swayfield Av. M13: Man 6L 95
Swaylands Dr. M33: Sale 7H 105
Sweet Briar Cl. OL12: Roch 3C 28
Sweetbriar Cl. OL2: Shaw 5M 45
Sweetbriar Ho. *OL2: Shaw* 5M 45
(off Glebe St.)
Sweet Briar La. OL12: Roch 3C 28
Sweetlove's Gro. BL1: Bolt 8F 22
Sweetlove's La. BL1: Bolt 8F 22
Sweetnam Dr. M11: Man 8N 79
Sweetstone Gdns. *BL1: Bolt* 8G 22
(off Stonyhurst Av.)
Swettenham Rd. SK9: Hand 1J 123
Swettenham St. SK11: Macc 5J 131
Swift Bank SK13: Glos 9B 100
Swift Cl. SK6: Wood 3N 109
Swift Rd. OL1: O'ham 7B 46
OL11: Roch 6L 27
Swift St. OL6: A Lyne 5A 82
WN5: Wig 4D 52
Swiftsure Av. M3: Sal 4B 4 (9C 78)
Swift Wlk. *M40: Man* 5A 80
(off Dakerwood Cl.)
Swinbourne Gro. M20: Man 1H 107
Swinburne Av. M43: Droy 7E 80
Swinburne Grn. SK5: Stoc 8B 96
Swinburne Way M34: Dent 1L 109
Swinburn Gro. WN5: Bil 1H 69
Swinburn St. M9: Man 1L 79
Swindells St. *M11: Man* 2C 96
(off Stanley St.)
SK14: Hyde 4B 98
Swindon Cl. M18: Man 4B 96
Swinfield Av. M21: Cho H 9M 93
Swinford Gro. OL2: O'ham 7L 45
Swinford Wlk. *M9: Man* 8K 61
(off Woodmere Dr.)
Swinhoe Pl. WA3: Cul 6F 88
SWINLEY 1F 52
Swinley Chase SK9: Wilm 5L 123
Swinley La. WN1: Wig 1F 52
Swinley Rd. WN1: Wig 1F 52
Swinley St. WN1: Wig 1F 52
Swinside WN1: Wig 2J 53
Swinside Cl. M24: Mid 1H 61
Swinside Rd. BL2: Bolt 4N 39
Swinstead Av. M40: Man 5K 79
SWINTON 2F 76
Swinton Ct. *M27: Swin* 3G 76
(off Park St.)
Swinton Cres. BL9: Bury 2N 59
Swinton Gro. M13: Man 4H 95
Swinton Hall Rd.
M27: Pen, Swin 2F 76
Swinton Ind. Est.
M27: Swin 2G 76
Swinton Leisure Cen. 2F 76
Swinton Library Art Gallery 2F 76
(off Station Rd.)
SWINTON PARK 3G 77
Swinton Pk. Golf Course 4G 77
Swinton Pk. Rd. M6: Sal 5H 77
Swinton Shop. Cen.
M27: Swin 2F 76
Swinton Sq. WA16: Knut 6G 133
Swinton Station (Rail) 1F 76
Swinton St. BL2: Bolt 5M 39
OL4: O'ham 6N 63
Swiss Cott. SK10: Macc 2F 130
Swiss Hill SK9: A Edg 4G 127
Swithemby St. *BL6: Hor* 8C 20
(off Mary St. W.)
Swithin Rd. M22: Wyth 7D 116
Swithland Rd. WA14: W Tim 7C 104
Swithun Wells Ct.
M38: Lit H 6H 57
Swythamley Cl. SK3: Stoc 8M 107
Swythamley Rd. SK3: Stoc 8M 107
Sybil St. OL15: Lit 8L 15
Sycamore Av. M26: Rad 3F 58
M29: Tyld 1C 74
M34: Dent 7K 97
OL4: O'ham 3A 64
OL9: Chad 8D 62
OL10: H'ood 4K 43
OL16: Miln 1L 45
WA3: Gol 9K 71
WA12: N Wil 6F 86
WA14: Alt 2A 114
WN2: Hin 8B 54
WN6: Wig 8C 34
Sycamore Cl. M20: Man 1H 107
OL6: A Lyne 7B 82
OL15: Lit 9K 15
SK9: Wilm 4G 123
SK16: Duk 1C 98
SK22: N Mil 6N 121
Sycamore Ct. M6: Sal 7N 77
M16: Whall R 6C 94
M33: Sale 2C 104
(off Carrington La.)
M40: Man 7K 79
PR7: Chor 1E 18
SK4: Stoc 5N 107
(off Heaton Moor Rd.)
Sycamore Cres. OL6: A Lyne 5N 81
SK11: Macc 6E 130
WA3: Rix 6C 102
(not continuous)
Sycamore Dr. BL9: Bury 7M 25
M26: Rad 7G 40
WN3: Wins 9M 51
Sycamore Gro. M35: Fail 3F 80
Sycamore Lodge SK7: Bram 8D 118
Sycamore Pl. M45: Whitef 5M 59
Sycamore Ri. SK11: Macc 6F 130
Sycamore Rd. BL8: Tot 8F 24
M30: Ecc 6A 76
M31: Part 5E 102
M46: Ath 8N 55
SK6: Bred 4L 109
WA16: Mob 9A 122
Sycamores, The M26: Rad 5B 58
M33: Sale 5J 105
(off Beaufort Av.)
OL4: Lees 3B 64
OL5: Mos 1H 83
SK13: Had 6B 100
SK15: Stal 1E 98
WA14: Alt 3B 114
Sycamore St. M33: Sale 4L 105
SK3: Stoc 8N 107
SK15: Stal 9C 82
Sycamore Wlk. BL6: Hor 2G 37
SK8: Chea 1K 117
Syddal Cl. SK7: Bram 1B 124
Syddal Cres. SK7: Bram 2B 124
Syddal Grn. SK7: Bram 1B 124
Syddall Av. SK8: H Grn 7J 117
Syddall St. SK14: Hyde 8A 98
Syddal Rd. SK7: Bram 1B 124
Sydenham St. OL1: O'ham 2L 63
(not continuous)
Sydenham Ter. OL12: Roch 2B 28
Syderstone Cl. WN2: Hin 7A 54
Sydney Av. M30: Ecc 8D 76
M90: Man A 7N 115
WN7: Lei 8F 72
Sydney Barnes Cl. OL11: Roch 2N 43
Sydney Gdns. OL15: Lit 5N 15
Sydney Jones Ct. M40: Man 1A 80
Sydney Rd. SK7: Bram 1D 124
Sydney St. M6: Sal 8L 77
M27: Swin 3D 76
M32: Stre 7K 93
M35: Fail 3C 80
OL5: Mos 2G 83
SK2: Stoc 9G 108
WN2: P Bri 8K 53
SYKE 1D 28
Syke Cft. SK6: Rom 5A 110
Sykefield Cl. WN2: Hin 8E 54
Syke La. OL12: Roch 1D 28
Syke Rd. OL12: Roch 1D 28
OL15: Lit 3N 29
Sykes Av. BL9: Bury 8A 42
Sykes Cl. OL3: G'fld 6L 65
Sykes Ct. *OL16: Roch* 7F 28
(off Sykes St.)
Sykes Mdw. SK3: Stoc 1B 118
Sykes St. OL16: Miln 9L 29
OL16: Roch 7F 28
SK5: Stoc 9D 96
SK14: Hyde 8C 98
(off Knight St.)
Sykes Wlk. *SK5: Stoc* 9D 96
(off Sykes St.)
Sylvan Av. M16: Whall R 6C 94
M33: Sale 5J 105
M35: Fail 5C 80
M41: Urm 6D 92
SK9: Wilm 9E 122
WA15: Tim 8F 104
Sylvan Cl. M24: Mid 1J 61
Sylvandale Av. M19: Man 8M 95
Sylvan Gro. WA14: Alt 2C 6 (2D 114)
Sylvan St. OL9: O'ham 4G 63
Sylvester Av. SK2: Stoc 1F 118
Sylvester Cl. WA16: Knut 7H 99
Sylvester Way M34: Dent 1L 109
SK14: Hat 7H 99
(off Sylvester Cl.)
Sylvia Ct. M40: Man 6H 79
Sylvia Gro. SK5: Stoc 1C 108
Symondley Rd. SK11: Sut E 9K 131
Symondley Vw. SK11: Sut E 9K 131
Symond Rd. M9: Man 6K 61
Symons Rd. M33: Sale 3H 105
Symons St. M7: Sal 3D 78
Syndall Av. M12: Man 3J 95
Syndall St. M12: Man 3J 95
Syresham St. WN2: P Bri 9L 53

T

Taberner Cl. WN6: Stan 3C 34
TABLEY 8A 132
Tabley Av. M14: Man 7G 95
Tabley Cl. SK10: Macc 4E 130
WA16: Knut 5E 132
Tabley Ct. WA14: Alt 2D 6
Tabley Gdns. M43: Droy 9F 80
SK6: Mar 3D 120
Tabley Gro. M13: Man 7L 95
SK5: Stoc 1C 108
WA15: Tim 7F 104
WA16: Knut 7E 132
TABLEY HILL 5C 132
Tabley Hill La. WA16: Tab 5A 132
Tabley House 8B 132
Tabley House Mus. 8A 132
Tabley La. WA16: Tab 7B 132
Tableymere Gdns. SK8: Chea H 4L 117
Tabley M. WA14: Alt 2D 6
Tabley Rd. BL3: Bolt 8C 38
M33: Sale 6L 105
SK9: Hand 1J 123
WA16: Knut 5D 132
Tabley Stables WA16: Tab 8A 132
Tabley St. M6: Sal 5A 78
OL5: Mos 2G 83
SK16: Duk 1B 98
Tabor St. M24: Mid 1L 61
SK11: Macc 6J 131
Tackler Cl. M27: Swin 3F 76
Tadcaster Dr. M40: Man 4J 79
Tadcaster Wlk. OL1: O'ham 1D 8
Taddington Pl. *SK13: Gam* 8A 100
(off Castleton Cres.)
Tadman Gro. WA14: Alt 1A 114
Tadmor Cl. M38: Lit H 7G 57
Tagge La. M6: Sal 4M 77
Tagg Wood Vw. BL0: Ram 9G 11
Tagore Cl. M13: Man 5K 95
Tahir Cl. M8: Man 3G 79
Tait M. SK4: Stoc 6L 107
Talavera St. M7: Sal 5C 78

Talbenny Cl. BL1: Bolt 4A 38
Talbot Av. BL3: Lit L 8A 40
Talbot Cl. OL4: O'ham 3N 63
Talbot Ct. BL1: Bolt 9G 22
M32: Stre 6L 93
Talbot Gro. BL9: Bury 7N 25
Talbot Pl. M16: Old T 4A 94
Talbot Rd. M14: Man 1K 107
M16: Old T 6L 93
M32: Stre 6L 93
M33: Sale 4L 105
SK9: A Edg 3G 126
SK13: Glos 7E 100
SK14: Hyde 4B 98
WA14: Bow 5B 114
(not continuous)
Talbot St. M24: Mid 1M 61
M30: Ecc 9E 76
OL6: A Lyne 7A 6 (7L 81)
OL11: Roch 7D 28
SK1: Stoc 2K 9
SK7: H Gro 3J 119
SK13: Glos 8E 100
WA3: Gol 1K 87
Talbot Vs. SK13: Glos 8E 100
Talford Gro. M20: Man 3F 106
Talgarth Rd. M40: Man 6H 79
Talkin Dr. M24: Mid 9K 43
Talland Wlk. *M13: Man* 4J 95
(off Plymouth Gro.)
Tallarn Cl. M20: Man 1H 107
Tallies Cl. WN2: Abr 3M 71
Tallis St. M12: Man 6M 95
Tallow Way M44: Irl 9H 91
Tall Trees M7: Sal 1C 78
Tall Trees Cl. OL2: O'ham 8G 44
Tall Trees Pl. SK2: Stoc 1G 118
Tally Cl. M27: Pen 3L 77
Tallyman Way M27: Pen 3L 77
Talman Gro. WN4: A Mak 7G 71
Talmine Av. M40: Man 5K 79
Tamar Cl. BL4: Kea 6B 58
M45: Whitef 3N 59
SK10: Macc 3C 130
Tamar Ct. M15: Man 3C 94
Tamar Dr. M23: Wyth 3N 115
Tamarin Cl. M27: Ward 1C 76
Tamar Way OL10: H'ood 1F 42
Tame Bank Cl. OL5: Mos 8G 65
Tame Barn OL16: Miln 8N 29
Tame Barn Cl. OL16: Miln 7L 29
Tame Cl. SK15: Stal 7F 82
Tame Ct. *SK15: Stal* 8E 82
(off Portland Pl.)
Tame La. OL3: Del 5F 46
Tamer Gro. WN7: Lei 2E 72
TAMER LANE END 2E 72
Tamerton Dr. M8: Man 4F 78
Tameside Bus. Pk. M34: Dent 6H 97
Tameside Ct. SK14: Hat 7H 99
SK16: Duk 2M 97
Tameside Gymnastics Cen.
Longdendale 6J 99
Tameside Pk. Ind. Est.
SK16: Duk 1M 97
Tameside Stadium 6J 81
Tameside Work Cen.
OL7: A Lyne 9K 81
(off Ryecroft St.)
Tame St. M4: Man 9J 79
M34: Aud 2K 97
M34: Dent 5J 97
OL3: Upp 3L 65
OL5: Mos 8H 65
SK15: Stal 9B 82
TAME VALLEY 9A 82
Tame Valley Cl. OL5: Mos 8H 65
Tame Vw. OL5: Mos 9F 64
Tame Wlk. SK9: Wilm 5J 123
TAME WATER 2J 65
Tamewater Ct. OL3: Dob 1J 65
Tamewater Vs. OL3: Dob 2J 65
Tamworth Av. M45: Whitef 4A 60
Tamworth Cl. M15: Man 4D 94
SK7: H Gro 7H 119
Tamworth Ct. M15: Man 4D 94
OL9: O'ham 6G 62
(off Tamworth St.)
Tamworth Dr. BL8: Bury 8J 25
WN2: Wig 1J 53
Tamworth Grn. SK1: Stoc 6F 108
Tamworth St. M15: Man 5D 94
OL9: O'ham 6G 62
SK1: Stoc 6F 108
WA12: N Wil 6D 86
Tandis Ct. M6: Sal 7G 77
Tandle Hill Country Pk. 6E 44
Tandle Hill Countryside Cen. 6E 44
Tandle Hill Rd. OL2: O'ham 6F 44
Tandle Hill Ter. OL11: Roch 4F 44
Tandlewood M. M40: Man 5A 80
Tandlewood Pk. OL2: O'ham 6F 44
Tanfield Dr. M26: Rad 4B 58
Tanfield Nook WN8: Par 2A 32
Tanfield Rd. M20: Man 8G 106
TANG 7M 109
Tang, The SK6: Rom 7M 109
Tanglewood Dr. SK10: Macc 9F 128
Tangmere Av. OL10: H'ood 5K 43
Tangmere Cl. M40: Man 8A 62
Tangmere Ct. M16: Whall R 6C 94
Tangshutts La. SK6: Rom 6A 110
Tanhill Cl. SK2: Stoc 1J 119
Tanhill La. OL8: O'ham 9L 63
TANHOUSE 2B 50
Tanhouse Av. M29: Ast 3E 74
Tan Ho. Cl. WN8: Par 1A 32
Tan Ho. Dr. WN3: Wins 9N 51
Tan Ho. La. WN3: Wins 9N 51
WN8: Par 2A 32
Tanhouse Rd. M41: Urm 6L 91
WN8: Skel 3A 50
Tanner Brook Cl. *BL3: Bolt* 8F 38
(off John Cross St.)
Tanner Bus. Cen., The
OL3: G'fld 7M 65
TANNERS 8H 11
Tanner's Brow BL6: Bla 3A 36
Tanners Cft. BL0: Ram 8H 11
Tannersfield Lodge M35: Fail 4C 80
Tanners Fold OL8: O'ham 9L 63
Tanners Grn. *M6: Sal* 7M 77
(off Nursery St.)
Tanner's La. WA3: Gol 1K 87
Tanners St. BL0: Ram 8H 11
M18: Man 4C 96
Tanner St. SK14: Hyde 6A 98
Tannery Way M18: Man 4C 96
WA14: Tim 9E 104
Tannock Ct. SK7: H Gro 6K 119
Tannock Rd. SK7: H Gro 6K 119
Tan Pit Cotts. WN3: Wins 9A 52
Tanpit Cotts. OL10: H'ood 9J 27
Tan Pit La. WN3: Wins 9A 52
Tan Pits Cl. M29: Ast 3D 74
Tanpits Rd. BL9: Bury 6J 7 (1L 41)
Tanpit Wlk. M22: Wyth 5B 116
Tansey Gro. M7: Sal 3E 78
Tansley Av. PR7: Cop 4A 18
Tansley Cl. BL6: Hor 2E 36
Tansley Rd. M8: Man 9G 60
Tansley Sq. WN5: Wig 6A 52
Tansybrook Way WA14: W Tim 7B 104
Tanworth Wlk. *BL1: Bolt* 2F 38
(off Wolfenden St.)
Tan Yd. Brow M18: Man 5C 96
Tanyard Cl. PR7: Cop 4A 18
Tanyard Dr. WA15: Haleb 9J 115
Tanyard Grn. SK5: Stoc 3D 108
Tanyard La. WA15: Ash 9G 114
Taper St. BL0: Ram 8H 11
Tapley Av. SK12: Poy 4J 125
Taplin Dr. M18: Man 4B 96
Taplow Gro. SK8: Chea H 5L 117
Taplow Wlk. *M14: Man* 6K 95
(off Binstead Cl.)
Tarbet Dr. BL2: Bolt 5N 39
Tarbet Rd. SK16: Duk 2N 97
Tarbet Wlk. M8: Man 4E 78
Tarbolton Cres. WA15: Hale 4J 115
TARDEN 2H 121
Target Fitness 1C 108
Target Life
Bramhall 7E 118
Cheadle Hulme 8N 117
Dialstone 1H 119
Kingsway 3H 117
Lapwing 2G 109
Marple 1C 120
Priestnall 5L 107
Werneth 6K 109
Tariff St. M1: Man 4K 5 (9G 78)
Tarland Wlk. *M11: Man* 9A 80
(off Kincraig Cl.)
Tarleton Av. M46: Ath 6K 55
Tarleton Cl. BL8: Bury 3F 40
Tarleton Ho. *M6: Sal* 6J 77
(off Moss Mdw. Rd.)
Tarleton Pl. BL3: Bolt 9B 38
Tarleton St. M13: Man 3J 95
Tarnbrook Cl. M45: Whitef 3B 60
Tarnbrook Dr. WN2: Asp 7L 35
Tarnbrook Wlk. *M15: Man* 4F 94
(off Wellhead Cl.)
Tarn Cl. WN4: A Mak 5E 70
Tarn Dr. BL9: Bury 6L 41
Tarn Gro. M28: Walk 1N 75
Tarn Ho. M15: Man 9B 4
Tarn Mt. SK11: Macc 7E 130
Tarnrigg Cl. WN3: Wig 8B 52
Tarns, The SK8: Gat 4G 117
Tarnside Cl. OL16: Roch 2G 29
SK2: Stoc 1K 119
Tarnside Fold SK13: Glos 9C 100
Tarnside Ho. M8: Man 9E 60
Tarnside Rd. WN5: Orr 5J 51
Tarnway WA3: Low 2B 88
Tarporley Av. M14: Man 9F 94
Tarporley Cl. SK3: Stoc 2B 118
Tarporley Wlk. *SK9: Wilm* 4K 123
(off Picton Dr.)
Tarran Gro. M34: Dent 8M 97
Tarran Pl. WA14: Alt 1E 114
Tarrant Cl. WN3: Wins 9A 52
Tarrington Cl. M12: Man 4M 95
Tartan St. M11: Man 8N 79
Tarves Wlk. *M11: Man* 9N 79
(off Kincraig Cl.)
Tarvin Av. M20: Man 1F 106
SK4: Stoc 1B 108
Tarvin Cl. SK11: Macc 7J 131
WA3: Low 2A 88
Tarvin Dr. SK6: Bred 4J 109
Tarvington Cl. M40: Man 4H 79
Tarvin Rd. SK8: Chea 2M 117
Tarvin Wlk. BL1: Bolt 2F 38
Tarvin Way SK9: Hand 1J 123
Tasle All. M2: Man 5G 4 (9E 78)
Tatchbury Rd. M35: Fail 3E 80
Tate St. OL8: O'ham 7M 63
Tatham Cl. M13: Man 6L 95
Tatham Gro. WN3: Wins 1A 70
Tatham St. OL16: Roch 8F 8 (6E 28)
Tatland Dr. M22: Wyth 4E 116
Tatlock Cl. WN5: Bil 5J 69
Tattenhall Wlk. *M14: Man* 9J 95
(off Ravenhead Cl.)
Tattersall Av. BL1: Bolt 2N 37
Tattersall St. OL9: O'ham 4A 8 (5H 63)
Tatton Bldgs. SK8: Gat 2G 116
Tatton Cl. SK7: H Gro 3K 119
SK8: Chea 3M 117
Tatton Ct. M14: Man 9J 95
SK4: Stoc 4A 108
WA16: Knut 6G 132
(off King St.)
Tatton Dr. WN4: A Mak 5C 70
Tatton Gdns. SK6: Wood 3A 110
Tatton Gro. M20: Man 2G 107
Tatton Ho. BL1: Bolt 5D 38
Tatton Lodge *WA16: Knut* 6G 133
(off Swinton Sq.)
Tatton Mere Dr. M43: Droy 9F 80
Tattonmere Gdns. SK8: Chea H 3M 117
Tatton Park 1G 133
Tatton Park Mansion 1E 132
Tatton Pl. M13: Man 5K 95
M33: Sale 3H 105
Tatton Rd. M33: Sale 3H 105
M34: Dent 8L 97
SK9: Hand 1K 123
Tatton Rd. Nth. SK4: Stoc 3A 108
Tatton Rd. Sth. SK4: Stoc 4A 108
Tatton Stile WA16: Mob 4N 133
Tatton St. M5: Sal 1A 94
M15: Man 9B 4 (3C 94)
SK1: Stoc 2L 9 (7D 108)
SK14: Hyde 1B 110
SK15: Stal 8E 82
WA16: Knut 6G 132
Tatton Ter. *SK16: Duk* 9M 81
(off Hill St.)
Tatton Vw. M20: Man 2G 107
TAUNTON 5J 81
Taunton Av. M30: Ecc 7B 76
M41: Urm 9B 92
OL7: A Lyne 6L 81
OL11: Roch 6N 27
WN7: Lei 9F 54
Taunton Av. E. SK5: Stoc 3G 108
Taunton Av. W. SK5: Stoc 3G 108
Taunton Brook La. OL7: A Lyne 5J 81
Taunton Cl. *BL1: Bolt* 3D 38
(off Valletts La.)
SK7: H Gro 5L 119
Taunton Dr. BL4: Farn 2G 56
Taunton Grn. OL7: A Lyne 5K 81
Taunton Gro. M45: Whitef 5N 59
Taunton Hall Cl. OL7: A Lyne 5K 81
Taunton Lawns OL7: A Lyne 5L 81
Taunton Pl. OL7: A Lyne 5K 81
Taunton Platting *OL7: A Lyne* 4K 81
(off Ney St.)
Taunton Rd. M33: Sale 4D 104
OL7: A Lyne 5B 6 (6L 81)
OL9: Chad 1E 62
Taunton St. M4: Man 9J 79
Taunton Wlk. *M34: Dent* 8L 97
(off Mancunian Rd.)
Taurus St. OL4: O'ham 3N 63
Tavern Ct. M35: Fail 3E 80
Tavern Ct. Av. M35: Fail 3E 80
Tavern Rd. SK13: Had 6A 100
Tavery Cl. M4: Man 3N 5 (8H 79)
Tavistock Cl. SK14: Hat 7H 99
Tavistock Dr. OL9: Chad 2D 62
Tavistock Rd. BL1: Bolt 6E 38
M33: Sale 3D 104
OL11: Roch 2D 44
WN2: Hin 7C 54
Tavistock Sq. *M9: Man* 3J 79
(off Grangewood Dr.)
Tavistock St. M46: Ath 8K 55
TAWD BRIDGE 4A 50
Tawd Rd. WN8: Skel 3A 50
Tawton Av. SK14: Hat 6H 99
Taxi Service Rd. OL11: Roch 9D 8
Tay Cl. OL8: O'ham 6J 63
Tayfield Rd. M22: Wyth 5B 116
Tayleur Ter. WA12: N Wil 7G 86
Taylor Av. OL11: Roch 5L 27
Taylor Bldgs. BL4: Kea 5B 58
Taylor Bus. Pk. WA3: Ris 7H 89
Taylor Grn. Way OL4: Lees 4C 64
Taylor Gro. WN2: Hin 8E 54
Taylor Ho. BL8: Bury 7J 25
Taylor La. M34: Dent 5H 97
Taylor Rd. M41: Urm 2E 92
WA11: Hay 3B 86
WA14: Alt 2A 114
WN2: Hin 8E 54
Taylor's La. BL2: Bolt 5B 40
M40: Man 5M 79
WN3: I Mak 8H 53
Taylorson St. M5: Sal 2A 94
Taylorson St. Sth. M5: Sal 3N 93
Taylors Pl. *OL12: Roch* 4D 28
(off Taylor St.)
Taylor Sq. *SK11: Macc* 6G 130
(off Slater St.)
Taylor's Rd. M32: Stre 5K 93
Taylor St. BL3: Bolt 4L 7 (6G 38)
BL6: Hor 1D 36
(off Emmett St.)
BL9: Bury 5N 7 (9M 25)
M14: Man 7H 95
M18: Man 3A 96
M24: Mid 3M 61
(not continuous)
M25: Pres 7B 60
M26: Rad 9G 40
M34: Dent 5K 97
M43: Droy 9D 80
M46: Ath 9N 55
OL1: O'ham 3N 63
OL2: O'ham 7T 45
OL4: Lees 5B 64
OL9: Chad 2H 63
OL10: H'ood 2H 43
OL12: Roch 2D 28
OL12: Whitw 6B 14
SK14: Holl 4N 99
SK14: Hyde 6C 98
SK15: Stal 9E 82
WA3: Gol 9M 71
(off Lowton Rd.)
WN3: Wig 8G 9 (3E 52)
WN7: Lei 2F 72
Taylor Ter. *OL15: Lit* 9N 15
(off Beswicke St.)
SK16: Duk 9M 81
(off Hill St.)
Tayton Cl. M29: Tyld 1D 74
Taywood Rd. BL3: Bolt 1M 55
Teak Dr. BL4: Kea 7D 58
Teak St. BL9: Bury 2A 42
Teal Av. SK12: Poy 2E 124
WA16: Knut 6H 133
Tealby Av. M16: Old T 5B 94
Tealby Ct. M21: Cho H 8B 94
Tealby Rd. M18: Man 5N 95
Teal Cl. SK2: Stoc 2K 119
WA14: B'ath 8B 104
WN3: Wig 7M 51
Teal Ct. OL11: Roch 6L 27
Teal St. BL3: Bolt 8G 38
Teasdale Cl. OL9: Chad 8C 62
Tebbutt St. M4: Man 1L 5 (7G 79)
Tebworth Dr. WN2: Hin 7A 54
Tedburn Wlk. M40: Man 9B 62
Tedder Cl. BL9: Bury 1A 60
Tedder Dr. M22: Wyth 8E 116
Teddington Rd. M40: Man 1A 80
Ted Jackson Wlk. *M11: Man* 1L 95
(off Newchurch St.)
Teer St. M40: Man 8J 79
Teesdale Av. M41: Urm 5A 92
Teesdale Cl. SK2: Stoc 1J 119
Teesdale Dr. WN7: Lei 5L 73
Teesdale Wlk. *M9: Man* 8K 61
(off Haverfield Rd.)
Tees St. OL16: Roch 7F 28
Tees Wlk. *OL8: O'ham* 6J 63
(off Lee St.)
Tegg's Nose Country Pk. 7N 131
Teggsnose La. SK11: Macc 6N 131
Tegsnose Mt. SK11: Lang 8N 131
Teignmouth Av. M40: Man 6H 79
Telegraphic Ho. M50: Sal 2N 93
Telegraph Rd. M17: T Pk 2G 92
Telfer Av. M13: Man 7K 95
Telfer Rd. M13: Man 7K 95
Telford Cl. M34: Aud 2J 97
SK10: Macc 3L 131
Telford Cres. WN7: Lei 2F 72
Telford M. OL3: Upp 3L 65
Telford Rd. SK6: Mar 3D 120
Telford St. BL6: Hor 2E 36
M8: Man 5H 79
M46: Ath 9J 55
Telford Wlk. M16: Old T 5C 94
Telford Way OL11: Roch 2E 44
Telham Wlk. M23: Wyth 2N 115
Tellers Cl. M46: Ath 8M 55
Tellson Cl. M6: Sal 4K 77
Tellson Cres. M6: Sal 4K 77
Tell St. OL12: Roch 7A 8 (6B 28)
Telryn Wlk. *M8: Man* 2H 79
(off Stakeford Dr.)
Temperance Sq. SK14: Mot 5K 99
Temperance St. BL3: Bolt 7F 38
M12: Man 7M 5 (1H 95)
(not continuous)
SK14: B'tom 9K 99
Temperance Ter. *SK6: Mar* 1C 120
(off Hollins La.)
Tempest Chase BL6: Los 8K 37
Tempest Ct. BL6: Los 8L 37
Tempest Rd. BL6: Los 9K 37
SK9: A Edg 4H 127
Tempest St. BL3: Bolt 8C 38
Templar Ct. SK10: Macc 3F 130
Temple Av. SK13: Had 4E 100
Temple Cl. OL4: Lees 3B 64
Templecombe Dr. BL1: Bolt 7E 22
Temple Dr. BL1: Bolt 1D 38
M27: Swin 3H 77
Templegate Cl. WN6: Stan 2C 34
Temple La. OL15: Lit 5N 15
Temple Rd. BL1: Bolt 1D 38
M33: Sale 4K 105
Temple Sq. M8: Man 5G 78
Temple St. M24: Mid 2N 61
OL1: O'ham 4M 63
OL10: H'ood 2J 43
SK13: Had 4E 100
Templeton Cl. BL5: W'ton 3G 54
Templeton Dr. WA14: Alt 1B 114
Templeton Rd. WN2: P Bri 9L 53
(not continuous)
Tempus Apartments M3: Man 1F 4
Temsbury Wlk. M40: Man 5K 79
Ten Acre Ct. M45: Whitef 4J 59
Ten Acre Dr. M45: Whitef 4K 59
Ten Acres Astro Cen. 5M 79
Ten Acres La. M40: Man 5M 79
Tenax Circ. M17: T Pk 1H 93
Tenax Rd. M17: T Pk 2H 93
Tenbury Cl. M6: Sal 7M 77
Tenbury Dr. M24: Mid 6M 61
WN4: A Mak 6C 70
Tenby Av. BL1: Bolt 3B 38
M20: Man 2G 106
M32: Stre 5M 93
Tenby Ct. *M15: Man* 3B 94
(off Cornbrook Pk. Rd.)
Tenby Dr. M6: Sal 5K 77
SK8: Chea H 6N 117
Tenby Gro. OL12: Roch 4A 28
Tenby Rd. OL8: O'ham 9F 62
SK3: Stoc 9N 107
SK11: Macc 6D 130
Tenby St. OL12: Roch 4A 28
Tenement La. SK7: Bram 4A 118
Tenement St. WN2: Abr 1L 71
Teneriffe St. M7: Sal 2C 78
Ten Foot Cl. SK13: Glos 7D 100
Tenham Wlk. *M9: Man* 8K 61
(off Ravenswood Dr.)
Ten Houses OL8: O'ham 9N 63
Tennis St. BL1: Bolt 1E 38
M16: Old T 5A 94
Tennyson Av. BL9: Bury 6M 41
M26: Rad 8E 40
M34: Dent 1L 109
SK16: Duk 2D 98
WN7: Lei 2E 72
Tennyson Cl. SK4: Stoc 6N 107
SK11: Macc 5C 130
Tennyson Dr. WN1: Wig 9F 34
WN5: Bil 1H 69
Tennyson Gdns. M25: Pres 8M 59
Tennyson Rd. BL4: Farn 5J 57
M24: Mid 1N 61
M27: Swin 2D 76
Tennyson Rd. M43: Droy 8E 80
SK5: Stoc 8B 96
SK8: Chea 1L 117
Tennyson St. BL1: Bolt 3E 38
M13: Man 4H 95
OL1: O'ham 2N 63
OL11: Roch 8E 28
Tennyson Wlk. *BL1: Bolt* 2F 38
(off Irving St.)
Tenpin
East Didsbury 7J 107
Stockport 4K 9 (8C 108)
Tensing Av. M46: Ath 6L 55
OL7: A Lyne 5M 81
Tensing Fold SK16: Duk 9M 81
Tensing St. OL8: O'ham 2L 81
Tenter Brow SK15: Stal 8C 82
Tentercroft OL1: O'ham 1C 8 (4J 63)
OL12: Roch 7A 8 (5C 28)
Tenterden St. BL9: Bury 8H 7 (2K 41)
Tenterden Wlk. *M22: Wyth* 4B 116
(off Poundswick La.)
Tenter Dr. WN6: Stan 5E 34
Tenterfield Cl. OL3: G'fld 5K 65
Tenterhill La. OL11: Roch 3J 27
TENTERSFIELD 8H 7 (2K 41)
Tenters St. BL9: Bury 8H 7 (2K 41)
Tenth St. M17: T Pk 3K 93
Terence St. M40: Man 5B 80
Terminal Rd. E. M90: Man A 8B 116
Terminal Rd. Nth. M90: Man A 8A 116
Tern Av. BL4: Farn 3G 56
Tern Cl. OL11: Roch 6L 27
SK16: Duk 2B 98
WA14: B'ath 8B 104
Tern Dr. SK12: Poy 2F 124
Ternhill Ct. BL4: Farn 3L 57
Terrace, The M25: Pres 8A 60
Terrace St. OL4: O'ham 4M 63
Terrington Cl. M21: Cho H 1D 106
Tetbury Cl. WN5: Wig 2A 52
Tetbury Dr. BL2: Bolt 4N 39
Tetbury Rd. M22: Wyth 6A 116
Tetley Bye Rd. OL3: Del 5A 48
Tetlow Fold SK14: Hyde 6E 98
Tetlow Gro. M30: Ecc 9C 76
Tetlow La. M7: Sal 2D 78
Tetlow St. M24: Mid 3M 61
M40: Man 5B 80
OL8: O'ham 4A 8 (5H 63)
SK14: Hyde 4B 98
Tetlows Yd. OL15: Lit 4A 16
Tetsworth Wlk. *M40: Man* 9B 62
(off Blandford Dr.)
Teviot St. M13: Man 5K 95
Tewkesbury Av. M24: Mid 9L 43
M41: Urm 5D 92
M43: Droy 7E 80
OL6: A Lyne 3N 81
OL9: Chad 1E 62
WA15: Hale 4J 115
Tewkesbury Cl. SK8: Chea H 9N 117
SK12: Poy 1H 125
Tewkesbury Dr. M25: Pres 9B 60
SK10: Macc 9J 129
Tewkesbury Rd. M40: Man 7J 79
SK3: Stoc 1N 117
WA3: Gol 1L 87
Texas St. OL6: A Lyne 9F 6 (8N 81)
Textile Apartments M3: Sal 3F 4
Textile M. OL15: Lit 4J 29
Textile St. M12: Man 2M 95
Textilis Ho. SK1: Stoc 3K 9
Textilose Rd. M17: T Pk 4H 93
Teynham Wlk. *M22: Wyth* 6B 116
(off Selstead Rd.)
Thackeray Cl. M8: Man 4F 78
Thackeray Gro. M43: Droy 8E 80
Thackeray Ho. *WN3: Wig* 6D 52
(off Thackeray Pl.)
Thackeray Pl. WN3: Wig 6D 52
Thackeray Rd. OL1: O'ham 2N 63
Thames Av. WN7: Lei 9H 73
Thames Cl. BL9: Bury 6M 25
M11: Man 1N 95
Thames Ct. *M15: Man* 3C 94
(off City Rd.)
Thames Dr. WN5: Orr 4K 51
Thames Ind. Est. M12: Man 2J 95
Thames Rd. OL16: Miln 7M 29
WA3: Cul 7H 89
Thames St. OL1: O'ham 3L 63
OL16: Roch 7F 28
Thames Trad. Cen. M44: Irl 1G 102
Thanet Cl. M7: Sal 5D 78
Thanet Gro. WN7: Lei 5J 73
Thankerton Av. M34: Aud 9H 81
Thatcher Cl. WA14: Bow 6C 114
Thatchers Mt. WA5: Coll G 8A 86
Thatcher St. OL8: O'ham 7L 63
THATCH LEACH 6D 62
Thatch Leach OL9: Chad 6D 62
Thatch Leach La. M45: Whitef 4N 59
Thaxmead Dr. M40: Man 6B 80
Thaxted Dr. SK2: Stoc 2L 119
Thaxted Pl. BL1: Bolt 4D 38
Thaxted Wlk. M22: Wyth 7B 116
The
Names prefixed with 'The' for example 'The Acorn Cen.' are indexed under the main name such as 'Acorn Cen., The'
Theatre Ho. *M6: Sal* 6L 77
(off Langworthy Rd.)
Theatre St. OL1: O'ham 2E 8 (4K 63)
Thekla St. OL9: O'ham 3H 63
Thelma St. BL0: Ram 8H 11
Thelwall Av. BL2: Bolt 4L 39
M14: Man 9E 94
Thelwall Cl. WA15: Alt 1F 6 (1E 114)
WN7: Lei 6D 72
Thelwall Ct. M14: Man 9F 94
Thelwall Rd. M33: Sale 5L 105
Theobald Rd. WA14: Bow 6D 114
Theta Cl. M11: Man 9N 79
Thetford OL12: Roch 6B 8 (5C 28)

Thetford Cl. BL8: Bury 8K **25**
SK10: Macc 1G **131**
WN2: Hin 7A **54**
Thetford Dr. M8: Man 3G **78**
THICKETFORD BROW 3K 39
Thicketford Brow BL2: Bolt 3L **39**
Thicketford Cl. BL2: Bolt 2K **39**
Thicketford Rd. BL2: Bolt 3J **39**
Thicknesse Av. WN6: Wig 9C **34**
Thimble Cl. OL12: Roch 1H **29**
Thimbles, The OL12: Roch 1H **29**
Third Av. BL1: Bolt 5C **38**
BL3: Lit L 8N **39**
BL9: Bury 9C **26**
M11: Man 7A **80**
M17: T Pk 4K **93**
(not continuous)
M27: Swin 5E **76**
M29: Ast 6C **74**
OL8: O'ham 9G **63**
SK12: Poy 5H **125**
SK15: C'ook 4H **83**
WN6: Wig 1D **52**
Third St. BL1: Bolt 9A **22**
WN2: Bam 3J **71**
Thirkhill Pl. M30: Ecc 8F **76**
Thirlby Dr. M22: Wyth 6C **116**
Thirlmere SK11: Macc 7D **130**
Thirlmere Av. BL6: Hor 2E **36**
M27: Swin 3G **76**
M29: Ast 3B **74**
M32: Stre 6J **93**
OL7: A Lyne 6K **81**
WN2: Abr 2L **71**
WN2: I Mak 4L **53**
WN4: A Mak 6F **70**
WN5: Orr 4K **51**
WN6: Stan 5D **34**
WN8: Uph 4F **50**
Thirlmere Cl. PR6: Adl 5L **19**
SK9: A Edg 4E **126**
SK15: Stal *6D* ***82***
(off Springs La.)
Thirlmere Dr. BL9: Bury 5L **41**
M24: Mid 1K **61**
M38: Lit H 6H **57**
WA13: Lym 4A **112**
Thirlmere Gro. BL4: Farn 3F **56**
OL2: O'ham 6H **45**
Thirlmere M. M24: Mid 9K **43**
Thirlmere Rd. BL5: O Hul 4A **56**
BL6: Bla 1M **35**
M22: Wyth 5A **116**
M31: Part 4F **102**
M41: Urm 6M **91**
OL11: Roch 9N **27**
SK1: Stoc 9F **108**
WA3: Gol 9M **71**
WN2: Hin 6A **54**
WN5: Wig 4M **51**
Thirlmere St. WN7: Lei 5G **73**
Thirlspot Cl. BL1: Bolt 7F **22**
Thirlstone Av. OL4: O'ham 8C **46**
Thirsfield Dr. M11: Man 8A **80**
Thirsk Av. M33: Sale 5C **104**
OL9: Chad 2D **62**
Thirsk Cl. BL8: Bury 8H **25**
Thirsk M. *M7: Sal* *4C* ***78***
(off Bury New Rd.)
Thirsk Rd. BL3: Lit L 1A **58**
Thirsk St. M12: Man 8M **5** (2H **95**)
Thirsk Way SK10: Macc 1G **131**
Thistle Bank Cl. M9: Man 1H **79**
Thistle Cl. SK15: Stal 2H **99**
Thistledown Cl. M30: Ecc 1C **92**
WN6: Wig 1D **52**
Thistle Grn. OL16: Miln 6J **29**
Thistle Ho., The *SK15: Mill* *6G* ***83***
(off Bramble Ct.)
Thistle Sq. M31: Part 6F **102**
Thistleton Cl. SK11: Macc 6H **131**
Thistleton Rd. BL3: Bolt 9A **38**
Thistle Wlk. *M31: Part* *6F* ***102***
(off Thistle Sq.)
Thistle Way OL4: O'ham 1A **64**
Thistlewood Dr. SK9: Wilm 7J **123**
Thistleyfield OL16: Miln 6J **29**
Thistley Flds. SK14: Hyde 9N **97**
Thomas Cl. M34: Dent 5L **97**
Thomas Ct. *BL7: Bro X* *6H* ***23***
(off Toppings Grn.)
M15: Man 9C **4**
Thomas Dr. BL3: Bolt 7E **38**
Thomas Garnet Ct. *BL4: Farn* *3K* ***57***
(off Glynne St.)
Thomas Gibbon Cl. *M32: Stre* *8J* ***93***
(off Mitford St.)
Thomas Henshaw Ct.
OL11: Roch 9A **28**
Thomas Holden St.
BL1: Bolt 1G **7** (4E **38**)
Thomas Ho. *OL2: O'ham* *8J* ***45***
(off Royton Hall Pk.)
Thomas Johnson Cl. *M30: Ecc* *9C* ***76***
(off Green La.)
Thomas More Cl. BL4: Kea 5N **57**
Thomason Sq. OL15: Lit 9L **15**
Thomas Regan Ct. *M18: Man* *3B* ***96***
(off Ansell Cl.)
Thomasson Cl. *BL1: Bolt* *3F* ***38***
(off Barnwood Dr.)
Thomasson Ct. BL1: Bolt 5C **38**
Thomas St. BL3: Bolt 7E **38**
BL4: Farn 3M **57**
(Frederick Ct.)
BL4: Farn 4M **57**
(Old Hall St.)
BL5: W'ton 9G **37**
M4: Man 3J **5** (8F **78**)
M8: Man 2E **78**
M26: Rad 9H **41**
M32: Stre 5K **93**
M46: Ath 8M **55**
OL2: O'ham 9K **45**
OL2: Shaw 6N **45**
OL4: Lees 6B **64**
Thomas St. OL12: Whitw 4B **14**
OL15: Lit 1K **29**
OL16: Roch 5E **28**
SK1: Stoc 9D **108**
SK6: Bred 5L **109**
SK6: Comp 6E **110**
SK13: Glos 8G **100**
WA3: Gol 1K **87**
WA15: Alt 3E **6** (3E **114**)
WN2: Hin 8D **54**
WN7: Lei 6K **73**
Thomas St. W. SK1: Stoc 9D **108**
Thomas Telford Basin
M1: Man 5M **5** (9H **79**)
Thompson Av. BL2: Ain 3D **40**
M45: Whitef 4N **59**
WA3: Cul 6G **88**
Thompson Cl. M34: Dent 6G **96**
WA12: N Wil 8F **86**
Thompson Ct. M34: Dent 6F **96**
SK15: Stal *8C* ***82***
(off Thompson Fold)
Thompson Dr. BL9: Bury 1B **42**
Thompson Fold
SK15: Stal 8C **82**
Thompson Ho. *M46: Ath* *8L* ***55***
(off Rosedale Av.)
Thompson La. OL9: Chad 7E **62**
Thompson Rd. BL1: Bolt 3C **38**
M17: T Pk 1E **92**
M34: Dent 6F **96**
Thompson St. BL6: Hor 1C **36**
M3: Man 7E **78**
M4: Man 1K **5** (8G **78**)
M40: Man 5L **79**
OL9: O'ham *4H* ***63***
(off Main Rd.)
WN1: Wig 5N **9** (2H **53**)
WN3: Wig 7D **52**
WN4: A Mak 6G **70**
WN7: Lei 5D **72**
Thomson Rd. M18: Man 5A **96**
Thomson St. M13: Man 3H **95**
SK3: Stoc 5K **9** (8C **108**)
Thoralby Cl. M12: Man 4M **95**
Thorburn Dr. OL12: Whitw 7N **13**
Thorburn Ho. WN5: Wig 4N **51**
Thorburn La. WN5: Wig 4A **52**
Thorburn Rd. WN5: Wig 5N **51**
Thoresby Cl. M26: Rad 7C **40**
WN3: Wig 8B **52**
Thoresway Rd. M13: Man 6K **95**
SK9: Wilm 9E **122**
Thorgill Wlk. *M40: Man* *3M* ***79***
(off Walderton Av.)
Thor Gro. M5: Sal 7A **4**
Thorlby Rd. WA3: Cul 6H **89**
Thorley Cl. OL9: Chad 9C **62**
Thorley Dr. M41: Urm 7D **92**
WA15: Tim 2H **115**
Thorley La. M90: Man A 6M **115**
WA15: Ring 6L **115**
WA15: Tim 1H **115**
Thorley M. SK7: Bram 8D **118**
Thorley Rd. WA15: Tim 2J **115**
Thorley St. M35: Fail 2D **80**
Thornaby Wlk. *M9: Man* *4J* ***79***
(off Kirklinton Dr.)
Thornage Dr. M40: Man 6H **79**
Thorn Av. M35: Fail 4C **80**
Thorn Bank SK15: C'ook 3J **83**
Thornbank M30: Ecc 7E **76**
Thornbank Cl. OL10: H'ood 5K **43**
Thornbank E. *BL3: Bolt* *6D* ***38***
Thornbank Est. *BL3: Bolt* *6D* ***38***
(off Thornbank E.)
Thorn Bank Lodge SK4: Stoc 4N **107**
Thornbank Nth. BL3: Bolt 6D **38**
Thornbank Sth. BL3: Bolt 6D **38**
Thornbank W. BL3: Bolt 6D **38**
Thornbeck Dr. BL1: Bolt 3A **38**
Thornbeck Rd. BL1: Bolt 3A **38**
Thornbridge Av. M21: Cho H 9A **94**
Thornbury OL11: Roch 7C **28**
Thornbury Av. SK14: Hat 6H **99**
WA3: Low 2A **88**
Thornbury Cl. *BL1: Bolt* *4F* ***38***
(off Prince St.)
SK8: Chea H 6A **118**
Thornbury Rd. M32: Stre 5L **93**
Thornbury Way M18: Man 4A **96**
Thornbush Cl. WA3: Low 9A **72**
Thornbush Way OL16: Roch 5G **28**
Thornby Wlk. M23: Wyth 2N **115**
Thorncliff Av. OL8: O'ham 8J **63**
THORNCLIFFE 3M 99
Thorncliffe Av. OL2: O'ham 6G **45**
SK16: Duk 2N **97**
Thorncliffe Gro. M19: Man 8A **96**
Thorncliffe Pk. OL2: O'ham 6G **45**
Thorncliffe Rd. BL1: Bolt 8F **22**
SK13: Had 5B **100**
Thorncliffe Va. SK14: Holl 3M **99**
Thorncliffe Wood SK14: Holl 4M **99**
Thorn Cl. OL10: H'ood 1G **43**
Thorncombe Rd. M16: Whall R 6D **94**
Thorn Ct. M6: Sal 8A **78**
SK15: Stal *8D* ***82***
(off Waterloo Rd.)
Thorncroft Av. M29: Ast 3A **74**
Thorncross Cl. M15: Man 9A **4** (2D **94**)
Thorndale Cl. OL2: O'ham 7J **45**
Thorndale Ct. *M9: Man* *9H* ***61***
(off Marshbrook Dr.)
WA15: Tim *2G* ***114***
(off Stockport Rd.)
Thorndale Gro. WA15: Tim 2G **114**
Thornden Rd. M40: Man 6J **79**
Thorn Dr. M22: Wyth 7F **116**
Thorndyke Gdns. *M25: Pres* *8A* ***60***
(off Bury New Rd.)
Thorndyke Wlk. M25: Pres 8A **60**
Thorne Av. M41: Urm 6A **92**
Thorne Cl. SK10: P'bury 8E **128**
Thornedge WA15: Tim 8F **104**
Thorne Ho. M14: Man 7J **95**
Thorneside M34: Dent 4K **97**
(not continuous)
Thorne St. BL4: Farn 2K **57**
Thorneycroft WN7: Lei 5L **73**
Thorneycroft Av. M21: Cho H 3A **106**
Thorneycroft Cl. WA15: Tim 2H **115**
Thorneycroft Rd. WA15: Tim 2H **115**
Thorney Dr. SK8: Chea H 9A **118**
Thorney Hill Cl. OL4: O'ham 5L **63**
Thorneyholme Cl. BL6: Los 6L **37**
Thorneyholme Dr. WA16: Knut 7H **133**
Thorneylea OL12: Whitw 5B **14**
Thornfield Cl. WA3: Gol 1M **87**
Thornfield Ct. *SK4: Stoc* *5M* ***107***
(off Thornfield Rd.)
Thornfield Cres. M38: Lit H 6G **57**
Thornfield Dr. M27: Swin 3E **76**
Thornfield Gro. M38: Lit H 6G **57**
OL6: A Lyne 7B **82**
SK8: Chea H 5M **117**
Thornfield Hey SK9: Wilm 6K **123**
Thornfield Ho. SK8: Chea H 5M **117**
Thornfield Rd. BL8: Tot 6D **24**
M19: Man 3K **107**
SK4: Stoc 5M **107**
Thornfield St. *M5: Sal* *9K* ***77***
(off Foster St.)
Thornfield Ter.
OL6: A Lyne 8F **6** (8N **81**)
Thornford Wlk. *M40: Man* *9B* ***62***
(off Blandford Dr.)
Thorngate Rd. M8: Man 5F **78**
Thorn Gro. M14: Man 9J **95**
M33: Sale 4H **105**
SK8: Chea H 9M **117**
WA15: Hale 4E **114**
Thorngrove Av. M23: Wyth 9K **105**
Thorngrove Dr. SK9: Wilm 8H **123**
Thorngrove Hill SK9: Wilm 8H **123**
Thorngrove Ho. M23: Wyth 9K **105**
Thorngrove Rd. SK9: Wilm 8H **123**
Thornham Cl. BL8: Bury 7J **25**
Thornham Ct. OL2: Roch 4G **44**
Thornham Dr. BL1: Bolt 7G **23**
THORNHAM FOLD 5D 44
Thornham La. M24: Mid 6B **44**
OL2: O'ham 4G **44**
Thornham New Rd. OL11: Roch 4B **44**
Thornham Old Rd. OL2: O'ham 5E **44**
Thornham Rd. M33: Sale 6E **104**
OL2: O'ham, Shaw 5H **45**
THORN HILL 7F 34
Thornhill WN1: Stan 7E **34**
Thornhill Cl. BL1: Bolt 1D **38**
M34: Dent 7E **96**
Thornhill Dr. M28: Walk 1M **75**
Thorn Hill Gdns. WN1: Stan 6E **34**
Thornhill Rd. BL0: Ram 4G **25**
M43: Droy 8F **80**
SK4: Stoc 6L **107**
WN4: Gars 6N **69**
Thornhill Ter. SK11: Macc 4F **130**
Thornholme Cl. M18: Man 6N **95**
Thornholme Rd. SK6: Mar 3C **120**
Thorn Ho. *SK15: Stal* *8D* ***82***
(off Waterloo Rd.)
Thorniley Brow M4: Man 3H **5** (8F **78**)
Thorn Lea BL2: Bolt 9L **23**
M46: Ath 9N **55**
Thornlea M9: Man 9M **61**
M43: Droy 9C **80**
WA15: Alt 3F **114**
Thornlea Av. M27: Swin 4D **76**
OL8: O'ham 1G **80**
Thorn Lea Cl. BL1: Bolt 5A **38**
Thornlea Dr. OL12: Roch 3N **27**
Thornlee Ct. OL4: Grot 6E **64**
Thornleigh Rd. M14: Man 8F **94**
Thornley Av. BL1: Bolt 2D **38**
Thornley Cl. OL4: Grot 6D **64**
Thornley Cres. OL4: Grot 6D **64**
SK6: Bred 4L **109**
Thornley La. OL4: Grot, O'ham 7D **64**
Thornley La. Nth.
M34: Dent, Stoc 6D **96**
SK5: Dent, Stoc 6D **96**
Thornley La. Sth.
M34: Dent, Stoc 7D **96**
SK5: Stoc 7D **96**
Thornley Pk. Rd. OL4: Grot 6D **64**
Thornley Ri. M34: Aud 2H **97**
Thornley Rd. M25: Pres 4B **60**
Thornleys Rd. M34: Dent 5L **97**
Thornley St. M24: Mid 2N **61**
M26: Rad 1H **59**
SK14: Hyde 8B **98**
Thornmere Cl. M27: Ward 9C **58**
Thorn Rd. M27: Swin 4E **76**
OL8: O'ham 8N **63**
SK7: Bram 1B **124**
Thorns, The M21: Cho H 1A **106**
Thorns Av. BL1: Bolt 1E **38**
Thorns Cl. BL1: Bolt 1E **38**
Thorns Clough OL3: Dig 7M **47**
THORNSETT 5N 121
Thornsett SK22: Bir V 5N **121**
Thornsett Cl. M9: Man 2K **79**
Thornsgreen Rd. M22: Wyth 7C **116**
Thorns Rd. BL1: Bolt 1E **38**
Thorn St. BL1: Bolt 2G **39**
BL9: Sum 2J **25**
WN2: Hin 7N **53**
Thorns Villa Gdns. M28: Wors 5H **75**
Thornton Av. BL1: Bolt 3A **38**
M34: Aud 1G **96**
M41: Urm 7A **92**
SK11: Macc 7E **130**
Thornton Cl. BL3: Lit L 9C **40**
BL4: Farn 4J **57**
M16: Old T 4B **94**
M28: Wors 3F **74**
WA3: Low 9C **72**
WN4: A Mak 6C **70**
WN7: Lei 9H **73**
Thornton Cres. M25: Pres 6M **59**
Thornton Dr. SK9: Hand 3J **123**
Thornton Ga. SK8: Gat 1F **116**
Thornton Pl. SK4: Stoc 4N **107**
Thornton Rd. M14: Man 7F **94**
M28: Wors 3F **74**
SK8: H Grn 6H **117**
Thornton Sq. SK11: Macc 7E **130**
Thornton St. BL2: Bolt 2N **7** (5H **39**)
M40: Man 6H **79**
OL4: O'ham 5E **8** (6K **63**)
OL11: Roch 8D **28**
Thornton St. Nth. M40: Man 5H **79**
Thorntree Cl. M9: Man 3K **79**
Thorntree Pl. OL12: Roch . . .5A **8** (5B **28**)
Thornvale WN2: Abr 3M **71**
Thorn Vw. BL9: Bury 1B **42**
Thorn Wlk. M31: Part 6F **102**
Thornway M28: Wors 3H **75**
SK6: H Lan 8C **120**
SK7: Bram 7A **118**
SK10: Boll 6L **129**
Thornway Dr. OL7: A Lyne 8K **81**
Thorn Well BL5: W'ton 4G **55**
Thornwood Av. M18: Man 5C **96**
Thornycroft St. SK11: Macc 5J **131**
Thornydyke Av. BL1: Bolt 8F **22**
Thorold Gro. M33: Sale 4L **105**
THORP 7H 45
Thorp Clough OL2: O'ham 8F **44**
Thorpe Av. M26: Rad 7K **41**
M27: Swin 1E **76**
Thorpebrook Rd. M40: Man 4M **79**
Thorpe Cl. M34: Dent 5K **97**
OL4: Aus 3D **64**
WA15: Tim 9J **105**
Thorpe Gro. SK4: Stoc 2B **108**
Thorpe Hall Gro. SK14: Hyde 3C **98**
Thorpe La. M34: Dent 4K **97**
OL4: Aus, Scout 3C **64**
Thorpeness Sq. M18: Man 3B **96**
Thorpe St. BL0: Ram 9H **11**
BL1: Bolt 2E **38**
M16: Old T 5B **94**
M24: Mid 4H **61**
M28: Walk 7L **57**
SK13: Glos 7G **100**
Thorp Rd. M40: Man 4M **79**
OL2: O'ham 8H **45**
Thorp St. M30: Ecc 1B **92**
M45: Whitef 1L **59**
SK10: Macc 4H **131**
Thorp Vw. OL2: O'ham 6G **44**
Thorsby Av. SK14: Hyde 7C **98**
Thorsby Cl. BL7: Bro X 5G **23**
M18: Man 4C **96**
Thorsby Rd. WA15: Tim 1F **6** (2E **114**)
Thorsby Way *M34: Dent* *8L* ***97***
(off Tatton Rd.)
Thorverton Sq. M40: Man 2A **80**
Thowler La. WA14: M'ton 9G **113**
Thrapston Av. M34: Aud 9H **81**
Threadfold Way BL7: Bolt 6G **22**
Threadmill La. M27: Swin 2D **76**
Threaphurst La. SK7: H Gro 7N **119**
Threapwood Rd. M22: Wyth 6D **116**
Three Acre Av. OL2: O'ham 8L **45**
Three Acres Dr. SK5: Stoc 3C **108**
Three Acres La. SK8: Chea H 8K **117**
Three Counties Rd. OL5: Mos 9G **64**
Three La. Ends M34: Dent 7K **97**
Three Pits M24: Mid 7A **44**
Three Sisters Enterprise Park, The
WN4: A Mak 4E **70**
Three Sisters Race Circuit 3F 70
Three Sisters Rd. WN4: A Mak 4E **70**
Threlkeld Cl. M24: Mid 2H **61**
Threlkeld Ct. M24: Mid 2H **61**
Threlkeld Rd. BL1: Bolt 7E **22**
M24: Mid 2H **61**
Thresher Cl. *M33: Sale* *5M* ***105***
(off Windmill Rd.)
Threshfield Cl. BL9: Bury 6M **25**
Threshfield Dr. WA15: Tim 9H **105**
Threxton Pl. *BL3: Bolt* *9A* ***38***
(off Cressingham Rd.)
Throstle Bank St. SK14: Hyde 5N **97**
Throstle Ct. OL2: O'ham 9H **45**
Throstle Gro. BL8: Bury 8J **25**
SK6: Mar 2A **120**
Throstle Hall Ct. M24: Mid 2L **61**
Throstle Nest HD7: Mars 1H **49**
Throstlenest Av. WN6: Wig 1D **52**
Throstles Cl. M43: Droy 7G **81**
Throstles Grn. M16: Old T 4N **93**
Thrum Fold OL12: Roch 2B **28**
Thrum Hall La. OL12: Roch 2B **28**
(not continuous)
Thrush Av. BL4: Farn 3G **57**
Thrush Dr. BL9: Bury 9A **26**
Thrush St. OL12: Roch 4A **28**
Thruxton Cl. M16: Whall R 6D **94**
Thurcaston Rd. WA14: W Tim 7C **104**
Thurland Rd. OL4: O'ham 5N **63**
Thurland St. OL9: Chad 3C **62**
Thurlby Av. M9: Man 6K **61**
Thurlby Cl. WN4: A Mak 6G **70**
Thurlby St. M13: Man 5J **95**
Thurleigh Rd. M20: Man 4G **106**
Thurlestone Av. BL2: Ain 3D **40**
Thurlestone Dr. M41: Urm 6C **92**
SK7: H Gro 5F **118**
Thurlestone Rd. WA14: Alt 1B **114**
Thurloe St. M14: Man 6H **95**
Thurlow WA3: Low 2A **88**
Thurlow St. M50: Sal 1M **93**
(not continuous)
Thurlston Cres. M8: Man 3F **78**
Thurlwood Av. M20: Man 1F **106**
Thurlwood Cft. BL5: W'ton 2G **55**
Thurnham St. BL3: Bolt 9D **38**
Thursby Av. M20: Man 2F **106**
Thursby Ho. *WN5: Wig* *4N* ***51***
(off Saddleback Rd.)
Thursby Wlk. M24: Mid 1H **61**
Thursfield St. M6: Sal 5A **78**
Thursford Gro. BL6: Bla 3N **35**
Thurstane St. BL1: Bolt 2D **38**
Thurstan St. WN3: I Mak 7H **53**
Thurston Av. WN3: Wig 8E **52**
Thurston Cl. BL9: Bury 1N **59**
Thurston Clough Rd.
OL3: Dob, O'ham 2F **64**
OL4: Scout 2F **64**
Thurston Grn. SK9: A Edg 4F **126**
Thurstons *BL5: W'ton* *3G* ***55***
(off Wigan Rd.)
Thyme Cl. M21: Cho H 4C **106**
Thynne St. BL3: Bolt 5L **7** (6G **39**)
BL4: Farn 2K **57**
Tiber Av. OL8: O'ham 1G **80**
Tib La. M2: Man 5G **4** (9E **78**)
Tib St. BL0: Ram 9H **11**
M4: Man 4J **5** (9F **78**)
M34: Dent 7K **97**
Tideswell Av. M40: Man 7J **79**
WN5: Orr 2L **51**
Tideswell Bank *SK13: Gam* *8A* ***100***
(off Edale Cres.)
Tideswell Cl. SK8: H Grn 7J **117**
Tideswell Rd. M43: Droy 7C **80**
SK7: H Gro 7J **119**
Tideswell Wlk. *SK13: Gam* *8A* ***100***
(off Riber Bank)
Tideswell Way M34: Dent 9L **97**
Tideway Cl. M7: Sal 2M **77**
Tidworth Av. M4: Man 3N **5** (8J **79**)
Tiefield Wlk. *M21: Cho H* *1D* ***106***
(off Marham Cl.)
Tiernan Lodge WN6: Wig 2D **52**
Tiflis St. OL12: Roch 5C **28**
Tig Fold Rd. BL4: Farn 3F **56**
Tilbury Gro. WN6: She 5H **33**
Tilbury St. OL1: O'ham 3J **63**
Tilbury Wlk. M40: Man 6J **79**
Tilby Cl. M41: Urm 7M **91**
Tildsley St. BL3: Bolt 8F **38**
Tilehurst Ct. M7: Sal 3A **78**
Tile St. BL9: Bury 1M **41**
Tilgate Wlk. *M9: Man* *8K* ***61***
(off Haverfield Rd.)
Tillard Av. SK3: Stoc 8N **107**
Tillerman Cl. M27: Pen 2K **77**
Tillhey Rd. M22: Wyth 5C **116**
Tillington Cl. *BL1: Bolt* *1F* ***38***
(off Eckersley Rd.)
Tilney Av. M32: Stre 8L **93**
Tilshead Wlk. *M13: Man* *3H* ***95***
(off Cavanagh Cl.)
Tilside Gro. BL6: Los 5K **37**
Tilson Rd. M23: Wyth 2L **115**
Tilstock Wlk. M23: Wyth 8L **105**
Tilston Wlk. SK9: Wilm 5K **123**
Tilton St. OL1: O'ham 2N **63**
Timberbottom BL2: Bolt 9K **23**
Timbercliffe OL15: Lit 5A **16**
Timberhurst BL9: Bury 2C **42**
Timbersbrook Gro. *SK9: Wilm* *4J* ***123***
(off Colshaw Dr.)
Timber St. SK10: Macc 3K **131**
Timber Wharf M15: Man 8B **4** (2C **94**)
Times Retail Pk. OL10: H'ood 2H **43**
Times St. M24: Mid 3N **61**
Timothy Cl. M6: Sal 7H **77**
TIMPERLEY 9F 104
Timperley Cl. OL8: O'ham 9L **63**
Timperley Cricket, Hockey, Tennis &
Lacrosse Club 2F **114**
Timperley Fold OL6: A Lyne 4N **81**
Timperley La. WN7: Lei 8K **73**
Timperley Rd. OL6: A Lyne 4M **81**
Timperley Stop (Metro) 8F 104
Timperley St. M11: Man 1A **96**
OL9: O'ham 1A **8** (4J **63**)
Timpson Rd. M23: Wyth 9L **105**
Timsbury Cl. BL2: Bolt 7N **39**
Timson St. M35: Fail 3D **80**
Tim's Ter. OL16: Miln 7K **29**
Tindall St. M30: Ecc 1B **92**
SK5: Stoc 6D **96**
Tindle St. M28: Walk 8N **57**
Tinkersfield WN7: Lei 3F **72**
Tinker's Pas. *SK14: Hyde* *7B* ***98***
(off Lumn Rd.)
Tinker St. SK14: Hyde 6A **98**
Tinline St. BL9: Bury 8N **7** (2N **41**)
Tinningham Cl. M11: Man 2C **96**
Tinsdale Wlk. M24: Mid 2H **61**
Tinshill Cl. M12: Man 4M **95**
Tinsley Cl. M40: Man 8K **79**
Tinsley Gro. BL2: Bolt 4N **39**
Tin St. BL3: Bolt 7F **38**
Tintagel Cl. SK10: Macc 4C **130**
Tintagel Ct. M26: Rad 7C **40**
SK15: Stal 8C **82**
Tintagel Rd. WN2: Hin 7C **54**
Tintagel Wlk. SK14: Hat 6H **99**
Tintern Av. BL2: Bolt 2J **39**
M20: Man 3E **106**
M29: Ast 3D **74**
M41: Urm 9A **92**
M45: Whitef 2M **59**
OL10: H'ood 9H **27**
OL12: Roch 2D **28**
OL15: Lit 7L **15**
WN4: A Mak 7G **71**
Tintern Cl. SK12: Poy 1H **125**
Tintern Ct. M20: Man 3E **106**
Tintern Dr. WA15: Hale 5J **115**
Tintern Gro. SK1: Stoc 7F **108**
Tintern Pl. OL10: H'ood 9H **27**
Tintern Rd. M24: Mid 9L **43**
SK8: Chea H 9N **117**
Tintern St. M14: Man 7G **95**
TINTWISTLE 2B 100
Tinwald Pl. WN1: Wig 2J **53**
Tipperary St. SK15: C'ook 5H **83**
Tipping St. WA14: Alt 4D **114**
WN3: Wig 5E **52**
Tipton Cl. M26: Rad 7D **40**
SK8: Chea H 3N **117**
Tipton Dr. M23: Wyth 6A **106**
Tiptree Wlk. *M9: Man* *2K* ***79***
(off Batley St.)

Tiree Cl. SK7: H Gro 6K 119
Tirza Av. M19: Man 9L 95
Tissington Bank SK13: Gam 8N 99
(off Youlgreave Cres.)
Tissington Grn. SK13: Gam 8N 99
(off Youlgreave Cres.)
Tissington Ter. SK13: Gam 8N 99
(off Youlgreave Cres.)
Titchfield Rd. OL8: O'ham 7N 63
Tithe Barn Cl. OL12: Roch 1H 29
Tithe Barn Ct. SK4: Stoc 4L 107
Tithe Barn Cres. BL1: Bolt 9J 23
Tithe Barn Rd. SK4: Stoc 4L 107
Tithebarn Rd. WA15: Haleb 7J 115
WN4: Gars 8N 69
Tithe Barn St. BL5: W'ton 2G 55
Tithebarn St. BL9: Bury 7L 7 (2M 41)
M26: Rad 8K 41
WN8: Uph 4F 50
Titian Ri. OL1: O'ham 7A 46
Titterington Av. M21: Cho H 7A 94
Tiverton Av. M33: Sale 5F 104
WN7: Lei 9F 54
Tiverton Cl. M26: Rad 7D 40
M29: Ast 3D 74
Tiverton Dr. M33: Sale 5F 104
SK9: Wilm 5J 123
Tiverton Ho. M6: Sal 7G 77
(off Devon Cl.)
Tiverton Pl. OL7: A Lyne 5L 81
Tiverton Rd. M41: Urm 5E 92
Tiverton Wlk. BL1: Bolt 3D 38
(off Valletts La.)
Tiviot Dale SK1: Stoc 1L 9 (6D 108)
Tiviot Way SK1: Stoc 5E 108
SK5: Stoc 5D 108
Tivoli St. M3: Man 5F 4
(off Stoney St.)
Tixall Wlk. M8: Man 9D 60
Toad La. OL12: Roch 6C 8 (5D 28)
OL15: Lit 5E 16
OL16: Roch 6C 8 (5D 28)
Toad Pond Cl. M27: Swin 4C 76
Tobermory Cl. M11: Man 9B 80
Tobermory Rd. SK8: H Grn 6H 117
Toddington La. WN2: Hai 4L 35
Todd St. BL9: Bury 9M 25
M3: Man 2H 5 (8F 78)
M7: Sal 4C 78
OL10: H'ood 2F 42
OL16: Roch 8E 8 (6E 28)
SK13: Glos 9F 100
Todmorden Rd. OL15: Lit 3N 15
Toft Rd. M18: Man 5A 96
WA16: Knut 7G 132
Toft Way SK9: Hand 2K 123
Toledo St. M11: Man 9B 80
Tolland La. WA15: Hale 7F 114
Tollard Av. M40: Man 5J 79
Tollard Cl. SK8: Chea H 9N 117
Toll Bar Av. SK11: Macc 5K 131
Toll Bar Rd. SK11: Macc 4D 130
Toll Bar St. M12: Man 3K 95
SK1: Stoc 4M 9 (8D 108)
Tollemache Cl. SK14: Mot 4K 99
Tollemache Rd. SK14: Mot 4K 99
Tollesbury Cl. M40: Man 6J 79
Toll Ga. Cl. M13: Man 5K 95
Tollgate Way OL16: Roch 5G 28
Tollgreen Cl. WN2: Hin 4N 53
Toll St. M26: Rad 8D 40
WN2: P Bri 1K 71
Tolver Rd. WN4: A Mak 4D 70
Tolworth Dr. M8: Man 3G 78
Tomcroft La. M34: Dent 7H 97
Tom Husband Leisure Complex . . .7B 78
Tom La. WA14: Rost 9M 113
Tomlinson Cl. OL8: O'ham 6J 63
Tomlinson St. BL6: Hor 1D 36
(not continuous)
M15: Man 3D 94
M40: Man 8A 62
OL11: Roch 9A 28
Tomlin Sq. BL2: Bolt 5K 39
Tom Lomas Wlk. M11: Man 8N 79
(off Frankland Cl.)
Tommy Browell Cl. M14: Man 6F 94
Tommy Johnson Wlk. M14: Man . . .6F 94
(off Up. Lloyd St.)
Tommy La. BL2: Ain 3C 40
Tommy Taylor Cl. M40: Man 5A 80
Tom Pendry Sq. SK15: Stal 9D 82
(off Melbourne St.)
Tom Shepley St. SK14: Hyde 7B 98
Tomwood Ri. SK13: Char 2M 111
TONACLIFFE 7A 14
Tonacliffe Rd. OL12: Whitw 9A 14
Tonacliffe Ter. OL12: Whitw 7A 14
Tonacliffe Way
OL12: Whitw 8A 14
Tonbridge Cl. BL8: Bury 6J 25
SK10: Macc 2F 130
Tonbridge Pl. BL2: Bolt 3H 39
Tonbridge Rd. M19: Man 9N 95
SK5: Stoc 9D 96
Tong Clough BL7: Bro X 5G 22
(not continuous)
Tonge Bri. Ind. Est. BL2: Bolt 4J 39
Tonge Bri. Way BL2: Bolt 4J 39
Tonge Bri. Workshop
BL2: Bolt 4J 39
Tonge Cl. M45: Whitef 2A 60
Tonge Ct. M24: Mid 3N 61
TONGE FOLD 5K 39
Tonge Fold Cotts. BL8: Haw 2C 24
Tonge Fold Rd. BL2: Bolt 5K 39
Tonge Grn. SK15: Mat 3H 99
Tonge Hall Cl. M24: Mid 3N 61
Tonge Mdw. M24: Mid 3N 61
TONGE MOOR 2J 39
Tonge Moor Rd. BL2: Bolt 3J 39
TONG END 4A 14
Tong End OL12: Whitw 4A 14
Tonge Old Rd. BL2: Bolt 5K 39
Tonge Pk. Av. BL2: Bolt 3K 39
Tonge Roughs M24: Mid 3B 62
Tonge St. M12: Man 2J 95
M24: Mid 5C 62
OL10: H'ood 2J 43
OL16: Roch 9E 8 (7E 28)
Tong Flds. BL7: Eger 5G 22
Tong Head Av. BL1: Bolt 9J 23
Tong La. OL12: Whitw 5A 14
Tongley Wlk. M40: Man 9B 62
(off Blandford Dr.)
Tong Rd. BL3: Lit L 8A 40
Tong St. BL4: Kea 6C 58
Tonman St. M3: Man 6E 4 (1D 94)
TONTINE 6H 51
Tontine Rd. WN5: Orr 5G 51
WN8: Uph 5G 51
Tontin St. M5: Sal 8A 78
Tooley Ho. M30: Ecc 1D 92
Toon Cres. BL8: Bury 7J 25
Tootal Dr. M5: Sal 8J 77
M6: Sal 7J 77
Tootal Gro. M6: Sal 8J 77
Tootal Rd. M5: Sal 8J 77
Toothill Cl. WN4: A Mak 5E 70
Top Acre Rd. WN8: Skel 4A 50
Topcliffe Rd. M9: Man 8N 61
Topcliffe St. WN2: Hin 5B 54
Topcroft Cl. M22: Nor 8D 106
Topfield Rd. M22: Wyth 3B 116
Topfields Gro. M7: Sal 3C 78
Topgate Brow M27: Pen 2K 77
Topham St. BL9: Bury 4N 41
(not continuous)
Topley St. M40: Man 4J 79
TOP LOCK .1L 53
TOP OF HEAP 2E 42
Top of Heap OL10: H'ood 2E 42
TOP OF HEBERS 9K 43
TOP OF LANE 8D 64
TOP OF MOOR 3A 64
Top of Wallsuches BL6: Hor 9H 21
TOP O' TH' BROW 2L 39
Top o' th' Brow BL2: Bolt 7M 23
Top o' th' Flds. M45: Whitef 4M 59
Top o' th' Gorses BL2: Bolt 7L 39
Top o' th' Grn. OL9: Chad 7G 62
Top o' th' La. BL3: Bolt 7L 39
TOP O' TH' MEADOWS 2D 64
Top o' th' Mdws. La. OL4: Wat 2D 64
TOP O' TH' WOOD 8G 26
Top Pk. Cl. WA13: Warb 7F 102
Topphome Ct. BL4: Farn 4M 57
(off Longcauseway)
Topping Fold Rd. BL9: Bury 1B 42
TOPPINGS .6J 23
Toppings, The SK6: Bred 5L 109
Toppings Grn. BL7: Bro X 6H 23
Topping St. BL1: Bolt 3F 38
BL9: Bury 1M 41
Topp St. BL4: Farn 4M 57
Topp Way BL1: Bolt 1J 7 (4F 38)
Top Schwabe St. M24: Mid 3H 61
Topsham Wlk. M40: Man 5B 80
(off Silverwell St.)
Top St. M24: Mid 2L 61
OL4: O'ham 3A 64
Torah St. M8: Man 6F 78
Tor Av. BL8: G'mount 4F 24
Torbay Cl. BL3: Bolt 6D 38
(off Blackshaw La.)
Torbay Dr. SK2: Stoc 9F 108
Torbay Rd. M21: Cho H 9B 94
M41: Urm 8E 92
Torbrook Gro. SK9: Wilm 4J 123
(off Bosley Cl.)
Torcross Rd. M9: Man 6G 60
Tor Hey M. BL8: G'mount 3F 24
TORKINGTON 5J 119
Torkington Av. M27: Pen 1F 76
Torkington Ho. SK7: H Gro 5K 119
Torkington La. SK6: H Gro 4A 120
Torkington Mnr. SK7: H Gro 4M 119
Torkington Rd. SK7: H Gro 5J 119
SK8: Gat 2G 117
SK9: Wilm 8H 123
Torkington St. SK3: Stoc 9B 108
Torksey Wlk. M9: Man 6G 61
Torness Wlk. M11: Man 9N 79
Toronto Av. M90: Man A 8A 116
Toronto Rd. SK2: Stoc 1E 118
Toronto St. BL2: Bolt 4M 39
Torpoint Wlk. M40: Man 1A 80
Torquay Cl. M13: Man 3J 95
Torquay Dr. WN5: Bil 2J 69
Torquay Gro. SK2: Stoc 3F 118
Torra Barn Cl. BL7: Eger 2F 22
Torrax Cl. M6: Sal 4H 77
Torre Cl. M24: Mid 9M 43
Torrens St. M6: Sal 5K 77
Torridon Cl. WN6: Stan 5D 34
Torridon Rd. BL2: Bolt 5N 39
Torridon Wlk.
M22: Wyth 7B 116
Torrin Cl. SK3: Stoc 2D 118
Torrington Av. BL1: Bolt 2F 38
M9: Man 9M 61
Torrington Dr. SK14: Hat 7G 99
Torrington Rd. M27: Pen 4H 77
Torrington St. OL10: H'ood 4K 43
Torrisdale Cl. BL3: Bolt 7C 38
Torr Rd. SK11: Macc 8G 131
Torrs Millennium Walkway 8L 121
(off Union Rd.)
Torrs Riverside Park, The 8K 121
Torrs Valley SK22: N Mil 8M 121
Torr Top St. SK22: N Mil 7M 121
Torrvale Rd. SK22: N Mil 8L 121
TOR SIDE .1E 10
Torside Cl. WN2: Hin 5N 53
Torside M. SK13: Had 4C 100
Torside Way M27: Pen 9F 58
SK13: Had 4C 100
Torver Cl. WN3: Wig 9D 52
Torver Dr. BL2: Bolt 4N 39
M24: Mid 1J 61
Torver Wlk. M22: Wyth 6A 116
Torwood Rd. OL9: Chad 2C 62
Total Fitness
Altrincham 4C 6
Bolton 3G 39
Walkden 7K 57
Whitefield 2L 59
Wigan 9C 52
Wilmslow 2L 123
Totland Cl. M12: Man 6N 95
Totley Av. SK13: Gam 8N 99
(off Youlgreave Cres.)
Totley Cl. SK13: Gam 8N 99
(off Youlgreave Cres.)
Totley Gdns. SK13: Gam 8N 99
(off Youlgreave Cres.)
Totley Grn. SK13: Gam 8N 99
Totley Lanes SK13: Gam 8N 99
(off Youlgreave Cres.)
Totley M. SK13: Gam 8N 99
Totley Pl. SK13: Gam 8N 99
(off Melandra Castle Rd.)
Totnes Av. OL9: Chad 2D 62
SK7: Bram 5E 118
Totnes Rd. M21: Cho H 9B 94
M33: Sale 3D 104
Totridge Cl. SK2: Stoc 2H 119
Tottenham Dr. M23: Wyth 9K 105
TOTTINGTON 6F 24
Tottington Av. OL4: Spri 4C 64
Tottington Fold BL2: Bolt 8M 23
(off Tottington Rd.)
Tottington La. M25: Pres 6L 59
Tottington Rd. BL2: Bolt 8M 23
BL7: Tur 3N 23
BL8: Bury 8H 25
Tottington St. M11: Man 8A 80
Totton Rd. M35: Fail 3D 80
Touchet Hall Rd. M24: Mid 8B 44
Touch Rd. BL9: Bury 6L 25
Touchstones 8B 8 (6C 28)
Toulston Rd. WN6: Wig 1C 52
Tourist Info. Cen.
Altrincham 3D 6 (3D 114)
Ashton-under-Lyne . . .6D 6 (7M 81)
Bolton 3K 7 (5G 38)
Bury 8K 7 (2L 41)
Glossop 9E 100
Macclesfield 4H 131
Manchester 5J 5 (9F 78)
Oldham 3E 8 (5K 63)
Rochdale 8B 8 (6C 28)
Salford Quays 2L 93
Stockport 1L 9 (6D 108)
Uppermill 3L 65
Tours Av. M23: Wyth 6N 105
Towcester Cl. M4: Man 9J 79
Tower Av. BL0: Ram 9G 11
Tower Bldgs. BL6: Hor 1J 37
Tower Ct. BL7: Tur 1K 23
BL8: G'mount 5F 24
Tower Dr. BL7: Tur 2K 23
Tower Ent. Pk. WN3: Wig . . .8H 9 (3E 52)
Tower Grange M7: Sal 2C 78
Tower Gro. WN7: Lei 4M 73
Tower Hill Rd. WN8: Uph 6D 50
Tower Ho., The SK11: Macc 4G 131
(off Bridge St.)
Tower La. WA13: Lym 5A 112
Tower Nook WN8: Uph 6E 50
Towers, The SK10: Macc 4D 130
Towers Av. BL3: Bolt 8B 38
Towers Bus. Pk. M20: Man 7H 107
Towers Cl. SK12: Poy 1K 125
Tower Sq. M13: Man 9M 5
Towers Rd. SK12: Poy 8K 119
Towers St. OL4: O'ham 2A 64
Tower St. BL7: Tur 1K 23
M26: Rad 9K 41
OL10: H'ood 3G 43
SK14: Hyde 3A 98
SK16: Duk 9A 82
Tower Ter. BL8: G'mount 5F 24
Tower Vw. BL6: Bla 1M 35
Towey Cl. M18: Man 3B 96
Towncliffe Wlk. M15: Man 3C 94
(off Shawheath Cl.)
Towncroft M34: Dent 5L 97
Towncroft Av. M24: Mid 1L 61
Towncroft La. BL1: Bolt 4N 37
Townend St. SK14: Hyde 7B 98
TOWNFIELD 4M 63
Townfield M41: Urm 8B 92
Townfield Av. WN4: A Mak 8E 70
Townfield Gdns.
WA14: Alt 1C 6 (2D 114)
Townfield La. WA13: Warb 2C 102
Townfield Rd. WA14: Alt . . .1C 6 (2D 114)
WA16: Mob 4N 133
Townfields WA16: Knut 6J 133
WN4: A Mak 7D 70
Townfields Cl. BL9: Bury . . .9L 7 (3M 41)
Townfield St. OL4: O'ham 4M 63
Townfield Wlk. M15: Man 3C 94
(off Shawgreen Cl.)
WA12: N Wil 5E 86
Town Fold SK6: Mar B 9E 110
Towngate Bus. Cen. M38: Lit H 6F 56
Town Ga. Dr. M41: Urm 7K 91
TOWN GREEN 7G 71
Towngreen Ct. M8: Man 9E 60
Town Hall La. M2: Man 4G 4
Town Hall Sq. OL16: Roch 7C 8
TOWN HEAD 5D 8 (4D 28)
Town Ho. Rd. OL15: Lit 7M 15
(not continuous)
TOWN LANE 6B 74
Town La. M34: Dent 8K 97
SK13: Char 2N 111
SK16: Duk 1A 98
WA16: Mob 4M 133
Town La. Ct. M34: Dent 7J 97
Townley Fold SK14: Hyde 5C 98
Townley Mill SK11: Macc 5H 131
(off Townley Pl.)
Townley Pk. Ind. Est. M24: Mid . . .2M 61
Townley Pl. SK11: Macc 5H 131
Townley Rd. OL16: Miln 7K 29
Townley St. M8: Man 5E 78
M11: Man 1L 95
M24: Mid 2M 61
SK11: Macc 5H 131
Townley Ter. SK6: Mar 1D 120
(off Canal St.)
Town Mdws. OL16: Roch 7B 8
Town Mill Brow OL12: Roch 7B 8
TOWN OF LOWTON 4L 87
Townrow St. OL10: H'ood 2J 43
Townscliffe La. SK6: Mar B 9E 110
Towns Cft. Lodge M33: Sale 2E 104
(off Green La.)
Townsend Farm La.
WA14: D Mas, Part 7K 103
Townsend Rd. M27: Pen 1F 76
Townsfield Rd. BL5: W'ton 4G 55
TOWNS GATE 7K 91
Townsgate Way M44: Irl 8J 91
Townside Row
BL9: Bury 9M 7 (3M 41)
Townsley Gro. OL6: A Lyne 5B 82
Townson Dr. WN7: Lei 9H 73
Town Sq. M33: Sale 4H 105
Town Sq. Shop. Cen.
OL1: O'ham 3D 8 (5K 63)
Town St. SK6: Mar B 9E 110
Towns Vw. SK15: Stal 9E 82
Towns Yd. OL2: O'ham 8J 45
(off Park St.)
Towton St. M9: Man 2K 79
Towyn Av. M5: Sal 8N 77
Toxhead Cl. BL6: Hor 1C 36
Toxteth St. M11: Man 2C 96
Tracey St. M8: Man 1F 78
Trackside App. BL5: W'ton 1G 55
Tracks La. WN5: Bil 8H 51
Tracy Dr. WA12: N Wil 6H 87
Traders Av. M41: Urm 3E 92
Trafalgar Av. M34: Aud 2G 97
SK12: Poy 3L 125
Trafalgar Bus. Pk. M8: Man 6D 78
Trafalgar Cen., The OL16: Roch 5F 28
Trafalgar Cl. SK12: Poy 3L 125
Trafalgar Ct. BL9: Bury 3L 41
(off Manchester Old Rd.)
M16: Whall R 7D 94
Trafalgar Gro. M7: Sal 5C 78
Trafalgar Ho. M34: Aud 2G 97
(off Audenshaw Rd.)
WA14: Alt 1D 114
Trafalgar Pl. M20: Man 4F 106
Trafalgar Rd. M6: Sal 8G 76
M33: Sale 2J 105
WN1: Wig 5J 9 (2F 52)
WN2: Hin 6N 53
Trafalgar Sq. OL5: Mos 1E 82
(off Wyre St.)
OL7: A Lyne 9K 81
(not continuous)
OL16: Roch 6F 8 (5E 28)
Trafalgar St. M7: Sal 5D 78
OL1: O'ham 1B 8 (3J 63)
OL7: A Lyne 1K 97
OL16: Roch 5F 8 (5E 28)
(not continuous)
Trafalgar Wlk. M11: Man 1M 95
(off Herne St.)
M15: Man 4D 94
Trafford Athletics Stadium 8M 93
Trafford Av. M41: Urm 6E 92
Trafford Bank Rd. M16: Old T 4B 94
Trafford Bar Stop (Metro) 4A 94
Trafford Boulevard M17: Urm 3C 92
Trafford Cen., The M17: Urm 3D 92
Trafford Ct. M15: Man 3C 94
(off Stretford Rd.)
Trafford Dr. M38: Lit H 6J 57
WA15: Tim 8H 105
Trafford Ecology Pk. 2J 93
Trafford Gro. BL4: Farn 2M 57
M32: Stre 8K 93
Trafford Ho. M32: Stre 4M 93
(off Chester Rd.)
Trafford Mans. M16: Old T 7A 94
Trafford Moss Rd. M17: T Pk 2F 92
TRAFFORD PARK 4J 93
Trafford Pk. Heritage Cen. 3J 93
Trafford Pk. Rd. M17: T Pk 1H 93
(Moorings Rd.)
M17: T Pk 3M 93
(Waters Reach)
Trafford Park Station (Rail) 6J 93
Trafford Pl. M15: Man 3C 94
SK9: Wilm 8J 123
Trafford Plaza M16: Old T 5A 94
Trafford Retail Pk. M41: Urm 4C 92
Trafford Rd. M5: Sal 3N 93
M30: Ecc 1D 92
M50: Sal 3N 93
SK9: A Edg 4F 126
SK9: Wilm 5G 122
WN2: Hin 6M 53
Trafford St. BL4: Farn 2L 57
M1: Man 7E 4 (1D 94)
OL8: O'ham 5C 8 (6J 63)
OL11: Roch 8C 28
Trafford Water Sports Cen. 2L 105
Trafford Way M17: Urm 2C 92
Trafford Wharf Rd. M17: T Pk 2K 93
Tragan Cl. SK2: Stoc 1H 119
Tragan Dr. SK2: Stoc 1H 119
Trail St. M6: Sal 8L 77
Trail Vw. SK13: Had 4D 100
Trajan Ho. OL1: O'ham 1D 8 (4K 63)
Tramore Wlk. M22: Wyth 5C 116
Tram St. M11: Man 1A 96
WN2: P Bri 1K 71
Tramway Rd. M44: Irl 1G 102
OL6: A Lyne 6E 6 (6N 81)
Tranby Cl. M22: Wyth 3E 116
Tranmere Cl. M18: Man 4N 95
Tranmere Dr. SK9: Hand 3K 123
Tranmere Rd. SK3: Stoc 8N 107
Trans Pennine Trad. Est.
OL11: Roch 1B 44
Transvaal St. M11: Man 9B 80
Travers St. BL6: Hor 3F 36
Travis Brow SK4: Stoc 2G 9 (7B 108)
Travis Ct. OL2: O'ham 8J 45
Travis St. M1: Man 7L 5 (1G 95)
OL2: Shaw 5M 45
OL16: Miln 9M 29
SK14: Hyde 7B 98
Trawden Av. BL1: Bolt 2D 38
Trawden Dr. BL9: Bury 5L 25
Trawden Grn. SK2: Stoc 3H 119
Traylen Way OL12: Roch 4M 27
Traynor Cl. M24: Mid 2L 61
Treacle Brow SK14: Hyde 9C 98
(off Mottram Old Rd.)
Trecastell Cl. WN1: Wig 2J 53
Tredcroft St. SK13: Glos 9D 100
Tredgold St. BL6: Hor 2E 36
Tree Av. M43: Droy 7E 80
Tree Ho. Av. OL7: A Lyne 4K 81
Treelands Wlk. M5: Sal 3A 94
Treen Cl. SK10: Macc 3B 130
Treen Rd. M29: Ast 2D 74
Tree Tops BL7: Bro X 7K 23
Treetops Av. BL0: Ram 2G 24
Treetops Cl. OL3: Dob 1J 65
SK6: Mar 9B 110
Tree Wlk. M32: Stre 8J 93
Tree Way WA16: Knut 9G 132
Trefoil Way OL15: Lit 8K 15
Tregaer Fold M24: Mid 3A 62
Tregaron Gro. WN2: Hin 8C 54
Tremain Wlk. M9: Man 3J 79
(off Stockwood Wlk.)
Trenam Pl. M5: Sal 8A 78
Trenant Rd. M6: Sal 5K 77
Trenchard Ct. M11: Droy 8B 80
M43: Droy 8B 80
Trenchard Dr. M22: Wyth 8E 116
Trencherbone M26: Rad 7E 40
Trencherfield Mill WN3: Wig 4E 52
Trencherfield Mill Engine 9H 9
Trencherfield Mill Leisure Arts &
Heritage Cen. 4E 52
(off Heritage Way)
Trengrove St. OL12: Roch 4A 28
Trent Av. OL9: Chad 3C 62
OL10: H'ood 1F 42
OL16: Miln 7L 29
Trent Bri. Wlk. M16: Old T 6N 93
Trent Cl. SK5: Stoc 3G 108
SK7: Bram 9A 118
WA3: Cul 7J 89
Trent Ct. M15: Man 3C 94
(off Johnson St.)
SK3: Stoc 9C 108
Trent Dr. BL9: Bury 5M 25
M28: Walk 9J 57
WN2: Hin 8E 54
Trent Gro. WN7: Lei 6E 72
Trentham Av. BL4: Farn 2K 57
SK4: Stoc 5L 107
Trentham Cl. BL4: Farn 2K 57
Trentham Gro. M40: Man 1M 79
Trentham Lawns M6: Sal 6N 77
Trentham Rd. M16: Old T 6N 93
Trentham St. BL4: Farn 2K 57
M15: Man 9A 4 (2B 94)
M27: Swin 1E 76
Trent Ind. Est. OL2: Shaw 4M 45
Trent Rd. OL2: Shaw 4L 45
WN4: A Mak 5H 71
WN5: Bil 6G 69
WN5: Wig 4N 51
Trent St. OL16: Roch 7F 28
Trent Wlk. M43: Droy 1F 96
Trent Way BL4: Kea 6B 58
(not continuous)
Tresco Av. M32: Stre 8L 93
Trescott M. WN6: Stan 4B 34
Treswell Cl. WN2: Hin 9N 53
Trevarrick Ct. BL6: Hor 2G 37
OL4: O'ham 3N 63
Trevelyan Dr. WN5: Bil 1H 69
Trevelyan St. M30: Ecc 8G 76
Trevone Cl. WA16: Knut 7G 132
Trevor Av. BL3: Bolt 9E 38
M33: Sale 6F 104
Trevor Dr. M40: Man 9C 62
Trevore Dr. WN1: Stan 3E 34
Trevor Gro. SK1: Stoc 8E 108
Trevor Rd. M27: Swin 4D 76
M30: Ecc 7B 76
M41: Urm 6N 91
Trevor St. M11: Man 2C 96
OL11: Roch 1N 43
Triangle, The M4: Man 3G 5 (8F 78)
WA15: Tim 9H 105
Tribune Av. WA14: B'ath 9B 104
Trident Rd. M30: Ecc 2N 91
Trident Way SK11: Macc 7E 130
Trillo Av. BL2: Bolt 6J 39
Trimdon Cl. M11: Man 8N 79
Trimingham Dr. BL8: Bury 8J 25
Trimley Av. M40: Man 5J 79
Tring Wlk. M9: Man 8G 60
Trinity Av. M33: Sale 4K 105
Trinity Bri. Ho. M3: Sal 3E 4
Trinity Bldgs. OL5: Mos 9G 64
Trinity Cl. SK16: Duk 1B 98
Trinity Ct. M3: Sal 3C 4
OL6: A Lyne 7A 6 (7L 81)
WA16: Knut 6G 132
(off Green St.)
Trinity Cres. M28: Walk 9M 57
Trinity Edge M3: Sal 3D 4
Trinity Gdns. M3: Sal 2C 4 (8C 78)
SK3: Stoc 4D 118
WN4: A Mak 6C 70
Trinity Grn. BL0: Ram 3H 25
Trinity Ho. OL1: O'ham 3J 63
Trinity La. SK11: Sut E 9K 131
Trinity Pl. BL5: W'ton 1G 55
Trinity Retail Pk.
BL2: Bolt 5N 7 (6H 39)
Trinity Rd. M33: Sale 4J 105

Trinity Sports Cen. 3F 94
Trinity Sq. SK10: Macc 3K 131
Trinity St. BL2: Bolt 5J 7 (6F 38)
BL3: Bolt 5J 7 (6F 38)
BL9: Bury 9L 7 (3M 41)
M24: Mid 3L 61
OL1: O'ham 3J 63
OL12: Roch 3K 27
SK6: Mar 2C 120
SK15: Stal 8D 82
(not continuous)
Trinity Wlk. *M14: Man* *6G 95*
(off Ellanby Cl.)
Trinity Way M3: Sal 4C 4 (8D 78)
Trippear Way OL10: H'ood 3G 42
Trippier Rd. M30: Ecc 1N 91
Tripps M. M20: Man 4E 106
Triscombe Way M16: Whall R 6D 94
Tristam Cl. M13: Man 9M 5 (3H 95)
Trojan Gdns. M7: Sal 5B 78
Trongate Wlk. *M9: Man* *3K 79*
(off Carisbrook St.)
Troon Cl. BL3: Bolt 9A 38
SK7: Bram 8E 118
Troon Dr. SK8: H Grn 6H 117
Troon Rd. M23: Wyth 1M 115
Trough Ga. OL8: O'ham 9H 63
Troutbeck Av. M4: Man 3N 5 (8J 79)
WA12: N Wil 5B 86
Troutbeck Cl. BL8: Haw 3B 24
Troutbeck Dr. BL0: Ram 6J 11
M29: Ast 3B 74
Troutbeck Gro. WA11: St H 8F 68
Troutbeck Ri. WN5: Wig 5M 51
Troutbeck Rd. SK8: Gat 4G 116
WA15: Tim 2K 115
WN4: A Mak 5F 70
Troutbeck Wlk. *OL2: O'ham* *8J 45*
(off Shaw St.)
Troutbeck Way OL11: Roch 9N 27
Trowbridge Dr. M40: Man 1A 80
Trowbridge Rd. M34: Dent 8L 97
Trows La. OL11: Roch 3B 44
Trowtree Av. M12: Man 3K 95
(not continuous)
Troydale Dr. M40: Man 5M 79
Troy Wlk. M5: Sal 2A 94
TRUB 4B 44
Trumpet St. M1: Man 7F 4 (1E 94)
Truro Av. M32: Stre 7L 93
OL6: A Lyne 3A 82
SK5: Stoc 3G 108
Truro Cl. BL8: Bury 1K 41
SK7: Bram 8D 118
SK10: Macc 3C 130
Truro Dr. M33: Sale 4D 104
Truro Rd. M29: Ast 2D 74
OL9: Chad 2E 62
Truro Wlk. M34: Dent 8K 97
Trust Rd. M18: Man 6A 96
Tucana Av. M7: Sal 1A 4 (7B 78)
TUCKER'S HILL 3L 35
Tuckers Hill Brow WN2: Hai 3L 35
Tudbury Way M3: Sal 2C 4 (7C 78)
Tudor Av. BL1: Bolt 5C 38
BL4: Farn 4J 57
M9: Man 1K 79
OL9: Chad 8B 62
SK15: Stal 7G 83
Tudor Cl. OL5: Mos 1H 83
SK5: Stoc 1C 108
Tudor Ct. BL1: Bolt 4F 38
M16: Old T *4B 94*
(off Stanley Rd.)
M25: Pres 8B 60
OL10: H'ood 3H 43
OL12: Roch 4F 28
SK7: Bram 9B 118
WN7: Lei 5L 73
Tudor Dr. SK10: P'bury 7B 128
Tudor Grn. SK9: Wilm 5K 123
Tudor Gro. M24: Mid 9J 43
WN3: Wins 9B 52
Tudor Hall St. OL11: Roch 2A 44
Tudor Ho. *M21: Cho H* *9E 94*
(off Mauldeth Rd.)
Tudor Ind. Est. SK16: Duk 3L 97
Tudor Rd. SK9: Wilm 5K 123
WA14: B'ath 9B 104
Tudor St. *BL3: Bolt* *8D 38*
(off Venice St.)
M24: Mid 3N 61
OL2: Shaw 5M 45
OL8: O'ham 6H 63
(not continuous)
Tuer St. M13: Man 3F 94
Tuffley Rd. M23: Wyth 4N 115
Tufton Wlk. M9: Man 3J 79
Tugford Cl. M16: Whall R 5D 94
Tuley St. M11: Man 2L 95
Tulip Av. BL4: Farn 2H 57
BL4: Kea 5N 57
Tulip Cl. M33: Sale 4C 104
OL9: Chad 4C 62
SK3: Stoc 2B 118
Tulip Dr. WA15: Tim 1F 114
WN6: Wig 9C 34
Tulip Gro. OL12: Roch 2C 28
Tulip Rd. M31: Part 6F 102
WA11: Hay 3C 86
Tulip Wlk. M7: Sal 6C 78
Tulketh St. Ind. Est. M40: Man 2L 79
Tulle Ct. M25: Pres 7N 59
Tully Av. WA12: N Wil 6B 86
Tully St. M7: Sal 3D 78
Tully St. Sth. M7: Sal 4D 78
Tulpen Sq. OL9: Chad 4F 62
Tulworth Rd. SK12: Poy 2H 125
Tumblewood Dr. SK8: Chea 3K 117
Tumbling Bank M9: Man 1J 79
Tumbling Bank Ter. OL4: Lees 6C 64
Tunbridge Sq. M5: Sal 9N 77
Tunnicliffe Rd. SK11: Sut E 9K 131
Tunnicliffe's New Row WN7: Lei 5E 72
Tunnicliffe St. SK10: Macc 3H 131
Tunshill Golf Course 6N 29
Tunshill Gro. OL16: Miln 7L 29
Tunshill La. OL16: Miln 6M 29
Tunshill Rd. M23: Wyth 7L 105
Tuns Rd. OL8: O'ham 9M 63
Tunstall Cl. BL9: Bury 5N 41
Tunstall La. WN5: Wig 6A 52
Tunstall Rd. OL4: O'ham 5N 63
Tunstall St. M11: Man 2C 96
SK4: Stoc 6C 108
TUNSTEAD 6N 65
Tunstead Av. M20: Man 2E 106
Tunstead La. OL3: G'fld 5M 65
Tupelo St. M13: Man 4J 95
Turbary Wlk. OL16: Miln 7H 29
Turf Cl. OL2: O'ham 9J 45
TURF HILL 9F 28
Turf Hill Rd. OL16: Roch 8F 28
Turf Ho. Cl. OL15: Lit 7K 15
Turfland Av. OL2: O'ham 9J 45
Turf La. OL2: O'ham 9J 45
OL9: Chad 8D 62
SK11: Macc 9G 131
TURF LEA 6E 120
Turf Lea Fold SK6: Mar 6E 120
Turf Lea Rd. SK6: Mar, Stri 5D 120
Turfnell Way M28: Wors 5A 76
Turf Pk. Rd. OL2: O'ham 9J 45
Turf Pit La. OL4: O'ham 9B 46
Turf Pits OL4: O'ham 9B 46
Turf St. M26: Rad 9F 40
Turf Ter. OL15: Lit 8L 15
Turfton Rd. OL2: O'ham 9K 45
Turing Cl. M11: Man 1M 95
Turing Ct. *M11: Man* *1M 95*
(off Turing Cl.)
Turks Rd. M26: Rad 7D 40
Turk St. BL1: Bolt 4D 38
Turley St. M8: Man 4G 79
TURN 5N 11
Turnberry BL3: Bolt 9A 38
Turnberry Cl. M29: Ast 2D 74
SK10: Macc 9G 129
Turnberry Dr. SK9: Wilm 6H 123
Turnberry Rd. SK8: H Grn 6H 117
Turnberry Wlk. *M8: Man* *2H 79*
(off Stakeford Dr.)
Turnbull Av. M25: Pres 4B 60
Turnbull Rd. M13: Man 7L 95
M18: Man 5D 96
WA14: W Tim 8B 104
Turnbury Cl. M33: Sale 2H 105
Turnbury Rd. M22: Shar 2D 116
Turncliff Cres. SK6: Mar 9A 110
Turncroft La. SK1: Stoc 3N 9 (7E 108)
Turncroft Way M28: Wors 3G 75
Turnditch Cl. WN6: Wig 8D 34
Turner Av. M35: Fail 4C 80
M44: Irl 6H 91
WN2: B'haw 1A 72
Turner Bri. Rd. BL2: Bolt 4K 39
Turner Dr. M41: Urm 7F 92
Turnerford Cl. BL7: Eger 4F 22
Turner Gdns. SK14: Hyde 5B 98
Turner La. OL6: A Lyne 5D 6 (6M 81)
SK6: Bred, Wood 1K 109
SK14: Hyde 4B 98
Turner Ri. SK10: Boll 5N 129
Turner Rd. SK6: Mar 1C 120
Turners Pl. OL12: Roch 2C 28
Turner St. BL1: Bolt 4H 39
BL5: W'ton 6G 54
M4: Man 3J 5 (8F 78)
M7: Sal 3D 78
M11: Man 9A 80
M16: Old T 3B 94
M18: Man 4B 96
M34: Dent 4J 97
OL4: Lees 3B 64
OL6: A Lyne 5D 6 (6M 81)
OL12: Roch 4C 28
SK1: Stoc 1L 9 (6D 108)
SK10: Boll 5M 129
WN1: Wig 7L 9 (2G 53)
WN2: Hin 4N 53
WN7: Lei 6J 73
Turners Yd. WN5: Orr 6H 51
Turnfield Cl. OL16: Roch 2H 29
Turnfield Rd. SK8: Chea 4H 117
Turnhill Rd. OL16: Roch 1F 44
Turnill Dr. WN4: A Mak 8E 70
Turnlee Cl. SK13: Glos 9E 100
Turnlee Dr. SK13: Glos 9E 100
Turnlee Rd. SK13: Glos 9D 100
Turn Moss Rd. M32: Stre 9M 93
Turnock St. SK11: Macc 5J 131
Turnough Rd. OL16: Miln 6K 29
Turnpike, The SK6: Mar 9A 110
Turnpike Cl. OL3: Dig 7M 47
OL12: Roch 3B 28
Turnpike Gallery *5H 73*
(off St Mary's Way)
Turnpike Grn. *M6: Sal* *7M 77*
(off Nursery St.)
Turnpike Wlk. *M11: Man* *9L 79*
(off Albert St.)
Turn Rd. BL0: Ram 6L 11
Turnstone Av.
WA12: N Wil 5F 86
Turnstone Cl. WN7: Lei 4J 73
Turnstone Rd. BL2: Bolt 6H 39
SK2: Stoc 2K 119
Turn St. OL6: A Lyne 6N 81
Turret Hall Dr. WA3: Low 1A 88
Turriff Gro. WN2: I Mak 3K 53
Turton Av. BL3: Lit L 8A 40
TURTON BOTTOMS 1L 23
Turton Cl. BL8: Bury 4G 40
OL10: H'ood 2F 42
Turton Community Leisure Cen. 6J 23
Turton Ct. BL1: Bolt 1M 7 (4H 39)
Turton Golf Course 4J 23
Turton Hgts. BL2: Bolt 7J 23
Turton La. M25: Pres 6M 59
Turton Rd. BL2: Bolt 7J 23
BL7: Bro X 7J 23
BL8: Tot 3A 24
Turton St. BL1: Bolt 4G 39
M11: Man 2B 96
WA3: Gol 1K 87
Turton Tower 2J 23
Turves Rd. SK8: Chea H 6K 117
Turville Ho. SK9: Wilm 4J 123
Turvin Rd. HX6: Ripp 5G 16
Tuscan Rd. M20: Man 8G 106
Tuscany Vw. M7: Sal 2A 78
Tutbury St. M4: Man 9J 79
Tutor Bank Dr. WA12: N Wil 6G 86
Tuxford Wlk. *M40: Man* *5J 79*
(off Palgrave Av.)
Tweedale Av. M9: Man 6H 61
(not continuous)
Tweedale St. OL11: Roch 8C 28
Tweedale Way OL9: Chad 9D 62
Tweed Cl. OL8: O'ham 6J 63
(not continuous)
WA14: Alt 1C 114
Tweedle Hill Rd. M9: Man 7G 61
Tweedsdale Cl. M45: Whitef 2A 60
Tweed St. WN7: Lei 6K 73
Tweed St. Ind. Est. WN7: Lei 6K 73
Tweenbrook Av. M23: Wyth 4N 115
Twelve Yards Rd. M30: Ecc 4G 90
(not continuous)
M44: Irl 5D 90
Twigworth Rd. M22: Wyth 5B 116
Twillbrook Dr. M3: Sal 1E 4 (7D 78)
Twinegate OL12: Roch 2C 28
Twingates Cl. OL2: Shaw 7M 45
Twining Brook Rd.
SK8: Chea H 3N 117
Twining Rd. M17: T Pk 1D 92
Twinnies Rd. SK9: Wilm 5G 122
Twin St. OL10: H'ood 3K 43
Twirl Hill Rd. OL6: A Lyne 1B 82
Twisse Rd. BL2: Bolt 5N 39
TWISS GREEN 5G 89
Twiss Grn. Dr. WA3: Cul 5G 88
Twiss Grn. La. WA3: Cul 5F 88
Twist Av. WA3: Gol 1M 87
Twist La. WN7: Lei 5F 72
Two Acre Av. M22: Wyth 2B 116
Two Acre Dr. OL2: Shaw 5K 45
Two Acre La. OL4: O'ham 1D 64
Two Bridges Rd. OL16: Miln 1M 45
Two Brooks La. BL8: Haw 3B 24
Two Mills La. OL5: Mos 1G 82
Two Trees La. M34: Dent 7K 97
Twyford Cl. M20: Man 5E 106
Tybyrne Cl. M28: Wors 3G 74
Tydden St. OL8: O'ham 8K 63
Tydeman Wlk. OL16: Miln 8L 29
Tyersall Cl. M30: Ecc 6E 76
TYLDESLEY 1A 74
Tyldesley Arc. WN1: Wig 7K 9
Tyldesley Old Rd. M46: Ath 9M 55
Tyldesley Pas. M29: Tyld 1A 74
Tyldesley Pool 1A 74
Tyldesley Rd. M46: Ath 8M 55
Tyldesley St. M14: Man 6F 94
Tyler St. SK9: A Edg 4F 126
Tymm St. M40: Man 2A 80
Tyndall Av. M40: Man 1M 79
Tyndall St. OL4: O'ham 5N 63
Tyne Ct. M28: Walk 8K 57
Tynedale Cl. SK5: Stoc 3C 108
SK11: Macc 4F 130
Tynesbank M28: Walk 9K 57
Tynesbank Cotts. *M28: Walk* *8K 57*
(off Tynesbank)
Tyne St. OL4: O'ham 4N 63
Tynwald St. OL4: O'ham 4N 63
Tynwell Wlk. *M40: Man* *5H 79*
(off Glendower Dr.)
Tyrer Av. WN3: Wig 6C 52
Tyrer Rd. WA12: N Wil 8F 86
Tyrer Wlk. WA3: Low 1B 88
Tyrone Cl. M23: Wyth 8K 105
Tyrone Dr. OL11: Roch 8L 27
Tyro St. OL8: O'ham 8K 63
Tyrrell Gro. SK14: Hyde 8D 98
Tyrrell Rd. SK5: Stoc 8D 96
Tysoe Gdns. M3: Sal 2C 4 (8C 78)
Tyson St. M8: Man 2E 78
TYTHERINGTON 1H 131
Tytherington Bus. Pk.
SK10: Boll 8H 129
(not continuous)
Tytherington Ct. SK10: Macc 2H 131
Tytherington Dr. M19: Man 8B 96
SK10: Macc 1H 131
Tytherington Golf Course, The 8G 129
Tytherington Grn. SK10: Macc 8G 128
Tytherington La. SK10: Boll 8H 129
Tytherington Pk. Rd.
SK10: Macc 1H 131
Tytherington Shop. Cen.
SK10: Macc 1H 131
Tywald Mt. OL2: O'ham 9J 45

U

Uganda St. BL3: Bolt 1D 56
Ukraine Rd. M7: Sal 4A 78
UKskate 4N 9 (8E 108)
Uldale Dr. M24: Mid 2K 61
Ullesthorpe OL12: Roch 6B 8
Ulleswater Cl. BL3: Lit L 9N 39
Ulleswater St. BL1: Bolt 2G 38
WN7: Lei 5G 73
Ullock Wlk. M24: Mid 1J 61
Ullswater SK11: Macc 7D 130
Ullswater Av. OL2: O'ham 6H 45
OL7: A Lyne 6L 81
OL12: Roch 4A 28
WN4: A Mak 6E 70
WN5: Orr 4K 51
Ullswater Dr. BL4: Farn 4F 56
BL9: Bury 5L 41
M24: Mid 1L 61
WN2: I Mak 4L 53
Ullswater Gro. OL10: H'ood 4J 43
Ullswater Ho. WA3: Gol 9M 71
Ullswater Mans. SK11: Macc 6D 130
Ullswater Rd. M22: Wyth 5A 116
M29: Ast 3B 74
M41: Urm 5M 91
SK1: Stoc 9F 108
SK9: Hand 2H 123
WA3: Gol 9M 71
Ullswater Ter. SK15: Stal 6D 82
Ullswater Wlk. *M9: Man* *8K 61*
(off Rockmead Dr.)
Ulster Av. OL11: Roch 8C 28
Ulundi St. M26: Rad 9G 40
Ulverston Av. M20: Man 1F 106
OL9: Chad 5E 62
Ulverston Rd. WN3: Wig 8C 52
Umberton Rd. BL5: O Hul 4A 56
Uncouth Rd. OL16: Roch 6J 29
Underhill SK6: Rom 6M 109
Underhill Rd. OL1: O'ham 2J 63
Underhill Wlk. M40: Man 6N 79
Under La. OL4: Grot 7E 64
OL9: Chad 8F 62
Underwood OL12: Roch 7B 8 (6C 28)
Underwood Cl. M18: Man 3D 96
SK10: Macc 3D 130
Underwood Rd. SK9: A Edg 4H 127
SK14: Hat 7F 98
Underwood St. SK16: Duk 1M 97
Underwood Ter. M29: Tyld 1B 74
Underwood Vs. *OL15: Lit* *1J 29*
(off Whitegate)
Underwood Wlk. SK14: Hat 7G 98
Underwood Way OL2: Shaw 4A 46
Undsworth Ct. OL10: H'ood 2J 43
Unicorn Gateway SK10: Macc 4H 131
Unicorn St. M30: Ecc 1B 92
Union Arc. BL9: Bury 7L 7 (2M 41)
Union Bank Chambers
SK15: Stal *8D 82*
(off Market St.)
Union Bldgs. BL2: Bolt 4L 7 (6G 39)
Union Cl. WN5: Orr 6J 51
Union Ct. BL2: Bolt 2H 39
Union Ind. Est. SK11: Macc 5J 131
Union Rd. BL2: Bolt 2H 39
OL6: A Lyne 6N 81
OL12: Roch 1J 29
SK6: Mar 1C 120
SK11: Macc 5J 131
SK22: N Mil 8L 121
Union St. BL0: Ram 8J 11
BL7: Eger 3E 22
BL9: Bury 7L 7 (2M 41)
M4: Man 3J 5 (8F 78)
M6: Sal 6N 77
M12: Man 8N 5 (2H 95)
M14: Man 6G 95
M18: Man 3C 96
M24: Mid 2M 61
M27: Pen 2G 77
M27: Swin 2E 76
M29: Tyld 1A 74
OL1: O'ham 3C 8 (5K 63)
OL2: O'ham 8H 45
OL4: Lees 5B 64
OL6: A Lyne 5D 6 (7M 81)
OL9: Chad 7F 62
OL12: Roch 5C 8 (5D 28)
OL12: Whitw 6A 14
OL16: Roch 6D 8 (5D 28)
SK1: Stoc 5L 9 (8D 108)
SK11: Macc 5G 131
SK13: Glos 9E 100
SK14: Hyde 7B 98
WN2: I Mak 3K 53
WN7: Lei 5H 73
Union St. W. OL8: O'ham 4B 8 (5J 63)
Union Ter. *M7: Sal* *2E 78*
(off Bury Old Rd.)
Union Yd. OL4: O'ham 5M 63
Unison Bus. Cen.
M41: Urm 2E 92
United Rd. M16: Old T 3L 93
United Trad. Est. M16: Old T 4L 93
Unity Cl. OL10: H'ood 3G 42
Unity Cres. OL10: H'ood 3G 42
Unity Dr. M7: Sal 4E 78
Unity Ho. WN3: Wig 5F 52
Unity St. OL10: H'ood 3G 42
Unity Wlk. SK13: Glos 9E 100
Unity Way SK1: Stoc 5M 9 (8D 108)
UNIVERSITIES 3F 94
University of Bolton
Deane Campus 5H 7 (6F 38)
University of Manchester
Beyer Building *3G 94*
(off Oxford Rd.)
Denmark Road Building 4G 95
Dryden St. *3H 95*
(off Dryden St.)
Ellen Wilkinson Building 4G 94
Institute of Science and Technology
....7K 5 (1G 94)
John Rylands University Library
....5F 4 (9E 78)
McDougall Sports Cen. 4F 94
Manchester Business School East
....9J 5 (3F 94)
Manchester Business School West
....3F 94
Sackville Street Building
....7K 5 (1G 94)
Stopford Building 4G 95
University Place *3G 94*
(off Wilton St.)
Up. Brook St. 9K 5 (3G 94)
University of Salford
Adelphi Campus 2B 4 (8C 78)
Adelphi House 3A 4 (8B 78)
Irwell Pl. 4A 4 (9B 78)
Newton Building 8A 78
Salford University Bus. Pk. 6A 78
Statham St. 7A 78
Technology House *7A 78*
(off Frederick Rd.)
University Rd. M5: Sal 7A 78
University Rd. W. M5: Sal 8A 78
UNSWORTH 9A 42
Unsworth Av. M29: Tyld 2C 74
WA3: Low 9A 72
Unsworth St. M26: Rad 8F 40
M29: Tyld 1C 74
WN2: Hin 7N 53
WN7: Lei 3G 72
Unsworth Ter. WN2: Hin 6M 53
Unsworth Way
OL1: O'ham 1C 8 (3J 63)
Unwin Av. M18: Man 5B 96
Unwin Ct. *M6: Sal* *8M 77*
(off Rosehill Cl.)
Upavon Ct. M7: Sal 4E 78
Upavon Rd. M22: Wyth 4E 116
Upcast La. SK9: A Edg, Wilm 2C 126
UP HOLLAND 4F 50
Upholland Rd. WN5: Bil 7H 51
Upholland Station (Rail) 7D 50
Upland Dr. M38: Lit H 5G 56
WN4: A Mak 6G 71
Upland Rd. OL8: O'ham 7J 63
Uplands M24: Mid 4M 61
Uplands, The OL5: Mos 1G 83
SK11: Macc 4E 130
Uplands Av. M26: Rad 1J 59
Uplands Rd. M41: Urm 9M 91
SK13: Glos 9F 100
SK14: Hyde 2D 110
Up. Brook St. M13: Man 9K 5 (3G 94)
SK1: Stoc 3M 9 (7D 108)
Up. Broom Way BL5: W'ton 1J 55
Up. Camp St. M7: Sal 5C 78
Up. Chorlton Rd. M16: Whall R 6B 94
Up. Cliff Hill OL2: Shaw 3N 45
Up. Conran St. M9: Man 2K 79
Up. Cyrus St. M40: Man 8K 79
Up. Dicconson St.
WN1: Wig 6K 9 (2F 52)
Upper Downs WA14: Alt 4C 114
Up. George St. M29: Tyld 2B 74
OL12: Roch 4D 28
Up. Gloucester St. M6: Sal 7N 77
Up. Hayes Cl. OL16: Roch 5G 28
Up. Helena St. M40: Man 8K 79
Up. Hibbert La. SK6: Mar 3C 120
Up. Kent Rd. M14: Man 6K 95
Up. Kirby St. M4: Man 4N 5
Up. Lees Dr. BL5: W'ton 2J 55
Up. Lloyd St. M14: Man 6F 94
Upper Mead BL7: Eger 4G 23
Up. Medlock St. M15: Man 3E 94
UPPERMILL 3L 65
Uppermill Dr. M19: Man 5K 107
Up. Monsall St. M40: Man 4K 79
Up. Moss La. M15: Man 3D 94
Up. Park Rd. M7: Sal 1C 78
M14: Man 5H 95
Up. Passmonds Gro.
OL11: Roch 5N 27
Up. St Stephen St. WN6: Wig 3E 52
Up. Stone Dr. OL16: Miln 7H 29
Up. West Gro. M13: Man 4J 95
Up. Wharf St. M5: Sal 4A 4 (9B 78)
Up. Wilton St. M25: Pres 7B 60
Uppingham Dr. BL0: Ram 7H 11
Upton OL11: Roch 7C 28
Upton Av. SK4: Stoc 4K 107
SK8: Chea H 7M 117
Upton Cl. M24: Mid 6M 61
WA3: Low 1N 87
Upton Dr. WA14: Tim 8E 104
Upton La. M29: Tyld 2D 74
Upton Rd. M46: Ath 7N 55
Upton Wlk. BL3: Bolt 8F 38
OL7: A Lyne *9L 81*
(off John St. E.)
Upton Way BL8: Bury 8F 24
SK9: Hand *1J 123*
(off Beeston Rd.)
Upwood Rd. WA3: Low 2N 87
Upwood Wlk. *M9: Man* *8K 61*
(off Sanderstead Dr.)
Urban Av. WA15: Alt 4F 6 (3E 114)
Urban Dr. WA15: Alt 4F 6 (3E 114)
Urban Rd. M33: Sale 4G 104
WA15: Alt 4F 6 (3E 114)
Urmson St. OL8: O'ham 8K 63
URMSTON 7D 92
Urmston Av. WA12: N Wil 4E 86
Urmston La. M32: Stre 8G 93
Urmston Leisure Cen. 7B 92
Urmston Pk. M41: Urm 7E 92
Urmston Station (Rail) 7D 92
Urmston St. WN7: Lei 5F 72
(not continuous)
Urquhart M. OL12: Roch 4L 27
Urwick Rd. SK6: Rom 7M 109
Usk Cl. M45: Whitef 4B 60
Utley Fld. Vw. WA15: Hale 4E 114
Uttley St. BL1: Bolt 2E 38
OL11: Roch 9A 28
Uvedale Ho. *M30: Ecc* *9D 76*
(off Adelaide St.)
Uxbridge Av. M11: Man 8A 80
Uxbridge St. OL6: A Lyne 7A 6 (7L 81)

V

Vaal St. OL8: O'ham 8G 63
Valance Cl. M12: Man 3M 95
Valdene Cl. BL4: Farn 4L 57
Valdene Dr. BL4: Farn 4L 57
M28: Walk 2L 75
Vale, The OL5: Mos 1E 82
WN6: App B 4H 33
Vale Av. BL6: Hor 1C 36
BL9: Bury 5K 41
M26: Rad 4C 58
M27: Pen 1G 77
M33: Sale 3L 105
M41: Urm 8M 91
SK14: Hyde 6D 98

Vale Cl. SK4: Stoc 6L 107
SK6: Rom 6C 110
SK7: H Gro 3J 119
WN6: App B 4J 33
Vale Coppice BL0: Ram 2J 25
BL6: Hor 1C 36
Vale Cotts. *BL6: Hor 2B 36*
(off Crown La.)
OL15: Lit 9L 15
SK14: Hyde 5N 97
(off Arnside Dr.)
Vale Cres. SK8: Chea H 5L 117
Vale Cft. WN8: Uph 5E 50
Vale Dr. M25: Pres 9N 59
OL9: O'ham 4A 8 (5H 63)
Vale Edge M26: Rad 7G 40
Vale Gdns. WN3: I Mak 6J 53
Vale Head SK9: Hand 4J 123
Vale Ho. SK4: Stoc 7K 107
Vale Ho. Dr. SK13: Had 3C 100
Vale La. M35: Fail 6E 80
Vale Mill Ct. BL0: Eden 1K 11
Valemount SK13: Had 4C 100
Valencia Rd. M7: Sal 4A 78
Valentia Rd. M9: Man 7J 61
Valentine Rd. WA12: N Wil 6C 86
Valentines Rd. M46: Ath 1J 73
Valentine St. M35: Fail 3C 80
OL4: O'ham 5N 63
Vale Pk. Ind. Est. M8: Man 3H 79
Vale Pk. Way M8: Man 3H 79
Valerie Wlk. M15: Man 9G 5
Vale Rd. M43: Droy 7F 80
OL2: Shaw 6A 46
SK4: Stoc 7L 107
SK6: Rom 7M 109
SK9: Wilm 6D 122
SK15: C'ook 4H 83
WA14: Bow 6B 114
WA15: Tim 2G 115
Vale Side OL5: Mos 2F 82
Vale St. BL2: Bolt 5A 40
BL7: Tur 1L 23
M11: Man 8A 80
M24: Mid 3N 61
OL7: A Lyne 4L 81
OL10: H'ood 2K 43
(not continuous)
Vale Top Av. M9: Man 3L 79
Valetta Cl. M14: Man 9G 94
Vale Vw. BL7: Bolt 6G 23
OL5: Mos 8H 65
WA14: Bow 6C 114
(off Vicarage La.)
Valewood Av. SK4: Stoc 7M 107
Valiant Rd. WN5: Wig 3A 52
Valiant Wlk. *M40: Man 1C 80*
(off Nuthurst Rd.)
Vallea Ct. M4: Man 1H 5 (7F 78)
Valletts La. BL1: Bolt 3D 38
Valletts Sth. Bldgs. BL1: Bolt 3D 38
Valley Av. BL8: Bury 9H 25
Valley Cl. OL5: Mos 9E 64
SK8: Chea 4K 117
WA16: Knut 9G 133
WN6: Wig 1B 52
Valley Ct. SK4: Stoc 7N 107
Valley Dr. SK9: Hand 3H 123
Valley Gdns. SK14: Hat 8H 99
Valley Ga. WN1: Wig 8G 34
Valley Gro. M34: Dent 7M 97
Valley M. OL3: G'fld 7M 65
Valley Mill BL7: Bolt 6G 22
Valley Mill La. BL9: Bury 3N 41
Valley New Rd. OL2: O'ham 9J 45
Valley Pk. Rd. M25: Pres 6M 59
Valley Ri. OL2: Shaw 3L 45
Valley Rd. M24: Mid 1N 61
M41: Urm 6L 91
OL2: O'ham 9J 45
SK4: Stoc 7L 107
SK6: Bred 4H 109
SK7: Bram 6D 118
SK8: Chea 4K 117
SK11: Macc 7E 130
SK13: Glos 9B 100
SK14: Hat 9H 99
WN5: Wig 6A 52
Valley Rd. Sth. M41: Urm 7K 91
Valley Vw. BL7: Bro X 6H 23
BL8: Bury 9J 25
OL12: Whitw 2B 14
SK14: Hyde 5D 98
WA12: N Wil 7E 86
Valley Wlk. M11: Man 9L 79
Valley Way SK15: Stal 9F 82
WA16: Knut 9G 132
Valpy Av. BL2: Bolt 1J 39
Vanbrugh Gro. WN5: Orr 2M 51
Vancouver Quay M50: Sal 2M 93
Vandyke Av. M6: Sal 7H 77
Vandyke St. OL12: Roch 4L 27
Vane St. M30: Ecc 8C 76
Vanguard Cl. BL8: Bury 1J 41
M30: Ecc 2N 91
(off Avroe Rd.)
Vantomme St. BL1: Bolt 9F 22
Vant St. OL8: O'ham 7N 63
Varden Gro. SK3: Stoc 2B 118
Varden Rd. SK12: Poy 3J 125
Varden Town Cotts.
SK10: O Ald 9M 127
Vardon Dr. SK9: Wilm 8J 123
Varey St. M18: Man 4B 96
Varley Bus. Pk. M40: Man 7K 79
Varley Rd. BL3: Bolt 8B 38
Varley St. M40: Man 6J 79
Varna St. M11: Man 2B 96
Vasser Rd. M18: Man 4N 95
Vauban Dr. M6: Sal 7H 77
Vaudrey Dr. SK7: H Gro 5J 119
SK8: Chea H 4M 117
WA15: Tim 8G 105
Vaudrey La. M34: Dent 7L 97
Vaudrey Rd. SK6: Wood 3L 109
Vaudrey St. SK15: Stal 9D 82
Vaughan Av. M40: Man 2M 79
Vaughan Gro. OL4: Lees 5C 64
Vaughan Ho. *M13: Man 4G 95*
(off Portsmouth St.)
Vaughan Ind. Est. M12: Man 2L 95
Vaughan Rd. M21: Cho H 9C 94
SK4: Stoc 5B 108
WA14: W Tim 7C 104
Vaughan St. M12: Man 2L 95
M30: Ecc 7B 76
OL2: O'ham 9J 45
Vauxhall Ct. *M40: Man 6H 79*
(off Hamerton Rd.)
Vauxhall Ind. Est. SK5: Stoc 2C 108
Vauxhall Rd. WN1: Wig 7M 9 (3G 53)
Vauxhall St. M40: Man 6G 79
Vauze Av. BL6: Bla 3N 35
Vauze Ho. Cl. BL6: Bla 2N 35
Vavasour Ct. OL16: Roch 7F 28
Vavasour St.
OL16: Roch 7F 28
Vawdrey Dr. M23: Wyth 6M 105
Vaynor OL12: Roch 5B 8 (5C 28)
Vega St. M8: Man 6D 78
Vela Wlk. M7: Sal 1A 4 (7B 78)
Velmere Av. M9: Man 6F 60
Velopark Stop (Metro) 9M 79
Velour Cl. M3: Sal 1B 4 (7C 78)
Velvet Ct. M1: Man 7J 5
Vendale Av. M27: Swin 4D 76
Venesta Av. M6: Sal 7H 77
Venetia St. M40: Man 5A 80
Venice Ct. *M1: Man 7J 5*
(off Samuel Ogden St.)
Venice St. BL3: Bolt 8D 38
M1: Man 7J 5 (1F 94)
Venlo Gdns. SK8: Chea H 6N 117
Ventnor Av. BL1: Bolt 1G 39
BL9: Bury 9M 41
M19: Man 9A 96
M33: Sale 2H 105
Ventnor Cl. M34: Dent 9M 97
Ventnor Rd. M20: Man 5H 107
SK4: Stoc 6M 107
Ventnor St. M6: Sal 6A 78
M9: Man 2J 79
OL11: Roch 8D 28
Ventura Cl. M14: Man 8F 94
Ventura Ct. SK22: N Mil 6N 121
Venture Ho. *SK11: Macc 6H 131*
(off Cross St.)
Venture Scout Way M8: Man 5E 78
Venture Way SK12: Poy 3K 125
Venwood Ct. M25: Pres 9M 59
Venwood Rd. M25: Pres 9M 59
Verbena Av. BL4: Farn 2H 57
Verbena Cl. M31: Part 5G 102
Verdant La. M30: Ecc 1N 91
Verdant Way OL16: Roch 1G 44
Verda St. WN2: Abr 2L 71
Verdun Av. M6: Sal 7H 77
Verdun Cres. OL11: Roch 5A 28
Verdun Rd. M30: Ecc 6B 76
Verdure Av. BL1: Bolt 4N 37
M33: Sale 7J 105
Verdure Cl. M35: Fail 3F 80
Vere St. M50: Sal 9M 77
Verity Cl. M20: Man 2G 107
OL2: O'ham 1H 63
Verity Wlk. M9: Man 8G 61
Vermont Gdns. SK8: Chea H 1N 123
Vermont St. BL1: Bolt 4E 38
Verna St. BL0: Ram 8J 11
Verne Av. M27: Swin 2E 76
Verne Dr. OL1: O'ham 7B 46
Vernet Gdns. OL9: O'ham 5G 63
Verne Wlk. WN4: A Mak 7G 70
Verney Rd. OL2: O'ham 1J 63
Vernham Wlk. BL3: Bolt 8F 38
Vernon Av. M30: Ecc 8F 76
M32: Stre 8K 93
SK1: Stoc 6F 108
Vernon Cl. SK8: Chea H 6K 117
SK12: Poy 4H 125
Vernon Ct. M7: Sal 1B 78
Vernon Dr. M25: Pres 9N 59
SK6: Mar 9N 109
Vernon Gro. M33: Sale 4L 105
Vernon Ho. SK1: Stoc 7F 108
Vernon Lodge *SK12: Poy 4H 125*
(off Copperfield Rd.)
Vernon Mill SK1: Stoc 6E 108
Vernon Pk. WA15: Tim 9G 105
Vernon Pk. Mus. 6F 108
Vernon Rd. BL8: G'mount 4F 24
M7: Sal 1B 78
M43: Droy 8C 80
SK6: Bred 6J 109
SK12: Poy 4H 125
Vernon St. BL1: Bolt 1H 7 (4F 38)
BL4: Farn 3M 57
BL9: Bury 9M 25
M7: Sal 5C 78
M9: Man 3K 79
M16: Old T 4B 94
OL5: Mos 9F 64
OL6: A Lyne 6N 81
SK1: Stoc 1L 9 (6D 108)
SK7: H Gro 4H 119
SK10: Macc 4K 131
SK14: Hyde 7B 98
WN7: Lei 5H 73
Vernon Vw. *SK6: Bred 5L 109*
(off Thomas St.)
Vernon Wlk. BL1: Bolt 1J 7 (4F 38)
SK1: Stoc 2K 9
Verona Dr. M40: Man 6A 80
Veronica Rd. M20: Man 5H 107
Verrill Av. M23: Wyth 7B 106
Verwood Wlk. *M23: Wyth 2N 115*
(off Beckfield Rd.)
Vesper St. M35: Fail 2E 80
Vesta St. BL0: Ram 8H 11
M4: Man 4N 5 (9H 79)
Vestris Dr. M6: Sal 7H 77
Vetch Cl. WA3: G'ook 3C 102
Vetchwood Gdns.
WA14: W Tim 7B 104
Viaduct Rd. WA14: B'ath 9D 104
Viaduct St. M3: Sal 2E 4 (8D 78)
M12: Man 9K 79
SK3: Stoc 3J 9 (7C 108)
WA12: N Wil 6D 86
Vibe, The M7: Sal 6C 78
Vicarage Av. SK8: Chea H 7N 117
Vicarage Cl. BL9: Bury 5L 25
M6: Sal 7H 77
OL4: Spri 4C 64
PR6: Adl 5K 19
SK16: Duk 1B 98
WN2: P Bri 9K 53
Vicarage Ct. SK14: Hyde 8A 98
Vicarage Cres. OL6: A Lyne 5A 82
Vicarage Dr. OL16: Roch 2G 29
SK16: Duk 1A 98
Vicarage Gdns. SK3: Stoc 8B 108
SK14: Hyde 7C 98
WN5: Orr 7H 51
Vicarage Gro. M30: Ecc 8F 76
Vicarage La. BL1: Bolt 1E 38
M24: Mid 4B 62
SK12: Poy 1H 125
WA14: Bow 6C 114
WN6: She 7L 33
Vicarage Rd. BL6: Bla 2M 35
M27: Swin 2E 76
M28: Walk 7K 57
M41: Urm 5B 92
M44: Irl 7H 91
OL7: A Lyne 5M 81
SK3: Stoc 1C 118
WN2: Abr 1L 71
WN4: A Mak 8D 70
WN5: Orr 7H 51
Vicarage Rd. Nth. OL11: Roch 3A 44
Vicarage Rd. Sth. OL11: Roch 3A 44
Vicarage Rd. W. BL6: Bla 2M 35
Vicarage Sq. WN7: Lei 5H 73
Vicarage St. BL3: Bolt 7E 38
M26: Rad 9G 41
OL2: Shaw 5M 45
OL8: O'ham 8G 62
Vicarage Vw. OL11: Roch 3B 44
Vicarage Way OL2: Shaw 6L 45
SK11: Macc 5D 130
Vicars Dr. OL16: Roch 8C 8 (6D 28)
Vicars Ga. OL16: Roch 8C 8 (6D 28)
Vicars Hall Gdns. M28: Wors 4G 74
Vicars Hall La. M28: Wors 5G 74
Vicars Rd. M21: Cho H 9N 93
Vicars St. M30: Ecc 8F 76
Viceroy Ct. M20: Man 6G 107
Vicker Cl. M27: Clif 9F 58
Vicker Gro. M20: Man 3E 106
Vickerman St. BL1: Bolt 2E 38
Vickers Cl. *BL3: Bolt 7E 38*
(off Vickers St.)
Vickers Dr. WN8: Skel 3C 50
Vickers Row *BL4: Farn 3J 57*
(off Mossfield Rd.)
Vickers St. BL3: Bolt 7E 38
M40: Man 7K 79
Victor Av. BL9: Bury 9L 25
Victor Cl. WN5: Wig 3A 52
Victoria Av. M9: Man 6F 60
M19: Man 9M 95
M20: Man 5F 106
M27: Swin 2G 76
M30: Ecc 7F 76
M45: Whitef 3N 59
SK6: Bred 5K 109
SK7: H Gro 4J 119
SK8: Chea H 5M 117
SK13: Had 4C 100
WA15: Tim 9E 104
WN2: B'haw 1A 72
WN6: Wig 2D 52
Victoria Av. E. M9: Man 7K 61
M40: Man 7K 61
Victoria Baths 5J 95
Victoria Bri. St. M3: Sal 3F 4 (8E 78)
Victoria Bldg., The M50: Sal 2M 93
Victoria Cl. M28: Wors 4H 75
SK3: Stoc 9C 108
SK7: Bram 9C 118
WN2: Asp 6L 35
Victoria Ct. BL4: Farn 1K 57
BL6: Hor 1E 36
BL8: Tot 7F 24
M11: Man 1A 96
(off Brigham St.)
M32: Stre 7J 93
M45: Whitef 4M 59
OL7: A Lyne 9L 81
SK13: Glos 9E 100
WN2: P Bri 8K 53
(off Neville St.)
Victoria Cres. M30: Ecc 7F 76
WN6: Stan 4B 34
Victoria Dr. M33: Sale 5K 105
Victoria Farm SK16: Duk 2A 98
Victoria Gdns. OL2: Shaw 5M 45
SK14: Hyde 5C 98
Victoria Grange *M20: Man 4F 106*
(off Barlow Moor Rd.)
Victoria Gro. BL1: Bolt 3D 38
M14: Man 9H 95
SK4: Stoc 3A 108
Victoria Hall *M13: Man 5H 95*
(off Up. Brook St.)
M15: Man 3F 94
(off Higher Cambridge St., not continuous)
Victoria Ho. M11: Man 1A 96
M30: Sal 6G 77
Victoria Ind. Est. WN7: Lei 3G 72
Victoria La. M27: Swin 2D 76
M45: Whitef 4M 59
Victoria Lodge M7: Sal 5B 78
Victoria M. BL9: Bury 1A 60
SK16: Duk 3N 97
Victoria Mill M43: Droy 9E 80
SK5: Stoc 9C 96
Victorian Lanterns BL9: Sum 3J 25
Victoria Pde. M41: Urm 7D 92
Victoria Pk. SK1: Stoc 8F 108
Victoria Pl. M34: Dent 9L 97
Victoria Plaza BL1: Bolt 3K 7
Victoria Point M13: Man 5J 95
Victoria Quay OL3: Dob 1L 65
Victoria Rd. BL1: Bolt 5M 37
BL4: Kea 5A 58
BL6: Hor 1E 36
M6: Sal 6G 77
M14: Man 9G 94
M16: Whall R 7C 94
M19: Man 8L 95
M22: Nor 8C 106
M30: Ecc 7E 76
M32: Stre 7K 93
M33: Sale 5K 105
M41: Urm 7B 92
M44: Irl 8G 91
SK1: Stoc 7F 108
SK9: Wilm 8F 122
SK10: Macc 3D 130
SK16: Duk 3N 97
WA12: N Wil 5F 86
WA15: Hale 4E 114
WA15: Tim 1G 114
WN2: P Bri 1K 71
WN4: Gars 7A 70
Victoria Sq. BL1: Bolt 3K 7 (5G 38)
M4: Man 2L 5 (8G 79)
M28: Walk 8L 57
(off Ellesmere Shop. Cen.)
M45: Whitef 4M 59
Victoria Station (Rail) 1H 5 (7F 78)
Victoria Sta. App.
M3: Man 2G 5 (8E 78)
Victoria Station Stop (Metro)
2H 5 (7F 78)
Victoria St. BL0: Ram 8H 11
BL2: Ain 3C 40
BL4: Farn 1J 57
BL5: W'ton 3H 55
BL6: Bla 2N 35
BL8: Bury 2K 41
(not continuous)
BL8: Tot 6E 24
M3: Man 3G 4 (8E 78)
M11: Man 1A 96
M24: Mid 3M 61
M26: Rad 9G 40
M28: Wors 4H 75
M34: Dent 6J 97
(not continuous)
M35: Fail 4B 80
OL2: Shaw 6M 45
OL4: Lees 4C 64
OL4: O'ham 3G 8 (5L 63)
OL7: A Lyne 9A 6 (9L 81)
OL8: O'ham 2K 81
OL9: Chad 4F 62
OL10: H'ood 3K 43
OL12: Roch 4D 28
OL12: Whitw 6A 14
OL15: Lit 9M 15
SK13: Glos 9E 100
SK14: Hyde 5B 98
SK15: Mill 6G 83
SK15: Stal 8C 82
SK16: Duk 1A 98
SK22: N Mil 9L 121
WA14: Alt 2D 6 (2D 114)
WA16: Knut 6F 132
WN2: P Bri 9K 53
WN5: Wig 6B 52
WN7: Lei 4G 72
Victoria St. E.
OL7: A Lyne 9B 6 (8L 81)
Victoria Ter. M12: Man 5L 95
M13: Man 5H 95
(off Hathersage Rd.)
OL2: O'ham 7H 45
(off Albert St.)
OL10: H'ood 9H 27
OL16: Miln 8L 29
WN2: B'haw 2B 72
Victoria Trad. Est. OL9: Chad 8F 62
OL9: O'ham 8F 62
(off Pennington St.)
Victoria Wlk. OL9: Chad 2G 62
Victoria Way OL2: O'ham 6G 45
SK7: Bram 9B 118
WN7: Lei 4G 72
Victor Mann St. M11: Man 2E 96
Victor St. M3: Sal 3C 4 (8C 78)
M40: Man 6H 79
OL8: O'ham 1F 80
OL10: H'ood 4K 43
VICTORY 4D 38
Victory Gro. M34: Aud 2G 96
Victory Pk. Ind. Est. M35: Fail 3B 80
Victory Rd. BL3: Lit L 8A 40
M44: Cad 4D 102
Victory St. BL1: Bolt 4D 38
(not continuous)
M14: Man 6H 95
Victory Trad. Est. BL3: Bolt 7H 39
Victory Way OL10: H'ood 2G 42
Vienna Rd. SK3: Stoc 1B 118
Vienna Rd. E. SK3: Stoc 1B 118
Viewfield Wlk. *M9: Man 3K 79*
(off Nethervale Dr.)
Viewlands Dr. SK9: Hand 4J 123
View St. BL3: Bolt 7E 38
Vigo Av. BL3: Bolt 9C 38
Vigo St. OL4: O'ham 6A 64
OL10: H'ood 3K 43
WN2: Asp 1J 53
Viking Cl. M11: Man 9L 79
Viking St. BL3: Bolt 8H 39
OL11: Roch 5A 28
Villa Av. WN6: Wig 8D 34
VILLAGE, THE 9N 91
Village M17: T Pk 4K 93
Village, The M41: Urm 8N 91
SK10: P'bury 7D 128
Village Circ. M17: T Pk 3K 93
Village Ct. M17: T Pk 3J 93
M41: Urm 9N 91
OL12: Whitw 5A 14
SK9: Wilm 5J 123
Village Grn. *OL3: Upp 3L 65*
(off New St.)
Village Leisure Club, The 3J 117
Village Mnr. OL3: Upp 2L 65
Village M. SK10: P'bury 7E 128
Village St. M7: Sal 5B 78
Village Vw. *SK15: Mill 6G 83*
(off Victoria St.)
WN5: Bil 5J 69
WN7: Lei 6K 73
Village Wlk. *M11: Man 9A 80*
(off Bob Massey Cl.)
Village Way M4: Man 3J 5
M17: T Pk 3H 93
SK9: Wilm 5J 123
Villa Rd. OL8: O'ham 7K 63
Villdale Av. SK2: Stoc 9G 109
Villemomble Sq. M43: Droy 9E 80
Villiers Ct. M45: Whitef 4N 59
Villiers Dr. OL8: O'ham 5B 8 (6J 63)
Villiers Ind. Est. M6: Sal 6N 77
Villiers St. BL9: Bury 1N 41
M6: Sal 6M 77
OL6: A Lyne 8G 6 (8A 82)
SK14: Hyde 7C 98
Vinca Gro. *M7: Sal 4C 78*
(off Hilton St. Nth.)
Vincent Av. M21: Cho H 8N 93
M30: Ecc 6D 76
OL4: O'ham 3N 63
Vincent Ct. BL3: Bolt 9F 38
Vincent St. BL1: Bolt 6E 38
M7: Sal 3C 78
M11: Man 1A 96
M24: Mid 1M 61
OL15: Lit 8L 15
OL16: Roch 8E 28
SK11: Macc 5H 131
SK14: Hyde 8C 98
Vincent Way BL3: Bolt 8J 39
WN5: Wig 3A 52
Vine Av. M27: Pen 2H 77
Vine Cl. M33: Sale 3C 104
OL2: Shaw 5M 45
SK11: Macc 7E 130
Vine Ct. M32: Stre 8K 93
OL16: Roch 6F 28
Vine Fold M40: Man 1D 80
Vine Gro. SK2: Stoc 1G 118
WN3: Wig 9J 9 (4F 52)
Vine Pl. OL11: Roch 8D 28
Viner Way SK14: Hat 6F 98
Vinery Gro. M34: Dent 6J 97
Vine St. BL0: Ram 1G 24
M7: Sal 2A 78
M11: Man 2C 96
M18: Man 2C 96
M25: Pres 6B 60
M30: Ecc 9C 76
OL9: Chad 8F 62
SK7: H Gro 4J 119
SK10: Boll 5M 129
WN1: Wig 5M 9 (2G 53)
WN2: Hin 5N 53
Vineyard OL12: Whitw 1C 14
Vineyard Cl. OL12: W'le 7G 15
Vineyard Cotts. OL12: W'le 7G 14
Vineyard Ho. *OL12: W'le 7G 14*
(off Knowl Syke St.)
Vineyards, The *M7: Sal 2B 78*
(off Nevile Rd.)
Vineyard St. OL4: O'ham 4M 63
Viola Cl. WN6: Stan 2A 34
Viola St. BL1: Bolt 1F 38
M11: Man 8B 80
Violet Av. BL4: Farn 2H 57
Violet Hill Ct. *OL4: O'ham 3B 64*
(off Howard St.)
Violet St. M18: Man 3D 96
SK2: Stoc 1D 118
WN3: I Mak 5H 53
WN4: A Mak 8E 70
Violet Way M24: Mid 4B 62
VIP Cen., The OL1: O'ham 2N 63
Virgil St. M15: Man 3B 94
Virgin Active
Bolton 1G 39
Castlefield 6F 4 (1E 94)
East Didsbury 7J 107
Manchester 3H 5
Virginia Chase SK8: Chea H 7L 117
Virginia Cl. M23: Wyth 9K 105
Virginia St. BL3: Bolt 8C 38
OL11: Roch 9C 28
Virginia Way WN5: Wig 3N 51
Viscount Dr. M24: Mid 4G 61
M90: Man A 8M 115
SK8: H Grn 8J 117
Viscount Rd. WN5: Wig 3A 52
Viscount St. M14: Man 6H 95
Vista, The M44: Cad 4D 102
Vista Av. WA12: N Wil 5D 86
Vista Cl. BL5: W'ton 9G 37
Vista Rd. WA11: Hay 2D 86
WA12: N Wil 2D 86
Vista Way WA12: N Wil 5D 86
Vivian Pl. M14: Man 5K 95
Vivian St. OL11: Roch 8C 28
Vixen Cl. M21: Cho H 1D 106
Voewood Ho. SK1: Stoc 8F 108
Voltaire Av. M6: Sal 7H 77
Vorlich Dr. OL9: Chad 3D 62
Vue Cinema
Bolton 4F 36
Salford Quays 2M 93
Vulcan Cl. WA12: N Wil 8F 86
Vulcan Dr. WN1: Wig 9M 9 (4G 52)
Vulcan Gym 7F 86
Vulcan Pk. Way WA12: N Wil 8G 86
Vulcan Rd. WN5: Wig 3A 52
Vulcan St. OL1: O'ham 2M 63

Vulcan Ter. OL15: Lit 9K 15
(off Spenwood Rd.)
VULCAN VILLAGE 9F 86
Vulcan Works M4: Man 5N 5 (9J 79)
Vyner Gro. M33: Sale 2F 104

W

Wadcroft Wlk. M9: Man 2K 79
(off Towton St.)
Waddicor Av. OL6: A Lyne 4B 82
Waddington Cl. BL8: Bury 2E 40
WA3: Low 1B 88
Waddington Fold OL16: Roch 2G 44
Waddington Rd. BL1: Bolt 3B 38
Waddington St. OL9: O'ham 3G 63
Wade Bank BL5: W'ton 3H 55
Wadebridge Av. M23: Wyth 9K 105
Wadebridge Cl. BL2: Bolt 3H 39
Wadebridge Dr. BL8: Bury 2F 40
Wadebrook Gro. SK9: Wilm 5J 123
(off Malpas Cl.)
Wade Cl. M30: Ecc 9D 76
Wadeford Cl. M4: Man 1M 5 (7H 79)
(not continuous)
Wade Hill La. OL3: Dob 3H 65
Wade Ho. M30: Ecc 9D 76
(off Wade Cl.)
Wade Row OL3: Upp 3L 65
Wade Row Top OL3: Upp 3L 65
(off Wade Row)
Wadesmill Wlk. M13: Man 9K 5
Wadeson Rd. M13: Man 8L 5 (2G 95)
Wadeson Way WA3: Cro 9D 88
Wade St. BL3: Bolt 9G 38
M24: Mid 5B 62
Wade Wlk. M11: Man 1M 95
(off Mill St.)
Wadham Gdns. SK6: Wood 3N 109
Wadham Way WA15: Hale 6F 114
Wadhurst Wlk. M13: Man 4H 95
(off Lauderdale Cres.)
Wadlow Cl. M3: Sal 1D 4 (7C 78)
Wadsley St. BL1: Bolt 1H 7 (4F 38)
Wadsworth Cl. SK9: Hand 3K 123
Wadsworth Dr. WN6: Wig 1C 52
Wadsworth Ind. Pk. BL3: Bolt 8F 38
Wadsworth M. M43: Droy 9D 80
Wagg Fold OL15: Lit 7K 15
Waggoners Ct. M27: Swin 3F 76
(off Wayfarers Way)
Waggon Rd. BL2: Bolt 3L 39
OL5: Mos 2F 82
Wagner St. BL1: Bolt 1E 38
Wagstaff Dr. M35: Fail 3D 80
Wagstaffe St. M24: Mid 2M 61
Wagstaff St. SK15: Stal 9B 82
Wagtail Cl. M28: Wors 2L 75
Waincliffe Av. M21: Cho H 4C 106
Wain Cl. M30: Ecc 8B 76
Wainfleet Cl. WN3: Wins 8B 52
Waingap Cres. OL12: Whitw 6B 14
Waingap Ri. OL12: Roch 1C 28
Waingap Vw. OL12: Whitw 7B 14
Wain Ho. WN7: Lei 7K 73
Wainman St. M6: Sal 5A 78
Wainscot Cl. M29: Ast 3C 74
Wainstones Grn. SK2: Stoc 1J 119
Wainwright Av. M34: Dent 6D 96
Wainwright Cl. OL4: Spri 4D 64
SK2: Stoc 9E 108
Wainwright Rd.
WA14: Alt 1A 6 (2B 114)
Wainwright St.
OL8: O'ham 5C 8 (6J 63)
SK16: Duk 9A 82
Waithlands Rd. OL16: Roch 7F 28
Wakefield Cres. SK6: Rom 7L 109
WN6: Stan 5D 34
Wakefield Dr. M27: Clif 7D 58
OL1: Chad 2G 62
Wakefield M. BL7: Bolt 6G 22
Wakefield Rd. SK15: Stal 8E 82
Wakefield St. M1: Man 8H 5 (2F 94)
OL1: Chad 2G 63
WA3: Gol 2K 87
Wakefield Wlk. M34: Dent 8L 97
(off Mancunian Way)
Wakeling Rd. M34: Dent 9J 97
Wakes Dr. M30: Ecc 6E 76
Walcot Pl. WN3: Wig 9C 52
Walcott Cl. M13: Man 4J 95
Wald Av. M14: Man 1K 107
Waldeck St. BL1: Bolt 4D 38
Waldeck Wlk. M9: Man 8K 61
(off Ravenswood Dr.)
Walden Av. OL4: O'ham 1A 64
Walden Cl. M14: Man 9F 94
WN2: Hin 7B 54
Walden Cres. SK7: H Gro 4G 119
Walden Flats OL10: H'ood 2H 43
(off Brunswick St.)
Walderton Av. M40: Man 3M 79
Waldon Av. SK8: Chea 2J 117
Waldon Cl. BL3: Bolt 8D 38
Waldon Rd. SK11: Macc 7E 130
Waldorf Cl. WN3: Wins 9A 52
Wales St. OL1: O'ham 2N 63
Walford Rd. WN4: A Mak 7F 70
Walford St. M16: Whall R 5D 94
Walk, The M46: Ath 8M 55
OL16: Roch 7C 8 (6D 28)
WALKDEN 8K 57
Walkden Av. WN1: Wig 1E 52
Walkden Av. E. WN1: Wig 1F 52
Walkden Ct. M28: Walk 7K 57
(off Mountain St.)
Walkdene Dr. M28: Walk 8J 57
Walkden Ho. WN4: A Mak 5C 70
Walkden Mkt. Pl. M28: Walk 8K 57
(off Ellesmere Shop. Cen.)
Walkden Rd. M28: Walk, Wors 9L 57
Walkdens Av. M46: Ath 9J 55
Walkden Station (Rail) 9L 57
Walkden St. OL12: Roch 4D 28
Walker Av. BL3: Bolt 9G 39
M35: Fail 4F 80
M45: Whitef 5N 59
SK15: Stal 8F 82
Walker Cl. BL4: Kea 5A 58
SK14: Hyde 7C 98
WALKER FOLD 8L 21
Walker Fold SK14: Hyde 7C 98
Walker Fold Rd. BL1: Bolt 1L 37
Walker Grn. M30: Ecc 5B 76
Walker Ho. M5: Sal 3N 93
M30: Ecc 9D 76
(off Barlow St.)
Walker La. SK11: Sut E 9J 131
SK14: Hyde 7B 98
Walker Rd. M9: Man 7K 61
M30: Ecc 6A 76
M44: Irl 8G 91
OL9: Chad 9D 62
WALKERS 5D 64
Walkers OL4: Spri 5D 64
Walkers Bldgs. M1: Man 5L 5
Walkers Cl. OL3: Upp 3L 65
Walkers Ct. BL4: Farn 3L 57
OL4: Spri 5D 64
Walker's Cft. M3: Man 2G 5 (8E 78)
Walkers Dr. WN7: Lei 5J 73
Walkers Fold OL5: Mos 1E 82
(off Barkwell La.)
Walker's La. OL4: Spri 5D 64
Walker's Rd. OL8: O'ham 9G 63
Walker St. BL1: Bolt 6E 38
BL5: W'ton 3G 54
BL9: Bury 4L 41
M24: Mid 4G 61
(not continuous)
M26: Rad 2J 59
M34: Dent 5J 97
OL8: O'ham 4A 8
OL10: H'ood 3H 43
OL16: Roch 8F 8 (6E 28)
SK1: Stoc 2K 9 (7C 108)
SK10: Macc 4G 130
SK13: Had 4C 100
Walkers Vw. OL4: Spri 5D 64
Walkerwood Dr. SK15: Stal 7G 82
Walkmill OL3: Dob 2J 65
Walk Mill Cl. OL12: Roch 1H 29
Walkway, The BL3: Bolt 7A 38
Wallace Av. M14: Man 6J 95
Wallace La. WN1: Wig 2H 53
Wallace St. OL8: O'ham 7K 63
Wallasey Av. M14: Man 8F 94
WALLBANK 7N 13
Wallbank Dr. OL12: Whitw 7N 13
Wall Bank La. OL12: Whitw 7N 13
Wallbank Rd. SK7: Bram 6E 118
Wallbrook Av. SK10: Macc 4C 130
WN5: Bil 1H 69
Wallbrook Cres. M38: Lit H 5H 57
Wallbrook Dr. M9: Man 1H 79
Wallbrook Gro. BL4: Farn 1J 57
Walled Garden, The
M16: Whall R 7D 94
M27: Swin 4D 76
Waller Av. M14: Man 9H 95
Waller St. SK11: Macc 6H 131
Walley St. BL1: Bolt 1F 38
Wallgarth Cl. WN3: Wins 9B 52
WALLGATE 9H 9 (4E 52)
Wallgate WN1: Wig 9J 9 (4F 52)
WN3: Wig 9G 9 (4D 52)
WN5: Wig 4D 52
Wallhead Rd. OL16: Roch 6H 29
WALL HILL 2H 65
Wall Hill Rd. OL3: Dob 2H 65
Wallingford Rd. M41: Urm 6E 92
SK9: Hand 1H 123
Wallis Av. OL16: Roch 8G 29
Wallis St. M40: Man 5A 80
OL9: Chad 7E 62
WALLNESS 1A 4 (8A 78)
Wallness Bri. M6: Sal 6B 78
Wallness La. M6: Sal 6A 78
Wallshaw Pl. OL1: O'ham 2G 8 (4L 63)
Wallshaw St. OL1: O'ham 1G 8 (4L 63)
(not continuous)
Walls St. WN2: Hin 9E 54
Wall St. M6: Sal 8M 77
OL8: O'ham 5D 8 (6K 63)
WN6: Wig 2C 52
WALLSUCHES 9G 21
Wallsuches BL6: Hor 9H 21
Wall Way M18: Man 5C 96
Wallwork Cl. OL11: Roch 4K 27
Wallwork Rd. M29: Ast 4E 74
Wallwork St. M11: Man 1C 96
M26: Rad 8G 40
SK5: Stoc 7D 96
Wallworth Av. M18: Man 4B 96
Wallworth Ter.
SK9: Wilm 6D 122
Wally Sq. M7: Sal 4D 78
Walmer Dr. SK7: Bram 6E 118
Walmer Rd. WN2: Hin 6C 54
WALMERSLEY 6L 25
Walmersley Ct. SK6: Mar 2C 120
Walmersley Golf Course 5A 26
Walmersley Old Rd.
BL9: Bury, Ram 5M 25
Walmersley Rd.
BL9: Bury, Ram 5M 7 (3L 25)
M40: Man 9C 62
Walmer St. M14: Man 6G 95
M18: Man 3C 96
Walmer St. E. M14: Man 6H 95
Walmesley Dr. WN2: I Mak 4L 53
Walmesley Rd. WN7: Lei 5G 73
Walmesley St. WN1: Wig 9L 9 (4G 53)
Walmley Gro. BL3: Bolt 9D 38
Walmsley Av. OL15: Lit 2K 29
Walmsley Gro. M41: Urm 7D 92
Walmsley St. BL8: Bury 9H 25
SK5: Stoc 5D 108
SK15: Stal 1D 98
WA12: N Wil 5G 87
Walney Rd. M22: Wyth 3C 116
WN3: Wins 9A 52
Walnut Av. BL9: Bury 1A 42
OL4: O'ham 3A 64
WN1: Wig 1G 53
Walnut Cl. M27: Clif 7D 58
SK9: Wilm 6K 123
SK14: Hyde 7D 98
Walnut Gro. M33: Sale 4G 104
WN7: Lei 2H 73
Walnut Rd. M30: Ecc 6A 76
M31: Part 5E 102
Walnut St. BL1: Bolt 2G 39
M18: Man 3B 96
Walnut Tree Rd. SK3: Stoc 8M 107
Walnut Wlk. M32: Stre 9J 93
Walpole Av. WN3: Wig 8C 52
Walpole St. OL16: Roch 8F 8 (6E 28)
Walsall St. M6: Sal 5N 77
Walsden St. M11: Man 8A 80
Walsh Av. M9: Man 9H 61
WALSHAW 9F 24
Walshaw Brook Cl. BL8: Bury 9F 24
Walshaw Dr. M27: Swin 3F 76
Walshaw La. BL8: Bury 9F 24
Walshaw Rd. BL8: Bury 9F 24
Walshaw Wlk. BL8: Tot 8F 24
Walsh Cl. WA12: N Wil 4F 86
Walshe St. BL9: Bury 8H 7 (2K 41)
Walsh Fold BL7: Tur 3M 23
Walsh Ho. M46: Ath 7M 55
(off Brooklands Av.)
Walsh St. BL6: Hor 9D 20
OL9: Chad 5F 62
Walsingham Av. M20: Man 4E 106
M24: Mid 6M 61
Walter Greenwood Ct. M6: Sal 7N 77
(off Belvedere Rd.)
Walter Leigh Way WA3: Low 9C 72
WN7: Lei 9C 72
Walter Scott Av. WN1: Wig 8E 34
Walter Scott St. OL1: O'ham 3M 63
Walters Dr. OL8: O'ham 8L 63
Walters Grn. Cres. WA3: Gol 8J 71
Walter St. M9: Man 2J 79
M16: Old T 5B 94
M18: Man 3C 96
M25: Pres 7M 59
M26: Rad 6F 40
M28: Walk 9L 57
OL1: O'ham 3E 8 (5K 63)
WN4: A Mak 5G 70
WN5: Wig 5A 52
WN7: Lei 5D 72
Waltham Av. WA3: G'ury 2L 89
WN6: Wig 9C 34
Waltham Dr. SK8: Chea H 9N 117
Waltham Gdns. M26: Rad 8E 40
WN7: Lei 7L 73
Waltham Rd. M16: Whall R 8D 94
Waltham St. OL4: O'ham 7N 63
WALTHEW GREEN 9G 33
Walthew Ho. La. WN5: Wig 2M 51
Walthew La. WN2: P Bri 8K 53
(not continuous)
WN5: Wig 1N 51
Walton Cl. M24: Mid 2H 61
OL10: H'ood 4J 43
Walton Ct. BL3: Bolt 8G 38
Walton Dr. BL9: Bury 5L 25
SK6: Mar 9A 110
Walton Hall Dr. M19: Man 8B 96
Walton Heath Dr. SK10: Macc 9F 128
Walton Ho. M35: Fail 2D 80
Walton Pk. Leisure Cen. 6G 104
Walton Pk. Miniature Railway 6G 104
Walton Pl. BL4: Kea 4M 57
Walton Rd. M9: Man 6J 61
M33: Sale 7F 104
WA3: Cul 6H 89
WA14: Alt 2B 114
Walton St. M24: Mid 1M 61
M46: Ath 7N 55
OL7: A Lyne 5L 81
OL10: H'ood 4J 43
PR7: Adl 7K 19
SK1: Stoc 9D 108
(off Brentnall St.)
Walton Way M34: Dent 8M 97
Walworth Cl. M26: Rad 4C 58
Walworth St. BL3: Bolt 8D 38
Walwyn Cl. M32: Stre 8L 93
Wanborough Cl. WN7: Lei 3H 73
Wandsworth Av. M11: Man 8B 80
Wanley Wlk. M9: Man 8L 61
Wansbeck Cl. M32: Stre 8L 93
Wansbeck Lodge M32: Stre 8L 93
Wansfell Wlk. M4: Man 8J 79
(off Pollard St.)
Wansford St. M14: Man 6F 94
Wanstead Av. M9: Man 8N 61
Wapping St. BL1: Bolt 2E 38
Warbeck Cl. SK5: Stoc 7E 96
WN2: Hin 8A 54
Warbeck Rd. M40: Man 9C 62
Warbreck Cl. BL2: Bolt 5N 39
Warbreck Gro. M33: Sale 5K 105
Warbrick Dr. M41: Urm 8B 92
WARBURTON 8C 102
Warburton Bri. Rd. WA3: Rix 7B 102
Warburton Bri Rd. WA13: Warb 7B 102
Warburton Cl. SK6: Rom 7L 109
WA13: Lym 3B 112
WA15: Haleb 9K 115
Warburton Dr. WA15: Haleb 9K 115
WARBURTON GREEN 9K 115
Warburton La. M31: Part 4G 102
M31: Part, Warb 8E 102
WA13: Warb 8E 102
Warburton Pl. M46: Ath 8M 55
Warburton Rd. SK9: Hand 2J 123
Warburton St. BL1: Bolt 2G 38
M5: Sal 3A 94
M20: Man 5G 106
M30: Ecc 1E 92
Warburton Vw. WA3: Rix 6B 102
Warburton Way WA15: Tim 9J 105
Warcock Rd. OL4: O'ham 4N 63
Wardale Ct. M33: Sale 4J 105
Ward Av. SK10: Boll 5L 129
Ward Ct. OL3: Dig 8M 47
Wardend Cl. M38: Lit H 5H 57
Wardens Bank BL5: W'ton 6G 55
Warden St. M40: Man 4N 79
Warde St. M15: Man 3D 94
Wardham Cl. BL5: W'ton 6H 55
Ward La. OL3: Dig 8M 47
WARDLE 8G 15
Wardle Brook Av. SK14: Hat 6F 98
Wardle Brook Wlk. SK14: Hat 6G 98
(off Wardle Brook Av.)
Wardle Cl. M26: Rad 7E 40
M32: Stre 7L 93
Wardle Edge OL12: Roch 2F 28
WARDLE FOLD 7G 15
Wardle Fold OL12: W'le 7G 14
Wardle Gdns. OL12: Roch 2G 28
Wardle Rd. M33: Sale 5H 105
OL12: Roch 9G 14
Wardle St. BL2: Bolt 7K 39
M40: Man 7K 79
OL4: O'ham 5M 63
OL15: Lit 8L 15
SK11: Macc 5H 131
WARDLEY 9D 58
Wardley Av. M16: Whall R 8D 94
M28: Walk 8J 57
Wardley Gro. BL1: Bolt 5C 38
Wardley Hall Ct. M27: Ward 9C 58
Wardley Hall La. M28: Wors 2A 76
(not continuous)
Wardley Hall Rd. M27: Ward 1B 76
M28: Wors 1B 76
Wardley Ho. M6: Sal 6J 77
(off Moss Mdw. Rd.)
Wardley Ind. Est. M28: Ward 1C 76
(not continuous)
Wardley Point M28: Ward 1C 76
Wardley Rd. M29: Tyld 2E 74
Wardley Sq. M29: Tyld 2E 74
Wardley St. M27: Swin 2F 76
WN5: Wig 6M 51
Wardlow Av. SK13: Gam 8N 99
(off Youlgreave Cres.)
WN5: Orr 2L 51
Wardlow Fold SK13: Gam 8N 99
(off Youlgreave Cres.)
Wardlow Gdns. SK13: Gam 8N 99
(off Youlgreave Cres.)
Wardlow Gro. SK13: Gam 8N 99
(off Youlgreave Cres.)
Wardlow M. SK13: Gam 8N 99
Wardlow St. BL3: Bolt 8C 38
Wardlow Wlk. SK13: Gam 8N 99
(off Youlgreave Cres.)
Wardour Cl. SK11: Macc 5D 130
Wardour St. M46: Ath 9L 55
(not continuous)
Ward Rd. M43: Droy 9F 80
WARDSEND 5L 125
Wardsend Wlk. M15: Man 3C 94
(off Shawgreen Cl.)
Wards Pl. WN7: Lei 6K 73
Ward St. M9: Man 9H 61
M20: Man 5G 106
M35: Fail 2C 80
M40: Man 2L 79
OL1: O'ham 3H 63
OL9: Chad 4G 62
SK1: Stoc 9E 108
SK6: Bred 5K 109
SK14: Hyde 7B 98
WN2: Hin 4N 53
Ware Cl. WN4: A Mak 6G 71
Wareham Cl. WA11: Hay 2A 86
Wareham Gro. M30: Ecc 7C 76
Wareham St. M8: Man 1G 78
SK9: Wilm 7G 123
Wareing St. M29: Tyld 2A 74
Wareing Way BL3: Bolt 4H 7 (6F 38)
Warfield Wlk. M9: Man 8K 61
(off Sanderstead Dr.)
Warford Av. SK12: Poy 4L 125
Warford Cres. SK9: A Edg 6A 126
Warford Hall Dr. SK9: A Edg 7A 126
(not continuous)
Warford La. SK9: A Edg 6A 126
WA16: Mob 6A 126
Warford St. M4: Man 6G 78
WARGRAVE 6F 86
Wargrave M. WA12: N Wil 8F 86
Wargrave Rd. WA12: N Wil 6E 86
WARHILL 6K 99
Warhurst Fold SK13: Had 4C 100
(off Old Hall Sq.)
Warke, The M28: Wors 4N 75
WARLAND 1A 16
Warland Ga. End OL14: Wals 1A 16
Warley Cl. SK8: Chea 1K 117
Warley Gro. SK16: Duk 2N 97
Warley Rd. M16: Old T 6N 93
Warley St. OL15: Lit 8M 15
Warlingham Cl. BL8: Bury 3H 41
Warlow Crest OL3: G'fld 7K 65
Warlow Dr. OL3: G'fld 7K 65
WN7: Lei 1F 72
Warmco Ind. Pk. OL5: Mos 9G 65
Warmington Dr. M12: Man 3K 95
Warminster Gro. WN3: Wins 9A 52
Warmley Rd. M23: Wyth 8K 105
Warncliffe St. WN5: Wig 6A 52
Warne Av. M43: Droy 8G 81
Warner Wlk. M11: Man 9L 79
(off Hopedale Cl.)
Warnford Cl. M40: Man 6B 80
Warnford St. WN1: Wig 1F 52
War Office Rd. OL11: Roch 7K 27
Warren, The WA12: N Wil 6D 86
Warren Av. SK8: Chea 2J 117
WA16: Knut 6E 132
Warren Bank M9: Man 8J 61
Warren Bruce Rd. M17: T Pk 3K 93
Warren Cl. M24: Mid 2L 61
M34: Dent 7H 97
M46: Ath 7N 55
SK7: Bram 5B 118
SK12: Poy 2F 124
WA16: Knut 6E 132
Warren Dr. M27: Swin 5D 76
WA12: N Wil 5J 87
WA15: Haleb 8K 115
Warrener St. M33: Sale 4K 105
Warren Hey SK9: Wilm 6K 123
Warren La. OL8: O'ham 7M 63
Warren Lea SK6: Comp 6E 110
SK12: Poy 1J 125
Warren Rd. M17: T Pk 3H 93
M28: Walk 8M 57
SK3: Stoc 1C 118
SK8: Chea H 5N 117
Warren St. BL8: Bury 3H 41
M7: Sal 2E 78
M9: Man 9H 61
SK1: Stoc 1L 9 (6D 108)
Warre St. OL6: A Lyne 6C 6 (7M 81)
Warrington La.
WA13: Lym 4E 112
WA14: Lit B 4E 112
WN1: Wig 8L 9 (3G 52)
Warrington Rd. M9: Man 7H 61
WA3: Cul, G'ury, Ris 8K 73
WA3: Gol 2K 87
WA3: Ris 9G 88
(not continuous)
WA12: N Wil 4K 87
WA16: Mere 1B 132
WN1: I Mak 4G 53
WN2: Abr, P Bri 9K 53
WN3: I Mak 4G 53
WN3: Wig 9C 52
WN4: A Mak 8E 70
WN5: Wig 9C 52
WN7: Lei 8K 73
Warrington Rd. Ind. Est.
WN3: Wig 6C 52
Warrington St. OL4: Lees 6B 64
OL6: A Lyne 6D 6 (7M 81)
SK15: Stal 9E 82
Warrington Ter. HD7: Mars 1G 48
Warsall Rd. M22: Shar 9D 106
Warslow Dr. M33: Sale 7L 105
Warsop Av. M22: Shar 2D 116
Warth Cotts. OL3: Dig 8M 47
WARTH FOLD 5K 41
Warth Fold Rd. M26: Rad 6J 41
Warth Ind. Pk. BL9: Bury 5K 41
Warth Rd. BL9: Bury 5K 41
Warton Cl. BL8: Bury 3F 40
SK7: Bram 8E 118
Warton Dr. M23: Wyth 2N 115
Warwick Av. M20: Man 4E 106
M27: Ward 9D 58
M34: Dent 8K 97
M45: Whitef 4A 60
WA12: N Wil 7G 87
WN4: A Mak 8G 70
Warwick Cl. BL8: Bury 9H 25
BL8: G'mount 4G 24
M24: Mid 6M 61
M45: Whitef 4N 59
OL2: Shaw 5K 45
SK4: Stoc 4B 108
SK8: Chea H 3M 117
SK11: Macc 6D 130
SK13: Glos 9H 101
SK16: Duk 3N 97
WA16: Knut 7J 133
Warwick Ct. M16: Old T 6N 93
M24: Mid 3M 61
M34: Dent 9L 97
(off Wordsworth Rd.)
SK4: Stoc 4B 108
Warwick Dr. M33: Sale 4K 105
M41: Urm 5B 92
SK7: H Gro 7H 119
WA15: Hale 6F 114
WN2: Hin 5B 54
Warwick Gdns. BL3: Bolt 1C 56
Warwick Gro. M34: Aud 9G 96
Warwick Ho. M19: Man 7M 95
(off Central Av.)
M33: Sale 4K 105
(off Temple Rd.)
Warwick Mall SK8: Chea 1J 117
Warwick M. SK11: Macc 6D 130
Warwick Rd. M16: Old T 4M 93
M21: Cho H 8A 94
M24: Mid 5N 61
M26: Rad 6F 40
M28: Wors 1K 75
M29: Tyld 9B 56
M35: Fail 5D 80
M44: Cad 3E 102
M46: Ath 6K 55
OL6: A Lyne 5N 81
SK4: Stoc 5A 108
SK6: Rom 6L 109
SK11: Macc 6C 130
WA15: Hale 6E 114
WN2: Asp 7M 35
Warwick Rd. Sth. M16: Old T 6N 93
Warwick St. BL1: Bolt 9F 22
M1: Man 3K 5 (8G 78)
M15: Man 4E 94
M25: Pres 7N 59
M27: Pen 1F 76
OL9: O'ham 7G 62
(not continuous)
OL12: Roch 3F 28
PR7: Adl 7J 19
WN7: Lei 7N 73
Warwick Ter. SK16: Duk 9M 81
(off Hill St.)
Warwick Wlk. SK11: Macc 6D 130
(off Warwick Rd.)
Wasdale Av. BL2: Bolt 3N 39
M41: Urm 6B 92
WA11: St H 9F 68

Wasdale Dr. M24: Mid 1K 61
SK8: Gat 4G 117
Wasdale St. OL11: Roch 3B 44
Wasdale Ter. SK15: Stal 6D 82
Wasdale Wlk. OL1: O'ham 3L 63
Washacre BL5: W'ton 4H 55
Washacre Cl. BL5: W'ton 4H 55
Washbrook OL9: Chad 7F 62
Washbrook Av. M28: Wors 1J 75
Washbrook Ct. OL9: Chad 7F 62
Washbrook Dr. M32: Stre 7H 93
Wash Brow BL8: Bury 9H 25
Washburn Cl. BL5: W'ton 1H 55
WASH END 1D 88
Wash End WA3: Low 1D 88
Wash Fold BL8: Bury 8H 25
Washford Dr. M23: Wyth 8K 105
Washington Cl.
SK8: Chea H 7L 117
Washington St. BL3: Bolt 6D 38
OL9: O'ham 4G 63
Wash La. BL9: Bury 6N 7 (1N 41)
WN7: Lei 4K 73
Wash La. Ter. BL9: Bury 2A 42
Wash Ter. BL8: Bury 8H 25
Washway Rd. M33: Sale 7E 104
Washwood Cl. M38: Lit H 5J 57
(off Wallbrook Cres.)
Wasnidge Wlk. M15: Man 4E 94
(off Crediton Cl.)
Wasp Av. OL11: Roch 1E 44
Wasp Mill Dr. OL12: W'le 8G 15
Wastdale Av. BL9: Bury 9N 41
Wastdale Rd. M23: Wyth 3M 115
WN4: A Mak 2D 70
Waste St. OL1: O'ham 1G 8 (4L 63)
Wast Water St. OL1: O'ham 2L 63
Watburn Rd. SK22: N Mil 6N 121
Watchgate SK7: H Gro 5G 119
Watchgate Cl. M24: Mid 9J 43
Waterbeck Cl. WN1: Wig 2J 53
Waterbridge M28: Wors 5N 75
Watercroft OL11: Roch 4J 27
Waterdale Cl. M28: Wors 4J 75
Waterdale Dr. M45: Whitef 3N 59
Water Dr. WN6: Stan 5E 34
Wateredge Cl. WN7: Lei 7F 72
Waterfield Cl. BL9: Bury 6M 25
Waterfield Way M35: Fail 4E 80
Waterfold Bus. Pk. BL9: Bury 3A 42
Waterfold La. BL9: Bury 3B 42
Waterfold Pk. BL9: Bury 3A 42
Waterfoot Cotts. SK14: Mot 5K 99
(off Rushycroft)
Waterford Av. M20: Man 5C 106
SK6: Rom 6C 110
Waterford Cl. PR6: H Char 4K 19
WN2: P Bri 9K 53
Waterford Pl. SK8: H Grn 7G 117
Waterfront, The M11: Man 8M 79
Waterfront Ho. M30: Ecc 7C 76
Waterfront Quay M50: Sal 2M 93
Watergate M34: Aud 1G 97
OL3: Upp 3L 65
Watergate Dr. BL5: O Hul 4D 56
Watergate La. BL5: O Hul 3D 56
Watergate Milne Ct. OL4: O'ham 3A 64
Watergrove Reservoir Vis. Cen. 5F 14
Water Gro. Rd. SK16: Duk 2C 98
WATERHEAD 3B 64
Waterhead OL4: O'ham 3B 64
WATER HEYES 6L 9 (2G 52)
Waterhouse Av. SK10: Boll 5K 129
Waterhouse Cl. OL12: W'le 9G 15
Waterhouse Ct. WN7: Lei 6H 73
(off Ellesmere St.)
Waterhouse Nook BL6: Bla 8K 19
Waterhouse Rd. M18: Man 5C 96
Waterhouse St.
OL12: Roch 6C 8 (5D 28)
Waterhouse Way SK5: Stoc 1C 108
Waterlake Cl. M22: Wyth 6A 116
Water La. BL0: Ram 4K 11
BL4: Kea 4M 57
M26: Rad 9F 40
M43: Droy 9C 80
(not continuous)
OL16: Miln 8L 29
SK9: Wilm 7F 122
SK13: Had 4N 99
SK14: Holl 4N 99
Water La. St. M26: Rad 8G 40
(Robert St.)
M26: Rad 9F 40
(Water La.)
WATERLOO 5L 81
Waterloo Cotts. SK6: Rom 6B 110
Waterloo Ct. BL9: Bury 4L 41
M20: Man 3F 106
(off Lapwing La.)
SK15: Stal 8C 82
(off Hully St.)
Waterloo Gdns. OL6: A Lyne 5B 82
Waterloo Ind. Est.
SK1: Stoc 3N 9 (7D 108)
Waterloo Ind. Pk. BL1: Bolt 4H 39
Waterloo Pl. SK1: Stoc 3M 9
(off Watson Sq.)
Waterloo Rd. M8: Man 5E 78
OL6: A Lyne 5M 81
OL11: Roch 2D 44
SK1: Stoc 3M 9 (7D 108)
SK6: Rom 6B 110
SK7: Bram 6D 118
SK12: Poy 4L 125
SK15: Stal 8D 82
Waterloo St. BL1: Bolt 3G 39
BL8: Bury 2K 41
M1: Man 6H 5 (1F 94)
M8: Man 2H 79
M9: Man 2H 79
OL1: O'ham 2E 8 (4K 63)
OL4: O'ham 4F 8 (5L 63)
OL6: A Lyne 6A 82
WN6: Wig 2D 52
Waterloo St. W. SK11: Macc 4G 131
Watermans Cl. BL6: Hor 9E 20
M9: Man 2L 79
Waterman Vw. OL16: Roch 5G 28
Watermead M33: Sale 7G 104
Watermead Cl. SK3: Stoc 3C 118
Water Mead Works BL1: Bolt 3H 39
Watermede WN5: Bil 8J 51
Watermeetings La. SK6: Rom 6B 110
Watermill Cl. OL16: Roch 7H 29
Water Mill Clough OL2: O'ham 1G 63
Watermill Ct. OL7: A Lyne 5L 81
Watermill Dr. SK11: Macc 5K 131
Watermillock Gdns. BL1: Bolt 9G 23
Watermint Way WA14: W Tim 7B 104
Waterpark Hall M7: Sal 1D 78
(off Montpellier M.)
Waterpark Rd. M7: Sal 2D 78
Water Rd. SK15: Stal 8C 82
Waters Edge BL4: Farn 1H 57
M24: Mid 5A 62
M28: Walk 9N 57
M40: Man 1D 80
OL3: G'fld 6K 65
OL6: A Lyne 5B 82
SK6: Mar B 8D 110
Waters Edge Bus. Pk. M5: Sal 3A 94
Watersedge Cl. SK8: Chea H 4N 117
Waters Edge Fold OL1: O'ham 8N 45
Watersfield Cl. SK8: Chea H 7L 117
Waters Grn. SK11: Macc 4H 131
WATERSHEDDINGS 2N 63
Watersheddings St. OL4: O'ham 2A 64
Watersheddings Way
OL4: O'ham 2A 64
Waterside BL3: Bolt 8K 39
M17: T Pk 3M 93
M33: Sale 3J 105
OL3: G'fld 7M 65
SK6: Mar 3C 120
SK11: Macc 5J 131
SK13: Had 3C 100
SK14: Hat 8G 98
Waterside Arts Cen. 3H 105
Waterside Av. SK6: Mar 2C 120
Waterside Bus. Pk. SK13: Had 3B 100
Waterside Cl. M21: Cho H 4C 106
M26: Rad 8K 41
OL1: O'ham 8N 45
SK14: Hat 7G 98
Waterside Ct. M41: Urm 7L 91
Waterside Dr. WN3: Wig 5E 52
Waterside Gdns. BL1: Bolt 1H 39
Waterside Ho. M28: Wors 5A 76
WN3: Wig 5F 52
(off Waterside Dr.)
Waterside Ind. Pk. BL3: Bolt 8L 39
Waterside La. OL16: Roch 5F 28
Waterside Plaza M33: Sale 3H 105
(off Tatton Rd.)
Waterside Rd. BL9: Sum 3H 25
SK12: Dis 8H 121
SK22: N Mil 8J 121
Waterside Trad. Est. WN7: Lei 6K 73
Waterside Vw. M43: Droy 1C 96
Waterside Wlk. SK14: Hat 7F 98
Waters La. OL3: Del 5L 47
Waterslea M30: Ecc 8C 76
Waterslea Dr. BL1: Bolt 4A 38
Watersmead Cl. BL1: Bolt 2G 38
Watersmead St. BL1: Bolt 2G 38
Watersmeet M32: Stre 5K 93
Waters Meeting Rd. BL1: Bolt 1G 38
WATER'S NOOK 2J 55
Waters Nook Cl. BL5: W'ton 2J 55
Water's Nook Rd. BL5: W'ton 3J 55
Waterson Av. M40: Man 3M 79
Waters Reach M17: T Pk 3M 93
OL5: Mos 7H 65
SK6: H Lan 8B 120
SK12: Poy 1K 125
WN1: I Mak 3J 53
Water St. BL0: Ram 9H 11
BL1: Bolt 2L 7 (5G 39)
BL7: Eger 3E 22
M3: Man 7B 4 (1C 94)
(not continuous)
M9: Man 2J 79
M12: Man 7N 5
M24: Mid 2L 61
(not continuous)
M26: Rad 9F 40
M27: Swin 4C 76
M34: Aud 2K 97
M34: Dent 5G 96
M46: Ath 8M 55
OL2: O'ham 8L 45
OL6: A Lyne 7C 6 (7M 81)
OL12: Whitw 6A 14
OL16: Miln 7K 29
OL16: Roch 7D 8 (6D 28)
PR6: H Char 1M 19
PR7: Adl 7K 19
SK1: Stoc 6D 108
SK10: Boll 5L 129
SK11: Macc 5G 131
SK13: Glos 7G 101
SK14: Hyde 6A 98
SK15: Stal 8D 82
WA12: N Wil 5F 86
WN1: Wig 7K 9 (3F 52)
Waters Way M28: Wors 5A 76
Waterton Av. OL5: Mos 9E 64
Waterton La. OL5: Mos 9E 64
Waterview Cl. OL16: Miln 1G 45
Waterview Pk. WN7: Lei 6M 73
Waterway Ent. Pk. M17: T Pk 3M 93
Waterworks Dr. WA12: N Wil 5J 87
Waterworks La. WA2: Win 9L 87
Waterworks Rd. OL3: Del 6K 47
OL4: O'ham 2B 64
Watfield Wlk. M9: Man 3J 79
(off Foleshill Av.)
Watford Av. M14: Man 7G 94
Watford Bri. Ind. Est.
SK22: N Mil 6N 121
Watford Bri. Rd. SK22: N Mil 6N 121
Watford Cl. BL1: Bolt 2F 38
(off Chesham Av.)
Watford La. SK22: N Mil 5M 121
Watford Lodge SK22: N Mil 6M 121
Watford Lodge Nature Reserve
5N 121
Watford Mt. SK22: N Mil 5M 121
(off Bridge St.)
Watford Rd. M19: Man 2M 107
SK22: N Mil 5M 121
Watkin Av. SK13: Had 5A 100
Watkin Cl. M13: Man 3H 95
Watkins Av. WA12: N Wil 6C 86
Watkins Dr. M25: Pres 8D 60
Watkin St. M3: Sal 1C 4 (7D 78)
OL16: Roch 9E 28
SK14: Hyde 4D 98
Watling Ga. WA14: Tim 7E 104
Watling St. BL8: Aff 3N 23
BL8: Bury 3F 40
Watlington Cl. OL1: O'ham 9A 46
Watson Av. WA3: Gol 9J 71
WN4: A Mak 7F 70
Watson Gdns. OL12: Roch 3B 28
Watson Rd. BL4: Farn 3G 57
Watsons M. SK9: Wilm 7G 123
Watson Sq. SK1: Stoc 3M 9 (7D 108)
Watson St. M3: Man 7F 4 (1E 94)
M26: Rad 8G 40
M27: Swin 1F 76
M30: Ecc 8C 76
M34: Dent 6M 97
OL4: O'ham 3N 63
Watton Cl. M27: Pen 9F 58
(off Hinchley Way)
Watts St. BL6: Hor 2D 36
M19: Man 9N 95
OL8: O'ham 9H 63
OL9: Chad 4F 62
OL12: Roch 5E 28
Waugh Av. M35: Fail 3D 80
Wavell Dr. BL9: Bury 2N 59
Wavell Rd. M22: Wyth 5C 116
Waveney Dr. SK9: Wilm 4J 123
WA14: Alt 1C 114
Waveney Flats OL10: H'ood 2H 43
(off Fox St.)
Waveney Rd. M22: Wyth 3D 116
OL2: Shaw 4L 45
Waverley OL12: Roch 5B 8
Waverley Av. BL4: Kea 5N 57
M32: Stre 6L 93
Waverley Cl. SK10: Macc 4L 131
Waverley Ct. M9: Man 6F 60
WN3: Wins 8A 52
Waverley Cres. M43: Droy 7E 80
Waverley Dr. SK8: Chea H 9N 117
Waverley Gro. WN7: Lei 4L 73
Waverley Pl. M26: Rad 9G 41
Waverley Rd. BL1: Bolt 1F 38
M9: Man 3L 79
M24: Mid 9M 43
M27: Pen 3J 77
M28: Wors 1J 75
M33: Sale 2J 105
SK3: Stoc 9A 108
SK14: Hyde 9A 98
WA3: Low 9N 71
WN2: Hin 6M 53
Waverley Rd. W. M9: Man 3L 79
Waverley Sq. BL4: Farn 5K 57
Waverley St. OL1: O'ham 3M 63
OL11: Roch 3A 44
Waverton Av. SK4: Stoc 1B 108
Waverton Rd. M14: Man 8F 94
Wavertree Av. M46: Ath 7L 55
Wavertree Ct. BL1: Bolt 4F 38
(off School Hill)
Wavertree Rd. M9: Man 7H 61
Waybridge Ind. Est. M50: Sal 1K 93
Wayfarers Dr. M29: Tyld 2B 74
WA12: N Wil 7H 87
Wayfarers Way M27: Swin 3E 76
Wayfaring BL5: W'ton 1H 55
Wayford Wlk. M9: Man 3H 79
(off Hendham Va.)
Wayland Rd. M18: Man 5B 96
Wayland Rd. Sth. M18: Man 6B 96
Wayne Cl. M43: Droy 6G 81
Wayne St. M11: Man 1C 96
Wayside Dr. SK12: Poy 2G 125
Wayside Gdns. SK7: H Gro 5L 119
Wayside Gro. M28: Walk 7M 57
Wayside Rd. SK10: Macc 4K 131
Weald Cl. M13: Man 3H 95
Wealdstone Gro. BL2: Bolt 2J 39
(off Scawfell Av.)
Weardale Rd. M9: Man 6G 61
Wearhead Cl. WA3: Gol 2K 87
Wearhead Row M5: Sal 9M 77
Wearish La. BL5: W'ton 6E 54
WEASTE 8K 77
Weaste Av. M38: Lit H 7J 57
Weaste Dr. M5: Sal 7K 77
Weaste La. M5: Sal 8K 77
M6: Sal 7J 77
Weaste Rd. M5: Sal 8K 77
Weaste Stop (Metro) 9K 77
Weaste Trad. Est. M5: Sal 8K 77
Weatherall St. Nth. M7: Sal 3E 78
Weatherley Cl. OL8: O'ham 1K 81
Weatherley Dr. SK6: Mar 1A 120
Weaver Av. M28: Walk 9H 57
Weaver Chase M26: Rad 3B 58
Weaver Cl. OL10: H'ood 3G 42
WA14: Bow 6C 114
Weaver Ct. M15: Man 3C 94
(off Johnson St.)
Weaver Dr. BL9: Bury 5M 25
Weaver Gro. WN7: Lei 6E 72
Weaverham Cl. M13: Man 6L 95
Weaverham Wlk. M33: Sale 5L 105
(off Mottram Rd.)
Weaverham Way SK9: Hand 2K 123
Weaver Ho. M7: Sal 5B 78
(off Victoria Lodge)
Weavermill Pk. WN4: A Mak 8F 70
Weaver Rd. WA3: Cul 7J 89
Weavers Ct. BL3: Bolt 7F 38
M24: Mid 2L 61
SK11: Macc 5G 130
SK14: Mot 5K 99
Weavers Grn. BL4: Farn 4L 57
Weavers La. SK7: Bram 9B 118
Weavers Rd. M24: Mid 2L 61
Weaver Wlk. M11: Man 2B 96
(off Ogden La.)
Webb Gro. SK14: Hat 8H 99
Webb La. SK1: Stoc 7E 108
Webb St. BL6: Hor 1E 36
BL8: Bury 6G 7 (1K 41)
Webb Wlk. SK14: Hat 8J 99
Webdale Dr. M40: Man 3M 79
Weber Dr. BL3: Bolt 7E 38
Webster Gro. M25: Pres 9M 59
Webster St. BL3: Bolt 8J 39
OL5: Mos 9F 64
OL8: O'ham 6K 63
WN2: P Bri 8K 53
Wedgewood Cl. OL16: Roch 7G 29
Wedgewood Dr. WN6: Stan 9A 34
Wedgewood St. M40: Man 6L 79
Wedgwood Rd. M27: Clif 9J 59
Wedhurst St. OL4: O'ham 4N 63
Wedneshough Grn. SK14: Holl 4M 99
Weedall Av. M5: Sal 3N 93
Weeder Sq. OL2: Shaw 4B 46
Weedon Av. WA12: N Wil 4E 86
Weedon St. OL16: Roch 5F 28
Weeton Av. BL2: Bolt 5N 39
Weighbridge Ct. M44: Irl 6K 91
Weint, The WA3: Rix 5C 102
Weir Rd. OL16: Miln 6J 29
Weir Side HD7: Mars 1H 49
Weir St. M15: Man 4D 94
M35: Fail 3C 80
Welbeck Av. M41: Urm 6E 92
OL9: Chad 8B 62
OL15: Lit 8L 15
WA12: N Wil 7G 87
Welbeck Cl. M45: Whitef 1M 59
OL16: Miln 7J 29
Welbeck Gro. M7: Sal 3D 78
Welbeck Ho. OL6: A Lyne 8A 6 (8L 81)
Welbeck Rd. BL1: Bolt 4B 38
M28: Wors 4B 76
M30: Ecc 6E 76
OL16: Roch 9F 28
SK5: Stoc 8D 96
SK14: Hyde 7C 98
WN3: Wig 8B 52
WN4: A Mak 5F 70
Welbeck St. M18: Man 3C 96
Welbeck St. Nth.
OL6: A Lyne 8A 6 (8L 81)
Welbeck St. Sth.
OL6: A Lyne 8B 6 (8L 81)
(not continuous)
OL7: A Lyne 9B 6 (8L 81)
Welbeck Ter. OL6: A Lyne 8A 6 (8L 81)
Welburn Av. M22: Wyth 4D 116
Welburn Cl. WN5: Orr 6J 51
Welburn St. OL11: Roch 8D 28
Welbury Rd. M23: Wyth 7M 105
Welby St. M13: Man 5J 95
Welch Hill St. WN7: Lei 6G 72
Welch Rd. SK14: Hyde 5C 98
Welcomb Cl. SK6: Bred 4K 109
Welcomb St. M11: Man 2N 95
Welcomb Wlk. M45: Whitef 4M 59
Welcome Pde. OL8: O'ham 8N 63
Welcroft St. SK1: Stoc 4M 9 (8D 108)
WELD BANK 1F 18
Weldbank St. PR7: Chor 1F 18
Weldon Av. BL3: Bolt 1B 56
Weldon Cres. SK3: Stoc 3C 118
Weldon Dr. M9: Man 6J 61
Weldon Gro. WN1: Wig 1H 53
Weldon Rd. WA14: Alt 1B 6 (1C 114)
Weld Rd. M20: Man 1J 107
Welfold Ho. OL4: O'ham 6M 63
Welford Av. WA3: Low 2M 87
Welford Cl. SK9: Wilm 6K 123
Welford Grn. SK5: Stoc 3D 108
Welford Rd. M8: Man 8E 60
Welford St. M6: Sal 6A 78
Welham Rd. WN3: Wig 8E 52
Welkin Rd. SK6: Bred 5G 108
Welkin Rd. Ind. Est. SK6: Bred 5G 108
Wellacre Av. M41: Urm 7L 91
Welland, The BL5: W'ton 3G 54
Welland Av. OL10: H'ood 1F 42
Welland Cl. M15: Man 3C 94
Welland Ct. M15: Man 3C 94
(off Welland Cl.)
Welland Gdns. WA12: N Wil 7F 86
Welland Rd. OL2: Shaw 4L 45
SK9: Wilm 4J 123
WN4: A Mak 5H 71
Welland St. M11: Man 1B 96
SK5: Stoc 8D 96
Wellbank M25: Pres 8M 59
SK15: Stal 1G 98
Wellbank Av. OL6: A Lyne 4B 82
Wellbank Cl. BL3: Lit L 9B 40
OL8: O'ham 7L 63
Wellbank Ct. BL8: Tot 7F 24
Wellbank St. BL8: Tot 7F 24
Wellbank Vw. OL12: Roch 4L 27
Wellbridge Rd. SK16: Duk 3M 97
Wellbrooke Cl. WN4: A Mak 7F 70
Well Brow OL3: Del 8J 47
(off King St.)
Well Brow Ter. OL12: Roch 4B 28
Wellbrow Wlk. M9: Man 8K 61
(off Haverfield Rd.)
Wellburn Cl. BL3: Bolt 1A 56
Well Cl. WN6: Stan 3B 34
Wellcroft Gdns. WA13: Lym 5B 112
Wellcross Rd. WN8: Uph 5F 50
Welldale M. M33: Sale 3L 105
Wellens Way M24: Mid 4H 61
Weller Av. M21: Cho H 1C 106
SK12: Poy 4H 125
Weller Cl. SK12: Poy 4H 125
Weller Gdns. M21: Cho H 1C 106
Wellesbourne Cl. SK10: Macc 3D 130
Wellesbourne Dr. M23: Wyth 9M 105
Wellesley Av. M18: Man 3B 96
Wellesley Cl. WA12: N Wil 4E 86
WN5: Wig 3B 52
Wellfield SK6: Rom 4N 109
Wellfield Cl. BL9: Bury 6L 41
Wellfield Gdns. WA15: Hale 4J 115
Wellfield La. WA15: Hale, Tim 3J 115
Wellfield Pl. OL11: Roch 8E 28
Wellfield Rd. BL3: Bolt 7D 38
M8: Man 2F 78
M23: Wyth 9N 105
SK2: Stoc 1G 119
WA3: Cul 5G 89
WN2: Hin 7C 54
WN6: Wig 8C 34
Wellfield St. OL11: Roch 8E 28
Wellgate SK13: Glos 7G 100
Wellgate Av. M19: Man 9N 95
WELL GREEN 4J 115
Wellgreen Cl. WA15: Hale 4J 115
Well Grn. Lodge WA15: Hale 4J 115
(off Wellfield La.)
Well Gro. M45: Whitef 1L 59
Wellhead Cl. M15: Man 4E 94
Wellhouse Dr. M40: Man 8A 62
Well-i-Hole Rd. OL3: G'fld 7H 65
Welling Rd. M40: Man 2C 80
Welling St. BL2: Bolt 3J 39
Wellington Av. M16: Whall R 7C 94
Wellington Cen.
OL6: A Lyne 9F 6 (8A 82)
Wellington Cl. M33: Sale 2J 105
WA12: N Wil 6D 86
WA16: Knut 4J 133
WN8: Skel 3C 50
Wellington Clough OL7: A Lyne 4K 81
Wellington Ct. BL8: Bury 3H 41
OL6: A Lyne 7F 6
OL8: O'ham 7H 63
(off Frederick St.)
Wellington Cres. M16: Old T 6B 94
Wellington Dr. M29: Tyld 1F 74
Wellington Gdns. BL8: Bury 3H 41
WA12: N Wil 6D 86
Wellington Gro. M15: Man 3C 94
SK2: Stoc 9D 108
WN3: I Mak 6G 53
Wellington Ho. BL8: Bury 3H 41
(off Haig Rd.)
M20: Man 1H 107
(off Wilmslow Rd.)
M32: Stre 8J 93
(off Sandy La.)
Wellington Lodge OL15: Lit 8M 15
(off Lodge St.)
Wellington M. BL7: Tur 1L 23
Wellington Mill SK3: Stoc 3K 9
Wellington Pde. SK16: Duk 9M 81
(off Queen St.)
Wellington Pl. M3: Man 6D 4
OL16: Roch 6F 8 (5E 28)
WA14: Alt 5C 6 (3D 114)
Wellington Rd. BL7: Tur 1K 23
BL9: Bury 4L 41
M8: Man 2G 78
M14: Man 1H 107
M16: Whall R 7D 94
M20: Man 1H 107
M27: Swin 2F 76
M30: Ecc 8E 76
M46: Ath 6A 56
OL3: G'fld 5L 65
OL6: A Lyne 6A 6 (7L 81)
(not continuous)
OL8: O'ham 7G 63
SK7: H Gro 7M 119
SK10: Boll 6K 129
WA15: Tim 1E 114
Wellington Rd. Nth.
SK4: Stoc 1H 9 (1N 107)
Wellington Rd. Sth.
SK1: Stoc 3K 9 (7C 108)
SK2: Stoc 7C 108
SK3: Stoc 3K 9 (7C 108)
Wellington Sq. BL8: Bury 3H 41
Wellington St. BL3: Bolt 4G 7 (6E 38)
BL4: Farn 3L 57
BL5: W'ton 1G 54
BL8: Bury 3J 41
M3: Sal 2C 4 (8C 78)
M18: Man 4B 96
M26: Rad 8J 41
(not continuous)
M32: Stre 8J 93
M34: Aud 3K 97
M35: Fail 1E 80
OL1: O'ham 3E 8 (5K 63)
OL4: O'ham 4D 8 (5K 63)
OL6: A Lyne 8C 6 (8M 81)
OL9: Chad 3F 62
OL12: Roch 4D 28
(not continuous)
OL15: Lit 9M 15
OL16: Miln 7L 29
SK1: Stoc 3K 9 (7C 108)
SK7: H Gro 4K 119
SK11: Macc 5H 131
SK14: Hyde 6N 97
WA12: N Wil 6D 86
WN1: Wig 8M 9 (3G 53)
Wellington St. E. M7: Sal 3C 78
Wellington St. W. M7: Sal 4C 78
Wellington Ter. HD7: Mars 1J 49
M5: Sal 8K 77
OL15: Lit 9M 15
(off Lodge St.)
SK16: Duk 9M 81
(off Queen St.)
Wellington Vs. BL8: Bury 3J 41
Wellington Wlk. BL3: Bolt 4H 7 (6F 38)

Well i' th' La. OL11: Roch 8E 28
Well La. HD7: Mars 2J 49
M45: Whitef 1M 59
SK15: P'bury 4G 128
SK10: Rain 2L 131
Well Mead SK6: Bred 5J 109
Wellmead Cl. M8: Man 5E 78
Well Mdw. SK14: Hyde 5A 98
Well Mdw. Ct. SK14: Hyde 5A 98
(off Well Mdw.)
Wellmeadow La. OL3: Upp 3M 65
Wellpark Wlk. M40: Man 5A 80
(off Langcroft Dr.)
Well Rd. WN7: Lei 1F 72
Well Row SK14: B'tom 9K 99
Wells Av. M25: Pres 9B 60
OL9: Chad 2E 62
WN5: Bil 4H 69
Wells Cl. M24: Mid 4H 61
M29: Ast 2D 74
M43: Droy 1D 96
SK8: H Grn 8H 117
Wells Ct. SK16: Duk 3N 97
Wells Dr. SK4: Stoc 6K 107
SK16: Duk 3N 97
WN2: Wig 1J 53
Wellside Wlk. M8: Man 4F 78
(off Dinnington Dr.)
Wells Pl. WN1: Wig 3H 53
Wells Rd. OL1: O'ham 7B 46
Wells St. BL9: Bury 3L 41
Wellstock La. M38: Lit H 5G 57
Well St. BL1: Bolt 2M 7 (5H 39)
BL2: Ain 3C 40
M4: Man 3H 5
M29: Tyld 2B 74
OL10: H'ood 3K 43
OL11: Roch 8E 28
SK22: N Mil 7L 121
WN1: Wig 3H 53
(off Caunce Rd.)
Well St. Nth. BL0: Ram 4J 11
Well St. W. BL0: Ram 9H 11
Wellwood Dr. M40: Man 3M 79
Wellyhole St. OL4: O'ham 5A 64
Welman Way WA15: Alt 4F 6 (3F 114)
Welney Rd. M16: Old T 6A 94
Welshpool Cl. M23: Wyth 6A 106
Welshpool Way M34: Dent 8L 97
Welsh Row SK10: N Ald 8D 126
Welton Av. M20: Man 6H 107
Welton Cl. SK9: Wilm 1E 126
WN7: Lei 5L 73
Welton Dr. SK9: Wilm 1D 126
Welton Gro. SK9: Wilm 1D 126
Welwyn Cl. M41: Urm 4B 92
Welwyn Dr. M6: Sal 5G 77
Welwyn Wlk. M40: Man 8J 79
(off Marcer Rd.)
Wembley Cl. SK3: Stoc 2B 118
Wembley Gro. M14: Man 9H 95
Wembley Rd. M18: Man 6A 96
Wembury St. M9: Man 2K 79
Wembury St. Nth. M9: Man 2K 79
Wembury Wlk. SK14: Hat 6H 99
(off Cambourne Rd.)
Wemsley Gro. BL2: Bolt 3J 39
Wem St. OL9: Chad 7E 62
Wemyss Av. SK5: Stoc 8D 96
Wendlebury Cl. WN7: Lei 9G 73
Wendlebury Grn. OL2: O'ham 7L 45
Wendon Rd. M23: Wyth 2A 116
Wendover Cl. WA11: Hay 2A 86
Wendover Dr. BL3: Bolt 7N 37
Wendover Ho. M5: Sal 9N 77
Wendover Rd. M23: Wyth 7K 105
M41: Urm 7C 92
Wenfield Dr. M9: Man 8N 61
Wenlock Av. OL6: A Lyne 5M 81
Wenlock Cl. BL6: Hor 7E 20
SK2: Stoc 1L 119
SK10: Macc 2F 130
Wenlock Ct. M12: Man 3L 95
(off Wenlock Way)
Wenlock Gro. WN2: Hin 7N 53
Wenlock Rd. M33: Sale 6G 104
WN2: Hin 7N 53
WN7: Lei 8G 73
Wenlock St. M27: Swin 2D 76
WN2: Hin 7N 53
Wenlock Way M12: Man 3L 95
Wenning Cl. M45: Whitef 2B 60
Wennington Rd. WN3: Wig 7N 51
Wenning Wlk. WN2: P Bri 9K 53
Wensley Ct. M7: Sal 1N 77
(off Wensley Rd.)
Wensleydale Av. SK8: Chea 1H 117
Wensleydale Cl. BL9: Bury 9N 41
M23: Wyth 4M 115
OL2: O'ham 7G 44
Wensleydale Rd. WN7: Lei 5L 73
Wensley Dr. M20: Man 3G 107
SK7: H Gro 8H 119
Wensley Rd. M7: Sal 2N 77
SK5: Stoc 4D 108
SK8: Chea 1H 117
WA3: Low 2A 88
Wensley Way OL16: Roch 7G 28
Wentbridge Rd. BL1: Bolt 1G 7 (4E 38)
Wentworth Av. BL4: Farn 4K 57
BL8: Bury 9H 25
M6: Sal 7J 77
M18: Man 3C 96
M41: Urm 8B 92
M44: Irl 6H 91
M45: Whitef 4K 59
OL10: H'ood 4J 43
SK11: Macc 6D 130
WA15: Tim 1G 114
Wentworth Cl. M24: Mid 3K 61
M26: Rad 8D 40
M34: Aud 8C 110
Wentworth Ct. M35: Fail 4D 80
M45: Whitef 3L 59
Wentworth Dr. M33: Sale 3F 104
SK7: Bram 8E 118
Wentworth Rd. M27: Swin 4D 76
M30: Ecc 6G 76
SK5: Stoc 8D 96
WN4: A Mak 5C 70
Wentworth Wlk. SK14: Hyde 4C 98
Werburgh Cl. WA13: Warb 8D 102
WERNETH 7G 63
Werneth Av. M14: Man 7G 95
SK14: Hyde 9C 98
Werneth Cl. M34: Dent 7K 97
SK7: H Gro 3J 119
Werneth Ct. SK14: Hyde 8B 98
(off Stockport Rd.)
Werneth Cres. OL8: O'ham 7G 63
Werneth Golf Course 1J 81
Werneth Hall Rd.
OL8: O'ham 6H 63
Werneth Hollow SK6: Wood 2M 109
Werneth Low Country Pk. 9E 98
Werneth Low Golf Course 2E 110
Werneth Low Rd. SK6: Rom 4A 110
SK14: Hyde 4A 110
Werneth Ri. SK14: Hyde 1C 110
Werneth Rd. SK6: Wood 3M 109
SK13: Glos 9C 100
SK14: Hyde 7C 98
Werneth St. M34: Aud 4K 97
SK1: Stoc 6F 108
Werneth Vw. SK7: H Gro 7M 119
Werneth Wlk. M34: Dent 7K 97
(off Werneth Cl.)
Wescoe Cl. WN5: Orr 6J 51
Wesham Rd. M11: Man 8M 79
Wesley Av. WA11: Hay 2C 86
Wesley Cl. BL5: W'ton 1G 55
OL12: Roch 2F 28
Wesley Ct. BL5: W'ton 1G 55
(off Wesley St.)
BL8: Tot 7E 24
M28: Walk 7K 57
(off Mountain St.)
OL15: Lit 2K 29
SK4: Stoc 6L 107
Wesley Dr. M28: Wors 2N 75
OL6: A Lyne 4A 82
Wesley Ho. BL8: Tot 6E 24
Wesley M. BL2: Bolt 3N 7 (5H 39)
Wesley Mt. SK4: Stoc 6C 108
(off Dodge Hill)
Wesleys, The BL4: Farn 3G 57
Wesley Sq. M41: Urm 7A 92
Wesley St. BL3: Bolt 7F 38
BL4: Farn 4M 57
BL5: W'ton 1G 55
BL7: Bro X 5H 23
BL8: Tot 6E 24
M11: Man 1M 95
M27: Swin 2F 76
M30: Ecc 8C 76
M32: Stre 6L 93
M35: Fail 1E 80
(not continuous)
M46: Ath 8N 55
OL2: O'ham 9J 45
OL10: H'ood 2H 43
OL12: Roch 2F 28
OL16: Miln 7J 29
SK1: Stoc 3M 9 (7D 108)
SK7: H Gro 4J 119
SK13: Glos 7G 101
SK13: Had 4C 100
WN5: Wig 6A 52
Wessen Ct. HD7: Mars 1H 49
Wessenden Bank E. SK2: Stoc . . .2H 119
Wessenden Bank W. SK2: Stoc . . .2H 119
Wessenden Head Rd.
HD9: Holme, Melt 7N 49
Wessenden Rd. HD7: Mars 3H 49
Wessex Cl. WN1: Stan 3E 34
Wessex Dr. WN3: I Mak 7J 53
Wessex Pk. Cl. OL2: Shaw 4M 45
Wessex Rd. WN5: Wig 2A 52
Wessington Bank SK13: Gam 7A 100
(off Hathersage Cres.)
Wessington Fold SK13: Gam 7A 100
(off Wessington M.)
Wessington Grn. SK13: Gam 7A 100
(off Wessington M.)
Wessington M. SK13: Gam 7A 100
Westage Gdns. M23: Wyth 9N 105
W. Ashton St. M50: Sal 9M 77
West Av. BL4: Farn 3J 57
M18: Man 4C 96
M19: Man 1L 107
M28: Walk 8K 57
M40: Man 2B 80
M45: Whitef 1L 59
OL12: Roch 2G 29
SK8: H Grn 6H 117
SK15: Stal 8D 82
WA3: Gol 9L 71
WA14: Alt 2A 114
WN7: Lei 7L 73
West Bank M11: Man 2E 96
SK9: A Edg 5F 126
W. Bank Rd. SK10: Macc 3F 130
Westbank Rd. BL6: Los 6M 37
M20: Man 3J 107
W. Bank St. M5: Sal 1B 94
M46: Ath 1N 73
W. Bond St. SK11: Macc 5G 130
Westbourne Av. BL3: Bolt 9H 39
M27: Clif 6D 58
M45: Whitef 2K 59
WN7: Lei 3G 73
(not continuous)
Westbourne Cl. WN3: I Mak 7H 53
Westbourne Dr. OL7: A Lyne 6L 81
SK9: Wilm 6J 123
Westbourne Gro. M9: Man 2J 79
M20: Man 2F 106
M33: Sale 4G 104
SK5: Stoc 9D 96
Westbourne Pk. M41: Urm 6D 92
Westbourne Range
M18: Man 5D 96
Westbourne Rd. M14: Man 9J 95
M30: Ecc 7B 76
M34: Dent 7J 97
M41: Urm 7D 92
Westbourne St.
OL9: O'ham 2A 8 (4H 63)
Westbridge M. WN1: Wig . . .9K 9 (4F 52)
W. Bridgewater St. WN7: Lei 6H 73
Westbrook Cl. OL11: Roch 4B 44
Westbrook Ct. BL2: Bolt 6H 39
M18: Man 6C 96
Westbrook Dr. SK10: Macc 3G 130
Westbrook Rd. M17: T Pk 2J 93
M27: Swin 3E 76
Westbrook Sq. M12: Man 3M 95
Westbrook St. BL2: Bolt 5M 7 (6H 39)
Westbrook Trad. Est.
M17: T Pk 2K 93
Westbrook Wlk. M20: Man 9F 94
Westbury Av. M33: Sale 7C 104
WN3: Wins 9A 52
Westbury Cl. BL5: W'ton 2J 55
BL8: Bury 3G 41
Westbury Ct. SK11: Macc 4E 130
Westbury Dr. SK6: Mar 1B 120
SK11: Macc 5E 130
Westbury Rd. M8: Man 1G 78
Westbury St. OL6: A Lyne . . .6E 6 (7N 81)
SK14: Hyde 4N 97
Westbury St. Ind. Est.
SK14: Hyde 4N 97
Westbury Way OL2: O'ham 1H 63
Westby Cl. SK7: Bram 8E 118
Westby Gro. BL2: Bolt 4K 39
W. Central Dr. M27: Swin 3H 77
Westchapel M. BL5: W'ton 9G 37
(off Dixon St.)
W. Charles St. M5: Sal 9A 78
W. Church St. OL10: H'ood 2H 43
Westcliffe Ho. OL12: Roch 1H 29
Westcliffe Rd. BL1: Bolt 7G 22
West Cl. BL9: Bury 8A 42
M46: Ath 1N 73
SK10: Boll 6K 129
Westcombe Building, The
OL11: Roch 2N 43
(off Sydney Barnes Cl.)
Westcombe Dr. BL8: Bury 9J 25
West Cotts. OL3: G'fld 6J 65
Westcott Av. M20: Man 2F 106
Westcott Cl. BL2: Bolt 8M 23
Westcott Ct. M15: Man 4C 94
Westcott Dr. WN3: Wig 7N 51
Westcott Gro. OL2: O'ham 7L 45
Westcourt Rd. BL3: Bolt 1E 56
M33: Sale 2F 104
Westcraig Av. M40: Man 8A 62
W. Craven St. M5: Sal 2A 94
West Cres. M24: Mid 4L 61
Westcroft WN2: P Bri 9L 53
West Cft. Ind. Est. M24: Mid 4J 61
Westcroft Rd. M19: Man 4J 107
M20: Man 4J 107
W. Crown Av. M5: Sal 1A 94
Westdale Gdns. M19: Man 3M 107
Westdean Cres. M19: Man 3L 107
W. Dean St. M5: Sal 5A 4 (9B 78)
Westdene WN8: Par 2A 32
(off Burnside)
WEST DIDSBURY 3E 106
Westdown Gdns. OL2: Shaw 4K 45
W. Downs Rd. SK8: Chea H 4L 117
West Dr. BL9: Bury 8L 25
M6: Sal 4L 77
M27: Swin 3H 77
M43: Droy 9D 80
SK8: Gat 3F 116
SK13: Tin 3A 100
W. Egerton St. M5: Sal 9A 78
West End SK14: B'tom 9J 99
West End Av. SK8: Gat 1F 116
Westend Av. PR7: Cop 4A 18
West End St. OL9: O'ham . . .2A 8 (4H 63)
West End Trad. Est.
M27: Swin 1F 76
Westerdale OL4: O'ham 5N 63
Westerdale Cl. M29: Tyld 2C 74
Westerdale Dr. BL3: Bolt 7B 38
OL2: O'ham 7G 45
Westerham Av. M5: Sal 9N 77
Westerham Cl. BL8: Bury 6J 25
SK10: Macc 2F 130
Westerhill OL7: A Lyne 2M 81
Westerhill Rd. OL8: O'ham 1L 81
Westerling Way
M16: Whall R 6D 94
Western Av. M27: Clif 9K 59
SK11: Macc 7G 130
Western Circ. M19: Man 2L 107
Western Dr. SK11: Macc 7G 130
Western Pk. M50: Sal 1L 93
Western Rd. M41: Urm 8M 91
Western St. M6: Sal 7L 77
M18: Man 3C 96
Westerton Ct. BL3: Bolt 7E 38
Westfield M6: Sal 6L 77
WA14: Alt 5A 6 (4C 114)
Westfield Av. M24: Mid 4M 61
WN4: A Mak 6D 70
Westfield Cl. OL11: Roch 4L 27
Westfield Dr. OL4: Gras 6H 65
SK6: Wood 3N 109
WA16: Knut 7E 132
Westfield Gro. M34: Aud 4J 97
WN1: Wig 9E 34
Westfield Rd. BL3: Bolt 1C 56
M21: Cho H 8A 94
M43: Droy 8C 80
M46: Ath 1N 73
SK8: Chea H 7L 117
Westfields WA15: Hale 7F 114
Westfields Av. SK10: Macc 3F 130
Westfield St. BL4: Farn 3J 57
M7: Sal 1C 78
OL9: Chad 6D 62
Westford Villa SK8: Chea 2H 117
Westgate M33: Sale 4G 104
M41: Urm 8B 92
OL12: Whitw 7N 13
SK9: Wilm 9F 122
WA15: Hale 5E 114
Westgate Av. BL0: Ram 3G 24
BL1: Bolt 5D 38
BL9: Bury 3L 41
M9: Man 9H 61
Westgate Ct. OL12: Whitw 7N 13
Westgate Dr. M27: Swin 4F 76
M29: Ast 4D 74
WN5: Orr 6H 51
Westgate Ho. OL8: O'ham 9H 63
(off Hollins Rd.)
West Ga. Rd. M90: Man A 9M 115
Westgate Rd. M6: Sal 5H 77
Westgate St. OL7: A Lyne 9L 81
WEST GORTON 3L 95
West Grn. M24: Mid 4G 61
West Gro. BL5: W'ton 5G 55
M13: Man 4J 95
M33: Sale 5H 105
OL5: Mos 2F 82
Westgrove Av. BL1: Bolt 7F 22
Westhead Av. WA3: Low 9A 72
West Heaton Bowling, Tennis &
Squash Club 4M 107
Westhide Wlk. M9: Man 1L 79
W. High St. M5: Sal 8N 77
West Hill OL11: Roch 9A 8 (7C 28)
West Hill Cl. SK15: Stal 8C 82
Westholm Av. SK4: Stoc 1N 107
Westholme Ct. SK9: A Edg 3F 126
(off Horseshoe La.)
Westholme Rd. M20: Man 3G 107
M25: Pres 4B 60
W. Hope St. M5: Sal 9A 78
Westhorne Fold M8: Man 9D 60
(off Counthill Dr.)
WESTHOUGHTON 3G 55
Westhoughton (Park & Ride) 1H 55
Westhoughton Golf Course 2F 54
Westhoughton Leisure Cen. 3H 55
Westhoughton Rd.
PR7: Adl, H Char 4J 19
Westhoughton Station (Rail) 1G 55
West Ho. Ct. SK10: Macc 3C 130
WEST HULME 2H 63
Westhulme Av. OL1: O'ham 2H 63
Westhulme St. OL1: O'ham 2H 63
Westhulme Way OL1: O'ham 2G 63
Westinghouse Cl. WN6: Wig 3D 52
Westinghouse Ind. Est.
M17: T Pk 4J 93
Westinghouse Rd. M17: T Pk 3G 93
W. King St. M3: Sal 2D 4 (8D 78)
Westlake Gro. WN2: Hin 7D 54
Westland Av. BL1: Bolt 3B 38
BL4: Farn 5K 57
SK1: Stoc 7F 108
Westland Dr. M9: Man 7J 61
Westlands M45: Whitef 5M 59
Westlands, The M27: Pen 4H 77
West La. WA13: Lym 8D 112
WA16: H Leg 9D 112
West Lea M34: Dent 6L 97
Westlea Dr. M18: Man 6B 96
WESTLEIGH 3F 72
Westleigh SK4: Stoc 4M 107
Westleigh Dr. M25: Pres 8C 60
Westleigh La. WN7: Lei 9F 54
Westleigh St. M9: Man 1K 79
Westleigh Vw. WN7: Lei 2G 72
Westlock WN3: Wig 5F 52
W. Malling Cl. OL10: H'ood 5L 43
Westmarsh Cl. BL1: Bolt 3F 38
(off Kentford Rd.)
W. Marwood St. M7: Sal 4D 78
Westmead WN6: Stan 4B 34
Westmead Dr. WA15: Tim 9H 105
West Meade BL3: Bolt 1E 56
M21: Cho H 1N 105
M25: Pres 9C 60
M27: Swin 4E 76
Westmeade Rd. M28: Walk 6K 57
West Mdw. SK5: Stoc 8E 96
Westmere Dr. M9: Man 4H 79
Westminster Av. BL4: Farn 3K 57
M16: Whall R 7B 94
M26: Rad 8D 40
M45: Whitef 3M 59
OL2: O'ham 6G 44
OL6: A Lyne 3A 82
SK5: Stoc 1C 108
Westminster Cl. M33: Sale 5D 104
OL2: Shaw 4M 45
SK6: Mar 9A 110
Westminster Dr. SK8: Chea H 9N 117
SK9: Wilm 1F 126
WA11: Hay 2C 86
WN7: Lei 3N 73
Westminster Ho. M3: Sal 2D 4
Westminster Rd. BL1: Bolt 8F 22
M28: Walk 9L 57
M30: Ecc 7E 76
M35: Fail 2F 80
M41: Urm 5D 92
SK10: Macc 2F 130
WA15: Hale 4G 114
Westminster St. BL4: Farn 3K 57
BL9: Bury 9K 7 (3L 41)
M15: Man 9A 4 (2B 94)
M19: Man 8N 95
M27: Swin 1D 76
OL1: O'ham 3M 63
OL11: Roch 8B 28
SK10: Macc 4G 131
WN5: Wig 5C 52
Westminster Wlk. BL4: Farn 3K 57
(off Westminster St.)
Westminster Way SK16: Duk 3M 97
Westmoor Gables SK4: Stoc 4M 107
Westmoreland Cl. WA14: Bow 7B 114
Westmoreland St.
WN1: Wig 6N 9 (2H 53)
Westmorland Av. OL7: A Lyne 6M 81
SK16: Duk 1B 98
Westmorland Cl. BL9: Bury 6L 41
SK5: Stoc 2G 108
SK10: Macc 2D 130
Westmorland Dr.
OL12: W'le 8H 15
SK5: Stoc 2F 108
Westmorland Rd. M20: Man 6F 106
M29: Tyld 9B 56
M30: Ecc 5G 76
M31: Part 6F 102
M33: Sale 6J 105
M41: Urm 8C 92
Westmorland Wlk. OL2: O'ham 8J 45
(off Royton Hall Wlk.)
W. Mosley St.
M2: Man 5H 5 (9F 78)
West Mt. OL3: G'fld 6J 65
(off Shaw Hall Bank Rd.)
WN1: Wig 2G 53
WN5: Orr 5K 51
Westmount Cl. M40: Man 4H 79
W. Oak Pl. SK8: Chea H 6M 117
WESTON 5D 130
Weston Av. M27: Clif 7E 58
M40: Man 1C 80
M41: Urm 8B 92
OL16: Roch 9F 28
Westonby Ct. WN4: A Mak 7G 70
Weston Ct. M14: Man 7J 95
Weston Dr. M34: Dent 6L 97
SK8: Chea H 3B 118
W. One Retail Pk. M50: Ecc 8G 77
W. One Way M50: Ecc 9G 76
Weston Gro. M22: Nor 8D 106
SK4: Stoc 2A 108
Weston Hall M1: Man 7J 5 (1F 94)
Weston Pk. WN6: Stan 9A 34
Weston Rd. M44: Irl 7H 91
SK9: Wilm 8J 123
Weston Sq. SK11: Macc 5D 130
Weston St. BL3: Bolt 8G 39
M46: Ath 7N 55
OL8: O'ham 7N 63
OL16: Miln 7J 29
(not continuous)
SK5: Stoc 4C 108
West Over SK6: Rom 8L 109
Westover Rd. M41: Urm 6C 92
Westover St. M27: Swin 1E 76
West Pde. M33: Sale 5C 104
West Pk. BL1: Bolt 5D 38
SK14: Hyde 1B 110
West Pk. Av. M34: Dent 7M 97
SK12: Poy 2E 124
West Pk. Dr. SK10: Macc 4F 130
West Pk. Rd. SK1: Stoc 6F 108
SK7: Bram 5B 118
West Pk. St. M5: Sal 2A 94
WEST PIMBO 7B 50
West Pl. M19: Man 1L 107
West Point M16: Old T 4B 94
(off Chester Rd.)
Westpoint Ent. Pk. M17: T Pk 2G 92
W. Point Lodge M19: Man 9L 95
(off Slade La.)
Westray Cres. M5: Sal 9L 77
Westray Rd. M13: Man 7K 95
Westrees WN7: Lei 3J 73
Westridge Chase OL2: O'ham 7H 45
West Rd. M25: Pres 6M 59
M41: Urm 2E 92
WA14: Bow 5C 114
West Row M25: Pres 1M 77
W. Starkey St. OL10: H'ood 1H 43
West St. BL0: Ram 9H 11
BL1: Bolt 5D 38
BL4: Farn 2M 57
M9: Man 8F 60
M11: Man 8N 79
M24: Mid 1M 61
M26: Rad 9G 41
M35: Fail 3C 80
M46: Ath 1N 73
OL1: O'ham 2C 8 (4J 63)
OL4: Lees 6B 64
OL6: A Lyne 6C 6
OL9: O'ham 5H 63
OL10: H'ood 2J 43
OL15: Lit 9N 15
OL16: Roch 5E 8 (5E 28)
(Buckley St.)
OL16: Roch 6H 29
(Cross St.)
SK3: Stoc 3G 9 (7B 108)
SK9: A Edg 4F 126
SK11: Macc 4F 130
SK13: Tin 2B 100
SK14: Hyde 4A 98
SK15: Stal 8C 82
SK16: Duk 9M 81
WN2: Hin 8D 54
WN2: I Mak 3K 53
WN6: Wig 2E 52
WEST TIMPERLEY 8C 104
W. Towers M. SK6: Mar 3D 120
W. Towers St. M6: Sal 9M 77
West Vale M26: Rad 7G 40
West Va. Rd.
WA15: Tim 1G 6 (1F 114)
West Vw. BL0: Ram 4J 11
BL6: Hor 8G 20
M34: Aud 2J 97
OL3: Del 6F 46
OL15: Lit 9N 15
SK22: N Mil 8L 121
WN8: Par 2A 32
West Vw. Gro. M45: Whitef 2K 59
West Vw. Rd. M22: Nor 8D 106
Westville Gdns. M19: Man 3K 107
Westwall Wlk. BL7: Eger 3E 22
Westward Ho OL16: Miln 7K 29
Westward Rd. SK9: Wilm 8E 122
West Way BL1: Bolt 1J 39
M38: Lit H 6H 57

Westway M9: Man 5G 60
M43: Droy 2E 96
OL2: Shaw 6M 45
OL4: Lees 6B 64
Westwell Gdns. BL1: Bolt 3G 38
(off Adisham Dr.)
Westwell Gro. WN7: Lei 2G 72
Westwell St. WN7: Lei 2G 72
Westwick Ter. BL1: Bolt 2F 38
(off Boardman St.)
WESTWOOD 4G 63
Westwood WA14: Alt 4A 6 (3B 114)
Westwood Av. M7: Sal 2D 78
M28: Walk 8H 57
M40: Man 1C 80
M41: Urm 8F 92
SK14: Hyde 6E 98
WA15: Tim 9F 104
Westwood Bus. Cen.
OL9: O'ham 5H 63
Westwood Cl. BL4: Farn 3L 57
Westwood Cres. M30: Ecc 7A 76
Westwood Dr. M27: Pen 4J 77
M33: Sale 6H 105
OL9: O'ham 4H 63
Westwood Ho. BL4: Farn 3L 57
(off Hesketh Wlk.)
Westwood Ind. Est. OL9: O'ham 4G 63
Westwood La. WN3: I Mak 6G 52
WESTWOOD PARK 6C 76
Westwood Pk. Dr.
WN3: Wig 5F 52
Westwood Rd. BL1: Bolt 4D 38
M32: Stre 7H 93
SK2: Stoc 3F 118
SK8: H Grn 7G 117
WN3: Wig 5F 52
Westwood St. M14: Man 5E 94
Westwood Ter. WN3: I Mak 6H 53
Westwood Trad. Est. SK6: Mar 2B 120
Westwood Way WN3: Wig 5F 52
W. Works Rd. M17: T Pk 5J 93
Westworth Cl. BL1: Bolt 1G 7 (4E 38)
Wet Earth Colliery 6F 58
Wet Earth Grn. M27: Pen 2K 77
Wet Ga. La. WA13: Lym 3D 112
Wetheral Cl. WN2: Hin 8E 54
Wetheral Dr. BL3: Bolt 8F 38
Wetherall St. M19: Man 8N 95
Wetheral Rd. SK10: Macc 2F 130
Wetherby Cl. WA12: N Wil 4F 86
Wetherby Dr. OL2: O'ham 7G 45
SK7: H Gro 5L 119
Wetherby St. M11: Man 2C 96
Wexford Cl. WA11: Hay 2A 86
Wexford Wlk. M22: Wyth 5D 116
Wexham Gdns. WN2: P Bri 8K 53
Weybourne Av. M9: Man 9M 61
Weybourne Dr. SK6: Bred 4K 109
WN3: Wig 8B 52
Weybourne Gro. BL2: Bolt 9J 23
Weybridge Cl. BL1: Bolt 4F 38
(off Prince St.)
Weybridge Dr. SK10: Macc 1F 130
Weybridge Rd. M4: Man 3N 5 (8H 79)
Weybrook Rd. M19: Man 1N 107
Weycroft Cl. BL2: Bolt 6A 40
Weydale Gro. WN2: Hin 7A 54
Weygates Dr. WA15: Haleb 8J 115
Weyhill Rd. M23: Wyth 2N 115
Weylands Gro. M6: Sal 5H 77
Weymouth Dr. WN2: Hin 7C 54
Weymouth M. OL6: A Lyne 4B 82
(off Kings Rd.)
Weymouth Rd. M30: Ecc 7B 76
OL6: A Lyne 4B 82
Weymouth St. BL1: Bolt 2F 38
Weythorne Dr. BL1: Bolt 9G 22
BL9: Bury 8E 26
Whalley Av. BL1: Bolt 1A 38
M16: Whall R 6C 94
M19: Man 7N 95
M21: Cho H 1B 106
M33: Sale 3J 105
M41: Urm 6E 92
OL15: Lit 8L 15
WA3: G'ury 2L 89
Whalley Cl. M45: Whitef 2M 59
OL16: Miln 7J 29
WA15: Tim 8F 104
WN3: Wig 8D 52
Whalley Cotts. BL6: Bla 4N 35
Whalley Dr. BL8: Bury 2F 40
Whalley Gdns. OL12: Roch 4N 27
Whalley Gro. M16: Whall R 7C 94
OL6: A Lyne 3N 81
WN7: Lei 1F 72
Whalley Hayes SK10: Macc 4G 131
WHALLEY RANGE 6C 94
Whalley Rd. BL0: Eden, Ram 5L 11
M16: Whall R 6B 94
M24: Mid 9L 43
M45: Whitef 2M 59
OL10: H'ood 2F 42
OL12: Roch 4N 27
SK2: Stoc 9G 108
WA15: Hale 5G 114
Wham Bar Dr. OL10: H'ood 2G 42
Wham Bottom La.
OL12: Roch 1B 28
Wham La. OL3: Dens 3G 46
Whams OL4: Spri 4C 64
Wham St. OL10: H'ood 2G 42
Wharf, The OL3: Dob 1K 65
Wharf Circ. M17: T Pk 2J 93
Wharf Cl. M1: Man 5L 5 (9G 79)
WA14: Alt 9D 104
(off Bridgewater Rd.)
Wharf Cotts. OL3: G'fld 5K 65
OL5: Mos 1G 82
Wharfdale WN7: Lei 6J 73
Wharfedale BL5: W'ton 1H 55
Wharfedale Av. M40: Man 1M 79
Wharfedale Rd. SK5: Stoc 9C 96
Wharf Pl. SK16: Duk 9M 81
(off Wharf St.)
Wharf Rd. M33: Sale 3J 105
WA12: N Wil 7B 86
WA14: Alt 9D 104
Wharfside BL8: Bury 9K 25
WN3: Wig 4E 52
Wharfside Av. M30: Ecc 1D 92
Wharfside Bus. Cen. M17: T Pk 3M 93
Wharfside Way M17: T Pk 3L 93
Wharf St. OL9: Chad 8F 62
SK4: Stoc 5C 108
SK16: Duk 9E 6 (9M 81)
Wharmby Rd. WA11: Hay 3B 86
WHARMTON 4J 65
Wharmton Ri. OL4: Gras 5G 65
Wharmton Vw. OL3: G'fld 5K 65
OL5: Mos 8H 65
Wharncliffe Cl. SK13: Had 5A 100
Wharncliffe St. WN2: Hin 6N 53
Wharton Av. M21: Cho H 1C 106
Wharton Hall Cl. M29: Tyld 1C 74
Wharton La. M38: Lit H 6E 56
Wharton Lodge M30: Ecc 7E 76
Wheat Cl. M13: Man 4H 95
Wheatcroft SK3: Stoc 2D 118
SK13: Had 5A 100
Wheaters St. M7: Sal 6C 78
Wheatfield SK15: Stal 2H 99
Wheatfield Cl. BL9: Bury 6M 25
SK6: Bred 4L 109
SK10: Macc 1G 131
Wheatfield Cres. OL2: O'ham 9H 45
Wheatfield St. BL2: Bolt 7J 39
Wheathill St. OL16: Roch 9E 28
Wheatlea Ind. Est. WN3: Wig 1C 70
Wheatlea Rd. WN3: Wig 9C 52
Wheatley Av. WA12: N Wil 4F 86
Wheatley Rd. M27: Ward 9D 58
Wheatley Wlk. M12: Man 3M 95
(off Woolfall Cl.)
Wheat Moss SK11: Chel 9A 126
Wheatsheaf Cen., The
OL16: Roch 6D 8 (5D 28)
Wheatsheaf Ind. Est. M27: Pen 1H 77
Wheatsheaf Wlk. WN6: Stan 3A 34
Wheeldale OL4: O'ham 5A 64
Wheeldale Cl. BL1: Bolt 2F 38
Wheel Forge Way M17: T Pk 2F 92
Wheelock Cl. SK9: Wilm 5J 123
Wheelton Cl. BL8: Bury 3G 40
Wheelwright Cl. OL11: Roch 9N 27
SK6: Mar 8C 110
Wheelwright Dr. OL16: Roch 2G 29
Whelan Av. BL9: Bury 5L 41
Whelan Cl. BL9: Bury 5L 41
Wheler St. M11: Man 1B 96
WHELLEY 2H 53
Whelley WN1: Wig 6N 9 (2H 53)
WN2: Wig 2H 53
Whelmar Est. SK8: Chea H 3N 117
Whelmar Ho. WN8: Skel 2A 50
Whernside Av. M40: Man 1M 79
OL6: A Lyne 3N 81
Whernside Cl. SK4: Stoc 5C 108
Whetmorhurst La. SK6: Mel 2H 121
Whetstone Hill Cl. OL1: O'ham 1M 63
Whetstone Hill La. OL1: O'ham 2N 63
(not continuous)
Whetstone Hill Rd. OL1: O'ham 1M 63
Whewell Av. M26: Rad 7K 41
Whewell St. M29: Tyld 1B 74
Whickham Cl. M14: Man 6G 95
Whiley St. M13: Man 5L 95
Whimberry Cl. M5: Sal 2A 94
Whimberry Dr. SK15: C'ook 5G 83
Whimberry Lee La. OL3: Del 4N 47
Whimberry Way M20: Man 2J 107
Whimbrel Av. WA12: N Wil 6F 86
Whimbrel Rd. M29: Ast 4C 74
SK2: Stoc 2L 119
Whinberry Rd. WA14: B'ath 8B 104
Whinberry Way OL4: O'ham 8B 46
Whinchat Av. WA12: N Wil 5F 86
Whinchat Cl. SK2: Stoc 3L 119
WA3: Low 2A 88
Whinfell Dr. M24: Mid 1K 61
Whinfield Cl. WN6: Wig 3D 52
Whingroves Wlk. M40: Man 4M 79
(off Halliford Rd.)
Whinmoor Wlk. M40: Man 3N 79
(off Bellscroft Av.)
Whins Av. BL4: Farn 3F 56
Whins Crest BL6: Los 5L 37
Whinslee Ct. BL6: Los 5L 37
Whinslee Dr. BL6: Los 5L 37
Whinstone Way OL1: Chad 2C 62
Whipney La. BL8: Haw 3D 24
Whipp St. OL10: H'ood 1G 43
Whirley Cl. SK4: Stoc 3B 108
WHIRLEY GROVE 1B 130
Whirley Rd. SK10: Hen, Macc 2A 130
Whistlecroft Ct. WN3: I Mak 5J 53
Whistley St. WN2: P Bri 8L 53
Whiston Cl. SK11: Macc 8F 130
Whiston Dr. BL2: Bolt 6K 39
Whiston M. SK11: Lang 8M 131
Whiston Rd. M8: Man 2G 78
Whiston St. SK11: Macc 5G 130
Whitbeam Gro. WN2: Hin 9A 54
Whitbrook Way M24: Mid 7B 44
Whitburn Av. M13: Man 7K 95
Whitburn Cl. BL3: Bolt 8N 37
WN4: Gars 6A 70
Whitburn Dr. BL8: Bury 8J 25
Whitburn Rd. M23: Wyth 3N 115
Whitby Av. M6: Sal 7J 77
M14: Man 9K 95
M16: Whall R 6C 94
M41: Urm 7E 92
OL10: H'ood 1H 43
Whitby Cl. BL8: Bury 2F 40
SK8: Chea 1H 117
SK12: Poy 2G 125
Whitby Rd. M14: Man 9J 95
OL8: O'ham 8N 63
Whitby St. M24: Mid 2A 62
OL11: Roch 8E 28
Whitchurch Dr. M16: Old T 4C 94
Whitchurch Gdns. BL1: Bolt 2F 38
(off Gladstone St.)
Whitchurch Rd. M20: Man 1E 106
Whiteacre WN6: Stan 2L 33
Whiteacre Rd.
OL6: A Lyne 6F 6 (7N 81)
Whiteacres M27: Swin 3D 76
Whiteacre Wlk. M15: Man 4D 94
(off Shearsby Cl.)
White Ash BL9: Bury 8D 26
White Ash Ter. BL9: Bury 7D 26
Whitebank Av. SK5: Stoc 4G 108
White Bank Rd. OL8: O'ham 1H 81
White Bank Stadium 1J 81
Whitebarn Av. M8: Man 3G 78
Whitebarn Rd. SK9: A Edg 5G 126
Whitebeam Cl. M6: Sal 7N 77
OL16: Miln 1L 45
WA15: Tim 2L 115
Whitebeam Ct. M6: Sal 7N 77
Whitebeam Wlk. BL5: W'ton 1H 55
M33: Sale 3D 104
(off Manor Av.)
White Bear Yd. WA16: Knut 6G 132
(off Canute Pl.)
Whitebeck Ct. M9: Man 7M 61
Whitebirk Cl. BL8: G'mount 3F 24
Whitebrook Ct. M33: Sale 5H 105
White Brook La. OL3: Upp 5N 65
Whitebrook La. OL3: Upp 3M 65
Whitebrook Rd. M14: Man 8G 95
White Broom WA13: Lym 3C 112
WHITE BROW 7M 41
White Brow BL9: Bury 7M 41
Whitecar Av. M40: Man 1C 80
White Carr La. BL9: Bury 4N 25
Whitecarr La. M23: Wyth 4K 115
WA15: Hale 4K 115
Whitechapel Cl. BL2: Bolt 5M 39
Whitechapel St. M20: Man 5G 106
White City Circ. M16: Old T 4N 93
White City Retail Pk.
M16: Old T 4N 93
White City Way M16: Old T 4N 93
Whitecliff Cl. M14: Man 6H 95
White Clover Sq. WA13: Lym 5B 112
White Ct. M27: Swin 3D 76
White Cft. BL1: Bolt 1H 7 (4F 38)
Whitecroft Av. OL2: Shaw 5A 46
WA3: Low 9A 72
Whitecroft Cl. SK10: Macc 2J 131
Whitecroft Dr. BL8: Bury 1F 40
Whitecroft Gdns. M19: Man 4K 107
Whitecroft Mdw. M24: Mid 3M 61
Whitecroft Rd. BL1: Bolt 3A 38
SK6: Stri 6F 120
WN3: Wig 9D 52
Whitecroft St. OL1: O'ham 2N 63
Whitecroft Vs. M31: Part 6F 102
White Cross Ct. WA12: N Wil 5E 86
WHITEFIELD 4M 59
Whitefield SK4: Stoc 5B 108
WA13: Lym 3B 112
Whitefield Av. OL11: Roch 5L 27
WA12: N Wil 7J 87
Whitefield Cl. WA3: Gol 1K 87
WA13: Lym 2B 112
Whitefield Ct. WA3: Ris 7H 89
Whitefield Golf Course 4L 59
Whitefield Gro. WA13: Lym 3B 112
Whitefield Rd. BL9: Bury 5K 41
(not continuous)
M33: Sale 3F 104
SK6: Bred 4J 109
Whitefield Stop (Metro) 2M 59
White Friar Ct. M3: Sal 1D 4
Whitefriars Wlk. M22: Wyth 7C 116
WHITE GATE 8E 62
Whitegate BL3: Bolt 1L 55
OL15: Lit 1J 29
Whitegate Av. OL9: Chad 7D 62
WA3: Cul 7H 89
Whitegate Bus. Cen. OL9: Chad 6D 62
Whitegate Cl. M40: Man 1C 80
Whitegate Dr. BL1: Bolt 8G 23
M5: Sal 7K 77
M27: Clif 9H 59
WHITE GATE END 8C 62
Whitegate Fold PR7: Char R 2B 18
Whitegate La. OL9: Chad 7D 62
(not continuous)
White Gate Mnr. OL10: H'ood 1J 43
Whitegate Pk. M41: Urm 7M 91
Whitegate Rd. OL9: Chad 8B 62
Whitegates BL7: Eger 4F 22
(off Turnerford Cl.)
OL4: Scout 1E 64
SK8: Chea 2J 117
SK14: B'tom 8K 99
Whitegates Cl. WA15: Tim 2H 115
Whitegates La. OL4: Scout 1D 64
Whitegates Rd. M24: Mid 8A 44
SK8: Chea 2J 117
Whitehall OL4: O'ham 8C 46
Whitehall Av. WN6: App B 4J 33
Whitehall Cl. SK9: Wilm 9F 122
Whitehall La. BL6: Bla 2N 35
OL4: O'ham 8C 46
Whitehall Rd. M20: Man 5H 107
M33: Sale 6H 105
Whitehall St. OL1: O'ham 1E 8 (3K 63)
OL12: Roch 4D 28
OL16: Roch 6D 8 (5D 28)
WN3: I Mak 5H 53
White Hart Mdw. M24: Mid 1M 61
White Hart St. SK14: Hyde 5A 98
Whitehaven Gdns. M20: Man 6F 106
Whitehaven Pl. SK14: Hyde 4N 97
Whitehaven Rd. SK7: Bram 1A 124
Whitehead Cl. OL3: G'fld 6H 65
Whitehead Cres. BL8: Bury 7J 25
M26: Rad 4C 58
Whitehead La. M29: Ast 5D 74
Whitehead Rd. M21: Cho H 9M 93
M27: Clif 9H 59
Whiteheads Pl. OL4: Spri 4C 64
Whitehead St. M24: Mid 2A 62
M28: Walk 7L 57
M34: Aud 2J 97
OL2: Shaw 4K 45
OL16: Miln 7J 29
White Hill Cl. OL12: Roch 1B 28
Whitehill Cotts. BL1: Bolt 7E 22
Whitehill Dr. M40: Man 3M 79
Whitehill Ind. Est. SK4: Stoc 2C 108
(not continuous)
Whitehill La. BL1: Bolt 7E 22
Whitehill St. SK4: Stoc 4C 108
SK5: Stoc 4C 108
Whitehill St. W. SK4: Stoc 4B 108
Whiteholme Av. M21: Cho H 4C 106
White Horse Cl. BL6: Hor 8E 20
White Horse Gdns. M27: Swin 4C 76
(off Worsley Rd.)
White Horse Gro. BL5: W'ton 1J 55
White Horse Mdws. OL16: Roch 2G 45
White Ho. Av. M8: Man 8D 60
Whitehouse Av. OL4: O'ham 5N 63
Whitehouse Cl. OL10: H'ood 5J 43
Whitehouse Dr. M23: Wyth 2N 115
WA15: Hale 7H 115
Whitehouse La. WA14: D Mas 9L 103
Whitehurst Dr. M11: Man 1M 95
Whitehurst Rd. SK4: Stoc 4L 107
Whitekirk Cl. M13: Man 9L 5 (3G 95)
White Lady Cl. M28: Walk 8G 57
Whitelake Av. M41: Urm 7N 91
Whitelake Vw. M41: Urm 6N 91
Whiteland Av. BL3: Bolt 7C 38
Whitelands OL6: A Lyne 9E 6 (8N 81)
Whitelands Ind. Est. SK15: Stal 8B 82
Whitelands Rd.
OL6: A Lyne 8E 6 (8N 81)
Whitelands Ter.
OL6: A Lyne 9E 6 (8N 81)
Whitelea Dr. SK3: Stoc 2B 118
Whiteledge Rd. WN8: Skel 5A 50
White Lee Cft. M46: Ath 8K 55
Whitelees M. OL15: Lit 9L 15
Whitelees Rd. OL15: Lit 9L 15
Whitelegge St. BL8: Bury 9H 25
Whiteleggs La. WA13: Lym 6C 112
Whiteley Dr. M24: Mid 4A 62
WHITELEY GREEN 3J 129
Whiteley Pl. WA14: Alt 1D 114
Whiteleys Pl. OL12: Roch 6B 8 (5C 28)
Whiteley St. M11: Man 8N 79
OL9: Chad 7F 62
White Lion Brow
BL1: Bolt 2H 7 (5F 38)
White Lodge Dr. WN4: A Mak 6G 71
Whitelow Rd. BL9: Bury 8L 11
M21: Cho H 9N 93
SK4: Stoc 5M 107
White Mdws. M27: Swin 3F 76
Whitemoss OL12: Roch 3N 27
White Moss Av. M21: Cho H 9B 94
White Moss Gdns. M9: Man 9M 61
White Moss Rd. M9: Man 8K 61
White Moss Vw. M24: Mid 6A 62
White Nancy 6M 129
Whiteoak Cl. SK6: Mar 9B 110
Whiteoak Ct. M14: Man 9H 95
Whiteoak Rd. M14: Man 9H 95
Whiteoak Vw. BL3: Bolt 7L 39
White Rd. SK22: N Mil 6M 121
Whites Cft. M27: Swin 2F 76
Whiteside Av. WN2: Hin 4N 53
WN6: Wig 2D 52
Whiteside Cl. M5: Sal 8K 77
Whiteside Fold OL12: Roch 4M 27
White Slack Ga. OL14: Wals 1K 15
Whitestar Ct. M44: Irl 7H 91
(off Ferry Rd.)
Whitestone Cl. BL6: Los 6M 37
Whitestone Ho. OL1: O'ham 1B 8
White St. BL8: Bury 3J 41
M6: Sal 9L 77
M15: Man 3C 94
SK11: Macc 6H 131
WN5: Wig 5M 51
WN7: Lei 6L 73
White Swallows Rd. M27: Swin 4G 77
White Swan Ind. Est.
OL1: O'ham 3N 63
White Ter. SK14: Hyde 9N 97
Whitethorn Av. M16: Whall R 6C 94
M19: Man 1L 107
Whitethorn Cl. SK6: Mar 9B 110
Whitewater Dr. M7: Sal 3M 77
Whiteway St. M9: Man 3K 79
Whitewell Cl. BL9: Bury 5K 41
OL16: Roch 5G 28
Whitewillow Cl. M35: Fail 4E 80
Whitewood Cl. WN4: A Mak 4D 70
WHITFIELD
OL2 2M 45
SK13 9E 100
Whitfield Av. SK13: Glos 9E 100
Whitfield Bottoms OL16: Miln 1M 45
Whitfield Brow OL15: Lit 7N 15
Whitfield Cres. OL16: Miln 1M 45
Whitfield Cross SK13: Glos 9F 100
Whitfield Dr. OL16: Miln 8J 29
SK11: Macc 7F 130
Whitfield Ri. OL2: Shaw 3L 45
Whitfields, The SK10: Macc 3E 130
Whitfield St. M3: Man 6F 78
WN7: Lei 6L 73
Whitfield Wells SK13: Glos 9F 100
Whitford Wlk. M40: Man 7J 79
(off Nuneaton Dr.)
Whithill Wlk. WN4: A Mak 5D 70
Whiting Gro. BL3: Bolt 6N 37
Whitington Cl. BL3: Lit L 8B 40
Whitland Av. BL1: Bolt 4A 38
Whitland Dr. OL8: O'ham 9F 62
Whit La. M6: Sal 4M 77
(not continuous)
WHITLE 6M 121
Whitle Bank Rd. SK22: N Mil 5L 121
Whitledge Grn. WN4: A Mak 5D 70
Whitledge Rd. WN4: A Mak 5D 70
Whitle Fold SK22: N Mil 5L 121
Whitle Rd. SK22: N Mil 6L 121
WHITLEY 8E 34
Whitley Cres. WN1: Wig 8E 34
WN2: Abr 3L 71
Whitley Gdns. WA15: Tim 9H 105
Whitley Pl. WA15: Tim 9J 105
Whitley Rd. M40: Man 6H 79
SK4: Stoc 5N 107
WN8: Roby M, Uph 9G 32
Whitley St. BL3: Bolt 1L 57
Whitley Wlk. SK13: Glos 9B 100
Whitlow Av. WA3: Gol 9J 71
WA14: B'ath 8B 104
Whitman St. M9: Man 2L 79
Whitmore Rd. M14: Man 8G 94
Whitnall St. M16: Whall R 5D 94
SK14: Hyde 4A 98
Whitney Ct. OL4: O'ham 3G 8
Whitney Cft. SK10: Macc 4L 131
Whitsand Rd. M22: Shar 2D 116
Whitsbury Av. M18: Man 6B 96
WN2: Hin 7N 53
Whitstable Cl. OL9: Chad 5F 62
Whitstable Rd. M40: Man 1A 80
Whitsters Hollow BL1: Bolt 1C 38
Whitstone Dr. WN8: Skel 4B 50
Whitsundale BL5: W'ton 1H 55
Whitswood Cl. M16: Whall R 6D 94
WHITTAKER 1A 30
Whittaker Cl. M25: Pres 7B 60
Whittaker Dr. OL15: Lit 3K 29
Whittaker Golf Course 1A 30
Whittaker Ho. M26: Rad 8G 41
Whittaker La. M25: Pres 7B 60
OL11: Roch 4J 27
OL15: Lit 1A 30
Whittaker St. M24: Mid 3L 61
M26: Rad 8H 41
M40: Man 2L 79
OL2: O'ham 7H 45
OL6: A Lyne 5A 82
OL11: Roch 4K 27
Whittingham Dr. BL0: Ram 1J 25
Whittingham Gro. OL1: O'ham 3H 63
Whittington St.
OL7: A Lyne 9B 6 (9L 81)
WHITTLE BROOK 9N 57
Whittle Brook Cl. BL9: Bury 7B 42
Whittle Brook Gro. OL10: H'ood 5K 43
Whittlebrook Ho. M28: Walk 9M 57
(off Trinity Cres.)
Whittle Ct. WN3: Wins 9B 52
Whittle Dr. M28: Walk 6K 57
OL2: Shaw 4A 46
Whittle Gdns. M28: Walk 9M 57
(off Whittle St.)
Whittle Gro. BL1: Bolt 3C 38
M28: Walk 8M 57
Whittle Hill BL7: Eger 2F 22
Whittle La. OL10: H'ood 7F 42
Whittles Av. M34: Dent 6L 97
Whittles Cft. M1: Man 5L 5 (9G 79)
(Peak St.)
M1: Man 5L 5
(Wharf Cl.)
Whittles Ter. BL5: W'ton 2G 55
(off Church St.)
OL16: Miln 9M 29
Whittle St. BL8: Bury 1J 41
M4: Man 3K 5 (8G 78)
M27: Swin 3E 76
M28: Walk 8L 57
OL15: Lit 9K 15
Whittles Wlk. M34: Dent 7L 97
Whittleswick Rd. M17: T Pk 1F 92
Whitton M. BL6: Hor 9D 20
(off Wright St.)
Whitwell Bank SK13: Gam 7N 99
(off Melandra Castle Rd.)
Whitwell Cl. SK13: Gam 7N 99
WN6: Stan 2A 34
Whitwell Fold SK13: Gam 7N 99
(off Hathersage Cres.)
Whitwell Gdns. BL6: Hor 8D 20
Whitwell Grn. SK13: Gam 7A 100
(off Hathersage Cres.)
Whitwell Lea SK13: Gam 7N 99
(off Calver M.)
Whitwell Wlk. M13: Man 5K 95
Whitwell Way M18: Man 4A 96
WHITWORTH 5A 14
Whitworth Art Gallery 5G 95
Whitworth Cl. OL6: A Lyne 6N 81
Whitworth La. M14: Man 8J 95
Whitworth Leisure Cen. 4B 14
Whitworth Mus. 5A 14
Whitworth Pk. Mans. M14: Man 5F 94
Whitworth Rake OL12: Whitw 6B 14
Whitworth Rd.
OL12: Roch 5D 8 (1B 28)
Whitworth Sq. OL12: Whitw 6B 14
Whitworth St. BL6: Hor 2E 36
M1: Man 7H 5 (1F 94)
(not continuous)
M11: Man 2M 95
OL16: Miln 7K 29
OL16: Roch 3G 28
Whitworth St. E. M11: Man 2A 96
Whitworth St. W.
M1: Man 7E 4 (1D 94)
Whitworth Water Ski Cen. 4A 14
Whitworth Way WN6: Wig 1B 52
Whixhall Av. M12: Man 3K 95
Whoolden St. BL4: Farn 2K 57
Whowell Fold BL1: Bolt 1D 38
Whowell St. BL3: Bolt 6F 38
Wibbersley Pk. M41: Urm 7N 91
Wichbrook Rd. M28: Walk 8G 57
Wicheaves Cres. M28: Walk 8G 57
Wicheries, The M28: Walk 8G 57
Wicken Bank OL10: H'ood 5K 43
Wickenby Dr. M33: Sale 4G 105
Wickenhall La. OL16: Miln 9C 30

Wicken St. SK2: Stoc 9G 109
Wickentree Holt OL12: Roch 3M 27
Wickentree La. M35: Fail 1D 80
Wicker La. WA15: Haleb 7H 115
Wicket Gro. M27: Clif 7E 58
Wickham Ter. M24: Mid 2M 61
Wickliffe Pl. OL11: Roch 9C 8
Wickliffe St. BL1: Bolt 1J 7 (4F 38)
Wicklow Av. SK3: Stoc 9N 107
Wicklow Dr. M22: Wyth 5D 116
Wicklow Gro. OL8: O'ham 8J 63
Wickmere Wlk. *M8: Man 4E 78*
(off Waterloo Rd.)
Widcombe Dr. BL2: Bolt 7N 39
Widdop St. OL9: O'ham 2A 8 (4H 63)
Widdow's St. WN7: Lei 6K 73
Widdrington Rd. WN1: Wig 1G 52
Widecombe Cl. M41: Urm 5B 92
Widford Wlk. BL6: Bla 3N 35
Widgeon Cl. M14: Man 9G 94
SK12: Poy 2F 124
Widgeon Rd. WA14: B'ath 8B 104
Wiend, The WN1: Wig 8K 9 (3F 52)
Wiend Hall BL5: W'ton 1H 55
WIGAN 8J 9 (3F 52)
Wigan Athletic FC 3C 52
Wigan Crematorium WN3: I Mak 7G 53
Wigan Enterprise Pk.
WN2: I Mak 5J 53
Wigan Gallery WN1: Wig 7J 9 (3F 52)
Wigan Golf Course 2G 35
Wigan Investment Cen.
WN3: Wig 5E 52
Wigan La.
PR7: Adl, Chor, Cop, H Char 7F 18
WN1: Wig 5L 9 (7E 34)
(not continuous)
Wigan Little Theatre 7L 9 (3G 52)
Wigan Lwr. Rd. WN6: Stan 8N 33
Wigan North Western Station (Rail)
9J 9 (4F 52)
Wigan Pier WN3: Wig 9G 9 (4D 52)
Wigan Rd. BL3: Bolt 1M 55
BL5: W'ton 4C 54
M46: Ath 8H 55
WA3: Gol 8L 71
WN1: Stan 6E 34
WN2: Asp, Wig 9K 35
WN2: Hin 5M 53
WN4: A Mak 2C 70
WN5: Bil 3K 69
WN6: She, Stan 6M 33
WN6: Stan 4C 34
WN7: Lei 2E 72
Wigan Sailing Club 7E 52
Wigan Sq. WN1: Wig 7J 9
Wigan St. WN2: P Bri 1K 71
Wigan Wallgate Station (Rail)
8J 9 (3F 52)
Wigan Warriors RLFC 3C 52
Wiggins Teape Rd. BL9: Bury 6A 42
Wiggins Wlk. *M14: Man 6H 95*
(off Bembridge Cl.)
Wightman Av. WA12: N Wil 4F 86
Wighurst Wlk. M22: Wyth 6C 116
Wigley St. M12: Man 2K 95
Wigmore Rd. M8: Man 3G 78
Wigmore St. OL6: A Lyne 6A 82
Wigsby Av. M40: Man 9A 62
Wigsey La. WA13: Warb 9B 102
WIGSHAW 7F 88
Wigshaw Cl. WN7: Lei 9H 73
Wigshaw La. WA3: Cul 7E 88
Wigwam Cl. SK12: Poy 2G 125
Wike St. BL8: Bury 1K 41
Wilberforce Cl. M15: Man 4D 94
Wilbraham Rd. M14: Man 8A 94
M16: Whall R 8A 94
M21: Cho H 8N 93
M28: Walk 8L 57
Wilbraham St. BL5: W'ton 3G 55
WN7: Lei 5E 72
Wilburn St. M5: Sal 6B 4 (1C 94)
(not continuous)
Wilby Av. BL3: Lit L 7A 40
Wilby Cl. BL8: Bury 9K 25
Wilby St. M8: Man 4G 79
Wilcock Rd. WA11: Hay 1D 86
Wilcockson Ho. *BL4: Farn 3L 57*
(off Hesketh Wlk.)
Wilcock St. M16: Whall R 5D 94
WN3: Wig 4D 52
Wilcott Dr. M33: Sale 3E 104
SK9: Wilm 1E 126
Wilcott Rd. SK8: Gat 2F 116
Wild Arum Cl. WA3: Low 1A 88
Wildbank Chase SK15: Stal 2H 99
Wildbrook Cl. M38: Lit H 8F 56
Wildbrook Cres. OL8: O'ham 8L 63
Wildbrook Gro. M38: Lit H 8F 56
Wildbrook Rd. M38: Lit H 7F 56
Wildbrook Ter. OL8: O'ham 9L 63
Wild Clough SK14: Hyde 8C 98
Wildcroft Av. M40: Man 1M 79
Wilders Moor Cl. M28: Wors 2K 75
WILDERSWOOD 8E 20
Wilderswood Av. BL6: Hor 9E 20
Wilderswood Cl. M20: Man 3H 107
Wilderswood Ct. BL6: Hor 8E 20
Wild Ho. OL8: O'ham 6K 63
Wildhouse Cl. OL16: Miln 6K 29
Wild Ho. La. OL16: Miln 6K 29
Wildings Old La. WA3: Cro 9C 88
Wilding St. WN3: I Mak 5H 53
Wildman La. BL4: Farn 3G 57
Wildmoor Av. OL4: O'ham 7B 64
Wildmoor Wood Cl.
SK15: C'ook 5G 83
Wilds Bldgs. OL16: Roch 6H 29
Wilds Pas. OL15: Lit 1J 29
(Oakley St.)
OL15: Lit 4A 16
(Roberts Pas.)
WN7: Lei 6H 73
Wilds Pl. BL0: Ram 9H 11
Wild's Sq. OL5: Mos 9F 64
Wild St. M26: Rad 8K 41
M34: Dent 6K 97
OL1: O'ham 4L 63
OL2: Shaw 6N 45
OL4: Lees 5B 64
OL10: H'ood 2K 43
SK2: Stoc 1E 118
SK6: Bred 6K 109
SK7: H Gro 5H 119
SK16: Duk 1A 98
Wildwood Cl. BL0: Ram 1G 24
SK2: Stoc 2E 118
Wileman Ct. *M5: Sal 8K 77*
(off Sheader Dr.)
Wilford Av. M33: Sale 6G 105
Wilfred Dr. BL9: Bury 9A 26
Wilfred Geere Ho., The
BL4: Farn 3F 56
Wilfred Rd. M28: Walk 9L 57
M30: Ecc 1A 92
Wilfred St. BL7: Bro X 6H 23
M3: Sal 6D 78
M40: Man 2M 79
OL4: O'ham 5M 63
WN5: Wig 4C 52
Wilfrid St. M27: Swin 2F 76
Wilham Av. M30: Ecc 9D 76
Wilkesley Av. WN6: Stan 4A 34
Wilkes St. OL1: O'ham 8A 46
Wilkin Cft. SK8: Chea H 6K 117
Wilkins La. SK9: Sty 1D 122
Wilkinson Av. BL3: Lit L 7A 40
Wilkinson Rd. BL1: Bolt 8D 22
SK4: Stoc 1J 9 (6C 108)
Wilkinson St. M24: Mid 3L 61
M33: Sale 4K 105
OL6: A Lyne 8A 6 (8L 81)
WN7: Lei 5G 73
Wilks Av. M22: Wyth 5E 116
Willand Cl. BL2: Bolt 6A 40
Willand Dr. BL2: Bolt 6A 40
Willan Ent. Cen. M17: T Pk 3J 93
Willan Ind. Est. M50: Sal 9M 77
Willan Rd. M9: Man 7H 61
M30: Ecc 8E 76
Willard Av. WN5: Bil 8H 51
Willard St. SK7: H Gro 4H 119
Willaston Cl. M21: Cho H 1N 105
Willaston Way *SK9: Hand 1J 123*
(off Sandiway Rd.)
Willbutts La. OL11: Roch 5A 28
Willdale Cl. M11: Man 8M 79
Willdor Gro. SK3: Stoc 1N 117
Willenhall Rd. M23: Wyth 6B 106
Willerby Cl. SK10: Macc 4G 130
Willerby Rd. M8: Sal 5D 78
Willert St. M40: Man 5J 79
Willesden Av. M13: Man 6K 95
Will Griffith Wlk. *M11: Man 1K 95*
(off Rylance St.)
William Chadwick Cl. M40: Man 7H 79
William Cl. M41: Urm 7C 92
William Coates Ct. M16: Whall R 5E 94
William Fairburn Way
M4: Man 3J 5 (8F 78)
William Ford Ho. SK14: Mot 5K 99
William Greenwood Cl.
OL10: H'ood 2H 43
William Henry St.
OL11: Roch 8E 28
William Jessop Ct. M1: Man 5M 5
William Kay Cl. M16: Whall R 5D 94
William Lister Cl. M40: Man 6B 80
Williams Av. WA12: N Wil 4F 86
Williams Ct. *M14: Man 5J 95*
(off Hope Rd.)
Williams Cres. OL9: Chad 8D 62
Williamson Av. M26: Rad 6F 40
SK6: Bred 4L 109
Williamson La. M43: Droy 1F 96
Williamson St. M4: Man 1K 5 (7G 78)
OL6: A Lyne 7C 6 (7M 81)
SK5: Stoc 1D 108
Williamson's Yd. OL1: O'ham 4M 63
Williams Rd. M18: Man 4A 96
M40: Man 3N 79
Williams St. BL3: Lit L 9B 40
M18: Man 4A 96
William St. BL0: Ram 5J 11
BL6: Hor 1C 36
M3: Sal 3D 4 (8D 78)
(not continuous)
M12: Man 1J 95
M20: Man 5G 107
M24: Mid 3N 61
M26: Rad 8H 41
M35: Fail 1E 80
OL7: A Lyne 9A 6 (8K 81)
OL11: Roch 9C 8 (7D 28)
OL12: Whitw 5A 14
OL15: Lit 9L 15
OL16: Roch 1H 29
SK10: Macc 4K 131
SK14: Hyde 7A 98
WN2: Hin 6A 54
WN3: I Mak 5G 53
WN7: Lei 5J 73
Williams Way SK11: Hen 4A 130
William Wlk. *WA14: Alt 4D 114*
(off Yarwood St.)
William Way WN7: Lei 9D 72
William Wroe Golf Course 8A 92
Willingdon Cl. BL8: Bury 6J 25
Willingdon Dr. M25: Pres 6A 60
Willis Rd. SK3: Stoc 1C 118
Willis St. BL3: Bolt 8D 38
Williton Wlk. M22: Wyth 4E 116
Willock St. M7: Sal 4E 78
Willoughby Av. M20: Man 4H 107
Willoughby Cl. M33: Sale 3G 104
Willow Av. M24: Mid 4A 62
M29: Ast 4B 74
M41: Urm 7E 92
SK5: Stoc 4D 108
SK8: Chea H 5L 117
WA12: N Wil 5G 87
Willow Bank *M9: Man 3K 79*
(off Church La.)
M14: Man 9H 95
OL3: Upp 3L 65
OL4: Lees 3B 64
SK8: Chea H 9M 117
WA12: N Wil 6J 87
WA15: Tim 1G 114
Willowbank M26: Rad 3F 58
Willowbank Av. BL2: Bolt 6J 39
Willow Bank Cl. SK2: Stoc 9H 109
Willow Bank Ct. M20: Man 8G 106
Willowbank Dr. SK10: Boll 5N 129
Willowbrook Av. M40: Man 3M 79
Willowbrook Dr. WN6: She 5M 33
Willowbrook Gdns. M22: Wyth 3B 116
Willow Cl. BL3: Bolt 8C 38
BL9: Bury 1A 60
PR6: And 5M 19
SK12: Poy 3J 125
SK16: Duk 2C 98
WA16: Mob 9A 122
Willow Ct. M14: Man 9H 95
M33: Sale 3L 105
SK6: Mar 2B 120
SK8: Gat 1F 116
SK10: Macc 1F 130
WA12: N Wil 5G 87
WN6: Stan 2B 34
Willow Cres. WN7: Lei 2G 73
Willowcroft Av. WN2: Asp 9B 36
Willowdale WA12: N Wil 6H 87
Willowdale Av. SK8: H Grn 5G 117
Willowdene Cl. BL7: Eger 5G 22
M40: Man 7H 79
(off Dalbury Dr.)
Willow Dr. BL9: Bury 1A 60
M33: Sale 6E 104
PR7: Char R 2A 18
SK9: Hand 3J 123
WN2: Hin 8B 54
Willowfield Gro. WN4: A Mak 8D 70
Willowfield Rd. OL4: O'ham 1A 64
Willow Fold M43: Droy 8F 80
Willowford Cl. M6: Sal 8M 77
Willow Grn. WA16: Knut 5F 132
Willow Gro. M18: Man 5G 96
M34: Dent 6J 97
OL9: Chad 3F 62
SK6: Mar 2C 120
WA3: Gol 9K 71
WN4: A Mak 5H 71
Willow Hey BL7: Bro X 6K 23
Willow Hill Rd. M8: Man 1F 78
Willow Lawn *SK8: Chea H 4M 117*
(off Vaudrey Dr.)
Willow Lodge WN2: Abr 1L 71
Willow Mead SK6: Rom 5A 110
Willowmead Dr. SK10: P'bury 8E 128
Willowmead Way OL12: Roch 3M 27
Willowmoss Cl. M28: Walk 1M 75
Willow Pk. M14: Man 9H 95
SK2: Stoc 9G 109
(off Wicken St.)
Willow Pk. Ho. M22: Wyth 4C 116
Willow Ri. OL15: Lit 2K 29
Willow Rd. M25: Pres 5N 59
M30: Ecc 6N 93
M31: Part 6F 102
OL3: Upp 4M 65
SK6: H Lan 8C 120
WA11: Hay 2B 86
WA12: N Wil 5H 87
WN6: Wig 8C 34
WILLOWS 8D 38
Willows, The BL2: Bolt 7A 40
M21: Cho H 1N 105
M31: Part 5G 102
M33: Sale 6D 104
M46: Ath 8M 55
(off Water St.)
OL4: Lees 6C 64
OL5: Mos 1H 83
OL12: Whitw 9A 14
(off Market St.)
PR7: Chor 2E 18
PR7: Cop 5B 18
SK4: Stoc 5M 107
WA12: N Wil 6H 87
Willows Cotts. OL16: Miln 7J 29
Willows Dr. M35: Fail 6D 80
Willows End SK15: Stal 7G 82
Willows La. BL3: Bolt 8C 38
OL16: Roch 7H 29
Willows Rd. M5: Sal 8K 77
Willow St. BL9: Bury 2A 42
(not continuous)
M8: Man 6D 78
M11: Man 9M 79
M27: Swin 5D 76
M28: Wors 3C 76
M46: Ath 7L 55
OL1: O'ham 1G 8 (4L 63)
OL10: H'ood 2J 43
WN2: Abr 1L 71
Willow Tree Cl. WN1: Wig 8E 34
Willow Tree Ct. *M30: Ecc 9C 76*
(off Aldred St.)
M33: Sale 5H 105
Willow Tree M. SK8: H Grn 7G 117
Willow Tree Rd. WA14: Alt 5D 114
Willow Wlk. M43: Droy 8G 80
Willow Way M20: Man 5H 107
SK7: Bram 8A 118
SK10: P'bury 8E 128
Willow Wood Cl.
OL6: A Lyne 7B 82
Wilma Av. M9: Man 7H 61
Wilmans Wlk. SK13: Had 3C 100
Wilmcote Cl. BL6: Los 6M 37
Wilmcote Gdns. SK6: Bred 5K 109
Wilmcote Rd. M40: Man 6J 79
Wilmers OL15: Lit 4A 16
Wilmington Rd. M32: Stre 7H 93
Wilmot Dr. WA3: Gol 2J 87
Wilmot St. BL1: Bolt 1D 38
Wilmott St. M15: Man 3F 94
(Cavendish St.)
M15: Man 9G 4 (2E 94)
(Chester St.)
WILMSLOW 7G 123
Wilmslow Av. BL1: Bolt 8F 22
Wilmslow By-Pass SK9: Wilm 1F 126
Wilmslow Ct. SK9: Hand 3J 123
Wilmslow Golf Course 4A 126
Wilmslow Leisure Cen. 7G 123
Wilmslow Old Rd.
SK10: Mot S A 3M 127
WA15: Ring 9M 115
WILMSLOW PARK 6J 123
Wilmslow Pk. Nth. SK9: Wilm 7H 123
Wilmslow Pk. Sth. SK9: Wilm 7H 123
Wilmslow Rd. M14: Man 5H 95
M20: Man 4G 106
SK7: W'ford 6N 123
SK8: Chea 2J 117
(Brooklyn Rd.)
SK8: Chea 4J 117
(Schools Hill)
SK8: Chea, H Grn 5J 117
SK9: A Edg 3F 126
SK9: Hand 1J 123
(not continuous)
SK9: Sty 4A 122
SK10: Mot S A 1M 127
SK10: Mot S A, P'bury 3N 127
SK10: P'bury 8A 124
WA15: Ring 9M 115
Wilmslow Station (Rail) 7H 123
Wilmslow Wlk. SK11: Macc 5J 131
Wilmur Av. M7: Sal 4D 78
M45: Whitef 4N 59
Wilpshire Av. M12: Man 6N 95
Wilsford Cl. WA3: Gol 9L 71
Wilsham Rd. WN5: Orr 6J 51
Wilshaw Gro. OL7: A Lyne 4L 81
Wilshaw La. OL7: A Lyne 5L 81
Wilshaw Pl. OL7: A Lyne 5L 81
Wilson Av. M27: Clif 9H 59
OL10: H'ood 2F 42
WN6: Wig 1E 52
Wilson Brook Ct. SK14: Hyde 6B 98
Wilson Cres. OL6: A Lyne 6B 82
Wilson Fold Av. BL6: Los 3H 37
Wilson Rd. M9: Man 1J 79
SK4: Stoc 4N 107
Wilsons Brow BL4: Kea 2N 57
Wilsons Pk. M40: Man 5K 79
Wilson's Ter. SK13: Glos 9D 100
Wilson St. BL4: Farn 3M 57
BL6: Hor 9C 20
BL9: Bury 9N 7 (3N 41)
M11: Man 1M 95
M13: Man 3H 95
M26: Rad 8F 40
M32: Stre 5L 93
M33: Sale 3H 105
OL3: G'fld 6K 65
OL8: O'ham 7J 63
OL12: Roch 5D 28
SK14: Hyde 7B 98
Wilson Way OL1: O'ham 1D 8
Wilsthorpe Cl. M19: Man 2A 108
Wilton Av. M16: Old T 6N 93
M25: Pres 9C 60
M27: Pen 3J 77
SK8: H Grn 8H 117
WN2: Wig 1J 53
Wilton Ct. M25: Pres 3D 60
M34: Dent 5E 96
Wilton Cres. SK9: A Edg 3E 126
SK11: Macc 6C 130
Wilton Dr. BL9: Bury 7N 41
WA15: Haleb 7J 115
Wilton Gdns. M26: Rad 7J 41
Wilton Gro. M34: Dent 5E 96
OL10: H'ood 3J 43
Wilton La. WA3: Cul 4C 88
Wilton Paddock M34: Dent 5E 96
Wilton Pl. M3: Sal 3B 4 (8C 78)
Wilton Polygon M8: Man 1E 78
Wilton Rd. BL1: Bolt 8F 22
M6: Sal 6H 77
M8: Man 9E 60
M21: Cho H 9A 94
WN6: She 6L 33
Wilton St. BL1: Bolt 1G 38
M13: Man 3G 94
M24: Mid 4G 61
M25: Pres 7B 60
M34: Dent 5J 97
M45: Whitef 4M 59
OL9: Chad 8F 62
OL10: H'ood 2G 43
SK5: Stoc 7D 96
WN1: Wig 9L 9 (4G 52)
WN4: A Mak 4D 70
Wilton Ter. OL12: Roch 5C 28
Wiltshire Av. SK5: Stoc 4G 109
Wiltshire Cl. BL9: Bury 4N 41
SK10: Macc 2C 130
Wiltshire Dr. SK13: Glos 9H 101
Wiltshire Pl. WN5: Wig 5N 51
Wiltshire Rd. M31: Part 6F 102
M35: Fail 4D 80
OL9: Chad 6F 62
Wiltshire St. M7: Sal 3D 78
Wiltshire Wlk. *SK10: Macc 2D 130*
(off Wiltshire Cl.)
Wilwick La. SK11: Macc 5D 130
Wimberry Cl. OL3: G'fld 6L 65
Wimberry Hill Rd. BL5: W'ton 9F 36
Wimbledon Cl. M30: Ecc 9B 76
Wimbledon Dr. OL11: Roch 8B 28
SK3: Stoc 9A 108
Wimbledon Rd. M35: Fail 2F 80
Wimbledon Ter. M40: Man 6N 79
Wimborne Av. M41: Urm 6D 92
OL9: Chad 2E 62
Wimborne Cl. BL6: Los 3H 37
SK8: Chea H 3A 118
Wimborne Rd. WN5: Orr 3L 51
Wimpenny Ho. OL8: O'ham 5C 8
Wimpole St. OL1: O'ham 2L 63
OL6: A Lyne 6E 6 (7N 81)
(not continuous)
Wimpory St. M11: Man 2B 96
Winbolt St. SK2: Stoc 3G 118
Winby St. OL11: Roch 8E 28
Wincanton Av. M23: Wyth 8K 105
Wincanton Dr. BL1: Bolt 6E 22
Wincanton Pk. OL4: O'ham 5A 64
Wince Brook M24: Mid 3M 61
Wince Brook Ct. M24: Mid 3N 61
Wince Cl. M24: Mid 5A 62
Wincham Cl. *M15: Man 3C 94*
(off Shawgreen Cl.)
Wincham Rd. M33: Sale 6E 104
Winchcombe Cl. WN7: Lei 9G 72
Winchester Av. M25: Pres 9B 60
M29: Ast 3D 74
M34: Dent 8K 97
OL6: A Lyne 2A 82
OL9: Chad 2D 62
OL10: H'ood 4H 43
PR7: Chor 2H 19
WN4: A Mak 7D 70
Winchester Cl. BL8: Bury 6J 25
OL11: Roch 6M 27
SK9: Wilm 9D 122
WN5: Orr 4K 51
Winchester Dr. M33: Sale 4D 104
SK4: Stoc 6N 107
SK10: Macc 4D 130
Winchester Gro. WN3: I Mak 5G 53
Winchester Pk. M20: Man 5E 106
Winchester Rd. M6: Sal 6J 77
M26: Rad 7D 40
M30: Ecc 6G 76
M32: Stre 6D 92
M41: Urm 6D 92
SK16: Duk 2D 98
WA11: Hay 9B 70
WA15: Hale 6J 115
WN5: Bil 9H 51
Winchester Way BL2: Bolt 3L 39
Wincle Av. SK12: Poy 4L 125
Wincombe St. M14: Man 7G 95
Windale M28: Walk 8J 57
Windermere Av. BL3: Lit L 8A 40
M27: Swin 3G 76
M33: Sale 6K 105
M34: Dent 7E 96
M46: Ath 6M 55
WA11: St H 9F 68
Windermere Cl. M11: Man 1M 95
M25: Pres 6M 59
M32: Stre 6J 93
Windermere Ct. *WN7: Lei 5G 73*
(off Windermere Rd.)
Windermere Cres. OL7: A Lyne 6K 81
Windermere Dr. BL0: Ram 7J 11
BL9: Bury 5L 41
PR6: Adl 4L 19
SK9: A Edg 4E 126
Windermere Gro. WN7: Lei 4G 73
Windermere Ho. *M28: Walk 9L 57*
(off Sandwich St.)
Windermere M. M24: Mid 9K 43
Windermere Rd. BL4: Farn 3E 56
M24: Mid 1H 61
M41: Urm 8C 92
OL2: O'ham 5H 45
SK1: Stoc 1F 118
SK6: H Lan 7B 120
SK9: Hand 2H 123
SK14: Hyde 4N 97
SK15: Stal 7D 82
SK16: Duk 1N 97
WN2: Abr 2L 71
WN2: Hin 6A 54
WN2: I Mak 4K 53
WN5: Orr 3K 51
WN7: Lei 5G 73
Windermere St. BL1: Bolt 2G 38
OL12: Roch 3D 28
WN1: Wig 6N 9 (2H 53)
Windermere Wlk. OL4: O'ham 3A 64
(not continuous)
Winder St. BL1: Bolt 4G 38
Winders Way M6: Sal 6A 78
Windfields Cl. SK8: Chea H 4N 117
Windgate Ri. SK15: C'ook 5G 83
Windham St. OL16: Roch 2G 28
Windle Av. M8: Man 8E 60
Windle Ct. SK2: Stoc 2J 119
WINDLEHURST 6B 120
Windlehurst Ct. SK6: H Lan 8A 120
Windlehurst Dr. M28: Wors 3J 75
Windlehurst Hall SK6: H Lan 6C 120
Windlehurst Old Rd. SK6: Mar 5C 120
Windlehurst Rd.
SK6: H Lan, Mar 7A 120
Windleshaw St. WN3: I Mak 5H 53
Windley St. BL2: Bolt 1N 7 (4H 39)
Windmill Av. M5: Sal 2A 94
Windmill Cl. M28: Walk 6K 57
M34: Dent 7F 96
OL2: O'ham 1H 63
WN1: Wig 7M 9 (3G 53)
Windmill Ct. OL16: Roch 7F 28
Windmill Hgts. WN8: Uph 3E 50
Windmill La. M29: Ast 6A 74
M34: Dent 7E 96
SK5: Stoc 8D 96
SK10: Kerr 6M 129
Windmill La. Ind. Est.
M34: Dent 6G 96
Windmill Rd. M28: Walk 6K 57
M33: Sale 5M 105
WN8: Uph 4D 50
Windmill Rdbt. WN8: Skel 4D 50
Windmill St. M2: Man 6F 4 (1E 94)
OL16: Roch 7F 28
SK11: Macc 6J 131
Windmill Trad. M34: Dent 6H 97
Windover Cl. BL5: O Hul 4A 56
Windover St. BL3: Bolt 8B 38

Windrush, The OL12: Roch 1A 28
Windrush Av. BL0: Ram 3G 25
Windrush Dr. BL5: W'ton 2H 55
M9: Man 3J 79
Windsor Av. BL3: Lit L 9A 40
M27: Clif 9G 59
M29: Ast 4B 74
M33: Sale 2H 105
M35: Fail 2F 80
M38: Lit H 6J 57
M41: Urm 7N 91
M44: Irl 6J 91
M45: Whitef 4N 59
OL9: Chad 7E 62
OL10: H'ood 2G 42
PR7: Adl 7J 19
SK4: Stoc 5M 107
SK8: Gat 2E 116
SK9: Wilm 7E 122
WA12: N Wil 7G 87
Windsor Bri. M5: Sal 8A 78
Windsor Cl. BL8: G'mount 4G 24
SK10: Boll 7J 129
SK12: Poy 2H 125
Windsor Ct. BL3: Bolt 1E 56
M9: Man 6F 60
M26: Rad 8H 41
M33: Sale 3F 104
(off Wentworth Dr.)
M34: Dent 9L 97
(off Wordsworth Rd.)
OL2: Shaw 4M 45
SK3: Stoc 9C 108
(off Castle St.)
Windsor Cres. M25: Pres 8D 60
WN2: Asp 7N 35
Windsor Dr. BL6: Hor 2G 36
BL8: Bury 4H 41
M34: Aud 9H 81
OL7: A Lyne 6K 81
SK6: Bred 5G 109
SK6: Mar 2B 120
SK15: Stal 7D 82
SK16: Duk 2C 98
WA11: Hay 2D 86
WA14: Bow 6N 113
WA14: Tim 8F 104
Windsor Gdns. SK7: Bram 9C 118
Windsor Gro. BL1: Bolt 3D 38
M26: Rad 4B 58
OL6: A Lyne 3N 81
SK6: Rom 6B 110
SK8: Chea H 7L 117
WN2: Hin 8D 54
Windsor Ho. *M21: Cho H 9E 94*
(off Mauldeth Rd.)
M34: Dent 6E 96
Windsor Rd. BL7: Bro X 6H 23
M9: Man 3K 79
M19: Man 8M 95
M25: Pres 9D 60
M34: Dent 6E 96
M40: Man 6C 80
M43: Droy 8B 80
OL8: O'ham 6H 63
(not continuous)
SK7: H Gro 5K 119
SK14: Hyde 1A 110
WA3: Gol 1M 87
WN4: A Mak 8E 70
WN5: Bil 5J 69
WN7: Lei 4N 73
WN8: Uph 3E 50
Windsor Sq. SK11: Macc 8H 131
Windsor St. M5: Sal 9A 78
M18: Man 5A 96
M35: Fail 2E 80
M40: Man 6C 80
M46: Ath 9N 55
OL1: O'ham 2L 63
OL11: Roch 8E 28
SK2: Stoc 1E 118
WN1: Wig 6M 9 (2G 53)
Windsor Ter. *OL16: Miln 7J 29*
(off Moorhouse Farm)
OL16: Roch 6G 29
SK2: Stoc 1E 118
(off Russell St.)
Windsor Wlk. SK2: Stoc 1D 118
Windsor Way WA16: Knut 6F 132
WINDY ARBOUR 2L 69
Windybank M9: Man 6H 61
Windy Bank Av. WA3: Low 1A 88
Windy Harbour La. BL7: Bro X 5J 23
Windyhill Dr. BL3: Bolt 9B 38
Winfell Dr. M40: Man 7J 79
Winfield Av. M20: Man 2J 107
Winfield Dr. M18: Man 3B 96
Winfield Gro. SK6: Mar B 7E 110
Winfield St. SK14: Hyde 7C 98
Winford Rd. M24: Mid 5A 62
Winford St. M9: Man 2K 79
Wingate Av. BL8: Bury 2H 41
Wingate Dr. M20: Man 6H 107
M45: Whitef 2L 59
WA15: Tim 2G 115
Wingate Rd. M38: Lit H 7J 57
SK4: Stoc 4A 108
WINGATES 9G 36
Wingates Gro. BL5: W'ton 9F 36
Wingates Ind. Est. BL5: W'ton 1E 54
Wingates Ind. Pk. BL5: W'ton 9F 36
Wingates La. BL5: W'ton 7G 36
Wingates Rd. WN1: Wig 7F 34
Wingates Sq. BL5: W'ton 9G 37
Wingate St. OL11: Roch 4K 27
Wingfield Av. SK9: Wilm 8D 122
Wingfield Cl. WN6: Wig 8D 34
Wingfield Dr. M27: Swin 4G 77
SK9: Wilm 8D 122
Wingfield Gro. SK13: Glos 9H 101
Wingfield St. M32: Stre 5K 93
Wingfield Vs. OL15: Lit 7N 15
Wingrave Ho. M5: Sal 8N 77
Wings Gro. OL10: H'ood 5J 43
Winhill Rd. SK22: N Mil 6M 121
Winifred Av. BL9: Bury 9E 26
Winifred Kettle Ho. BL5: W'ton 4H 55
Winifred Rd. BL4: Farn 2H 57
M20: Man 5G 107
M40: Man 3N 79
M41: Urm 7C 92
SK2: Stoc 2E 118
Winifred St. BL0: Ram 9H 11
M30: Ecc 9B 76
OL12: Roch 4N 27
SK14: Hyde 1B 110
WN3: I Mak 5H 53
Winmarith Dr. WA15: Haleb 8K 115
Winmarleigh Cl. BL8: Bury 3F 40
Winmarleigh Gdns. WN7: Lei 7G 73
Winnall Wlk. *M40: Man 4A 80*
(off Rothman Cl.)
Winnard St. WA3: Gol 8L 71
Winnats Cl. SK13: Glos 9H 101
Winnie St. M40: Man 2M 79
Winning Hill Cl. M18: Man 5B 96
Winnington Grn. SK2: Stoc 1H 119
Winnington Rd. SK6: Mar 8C 110
Winnipeg Quay M50: Sal 2M 93
Winnows, The M34: Dent 6H 97
Winscar Rd. WN2: Hin 5N 53
Winscombe Dr. M40: Man 6H 79
Winser St. M1: Man 7H 5 (1F 94)
Winsfield Rd. SK7: H Gro 7H 119
Winsford Cl. WA11: Hay 2C 86
Winsford Dr. OL11: Roch 8L 27
Winsford Gro. BL3: Bolt 7A 38
Winsford Rd. M14: Man 8F 94
Winsford Wlk. *M33: Sale 5L 105*
(off Mottram Rd.)
Winskill Rd. M44: Irl 9H 91
Winslade Cl. OL4: O'ham 2A 64
SK7: H Gro 5E 118
Winslade M. BL4: Farn 2L 57
Winsley Rd. M23: Wyth 6M 105
Winslow Av. SK14: Mot 7J 99
Winslow Pl. M19: Man 2L 107
Winslow Rd. BL3: Bolt 9L 37
Winslow St. M11: Man 1M 95
Winsmoor Dr. WN2: Hin 7A 54
Winson Cl. BL3: Bolt 8F 38
WINSTANLEY 9A 52
Winstanley Cl. M6: Sal 5K 77
Winstanley Ho. WA16: Knut 6F 132
Winstanley Pl. WN3: I Mak 6H 53
Winstanley Rd. M33: Sale 3J 105
M40: Man 7J 79
WN2: Bam 2J 71
WN4: A Mak 4M 69
WN5: Bil 7J 51
Winstanley Shop. Cen.
WN3: Wins 9A 52
Winstanley St. WN5: Wig 5C 52
Winstanley Tennis Club 7K 51
Winster Av. M7: Sal 4A 78
M20: Man 4D 106
M32: Stre 6G 93
Winster Cl. BL2: Bolt 3N 39
M45: Whitef 3A 60
Winster Dr. BL2: Bolt 3M 39
M24: Mid 1K 61
Winster Grn. M30: Ecc 1B 92
Winster Gro. SK2: Stoc 1E 118
Winster Ho. M41: Urm 6N 91
WN5: Wig 4N 51
(off Helvellyn Rd.)
Winster M. *SK13: Gam 7A 100*
(off Melandra Castle Rd.)
Winster Rd. M30: Ecc 1B 92
Winston Av. BL3: Lit L 9C 40
OL11: Roch 7K 27
WA12: N Wil 6F 86
Winston Cl. M26: Rad 7E 40
M33: Sale 3F 104
SK6: Mar 9A 110
Winston Rd. M9: Man 2L 79
(not continuous)
Winswell Cl. M11: Man 8N 79
Winterbottom Gro. SK14: Mot 7J 99
Winterbottom St.
OL9: O'ham 2A 8 (5H 63)
Winterbottom Wlk. *SK14: Mot 7J 99*
(off Winterbottom Gro.)
Winterburn Av. BL2: Bolt 7J 23
M21: Cho H 4B 106
Winterburn Grn. SK2: Stoc 2J 119
Winterdyne St. M9: Man 3K 79
Winterfield Dr. BL3: Bolt 9B 38
Winterford Av. M13: Man 4J 95
Winterford La. OL5: Mos 9G 65
Winterford Rd. M7: Sal 3E 78
M8: Man 3E 78
OL5: Mos 9G 64
Winter Gdn. M4: Man 3H 5
Wintergreen Cl. WN7: Lei 6F 72
Wintergreen Wlk. *M31: Part 5G 103*
(off Wychelm Rd.)
Winter Hey La. BL6: Hor 1D 36
WINTER HILL 3H 21
Winter Hill Vw. BL7: Eger 2E 22
Wintermans Rd. M21: Cho H 1D 106
Winterslow Av. M23: Wyth 7K 105
Winter St. BL1: Bolt 1E 38
Winterton Cl. BL5: W'ton 2J 55
Winterton Rd. SK5: Stoc 8E 96
Winterton Way SK11: Lym G 9G 131
Winthrop Av. M40: Man 5J 79
WINTON .8B 76
Winton Av. M34: Aud 2H 97
M40: Man 1B 80
WN5: Wig 6A 52
Winton Cl. SK7: Bram 6B 118
Winton Ct. WA14: Bow 5C 114
Winton Grn. BL6: Los 4H 37
Winton Gro. BL3: Bolt 8N 37
Winton Rd. M6: Sal 4K 77
WA3: Low 3A 88
WA14: Bow 5C 114
Winton St. OL6: A Lyne 6C 6 (7M 81)
OL15: Lit 9M 15
SK15: Stal 9E 82
Winward St. BL3: Bolt 8B 38
BL5: W'ton 2G 55
WN7: Lei 5D 72
Winwick La. WA3: Cro, Low 8N 87
WA3: Low 4A 88
Winwick Link Rd. WA2: Win 9M 87
Winwick Rd. WA12: N Wil 7H 87
Winwick Vw. WA5: Coll G 8A 86
Winwood Dr. M24: Mid 1N 61
Winwood Fold M24: Mid 8L 43
Winwood Rd. M20: Man 8H 107
Wirksmoor Rd. SK22: N Mil 8L 121
Wirral Cl. M27: Clif 9G 58
WA3: Cul 6G 89
Wirral Cres. SK3: Stoc 8M 107
Wirral Dr. WN3: Wins 9N 51
Wisbech Dr. M23: Wyth 7M 105
Wisbeck Rd. BL2: Bolt 4K 39
Wiseman Ter. M25: Pres 7B 60
Wishaw Sq. M21: Cho H 1D 106
Wisley Cl. SK5: Stoc 9E 96
Wistaria Rd. M18: Man 4B 96
Witham Av. M22: Shar 2D 116
Witham Cl. OL10: H'ood 1F 42
WN6: Stan 3A 34
Witham St. OL6: A Lyne 6B 82
Withenfield Rd. M23: Wyth 8M 105
Withens Grn. SK2: Stoc 1J 119
Withern Flats *OL10: H'ood 2H 43*
(off Hill St.)
Withies, The *M30: Ecc 8B 76*
(off Worsley Rd.)
WITHINGTON 2F 106
Withington Av. WA3: Cul 5J 89
Withington Cl. M46: Ath 7K 55
Withington Dr. M29: Ast 3D 74
Withington Golf Course 6E 106
Withington Grange WN2: Asp 1L 53
Withington Grn. M24: Mid 8M 43
Withington La. WN2: Asp 9K 35
Withington Leisure Cen. 2G 106
Withington Rd. M16: Whall R 5C 94
M21: Cho H 9C 94
Withington St. OL10: H'ood 4K 43
Withinlea Cl. BL5: W'ton 1J 55
WN2: Hin 8E 54
Withinlee Rd. SK10: P'bury 7N 127
Withins Av. M26: Rad 7J 41
Withins Cl. BL2: Bolt 4M 39
Withins Community Leisure Cen.
. . . . .2M 39
Withins Dr. BL2: Bolt 4M 39
Withins Gro. BL2: Bolt 4M 39
Withins Hall Rd. M35: Fail 4F 80
Withins La. BL2: Bolt 4M 39
M26: Rad 7J 41
Withins Rd. OL8: O'ham 9F 62
WA3: Cul 6H 89
WA11: Hay 1B 86
Withins St. M26: Rad 8J 41
Withnell Cl. WN6: Wig 1D 52
Withnell Dr. BL8: Bury 3G 40
Withnell Rd. M19: Man 5J 107
Withycombe Pl. M6: Sal 5N 77
Withyfold Dr. SK10: Macc 3H 131
Withy Gro. M4: Man 3H 5 (8F 78)
Withypool Dr. SK2: Stoc 2F 118
Withy Tree Gro. M34: Dent 7L 97
Witley Dr. M33: Sale 2D 104
Witley Rd. OL16: Roch 6F 28
Witney Cl. *BL1: Bolt 2F 38*
(off Draycott St.)
Wittenbury Rd. SK4: Stoc 6N 107
Wittenham Ho. SK9: Wilm 4J 123
Witterage Cl. M12: Man 3L 95
Witton Wlk. *M8: Man 4E 78*
(off Cranlington Dr.)
Wizard Caravan Pk.
SK10: N Ald 7H 127
Woburn Abbey OL3: Upp 2K 65
Woburn Av. BL2: Bolt 1K 39
WA12: N Wil 7G 87
WN7: Lei 1F 72
Woburn Cl. OL16: Miln 7J 29
SK10: Macc 2G 130
WA11: Hay 2C 86
Woburn Ct. SK12: Poy 2K 125
Woburn Dr. BL9: Bury 7M 41
WA15: Hale 5H 115
Woburn Grn. M24: Mid 1M 61
Woburn Rd. M16: Old T 7N 93
Woburn St. M16: Whall R 6E 94
Woden's Av. M5: Sal 8A 4 (2B 94)
Woden St. M5: Sal 8A 4 (2B 94)
Woking Rd. SK8: Chea H 9L 117
Woking Ter. *BL1: Bolt 3F 38*
(off Woking Gdns.)
Wolfe Cl. WA16: Knut 5J 133
Wolfenden Cres. BL4: Farn 2F 56
Wolfenden St. BL1: Bolt 2F 38
Wolfenden Ter. *BL1: Bolt 2F 38*
(off Wolfenden St.)
Wolf Grange WA15: Hale 6E 114
Wolford Dr. M29: Tyld 1D 74
Wolfreton Cres. M27: Clif 8G 58
Wolfson Sq. WN4: A Mak 6C 70
Wollaton Wlk. M34: Dent 8J 97
Wolmer St. WN4: A Mak 6D 70
Wolseley Ho. *M33: Sale 2J 105*
(off Dargle Rd.)
Wolseley Pl. M20: Man 3G 106
Wolseley Rd. M33: Sale 2H 105
Wolseley St. BL8: Bury 3H 41
OL16: Miln 9M 29
Wolsey Cl. M26: Rad 9G 40
WN4: A Mak 5D 70
Wolsey Dr. WA14: Bow 6A 114
Wolsey St. M26: Rad 9G 40
OL10: H'ood 3H 43
Wolstenholme Av. BL9: Bury 7M 25
Wolstenholme Coalpit La.
OL11: Roch 3G 27
WOLSTENHOLME FOLD 3H 27
Wolstenholme La. OL12: Roch 3H 27
Wolstenvale Cl. M24: Mid 2N 61
Wolver Cl. M38: Lit H 5J 57
Wolverhampton Ho. *SK9: A Edg . . .4F 126*
(off George St.)
Wolverton Av. OL8: O'ham 8H 63
Wolverton Dr. SK9: Wilm 5H 123
Wolverton St. M11: Man 2L 95
Wolvesey *OL11: Roch 7C 28*
(off Boundary St.)
Woodacre M16: Whall R 8D 94
Woodacre Cl. M33: Sale 6G 104
Woodacres Ct. SK9: Wilm 8E 122
Woodall Cl. M33: Sale 4K 105
Woodark Cl. OL4: Spri 6C 64
Woodbank BL2: Bolt 2L 39
OL14: Wals 1A 16
SK1: Stoc 7F 108
SK9: A Edg 3F 126
Woodbank Av. SK1: Stoc 8G 108
SK6: Bred 5J 109
Woodbank Ct. M41: Urm 6B 92
Woodbank Dr. BL8: Bury 9J 25
Woodbank Pk. Athletic Track 7G 109
Woodbank Rd. OL15: Lit 2L 29
Woodbank Ter. OL5: Mos 9G 64
Woodbank Works Ind. Est.
SK1: Stoc 6F 108
Woodbine Av. M44: Cad 4E 102
Woodbine Cres. SK2: Stoc 9D 108
Woodbine Pas. *OL15: Lit 9L 15*
(off Featherstall Rd.)
Woodbine Rd. BL3: Bolt 9D 38
(not continuous)
WA13: Lym 3C 112
Woodbine St. M14: Man 5F 94
OL16: Roch 8E 28
Woodbine St. E. OL16: Roch 8F 28
Woodbine Ter. M44: Irl 7J 91
Woodbourne Ct. M33: Sale 6H 105
Woodbourne Rd. M33: Sale 6G 104
SK4: Stoc 2A 108
SK22: N Mil 9K 121
Woodbray Av. M19: Man 3K 107
Woodbridge Av. M34: Aud 2H 97
Woodbridge Dr. BL2: Bolt 3J 39
Woodbridge Gdns. OL12: Roch 3A 28
Woodbridge Gro. M23: Wyth 7N 105
Woodbridge Rd. M41: Urm 6L 91
Woodbrook Av. OL4: Spri 4E 64
Woodbrook Dr. WN3: Wig 7A 52
Woodbrooke Av. SK14: Hyde 7C 98
Wood Brook La. OL4: Lyd, Spri 4E 64
Woodbrook Rd. OL4: Spri 4D 64
SK9: A Edg 4G 126
Woodburn Dr. BL1: Bolt 1C 38
Woodburn Rd. M22: Nor 8C 106
Woodburn Row M29: Ast 7D 74
Woodbury Cres. SK16: Duk 2M 97
Woodbury Pk. SK7: H Gro 4L 119
Woodbury Rd. SK3: Stoc 9N 107
Woodchurch WN1: Wig 2J 53
Woodchurch Cl. *BL1: Bolt 3F 38*
(off Kentford Rd.)
Woodchurch Wlk. *M33: Sale 5M 105*
(off Mottram Rd.)
OL9: Chad 5F 62
Woodcliffe Lodge M25: Pres 9A 60
Woodcock Cl. M43: Droy 7G 81
OL11: Roch 6L 27
Woodcock Dr. WN2: P Bri 9L 53
Woodcock Gro. SK13: Glos 8H 101
Woodcock Ho. WN1: Wig 8L 9 (3G 52)
Woodcock Rd. SK13: Glos 8J 101
Woodcock Sq. WN1: Wig 7J 9
Woodcote Av. SK7: Bram 5A 118
Woodcote Rd. M31: C'ton 6A 104
WA14: D Mas 6A 104
WA14: W Tim 7D 104
Woodcote Vw. SK9: Wilm 5L 123
Woodcote Wlk. *M8: Man 2H 79*
(off Nunthorpe Dr.)
Wood Cott. Cl. M28: Walk 8G 57
Wood Cotts. SK6: Wood 2L 109
Woodcott Bank BL1: Bolt 9F 22
Woodcott Gro. *SK9: Wilm 5K 123*
(off Picton Dr.)
Woodcourt WN3: Wig 5E 52
Wood Cres. OL4: O'ham 8B 64
Woodcroft SK2: Stoc 1H 119
WN6: She 6J 33
Woodcroft Av. M19: Man 4K 107
Wood Dagger Cl. WN2: Hin 6B 54
Woodeaton Cl. OL2: O'ham 8L 45
Wooded Cl. BL9: Bury 8M 25
Woodedge WN4: A Mak 7C 70
Wood Edge Cl. BL3: Bolt 1K 57
WOOD END 4M 45
WOODEND
OL5 . . . . .9G 65
SK6 . . . . .7G 121
SK9 . . . . .2G 122
Wood End WN7: Lei 4K 73
Woodend OL2: Shaw 4N 45
SK7: Bram 5B 118
Woodend Cen. Ind. Pk.
OL5: Mos 9G 65
Woodend Ct. SK14: Hyde 8A 98
Woodend Dr. SK15: Stal 3G 99
Woodend La. OL12: W'le 8H 15
SK14: Hyde 8N 97
SK15: Stal 3G 99
Woodend Mill OL5: Mos 9G 65
Woodend Mills Ind. Est.
OL4: Spri 6C 64
Woodend Rd. M22: Wyth 3C 116
SK3: Stoc 3D 118
Woodend St. OL1: O'ham 2J 63
OL4: Spri 6C 64
Woodend Vw. OL5: Mos 9G 64
Woodfield M22: Wyth 4C 116
Woodfield Av. OL12: Roch 3C 28
SK6: Bred 4L 109
SK14: Hyde 9A 98
Woodfield Cl. OL8: O'ham 7G 63
SK13: Had 4B 100
Woodfield Ct. SK2: Stoc 3E 118
Woodfield Cres. SK6: Rom 6K 109
WN4: A Mak 8D 70
Woodfield Dr. M28: Wors 4J 75
Woodfield Gro. BL4: Farn 5K 57
M30: Ecc 9C 76
M33: Sale 2G 105
Woodfield M. SK14: Hyde 9A 98
Woodfield Rd. M6: Sal 6K 77
M8: Man 1F 78
M24: Mid 5K 61
SK8: Chea H 8N 117
WA14: Alt 1C 114
WOOD FIELDS 5K 7 (1L 41)
Woodfields Retail Pk.
BL9: Bury 6K 7 (1L 41)
Woodfields Ter. BL9: Bury 1L 41
Woodfield St. BL3: Bolt 9H 39
WN2: Asp 9K 35
Woodfield Ter. OL10: H'ood 1K 43
Wood Fold BL7: Bro X 7K 23
Woodfold Av. M19: Man 7M 95
WOODFORD 4C 124
Woodford Av. M30: Ecc 8B 76
M34: Dent 5L 97
OL2: Shaw 5A 46
WA3: Low 2N 87
Woodford Ct. M43: Droy 1F 96
WN2: Hin 5A 54
(off Woodford St.)
Woodford Dr. M27: Swin 9E 58
Woodford Gdns. M20: Man 6F 106
Woodford Gro. BL3: Bolt 8D 38
Woodford La. SK10: P'bury 8A 124
Woodford Rd. M35: Fail 2E 80
SK7: Bram, W'ford 1C 124
SK9: Wilm 6N 123
SK12: Poy 2E 124
Woodford St. WN2: Hin 5A 54
WN5: Wig 5M 51
Wood Gdns. SK9: A Edg 2G 126
Woodgarth WN7: Lei 5E 72
Woodgarth Av. M40: Man 5B 80
Woodgarth Dr. M27: Swin 4E 76
Woodgarth La. M28: Wors 5N 75
Woodgate Av. BL9: Bury 9C 26
OL11: Roch 7M 27
Woodgate Cl. SK6: Bred 5K 109
Woodgate Dr. M25: Pres 5B 60
WOODGATE HILL 9C 26
Woodgate Hill Rd. BL9: Bury 1B 42
(Ferngrove East)
BL9: Bury 9C 26
(Woodgate Av.)
Woodgate Rd. M16: Whall R 8D 94
Woodgate St. BL3: Bolt 9H 39
Woodgrange Cl. M6: Sal 8L 77
Woodgreen Cl. WN2: Hin 7N 53
Woodgreen Dr. M26: Rad 3G 59
Wood Grn. Gdns. WN5: Wig 2M 51
Wood Gro. M34: Dent 5K 97
M45: Whitef 9L 41
SK6: Wood 3L 109
Woodhall Av. M20: Man 1F 106
M45: Whitef 5K 59
Woodhall Cl. BL2: Bolt 2K 39
BL8: Bury 8K 25
SK7: W'ford 3C 124
Woodhall Cres. SK5: Stoc 4E 108
Woodhall Rd. SK5: Stoc 4D 108
Woodhall St. M35: Fail 2D 80
Woodhalt Rd. M8: Man 2F 78
Woodham Rd. M23: Wyth 7M 105
Woodham Wlk. BL3: Bolt 7E 38
Woodhead Cl. BL0: Ram 1J 25
OL4: Lees 4B 64
Woodhead Dr. WA15: Hale 6F 114
Woodhead Gro. WN3: Wig 9E 52
Woodhead Rd. SK13: Glos 7F 100
SK13: Tin 2C 100
WA15: Hale 6F 114
Woodhead St. M16: Whall R 5D 94
WOODHEY 2H 25
Wood Hey Cl. M26: Rad 9D 40
Woodhey Ct. M33: Sale 7E 104
Wood Hey Gro. M34: Dent 7L 97
OL12: Roch 1D 28
Woodhey Rd. BL0: Ram 2G 24
Woodheys SK4: Stoc 5L 107
Woodheys Cotts. SK6: Mar B 4H 111
Woodheys Dr. M33: Sale 7D 104
Woodheys Rd. OL15: Lit 3L 29
Woodheys St. *M6: Sal 8M 77*
(off Derg St.)
WOODHILL 1K 41
Woodhill M24: Mid 1L 61
Woodhill Cl. BL8: Bury 9K 25
M12: Man 5N 95
M24: Mid 1L 61
Woodhill Dr. M25: Pres 9A 60
WOODHILL FOLD 5H 7 (1K 41)
Woodhill Fold
BL8: Bury 5H 7 (1K 41)
Woodhill Gro. M25: Pres 8A 60
Woodhill Rd. BL8: Bury 5G 7 (7K 25)
Woodhill St. BL8: Bury 9K 25
Woodhill Va. BL8: Bury 1K 41
Woodhouse Ct. *M41: Urm 5A 92*
(off Davyhulme Rd.)
Woodhouse Dr. WN6: Wig 9B 34
Woodhouse Farm Cotts.
OL12: Roch 3J 27
WOODHOUSE GREEN 3G 81
Woodhouse Knowl OL3: Del 8H 47
Woodhouse La. M22: Wyth 3C 116
M33: Sale 6C 104
(Glencoe Dr.)
M33: Sale 7B 104
(Riley Cl.)
M90: Man A 8C 116
OL12: Roch 3J 27
WA14: D Mas 3J 113
WN6: Wig 1B 52
(not continuous)
Woodhouse La. E. WA15: Tim 7G 104
Woodhouse La. Nth.
M22: Wyth 7C 116
WOODHOUSE PARK 6A 116
Woodhouse Pk. Lifestyle Cen. . . .6A 116

Woodhouse Rd. M22: Wyth 7C 116
M41: Urm 5N 91
OL2: Shaw 3N 45
WA14: D Mas 3L 113
WOODHOUSES
M33 6C 104
M35 4F 80
Woodhouse St. M18: Man 4C 96
M40: Man 5L 79
M46: Ath 9M 55
Woodhurst Dr. WN6: Stan 3A 34
Wooding Cl. M31: Part 4H 103
Woodlake Av. M21: Cho H 4B 106
Woodland Av. BL3: Bolt 1J 57
M18: Man 5C 96
SK7: H Gro 6J 119
WA12: N Wil 6J 87
WA13: Lym 5B 112
WN2: Hin 8C 54
Woodland Cl. BL2: Bolt 2M 39
Woodland Cres. M25: Pres 9A 60
Woodland Dr. WA13: Lym 5A 112
WN4: A Mak 5E 70
WN6: Stan 2B 34
Woodland Gro. BL7: Eger 3E 22
WN1: Wig 1G 53
Woodland Pk. OL2: O'ham 6F 44
Woodland Rd. M18: Man 5C 96
M19: Man 9M 95
OL10: H'ood 1K 43
WOODLANDS
M41 8K 91
SK15 2G 98
Woodlands M35: Fail 6C 80
M41: Urm 6C 92
SK14: Hyde 7C 98
SK15: Stal 2F 98
Woodlands, The BL6: Los 4L 37
BL8: Bury 8K 25
M25: Pres 1M 77
M27: Swin 3H 77
M43: Droy 7C 80
OL10: H'ood 4K 43
WN1: Wig 9G 34
Woodlands Av. M27: Swin 4C 76
M30: Ecc 1A 92
M32: Stre 7K 93
M41: Urm 7K 91
M44: Irl 6H 91
M45: Whitef 2L 59
OL11: Roch 7M 27
SK6: Wood 3L 109
SK8: Chea H 5M 117
WN3: I Mak 5J 53
WN7: Lei 7H 73
Woodlands Cl. M28: Wors 3M 75
SK8: Chea H 7M 117
SK13: Tin 3B 100
SK14: B'tom 8J 99
SK15: Stal 2G 98
Woodlands Ct. SK2: Stoc 8J 109
SK9: A Edg 5F 126
WA15: Tim 1F 6
WA16: Knut 6H 133
Woodlands Dr. M33: Sale 7J 105
M46: Ath 6N 55
SK2: Stoc 8G 109
SK6: Wood 3L 109
WA16: Knut 6H 133
WN6: She 8K 33
Woodlands Gro. BL8: Bury 1H 41
SK14: B'tom 8J 99
Woodlands La.
WA15: Tim 1F 6 (2F 114)
Woodlands Mdw. PR7: Chor 2F 18
Woodlands on Stamford, The
OL6: A Lyne 8A 82
(off Stamford St. E.)
Woodlands Pk. SK14: Hyde 7D 98
WA12: N Wil 3F 86
Woodlands Pk. Cl. WN1: Wig 7F 34
Woodlands Pk. Rd. SK2: Stoc 8H 109
Woodlands Parkway
WA15: Tim 1F 6 (1E 114)
Woodlands Rd. BL0: Ram 4K 11
M8: Man 2F 78
M16: Whall R 8D 94
M28: Wors 3M 75
M29: Ast 3C 74
M33: Sale 3J 105
OL6: A Lyne 4B 82
OL16: Miln 8J 29
SK4: Stoc 6J 107
SK9: Hand 3K 123
SK9: Wilm 5E 122
SK11: Macc 6G 130
SK12: Dis 9D 120
SK15: Stal 2G 98
SK22: N Mil 7K 121
WA14: Alt 1D 6 (2D 114)
WA15: Alt 1D 6 (2E 114)
Woodlands St. M8: Man 2F 78
Woodland St. M12: Man 4N 95
OL10: H'ood 2J 43
OL12: Roch 3E 28
Woodlands Vw. OL16: Roch 5G 28
Woodlands Way M24: Mid 5L 61
Woodland Ter. M7: Sal 5C 78
M31: Part 5F 102
Woodland Vw. BL7: Bro X 5J 23
SK14: Hyde 6C 98
Wood La. BL0: Ram 4K 11
M24: Mid 4N 61
M31: Part 5E 102
OL6: A Lyne 5M 81
SK6: Mar 2A 120
WA15: Tim 2G 114
WN8: Par 2B 32
Wood La. E. SK10: Adl 6M 125
WOOD LANE END 5M 125
Wood La. Nth. SK10: Adl 6M 125
Wood La. Sth. SK10: Adl 7L 125
Wood La. W. SK10: Adl 6K 125
Woodlark Cl. M3: Sal 4C 4
Woodlark Dr. PR7: Chor 1C 18
Woodlawn Ct. M16: Whall R 6B 94
Woodlea M28: Wors 2M 75
M30: Ecc 6C 76
OL9: Chad 4B 62
WA15: Alt 3F 114
Woodlea Av. M19: Man 2K 107
Woodlea Chase M27: Clif 6D 58
Woodlea Dr. SK10: Boll 5J 129
Woodlea Rd. SK13: Glos 9D 100
Woodleigh WA14: Alt 2A 114
Woodleigh Ct. SK9: A Edg 3F 126
Woodleigh Dr. M43: Droy 6G 80
Woodleigh Rd. OL4: Spri 4D 64
Woodleigh St. M9: Man 1L 79
WOODLEY 3L 109
Woodley Av. M26: Rad 2H 59
Woodley Bank SK14: Hyde 2N 109
Woodley Cl. SK2: Stoc 9H 109
Woodley Gro. WN7: Lei 5F 72
Woodley Pct. SK6: Wood 3L 109
Woodley Station (Rail) 3M 109
Woodley St. BL9: Bury 4M 41
Woodliffe St. M16: Old T 4B 94
Woodlinn Wlk. M9: Man 3J 79
(off Ravelston Dr.)
Woodman Dr. BL9: Bury 7L 25
Woodman St. SK1: Stoc 1K 9 (6C 108)
Woodmeadow Ct. OL5: Mos 9F 64
Woodmere Dr. M9: Man 8K 61
Wood Mt. WA15: Tim 2H 115
Woodmount Cl. SK6: Rom 6B 110
Woodnewton Cl. M18: Man 5A 96
Woodnook Rd. WN6: App B 4J 33
WOOD PARK 2J 81
Woodpark Cl. OL8: O'ham 8L 63
Woodpecker Pl. M28: Wors 2L 75
Woodridings WA14: Bow 4B 114
WOOD ROAD 4J 25
Wood Rd. M16: Whall R 6B 94
M33: Sale 7H 105
WA15: Tim 7G 105
Wood Rd. La. BL8: Bury 5H 25
BL9: Bury 5H 25
Wood Rd. Nth. M16: Old T 6B 94
Woodrow Wlk. M12: Man 3L 95
(off Clowes St.)
Woodrow Way M44: Irl 1G 103
Woodroyd Cl. SK7: Bram 6B 118
Woodroyd Dr. BL9: Bury 1B 42
Woodruffe Gdns. SK6: Rom 8L 109
Woodruff Wlk. M31: Part 5G 103
Woodrush Rd. WN6: Stan 9A 34
Woods, The OL4: Grot 5E 64
OL11: Roch 9A 28
WA14: Alt 1E 114
Woods Ct. BL1: Bolt 2L 7 (5G 39)
M24: Mid 3H 61
WOODSEATS 2K 111
Woodseats La. SK13: Char 1K 111
Woodseaves Cl. M44: Irl 8J 91
WOODS END 5L 91
Woodsend Circ. M41: Urm 6L 91
(not continuous)
Woodsend Cres. Rd. M41: Urm 7L 91
Woodsend Grn. M41: Urm 6L 91
Woodsend Rd. M41: Urm 5M 91
Woodsend Rd. Sth. M41: Urm 7M 91
(not continuous)
Woods Gro. SK8: Chea H 8N 117
Woodshaw Gro. M28: Wors 2K 75
Woodside OL2: Shaw 4A 46
OL16: Miln 8N 29
PR7: Chor 1H 19
SK4: Stoc 7L 107
SK12: Poy 2K 125
WA16: Knut 7H 133
Woodside Av. M19: Man 3L 107
M28: Walk 9N 57
WA11: St H 9D 68
WN4: A Mak 2D 70
Woodside Cl. OL4: Lees 5B 64
WN8: Uph 3G 50
Woodside Dr. BL0: Ram 9G 11
(off Hillside Rd.)
M6: Sal 7J 77
SK6: H Lan 8B 120
SK11: Macc 6G 130
SK14: Hyde 8B 98
Woodside Gdns. M31: Part 4G 102
(off Lock La.)
Woodside La. SK12: Poy 2J 125
WA13: Lym 6C 112
Woodside M. SK7: Bram 5A 118
Woodside Pl. BL2: Bolt 7K 39
Woodside Rd. M16: Whall R 7A 94
WA11: Hay 2B 86
Woodside Sq. BL2: Bolt 7K 39
Woodside St. SK15: C'ook 4H 83
SK22: N Mil 9L 121
Woodside Tennis Club 9B 120
Woodside Vw. M46: Ath 6N 55
Woods La. OL3: Dob 2K 65
SK8: Chea H 8N 117
WN4: A Mak 5F 70
Woods Lea BL1: Bolt 5A 38
Woodsleigh Coppice BL1: Bolt 5A 38
Woodsley Rd. BL1: Bolt 2A 38
WOODS MOOR 3F 118
Woodsmoor La. SK2: Stoc 3E 118
SK3: Stoc 3E 118
Woodsmoor Rd. M27: Swin 3D 76
Woodsmoor Station (Rail) 3F 118
Woods Mt. HD7: Mars 1K 49
Wood Sorrel Way WA3: Low 1A 88
Woods Pas. OL15: Lit 9K 15
Wood Sq. M43: Droy 1E 96
OL3: G'fld 5L 65
Woods Rd. M44: Irl 9G 91
WN2: Asp 8M 35
Wood's St. WN3: Wig 4F 52
Woodstock Av. SK5: Stoc 3D 108
SK8: Chea H 8M 117
WA12: N Wil 7G 87
Woodstock Bus. Pk. OL2: O'ham 9L 45
Woodstock Cl. OL10: H'ood 2K 43
SK10: Macc 2D 130
WN7: Lei 9G 72
Woodstock Ct. SK9: Hand 1K 123
Woodstock Cres. SK6: Wood 3L 109
Woodstock Dr. BL1: Bolt 3B 38
BL8: Tot 6D 24
M27: Swin 4G 77
M28: Wors 5A 76
Woodstock Grn. OL8: O'ham 8L 63
SK5: Stoc 2E 108
Woodstock Rd. M16: Old T 6A 94
M40: Man 1A 80
SK6: Wood 3L 109
WA14: B'ath 8C 104
Woodstock St.
OL4: O'ham 5E 8 (6K 63)
OL12: Roch 4A 28
Wood St. BL0: Ram 9H 11
BL1: Bolt 3L 7 (5G 39)
BL5: W'ton 3G 55
BL6: Hor 1E 36
BL8: Bury 1J 41
M3: Man 5E 4 (9D 78)
M11: Man 1N 95
M24: Mid 1J 61
M26: Rad 3E 58
M29: Tyld 2C 74
M30: Ecc 9F 76
M34: Dent 5K 97
M46: Ath 7K 55
OL1: O'ham 3M 63
OL2: Shaw 4J 45
OL6: A Lyne 8C 6 (8M 81)
OL10: H'ood 2J 43
OL15: Lit 9M 15
OL16: Miln 9N 29
OL16: Roch 9E 8 (7E 28)
SK3: Stoc 4G 9 (8B 108)
SK8: Chea 1J 117
SK11: Macc 5H 131
(not continuous)
SK13: Glos 9E 100
SK14: Holl 4N 99
SK14: Hyde 7B 98
SK15: Stal 8D 82
SK16: Duk 3N 97
SK22: N Mil 8L 121
WA3: Gol 1L 87
WA14: Alt 3D 6 (3D 114)
WN2: Hin 8D 54
WN3: Wig 4F 52
WN5: Wig 4C 52
Wood Ter. BL2: Ain 3D 40
Woodthorpe Ct. M25: Pres 9C 60
Woodthorpe Dr. SK8: Chea H 5M 117
Woodthorpe Grange M25: Pres 9C 60
Wood Top BL0: Ram 7H 11
(off Glen St.)
HD7: Mars 1H 49
Wood Top Av. OL11: Roch 8L 27
Wood Top Cl. SK2: Stoc 9J 109
Woodvale M24: Mid 8M 43
WA14: Bow 5D 114
Woodvale Av. BL3: Bolt 1E 56
M46: Ath 6K 55
WN2: Asp 9B 36
Woodvale Dr. BL3: Bolt 1E 56
WA3: Low 9A 72
Woodvale Gdns. BL3: Bolt 1E 56
Woodvale Gro. BL3: Bolt 1E 56
Woodvale Pk. SK15: Stal 8C 82
(off Stamford St.)
Woodvale Rd. M26: Rad 2H 59
WA16: Knut 8G 133
Woodvale Wlk. M11: Man 9L 79
(off Redfield Cl.)
Wood Vw. M22: Nor 7C 106
OL10: H'ood 9H 27
Woodview WN6: She 6M 33
Woodview Av. M19: Man 3L 107
Woodville Dr. M33: Sale 3G 104
SK6: Mar 2A 120
SK15: Stal 7G 82
Woodville Gro. SK5: Stoc 2D 108
Woodville Rd. M33: Sale 3G 104
PR6: H Char 1J 19
WA14: Alt 4A 6 (3C 114)
WN3: I Mak 7J 53
Woodville Ter. M40: Man 1L 79
Woodward Cl. BL9: Bury 8M 25
Woodward Ct. M4: Man 2N 5 (8J 79)
Woodward Pl. M4: Man 3N 5 (8H 79)
Woodward Rd. M25: Pres 9M 59
Woodwards Rd. BL5: W'ton 5H 55
Woodward St. M4: Man 3N 5 (8H 79)
Woodwise La. M23: Wyth 7L 105
Wood Yd. OL16: Roch 3H 45
Woodyates St. WN5: Wig 5C 52
Woolden Rd. M44: Cad 1B 102
Woolden St. M30: Ecc 7B 76
WN5: Wig 5C 52
Wooler Gro. WN2: Hin 9N 53
Woolfall Cl. M12: Man 3M 95
WOOLFOLD 9H 25
Woolfold Trad. Est. BL8: Bury 9H 25
Woollacot St. OL1: O'ham 2E 8 (4K 63)
Woollam Pl. M3: Man 6C 4 (1C 94)
Woolley Av. SK12: Poy 4H 125
WOOLLEY BRIDGE 5N 99
Woolley Bri. SK13: Had 5A 100
Woolley Bri. Rd. SK13: Had 5A 100
Woolley Cl. SK14: Holl 3N 99
Woolley La. SK14: Holl 3N 99
(Meadowbank)
SK14: Holl 5M 99
(Samuel St.)
Woolley Mill La. SK13: Tin 2N 99
Woolley St. M8: Man 6E 78
OL6: A Lyne 4B 82
Woolley Ter. SK16: Duk 9M 81
(off Queen St.)
Woolmore Av. OL1: O'ham 2J 63
Woolpack Grn. M6: Sal 7M 77
(off Arbour Cl.)
Wool Rd. OL3: Dob 1L 65
Woolston Dr. M29: Tyld 2D 74
Woolston Ho. M6: Sal 6J 77
(off Moss Mdw. Rd.)
Woolston Rd. WA11: Hay 2A 86
Woolton Cl. M40: Man 9A 62
(off Pleasington Dr.)
WN4: A Mak 5C 70
Woolton Hall M14: Man 8J 95
Wootton St. SK14: Hyde 5A 98
Worcester Av. M23: Wyth 8M 105
M34: Dent 8L 97
SK5: Stoc 3G 109
WA3: Gol 1L 87
WN2: Hin 5B 54
Worcester Cl. BL9: Bury 4N 41
M6: Sal 6J 77
OL6: A Lyne 2A 82
SK6: Rom 7L 109
Worcester Gro.
SK13: Glos 9H 101
Worcester Pl. PR7: Chor 2H 19
Worcester Rd. BL3: Lit L 9N 39
M6: Sal 6J 77
M24: Mid 6L 61
M27: Ward 9D 58
M33: Sale 5D 104
SK8: Chea H 3M 117
Worcester St. BL1: Bolt 3F 38
BL8: Bury 9K 25
OL9: O'ham 6F 62
OL11: Roch 9C 28
Wordsworth Av. BL4: Farn 4J 57
BL9: Bury 6M 41
M8: Man 4F 78
M26: Rad 9E 40
M43: Droy 8E 80
M46: Ath 6N 55
WN1: Wig 9F 34
WN5: Bil 1H 69
WN5: Orr 5K 51
WN7: Lei 3F 72
Wordsworth Cl. SK16: Duk 2D 98
Wordsworth Cres. OL7: A Lyne 5J 81
OL15: Lit 3K 29
Wordsworth Gdns. M25: Pres 8M 59
Wordsworth Ho. SK10: Macc 3D 130
(off Priory Ct.)
Wordsworth Ind. Est. BL1: Bolt 2E 38
(off Wordsworth St.)
Wordsworth Rd. M16: Old T 6A 94
M24: Mid 1N 61
M27: Swin 1D 76
M34: Dent 1L 109
M38: Lit H 6J 57
OL1: O'ham 2M 63
SK5: Stoc 8B 96
Wordsworth St. BL1: Bolt 3E 38
Wordsworth Way OL11: Roch 7K 27
Workesleigh St. M40: Man 5A 80
World Trade Cen. M5: Sal 3N 93
World Way M90: Man A 7A 116
Worrall St. M5: Sal 8A 4 (2B 94)
M40: Man 4M 79
OL12: Roch 3B 28
SK3: Stoc 9C 108
(not continuous)
Worrell Cl. M26: Rad 8F 40
Worsbrough Av. M28: Walk 9K 57
Worsefold St. M40: Man 2M 79
Worsel St. BL3: Bolt 8D 38
WORSLEY 3M 75
Worsley Av. M28: Walk 8H 57
M40: Man 1L 79
Worsley Brow M28: Wors 4N 75
Worsley Bus. Pk. M28: Wors 2G 74
Worsley Cl. WN5: Wig 6N 51
Worsley Ct. M14: Man 7H 95
M28: Walk 8L 57
Worsley Cres. SK2: Stoc 9G 108
Worsley Gdns. M28: Walk 7K 57
(off Mountain St.)
Worsley Golf Course 6C 76
Worsley Grn. WN5: Wig 6M 51
Worsley Gro. M19: Man 8M 95
M28: Walk 9H 57
WORSLEY HALL 4C 52
WORSLEY MESNES 7D 52
Worsley Mesnes Dr. WN3: Wig 6C 52
Worsley Mill M3: Man 8C 4 (1C 94)
Worsley Pk. Golf Course 3M 75
Worsley Pl. OL2: Shaw 6L 45
OL16: Roch 8G 8 (6F 28)
Worsley Point M27: Swin 4E 76
Worsley Rd. BL3: Bolt 8B 38
BL4: Farn 5L 57
M27: Swin 4C 76
M28: Wors 5N 75
M30: Ecc 6A 76
Worsley Rd. Ind. Est. BL4: Farn 5L 57
Worsley Rd. Nth. M28: Walk 6L 57
Worsley St. BL3: Bolt 7F 38
BL8: Tot 6E 24
M3: Sal 3E 4 (8D 78)
M15: Man 8B 4 (2C 94)
M27: Pen 9F 58
M27: Swin 3G 77
OL8: O'ham 6M 63
OL16: Roch 9G 8 (6F 28)
WA3: Gol 1K 87
WN5: Wig 6M 51
Worsley Ter. WN1: Wig 6K 9 (2F 52)
Worsley Trad. Est. M38: Lit H 6F 56
Worsley Vw. M29: Ast 5D 74
Worston Av. BL1: Bolt 1A 38
Worth Ct. SK12: Poy 4G 125
Worthenbury Wlk. M13: Man 6K 95
Worthing Cl. SK2: Stoc 1H 119
Worthing Gro. M46: Ath 8K 55
Worthing St. M14: Man 7G 95
Worthington Av. M31: Part 5G 103
OL10: H'ood 5K 43
Worthington Cl. OL7: A Lyne 5L 81
SK11: Hen 4A 130
SK14: Hat 7H 99
Worthington Ct. M33: Sale 4L 105
Worthington Dr. M7: Sal 1C 78
Worthington Fold M46: Ath 8K 55
Worthington Lakes Country Pk. 2F 34
Worthington Lakes Vis. Cen. 3F 34
Worthington Rd. M33: Sale 4L 105
M34: Dent 8M 97
Worthington St. BL3: Bolt 9D 38
M16: Old T 5B 94
M40: Man 2A 80
OL7: A Lyne 5L 81
SK15: Stal 9C 82
WN2: Hin 5N 53
Worthington Way M34: Dent 5J 97
WN3: Wig 9B 52
Worth's La. M34: Dent 1L 109
Wortley Av. M6: Sal 7J 77
Wortley Gro. M40: Man 9N 61
Wotton Dr. WN4: A Mak 7G 70
Wragby Cl. BL8: Bury 8K 25
Wrath Cl. BL2: Bolt 8J 23
Wraxhall Cres. WN7: Lei 3F 72
Wray Cl. M22: Wyth 3C 116
Wray Gdns. M19: Man 9A 96
Wray Pl. OL16: Roch 7G 28
Wraysbury Wlk. M40: Man 4M 79
(off Hugo St.)
Wray St. WN1: I Mak 3H 53
Wrayton Lodge M33: Sale 5H 105
Wrekin Av. M23: Wyth 4N 115
Wren Av. M27: Clif 8H 59
Wrenbury Av. M20: Man 1E 106
Wrenbury Cl. WN5: Wig 6M 51
Wrenbury Cres. SK3: Stoc 1A 118
Wrenbury Dr. BL1: Bolt 7G 23
OL16: Roch 1G 44
SK8: Chea 1K 117
Wrenbury Wlk. M33: Sale 5L 105
(off Mottram Rd.)
Wren Cl. BL4: Farn 3G 56
M34: Aud 9G 81
SK2: Stoc 2K 119
SK10: Macc 3E 130
WN5: Orr 2M 51
Wren Dr. BL9: Bury 9A 26
M44: Irl 5H 91
Wren Gdns. M24: Mid 2L 61
Wrengate Ho. M20: Man 5E 106
Wren Grn. OL16: Roch 7G 28
Wren Nest Cl. SK13: Glos 9D 100
Wren Nest Mill SK13: Glos 8D 100
Wren Nest Rd. SK13: Glos 8D 100
Wren Nest Ter. SK13: Glos 8D 100
Wrenshot La. WA16: H Leg 9D 112
Wrens Nest Av. OL2: Shaw 4N 45
Wren St. OL4: O'ham 5N 63
Wrenswood Dr. M28: Wors 2K 75
Wren Way M11: Man 1K 95
OL16: Roch 7G 29
Wrexham Cl. OL8: O'ham 9F 62
Wrigglesworth Cl. BL8: Bury 1F 40
Wrightington St.
WN1: Wig 6J 9 (2F 52)
Wright Robinson Cl. M11: Man 1K 95
Wright Robinson Hall M1: Man 7K 5
Wrights Bank Nth. SK2: Stoc 2J 119
Wright St. BL6: Hor 9D 20
M16: Old T 3B 94
M26: Rad 9F 40
M34: Aud 1J 97
M35: Fail 2D 80
OL1: O'ham 2F 8 (4L 63)
OL6: A Lyne 6A 82
OL9: Chad 6F 62
WA14: B'ath 9C 104
WN1: Wig 5N 9 (2H 53)
WN2: Abr 3L 71
WN2: P Bri 8K 53
WN4: A Mak 4C 70
Wright St. W. BL6: Hor 9D 20
(off Julia St.)
Wright Tree Vs. M44: Cad 3E 102
Wrigley Cres. M35: Fail 3D 80
Wrigley Fold M24: Mid 9H 43
Wrigley Head M35: Fail 2D 80
Wrigley Head Cres. M35: Fail 2D 80
Wrigley La. SK10: O Ald 9M 127
Wrigley Pl. OL15: Lit 2K 29
Wrigley Rd. WA11: Hay 3B 86
Wrigley's Pl. OL8: O'ham 8J 63
Wrigley Sq. OL4: Lees 5C 64
SK14: Hyde 1B 110
(off Rowbotham St.)
Wrigley St. OL4: Lees 5B 64
OL4: O'ham 4M 63
OL4: Scout 3E 64
OL6: A Lyne 6M 81
Wrington Cl. WN7: Lei 2F 72
Wroe St. M3: Sal 4B 4
M27: Pen 8F 58
OL4: Spri 5C 64
Wroe Ter. M27: Clif 8F 58
Wrotham Cl. M5: Sal 9N 77
Wroxeter Wlk. M12: Man 3L 95
(off Witterage Cl.)
Wroxham Av. M34: Dent 6E 96
M41: Urm 6B 92
Wroxham Cl. BL8: Bury 8K 25
Wroxham Rd. M9: Man 8G 61
WUERDLE 1J 29
Wuerdle Cl. OL16: Roch 2J 29
Wuerdle Farm Way OL16: Roch 1J 29
Wuerdle Pl. OL16: Roch 1J 29
Wuerdle St. OL16: Roch 1J 29
Wyatt Av. M5: Sal 2A 94
Wyatt Gro. WN4: A Mak 7G 71
Wyatt St. SK4: Stoc 1H 9 (6C 108)
SK16: Duk 1N 97
Wybersley Rd. SK6: H Lan 7D 120
Wychbury St. M6: Sal 6L 77
Wychelm Rd. M31: Part 5G 102
Wycherley Rd. OL12: Roch 3N 27
Wych Fold SK14: Hyde 1B 110
(not continuous)
Wych La. SK10: Adl 9H 125
Wych St. OL6: A Lyne 8C 6 (8M 81)
Wychwood WA14: Bow 6B 114
Wychwood Cl. M24: Mid 4N 61
Wycliffe Av. SK9: Wilm 7F 122
Wycliffe Ct. M41: Urm 7C 92
(off Flixton Rd.)

Wycliffe Rd. M41: Urm 7C 92
WA11: Hay 2B 86
Wycliffe St. *M30: Ecc* *8C 76*
(off Watson St.)
SK4: Stoc 1H 9 (6B 108)
Wycombe Av. M18: Man 3C 96
Wycombe Cl. M41: Urm 4C 92
Wycombe Dr. M29: Ast 3C 74
Wye Av. M35: Fail 3D 80
Wyecroft Cl. SK6: Wood 3M 109
Wye St. OL8: O'ham 6H 63
Wye Wlk. BL8: Bury 7G 25
Wykeham Chase SK11: Macc 5D 130
Wykeham Cl. WN3: I Mak 5J 53
Wykeham Gro. OL12: Roch 4N 27
Wykeham M. BL1: Bolt 5B 38
Wykeham St. M14: Man 6F 94
Wyke Pk. OL4: O'ham 5A 64
Wylam Wlk. M12: Man 6N 95
Wylde, The BL9: Bury 7K 7 (2L 41)
Wynard Av. WN1: Wig 5M 9 (2G 53)
Wynchgate Rd.
SK7: H Gro 4L 119
Wyndale Dr. M35: Fail 5D 80
Wyndale Rd. OL8: O'ham 8K 63
Wyndcliffe Dr. M41: Urm 8M 91
Wyndham Av. BL3: Bolt 1B 56
M27: Clif 9F 58
Wyndham Cl. SK7: Bram 8C 118
Wyne Cl. SK7: H Gro 4L 119
Wynfield Av. M22: Wyth 8E 116
Wynford Sq. M50: Sal 9M 77
Wyngate Rd. SK8: Chea H 6L 117
WA15: Hale 7F 114
Wynne Av. M27: Clif 8F 58
Wynne Cl. M11: Man 1L 95
M34: Dent 8K 97
Wynne Gro. M34: Dent 8K 97
Wynne St. BL1: Bolt 2F 38
M6: Sal 7A 78
M29: Tyld 1A 74
M38: Lit H 7H 57
Wynnstay Gro. M14: Man 9H 95
Wynnstay Rd. M33: Sale 3H 105
Wynn St. M40: Man 1C 80
Wynton Cl. WN7: Lei 8G 72
Wynyard Cl. M33: Sale 6K 105
Wynyard Rd. M22: Wyth 4B 116
Wyre Av. WN2: P Bri 9K 53
Wyre Cl. M45: Whitef 2A 60
Wyredale Cl. WN2: P Bri 9J 53
Wyre Dr. M28: Wors 3J 75
Wyresdale Rd. BL1: Bolt 4D 38
Wyre St. M1: Man 7L 5 (1G 95)
OL5: Mos 1F 82
Wyrevale Gro. WN4: A Mak 7F 70
Wythall Av. M38: Lit H 5J 57
Wythburn Av. BL1: Bolt 3B 38
M8: Man 4H 79
M41: Urm 6B 92
Wythburn Cres. WA11: St H 9F 68
Wythburn Rd. M24: Mid 9K 43
SK1: Stoc 9F 108
Wythburn St. M6: Sal 8L 77
WYTHENSHAWE 5C 116
Wythenshawe Community Farm 8N 105
Wythenshawe Hall 8A 106
Wythenshawe Pk. 8N 105
Wythenshawe Rd. M23: Wyth 8L 105
M33: Sale 4L 105
Wythens Rd. SK8: H Grn 7G 116
Wythop Gdns. M5: Sal 9N 77
Wyvern Av. SK5: Stoc 3C 108
Wyverne Rd. M21: Cho H 8C 94
Wyville Cl. SK7: H Gro 4L 119
Wyville Dr. M6: Sal 7M 77
M9: Man 5G 60
M27: Swin 4E 76
Wyvis Cl. OL9: Chad 2E 62

X

XQ7 Building M5: Sal 3N 93

Y

Yale Rd. M18: Man 4N 95
Yarburgh St. M16: Whall R 6D 94
Yardley Av. M32: Stre 7G 93
Yardley Cl. M32: Stre 7G 93
Yarmouth Dr. M23: Wyth 7A 106
Yarn Cft. M29: Ast 2C 74
Yarnton Cl. OL2: O'ham 7L 45
Yarrow Cl. OL11: Roch 8D 28
Yarrow Gro. BL6: Hor 9D 20
Yarrow Pl. BL1: Bolt 3F 38
Yarrow St. WN2: Hin 7M 53
Yarrow Valley Country Pk. 3C 18
Yarrow Valley Vis. Cen. 2D 18
Yarrow Valley Way PR7: Chor 1C 18
Yarrow Wlk. M45: Whitef 2B 60
Yarwell OL12: Roch 5B 8
Yarwood Av. M23: Wyth 9M 105
Yarwood Cl. OL10: H'ood 1K 43
Yarwoodheath La. WA14: Rost 7M 113
Yarwood St. BL9: Bury 7N 7 (2N 41)
WA14: Alt 4D 114
Yasmin Gdns. OL1: O'ham 2H 63
Yates Dr. M28: Walk 8H 57
Yates Gro. WN6: Wig 8C 34
Yates Rd. SK22: N Mil 8M 121
Yates St. BL2: Bolt 3H 39
M24: Mid 4H 61
OL1: O'ham 3L 63
SK1: Stoc 5F 108
WN3: Wig 4D 52
WN7: Lei 3G 73
Yattendon Av. M23: Wyth 8K 105
Y Club, The 6D 4 (1D 94)
Yeadon Rd. M18: Man 6B 96
Yea Fold OL15: Lit 2J 29
Yealand Av. SK4: Stoc 5B 108
Yealand Cl. OL11: Roch 7N 27
Yealand Gro. WN2: Hin 6C 54
Yeardsley Cl. SK7: Bram 4C 118
Yeargate Ind. Est. BL9: Bury 2C 42
Yellow Brook Cl. WN2: Asp 6M 35
Yellow Lodge Dr. BL5: W'ton 2K 55
Yeoford Dr. WA14: Alt 1B 114
Yeoman Cl. SK7: H Gro 4H 119
Yeomanry Ct. M16: Whall R 6C 94
Yeoman's Cl. OL16: Miln 6K 29
Yeoman Wlk. M11: Man 9L 79
Yeovil St. M16: Whall R 6E 94
Yewbarrow Cl. M29: Ast 3C 74
Yewbarrow Rd. OL1: O'ham 3L 63
Yew Cl. BL3: Bolt 8D 38
Yew Ct. OL12: Roch 3F 28
Yew Cres. OL4: O'ham 3A 64
Yewdale M27: Clif 9H 59
WN6: She 6M 33
Yewdale Av. BL2: Bolt 2N 39
WA11: St H 9F 68
Yewdale Cres. WN1: Wig 9E 34
Yewdale Dr. M24: Mid 2K 61
M35: Fail 2G 80
Yew Dale Gdns.
OL11: Roch 9N 27
Yewdale Gdns. BL2: Bolt 2N 39
Yewdale Rd. SK1: Stoc 1F 118
WN4: A Mak 3D 70
Yew Gro. WN6: Wig 9C 34
Yewlands Av. M9: Man 6J 61
Yewlands Dr. WA16: Knut 7J 133
Yew St. BL9: Bury 1B 42
M7: Sal 4B 78
M15: Man 4D 94
M34: Aud 4K 97
OL10: H'ood 2G 43
SK4: Stoc 8N 107
YEW TREE 2C 98
Yew Tree Av. M14: Man 7F 94
M19: Man 8M 95
M22: Nor 7C 106
M46: Ath 7L 55
SK7: H Gro 6K 119
WA12: N Wil 5D 86
Yew Tree Cl. OL7: A Lyne 4L 81
OL11: Roch 3F 44
SK6: Mar 2B 120
SK9: Wilm 7J 123
SK10: P'bury 6F 128
SK11: Macc 6E 130
Yewtree Cl. PR7: Chor 2F 18
Yew Tree Cotts. OL3: Dig 6M 47
SK6: Comp 5E 110
Yew Tree Cres. M14: Man 8G 95
Yew Tree Dr. BL6: Los 6K 37
M22: Nor 7C 106
M25: Pres 7A 60
M33: Sale 4L 105
M41: Urm 5N 91
OL9: Chad 4B 62
SK6: Bred 5H 109
Yew Tree Gro. SK8: H Grn 4F 116
Yew Tree La. BL1: Bolt 8H 23
M22: Nor 7C 106
M23: Wyth 6A 106
(not continuous)
SK12: Poy 4J 125
SK16: Duk 2B 98
Yew Tree Pk. Rd. SK8: Chea H 9N 117
Yew Tree Rd. M14: Man 6G 94
M20: Man 1G 106
M34: Dent 8J 97
SK3: Stoc 4D 118
SK10: Adl 5M 125
Yew Tree Trad. Est.
WA11: Hay 1C 86
Yew Tree Way SK10: P'bury 7F 128
WA3: Gol 2L 87
Yew Wlk. M31: Part 6F 102
York Arc. *M1: Man* *5J 5*
(off Parker St.)
York Av. BL3: Lit L 9A 40
M16: Whall R 7B 94
M25: Pres 9C 60
M27: Swin 9D 58
M29: Tyld 9A 56
M33: Sale 3H 105
M41: Urm 6E 92
OL8: O'ham 7H 63
OL11: Roch 7M 27
WA3: Cul 7H 89
York Chambers
WN1: Wig 8J 9
York Cl. M34: Dent 5K 97
SK8: Chea 2M 117
York Cres. SK9: Wilm 7H 123
Yorkdale OL4: O'ham 4A 64
York Dr. BL0: Ram 1G 25
M90: Man A 8M 115
SK7: H Gro 5L 119
WA14: Bow 6D 114
York Ho. M33: Sale 3H 105
York Pl. OL6: A Lyne 9A 6 (8L 81)
PR6: Adl 5K 19
York Rd. M21: Cho H 9A 94
M33: Sale 3G 105
M34: Dent 5J 97
M43: Droy 7D 80
M44: Cad 3E 102
OL9: Chad 3D 62
SK4: Stoc 3N 107
SK14: Hyde 9B 98
WA14: Bow 6C 114
WN2: Hin 6B 54
WN4: A Mak 7E 70
York Rd. E. M24: Mid 6A 62
York Rd. Sth.
WN4: A Mak 8F 70
York Rd. W. M24: Mid 6A 62
Yorkshire Rd. M31: Part 6F 102
Yorkshire St. M3: Sal 3E 4 (8D 78)
OL1: O'ham 2D 8 (4K 63)
OL6: A Lyne 5C 6 (6M 81)
(not continuous)
OL12: Roch 5E 8 (5E 28)
OL16: Roch 7C 8 (6D 28)
(not continuous)
Yorkshire Ter. *OL5: Mos* *1F 82*
(off Mill St.)
Yorkshire Way SK13: Glos 9H 101
York St. BL4: Farn 3M 57
BL9: Bury 7N 7 (2N 41)
M1: Man 7H 5 (1F 94)
M2: Man 4H 5 (9F 78)
York St. M9: Man 2K 79
(not continuous)
M13: Man 9J 5 (2F 94)
M19: Man 9M 95
M20: Man 5G 106
M26: Rad 7K 41
M34: Aud 1J 97
M45: Whitef 3M 59
M46: Ath 8M 55
OL9: O'ham 3B 8 (5J 63)
OL10: H'ood 2J 43
OL16: Roch 7F 28
SK3: Stoc 4J 9 (8C 108)
SK10: Macc 4J 131
SK13: Glos 8G 100
WA3: Gol 9K 71
WA15: Alt 5D 6 (4E 114)
WN3: Wig 8G 9 (3E 52)
WN7: Lei 6M 73
York Ter. *BL1: Bolt* *2F 38*
(off Boardman St.)
M33: Sale 2G 105
SK13: Glos 9E 100
Youd St. WN7: Lei 5H 73
Youlgreave Cres. SK13: Gam 8N 99
Young St. BL0: Ram 8H 11
BL4: Farn 4M 57
M3: Man 5E 4 (9D 78)
M26: Rad 7F 40
WN7: Lei 6N 73
Yulan Dr. M33: Sale 4C 104
Yule St. SK3: Stoc 5G 9 (8B 108)
Yvonne Cl. WN4: A Mak 5G 71

Z

Zama St. BL0: Ram 1G 25
Zandra Ho. *M16: Whall R* *6C 94*
(off Dudley Rd.)
Zealand St. OL4: O'ham 3N 63
Zedburgh
OL12: Roch 5B 8 (5C 28)
Zeta St. M9: Man 3L 79
Zetland Av. BL3: Bolt 1C 56
Zetland Av. Nth. BL3: Bolt 1C 56
Zetland M. *SK16: Duk* *9N 81*
(off Zetland St.)
Zetland Pl. OL16: Roch 5F 28
Zetland Rd. M21: Cho H 9A 94
Zetland St. SK16: Duk 9N 81
Zinc Ct. *M25: Pres* *6N 59*
(off Longfield Cen.)
Zinnia Dr. M44: Irl 9F 90
Zion Arts Cen. 3D 94
Zion Cres. *M15: Man* *3D 94*
(off Stretford Rd.)
Zion Ter. OL12: Roch 3K 27
Zorbit M. SK14: Hyde 5A 98
Zulu St. BL2: Bolt 5J 39
Zurich Gdns. SK7: Bram 4C 118
Zyburn Ct. M6: Sal 7G 77

HOSPITALS, HOSPICES and selected HEALTHCARE FACILITIES covered by this atlas.

N.B. Where it is not possible to name these facilities on the map, the reference given is for the road in which they are situated.

ALEXANDRA BMI HOSPITAL 1J **117**
Mill Lane
CHEADLE
SK8 2PX
Tel: 0161 4283656

ALPHA HOSPITAL, BURY 3J **41**
Buller Street
BURY
BL8 2BS
Tel: 0161 762 7200

ALTRINCHAM GENERAL HOSPITAL 3C **6** (3D **114**)
Market Street
ALTRINCHAM
WA14 1PE
Tel: 0161 9348464

ALTRINCHAM PRIORY HOSPITAL 8G **115**
Rappax Road
Hale
ALTRINCHAM
WA15 0NX
Tel: 0161 9040050

BEALEY COMMUNITY HOSPITAL 8K **41**
Dumers Lane
Radcliffe
MANCHESTER
M26 2QD
Tel: 0161 7259800

BEAUMONT BMI HOSPITAL 4L **37**
Old Hall Clough
Chorley New Road
Lostock
BOLTON
BL6 4LA
Tel: 01204 404404

BEECHWOOD CANCER CARE CENTRE .2B **118**
Chelford Grove
STOCKPORT
SK3 8LS
Tel: 0161 4760384

BIRCH HILL HOSPITAL 9J **15**
Union Road
ROCHDALE
OL12 9QB
Tel: 01706 377777

BOLTON HOSPICE 5E **38**
Queens Park Street
BOLTON
BL1 4QT
Tel: 01204 663066

BRIDGEWATER HOSPITAL 5E **94**
120 Princess Road
MANCHESTER
M15 5AT
Tel: 0161 227 0000

BURY HOSPICE 8K **41**
Dumers Lane
Radcliffe
MANCHESTER
M26 2QD
Tel: 0161 7259800

CHERRY TREE HOSPITAL 2G **119**
Cherry Tree Lane
STOCKPORT
SK2 7PZ
Tel: 0161 4831010

CHRISTIE HOSPITAL 2G **107**
Wilmslow Road
MANCHESTER
M20 4BX
Tel: 0161 446 3000

DR. KERSHAW'S HOSPICE 9K **45**
Turf Lane
Royton
OLDHAM
OL2 6EU
Tel: 0161 6242727

EAST CHESHIRE HOSPICE 3D **130**
Millbank Drive
MACCLESFIELD
SK10 3DR
Tel: 01625 610364

EMERGENCY CARE WALK-IN CENTRE 1J **117**
The Alexandra BMI Hospital
Mill Lane
CHEADLE
SK8 2PX
Tel: 0161 4282161

FAIRFIELD GENERAL HOSPITAL 9D **26**
Rochdale Old Road
BURY
BL9 7TD
Tel: 0161 6240420

FAIRFIELD INDEPENDENT HOSPITAL 8C **68**
Crank Road
Crank
ST. HELENS
WA11 7RS
Tel: 01744 739311

FRANCIS HOUSE CHILDREN'S HOSPICE 6H **107**
390 Parrs Wood Road
MANCHESTER
M20 5NA
Tel: 0161 4344118

GREATER MANCHESTER SURGICAL CENTRE 6A **92**
Trafford General Hospital
Moorside Road
Urmston
MANCHESTER
M41 5SL
Tel: 0161 746 2828

HIGHBANK PRIORY CENTRE (EATING DISORDERS) 3L **25**
Walmersley Road
BURY
BL9 5LX
Tel: 01706 829540

HIGHBANK PRIORY REHABILITATION CENTRE (ELTON UNIT) . . .9F **24**
Walshaw Road
Elton
BURY
BL8 3AL
Tel: 01706 829540

HIGHFIELD BMI HOSPITAL 8B **28**
Manchester Road
ROCHDALE
OL11 4LZ
Tel: 01706 655121

KNUTSFORD DISTRICT COMMUNITY HOSPITAL 7F **132**
Bexton Road
KNUTSFORD
WA16 0BT
Tel: 01565 757220

LEIGH INFIRMARY 3J **73**
The Avenue
LEIGH
WN7 1HS
Tel: 01942 244000

MACCLESFIELD DISTRICT GENERAL HOSPITAL 4F **130**
Victoria Road
MACCLESFIELD
SK10 3BL
Tel: 01625 421000

MANCHESTER ROYAL EYE HOSPITAL .4H **95**
Oxford Road
MANCHESTER
M13 9WL
Tel: 0161 276 1234

MANCHESTER ROYAL INFIRMARY 4H **95**
Oxford Road
MANCHESTER
M13 9WL
Tel: 0161 276 1234

MANCHESTER SPIRE HOSPITAL 6C **94**
Russell Road
Whalley Range
MANCHESTER
M16 8AJ
Tel: 0161 2260112

MEADOWS HOSPITAL 9J **109**
Owens Farm Drive
STOCKPORT
SK2 5EQ
Tel: 0161 419 6000

NEIL CLIFFE CANCER CARE CENTRE .3M **115**
Wythenshawe Hospital
Southmoor Road
MANCHESTER
M23 9LT
Tel: 0161 2912912

NEWTON COMMUNITY HOSPITAL 7E **86**
Bradlegh Road
NEWTON-LE-WILLOWS
WA12 8RB
Tel: 01925 222731

NHS WALK-IN CENTRE (BOLTON) 4K **7**
Lever Chambers
27 Ashburner Street
BOLTON
BL1 1SQ
Tel: 01204 462787

NHS WALK-IN CENTRE (BURY) .6N **7** (1N **41**)
Moorgate Primary Care Centre
22 Derby Way
BURY
BL9 0NJ

NHS WALK-IN CENTRE (CENTRAL MANCHESTER PCT) 4H **95**
Oxford Road
MANCHESTER
M13 9WL

NHS WALK-IN CENTRE (LEIGH) 3J **73**
Leigh Infirmary
The Avenue
LEIGH
WN7 1HS
Tel: 01942 483453

NHS WALK-IN CENTRE (LITTLE HULTON) 7H **57**
Haysbrook Avenue
Worsley
MANCHESTER
M28 0AY

NHS WALK-IN CENTRE (MANCHESTER, MARKET STREET) 4G **5**
32 Market Street
MANCHESTER
M1 1PL
Tel: 0161 8396227

NHS WALK-IN CENTRE (OLDHAM) 3B **8** (4J **63**)
New Radcliffe Street
OLDHAM
OL8 1NL
Tel: 0161 621 3737

NHS WALK-IN CENTRE (PRESTWICH) 6N **59**
Fairfax Road
Prestwich
MANCHESTER
M25 1BT

NHS WALK-IN CENTRE (ROCHDALE) 4D **28**
90 Whitehall Street
ROCHDALE
OL12 0ND

NHS WALK-IN CENTRE (SKELMERSDALE) 2A **50**
116-118 The Concourse Shopping Centre
SKELMERSDALE
WN8 6LJ
Tel: 01695 554260

NHS WALK-IN CENTRE (WYTHENSHAWE FORUM) 5B **116**
Forum Centre
Forum Square
Simonsway
Wythenshawe
MANCHESTER
M22 5RX
Tel: 0161 435 3694

NORTH MANCHESTER GENERAL HOSPITAL 1G **79**
Delaunays Road
MANCHESTER
M8 5RB
Tel: 0161 795 4567

OAKLANDS PRIVATE HOSPITAL 6H **77**
19 Lancaster Road
SALFORD
M6 8AQ
Tel: 0161 7877700

ORCHARD HOUSE DAY HOSPITAL 8J **45**
Milton Street
Royton
OLDHAM
OL2 6QX
Tel: 0161 6336219

PRESTWICH SITE (GREATER MANCHESTER WEST TRUST) . . .6M **59**
Bury New Road
Prestwich
MANCHESTER
M25 3BL
Tel: 0161 773 9121

PRIORY CHEADLE ROYAL HOSPITAL 5H **117**
100 Wilmslow Road
CHEADLE
SK8 3DG
Tel: 0161 4289511

REGENCY SPIRE HOSPITAL 4F **130**
West Street
MACCLESFIELD
SK11 8DW
Tel: 01625 501150

ROCHDALE INFIRMARY 4C **28**
Whitehall Street
ROCHDALE
OL12 0NB
Tel: 01706 377777

ROYAL ALBERT EDWARD INFIRMARY 9F **34**
Wigan Lane
WIGAN
WN1 2NN
Tel: 01942 244000

ROYAL BOLTON HOSPITAL 2G **56**
Minerva Road
Farnworth
BOLTON
BL4 0JR
Tel: 01204 390390

ROYAL MANCHESTER CHILDREN'S HOSPITAL 5H **95**
Oxford Road
MANCHESTER
M13 9WL
Tel: 0161 276 1234

ROYAL OLDHAM HOSPITAL 2H **63**
Rochdale Road
OLDHAM
OL1 2JH
Tel: 0161 624 0420

ST ANN'S HOSPICE (HEALD GREEN) 5H **117**
St Ann's Road North
Heald Green
CHEADLE
SK8 3SZ
Tel: 0161 4378136

ST ANN'S HOSPICE (LITTLE HULTON) 7H **57**
Meadowsweet Lane
(Off Peel Lane)
Worsley
MANCHESTER
M28 0FE
Tel: 0161 702 8181

ST MARY'S HOSPITAL (FOR WOMEN & CHILDREN) 5H **95**
Oxford Road
MANCHESTER
M13 9WL
Tel: 0161 276 1234

SALFORD ROYAL HOSPITAL 7H **77**
Stott Lane
SALFORD
M6 8HD
Tel: 0161 7897373

SHIRE HILL HOSPITAL 6G **100**
Bute Street
GLOSSOP
SK13 7QP
Tel: 01457 850400

SPRINGHILL HOSPICE 1F **44**
Broad Lane
ROCHDALE
OL16 4PZ
Tel: 01706 649920

STEPPING HILL HOSPITAL 3G **118**
Poplar Grove
STOCKPORT
SK2 7JE
Tel: 0161 4831010

STRETFORD MEMORIAL HOSPITAL 6A **94**
226 Seymour Grove
MANCHESTER
M16 0DU
Tel: 0161 8815353

TAMESIDE GENERAL HOSPITAL 6B **82**
Fountain Street
ASHTON-UNDER-LYNE
OL6 9RW
Tel: 0161 3316000

THOMAS LINACRE CENTRE 6H **9** (2E **52**)
Parson's Walk
WIGAN
WN1 1RU
Tel: 01942 244000

TRAFFORD GENERAL HOSPITAL 6A **92**
Moorside Road
Davyholme
MANCHESTER
M41 5SL
Tel: 0161 7484022

UNIVERSITY DENTAL HOSPITAL OF MANCHESTER 3F **94**
Higher Cambridge Street
MANCHESTER
M15 6FH
Tel: 0161 275 6666

WALK-IN CENTRE (HAWTHORN MEDICAL CENTRE) 9L **95**
Fallowfield Retail Park
Birchfields Road
MANCHESTER
M14 6FS
Tel: 0161 220 6080

WIGAN & LEIGH HOSPICE 6M **53**
Kildare Street
Hindley
WIGAN
WN2 3HZ
Tel: 01942 525566

WILLOW WOOD HOSPICE 7B **82**
Willow Wood Close
ASHTON-UNDER-LYNE
OL6 6SL
Tel: 0161 3301100

WITHINGTON COMMUNITY HOSPITAL 3E **106**
Nell Lane
MANCHESTER
M20 2LR
Tel: 0161 434 5555

WOODLANDS HOSPITAL 7G **57**
Peel Lane
Worsley
MANCHESTER
M28 0FE
Tel: 0161 7031040

WOODS DAY HOSPITAL 6E **100**
Park Crescent
GLOSSOP
SK13 7BQ
Tel: 01457 860783

WRIGHTINGTON HOSPITAL 2H **33**
Hall Lane
Appley Bridge
WIGAN
WN6 9EP
Tel: 01942 244000

WYTHENSHAWE HOSPITAL 2M **115**
Southmoor Road
Wythenshawe
MANCHESTER
M23 9LT
Tel: 0161 998 7070

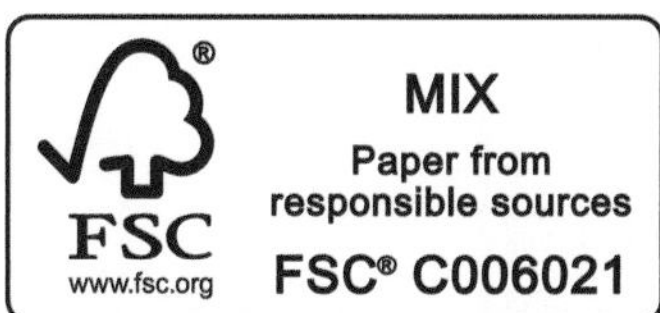

MIX
Paper from responsible sources
FSC
www.fsc.org
FSC® C006021

SAFETY CAMERA INFORMATION

Safety camera locations are publicised by the Safer Roads Partnership which operates them in order to encourage drivers to comply with speed limits at these sites. It is the driver's absolute responsibility to be aware of and to adhere to speed limits at all times.

By showing this safety camera information it is the intention of Geographers' A-Z Map Company Ltd., to encourage safe driving and greater awareness of speed limits and vehicle speed. Data accurate at time of printing.

Printed and bound in the United Kingdom by Polestar Wheatons Ltd., Exeter.

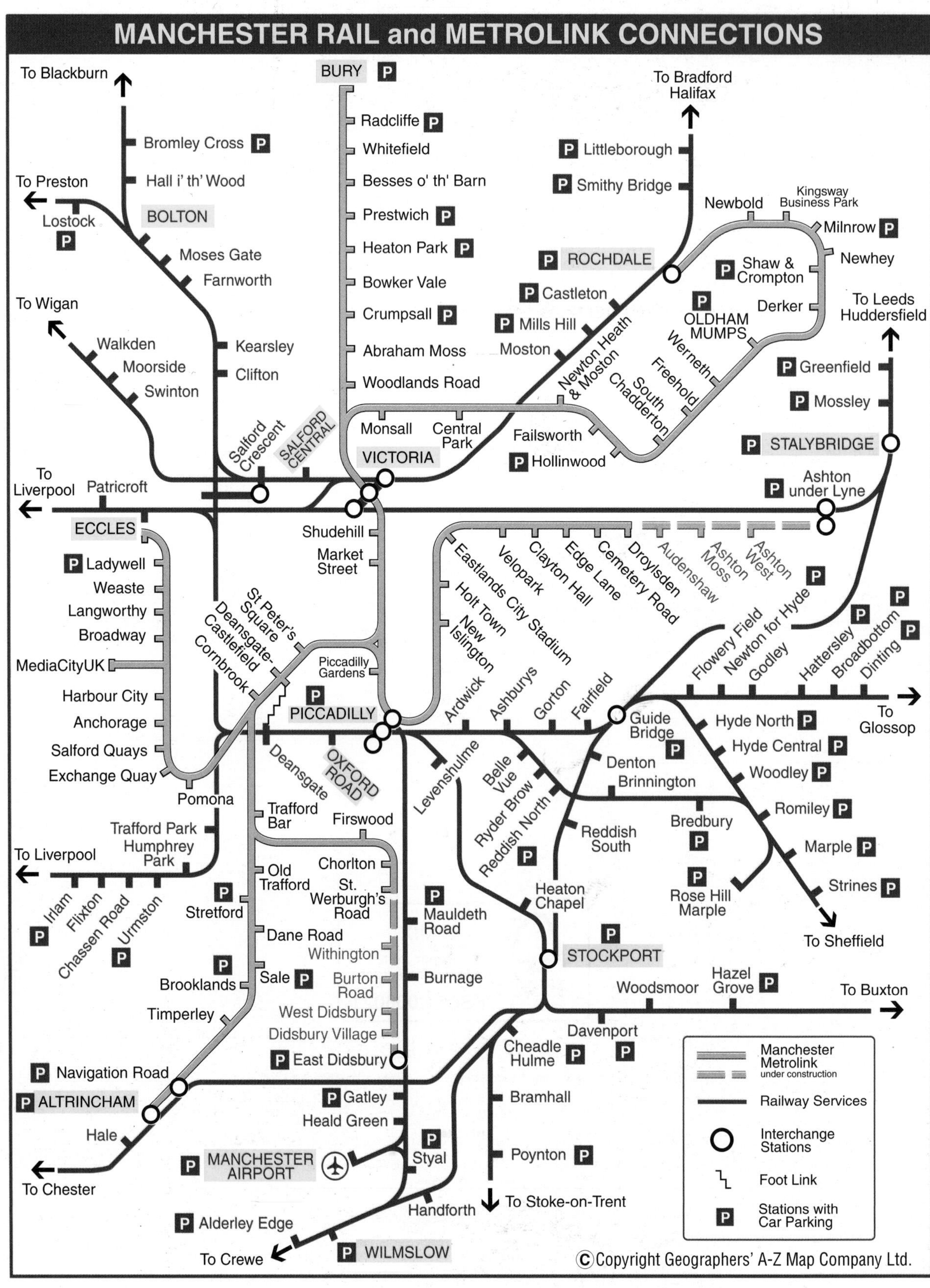

MANCHESTER RAIL and METROLINK CONNECTIONS
To Blackburn
Bromley Cross
Hall i' th' Wood
BOLTON
To Preston
Lostock
Moses Gate
Farnworth
To Wigan
Walkden
Moorside
Swinton
Kearsley
Clifton
Salford Crescent
SALFORD CENTRAL
To Liverpool
Patricroft
ECCLES
Ladywell
Weaste
Langworthy
Broadway
MediaCityUK
Harbour City
Anchorage
Salford Quays
Exchange Quay
Pomona
Trafford Park
Humphrey Park
To Liverpool
Irlam
Flixton
Chassen Road
Urmston
Stretford
Brooklands
Timperley
Navigation Road
ALTRINCHAM
Hale
To Chester
BURY
Radcliffe
Whitefield
Besses o' th' Barn
Prestwich
Heaton Park
Bowker Vale
Crumpsall
Abraham Moss
Woodlands Road
Monsall
Central Park
VICTORIA
Shudehill
Market Street
St Peter's Square
Deansgate-Castlefield
Cornbrook
Piccadilly Gardens
PICCADILLY
Deansgate
OXFORD ROAD
Trafford Bar
Firswood
Old Trafford
Chorlton
St. Werburgh's Road
Dane Road
Withington
Sale
Burton Road
West Didsbury
Didsbury Village
East Didsbury
Mauldeth Road
Burnage
Gatley
Heald Green
MANCHESTER AIRPORT
Styal
Handforth
Alderley Edge
To Crewe
WILMSLOW
To Bradford Halifax
Littleborough
Smithy Bridge
ROCHDALE
Newbold
Kingsway Business Park
Milnrow
Newhey
Shaw & Crompton
Castleton
Mills Hill
Moston
OLDHAM MUMPS
Derker
Newton Heath & Moston
Werneth
Freehold
South Chadderton
Failsworth
Hollinwood
To Leeds Huddersfield
Greenfield
Mossley
STALYBRIDGE
Ashton under Lyne
Eastlands City Stadium
Holt Town
New Islington
Velopark
Clayton Hall
Edge Lane
Cemetery Road
Droylsden
Audenshaw
Ashton Moss
Ashton West
Newton for Hyde
Flowery Field
Godley
Hattersley
Broadbottom
Dinting
To Glossop
Ardwick
Ashburys
Gorton
Fairfield
Guide Bridge
Levenshulme
Belle Vue
Ryder Brow
Reddish North
Denton
Brinnington
Reddish South
Hyde North
Hyde Central
Woodley
Romiley
Bredbury
Marple
Strines
Rose Hill Marple
To Sheffield
Heaton Chapel
STOCKPORT
Woodsmoor
Hazel Grove
To Buxton
Davenport
Cheadle Hulme
Bramhall
Poynton
To Stoke-on-Trent
Manchester Metrolink
under construction
Railway Services
Interchange Stations
Foot Link
Stations with Car Parking